W9-BIK-158

CONTENTS AT A GLANCE

SPECIAL EDITION

USING
FileMaker 7

Steve Lane

Bob Bowers

Scott Love

Chris Moyer

800 East 96th Street
Indianapolis, Indiana 46240

SPECIAL EDITION USING FILEMAKER 7

Copyright © 2005 by Que Publishing

International Standard Book Number: 0-7897-3028-6

Library of Congress Catalog Card Number: 2004104262

Printed in the United States of America

First Printing: August 2004

07   06   05   04   4   3   2   1

Trademarks

Warning and Disclaimer

Bulk Sales

Que Publishing offers excellent discounts on this book when ordered in quantity for bulk purchases or special sales. For more information, please contact

> **U.S. Corporate and Government Sales**
> **1-800-382-3419**
> **corpsales@pearsontechgroup.com**

For sales outside of the U.S., please contact

> **International Sales**
> **international@pearsoned.com**

Associate Publisher
Greg Wiegand

Acquisitions Editor
Stephanie J. McComb

Development Editor
Laura Norman

Managing Editor
Charlotte Clapp

Project Editor
Tonya Simpson

Copy Editor
Margo Catts

Indexer
Ken Johnson

Proofreader
Elizabeth Scott

Technical Editors
Debi Fuchs
Jay Weischofer

Publishing Coordinator
Sharry Lee Gregory

Multimedia Developer
Dan Scherf

Designer
Anne Jones

Page Layout
Eric S. Miller

TABLE OF CONTENTS

III Developer Techniques

About the Authors

Steve Lane has worked with relational databases for 15 years. He has written for *FileMaker Advisor* magazine, and co-authored *Advanced FileMaker Pro 6 Web Development*. He is a vice president with the Moyer Group and has led training classes in FileMaker technologies all over the country, both in open sessions and in on-site client engagements. He regularly speaks at the annual FileMaker Developer's Conference, where in 2003 he was awarded the FileMaker Fellowship Award for "pushing the boundaries of FileMaker Pro."

Bob Bowers is a columnist and contributing editor for *FileMaker Advisor* magazine and has co-authored two other books: *Advanced FileMaker Pro 5.5 Techniques for Developers* and *Advanced FileMaker Pro 6 Web Development*. He is president of the Moyer Group. At the 2002 FileMaker Developer's Conference, where he is a perennial speaker, he was awarded the FileMaker Fellowship Award for "developing outstanding technical and educational resources for FileMaker."

Scott Love has been working with FileMaker at leading technology firms for over a decade. Currently a vice president with the Moyer Group, he served at *MacUser/MacWEEK* as an online Managing Editor, at Apple Computer as its Web Publishing Technology Evangelist, followed by directing the Technical Marketing team at Macromedia. He has written dozens of feature and review articles on FileMaker and Internet/Web topics for a wide range of computer publications, including *Macworld* magazine.

Chris Moyer has been designing and implementing database solutions for Fortune 500 companies for more than 13 years. He is CEO of the Moyer Group. Before founding the Moyer Group in 1995, he worked as a Sales Engineer for the Claris Corporation (now FileMaker, Inc.). He was one of three trainers selected by Claris to train the FileMaker developer community in the United States and abroad when FileMaker 3.0 was released. Chris subsequently authored *Special Edition Using FileMaker Pro 3 for Macintosh*. In 1998, he was awarded the FileMaker Solutions Alliance Award of Excellence. Chris is a co-author of *Advanced FileMaker Pro 5.5 Techniques for Developers*. Today Chris serves as a technical editor for the *FileMaker Advisor* magazine, and is a regular presenter at the FileMaker Developer Conference.

DEDICATION

To Signe, Erlend, and Rona, who hopefully still think that books are, in general, a good idea.

—Steve Lane

To Rebecca and Nate, the most important people in my world.

—Bob Bowers

To my son Kai and to my fellow authors. I'm extremely fortunate to have found a place in the world where I can work each day with such friends.

—Scott Love

To my wife Laura, my sons Devlin and Conrad, and to the memory of my grandmother, Gertrude Moyer, who passed away in December at the age of 96.

—Chris Moyer

ACKNOWLEDGMENTS

Anyone who's ambitious (or foolish) enough to sit down and write a book accumulates many debts along the way. It's our pleasure to acknowledge those here.

The team at Que—senior editor Stephanie McComb, development editor Laura Norman, copy editor Margo Catts, and production coordinator Tonya Simpson—have been outstanding. It's hard enough to shepherd a single author through the exacting process of technical publishing, let alone four. Stephanie and her crew have doubtless been taxed by our unruliness (we imagine the term "skunk herders" has come up now and again) but have remained unfailingly patient and gracious. Their hard work and expertise has smoothed away a thousand rough edges, has made murky ideas clear, and clear ones transparent.

We had able assistance from many friends and colleagues along the way. In particular, Greg Lane, Roger Jacques, Liz Chilton, Carlos Ramirez, Jan Jung, Aaron Holdsworth, and Thomas Andrews all made important technical contributions. Numerous other friends and family provided moral support and listened to our lamentations along the way, including Rebecca Moore, Molly Connolly, John Overton, Adrienne Vasquez, Bill Bennett, Kim Fenn, and Bethany Albertson.

Working with a new version of a product, especially one with as many changes as FileMaker Pro 7, provides many challenges. We are grateful to the participants of several early testing groups for sharing their ideas and discoveries, some of which have been the basis for ideas and examples contained herein. Many individuals at FileMaker, Inc. are deserving of thanks for answering questions ("Is that a bug or a feature?") and going out of their way to help make sure we had the latest, greatest versions to work with. We'd like to make special mention of the FileMaker documentation group, who produced some superb documentation for the new version.

We were also fortunate to have an extremely talented crew of technical editors. Jay Welshofer, Andrew LeCates, and Debi Fuchs all brought their prodigious talents to bear in picking over our facts and technical details one by one. Any errors or omissions that remain are our own.

In addition, Chris would like to thank Steve Lane for quarterbacking this project through to completion. It was a long, hard trip, and Steve carried the largest load and really made it happen.

The most important debt, though, is to our families, who endured the sight of far too many closed office doors and late nights over the time it took to write this book. We promise not to do it again soon.

WE WANT TO HEAR FROM YOU!

As the reader of this book, *you* are our most important critic and commentator. We value your opinion and want to know what we're doing right, what we could do better, what areas you'd like to see us publish in, and any other words of wisdom you're willing to pass our way.

As an associate publisher for Que Publishing, I welcome your comments. You can email or write me directly to let me know what you did or didn't like about this book—as well as what we can do to make our books better.

Please note that I cannot help you with technical problems related to the topic of this book. We do have a User Services group, however, where I will forward specific technical questions related to the book.

When you write, please be sure to include this book's title and author as well as your name, email address, and phone number. I will carefully review your comments and share them with the author and editors who worked on the book.

Email: feedback@quepublishing.com

Mail: Greg Wiegand
           Associate Publisher
           Que Publishing
           800 East 96th Street
           Indianapolis, IN 46240 USA

For more information about this book or another Que Publishing title, visit our Web site at www.quepublishing.com. Type the ISBN (excluding hyphens) or the title of a book in the Search field to find the page you're looking for.

WELCOME TO FILEMAKER PRO 7

In this introduction

WAITER, THERE'S A SOFTWARE DEVELOPMENT TOOL IN MY PRODUCTIVITY APPLICATION!

Welcome to the world of FileMaker Pro. By simply standing in this section of your local bookstore, you're sure to have heard the word "database." We'll cover what databases are ad nauseam in the rest of this book—so go ahead and take it up to the counter...we'll wait—but one of the first things you'll need to understand about FileMaker Pro is that it is far more than just a database.

FileMaker Pro is nearly unique in the world of software. It is a powerful database system that can manage and store a wide range of information; it's an application for end users (like Microsoft Excel or Intuit's Quicken), and it's also a robust rapid application software development platform.

When you hear someone speak about FileMaker, keep in mind they may be viewing it from one of these different perspectives or another. An IT professional likely sees it as a database engine that fits into a greater security and network infrastructure. An end-user probably is thinking about a specific solution built in FileMaker Pro and how that solution helps (or doesn't help) make work more efficient. A software developer may see it as one of many tools he employs in building a wide range of applications.

However you approach FileMaker Pro, some core strengths of the platform are important to all types of users.

- **Flexibility**—Working with FileMaker Pro is inherently open-ended. It is simple to create ad hoc data queries, quickly manage data entry, add functionality to a live system, or deploy to the Web in minutes.

- **Ease of Use**—The folks at FileMaker, Inc., have labored hard to make FileMaker as approachable as humanly possible. Day-to-day users can easily learn how to add fields to a database, create reports, add form layouts, and more. With FileMaker Pro, organizations need not be dependent on mysterious software engineers and their arcane knowledge or, even worse, consultants like us!

- **Interoperability**—FileMaker Pro supports many common, open standards for data exchange (SQL, ODBC, JDBC, XML) and allows users to connect their database solutions to the greater world of applications—both within their organizations and online on the Web.

- **Modern Data Architecture**—FileMaker Pro, despite being "just" a productivity application that lives on your computer along with Microsoft Word and Solitaire, allows users to create fully relational data structures for information and to properly build architectures that rightly manage real-world data.

We'll cover the right and wrong ways to build solutions in FileMaker throughout the book; for now the point we're making is that FileMaker Pro is both something you use (a productivity application) and something with which you build things (a development tool).

RAPID APPLICATION DEVELOPMENT

In the world of software development, flexibility and speed are critical. We live in the world of Internet time—burst bubbles notwithstanding—and businesses usually embark on a development project only when they need something yesterday.

In addition to simple impatience, the practices and experiences of the past two decades have proven software development to be a risky, unpredictable business. NASA's travails are painful reminders that this stuff is, in some ways, truly rocket science. New job functions have been developed in software quality assurance and project management. Certification programs exist to sift the wheat from the chaff.

FileMaker Pro exists in many respects to help organizations take on less risk and navigate the waters of software development without having to reinvent the boat, the oar, the sail, and the steam engine. Because it is a rapid application development platform, it is possible to build a system in FileMaker Pro in a fraction of the time it takes to build the same system in more classic, compiled software languages.

LOW TOTAL COST OF OWNERSHIP

FileMaker Pro is focused around offering a low total cost of ownership for organizations. In October 2001, the Aberdeen Group, an independent research firm in Boston, found that, "Under conservative assumptions, FileMaker Pro was superior, with an average ratio of 5:1 in [cost of ownership] over the industry average database." (Quote taken from the Aberdeen Group Executive White Paper "FileMaker Low-IT Database Cost-of-Ownership Study," October 2001.)

Both the cost of the software itself and the rapidity with which systems can be built mean that IT organizations have a viable alternative to the massive enterprise-level systems of the past.

FILEMAKER IS A SEASONED PRO

The history of FileMaker Pro reveals that the software is nearing its 20th birthday, though its first years are a bit fuzzy: Sometime between 1983 and 1985, Nashoba Systems created an initial version that was acquired and published by Forethought, Inc., in April of 1985. Nashoba then reacquired the rights to their software and published FileMaker Plus in 1986 and FileMaker 4 in 1988.

Claris Corp., which was then being formed by Apple Computer and was to become FileMaker's guiding parent, purchased Nashoba and published FileMaker II in 1988 and 1989. Finally in October 1990 FileMaker Pro 1.0 made its debut and set the product line on the course it has largely followed to this day. In December of 1995 Claris shipped FileMaker Pro 3.0, which saw the introduction of relational data modeling to the platform and even more importantly a completely seamless cross-platform application that's virtually identical between the Mac OS and Microsoft Windows. Today a majority of FileMaker's audience lives on the Windows side.

Other major innovations have occurred along the way, but nearly everyone in the community recognizes that it was the watershed version 3.0 that broke open the gates for

FileMaker. Version 4.0 introduced Web publishing to the platform and version 6.0 offered significant support for XML-based data interchange.

In 1999, at the time of version 4.1, Claris Corp. rechristened itself FileMaker, Inc., and focused all its energy around its flagship product.

FileMaker has been profitable every quarter since changing its name from Claris Corporation to FileMaker, Inc., in 1998 (an extraordinary feat considering the climate in Silicon Valley for the past few years) and continues to enjoy the backing (as a subsidiary) of a cash-flush Apple Computer, Inc.

YOU'RE NOT ALONE

FileMaker, Inc., has sold more than 8.5 million units worldwide as of this writing. Users range from a single magician booking gigs in Denver, Colorado, to Fortune 500 companies such as Citibank and Genentech. Just like any tool, FileMaker is noteworthy only when it has been employed to build something...and its builders come in all shapes and sizes. The only true common element seems to be that they own computers (but not always!).

There are some trends: FileMaker Pro is widely used in the world of both K-12 and higher education. Of the 50 top Universities in the United States, 49 use FileMaker Pro. The non-profit industry is also a key focal point for FileMaker. Ultimately these trends have more to do with FileMaker Pro's price tag than with any inherent advantage the software offers. FileMaker Pro truly is like a hammer: You can build a birdhouse or the Golden Gate Bridge. It's just a question of the skill of the craftsman and the time you're willing to devote to your system.

HOW THIS BOOK IS ORGANIZED

Special Edition Using FileMaker 7 is divided into five parts, organized into something like a tree. Part I, "Getting Started with FileMaker 7," and Part II, "Developing Solutions with FileMaker," constitute the "trunk" of the tree; they cover central material that we recommend everyone read. If you're familiar with previous versions of FileMaker, you may only need to glance through Part I, but we still recommend you read Part II carefully.

Subsequent parts branch out from this base. Part III, "Developer Techniques," focuses on using FileMaker's features to develop complete, robust database applications. Part IV, "Data Integration and Publishing," covers getting data into and out of FileMaker. And Part V, "Deploying a FileMaker Solution," covers options for making a FileMaker solution accessible to others.

The five parts of *Special Edition Using FileMaker 7*, and the topics they cover, are described in the following sections.

PART I: "GETTING STARTED WITH FILEMAKER 7"

The chapters in Part I introduce you to FileMaker, its uses and features, and get you started with basics of defining databases.

- Chapter 1, "FileMaker Overview," situates FileMaker Pro within the wider world of database and productivity software. It provides an overview of the new FileMaker 7 product line, and mentions the most important new features in FileMaker 7. This chapter is appropriate both for those who are new to FileMaker Pro, and for those who may have used previous versions and want a quick tour of the major innovations.

- Chapter 2, "Using FileMaker Pro," is intended as an introduction to the software from the perspective of a database user rather than a database developer. We introduce the major components and functions of the FileMaker interface, such as the Status Area, layouts, FileMaker's modes, and the basics of record creation, editing, and deletion.

- Chapter 3, "Defining and Working with Fields," provides a thorough overview of all of FileMaker Pro's field types and field options, including lookups, validation, storage types, and indexing. This chapter is intended to help lay the groundwork for talking about database development, and to serve as a thorough reference on FileMaker field types and options.

- Chapter 4, "FileMaker Fundamentals: Working with Layouts," covers all of FileMaker's layout-building options in detail. We cover all aspects of layout building, and offer guidelines for quicker and more efficient layout work.

PART II: "DEVELOPING SOLUTIONS WITH FILEMAKER"

Part II is intended to introduce you to the fundamental techniques of database application development using FileMaker Pro. Chapters 5–7 cover the theory and practice of designing and building database systems with multiple data tables. Chapters 8–10 introduce you to foundational concepts in application and reporting logic.

- Chapter 5, "Relational Database Design," introduces you to relational database design concepts. We proceed by working "on paper," without specific reference to FileMaker, and introduce you to the fundamental vocabulary and techniques of relational database design (keys and relationships), through a series of modeling exercises based on fictional business and organizational problems.

- Chapter 6, "Working with Multiple Tables," begins the task of translating the generic database design concepts of Chapter 5 into specific FileMaker techniques. We show how to translate a paper diagram into an actual FileMaker table structure. We show how to model different relationship types in FileMaker using multiple data tables, and how to create fields that function effectively as relational keys.

- Chapter 7, "Working with Relationships," builds on the concepts of Chapter 6. Rather than focusing on FileMaker's relationships from the standpoint of database design, we focus on their practical use in FileMaker programming. We look in detail at the new capabilities of FileMaker 7, and discuss non-equijoin conditions, file references, and some strategies for organizing a multi-table system.

- Chapter 8, "Getting Started with Calculations," introduces FileMaker's calculation engine. The chapter delves into the major types of FileMaker calculations (though it's not an exhaustive reference—you'll find that in Appendix B, "Calculation Function

Reference"). We cover a number of the most important functions, and discuss general strategies and techniques for writing calculations.

- Chapter 9, "Getting Started with Scripting," introduces FileMaker's scripting engine. Like the previous chapter, this one covers the fundamentals of an important skill for FileMaker developers. We cover some common scripting techniques and show how to use triggered scripts to add interactivity to a user interface.

- Chapter 10, "Reporting with Grouped Data," illustrates the fundamental techniques of FileMaker Pro reporting, such as list views and subsummary reports, as well as some more advanced subsummary techniques, and some design techniques for improving the look and usability of your reporting layouts.

PART III: "DEVELOPER TECHNIQUES"

The chapters in Part III delve deeper into individual topics in advanced FileMaker application development. We build on earlier chapters by exploring more complex uses of portals, calculations, and scripts. We also offer chapters that help you ready your FileMaker solutions for multi-user deployment, and we examine the tricky issue of conversion from previous versions.

- Chapter 11, "Developing for Multi-User Deployment," explores the issues and challenges of designing FileMaker systems that will be used by several or many people at once. We discuss how FileMaker handles concurrent access to data and discuss the concept of user sessions.

- Chapter 12, "Implementing Security," is a thorough overview of the new FileMaker 7 security model. We cover the new role-based Accounts feature, the new Extended Privileges, and many of the complexities of server-based external authentication (against Windows or Mac OS user directories, for example).

- Chapter 13, "Advanced Layout Techniques," provides detailed explanations of a number of more complex, applied techniques for working with layouts and data presentation in a FileMaker application. We look at different options for where and how to build interface layouts, and explore an advanced, script-based navigation scheme and discuss FileMaker's new tools for building multi-window interfaces.

- Chapter 14, "Specialized Calculation Functions," looks closely at some of the more advanced or specialized types of FileMaker calculations, including the new Let and Evaluate functions, as well as the new functions for text formatting and for array manipulation. The chapter finishes with an examination of custom functions, another important new feature in the FileMaker 7 product line.

- Chapter 15, "Advanced Scripting," like the preceding chapter, is full of information that is specific to new features of FileMaker 7. Here we cover programming with script parameters, programming in a multi-window system, and the complexities of scripted navigation among multiple tables and record sets.

- Chapter 16, "Working with Portals," looks at FileMaker's portal elements from two perspectives. First, we examine more advanced uses of portals for creating and viewing database records. Second, we examine the ways in which portals can be used to create new types of interface elements, such as filtered record browsers or pick lists.

■ Chapter 17, "Troubleshooting," is a broad look at how to find, diagnose, and cure trouble in FileMaker systems—but also how to prevent it. We look at some software engineering principles that can help make systems more robust, and can reduce the incidence and severity of errors. The chapter also includes detailed discussions of how to troubleshoot difficulties in a variety of areas, from multi-user record lock issues to performance difficulties over large networks.

■ Chapter 18, "Converting Systems from Previous Versions of FileMaker Pro," explores the complex issues involved in moving to FileMaker 7 from a previous version. We begin by discussion migration scenarios that help you decide how much you stand to benefit from moving to 7. For certain systems, the choice to move to 7 will be clear; for others it may be less so. We then discuss the mechanics of conversion in detail, and discuss some of the more significant pitfalls to be aware of.

PART IV: "DATA INTEGRATION AND PUBLISHING"

Part IV covers technologies and capabilities that allow FileMaker to share data, either by exchanging data with other applications, or by exporting and publishing data, for example via ODBC, JDBC, and the Web.

■ Chapter 19, "Importing Data into FileMaker Pro," looks at all the different means by which you can import data into FileMaker. It covers how to import data from flat files, how to batch imports of images and text, how to import images from a digital camera, and how to import data from ODBC and XML data sources. (The full treatment of XML import is reserved for Chapter 22.)

■ Chapter 20, "Getting Data Out of FileMaker," is in some respects the inverse of Chapter 19. It covers almost all the ways by which you can extract or publish data from FileMaker, including simple export, XML export, and pushing data into SQL databases via ODBC, as well as means by which others can query FileMaker data over ODBC.

■ Chapter 21, "Instant Web Publishing," looks at the features of the new FileMaker 7 Instant Web Publishing model. IWP is vastly improved in FileMaker 7. Anyone interested in making FileMaker data available over the Web should begin with this chapter.

■ Chapter 22, "FileMaker and Web Services," introduces you to FileMaker's XML capabilities. XML is the backbone of FileMaker's Custom Web Publishing technologies. This chapter introduces XML and its companion technology XSLT as they relate to FileMaker's XML import capability. Though no substitute for a book devoted to XML and XSLT, this chapter should teach enough for you to begin to get your footing with these technologies as they relate to FileMaker.

■ Chapter 23, "Custom Web Publishing," covers FileMaker 7's new advanced Web publishing technology. The new technology, which is XML- and XSLT-based, replaces CDML. This chapter discusses how to configure the FileMaker Web Publishing

Engine (WPE), and how to write XSLT stylesheets that exploit the WPE's capabilities to build FileMaker-backed Web applications.

Part V: "Deploying a FileMaker Solution"

Part V delves into the different choices you have for how to deploy a FileMaker database, including deployment via FileMaker Server and via kiosk or runtime mode using FileMaker Developer.

- Chapter 24, "FileMaker Deployment Options," is a short chapter that provides an overview of the different ways you can distribute a FileMaker database to one or more users. Read this chapter for a quick orientation toward your different deployment choices.
- Chapter 25, "FileMaker Server," tells you everything you need to know to deploy solutions to FileMaker Server, for distribution to many users. The chapter covers setup, configuration, and tuning of Server, as well as managing server-side plugins and authentication.
- Chapter 26, "FileMaker Developer and Plug-ins," looks at some of the special features of FileMaker Developer, such as the creation of bound runtime solutions and kiosk solutions. We also explore FileMaker plugins in this chapter, from the standpoint of a developer rather than a plugin programmer.

Special Features

This book includes the following special features:

- **Chapter roadmaps**—At the beginning of each chapter, you will find a list of the top-level topics addressed in that chapter. This list enables you to quickly see the type of information the chapter contains.
- **Troubleshooting**—Many chapters in the book have a section dedicated to troubleshooting specific problems related to the chapter's topic. Cross-references to the solutions to these problems are placed in the context of relevant text in the chapter as Troubleshooting Notes to make them easy to locate.
- **FileMaker Extra**—Many chapters end with a section containing extra information that will help you make the most of FileMaker Pro. In some cases we offer expanded, fully-worked examples of tricky database design problems; in others, we offer shortcuts and maintenance techniques gleaned from our collective experience with developing production FileMaker systems (creating custom function libraries, or getting the most out of team development); and in others we delve all the way to the bottom of tricky but vital FileMaker features such as the process of importing records.
- **Notes**—Notes provide additional commentary or explanation that doesn't fit neatly into the surrounding text. You will find detailed explanations of how something works, alternative ways of performing a task, and other tidbits to get you on your way.

- **Tips**—This element will identify some tips and tricks we've learned over the years.

- **Cautions**—Here we'll let you know when there are potential pitfalls to avoid.

 - **The new version icon**—This icon will identify things that are new in FileMaker 7. In one sense we could just put this icon on the front of the book and be done with it, but instead we've used it to call out areas that are particularly new and noteworthy in 7, or things that are particularly different from the way things would have been done in earlier versions.

- **Cross-references**—Many topics are connected to other topics in various ways. Cross-references help you link related information together, no matter where that information appears in the book. When another section is related to one you are reading, a cross-reference directs you to a specific page in the book on which you will find the related information.

Typographic Conventions Used in This Book

This book uses a few different typesetting styles, primarily to distinguish among explanatory text, code, and special terms.

Key Combinations and Menu Choices

Key (and possibly mouse) combinations that you use to perform FileMaker operations from the keyboard are indicated by presenting the Mac command first in parenthesis followed by the Windows command in brackets: (⌘-click) for Mac and [Ctrl+click] for Windows, for example.

Sub-menu choices are separated from the main menu name by a comma: File, Define, Value Lists.

Typographic Conventions Used for FileMaker Scripts

Monospace type is used for all examples of FileMaker scripting. FileMaker scripts are not edited as text, but are instead edited through FileMaker's graphical script design tool, called ScriptMaker. As a result, scripting options that are presented visually in ScriptMaker need to be turned into text when written out. We follow FileMaker's own conventions for printing scripts as text: The name of the script step comes first, and any options to the step are placed after the step name, in square brackets, with semicolons delimiting multiple script step options, as in the following example:

```
Show All Records
Go to Record/Request/Page [ First ]
Show Custom Dialog [Title: "Message window"; Message; "Hello, world!";
➥ Buttons: "OK"]
```

Who Should Use This Book

Like FileMaker Pro itself, this book has several audiences. If you work with structured data a lot (Excel spreadsheets, for example), but are new to databases, this book will provide you with a solid foundation in the world of databases, in the basics of database theory, and in the practical skills you need to become a productive database user or developer. The book's more introductory chapters tell you what you need to know to get started building basic databases for your own use (we like to call these "spreadsheet-plus"). Later chapters introduce you to the world of multi-user database design, and to some of FileMaker's more advanced application design features.

If you've worked with other database systems—either server-side relational database engines based on SQL, or desktop development environments such as Access—this book will help you see how FileMaker Pro fits into the universe of database software. Look over the section in this Introduction titled "How This Book Is Organized" to get a sense of which chapters will get you started quickly with FileMaker.

If you're a Web developer wondering how FileMaker might fit into your toolkit, we have extensive coverage of the new FileMaker Web technologies in Chapters 21, 22, and 23.

And if you're an old hand with FileMaker and are wondering what's new, the answer is...more than you think! We've called out some notable differences between FileMaker 7 and previous versions, but in some sense, it's *all* new. The application has been significantly redesigned. Chapters 6 and 7 (which cover the new relational model), Chapters 14 and 15 (which cover important changes to FileMaker scripting and calculations), and Chapter 18 (covering conversion from previous versions) contain a lot of information about new features, but there are changes, large and small, lurking everywhere.

A Brave, New World

Without wanting to resort to hyperbole, we feel that FileMaker Pro 7 represents a dramatic step forward for FileMaker. This version includes a wide range of impressive changes to the platform, and this book is being written while the software is still in an alpha and beta state. We have done our best to research and double-check everything we present here, but do please keep in mind that some aspects of the software may change by the time this book reaches your hands. We encourage you to use Appendix A, "Additional Resources," as a means of finding online information about FileMaker Pro...and if you're new to the platform, welcome to a great community!

GETTING STARTED WITH FILEMAKER 7

CHAPTER 1

FileMaker Overview

In this chapter

1

INTRODUCTION TO DATABASE SOFTWARE

FileMaker Pro is database software. If you need to keep track of more than one of anything, you could probably benefit from using a database. Databases are useful for keeping track of contacts and their addresses and phone numbers, the students in a school, the sales and inventory in a store, or the results of experimental trials. You can also keep that kind of information in a word processor or on paper, but a database will make it much easier to

- **Organize your data into reports**—You can organize your data into reports that are sorted by city, last name, price, or any other criteria that you're tracking.

- **Find one or several items in your collections**—If you have a list of twenty names, it's not too difficult to find Jane Smith. If you have 500,000 though, it takes too long to do a visual search.

- **Quickly categorize records based on some criteria**—For example, customers who buy a certain amount of merchandise can be grouped into categories of A, B, and C customers. This would make it easy to target marketing at a certain segment of your customers.

- **Share data with other systems**—If you need to import data from another source or send information to a charting program or to merge with a desktop publishing package to do catalog publishing, having all of your information in a database makes those tasks much simpler.

The rest of this book gets into detail on how to do everything just mentioned and much more as well. You'll get a more detailed look at what a database is and how it works, but first let's consider how a database product such as FileMaker Pro fits into the universe of software products.

TYPES OF DATABASE SOFTWARE

A huge variety of software is on the market today. At the top level are broad software categories such as games, multimedia, and educational software. The category that FileMaker generally fits into is business productivity software. We say "generally" because lots of people use FileMaker for non-business activities such as managing wedding invitation lists or keeping track of their hobbies or collections.

The idea of managing a collection of something is what database software is all about. Some database products on the market manage specialized collections such as business contacts. Products such as Act or Goldmine are good examples of those. Quicken, QuickBooks, and Microsoft Money manage collections of financial transactions.

FileMaker and other non-specialized database products such as Microsoft Access are used to create database systems just as word processing software is used to create specific documents and Microsoft Excel is used to create spreadsheets. In fact, Microsoft Excel is often used as a database because it has several strong list management features. It works well for managing simple databases, but doesn't work well in managing multiple lists that are related to each other.

A quick example of two lists that are related to each other is a list of companies and a list of contacts at those companies. If you were to keep these two lists as a single list, the company information would have to be repeated for each employee that worked at the company. That doesn't sound like a big deal, and it isn't for small databases, but suppose the list contained dozens of contacts for each company. If a company name or address ever changed (which happens) you would have to find each contact for that company and update the name or address information over and over again. There are other problems with this kind of a simple list structure, or *flat file*, but we'll get into those later in the book.

OFF-THE-SHELF SOFTWARE

For now, let's stay with the idea of a collection of collections, or multiple lists that have some relationship to other lists, like employees to companies. This idea of relatedness is why you may have heard the term *relational database*. There are many relational database products on the market, and FileMaker Pro is one of them. Specialized products such as Act or Quicken are also relational database products, but the difference is that those products are finished systems, whereas products such as FileMaker are used to create such systems.

If you wanted to, you could re-create the functionality in Act or Quicken by using FileMaker, and some people do. They do so because the problem with specialized products is that they're relatively inflexible. If your organization has some non-standard ways of doing things, you may find it difficult to work with these specialized products. Another term for these products, by the way, is *off-the-shelf software*, which just means that they're ready to use right off the shelf. That contrasts with database authoring tools such as FileMaker Pro. Although FileMaker Pro does come with several database templates that might be perfectly suitable for you to use off the shelf, most people instead use FileMaker Pro to create a custom database system that exactly matches how their organization operates.

CUSTOM DEVELOPMENT SOFTWARE

Ideally, a database system should work exactly as your organization does, and your organization should not have to adapt its procedures to work with the database system. It should be the other way around, with the database system adapting to fit the needs of an organization. That's the drawback of off-the-shelf software. Except for some limited customization features, you don't have the ability to make major changes to its functionality.

With custom development database software such as FileMaker Pro, you can build a system to be exactly what you need. It's the difference between buying a house that is a pretty good match for you and having a custom home built that has all the features that you want (or at least can afford).

Building a house is actually a great analogy for building a database, because they follow similar trajectories. You need to design your database before you build it. You need to wait for it to be built before you can move in, and questions or issues often arise during the construction process. After it's built, your needs may change and you may need to make an addition to accommodate your changed circumstances.

This last point is an important one, because business environment changes and resulting organizational changes happen much more rapidly than in years past. One of the key advantages to developing database systems in FileMaker Pro is that it can be rapidly redesigned, even while the system is in use by other users. You can change any aspect of the system while it's "live" if need be, although that may not always be advisable. This was true in previous versions of FileMaker, but that flexibility is even greater with FileMaker Pro 7. In FileMaker Pro 7, you can make changes to field definitions and security settings even while users are logged in to the system.

WHAT DATABASE SOFTWARE DOES

Now that we've taken a general look at different types of database software, let's circle back to the functionality of database software. We'll start with the concept of a collection—a list.

The simplest kind of database is a list. It could be a list of employees or products or soccer teams. Consider an employee example. The information that you want to keep track of might look the table shown in Table 1.1.

TABLE 1.1   EMPLOYEE TABLE

First Name	Last Name	Department	Extension
Jane	Smith	Marketing	327
Calvin	Russell	Accounting	231
Renee	Frantz	Shipping	843

In database parlance, a list like this is called a *table*. Many database systems start off like this. Someone got organized and gathered information into one place. As soon as other people notice this, the idea gets extended, and soon the table grows to keep track of other phone numbers as well. The result is shown in Table 1.2.

TABLE 1.2   THE GROWING PHONE DIRECTORY

First	Last	Department	Ext.	Home	Cell
Jane	Smith	Marketing	327	555-1234	555-4453
Calvin	Russell	Accounting	231	555-8760	555-3321
Renee	Frantz	Shipping	843	555-9877	555-1122

As mentioned earlier, this type of database is called a *flat file* database because everything is in one table. Although it's nice to have everything in one place, this kind of structure has shortcomings. In this case, every time someone thinks up a new type of phone number to track, another field needs to get added to the table. If someone doesn't have a particular type of phone number, that field is blank, resulting in a Swiss cheese look to the table. Unused fields take up space in the database and slow things down for larger data sets.

In a relational structure (which is the opposite of flat file), only the first three columns would be in the employee table. The last three columns, which are all essentially just phone numbers, would be moved out to their own table. A label field could be added to identify each type of phone number, with the resulting two tables looking something like those shown in Tables 1.3 and 1.4.

TABLE 1.3   THE REVISED EMPLOYEE TABLE

Emp ID	First	Last	Department
1	Jane	Smith	Marketing
2	Calvin	Russell	Accounting
3	Renee	Frantz	Shipping

TABLE 1.4   THE NEW PHONE TABLE

Emp ID	Label	Number
1	Extension	327
1	Home	555-1234
1	Cell	555-4453
2	Extension	231
2	Home	555-8760
2	Cell	555-3321
3	Extension	843
3	Home	555-9877
3	Cell	555-1122

Note than an additional field has been added: an Employee ID field. This field is used to match up the employees with the phone numbers for each employee, and in relational database terminology, it's called a *key field*. The FileMaker Pro help system refers it as a match field, but they are one and the same. Key fields are used to locate specific records. You'll learn more about key fields later in the book, but for now it's enough to know that key fields are used to link records in different tables.

Although FileMaker Pro can be used to build simple flat file database systems (see Figure 1.1), it really shines at creating relational database systems (see Figure 1.2). Other database products can do this as well, but FileMaker Pro stands alone in the speed and elegance with which you can create such systems. It is truly a rapid application development (RAD) tool.

→ For a thorough introduction to database application development with FileMaker Pro, **see** Chapter 3, "Defining and Working with Fields," **p. 63** and Chapter 4, "FileMaker Fundamentals: Working with Layouts," **p. 89**.

Figure 1.1
FileMaker can be used to construct simple flat-file databases.

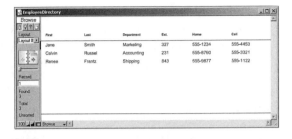

Figure 1.2
The two-table Employee/Phone example can look something like this when implemented in FileMaker.

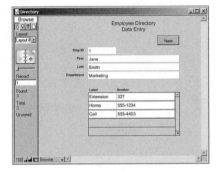

OVERVIEW OF THE FILEMAKER 7 PRODUCT LINE

FileMaker Pro is just one product in a broader product line. It's worth noting the differences between the different products and how they work together.

- **FileMaker Pro 7**—This is the regular desktop version of FileMaker. It can be used to author new database systems, to host systems for a limited number of guests, or to serve as a guest of a hosted system. It can also publish as many as 10 database files to up to 5 users with Instant Web Publishing.

- **FileMaker Server 7**—This is for hosting only databases for FileMaker Pro. FileMaker Server 7 can host a maximum of 125 database files and 250 FileMaker Pro 7 or FileMaker Pro Developer 7 client connections. In addition, it can manage database backup schedules, log usage statistics, disconnect idle users, and manage FileMaker plug-in updates.

- **FileMaker Server 7 Advanced**—FileMaker Server 7 Advanced has all the features of FileMaker Server 7, and can also host ODBC/JDBC and Web-based client connections. It has the same limit of 250 connections for FileMaker Pro and ODBC/JDBC client connections, but Web connections can have an additional 100 client connections (see Figure 1.3).

- **FileMaker Pro Developer 7**—This is similar to the regular version of FileMaker Pro, except that it has additional functionality aimed at application developers. A Script Debugger feature allows developers to walk through scripts one step at a time, and to watch the effect of each script step. The Database Design Report (DDR) feature enables developers to document and troubleshoot development issues from a system-wide perspective. The developer version also enables you to define custom functions that can be used in calculations.

The Developer Edition also comes with a run-time binder that allows developers to bundle database solutions with the FileMaker engine so that users won't need to own FileMaker to run the database solution. The Developer Edition also comes with sample code to assist developers in working with ODBC, XML, and so on.

Figure 1.3
You can mix and match the maximum number of different types of client connections with FileMaker Server 7 Advanced.

- **FileMaker Mobile**—FileMaker Mobile is a slimmed down version of FileMaker designed to run on Palm and Pocket PC PDAs. FileMaker Mobile can synchronize with the regular version of FileMaker so that portions of system data can be taken out on a Palm or Pocket PC device. When that device reconnects with the network, any changes that have been made can be synchronized into the main system.

FILEMAKER DEPLOYMENT OPTIONS

After a database application has been developed in FileMaker Pro, it can be deployed in a variety of ways, and on a variety of operating systems. FileMaker Pro 7 runs on Mac OS X 10.2 or later and on Microsoft Windows 2000 or later. The following sections describe different ways to configure a FileMaker database system deployment.

SINGLE USER

Many people get their start in FileMaker development by building a small application for their personal use. Although FileMaker Pro is inherently a networkable application, there's nothing wrong with a single user working with a system on his or her computer.

PEER-TO-PEER HOSTING

The next stage in a typical system evolution is that other people notice the system that a single person made, and they want to use it also. It's a simple matter to enable FileMaker Network Sharing on a file, and after that's been done, other FileMaker users can become guests of one user's shared file. This kind of FileMaker hosting is called peer-to-peer because the database host and the database clients are all using the same application—desktop versions of FileMaker Pro.

1

You should keep some considerations in mind with this type of hosting. Only 5 files at a time can be hosted on a single machine this way. Up to 10 users can be guests of a file hosted in this fashion. Another consideration is that if you're the host of a file, you can't close the file while other users are working with it.

FILEMAKER SERVER HOSTING

If a FileMaker database needs to be shared by multiple FileMaker users, using FileMaker Server is the best way to host it. FileMaker Server is optimized for hosting, and it can host more files (125) to more users (250) than FileMaker Pro can. It has several other features that make it a better database host. You can remotely administer the server, create schedules for automated database backups, set the server to encrypt the network traffic between the server and the clients, and log server actions.

→ For more information about hosting database files with FileMaker Server, **see** Chapter 25, "FileMaker Server," **p. 737**.

FILEMAKER SERVER ADVANCED HOSTING

FileMaker Server Advanced can host files for FileMaker users just as FileMaker Server can, but it can also allow ODBC/JDBC clients to access hosted files. ODBC/JDBC count against the 250 user limit. FileMaker Server Advanced can also act as a Web host, allowing up to an additional 100 user connections for Web clients.

→ For more information about hosting database files for ODBC/JDBC access, **see** Chapter 20, "Getting Data Out of FileMaker," **p. 563**.

KIOSK MODE

Using FileMaker Developer, you can configure FileMaker databases to run without the menu bar. This mode is called *kiosk mode*, and it's ideal for information or data entry kiosks. Some extra programming is required because the menu items are no longer available in this mode. If you want the user to be able to search or make new records, scripts and buttons have to be created to make up for the lost menu functionality.

EXTENDING THE FUNCTIONALITY OF FILEMAKER PRO

Your deployment can be enhanced by incorporating plug-ins that extend the functionality of FileMaker Pro. Certain specialized math functions such as those used in financial services or chemistry are not standard in FileMaker's function list. Developers can create custom plug-ins to add these functions to FileMaker's repertoire. Some plug-in developers have gone way beyond math functions to create plug-ins that talk to the serial port or authenticate credit card transactions or even work with biometric devices to authenticate users by their thumb prints.

→ For a list of Web sites that list available FileMaker plug-ins, **see** Appendix A, "Additional Resources," **p. 799**.

WHAT'S NEW IN FILEMAKER PRO 7

FileMaker, the database product, has been around since 1985, and it has undergone a lot of evolution during that time. The immediate predecessor product to FileMaker Pro 7, FileMaker Pro 6, was already a very mature and time-tested application. As mature as the product was, though, FileMaker Pro 7 represents a quantum leap in functionality. We'll do some quick technical specification comparisons to give you an idea of the significance of the changes.

TECHNICAL SPECIFICATIONS

One of the easiest ways to see what's changed in the product is to compare specifications between FileMaker Pro 6 and FileMaker Pro 7 (see Table 1.5).

TABLE 1.5   FILEMAKER PRO 6 AND 7 FEATURE COMPARISON

Feature	FileMaker Pro 6	FileMaker Pro 7
Number of tables per file	1	1,000,000
Maximum file size	2 gigabytes	8 terabytes
Maximum amount of data in a text field	64,000 characters	2 gigabytes of data
Number of significant digits in a number field	14	The first 400 significant digits are indexed, including integers, decimals, and signs. Nonnumeric data, such as letters, is available in the index (for find requests) but is not evaluated in calculations and relationships.
Number of characters in a number field	120	800: 400 on either side of the decimal
Maximum number of files allowed open on the client	50	Limited only by memory
Maximum records per file (theoretical limit)	100 million	64 quadrillion over the lifetime of the file
Maximum amount of data allowed in a container field	2 gigabytes theoretically. This is the file size limit.	4 gigabytes
Maximum number of fields in a table	5,900, depending on the length of field names	256 million over the lifetime of the file
Number of script steps supported by Instant Web Publishing	10	74
Number of FileMaker clients hosted by FileMaker Server	250	250
Number of Web clients hosted by FileMaker Server Advanced	N/A	100

FILE FORMAT

The file format for FileMaker 7 is radically different from earlier versions of FileMaker Pro. Earlier versions of the product were limited to one table per file, whereas FileMaker 7 allows one million tables per file. Not only is the file format different, but the network protocol that FileMaker uses to communicate between hosts and guests is different as well. That means that if you need to, you can run both FileMaker 6 and FileMaker 7 on the same network and the two versions won't "see" each other on the network. After you convert FileMaker 6 files into FileMaker 7, the FileMaker 7 versions will no longer be readable by FileMaker 6. "Conversion" in this sense is actually a misnomer, because when FileMaker 7 converts a FileMaker 6 file, the original file is left untouched. Instead, FileMaker 7 uses the original to create a new version of the file.

Along with the file format change comes some dramatic benefits. Our favorite one is that if your database crashes, files no longer become corrupted (we can vouch for this). Also, you can now make changes to everything—field definitions, table definitions, access privileges—while the database is being hosted with guests logged on.

RELATIONSHIPS GRAPH

The Relationships Graph is a graphical representation of the relationships between table occurrences. We say "table occurrences" because there can now be only a single relationship between two table occurrences. If you need to have multiple relationships between two tables, you need to display those tables multiple times on the Relationships Graph—hence the term *table occurrence*.

In Figure 1.4, the Relationships Graph shows that because there are two different relationships between Person and Team Member, the Person table has two occurrences on the chart.

Figure 1.4
This Relationships Graph shows two occurrences of the Person table, each with a different relationship.

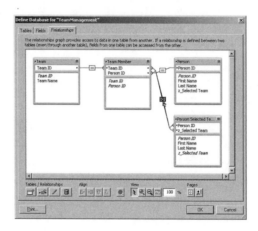

→ For more on the Relationships Graph, **see** "Adding a Relationship," **p. 157**.

ENHANCED RELATIONSHIP FUNCTIONALITY

In previous versions of FileMaker Pro, relationships could be constructed only on the basis of a key field (match field) in one file being equal to a key field in another file. These relationships, or joins, are known as *equijoins* in relational database terminology. FileMaker Pro 7 supports multiple join types. Now relationships can be constructed where one value is less than, greater than, or not equal to the other value.

In addition to the multiple join types, FileMaker 7 also supports complex joins, or joins with more than one criteria. In Figure 1.5, the new Edit Relationship dialog clearly shows the different join types and the multiple join criteria.

Figure 1.5
This relationship shows all team members for the selected Team ID, excluding the current person's record.

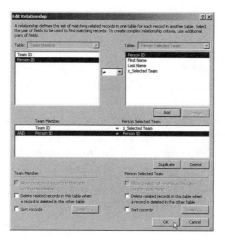

MULTIPLE WINDOWS PER FILE

For the first time, a user can have more than one window open per file, and more importantly, more than one window open per table (because it is now possible to have multiple tables per file). Imagine that you're looking at a list of customers to review unpaid orders when the phone rings. A different customer is on the line, and he wants to discuss his last statement. In earlier versions of FileMaker, you would lose the found set of unpaid order customers while you went and found the record for the calling customer. In FileMaker Pro 7, you can just create a new window while still in the customer table. You can find the caller's record in that window while still preserving your found set in the original window. This feature alone has significant implications in how FileMaker database developers need to think about the system interface.

SECURITY

Security administration in previous versions of FileMaker had several shortcomings. The biggest problem was that you couldn't revise security settings without kicking all users out of the system. Mission-critical database systems, however, can't be brought down without disrupting the organization that they serve. In FileMaker 7, database administrators can change any security settings while the system is up and running and while users already logged in.

The next biggest problem was that security settings were local to each file, and because each file could contain only a single table, this meant that complex systems with several tables were onerous to maintain in regard to security settings. There was no way to have centralized security administration without constructing your own secure login system, which many developers did. FileMaker 7 centralizes security in that all security settings for a particular file control access for all tables in that file. However, to the extent that tables are separated into separate files, multiple security settings still need to be maintained. For example, some developers advocate having separate files for tables and for the interface that controls the data in those files. In that case, the database administrator has to create two sets of security settings: one set for the file containing the data tables and one set for the file containing all the interface elements.

There were other, more minor problems as well, such as the inability to use the user's network login information to authenticate the user to the database. The result was that users had to log in to the computer and then log in to the database system. From a pure security standpoint, that was an added level of security, but from the user standpoint, it was irritating, and another password that had to be remembered. FileMaker 7 has the capability to authenticate in different ways. The standard way is for the usernames and passwords to be stored in the database. FileMaker Pro can also authenticate through FileMaker Server, which can refer to external authentication resources. Such resources might be an LDAP server on the network, or just the Windows workgroup server that controls access to the network.

NOTE

LDAP stands for *Lightweight Directory Access Protocol*. A LDAP server acts as a centralized list of resources on the network. The LDAP server determines whether a particular logged-in user's computer can "see" network resources such as printers, file servers, and hosted FileMaker databases, and presents them to the user as selectable options. In the case of FileMaker servers, however, that doesn't prevent a user from locating the server independently of the LDAP server.

Another problem with previous versions of FileMaker was that passwords couldn't be given expiration dates. In FileMaker 7, passwords can be set to expire every *x* number of days. In addition, they can also be specified to have a required number of characters, and users can be required to change their passwords at the next logon.

These are just a few of the changes to FileMaker's security features. There are too many to describe them all here.

→ For a complete overview of FileMaker's new security features, **see** Chapter 12, "Implementing Security," **p. 315**.

1

CALCULATIONS

The calculation functionality has changed considerably in FileMaker Pro 7. One of our favorite changes is the ability you now have to comment anywhere within the formula of a calculation. Almost every FileMaker developer has had the experience of revisiting a calculation that was devised months before. It always takes time to re-familiarize yourself with a complex formula, and this commenting feature helps out immensely.

For the first time ever, FileMaker can format text as the result of a calculation. There's a new class of functions called *text formatting functions*, and they enable you to manipulate the size, color, font, and style of text.

FileMaker has also now enabled you to create your own custom functions by using FileMaker Developer 7. In previous versions of FileMaker Pro, you needed to author a plug-in to add custom functions. Now you can use FileMaker Developer to add them to a file, and reference those functions in calculations while using a regular version of FileMaker Pro 7.

SCRIPTS

Scripts can now be set to run with full access privileges on a script-by-script basis. This is extremely useful if you have users with a low level of system access who need to run scripts that perform actions (such as deleting or modifying records) that require a higher level of access. The script itself can be authorized to do what the user cannot.

Scripts can also be set to be available for execution from the Web. In conjunction with custom extended privileges (yet another new feature in the revised security system), scripts can also check the privileges of the current user and conditionally perform actions based on the privilege set or extended privileges that have been assigned to that user.

LAYOUTS

Layouts have changed as well, especially the controls on the table view. You now have control over the user's ability to reorder columns, resize columns, and sort data when a column header is clicked.

On a layout-by-layout basis, you can decide whether record changes will be automatically saved, as they were in previous versions of FileMaker Pro, or whether the user needs to deliberately commit the record to save changes.

For each layout, you can specify whether the Tab, Return, or Enter key advances the user from field to field, and you can also allow fields to be entered in find mode but not in browse mode (or vice versa).

WEB

Instant Web Publishing has been greatly enhanced, and is much more powerful than ever before. FileMaker Pro 7 can still host it on a limited basis, and FileMaker Server 7 Advanced can host up to 100 Web connections.

SERVER

FileMaker Server can now host up to 250 FileMaker client users at once, and when using FileMaker Server Advanced, it can host Web connections and ODBC/JDBC (Windows only) connections as well. One of the server administration options is to encrypt the network traffic between FileMaker Server and the FileMaker Pro clients or Web Publishing Engine clients.

FileMaker Server can also be the authentication authority for hosted systems, and it can in turn authenticate users with domain or workgroup servers.

## CHAPTER 2

USING FILEMAKER PRO

In this chapter

GETTING STARTED

It's time to roll up your sleeves and actually put FileMaker Pro to use. Most of this book deals with being a FileMaker Pro developer—someone who is focused on the programming side of creating and managing FileMaker Pro solutions. However, ironically, development comprises only a small percentage of the overall time a given database gets used. Much of the time a FileMaker solution will simply "be in use," and its users will care nothing for scripting, calculations, or the vagaries of user-interface design. They will simply be involved with working with your creation and will not need to know anything of the development side of FileMaker Pro.

Becoming facile in working with FileMaker Pro databases will prove quite helpful in allowing you to quickly access the information you want and to understand the underpinnings of any database, regardless of user interface.

This chapter introduces you to how to make the most of FileMaker databases that have already been built. All FileMaker databases—often called *solutions*, *systems*, or *applications*—have certain common elements, and becoming adept in developing FileMaker Pro solutions will not only help you manipulate and analyze data better, but will assist you in extending what you can accomplish with that data. We'll cover some broad concepts at first, move into the nuts and bolts of working with databases, and finally wrap things up with some techniques to help you become a FileMaker Pro power user.

One quick note before we begin: This chapter assumes you bought this rather hefty tome for a reason (unless of course you're one of the authors' mothers), namely that you want to learn as much as you can about FileMaker Pro. Although the concepts and functions described in this chapter can be fairly basic (how to open a database, for example), it also covers a fair number of advanced topics as well. This chapter is a good place to start if you're unfamiliar with FileMaker Pro, or if you still don't quite feel comfortable using a FileMaker Pro database.

Before going much further, we need to be clear on some basic FileMaker Pro vocabulary. *Databases* store collections of information, and one of their primary functions is to properly identify the information they store. It's not enough to simply save the text strings "Pink Floyd" and "Dark Side of the Moon" in a file. For a database to be useful, you need to know that Pink Floyd is a band and that the *Dark Side of the Moon* is an album (one of the greatest of all time!).

For a database to fulfill its primary function, a developer needs to have properly identified all the appropriate elements of information you or your organization wishes to store and use. It is in these identifications that information becomes meaningful.

RECORDS AND FIELDS

Databases store information about one or more different kinds of "items." For example, a database might store information about music albums, or musicians, or guitar manufacturers. In FileMaker, each individual item is referred to as a *record*. So in a database of music CDs, each record represents an individual CD.

To track the attributes of items or specific information—for example, *Dark Side of the Moon*'s release date of March 24, 1973—*fields* are defined, specific to each type of item. These fields hold and also identify the type of information found for each record. Examples of fields that might be found in the music CD database are release date, recording studio, and so on.

In FileMaker Pro you will be working with a specific individual record at a time and will be viewing (and storing) information from that record's fields.

NOTE

> For those of you familiar with SQL, a *row* corresponds to a *record* in FileMaker Pro, and a *column* corresponds to a *field*.

→ For more information on SQL and how it relates to FileMaker Pro, **see** "Importing from an ODBC Data Source," **p. 552**.

TABLES

It's important to have a grasp of what a table is when working with FileMaker Pro.

Simply stated, a *table* is a collection of like records. You might have a table of automobile model records and another table of manufacturer records. Miata would belong in the automobile table, and Mazda in the manufacturer table. From the music example, music albums would belong to a table, musicians to another, and genres to another. An album isn't a genre, and nor are musicians the same as the albums they create.

For the purposes of using FileMaker Pro, you really need to remember one thing: every layout (a view or form for data) in FileMaker Pro is associated with a specific table. If you look at a layout with a picture of a Mazda Miata, and fields that break out the attributes of that car, more than likely you're in an automobiles table. If you see a layout with "Mazda" at the top and multiple car models listed, you're more than likely in the manufacturer table. This will come into play later in the chapter when you begin working with multiple records and found sets.

→ To explore working with multiple record sets, **see** "Working with a Found Set," **p. 47**, later in this chapter.

NOTE

NEW

> In FileMaker Pro, you can have as many tables in a single file (`.fp7` document) as you need, and FileMaker Pro 7 is a fully relational database platform. Versions of FileMaker since version 3's introduction in 1995 were also fully relational, but prior versions allowed only one table per file.
>
> Database solutions would often be collections of files and require that you open all these multiple files at once to use a solution. Now in FileMaker 7, you can consolidate solutions into single files with multiple tables.

→ To dig deeper into working with multiple tables and understanding relational data models, **see** Chapter 6, "Working with Multiple Tables," **p. 153**, and "Understanding Relationships," **p. 130**.

2

FILEMAKER PRO NAVIGATION

One of the first things you'll want to do when you open a database in FileMaker Pro is navigate the various screens, called *layouts*, that the developer designed as the interface for the database. Using these layouts, you can view records, enter data into fields, see reports, run scripts, and more.

There are two important work areas to distinguish from one another in a FileMaker Pro database: the Status Area on the left and the Layout area on the right (see Figure 2.1).

Layout area—this is just one example of many
possible layouts in FileMaker Pro. It is your work area.

Figure 2.1
These are the primary areas of all FileMaker Pro databases; in some cases, however, a developer might have hidden the Status Area.

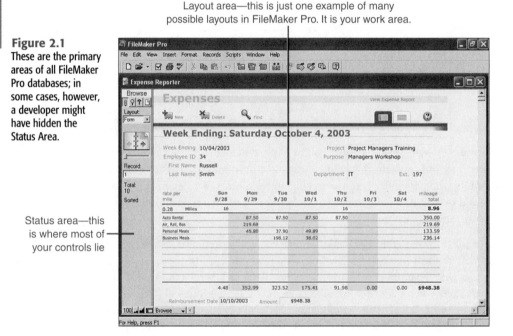

Status area—this is where most of your controls lie

LAYOUTS

Most FileMaker Pro databases open to a data entry layout. Generally you have access to fields, commonly designated by a field border or embossing of some kind (again depending on the design or dementia of the database's developer), or you may come across a layout used for reporting purposes only. Figures 2.2, 2.3, and 2.4 illustrate just a few examples of layouts that you might find with databases created in FileMaker Pro.

THE STATUS AREA   The Status Area serves as a primary control center for FileMaker Pro. In *Browse mode*—the state in which all data entry and general use occurs—the Status Area displays a book icon and other elements for navigating a database solution.

Figure 2.2
FileMaker's built-in templates offer a simple, clean interface. Shown here are a *form layout* (one record per screen) and a *list layout* (multiple records per screen).

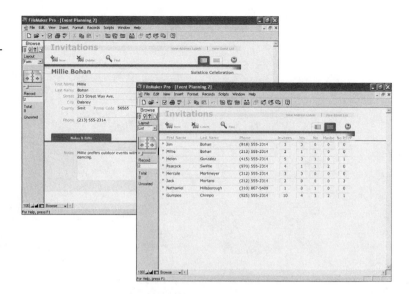

Figure 2.3
FileMaker Applications—commercially available database solutions from FileMaker, Inc.—demonstrate the possibilities of more feature-rich systems. (Screenshots provided by permission of FileMaker, Inc.)

Figure 2.4
Here's a departure from the staid designs of typical productivity applications!

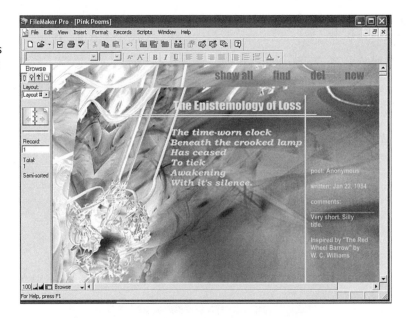

FileMaker Pro has four modes, which we'll explain later in this chapter. For now, note that the Status Area changes depending on which mode you're using. In Find mode it allows access to search functions and special search wildcard characters. In Layout mode the Status Area contains most of the tools used for controlling the look and feel of your database.

Figure 2.5 details the various elements of the Status Area, as it appears in Browse mode.

Figure 2.5
Note the various functions of the Status Area in Browse mode. To jump to a specific record, type a number into the record number field and press Enter.

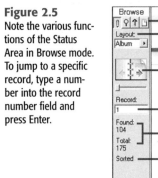
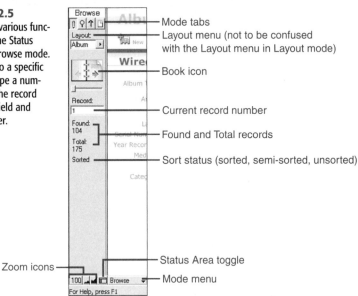

- Mode tabs
- Layout menu (not to be confused with the Layout menu in Layout mode)
- Book icon
- Current record number
- Found and Total records
- Sort status (sorted, semi-sorted, unsorted)
- Status Area toggle
- Zoom icons
- Mode menu

The elements of the Status Area include:

- **Layout Pop-up Menu**—Enables you to navigate from layout to layout in your database.

- **Book Icon**—The book icon enables you to page through each record in your database. You stay on the same layout, but you see the information for each record in your database as you click through your records. The slider below enables you to jump ahead and back by multiple records.

- **Current Record Number**—Not to be confused with a record identifier, key, or ID, this number indicates which record in your current set you're viewing. FileMaker Pro allows you to establish *found sets*—groups of records with which you're currently working—and this number shows where your current record lies relative to the found set.

- **Found and Total Records**—These numbers show how many records are in your found set compared to the total in your entire database. Found sets are covered in more detail later in the chapter.

- **Sort Status**—FileMaker Pro allows you to order your records based on some criterion. Depending on how your found set has been sorted, the Status Area shows "sorted," "semi-sorted," or "unsorted." A semi-sorted state would occur if you were to sort the records in your database and then created a new record.

- **Zoom Icons**—These allow you to zoom in and out on a given layout.

- **Status Area Toggle**—Allows you to show and hide the Status Area.

- **Mode Menu**—This pop-up menu functions in the same way as the mode icons.

CAUTION

> You'll notice something missing from FileMaker Pro: back and forward buttons. It's important that you not confuse the book icon with such. The book icon enables you to page back and forward through your *data* as opposed to paging through your layouts in Browse mode.
>
> Some users familiar with the Web might expect the book icon to step forward and back through their navigation history within a database.

FILEMAKER PRO MODES

You'll interact with your FileMaker Pro databases via one of four modes. At times, developers choose to tailor a layout for use with a specific mode, but more often than not layouts can be effectively used with all four.

To familiarize you with the four modes, here's a simple description of each. To switch between modes, use the View menu.

- **Browse Mode**—Browse mode is FileMaker Pro's "primary" mode, where all data entry occurs, and generally the one that you'll primarily interact with in a given solution.

- **Find Mode**—Here one creates and then performs *find requests* to search for specific sets of records or information in a given solution.

- **Preview Mode**—When preparing to print from FileMaker Pro, you may opt to switch to Preview mode to see what a given layout will look like after it is printed. Developers may also build Preview mode steps into their reporting functions so that you can review a document before sending it to a printer.

- **Layout Mode**—It is in Layout mode that most development occurs. Here developers can manipulate all the elements of a given layout, including controlling all the things that appear on that layout.

NOTE

You can change modes in three other ways: Use the menu at the lower left of your screen, use the mode tabs at the top of the Status Area, or a developer may program a number of different functions and/or buttons that switch modes.

VIEWS

In addition to the modes of FileMaker Pro, there are three *views* as well. To change between them, use the View menu as well.

- **Form view**—Allows you to see and manipulate only one record at a time (see Figure 2.6).

Figure 2.6
Form view is usually where most data entry is performed.

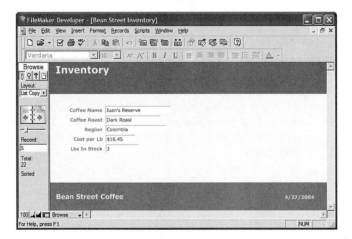

- **List view**—Here you can display multiple records. At any given moment, you still are working with only one specific record while still being able to view the rest (see Figure 2.7).

- **Table view**—Table view simply displays the raw data for a given record (depending on what fields have been placed on a layout). It looks quite similar to a spreadsheet application (see Figure 2.8). This is extremely handy for reviewing large groups of data quickly without pesky user interface elements getting in the way. A developer has little control over how a Table view appears.

Figure 2.7
List views can also include summary data.

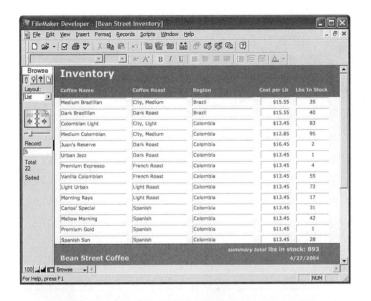

Figure 2.8
In Table view you can automatically resize, move, and sort with column headers.

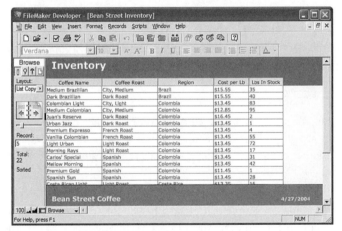

BUTTONS

Notice we've largely been talking about fields on layouts. Most FileMaker Pro solutions also include buttons. Figure 2.9 shows a few examples.

Buttons trigger actions—often by launching scripts that developers write—and are specific to a given FileMaker Pro database. Buttons can perform dozens of actions, such as creating a new record, deleting a record, navigating to another layout, performing a calculation, performing a find request, controlling windows, even spell-checking and emitting a simple "beep." The possibilities are nearly endless.

You'll need to become familiar with the specifics of a given FileMaker Pro solution to come to understand what its buttons do. The person who built the system should have those details, or should have provided some form of training or documentation.

Figure 2.9
Buttons can come in all shapes and sizes in FileMaker Pro. Text can be a button, a field can be a button, and even just a mysterious blank area in the middle of a layout can be a button.

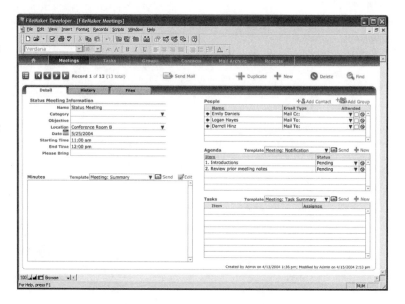

WORKING IN FILEMAKER PRO

It's time to dive in. This next section walks you through working in some typical FileMaker Pro situations and addresses many of the common tasks you need to be able to perform.

OPENING A DATABASE

The first step, obviously, is opening a database. FileMaker Pro databases can live in various places. They can sit on your own computer, just as any other document might, they can be hosted by another computer, or they can be served by FileMaker Server.

LOCAL FILES

Opening a local file is a simple matter of either double-clicking its icon in either your Windows environment or in the Mac OS X Finder. You may also use FileMaker Pro's File, Open command.

REMOTE FILES

Working with remote files requires connecting to a server—which could be a database hosted on *FileMaker Server* (the software that allows you to host a FileMaker database for use across a LAN or WAN by up to 250 users)—or simply to a file set to multi-user on another person's workstation. To a client computer, there's no distinction. FileMaker Pro treats both cases as a remote connection.

To open a remote database, click the Remote button in the open dialog, or choose Open Remote from the File menu.

As shown in Figure 2.10, you may choose from those hosts available to you locally (those on your network, within your domain in corporate environments, or accessible on the Internet), or you can opt to access files via a secure LDAP server.

Figure 2.10
Use the Open Remote File dialog to open a database on a LAN, in a corporate domain, or (with a proper IP address) across the Internet.

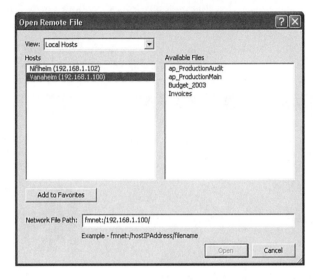

NOTE

Note that some solutions contain multiple files. A developer can opt to hide some files from the remote hosts dialog and therefore present only a "launch" or menu file as needed.

TIP

If you work in a large organization, your server list can become quite cluttered. Use the Favorite Hosts menu option for those you most frequently use. It enables you to add all the files from a server or just those you want.

CAUTION

Opening a FileMaker database across an Internet connection is entirely possible, but you should be aware that connection speeds will vary, depending on your network, hardware, and the specific FileMaker Pro database. Don't plan on making this a deployment strategy until you've properly tested both your solution itself and your users' connections to it.

 If you've run into what might appear to be a corrupted file, refer to "File Corruption and File Recovery" in the Troubleshooting section at the end of this chapter.

2

CREATING A NEW DATABASE FROM A TEMPLATE

Because this could be your first foray into FileMaker Pro, you may not yet have a database to tinker with. FileMaker Pro's templates are a great place to start. Ordinarily, you'd likely be working with a database either you or some other developer created; however, for our purposes, let's walk through how to open and use one of FileMaker Pro's existing templates.

Navigate to File, New Database. Then select Create a New File Using a Template. The New Database dialog box shown in Figure 2.11 appears.

Figure 2.11
Dozens of templates ship with FileMaker Pro, ranging from an invoicing system to a tool to organize your personal DVD collection.

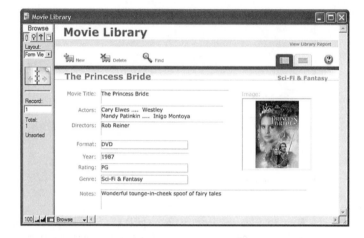

You are encouraged to explore FileMaker's templates. They are fairly simple databases that show by example how FileMaker Pro can be used, and can also give you a jump-start on creating your own database solutions.

CREATING AND DELETING RECORDS

Creating and deleting records in FileMaker Pro is simple. Under the Records menu, choose New Record, Delete Record, or Duplicate Record. Notice also there's a Delete All Records option. For now, let's explore how to take care of simple data entry.

CAUTION

Keep in mind, even though there's an Undo command in the Edit menu, it doesn't work at the record level. After a record is committed, it is a part of your database. After you delete a record, it's gone forever.

If you are in the midst of entering data in a record and want to undo the entry, use the Revert Record command under the Records menu. A record is saved—or *committed*—automatically when you click outside a field for the first time, change modes, change layouts, or press the Enter key. FileMaker Pro uses the term *commit* to indicate when a record is posted, or saved, to your database.

If Revert Record doesn't seem to do anything, refer to "Reverting Records" in the Troubleshooting section at the end of this chapter.

NOTE

> You never need to save a FileMaker Pro database. As users commit records, those records are automatically stored in the database file. If you want to save a copy of your database or create a duplicate for backup purposes, the Save As option under the File menu will serve.

If you have trouble with apparently lost data, refer to "Data Loss" in the Troubleshooting section at the end of this chapter.

WORKING WITH FIELDS

If you're used to other productivity applications or have ever filled out a form on the Web, you should find data entry quite familiar in FileMaker Pro.

Fields generally look like embossed or bordered areas with labels off to one side or the other. Keep in mind: developers control the look and feel of their systems, so it's entirely possible that someone could build a database with no labels, fields that are the same color as their background, and white text on a white background. Thankfully, when a field is being actively edited, the other fields on a given layout are highlighted by a dotted border, indicating you're in the midst of editing a record (see Figure 2.12). That at least will help you see which fields allow entry and which don't.

Dotted line indicates that the record is currently being edited.

Figure 2.12
FileMaker's field borders indicate the edit state of a record.

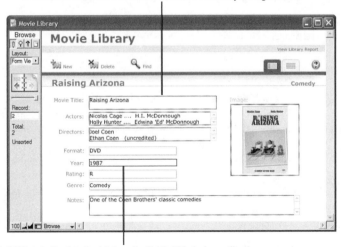

Solid line indicates that this specific field is being edited.

Editing fields is as easy as clicking into them, typing some text, and clicking out again.

NOTE

> Moving from field to field can be managed on your keyboard if you simply press the Tab key. Some solutions may also support the Return and Enter keys.

→ For discussion on how to control this behavior from a development perspective, **see** "Working with Fields," **p. 114**.

You'll work with a few different formats of fields in FileMaker Pro:

- **Edit Box**—Allows standard keyboard entry and sometimes includes a scrollbar.
- **Pop-Up List**—When first clicking into the field, you are presented with a list of options from which you may select, or alternatively you may type directly into the field.
- **Pop-Up Menu**—A pop-up menu is similar to a pop-up list, except that a pop-up menu does not allow typing directly into the field and thus allows values from only the menu in question.

CAUTION

> Just as on the Web, it is possible to Shift-click multiple values in a pop-up list; however, only one value (the first selected) will be visible, and you may get unexpected results from using this technique.

- **Check Box Set**—Check boxes allow multiple values per field.
- **Radio Button Set**—Similar to check boxes, with the exception that they are mutually exclusive. A user can select only one value at a time.

CAUTION

> We lied. Shift-clicking allows a user to select multiple values in a radio button set. Unless field validation is set up to check for it, selecting multiple values in a pop-up menu or in radio button sets is generally a bad idea. Again, you will end up with unpredictable results because you're making an exception to a formatting choice meant to allow for only one value in a given field.

Figure 2.13 contains examples of these field formats.

DATA IN FORMATTED FIELDS

You might find it helpful to understand *how* multiple-value data is stored in fields: remember that check boxes, radio buttons, pop-up lists, and pop-up menus are all nothing more than data-entry assistants. The actual data stored is a collection of values delimited by line returns. This means that you can accomplish the same result, from a data perspective, by simply entering a return-delimited list of values into your fields. This is an important thing to remember when performing find requests, which we'll cover later in this chapter.

Figure 2.13
Using field formatting can make data entry more intuitive. Notice that all four types are present, though in a real database only one field would be active at a time.

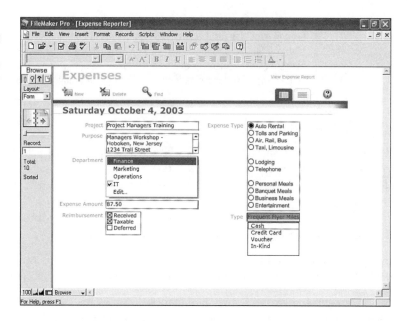

→ To understand more about how multiple values in a field can lead to relational data structure problems, **see** Chapter 5, "Relational Database Design," **p. 123**.

MODIFYING VALUE LISTS

Often, you might need to add new values to a value list—the list that is used to create pop-up lists and menus, check boxes, and radio button items. Developers have the option of including an Edit option at the bottoms of their menu fields. Selecting Edit then brings up a dialog that you may change or add to a list as needed (see Figure 2.14).

Figure 2.14
Editing value lists is a simple way to fine-tune a database to your specific needs without having to dig into programming.

To edit the items in a value list, simply type text into the Edit Value List dialog, followed by a carriage return. A hyphen adds a separator to the list.

NOTE

Keep in mind that just because you replaced an old menu item with a new category—for example, "autos" becomes "cars"–it won't change the actual values stored in your database's records. Remember that field formatting is nothing more than a data entry assistant. By changing the assistant menu, you have *not* changed any data in your database.

USING THE "OTHER" VALUE IN VALUE LISTS

Radio button sets and check boxes work a bit differently. Developers do not have the choice to add an edit function to these formats; rather, they may include an Other option. This allows a user to enter virtually any custom text they want, from a single value to Grandmother's recipe for apple pie. Regardless of the value, the check box or radio button option that would be visibly displayed is Other; however, the data stored and included in the field's index includes whatever your other data is.

In contrast to adding values to a value list and changing the options available on all records, the Other function simply enables you to enter custom text into a specific record's field.

As you can guess, developers often disable these features. Just remember that all you're doing is using field formatting to help in entering consistent data.

FIELD TYPES

In addition to enabling you to control how data gets entered into a field, FileMaker Pro databases use specified kinds of fields for different types of information.

Field formatting is independent from field types. For example, it's entirely possible to format a calculation field as a check box. Although you as a user may expect to be able to click on a check box, FileMaker Pro will then prompt you and explain that calculation fields are not modifiable.

It's incumbent on the developer to sensibly identify for a given system's users which fields expect what sort of data. Often field labels make this clear. For example, you can often expect a Price field to be a number, and an Invoice Date field will no doubt be a date type.

The following list describes the field types available in FileMaker Pro:

- **Text**—Allows a user to enter approximately 2GB of information, including carriage returns. Sorting by a text field is alphabetical.
- **Number**—Stores up to 800 digits and sorts as typical numbers.
- **Date**—Gregorian calendar, 1/1/0001 through 12/31/4000. It's a good practice, but not required, to use four-digit years when doing data entry. Sorting is by year, month, and day, as one would expect.
- **Time**—Hours, minutes, and seconds. Again, sorting is based on a typical 24-hour clock.
- **Timestamp**—Timestamps are a tool generally used by database developers to identify exactly when a record has been created or modified. It combines a date with a time and

looks like "6/28/1998 2:00 AM." For the user, occasionally you may want to use a time-stamp for performing a find.

- **Container**—Container fields hold just about any binary information, be it an image, a movie, a PDF document, a Word document, or a file archive. These fields cannot be used for sorting purposes.

The use of container fields should be immediately obvious. Capable of holding up to 4GB files, one can use FileMaker Pro for managing all sorts of digital assets.

Data entry for container fields is slightly different from other types: You need to either paste a file or image into the field or use the Insert menu.

TIP

One extremely valuable feature is FileMaker Pro's ability to store just references to digital assets in a container field. For all intents and purposes, the application treats that item as though it were stored within FileMaker Pro, while gaining a boost in performance by leaving it outside FileMaker Pro's internal files.

- **Calculation**—A calculation field stores the result of a formula, based on other fields or related information in your system. The resultant data is specified by type so that one can return a date, time, and so on. It's even possible for a calculation field to be a container.

NOTE

Calculation fields by definition are not modifiable by an end user; however, don't forget that you can access them for performing finds, sorts, and so on.

- **Summary**—Summary fields are similar to calculations, but return information from your found set, or current group, of records. A total, for example, totals a field across your current set of records. Other functions include averaging, totals, maximum, minimum, and so on.

GLOBAL STORAGE

Fields in your database generally pertain to a specific, individual record. The baseball team field for your San Francisco record holds "The Giants," whereas for Chicago it's "The Cubs."

In some cases, however, a developer opts to define a field as global. The value in that field, then, is constant throughout the database. Some common examples might be fiscal year start and end dates, your company name, report headers, or a fixed commission rate.

As a user, you might not always be able to tell which fields in your database have been defined to store global values and those that are record specific.

An important thing to keep in mind about global fields is that their behavior varies depending on how you're hosting a database. If you're using a database on your own local machine, with sharing set to single user, all global data is preserved from session to session. In other words, the next time you open the database, your global details remain from the last time you worked with the system.

If you're working with a database hosted on a server, all global information is session specific. It may contain default values, but if you change some data in a global field, other users of the system do not see that change, nor is it preserved for the next time you use the database.

There are often cases where you need those values to "stick" across sessions and for all people. You've got two options: either take the files down from the server and open them locally on a single user machine, or, as a developer, write a script that sets your global information whenever the system is opened.

DATA VALIDATION

Data integrity is one of the primary concerns of any database developer or of the team using a given system. If duplicate records appear, or misspellings and typos plague your database, or worse yet the wrong data is entered into the wrong fields, your system will soon become essentially unreliable. For example, if you run a monthly income report, but in a few of your transaction records someone has entered a date where a transaction amount belongs, your monthly totals will be incorrect.

FileMaker Pro—or any application, for that matter—cannot read users' minds and fully safeguard against bad data, but developers do have a wide range of tools for validating information as it is entered. If your organization can come up with a business rule for validation, a developer can apply that rule to a given field.

Consider the following examples:

- Transaction amounts can be only positive numbers, can have only two decimal places, and cannot exceed 100,000.
- Employee hire dates may be only equal to or later than 1/1/2001.
- Data in a given field must match a value in a given value list and the field does not accept any custom information.
- Company names in the database must be unique.

Understanding that these rules are in place will help you understand the underpinnings of your database application. When a validation check occurs, the system may prompt you with an appropriate message (see Figure 2.15).

In addition to the default dialog in Figure 2.15, a developer can create his or her own custom text: for example, "This transaction amount must be a positive value greater than 99 cents."

If you choose Yes rather than Revert Record, your data is accepted as is and overrides the validation requirement. In some cases you may not have the option of posting an override.

Figure 2.15
This is an example of a default validation message. If you choose Revert Record, whatever data you've entered into the field reverts to its prior state before you started editing.

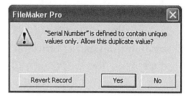

 To explore initial thoughts on addressing data problems, refer to "Data Integrity" in the Troubleshooting section at the end of this chapter.

MANIPULATING RECORDS IN PORTALS

By now you've probably read the word "relational" a few hundred times already in this book. Get used to it. One of FileMaker Pro's core strengths is how it allows you to view and work with related information from a different but connected contextual set of records from other tables.

For example, in a table of car manufacturers you would likely have records for "Audi, BMW, Chrysler, Mazda," and so on. Imagine that you also have a table for car models: "Mazda 6, MX-5 Miata, Protege5," and so on. FileMaker Pro allows you to view a car manufacturer, and on the same layout also see the models specific to that manufacturer (see Figure 2.16).

Figure 2.16
You are in the manufacturer's table, looking at a record for Mazda, while also being able to see records from the car models table.

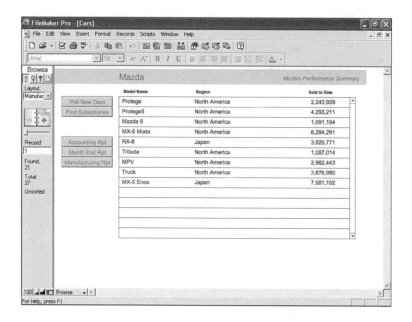

FileMaker Pro allows developers to build *portals* in which related information can be displayed.

UNDERSTANDING THE MECHANICS OF A PORTAL

A *portal* is simply a view into another table and includes specific related records. Developers determine the rules by which records appear in portals and at times these can become dynamic or even display other records in the same table you're currently viewing.

→ To explore the depths of advanced portal development techniques, **see** Chapter 16, "Working with Portals," **p. 445**.

Most portals have a scroll bar on the right. They feel a bit like list views, and act much the same way. To browse through your related records, simply scroll up and down through the list. Data entry works the same way it does in other areas of FileMaker: Simply click into a field and enter whatever data is appropriate.

At times developers include buttons in portals. In this case there appears one identical button in each portal row, and each button acts on the row whose button you clicked.

CREATING AND DELETING PORTAL ROWS

Often, a developer disables the behaviors we're about to describe; however, they're handy to understand and to look for when they are available.

To create a new portal row—which then creates a new child record—scroll to the bottom of a portal and click into the blank row. *Child records* is a term often used to describe related, hierarchically dependent records—for example, Company and Employee. Employees would be considered "children" of a Company.

> **NOTE**
>
> Your developer might have turned off the ability to add or delete portal rows, in which case he or she has likely provided an alternate means of adding related records.

If a developer has allowed for such, you can delete a portal row by following these steps:

1. Click outside the fields of a given portal on the row background. (You might have to mouse around a bit.) You should see the row become highlighted (see Figure 2.17).

2. To delete a portal row, click outside the fields, yet still *within* the portal row. You may then press either the Delete or Backspace keys on your keyboard.

3. You are prompted as to whether or not you want to delete that child record. Click Yes, No, or Cancel to close the dialog box.

PORTAL SORTING

Sorting records is covered later in the chapter. For now, simply note that a developer determines by what means a portal is ordered and that there is no "built-in" portal sorting command in standard FileMaker Pro portals. There are a number of ways a developer can build a dynamically sortable, command-driven portal, but this is not default behavior in FileMaker Pro.

→ To learn how to build sorting portals, **see** "Dynamic Portal Sorting," **p. 468**.

Figure 2.17
Notice that the sixth row in the displayed portal is highlighted. The Delete dialog then pertains to it.

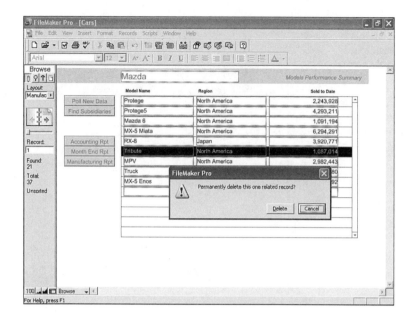

WORKING WITH A FOUND SET

Up to this point, we've discussed working with a single record and the fields on a given form layout. Refer to the Status Area on the left of your screen again. Notice the Found: and Total: numbers.

At every moment of working with an open FileMaker Pro database, you are working with some number of "found" records. Notice the plural. It's also possible that your *found set* contains only one record, or even none; however, generally speaking, you are likely to have many records in your found set.

This is an important point to remember. Even though you may be able to see the contents of only one record's fields (more than likely in Form view), you can still work with either all the records in your table or a subset of such.

Think of it as working with a deck of cards. There are 52 total cards in your deck, some of which are in your hand, and one of which is front-most—visible. Your current record would be akin to that front card and your found set like those cards in your hand.

In FileMaker Pro many functions apply to a found set. A good example is sorting: You are organizing only those records in your found set.

Many FileMaker Pro databases offer layouts tailored to be viewed either in Form view, where one record encompasses the information on the screen, or in List view, where layouts resemble spreadsheets or tables and display multiple records at once. To grasp visually what we're discussing, see Figure 2.18.

Figure 2.18
List views pull data from multiple records. There is a black bar in the left margin that indicates which record is current. The active field and the dotted lines indicate you're currently editing this record.

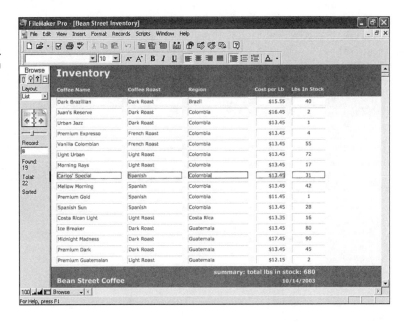

Working with groups of records is important mainly for comprehension and processing of your information. Data entry usually occurs on one individual record at a time, unless you're importing or performing some other function that applies across multiple records. It's in the reporting and analyzing stage that working with multiple records becomes necessary.

One of the first ways to work with a group of records is to simply scan the list. Nothing beats the human brain for processing information.

Summary fields often lie at the bottom of a list view, as shown previously in Figure 2.18, and can total numeric data based on a current found set.

For a quick example of how this might work, imagine a sales database. If you were to find (or search) for all records in January, your summary fields could then total January's sales. If you find again for the year 2003, your totals are annual. The value of the summary field varies depending on your found set.

If you perform different find requests, the information on your screen can deliver different results, specific to a given group of records.

NOTE

> Summary fields are quite powerful, but they do require processor time. If you have a large found set of thousands of records, waiting for a summary field to evaluate can take some time. You can press the Esc key to cancel the summary, or simply avoid scrolling or viewing that portion of a layout. Summary fields evaluate only when they are visible on the screen.

One last important note about found sets: They can be comprised of records from only one table. You cannot display records from an automobile table and a manufacturer table in the same List view or Table view.

USING FIND MODE TO PERFORM A FIND REQUEST

For performing search queries in FileMaker Pro, you need to use one of three options to change to Find mode: the tabs at the top of the Status Area, the menu on the bottom left of your application window, or the View menu. Developers may also opt to put various Find buttons into their systems.

After you're in Find mode, FileMaker Pro waits for you to enter data for your *find request*. A find request is a single entry in Find mode that encapsulates the criteria by which you want to perform a search. It behaves and looks much like a record. You enter data into fields just as you would in Browse mode, but instead of saving records, these requests serve as a means of matching to your actual data. You can add a new request, create multiple requests, and delete requests.

A Find button appears in the Status Area in Find mode. FileMaker Pro enables you to search for any number of criteria throughout your database. Enter whatever fraction of words or data you want on the same layouts you've used in Browse mode, then click the Find button. Any records that match your request are then placed in your found set, replacing the set you had before performing the find.

Figure 2.19 shows the full data set in a database of coffee beans (an inventory database).

Figure 2.19
Notice this is the full found set. There's no "Found:" record count, just a total.

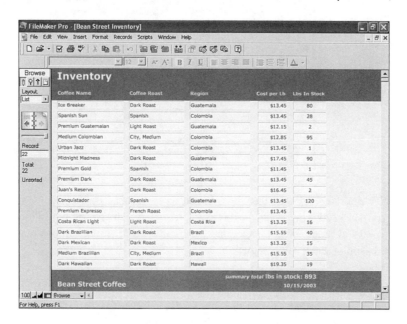

To find a specific set of records, a user would enter Find mode (choose View, Find mode) and type a criteria by which to search. Refer to Figure 2.20. As an example, a user might have typed **dark roast** in the Roast column and then would click Find in the Status Area.

Figure 2.20
FileMaker matches the find criterion "dark roast" against the data in the database after a user clicks Find.

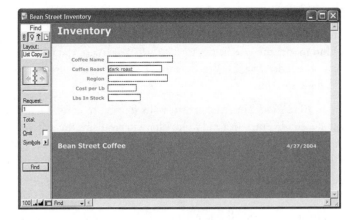

Notice in Figure 2.21 that there are eight records in the resultant found set, all of which are dark roasts. Notice also that the summary total changed appropriately.

Figure 2.21
Note that the first record in the set is always the active, or current, record after a find is performed.

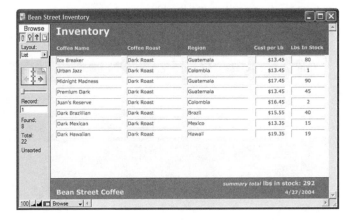

If you perform another find, your found set is replaced by the records matching your new requests (see Figure 2.22). In this example, the search criteria was all coffees with "<3" in the Lbs in Stock field. The result is four coffees that are almost out of stock. (We cover special symbols such as "<" shortly.)

SEARCH SYMBOLS

To create the found set seen in Figure 2.22, a < (less than) symbol was used to act as an operator on the find request. Switch to Find mode again and notice the symbol menu on the left (see Figure 2.23).

Figure 2.22
This figure shows a new found set: These four records are of different roasts, but all are low in inventory with less than 3 lbs. in stock.

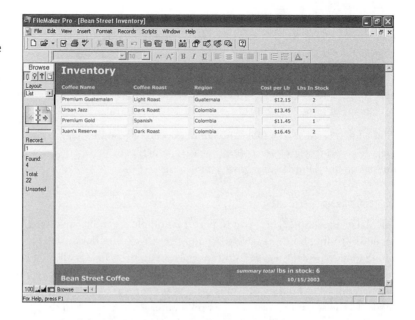

Figure 2.23
Special symbols enable you to search for a wide range of match criteria.

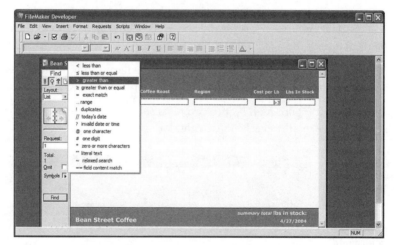

The less than, less than or equal, greater than, greater than or equal, and exact match symbols should be fairly obvious. ">3" finds all records with a value 4 and above. "<=100" finds all records with values of 100 or lower (including zero and negative numbers).

NOTE

> You need not use the symbol menu at all: A < and = typed from your keyboard work just as well as inserting the symbol from the pop-up menu in the Status Area.

The ellipsis (…) for ranges is a commonly used search symbol. "1/1/2003…12/31/2003" returns all records for the year of 2003. (If you're lazy, just type two or three periods from your keyboard.)

Use * and # for wildcards. The # symbol is for one digit exactly. "5#" finds all whole numbers from 50 to 59. The # alone finds just those numbers 1–9. "1#1" finds 101, 121, 131, and so on, but not 211 or 1211.

The ~ for relaxed search looks intriguing, doesn't it? Some fuzzy logic, perhaps? No such luck. It's used to search for common base characters in two-byte Asian phonetic alphabets. It doesn't do anything for any other languages.

MULTIPLE FIND REQUESTS

FileMaker Pro also enables you to perform complex searches involving multiple find requests. To find both the dark roast and French roast coffees, a user would simply enter Find mode, type **dark roast** into the appropriate roast field, and then create a new record/request. Just as you can create new records in Browse mode, you can create and delete requests in Find mode. This process is identical to creating a new record in Browse mode. In the second record, a user would enter **French roast** in the roast field.

A user can flip between requests, using the book icon in the Status Area, and can delete requests as necessary. As soon as the user is satisfied with a series of requests, clicking Find on the left performs the Find and returns the user to Browse mode with a new found set.

Multiple Find Requests can also include requests meant to be omitted. Say that a user wanted to find all the coffees from Colombia but exclude the premium coffees.

Take a look at Figure 2.24. Notice two requests appear in List view, the second of which is active. Notice too the checked Omit check box in the Status Area.

Figure 2.24
Notice which request is applying an Omit request. The prior request is a normal find request with the Omit function turned off. Your result will be all records from Columbia excluding those with "premium" in their names.

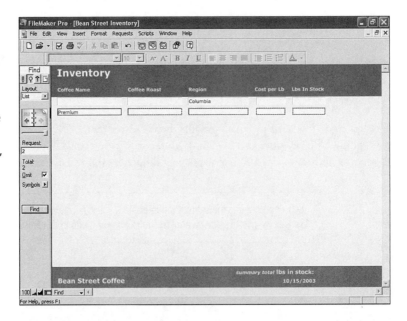

CONSTRAIN AND EXTEND REQUESTS

Performing find requests is all well and good, and as you can imagine they can become quite complex. For example, you could search for all coffees with "roast" in their names, with 10–14 or >20 lbs in stock, excluding those of premium quality from Colombia. Now imagine if, after getting all that put together, you forgot you'd wanted to omit Brazilian coffees as well.

Rather than re-create your find requests, enter Find mode again, create one request: omit Brazilian. Now instead of clicking the Find button in the Status area, choose Requests, Constrain Found Set. This new find request will be performed only on the existing found set rather than on the entire database.

Using Requests, Extend Found Set works in a similar fashion by retaining the existing records and simply adding more to them.

For example, if you have a found set of all French roast coffees and decide you want add Italian Roast to this found set of records, you don't have to start the find process over. You simply switch back to Find mode, type **Italian roast** in the Coffee Roast column, and choose Requests, Extend Found Set. The resulting found set would include both French and Italian roasts: French from your original found set, and Italian from the results of your second find.

MODIFY LAST FIND

Modify Last Find is a great feature for find requests. In Browse mode, choose Records, Modify Last Find. You are placed in Find mode with the last set of Find requests you performed. This is handy if you want to continue to play with a particularly complex set of find requests, or simply are performing a series of similar requests.

FINDING ON MULTIPLE LAYOUTS

FileMaker Pro's find functionality really is quite flexible. While you are in Find mode, it is entirely possible to change layouts. As long as the layouts on which you enter your requests are all associated with the same base table, your find performs just as though you had a layout with all the fields on it you needed. Finding is not layout specific.

Finding is, however, always table specific. Some more advanced FileMaker Pro solutions comprise multiple tables. Although it is possible to search across related information in FileMaker Pro, your find results will always display a found set of records from a single table.

→ To learn more about working with multiple tables, **see** Chapter 6, "Working with Multiple Tables," **p. 153**.

Each layout in your database is associated with a given table. When you perform a find, FileMaker Pro returns your set of records on the layout, from which you may choose Requests, Perform Find, Constrain Found Set or Extend Found Set.

OMIT AND SHOW ALL RECORDS

After performing a find, you can opt to omit individual records from a resultant found set. Choose Records, Omit Record (to omit a single record), or Omit Multiple (to omit a specified number of records).

To restore your found set to the full set of records in your current table, choose <u>R</u>ecords, Sho<u>w</u> All Records.

SORTING

When working with multiple records, an obvious requirement is the ability to sort. FileMaker Pro doesn't store its records in a sorted order—it stores them in the order in which they were created. When you first open an unsorted table, the records follow that order. There aren't any real mysteries here; for a view of the Sort dialog, see Figure 2.25.

To sort the records from a table in your database, move fields from the right side of the dialog into the left. There you can choose to have a field sort ascending, descending, or based on the order in which values appear in a specific value list. (Choosing descending, for example, sorts a number field from largest to smallest.)

If you move multiple fields into the dialog, FileMaker sorts all records by the first field, and in cases where records contain the same values, the first field then uses the second as an additional criterion.

Figure 2.25
You can control how a field is sorted: ascending by type (alpha or numeric generally), descending, or in custom order by value list.

TIP

Sorting by value list enables you to set up your own order in which things should appear. For example, if you have a workflow process that flows from "Pending" to "Approved" to "Complete," you can have your records sort in that order rather than alphabetically.

By adding multiple fields to your sort criteria, you are specifying secondary sorts: First sort by last name, then by first name, for example.

→ Sorting by Summary field is a bit tricky. **See** "Summarized Reports," **p. 281**.

PRINTING

Printing is fairly straightforward in FileMaker Pro. Choose File, Print. In the subsequent dialog that appears, you have the choice to print your found set, just the current record, or a blank record showing field names.

If you'd like to see what something will look like before wasting paper on something you don't want, use Preview mode (via the mode tabs at the top of the Status Area, or the View menu). Choose the layout from which you want to print and change to Preview mode.

After you're there you can see where page margins will fall, and the Book icon enables you to step through the pages you will send to the printer. Keep in mind that Preview mode shows you what will be sent to the printer if you choose to print current records.

PRESENTING DATA WITH SUBSUMMARY REPORTS

One prevalent type of report is a subsummary report. A subsummary report enables you to group records that share some bit of common data.

Let's start with a non-summarized report. For example, a standard list view report might look like the one shown in Figure 2.26.

Figure 2.26
Notice that this report has been formatted for paper: It is black and white, vertically oriented, ready for print.

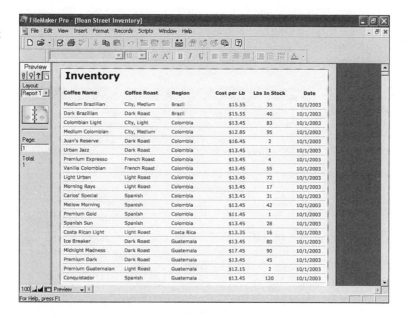

The records are sorted by region. Instead of having a report like this, where a column simply repeats for dozens of rows, a subsummarized view of this data enables you to "collapse" the information under a header that represents the group (see Figure 2.27).

Figure 2.27
Visually, this report is far more comprehensible. Your eye can see the delineation between regions instantly.

It's possible for a developer to create quite complex reports. More often than not, he or she will also provide scripts to drive those reports. As a user, it's valuable for you to understand that subsummary reports act on one's found set, and depending on sort criteria, some elements can collapse and be summarized (see Figure 2.28).

Figure 2.28
This somewhat more complex report, complete with formatting, should give you an idea of what's possible in FileMaker Pro.

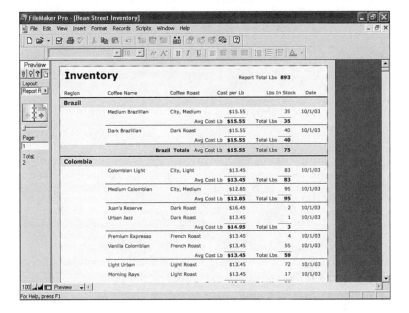

Notice in Figure 2.28 that the data fields with Brazil as a region have been collapsed into sub-headers for individual rows.

IMPORTING AND EXPORTING DATA

Having to manually type every bit of data into a database can be an excruciating experience (almost as bad as having to write a book about it). Fortunately FileMaker Pro has excellent capabilities for importing data from a wide variety of sources.

Integration with other systems is covered in later chapters. For now, keep in mind that there are options other than spending all day at the keyboard.

Importing and exporting data isn't necessarily for the faint of heart. Depending on how complex your data structure is, you may be somewhat baffled as to how to match the fields of your incoming data with that of your FileMaker system. This is a primary problem all database developers face: getting the information from two different systems to integrate properly.

→ To explore how to bring data, including a directory of images, into your FileMaker Pro solution, **see** Chapter 19, "Importing Data into FileMaker Pro," **p. 537**.

→ To learn about ODBC connectivity and SQL imports, **see** Chapter 20, "Getting Data Out of FileMaker," **p. 563**.

TROUBLESHOOTING

Most of the trouble you'll run into as a user will be with the issues specific to your own database solutions. The best advice we can offer both developers and users is to work together!

When you run into problems, knowing your developer will be a great first step.

DATA LOSS

I've noticed that I'm suddenly missing some data. What happened? What can I do?

One of the most critical aspects of your database is its namesake: your data. There's a wide range of possible problems that can impact your data, but the most dangerous is accidentally deleting a record… or worse yet, discovering you had the wrong found set when performing a Delete All Records command. FileMaker Pro doesn't have an undo function, so if a record gets deleted, it's gone forever.

Be sure you haven't simply altered your found set to exclude the records you're looking for. Go to Records, Show All Records to recall all the data in your table.

Back up your data. We can't stress this enough. FileMaker Server 7 deployment best practices and back-up routines are easy to learn. If you're not using FileMaker Server, then just make dated copies of your files and store them on CD or on another computer.

DATA INTEGRITY

How do I ensure that the data I have in my database is "good" data?

Making sure good data is entered into your database is vital. If you properly put people's names in the first name and last name fields of a contact database, but your office assistant decides to enter nicknames and other random tidbits, your data will be compromised.

Also, duplicate data is a problem that plagues all databases everywhere. If you've already created a record for, say, Conrad Moyer, you won't want to create a second record for him. What happens if his phone number changes? You'll change one record, but not the other.

Dealing with bad data is a challenge and almost always requires the power of the human brain. Get adept with running find requests. Use the ! mark to find duplicates and use * characters for wildcard characters.

You can also work with your developer to put validation in place, or even build an approval process by which new data is added to your system.

REVERTING RECORDS

What does Revert Record do?

As you enter data into fields, that information is not saved—committed—until you exit the record in question. You do so by clicking outside any fields or by changing modes, changing layouts, and so on. Before the record is committed, you can choose Records, Revert Record. This undoes all the data you've entered while working with active fields. If you've tabbed from field to field, it reverts all those not yet saved. If you have created a new record, it even reverts the entire new record if you've not yet committed it.

FILE CORRUPTION AND FILE RECOVERY

What do I do if a file won't open or says it needs to be recovered?

In the rare case that a file is corrupted, you can attempt to recover it by using the File, Recover command. By recovering a file, FileMaker attempts to create a new copy of your database and rebuild its information, structure, and indices. Generally speaking, this is necessary only in drastic circumstances. It is extremely difficult to corrupt a FileMaker Pro 7 file.

Be careful: You should *never* use a file that has been recovered. The purpose of recovery is to give you access to your data in the case of file corruption. You should immediately import your data into an empty copy of your database backed up prior to when corruption was evidenced. Then be sure to discard both the corrupted and recovered files.

FILEMAKER EXTRA: BECOMING A FILEMAKER PRO POWER USER

Manipulating data can illuminate a wide range of information and can allow business users to draw conclusions they may not have been able to anecdotally. For example, in our consulting firm, we were able to analyze our time entry data and calculate the average amount of time we need for testing. This helped greatly for future estimating.

Becoming adept at using FileMaker Pro enables you to understand what information you can pull from the system, but most importantly it enables you to know what to ask for. In working with a developer, you can guide that person's priorities (or your own), based on a solid understanding of the platform.

TECHNIQUE 1: USE YOUR KEYBOARD FOR MORE SPEED

This one's obvious. Entering (⌘-F) [Ctrl+F] brings you into Find mode. Tabbing takes you from field to field. The (Return) [Enter] key executes default values in dialog boxes, performs finds, and so on. Ctrl-up arrow and -down arrow pages through your data. You'll become much faster with FileMaker Pro if you take the time to learn your key commands. FileMaker's online help details all the key commands available.

TECHNIQUE 2: WORK WITH TABLE VIEW

User interfaces have their purpose, and more often than not greatly assist data entry and working with a given solution, but if you just need to look at the raw data in your system, you can opt to change to Table view from any layout in FileMaker Pro (assuming your developer hasn't disabled the option). This gives you a "bird's eye view" of your information. Don't forget that clicking on a column header sorts for that column. A second click re-sorts descending.

TECHNIQUE 3: REPLACING DATA

Fairly often you'll run across cases where you need to globally replace some data with other data. For example, perhaps you've changed a value list of vehicles to read "auto, bike, boat, plane," rather than "bike, boat, car, plane." If you leave things alone after changing the value list, you'll have both "car" and "auto" data in your system. Enforcing the consistent use of terms is important in maintaining your data integrity. To quickly take care of migrating from an old value to a new one, follow these steps:

1. Choose <u>R</u>ecords, Sho<u>w</u> All Records. (Otherwise your change is applied to only your current found set.)
2. Place your cursor into the field in question.

NOTE

> In the case of a pop-up menu, you're out of luck. FileMaker Pro doesn't recognize a cursor in a pop-up menu. You need to do a little development (to be covered in Chapter 3, "Defining and Working with Fields"), copy the field to an open spot on your layout, and change its formatting to a pop-up list. Then don't forget to delete the field when you're finished.

3. Choose Edit, Find/Replace to open the Find/Replace dialog box (see Figure 2.29).

Figure 2.29
Find/Replace can step through your records, or can be applied across the entire database. Be careful: These functions cannot be undone!

4. Type your old and new values.

5. Choose All from the Direction drop-down menu (so that your entire database will be covered).

6. Depending on your preferences, choose Current Field or apply your change to entire records. We recommend just the selected field because that's much safer than accidentally changing all instances of a text string.

7. Click Replace All.

CAUTION

> It's important to note: This is a function that cannot be undone! Be sure you know what you're doing with your data.

TECHNIQUE 4: INSERTING SPECIFIC INFORMATION

The Insert menu is an oft-ignored source of handy time-saving commands. From a single menu choice or keyboard command, you can insert the current time, current date, or your username into an active field.

In addition to that, Insert, From Index allows you to select from all the values in a given field from all records in a database. If you can't quite remember the spelling of a given item, or simply want to be perfectly consistent, this is a great way to see the data in your system and make a compatible selection. (This works only if the field in question allows indexing.)

→ To learn about field indexing, **see** "Storage and Indexing," **p. 82**.

Finally, there's a handy way to pull data from another record in your database. If three or four fields need to contain identical data to another record in your database, visit the "source" record first, then via a List view or Table view jump (by clicking on the appropriate row) to the "destination" record. Click into the specific fields you want and choose Insert, From Last Visited Record.

TECHNIQUE 5: GET TO KNOW YOUR ENTIRE DATABASE

One of the best ways to make the most of a FileMaker Pro database is to learn how to navigate around it and to understand its core data structure. Even if you're working with just one screen or process, it's good to explore further.

Review the other layouts in your system, take a look at the fields you see, and explore other files (if there are others) in the solution. Be sure to discuss with your developer how the information fits together.

TECHNIQUE 6: MULTI-TIERED SORTS

Sorting can be a fairly powerful way to derive meaning and see patterns in data. To make the most of the Sort dialog, don't forget that you can provide additional sort criteria. For example, in a contacts database you could sort by Last Name, First Name, City, descending by Age, and finally by Pet name.

You can also sort by the custom order of a value list. If you have, say, a status field that is managed by a value list of "open, pending, closed," you can sort by that order.

TECHNIQUE 7: USE MULTIPLE WINDOWS

FileMaker Pro provides you with a Window menu. If you'd like to work with multiple layouts at once, choose Window, New Window, then navigate to the second layout in question (using either the Layout Pop-up Menu in the Status Area or the buttons a developer may have provided).

Multiple windows are also useful when you open two windows looking at the same list view layout: It's possible for you to have two separate found sets. Imagine finding all the invitees of an event in one window and all the people whom you've not yet invited in the other.

TECHNIQUE 8: TEXT STYLING AND TABS

You can apply a wide range of formatting options to text within FileMaker Pro fields: bold, italic, font choice, color choice, and so on (see Figure 2.30). This information is preserved within FileMaker Pro, and you can copy and paste formatted text with other applications. For formats that support it, such as XML, you can export formatting as well.

There is another neat trick in FileMaker Pro: In any field you can establish an internal tab placement and apply tabs by using (⌘-Tab) [Ctrl+Tab]. Choose View, Text Ruler. When you click into a field, a horizontal ruler appears above it, into which you can click to establish tabs. Double-click on a tab to set its properties: left, center, right, align to character, and whether to use a fill character.

Figure 2.30
You have a wide range of control over text appearance in FileMaker Pro.

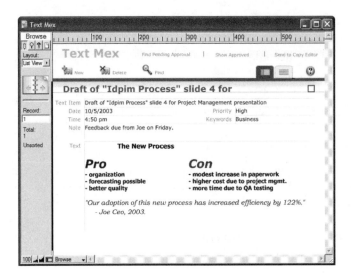

CHAPTER 3

DEFINING AND WORKING WITH FIELDS

In this chapter

WORKING UNDER THE HOOD

Fields are the heart of any database. By storing information in properly categorized fields, you impart both function and meaning to what would otherwise be an incomprehensible pile of raw data.

We'll spend much of this chapter describing what kinds of fields exist in FileMaker Pro, how they store information, and how to ensure proper data integrity in your database solutions.

If you're new to development in FileMaker Pro, this chapter is a good place to start. No doubt some of the topics we cover will lack a certain context, but establishing a solid foundation in field definition is a vital part of becoming a practiced developer.

If you have built a few FileMaker Pro databases, you may need to only skim this chapter. Of the topics we cover, indexing is likely the most advanced; our discussion explores some subtle differences from prior versions of FileMaker Pro.

NEW DATABASES BEGIN WITH FIELD DEFINITIONS

To create a new database, simply launch FileMaker Pro and then choose File, New Database. You'll be presented with the option to start with a template or to create a new, empty file. To create a file of your own, select the Create A New Empty File option and click Okay.

After you've stepped through these first tasks, you'll be taken to the Define Fields dialog.

> **TIP**
>
> If you don't want to see this dialog every time you create a new database, click the No Longer Show This Dialog check box. Subsequently, selecting File, New Database takes you directly to a New File dialog.

Working with Templates

We recommend that you go back at some point and work with FileMaker's built-in templates. They're a good learning tool, and you will be able to see how fields are defined in these finished solutions. There are dozens of them, they're not all that complicated, and they'll give you some good ideas for designing your own solutions. From them you can learn about simple user interfaces and calculation functions and can see some basic scripts in action.

USING THE DEFINE DATABASE DIALOG

When you choose to start on a new, empty database, FileMaker Pro creates a file for you and automatically opens the Define Database dialog (shown in Figure 3.1). As a developer, you'll spend a good bit of time in the three tabs in this dialog. FileMaker Pro's Define Database dialog allows you to create the fields, tables, and relationships you need to form your database. It also enables you to modify a wide range of attributes associated with fields, such as auto-entry functions, validation, storage, and calculation formulas. It is these elements that comprise a database's "structure" or "schema." It is here where you form your database behind the scenes.

Figure 3.1
The three tabs allow you to switch between defining fields, tables, or relationships.

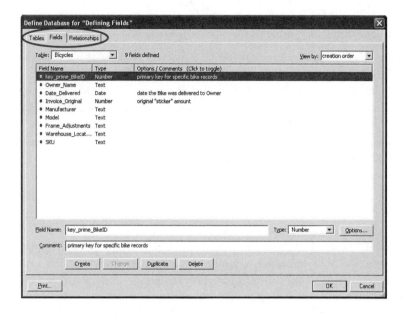

NOTE

> Notice the active table in Figure 3.1: The fields you define are associated with this selected table.

FileMaker Pro will have already created a default table for you, named the same as the file itself. Notice the Table menu selection on the Fields tab of the dialog in Figure 3.1. Any fields you create will then be created in that table.

→ For some basic information on tables, **see** "Tables," **p. 29**.

→ For a detailed discussion of multiple-table solutions, **see** Chapter 6, "Working with Multiple Tables," **p. 153**.

Notice the third tab in the Define Database dialog: Relationships. We won't be covering multi-table relational databases in this chapter, but it is on that tab that you'd create the relational associations between tables in your solution.

→ For information on relational data modeling, **see** Chapter 5, "Relational Database Design," **p. 123**.

TIP

> Commenting is a vital discipline to develop. Spending a few moments to add information to the Comment text box, below the field name, as you create something will save time later in trying to figure out what you were thinking at the time.
>
> To view comments, toggle between options and comments at the top of your field list.

Working with Fields

Every table in any database—FileMaker Pro or otherwise—is a collection of information stored in fields (or columns, if you're familiar with that terminology.) It is by storing like information in appropriate fields that a database is given meaning.

For example, by entering "124 Main Street" in a field called Address, we've identified what "124 Main Street" is. In the case of a street address, it's fairly easy to identify without a field definition, but what about "912.5" all on its own? That could be a price, a number of units, a chapter heading, or a thousand other things. When you place that number into a named column or field, your data becomes meaningful. If "912.5" sat in a field named Temperature, you'd likely conclude that such is pretty darn hot. Conversely, if it sat in a Kilobytes Available field, you'd look to be buying a new hard drive. Keep this ultimate goal of imparting meaning in mind as you create and name fields, and assign appropriate data types to them.

Field Naming Conventions

One of the nice things about FileMaker Pro development is the freedom developers have in naming fields. (FileMaker Pro is not unique in allowing developers field naming freedom, by the way.) That freedom also, unfortunately, gives rise to confusion and arbitrary naming conventions. "Name_xTJm2" may mean something to someone, or "Name" might also, but both examples—the overly specific and the overly general—require a strong familiarity with a given system. If you ever return to a database months after building it, odds are you will have forgotten your clever abbreviations.

We encourage you to take advantage of FileMaker's allowance for long field names of up to 100 characters. Use full text names (like "Street Address line1"), avoid abbreviations (or if you use them be sure to provide an obvious key!), and try to group things logically.

Here's an example of what we'd consider a fairly reasonable approach to naming fields:

- Address_City
- Address_Postal_Code
- Address_State
- Address_Street_line1
- Address_Street_line2
- Person_Name_First
- Person_Name_Last
- Phone_Home
- Phone_Work

These fields are quite simple to identify and are neatly grouped together when sorted alphabetically. This isn't such a big deal for small databases, but if you ever work on a large database, with multiple developers, a well established naming convention is vital. Right from day one we encourage you to adopt good programming habits.

Another common approach many developers use includes abbreviations for data types. Often it's handy to know the data type of a given field when working with it without having to refer to the Define Database dialog. (Here we've used "t" for text, "n" for number, and "c" for calculation):

- ProductName_t
- Price_n
- TaxRate_n
- Tax_c

We'll cover indexing later in the chapter, but some developers also note whether a field is indexed or not (x for indexed, n for unindexed):

- Location_Name_tx
- Location_Desc_tn
- Location_Size_nn

Some naming conventions also break out a division between data fields and what are commonly referred to as *developer fields*—those fields that one needs only to make one's FileMaker Pro solution work. If you ever went to import your database wholesale into another system, these fields would be left behind. Here we have two abbreviations: k for key (or match field), and z (so that it sorts to the bottom of the list) for developer utility fields.

- AlbumName
- Date
- k_primary_AlbumID
- k_foreign_ArtistID
- z_SelectedPortalRow
- z_UserColor_Preference
- z_UserGenre_Preference

Finally, here's a real example from a database we recently were hired to modify (used with permission and good humor!):

- Bike Type
- Wheel Diam
- Bike Name
- Model
- Temp
- Date
- Bike

- Sp.99 Meas
- Tire Diam
- Bikeid
- Sku
- 2002 Tire Diam
- 1999 Tire Diam
- BikeMODEL
- SUMMARY
- zTempzzz
- Phils field (no lie!)

We're sure we've belabored the point, but this database was difficult to modify not because it was complex, but because it was hard to read. As in all things, a little planning goes a long way.

If you're planning on using FileMaker Pro as a Web backend, refer to "Problematic Field Names" in the Troubleshooting section at the end of this chapter.

→ For more information on using databases on the Web, **see** "Designing for IWP deployment," **p. 619** (Chapter 21), as well as Chapter 23, "Custom Web Publishing," **p. 671**.

There are some restrictions to field naming in FileMaker Pro: A field name must be unique and must be less than 100 characters.

You can opt to use special characters, numbers, spaces, even the names of functions, but we recommend against using them. If you use: ,(comma), +, -, *, /, ^, &, =, ≠, >, <, (,), ", ;(semicolon), :(colon), ::(double colon relationship indicator), you need to enclose such special characters with a $() in calculation formulas to have them interpreted as field names. For example, the calculation $(Tax,special) returns the value of a field named Tax,special.

We recommend strongly that you name fields without using special characters, the names of functions, or operators (AND, OR, NOT, XOR, TRUE, FALSE).

The same is true for fields that begin with a space, a period, or a number: You'll have to contort your calculations to deal with them. Don't use them. Begin each field with a standard alphabetical letter or at least an underscore.

ADDING FIELD COMMENTS

Notice also that you can add comments to your field definitions. We don't mean to be pedantic, but want to drive home that establishing good programming habits will serve you well for the rest of your life as a developer. Use the field comments feature. Explain to yourself a year from now why a field exists, any dependencies or assumptions you made, and possibly how you intend to use it.

CREATING NEW FIELDS

To create fields in FileMaker Pro, you need to enter some text in the Field Name area of the Define Database dialog and click Create.

One important aspect to databases to keep in mind is that it's important to establish a discrete field for each bit of information you want to store. If you create a field called Contact Information and cram an entire address and set of phone numbers into it, technically it will work fine, but if it ever comes time to export that information, sort by area code, or run a report by city, you won't be able to cull the information you want from the field without suffering from a good headache.

→ To database wonks, the Contact Information example would be a violation of "first normal form," or more colloquially, "one fact, one field." For information on relational data modeling and defining fields, **see** "Relationship Types," **p. 131**.

WORKING WITH FIELD TYPES

One of the most important aspects of understanding FileMaker Pro is understanding field types, how they're different from one another, and how to use them effectively.

Simply stated, field types identify what kind of information each field of your database is expected to hold. A person's name is text, the dollar amount for a transaction is a number, a birthday is a date, and so on. Generally it should be quite clear to you what each needs to be.

Field types determine what types of operations can be performed on a given field, what information a field can accept, and the rules by which a field is sorted. It's the combination of a proper identifying field name and a data type definition that gives a database its context and meaning.

TEXT

Text fields are the most freeform of the field types. Users can enter any range of information in them, including carriage returns, and there's no expectation of what form or sort of information a text field will hold. The only requirement is that it be text—in other words, you can't place a picture in a text field. A text field can store up to 2GB of information, limited by RAM and hard drive space, of course, and indexes up to approximately 100 characters, depending on what language you're using. We'll cover indexing in more depth later in the chapter. For now, simply remember that each field type has different limits and approaches on indexing.

NUMBER

Number fields can store values from 10^{-400} up to 10^{400}, and negative values in the same range. FileMaker Pro indexes the first 400 significant digits (numbers, decimal points, or signs) of a number field, ignoring letters and other symbols. Number fields can accept text (though not carriage returns), but any text in a numeric field is ignored. FileMaker interprets "12ax3" as 123 if you enter it into a numeric field, for example.

Something to keep in mind with FileMaker Pro: A number field can be expressed as a Boolean. A Boolean value is either true or false, and is often used to test the condition of something. A zero or null value is false; any other data is true. You will often run across number fields being used in such a manner.

The primary distinction between a number and text field lies in how they're sorted: a text field sorts 1, 10, 2, 20, 3, 4, 5, whereas a number field sorts 1, 2, 3, 4, 5, 10, 20.

DATE

Date fields accept Gregorian calendar dates only. FileMaker Pro honors whatever date standard your country follows by taking the standard your operating system uses at the time a new file is created. Date formats—the order of year, month, and day—are common for a given file. Although it's possible to change the way dates are displayed, it is this basic ordering that is fixed at the time of file creation.

Dates in FileMaker Pro are internally stored as the number of days since 01/01/0001. January 1, 2004, for instance, is 731581. If you need to compare dates or perform any functions on them, remember that behind the scenes they're really just numbers. This feature is actually quite handy. To switch a date to a week prior, all you need to do is subtract seven.

Date fields can store values from January 1, 0001 to December 31, 4000.

If your fields are sorting or displaying oddly, refer to "Mismatched Data Types" in the Troubleshooting section at the end of this chapter.

TIME

Time fields hold HH:MM:SS.ddd information. Notice that a decimal may be added to the end. Also useful: If a user enters "25:00," FileMaker Pro rightly interprets such as 1:00 a.m. 99:30 becomes 3:30 a.m. The clock simply keeps rolling over. This behavior is useful when you need to add, say, 30 hours to a time, and don't want to be bothered with calculating what hour that becomes. Likewise, if you are doing data entry in a time tracking system and don't want to create two entries for a case where you worked from 2:00 p.m. until 2:00 a.m. on Monday (really Tuesday), entering 26:00 in your system rightly calculates to 12 hours.

As in dates, FileMaker Pro stores time internally as the number of seconds from 12:00:00 on the current day. "1" is 12:00:01, and "43200" is 12:00 p.m. Likewise, your time format is established during the creation of the file, based on system OS settings.

The maximum time value you can store in FileMaker Pro is 2,147,483,647. That's a lot of time.

TIMESTAMP

Timestamp combines date and time information. It appears as a field with both date and time values, separated by a space: 1/1/2004 12:00:00. As in date and time formats, timestamps are stored also as numbers: the count of seconds from 1/1/0001 00:00:00. Be prepared to work with large numbers when using this field type. Timestamps are an important aid to interoperability with other databases (such as those powered by the SQL language), which often store date and time information in a single timestamp field.

The maximum value of a timestamp is 12/31/4000 11:59:59.999999 p.m. or 126,227,764,799.999999 seconds.

CONTAINER

Container fields are different from the four above: They store binary information. Information, such as it is, is often inserted into them rather than being entered manually (you can copy and paste). You can place any sort of digital document in your database, limited again by the practical limits of your computer hardware, up to 4GB.

Container fields also support displaying/playing three native types of media: pictures, QuickTime movies, and sounds. Refer to the FileMaker help system for supported formats, but most common image formats are included...as well as some you won't expect. For example, by using QuickTime, it's possible to display and play a Macromedia Flash 5 .swf file.

Last, on Windows, a wide range of OLE objects are supported, including Microsoft Excel documents, PDF, and more.

One important thing to remember about using container fields: You can store either the file or media in FileMaker itself—requiring disk space—or simply store the path reference to the file. If you choose to store just a reference to the file, FileMaker Pro, somewhat like a Web browser, displays the image or file icon as necessary, but does not hold the actual document itself. A nice feature of storing references is that you can then double-click documents in your container fields to launch them in your operating system.

> **CAUTION**
>
> Keep in mind that if you move the source document, the FileMaker Pro reference remains but is no longer valid.

CALCULATION

Calculation fields evaluate formulas and display the requisite results. When you create a calculation field, the Specify Calculation dialog opens.

→ Be sure to refer to FileMaker Pro's online help or this book's Appendix B, "Calculation Function Reference," **p. 807**, for a complete list of functions.

The features of the Specify Calculation dialog box include

- **Field list**—Select fields to include in your calculation from the list below the table menu. Use the drop-down menu to change from table to table. Note that double-clicking inserts a field into your calculation where your cursor currently sits.

- **Operators**—Use these buttons to insert math and special operators.

- **Function list**—Just below the View drop-down menu is a list of functions. Here you're able to scroll through all of FileMaker Pro's various functions and then double-click to insert. It's a good idea to start here to get your syntax correct.

Figure 3.2
Calculations form an essential pillar of FileMaker Pro development.

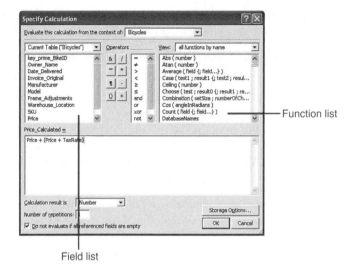

Function list

Field list

The menu above enables you to filter your list by category to show the functions as you need.

- **Formula text box**—This is where you assemble your actual formula. This is a simple text entry area: If you wish, work in a text editor and paste calculations here.

- **Calculation Result Is**—Calculations return varying information, depending on what data/field type is required. If you want the field to be sortable by alphabet, return Text. If you have a field returning, say, a price, then set the type to Number.

Examples of calculations include

- `3 + 4` always displays its result of 7.
- `Sale + Tax` displays the sum of two fields named `Sale` and `Tax`.
- `Position ( Notes; "a"; 1; 1)` returns a numeric position, starting from the first character in the field `Notes`, for the first "a" found.
- `IsEmpty ( MyField )` returns a zero or one (Boolean) depending on whether or not "MyField" has a value in it, including zero. If a zero is entered, the field is technically not empty. Only a null value is considered empty.
- `If ( MyDate > 900; "yes" ; "no" )` displays a yes for dates entered in `MyDate` greater than 6/19/0003; otherwise it will display no . (Remember that you've just tested for the number of days past 1/1/0001.)

Calculations are fundamental to FileMaker programming, and it's worth your while to master them fully.

→ For more detail on Calculations, **see** Chapter 8, "Getting Started with Calculations," **p. 213**, Chapter 14, "Specialized Calculation Functions," **p. 381**, and Appendix B, "Calculation Function Reference," **p. 807**.

If your calculation formula looks correct, but FileMaker is returning an odd result or "?", refer to "Mismatched Calculation Results" in the Troubleshooting section at the end of this chapter.

SUMMARY

Summary fields allow you to evaluate information across a found set of records. Sum, Average, Max, Min, and Count are among the summaries you can establish. Don't forget that they apply to found sets: Change your found set, and the result changes.

For example, say you have a table called Transaction, which contains Tranaction_Date and Transaction_Amount fields. You can then define and place on a layout a summary field to total the Transaction_Amount field. The summary field adds the values of the Transaction_Amount field for whatever set of records is currently active. If you perform a find, by date, on 10/1/2003–10/31/2003, your found set will be all the transactions for the month of October and the summary field would show just the aggregate monthly transaction amount. Perform a different find request and your total changes, reflecting the aggregate of the new found set.

Table 3.1 contains a list of Summary field functions.

TABLE 3.1   SUMMARY FIELD FUNCTIONS

Function	Summary Behavior
Total of	Adds values from the specified field in your found set. Think of it as a subtotal or grand total from a column of numbers. You may also enable the option to display a running total for your record set. This then shows a running tally of your total if you place the summary field in the body area of a list.
Average of	Averages the values from the specified field in your found set. The weighted average option enables you to specify a second field to act as a weight factor for calculating the average. The field you choose must be a number or a calculation with a number result.
Count of	Counts the number of records in your found set that have valid data in the specified field. For example, if 18 of the 20 current found records have data, your summary field will display "18." A running count functions similarly to a running total: It displays the incremented count of each record in your found set.
Minimum	Returns the lowest number, date, time, or timestamp in a given found set from the referenced field.
Maximum	Returns the highest number, date, time, or timestamp in a given found set from the referenced field.

continues

TABLE 3.1   CONTINUED

Function	Summary Behavior
Standard Deviation of	Determines how widely the values in the referenced field differ. Returns the standard deviation from the mean of the values in your found set. The standard deviation formula is n-1 weighted, following the normal standard deviation. Standard deviation comes in two flavors: to perform a biased or n-0 evaluation, select the By Population option.
Fraction of Total of	Returns the ratio of a total for which a given record (or set of records, when the field is placed in a sub-summary part) is responsible. For example, you can track what percentage of sales are attributable to a given person. The subtotaled option enables you to specify a second field by which to group your data.

When you create a summary field, the Options for Summary Fields dialog opens, prompting you to choose the function you want to use and the field for which you want a summary (see Figure 3.3).

Figure 3.3
Summary fields are useful for performing functions across sets of records, but use them with care. They can slow down the time it takes to load any given layout.

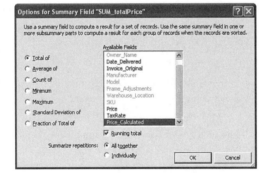

It's generally a good idea to place Summary fields on their own layouts so that a user deliberately chooses to have them evaluate a found set.

ASSIGNING FIELD OPTIONS

In addition to establishing fields and assigning data types, you may assign options to your fields as well. These range in function from managing auto-entry of default data to validation checks and internal storage settings. They can vary for each field type.

After you have named a field and chosen its type on the Fields tab of the Define Database dialog box, click Create to save it to your database. You may then opt to apply further behaviors via the Options button on the right. The first set of options is the auto-entry behaviors.

AUTO-ENTRY FIELD OPTIONS

When defining non-calculation fields in FileMaker Pro, you can choose to apply a range of options as records are created and/or modified. The applications for this can range from assigning default values to fields, to automatically reformatting data, or inserting values from other fields based on certain "trigger" events.

In some cases you might not even allow users to modify these auto-generated values, such as when tracking a serial ID or applying a date you don't want adjusted afterward (see Figure 3.4).

Figure 3.4
Auto-entry of data allows you to define rules for automatically populating data into fields in your database.

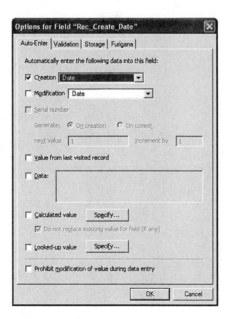

Auto-entry data is inserted into a field based on some trigger event. The most common event is record creation: When a user clicks New Record, data can be pre-populated into the record and then be accessible for changes to be made. Each Auto-Entry function has its own particular rules for what trigger event applies.

In addition to new record creation, other trigger events include record modification and modification of a particular field.

CREATION AND MODIFICATION

The first two options on the Auto-Entry tab deal with tracking and applying certain values as a record is committed to your database. They behave essentially the same way, with Creation values being applied the first time a record is committed, and Modification values applied thereafter as it is subsequently modified (committed again).

Values you can opt to apply comprise the Date, Time, Timestamp, Name (from the General Preferences dialog under the Edit menu), or Account Name (that which the user validated during login.)

CAUTION

Name is something users can modify as they will via the Preferences dialog, so you generally shouldn't depend on it for anything vital. If you want to depend on knowing who has created or modified a given record using auto-entry functions, always use the Account Name option.

NOTE

If you do not change any of the account settings of a new file, FileMaker will have established two default accounts for you: Guest and Admin. Both begin with full access to the database.

SERIAL NUMBER

Here you're able to set a number that increments every time a new record is added to the table. Often this is used to uniquely identify individual records in a table. The value can be generated either when the record is created or when it is committed. The difference is subtle: In the case of incrementing on creation, your number increments even if a user then reverts and effectively cancels a record's creation. The next record will then have "skipped" a number in your sequence. This doesn't have much of an effect on your database unless your business requires strict tracking of each serial number, even those voided. In those cases, choosing On Commit helps avoid spaces in the sequence.

It is possible to include text characters in addition to a number as the starting value if you wish. This enables you to create serial numbers that look something like "a1, a2, a3, a4..." Only the numeric portion of the value is incremented; the text portion remains unchanged.

One of the common uses of auto-entry options is in establishing serialized key values, or IDs. This is a vital element of your database structure when working with more than one table, but regardless of how complex or simple your plans are, we encourage you to adopt some best practices.

For every table in your database, the first field you should create is a "primary key" or ID field. It is these IDs that uniquely identify each record in your database. There are several ways one could go about having the system establish unique IDs automatically; our recommendation in most cases is to use a serial number set to increment automatically.

We can't stress this practice strongly enough. If you ever want to tackle relational data structures, these serial IDs are a vital element in doing so. Further, if you ever export your data to another system or need to interact with other databases, having a key field that uniquely identifies each record in your database will make keeping track of your data possible.

To create a serial key field, use the following steps:

1. Define a number field. (It is generally advisable to use number-based serial keys, but it is possible to use text as well; the important thing is to make certain your keys are unique and un-modifiable.)

2. Go into the Options for that field and select the Serial Number option.

3. Click the Prohibit Modification of Value During Data Entry option at the bottom of the dialog. This is an important step: If you establish unique identifiers that your users can then override, you're risking the chance that they'll introduce duplicate IDs.

If you need an ID field for a business purpose (SKUs, Student IDs, Employee IDs from your organization, and so on) we recommend that you create separate fields for such cases. Generally, users should never need to access this serialized ID field, but you may opt to put it on a layout and allow entry in Find mode so that they may search if they choose.

→ For a full discussion of the use of keys (or *match fields*), **see** the discussion in "Working with Keys and Match Fields," **p. 158**.

VALUE FROM LAST VISITED RECORD

Used most often as a way to speed data entry when information is often repeated for groups of records, this function copies the value from a prior record into a given new record. Bear in mind: "Visited" means the last record in which you entered data. If you enter data in a record, then view a second record without clicking into a field and activating it, it is the data from the first, edited record from which a new record obtains its value.

DATA

Here you may specify literal text for auto-entry. This is frequently used to set default states for field entry. For instance, in an Invoice table, you might have a text field called Status where you want to enter "Not Paid" as a default. Being a regular text field, the value is fully modifiable by a user.

CALCULATED VALUE

In addition to establishing a field as a calculation field, where its value will always be controlled by its defined formula, it is possible to insert the results of a calculation into any other field—including a container field—as an auto-entry option.

Further, if you uncheck the, Do Not Replace the Existing Value For Field (If Any) option, the results of the calculation formula are entered into the field (overriding any existing value) any time a field reference by the calculation changes.

In other words, a referenced field in your calculation statement acts as a trigger—including the auto-entry field itself. This enables you to apply calculations to data entry on the fly. One great example of this is a phone number field. You may always want phone numbers formatted as "(123) 456-7890" regardless of how a user entered the data. By using this triggered auto-entry function, you can apply the results of a calculation whenever a field is modified.

3

For an example of this technique, refer to Figure 3.5.

Figure 3.5
By using a self-referencing calculation, FileMaker Pro is able to replace and correct data as it is entered by the user.

"123" entered.   "555.123.4567 x-11" entered.

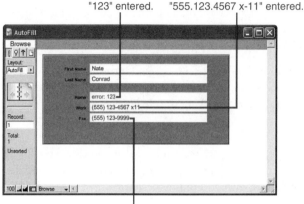

"fax:5551239999" entered.

The actual calculation for this Auto-Fill option looks like this (returned as text):

```
Let (
    //define variables:
[

rawNumber = Filter (Phone_Number; "0123456789") ;
length = Length (rawNumber);
red = RGB (160;0;0);

    //set error flag for a phone number that's too short
error = If ( length < 10 ; TextColor ("error: " & Phone_Number; red); "")

];
    // now apply the phone formatting and return results

    If ( error ≠ ""; error;

        "(" & Left (rawNumber; 3) & ") " & Middle (rawNumber; 4; 3) &
        "-" & Middle (rawNumber; 7; 4) &

        // this condition tests for extra digits
        // that we'll treat as an extension
        If ( length > 10; " x" & Middle (rawNumber; 11; length - 10); "")

    )
)
```

→ To learn more about advanced calculation functions, **see** Chapter 14, "Specialized Calculation Functions" **p. 381**.

LOOKED-UP VALUE

This auto-entry option copies a value from a related record into a field. Any time the field controlling your association to that related record changes, FileMaker Pro updates the value in the lookup field.

For example, if a user enters a ZIP code into a given record, it's possible you could have another table then auto-populate your city and state fields with the appropriate information.

When a user enters a ZIP code in the highlighted field in Figure 3.6, the city and state fields below are triggers to pull values from the ZipCodes table. An important fact to keep in mind is that FileMaker has copied the values from the ZipCodes table. If the source data changes or is deleted, this record remains unmodified until it is re-triggered by someone editing the ZIP code field again.

Figure 3.6
Lookup functions work somewhat like relational data, but instead of displaying values from a related record, their information is copied and stored when a trigger event occurs.

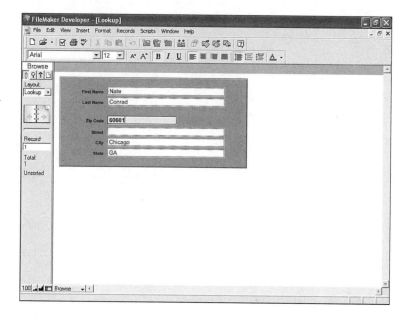

Take special note that lookup auto-entry functions work just as all auto-entry functions do: They copy or insert information into a field. You are not displaying related information, nor are you controlling content by calculation. Thus lookup values are not live links to related data: If you were to delete the records in the ZipCode table in the previous example, all your people records would remain untouched, preserving your city and state data.

This is an important distinction to understand, especially as we get into indexing later in this chapter.

To see how to create a lookup field, refer to Figure 3.7.

Remember that anytime your match field changes, your lookup refreshes. In this case, the auto-entry function does not act on record creation, but rather on committing/triggering.

When performing a lookup, it is possible to apply close matches. In the case of the ZIP codes example, obviously you'd only want an exact match or you might end up with incorrect data. In a different case, however, you need not be so strict. Consider a scheduling system that automatically finds the closest available appointment: Enter a target date into a field, and the lookup function could return the closest match. Another application might be a parts database with units of measurement. You may not be able to find a .78" wrench, but a .75" might work.

Figure 3.7
Often you'll want only exact matches, but in some cases you can use the closest value based on a comparison of the trigger values in your related table.

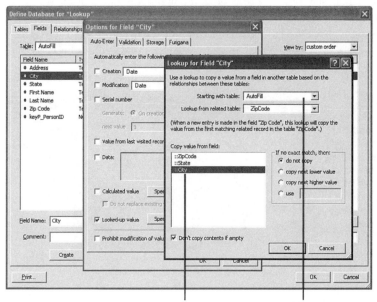

Choose source field   Choose the relationship

How you set up your trigger values is important here. It's easy to compare numbers and come up with the next closest value. If your trigger field is text, FileMaker Pro uses ASCII value rules to compare and determine order.

→ For further discussion of lookups, **see** Chapter 6, "Working with Multiple Tables," **p. 153**.

Housekeeping Creation and Modification Fields

As a best practice, we also recommend that you create another set of fields in all tables that help track changes. Create a timestamp field and in the Auto-Enter options, choose `Creation Timestamp`. Define another for `Modification Timestamp`, and text fields for Creation and Modification Account Names.

These four fields tell you exactly when a record was created or modified and by whom (assuming you assign an account to each individual person using your database). If you ever need to identify problem records for a given day range, time, or account, these fields allow such. We strongly recommend you add them every time you create a new table.

The only downside to following this practice is that additional storage space is required for this data, and in this version of FileMaker Pro, only in the most extreme case is that an issue.

FIELD VALIDATION

Storing correct and complete information is critical for generating accurate reports, establishing proper, expected conditions on which other functions and calculations are performed, and ensuring overall data integrity. Unfortunately, most data applications suffer from a chronic condition of having humans interacting with them; although some humans are worse than others (like developers), none are perfect. We all make mistakes.

As data is entered into FileMaker Pro, you may opt to apply one or more validation checks to test that certain conditions are met before allowing users to commit the record to your system. This can be as simple as ensuring that a field isn't empty, or as complex as making sure that an invoice total doesn't contain multiple entries for the same product.

To review the various validation options available, see Figure 3.8.

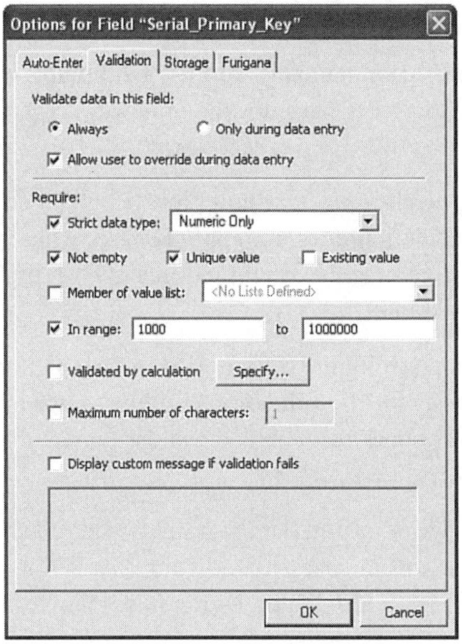

Figure 3.8
These are common validation settings for a numeric key value meant to always remain unique and unmodified by users. Even if your users can't access a given field on any layout, it's still a good policy to validate.

This example demonstrates a common approach to ensuring that your primary keys are properly maintained. This may be overkill if you've enabled the Prohibit <u>M</u>odification of the Value During Data Entry option on the Auto-Entry tab, but on the chance that a developer turns that option off for some reason, or that users import records into your database, this is a handy bit of insurance.

→ Importing records can circumvent your carefully designed field validation rules. For a full discussion, **see** Chapter 19, "Importing Data into FileMaker Pro," **p. 537**.

VALIDATION CONDITIONS AND FAILURE

Field Validation simply tests whether one or more conditions, as defined in your Validation dialog, is false. In the case where all tests are true, the user is not interrupted or prompted for action.

Figure 3.9 shows an example of what your users will see in cases where validation fails.

Figure 3.9
The Yes option appears only in cases where a user has the option to override the validation warning.

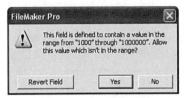

In this case, the check box allowing users to override has been left enabled, so they do have the option to ignore the warning. When that function is disabled, the field does not allow "bad" data to be committed and the system forces users to deal with the problem. They can choose either to revert the field to its previous state or to clear it.

WHEN VALIDATION OCCURS

Validation occurs when users enter data manually into the field being validated and then commit the record. Remember, however, that's not the only way to get information into a field. You can also import records or use various script steps, such as Set Field().

Validation isn't triggered simply by clicking or tabbing into a field; a change needs to be attempted. And keep in mind: Validation does not apply in cases where users modify other fields of a given record. A new value must be attempted in a given, respective field for that field's validation check to be performed.

At the top of the validation dialog (see Figure 3.8), notice the Always versus Only During Data Entry choices. The latter tests for the validation conditions when users modify the field in question. When the Always option is enabled, validation occurs during scripts and imports as well as during data entry.

If an import process attempts to write invalid data to a field, FileMaker Pro simply ignores the improper entry. The field remains unchanged and your data is not imported. You will see a note in the Import Records Summary dialog listing how many errors were encountered.

In the case where the Only During Data Entry option is used, that improper data would be inserted into your database.

 If you get trapped in a series of validation dialogs, refer to "Validation Traps" in the Troubleshooting section at the end of this chapter.

STORAGE AND INDEXING

Field storage and indexing is found on the Storage tab in your Field Options dialog and deals with how FileMaker Pro manages the contents of your data internally.

GLOBAL STORAGE

A developer can designate a field to have *global* storage on the Storage tab of the Field Options dialog. Commonly fields with this option are simply referred to as "global fields" and collectively they're usually referred to as "globals." Global fields live independently from any specific record in the database and hold one value per user-session.

Global fields are often used by developers to establish variables during scripts, to display programmatic field labels (as opposed to simply leaving text on a layout), or to maintain system preferences. Globals have a wide range of applications.

One vital element to learn is when data is committed and stored for globals: In a single-user environment, any change to a global field is permanent and is saved across sessions. In the case of a multi-user environment—where a FileMaker Pro solution is hosted on FileMaker Server or via multi-user hosting—global values for each guest default to the value from the last time the database was in single-user mode; any change made to these defaults will then be specific only to a given user's session. Other users continue to see the default values, and after the database session is closed it reverts to its original, default state.

Using globals is a great way to keep track of certain states of your database. For example, you could use a global field to store which row of a portal was last selected. This field could then be used in scripts or calculation formulas.

→ For an example of using a global to drive portal behaviors, **see** "Selection Portals," **p. 454**.

Another common use of globals is for storing system graphics. Establish a container field, set it for global storage, and paste a favorite company logo, a custom button graphic, or any number of elements that you can then control globally in a field rather than having to paste discrete elements on each and every layout.

A third use for globals takes advantage of their being user-session specific. A developer can set a global with user account information and refer to such via scripts, confidant that the same script will work for each individual user of the system. Person A's global field relates to him or her, and Person B's field holds his or her relative data.

REPEATING FIELDS

The second section of the Storage tab on the Field Options dialog lets developers allow a field to contain multiple values. Such fields are known as *repeating fields*. On a given layout the developer can array repetitions either horizontally or vertically, and in scripts can refer to specific repetitions within the field.

Repeating fields can be problematic. They behave just as individual fields might and are really just a shortcut for having to define multiple instances of a given type of field. It's possible, for example, to have no values in the first and second repetitions, but to have a value in the third. This sounds convenient and intuitively makes common sense, but imagine having to write a script that references that field. How do you know which repetition of the field to reference? Unlike an array in other programming languages, a repeating field cannot be manipulated as a whole. You can reference only one specific repetition at a time.

Repeating fields do have their place, however. Imagine a spreadsheet. Even though an entire row may be blank, the cells are there, ready and waiting for input. If your users are familiar with Microsoft Excel or have been using a paper form for years, it may make sense for you to duplicate the look-and-feel in question, using repeating fields.

In addition to facilitating data entry, one could simulate a related child table with repeating fields.

→ For a detailed discussion of multiple-table solutions, **see** Chapter 6, "Working with Multiple Tables," **p. 153**.

INDEXING

Databases store data by definition, of course, but they are also required to perform functions such as searches and sorts with that data. FileMaker Pro, like many databases, can *index* some of the data in a file to increase the speed at which it performs some of these functions and to enable it to relate data across tables.

An index is somewhat like a database within a database. FileMaker Pro can store, along with a specific value in a given field, all the records in which that exact data is used. This then enables FileMaker to recall those records quickly without having to resort to a linear scan of your file. Aptly named, these indexes work just as a book index works: They facilitate finding all the locations in which a given item is used.

To familiarize yourself with the concept, take a look at a given field's index. Click into a field and select Insert, From Index. If the field is indexable, and has already been indexed, you are presented with a dialog box showing all the discrete values indexed for a given field. Just as with selecting from a value list, you may opt to choose from this list rather than type.

Allowing a user to select from an index is only one of the reasons for having them. Indexes enable FileMaker Pro to perform find requests, sort records, and establish relationships.

 New in this version of FileMaker are two kinds of indexes: value indexes and word indexes. *Value indexes* apply to all field types, with the exception of container or summary fields; *word indexes* only apply to text fields and are based on a given language or character set. The difference between the two, and when either is specifically enabled, lies in their applications.

FileMaker Pro's default setting (found on the Storage tab of the Field Options dialog, displayed in Figure 3.10) is None, with the check box for Automatically Create Indexes As Needed enabled. Most developers, even the more advanced, should find that this setting serves their needs.

Value indexes are established by a database's schema definition—as a developer defines fields and builds relationships—and allow for relationship matches and value lists. If a developer creates a serial ID and joins a relationship via such a field, a value index is created for the serial ID field.

Unless a developer explicitly sets a field to generate one, Word indexes are created as users are interacting with and using a given database. They are utilized for find requests, or created when a user explicitly chooses Insert, From Index. If a user enters data in a find request for a field that lacks a word index, FileMaker Pro enables indexing for that field and builds one (unless its explicitly unindexed, or an unindexable calculation).

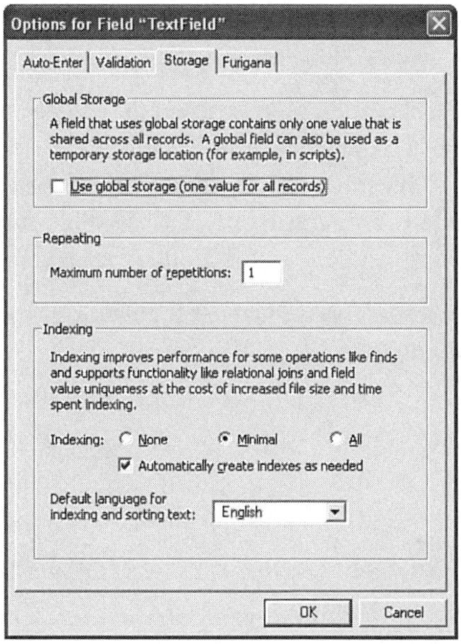

Figure 3.10
FileMaker creates either one type of index or both, depending on how a field is defined and used by users.

At this point you may be wondering what all the fuss is about. Why not index every field in a database and be done with it? The downside to indexes is increased file size and the time it takes FileMaker to maintain the indexes. Creating new records, deleting, importing, and modifying them all take more time, in addition to the fact that the indexes themselves take up more file space.

Notice that FileMaker doesn't allow you to explicitly control word and value indices. Value indices are possible for all field types: Word indices apply only to text fields. Minimal prevents a word index from being created—thus forcing any find requests to be processed through unindexed fields.

Only a subset of the fields in your database will ever need to be indexed, and FileMaker's "on demand" approach makes things fairly simple for developers. Generally speaking, it's best if a field is indexed only when necessary.

→ To explore the vagaries of storage and indexing considerations for calculation fields, **see** "Other Options," **p. 220**.

An important point to remember is that some fields are not indexable. This means than they will be slow when used in sorts and find requests, but most importantly they cannot be used to establish relationships.

A field is unindexable if it is a calculation based on a related field, a summary field, or a global field, or if it references another unindexed, unstored calculation field.

FURIGANA

The fourth tab in the Field Options dialog is one that many English-speaking developers will have trouble properly pronouncing, let alone using. Because of the adoption of Unicode support in FileMaker Pro 7, it is now possible to offer Asian-language double-byte language support. As a result, you can now manage Japanese.

Japanese has four alphabets. One is based on glyphs from Chinese, known as Kanji, two are based on phonetic syllables known as Hiragana and Katakana, and the last is our own Roman alphabet, adopted in the 19th century for foreign words. When working in Japanese, it is possible to render the phonetic equivalents to a Kanji-based block of text. Quite useful when one doesn't quite know how to read one of the 20,000+ characters in Kanji.

Suffice it to say that unless you're a student of Japanese (native or otherwise), this tab will likely not attract much of your attention.

TROUBLESHOOTING

MISMATCHED DATA TYPES

My data isn't sorting properly. Where should I look first to diagnose the problem?

One of the most common bugs you'll run into in FileMaker Pro is confusion stemming from mismatched data types. If your users are entering text data into a field you have defined as numeric, you're bound to get unexpected results, and sorting will be unpredictable. Check your field types when your data appears to be misbehaving.

MISMATCHED CALCULATION RESULTS

One of my date calculations looks like an integer. What's going on?

Some of the more subtle extensions of the data type problem are calculation fields. Note that their result is both the determination of their formula and a data type you set at the bottom of the Specify Calculation dialog. If you're working with dates and return a number, for example, you'll get an entirely valid calculation that will look nothing like "12/25/2003."

PROBLEMATIC FIELD NAMES

My Web programmers are complaining about my field names in FileMaker Pro, and that I keep changing them. What should I consider when naming fields?

Other systems are not as flexible as FileMaker Pro—this is especially true for URLs and the Web. Spend some time with Chapters 21 and 23 if you ever plan to publish your database to the Web. FileMaker Pro breeds a certain freedom when it comes to changing field names as the need arises, but you'll send your XSLT programmer into fits every time you do.

Also be sure to check the restrictions of various SQL databases in your organization. In the case that you need to interoperate with them, you might need to have your field names conform to stricter naming standards. You'll be safe if you never use spaces or special characters and start each field with a letter of the alphabet.

VALIDATION TRAPS

My field validation seems to have gone haywire. I defined a field that now simply throws up one error message after another. What's the problem?

At the end of the day, field validation is only a helpful bank of sandbags against the storm of human interaction your database will suffer. And as in all aspects of your database, the first and worst human in the mix is the developer. Just as with any programming logic, carefully test your validation conditions. FileMaker Pro can't totally prevent you from illogically conflicting restrictions. For example, if you set a field to be unique and non-empty, but also prohibit modification in the auto-entry options, the first record you create will trap your system in an irresolvable conflict.

It's a good idea to leave the Allow User to Override During Data Entry option enabled while you're building a solution and turn it off only when you have completely tested the field in question.

FILEMAKER EXTRA: INDEXING IN FILEMAKER PRO 7

One of the more impactive changes in FileMaker Pro 7 revolves around indexing. In prior versions, indexing was restricted to 60 characters total, broken into blocks of up to 20-character words. Relationships had to be built around match fields, or keys, that were relatively short and generally non-descriptive. This is one of the reasons why we generally advocate using simple serial numbers for indexing purposes. It's rare that you'd need more than 20 digits to serialize the records in a data table.

In this new version of FileMaker Pro, words can be indexed up to approximately 100 characters. Text fields can be indexed to a total of 800 characters and numbers can be indexed up to 400 digits. The limits to indexing have been effectively removed.

What this means to developers is that we can now use far more complex concatenated key combinations (ironically there will be less of that in FileMaker 7, given that data can be related in multiple table depths), longer alphanumeric keys, or as we suggested earlier, introduce a descriptive elements to keys.

In the past, FileMaker Pro would identify "Special_Edition_Using FileMaker_7" (32 characters) as identical to "Special_Edition_Using_MS_Access"...clearly a terrible association to get confused. It's now possible to match against paragraphs of text or very large numbers. Determining matches will be more exact and finds and sorts more robust.

CHAPTER 4

FILEMAKER FUNDAMENTALS: WORKING WITH LAYOUTS

In this chapter

WHAT'S A LAYOUT?

In the previous chapter, we discussed how to define fields for holding the data that you want to store in your database. In this chapter, we discuss the tools at your disposal for creating user interfaces to manage that data.

You use *layouts* to create user interfaces in FileMaker Pro. Layouts are similar in some ways to Web pages, though they're structured quite differently. If you're familiar with SQL-based database development, it might help to think of layouts as being similar to views.

A layout is a collection of graphical objects that a user interacts with to view and modify data. These objects include things such as fields, buttons, static text blocks, graphic elements (such as lines or rectangles), and images. FileMaker Pro contains a rich set of tools for manipulating these objects, allowing you to create attractive and functional interfaces for your users easily.

You can create many different kinds of layouts in FileMaker. Form layouts are useful for data entry; list layouts are generally used for reports and often contain summary parts. Some layouts may be designed for system administrators to clean up data quickly. Still others can serve as user navigation menus and contain no data at all.

One of the things that makes FileMaker unique among database products is that the layouts themselves are stored in a file, right along with data, scripts, access privileges, and other elements of application logic. Every FileMaker Pro file must have at least one layout; there is no practical limit to the number of layouts that a file can contain. It's not unheard of, nor undesirable, to have anywhere from a dozen to a hundred or more layouts in a file.

Layouts are created and managed in what's known as *Layout mode*. To get to Layout mode, choose <u>V</u>iew, <u>L</u>ayout Mode, or simply type (⌘-L) [Ctrl+L]. Almost all the material in this chapter deals with tools and functions that require you to be in Layout mode to access them, but for simplicity and brevity, we will not specifically mention that fact in conjunction with every tool and tip. Consider yourself warned.

In this chapter, we take a "top-down" approach to learning about layouts. We begin by discussing layout creation and layout configuration options. We then move down to the level of the part, and finally down to the level of objects. Learning about layouts can entail "chicken-and-egg" problems: Most topics are intertwined to the extent that there's no convenient linear approach through the material. We therefore encourage you to skip around from topic to topic as necessary to fill out your knowledge.

Finally, this chapter does not comprehensively cover every layout tool or configuration option. Rather, our approach has been to cover details that you might not otherwise discover on your own, and to present what we consider to be "best practices" for working with layouts.

CREATING AND MANAGING LAYOUTS

Creating and managing layouts is one of the most important tasks required of a FileMaker Pro developer. It's also one of the most intuitive. There are, nonetheless, numerous subtle facts and details that you need to know. We encourage you to have a test file open as you go through the following sections so you can try things firsthand.

CREATING A NEW LAYOUT

Every time you create a new table in a file, FileMaker automatically creates a new layout for you as well. The layout is given the same name as your table, and all the fields that you defined at the time of table creation are placed on the layout for you. Figure 4.1 shows an example of what this default layout looks like.

Figure 4.1
The default layout created when you add new tables to a file.

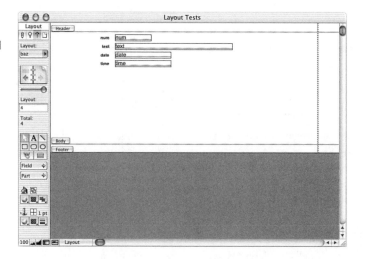

You can create new layouts any time you want while in Layout mode simply by choosing Layouts, New Layout/Report, or by pressing (⌘-N) [Ctrl+N]. You are then taken to a set-up wizard that can help you configure a layout according to one of a handful of types of common layout designs. Figure 4.2 shows the first screen of the Layout Wizard, on which you specify a name for the layout and choose a layout type. You also specify a layout's *context* here; that topic is covered in the next section.

You can create the following six types of layouts:

- **Standard Form**—Useful for data entry layouts, Standard Form generates a basic form view layout with a set of fields you specify. You can select a theme for the layout as well; themes specify the default background color and text styles that will be applied to the layout.

- **Columnar List/Report**—As the name implies, this type is used for creating basic list and subsummary reports. If you don't already have the necessary summary fields in your database, you can create them right from within the wizard.

Figure 4.2
This is the first screen of the wizard for creating new layouts.

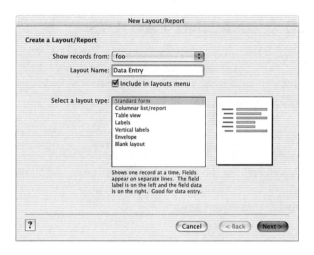

- **Table View**—Table view gives you a spreadsheet-like view of your data. When you select Table view as your layout type, you can select the fields you want to appear on your new layout. They are then displayed according to your selected theme in Table view. Table view is quite useful for behind-the-scenes data manipulation, but may not be suitable as an end-user interface.

- **Labels**—This type of layout is used for printing sheets of labels in standard or custom sizes. The Layout Wizard prompts you to specify the type of labels you will be using—Avery 5160/5260 are the labels used most commonly. If you don't see your label type listed, you can specify custom measurements. See the "Multi-Column Layouts" section later in this chapter for some tips that will come in handy for working with label layouts.

- **Envelope**—You are prompted to select fields you want to use for the address portion of the envelope. The default layout is sized for standard business envelopes. You may need to do some testing and tweaking of the layout to get things just right for your envelopes and printer.

- **Blank Layout**—Choosing Blank Layout gives you just that: a completely blank layout, which you can then manipulate any way you want, free of wizards.

We do not discuss all the screens of the New Layout/Report Assistant here; they're quite intuitive, even for rookie developers. Besides, if you are new to FileMaker, nothing beats spending an hour just playing around with the assistant to see first hand what the various configuration options do for you. You won't cause harm to any existing layouts by doing so, nor can you hurt the database even if you mess up the creation of a new layout.

After a layout has been created, it can be completely modified and turned into whatever you need it to be. Much of the remainder of this chapter is devoted to the tools at your disposal to do just that.

TIP

> There is no tool available for importing layouts from one file to another. If you ever need to do this, the best method is to set up a new, blank layout with parts sized the same as the source layout. Then, copy all the objects from the source file and paste them into the new file. Fields, buttons, and portals need to be respecified to point to their correct referents, but at least all your formatting will be retained.

Within a file, you can duplicate layouts by choosing Layouts, Duplicate Layout. Often, this is a preferred method for creating new layouts, even if they end up looking significantly different from the original. Part sizes, graphic elements, and formatting options are all retained, so modifying as necessary with these as a starting point is usually much faster than creating new layouts from scratch.

TIP

> Create a template layout for yourself that has examples of all the necessary bits and pieces specified (portals, fields, field labels), along with color squares and grid lines. Then you can simply duplicate your template when you need to create a new layout and you'll be well on your way to a finished product.

LAYOUT CONTEXT

In FileMaker Pro 7, every layout is linked to a table occurrence from the Relationships Graph. Many layouts can be linked to a particular table occurrence, but each layout must be tied to one, and only one, table occurrence.

→ For more information on table occurrences, **see** "Adding a Table Occurrence to the Relationships Graph," **p. 183**.

The reason layouts need to be associated with table occurrences is because in a multi-table file, FileMaker needs some way of knowing which records to display in a given layout. In the old days when FileMaker allowed only one table per file, it was always clear that layouts in file X should display records from table X. Now, layouts in file X can be configured to display records from table A, B, or C. The *context* of a layout is determined by the table occurrence to which it is tied.

The concept of layouts being tied to table occurrences can be a bit confusing. See "Determining Which Records Will Be Displayed on a Layout" in the Troubleshooting section at the end of this chapter.

You might wonder why layouts need to be associated with *table occurrences* and not base tables themselves. If you were concerned only with displaying records from the base table, you wouldn't need to worry about table occurrences. But layouts also need to be able to contain records from related tables (that is, portals), and relationships are built between table occurrences, not between base tables. Having a layout linked to a table occurrence makes it unambiguous what context should be used to access related records.

When you define a new layout, the very first prompt of the New Layout/Report Assistant is for where to Show Records From. The options in the pick list are all the table occurrences from the current file's Relationships Graph. At any time, you can go into the Layout Setup dialog to see what context has been set or to change it, though this isn't advisable unless you're an experienced multi-table developer.

If you do have multiple occurrences of any of your base tables, the selection of a particular occurrence in no way affects your ability to see and/or edit field data in the base table itself. That is, if you don't intend to put any related fields on the layout, then it's likely to be inconsequential which occurrence of that base table you select. Do realize, however, that context for scripts is determined by the currently active layout, so some scripts might behave differently if one or another occurrence is used.

→ The implications of context for scripting are discussed elsewhere; **see** "Script Context and Internal Navigation," **p. 253**.

LAYOUT SETUP

The Layout Setup dialog, accessed under the <u>L</u>ayouts menu, allows you to edit many of the fundamental characteristics of a layout, such as the name of the layout, its context, and how it can be viewed (see Figure 4.3).

Figure 4.3
The Layout Setup dialog is where you go to change things such as the name of a layout and its context.

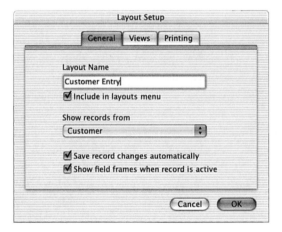

LAYOUT NAMES

You have a great deal of flexibility in how you name layouts. Layout names do not need to be unique and can be up to 100 characters long. They can include numbers, symbols, spaces, and pretty much anything else you want to use.

Though flexibility is a good thing, we suggest you follow a few guidelines:

■ If a layout will potentially be accessed via ODBC or Custom Web Publishing, you should avoid symbols and spaces in the layout name.

- Only the first 8–12 characters of a layout name are visible in the layout selection pop-up (near the top of the status area). The full name is visible when a user clicks on the pop-up, but it can be helpful to use short, unique names for easy identification.

- Try to use names that are somewhat descriptive of the purpose of the layout. Names like "List" and "Layout #3" may not convey much meaning to users.

- In a multi-table file, consider having the base table name as part of the layout name. For instance, "Customer:Data Entry" or "Data Entry (Customer)" may be good names if you need to differentiate among multiple data entry layouts.

- Finally, if you use a single hyphen (-) as a layout name, this appears in the layout pop-up list as a divider. Users can't select divider layouts, which merely serve to help organize what might otherwise be an unwieldy list. Typically, such layouts would be left completely blank, but this isn't a requirement.

TIP

> The single hyphen naming trick works in other areas of FileMaker as well, such as within value lists and as a script name.

VIEW OPTIONS

Every layout you develop can potentially be viewed in three different ways: as a form, as a list, or as a table. A user with access to menu commands can use the <u>V</u>iew menu in Browse mode to switch between them. When you navigate to a layout, you will see it in whatever state in which it was last saved, so bear in mind that switching from layout to layout may also change the view setting as well.

The differences between the three view types are quite straightforward:

- **View as Form**—This view type always shows one record at a time. Any header and footer parts are not fixed on the layout; if the layout has a long body, a user might need to scroll to see the footer. If the body part is short, the last part on the layout expands to fill the empty space. Subsummary parts are visible in Browse mode, but any summary fields in them represent summaries of all the records in the found set. The maximum height and width of a layout is just over 111 inches. For some long forms, such as legal contracts, you may need to split the form into two separate layouts.

- **View as List**—With View as List, the number of records displayed is determined by the height of the layout body part and the height of the window. If more records are present in the found set than can be displayed on screen, the vertical scroll bar enables users to see additional records. Any header and footer parts are fixed on screen at all times, even when a user scrolls to see additional records. Subsummary parts are never visible in Browse mode with View as List. If fields are placed in the header or footer parts, they take their values from the currently active record. Any modification to a field in the header or footer part likewise affects the currently active record.

- **View as Table**—In Table view, all the fields in the layout's body are presented in a spreadsheet-like grid. The initial order of the fields is determined by their top-to-bottom position on the layout. That is, the first column is the top-most field on the layout. No non-field elements (for example, buttons, text, graphics) from the body of the layout are rendered in Table view. Field formatting (for example, color, font, font size, and so on) is honored, however. Oddly, the column headers conform to the format of the first field. Other properties of the Table view can be specified under the Views tab of the Layout Setup dialog. As shown in Figure 4.4, you can specify whether header and footer parts should be visible and whether columns can be sorted, reordered, and resized.

Figure 4.4
You can alter the look and functionality of the table view by using the Table View Properties dialog.

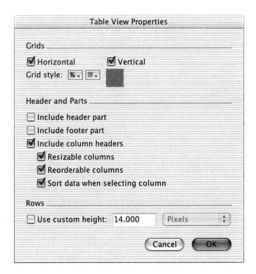

Using the Views tab of the Layout Setup dialog, you can disable user access to certain view types. Although usually not necessary, this can be a good precaution to take to keep adventurous users on the right track. Accessing an inappropriate view type is likely not going to cause much harm, but it certainly can confuse users.

MULTI-COLUMN LAYOUTS

When printing labels and certain types of reports, you might want to present your data in multiple columns. You can specify the number of columns to display on the Printing tab of the Layout Setup dialog; this is shown in Figure 4.5.

In Layout mode, dashed vertical lines represent the boundaries between columns. Columns other than the first are grayed out; the idea is that you need to place any objects you want displayed in the first column, and these objects are replicated to the other columns as necessary. Figure 4.6 shows an example of a 3-column layout used to display a phone directory. Notice that the header and footer part are not divided into columns. This means that if you want headers to appear above the second and third columns, you need to add those explicitly, as we've done in Figure 4.6.

Figure 4.5
You can customize the print settings for a particular layout on the Print tab of the Layout Settings dialog.

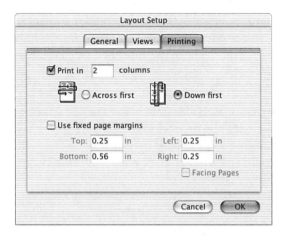

Figure 4.6
This example shows how a layout for a 3-column phone directory might appear in Layout mode.

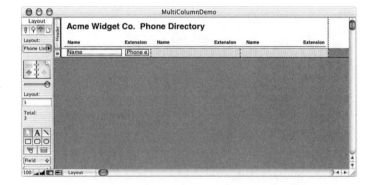

It's not possible to have columns of differing widths; every column is the same width as the first one. You can manually adjust the column width by clicking on the dashed divider between the first and second column and dragging left or right as appropriate.

Subsummary parts and leading and trailing grand summaries can be used on multi-column layouts, but they behave slightly differently depending on whether you've chosen to display data Across First or Down First. If you chose Down First, then any summary parts are also columnar. On the other hand, if the data is displayed Across First, then summary parts span the full width of the layout, just as the header and footer parts do.

→ Subsummary parts are covered in depth in "Working with Parts," **p. 99**.

The effects of a multi-column layout can be viewed only in Preview mode. In Browse mode, a user sees only a single column of data.

HIDING AND REORDERING LAYOUTS

In Browse mode, layouts can be either accessible or inaccessible via the layout pull-down menu in the status area. If a layout is accessible, users can see it and navigate to it at will. If it is inaccessible, users can navigate to it only by running a script that takes them there. In Layout mode, all layouts are accessible.

Typically, layouts are set to be inaccessible when you need to prevent users from manually navigating to a layout. For instance, you might have report layouts or find screens that require certain preparation before they become useful. There may be unanticipated and/or undesired results if a user is able to bypass the scripts you've created and navigate directly to a layout.

The option to have a layout be accessible or not is on the first screen of the New Layout/Report Assistant; it can also be set through the Layout Setup dialog. The Set Layout Order dialog, shown in Figure 4.7, also has a check box on each line that can be toggled to change a layout from visible to hidden and vice versa. Using this method is the quickest way to hide (or show) a number of layouts at once.

Figure 4.7
Use the Set Layout Order dialog to set the accessibility and order of layouts.

The Set Layout Order dialog, as you might guess from its name, also enables you to change the order in which layouts appear in the layout pop-up list. You can use the double-arrowed selection tool to move a layout up or down in the order. You can accomplish the same thing by selecting a line and pressing (⌘) [Ctrl] and either the up or down arrow.

NOTE

In previous versions of FileMaker, you were required to be the host of a file to access the Set Layout Order dialog. It can now be managed even as a client of FileMaker Server.

Restricting Access to Layouts

Using the methods discussed in the previous section to hide layouts is a good way of keeping users from going places they shouldn't, but it's not adequate security if you truly need to restrict access to layouts. Plus, making layouts inaccessible affects all users; you can't set up rules for which layouts are accessible for which users.

Added protection for layouts can be achieved by restricting access via privilege sets. A privilege set can be defined to provide either All No Access, All View Only, or All Modifiable control over layouts. Alternatively, you can specify custom layout privileges, as shown in Figure 4.8. You can protect both editing the layouts themselves as well as the data displayed on them. Any user who has no access to a layout, doesn't see that the layout exists, even in Layout mode.

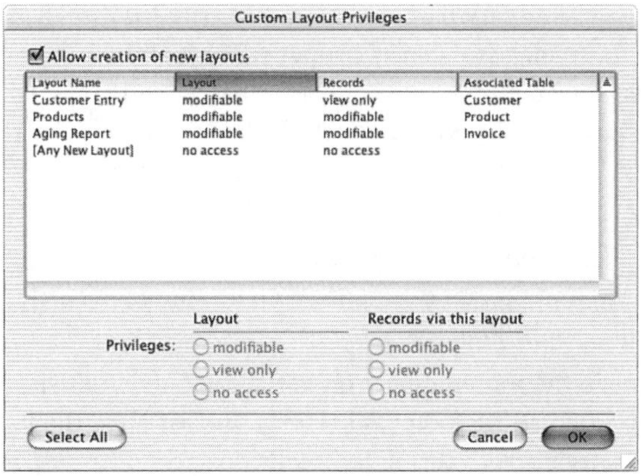

Figure 4.8
Custom Layout Privileges enable you to restrict certain users from modifying or viewing certain layouts.

→ For more information about setting up privilege sets, **see** "Privilege Sets," **p. 325**.

If you want to prevent certain users from creating new layouts, leave the Allow Creation of New Layouts option at the top of the Custom Layout Privileges dialog unchecked. Additionally, you can set default privileges that users will have for new layouts by editing the options for the [Any New Layout] line.

WORKING WITH PARTS

Layouts are made up of parts. Depending on your objectives, your layout may contain header and footer parts, a body part, one or more subsummary parts, and maybe even a leading or trailing grand summary. Every layout must contain at least one part.

Briefly, the purpose and some characteristics of each type of part are as follows:

■ **Title Header**—Title headers are used when you need a header on the first page of a multi-page printout that differs from the header on subsequent pages. In Form view, a user sees only a title header while in Browse mode, but not in List or Table view.

■ **Header**—Objects in the header part appear at the top of each page of a multi-page report (except the first when a title header is present). A header part remains fixed on screen in List or Table views, even when a user scrolls to see additional records. Fields placed in a header part can be modified; they always represent data in the currently active record.

■ **Leading Grand Summary**—Typically used on report layouts, a leading grand summary appears between the header and any subsummary or body parts. Summary fields placed in this part aggregate across the entire found set.

→ For more information about using summary fields and summary parts to create reports, **see** "Summarized Reports," **p. 281**.

■ **Body**—The body part is used to display record data. A data entry layout often consists of nothing other than a body part. Most every layout you create will have a body part.

- **Subsummary**—Subsummary parts are used primarily for displaying subtotals on reports. For a subsummary to display properly, the found set must be sorted by the same field as that on which the subsummary is based, and you must be in Preview mode. Subsummaries can be placed either above or below the body part, depending on whether you want the subtotals displayed before or after the data they summarize.

- **Trailing Grand Summary**—Similar to leading grand summaries, a trailing grand summary is typically found on report layouts and is used to display aggregate summaries. When printed, the trailing grand summary report appears directly following the body part and any trailing subsummaries.

- **Footer**—Objects in the footer appear on every page of a multi-page print out (except on the first page when a title footer is present). In List view, the footer remains fixed on the layout when a user scrolls through records.

- **Title Footer**—A title footer part is used when you want to display a different footer on the first page of a multi-page printout.

ADDING AND ORDERING PARTS

There are two ways of adding parts to a layout. The first is by clicking and dragging the Part button in the status area to the point where you want the new part to appear. You are prompted to select a part type when you let up the mouse. Although it is convenient, we discourage this method of adding new parts. New parts, except when added to the very bottom of the layout, always come at the expense of existing parts. That is, if you have a 50-pixel header followed by a 200-pixel body, and you attempt to add a subsummary between these parts, the body part shrinks by the size of the subsummary part. Moreover, fields that were in the body part may now be part of the subsummary part.

The other option for adding new parts, which we prefer in almost every circumstance, is to use the Part Setup dialog (shown in Figure 4.9), which can be found under the Layouts menu. When parts are added with this tool, it's not at the expense of any existing part; the total height of the layout increases.

Figure 4.9
You can add, edit, delete, and reorder the parts on a layout from the Part Setup dialog.

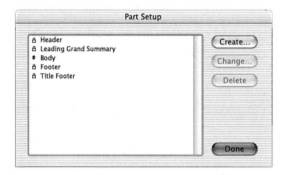

The Part Setup dialog can also be used to reorder, edit, and delete parts. The only types of parts that can be reordered are the body and subsummary parts. To reorder these, click the arrow in front of the part name and drag it to the desired position. Other part types appear with a lock in front of them, indicating that they are fixed in a certain order by definition.

You can delete a part from a layout either by selecting it from the Part Setup dialog and clicking Delete, or by clicking the part label while in layout mode and pressing the Backspace or Delete key on your keyboard. Either way, when you delete a part, any objects contained in that part are also deleted.

FORMATTING A PART

You can configure a few attributes of parts directly from Layout mode itself. First, you can set a background color and/or fill pattern for a part by clicking on the part label, then selecting a color and/or fill pattern. (Control-clicking) [right+clicking] on the part label similarly pulls up a contextual menu with access to these attributes.

You can achieve much the same effect simply by drawing a large rectangle on the layout, sending it to the back, and locking it. Setting a background color for the part is preferred, though, because the color extends to the right and downward if the user expands the window beyond the boundaries of your rectangle.

> **TIP**
>
> For users with monitors set to higher resolutions than your database was designed for, consider adding a footer with a background color different from your body part so that users can visually see where the layout "ends" and size their windows appropriately.

You can also change a part's size. To do this, simply click on the dividing line between two parts and drag either up or down. When making a part smaller, you can remove whitespace from the part, but you are prevented from dragging through any objects in the part. Any expansion of a part increases the overall size of the part.

Holding down (Option) [Alt] as you resize a part changes the rules slightly. First, any expansion or contraction comes at the benefit or expense of the neighboring part; the overall length of the layout remains the same (except, of course, when lengthening the last part on the layout). Also, you can "run over" objects this way; an object that was in one part may end up belonging to another part after you've resized things. An object that ends up straddling two (or more) parts belongs to the part that contains its upper left-hand corner.

The Size palette can also be used to see and set a part's length. This is the best way to precisely set part lengths, especially when trying to duplicate complex layouts from one file to another. Click the part label to display that part's data in the Size palette.

→ For more information about the Size palette, **see** "Positioning Objects on a Layout," **p. 106**.

PART DEFINITION

Beyond the size and background color of a part, some part attributes can be set only in the Part Definition dialog, which is shown in Figure 4.10. You can get to this dialog either from the Part Setup dialog (clicking Create or Change), or by double-clicking on the part label itself.

Figure 4.10
The Part Definition dialog is used to specify a part's type and attributes.

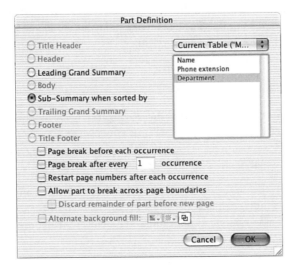

The type of part is indicated by the radio buttons on the left side of this dialog. You can change the type of a part simply by selecting a different radio button. If a type is grayed out, that means you already have a part of that type. The only part type for which you can have multiples is subsummary.

The fields on the right side of the dialog apply only to subsummaries. When you make a subsummary part, you must specify what field will act as the break field for the summary. The break field doesn't need to actually appear in that part, but the found set must be sorted by the break field for the subsummary part to show up on a report.

→ For more information on break fields and subsummary reports, **see** "Summarized Reports," **p. 281**.

At the bottom of the dialog are a number of options for configuring page breaks and page numbers. Often in subsummary reports, you'll want each new sub-section to start on a new page. To do this, you would edit the part definition of the subsummary part to include the Page Break Before Each Occurrence option. As you would expect, it's actually only each occurrence *after the first one* that's preceded by a page break.

One of the new features of FileMaker Pro 7 is the option to Alternate Background Fill. This option is available only on body parts. Any color and/or fill that you specify is used as the background for every other record. It alternates with any background color that has been specified for the part itself. Often, a slight shading of alternate rows on a report makes it easier to read.

WORKING WITH OBJECTS ON A LAYOUT

As stated previously, a layout is essentially a collection of objects that is manifested as a "screen" that allows users to see and/or modify data. We'll refer abstractly to anything that can be placed on a layout as a *layout object*. There are many tools and techniques for configuring and manipulating layout objects. Some of these apply only to specific types of objects, whereas others are more general in nature. The better you know how to work with the tools for crafting layouts, the better your user interface will be.

ADDING OBJECTS TO A LAYOUT

The status area in Layout mode provides a rich set of design tools for adding and manipulating layout objects. These tools are shown in Figure 4.11.

Figure 4.11
The status area contains most of the tools you need for designing layouts.

4

TIP

In Layout mode, the flip book can be used to move from layout to layout. The keyboard shortcut for this, (Ctrl-Up Arrow) [Ctrl+Up/Down arrow], is the same one used in Browse mode to move from record to record, and in Preview mode to move from page to page.

The layout tools in the middle of the status area are used to add new objects to a layout. There are tools for adding text blocks, lines, rectangles, rounded rectangles, ovals, buttons, and portals. With each, you can simply click on the tool to activate it, then click and drag on your layout where you want the object to appear.

Normally, when you are finished creating an object, the pointer tool is reselected automatically. There are times, however, when you want to create multiple objects of the same type at once. In these cases, it's useful to "lock in" the selection of a particular tool. You can do this by double-clicking on the tool in the status area. There's also a preference on the Layout tab of the application preferences screen to Always Lock Layout Tools, though we generally advise against enabling it. You can tell when a tool is locked because its image turns white instead of black.

The Insert menu provides another means for adding objects to a layout. At the top of this menu you'll find selections for adding all the object types found in the status area.

CAUTION

Unless your status area is closed and locked for some reason, we prefer not to use this menu because it doesn't give you an opportunity to specify location or size during object creation. Either duplicate existing objects or use the tools from the status area when at all possible.

To insert a picture or other graphic element developed externally, you can use the Insert, Graphic menu command. Or you can simply cut and paste objects from many other applications directly into your FileMaker layouts.

Specifying Object Attributes

You have a great deal of control over the attributes of any object that you place on a layout. Different object types may have different attribute options. You can always tell what attributes of an object can be configured by (Control-clicking) [right+clicking] the object. A contextual menu appears, listing any formatting options that are appropriate to that particular object type. There are menu commands and status area tools that provide access to the same attribute settings, but the most efficient way to set an object's attributes is to use the contextual menus.

The Format Painter Tool

You can copy the formatting attributes from one object to other objects on your layout by using the Format Painter tool. The Format Painter can be found under the Format menu and in the Standard toolbar, which you can enable from the View, Toolbars menu.

To use the Format Painter, you simply select an object that has the formatting attributes you want to propagate, then turn on the Format Painter, using either of the two methods just mentioned. A small paintbrush appears next to your mouse pointer, indicating that the Format Painter tool is active. Then simply select an object (or set of objects) to which you want to apply the formats. You can "lock in" the Format Painter tool by double-clicking its icon from the Standard toolbar. This enables you to click on several objects, applying formats as you go.

SETTING DEFAULT OBJECT ATTRIBUTES

The default format attributes include such things as the font, font size, font color, text style (for example, bold, italics), pen width, alignment, shading, and object effects. In short, any configurable attribute of a layout object has a default setting. Not all objects, of course, have all the potential attributes. Rectangles, for instance, have shading and pen width attributes, but don't have any font attributes. When a new object of any sort is added to a layout with the layout tools, the applicable attributes of that object inherit the current default settings.

NOTE

You can, of course, change the attributes of an object after it has been placed on a layout.

The default format attributes are stored at the file level. This means that as you move from layout to layout within a file, the defaults stay the same, but if you're working with multiple files, each may have its own defaults.

When you first create a file, the default text format is fairly vanilla: 12-point black Helvetica (Mac), 12-point Arial (Windows), no object effects, no text styles, no field borders, and no shading. You can change the default settings in one of two ways:

- In Layout mode, if you have no objects selected, any formatting options you change are applied to the default text attributes. Only the attributes you change are affected.
- If you (⌘-click) [Ctrl+click] on an object, that object's characteristics become the default. This is the easiest way to set the default; you can simply format one object with the settings you want and then click it. All that object's attributes together become the new default; any attributes that the object doesn't possess are not affected.

TIP

If multiple layout objects are selected and you (⌘-click) [Ctrl+click] on any one of them, the front-most object's characteristics become the default.

If you have opened a file as a guest (either of FileMaker Pro or of FileMaker Server), any changes that you make to the default attributes persist only until you close the file; those defaults aren't stored in the file and don't affect other developers in the system. As the host of a file, any changes that you make to the default attributes are stored and persist until you change them again, even if you close and reopen the file.

DUPLICATING LAYOUT OBJECTS

Any object on a layout can be duplicated in one of two ways. When you duplicate an object (or set of objects), the new objects have all of the same attributes of the source objects. It therefore is often faster and more efficient to create a new object by duplicating an existing one and modifying it rather than adding a new one using the layout tools.

The first way is simply to select some set of objects and to choose Edit, Duplicate or press (⌘-D) [Ctrl+D]. The entire set of objects is duplicated, with the new objects appearing 6 pixels to the right and 6 pixels lower than the original set. The new objects are selected (as opposed to the original set) so you can easily move them to wherever you want.

There's a useful technique for creating multiple copies of an object, spaced out at consistent intervals. Begin by selecting a set of objects, which we'll call set A, and duplicate it as described, creating set B. Without deselecting any of the objects in set B, move them to some desired place on a layout. Choose Edit, Duplicate again, and the new copy, set C, instead of having the 6 pixel to the right, 6 pixel down relationship to its source, is spaced an equal distance from set B as B is from A. Continued selection of Edit, Duplicate results in additional new sets, each positioned a consistent distance from its source. This technique is very useful when creating columnar lists and grids of equally spaced lines.

The second way to duplicate layout objects is to (Option-drag) [Ctrl+drag] them. Simply select a set of objects, then start to drag them as if you intended to move them to a new location on the layout. As you're moving the objects, however, hold down the (Option) [Ctrl] key. Continue to hold this key down until after you have released the mouse click; the objects are not moved, but a copy of them is placed at the new location.

TIP

> You can also hold down the Shift key as you're dragging the objects to constrain movement to a vertical or horizontal axis. This is generally our preferred method for duplicating layout objects.

POSITIONING OBJECTS ON A LAYOUT

Much of layout design is simply moving things around until they look just right. This is also one of the most intuitive things for new developers to learn. So much so, in fact, that many never learn some of the fine points of working with objects on a layout. We will attempt to remedy that here.

SELECTING OBJECTS ON A LAYOUT

Most all formatting and positioning of objects on a layout begins with the selection of a set of objects to work with. You can go about selecting objects in several different ways; knowing these methods can greatly increase your efficiency at designing layouts.

- **Click on an object**—You can select any object simply by clicking on it. When you do so, small squares, called handles, appear at the four corners of the object, indicating that the object is indeed selected.

- **Shift+click**—When you have one or more objects selected, you can Shift+click on an additional object to add it to the selected set. Similarly, Shift+clicking on an object that is already selected removes it from the selected set.

- **Selection box**—If you click on the background of the layout (that is, any place there's not an object), and drag a rectangle across the screen, when you release the mouse, any objects that were completely contained within your selection box are selected. This is typically the easiest and quickest way to select multiple objects.

NOTE

> If you hold down the (⌘) [Ctrl] key while dragging a selection box on the screen, then any objects *touched* by (instead of contained by) the box are selected. This technique works well for selecting objects that might partially overlap other objects, where using the enclosing method would result in too many selected objects.

- **Select all objects**—To select all the objects on a layout, choose Edit, Select All, or use the (⌘-A) [Ctrl+A]) keyboard shortcut.
- **Select all instances of a type of object**—It's also possible to select all instances of a particular type of object, such as all the text objects, or all the fields, or all the rectangles. There are several ways to do this. If the Arrange toolbar is visible, you can select an object, then click the Select Objects by Type button in that toolbar to select all similar objects. Or, you can select an object, then press (⌘-Option-A) [Ctrl+Alt+A] to accomplish the same thing. Finally, if you have a tool (other than the Button or Portal tool) selected from the layout tools, you can select all the objects of that type by performing an Edit, Select All.

MOVING OBJECTS

After you have selected a set of objects, you can move those objects around on the layout—provided they are not locked—in a few different ways. First, you can click on the interior of any object in the selected set and drag the set to a new location. You can also use the arrow keys on your keyboard to move a selected set of objects pixel by pixel.

Using the click and drag method, hold down the Shift key after you start dragging the objects and the movement will be constrained to either the vertical or the horizontal plane. That is, there would be no way of moving the objects other than up and down or from side to side. This is very useful for keeping objects properly aligned as you reposition them.

RESIZING OBJECTS

When you select an object, four small black or gray squares appear at the corners of the object. These define the object's boundaries; they are called the object's *handles*. All objects, even circular ones, have a rectangular "footprint" defined by the four handles. If the handles are gray, that indicates the object is locked; it can't be moved or resized in this state. (Refer to the "Locking Objects" section later in this chapter.)

You can resize an object by clicking on one of the four handles and dragging in the desired direction. Unlike some other graphic applications, FileMaker does not enable you to click on the sides of the object to change just the height or width of the object. You must always use the object's corners. Just as when moving objects, you can, however, constrain movement to the vertical or horizontal plane by holding down the Shift key as you drag to resize the object.

If you have selected multiple objects, resizing any one of them causes all the objects to resize by a similar amount. This is very useful in cases where you want to select, for instance, five fields and make them all slightly longer or shorter. Resizing them as a set ensures that they will all be changed by the same absolute amount.

THE OBJECT GRID

You have the option, when working with layouts, of enabling or disabling an *object grid*. You can change the status of the object grid by toggling the <u>O</u>bject Grids command, found at the bottom of the <u>A</u>rrange menu. You can also toggle the status of the object grid by pressing (⌘-Y) [Ctrl+Y].

When object grids are enabled, then all movement and resizing of objects takes place against a virtual grid. Each "square" of the grid measures 6 pixels by 6 pixels. The effect of this is that when you are moving or resizing objects, movement happens in 6-pixel chunks. When the object grids are disabled, movement happens in 1-pixel units, resulting in fluid motion.

> **TIP**
>
> You can change the default grid spacing to something other than 6 pixels by using the Layouts, Set <u>R</u>ulers menu.

The object grids are defined relative to each object. That is, there's not a static grid to which everything snaps. If object A and object B are 2 pixels apart, with object grids enabled, you could move each object one "chunk" in any direction and they'd still be 2 pixels apart, each having moved 6 pixels from its original location.

Whether or not you choose to have object grids enabled as you design layouts is purely a personal preference. Some developers love object grids; others loath them. Even the authors of this book are passionately divided on this subject. The benefit of using the object grids is that it's easy to keep things arranged and sized nicely. It's much easier to notice visually when an object is 6 pixels off-line rather than 1 pixel. Plus, if you ever need to move things in finer increments, you can simply use the arrow keys to "nudge" the objects into line. Also, you can temporarily suspend the object grids by holding down the (⌘) [Alt] key as you are moving or resizing an object.

The object grid's status is a file-level setting. That is, as you work on different layouts within a file, the grid status carries through to them all, but if you have multiple files in a solution, you can conceivably have the object grid enabled in some and not in others.

THE SIZE PALETTE

The Size palette is a floating toolbox that can be used to see and set very precise object positions. It's shown in Figure 4.12. To make the palette appear, choose <u>V</u>iew, Object Si<u>z</u>e.

It's an application-level setting, so after you have the palette onscreen, it is available no matter with what layout you are working. You can move the palette around on your screen so that it's positioned optimally for whatever task you need it for.

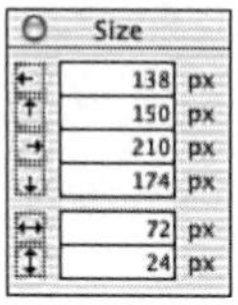

Figure 4.12
The Size palette is quite useful for positioning and sizing objects on a layout.

The Size palette provides six pieces of data about the position and size of a selected object (or set of objects). From top to bottom, these data points represent:

- The distance from the left edge of the object to the left edge of the layout
- The distance from the top edge of the object to the top edge of the layout
- The distance from the right edge of the object to the left edge of the layout
- The distance from the bottom edge of the object to the top edge of the layout
- The object's width
- The object's height

In these definitions, the left edge and top edge of the layout may be outside the area you can actively work with. Most layouts have a default page margin, usually .25 inches on each side. You can make your layout's page margins visible by choosing View, Page Margins. Fixed page margins can be set under the Printing tab of the Layout Setup dialog.

CAUTION

It's important to know that page margins are factored into the distances displayed in the Size palette. You can't move or position an object in the page margin. If you are trying to use absolute positioning to align objects on different layouts, any differences in page margins need to be taken into consideration.

The Size palette can measure distance as inches, centimeters, or pixels. You'll see the unit prominently displayed on the palette itself. You can toggle between the three available units simply by clicking on any of the unit labels.

TIP

We find that setting the Size palette to display pixels is much more intuitive and useful than using inches or centimeters.

The Size palette doesn't merely report on the position and size of a selected object; it can also be used to set these attributes. With an object selected, you can click into and edit any of the six data points. Pressing the Tab or Return keys moves you through the palette's fields; pressing the Enter key exits the palette. As you change the numbers in the palette, the selected object moves or resizes as you have specified. This makes it very easy to precisely align, position, and size objects on a layout.

ARRANGING OBJECTS

FileMaker provides many tools to help you organize and arrange objects on a layout. This section discusses some of these tools.

GROUPING OBJECTS

Objects can be grouped together to form a new object. You do so by selecting the desired objects and choosing Arrange, Group or pressing (⌘-R) [Ctrl+R]. The resulting object behaves just like any other object. It has a single set of selection handles, and it can be moved and resized as described in the previous sections. Any formatting applied to the grouped object is applied to each of the elements of the group, as if you had simply selected all the elements individually. Grouped objects can be further grouped with other objects to form yet new objects.

To ungroup an object, select the object, then choose Arrange, Ungroup or press (⌘-Shift-R) [Ctrl+Shift+R]. If an object was formatted as a button, ungrouping it deletes the button definition.

> **TIP**
>
> Ungrouping an object is the easiest way to remove a button definition from an object. This works even if the object in question isn't a grouped object.

LOCKING OBJECTS

To prevent an object from being moved, resized, reformatted, or deleted, you can lock it by selecting it and choosing Arrange, Lock or pressing (⌘-Option-L) [Ctrl+Alt+L]. When you select a locked object, its handles appear grayed out rather than black.

When you select a combination of locked and unlocked objects, if you attempt to move or resize them as a set, only the unlocked objects are affected. If you attempt to change the formatting of the selected set, you see an error that the formatting can't be applied to some objects in the set because they are locked.

Locking objects is very useful when you have objects stacked on top of or overlapping one another. It's as if the locked objects become a backdrop against which you do your work. Whether you leave the objects permanently or temporarily locked, it becomes much easier to select and work with certain objects when the objects behind them are locked.

To unlock an object, choose Arrange, Unlock, or press (⌘-Option-Shift-L) [Ctrl+Option+Shift+L].

ALIGNING OBJECTS

It's often desirable to align objects on a layout relative to one another, and FileMaker has some built-in tools to make this easy to do. For instance, say you have 10 fields on a layout and you want to make sure that they are aligned along their left edges. Figure 4.13 shows the Set Alignment dialog, which you can access either by choosing Arrange, Set Alignment or by pressing (⌘-Shift-K) [Ctrl+Shift+K].

Figure 4.13
The Set Alignment dialog enables you to specify the relative alignment of a set of objects.

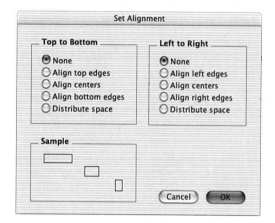

You can specify either a Top to Bottom alignment, or a Left to Right alignment, or both. If you have selected a set of objects before coming to this dialog, they will be aligned according to your instructions, and that alignment will be remembered as the active configuration. If you have subsequent alignment operations to perform that need to use that same active configuration, rather than come back to the Set Alignment dialog each time, you can just select Arrange, Align, or press (⌘-K) [Ctrl+K].

When you align a set of objects relative to one another, one of the objects usually serves as the reference point. For instance, when you left-align a set of objects, the left-most object is the reference point. The other objects move left while the left-most object remains in place. Similar results are obtained for aligning to the right, top, and bottom. The exception to this is when one or more of the selected objects is locked. If this is the case, and you want to, say, left-align a set of objects, the left-most *locked* object becomes the reference point.

The rules for centering are slightly different. When centering left to right, the objects are centered on the midpoint between the left-most and right-most selection points. For top-to-bottom centering, they are aligned on the midpoint between the top-most and bottom-most selection points.

The option to distribute space is useful when you want to be sure that objects in a set are equidistant from one another. The two outer-most objects, whether left-to-right or top-to-bottom, act as anchors for the distribution: The selected objects in between them are spaced apart evenly.

LAYERING OBJECTS

FileMaker maintains a *stacking order* for objects on a layout. When a new object is added to a layout, it becomes the front-most item in the stacking order. The stacking order becomes important when objects overlap one another. If two objects overlap, object A appears in "front" of object B if it is forward in the stacking order. Also, if object B is completely behind object A, it is impossible to select object B simply by clicking on it. When you click on a spot on a layout where multiple objects overlap, you select the front-most of the objects.

There is no way to see the stacking order of the objects on a layout, but you can manipulate it by using the Bring to Front, Bring Forward, Send to Back, and Send Backward functions, all of which can be found under the Arrange menu.

→ The stacking order also determines the tab order of layouts published to the Web with Instant Web Publishing. For more on IWP, **see** "Layout Design," **p. 623**.

NOTE

> The stacking order also determines the order in which objects draw on the screen. With a local file or on a fast network, it's probably imperceptible, but on slow networks, you will sometimes see the objects draw one by one, from back to front.

SLIDING OBJECTS

If you are developing layouts that are intended to be printed, and you have variable amounts of text in certain fields, you may want to configure some objects on your layout to slide. Sliding eliminates excess white space from an object, allowing it to appear closer to its neighboring objects. You can configure an object to slide either up or to the left, using the dialog shown in Figure 4.14, which you open by selecting a set of objects and choosing Format, Sliding/Printing or by pressing (⌘-Option-T) [Ctrl+Alt+T].

Figure 4.14
You can configure an object to slide either up or to the left by using the Set Sliding/Printing dialog.

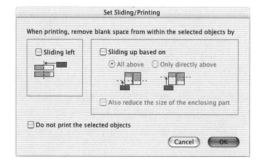

The effects of sliding can't be seen unless you are in Preview mode (or you actually print). If you set a field to slide, then any whitespace in the field is removed in preview mode. One caveat to know is that the contents of a field must be top-aligned to slide up and left-aligned to slide left.

Sliding does not reduce the amount of space between objects. Say you have a large text field, as in Figure 4.15, with a horizontal line located 10 pixels below the bottom of the field. If you set both objects to slide up, empty space in the field will be removed, and the line will slide up until it is 10 pixels away from the bottom of the field. Figure 4.16 shows how the record in Figure 4.15 looks in Preview mode. All objects on the layout have been set to slide up.

Figure 4.15
You can't see any effects of sliding while in Browse mode.

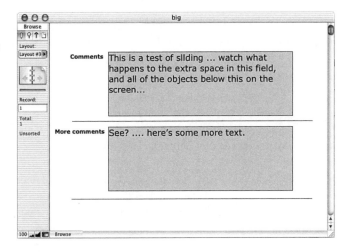

Figure 4.16
In Preview mode, objects slide either up or to the left, removing whitespace within fields.

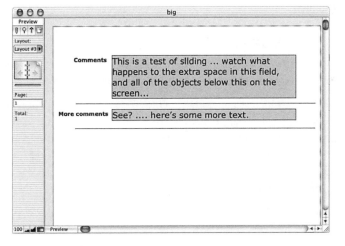

The option to Also Reduce the Size of the Enclosing Part is useful when you have a list of variable-length records. Set the layout to accommodate the longest possible record, then turn on sliding for all the fields in the body and reduce the size of the enclosing part. The rows of the list will then have a variable length when they are previewed and printed. You must be sure to set all the objects in the list to slide; a single non-sliding object may cause the part to not reduce properly. Objects such as vertical lines do not shrink in size to accommodate variable record widths, so if you need this effect, use left or right field borders, which do shrink appropriately.

Sliding can be applied to portals as well, but objects in a portal can't slide. If a portal is set to slide up, then any blank rows of the portal are suppressed, but there's no way to make the height of the individual rows of the portal variable. Portal sliding is useful and necessary in reports that must pull in data from related files. Typically, if there's a portal on a printable report, you should set the portal to display a large number of records and not to have a vertical scroll. If you enable sliding as well, any unneeded portal rows simply disappear.

The Set Sliding/Printing dialog also has an option to make a layout object non-printing. As with sliding, this setting is apparent only in Preview mode. Typically, you use this option to allow buttons, background images, and data entry instructions—items you typically wouldn't want to have on a printout—to be visible only in Browse and Find modes.

WORKING WITH FIELDS

The primary purpose of a layout is to allow users to interact with data. By *interact*, we mean everything from viewing, editing, and formatting to finding and sorting. Although a field is at some level just another type of layout object and can be manipulated using the same tools as other layout objects, a number of tools are designed specifically for working with fields. These provide you with a great deal of freedom and flexibility for creating the interfaces that work best for your users and your solution. We don't cover every option of every tool here, but rather try to give you a sense of what the tools are and some of the situations in which to use them.

ADDING FIELDS TO LAYOUTS

There are essentially two different ways that you can add fields to a layout: by using the Field button in the status area and by duplicating an existing field.

The first of these—which is generally also the first method that people learn—involves clicking and dragging the Field button in the status area out to the section of the layout where you want to place the field. The attributes of a field added this way are governed by the current default format attributes. However, the field's width is always 79 pixels. Its height is determined by a combination of the default font, font size, pen width, and object effects (for example, embossing, engraving, drop shadow).

As with other layout objects, when you duplicate an existing field, the new field has all the attributes of the previously existing field. Remember, you can duplicate any layout object either by selecting it and choosing <u>E</u>dit, <u>D</u>uplicate or pressing (⌘-D) [Ctrl+D], or you can select it, then (Option-drag) [Ctrl-drag] to a new location. In either case, if you have selected a single field, when you duplicate it, you see the Specify Field dialog and can identify the new field. On the other hand, if you have selected multiple objects, when you duplicate them, you get just the duplicated objects.

 There are some issues to be aware of when copying and pasting fields from a layout in one file to a layout in another file. See "Copying and Pasting Fields Between Files," in the Troubleshooting section at the end of this chapter.

Each field object on a layout is defined to display data from a particular field. Unless you have selected Sample Data in the View, Show menu, you see the field's name on the object when you're in Layout mode. If the field name begins with ::, that's an indication that the object is linked to a related field. To know what relationship is used, you need to go into the Specify Field dialog. That's also where you can re-define a field object to display the contents of a different field. You can get to the Specify Field dialog either by (⌘-clicking) [right+clicking] the object, or by double-clicking the object.

TIP

> If a field has been defined as a button, then double-clicking it takes you to the Button Definition dialog, not the Specify Field dialog. Similarly, if multiple fields are grouped together, then right-clicking doesn't offer you the option to go to the Specify Field dialog.

FIELD FORMATTING

You can apply several field formatting options to the fields on a layout. To get to the field format dialog, which is shown in Figure 4.17, select a field, then choose Format, Field Format. You can also (Control-click) [right+click] a field and select Field Format.

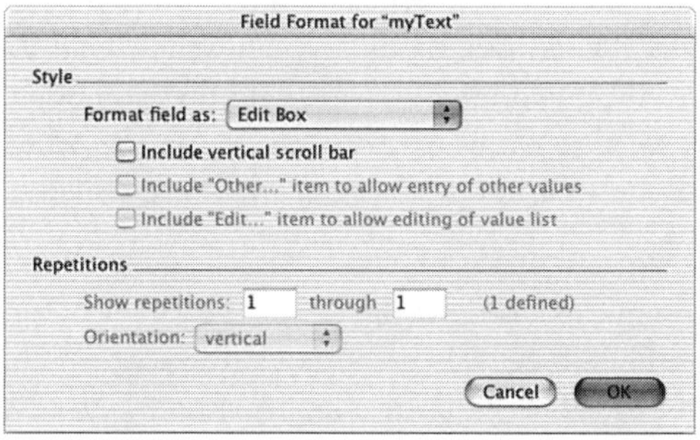

Figure 4.17
The Field Format dialog enables you to format a field as a pop-up list, pop-up menu, check box set, or radio button set. It also includes settings for how to display repeating fields.

For standard fields where a user will be manually entering and editing data, the Edit Box format is appropriate. The option to include a vertical scroll box is usually used only when a user is able and/or expected to type in multiple lines of text.

→ For more information on creating value lists, **see** "Working with Fields," **p. 39**.

The options to format a field as a Pop-up List, Pop-up Menu, Checkbox Set, or Radio Button Set require that you specify a value list that will provide the content for the selection values.

The bottom half of the Field Format dialog is relevant only for fields that have been defined to allow multiple repetitions. You can hard-code the starting and ending repetitions and specify whether a vertical or horizontal orientation should be used.

FIELD BEHAVIOR

 The Field Behavior dialog, new to FileMaker Pro 7, contains controls for setting when a field is enterable and how a user can exit it. To access this dialog, select one or more fields on a layout, then choose Format, Field Behavior. You can also (Control-click) [right+click] a field, or simply use the (⌘-Option-K) [Ctrl+Alt+K] keyboard shortcut. The Field Behavior dialog is shown in Figure 4.18.

Figure 4.18
Using the Field Behavior dialog, you can specify in which modes a field can be entered, as well as the keystrokes that can be used to exit a field.

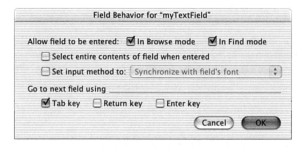

In this dialog, you can control whether a user is able to enter a particular field while in Browse or Find mode. In previous versions of FileMaker, there was no distinction between modes; a field was either enterable or not. Typically, a user should be able to enter a field in both Browse and Find mode. Sometimes, though, you'll want a field to be enterable in only one of these modes. For instance, you might have a field that you don't want users to manually edit, but that they may need to use as part of a query. On the other hand, there may be unindexed fields on your layout that, for performance reasons, you don't want users to search on.

 The other important setting in this dialog is the Go to Next Field Using option. By default in FileMaker Pro, pressing the Tab key lets users move to the next field on the layout. New to FileMaker 7 is the option to allow the Return and/or Enter keys to also perform this function. This is desirable in some cases to allow rapid data entry and to prevent data entry mistakes. For instance, by setting a text field to use the Return key to go to the next field, you prevent users from accidentally adding stray returns at the ends of fields. Obviously, if a user needs to be able to enter carriage returns in a text field—say in a Comments field—you wouldn't set the Return key to go to the next field.

CAUTION

> Normally, the Enter key serves to commit a record and exit all fields. If you change all your field behavior to have Enter go to the next field, be aware that users need to explicitly click on the background of a layout or perform some script or navigation routine to commit record changes.

SETTING THE TAB ORDER

When moving from field to field on a layout with the Tab key (or (Return) and/or [Enter], as described in the previous section), the order in which the fields are activated is known as the *tab order*. The default tab order is the order the fields appear on the layout from top to bottom. Rearranging fields changes the tab order.

Anyone with the ability to modify a layout can change its tab order; do so by selecting Layouts, Set Tab Order. Tab order is stored with the layout, so there's no opportunity to customize the tab order for different users. The Set Tab Order dialog is shown in Figure 4.19. After the tab order has been edited manually, rearranging fields doesn't change the tab order. New fields are added to the end of the tab order automatically, regardless of position.

Figure 4.19
You can change the tab order of a layout to make data entry flow in a logical progression for end users.

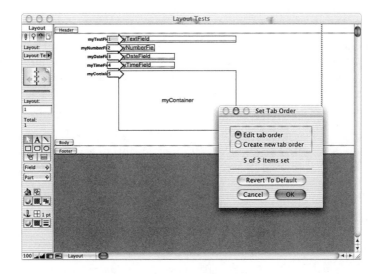

MERGE FIELDS

If you've ever done a mail merge, then the concept of merge fields should be familiar to you. Merge fields give you a way of incorporating field data within text blocks on a layout. This is very useful when creating form letters, labels, and reports.

Merge fields display field data, but they don't behave like or have all the properties of normal fields. A user can't click into a merge field to do data entry, for instance.

To add a merge field to a layout, choose Insert, Merge Field, or press (⌘-Option-M) [Ctrl+Alt+M]. You are then prompted to specify a field. After you make your selection, the field name shows up on your layout surrounded by angle brackets, as shown in Figure 4.20.

Figure 4.20
Merge fields allow field data to be displayed inline with text and avoid the need for sliding fields.

The primary benefit of merge fields is that field data can be flexibly placed within a text block; text before and after the merge field is repositioned to close up any extra space. Thus, within a text block, you could have "Hi <<First Name>>, How are you?" On one record, that would come out as "Hi Joe, How are you?", whereas on another it might be "Hi Frederick, How are you?"

Text, number, date, and time formatting applied to a text block are applied to any appropriate merge field within the text block. It is not possible to have a single text block that contains multiple merge fields that have different number formats applied to them.

TROUBLESHOOTING

COPYING AND PASTING FIELDS BETWEEN FILES

When I copy and paste fields from a layout in one file into another file, sometimes the fields retain their proper identity, sometimes they have no identity, and sometimes they have the wrong identity. Why is that?

When you copy fields from a layout in one file and paste them into another file, they may or may not retain their identity, as you've discovered. A field retains its identity when there exists a field in the destination file that has the same name as the source field. Additionally, the layouts must be based on identically named table occurrences. (It's not enough for the base tables to be named the same.) If the table occurrences match, but no similarly named field is found in that table, then the field displays <field missing> when it's pasted into the destination file. If the table occurrence names don't match, then the field shows up without any identity in the destination file.

Fields in portals behave a bit differently. For them, it's not the field names that must match, but rather the field creation order. If a field displayed in a portal displays the eighth field created in some file, then the portal identifies the pasted field as the eighth field created in the related table in the destination file. This explains why sometimes fields have a new identity. For fields in portals to retain their proper identity, both the table occurrence of the layout and the table occurrence of the related field must be the same in both files, and the fields must have an identical creation order.

Determining Which Records Will Be Displayed on a Layout

I created a table occuurrence that's supposed to display only invoices that are more than 60 days overdue. However, when I build a layout based on this table occurrence, I still see all the invoice records. What did I do wrong?

The problem here isn't anything you've done or haven't done, but rather your expectations. The table occurrence to which a layout is tied never determines what records from the base table are displayed on that layout. It merely determines the starting point on the Relationships Graph from which any action or object involving a relationship is evaluated.

If you have a layout that's tied to an occurrence—*any* occurrence—of an Invoice base table, then all the records from the Invoice table can be viewed from the context of that table occurrence. Think of it this way: A layout's table occurrence doesn't determine what records *you* can view from that layout, but rather, it determines what records the *records* of that table can view. So in the case of your table occurrence, which is supposed to show only invoices that are more than 60 days overdue, you'd need to view those via a portal from a layout tied, say, to a Customer table.

FileMaker Extra: Designing Cross-Platform—Friendly Layouts

One of the things that sets FileMaker apart from other database applications is that it runs on both Windows and Macintosh operating systems. You can even have a mixed platform of client machines. If you are developing a system that needs to run on both platforms, there are a few design considerations you'll need to keep in mind.

First, text blocks may be rendered slightly differently between platforms because of differences in the dots per inch (dpi) that each supports. Macintosh operating systems use 72 dpi, whereas Windows is built at 96 dpi. Font sizes are always described as 72nds of an inch regardless of platform, which means that a 12-point font takes up 12 pixels (12/72nds of 72) on a Macintosh monitor, but 16 pixels on a Windows monitor (12/72nds of 96). In either case, this represents 1/6th of an inch.

The problem is that graphics and other layout objects are set to be a precise number of pixels tall and wide. If, for instance, you have a text block or field on a layout that's set to be 72 pixels wide, you'd be able to see fewer characters in that space on Windows. To account for this, you should make text blocks and buttons slightly oversized so that you don't truncate characters on Windows.

Not all fonts available on one platform are supported on the other; platform-specific fonts should be avoided. Some fonts display different baselines on Mac and PC. Trebuchet, for example, is a particularly bad culprit. The text baseline determines where the "bottom" of a font appears within a text block. Different baselines may mean that letters that hang below the baseline (such as g, y, j, p) have their tails cut off. Verdana tends not to be so bad. The combination of font and field box size is tricky and you'll just have to experiment. 10-point Verdana with a 16-pixel field height tends to work well on both platforms, but it's a very wide font. Use Arial/Helvetica if you're pressed for space.

The other big cross-platform layout problem is the viewable size of your layouts. It's generally desirable to create layouts where users won't need to scroll to see important information. Different operating systems, even within a platform, may have different viewable layout areas, even at the same monitor resolutions. The problem is compounded by users who position their Dock or Start menu bar in different places. Windows XP tends to be the "piggiest" consumer of screen real estate and represents your lowest common denominator for a given resolution.

In the end, of course, the best advice when developing cross-platform applications is simply to test everything *early in your development process* on all operating systems that you plan to support.

4

PART

II

DEVELOPING SOLUTIONS WITH FILEMAKER

CHAPTER 5

RELATIONAL DATABASE DESIGN

In this chapter

UNDERSTANDING DATABASE DESIGN

By now you've designed a simple FileMaker database, and built some nice data entry screens and some reports. Your friends and co-workers are clamoring for you to add features. Can it do invoicing? Inventory tracking? Bar-coding?

Well, it can probably do all those things. But it's going to take some planning. If this is your first time out with FileMaker, you're like the home carpenter who's just built her first birdhouse. It's a nice birdhouse, but your kids want a tree fort. That's not just going to take more work; it's going to take more thought as well.

FileMaker is a tool for building database applications. Both parts of that term are important. By "applications" we mean coherent pieces of software with which users can interact in defined and predictable ways. And by databases, of course, we mean databases, pointing to the fact that FileMaker applications are, in the end, designed to help generate, store, and retrieve data.

Much of the rest of this book concentrates on either the application angle or the database angle. In this chapter, we're going to lay out for you the fundamentals of database design. When you're designing a simple contact manager or recipe book, the database structure is pretty clear. You know what fields you need to track and what kinds of fields they are. But when you get into tracking additional categories of data in the same database, things get trickier. If you want to build bigger and better databases, you'll need a firm grounding in database analysis and database design. Don't worry if that sounds ominous. It's easier than it appears.

DATABASE ANALYSIS

One of the great beauties of FileMaker is that it's very easy to just jump right in and start building things that work. And this is fine, as long as you can keep the whole plan in your head.

Earlier chapters have looked at some practical techniques for separating and organizing data in a FileMaker database system. This chapter takes that work another step. Here you'll learn some tools for analyzing database problems and translating them into buildable designs.

This chapter approaches the idea of things and their relationships somewhat abstractly. Your goal here won't be a finished FileMaker system, but rather a more general design document. You'll learn a simple but powerful design process to help you take a real-world problem description and translate it into a blueprint that a database designer could use to build the database in a real-world database development system. This design document is known as an *entity-relationship diagram*. The process for creating an entity-relationship diagram, somewhat simplified, looks like this:

1. Identify all the different types of things that are involved in the problem that's being modeled (customers and sales, for example, or trucks, drivers, and routes).

2. For each type of "thing," identify its attributes (customers have first and last names, truck routes have a beginning and an end).

3. Looking across all the different types of "things," determine the fundamental relationships between them (truck drivers have routes, trucks have drivers).

4. Draw up your findings into an entity-relationship diagram (ERD).

The ERD, again, is an abstract document, that you could implement (build) with FileMaker or some other database tool. The sections that follow examine each of the steps of this process in much more detail.

WORKING WITH ENTITIES AND ATTRIBUTES

When you set out to design a database system, there are two concepts you simply must be familiar with before you can say you have a solid planning foundation. You need to know the different types of "things" your system will track, and you need to know the characteristics of each of those "things." In a recipe list, for example, you track one kind of thing: recipes. A recipe's characteristics are, for example, recipe name, recipe type, calories, ingredients, and cooking time. You could draw it out like this:

Recipe
- Name
- Type
- Ingredients
- Cooking Time
- Calories
- Directions

Here is one "thing" followed by a collection of its characteristics. A bigger database system may store information about several different kinds of "things," each with its own set of characteristics. For example, if I want to write a database system for a motorcycle company, I might want to track information about motorcycles, customers, and sales. Now I have three kinds of "things," each with its own set of characteristics (see Table 5.1).

In database design terminology, the "things" in your database system are called *entities*. Each entity is a specific, distinct kind of "thing," about which you need to track information. This system tracks data about three distinct kinds of "things." And each kind of "thing" has certain characteristics, which in the technical jargon are called *attributes*. The motorcycle example includes three entities, and each has some specific number of attributes (see Table 5.1).

TABLE 5.1   SIMPLE ANALYSIS OF A DATABASE STRUCTURE

Motorcycle	Customer	Sale
Model Number	First Name	Customer Name
Model Year	Last Name	Date
Vehicle ID Number	Birth Date	Amount
Factory Serial Number	Street Address	
Accessories	City	
Manufacturer	State	
Model Name	Zip	

The first indispensable step in solid database design is to determine what entities (things) your proposed system needs to track, and what the attributes (characteristics) of each entity are. It's not just the first step, though—it's also the third, fifth, seventh, and so forth. Your list of things and their characteristics will inevitably change during your analysis, sometimes quite frequently. This is not a bad thing. It's a natural part of database design. You'll inevitably revisit and refine your list of entities and their attributes several times in the course of designing the system.

Roughly speaking, an entity is a class of things that all look more or less alike. In other words, from a database standpoint, you track many instances of an entity, and you track the same kind of information about each one. In a banking system, you'd probably have an entity called Customer because a banking database wants to keep track of many different customers, and wants to record roughly the same kinds of data about each one. (You'll always want to know a customer's birth date, Social Security number, home address, and the like.)

Attributes, on the other hand, refer to the kinds of information you track about each entity. If Customer is an entity in our banking database, then birth date, home address, and Social Security number are among the attributes of a customer.

It won't surprise you to learn that entities often correspond to actual database tables, and attributes often correspond to database fields or columns. More likely than not, a banking database will have a Customer table with fields for date of birth, address, and Social Security number.

NOTE

> The entities in these diagrams are purely abstract things. They may or may not translate directly into database tables. Your FileMaker solution may (and almost certainly will) end up with tables that aren't represented on your diagram.

It's fairly easy to represent entities and attributes in the graphical notation of an ERD. Sometimes it's more convenient to draw an entity without showing any of its attributes, in which case you can draw it in a simple box, as shown in Figure 5.1.

Figure 5.1
Simple preliminary ERD showing entities for customers and accounts, with no attributes shown.

| Customer |

| Account |

Sometimes it's appropriate to show entities with some or all of their attributes, in which case you can add the attributes as shown in Figure 5.2.

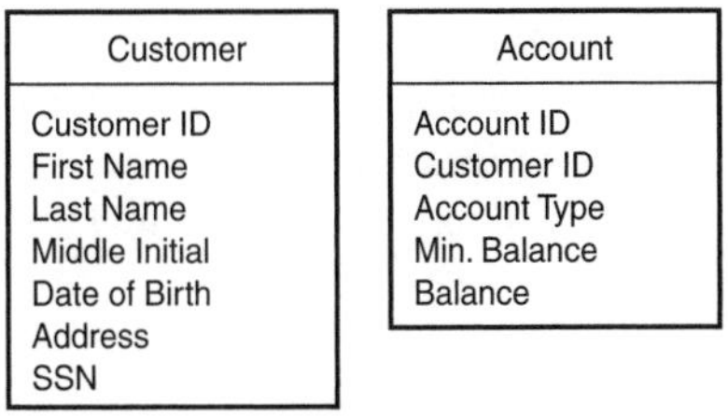

Figure 5.2
An ERD showing entities for customers and accounts, with attributes shown.

Customer
Customer ID
First Name
Last Name
Middle Initial
Date of Birth
Address
SSN

Account
Account ID
Customer ID
Account Type
Min. Balance
Balance

ENTITIES VERSUS ATTRIBUTES: A CASE STUDY

The focus of this chapter is in taking descriptions of real-world problems and turning them into usable ERDs. As was noted earlier, your first step in trying to model a problem into an ERD is sorting out the entities from the attributes. To see how to tackle this, let's begin with an example of a simple process description.

Maurizio's Fish Shack is ready to go digital. Maurizio sells fish out of his storefront but he's not worried about electronically recording his sales to consumers just yet. He just wants to keep track of all the fish he buys wholesale. Every time he buys a load of fish, he wants to know the kind, the quantity, the cost of the purchase, and the vendor he bought it from. This will give him a better handle on how much he's buying and from whom, and may help him negotiate some volume discounts.

Now you know the basics of Maurizio's business. Next you need to develop a list of potential entities. Here are some possibilities:

Fish

Storefront

Sale

Consumer

Load of fish

Variety

Quantity

Cost

Purchase

Vendor

Volume discount

TIP

> Usually the rule of thumb to apply when coming up with a list of possible entities is to pull out every word that's a noun, in other words, every word that represents a specific "thing."

These are typically referred to as *candidate entities*, in that they all represent possible entities in the system. But *are* they all entities? You can immediately cross "storefront," "sale," and "consumer" off the list, for the simple reason that the process description already says that these are parts of his business that Maurizio *doesn't* want to automate at this time. That leaves us with

Fish

Load of fish

Variety

Quantity

Cost

Purchase

Vendor

Volume discount

Well, "fish" and "load of fish" look like they refer to the same thing. According to the process description, a load of fish is actually a quantity of fish that Maurizio bought to resell. Put in those terms, it's clearly the same thing as a purchase. Now the list looks like this:

Purchase (of fish)

Variety

Quantity

Cost

Vendor

Volume discount

These all seem like reasonable things to track in a database system. But are they all entities? Remember that an entity is a *kind of thing*. The thing will probably appear many times in a database, and the system will always track a coherent set of information about the thing. Put that way, a purchase of fish sounds like an entity. You'll record information about many fish purchases in Maurizio's database.

What about something like "cost"? The "cost" in the process description refers to the price Maurizio paid for a load of fish, so cost isn't really an entity. It's the price paid for one load of fish. It's actually a piece of information *about* a fish purchase because each fish purchase has an associated cost. The same is also true for "variety" and "quantity." These are all attributes of the "purchase" entity.

Then you get to "vendor." A vendor is clearly a category of thing; you'll probably want to store information about many vendors in this database, so you can consider a vendor to be an entity. This leaves "volume discount." Well, that one's a bit tricky. It probably applies to a vendor, and might reasonably be called an attribute of a vendor. If you assume that each vendor may offer a discount of some kind, it makes sense for it to be an attribute of a vendor.

Figure 5.3 shows what the fledgling ERD for this system might look like, with the two entities from the process description and their various attributes.

Figure 5.3
An ERD showing entities for fish purchases and vendors, with attributes shown.

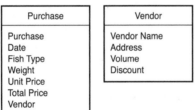

A few things are noteworthy about this diagram. Notice that the entities are called Purchase and Vendor, instead of Purchases and Vendors. When naming entities, it's preferable to name them in the singular, rather than the plural. (You're trying to answer the question "each instance of this thing is a …".) In FileMaker, we usually extend that convention to the database tables that end up being built for each entity.

DESIGN AS AN ITERATIVE PROCESS

Your general task, when designing a database (or indeed any piece of software), is to take a set of things in a real-world *problem domain* and translate them into corresponding things in the *software domain*. In your software, you create a simplified model of reality. Concepts like "fish purchase" and "fish vendor" in the problem domain turn into concepts like "purchase entity" and "vendor entity" in a design, and may ultimately turn into things like "purchase table" and "vendor table" in the finished database.

But this translation (from problem domain to software) is rarely a one-way street. It's rare that there's a single, unambiguous software model that corresponds perfectly to a real-world problem. Usually, your software constructs are approximations of the real world, and how you arrive at those approximations depends a lot on the goal toward which you're working.

In general, software design follows an *iterative* path, meaning you perform a similar set of steps over and over again until you end up with something that's "close enough." For example, in your initial reading of the design problem, you might miss an entity or two. Or you might create entities you don't really need on later examination. Later, as you do more work on the project and learn more about the problem domain, you may revise your understanding of the model. Some entities might disappear and become attributes of other entities. Or some attributes can turn out to be entities in their own right. You might find it's possible to combine two similar entities into one. Or you might find out that one entity really needs to be split in two. We're not trying to make you feel uncertain or hesitant about your design decisions. Just recognize that it's not imperative, or necessarily even possible, to get the design exactly right the first time. You'll revisit your design assumptions frequently over the course of the design process, and this is a natural part of the process.

UNDERSTANDING RELATIONSHIPS

We've dealt with the first two steps of the design process now: the sorting out of entities and attributes. After you have what you think is a decent draft of a set of entities and attributes, the next thing to do is to start to consider how these entities relate to one another. You need to become familiar with the fundamental types of entity relationships, and also with a simple notation for representing relationships graphically in a diagram.

REPRESENTING RELATIONSHIPS IN A DIAGRAM

Consider a system that stores information about farmers and pigs, among other things. Farmers and pigs are each entities, and these two entities have a direct relationship, in that each pig ties back to a single farmer.

There's a name for the farmer-pig relationship. It's called a *one-to-many* relationship, meaning that for each farmer there may be any number of pigs. "One farmer," as we usually put it, "can sell many pigs."

Now you can expand on the entity-relationship notation. You already have a graphical shorthand for depicting the entities and attributes in a database system. Next you should add some conventions for showing the relationships among them. Each entity can be represented by a box, as before, and each relationship can be represented by a line that indicates the relationship type. In this simple notation, you'd depict the relationship between farmers and pigs along the lines of Figure 5.4.

Figure 5.4
Entity-relationship notation for a database that stores information about farmers and pigs.

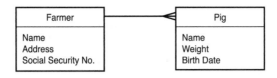

Notice the line between the two entities that depicts their relationship branches out where it touches the Pig entity. In a one-to-many relationship, this fork or branch indicates the "many" end of the relationship. So this notation tells us that one farmer may be linked to many pigs. If the fork were on the other end, this would imply that one pig could be associated with many farmers, which would be a very different assertion about the data we're trying to model.

RELATIONSHIP TYPES

Those simple graphical conventions are the foundation of what you need to draw your entity-relationship diagrams (ERDs). Another important concept is an understanding of the different relationship types that you could encounter. You need to reckon with four types: the one-to-many and many-to-one relationships (the latter is simply a one-to-many relationship looked at from the other direction); the one-to-one relationship, which is a rare case you probably won't encounter much; and the many-to-many relationship, a common but more complicated relationship to which we'll need to devote special attention.

We'll consider each of these relationship types in turn, and show how to represent them in the ERD notation.

ONE-TO-ONE RELATIONSHIPS

This relationship type is rather rare in practice. For example, consider a dataset concerning children and their birth records. Let's say that for now, you've decided that children and birth records should represent separate entities.

In a standard analysis sequence, after you've decided on entities and attributes, you'll start to ask questions about relationships. What's the relationship between children and birth records? Can one child have many birth records? No, each child is born only once. And can one birth record pertain to more than one child? Again, probably not. So the relationship between a child and a birth record appears to be one-to-one. You can depict that as shown in Figure 5.5.

In general, as we said, it's rare to let the two sides of a one-to-one relationship stand as separate entities. In general, you'll fold one of the entities into the other. In this case, you might decide to move all the attributes of a birth record into the Child entity and get rid of Birth Record as a separate entity.

Figure 5.5
This ERD shows the one-to-one relationship between children and birth records. A single line with no "crows-feet" is used.

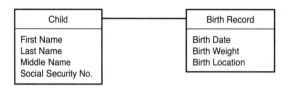

When Is One to One the Right Choice?

There are some circumstances that would justify keeping two separate entities, even when the relationship between them is one to one. Probably the clearest case occurs when one of the entities represents data that's filled out only in infrequent cases. Such could be the case in a database that stores information about spacecraft. For simplicity, assume that all the relevant information on a spacecraft can be represented by a single entity, called Craft.

Now further suppose that when a spacecraft reaches the end of its useful life, it's formally decommissioned, and at that point a huge amount of data is gathered—once and only once—as part of the decommissioning process. For this example, assume there are an additional three hundred attributes you need to track when a craft is decommissioned. You could add all those attributes to the Craft entity. But in actual use, those columns are almost always going to be empty. They won't be filled until a craft is taken out of service. This leads to the potential for large "holes" in the actual, physical database. In other words, at the implementation level, it could be very wasteful to have those three hundred data slots ready and waiting when they're used very infrequently.

One solution here would be to have Craft and Decommission as two separate entities in a one-to-one relationship. You would create a Decommission entry for a Craft only when you actually needed it, and your view of the data would be a little cleaner. For example, to find all ships that had been decommissioned, you'd just run a search in the Decommission table. If the system contained only a Craft entity, you might end up needing some special additional attribute to signify that a ship had been decommissioned, or else you'd have to rely on certain specific attributes, such as "decommission date" being empty if the ship hadn't been decommissioned yet.

5

ONE-TO-MANY RELATIONSHIPS

We've already devoted some attention to the one-to-many relationship. The relationship of a customer to sales, of a farmer to pigs, and of a passenger to trips are all examples of one-to-many relationships. And you've seen the "crow's-foot" notation for indicating these relationships, where the fork notation indicates the "many" side of the relationship.

There's another piece of terminology for one-to-many relationships that's helpful to know. You'll frequently see the entity that represents the "one" side of the relationship referred to as the *parent* entity, whereas the "many" side is often referred to as the *child* entity. If you hear a database architect blurt out a reference to a "child" table, odds are she's referring to the entity on the "many" side of a one-to-many relationship.

MANY-TO-ONE RELATIONSHIPS

There's no difference at all between the concepts of a one-to-many and a many-to-one relationship. They're the same idea, just seen from different points of view. If the relationship between customers and sales is one to many, then it's equally true that the relationship between sales and customers is many to one. Customer is the parent of Sale, Sale is the child of Customer. These statements are equivalent. Figure 5.6 shows the Customer-Sale relationship. Whether you choose to describe this as a one-to-many or a many-to-one depends on which "side" you start from in your description. The relationship of a customer to a sale is one to many; the relationship of a sale to a customer is many to one. One-to-many and many-to-one are two sides of the same coin; a relationship can't be one without being the other.

Figure 5.6
The Customer-Sale relationship drawn as both a one-to-many and a many-to-one relationship.

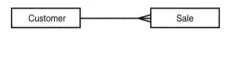

MANY-TO-MANY RELATIONSHIPS

Consider the relationship between actors and movies. One actor may play roles in many movies. One movie involves roles played by many actors. Each actor can relate to many movies. Each movie may be associated with many actors. This is a classic many-to-many relationship. You can depict it as shown in Figure 5.7.

Figure 5.7
Entity-relationship notation for a many-to-many relationship.

Many-to-many relationships are extremely common in relational database systems. Here are examples of some other many-to-many relationships.

- **Attorney—Case**—One attorney may serve on many cases, and one case may involve many attorneys.
- **Player—Game**—One player may play in many games, and one game involves many players.
- **Product—Invoice**—One invoice may contain orders for many products, and one product may be ordered on many different invoices.
- **Student—Class**—One student may participate in many classes, and one class may have many students enrolled.

You can probably think of your own examples pretty easily as well.

Many-to-many relationships are a bit trickier than the others to actually implement in real life. When we get to the details of how to build a FileMaker database based on an ERD, you'll see the specific techniques you need to bring a many-to-many relationship to life in FileMaker. For now, though, we'll just use the ERD as an analysis tool, and not worry about implementation.

RELATIONSHIP CARDINALITY

You've seen how to filter a process description into a list of entities and their attributes, and you've seen a useful language for describing the relationships between those entities. So far, in describing these relationships, we've been mainly concerned with the question "how many?" How many purchases can relate to a customer? One, or many? And how many customers can participate in a purchase?

The answers to these questions tell you into which of the three (or four) relationship types a given relationship falls. This information is sometimes referred to as the *cardinality* of the relationship. Cardinality specifies whether a relationship is one to one, one to many, many to one, or many to many.

RELATIONSHIP OPTIONALITY

Relationship cardinality answers a fairly simple question: Given an entity A, how many instances, at most, of another entity B might potentially be linked to a given instance of A? The answer could be "zero" (in which case there's actually no relationship), but in general the answer is either "one" or "many" (in other words, more than one).

It can be useful to know one additional piece of information about a relationship. This is what's called the relationship's *optionality*. This information is not strictly necessary for a complete ERD, but it can be very useful information to gather.

Cardinality allows you to answer the question, "How many?" What is the maximum number of orders with which a customer may be linked? One, or many? Optionality, by contrast, answers the question, "How few?" What is the *minimum* number of orders with which a customer may be linked? Is it permissible to have a customer with no recorded orders? Answering such questions about the data can provide considerable additional precision to your model.

OPTIONALITY IN MANY-TO-MANY RELATIONSHIPS

Suppose you have a database system designed to track information about college students (including their high school, transcripts and grades from other schools, sports, student organizations, and classes). Two of the entities in this system are a Student entity (of course) and a Class entity. The relationship between these two entities is many to many. So you know that one student record can potentially be linked to many class records, if a student is enrolled in many classes. But is there a *minimum* number of classes that a student must be associated with at any time? Put differently, is it permissible to have a student record in the system that's not associated with *any* class records?

Your first instinct might be to say no. After all, students have to take at least one class, don't they? But that's not quite the question that's being asked. The question is not whether all student records *eventually* have to be associated with at least one class record. Presumably they do. The question is, must a student record, always and at all times in its existence, be associated with at least one class record? And the answer to this question is clearly no. New students, or transfers, are not associated with class records until they first enroll for classes. But their records might be entered into the system weeks or even months prior to enrollment. So the answer here is that it's acceptable for student records to have no associated classes.

Here's how to show this rule in the ERD notation. Take a look at Figure 5.8 and notice that we've added some adornment to the "Class" end of the Student-Class relationship. In addition to the crow's foot, which shows the fact that, potentially, multiple class records can be associated with a single student, we now also have an open circle to indicate that it's all right for a student to have *no* associated class records.

Figure 5.8
Entity-relationship notation for the Student–Class relationship, with optionality shown at the Class side.

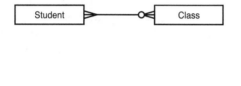

In an ERD where you fully diagram all the optionalities, each "end" of a relationship line has two notations: one to show the smallest number of records that *have* to exist in the related entity (the optionality) and the other to show the largest number that *can* exist (the cardinality). The graphical notation closest to the entity specifies the cardinality, and the one farther away specifies the optionality. So the way to read the notations at the Class end of the diagram in Figure 5.8 is something like this: "one student record may be associated with as few as zero class records or with many class records."

Now consider the other end of the relationship, the Student side. What's the fewest number of students with which a class may be associated? Well, before anyone enrolls for the class, the answer is zero. And what's the largest number of students with which the class may be associated? There's no maximum (that we know of), so you can just use the generic term "many" again. The Student end of this relationship is drawn as shown in Figure 5.9.

This diagram now provides a bit more information than a plain, unadorned ERD would have. Now you've specified not only that the relationship of Class to Student is many to many, but also that it's permissible to have classes with no associated students, and students with no associated classes.

Figure 5.9
Entity-relationship notation for the Student–Class relationship, with optionality shown at both sides.

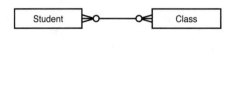

OPTIONALITY IN ONE-TO-MANY RELATIONSHIPS

When dealing with one-to-many (and by extension with many-to-one) relationships, there are two broad scenarios, which can be called "loose binding" and "tight binding."

OPTIONALITY IN ONE-TO-MANY RELATIONSHIPS: LOOSE BINDING

Consider the relationship between the entities "Customer" and "Sale." It seems to be one to many: One customer may have many sales. That's the cardinality. What about the optionality? Take it one side at a time. Is it permissible to have a customer with no associated sale records? It seems likely that this would be all right. Until they actually buy something, they're more of prospects than customers, but we probably still want to allow them in the database without a sale. So a customer can have anywhere from zero to "many" sale records.

Now look from the other side. Is it permissible for a sale record to be missing an associated customer? No, this seems unlikely to be allowable. You'd want to tie each sale to a customer. So it seems best to say that a sale must be associated with at least one customer. Zero customers on a sale is not permitted.

What's the largest number of customers to which a sale can be related? The answer again is "one." If a sale could be associated with more than one customer, then the relationship of Sale and Customer would be many to many, rather than the many to one that we've already settled on.

Figure 5.10 shows this relationship with all the optionalities drawn in on both sides. This optionality pattern is very typical of one-to-many or many-to-one relationships: the "many" side may range from zero to many associated items, whereas on the "one" side each "child" record must have exactly one parent, no more, no less. The double lines on the Customer side indicate the cardinality and optionality of a Customer seen from the perspective of a Sale: Each Sale must have a minimum of one Customer, and a maximum of one Customer. Put more succinctly, a sale is associated with one and only one customer.

We call this optionality configuration a "loose binding" because it's permissible to have Customer records with no associated Sales. A given customer may have one or more sale records—then again, she may not.

OPTIONALITY IN ONE-TO-MANY RELATIONSHIPS: TIGHT BINDING

There is another common business model: the model for an order of some kind. Each order can contain requests for multiple different kinds of goods. You would put each different request on its own order line: five kumquats on the first line, three bass lures on the second, and so on. Each order can have as many order lines as it needs to list everything that was ordered.

Figure 5.10
Entity-relationship notation for the Customer–Sale relationship. This is a very typical optionality pattern for one-to-many and many-to-one relationships.

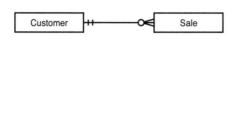

So, clearly, you have a one-to-many relationship from order to order line. If you look at the "one" side first, you'll see that, as with other one-to-many relationships you've seen, the "one" side is pretty hard and fast: Each order line must be tied to one and only one order. On the other side, we know that an order can possibly contain many order items. But what's the fewest items an order may contain? Should it be permissible to leave an order sitting there with no items on it?

This may end up being a question about business rules that a database designer may not be able to decide on his own without conferring with someone involved on the business side of the process that's being modeled. But let's assume that you learn that it should not be permissible to create an order with no associated order items. Every order has to be an order *for* something. You can't leave it blank. So an order needs a minimum of one associated order line, and the ERD with optionalities will look like Figure 5.11.

Figure 5.11
Entity-relationship notation for the Order/Order Line relationship. This shows a "parent" entity that must always have at least one "child."

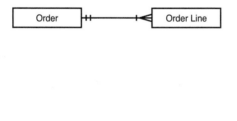

NOTE

This kind of tight binding between a parent and a child entity is not as common as the looser type of one-to-many relationship, in which it's permissible for the parent to be childless, so to speak. But it does happen, so it's worth being familiar with it.

OPTIONALITY IN ONE-TO-ONE RELATIONSHIPS

Optionality is a concept that's easily learned by example, so let's look at a few more. Look again at the earlier example of a legitimate one-to-one relationship. The scenario that was previously discussed included spacecraft that would have an associated Decommission record created at the end of their lives. So a Craft spends most of its time without an associated Decommission record. As a result, the minimum number of Decommission records associated with a craft is zero: It's fine to have a Craft with no associated Decommission record. And a Craft may have at most one Decommission record.

From the other side, it's not possible to have a Decommission record without an associated Craft. Having a Decommission record that stood alone would be meaningless. At the same time, a Decommission record can't be associated with *more* than one Craft; by definition, one decommissioning applies to only one craft. So your optionalities for this relationship appear as in Figure 5.12. The optionalities tell a lot in this case. With the optionalities added to the ERD, you can easily tell which of these two is the "strong" entity, and which is the "weaker" or optional one. This diagram reveals clearly that there will *always* be a Craft record, and there will *sometimes* be an associated Decommission record.

Figure 5.12
Entity-relationship notation for the Craft/Decommission relationship. This is a typical optionality pattern for one-to-one relationships.

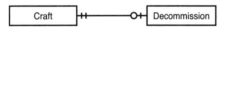

Optionality Recap

Not everyone uses optionality in ER diagrams, but we think it's a good habit to cultivate. After you do it for a while you might start to omit it except in cases where the optionality is a little different from what you might expect. Most one-to-many relationships, for example, are of the "loose binding" type, where the children are optional. With sufficient practice, you may find you want to write in the optionality of a one-to-many relationship only when the binding is tight (that is, when at least one child record must always be present). Likewise, it's rather rare to find a many-to-many relationship that isn't "loose" on both sides. So you may eventually decide to annotate only the exceptional cases.

UNDERSTANDING THE ROLE OF KEYS IN DATABASE DESIGN

So far, this chapter has presented quite a few ERDs. Many of them depict relationships, but so far there's been no discussion of exactly *how* a relationship between two entities is created and maintained. The answer is simple: We create fields in each entity called *keys*, which allow instances of one entity to be associated with instances of another. You might relate orders to customers, for example, by using a customer's Social Security number as a key. Each order would then contain the Social Security number of the related customer as one of its attributes. The following sections explore the concept of keys in more detail.

KEYS THAT DETERMINE UNIQUENESS

One of the crucial tenets of relational database theory is that it has to be possible to identify any database row, anywhere, without ambiguity. Put differently, every row in every table should have a unique identifier. If I have a record in a table of orders, I want to be able to ask it "what customer do you tie to?" and get an unambiguous answer. I need a simple answer: "customer 400." End of story.

A piece of data that is capable of uniquely identifying a database row is known as a *primary key*. A primary key, is an attribute that is (and always will be) unique for every single row in the database. It's a unique identifier, like a Social Security number, an ISBN number for a book, or a library card catalog number.

We recommend that *every database table you design* have a primary key, without exception. Some database systems force you to create a primary key for each new table. FileMaker Pro doesn't, but we strongly recommend you do so anyway. There's very little to lose and a great deal to gain by following this practice.

The discussions in this chapter assume that every table you design, without exception, has a primary key.

What Makes a Good Primary Key?

So far, we've mentioned that every database table should have a primary key, and that those keys have to be unique, to distinguish one row from another absolutely. There's one other important rule: Primary keys are best (in our opinion) if they're *meaningless*.

The important idea here is that data chosen to act as a primary key should be free of real-world meaning or significance. When data has meaning in the "real" world, such meaning is subject to change. In simple terms, data that is supposedly unique may turn out not to be.

Here's an example. You're designing a database that holds information about the different offices of a company. Offices are stored in their own table. You decide that, because there's no more than one office in a city, the City field in the Office table will make a great primary key. It's unique, after all, and every Office record has a City value.

Just to be sure, you check with someone highly placed in the firm, and they assure you that, no, the company will never need to open more than one office in any one city. So you go ahead and build a database structure around the assertion that the City field in the Office table is unique.

Seven months later the company announces plans to open its second office in New Delhi, and you're left to explain why an important part of the database structure needs to be rewritten.

Imagine instead that you'd decided that the database system itself should generate a primary key. Offices will be numbered sequentially starting from 1. The important thing about this data is that it has meaning only to the database system itself. No one else cares, or even knows, that the New Delhi office is office number 14. The number 14 has no business significance.

5

The critical difference here is that when you used the City field as a primary key, you were relying on the stability of an assertion about the real world (a place notoriously subject to change). By contrast, when you create your own key, you're working in an environment that no one but the database programmers care about, so you're at liberty to design uniqueness rules that won't be affected by decisions beyond your control.

Keys That Refer to Other Tables

Keys are essential to specifying relationships between tables. Going back to the example of customers and orders, the relationship between these entities is one to many: One customer may have many orders.

If you've followed the rule about always having a primary key, your Customer entity has a primary key, which you might call Customer ID. Now, each unique customer may have many related orders. To forge that relationship, each record in the order table needs to store the Customer ID (the primary key) of the related customer. This value, when it's stored in the order table, is known as a *foreign key*. The reason for the term is simple: The value in the order table refers to a primary key value from a different ("foreign") table.

Figure 5.13 demonstrates how primary and foreign keys work together to create relationships between database tables.

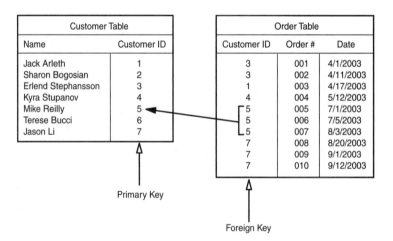

Figure 5.13
A one-to-many relationship between customers and orders, showing primary and foreign keys.

→ FileMaker Pro has several built-in capabilities that help you add strong key structures to your FileMaker databases. To see how to best define key fields in FileMaker Pro, **see** "Working with Keys and Match Fields," **p. 158**.

Many-to-Many Relationships: Solving the Puzzle

It was mentioned earlier that many-to-many relationships are slightly tricky. After you have an understanding of keys and have seen how they work in a simple ERD, the solution to the many-to-many problem becomes clearer. But first you should understand why it's a problem.

Assume you're building a class registration database. It's intended to show which students are enrolled in which classes. It sounds as if you just need to deal with two entities: students and classes.

Students and classes have a many-to-many relationship. One student may participate in many classes, whereas one class may contain many students. That sounds fine, but how would you actually construct the relationship?

Based on the fundamental rule mentioned earlier, you need a primary key for each entity. Student needs a Student ID, and Class needs a Class ID. If you look at things from the student side for a moment, you know that one student can have many classes. Accordingly, from that viewpoint, Student and Class have a one-to-many relationship. If that's the case, from what you now know about foreign keys, each Class record should store a Student ID to indicate the student record to which it relates.

This won't work, though, for the simple reason that one class can contain many students. This means that the Student ID attribute in Class would have to contain not just one student ID, but a list of student IDs—one for each enrolled student. The same would be true in the other direction: Each student record needs a Class ID attribute that stores a list of all classes in which the student is enrolled.

One rule of relational database design that has already been touched on is that it's almost always a bad idea to store *lists* of things in database fields.

As a general rule, when you find you're using a field to store a list of some kind, that's a sign that you need to add another entity to your system where you can then store the list items as single records. This should suggest to you that the many-to-many problem can't be solved without some kind of additional entity. This is true, and it leads to a simple rule:

Resolve a many-to-many relationship by adding an additional entity "between" the two in question.

Figure 5.14 shows an ERD for students and classes with an additional entity to solve the many-to-many problem.

Figure 5.14
An ERD for students and classes.

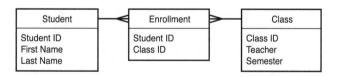

This middle entity is often called a *join table*. Each of the "outer" entities now has a one-to-many relationship with this middle entity. Not surprisingly, then, the middle entity has *two* foreign keys, because it's on the "many" side of two different relationships. It needs to hold both a student ID *and* a class ID.

NOTE

In previous versions of FileMaker, where each database table was a separate physical file, the term *join file* was also widely used.

What, if anything, does this entity represent in the real world, and what should it be called? One useful exercise, after you've diagrammed a one-to-many relationship, is to say to yourself (for a join table that resolves a many-to-many relationship between entities A and B), "This entity represents the association of one A with one B." In the example of students and classes, the middle entity represents the association of a specific student with a specific class. If you think of the entity as a database table (which it will almost certainly become), then each row of the table holds one student ID and one class ID. If such a row holds the student ID for student number 1009023 (Sam Tanaka) and the class ID for class H440 (History of the Sub-Sahara), then this record tells us that Sam is enrolled in History 440. This also suggests a good name for the entity: Enrollment. Each record in this table records the enrollment of one student in one class.

ATTRIBUTES IN A JOIN ENTITY

You've seen that this "join entity" needs, at the very least, two foreign keys: one pointing to each "side" of a many-to-many relationship. What other attributes does it need?

We emphasized earlier that "every entity, without exception, should have a primary key." Does this mean you should be adding an Enrollment ID to the Enrollment entity? Well, not necessarily. Often the two foreign keys, taken together, constitute a unique key in themselves. In the enrollment example, it wouldn't make sense to have a student enrolled twice in the same class. So student ID 1009023 and class ID H440 should never both occur in the same record more than once. This is an example of something we haven't discussed much: a *multi-column key*. Often, the two foreign keys in a join entity constitute a primary key when taken together.

You'll need to assess this situation for yourself. If the two foreign keys together constitute a primary key, you're off the hook. But if the combination of those two keys isn't unique, then you need an additional primary key in the join entity.

Besides primary and foreign keys, are there other attributes that are appropriate in a join entity? Well, looking at the example of students and classes, you might wonder where you'd store an important piece of information such as a student's GPA. A student has only one GPA at one time, so you should store that as an attribute of the student. But what about course grades? Where do you record Sam's grade for H440? Well, Sam can be enrolled in many courses, and so can receive many grades. So it's not appropriate to try to store the grade somewhere on Sam's student record. It belongs instead on the enrollment record for that specific course. And, if attendance were being taken, Sam's attendance would logically go on his enrollment record as well.

ADDITIONAL MANY-TO-MANY EXAMPLES

Resolving many-to-many relationships correctly is something that becomes easier with practice. We'll present a few more examples here, just to make the concepts clearer.

ACTORS AND MOVIES

One actor may be in many movies, and one movie generally involves several actors. To resolve this, you need a join entity containing an Actor ID and a Movie ID. This entity records the participation of one actor in one movie: an appropriate name might be Role or Casting. Do Actor ID and Movie ID together form a primary key? Put differently, can a single actor appear more than once in the same movie? Well, yes—some virtuoso actors occasionally take several roles in a movie. So you'd want a Role ID in addition to the other two keys.

BOOKS AND LIBRARIES

One library obviously holds many books. But can one book be in many libraries? It depends. If you mean a physical copy of a book, the answer is no. If by "book" you mean something more like a "title," the answer is yes. Only one library can hold a given physical copy of Ole Rolvaag's *Giants in the Earth*. But as a book title, it can be held by many libraries.

Let's concentrate on the idea of the book as a title. In this case, the relationship of Titles to Libraries is many to many. The join entity contains a Title ID and a Library ID. Is this combination of keys unique? No, it isn't. One library may hold several physical copies of *Giants in the Earth*. So, if you call your join entity a Holding, you can either add a special Holding ID, or add something else, such as a copy number, as an additional attribute. In the latter case, the combination of Title ID, Library ID, and Copy Number would be unique, and would constitute a primary key.

> **TIP**
>
> Good names for join entities can greatly increase the clarity of your designs. If you can find a descriptive name like Role, Enrollment, or Holding, you should use it. If no clearer name presents itself, we recommend naming the join entity by a combination of the names of the entities it's joining: AttorneyClient, for example.

THE BASICS OF PROCESS ANALYSIS

So far this chapter has illustrated the principles of relational database design, and provided examples of a notation (the ERD notation) that can be used to produce a compact visual representation of a database structure. But this activity needs to fit into a broader type of activity that we refer to as *process analysis*.

Process analysis (in this book, anyway) refers to the act of deriving a database design from a real-world problem. In a sense, almost all database design needs be preceded by some form of analysis, to determine the scope of the problem being solved and focus on what needs to be built and why. Process analysis begins with a process description and ends with an ERD. That ERD will be the basis for implementing a real solution in FileMaker, a process covered in more detail in Chapter 6, "Working with Multiple Tables." To perform such analysis, you need a firm grip on entities, attributes, and relationships. Understanding relationship optionality is also a helpful tool.

Here again is the strategy for going from a problem to an ERD:

1. Capture the problem in a process description of some kind. (You might already have one, or might need to interview one or more people and write one up yourself.)

2. Boil the process description down into a list of candidate entities.

3. Figure out which of the candidate entities are "real" entities.

4. Figure out the attributes of each entity.

5. Determine the important relationships that link the entities together. Include cardinality information.

6. For greater clarity, determine the optionalities of the relationships from step 5.

PROCESS ANALYSIS: LEGAL DOCUMENTS

Karen Schulenberg's law office handles a great many estate issues. In particular they handle a lot of wills. They need a software system to track individual wills. For each will, they need to know the identities of the testator, the executor, the beneficiaries, and any witnesses. They need to know the date of the will itself and, if applicable, the testator's date of death. This information constitutes your process description.

DETERMINING ENTITIES

Next, you need a list of candidate entities. One rule of thumb, you might remember, is to pull out anything that looks like a noun.

Doing so, you'd get the following list: law office, estate issue, will, testator, executor, beneficiary, witness, date of will, and date of death.

The challenge here is to decide which of these are *types of things*, and which are *characteristics of things*. For example, "date of will" and "date of death" both seem like characteristics of things (characteristics of a will and a testator, respectively). Witnesses and beneficiaries, by contrast, look like types of things—you could store additional information about witnesses and beneficiaries (name, address, height, and so on).

As far as the rest of the entity list, you can discard "law office" and "estate issue" because these pertain to the running of the law office, which is not what the desired database is about. "Will" is clearly an entity; in fact, it's the central entity of the proposed system.

What about "testator" and "executor"? By the logic we applied to witnesses and beneficiaries, these could both be entities: you could track plenty of additional information about them. So for now, leave them as entities.

The current universe of entities is shown in Figure 5.15.

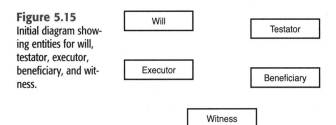

Figure 5.15
Initial diagram showing entities for will, testator, executor, beneficiary, and witness.

With this entity list in place, you need to fill in the attributes. Some of these may arise from the process description, whereas you may need to fill in others based on common sense or further investigation. Take a look at the entities one by one.

For the will, you know that the date is one important attribute. Witnesses and beneficiaries are important too, but you've decided these are entities in their own right. So for now leave the will entity with just a date.

The testator is a person, so even though nothing lengthy was specified in the process description, you can reasonably assume you'd want to capture the name and address. The process description states that you need to capture the death date, and you might as well ask for birth date as well.

Similar logic applies to the executor, witness, and beneficiary entities. All are people, so you'd presumably want their names and probably addresses as well. For witnesses, you'd also like to know the date on which they witnessed the will.

Figure 5.16 shows the developing diagram with these attributes added.

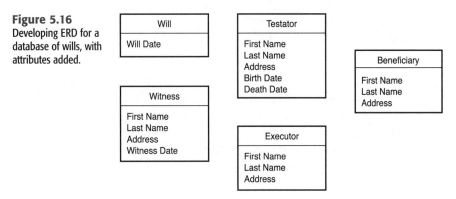

Figure 5.16
Developing ERD for a database of wills, with attributes added.

With this done, you need to consider the relationships that apply among these entities. Because the will is the critical entity, the instinct here is to look first at the way wills relate to the things around them. For each entity pair you examine, you should determine the relationship type: one-to-one, one-to-many, or many-to-many.

Consider first the relationship between a will and its witnesses. This is clearly a one-to-many relationship: a will might have only one witness, but it could certainly have several as well. The same is true of the relationship of a will to its beneficiaries. What about the relationship of a will to an executor? Well, there is generally only one executor, but in extraordinary cases there might be more than one. Again you have a one-to-many relationship.

And finally, what about the relationship of a will to a testator? Well, a will can apply to only one testator, so you might first be tempted to call this a one-to-one relationship. But one person (testator) could in theory have several wills, one superseding the other over time. To retain that flexibility, you might be better off thinking of this as a one-to-many relationship.

What about other relationships? Is it meaningful to talk about a relationship between witnesses and beneficiaries, for example? Probably not. In any case, you now have an ERD that connects all the entities together: Each entity is now related to every other entity through the "main" entity, which is the will. The resulting ERD is shown in Figure 5.17.

Figure 5.17
The "wills" ERD with all relationships drawn.

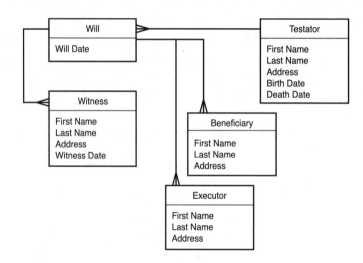

The last step in the process, though not a mandatory one, is to add the optionalities to the existing relationships. There won't be too many surprises with this system. The couplings here are fairly loose. It might well be permissible to have a testator with no wills in the system, for example. It's not likely that a will would have no beneficiaries, but it is possible. And a will need not have associated witnesses, at least not until it's signed. A will might even sit in limbo for a while with no executor assigned. So these relationships are all fairly loose. The ERD with optionalities might appear as in Figure 5.18.

We've made a slight simplification here, for the purpose of clarity. The diagram indicates that one witness can only ever witness one will. In truth, one person could witness quite a number of wills, which would entail a many-to-many relationship between witnesses and wills. Here, we're effectively presuming that we'll make a new Witness record every time someone witnesses a will, whether or not that person has already done so.

Figure 5.18
The "wills" ERD with optionalities added.

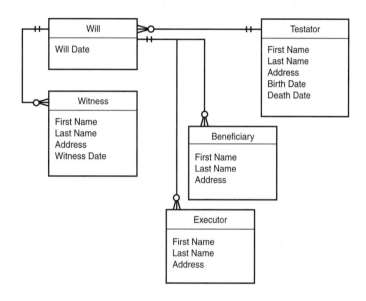

ADDING ATTRIBUTES

Now you have a pretty good list of entities, but they still need attributes. (These, again, are likely to turn into database fields when you actually build the system.)

ADD THE PRIMARY KEYS   You might remember that earlier it was recommended that every entity, without exception, have a primary key. So the first thing to do is add a primary key to each entity in the diagram. Figure 5.19 shows the result.

ADD THE FOREIGN KEYS   Foreign keys, you'll remember, tie the rows of one table to the primary key of another table. Anywhere you have a one-to-many relationship indicated on your ERD, you need two things: a primary key on the "one" side, and a foreign key on the "many" side. In the current example, beneficiaries and witnesses both have a many-to-one relationship with wills. So, in addition to their own primary keys (Beneficiary ID and Witness ID, which you've already added), they each need to store a foreign key called Will ID, that ties each beneficiary or witness record back to a unique record in the Will table. Figure 5.20 shows the ERD with foreign keys added.

5

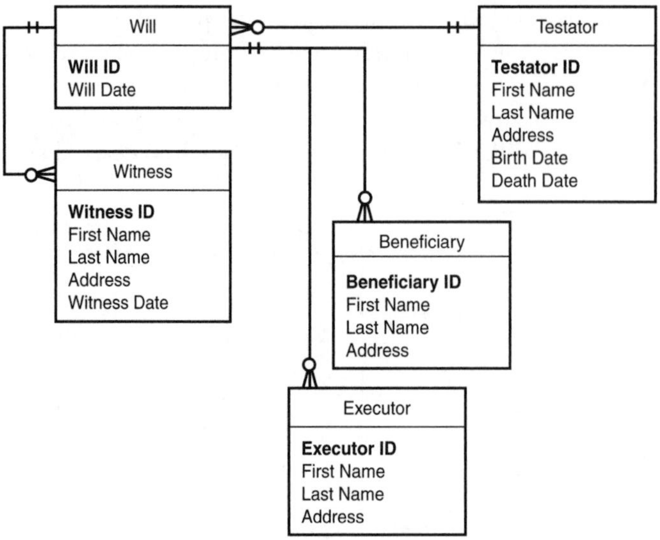

Figure 5.19
The "wills" ERD with primary keys added.

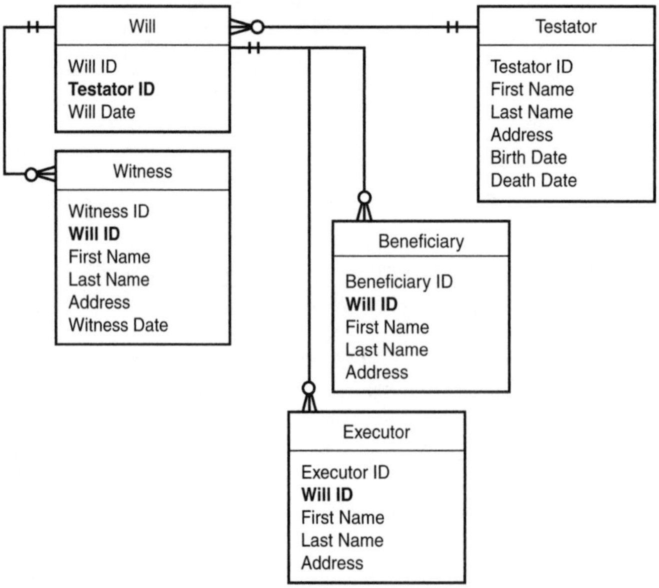

Will

Will ID
Will Date

Witness

Witness ID
First Name
Last Name
Address
Witness Date

Testator

Testator ID
First Name
Last Name
Address
Birth Date
Death Date

Beneficiary

Beneficiary ID
First Name
Last Name
Address

Executor

Executor ID
First Name
Last Name
Address

Figure 5.20
The "wills" ERD with foreign keys added.

Will

Will ID
Testator ID
Will Date

Witness

Witness ID
Will ID
First Name
Last Name
Address
Witness Date

Testator

Testator ID
First Name
Last Name
Address
Birth Date
Death Date

Beneficiary

Beneficiary ID
Will ID
First Name
Last Name
Address

Executor

Executor ID
Will ID
First Name
Last Name
Address

ADD THE "OTHER" ATTRIBUTES The keys you've just added represent the ERD's structural attributes. These are the minimal attributes needed to create the relationships you identified in earlier steps. What's left, of course, is all the "actual" data—the information a user of the system expects to work with.

You will have identified some of these attributes during the initial design process, and may have wrestled with the question of whether they should appear as attributes or entities (as with testator and executor in this example, both of which we're calling entities in this design). You'll find out about others as you dig deeper into the requirements for the particular system you're building. In the current example, there may be many other pieces of data about a will that these lawyers want to track. All that information would appear as additional attributes of the Will entity.

Strictly speaking, attributes don't need to appear in an ERD. An ERD, after all, is mostly about entities and relationships. In a system with complex entities, showing all the attributes on the ERD would be unwieldy and would obscure the main structure of the ERD. Just make sure that an attribute list for each entity appears *somewhere* in your design documents.

TIP

> When you first start sketching your ERD, you might just be scribbling on the back of envelope. But sooner or later, especially for large projects, you'll want to turn your ERD into an electronic document of some kind. We recommend you find a suitable tool for doing this. If you want to go with a dedicated diagramming tool, Visio is popular for the PC platform, and on the Mac, OmniGraffle is an excellent tool.
>
> But if you don't want to spring for (or worse, spend time learning) a new tool, well, FileMaker's Layout Mode also makes a great ERD tool! It's easy to whip up a small library of ERD adornments and cut and paste them where needed. That way, each of your FileMaker solutions can contain its own ERD, squirreled away in a hidden layout somewhere.

FILEMAKER EXTRA: COMPLEX MANY-TO-MANY RELATIONSHIPS

5

Most of the examples in this chapter involved fairly simple, commonly found data modeling problems. But in the real world, matters can get quite complex. Some problems are hard to model in the language of relational databases. Others involve concepts you've already seen, but in more complex ways.

Let's say you've been asked to sketch out a database system for a trucking company. The company needs to track which drivers are driving which trucks, and where they're driving them. After some thought, you decide you're dealing with three entities: Driver, Truck, and Route. A route consists of a start location, a destination, and a number of miles driven.

With the entities fixed, you start to think about relationships. Driver and Truck seem to have a many-to-many relationship: one driver can (over time) drive many different trucks for the company, and one truck will be driven by many drivers (again, over time). Driver and Route also seem to have a many-to-many relationship. Route and Truck also are many-to-many, for similar reasons.

A first sketch of the system might look like Figure 5.21.

Figure 5.21
Initial ERD for a trucking system.

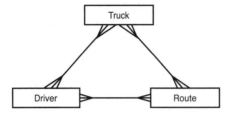

Earlier you learned how to resolve a many-to-many relationship. For any two entities that have a many-to-many relationship, you add a join entity between them that holds a primary key from each side of the relationship. You relate each "side" to the new join entity in a one-to-many relationship. If you "fix" the diagram of Figure 5.21 using those rules, you end up with something that looks like Figure 5.22.

Figure 5.22
The trucking system ERD with the many-to-many relationships resolved.

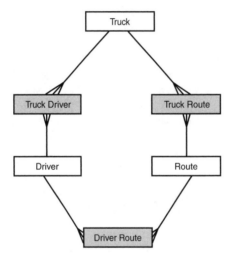

5

This diagram seems to be following the rules, but it's hard to know what it means or how it would work. What happens when trucker Samson drives truck T14302-B from Lubbock to Odessa? You need to record this fact by making entries in three different places—once in each of the join entities. You note the association of the truck and driver in one place, the association of the driver and the route in a second place, and the association of the truck and the route in a third place. What's more, it's possible to make an incomplete entry. What if you make additions to only two of the three join tables? It seems very confusing.

Let's say that the trip starts on Monday and ends on Wednesday and you want to record that fact. With three join entities, where do you put that data? In theory, you'd need to put it into each of the three join records. That amounts to repetitive data entry, and in relational database modeling, a design that promotes redundant data entry is usually a sign that something's not quite right.

One clue is that these three associations (truck-driver, truck-route, driver-route) are not independent of each other. They all happen at the same time. When a trucker drives a truck from point A to point B, all three associations happen at once. Why not put them all into just one record? That's the right answer, as it turns out, and it implies the structure shown in Figure 5.23.

Figure 5.23
The trucking system ERD with a single central join entity.

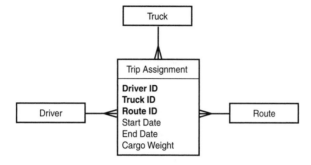

What you're dealing with here is not three many-to-many relationships, but a single "many-to-many-to-many" relationship. This kind of structure is sometimes referred to as a *star join*. The central entity in a star join (which in the example stores information about the association between a truck, a driver, and a route) is sometimes called a *fact table*. If you see a number of join entities in your diagram that are "symmetrical," as they are here, and seem to capture different pieces of the same data, you might want to think about whether you have a star join of some kind on your hands.

5

WORKING WITH MULTIPLE TABLES

MULTI-TABLE SYSTEMS IN FILEMAKER PRO

Chapter 5, "Relational Database Design," laid a heavy dose of abstract database theory on you. This chapter shows you how to take those essential ideas and use them to build more complex FileMaker database systems. You'll learn how to use FileMaker to create database systems that model the types of relationships covered in Chapter 5. In general, we don't like to prescribe a linear path through this book, but for this chapter (and really the one following, as well), we're going to assume you've either read Chapter 5 already, or have a reasonable familiarity with the terms and concepts of relational database design. If terms such as *entity-relationship diagram*, *primary key*, *foreign key*, and *one-to-many relationship* are unfamiliar to you, we recommend you review Chapter 5 before proceeding here.

Chapter 5 laid out a set of design concepts that centered around the ideas of *entities*, their *attributes*, and the *relationships* between entities. In FileMaker Pro, you'll generally represent a database entity ("student," for example) as a *table*. You'll generally represent an entity's attributes ("first name," "year of graduation," for example) by the *fields* of that table. And you'll create relationships among tables with FileMaker's Relationships Graph, a new tool that we'll be showing you in this chapter.

Before you get into the meat of this chapter, it's a good idea to review FileMaker's default behavior when you create a new database. When you create a new database, FileMaker creates a database with just one table in it, and that table initially has the same name as the name you gave the database as a whole. This is a sensible default behavior if you only ever intend to work with one table in the given database.

But FileMaker also has facilities for adding more tables to a system, adding different fields to each table, and creating many kinds of relationships between tables. We explore these tools in the context of some of the fundamental relationship types discussed in Chapter 5.

CREATING A ONE-TO-MANY RELATIONSHIP IN FILEMAKER

Let's consider a simple case. We're doing a database for a municipal government. The database is intended to store information on all the towns in an area, as well as a list of government officials such as mayors, commissioners, and the like. If we follow the principles mentioned in Chapter 5 and try to think of this in entity-relationship terms, it should be clear that we have two different entities here: "town" and "town official." The two have a one-to-many relationship: one town may have many officials. (We'll assume for the sake of simplicity that single person can't hold more than one town official post at once.)

Each entity on an entity-relationship diagram (ERD) generally translates into one table in a FileMaker system. To make this happen for our example, begin by creating a database that initially contains just the Town table, then add a TownOfficial table and join the two in a relationship. The following sections describe how.

CREATING THE FIRST TABLE IN A MULTI-TABLE SYSTEM

Again, when you create a FileMaker database for the first time, you get a single table with the same name as the database. If you create a new database called Town, you'll also get within it a single table, also called Town, and the option to add fields to that table. The initial field definition might look like Figure 6.1.

Figure 6.1
Field definitions for an initial table in a database of town information.

We've defined a number of basic fields containing town information. You should notice two things here. First, there is a field called Town ID. That field will be the *primary key* field, which will be essential when it's time to build a relationship to another table. Notice also the small menu at the top left of the Define Database dialog called Table. In a multi-table system, this menu shows on which table you're currently working, and lets you switch easily among field definitions for different tables.

→ For a refresher on the details of creating fields within a single table in FileMaker, **see** Chapter 3, "Defining and Working with Fields," **p. 63**.

ADDING A TABLE TO A MULTI-TABLE SYSTEM

That takes care of the Town table. To add a table for TownOfficer, stay in the Define Database dialog, but switch to the Table tab. You'll see just one table, which in this example is called Town. To add a new Table, type the name in the Table Name box, click Create, and the new table is added to the list, as shown in Figure 6.2.

You're now free to add fields to the new table. Figure 6.3 shows a suggested field list for the TownOfficer Table.

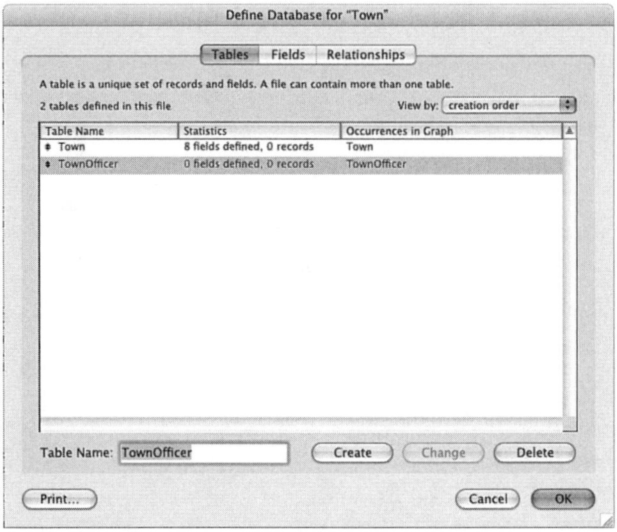

Figure 6.2
FileMaker's Tables view, showing a database with multiple tables.

Figure 6.3
Field structure for a table of town officers.

Pay attention to two fields here. The first is TownOfficerID. Like TownID in the Town table, this is the primary key for TownOfficer. Notice also the field called TownID. This is the *foreign key* that makes it possible to specify in *which* town this particular town officer serves. The foreign key will be crucial to making the relationship back to the Town table. Later in this chapter we discuss the principles of making effective key fields in FileMaker.

→ For a refresher on primary and foreign keys, **see** "Understanding the Role of Keys in Database Design," **p. 138**

ADDING A RELATIONSHIP

There are now two tables, as well as the primary and foreign keys that good database design demands. To create a relationship between these two tables, move to the Relationships tab of the Define Database dialog. This window, known as the Relationships Graph, should have a couple of graphical elements already displayed. Each one represents one of the database tables that exist in this database. These elements are known as *table occurrences*. Each shows the name of the table it represents, along with that table's fields. Figure 6.4 shows the Graph with the two tables presented there.

Figure 6.4
FileMaker's Relationships Graph, with table occurrences for two tables.

Adding a relationship between these two table occurrences is simple: Position the mouse over the TownID field in the Town table occurrence, and drag until the mouse is over the corresponding TownID field in the TownOfficer table occurrence. You should see a line extend from one table to the other, and when you release the mouse, FileMaker creates the relationship and displays it as a link between one or more match fields at the top of the table occurrence pair. Figure 6.5 shows how the Graph will look as a result.

You might have noticed the "crow's-foot" at the end of the relationship line, where it touches TownOfficer. This is none other than the indicator that you're accustomed to seeing on the ERDs from the last chapter. It's intended to indicate the "many" side of a one-to-many relationship. Be warned, though! FileMaker provides this graphical adornment as a kind of a hint or guess about the relationship—it may not always be accurate, though in this case it is. We explain that point fully in the next section, where we discuss the creation of key fields in FileMaker.

6

Figure 6.5
FileMaker's Relationships Graph, with a relationship between two table occurrences.

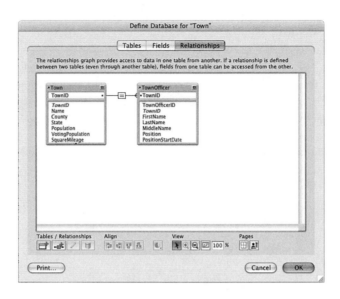

At this point you've seen how to add a new table to FileMaker's default one-table database configuration and how to define a one-to-many relationship between two FileMaker tables. The next sections clarify some important points about multi-table systems.

WORKING WITH KEYS AND MATCH FIELDS

You should remember from Chapter 5 that keys are table fields—fields that are essential elements in forming the relational structure of a multi-table system. FileMaker takes a somewhat broader view of keys, as you'll see, and for that reason these fields are referred to as *match fields* when you're working in a FileMaker context. A match field in FileMaker is any field that participates in a relationship between two FileMaker tables. Primary keys and foreign keys fit this definition, of course, but so do a number of other types of fields that are explored more in the next chapter.

→ For more on the broader uses of match fields in FileMaker Pro, **see** "Relationships as Queries," **p. 180**, as well as other sections of Chapter 7.

Key fields (which form the structural backbone of the system) need to play by some special rules—especially primary keys. Consider the current example, the Town database system, and consider the TownID field in the Town table. This field has been identified as the primary key for the Town table. To play the role of primary key, there are a few rules the field has to follow. In the first place, the value in it has to be *unique* within the given table. In the example, this means that no two towns should share the same TownID (though it's fine if there's a town official with an ID of 27, as well as town with an ID of 27—they're in two different tables, so you won't get them mixed up). The reasons for this are fairly obvious: A TownID isn't much use if two towns can share a single TownID; we'd have no way to identify one single town uniquely. And by the same token, we never want the TownID field to be empty. FileMaker helps us work within these constraints.

To make a field suitable for use as a primary key, use FileMaker's field options to add some important restrictions to the field definition. You do this in the Options dialog that's available when you have a field selected in the Define Database dialog.

On the Auto-Enter tab of the Options dialog, click the Serial Number check box (see Figure 6.6). (Leave the specific serial number options alone for now.) This instructs FileMaker to enter a new, unique number into the field every time a record is created, starting at whatever number you specify and going as high as necessary.

Figure 6.6
Use a serial numbering auto-entry option to populate a primary key field.

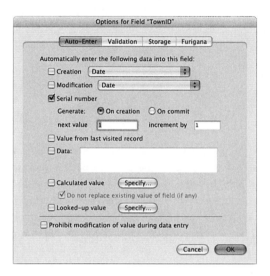

Click the Validation tab, and then click to check the Not Empty and Unique Value check boxes, found in the Require section. This ensures the field follows the earlier criteria for a good primary key field: never empty, always unique. Lastly, in the upper portion of the box, uncheck the choice that says Allow User to Override During Data Entry. With that box checked, the user could enter her own data values in the field, possibly breaking the established uniqueness rules, or creating incorrect associations between records. You certainly don't want this to be possible. Figure 6.7 shows the Validation tab in use.

Primary Key Options

Using an automatically-entered serial number is one of the simplest ways to create a primary key, but there are other schools of thought. These serial numbers are not globally unique, or even unique in the context of a single database. As we mentioned earlier, two records in different tables can share the same primary key when this kind of record numbering is used. The odds of any kind of mix-up are slight, but you may want to avoid the concern entirely. Some developers create a key based on complex random criteria, such as the current timestamp or current userid, for example. A simpler scheme we've seen used involves still using FileMaker's serial numbers, but adding a prefix to them, so that invoices are numbered INV1, INV2, and so on. FileMaker's serial numbering option accepts text prefixes and suffixes of this sort, and such a scheme can add a useful descriptive dimension to your keys while also better ensuring uniqueness (assuming you never use duplicate prefixes within one database).

Figure 6.7
These validation options are appropriate for a primary key field.

We consider these settings to be essential for any field used as a primary key. For a *foreign key*, the constraints are less severe. Consider the TownID field in the TownOfficers table. First, there doesn't need to be a uniqueness constraint. For example, many town officers should be permitted to have the same TownID. And the TownID in the TownOfficer table shouldn't be a sequential serial number, either. That's a characteristic of a primary key. The main thing is that it not be empty. So you can simply apply the "not empty" validation rule to a foreign key field and leave it at that.

NOTE

There's another important constraint you may want to place on a foreign key field. It's called a *referential integrity rule*, and it's discussed later in this chapter in the section titled "Relational Integrity."

Cardinality in the Relationships Graph

This discussion provides an opportune moment to look again at that crow's-foot that FileMaker so cleverly applied to the Town/TownOfficer relationship created earlier. FileMaker looks at the field definition options to try to determine the cardinality of a relationship. Any field that is either defined to be unique or has an auto-enter serial-number is assumed by FileMaker to be the "one" side of a relationship. Lacking either of those characteristics, it's assumed to represent the "many" side. That, in brief, is how FileMaker determines how to draw the cardinality indicators (that is, the crow's-foot) in the Relationships Graph. It's a useful indicator, to be sure, but not bulletproof, and is really just advisory. The cardinality indicator neither creates nor enforces any rules, and can't be changed from FileMaker's default "guess" value. It simply tells you what FileMaker thinks is going on.

→ For a discussion of cardinality, **see** "Relationship Cardinality," **p. 134**.

UNDERSTANDING TABLE CONTEXT

FileMaker 7 differs greatly from previous versions in its capability to work with many database tables in a single physical file. But there's a bit of a price to be paid for this power. Many, if not most, actions in FileMaker 7 assume that some particular table is somehow the "active" table. Say you reach up to the Records menu and select Delete Record. Which table does that command affect? It affects the "current" table—but how does FileMaker decide which table is "current"? The answer is that FileMaker determines this from what's called the *table context*.

Table context, it turns out, is determined by the currently active layout. Let's continue to refer to the Town/TownOfficer example. The steps to add the new table were simple, but there's some complexity underneath. After you're back in the Town database, you're still probably looking at the town entry layout, the one where you can view basic town information. But FileMaker has silently added another layout to the database.

In Layout mode, make sure the status area is showing and click on the layout popup list near the top of the Status Bar. There are now two layouts: one called Town, the other called TownOfficer. The new layout is named for the second table you added. You've already learned how the displays in the Status Area work. Add a few records while you're on the Town layout, and you'll see the total number of records, as listed in the status area, grow. More towns, more records—no big surprise there.

But if you use the layout popup list to switch to the TownOfficer layout, a surprise *is* in store: The record total drops back to zero. Why?

The simple answer is that each layout is showing something different. The Town layout shows records from the Town table, and the TownOfficer layout shows records from the TownOfficer table. These tables can, and probably will, have different numbers of records. To make the concept still clearer, go ahead and add a bunch of records while you're on the TownOfficer layout. For TownID, pick some of the IDs of towns you've already created—they'll probably be low numbers such as 1–5. You may want to choose View, View as Table to see the list in its entirety as it grows. Now switch back and forth between the two layouts to see the record totals shift.

In FileMaker 7, each layout represents a view into a particular database table. If you think back to the analogy of a database table as a card file, you can think of each table as a file containing a different kind of card. In the Town card file, each card holds information about one particular town. In the TownOfficer card file, each card holds information about a town officer in one of those towns. When you move from one layout to another in FileMaker, it's as though you're closing one card file and opening up another. Each new card file you open may have a different number of cards, with different information on each card.

FileMaker keeps track of all this by storing a *table context* with each layout. To see this, drop into Layout mode on the Town layout and choose Layouts, Layout Setup. Notice the menu that says Show Records From (you can see it in Figure 6.8). If you click on that menu, it lists all the tables for this database and shows that the layout is currently linked to the Town table.

6

Figure 6.8
This is the Layout Setup dialog, showing the table context for the TownOfficer layout.

In practice, you're unlikely to need to change the table context of a layout after it's been established. When you create a new table in a database, FileMaker adds the new table to the Relationships Graph, and also adds a new layout based on the table. You may, though, want to create additional layouts that refer to the same underlying table. In that case, you need to set the table context for the layout in the course of creating the layout. Again, you're unlikely to need to change this after it's been set. If you have a working layout that's displaying data from a particular table, you're likely to discover odd consequences if you change the table context.

NOTE

There's some simplification in that last paragraph. Here's a more accurate rendition of the second sentence: "When you create a new table in a database, FileMaker adds a *table occurrence* for the new table to the Relationships Graph, and also adds a layout based on that table occurrence." The full importance of the distinction is made clear in the next chapter.

→ For a discussion of table occurrences, **see** "Adding a Table Occurrence to the Relationships Graph," **p. 183**.

WORKING WITH RELATED DATA

So far in this chapter you've learned how to create additional tables in a FileMaker system and how to build relationships between those tables based on well-constructed match fields. This section shows you how to begin to *use* your relationships to work with and create data in multiple tables at once.

USING A PORTAL TO VIEW RELATED CHILD DATA

The town records database system has two tables in it now. But how do we use them? Say there's a record for a town called Gorre, with a TownID of 1, and you want to enter information about the mayor and town councilors of Gorre. One way would be to navigate to the

TownOfficer layout and create a record for each official, assigning a `TownID` of 1 to each. That seems like a tedious way to create data, and it's potentially error-prone because a user must know and correctly enter the `TownID` of every town. Additionally, there's no way to see a list of town officials when looking at the master town record in the Town table.

FileMaker solves both these problems with a tool called a *portal*. A portal is a special FileMaker layout element that lets you work with data across two (or sometimes more) tables at once. In the case of the Towns database, a portal lets you look at records in the TownOfficer table while you're sitting on the "parent" Town record.

→ For addition discussion of the "parent/child" naming convention, **see** "One-to-Many Relationships," **p. 132**.

To see a portal in action, navigate to a layout that has the parent table (Town, in this case) as its *table context*. After you're on this layout, drop into Layout mode and you'll see the portal tool among the available tools in the status bar (see Figure 6.9).

NOTE

> You should be able to tell the table context by the fields on the layout, but you'll recall that the Layout setup dialog, accessible in the Layouts menu while in Layout mode, gives the definitive answer.

Figure 6.9
This is a layout in Layout mode, showing the FileMaker portal tool.

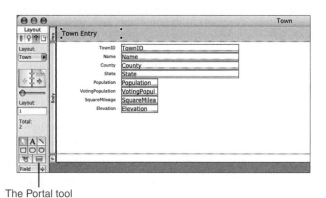

The Portal tool

Click once on the tool, and then, on the layout, drag out a box wide enough to show an entire town officer's name and release the mouse. You'll get a dialog box asking for details about the portal's contents, behavior, and display. The dialog is shown in Figure 6.10.

In general, when you set up a portal for the first time, you'll need to do the following:

- Choose a table occurrence from which to display data
- Choose additional portal options
- Choose data fields for display in the portal

More details on each of these steps follow.

Figure 6.10
FileMaker's Portal
Setup dialog.

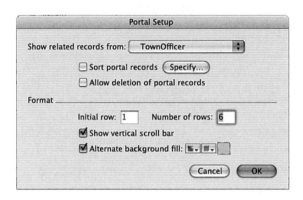

First, you need to specify where the portal gets its data. In the Portal Setup dialog, the Show Related Records From list enables you to choose from which table to draw data. The list is divided into sections: one for related tables and one for unrelated tables. (The question of whether a table is "related" or "unrelated" is determined by the Relationships Graph.) In the current example, for a portal on a layout where the table context is the Town table, there should be only one available choice in the menu: the TownOfficer table, which is the only other table related to Town in the Relationships Graph. By choosing TownOfficer from this menu, you're instructing FileMaker to show you all town officer records that are related to the currently-visible town record (in other words, all that share the same TownID).

The Portal Setup dialog contains a number of other choices as well. For now, you can opt to display just twelve portal rows, and put a vertical scroll bar on the portal so that you can scroll down if a town has more than twelve officers. You can also apply coloring or striping to the portal if you chose.

FileMaker also displays a dialog at the end of the portal creation process, asking which fields from the related table you want to show in the portal. For this example, we chose to show FirstName, LastName, Position, and PositionStartDate from the TownOfficer table.

Back in Browse mode, you should see a list of town officers in the portal (assuming you created some and they're still around), as shown in Figure 6.11. It would be ideal if you could type right into the rows of the portal and enter your data that way. By default, this isn't possible (try it and see), but it's easy to add this capability to the portal.

 If you don't see the records you expect to see in the portal, you might need to check your portal settings. See "Repeating Portals" in the Troubleshooting section at the end of this chapter.

USING A PORTAL TO ADD RELATED RECORDS

Portals can be used for data entry, as well as data viewing. It's possible to configure the portal and its underlying relationship so that a user can add officers to a town record by typing directly into the portal rows.

To accomplish this, you need to edit the relationship between Town and TownOfficer. On the Relationships Graph, double-clicking on the relationship line between the two tables brings up the Edit Relationship dialog, shown in Figure 6.12.

Figure 6.11
A portal can display multiple records from a related table.

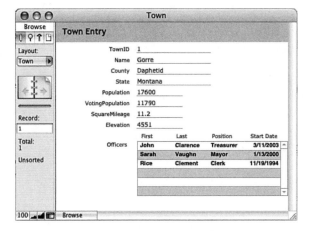

Figure 6.12
The Edit Relationships dialog is where you can edit individual relationships in the Relationships Graph.

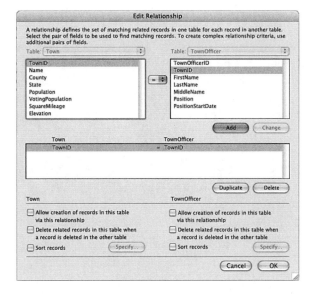

For each of the tables participating in the relationship, there's a check box underneath it called Allow Creation of Records in This Table via This Relationship. If you check this box on the TownOfficer side of the dialog, it becomes possible to create TownOfficer records via this relationship.

If you check this option, and return to the Town layout in the parent table, you'll discover that you can now click on an empty row of the portal and type in an officer for this town.

This is all good in its own right, but another payoff comes if you flip over to the TownOfficer layout to get a direct look at the records in the TownOfficer table. You'll notice that there are new records in TownOfficer, corresponding to those you entered in the portal. Notice in particular that the TownID has been set automatically to the ID of the town record from which you were performing the data entry. FileMaker has created the foreign keys in TownOfficer for you automatically. Figure 6.13 shows a possible view of the TownOfficer table after portal-based record creation.

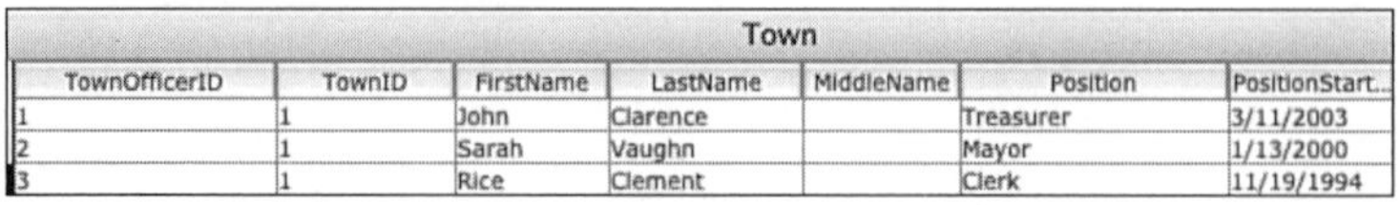

Figure 6.13
Adding records to the portal on the Town layout creates linked records in the TownOfficer table.

Town						
TownOfficerID	TownID	FirstName	LastName	MiddleName	Position	PositionStart...
1	1	John	Clarence		Treasurer	3/11/2003
2	1	Sarah	Vaughn		Mayor	1/13/2000
3	1	Rice	Clement		Clerk	11/19/1994

With portals, it's easy to view, create, and manipulate records on the "many" side of a one-to-many relationship.

WORKING WITH RELATED PARENT DATA IN A CHILD FILE

You've seen how to use a portal to add related ("child") records to a master ("parent") record. Suppose you want to turn the problem around, and see information about the *town*, on the *officer's* data record. Figure 6.14 shows a somewhat bare-bones rendition of the TownOfficer layout. In addition to information about the town officer, you can see the TownID, but you can't tell what the name of that town is, much less any other information about it. Given a record for John Samuels, who's the Sheriff of the town of Gorre, you'd like to be able to view the town's name, county, and population on John's data record. So far, this database doesn't do that. But it's not hard to configure.

Figure 6.14
A simple view of a town officer record. No information about the associated town is shown, other than the TownID.

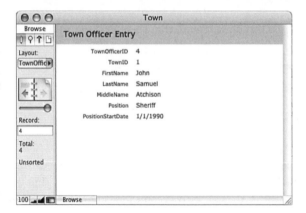

To make this happen, you need to edit the TownOfficer layout a bit. Enter Layout mode and shrink the TownID field so there's some room to the right of it. Drag another field to the right of TownID. You'll see the Specify Field dialog, as shown in Figure 6.15. If you inspect the menu at the top of the box, you can see that it indicates that the box is currently allowing you to choose fields from the TownOfficer table (the current table). But you can change the menu to show fields from a related table; in this case, Town is your only choice. Figure 6.15 shows the dialog after the user has chosen to show fields from the related Town table.

Figure 6.15
It's possible to display individual fields from related records on a FileMaker layout.

Change the menu to read Town, and select the Name field you find there. Back in Layout mode, you'll see a subtle change in the display. The field name now has two colons preceding it, as Figure 6.16 shows. This is FileMaker's cue that the field doesn't come from the current table, but from a related table. At this time, you can use the same technique to bring in the County and Population fields from the Town table.

Figure 6.16
Fields from related tables are displayed with a preceding double colon in Layout mode.

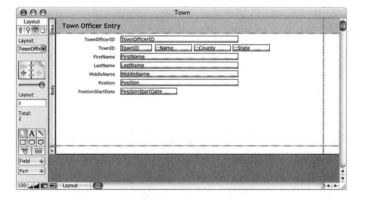

Drop back into Browse mode and you'll see that the name field now shows the name of the town of Gorre, along with its county and population. Just to understand the point, clear out the TownID field. Notice that the town name and other information disappear. Reset the TownID field to 1 again, and back comes the town data.

Editing Related Fields
One thing to be aware of is that the data you see in these related fields is not in any sense a "copy" of the related data. Displaying related fields gives the user direct access to the data on the master record (the town record in this case). To see this, edit the data in a related field, say by changing the town name. Now shift to a layout that shows you the master town record. You'll see that the town record itself has a new name!

In some situations, you probably don't want to let this happen. Those fields are intended to *show* information from the master record, not necessarily to allow it to be edited. To prevent the data in a layout field from being edited, you can drop into Layout mode, then select the field in question and choose Format, Field Behavior. At the top of this box uncheck the box that says Allow Field to be Entered in Browse Mode. That way, on this layout, users cannot enter the field in Browse mode.

This restriction applies only to the current field (though you can apply it to as many layout fields as you like) and *applies only on the current layout.*

To repeat: Related data is the "real" data, not a copy, and unexpected things can happen if you allow users to edit related fields.

PORTALS VERSUS RELATED FIELDS: WHICH IS WHICH?

You might be puzzled that previously we used a portal to access and view related data, and here we're using this seemingly quite different technique. Which is which, and how do you know when to use each one?

The answer is actually quite simple:

> Use a portal to view multiple related child records from the perspective of a parent record. Use related fields to see a single parent record's information from the perspective of a child record.

In the town example, we used a portal on the parent record (the town) to view multiple related child records (the town's officers). Looking from the other side, we used individual related fields on a child record (the town officer) to view information from the single parent record (the town).

To put this in terms of the "one-to-many" language we've been using, a portal is used to look at the "many" from the perspective of the "one," and single related fields are used to look at the "one" from the perspective of the "many."

CREATING A MANY-TO-MANY RELATIONSHIP

The preceding sections introduced you to most of FileMaker's fundamental tools for working with multiple related tables. Now it's time to extend those concepts and see how to use them to create a many-to-many relationship structure.

BUILDING THE STRUCTURE

Let's say that you've been asked to create a database for a town militia. You need to keep track of militia members in their own right, and you also need to be able to assign them to different guard shifts. An ERD for the proposed system is shown in Figure 6.17. On the one hand there are guard shifts, each of which can be staffed by several militia members. On the other hand, there are militia members, each of whom can work many shifts. This is a classic many-to-many relationship. You'll recall from Chapter 5 that such relationships are resolved with an intermediate *join entity*. In this case, we'll call the join entity a "shift assignment." Each shift assignment records the posting of a single person to a single shift.

Figure 6.17
An ERD for a system that tracks guard shifts and shift assignments.

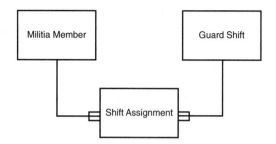

As before, we map the abstract entities directly onto FileMaker tables. This produces a three-table system. The appropriate key structure is essential: primary keys in the Shift and MilitiaMember tables, and *two* foreign keys (ShiftID and MilitiaMemberID) in the middle ShiftAssignment table.

→ For additional discussion of the key structure of join tables, **see** "Many-to-Many Relationships: Solving the Puzzle," **p. 140**.

We're going to assume that you're familiar enough with the field and table definition process by now that we can skip over the details. We'll take you straight to the Relationships Graph. Figure 6.18 shows the Graph after we've created all three tables and established the two relationships into the ShiftAssignment table.

Figure 6.18
The FileMaker Relationships Graph with three related table occurrences representing a many-to-many relationship.

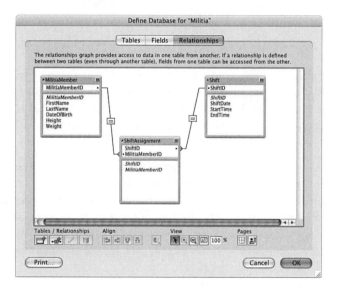

CREATING A DATA ENTRY INTERFACE

As before, the structural part is not so hard. But it takes some work to make data entry easy. Creating and editing militia members or guard shifts is pretty straightforward: the user navigates either to the Shift layout or the MilitiaMember layout and adds, edits, and deletes records there.

But what about shift assignments? As with the earlier example of town officers, shift assignments are a type of child record that you want to create in association with a parent record of some kind. In the town/officer example, the data entry interface we discussed enables users to add officers to a particular selected town. In the guard system under discussion, the intent is to be able to choose a shift, view that shift record, and assign militia members to that specific shift. In a similar vein, users should also be able to choose a militia member, view her record, and see on the same screen a list of all of her current shift assignments.

Let's assume that you've created records for a few militia members and a few shifts already. You'd like to edit the Shift layout so as to be able to view and create shift assignments from the Shift layout itself. You can add a portal to the layout: It'll be a portal showing records—*not* from the MilitiaMember table, but from the ShiftAssignment table. We want users to be able to add multiple assignments to this shift and specify a militia member for each assignment.

Recall the data structure from Figure 6.17. There's no way to record a member's *name* in the shift assignment table—only her primary key. That's not a very friendly data entry mechanism. The watch commander is more likely to know his staff by name, not by database ID. We can fall back on a familiar FileMaker tool for this data entry task: the value list.

Before doing this, by the way, you're going to want to make sure that the relationship between Shift and ShiftAssignment is configured to allow creation of related ShiftAssignment records. This is necessary if the portal is to be used as a data entry tool.

USING A VALUE LIST FOR DATA ENTRY

Even though users know militia members by name, the key structure of the data is rigid (as it should be). What the user needs to enter into each shift assignment record is a member's primary key, not her name. But it's not realistic to memorize member IDs. You need some kind of data entry mechanism that will give a hint as to which member ID goes with which member.

FileMaker's value lists are the right tool for this. Chapter 4, "FileMaker Fundamentals: Working with Layouts," discussed creating value lists from a hand-entered list of custom values. In the current example, to speed the assignment of members to shifts, what you need is a way to build a value list dynamically, based on the contents of the MilitiaMember Table, so that the value list has one entry for each member in the database. And each entry should show two pieces of data—not only the member ID, but also the member's name.

DEFINING A VALUE LIST TO DRAW DATA FROM A TABLE

Choose File, Define, Value Lists, and create a new value list. In the Edit Value List dialog, rather than choose the third radio button (Custom), choose the first one, Use Values From Field, as shown in Figure 6.19.

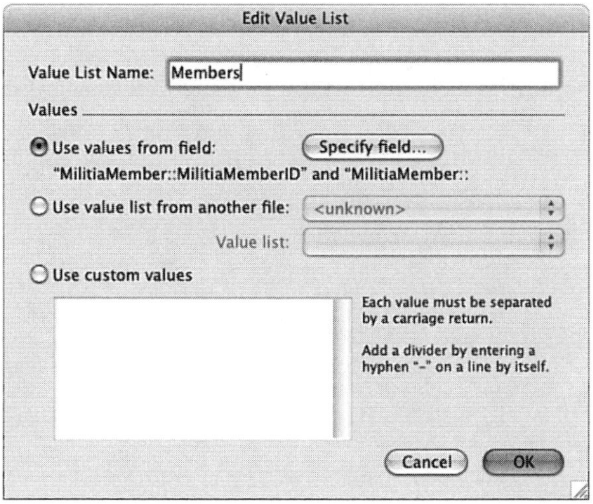

Figure 6.19
This is the first of two dialogs you use to create a new value list.

Edit Value List

Value List Name: Members

Values

⦿ Use values from field: [Specify field...]
"MilitiaMember::MilitiaMemberID" and "MilitiaMember::

◯ Use value list from another file: <unknown>

Value list:

◯ Use custom values

Each value must be separated by a carriage return.

Add a divider by entering a hyphen "-" on a line by itself.

[Cancel] [OK]

When you do this you'll get a second dialog box. Go to the menu that says Use Values from First Field. This lets you pick first a table, and then a field from that table. Choose `MilitiaMemberID` from the field list in the first column. In the second column, choose the check box that says Also Display Values from Second Field, then choose `LastName` from the list of fields in that table. At the bottom left, choose the Include All Values radio button. You can also choose the button at the bottom right that instructs FileMaker to sort the value list by the second field. This assures that the list will be sorted in order of last name, rather than in order of the member ID. This second dialog box is shown in Figure 6.20.

Figure 6.20
The second value list dialog, allowing you to specify an additional field to display in the value list.

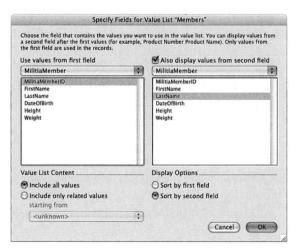

Specify Fields for Value List "Members"

Choose the field that contains the values you want to use in the value list. You can display values from a second field after the first values (for example, Product Number Product Name). Only values from the first field are used in the records.

Use values from first field | ☑ Also display values from second field

MilitiaMember | MilitiaMember

MilitiaMemberID / FirstName / LastName / DateOfBirth / Height / Weight | MilitiaMemberID / FirstName / LastName / DateOfBirth / Height / Weight

Value List Content | Display Options
⦿ Include all values | ◯ Sort by first field
◯ Include only related values | ⦿ Sort by second field
starting from
<unknown>

[Cancel] [OK]

6

With the value list created, it's time to return to the ShiftAssignment layout and build the data entry portal. The first step is, of course, to use the Portal tool to draw the portal. Choose whatever features you like, such as vertical scroll bar or row striping. When you're finished, FileMaker prompts you to choose fields to put into the portal.

Figure 6.21 shows the Add Fields to Portal dialog. Notice that the table selection menu at the left lets you choose fields from either of two different tables: You can choose fields from the intermediate ShiftAssignment table or from the more "distant" MilitiaMember table itself.

Figure 6.21
In FileMaker 7, a portal can display records from tables that are more than one "hop" distant from the current table.

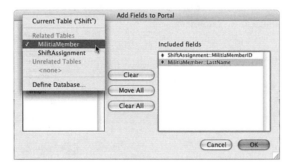

In this case, you need to do both. Choose the MilitiaMemberID field from ShiftAssignment. You need to fill that field in with a member ID, so it needs to be in the portal. But when you're viewing the portal, you're really more interested in the member's name. Well, that field isn't in the join table, so you just need to reach "farther down" to get to it. Switch the Available Fields menu to show fields from the MilitiaMember table and select LastName.

NOTE
NEW

> If you're used to previous versions of FileMaker, you'll recognize that this ability to reach more than one relationship "deep" is a huge advance. Making this happen was possible in previous versions, but did require setting up additional calculations in the join table to "pipeline" data through to the portal. In FileMaker 7, it's possible to look several levels deep, if necessary, to bring back related information.

With the portal created on the layout, you're almost finished. You still need to apply the value list to aid in record creation. In Layout mode, select the MilitiaMemberID field in the portal. Choose Format, Field Format. In the Field Format dialog box, choose Format Field as Pop-up List and choose Display Values from Members, since "Members" is the name of the member value list you created.

Back in Browse mode, if you click into the ID field, you should see a neatly-formatted list of possible members to add to the shift. Figure 6.22 illustrates the behavior.

CAUTION

> As before, you should use the Field Behavior dialog box to prevent users from entering into that LastName field while in Browse mode. If they edit the name there, the name on the original MilitiaMember is changed.

Figure 6.22
Using value lists built on table data is a powerful way to aid data entry in related tables.

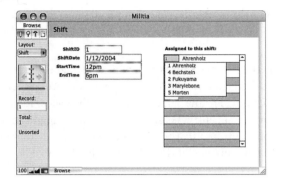

RELATIONAL INTEGRITY

I'm sure the topic of this section sounds suspiciously like some form of couples therapy. Not to fear—it's a good deal less interesting than that, unless you're a database designer, in which case it's endlessly fascinating.

Relational integrity, also known as *referential integrity*, speaks to the notion that a database structure, as expressed in an ERD, also implies certain rules about what can and cannot happen in a database. If you read Chapter 5, you encountered the concept of *optionality rules*. An optionality rule may, for example, assert that an order must have at least one order line item. Or it may assert the more obvious truth that an order line item that doesn't relate to an existing order is an error.

Consider the example of shift assignments again. Suppose there's a record in the ShiftAssignment table that references a militia member with an ID of 1002, when in fact there is no member with that ID. This could have happened because of data entry error (again, a great reason to use a value list in the way we demonstrated in the previous section). It could also happen if that member had existed once upon a time and has since been deleted. In that case, without integrity rules to protect against this, the member's assignment records would be left dangling in the ShiftAssignment table. Database analysts usually refer to such records as "orphans," and their existence is a violation of referential integrity.

This state of affairs clearly looks like an error that you should avoid. There are a couple of things you can do to prevent this. To prevent erroneous entry of a non-existent member ID, you can use field validation. To prevent the creation of orphaned records as a result of deletion, you can use an *integrity rule*.

USING A VALUE LIST TO ENSURE RELATIONAL INTEGRITY

We'd like to add a validation rule to the ShiftAssignment table that says it's not valid to create a record with an nonexistent `MilitiaMemberID`. The best way to do this in FileMaker is to create a value list containing all the extant `MilitiaMemberID` numbers, and apply validation that allows only IDs from that list to be used. You'd do that as follows.

1. Define a new value list, called `MemberIDs`. You can make it by duplicating the Members list you already created. This differs from the earlier list only in that it does not use

values from a second field, so that box should remain unchecked. (Because the earlier value list sorts based on the Name field, it cannot be used to validate based on the contents of the ID field.)

2. Go to Define Database, edit the ShiftAssignment table, and edit the field options for the MilitiaMemberID field. Choose the Validation tab, and on that screen check the Member of Value List box. For the value list, choose the MemberIDs value list you created earlier to help with data entry. While you're here, you might as well also stipulate that the field can't be empty and that the user may not override these restrictions. You can also provide a custom message if the validation should fail. These options are shown in Figure 6.23.

Figure 6.23
Use FileMaker's validation options to enforce a referential integrity rule between two tables.

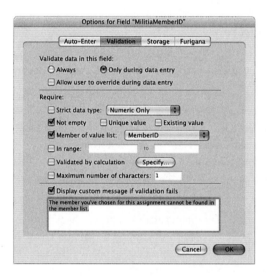

Now, if you were to try to enter a member ID that didn't exist in the MilitiaMember table, you'd get a warning that the action was disallowed.

PRESERVING REFERENTIAL INTEGRITY DURING DELETION

Deletion is another pitfall if you're picky about keeping your database consistent. What happens if you want to delete a member, and he already has shift assignments? Well, you have two choices: either forbid the deletion on the grounds that the assignments exist, *or* delete all the shift assignments along with the member himself.

These two options are known in database parlance as a *restricted delete* and a *cascading delete*, respectively. A restricted delete ensures that parent records with related children can't be deleted—an attempt to do so produces an error. A cascading delete, on the other hand, deletes all the associated shift assignment records along with the member. FileMaker doesn't at this point support restricted delete directly, although the effect can be achieved in other ways.

To add a cascade-delete rule to a relationship, simply edit the MilitiaMember-ShiftAssignment relationship in the Relationships Graph. On the ShiftAssignment side of the dialog box, look for a check box that says Delete Related Records in This Table When a Record Is Deleted in the Other Table.

CAUTION

Be sure not to check the corresponding box under MilitiaMember. This would have the effect of deleting a member record any time a corresponding shift assignment was deleted. This is the wrong direction in which to cascade! Also be aware that "cascade" effects are cumulative. If you define multiple cascade-deletion rules in a system, a single deletion can sweep across multiple tables. Pay careful attention to the details of this feature until you're comfortable working with it. As with other mass-update operations in FileMaker, such as Replace Field Contents, or a data import, there is no way to undo such deletions.

It's possible to configure FileMaker's security privileges in a way that interferes with the enforcement of integrity rules. See "Accidental Delete Restrictions" in the Troubleshooting section at the end of this chapter.

TROUBLESHOOTING

REPEATING PORTALS

I've created a portal, but instead of seeing a set of different records, I see that every single row of the portal shows exactly the same data.

This indicates a mismatch of table occurrences. Specifically, it suggests that although the portal is set to look at records from table occurrence A, the fields you've chosen to display in the portal are actually from table occurrence B. Because it's possible to have several different table occurrences that are based on the same underlying table, it's possible to see the same field list for several different table occurrences. Nevertheless, if the portal and the fields displayed in it draw from different table occurrences, you probably won't get a meaningful display, even if the different table occurrences are all based on the same underlying table.

ACCIDENTAL DELETE RESTRICTIONS

I set up a cascade-delete relationships between my Customer table and my Invoice table, so that when I delete a customer, all related invoices are deleted as well. But when I try to delete a customer, it tells me I don't have sufficient privileges. I checked my privileges and I do have delete privileges in the Customer table.

Check to make sure you also have delete privileges on the Invoice table as well. To perform a delete operation successfully in FileMaker, a user needs delete access to any and all records that are to be deleted. If you have delete privileges for customers but not for invoices, the entire deletion operation is forbidden.

FILEMAKER EXTRA: BUILDING A THREE-WAY JOIN

In the "Extra" section at the end of Chapter 5, we sketched out the ERD for a many-to-many-to-many relationship among truckers, trucks, and truck routes. We follow up on that discussion here and show you how you might build such a thing in FileMaker.

Structurally, it's not too complex—we already worked out the relationships at the end of Chapter 5. You need a four-entity system: Trucker, Truck, Route, and the central three-way join entity, called in this case RouteAssignment. The Relationships Graph for such a structure might look like Figure 6.24.

Figure 6.24
The FileMaker Relationships Graph showing table occurrences and relationships for a three-way join.

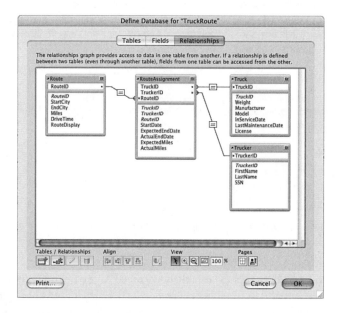

What about data entry? This is a bit more challenging. In theory, you could have a portal in any of the "parent" tables that would enable you to create RouteAssignment records. If the portal were in the Trucker table, you'd be entering a Truck and a Route on each portal row to make the assignment. If the portal were in the Truck Table, you'd enter a Trucker and a Route on each row. If the portal were in the Route table, you'd enter a Truck and a Trucker on each row.

Well, these portals are probably useful for data viewing. Certainly, if I'm on a trucker record, I'd like to see a portal with all that trucker's route assignments. Same for a truck: I'd like to see a list of all the routes over which the truck has been driven in its service lifetime. But none of these is obviously the "right" place from which to do data entry.

In a case like this, it may be best to set aside the portal-based method for entering data in a related field and allow the user to create the assignment records directly. You still want to use value lists to assist data entry; if it's hard to remember one set of keys, it's surely impossible to remember three! So you'd define three value lists, one based on each table, with the first field in the value list being the primary key for the table, and the second field being some nice identifying field from the rest of the table. Such a set of value lists is shown in Figure 6.25.

TIP

> This last point raises a difficulty with two-field value lists. You're limited to a total of two fields, so if the first field is a key field of some kind, that leaves you a total of one field of identifying data. Sometimes that's not enough. For the truckers, last name may be enough for the second field. For trucks, the license plate number might suffice. But for routes, we'd really like to see both the start and the end city of the route. The only way to do this is to create a calculation field to display the start and end nicely—such as Poughkeepsie-Hopalong. You can then use this calculation as the second field in the value list.

Figure 6.25
These value lists speed data entry into the join table in the midst of the three-way join.

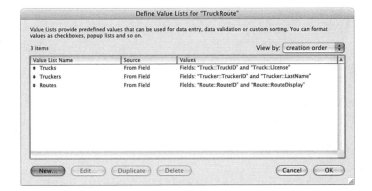

After you have the three value lists, you can create a layout, based on the RouteAssignment table, where users can easily create a new route by using the value lists to populate the three key fields. You could set things up so that the data entry would take place in Table View, as shown in Figure 6.26.

Figure 6.26
You can use value lists, as well as the display of appropriate related fields, to create a usable data entry interface for this complex three-way join setup.

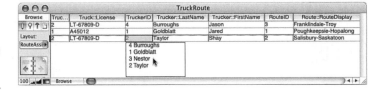

6

Notice that related fields have been added from each of the three main tables to make the display more intelligible.

Although FileMaker excels at modeling and implementing the standard one-to-many and many-to-many relationships, it's equally capable of working with more esoteric structures as well. In such cases you're likely to find that modeling and building the relationships is relatively straightforward, whereas designing the data entry interface takes some more thought. The techniques described in this section may be instructive, or you may find you need a different solution, depending on the nature of the problem and the needs of your users.

6

CHAPTER

7

WORKING WITH RELATIONSHIPS

In this chapter

RELATIONSHIP GRAPHS AND ERDs

Chapter 5, "Relational Database Design," outlined some database theory that helps produce an ERD—an *entity-relationship diagram* that shows the fundamental building blocks of a database system and the ways in which they relate. In Chapter 6, "Working with Multiple Tables," we showed how to use FileMaker's Relationship tools to turn an ERD into a working FileMaker database. This might lead you to think that the Relationships Graph is really the same thing as an ERD, and that the relationships you build there match one-to-one with the relationships you sketch out on your ERD.

In fact, there's a lot more to relationships in FileMaker. The Relationships Graph certainly handles all the structural relationships present on an ERD. But there are many other ways to use relationships in FileMaker. The ERD-based relationships are the structural core of any FileMaker database (or *any* relational database), but this chapter takes you beyond the core and shows you some other ways you can use relationships in FileMaker. It also delves further into the features of the Relationships Graph, and discusses different ways of organizing files, tables, and table occurrences in a FileMaker system.

Bottom line: The Relationships Graph is actually a *superset* of your ERD. It certainly has the ERD wrapped up in it, but it may well contain other important structures and relationships as well. Those techniques are the subject of this chapter.

RELATIONSHIPS AS QUERIES

We want to introduce you to the idea of a relationship as a kind of query. Consider a database that stores information about customers and their invoices. On a layout specific to the Customer entity, you can add a portal of invoice information. Figure 7.1 shows that layout.

Figure 7.1
Using a portal to look for a particular customer's invoices.

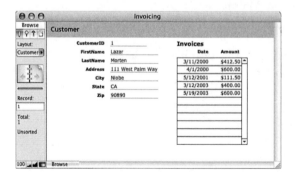

The portal looks into a table of invoices, and is based on the fundamental one-to-many relationship between a customer and an invoice, based on a shared key called CustomerID (see Figure 7.2). But the portal also represents a kind of query, which says, "Show me all invoices that have the same CustomerID as this customer."

Figure 7.2
Relationships
Graph for a simple
customer-invoice
system.

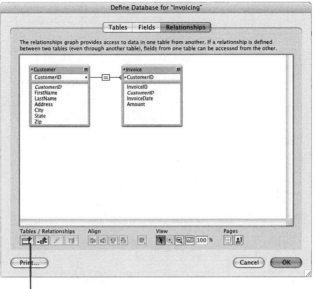

Add Table Occurrence button

That's all well and good, but suppose a user comes to you and asks for a portal that shows only this year's invoices for that customer. That's a different query than before, and therefore requires a different relationship. Well, FileMaker can do that. Creating this new query requires delving into three new concepts in FileMaker relationships: the concept of *non-equijoins*, the concept of a *table occurrence*, and the concept of a *multiple match*.

NON-EQUIJOINS

Don't let the scary terminology throw you. The concept is simple. Refer back to Figure 7.2, which illustrated the relationship between Customer and Invoice. Notice that the line representing the relationship has an "equals" sign right in the middle. To explore what that means, you would double-click on the relationship line to edit the relationship. The Edit Relationship dialog is shown in Figure 7.3.

The middle-most box shows the match field or fields defined for this relationship. This current relationship is built between a `CustomerID` in Customer and a `CustomerID` in Invoice. The match criterion is based on equality, meaning that invoices match (and hence are displayed in a portal that shows records from this relationship) if and only if the `CustomerID` in Invoice is exactly equal to the `CustomerID` in Customer. This is the correct behavior for the structural relationship represented on the ERD. Such a relationship, based on equality, is often called an *equijoin*.

7

Figure 7.3
FileMaker can use any of seven different operators to compare match fields.

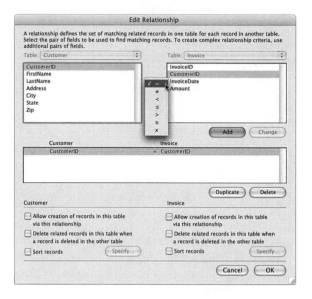

The upper part of the Edit Relationship dialog is where the match actually gets defined. And you'll notice, in Figure 7.3, that equality is not the only operator available for defining a match. In fact, in FileMaker 7, you can build relationships based on combinations of any of the seven different comparison operators.

How does this help you with that user who wants to see a portal of invoices for this customer for the current year only? Well, it implies you need to extend the match criteria somewhat. In addition to matching on the CustomerID, you also need to restrict the match to just those invoices where the date is *greater than* the start of the current year.

The Edit Relationships dialog enables you to build matches between fields in different tables. You know you want to build a match that incorporates the InvoiceDate, but you need to somehow compare that to the start of the current year, and the database doesn't have a field for that at present.

You can solve that problem by defining a *calculation* field that gives you the start of the current year. The definition for such a calculation is shown in Figure 7.4. It's a simple formula that returns the first day of the current year, expressed as a date.

NOTE

The figure doesn't show the storage options, but we've chosen to make the calculation unstored so that it updates properly as the current date changes.

Figure 7.4
CurrentYearStart is a calculation that you'll be able to incorporate into a relational match for invoices within a certain date range.

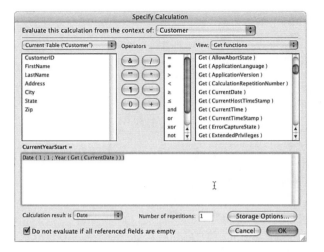

→ For more on calculations and storage options, **see** "Storage Options," **p. 221**.

With the calculation in hand, you can proceed to build the "this-year-only relationship." You could certainly just edit the relationship you originally created between the two tables, but it's more likely that you'll want to keep that structural relationship intact and add a new one to represent this new query.

ADDING A TABLE OCCURRENCE TO THE RELATIONSHIPS GRAPH

We used the term *table occurrence* sporadically throughout Chapter 6 when referring to the graphical table representations in the Relationships Graph. Why not just call them tables and be done with it? Well, they're not the same thing. An underlying table (or *base table*, meaning those tables that appear in the Tables tab of the Define Database screen) can appear multiple times in the Relationships Graph. In fact, any time you want to have more than one relationship between two base tables, you need to add an additional *occurrence* of at least one of the base tables to the Graph. You cannot create multiple relationships between two table occurrences in the Graph. If you want to relate table A to table B in two different ways, you need two occurrences of at least one of the tables.

In the current example, you want a new view of invoices from the perspective of a customer. Therefore you need to add a new occurrence of the Invoice table to the Graph. So far, FileMaker has created all table occurrences for you automatically. Any time you add a new table to a database, FileMaker adds a corresponding table occurrence to the Graph, and gives it a name identical to the underlying table. Now you need to add a new occurrence of Invoice to the Graph by hand. To do this, open the Relationships Graph in the Define Database dialog box and click the Add Table Occurrence icon in the lower left corner. Figure 7.5 shows the resulting Specify Table dialog box.

7

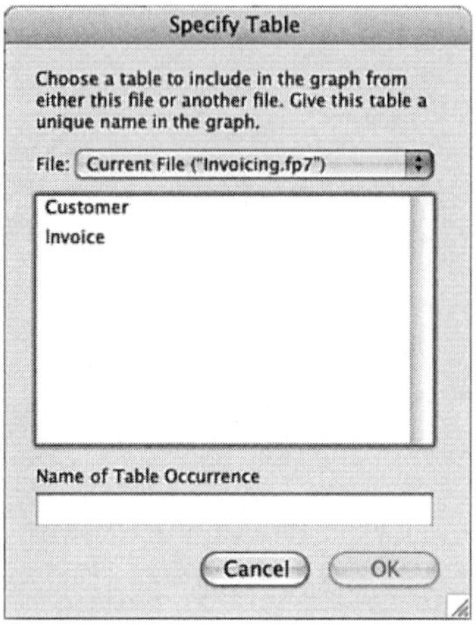

Figure 7.5
You can add a new table occurrence to the Relationships Graph.

Specify Table

Choose a table to include in the graph from either this file or another file. Give this table a unique name in the graph.

File: Current File ("Invoicing.fp7")

Customer
Invoice

Name of Table Occurrence

Cancel   OK

In the Specify Table dialog, choose a base table to include in the Graph. In this case, you want to add another occurrence of Invoice. Notice that FileMaker instructs you to "Give this table [occurrence] a unique name in the graph." At the bottom of the box is a place for you to name the table occurrence. Because the original occurrence of the Invoice table is already named Invoice, you need a new name. We recommend a name that says something about the way the new relationship is used. In this case, something like InvoiceThisYear should fit the bill. Figure 7.6 shows the Relationships Graph with the new table occurrence, as well as the CurrentYearStart field you added to Customer.

Figure 7.6
A second occurrence of the Invoice table has been added to the Graph.

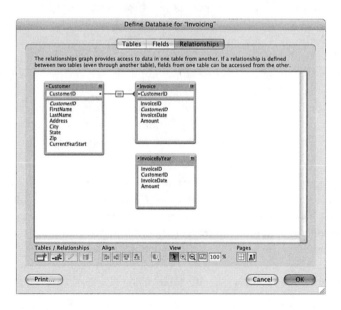

All that's left is to create a relationship from Customer to this new table occurrence, which will incorporate the CurrentYearStart field into the match criteria.

DEFINING A RELATIONSHIP WITH MULTIPLE MATCH CRITERIA

Chapter 6 showed you how to define new relationships in the Relationships Graph with a graphical technique consisting of dragging from one match field to another. You can also, though, add a new relationship just by clicking the small Add Relationship icon, which is the second icon in the Tables/Relationships icon group at the lower left of the Relationships Graph. Clicking that icon brings you the familiar Edit Relationship dialog, but it's initially completely empty.

Begin by selecting the two tables that are to participate in the relationship. Choose Customer on the left, and InvoiceByYear on the right. Then define the first match criterion. Select the CustomerID field under each table name, make sure the menu of operators in the middle shows an equals sign, and press the Add button. So far it looks exactly like the Edit Relationship screen for the original Customer-Invoice relationship, as shown in Figure 7.3, except that the table occurrence on the right is now InvoiceByYear instead.

But you still need to tell FileMaker to consider only those invoices where the invoice date is greater than the start of the current year. To make this happen, you can add another criterion. Select CurrentYearStart on the left, InvoiceDate on the right, and from the operator menu in the middle, select the "less than or equal to" sign. (This signifies that January 1st of the current year must be less than or equal to the invoice date.) Press Add, and the new match criterion is added in the middle-most box, as shown in Figure 7.7.

Figure 7.7
Using a non-equality condition to build a relationship.

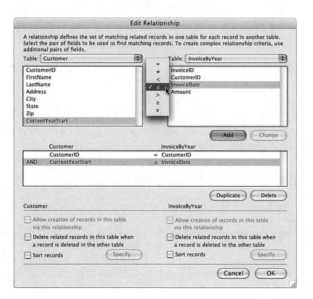

Notice what that middle box is saying now. There's a large "AND" in the left margin, which says that this relationship pulls back only those invoices where the CustomerID matches, *and* the invoice date is sometime this year.

7

You might be wondering how to create a multiple-match relationship that works if any of the criteria are true, as opposed to those that work only if all the criteria are true. This isn't possible, unfortunately. To learn more, see "No OR Conditions with Multiple Match Criteria" in the Troubleshooting section at the end of this chapter.

Notice also how FileMaker represents this new relationship in the Relationships Graph. Each end of the relationship line forks, to indicate the multiple match criteria—and the operator symbol in the middle of the line is a curious kind of X, indicating a complex match with multiple operators at work. Figure 7.8 shows the Graph with the new relationship.

Figure 7.8
The Graph indicates when a relationship is based on multiple match fields. The [X] comparison operator shows that multiple operators are in use as well.

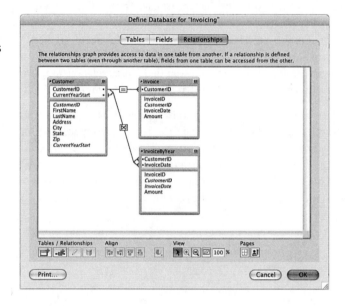

To use the new relationship, you could draw another portal on the Customer layout. Base it on `InvoiceThisYear` instead of plain `Invoice`, and use the same data fields from the base table. The result should be similar to what you see in Figure 7.9.

Figure 7.9
More complex relationships can produce sophisticated views, such as the Invoices This Year view shown here.

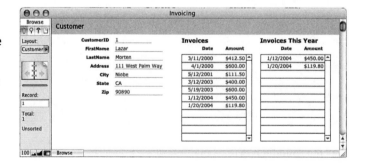

These three concepts—non-equijoins, multiple table occurrences, and multiple match criteria—afford you extraordinary flexibility as a database developer. The sections ahead explore examples that show how to use these tools to solve particular problems of database design.

CREATING SELF-RELATIONSHIPS

A self-relationship sounds like another dubious (if not illegal) concept. We assure you it's just one more tool in the database developer's arsenal. Self-relationships are an important tool even at the ERD level, though we didn't explore them in Chapter 5. We'll go into some detail here on how to create and use them.

MANAGERS AND EMPLOYEES: A "STRUCTURAL" SELF-RELATIONSHIP

Suppose you want to create a database system that models a company's organization chart. Your process description tells you that the system should show, for each employee, who that employee's manager is, and for each manager, a list of all that manager's direct reports. On the strength of this, you draw an ERD like that in Figure 7.10, with two separate entities, Manager and Employee, in a one-to-many relationship.

Figure 7.10
ERD for a system that models an organizational chart.

This diagram seems fine, until you come to list attributes for each entity. Besides the difference in "type" (manager versus employee), it appears that managers and employees look pretty much alike. They each have a first and last name, a department, an employee ID, and so on. Worse, as you think about it, many people in the chart are *both* a manager and an employee—they manage several others as managers, but also report to their own superiors.

It turns out that the correct way to solve such a problem is to collapse the two entities into one. The trick here is that the relationship of managers to employees doesn't quite fit the regular one-to-many or many-to-many criteria. The relationship is *hierarchical*, in the sense that one person can have many levels below her, and many above, similar to a family tree in some ways. A more accurate ERD for the system looks like Figure 7.11.

Figure 7.11
An ERD for an organization-chart system, with attributes shown.

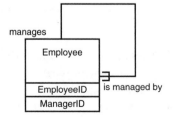

Each instance of the Employee entity has an `EmployeeID`, but also a `ManagerID`, which points to the particular employee who is this employee's manager.

NOTE

> This does beg the question of what to enter into the `ManagerID` field when you get to the CEO's record. This can be solved by adopting some convention, either leaving the field empty, or (probably better) setting it equal to the CEO's own `EmployeeID`.

USING VALUE LISTS TO SPEED UP SELF-JOIN DATA ENTRY

How would you implement this in FileMaker? You'd begin with a one-table system matching the ERD. The structure is shown in Figure 7.12. You'll also find it useful to create a couple of value lists, based on field data from the Employee table. The first should be a two-field value list, where the first field is the `EmployeeID`, and the second field is either the employee's last name or a calculation that shows both the last and first names together. You'll use that value list for data entry. The other list should be just alike, but contain only the `EmployeeID`—you can use this value list to validate the contents of the `ManagerID` field. Figure 7.13 shows the value list definitions.

→ For a discussion on using value lists to speed data entry in related files, **see** "Using a Value List For Data Entry," **p. 170**.

Figure 7.12
FileMaker field structure for an organization chart system.

At this point, without even touching the Relationships Graph, you've done enough work to begin data entry. If you apply the `EmployeeIDNames` value list to the `ManagerID` field on the Employee layout, you can begin entering data. Of course, the list is initially empty, so you need to either begin with the CEO and work your way down, or enter a bunch of other employees and come back and fill their managers in later. Figure 7.14 shows how the system might look during data entry.

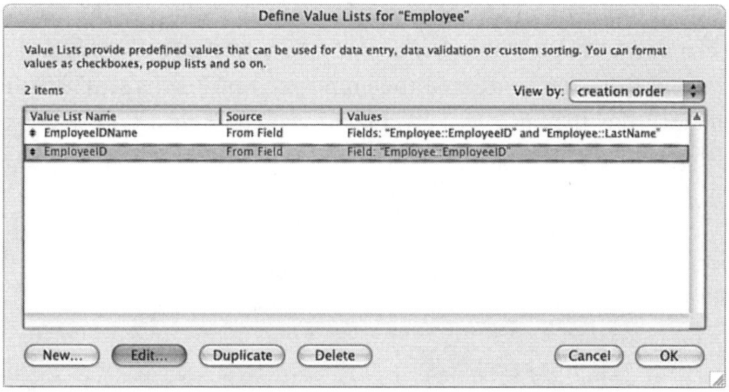

Figure 7.13
Two value lists are defined in the system to aid with data entry.

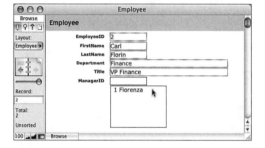

Figure 7.14
Using a value list to select an employee's manager.

CREATING ADDITIONAL TABLE OCCURRENCES TO DISPLAY RELATED DATA

The setup shown in Figure 7.14 works fine, but soon you'll find a few things missing. When you enter a manager ID, you probably want the manager's name to somehow appear as well. Likewise, on the layout for an employee who manages others, you'd probably like to see a list of those who report to the current employee.

These problems sound quite similar to the ones we covered in the last chapter (see Chapter 6, the section titled "Working With Related Data"). Whether you want to see a manager name when you choose a manager ID, or see a list of managed employees in a portal, some kind of relationship appears to be called for.

To make this work, you need to relate your single Employee table to *itself*. To do this, you need to add it to the Relationships Graph—*twice* more, in the form of two separate table occurrences. To do this, open the Relationships Graph and click the Add Table Occurrence button at lower left. Add another table occurrence for Employee and name it Manager.

Now relate the two table occurrences by dragging a relationship line from the EmployeeID field in the Manager table occurrence to the ManagerID field in the Employee table occurrence. If the significance of that isn't obvious right away, think about it for a bit. If I'm an employee, then my manager is the person with an EmployeeID equal to my ManagerID.

That handles the employee-manager relationship. What about the relationship between an employee and those she manages? (Let's call them, clumsily, "managees"). To capture that relationship, you need to add another table occurrence. Once again, the table occurrence is

7

based on the Employee table. Name it Managee and add it to the Graph. Then define an employee-managee relationship between `Employee::EmployeeID` and `Managee::ManagerID`. Looking again from the context of the employee, the "managees" are all those employees whose `ManagerID` is the same as a given `EmployeeID`. Figure 7.15 shows the resulting Relationships Graph.

Figure 7.15
This is the Relationships Graph for the employee-manager system.

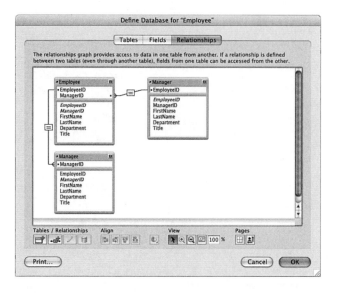

With that relationship in place, adding the remaining data views you want is easy. To view the name of the employee's manager, alongside the `ManagerID`, drag a couple of additional fields onto the Employee layout. You would choose to look at fields from the Manager table occurrence, and choose to show first and last name.

Finally, on the same layout, you want a portal of "managed employees." To do this, you'd add a portal to the layout, and this time you'd base it on the Managee table occurrence, bringing in (say) the `FirstName`, `LastName`, and `Title` fields. The resulting layout is shown in Figures 7.16 and 7.17 in Layout and Browse modes.

Figure 7.16
Adding a portal to the Employee layout to show managed employees.

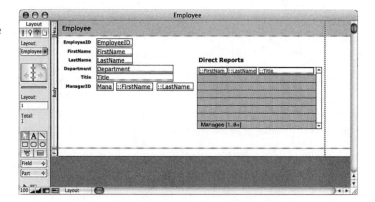

Figure 7.17
Viewing the new Reports portal in Browse mode.

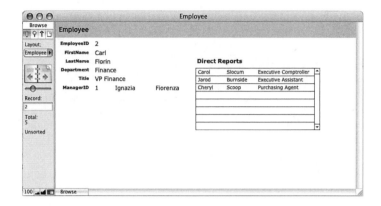

The manager-employee relationship is "structural," in the sense that you'd find it on a good ERD of this system. But, as you've just seen, to implement this structure in FileMaker, you need to add a couple of table occurrences to your system. From the standpoint of an employee, there exist both upward relationships (to your manager) and downward relationships (to your direct reports), and in each direction, Employee is relating back to itself. So one additional table occurrence is required for each relationship, for a total of three.

We recognize that this example is a little tricky, and we encourage you to work through it and think about it until it makes sense.

> **NOTE**
>
> Strictly speaking, you could accomplish much of what's described here with just two table occurrences, rather than the three we advocate. But you'd lose the ability to display both the name of an employee's manager *and* a list of his direct reports on the same layout. You'd need to view the manager name from one layout, and the data on managees from another layout, which is not very desirable.

AN "EXCLUSIONARY" SELF-RELATIONSHIP

The previous section looked at a fairly straightforward self-relationship (believe it or not). But, in the same way that it's possible to add complex criteria to relationships between different tables (as shown in an earlier example that displayed a portal of this year's invoices), it's also possible to design more complex self-joins. In this section we describe a useful form of relationship that we call an "exclusionary" relationship (also known as the "everyone but me relationship"). This type of relationship was rather challenging to create in previous versions of FileMaker, but is quite straightforward in FileMaker 7.

Suppose you have a database containing information about model railroad hobbyists. One of the goals of the system is to give people who live near each other the chance to meet. Suppose that for any given railfan (call her Antigone), you'd like to display a list of the other railfans in her state. You'd specifically like to exclude Antigone's record from the list; you *know* she lives in Montana, and you're really just interested in pairing her up with her fellow Montanans for a few evenings of tracklaying and dispatching.

Let's say the basic data of your Railfan database looks like what's depicted in Figure 7.18.

Figure 7.18
This database needs to perform some sophisticated filtering of this list of railfans.

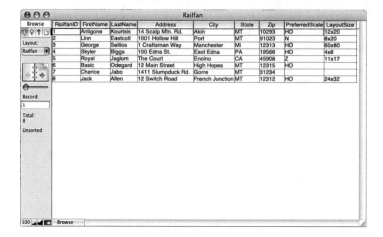

If you want to view other Montanans in a portal from Antigone's record, you need to create a relationship that somehow looks for "others in the same state." If you think about that more precisely, from the viewpoint of Antigone's record, you want to see all other railfans that live in the same state as she does, but that do *not* have the same RailfanID—all Montanans except Antigone. This, again, is a kind of query, and you can implement it with a relationship.

To make this happen, go to the Relationships Graph and add a new table occurrence. Base it on Railfan and call it OthersInState. You need to create a relationship from Railfan to OthersInState based on multiple match criteria. Select State=State in the upper boxes and then click Add. Then select Railfan ID ≠ Railfan ID, and then click Add again. Figure 7.19 shows the Edit Relationship dialog as it will appear after this step.

Figure 7.19
This relational match finds all other railfans in the same state as the current record.

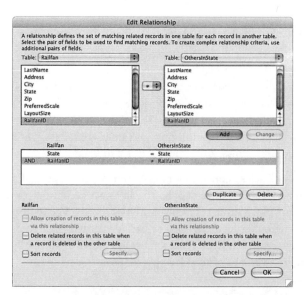

You can now create a portal on your main Railfan layout that uses this new relationship. The resulting display might look like Figure 7.20.

Figure 7.20
The portal on this layout shows all other records that share the current record's State. The current record will always be excluded from the list.

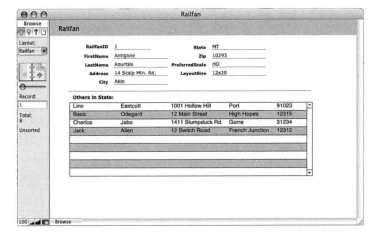

 If you work with non-equijoins, you might notice that the option to "allow creation of related records" has disappeared from the Edit Relationship dialog. To learn more about why, see "Trouble Creating Related Records with Non-Equijoins" in the Troubleshooting section at the end of this chapter.

CREATING RANGED RELATIONSHIPS

FileMaker Pro's new non-equijoin feature has a great number of uses—too many to cover exhaustively. We'll touch on a couple more before moving on. An earlier example, looked at a relationship that let you look at a customer's invoices for the current year only. What if you wanted to refine those criteria further, and look at invoices for just the first fiscal quarter (January through March)?

Let's return to the Invoicing example (shown in Figures 7.4-7.9). The first "date-filtering" relationship was created when a calculation field was added in the Customer table to produce the start of the current year. For this new query, you need to add one more calculation field—one that will give you the end of the first quarter. This one is also quite simple; the new calculation is shown at the end of the field list in Figure 7.21.

To factor this new calculation into the query logic, you need a new relationship. That in turn means a new table occurrence in the Relationships Graph. Open the Relationships Graph and add a new table occurrence called InvoiceFirstQuarter. Then add a new relationship. Define it to have Customer on the left, and InvoiceFirstQuarter on the right. You need three match criteria in this case: CustomerID = CustomerID, CurrentYearStart ≤ InvoiceDate, FirstQuarterEnd ≥ InvoiceDate. All three have to be true for a match to exist. Figure 7.22 shows the Edit Relationships dialog for this new relationship, and Figure 7.23 shows the Customer layout with a third portal added to show just the first-quarter invoices.

7

Figure 7.21
This table of customer data also contains two calculation fields for performing ranged relational comparisons.

Figure 7.22
This complex relationship is intended to find all of a customer's invoices between two dates.

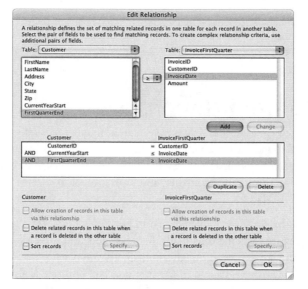

Figure 7.23
FileMaker's multiple match criteria can easily be used to create relationships that pick out ranges of related records.

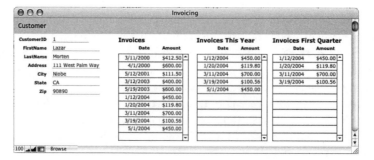

→ For a range of additional techniques for doing interesting things with portals and non-structural relationships, **see** Chapter 16, "Working with Portals," **p. 445**.

CREATING CROSS-PRODUCT RELATIONSHIPS

In working with non-equijoin relationship matches, you may have noticed one oddball operator in the little menu of match criteria. Most of them are familiar comparison operators—but what about the last one, the one that looks like an X?

That operator is known as a *cross product* (or *Cartesian product* if you really want to show off). The cross product does one and only one thing: It provides a "universal match" between the records in two tables. What this means is that it does no limiting of any kind. If you think of a relationship again as a kind of query, a cross-product relationship is a "find all" query. If you define a cross-product relationship from Customer to Invoice, a portal based on that relationship would always show all invoices, no matter which customer record was being viewed. The choice of fields on the left and right sides is more or less unimportant; this "all to all" relationship is fulfilled regardless of the choice of match fields.

Cross products really make sense only by themselves, in single-match relationships. They have no effect at all if they're added into multi-match criteria sets. A cross product match condition is always true, so it can never further limit the potential matches of other criteria. Of course, if that makes your head spin, you can just take our word for it.

> **NOTE**
> Savvy users of previous versions of FileMaker may recognize that the cross product operator replaces the technique that used to be known as a "constant" or "always-true" relationship. In that technique, you had to define specific fields on either side that explicitly matched each other (generally a pair of calculations that each evaluated to 1) and build a relationship between the two fields. FileMaker 7's cross products provide the same feature in a more integrated fashion.

Well, that explains what a cross product relationship is, but not how you might want to use one. The cross product is the ultimate nonstructural relationship. After all, its purpose is to show *all* of something. These are generally used for a variety of user interface purposes. Sometimes you might want users to pick from a list of things, for example, and it's more pleasing to allow them to pick from a scrolling list in a portal than from a dropdown list or menu. Generally such techniques need to be coupled with some scripting to react to users' choices.

WORKING WITH DATA FROM DISTANT TABLES

The new relational model of FileMaker 7 has significant improvements in its ability to handle a relational "tree." As an example, suppose you have a classic Customer-Product-Invoice system with a Relationships Graph like the one shown in Figure 7.24.

Figure 7.24
Relationships Graph for a system that tracks customers, products, and invoices.

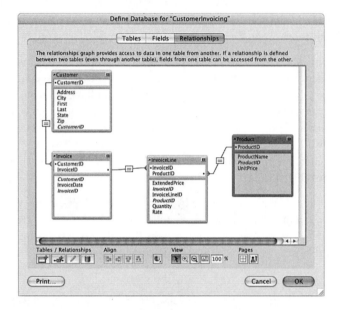

You might want to do a number of things in this system that would have been slightly cumbersome in previous versions of FileMaker. Suppose, for example, that you'd like a portal on a customer layout showing all the products that customer had ever purchased. Previously, you might have used a somewhat complicated technique involving global fields and the Copy All Records script step to "hop" from a customer record to the customer's related invoices, then again from the invoices to their related line items, and finally from the line items over to products. Scripting this process was relatively slow, and the technique was not guaranteed to work for large data sets.

By contrast, in FileMaker 7 it's as simple as creating a portal on the Customer layout and choosing the Product table occurrence as your data source. FileMaker 7 correctly navigates the Relationships Graph from Customer to Product and brings you back a listing of all products ever purchased by a given customer. Though this is somewhat difficult to illustrate concisely (we'd need to show the intervening invoices), Figure 7.25 shows what the result might look like. Even though some of the products have been entered on several invoices for this customer already, each one appears only once, as you would expect.

The technique could be reversed. For example, from the viewpoint of a Product record, you could just as easily see a portal of all customers who had ever purchased that product.

Figure 7.25
FileMaker 7 lets you perform a "deep" relational view, allowing you to display, for example, all products a customer has purchased in a given year.

This capability to perform multi-step relational navigation in a single swoop is a powerful new feature of FileMaker 7. Combined with some of the multi-match and non-equijoin relationships you saw earlier, this technique can produce quite sophisticated queries. Think back to the example that used a relationship to isolate a customer's invoices in the first quarter. Well, if those invoice records eventually contained a link back to a products table, you could use a "deep" relationship (as we sometimes call them) to produce a portal of just those *products* purchased by a given customer in the first quarter.

WORKING WITH MULTIPLE FILES

In all the discussions of multi-table systems in Chapters 5, 6 and so far in this chapter, we've assumed that all the tables you want to work with live within a single FileMaker file. The capability to have many tables in a single physical file is, after all, one of the greatest new features of FileMaker 7. But there are still many reasons to build systems that are multi-*file*, in addition to being multi-table. This section reviews the mechanics of working with several files at once, and then discusses different design strategies that use a multi-file structure.

So far we've looked just at relationships between tables within the same file. But it's also possible to build relationships between tables in different files. As an example, suppose you're (again!) being called on to build an invoicing system of some kind. Naturally you'll want to start with some set of customer data and a place to hold it. Well, it may happen that a FileMaker file already exists with a bunch of tables of customer information: a table of companies, a table of individual contacts at each company, and a table of company addresses, to name a few. There's no need to redo all that work—all you need is the data. But let's assume that the designer of the Customer file is not eager to have you in there adding things to her file. She'd rather you kept the invoicing tables separate, in their own file.

Well, you might find her lack of faith disturbing, but it won't create any actual technical hurdles for you. To reference her customer file from your new invoicing file, you only need to create a *file reference* to her file. You can then use that file reference to create new table occurrences for her customer tables, inside your invoicing file.

7

CREATING A FILE REFERENCE

File references are an extremely important topic in FileMaker 7. In a number of places in FileMaker, you might want to refer to or work with another file. Here are some of the things you can do with other files in FileMaker 7:

- Call a script in the other file.
- Use a value list that's defined in the other file.
- Refer to one or more tables from the other file in your Relationships Graph.

To do any of these things, you first need to create a reference to the other file. A file reference simply tells FileMaker where and how to find another file. FileMaker is capable of working with external files that are present on a local hard drive, that are present on a shared network volume, or that are present on an available FileMaker Server. You can also specify multiple search locations for a file, and the priority in which they should be searched. You can, for instance, create a file reference that says "First search for the invoicing file on the FileMaker server at 192.168.100.2. If you don't find it there, look on the FileMaker server at 10.11.1.5. If you don't find it there, give up."

Previous versions of FileMaker used file references as well. But these earlier versions kept track of these references behind the scenes, and didn't let you alter the order in which FileMaker searched for a given file. Problems with file references were harder to spot in previous versions, and could occasionally give rise to a problem called *crosstalk*, in which the wrong copies of files could be accessed by mistake.

→ For more on the concept of crosstalk and its relationship to file references, **see** "Crosstalk," **p. 496**.

In FileMaker 7, each physical file maintains its own list of file references. You can work with these references centrally, and also create them on the fly as needed. Let's see how this works in practice.

Going back to the invoicing example, say you have your own invoicing file, called InvoicingSeparate. The aforementioned untrusting colleague has a file called CustomerSeparate, with a Customer table. You want to use that Customer table from the CustomerSeparate file in InvoicingSeparate.

Your first step is to define a file reference to the external file. To do this, choose File, Define, File References. Click the New button on the next screen, and you'll see the Edit File Reference dialog, shown in Figure 7.26.

A file reference is a more complex object than it sounds at first. A file reference is really a name given to a series of file paths. (See Figure 7.28 for an example of a file path with several entries). FileMaker resolves the file reference by searching through the path list in the specified order. In general, the point is to use a file reference to tell FileMaker the "best" (or perhaps the only) place for FileMaker to look for a file.

7

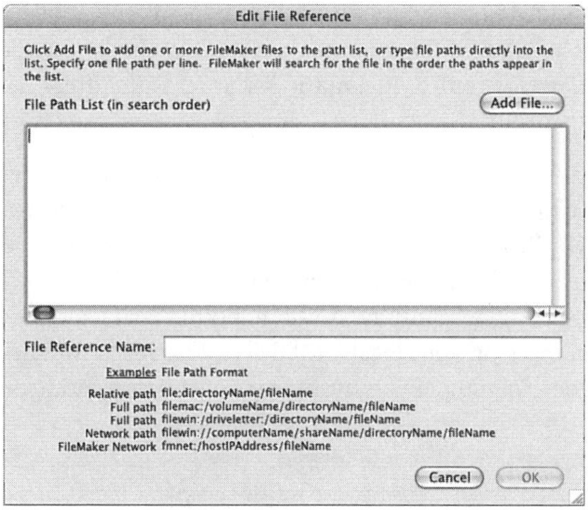

Figure 7.26
You can add search paths to a file reference by typing them manually, or by using the Add File button to choose a specific file.

NOTE

In general, all the different file paths in the path list point to the "same" file, that is, a file with the same name and contents. In theory, you could also use a single path list to point to a number of different files, indicating that the later ones should be used if the earlier ones can't be found. You could perhaps use this feature to "fall" back to other versions of a file or system if necessary.

In the case of the external Customer file to which you want to relate, say that file is being hosted under FileMaker Server. One way to build the file reference is simply to click the Add File button in the Edit File Reference dialog. This brings you to a standard Open File dialog, from which you can click the Remote button to look for servers on your network. When you find the server hosting the Customer file, you can select and open the Customer file. After you do this, FileMaker adds an element to the file path list that looks something like `fmnet:/192.168.101.66/Customer`, as shown in Figure 7.27.

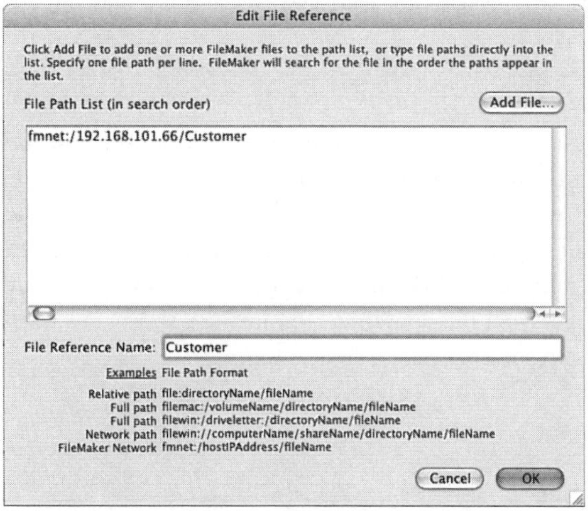

Figure 7.27
File references tell FileMaker where to look to find externally referenced files.

There's nothing magical about the text FileMaker added to create this file path. The file path list is a free text area, so you're free to add entries to the list yourself by hand, separating each one with a carriage return. Again, the list order is the order in which FileMaker looks for the file.

Suppose that your colleague had also given you a copy of the file to use "offline" while you were doing your development work. You'd want the file reference to resolve to a copy on your local disk instead. But after the file was hosted on FileMaker Server, you'd want to avoid that local copy being found by accident. One way to do this is to add another element to the file path list, possibly by using the Add File button again and navigating to the copy of CustomerSeparate that's on your local hard drive. This places the new path element second in the list, but you can cut and paste it in front of the first path (see Figure 7.28).

Figure 7.28
A search path can contain multiple search locations. FileMaker scans them in the specified order.

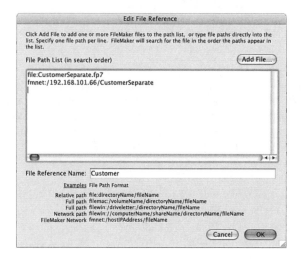

NOTE

If you've inserted a "local" reference to the file to aid offline development, you need to remember to remove that reference later, or perhaps move it lower on the list. Otherwise, FileMaker continues to search your local drive first, which is probably not desirable.

The file reference displayed in Figure 7.28 instructs FileMaker first to look for the file locally, and if it can't be found locally, to look for it on the server at 192.168.101.66. If FileMaker searches the entire file path and can't find a file at any of the specified points, it presents a dialog telling you that it's failed to find the file, and then throws up an Open File dialog inviting you to find the file by hand. If you find and specify a file by hand, that file is used for the current external file operation. Figure 7.29 shows the warning you see when a file reference can't be resolved.

Figure 7.29
If FileMaker cannot find a referenced file after searching the specified search path, it displays an error dialog.

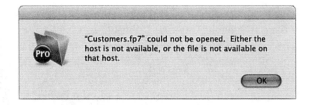

 In previous versions of FileMaker, when an external file reference failed, FileMaker would also prompt the user to find the referenced file by hand. But in previous versions, FileMaker would remember this choice and add it into the internally stored file path list. This was not always the right thing to do; the path could easily be reset by a flustered user just trying to close the ominous dialogs on her screen. When FileMaker 7 fails to resolve a file reference, and prompts the user to find the file, any selected file choice is valid for the current action, but FileMaker doesn't alter the stored file reference in any way based on this choice.

ADDING AN EXTERNAL TABLE TO THE RELATIONSHIPS GRAPH

If you've followed along with the example to this point, you've now built a file reference that points to the CustomerSeparate file, that looks for it first on your local hard drive, and next on a networked FileMaker Server. You can now use this reference to add tables from the external file to the Relationships Graph in your InvoicingSeparate file. If you open the Relationships Graph and click the Add Table Occurrence icon, you'll notice something we didn't highlight before. In the resulting Specify Table dialog, there's a menu that lets you choose which file you want to browse for table choices. This menu always includes the current file, and also includes any file references you have defined using the techniques covered in the previous sections of this chapter. Figure 7.30 illustrates this point.

Figure 7.30
When adding a table occurrence to the Relationships Graph, it's possible to base the new occurrence on a table in another file.

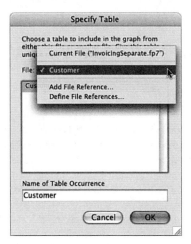

With the file reference in place, you can choose the Customer file reference (remember that the name of the file reference can be different from the name of the file to which it resolves, much as the name of a table occurrence can differ from the name of the underlying base table), and from the resulting table list you can choose the Customer table. The table is then added to the Relationships Graph, much as all the other tables we've seen, and you can create the usual relationship between the customer table and the invoice table based on CustomerID. The result is shown in Figure 7.31. There's one subtle visual indication that the Customer table occurrence is based on a table from another file: The table occurrence name for Customer is italicized. Otherwise it's just as though you were working with a table in the same file.

Figure 7.31
In this Relationships Graph, the italicized title of the Customer table occurrence shows that the base table exists in an external file.

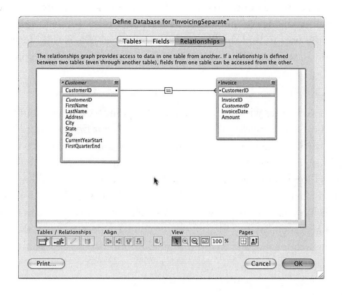

So that's all there is to using external tables in your Relationships Graph. Add a file reference that points to the appropriate file, and use that reference to pull in tables from the external file.

TIP

File references, like tables, table occurrences, fields, layouts, and scripts, can also benefit from a consistent naming scheme. Here, as elsewhere, the naming scheme you choose is less important than the consistency with which you apply it. By default, FileMaker names a file reference after the actual file to which it points. You may feel, though, that you want some added information in the name—an "Ext" prefix or the like, for example, to show that the file is external. This may be even more helpful when naming table occurrences from external files. In the Relationships Graph, the only clue that a table occurrence is external is the fact that the name is italicized. If an occurrence of an Employee table from an external file is named ExtEmployee, this may be a helpful clarification.

HOW AND WHEN TO USE MULTIPLE FILES

The preceding section showed the mechanics of creating a FileMaker system that uses tables from different files. It didn't say much about the reasons why, in general, you might want to do such a thing. We offered the example of needing to work with a pre-existing file "owned" by someone else. This is certainly a relevant case, but there are also reasons why you might choose to build your own systems with multiple files from the start. This section looks over some of the major reasons for using multiple files in a single database solution.

WORKING WITH CONVERTED FILES

FileMaker 7 represents a very new way of building FileMaker databases. The differences between FileMaker 7 and previous versions are significant enough that converting a system from a previous version to 7 is not quite the easy, nearly transparent process that conversions between different versions of the product have been in the past.

→ For greater detail on the conversion process, **see** Chapter 18, "Converting Systems from Previous Versions of FileMaker Pro," **p. 507**.

In previous versions of FileMaker, each database table was represented by a single physical disk file. A ten-table system would use ten different FileMaker files. In FileMaker 7, if you build that ten-table system from scratch, you could choose to put all ten tables into a single physical file. But if you're converting that system from, say, FileMaker 6 to FileMaker 7, you won't have that option. The conversion process cannot roll separate files together into a single new FileMaker 7 file. Your ten-file (that is, ten-table) FileMaker 6 system becomes a ten-file FileMaker 7 system as well. The conversion process brings forward all the appropriate file references into each of the new FileMaker 7 files, and populates the Relationships Graphs of each file appropriately, but structurally you'll still have a set of ten interlocking files, just as you did before. From that point, of course, you might be able to start rolling the different tables together, but the process is largely a manual one.

Any system converted from previous versions of FileMaker is sure to have a large number of external file references. Many of these may be to the same file, but in different forms (with different directory paths, for example). The new system will probably work perfectly well like this. And if it's working, you're likely to leave it alone. At most you may consider adding any new tables into existing files, when and if new tables become necessary.

NOTE

> The presence of multiple redundant file paths in a single file reference is characteristic of files converted from FileMaker 6 and earlier to FileMaker 7. In previous versions, if you worked with a file in multiple places over time, many or all of those places might end up in the file path list. Because FileMaker needs to search the entire file reference, item by item, all the unused file paths can cause significant slowdown in opening files.

→ For more information on this problem, and on approaches to solving it, **see** "Fix File References," **p. 518**.

7

SEPARATION OF A SYSTEM INTO MODULES

FileMaker 7 makes it possible, even tempting, to put all the tables for a database system into a single file and be done with it. But is that always the best choice? Well, there are still several reasons to suggest that breaking things into multiple files may sometimes be a more suitable choice. The sections that follow examine a number of potential benefits to using multiple tables. We're not presuming anything about *how*, exactly, you might choose to split your tables up. There are a few possibilities. If your system falls cleanly into several different "modules," for example (let's say Accounting, Orders, and Inventory), it may make sense to take the tables that comprise each module and group each set in its own file. You may also want to split your system into a file of data tables and another file dedicated to interface layouts and application logic such as scripts; this possibility is discussed later in this chapter in "Separation of Data and Application Logic."

EASE OF SHARED DEVELOPMENT

FileMaker has always been a great Rapid Application Development (RAD) tool, but the product has tended to retain an emphasis on the single developer. It's often been challenging for multiple people to work on the same FileMaker system simultaneously without getting in each other's way. In previous versions of the product, only one person could open the ScriptMaker at a time, and only one person could access the Define Fields dialog at once.

NEW Things are much improved in FileMaker 7. Anyone with sufficient privileges can open the ScriptMaker. If others have ScriptMaker open as well, you'll be inhibited from editing only any scripts they have open, and any subscripts called by those scripts. But in other ways FileMaker 7 exacerbates the earlier problem, in that scripts in FileMaker 7 can span multiple tables within a single file, aggregating together scripts that would have been separated into different files in earlier versions. The more tables you group into a single file, the more likely it may be that multiple developers will interfere with each other when editing scripts.

Things are a bit tougher with the database definition tools. In another advance from previous versions, multiple developers can open the Define Database dialog at once. But only one at a time can be "in control" of the database definition. The others can view any aspect of the structure, but cannot change it.

So if you expect you'll often have more than one person making script or database definition changes inside your system, it may make sense to try to separate your tables into groups and put each group in its own file to minimize the chances of developers getting in each other's way.

EASE OF MAINTENANCE

Every database system needs maintenance. Files become fragmented, which makes access to them slower. Lost space needs to be reclaimed; indexes need to be optimized. FileMaker is no different. It's a good idea to perform periodic file maintenance on your FileMaker files.

→ For a discussion of file maintenance, **see** "File Maintenance and Recovery," **p. 503**.

One thing to consider is that the larger your file, the longer it takes to perform this periodic maintenance. The same is true for other maintenance tasks, such as backing up. If your system is particularly large, say in the hundreds of megabytes or into the gigabyte range, your backups will take a long time to run. This may not be a problem if you run your backups at night, but in many mission-critical systems the data is backed up periodically during the day, sometimes as often as hourly. If all your tables are in a single file, your choices are to back up all, or nothing. There's no way to back up only a few tables from a single file. Suppose further that this system had one massive table of fairly static data, which changed on the order of only once a week, as well as many smaller tables of critical, highly changeable data. In the best of all worlds you'd back the huge table up daily or weekly, the smaller ones perhaps as often as hourly. If all the tables are in one file, you're out of luck. Each backup has to copy the single massive table again, even though it's unlikely to have changed.

In the worst case, consider the problem of file recovery. In rare circumstances, a FileMaker file can become damaged or unusable due to a crash. If all your tables and data are in that one file, the consequences of a crash are potentially catastrophic. One bad event can in theory compromise your entire system.

Even if the worst doesn't happen, you may still need to run a recovery on such a file. As with maintenance and backups, the time it takes to recover the file is in proportion to its size. And you need to recover everything—all the tables—even if the massive ones were undamaged and only the little ones were damaged in some way. Had the tables been separated into additional files, the consequences of a crash could have been mitigated.

None of this is to suggest that you should go back to the one-file-per-table model of previous versions, necessarily. It does mean that you should think carefully about how your database is going to be used, and whether there will be wide variation in size or usage pattern among tables. If such differences exist and can be predicted, it may be worthwhile to isolate certain tables in their own file or files.

Separation of Data and Application Logic

In FileMaker 7, as in previous versions, data and application logic are mixed together in a single file. Not only does a physical file contain a system's data (the "database" portion of things), but also all the scripts, layouts, value lists, and the like that make up the "user application" portion of things. After a system has been rolled out and is in use, if you want to continue to make changes to it, you have a limited range of choices.

One possibility is to work directly on the running copy. FileMaker permits this; you can edit scripts, add layouts, even add entire tables to a running system. Still, just because you can doesn't mean you should. What if you make a mistake? (They do happen from time to time—in fact we devote an entire chapter to avoiding and repairing them.) That mistake will impact users who are probably trying to get work done. It may be merely annoying, or it may be catastrophic. If the changes are small and you know what you're doing, you may be fine making the changes on-line, so to speak. For more extensive changes, it's not a great idea.

7

Another possibility is to work on a copy of the system. Make all your changes, test them every which way, and when they're all ready, integrate them into the current live system. But here's where the data-and-logic problem rears its head. You can't just replace the existing production files with your development copy—the production files almost certainly contain a different data set. And there's no convenient way to merge your structural changes with the data in the live copy. In previous versions of FileMaker, you needed to shut down the live file and import its data into your development copy. Depending on the size of the data, this was often a long process, and there were several small potential pitfalls along the way, such as accidental generation of overlapping serial numbers, or forgetting to reset global fields to default values.

Things are not really better on this front with FileMaker 7. In fact, things are a bit tougher still. Because a file can contain multiple tables, performing an update on a file may mean importing data into a great many tables, even if only a small area of the system has really changed. Separating the tables into several modules, as discussed previously, can help, but the problem remains.

Ideally, we'd be able to take a given data set and just swap a new interface in on top of it without all this talk of mass imports. In FileMaker 7, this is now a reasonable possibility if you separate your data and your interface into two or more separate files.

Let's consider a library book tracking system. It has two main entities, called Item and Patron. An Item is anything the library holds, such as a book, movie, DVD, CD, and so on. There is a many-to-many relationship between Item and Patron, so you also need a join entity, which we'll call Checkout.

This is a thriving public library, and the tables are very large: hundreds of thousands of Items, tens of thousands of Patrons, and literally millions of Checkout records. If you have to reload that data when we make programming changes to the system, you're in for some misery.

Figure 7.32 shows the Relationships Graph for a file called Library. Here you can see the entities, related in the way you'd expect.

There's one slight difference here. As you can tell from the italicized table occurrence names, *all* these table occurrences are from externally-related files. The three data tables now have a separate physical file of their own.

In theory, you can now do all your interface work in the Library file. You can create all your scripts and user screens in the Library file, leaving the file containing the three data tables alone. If you update a screen or change a script's logic, rather than tinkering with the massive data file, you can just swap in a new Library file (the "viewer" file, if you will) and you'll be all set. And if Library 2.1 has a problem, it's easy enough to roll back to Library 2.0 until you can get 2.1 fixed up.

This is all true and good so far. In all fairness, though, we have to point out that there are some limitations to this technique, as follows:

Figure 7.32
A Relationships Graph for a system that models a many-to-many relationship between library patrons and library items, via a join file that records each checkout of an individual item.

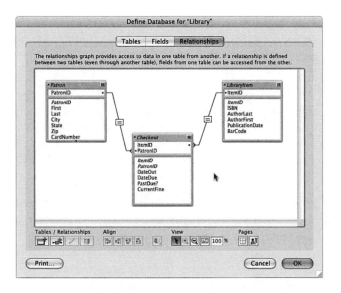

- **Security**—Accounts and privileges are maintained separately in each file. It's not possible to instruct one FileMaker 7 file to draw its accounts and privileges from another FileMaker file. It's possible to use external authentication methods to offload a lot of the work to an external authentication server, but it's still necessary to create group-to-privilege mapping information in each separate FileMaker file. (For more information on security matters, please see Chapter 12, "Implementing Security.") So in this example, privileges would have to be created and maintained in parallel in both the interface and data files.

- **Multiple Relationships Graphs**—Even in this kind of scenario, the data file is still going to need to be aware of most or all of the structural relationships between data tables. If, for example, you want to create a calculation field that tells you how many items a given patron currently has checked out, that calculation field, which lives in a data table, needs to use a relationship between Patron and Checkout to compute that number. So it isn't possible to build a Relationships Graph in just the "interface" file—substantial portions of it may need to be replicated in the "data" file as well.

- **"Stickiness" of the data tables**—In theory, changes to scripts or layouts can be accomplished just by swapping out the interface file. But in our experience, many if not most significant updates end up touching the data side as well, even if only to add certain new calculations. The separation methodology described here still doesn't give you a means to avoid making these additions to the data file. However, data file changes are quite a bit easier to write down and replicate than wide-ranging script and layout changes. Manual work may still be necessary in many updates, but it is still much less onerous than doing a massive import of one or more tables.

FileMaker 7 is new enough—and different enough from its predecessors—that best practices in these design areas are still emerging. We think, based on early use of the software, that the idea of separation of data and interface is likely to turn out to be a useful one. It won't cure all woes, and it won't always be the right thing to do, but it clearly has the potential to address some vexing problems and open some new doors.

WORKING TOWARD REUSE

As a final reason to consider a multi-file structure, consider the idea of reuse. This is in some ways an extension of the earlier discussion of the idea of separating a system into modules. Suppose there's a module that you want to use in several or many different FileMaker systems. You may want to consider isolating the functionality of the module in a single file and including that file in solutions that need the functionality.

As an example, suppose you have a custom-built user management system that keeps track of users, passwords, and privileges. FileMaker 7's new account management features are great, but you still might want to roll your own sometimes.

NOTE

> This is especially true in multi-file situations. FileMaker's access privilege system is still slightly hampered because each separate file stores its own account and privilege information, as we discussed above.

You could create a User file that would include a table for user information, as well as tables for user groups—or even sub-groups, if applicable. If records of user activity, such as logon and logoff times, were required, that information could be stored here as well.

To promote a module's reusability, you could take advantage of a number of new FileMaker features that promote abstraction, such as custom functions and script parameters. Suppose you wanted to create a somewhat generic logging facility (that is, the ability to log user actions to a database table). You could create a Log table with fields for user ID, timestamp, and a textual description of the event. You could then create a logging script that takes a script parameter containing the text to be written to the log, and writes out a log record with this text, the current user ID (presumably stored in a global), and the current timestamp. With planning and forethought, it's possible to create a module in FileMaker 7 with a high degree of reusability.

Let's think about how you might use such a module. First suppose that you're pursuing a strategy of data/interface separation such as the one described earlier in this chapter. Your "main" system consists of two files, MainData (containing all the data tables, but no scripts or interface) and MainViewer (the interface file that contains scripts, layouts, and interface logic). You also have your user module, which is split into two files, UserData and UserAdmin.

You need to create a file reference from MainViewer to UserAdmin. You probably should *not* need to create a file reference from MainView to UserData. All the main system's interactions with the UserData file should ideally be calls to scripts in UserAdmin; adding log records or checking a user's privileges should not be done by checking the UserData tables directly, but by asking UserAdmin to do this and report on the success or failure of the request.

You would especially want to avoid any logic that would force you to create a table reference *from* UserAdmin to MainViewer or MainData. UserAdmin shouldn't care about the nature or internals of any files or system that wants to use its services.

Not every group of related tables is likely to be suitable for this kind of "modularization." But you might want to consider splitting out any subsystems that provide somewhat non-specific functions, such as logging or user management, and making them into their own, semi-connected modules. Careful planning and exploitation of new features such as script parameters can help you create modules that can be smoothly integrated with a variety of different FileMaker systems.

TROUBLESHOOTING

TROUBLE CREATING RELATED RECORDS WITH NON-EQUIJOINS

I want to create a relationship that allows creation of related records on one side of the relationship, but the box that enables that capability is grayed out.

You might have noticed (for example, in Figure 7.19) that the option to "allow creation of related records" has mysteriously been disabled. This suggests that you have one or more non-equality conditions in your relationship match criteria. The rule is this: FileMaker can allow creation of related records only if the relationship in question consists only of equijoin conditions.

Multiple match criteria are fine, as long as they're all based on the equals operator. (This can actually be rather useful: A multi-match relationship that allows creation of related records automatically fills in *all* the key fields of the related record.) But as soon as any non-equality condition becomes involved in the match, the capability to create related records goes away.

This makes sense if you think about it. FileMaker can create a record via an equijoin because there's only one condition that satisfies the match criteria for the current record. Suppose you're on a Customer Layout, looking at customer number 17, and you have a portal into Invoices, where the relationship to Invoices is an equijoin on CustomerID. FileMaker can create a new record in the portal by creating a new invoice record and setting the CustomerID to 17. But suppose the relationship instead were based on a "not-equal-to" relationship? To create a record on the other side, FileMaker would need to create an Invoice record with a customer ID *other than* 17. Fine, but what customer ID should it use? There's really no way to say. Similar reasoning holds for other non-equijoin types: There's no sensible way for FileMaker to decide what match data should go into the related record.

NO OR CONDITIONS WITH MULTIPLE MATCH CRITERIA

Whenever I add multiple match criteria to a relationship, FileMaker always tells me the match will work if condition 1 AND condition 2 AND condition 3 are true. But I have a match that needs to work if 1 OR 2 OR 3 is true. Where do I set that up?

You don't, unfortunately. Using the native FileMaker relationship features, relational matches are always AND matches whenever multiple match criteria are specified. If you want to mimic the effect of an OR search in another table, you need to find another means of doing that. Say, for example, that you have a database with tables for teachers, classes, enrollments, and students. From the viewpoint of a teacher, you want to be able to view all students who are outside the norm—they have either a very low GPA or a very high GPA. You could try to do this with two match criteria, but that would necessarily be an AND match, which would never be fulfilled (no student would have both low AND high GPA at once).

The solution here would be to create a stored calculation in the student table called something like ExceptionalGPA, defined as

```
If ( GPA < 2 or GPA > 3.75; 1; 0)
```

The calculation will have the value 1 when the student's GPA is exceptionally high or low, and a value of 0 otherwise.

You could now create a field in the teacher table called Constant, and define it as a calculation that evaluates to 1. Then specify a relationship between the teacher table and the student table, with multiple match criteria: TeacherID=TeacherID, and Constant=ExceptionalGPA, meaning, "Find me all students with the same teacher ID and an exceptional GPA."

FILEMAKER EXTRA: MANAGING THE RELATIONSHIPS GRAPH

The new Relationships Graph in FileMaker 7 is a nice answer to developers who've clamored for years for a visual representation of relationships in FileMaker systems. But for large or complex systems, with many table occurrences, the Graph has the potential to be a bit unwieldy. Table occurrences in the Graph take up a fair amount of space, and it can be difficult to organize the occurrences without creating a web of overlapping relationship lines.

You can use a number of tools for Graph management. For one thing, the small "window-shade" icon at the top right of a table occurrence can be used to hide the fields in the table occurrence, leaving only the match fields used in relationships. This can save valuable space (though there's no "all-off" or "all-on" switch you can toggle). Figure 7.33 shows a Relationships Graph in "windowshade" mode.

Figure 7.33
Individual table occurrences can be made into "windowshades" that display only the match fields that participate in relationships.

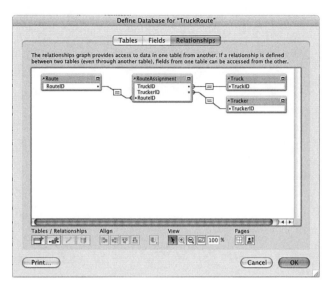

You can also resize an individual table occurrence manually to save space. This, again, needs to be done one table occurrence at a time. It's also possible to zoom out from the Graph as a whole and view it at 75% or 50% of regular size, or smaller.

It might also be useful to you to organize your table occurrences into logical groups of some kind within the Relationships Graph. Let's say you're working on a trucking module with four table occurrences, and you also have a file reference to an external user-management module and you've used that to bring a number of user-oriented table occurrences into the Graph. FileMaker enables you to color-code table occurrences in the Graph, so it's possible to give each group of table occurrences its own color. It's even possible to create "dummy" table occurrences strictly for purposes of naming and separating, much as is occasionally done with scripts.

Figure 7.34 shows a Relationships Graph with table occurrences both from the trucking module and the user module. The trucker tables are colored red here, the user tables blue, and each group has a "header" of a sort, formed by a dummy table occurrence. (We owe this labeling idea to Danny Mack and Todd Geist of New Millennium Communications). In addition, in the figure, the Graph has been reduced to 75% of its normal size.

All these techniques can help make your Graph more manageable. Still, if you have a system with a hundred table occurrences, your Graph will be crowded, without question. It's been suggested that offering a list view of relationships as well, in a manner similar to previous versions of FileMaker, would be helpful, and it's possible we may see such a list view in future versions of the product.

→ For some more discussion of using the Relationships Graph as a kind of documentation tool, **see** "Documenting the Relationships Graph," **p. 1026**.

7

Figure 7.34
Use color coding and group naming to help organize the Relationships Graph.

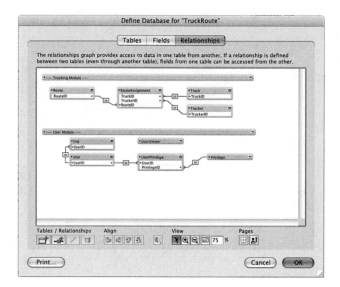

## CHAPTER 8

GETTING STARTED WITH CALCULATIONS

In this chapter

UNDERSTANDING HOW AND WHERE CALCULATIONS ARE USED

Calculation functions are among the most important and powerful tools at your disposal in the development of FileMaker Pro applications. Some find learning calculations to be an easy task. Others find writing complex calculations to be a terrifying experience. Whichever camp you fall into, becoming a master of calculation formulas is a worthy goal to have, and we'll get you started on the path.

This chapter focuses on basic calculation functions and techniques for using them well. Chapter 14, "Specialized Calculation Functions," looks at more advanced calculation formulas and techniques. If you're new to FileMaker, you should start here. Those who have been using FileMaker for years may want to just skim this chapter. (There are probably a few nuggets of info that will make it worth your while.) We've also included a complete function reference in Appendix B, "Calculation Function Reference." That's intended to be a reference when you need specific or comprehensive information. Here, we take more of a tutorial approach.

From the outset, it's important to understand the difference between calculation fields and calculation formulas. The term *calculation* is often used ambiguously to denote both concepts ("That table has more than 100 calculations!" or "What's the calculation used to determine access to this record?"). *Calculation fields* are a particular type of field whose value is determined through the evaluation of a calculation formula. *Calculation formula* is a broader concept that refers to any use of a formula to determine an output. When you learn "calculations," you're really learning calculation formulas. It so happens that calculation formulas are most frequently encountered in the construction of calculation fields, but try not to let that fact confuse you.

WRITING CALCULATION FORMULAS

Essentially, the purpose of a calculation formula is to evaluate an expression and return a value. In Figure 8.1, for example, you can see the field definition for a calculation field called Mileage Calc. The value of this field is defined to be the result of multiplying the contents of the Mileage field by .37, which is a typical mileage reimbursement rate.

Most of the expressions you use in calculation formulas are intended to return a value, and that value might be a number, a text string, a date or time, or even a reference to a file to place in a container field. Another class of formulas, however, is intended to evaluate the truthfulness of an equation or statement. The "value" returned by these formulas is either a 1, indicating the equation or statement is true, or 0, indicating that the equation or statement is false. Typically, calculations are used in this manner in If script steps, in calculated validations, and for defining field access restrictions.

In Figure 8.2, for instance, you can see a calculation dialog that specifies the condition for an If script step. When the script executes, FileMaker evaluates whether the number of hours is in fact greater than 8 (based on the current record's data). Depending on the value of the Hours field for any particular record, the statement may be either true or false.

Figure 8.1
When defining calculation fields, you specify an expression to evaluate in the calculation dialog.

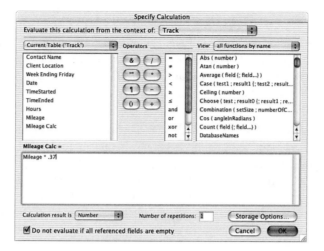

Figure 8.2
Calculation formulas are often used to determine the truthfulness of an equation or statement.

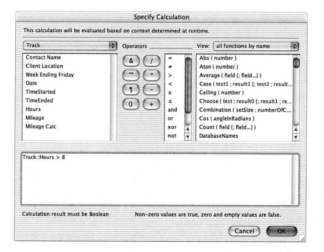

For certain uses, then, the purpose of a calculation formula is to return a value; for other uses it's simply to evaluate the truthfulness of an equation or statement. In situations where FileMaker is expecting a formula that returns a true/false result, you see the words "Calculation results must be Boolean" near the bottom of the calculation dialog. The If script step shown earlier is a typical example of this situation. *Boolean* is a fancy term for a simple concept: The formula you provide evaluates as being either true or false. Any value returned other than 0 or a null value (for example, an empty string) is considered true.

USES FOR CALCULATION FORMULAS

This chapter focuses on the use of calculation formulas in field definitions, but it's important that you understand that there are a number of other places where calculation formulas are used.

Briefly, these include:

- **Script Steps**—Calculation formulas come into play in many script steps. The If and Set Field script steps are notable examples. Many other script steps allow you to use a calculation formula to act as a parameter. These include Go to Layout, Go to Field, Go to Record, Pause/Resume Script, and Omit Multiple. Additionally, calculation formulas can be used to define script parameters.

- **Field Validation**—One of the options available to you for validating data entry is validating by calculation. This, in effect, lets you define your own rules for validation. The equation you provide is evaluated every time a user modifies the field. If it evaluates as true, the user's entry is committed. If it doesn't, the user is presented with an error message. For instance, if a user is supposed to enter a call-back date on a contact record, you might want to validate that the entry is a future date. To do this, you might use the formula Call_Back_Date > Get (CurrentDate) as the validation for the Call_Back_Date field.

- **Record-level Security**—When you define privilege sets, you have the option of limiting a user's access to view, edit, and delete records based on a calculation formula you provide. If the equation you provide evaluates as true, then the user can perform the action; if not, the action is prohibited. For instance, you might want to prevent users from inadvertently modifying an invoice that has already been posted. So, you'd set up limited access for editing records based on the formula Invoice_Status <> "Posted". Only records where that is a true statement would be editable.

- **Auto-Entry Options**—When defining text, number, date, time, and timestamp fields, several auto-entry options are available for specifying default field values. One of these options is to auto-enter the result of a calculation formula. For instance, in a contact management database, you might want a default call-back date set for all new contact records. The formula you'd use for this might be something like Get(CurrentDate) + 14, if you wanted a callback date two weeks in the future.

- **Calculated Replace**—A calculated replace is a way of changing the contents of a field in all the records in the current found set. It's particularly useful for cleaning up messy data. Say, for example, that your users had sometimes entered spaces at the end of a name field as they were doing data entry. You could clean up this data by performing a calculated replace with the formula Trim (First Name).

EXPLORING THE CALCULATION DIALOG BOX

Now that you know something about how and where calculation formulas are used, it's time to turn next to the anatomy of the calculation dialog box itself. There are some small differences among the calculation dialogs you find in particular areas within FileMaker Pro. We'll focus our attention on the dialog used for defining calculation fields because it's the most complex. Figure 8.3 shows the calculation dialog for a field called FullName, which serves as the model for this anatomy lesson.

8

Figure 8.3
When creating calculation fields, it helps to know your way around the Specify Calculation dialog box.

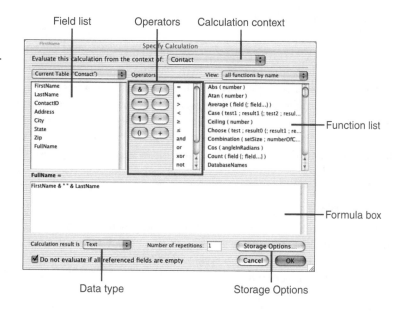

Field list   Operators   Calculation context

Function list

Formula box

Data type   Storage Options

SPECIFYING CONTEXT

Across the very top of the dialog, you're asked to specify the context from which to evaluate this calculation. This choice, new to FileMaker Pro 7, is necessary only in those cases where the base table you are working with appears in your Relationship Graph more than once. And even in those cases, it really matters only when your calculation formula involves related fields. In such cases, the calculation may return different results, depending on from which context it's evaluated.

WRITING THE FORMULA

The large box in the middle of the Specify Calculation dialog is where you define the formula itself. If you know the syntax of the functions you need and the names of the fields, you can simply go ahead and type the formula in by hand. In most cases, though, you'll want to use the lists of fields and functions above the text box. Double-clicking on an item in those lists inserts that item into your formula at the current insertion point.

NOTE

On a Macintosh, after an item is highlighted, you can also press the space bar to insert it into your formula. On Windows, the Insert key functions similarly.

Every calculation formula is made up of some combination of fields, constants, operators, and functions. All the following are examples of formulas that you might write:

```
2 + 2
FirstName & " " & LastName
Get(CurrentDate) + 14
Left(FirstName; 1) & Left(LastName; 1)
```

```
"Dear " & FirstName & ":"
LastName = "Jones"
```

In these examples, FirstName and LastName are fields. Get(CurrentDate) and Left are functions. The only operators used here are the addition operator (+) and the concatenation operator (&). (*Concatenation* means combining two text strings to form a new text string.) There are also numbers and text strings used as constants (meaning that they don't change), such as 14, "Dear", and "Jones". Text strings are the only things that need to be placed within quotes. FileMaker assumes that any unquoted text in a formula is a number, a function name, or a field name. If it's none of these, you get an error message when you attempt to exit the dialog.

SELECTING FIELDS

Above the formula box to the left is a list of fields. By default, the fields in the current table are listed. You can see the fields in a related (or unrelated) table by making a selection in the pop-up above the field list. Double-click a field name to insert it into your formula. You can also type field names directly.

CAUTION

Be aware that the only fields you can use from an unrelated table are those with global storage. There's no way FileMaker could determine which record(s) to reference for non-globally stored fields. You get an error message if you attempt to use a non-global field from an unrelated table in a formula.

If you have difficultly typing field names directly into formulas within ScriptMaker, see "Formulas in Scripts Require Explicit Table Context" in the Troubleshooting section at the end of this chapter.

CHOOSING OPERATORS

In between the field and function areas in the calculation dialog is a list of operators that you can use in your formulas. Operators are symbols that define functions, including math functions such as addition, subtraction, raising to a power, and so on.

NOTE

Strictly speaking, not all the symbols listed here are operators. The paragraph symbol (¶), for instance, is used to represent a literal return character in strings.

There is often some confusion about the use of &, +, and the and operator. The ampersand symbol (&) is used to concatenate strings of text together, as in the previous example where we derive the FullName by stringing together the FirstName, a space, and the LastName. The + symbol is a mathematic operator, used, as you might expect, to add numbers together. The and operator is a logical operator used when you need to test for multiple conditions. For instance, you might use a formula Case (Amount Due > 0 and Days Overdue > 30, "Overdue"). Here, the and indicates that both conditions must be satisfied for the test to return true.

The other operators are quite intuitive, with the exception of XOR. XOR, which stands for "exclusive or," is used to test if either of two statements is true, but not both of them. That is, (A xor B) is the same thing as (A or B) and not (A and B). The need for such logic doesn't come up often, but it's still handy to know.

SELECTING FUNCTIONS

The upper-right portion of the calculation dialog contains a list of the functions you can use in your formulas. By default, they are all listed alphabetically, but you can use the View pop-up menu above the list to view only formulas of a certain type. The Get functions and External functions, in fact, will display only if you change to View By Type.

Double-clicking a function inserts the function into your formula at the current insertion point. Pressing the space bar (Macintosh) or the Insert key (Windows) while the function is highlighted also adds the function to your formula. The "guts" of the function—the portion in between the parentheses—is highlighted so that you can begin typing parameters immediately.

→ You can learn more about how to read and use functions later in this chapter in the section titled "The Parts of a Function," **p. 223**.

WRITING LEGIBLE FORMULAS

Whether you're typing in a formula by hand, or are using the selection lists to insert fields and functions, we have a few general comments about how to make your functions easy to read.

First of all, when writing functions, spacing doesn't matter at all. You can put spaces and returns just about anyplace you want without changing how the formula evaluates. For legibility, it's therefore often helpful to separate the parameters of a function on separate lines, especially when you have nested functions.

 Also, one of the new features of FileMaker Pro 7 is the capability to add comments to calculation formulas. You can use either C or C++–style comments. Using C-style comments, you can type // and anything that follows on that line is considered a comment. C++–style comments use /* and */ to set off commented sections. This type of comment can appear in the middle of a line or can span multiple lines.

Compare, for example, the legibility of a complex function written two different ways. In Figure 8.4, you can see a mildly complex function with no commenting or spacing. In Figure 8.5, that exact same formula has been rewritten with comments and extra spacing to make it more legible. Legibility isn't merely an idle concern; it has real value. If you, or someone else, ever need to debug or alter one of your formulas, it will take much less time and effort if you've formatted your formula well in the first place.

Figure 8.4
A complex formula written without adequate spacing can be very difficult to understand and troubleshoot.

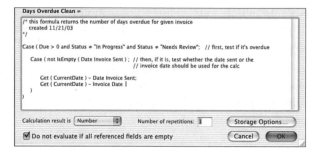

Figure 8.5
Adding spaces, returns, and comments to a formula can make it much more legible, and hence, easier to maintain in the future.

OTHER OPTIONS

Before ending this calculation dialog anatomy lesson, we must cover the miscellaneous options you can see at the bottom of the calculation dialog. These options pertain only to defining calculation fields; you don't see them in any of the other calculation dialogs.

DATA TYPE

The first of these miscellaneous options is to specify the type of data that the calculation will return. Usually, it's quite obvious. If you're concatenating the FirstName and LastName fields to form the FullName field, your calculation result will be a text string. If you're adding the SalesTax to an InvoiceSubTotal to generate the InvoiceTotal, the result will be a number. Adding 14 days to the current date to generate a call-back date will result in a date. Simply ask yourself what the formula will produce and select the appropriate result.

 If you do choose the wrong data type for a calculation field, you may experience some unexpected results. See "Errors Due to Improper Data Type Selection" in the Troubleshooting section at the end of this chapter.

NUMBER OF REPETITIONS

The only time you'll ever have to worry about the number of repetitions in a calculation field is when your formula references one or more repeating fields. If it does, then you'll typically define your calculation to have the same number of repeats as the fields it references. The formula that you define is applied to each repetition of the source fields, resulting in different values for each repetition of your calculation field.

If you reference non-repeating fields in your calculation, they affect only the first repetition of output. You can, however, use the Extend function to allow a non-repeating field to be applied to each repetition of output.

For instance, in Figure 8.6, Quantity and ItemCost are both number fields defined to allow 10 repetitions. TaxRate is a regular number field. The formula used to determine the LineTotal is as follows:

```
Quantity * ItemCost * (Extend(TaxRate) + 1)
```

LineTotal itself is defined to allow 10 repetitions.

Figure 8.6
Calculations fields can be defined to allow multiple repetitions.

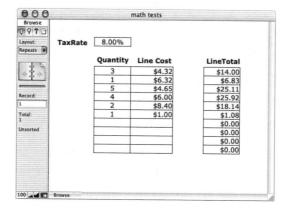

DO NOT EVALUATE

By default for new calculation fields, the Do Not Evaluate If All Referenced Fields Are Empty box is checked. This means that the calculation will return a null (empty) value as long as all the fields it refers to are empty. The difference in behavior caused by unchecking this box is subtle, but sometimes important. For instance, say you had a StatusCode field in an invoice database and wanted to use it to generate a status message, the formula of which was If (StatusCode = "P"; "Paid"; "Not Paid"). If you left the Do Not Evaluate... box checked, then invoices with no status code would have no status message. If it were unchecked, then their status message would be "Not Paid."

There's no simple rule we can provide as to when you want to check or uncheck this option. You need to look at your formula and determine whether or not the inputs to the formula (those fields referenced in the formula) could all ever be blank, and if so, whether or not you would still want the formula to evaluate. Typically, if your formulas have default results (as in the StatusCode example) rather than use explicit logic for determining results, you probably want to uncheck the box.

STORAGE OPTIONS

The last things we'll touch on in this anatomy lesson are the storage options available to you when defining calculation fields. Be aware that the output of your calculation formula may differ depending on the storage method selected. The Storage Options dialog box is shown in Figure 8.7.

8

Figure 8.7
The Storage Options dialog enables you to set calculation fields so that they have global results and to specify indexing options.

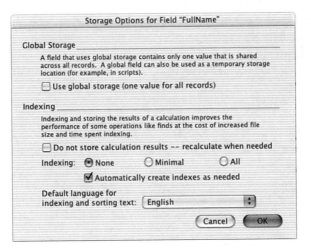

In the top portion of the dialog, you may specify *Global Storage* as an option. This is a concept new to FileMaker Pro 7, and one perhaps not immediately intuitive even for long-time FileMaker developers. Global storage for regular fields (that is, text, number, date) is typically used when you need a temporary storage location for a value or for infrequently changing, solution-wide values such as your company's name and address. For instance, globally stored text fields are often used in scripts as variables or as a place to hold users' preferences or selections as they navigate through your interface.

→ For more information on global storage of field data, **see** "Storage and Indexing," **p. 82**.

If you set a calculation field to be stored globally, then the results of the calculation formula will be available to you from any record, and indeed, any table, in your system. The formula isn't evaluated for each record in the system; it is evaluated only when one of the inputs of the formula changes or when you modify the formula. So picture a scenario in which you have a table called SystemPrefs that contains a single record with system-wide information, such as your company name. This field is a regular text field so that the company name can be stored from session to session and updated without the system having to be taken offline. If you have another field, gCompanyName, that's set to be the value of the company name field, but that has global storage, that field could be placed on any layout or in any script without needing a relationship to the SystemPrefs table. Whenever the company name field is updated, however, the calculation formula re-evaluates. The moment you make the change, all the system's users will see the new value.

The example given here makes the assumption that the SystemPrefs table would only ever have one record. If in fact it was allowed to have more, the value of gCompanyName would be the value of the last modified record.

→ For another example of when to use global storage for calculation fields, **see** "Sortable Column Headers," **p. 278**.

The bottom half of the Storage Options dialog enables you to specify indexing options. *Indexing* a field speeds up searches based on that field, but it results in larger files. FileMaker also uses field indexes for joining related tables.

→ For more detailed information on indexing, **see** "Storage and Indexing," **p. 82**.

In most cases, the default indexing option for a calculation field will be set to None, and the Automatically Create Indexes As Needed box will be checked. For most calculations you write, this configuration is perfect. FileMaker determines whether an index is needed and creates one if it is. Performing a find in the field or using the field in a relationship are both actions that trigger the automatic indexing of a field.

For some calculation formulas, the default storage option is to have the Do Not Store Calculation Results option checked and for everything else to be grayed out. This is an indication that the field is unindexable. Calculation fields that return text, number, date, time, or timestamp results can be indexed so long as they are stored. Calculations can be stored so long as they don't reference any unstored calculations, globally stored fields, related fields, or summary fields.

There are a few circumstances in which you'll want to explicitly turn off storage. For instance, when you use any of the Get functions in a calculation, you should make sure the calculation result is unstored. If you do so, the calculation is forced to evaluate based on the current environment each time it's displayed (as opposed to the environment at the time the record was created or modified). Let's say that you defined a calculation to return the number of records in the current found set by using the Get(FoundCount) formula. If you don't explicitly set the results to be unstored, then for a given record the formula evaluates once and keeps that value, regardless of changes to the size of the found set—it's stored there. As their name implies, unstored calculations do not make your files larger, but because they must evaluate each time you view them, they can slow down a system if they're based on complex formulas.

As a rule of thumb, you should usually stick with the default storage options unless you know for sure that you need the result to be unstored. You'll almost never need to explicitly turn indexing on; let FileMaker turn it on as necessary. Very seldom, you should uncheck the option to have FileMaker turn on indexing as needed. Be aware that indexing increases the size of your files, sometimes by a great deal. By unchecking the option to have FileMaker turn on indexing as needed, you can ensure that the certain fields won't be indexed accidentally just because a user performs a find on them.

ESSENTIAL FUNCTIONS

Now that you know your way around the calculation dialog itself, it's time to start learning more about particular calculation functions. Here we'll present an in-depth tutorial on what we feel are the most essential functions and techniques. These will form a solid base for your own work and for assembling complex formulas. As a reminder, Chapter 14, "Specialized Calculation Functions," covers advanced calculation formulas and techniques, and there's a complete function reference in Appendix B, "Calculation Function Reference."

THE PARTS OF A FUNCTION

Let's begin with a general discussion about what functions do and how to learn about them. Functions are amazing creatures. Their sole mission in life is to act on some set of inputs

8

and produce an output. The inputs are usually referred to as parameters; the function's syntax specifies the number of parameters it expects to be fed, and provides a clue about what the nature of each of those parameters is.

An example will help clarify this. Look at the syntax of the Position function as it's taken directly from the function list in the calculation dialog:

```
Position ( text ; searchString ; start ; occurrence )
```

A function's parameters are always placed in parentheses directly after the name of the function itself. They are separated from one another by semicolons.

NOTE

NEW

In previous English versions of FileMaker, the parameter separator was a comma, and in fact, if you use commas in FileMaker Pro 7, they are transformed into semicolons for you.

You can see that the Position function has four parameters. Any function reference (the Help system, Appendix B of this book) will tell you that the first parameter should be a text string in which you want to search, and the second should be a text string that you want to find within it. The third parameter is a number that specifies the character number to begin searching. The final parameter is also a number; it specifies which occurrence of the search string to find.

Besides knowing what to "feed" a function (here, two text strings and two numbers), you also need to know what type of output the function produces. Again, you first learn this by consulting some reference source or the help system. There, you'd learn that the Position function returns a number—not just any number, of course, but the character number where the search string was found within the initial text string. If the string was not found at all, it returns a 0. So, for example, if you had the following function:

```
Position ("Mary had a little lamb"; "a"; 1; 1)
```

the function would return 2 because the first occurrence of the letter *a* is at character 2 of the initial string. If you change the function slightly, to

```
Position ("Mary had a little lamb"; "a"; 1; 2)
```

you'd now expect a value of 7 because that's the position of the second occurrence of the letter *a*.

In these examples, all the parameters were "hard coded" with constant values. More typically, the parameters that you feed a function will be either fields or the outputs of other functions. For instance, if you had a field called PoemText and another called SearchCharacter, you might end up using the Position function as follows:

```
Position (PoemText; SearchCharacter; 1; 1)
```

Now, each record in your database will contain a different result, dependent on the contents of those two fields.

8

Using functions as parameters of other functions is called *nesting*. In those cases, the inner functions evaluate first, and their results are used as the inputs for the outer functions. For instance, you might have the following function:

```
Position (PoemText; SearchCharacter; Length(PoemText) - 5; 1)
```

Notice that the third parameter of the `Position` function here is the expression `Length(PoemText) - 5`. The `Length` function (which we discuss more shortly) takes a single parameter, a text string, and returns the number of characters in the string. So, in the preceding function, the length of the `PoemText` field will be determined, and that value less 5 will be used as the third parameter of the position function. There is no practical limit on the number of layers you can use to nest functions within one another. Just remember that readability becomes very important as your calculations become more complex.

At this point, you know quite a bit about the `Position` function. You know about its inputs and outputs; you've developed proficiency with a tool. Eventually, you'll want to memorize the inputs and outputs of a core set of functions. For lesser-used functions, you can look up the parameters and usage on an as-needed basis. There's still a difference between proficiency with a function and mastery of it. For instance, to truly master the `Position` function, you'd need to know such things as whether it's case sensitive (it's not), and what happens if you supply a negative number for the occurrence (it searches backward from the specified start character). Over time and with use, you'll learn about the subtle and esoteric usage of various functions, thereby moving from mere proficiency to mastery.

Let's turn now to a close look at those functions and techniques that should form the "core" of your calculation knowledge.

TEXT OPERATIONS

Text functions enable you to interrogate and manipulate text strings. If you haven't done much programming before, the concept of a string may need some explanation. Essentially, a *string* is a series of characters. Think about threading characters on a string like you do popcorn to make holiday decorations and you'll have a good mental image of a text string. The characters can be anything from letters and numbers to spaces and punctuation marks.

NOTE
NEW

> In previous versions of FileMaker, the size limit for text strings was 64,000 characters. In FileMaker 7, it's been expanded to a whopping 2GB!

Typically in FileMaker, text strings are found in text fields, but be aware that you can treat any numeric, date, and time data as a text string as well. When you do that, it's called *coercing* the data. FileMaker automatically coerces data into the type expected for a given operation. If you ever need to override the automatic coercion for any reason, you can use the "GetAs" functions. These include `GetAsDate`, `GetAsNumber`, `GetAsTime`, and `GetAsText`.

8

The simplest text operation you can perform is concatenation. *Concatenation* means taking two or more text strings and placing them beside each other to form a new, longer text string. As an example, consider the following formula:

```
FirstName & " " & LastName
```

Here, we're taking three strings, two of which happen to be field data, and we're concatenating them into a full name format.

Let's look next at several functions that can be used to interrogate text strings. By *interrogate*, we mean that we're interested in answering a specific question about the contents of a text string. For the examples in this section, assume that you have a field called `myData` with the string "Fred Flintstone" and the field `someString` which contains "The quick brown fox jumped over the lazy dog". The following is a list of some of the core calculation functions with examples that apply to the `myDate` and `someString` fields:

- `Length(string)`—The `Length` function takes a single argument and simply returns the number of characters in the string. Remember that spaces and return characters are considered characters. So, `Length(myData)` would return 15.

- `PatternCount(text; searchString)`—The `PatternCount` function tells you the number of times a search string occurs within some string. As an example, `PatternCount(someString; "the")` would return 2. Note that this function is *not* case sensitive. If the search string is not found, the function returns 0. Although the function returns an integer, it's often used as a true/false test in cases when you just want to know whether or not something is contained in a string. That is, you don't care where or how many times the string is found—you just care that it's there somewhere. Recall that any non-zero value represents "true" when being used as a Boolean value.

- `Position(text; searchString; start; occurrence)`—You've already looked in depth at the Position function. To recap, it returns an integer that specifies the place where one string is found in another. The `start` argument specifies where to begin the search; the `occurrence` argument specifies whether you want the first occurrence, the second, and so on. 94.5% of the time, you'll simply use 1 for both the `start` and `occurrence` parameters.

- `WordCount(string)`—`WordCount` is similar to the `Length` function, except that instead of counting every character, it counts every word. So, `WordCount(someString)` would return 9, as there are 9 words in the phrase. Be careful if you use `WordCount` that you have a good understanding of what characters FileMaker considers being word delimiters.

What's in a Word?

Several FileMaker functions, such as `WordCount`, `LeftWords`, `RightWords`, and `MiddleWords`, treat text strings as collections of words rather than as collections of characters. But how does FileMaker determine what constitutes a word? It's actually quite simple. There are a handful of characters that FileMaker recognizes as word separators. Spaces and carriage returns are both word separators, as you'd probably expect. Additionally, just about every punctuation symbol or other special character is considered a word separator. The two exceptions are worth knowing: neither a period (.) nor an apostrophe (') is a word separator. Also, in previous versions of FileMaker, hyphens (-) were *not* considered word separators, but they are in FileMaker Pro 7. If you have multiple word separators right next to each other, they're considered together as a single delimiter. For instance, the string " hello ,-, world " is considered to have two words, even though there are a total of nine word separators in the string.

- Exact(string1, string2)—The Exact function takes two strings as its inputs, and it compares them to see whether they are exactly the same string. It returns a 1 if they are, a 0 if not. By "exactly," we mean *exactly*; this function is case sensitive. The order of the two input arguments is irrelevant.

The other broad category of text operators consists of those functions that enable you to manipulate a string. Where the interrogatory functions returned a number, these functions all return a string. You feed them a string; they do something with it and spit back another string. The text operators that fall into this category are explained in the following sections.

Trim

The simplest of these functions is the Trim(string) function. Trim takes a string and removes any leading or trailing spaces from it. Spaces between words are not affected; no other leading or trailing characters other than a space (that is, return characters at the end of a field) are removed.

There are two common uses of Trim. The first is to identify data entry problems. Imagine you have a field called FirstName, and that some users have been accidentally typing spaces after the first name. You might want to display a message on such records, alerting users to that error. You'd define a new calculation field, called something like SpaceCheck. Its formula could be one of the following:

```
Case (FirstName <> Trim (FirstName), "Extra Space!")
Case (not Exact(FirstName, Trim (FirstName)), "Extra Space!")
Case (Length(FirstName) > Length(Trim(FirstName)), "Extra Space!")
```

→ The use and syntax of the Case function is covered in detail in the section titled "Using Conditional Functions," **p. 234**, later in this chapter.

The other common usage of Trim is in a calculated replace to clean up fixed-length data that's been imported from another application. "Fixed-length" means that the contents of a field are padded with leading or trailing spaces so that the entries are all the same length. After importing such data, you'd simply replace the contents of each field with a trimmed version of itself.

Substitute

The next text manipulation function we'll explore is the Substitute function. Substitute(string; searchString; replacementString) is used to replace every occurrence of some substring with some other substring. So, Substitute(myData; "Fred"; "Wilma") would return the string "Wilma Flintstone". If the initial substring were not found, then the Substitute function would simply return the original string. You should be aware that the Substitute function is case sensitive.

8

One common use of Substitute is to remove all occurrences of some character from a string. You just substitute in an empty string for that character. For instance, to remove all occurrences of a carriage return from a field, you could use Substitute(myString; "¶"; ""). If there are multiple substitutions you want to make to a string, you simply list them all as bracketed pairs in the order in which they should be performed. Let's say you have a PhoneNumber field where you want to strip out any parentheses, dashes, or spaces that users might have entered. One way to do this would be to use the following formula:

Substitute(PhoneNumber; ["("; ""] ; [")"; ""] ; ["-"; ""] ; [" ", ""])

Be aware when performing multiple substitutions like this that the substitutions happen in the order they are listed, and that each subsequent substitution happens on an altered version of the string rather than on the original string. Say you had the string "xxyz" and you wanted to put z's where there are x's, and x's where there are z's. The formula Substitute("xxyz"; ["x"; "z"]; ["z"; "x"]) incorrectly returns "xxyx". First, the two leading x's are turned to z's, yielding "zzyz"; then all three z's are turned into x's. If you ever want to swap two characters like this, you need to temporarily turn the first character into something that you know won't be found in your string. So, to fix this example, we could use the formula Substitute("xxyz"; ["x"; "**TEMP**"]; ["z"; "x"]; ["**TEMP**", "z"]). That would correctly yield "zzyx".

CASE ALTERING FUNCTIONS

There are several text functions you can use to alter a string's case. These are Lower(string), Upper(string), and Proper(string). It's quite intuitive how these act. Lower("Fred") returns "fred"; Upper("Fred") returns "FRED". Using Proper returns a string in which the first letter of each word is capitalized. For instance, Proper("my NAME is fred") returns "My Name Is Fred".

TEXT PARSING FUNCTIONS

The final category of text operators we'll look at here is text-parsing functions. Text parsing functions enable you to extract a substring from a string. The six text parsing functions are Left, Middle, Right, LeftWords, MiddleWords, and RightWords. The first three operate at the character level; the other three operate at the word level.

The Left function extracts a substring of length N from the beginning of some string. For example, Left("Hello"; 2) returns the string "He"; it simply grabs the first 2 characters of the string. If the number of characters you ask for is greater than the length of the string, the function simply returns the entire string. A negative or zero number of characters results in an empty string being returned.

The Right function is similar, except that it grabs characters from the end of the specified string. Right("Hello"; 2) would return "lo". Middle, as you might expect, is used to extract a substring from the middle of a string. Unlike the Left and Right functions, which require only a string and a length as parameters, the Middle function requires a starting position. The syntax is Middle(string; startingPosition; numberOfCharacters). For example, Middle("Hello"; 2; 3) yields "ell".

The LeftWords, RightWords, and MiddleWords functions all operate exactly as Left, Middle, and Right functions, except that they operate at the word level. One typical use of these functions is to parse apart names or addresses that you've imported from some other application. Say that your import resulted in contact names coming in as full names. You might want to create a LastName calculation field so that you could sort the records. If you knew that the last name was always the last word of the FullName field, you could use the formula RightWords(FullName; 1).

NESTED FUNCTIONS

The text operators we have discussed often appear nested within each other in formulas. Writing nested formulas can be tricky sometimes. One thing that helps is to think of a particular example rather than trying to deal with it abstractly. For instance, let's say that you have a big text field, and you need a formula that extracts just its first line—that is, everything up until the first carriage return. So, imagine that you had the following text:

```
The quick
brown fox
jumped over the
lazy dog
```

Think first: What text parsing formulas would potentially yield "The quick" from this text? Well, there are several of them:

```
Left(myText; 9)
LeftWords(myText; 2)
Middle(myText; 1; 9)
```

Of course, at this point these formulas apply only to this particular example. Think next: Could one of these be extended easily to *any* multi-line text field? If there were a constant number of words per line, the LeftWords formula would work. And if not? What do the text interrogation formulas tell us about this field? Length(myText) is 44. Not particularly helpful. PatternCount(myText; "¶") is 3. That indicates there are 4 lines total. Interesting, but not obviously helpful for extracting the first line. WordCount(myText) is 9. It's just coincidence that this is the number of characters in the first line; be careful not to be misled. Position(myText; "¶"; 1; 1) is 10. Finally, something interesting. In this example, the length of the first line is 1 less than the position of the first carriage return. Is that true in all cases? At this point, if you write out a few more examples, you'll see that indeed, it is. Therefore, a general formula for extracting the first line of text is:

```
Left(myText; Position(myText, "¶"; 1; 1) - 1)
```

How about extracting the *last* line from any multi-line text field? You should approach this problem the same way, working from a specific example. Counting characters by hand, assemble a list of options:

```
Middle(myText; 36, 8)
Right(myText; 8)
RightWords(myText; 2)
```

8

What clues do the interrogatory functions yield? If you spend a few minutes thinking about it, you'll realize that 36 is the position of the last return character. You can derive that by using the number of returns as the occurrence parameter in a `Position` function, like this:

```
Position(myText; "¶"; 1; PatternCount(myText; "¶"))
```

After you have the 36 figured out, recall that the length of the string is 44 characters, and notice that 44–36 = 8. Given these discoveries, you'll soon see that a simple and elegant generalized formula for grabbing the last line of a text field is

```
Right(myText; Length(myText) - Position(myText; "¶"; 1;
➡ PatternCount(myText; "¶")))
```

Take a moment to convince yourself that this works for any multi-line text field that you feed it.

NUMBER FUNCTIONS

In general, most people find working with math functions simpler and more intuitive than working with string functions. Perhaps this is because they remind us of various high school math courses. Or it could be they typically have fewer parameters. Regardless, you'll find yourself using number functions on a regular basis. This chapter focuses not so much on what these functions do, but rather on some interesting applications for them.

The first set of functions that we'll look at are `Int`, `Floor`, `Ceiling`, `Round`, and `Truncate`. Each of these can be thought of as performing some sort of rounding, making it sometimes difficult to know which one you should use. You can look up these functions in Appendix B for complete syntax and examples, but it's helpful to consider the similarities and differences of these functions as a set.

- `Int(number)`—The `Int` function returns the integer portion of the number that it's fed—that is, anything before the decimal point. `Int(4.5)` returns 4. `Int (-2.1)` returns -4.

- `Floor(number)`—Floor is similar to `Int`, except that it returns the next lower integer of the number it's fed (unless that number is an integer itself, of course, in which case `Floor` just returns that integer). For any positive number, `Floor(number)` and `Int(number)` returns the same value. For negative numbers, though, `Floor(number)` and `Int(number)` don't return the same value unless *number* is an integer. `Floor (-2.1)` returns -3, whereas `Int (-2.1)` returns -2.

- `Ceiling(number)`—The `Ceiling` function is complimentary to the `Floor` function: It returns the next higher integer from the number it's fed (unless, again, that number is already an integer). For example, `Ceiling (5.3)` returns 6.

- `Round(number, precision)`—Round takes a number and rounds it to the number of decimal points specified by the precision parameter. At the significant digit, numbers up to 4 are rounded down; numbers 5 and above are rounded up. So, `Round(3.6234; 3)` returns 3.623, whereas `Round(3.6238; 3)` returns 3.624. Using a precision of 0 rounds to the nearest whole number. Interestingly, you can use a negative precision. A precision of -1 rounds a number to the nearest 10; -2 rounds to the nearest hundred, and so on.

- Truncate(*number, precision*)—Truncate is similar to Round, but Truncate simply takes the first n digits after the decimal point, leaving the last one unaffected regardless of whether the subsequent number is 5 or higher. Truncate(3.6238; 3) returns 3.623. For any number, Truncate(number; 0) and Int(number) return the same value. Just as Round can take a negative precision, so can Truncate. For example, Truncate(258; -2) returns 200.

Which function you use for any given circumstance depends on your needs. If you're working with currency and want to add an 8.25% shipping charge to an order, you'd probably end up with a formula like Round(OrderTotal * 1.0825 ; 2). Using Truncate might cheat you out of a penny here or there.

Floor, Ceiling, and Int have some interesting uses in situations where you want to group numeric data into sets. For instance, imagine you have a list report that prints 10 records per page, and that you have a found set of 57 records to print. If you wanted, for whatever reason, to know how many pages your printed report would be, you could use Ceiling(Get(FoundCount)/10). Similarly, if you wanted to know what page any given record would print on, you would use the formula Floor((Get(RecordNumber)-1)/10)+1. The Int function would yield the same result in this case.

Another common use of these functions is to round a number up or down to the multiple of some number. As an example, say you had the number 18, and you wanted to know the multiples of 7 that bounded it (…14 and 21). To get the lower bound, you can use the formula Floor(18/7)*7; the upper bound is Ceiling(18/7)*7. These generalize as

```
Lower bound:  Floor (myNum / span) * span
Upper bound:  Ceiling (myNum / span) * span
```

The span can be any number, including a decimal number, which comes in handy for rounding currency amounts, say, to the next higher or lower quarter.

You should know a few other number functions:

- Abs(*number*)—The Abs function returns the absolute value of the number it's fed. There's nothing tricky to understanding the function itself, but there are a few handy uses that you might not think of. One is to toggle a flag field between 0 and 1. The formula Abs(Flag-1) always "flips" the flag. If Flag is 0, then Flag-1 is -1, and Abs(-1) is 1. If Flag is 1, then Flag-1 is 0, and Abs(0) is 0.

- Mod(*number*; *divisor*)—The Mod function returns the remainder when a number is divided by a divisor. For instance, Mod (13; 5) returns 3 because 13 divided by 5 is 2, remainder 3.

- Div(*number*; *divisor*)—The Div function, new to FileMaker 7, is complimentary to the Mod function. It returns the whole number result of dividing a number by a divisor. For instance, Div (13; 5) would return 2. In all cases, Div(number; divisor) and Floor(number/divisor) return exactly the same value; it's a matter of personal preference or context which you should use.

8

■ Random—The Random function returns a random decimal number between 0 and 1. Usually, you'll use the Random function when you want to return a random number in some other range, so you'll need to multiply the result of the function by the span of the desired range. For instance, to simulate the roll of a six-sided die, you'd use the formula Ceiling(Random * 6). To return a random integer between, say, 21 and 50 (inclusive), the method would be similar: First you'd generate a random number between 1 and 30, then you'd add 20 the result to translate it into the desired range. The formula would end up as Ceiling(Random * 30) + 20.

WORKING WITH DATES AND TIMES

Just as there are functions for working with text and numbers, FileMaker Pro provides a number of functions that enable you to manipulate date and time fields. This section introduces you to the most common and discusses some real world applications that you'll be likely to need in your solutions.

The most important thing to understand at the outset is how FileMaker itself stores dates, times, and timestamps. Each is actually stored as an integer number. For dates, this integer represents a serialized number beginning with January 1, 0001. January 1, 0001 is 1, January 2, 0001 is 2, and so on. As an example, October 19, 2003 would be stored by FileMaker as 731507. FileMaker understands dates from January 1, 0001 until December 31, 4000.

Times are stored as the number of seconds since midnight. Midnight itself is 0. Therefore, times are typically in the range of 0 to 83999. It's worth knowing that time fields can contain not only absolute times, but also elapsed times. That is, you can type **46:18:19** into a time field, and it will be stored as 166699 seconds. Negative values can be placed in time fields as well. FileMaker doesn't, however, have the capability to deal with microseconds.

 Timestamps are a new field type in FileMaker Pro 7. A timestamp contains both a date and time. For example, "10/19/2003 8:55:03 AM" is a timestamp. Internally, timestamps are converted to the number of seconds since midnight on January 1, 0001. You could derive this number from date and time fields with the formula ((myDate-1) * 86400) + myTime.

The easiest way to begin learning date, time, and timestamp functions is to split them into two categories: those that you feed a date or time and that return a "bit" of information back, and those that are *constructors*, where you feed the function bits and you get back a date, time, or timestamp. Neither of these are formal terms that you'll find used elsewhere, but they're nonetheless useful for learning date and time functions.

The "bit" functions are fed dates and times, and they return numbers or text. For instance, say that you have a field myDate that contains the value "10/19/2003". Here's a list of the most common "bit" functions and what they'd return:

```
Month(myDate) = 10
MonthName(myDate) = October
Day(myDate) = 19
DayName(myDate) = Sunday
DayOfWeek(myDate) = 1
Year(myDate) = 2003
```

Similarly, a field called `myTime` with a value of `"9:23:10 AM"` could be split into its bits with the following functions:

```
Hour(myTime) = 9
Minute(myTime) = 23
Seconds(myTime) = 10
```

You need to know only three constructor functions. Each is fed bits of data and returns, respectively, a date, time, or timestamp. When using these formulas in calculation fields, be sure to check that you've set the calculation result to the proper data type.

```
Date(month; day; year)
Time(hours; minutes; seconds)
TimeStamp(date; time)
```

For example, `Date(10; 20; 2003)` returns `"10/20/2003"`. `TimeStamp(myDate; myTime)` might return `"10/19/2003 9:23:10 AM"`.

One very interesting and useful thing to know about these constructor functions is that you can "overfeed" them. For example, if you ask for `Date(13; 5; 2003)`, the result will be `"1/5/2004"`. If the bits you provide are out of range, FileMaker automatically adjusts accordingly. Even zero and negative values are interpreted correctly. `Date (10; 0; 2003)` returns `"9/30/2003"` because that's one day before 10/1/2003.

There are many practical uses of the date and time functions. For instance, the "bit" functions are often used to generate a break field that can be used in subsummary reports. Say that you have a table of invoice data, and you want a report that shows totals by month and year. You would define a field called `InvoiceMonth` with the formula `Month(InvoiceDate)` and another called `InvoiceYear` with a formula of `Year(InvoiceDate)`.

A common use of the constructor functions is to derive a date from the bits of a user-entered date. Say, for example, that a user entered **"10/19/2003"** into a field called `myDate`, and you wanted a calculation formula that would return the first of the next month, or `"11/1/2003"`. Your formula would be `Date(Month(myDate)+1; 1; Year(myDate))`.

If you're importing dates from other systems, you may need to use text manipulation functions in conjunction with the constructor functions to turn the dates into something that FileMaker can understand. Student information systems, for example, often store students' birth dates in an 8-digit format of MMDDYYYY. To import and clean this data, you'd first bring the raw data into a text field. Then, using either a calculated replace or a looping script, you would set the contents of a date field to the result of the formula:

```
Date(Left(ImportedDate;2); Middle(ImportedDate;3;2); Right(ImportedDate;4))
```

Timestamps are quite useful for logging activities, but sometimes you'll find that you want to extract either just the date or time portion of the timestamp. The easiest way to do this is via the `GetAsDate` and `GetAsTime` functions. When you feed either of these a timestamp, they return just the date or time portion of that timestamp. Similarly, if you have a formula that generates a timestamp, you can set the return data type of the calculation result to date or time to return just the date or just the time.

USING CONDITIONAL FUNCTIONS

Conditional functions are used when you want to return a different result based on certain conditions. The most basic and essential conditional function is the If function. If takes three parameters: a test, a true result, and a false result. The test needs to be a full equation or expression that can be evaluated as true or false.

Let's look at an example. Suppose you have a set of records containing data about invoices. You'd like to display the status of the invoice—"Paid" or "Not Paid"—based on whether the AmountDue field has a value greater than zero. To do this, you'd define a new field, called InvoiceStatus, with the following formula:

```
If ( AmountDue > 0, "Not Paid", "Paid")
```

For each record in the database, the contents of the InvoiceStatus field will be derived based on the contents of that record's AmountDue field.

The test can be a simple equation, as in the preceding example, or it can be a complex test that uses several equations tied together with "and" and "or" logic.

```
If ( A and B;"something"; "something else") - both A and B have to be true
➥to return the true result
If ( A or B; "something"; "something else") - if either A or B is true,
➥ it will return the true result
```

The true or false result arguments can themselves be If statements, resulting in what's known as a nested If statement. This allows you to test multiple conditions and return more than two results. For instance, let's revise the logic of the InvoiceStatus field. Say that we wanted invoices with a negative AmountDue to evaluate as "Credit Due". We could then use the following field definition:

```
If ( Amount Due > 0; "Not Paid"; If (Amount Due < 0; "Credit Due"; "Paid"))
```

The other commonly used conditional function is the Case statement. The Case statement differs from the If statement in that you can test for multiple conditions without resorting to nesting. For instance, say that you have a field called GenderCode in a table that contains either "M" or "F" for a given record. If you wanted to define a field that would display the full gender, you could use the following formula:

```
Case(GenderCode = "M"; "Male"; GenderCode="F"; "Female")
```

A Case statement consists of a series of tests and results. The tests are conducted in the order they appear; if a test is true, then the following result is returned; if not, then the next test is evaluated. FileMaker stops evaluating tests after the first true one is discovered. You can include a final optional result that is returned if none of the tests come back as true. The gender display formula could be altered to include a default response as follows:

```
Case(GenderCode = "M"; "Male"; GenderCode="F"; "Female"; "Gender Unknown")
```

Without the default response, if none of the tests are true then the Case statement returns a null value.

8

AGGREGATE FUNCTIONS

Another important category of functions are those known as aggregate functions. These include Sum, Count, Min, Max, and Avg. These all work in similar, quite intuitive ways. They each operate on a set of inputs (numeric, except for Count) and produce a numeric output. The name of the function implies the operation that each performs. Sum adds a set of numbers, Min and Max return the smallest and largest items of a set, Avg returns the arithmetic mean of the numbers, and Count returns the number of non-null values in the set.

The inputs for an aggregate function can come from any one of three sources:

- **A series of delimited values**—For example, Sum(6; 4; 7; 2) yields 19. Average (6; 4; 7; 2) yields 4.75. An interesting use of the Count function is to determine the number of fields in a record into which a user has entered values. For instance, Count (FirstName; LastName; Phone; Address; City; State; Zip) would return 2 if the user had entered values into only those two fields.

- **A repeating field**—Repeating fields enable you to store multiple values within a single field within the same record. For instance, you might have repeating fields within a music collection database for listing the tracks and times of the contents of a given disc. The functions Count(Tracks) and Sum(Times) would produce the number of tracks and the total playing time for a given disc.

- **A related field**—By far, this is the most common application for aggregate functions. Imagine that you have a Customer table and an Invoice table and you want to create a field in Customer that totals up all the invoices for a particular customer. That field would be defined as Sum(Invoices::InvoiceTotal). Similarly, to tell how many related invoices a customer had, you could use the formula Count(Invoices::CustomerID).

NOTE

> When using the Count function to count related records, it usually doesn't matter what field you count, so long as it's not empty. The count will not include records where the specified field is blank. Typically, you should count either the related primary key or the related foreign key, as these by definition should contain data.

LEARNING ABOUT THE ENVIRONMENT

FileMaker has two categories of functions whose job it is to tell you information about the environment—the computing and application environment, that is. These are the Get functions and the Design functions. There are over 70 Get functions, and 20 Design functions, all of which are presented in detail in Appendix B. Here, our goal is to give you an overview of the types of things these functions do and some of the most common uses for them.

Get FUNCTIONS

In previous versions of FileMaker, these functions were known as the Status functions. Now known as Get functions, they provide a broad array of information about a user's computing environment and the current state of a database. None of the Get functions take parameters; each simply gives you some tidbit of information that you can use however you wish.

As an example, the Get(TotalRecordCount) function returns the total number of records in some table. One typical use for this is as the formula for a calculation field. If you have hidden the status area from users, this field could be used as part of constructing your own "Record X of Y" display. If you're using this function in a script—or any Get function, for that matter—be sure that you're aware that the active layout determines the context in which this function is evaluated.

Whenever you use a Get function as part of a field definition, you need to be acutely aware of the storage options that have been set for that field. For Get functions to evaluate properly, you must explicitly set the calculation to be unstored. If it not set this way, then the function evaluates only once when the record is created; it reflects the state of the environment at the time of record creation, but not at the current moment. Setting the calculation field to be unstored forces it to evaluate every time the field is displayed or used in another calculation, based on the current state of the environment.

Although you don't need to memorize all the Get functions, a handful are used frequently and should form part of your core knowledge of functions. To remember them, it's helpful to group them into subcategories based on their function.

The first subcategory includes functions that reveal information about the current user:

```
Get ( AccountName )
Get ( ExtendedPrivileges )
Get ( PrivilegeSetName )
Get ( UserName )
Get ( UserCount )
```

Another subcategory includes functions that are frequently used in conditional tests within scripts to determine what actions should be taken:

```
Get ( ActiveModifierKeys )
Get ( LastMessageChoice )
Get ( LastError )
Get ( ScriptParameter )
```

There are four functions for returning the current date and time:

```
Get ( CurrentDate )
Get ( CurrentHostTimeStamp )
Get ( CurrentTime )
Get ( CurrentTimeStamp )
```

Many Get functions tell you where the user is within the application and what the user doing:

```
Get ( FoundCount )
Get ( LayoutNumber )
Get ( LayoutName )
Get ( LayoutTableName )
Get ( PageNumber )
```

8

```
Get ( PortalRowNumber )
Get ( RecordNumber )
```

And finally, another group of functions reveal information about the position, size, and name of the current window:

```
Get ( WindowName )
Get ( WindowTop )
Get ( WindowHeight )
Get ( WindowWidth )
```

Finally, to see the list of `Get` functions in the calculation dialog, you need to toggle the view to either All Functions By Type or to just the `Get` functions. They don't show up when the view is All Functions By Name. Be aware that there are a number of functions with "Get" in their name that aren't `Get` functions. These include things like `GetRepetition`, `GetField`, `GetAsText`, and `GetSummary`. These are not functionally related in any way to the `Get` functions that have just been discussed.

DESIGN FUNCTIONS

The `Design` functions are used to get information about the structure of a database file itself. With just two exceptions (`DatabaseNames` and `WindowNames`), none of the `Design` functions are session-dependent. That is, the results returned by these functions won't differ at all based on who is logged in or what they're doing. Unlike the `Get` functions, `Design` functions often take parameters.

Fully half of the `Design` functions simply return lists of names or IDs of the major structural components of a file. These include

```
FieldIDs
FieldNames
LayoutIDs
LayoutNames
ScriptIDs
ScriptNames
TableIDs
TableNames
ValueListIDs
ValueListNames
```

Six other `Design` functions return information about a specified field:

```
FieldBounds (fileName ; layoutName ; fieldName)
FieldComment (fileName ; fieldName)
FieldRepetitions (fileName ; layoutName ; fieldName)
FieldStyle (fileName ; layoutName ; fieldName)
FieldType (fileName ; fieldName)
GetNextSerialValue (fileName ; fieldName)
```

The `DatabaseNames` function returns a list of the databases that the current user has open. The list doesn't include file extensions, and it doesn't distinguish between files that are open as a host versus those that are open as a guest.

Similarly, the `WindowNames` function returns a list of the window names the current user has open. The list is ordered by the stacking order of the windows; it includes both visible and hidden windows across all the open database files.

Typically, the `DatabaseNames` and `WindowsNames` functions are used to check whether a user has a certain database file or window open already. For instance, if you have a navigation window that you always want to be open, you can have a subscript check for its presence and open it if it has been closed by the user. To do this, you would use the formula `PatternCount(WindowNames; "Nav Window")`. This would return a `0` if there was no window open whose name included the string `"Nav Window"`.

The final `Design` function is `ValueListItems (fileName ; valueList)`. This function returns a list of the items in the specified value list. As with most of the `Design` functions, the primary purpose of this function is to help you catalog or investigate the structure of a file. There's another common usage of `ValueListItems` that is handy to know. Imagine that you have a one-to-many relationship between a table called Salespeople and a table called Contacts, which contains demographic information about all of a salesperson's contacts. For whatever reason, you might want to assemble a list of all the cities where a salesperson has contacts. You can do this by defining a value list based on the relationship that shows the `City` field, and then creating an unstored calculation field in Contacts with the formula `ValueListItems("Contacts"; "CityList")`. For any given salesperson record, this field will contain the "sum" of all the cities where she has contacts.

TROUBLESHOOTING

FORMULAS IN SCRIPTS REQUIRE EXPLICIT TABLE CONTEXT

I'm used to being able to type field names into calculation formulas rather than select them from the field list. Sometimes, even if I've typed the field name correctly, I get a "Field not found" message when trying to leave the calc dialog. It seems that sometimes calcs need the table occurrence name before the field name, and sometimes they don't. What are the rules for this?

When you define calculation fields, any fields within the current table can be entered into the formula without the table context being defined. For instance, you might have a `FullName` field defined to be `FirstName & " " & LastName`.

All formulas that you write anywhere within ScriptMaker require that the table context be explicitly defined for every field, even when there's only a single table in the file. For instance, if you wanted to use a Set Field script step to place a contact's full name into a field, you wouldn't be able to use the formula above as written. Instead, it would need to be something like `Contact::FirstName & " " & Contact::LastName`.

If you're used to being able to manually type field names into formulas, be aware that the table context must be included for every field referenced in the formula.

The reason for this is that the table context for a script is determined by the active layout when the script is executed. `Contact::FirstName` may have a very different meaning when evaluated on a layout tied to the Contact table than it would, say, on one tied to an Invoice table.

ERRORS DUE TO IMPROPER DATA TYPE SELECTION

I've heard that the data type selection for calculation fields is important. What kind of problems will I have if I select the wrong data type, and how do I know what type to choose?

Every time you define a calculation field, no matter how simple, be sure to check the data type that the formula is defined to return. The default data type is "Number", unless you're defining multiple calculations in a row, in which case the default for subsequent fields will be the data type defined for the previous calculation.

A number of errors can result from selecting the improper data type. For instance, if your formula returns a text string but you leave the return data type as number, any finds or sorts you perform using that field will not return expected results.

Be especially aware that formulas that return dates, times, and timestamps are defined to have date, time, and timestamp results. If you leave the data type as number, your field displays the internal serial number that represents that date and/or time. For instance, the formula Date (4 ; 26 ; 2004) returns 731697 if the date type is improperly set to number.

FILEMAKER EXTRA: TIPS FOR BECOMING A CALCULATION MASTER

As we mentioned at the outset of this chapter, it takes time to master the use of calculation formulas. We thought it would be helpful to compile a list of tips to help you get started on the path.

- **Begin with a core**—Don't try to memorize everything at once; chances are you'll end up frustrated. Instead, concentrate on building a small core of functions that you know inside and out and can use without having to look up the syntax or copy from examples. Then, gradually expand the core over time. As you have a need to use a new function, spend a few minutes reading about it or testing how it behaves in various conditions.

- **Work it out on paper first**—Before writing a complex formula, work through the logic with pencil and paper. This way you can separate the logic from the syntax. You'll also know what to test against and what to expect as output.

- **Search for alternative methods of doing the same thing**—It's uncommon to have only one way to approach a problem or only one formula that will suit a given need. As you write a formula, ask yourself how else you might be able to approach the problem, and what the pros and cons of each method would be. Try to avoid the "if your only tool is a hammer, than all your problems look like nails" situation. For instance, if you always use If statements for conditional tests, be adventurous and see whether you could use a Case statement instead.

■ **Strive for simplicity, elegance, and extensibility**—As you expand your skills, you'll find that it becomes easy to come up with multiple approaches to a given problem. So how do you choose which to use? We suggest that simplicity, elegance, and extensibility are the criteria to judge by. All other things being equal, choose the formula that uses the fewest functions, has tightly reasoned logic, or can be extended to handle other scenarios or future needs most easily. This doesn't mean that the shortest formula is the best. The opposite of simplicity and elegance is what's often referred to as the "brute force" approach. There are certainly situations where that's the best approach, and you shouldn't hesitate to use such an approach when necessary. But if you want to become a calculation master, you'll need to have the ability to go beyond brute force approaches as well.

■ **Use comments and spacing**—Part of what makes a formula elegant is that it's written in a way that's logical and transparent to other developers. There may come a time when someone else needs to take over development of one of your projects, or when you'll need to review a complex formula that you wrote years before. By commenting your formulas and adding white space within your formulas, it becomes easier to expand upon and troubleshoot problems in the future.

■ **Be inquisitive and know where to get the answer**—As you write formulas, take time to digress and test hunches and learn new things. Whip up little sample files to see how something behaves in various conditions. Also, know what resources are available to you to get more information when you get stuck or need help. The Help system, the function reference found in Appendix B of this book, and online discussion groups are all examples of resources you should take advantage of.

CHAPTER 9

GETTING STARTED WITH SCRIPTING

SCRIPTS IN FILEMAKER PRO

Scripts are sets of stored instructions that specify a series of actions FileMaker should perform when they're initiated; they're programs that run within FileMaker Pro solutions. They can be just one command attached to a button, or they can be hundreds of commands long.

Scripts do two important things in FileMaker Pro: They automate internal processes, and they are used to add interactivity to custom user interfaces. Internal functions are often critical and specific, used for such things as a monthly run at creating invoices, setting the status of sales leads, exporting data for an aggregated report, and so on. Central to making a database application usable is the ability to create interface elements (such as buttons or icons) and then have them *do something* in response to user actions. Scripts can help with both of these.

Scripts are written in FileMaker Pro's ScriptMaker, a point-and-click interface. They allow routines to perform tasks ranging from simple things (such as beeping at the press of a button) to complex automated import/export processes, multi-table reporting, data reconciliation, and really anything that can be expressed as a programmed series of FileMaker steps.

> **N O T E**
>
> If you're new to FileMaker Pro, we suggest you read this chapter from start to finish because we will be covering some important fundamentals. If you're familiar with previous versions of FileMaker Pro, we suggest you take a look at the discussion of access privileges and skim the functions section for those you might not be familiar with. We'll be covering some new script steps.

After a script is initiated through some user action or external prompt (we'll cover how scripts get initiated later in the chapter), it runs in sequence from its first step to the last, exiting or ending after it is complete. Here's a simple example:

```
Show All Records
Go to Record/Request/Page [ First ]
Beep
Show Custom Dialog [ Title: "First Record";
Message: "This is your first record."; Buttons: "OK" ]
```

As you can see from this short example, FileMaker Pro scripts are very easy to read and comprehend. This script resets the found set of the current layout/window to all the records in a given table, takes the user to the first record in that set, beeps, and shows a dialog with an OK button. Each step of the script is executed in order: Show All Records is completed, and then Go to Record/Request/Page is dealt with.

It's possible to create branching scripts by using logical If[] statements, and it's also possible to construct scripts that execute other scripts (hereafter referred to as *subscripts*). We'll get into both such techniques later in the chapter.

CREATING SCRIPTS

Creating and editing scripts in FileMaker is fairly straightforward. Simply choose Scripts, ScriptMaker and the Define Scripts dialog opens. Keep in mind you'll need to have signed in with an account that allows script access.

Before getting into the exact mechanics of creating a script, you'll want to consider the process conceptually. A script steps through a series of instructions, one at a time, until the script either reaches its last instruction or until it reaches some exit condition. Exit conditions can vary, and many of their implementations are covered in this chapter.

→ To delve into common scripting techniques including exit conditions, **see** "Common Scripting Techniques," **p. 249**, later in this chapter.

Here's a simple example of the logical outline of a script that you might use to take users to a Main Menu layout after they log in. This script would be set up to run when a file is opened. Assume that someone named Kim has just logged in.

After valid login:

1. In a table of users, set the `LastLoginDate` field in Kim's record to today's date.

2. Set the `gUserNameDisplay` field to "Kim."

3. Set the `gUserMessage` field to "Welcome back, Kim."

4. Go to layout: `Main_Menu`

This simple four-step process takes care of some background tasks first, then from a user's standpoint navigates to the main menu on which, presumably, a welcome message sits.

TOPOLOGY OF SCRIPTMAKER

The Define Scripts dialog (see Figure 9.1) allows you to manage all the scripts in your current file. To reorder scripts, simply drag individual scripts up or down along the list. Unfortunately, there's no means of sorting scripts, so you need to do your best to stay organized.

Figure 9.1
The Define Scripts dialog box allows you to create, edit, and organize your scripts, and to decide which ones to display in FileMaker's Script menu.

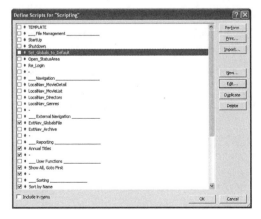

TIP

> Use (⌘-up/down arrow) [Ctrl+up/down arrow] to move scripts via your keyboard.

You can perform various actions in the Define Scripts dialog box as outlined in the following list:

- You can create new scripts, edit existing scripts, or delete those you no longer need.
- By selecting a given script and clicking Perform you can execute scripts directly from this dialog. Using this button to initiate scripts saves you the extra step of having to close the dialog and launch them from within your database.
- You can use the Print button to print a script. Printing a script is a good way to create documentation—especially in combination with Adobe Acrobat's capability to create PDFs—or spot problems more easily.
- You can import scripts. You are likely to find yourself writing scripts that may be similar to those you've written before, or needing to migrate from an older file into a newer. Luckily, you need not reassemble all your scripts by hand. It's possible to import a script from another file. In this latest version of FileMaker, imported scripts match field, relationship, layout, and other references by name (as opposed to prior versions' behaviors of matching by internal object IDs). Naturally, it's necessary to double-check whether a script imported rightly. It's a good idea to look at any script steps that refer to fields, layouts, subscripts, related records, or anything that is layout-driven and assumes the object in question is on a given layout.

TIP

> If you use FileMaker Developer, one of the easiest ways to confirm that a script has imported well is to run it the first time with the Script Debugger turned on.

- The Edit button opens the Edit Script dialog for any given selected script. A much faster way to work is to simply double-click the script you want to edit.
- The Duplicate button can be used to duplicate a script so that you need not start from scratch when writing a new script. We recommend creating a script template and duplicating such to begin new scripts.
- The check box column along the left of the dialog controls whether or not a given script appears in FileMaker's Script menu. If you hide a script by unchecking its check box, you need to provide the user with another means of performing, or executing, the script. Typically, you include a button in the user interface that executes the script. In fact, quite often this is the preferred means of managing scripts. Attached to buttons, scripts become an integral part of your user experience.

Note also that just as in other areas of FileMaker Pro, a single hyphen becomes a menu divider. If you create a script named "-", you insert a divider in your list. This is useful in organizing your scripts visually. Plan to have a good many scripts; it is a good idea to keep them well organized.

TIP

> Notice that by using (⌘-click) [Ctrl+click] you can select multiple, non-contiguous scripts and then delete, duplicate, or print as you need.

SCRIPT NAMING PRACTICES

Keeping your scripts well organized and following good script naming practices is even more important in FileMaker 7 than it was in previous versions of the product. Prior versions of FileMaker Pro generally involved more individual files than FileMaker 7, and hence scripts tended to be naturally distributed throughout a given system. In this version, all your scripts may very well live in a single file.

NOTE

> FileMaker 7's capability to store many tables in one file has many implications, but in particular with scripts, you won't be constantly closing and reopening ScriptMaker in different files. Fewer scripts are also required in many cases: Many operations that would have required executing a series of external subscripts can now be accomplished by a single script in FileMaker Pro 7.

Script naming practices vary quite widely from developer to developer; even the authors of this book find it difficult to agree to a common standard. It's less important that you follow any particular naming convention than that you use a logical and consistent system. We do, nonetheless, recommend you consider some of the following ideas:

- Use hyphens, underscores, and so on to divide your scripts into logical groupings. As in other areas of FileMaker Pro, a single hyphen displays as a menu separator in the Scripts menu.

- Don't show all your scripts to your users. Surely most can be turned off! Choose deliberately which scripts you want to make available to users in the Scripts menu.

- Think of adding headers as shown previously in Figure 9.1. Organize your scripts into groups and then label them accordingly.

- When using subscripts (this topic is covered later in the chapter), you might consider indenting the names of subscripts with underscores or using a prefix naming style to indicate that a given script belongs to another "parent" script.

- Scripts are often intended to operate on a specific table occurrence (for example, if you're using a script to control the creation of a new record). It's a good idea to use short table prefixes or suffixes when a script applies to only a given table and "all" when it doesn't—for example, `New_Record_contact_to`, `Report_invoices_to`, or `Resize_Window_all`.

- If you plan on using Custom Web Publishing, we encourage you to avoid spaces and special characters in your script names. They're a pain to parse if you plan on calling these scripts from the Web. (Clearly those scripts you allow to be displayed in the Scripts menu need to follow user-friendly naming conventions.)

SCRIPT EDITING

After you create a new script in ScriptMaker, or edit an existing script, the Edit Script dialog opens (see Figure 9.2). Here you construct the actual script by inserting script commands from the list on the left into the window on the right. Nearly every script step has additional options you need to specify, such as the name of a layout to go to, or the name of a file from which to import. These options appear underneath your script when you highlight a given step in your script.

Figure 9.2
The Edit Scripts dialog presents you with additional dialogs as needed to configure settings for specific steps in your script.

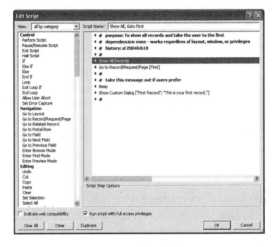

> **TIP**
>
> You can (⌘-click) [Ctrl+click] multiple script steps at once and insert the batch into a script in one move.

To reorder script steps, simply drag them by the two-headed arrow icon located to the left of the step. It's often handy to assemble a series of Loop steps or If steps and then click Duplicate to duplicate the batch as needed.

If Indicate Web Compatibility is enabled, script steps that are incompatible with Web publishing display in gray.

As an example, Go to Layout is a common step you'll use quite often. Notice that when you insert it into a script, a menu appears in the Script Step Options area at the lower right, from which you can choose an existing layout, the layout on which the script began, or one determined by calculation.

FULL ACCESS PRIVILEGES

Notice the Run Script With Full Access Privileges check box at the bottom of the Edit Script dialog. Designating that a script run with full access privileges means simply that for the duration of that script, FileMaker will override all security restrictions. When this option is *not* enabled, scripts run subordinate to whatever privilege set the currently signed-in user has. For instance, if a script makes a call to delete a record and the user who is running that script cannot do so based on his current security privileges, the script usually presents an alert message to the user and ignores that step of the script. The rest of the script is still performed.

→ Error management in scripts is an important element in all scripting. For more detail, **see** "Set Error Capture," **p. 250**, later in this chapter.

COMMENTING SCRIPTS

Keeping track of what scripts do is a difficult task. What seemed perfectly intuitive at the time you wrote a given script may become hopelessly obscure a few weeks—or sometimes even hours—later. Although developers vary in how they use comments, nearly all recognize their value.

Also remember that you're not coding in a vacuum. We can virtually guarantee that although you may never intend that a given database be seen by someone else's eyes, if it stands the tests of time and proves useful, at some point you'll crack it open with the infamous words, "Let me show you how I did this…." Likewise, professional-grade systems are nearly all collaborative efforts. Comments exist to help your peers understand what your caffeine-sodden brain was thinking at the time you wrote a particular routine.

A simple example of a commented script is seen in Listing 9.1.

LISTING 9.1   SCRIPT WITH COMMENTS

```
#   Purpose: initiate the running of a report while allowing users to choose
➥what sort order they want
#   History: sl 2004 02 04; bb 2004 02 05
#   Dependencies: Invoices: Monthly Report layout
#
#           prompt user for sort order
Show Custom Dialog [ Title: "Sort Order"; Message: "Do you want to sort by
➥amount or date?"; Buttons: "Date", "Amount", "Cancel" ]
#
#           check for cancel first
If [ Get (LastMessageChoice) = 3 ]
Go to Layout [ original layout ]
Halt Script
#
#           sort by Amount
Else If [ Get (LastMessageChoice) = 2 ]
Go to Layout [ "Monthly Report" ]
Perform Script [ "Sort by Amount" ]
#
#           sort by Date
Else If [ Get (LastMessageChoice) = 1 ]
Go to Layout [ "Monthly Report" ]
Perform Script [ "Sort by Date" ]
#
End If
```

Notice that in FileMaker Pro comments are prefixed by the "#" symbol.

USING A SCRIPT TEMPLATE

It is often helpful to create a template script that you can duplicate when you need to create a new script. In our templates, we include several comment lines at the top where we record information about the purpose and revision history of the script. A template script looks something like this:

```
# purpose: TYPEHERE
# dependencies: TYPEHERE
# history: XXX DATE
#
#
Allow User Abort [ Off ]
Set Error Capture [ On ]
#
#   establish context
Go to Layout [ Original Layout ]
#
#
```

Although it is simple, this template does save time and promotes good code. We recommend placing the Go to Layout step in your template, regardless of whether or not you'll need it in all scripts. In many cases you may simply delete it.

This final step ensures that the script begins on the correct layout and is associated with the proper base table attached to that layout. Including it in the template prompts developers to make a conscious decision and will remind you that context needs to be managed.

USING SUBSCRIPTS

One of the most useful things in ScriptMaker is the Perform Script step itself. One FileMaker script can call another script, which is then known as a subscript. This then allows you to divide scripts into smaller logical blocks and also break out discrete scripts for anything that you are likely to want to use again. This allows a degree of abstraction in your system that we very much recommend. Abstraction makes scripts easier to read, easier to debug, and modular—in that a subscript may be generic and used in a variety of scripts. Here's an example:

```
Sales_Report
# purpose: to run the Sales Report, weekly or monthly
# history: scl 2-5-2004
#
#
Perform Script [ "CheckPermission_forSales" ]
#
Perform Script [ "Find_CurrentSales" ]
#
Show Custom Dialog [ Title: "Run Report"; Message: "Would you like this
➥report broken out by Weekly or Monthly subtotals?"; Buttons:
"Monthly", "Weekly", "Cancel" ]
#
If [ Get (LastMessageChoice) = 1 ]
Perform Script [ "Monthly_Report" ]
#
```

```
Else If [ Get (LastMessageChoice) = 2 ]
Perform Script [ "Weekly_Report" ]
#
End If
```

Notice that the script offers a branch where one or another subscript will be run, but not both. It also has the `Find_CurrentSales` and `CheckPermission_forSales` scripts broken out—which means they can be called from a variety of scripts and are not necessarily specific to only this `Sales_Report` script.

As an example of script abstraction, imagine sorting a contacts database by last_name then first_name for a given report. If you've written a script to produce that report, sorting is a step in the process; however, odds are that you'll want to be able to sort by last_name, first_name again—perhaps for a different report, perhaps as a function that lives on a list view or in the Script menu, or perhaps prior to running an export script. Whenever is reasonable, we recommend looking for ways to abstract your code and foster reuse. It saves time and complexity if suddenly your client (or boss) comes to you and says you need to now present everything by first name. If that logic lives in one place, it's a one-minute change. If you have to hunt for it, it could take days and require extensive debugging.

Even if you're not planning on reusing blocks of code, it's still a good idea to break scripts into subscripts. They're easier to read, easier to turn on and off during testing, and allow you to name them in logical (even numeric, if you wish) ways that are comprehensible even at the Define Scripts dialog level.

Some other good candidates for subscripts are sort and find routines; these are often reusable by a wide range of scripts or by users as stand-alone functions. Other uses of subscripts might be for the contents of a loop or `If[]` function. Sometimes it's easier to separate logic into separate "paths" by dividing logical groups into separate scripts. When you have a branching script (covered later in the chapter) it's helpful to encapsulate a single branch in a subscript. This allows you to see the flow of logic in the parent script and cover each branch in its own respective subscript.

COMMON SCRIPTING TECHNIQUES

We will now delve into some useful and common scripting techniques. This is not meant to be a comprehensive list—the Beep script step should be fairly obvious to you—but rather these are the important areas to understand. They will help you establish a solid foundation in scripting.

→ For a reference to all the script steps in FileMaker 7, **see** Appendix C, **p. 927**.

ERROR MANAGEMENT

Error management is an important part of the scripting process. Frequently scripts make assumptions about the presence of certain data, the existence of certain objects, or depend on layout to establish context. If any of a given script's assumptions are not met, it either might not work or might produce unintended results. Error management involves identifying these assumptions and creating ways of dealing with them. You can bank on users finding odd, unpredictable ways to break your system. Applying some thought to how to manage such situations will serve you well in the long run.

FileMaker Pro's error handling is somewhat limited, but you do have some tools at your disposal.

→ For further discussion of error handling, **see** "Handling Errors in Scripts," **p. 486**.

To explore problems with error messages you think are being wrongly suppressed in scripts, refer to "Lost Error Messages in Script" in the Troubleshooting section at the end of this chapter.

Allow User Abort

`Allow User Abort` enables and disables a user's ability to hit the Esc key (or ⌘-period on a Mac) to cancel a script in midstream. Generally speaking it's the rare script that's designed to be cancelled gracefully at any time in its process. There's really no reason to ever turn `Allow User Abort` on, unless you're testing a loop script or some other long-running process. Any script without `Allow User Abort disabled` allows users to cancel a script in progress, with consequences that you may not intend.

The other thing `Allow User Abort` does is take away the Cancel button when a script pauses, giving users only the option to continue. There are many cases where canceling a script would leave them stuck on a report layout or stranded midstream in some extended process.

To learn more about how to deal with incomplete script completion (atomicity in database lingo), refer to "Unfinished Scripts" in the Troubleshooting section at the end of this chapter.

Set Error Capture

The `Set Error Capture` script step either prevents or allows error messages to be displayed to the user. When turned on, the script in question captures errors before presenting them to the user.

→ Handling errors well in scripts is a black art: It's difficult to always anticipate what errors will crop up. For more information on using the Set Error Capture script step, **see** Chapter 17, "Troubleshooting," **p. 475**.

It is possible, and very much preferable, to use the `Get(LastError)` calculation function to programmatically deal with errors within your script. The technique you'll need is to use the `If` function to test `Get(LastError)` and present dialogs to the user as appropriate. Refer to FileMaker Pro's online help system for a list of error codes.

Be careful with this script step. It certainly doesn't prevent errors from happening—it simply and rightly doesn't show the user a message about one that did. An error may happen, but the user's experience won't be interrupted to deal with it. This allows you to control how errors are managed within your script itself. You should not turn error capture on unless you have also added steps to identify and handle any errors that may arise.

If you have set up your own custom error handling routines, you'll clearly prefer to turn FileMaker Pro's standard alerts off.

SETTING AND CONTROLLING DATA

One of the primary uses of scripts lies in manipulating, moving, and creating data. Most of the script steps for manipulating field data are found in the Fields category.

Essentially these Fields steps allow you to insert data into a given field programmatically, just as a user otherwise would. This can mean setting the field contents to the result of a calculation, copying the contents of one field into another, or simply inserting whatever is on the user's clipboard.

As an example, imagine that you wanted to give users a button that would insert their name, the current date, and the current time into a "comments" field, then place the cursor in the proper place for completing their comment:

```
# purpose: To insert user and date/time data into a comment field, preserving
➡the existing information, and place the cursor in the correct position
➡for the user to begin typing.
# dependencies: Need to be on the Main_Info layout, with the Comment field
➡available. The script takes the user there.
# history: sl 2004 jan 25
#
#
Allow User Abort [ Off ]
Set Error Capture [ On ]
#
#
Go to Layout [ "Main_Info" (Movie) ]
#
#    this next step applies the comment info in italics.
Set Field [ Movie::Comment; TextStyleAdd (
Movie::Comment & "¶¶" & Get ( AccountName ) & " " &
Get ( CurrentDate) & " " & Get ( CurrentTime);
Italic)
& "¶" ]
#
Go to Field [ Movie::Comment ]
Commit Records/Requests [ No dialog ]
```

NOTE

> This script includes the full commenting approach described in this chapter and the two `Allow User Abort` and `Set Error Capture` steps. From here on out, we'll forego those details in the interest of brevity.

When using a `Go to Field` step, FileMaker Pro places the cursor at the end of whatever content already exists in the field, unless the Select/Perform option is enabled, in which case the entire field will be selected.

Notice that the comment info is nested within a `TextStyleAdd()` function so that it will be displayed in italics.

→ For more information on calculation functions, including text formatting, **see** Chapter 8 "Getting Started with Calculations," **p. 213**, and Chapter 14, "Specialized Calculation Functions," **p. 381**.

Set Field is by far the most used of the field category steps. The other functions in this category nearly all depend on the field in question being on the layout from which the script is being performed. You should get into the habit of using the Set Field command whenever possible. It doesn't depend on a field being on a specific layout—or any layout, for that matter—and it usually can accomplish what you're trying to do with one of the other steps.

You'll generally need the insert script steps only when you expect user input. For example, you might place a button next to a field on a given layout called "index" that then calls up the index for a given field and waits until the user selects from its contents.

That script could often be a one-step script: Insert from Index (table::fieldname). As always, you'd use your template for clarity, but this script would open the index for a given field and wait for the user to select a value. Again, you should tend to think of scripts as evolutionary. Consider writing a script even for one-step processes.

 To manage cases where your script seems to be affecting the wrong portal row or related record, refer to "Editing the Correct Related Records" in the Troubleshooting section at the end of this chapter.

➔ For more discussion on indexes, **see** "Storage and Indexing," **p. 82**.

CAUTION

> You may also discover the Copy, Cut, and Paste script steps. These work as you would expect. Copy and Cut place data onto the user's clipboard and Paste inserts from it. Cut and Copy overwrite anything already on the user's clipboard. Furthermore, Copy, Cut, and Paste depend on having access to the specified fields, and are therefore layout dependent. If, for some reason, you remove those fields from the specific layout in the future, your script will stop working. You should almost never use copy and paste for these reasons, and should defer instead to Set Field.

➔ For further discussion of layout dependencies, as well as other types of dependencies that can get your scripts into trouble, **see** "Context Dependencies," **p. 498**.

Another example of using the Set Field script step details how you might work with totaling child record data calculations. Often a simple calculation field with a Sum (related field) function works, but consider that with a large related data set, performance can become a problem. Furthermore, you cannot index that sort of a calculation field—which might prove problematic for users performing Find requests or for your needs as a developer. Consider instead creating a script to calculate your totals and calling that script only on demand.

PROVIDING USER NAVIGATION

You might have noticed in FileMaker's Edit Script dialog a subsection broken out for navigation. One of the most common uses of scripts is to provide a navigation scheme to users whereby they can navigate from layout to layout, record to record, or window to window by using buttons or some other intuitive means.

There's not too much magic here: By using the `Go to Layout` script step, you'll get the fundamentals. Consider placing buttons along the top of each layout that offer a means of navigating to all user-facing layouts in your solution with a `Go to Layout` script attached.

By building complete navigation scripts, you can control the entire user experience of your solutions and can opt to close the status area if you wish. Armed with find routines, sort buttons, reporting scripts, and a navigation interface, it is possible to build a complete application with a look and feel all its own.

Navigation can become quite complex. At the simplest level, a script attached to a `Go to Layout` command qualifies, but it's also possible to abstract a system by using the Go to Layout Name by Calculation options. It is now possible in this latest version of FileMaker to write one global navigation script for your system and control things by the attributes that you feed it.

→ For an explanation of advanced navigation techniques, **see** Chapter 13, "Advanced Layout Techniques," **p. 353**.

SCRIPT CONTEXT AND INTERNAL NAVIGATION

Consider that FileMaker uses layouts to determine script context: For any script step that depends on a specific table, you need to use `Go to Layout` steps to provide that context. If, for example, you need to create a related record in a child table, your script acts on context. Consider the following:

```
New Line Item
# assumes that the tempInvoiceID holds the key value the system needs
➥to establish a relationship from LineItems to Invoices
#
Go to Layout [ "LineItems" (LineItems) ]
New Record/Request
Set Field [ LineItems::keyF_invoiceID; Globals::tempInvoiceID ]
Commit Records/Requests
[ No dialog ]
Go to Layout [ original layout ]
```

The script takes itself to the LineItem layout, executes some steps (in this case creating a record and then setting a key field) and then returns to the original layout.

NOTE

> One technique is used in the script that helps make the script more portable: Notice that it doesn't assume anything about where it originated. You could call this script from anywhere in your system and, assuming your `tempInvoiceID` held either a proper value or intentionally did not, the script would perform just as you need.

The point here is that you'll need to bring a script to a specific layout to establish a different context. The user might never see this going on, but if you were to walk through the script step by step, you'd see the system go to the LineItem layout and then return to the layout from which the script originated.

MULTI-FILE NAVIGATION

Navigation becomes a bit more complex when you're working with multiple files. In general, placing all your user interface layouts in just one of your files is a good idea, but that doesn't save you from having to manage script context. To navigate to layouts external to your current file, you need to create "go here" scripts (that utilize a `Go to Layout` step) to be called as subscripts in your destination files. Also remember that if you want the user to visually see the new layout, you'll need a second step in your `Go Here` script: `Select Window ("current")`.

→ For a discussion of data-separation strategies, whereby you isolate your interface elements in one file, **see** "Separation of Data and Application Logic," **p. 205**.

It is helpful to distinguish scripts that reference external navigation as a reminder that the user might end up in a different file. Use a suffix such as _ext to distinguish those scripts.

SAVED SCRIPT OPTIONS

Scripts tend to mirror the actions a user could perform manually, but, obviously, do so without human intervention. It is possible in FileMaker to save Find, Sort, Export, and other actions in a script (hard-coding them, if you will), or to prompt the user for some input to help perform these steps.

The advantages of hard-coding requests should be fairly obvious. If, for example, you need to prepare a report on "active" real estate listings, it makes sense to have one of your script steps be a `Perform Find` that returns all the records with a status of "active." The requirements of your report will rarely change, so you'll save users time (and possible errors) if you hard-code the find request.

On the other hand, allowing the user to provide input is a great way to make scripts more flexible. Continuing the example, you might create a "real estate listings" report and then in your script prompt the user for some search criteria. This can be done by either using a dialog that gives them one or two choices (we'll cover that later in the chapter in the "Working with Custom Dialogs" section), or simply allowing the report to act on the current found set and sort.

You will often find it helpful to build pre-canned find and sort routines. For example, you might want a script for finding overdue invoices, or easy-access buttons for sorting by first name, last name, or company.

FileMaker allows you to save complex find, sort, export, and import requests as necessary, and allows you to edit these requests within ScriptMaker.

FileMaker 7 has a wide range of dramatic scripting improvements: script parameters, window management, account management, but among some of the most noteworthy improvements is the ability to create explicit, editable find, sort, and export script steps. This alone is worth the price of admission.

FIND SCRIPT STEPS

FileMaker allows you to assemble and store complex find requests within scripts. In Figure 9.3, the script finds all overdue invoices over $500 and, in the same Perform Find step, omits invoice number 2004.1.1; the result replaces the found set.

Figure 9.3
Assemble as many find requests as necessary.

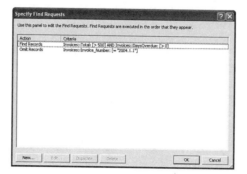

Notice that multiple requests have been added; this enables you to perform Or finds where you will be left with records that match either the first condition *or* the second.

A single Find request is assembled via the Edit Find Request dialog (see Figure 9.4).

Figure 9.4
By adding multiple criteria to a single find request, you will be performing an And search.

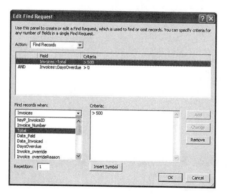

Note in Figure 9.3, however, that we have opted to omit records that match the second request. Setting a request to omit records simply means that FileMaker will find those records that match the overall request and then take out or ignore those that meet the omit criteria. If you create a find request that does nothing but omit records, it replaces your existing found set with all records that don't match your request. (How's that for a double negative?)

```
Find_Overdue_Invoices
Perform Find [ Specified Find Requests: Find Records; Criteria: Invoices::Total:
➥"> 500"
AND Invoices::DaysOverdue: "> 0"
Omit Records; Criteria: Invoices::Invoice_Number: "= "2004.1.1"" ]
[ Restore ]
```

Other search-related script steps include Constrain Found Set and Extend Found Set. Just as though a user had chosen each command from FileMaker's menu-driven interface, Constrain reduces the current found set, eliminating any records that don't match the search criteria, and Extend adds those records from outside the set that match its criteria to the current found set.

SORT SCRIPT STEP

Establishing saved sort orders in the Sort dialog works, happily, just as it does for users performing a manual sort (see Figure 9.5).

Figure 9.5
It's generally quite helpful to create sorting scripts for users. Sorting needs are usually fairly predictable and always needed more than once.

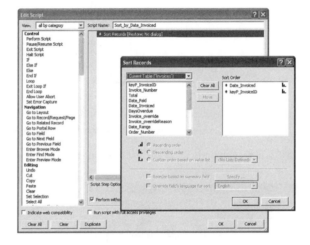

One of the most common applications of sort scripts is in building column header buttons. Simply create a series of sort scripts and apply them to the buttons along the top of a list view (see Figure 9.6).

Figure 9.6
Scripting is often employed in creating more intuitive user interfaces for users.

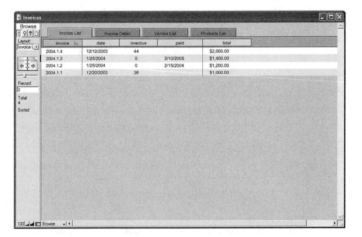

Keep in mind that many of your reports depend on sorting, especially as you get into reporting by summary data. It's a good idea to create sort scripts for your reports and call them as subscripts, rather than hard-coding sort routines into your report scripts themselves.

You may well create reports that behave differently depending on different sort orders—by setting up different, multiple subsummary parts on one report layout, for example—so you'll want to factor the sorting logic into its own script or subscripts. A report with both a week-of-year sub-summary part and a month sub-summary part will display by week, by month, or by week and month depending on the sort options your script establishes. This is a handy technique for reducing the number of layouts you need in a system—with a little bit of scripting you can use a single layout for three different reports.

→ For more on summary reporting, **see** Chapter 10, "Reporting with Grouped Data," **p. 269.**

USING CONDITIONAL LOGIC

Another important element of scripting is the ability to branch scripts based on various conditions. To manage logically branching scripts, you use the If, Else, Else If, and End If script steps.

These conditional script steps work by performing a logical test, expressed as a calculation. If that calculation formula resolves to a true statement, FileMaker then executes all the script steps subordinate to (that is, nested within) an If or Else If statement.

Here's the idea, without troubling with FileMaker syntax:

```
If person is a student

   Go to school

Else

   Go to work

End If
```

In this simple logic, when you test to see whether a particular person is a student, he either will be or won't be. The test resolves to either a true condition or a false condition. This simple branch assumes that anyone who isn't a student should be going to work.

Let's add some complexity—choose four possible avenues for, say, a family of four:

```
If person is "Dad"

    Go to work

Else If person is "Mom"

    Go to work after dropping kids off

Else If person is a "kid"

    Get dropped off at school
```

```
Else If person is "Grandparent"

    Start third career

End If
```

Okay, your family might not be quite so well organized, but this should give you the gist of things.

Logical conditions can be nested as well. Nesting allows you to define trunk-branch logic trees: What if it's Saturday?

```
If today is a weekday

    If person is "Dad"

        Go to work

    Else If person is "Mom"

        Drop kids off at school

        Go to work

    Else If person is "kid"

        Get dropped off at school

        Learn

    Else If person is "Grandparent"

        Start third career

    End If

Else If today is a weekend

    If person is "Dad"

        Sleep in the hammock

    Else If person is "Mom"

        Visit friends

    Else If person is "kid"

        Spend the day with grandparents

    Else If person is "Grandparent"

        Watch the kids

    End If

End If
```

These concepts should be fairly intuitive to follow. By using these sorts of nests and branches, it's possible to create some dramatically complex scripts. Don't forget that comments and breaking things into subscripts help with clarity.

Figure 9.7 shows an example of a real-world conditional script.

Figure 9.7
Notice that scripts within FileMaker's Script Editor are automatically indented. Liberal use of comments will help make scripts readable.

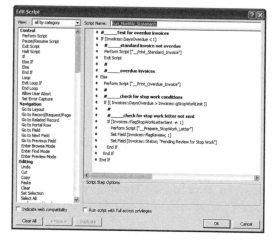

To learn how to bake error checking into your conditional tests, refer to "Conditional Error Defaults," in the Troubleshooting section at the end of this chapter.

USING LOOPS

Another key scripting technique is looping. Looping allows you to execute a series of script steps over and over until some exit condition is met.

A simple example of this might be stepping through each record in an invoice table's found set and generating a new invoice for any that remain unpaid or that somehow need to be sent out again. The logic, again without worrying about syntax, looks like this:

```
Go to first record in found set.

Begin Loop.

    Check whether the invoice is closed. (We'll assume
    unclosed invoices are those that need to be resent.)

    If CLOSED

        Go to next record.

        If there is no next record (you're at the end of
        your found set), then exit the loop (go to step 3).

        Else begin loop again (go to step 2).
```

```
If NOT CLOSED

    Close current invoice.

    Create/duplicate new invoice. (In a real system,
    there would likely be more steps involved here.)

    Go to next record.

    If there is no next record (you're at the end of
    your found set), then exit the loop (go to step 3).

    Else begin loop again (go to step 2).

End Loop

Exit Script
```

Notice that an exit condition is established. The system tests, in steps, both `If` steps whether or not you're at the end of a found set.

Imagine you're a user doing this manually. You'd start at the top of a found set, use the book icon to page through each record one at a time, and then stop the process after you reach the end of your record set.

Here's another example, this time in FileMaker's syntax. It creates a series of 10 new order records.

```
NewOrdersBatch
Set Field [ Invoices::gLoopCounter; 0 ]
Loop
    Set Field [ Invoices::gLoopCounter; Invoices::gLoopCounter + 1 ]
    Perform Script [ "__NewOrder" ]
    Exit Loop If [ Invoices::gLoopCounter = 10 ]
End Loop
```

This simple example demonstrates all the essential logic for working with loops. First, some condition by which the script exits the loop must be established. In this case a hard-coded number (10) is used to exit the script.

Second, notice that a field was created to keep track of the iterations through the loop. Often called a *loop counter*, it is initialized (set to an initial value) just in case it was left at some different number from another script or, as is the case here, at the end of this script. An improper starting condition for a loop is a common source of bugs.

Third, the counter is incremented as you go. A loop exit condition is almost always useful only if something changes during the course of a script. (It's possible you might be sitting in a loop, waiting for something elsewhere to change and checking periodically, but this kind of "polling" activity is not commonly needed in FileMaker Pro.)

Notice too where the commands are placed. It is not until after the __NewOrder script is performed that the exit loop condition is tested. This ensures that the script does, in fact, run 10 times. If the __NewOrder script were placed below the `Exit Loop If` step, this script would still be perfectly valid, but it would generate only 9 new orders.

Loops get more interesting when combined with conditional logic more complex than checking for an incremented counter. The first example for closed invoices did just this. It is possible to build a loop that tests for certain conditions within your system and exits only when those conditions are met—for example, a loop that processes all unclosed invoices, checking at the end of each cycle whether it has reached the end of a found set.

Loops can be exited in a variety of ways. The simple conditional in the script example shown earlier is quite common. Another common technique is to use the Go to Record/Request/Page [Next, Exit After Last] script step. It enables you to step through a found set and exit a loop after the last record is reached.

Another way to exit a loop is to exit or halt the script altogether. You have two processes running: the script itself, which can be terminated, and the internal loop.

To cope with endless loop problems, refer to "Testing Loops" in the Troubleshooting section at the end of this chapter.

WORKING WITH CUSTOM DIALOGS

One of the most common user interactions necessary for a system is to capture a response to a question. "Are you sure you want to delete all records?" "Do you want to report on all records, or just your found set?" "Would you like fries with that?"

The Show Custom Dialog script step is a great, built-in way to capture this sort of interaction. (There are ways to create layouts that act and behave like dialog boxes, but they're a good bit more work.) Custom Dialogs allow you to present some descriptive text or a question to a user and capture a response (see Figure 9.8).

Figure 9.8
Here's an example of a custom dialog. Notice that it has an appropriate title and specific, data-derived text.

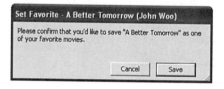

→ To learn how to create pop-up layouts that behave as modal dialogs, **see** "Multi Window Interfaces," **p. 367**.

Naturally, after you've created a custom dialog, you then need to deal with the results. FileMaker Pro stores the user's button choice until the end of the current script or until you present another custom dialog. Think of these dialogs as existing solely within the space of a given script.

To identify which response the user chose to your dialog, use the Get (LastMessageChoice) function. This function returns a 1, 2, or 3 based on which button was clicked, from right to left. The right-most button is identified as 1. The label you assigned to the button is not consequential.

Conditional scripting similar to what was covered previously allows you to test the choices a user made and respond accordingly. Here's an example:

```
Report_Revenue_Start
Show Custom Dialog [ Title: "Revenue Report"; Message:
"Do you want to view a Revenue
➥Report by month, year, or a date range?";
Buttons: "Range", "Year", "Month"; Input #1:
➥Invoices::Date_Range, "Date Range (e.g., 1/1/2004...2/15/2004)" ]
If [ Get ( LastMessageChoice ) = 1 ]
    Perform Script [ "__Report_DateRange" ]
Else If [ Get ( LastMessageChoice ) = 2 ]
    Perform Script [ "__Report_YearSummary" ]
Else If [ Get ( LastMessageChoice ) = 3 ]
    Perform Script [ "__Report_MonthSummary" ]
End If
```

Custom Message dialogs can also be used to guard against data problems and help offer users a somewhat richer data entry process. Figure 9.9 presents an idea of what this might look like. Instead of going with FileMaker's standard "Revert Field" response to a validation error, you might instead want to build a script that checks your data either on demand or as part of a scripted data entry routine. This completely skips the standard field validation options in FileMaker and instead offers users the chance to correct their data in a dialog. Keep in mind that they'd need to perform this script somehow.

Figure 9.9
This custom dialog offers a graceful alternative to FileMaker's native validation dialogs, but would need to be prompted by a script.

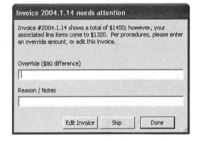

Here's an example of how you might handle validation in a scripted way:

```
Validation_Prompt
#
# Assume this next step checks some condition and sets the gInvalidFlag
# to a value if there is an error.
    Perform Script [ "__Validation_Check" ]
#
If [ Invoices::gInvalidFlag > 0 ]
#
# Notice in this next step that a case statement analyzes the error message
# passed to it.
    Show Custom Dialog [ Title: "Shipping Correction"; Message: Case (
    Invoices::gInvalidFlag = 1;
    "You have entered a shipping date that precedes order fulfillment. Please
enter a corrected ship date.¶¶
    Order " & Invoices::Order_Number & "¶Date to be fulfilled: " &
    ➥Invoices::Order_Date_Fulfillment;
```

```
    Invoices::gInvalidFlag = 2;
    "Your ship date cannot be more than 14 days past your fulfillment date.
Please enter a corrected ship date.¶¶
       Order " & Invoices::Order_Number & "¶Date to be fulfilled: " &
       ➧Invoices::Order_Date_Fulfillment;
    Invoices::gInvalidFlag = 3;
    "Your ship date is set for the same day of fullment, but this is not marked
as a rush order. Please enter a corrected ship date.¶¶
       Order " & Invoices::Order_Number & "¶Date to be fulfilled: " &
       ➧Invoices::Order_Date_Fulfillment;
       "The system has posted an invalid internal error message [error code: " &
    Invoices::gInvalidFlag & "] ; please contact the database developer, and
    reference the 'Validation Prompt' script routine. We apologize for the
    inconvenience." ); Buttons: "Done", "Edit Order"; Input
       #1: Invoices::Order_Date_Shipping, "Ship Date" ]
    If [ Get ( LastMessageChoice) = 2 ]
        Perform Script [ "__Edit_Order" ]
        Exit Script
    Else
        #
        # Here we're employing some recursion. After the user inputs a new Ship
Date, we'll run this script again until it validates. Notice that the exit
condition is an error message of < 1 at the top of the script. The inner IF
statement will only proceed if gInvalidFlag >0.
        Perform Script [ "Validation_Prompt" ]
        End If
End If
```

A better way to handle this script would be to better abstract your error messages and conditions. Imagine a table of error ID numbers followed by explanation text. Simply reference a table of related values, and the very long, hard-coded case statement goes away.

Custom dialogs are fairly flexible, but they do have limitations. The most obvious limitation is that their appearance cannot be altered. In a FileMaker layout you're able to apply images, background color fills, and other graphical attributes of the screen. Not so in a custom dialog. You are limited to a system-style dialog.

Second, and more importantly, if you provide input fields (as was shown in Figure 9.7), data entered is posted to your database only if the user clicks the first, right-most button in the dialog. You do not have programmatic control of the input field behaviors. This then means your users will have "post to database" as their default. Not optimal, but there you have it.

The third limitation of the dialog lies in scope: You're limited to three input fields and three buttons. If you need anything more complex, you need to use a standard FileMaker layout to build a custom pop-up layout.

TIP

> One alternative to keep in mind is a range of plug-ins available that also offer dialogs. Visit FileMaker's Web site to explore those options.

TRIGGERING SCRIPTS

There are six ways to initiate—or "perform"—scripts:

- By selecting them via the Scripts menu
- By opening the Scripts Dialog, selecting a script, and clicking Perform
- By calling them from another FileMaker script (within the same file or externally)
- By calling them from an external Web source
- By attaching them to a layout element, which a user then clicks
- By attaching them to the startup or shutdown routines in the file preferences dialog

FileMaker Pro lacks most procedural triggers—functions that fire automatically when certain events, such as creating or editing a record, occur. (An exception is that you may configure a file to run a specific script when the file is opened or closed.) For a script to be performed, the user needs to click something. Scripts can be attached to layout objects, so that they are triggered by a user clicking on the object, or they can be activated directly from the Scripts menu, if you've chosen to make particular scripts visible there. There are other ways to call scripts externally through Web publishing as well.

→ To call scripts externally through Instant Web Publishing, **see** Chapter 21, "Instant Web Publishing," **p. 605**.

WORKING WITH BUTTONS ON LAYOUTS

More often than not, clickable layout objects are graphical buttons, but it is possible to attach a script to anything you can place on a layout: a field, a graphic, even a portal. These layout objects then become "button-like," so that when a user clicks such an object, the object's associated script runs.

Creating buttons on FileMaker layouts is fairly straightforward. You can opt to use the button tool to draw a 3D-esque button, or you can attach a button behavior to any object on a layout (including fields, merge fields, text, images, and even binary files pasted onto layouts).

Apply button behaviors to an object by either right-clicking and choosing Specify Button, or, with a layout object selected, navigate to the format menu and choose Button.

We've talked about buttons as a tool for triggering scripts. This is actually a little inaccurate. A button, when clicked, can perform any single script step: Go To Layout, for example, or Hide Window. Of course, one of the available script steps that you can attach to a button is Perform Script. Choose that option, and your button can perform a script of any length or complexity.

Given that fact, when adding interactivity to a button, why use any of the other single script steps other than Perform Script itself? Well, we're going to argue that you shouldn't. If you use single script steps, you're out of luck if you ever want a button to do two things, and you're out of luck if you create a bunch of buttons that perform the same step (such as Go to Layout) and you need to change them all—it's insufficient abstraction to not allow the same button behavior to be reused elsewhere. Because it's likely that you will want to add steps, or duplicate a button and edit its behavior globally, you should ignore every button behavior other than Perform Script. Even if a script is one step long and is likely never to be reused, still take the few extra seconds to create a script. If the button performs a script, you can easily add steps whenever you need them, and all the buttons that need to go to, say, the Invoice layout can be changed at once. After you've selected the script in question, you can opt to modify the behavior of the script that may or may not be currently running.

→ For more details on controlling script flow via button attributes, **see** "Script Parameters," **p. 422**.

TROUBLESHOOTING

LOST ERROR MESSAGES IN SCRIPTS

My script is not working properly, but I'm not getting any error messages. Where do I start?

Be sure that you properly account for potential errors if you turn error capture on. What if a find request returns zero records? What if a user doesn't have access to a given layout, which is needed for a script? To manage debugging, turn error capture off while you're testing. Some developers write scripts that toggle error capture for all scripts in a system. This is a convenient way to turn on and off a debugging mode.

UNFINISHED SCRIPTS

I need a script to run to completion without fail. I set Allow User Abort [off], but it appears that the script was aborted at some point by a user. How can I make sure users can't muck with my scripts?

Remember that turning Allow User Abort off doesn't always save you from errors in the script itself, power outages, the user closing FileMaker Pro, or other random acts of unpredicted computer wonkiness. You can never absolutely depend on a script completing in FileMaker Pro. If need be, write a "check conditions" script in your system and run it when appropriate. Another way to deal with this problem is to write a script log that saves a record when a script starts and another when it ends. You can check for incomplete pairs.

EDITING THE CORRECT RELATED RECORDS

My Set Field script step is just continually changing the first record in a portal instead of the one I want. How do I get the script to act on the proper row?

Be careful when setting fields through relationships. It's possible to think that you're pointing to a single record when you're really pointing to the first of many. In that case, FileMaker blithely applies your script steps to the first valid related record it finds. Either put a button directly in a portal—in which case the script will apply to that row—or use a Go To Related Record script step to explicitly control both the context and the record against which a script operates.

CONDITIONAL ERROR DEFAULTS

My case statement isn't returning the proper result. How can I test what's going on?

Be sure to account for all variations of logic in your conditional scripts. It is strongly recommended that you build If routines that end with an option that you think will never occur. Here's a quick example:

```
If [Invoices::Total > 0]
    Do something
Else If [Invoices::Total = 0]
    Do something
Else If [Invoices::Total < 0]
    Do something
Else
    Handle error conditions here
End
```

This function should *never* return the default error but you cannot perfectly predict all such behaviors. For example, what if a calculation for Total is wrong and returns a null or empty value? Or perhaps a calculation you expect to be numeric returns text in some cases?

TESTING LOOPS

My loop seems to be stuck endlessly looping. How do I debug the problem?

The rare developer gets everything right the first time, but if you don't, you might find yourself in the middle of an endless loop. A handy trick is to always create an exit condition that tests whether the Shift key is held down by using the Get(CurrentModifierKey) function. It's a backdoor out of your loop that's quite handy if you have an error in logic. A much easier way to go if you own FileMaker Developer is to simply turn on the script debugger the first time you test a new loop.

FILEMAKER EXTRA: CREATING A SCRIPT LIBRARY

You might consider having a utility file sitting around your hard drive with all the basic scripts each of your solutions will need. You can then import these scripts into your own solution files as needed. We always have the following in our databases:

- Relogin—This script should be the first you have in every file. Press (⌘-1) [Ctrl+1] (if it's turned on in the menu) and you'll be able to relogin and test how things work for your end users. This is a critically useful script to have access to during development and testing.

- StartUp—Here's a script we use to open all the files of a given solution at once, to set default values for globals, to set a login history record if need be, and so on.

- ShutDown—The partner for StartUp, ShutDown can close out your user session by setting any tracking info and can close all the files in a solution so that FileMaker Pro need not be quit.

- ToggleAllStatusAreas—This is another critical script for developers working in multiple files or windows. Very often we'll close and lock the status area to maintain control and keep users from accessing records or layouts we have carefully scripted around. This handy script re-opens the Status Area for development.

- **ToggleMultiUser**—A script that simply turns on or off peer-to-peer sharing. It is useful to use the Set Multi-User [on/off] script step when you need to isolate your system during testing.

- **InitializeGlobals**—Often a subscript of StartUp, but best abstracted as it is here, this script sets all the initial values of globals in your system, ensuring that they all start out user sessions in a predictable state. You need to add explicit steps for each global you add to your system as you work, but you'll find it invaluable to have a "global" global initializer.

- **ScriptTEMPLATE**—This is the template we duplicate for new scripts. It has initial comment headers and default script steps as needed.

- **- **—Okay, maybe it only saves you a single keystroke, but having an already-ready hyphen handy just means a quick click on the duplicate button. (And a nice touch from the engineers at FileMaker: In this version, hyphens simply duplicate and don't get suffixed with a "copy!")

- **PrintSetUp_landscape** and **PrintSetUp_portrait**—Every printer-bound output of your system needs page properties established. Write them once.

- **___ScriptHEADER_____**—Here's an empty script for dividing your script menu into logical subsections. Again, clicking the Duplicate button means you don't need to count how many underscores to use.

If you find yourself writing certain scripts time and time again, add them to your library. Using FileMaker 7's import script capability enables you to more easily leverage prior work.

CHAPTER **10**

REPORTING WITH GROUPED DATA

In this chapter

DERIVING MEANING FROM DATA

Reporting is an important component in almost every database project. Indeed, the need to create reports that summarize or synthesize data is often the reason many databases exist in the first place. No matter what your database does, it's a fair bet that you have many reporting needs.

Reports come in many shapes and sizes: There are simple list reports, summarized reports, workflow reports, cross-tabulated reports, variance reports, and graphic reports (to name but a few). There are standard reports that need to be generated periodically; there are ad hoc reports where the report criteria need to be defined on the fly. Some reports need to be printed and distributed, whereas others are meant to be viewed on screen.

Despite the wide range of "things" that can be classified as "reports," most reports tend to have a few characteristics in common:

- Reports are generally used for viewing data rather than creating or editing data.
- Reports generally display (or draw on data contained in) multiple records from a table. They are usually designed to provide an overview or higher-level understanding of a data set than you would obtain by looking strictly at data entry screens.
- Reports capture a snapshot in time and reflect the database's current state. Running the same report at different times may yield different results if the data in the system has changed.

To generate meaningful reports, you should learn several standard reporting techniques. From there, it's just a matter of coming up with variations that suit your particular needs. This chapter covers working with lists of data and reporting with grouped data (also known as *sub-summary reports*).

BEGIN WITH THE END IN MIND

In our experience, one of the keys to creating successful reports is beginning with the end in mind. By this, we mean that you should begin thinking about the reports that a system will need to generate right at the beginning of a project. A system's intended outputs can have a profound impact on its design and implementation.

A few simple illustrations will help clarify this point. Say that you've been asked to design a contact management system, and that the client mentions that he wants the system to be able to track a history of conversations and interactions with each of his clients. From a data entry standpoint, you could create this sort of functionality either by having a single long "Notes" field in the Contact table, or you could set up a related "Contact History" table and use a portal to capture information about each interaction separately.

All other considerations aside (for example, time/cost to implement, rules of normalization), the reporting needs of the client may influence your decision about how to implement this feature. If you don't ask the right questions up front, you may find out in two months that the client expects to be able to generate a report of call activity summarized by account representative. This report would be relatively simple to generate if you had chosen the route of the related Contact History table; it would be virtually impossible to generate from a single undifferentiated "Notes" field.

Another typical example of reporting needs driving feature implementation is the decision to use check boxes to capture data. Check boxes are fantastic from a data entry standpoint, but may limit your reporting capabilities because they store multiple pieces of data in the same field. For instance, imagine that in the contact management system you're building, the client asks you to put a check box field on the layout so that users can select one or more "Sources" for the contact (such as "Referral," "Conference attendee," "Web site").

If you know that one of the reports the client wants is a "Contact Source Summary" that lists the various sources and the total number of contacts each has generated, one would hope that you'd not implement the feature as a check box field. With potentially multiple sources selected for a given contact, it's not straightforward to split the selections apart. Instead, if you set up a Source table and a ContactSource table (as a join table between Contact and Source), then you could display and maintain the contact's sources via a portal from Contact into ContactSource. The desired report could easily be generated from the ContactSource table. The point here is simply that the reporting requirement informs both the table structure and the user interface.

In both of the previous examples, choosing a more fully normalized data structure happened to provide the more robust reporting capabilities, but there are certainly just as many occasions where you'll find that opting for a de-normalized data structure makes for better, faster reporting. For example, imagine you're a teacher creating a system that will track the scores on eight quizzes you plan to give to your class. You could set up a Student table and a related Quiz table (which would eventually contain eight related records for each student record), or you could just create a Student table with eight QuizScore fields. If one of your goals was to get a spreadsheet-like report that listed students down the side and quizzes going across, you'd have a significantly easier time using a "flat file" than you would if quiz scores were broken out into their own table. Of course, the flat file approach is not without its own problems and limitations. By "hard coding" the number of quizzes, you restrict possible future expansion. Similarly, a seemingly simple ad hoc question, like "Which students scored a perfect 100 on at least one of the quizzes?" would be difficult to answer with the scores spread across eight fields.

The point of both of these examples is simply to demonstrate what we mean by "begin with the end in mind." Over the course of this chapter, you'll learn more about these types of reports. For now, what's important is that as you define the requirements for any database system, be sure to think carefully about the reporting needs. If you don't, you may end up having to rewrite sections of your system and/or create more complex reporting routines later on.

DETERMINE REPORT REQUIREMENTS

Just as a system's reporting requirements influence its design, an organization's business needs influence the design of the reports themselves. When thinking about how you'll go about generating any given report, ask yourself (or your client/users) the following types of questions:

10

- What questions is this report trying to answer? Focus first on the purpose the report will serve, not on its design. Is it trying to monitor progress toward a goal? To be an early warning of potential problems? To help spot business trends? The more you know about how a report will be used, the more effective you can make it.

- Who will read this report? Is it going to be used strictly for internal purposes, or might it be presented to customers or vendors? Should the report be accessible to everyone, or should certain users be prohibited from viewing it?

- How will be it read? Will it be distributed in hard copy, emailed to a group of people, or read on screen 18 times a day?

- Is this a one-time report, or will it be used on a regular basis? For one-time or special occasion reports, you probably won't go to the trouble of setting up scripts and/or find screens, but you should do so for reports that are intended to be run regularly.

- What level of granularity is appropriate? Will the consumers of the report be interested in seeing details, or just the big picture?

After you've collected answers to questions like these, we strongly recommend writing out a sample report (using whatever tools you choose…pencil and paper and white boards are our favorites) and showing it to its appropriate consumers for feedback.

GENERIC VERSUS SPECIFIC REPORT STRUCTURES

Another part of report planning is determining whether the report is to meet a specific or a generic need. That is, should users be able to select a data set to feed into a report "shell," or should the search criteria for the report be hard-coded?

For example, say you have a list view layout that displays customer data. If you feed it a found set of customers obtained since a certain date, then it becomes a "New Customers" report. If you feed it a set of inactive customers, the same shell is transformed into an "Inactive Customers" report.

In instances like this, it's often helpful to think of a report as consisting of two distinct components: its format and its content. If you can create a generic multi-purpose format, then simply by sending in different content, you "create" different reports. The point is that in planning out reports, you should have the distinction between format and content in mind. You can sometimes save yourself a lot of work if you recognize when a report can be created by simply feeding new data into an existing format.

As a classic example of this separation between format and content, we had a client who wanted a 10 a.m. activity report and a 2 p.m. activity report. Now, the reports showed the same sort of information; they just contained different sets of data. But in discussing these reports, it was very clear that to the client these were two different reports. Any time we made a change to the 10 a.m. report, he would always remind us to be sure to change the 2 p.m. report also. We tried to explain why that wasn't necessary, but it never really sank in.

WORKING WITH LISTS OF DATA

Many reports are nothing more than simple lists of data. Examples include such things as task lists, customer lists, overdue invoice reports, student test scores, and phone directories. Besides being the most frequently encountered types of reports, lists of data are also the easiest types to create. As such, they provide us with a good starting place to begin delving into report creation.

List view layouts can be created with the Layout Wizard or by hand. Figure 10.1 shows an example of a basic list view layout that displays student names and quiz scores. Depending on your needs and aesthetics, this alone might serve as a report.

→ For more on creating layouts and working with layout tools, **see** "Working with Objects on a Layout," **p. 103**.

Figure 10.1
Basic list view layouts are the simplest types of reports you can create.

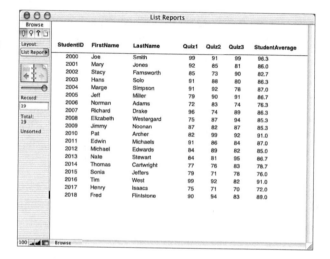

Beyond being simple to create, list views make nice reports for several other reasons. The first is that they're very flexible. You can allow users to perform ad hoc finds, or you can program scripts with "canned" searches, and then simply display the results using your list view.

Users can also view list reports while in Browse mode. This isn't the case with subsummary reports, which can be viewed only in Preview mode. The key benefit of being able to work with a report in Browse mode is that you can place buttons on your report that give the user additional functionality, such as drilling down to additional levels of detail, or re-sorting the data without having to regenerate the report. There may be buttons (or other objects) on your layout that you wouldn't want to appear when the report is printed (such as navigation buttons). While building the report in Layout mode, select those objects and then choose Format, Sliding/Printing to open the Sliding/Printing dialog, then select Do Not Print the Selected Objects.

NOTE

> If your users are likely to print from a list view, be sure that you constrain your report to the width of the printed page rather than the monitor screen width. You'll also find that although 10–12 point fonts generally work well for reports that will be viewed onscreen, 8–10 point fonts are more appropriate for printed reports. Be sure to actually print out your reports to proof them rather than simply rely on what you see on screen.

If you have problems printing your reports, see "Printed Reports Show Only a Single Record" in the Troubleshooting section at the end of this chapter.

Of course, you can make your list view layout as crafted and fancy as you desire. You might consider employing some common techniques, however, for enhancing list view reports.

TRAILING SUMMARIES

A list report in and of itself does little synthesizing of data; it just organizes data for easy review. The main tools at your disposal for synthesizing a set of data are summary fields. Summary fields enable you to perform aggregations across a set of records, including counting, totaling, and averaging.

→ For more information about creating summary fields, **see** "Working with Field Types," **p. 69**.

Adding a trailing grand summary part to a basic list report gives you a place to put summary information about the set of records in your report. For example, in a list report that displays invoice data, you might choose to put the total amount invoiced in the trailing grand summary part.

→ For more information about working with layout parts, **see** "Working with Parts," **p. 99**.

Summary fields placed in a leading or trailing grand summary part summarize the entire found set of data, so as you feed different sets of records into a report, your totals change accordingly. Figure 10.2 shows the same report as Figure 10.1, except that here four summary fields (Average_Quiz1, Average_Quiz2, Average_Quiz3, Average_Overall) have been added to the database and placed in a trailing grand summary.

Figure 10.2
Summary fields placed in a trailing grand summary part act upon the entire current found set.

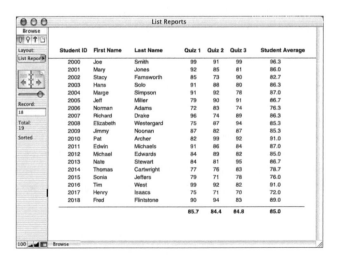

ALTERNATING ROW COLOR

NEW Another enhancement that you may wish to make to a list report is to alternate the row color. This is a new feature in FileMaker Pro 7, and it can make reports much easier to read and more aesthetically pleasing. The option to alternate row color is found in the Part Definition dialog, which is shown in Figure 10.3; the quickest way to get there is by double-clicking on the body part label while in Layout mode. Figure 10.4 shows the effect that this feature can have on a list report.

Figure 10.3
The option to alternate row colors can be applied only to body parts; it is grayed out as an option for any other type of part.

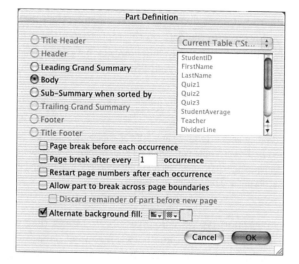

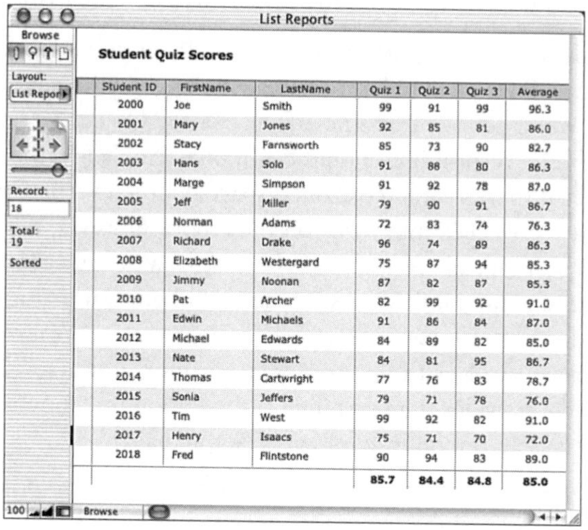

Figure 10.4
Adding a subtle alternate row color can make a list report much easier to read.

Alternating the row color is more appropriate for use in reports that are to be viewed onscreen rather than printed, but if you use a light enough color, it may still print well. If you have a need for both print and onscreen versions of the same report, you may end up creating two different layouts, each optimized for a particular usage. This is more work, of course, but is certainly the best solution in many cases.

HORIZONTAL AND VERTICAL DIVIDERS

Another method of increasing the readability of a list report is to add horizontal and/or vertical lines between the columns and rows. When both are used, the resulting report may resemble a spreadsheet; your perception of whether this is good or bad should guide your use of dividers.

We find that using thin gray lines as dividers is more effective than using solid black lines. That way, it's easier to differentiate the data on the report from the grid. There's a risk, though, that too many grid lines, especially in a complex list report, can actually obscure the data. Try to use just as many lines and/or field borders as necessary to increase the readability of your report, but no more.

Report Aesthetics
In some sense, the use of dividing lines is certainly an aesthetic choice. But there's a sense where it's not: The well-respected design expert Dr. Edward Tufte wrote in the *Visual Display of Quantitative Information* about the concept of data-ink ratio. Eliminating "chart junk," such as most borders, frames, and gridlines, gives the data room to breathe without sacrificing any readability or meaning.

Placing dividers into your report typically involves nothing more than drawing some lines on the layout. When adding a horizontal line between rows of data, we generally put it beneath the data as a baseline rather than above it. You can then add whatever effect you need beneath your column headers to set them apart from the first row of data.

Adding vertical dividers to a list report can be a bit tricky until you get the hang of it. The key is that your vertical lines need to be the same height as the height of the body part itself. If they're too small, you'll get a dotted-line effect. Use the Object Size palette to ensure an exact fit. The top of your vertical line should begin one pixel below the top of the body part. It usually looks better if there's some horizontal space between vertical lines and your data cells. If users are allowed to click into fields on the report, however, the field frames that appear may not look aesthetically pleasing. If your list view is truly acting as a report, then you should turn off entry into all fields (using the Field Behavior dialog). That also means that your field frames will never be visible, which is a good thing. Your vertical lines can define the space between fields without interference from field frames. If users need to be able to click into fields, consider then turning off the option to "Show Field Frames When a Record is Active"; this is an option in the Layout Setup dialog.

→ For more on the Layout Setup dialog, **see** "Creating and Managing Layouts," **p. 91**.

If you find that horizontal lines between every row of your report makes the report look too cluttered, it's possible also to add horizontal lines that just appear, say, every fifth row. The effect of this is illustrated in Figure 10.5.

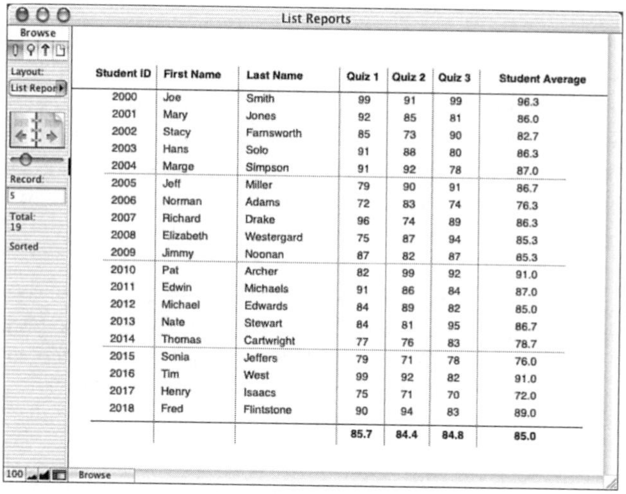
List Reports
Browse
Layout:
List Report
Record:
5
Total:
19
Sorted
Student ID | First Name | Last Name | Quiz 1 | Quiz 2 | Quiz 3 | Student Average
2000 | Joe | Smith | 99 | 91 | 99 | 96.3
2001 | Mary | Jones | 92 | 85 | 81 | 86.0
2002 | Stacy | Farnsworth | 85 | 73 | 90 | 82.7
2003 | Hans | Solo | 91 | 88 | 80 | 86.3
2004 | Marge | Simpson | 91 | 92 | 78 | 87.0
2005 | Jeff | Miller | 79 | 90 | 91 | 86.7
2006 | Norman | Adams | 72 | 83 | 74 | 76.3
2007 | Richard | Drake | 96 | 74 | 89 | 86.3
2008 | Elizabeth | Westergard | 75 | 87 | 94 | 85.3
2009 | Jimmy | Noonan | 87 | 82 | 87 | 85.3
2010 | Pat | Archer | 82 | 99 | 92 | 91.0
2011 | Edwin | Michaels | 91 | 86 | 84 | 87.0
2012 | Michael | Edwards | 84 | 89 | 82 | 85.0
2013 | Nate | Stewart | 84 | 81 | 95 | 86.7
2014 | Thomas | Cartwright | 77 | 76 | 83 | 78.7
2015 | Sonia | Jeffers | 79 | 71 | 78 | 76.0
2016 | Tim | West | 99 | 92 | 82 | 91.0
2017 | Henry | Isaacs | 75 | 71 | 70 | 72.0
2018 | Fred | Flintstone | 90 | 94 | 83 | 89.0
85.7 | 84.4 | 84.8 | 85.0
100
Browse

Figure 10.5
Having lines appear less often provides the visual guide necessary to follow a row across but doesn't overpower the data itself.

You need to add two new fields to your table to achieve this effect. The first is a global container field, which we'll call `gLine`. Place this field on a layout that you can use as a scratch pad (we generally refer to these as "utility layouts"), then draw a horizontal line on your layout. Copy the line to your clipboard, switch back to Browse mode, and paste the line into the `gLine` field.

The other field you need is a calculation field (set to return a container result) with the following formula:

```
Case ( Mod ( Get (RecordNumber) ; 5 ) = 0 ; gLine )
```

In effect, this formula says that for any record that's a multiple of five, be the contents of `gLine`, or else be nothing.

On your list layout, finally, you'd place the calculation field as a long, thin object along the bottom of your body part. You need to reduce the field's font size to make the object thin. Also, go into the Graphic Format options for the field (by right-clicking it in Windows, Control-clicking it on Mac): select the Reduce or Enlarge Image to Fit Frame option, uncheck the Maintain Original Proportions option, and set the alignment to be Left, Bottom.

NOTE

> You might be wondering whether you can just use Table view for your list reports; it provides a lot of the functionality discussed here (gridlines, sortable headers) for free. In general, though, Table view isn't suitable for reports, especially those that need any degree of "polish" to them. For one thing, the column labels must be the names of your fields; if you use any naming conventions your field names may not be terribly user friendly. Another issue in some reports is that you can't have multiple lines of data per row or any objects that overlap one another. Finally, one of the major drawbacks to Table view is that buttons and other layout objects don't show up.

10

SORTABLE COLUMN HEADERS

An interface convention that's been widely adopted by software applications is that clicking on the various column headers of a list report sorts the set of records by that column. It's relatively easy (especially after you've done it a few times!) to add this sort of functionality to your list reports in FileMaker Pro. There are several ways you can go about this, but they're all essentially variations on the same basic theme, so we present a relatively "vanilla" method that you can spice up as you see fit.

NOTE

> Another easy way to sort a set of records is to (Control-click) [right+click] on any field and choose Sort Ascending or Sort Descending. You don't need to know the name of the field or fret about finding it in a long list of available fields.

The two components of a sortable column header routine are a script (which does the actual sorting) and a graphic indicator to let the user know by which column the list is sorted. You can use whatever graphic indicator you want for this purpose. The simplest, and what we use here, is simply a special background color, but you can also use other indicators if you prefer. Figure 10.6 shows an example of what a list layout might look like after sortable column headers have been implemented. In the example, the set of records has been sorted by the values in the Quiz1 field.

TIP

> An alternative to indicating the sort column graphically is to use text formatting functions to change the appearance of the column labels. It's quite similar to the approach discussed here, except that you would use calculated text fields rather than calculated container fields.

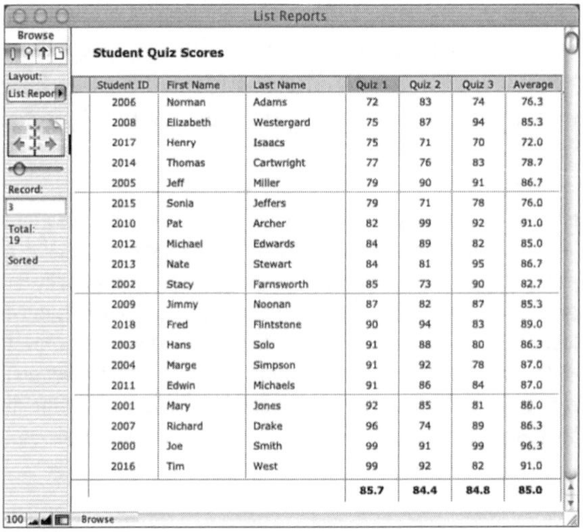

Figure 10.6
Users can re-sort this list report any way they want by clicking on the column headers.

Several fields need to be added to your database to make the graphic indicators for this routine. These fields can be added to whatever table you're working with (here, Student), but it's also possible (and arguably better) to place these new fields into a separate table. This allows them to be reused in other places, and it also helps keep your data tables free of clutter. In this example, the utility table is called globals.

The following fields need to be created in the globals table:

```
gHighlight - Container - Global

gSortField - Text - Global

Highlight_Quiz1 - Global Calculation - Case (gSortField = "Quiz1" ; gHighlight)

Highlight_Quiz2 - Global Calculation - Case (gSortField = "Quiz2" ; gHighlight)

Highlight_Quiz3 - Global Calculation - Case (gSortField = "Quiz3" ; gHighlight)

Highlight_Average - Global Calculation - Case (gSortField = "Average" ;
➥gHighlight)

Highlight_FirstName - Global Calculation - Case (gSortField = "FirstName" ;
➥gHighlight)

Highlight_LastName - Global Calculation - Case (gSortField = "LastName" ;
➥gHighlight)

Highlight_StudentID - Global Calculation - Case (gSortField = "StudentID" ;
➥gHighlight)
```

Notice that all the calculation fields have been set to use global storage. This is so they can be used on any layout, even by those attached to unrelated tables. They should also be set to return a container result. After gSortField has been set to the name of a field from the quiz score report (this happens in the script shown in Listing 10.1), one of the seven calculations will resolve to the contents of gHighlight; the other six will be empty.

After these fields have been defined, you need to put a swatch of color into the gHighlight field. Switch to Layout mode and draw a colored rectangle. Copy it to your clipboard, return to Browse mode, and paste it into the gHighlight field.

There's still a little layout work to be done on the report itself.

1. Position a single gray rectangle behind all the column labels.
2. Place horizontal lines on top of the gray bar as necessary to segment the header row.
3. Then, on top of the gray bar (but beneath the column labels), place the seven Highlight calculation fields from the globals table. Each should be sized to fit its particular label.
4. Define each to be a button that calls a script called "List Report - Sort" (which is shown in Listing 10.1; you need to create the script before defining the headers as buttons).

Although all seven buttons call the same script, each passes that script a unique parameter. In this example, the parameters are simply the names of the fields themselves. That is, clicking on the Quiz 1 header sends the parameter Quiz1, and clicking on the First Name field sends the parameter FirstName. You can also choose to pass a numeric code instead of the field name. This type of abstraction makes the buttons more reusable and means that you don't have to edit the parameter if your field names change, but we think it's more intuitive when learning this routine to use the actual field names.

→ For more information about using script parameters, **see** "Script Parameters," **p. 422**.

LISTING 10.1   LIST REPORT-SORT SCRIPT

```
Set Field [globals::gSortField; Get(ScriptParameter)]
If [Get (ScriptParameter) = "Quiz1"]
    Sort Records [Restore; No dialog]
Else If [Get (ScriptParameter) = "Quiz2"]
    Sort Records [Restore; No dialog]
Else If [Get (ScriptParameter) = "Quiz2"]
    Sort Records [Restore; No dialog]
Else If [Get (ScriptParameter) = "Average"]
    Sort Records [Restore; No dialog]
Else If [Get (ScriptParameter) = "FirstName"]
    Sort Records [Restore; No dialog]
Else If [Get (ScriptParameter) = "LastName"]
    Sort Records [Restore; No dialog]
Else If [Get (ScriptParameter) = "StudentID"]
    Sort Records [Restore; No dialog]
End If
```

Each of the Sort Records steps is defined to sort by the appropriate field. Also, because gSortField is set in the first step, the correct Highlight field will be turned "on" in the globals table; after the sort is performed, the column heading will therefore accurately reflect the sort order.

> **TIP**
>
> If you have your list report displayed simultaneously in multiple windows, each report can be sorted differently, but the graphic sort indicator highlights the same field in all the windows. That is, if you were to click on the "Last Name" header in the active window, that window's found set would be sorted appropriately, but all open windows would have "Last Name" highlighted as the sort order, even when they may in fact be sorted differently.

You can easily extend this example on your own to allow for both ascending and descending sorts. To do so, you would need another field in the globals table (something like gSortDirection) to indicate the direction of the sort. Then add more conditional statements to the script so that a combination of field name and direction determines how to sort the records. Finally, alter the Highlight calculations in the globals table so that they display different images for ascending and descending sorts. You can either create a separate global container field to house the descending image, or simply turn gHighlight into a repeating field and have a conditional statement in the calculation resolve to the appropriate repetition. As an example, the definition for Highlight_Quiz1 might end up as the following:

```
Case (gSortField = "Quiz1" Case (gSortDirection = "Ascending" ; gHighLight[1] ;
➡ gHighLight[2] )
```

Finally, because the sort order and the column images are all based on global fields, this routine is multi-user friendly. Two different users can be viewing the same report but have it sorted differently.

GO TO DETAIL

No matter whether the set of records displayed in your list report is the result of an ad hoc find by a user or a canned report routine, you'll probably want to enable users to see additional details for a particular record. Typically, if you allow users to enter into fields in the list report, then you have a discrete button at the beginning or end of the row that a user can click on to get to a detail view. If you don't allow data entry, then it's common to let a user click anywhere on the row to be taken to a detail screen. To achieve the latter result, place a long transparent rectangle (to which you attach a navigation script) on top of the row. It should be the same height as the body itself so that there aren't any dead spaces between rows.

You have a few choices about how to display the detail record. The easiest thing to do is have the script navigate to a form view data entry layout. Another option to consider is to have the detail record pop up in its own window. This enables users to go back and forth more easily between detail and list layouts.

→ For more on scripting techniques like this, **see** "Window Management Techniques," **p. 430**.

SUMMARIZED REPORTS

Subsummary reports are perhaps the most useful and durable of all the reporting techniques in FileMaker Pro. It takes but little effort to extend a list report into a summary report, but the additional amount of information they can convey is significant. After you become comfortable with the basic techniques for creating subsummary reports, you'll find that they form an important part of your reporting repertoire.

As a good place to start thinking about subsummary reports, consider the sample data set in Table 10.1.

TABLE 10.1   STUDENT DEMOGRAPHIC DATA

Gender	Name
Male	Conrad
Female	Jasper
Male	Nate
Male	Kai
Female	Rona

If this data set were to be presented in FileMaker Pro as a subsummary report, it might be structured something like the following:

Female

    Rona

    Jasper

Male

    Conrad

    Nate

    Kai

You can easily see that the difference in the subsummary version is that the data has been grouped by gender. The heading for each particular group of data only appears once instead of redundantly on each record of the list.

USING A BREAK FIELD

In this example, the Gender field is acting as the *break field*. Understanding break fields is crucial for understanding subsummary reports. The break field is the column of data that determines what records appear with what grouping of information. The number of unique entries in the break field for the current found set of data (here, two: Male and Female) determines the number of groupings, or subsummaries, that will be present on the report.

The purpose of a break field is to segment your data into useful subdivisions. As such, break fields are almost always categorical (rather than continuous) data elements. As an example, in a billing system you probably wouldn't choose to use an invoice total or invoice date field as a break field, but you might use an invoice type, invoice status, or invoice month field. The main purpose of subsummary reports is to enable you to "roll up" data to a less granular level, so that you see larger trends in your data that may be obfuscated when looking at simple lists. The break field defines how those larger trends will be manifested on your report. Thus, it makes no sense to use a field with unique values (that is, a primary key) as a break field because there's no grouping of records by common values that could possibly take place in such a situation.

NOTE

> Break fields can be text, number, time, date, or timestamp fields, or a calculation that returns one of these data types. Fields with global storage should not be used as break fields because they provide no categorization of the data.

CREATING A SUBSUMMARY REPORT

The physical creation of a subsummary report is quite similar to the creation of a simple list report. The Layout Wizard, in fact, has an option within the Columnar List/Report type to make your list a Report with Grouped Data. For our purposes here, we discuss how to turn a list report into a subsummary report. You can explore the wizard's capabilities on your own.

→ For more on the layout wizard, **see** "Creating a New Layout," **p. 91**.

Earlier in the chapter, we developed a Student Quiz Scores list report. Now that example will be extended into a subsummary report. Assume that each of the students has been assigned to a teacher (Donovan, Ferris, or Young); the present goal is to produce a subsummary report of the scores by teacher. Figure 10.7 shows the data from which the report will be generated (as a simple list).

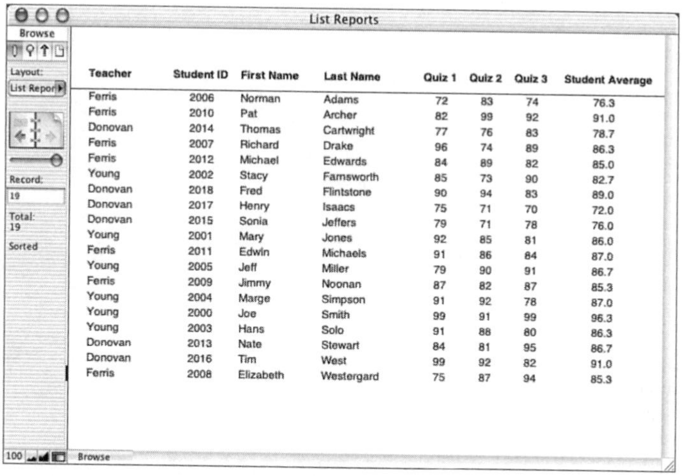

Figure 10.7
Any time data can be grouped according to a common element, you have the potential for a subsummary report.

Teacher	Student ID	First Name	Last Name	Quiz 1	Quiz 2	Quiz 3	Student Average
Ferris	2006	Norman	Adams	72	83	74	76.3
Ferris	2010	Pat	Archer	82	99	92	91.0
Donovan	2014	Thomas	Cartwright	77	76	83	78.7
Ferris	2007	Richard	Drake	96	74	89	86.3
Ferris	2012	Michael	Edwards	84	89	82	85.0
Young	2002	Stacy	Farnsworth	85	73	90	82.7
Donovan	2018	Fred	Flintstone	90	94	83	89.0
Donovan	2017	Henry	Isaacs	75	71	70	72.0
Donovan	2015	Sonia	Jeffers	79	71	78	76.0
Young	2001	Mary	Jones	92	85	81	86.0
Ferris	2011	Edwin	Michaels	91	86	84	87.0
Young	2005	Jeff	Miller	79	90	91	86.7
Ferris	2009	Jimmy	Noonan	87	82	87	85.3
Young	2004	Marge	Simpson	91	92	78	87.0
Young	2000	Joe	Smith	99	91	99	96.3
Young	2003	Hans	Solo	91	88	80	86.3
Donovan	2013	Nate	Stewart	84	81	95	86.7
Donovan	2016	Tim	West	99	92	82	91.0
Ferris	2008	Elizabeth	Westergard	75	87	94	85.3

The first step to turning this into a subsummary report is to add a new part to the layout. It's possible to do this simply by clicking on the Part tool in the status area (in Layout mode, of course) and dragging a new part into existence. We prefer, however, to use the Part Setup dialog (select Layouts, Part Setup) to create new parts.

→ For a discussion of why it's better to use the Part Setup dialog than to drag from the status area, **see** "Working with Parts," **p. 99**.

When you add a subsummary part to a layout, you must specify what break field should be represented by that part. In this example, shown in Figure 10.8, the Teacher field has been selected as the break field. Subsummary parts can be placed either above or below the body part. You can change the order of parts from the Part Setup dialog. Place a summary part above the body if you want it to act as a header for the data set; place it below if you want summary information about a subset of records to appear below the data set. You can (and indeed often will) place both a leading and a trailing subsummary part on a layout as well.

After you've added a subsummary part to the layout, you next place fields, texts, and/or graphic elements in the part. Any objects that you place in the subsummary part appear on your report once for each group of data. You will typically place the break field itself in the subsummary part, but this isn't required. As is discussed shortly, any other fields that you place in the subsummary part are usually summary fields. Figure 10.9 shows what the new Quiz Scores by Teacher report looks like in Layout mode; the Teacher field and a horizontal line have been placed in the subsummary part. Notice also that the Teacher field has been removed from the body part, as it would be redundant.

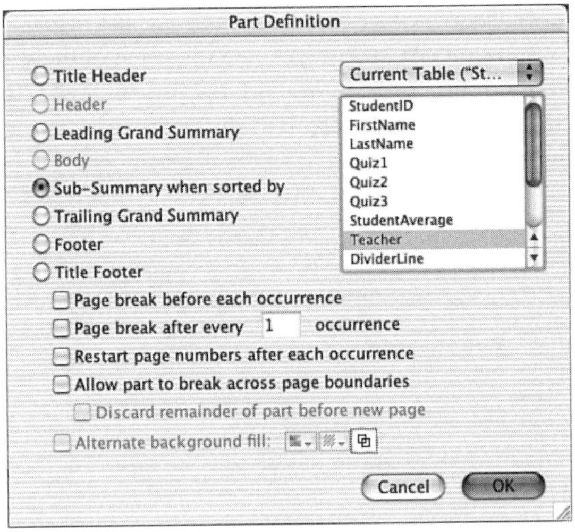

Figure 10.8
The only time you'll be able to select from the field list in the right side of this dialog is when you choose the Sub-Summary When Sorted By option.

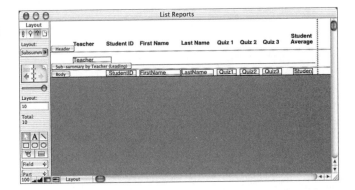

Figure 10.9
A subsummary part is used to display data relating to a set of records.

> **TIP**
>
> In Layout mode, the part labels can either appear as they do in Figure 10.9—as horizontal blurbs at the lower-left corner of the part—or as rotated text along side of the part. Labels are easier to read as horizontal text, but they tend to get in the way, so we usually leave them along side of the parts. You can toggle between the two settings either by clicking on the part label orientation button (the 5th button in from the left at the bottom of your window) or by (⌘-clicking) [Ctrl+clicking] on any of the part labels themselves.

Before looking at the actual report, you must keep two points in mind at all times when working with subsummary reports. First, the found set of records must be sorted by the break field to be presented properly. In the quiz score report, this means sorting by the Teacher field before viewing the report. (It doesn't matter how it's sorted...ascending, descending, or by the contents of a value list.) Second, you must be in Preview mode to view a subsummary report. Subsummary parts are simply not visible while you're in Browse mode. One of the implications of needing to be in Preview mode is that the user can't directly interact with the report in any way; buttons aren't functional in Preview mode. Users can, however, still run scripts from the script menu.

TIP

> If you ever have problems with getting a subsummary report to work correctly, the first thing you should check is that you have the data sorted by the same field(s) that you're summarizing by and that you're in Preview mode.

Figure 10.10 shows the completed (for now) subsummary report. Comparing this to Figure 10.7, it's easy to see how simply grouping data together according to a common data element makes it much easier to read.

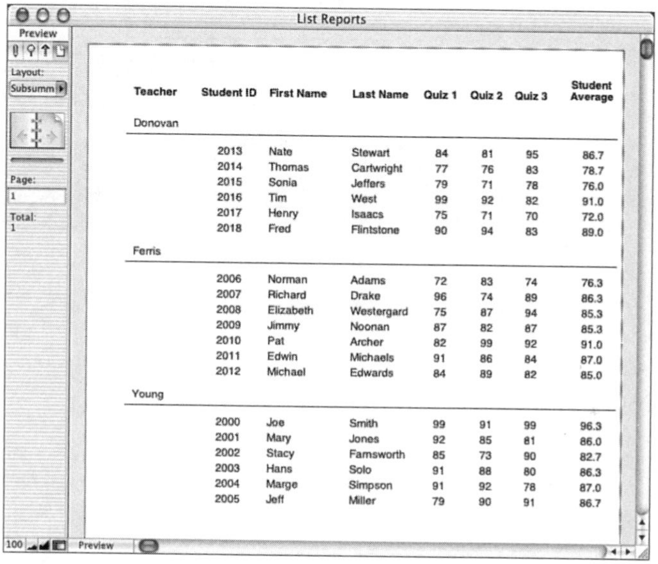

Figure 10.10
This subsummary report groups records together based on the contents of the Teacher field.

Teacher	Student ID	First Name	Last Name	Quiz 1	Quiz 2	Quiz 3	Student Average
Donovan							
	2013	Nate	Stewart	84	81	95	86.7
	2014	Thomas	Cartwright	77	76	83	78.7
	2015	Sonia	Jeffers	79	71	78	76.0
	2016	Tim	West	99	92	82	91.0
	2017	Henry	Isaacs	75	71	70	72.0
	2018	Fred	Flintstone	90	94	83	89.0
Ferris							
	2006	Norman	Adams	72	83	74	76.3
	2007	Richard	Drake	96	74	89	86.3
	2008	Elizabeth	Westergard	75	87	94	85.3
	2009	Jimmy	Noonan	87	82	87	85.3
	2010	Pat	Archer	82	99	92	91.0
	2011	Edwin	Michaels	91	86	84	87.0
	2012	Michael	Edwards	84	89	82	85.0
Young							
	2000	Joe	Smith	99	91	99	96.3
	2001	Mary	Jones	92	85	81	86.0
	2002	Stacy	Famsworth	85	73	90	82.7
	2003	Hans	Solo	91	88	80	86.3
	2004	Marge	Simpson	91	92	78	87.0
	2005	Jeff	Miller	79	90	91	86.7

After you have a good grasp of the concepts at work in a basic subsummary report (like the one presented in this section), you can extend them in a number of ways to produce even more interesting and/or meaningful reports.

If you are experiencing performance issues when generating subsummary reports, see "Slow Generation of Subsummary Reports" in the Troubleshooting section at the end of this chapter.

USING SUMMARY FIELDS IN SUBSUMMARY REPORTS

Earlier in this chapter, we discussed how you could add summary fields to a leading or trailing grand summary part to enhance a basic list report. Summary fields, not surprisingly, are also quite appropriate for use in subsummary reports.

A summary field placed in a subsummary part generates aggregate results for each group of data presented in the report. You need to do nothing in terms of field definitions to make it work this way. After you've defined a summary field, you can place it in any subsummary part and it will be intelligent enough to act upon the correct group of records.

In the example file we've been discussing, for instance, the summary field Average_Quiz1 is defined to be the average of the Quiz1 field. When this field is placed in a trailing grand summary, it displays the average of that field across the entire current found set. When it's placed in a subsummary (by teacher) part, it displays the average for each teacher's set of students. In Figure 10.11, a trailing subsummary by teacher and a trailing grand summary part have been added to the layout shown previously in Figure 10.9. The same four summary fields appear in both parts. The report generated by this layout is shown in Figure 10.12.

Figure 10.11
Summary fields placed in a subsummary part calculate aggregate results for each group of data presented in the report.

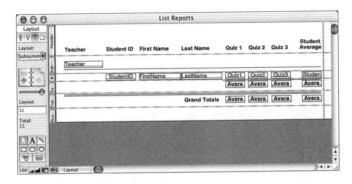

Figure 10.12
The leading and trailing subsummary parts can be thought of as providing a header and footer for each group of data presented in the report.

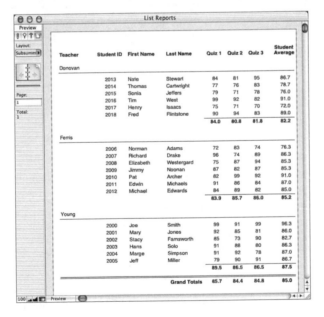

If another subsummary report were built that summarized on, say, students' genders or favorite pizza toppings, the same summary fields could be used in that report. Summary fields are thus quite versatile and powerful creatures. You'll find that after you've developed one subsummary report it's quite easy to duplicate the layout and change the break field specified for the summary part(s), thereby creating an entirely new and different report. For example, the layouts needed to generate Quiz Scores by Teacher, Quiz Scores by Gender, and Quiz Scores by Favorite Pizza Topping would be nearly identical to each other; you wouldn't need to modify the definitions of the summary fields in any way.

CAUTION

> If you ever put a summary field into the body part on a layout, it displays, for every record, the aggregated result for the entire found set.

CALCULATIONS INVOLVING SUMMARY FIELDS

After you begin using summary fields on reports, you're likely to come across situations where you need to perform some sort of calculation involving a summary field. For instance, in the Student Quiz database, imagine that Quiz 1 was a pre-test for a unit and that Quiz 3 was a post-test for the same unit. You might want to find out the change in scores from the pre-test to the post-test.

For an individual student, you could generate this by simply adding a calculation field called something like ScoreIncrease, defined as Quiz3 - Quiz1. But what if you wanted to find out the average increase for each class? Can you do math with summary fields?

The answer to the last question is both yes and no. Summary fields shouldn't be used directly in calculation formulas. There's nothing to prevent you from doing so, but it's usually nonsensical to do so. Inside a calculation formula, a summary field is evaluated as the aggregate result of the entire found set. Thus, if you were to define a field called Average_ScoreIncrease as Average_Quiz3 - Average_Quiz1, the result would be -0.84 no matter what record you were viewing or in what layout part you placed the field. This formula doesn't properly generate subsummary values.

The solution to the problem is to use the GetSummary function. GetSummary takes two parameters: a summary field and a break field. When the current found set is sorted by the break field, this function returns the same value that would appear if the summary field were used in a subsummary layout part (based on the same break field, of course). If the found set is *not* sorted by the break field, the function returns the value of the summary field over the entire found set, which the astute reader should recall (from the preceding paragraph) is the same value returned by simply putting a summary field in a calculation without the GetSummary function.

In the current situation, to produce a summary ScoreIncrease at the teacher level, the following calculation (called Average_ScoreIncrease_Teacher) would be necessary:

```
GetSummary (Average_Quiz3 ; Teacher) - GetSummary (Average_Quiz1 ; Teacher)
```

This field could then be placed in the trailing subsummary part to display the results for each teacher.

The fact that you must name a break field explicitly means that calculations involving summary fields aren't as re-usable as summary fields themselves. If you were making another report showing quiz scores by gender, you would need a new calculation field called Average_ScoreIncrease_Gender that specified Gender as the break field instead of Teacher. Similarly, for use in a trailing grand summary, you'd need yet another version of the formula that didn't use GetSummary at all.

If this lack of reusability is a problem for you, then there actually is a way around the break field problem. The solution is to make a new field—a global text field—that you set (either manually or via script) to be the name of the break field that you need. Then you can dynamically assemble an appropriate GetSummary function and use the Evaluate function to return the proper value. Using this technique in the present example, you would just define a single Average_ScoreIncrease field with the following formula:

```
Evaluate ( "GetSummary(Average_Quiz3; " & gSortValue & ")") -
➥Evaluate ( "GetSummary(Average_Quiz1; " & gSortValue & ")")
```

Although the purpose of using a GetSummary function is to produce a value appropriate for display in a subsummary part, the values also display "properly" when placed in a body part. That is, each of the records of the subgroup knows the aggregate value for its particular set. This is distinctly different than the result of simply placing a summary field into a body part, in which case the value displayed represents an aggregation of the entire found set.

SUMMARIZING ON MULTIPLE CRITERIA

All the examples thus far in this chapter have had a single summary criterion. It's but a small additional effort to produce a report that summarizes on multiple criteria. In fact, there's no practical limit to the number of subsummary parts that you can add to a layout, except perhaps your ability to make sense of the results.

Summarizing based on multiple criteria is simply another way of categorizing a set of data. In the examples you've seen here, the student quiz scores have been grouped by teacher—a single criterion. What if within each teacher's group of students, you wanted to subcategorize by gender?

To accomplish this, you would add another summary part to your report layout. The subsummary part by gender would be positioned between the subsummary by teacher and the body. If you wanted trailing summary information as well, a second subsummary by gender would be placed between the body and the trailing summary by teacher. Figure 10.13 shows what such a layout would look like.

Figure 10.13
To summarize on multiple criteria, create additional subsummary parts on your layout.

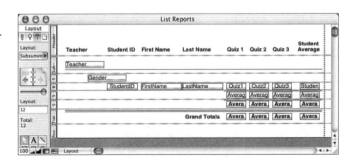

To properly generate this report, you would need to make sure that your found set was sorted first by `Teacher` and then by `Gender`. The finished report is shown in Figure 10.14. If it were sorted by only one of those fields, then you would end up with a single criteria sub-summary report; the other part would not be displayed on the report. This means that a single layout can generate several different reports, if just the sort criteria is changed.

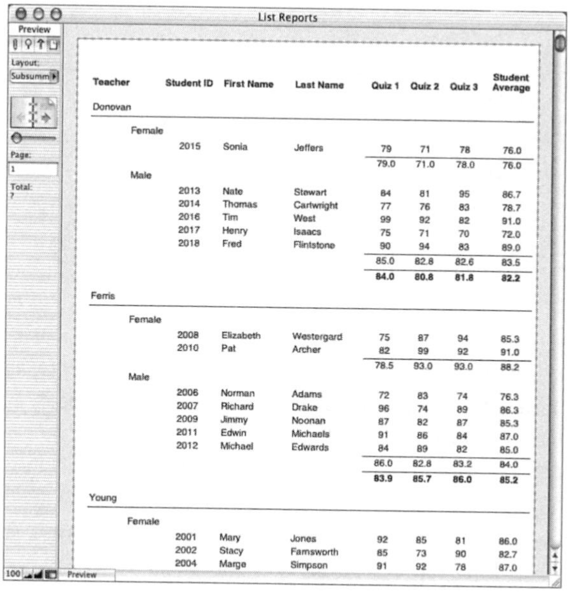

Teacher	Student ID	First Name	Last Name	Quiz 1	Quiz 2	Quiz 3	Student Average
Donovan							
Female							
	2015	Sonia	Jeffers	79	71	78	76.0
				79.0	71.0	78.0	76.0
Male							
	2013	Nate	Stewart	84	81	95	86.7
	2014	Thomas	Cartwright	77	76	83	78.7
	2016	Tim	West	99	92	82	91.0
	2017	Henry	Isaacs	75	71	70	72.0
	2018	Fred	Flintstone	90	94	83	89.0
				85.0	82.8	82.6	83.5
				84.0	**80.8**	**81.8**	**82.2**
Ferris							
Female							
	2008	Elizabeth	Westergard	75	87	94	85.3
	2010	Pat	Archer	82	99	92	91.0
				78.5	93.0	93.0	88.2
Male							
	2006	Norman	Adams	72	83	74	76.3
	2007	Richard	Drake	96	74	89	86.3
	2009	Jimmy	Noonan	87	82	87	85.3
	2011	Edwin	Michaels	91	86	84	87.0
	2012	Michael	Edwards	84	89	82	85.0
				86.0	82.8	83.2	84.0
				83.9	**85.7**	**86.0**	**85.2**
Young							
Female							
	2001	Mary	Jones	92	85	81	86.0
	2002	Stacy	Farnsworth	85	73	90	82.7
	2004	Marge	Simpson	91	92	78	87.0

Figure 10.14
Typically when you develop a subsummary report based on multiple criteria, you should use dividing lines and/or indentation to clarify the report structure.

TIP

> If you were to sort the found set first by `Gender` and then by `Teacher`, your report might look a bit strange. That would have the effect of reversing the placement of the two subsummary parts; the data set would be separated first by gender, then within each gender by teacher. If you've built your report with any sort of indentation (as in these examples), then reversing the summary hierarchy would mean that the wrong headings would be indented.

REORDERING A REPORT BASED ON SUMMARY DATA

When you create a subsummary report, the groups are ordered according to how you have sorted the break field. For example, in the Quiz Scores by Teacher reports, the groups are ordered as Donovan, Ferris, Young. A descending sort would have resulted in the groups being ordered as Young, Ferris, Donovan.

NEW It's possible also to reorder the groups based on a summary field. To do this, when you sort the found set, click one of the sort criteria and then select the Reorder Based on Summary Field option. Figure 10.15 shows the Sort Records dialog with this option specified.

Figure 10.15
A new option in the Sort Records dialog in FileMaker Pro 7 is the capability to reorder the set based on a summary field. This enables you to generate ranking reports at a group level.

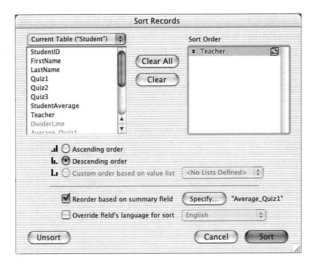

NOTE

The interface for reordering a sort based on a summary field is different in FileMaker Pro 7 than in previous versions. In FileMaker Pro 7, you can specify a reordering at any level of a multi-criteria subsummary report.

The typical reason you would want to reorder your report based on a summary value is to produce group-level ranking reports. As an example, if the Quiz Scores by Teacher report used the sort shown in Figure 10.15, where the Teacher sort criteria is reordered by the value of Average_Quiz1, the results would be the report shown in Figure 10.16. Notice that Young is the first group; her student average on Quiz 1 was 89.5. Donovan is next with a student average of 84.0, followed by Ferris at 83.9.

If you have a subsummary report with multiple summary levels, you can reorder the subgroups at any level of the report. When you do this, keep in mind that you can (and probably will) end up with a situation where the subgroups are ordered differently within the groups. That is, if you did a secondary sort by Gender (reordered by one of the summary fields) on the data in Figure 10.16, you would find that sometimes Male appeared before Female and that other times Female appeared first; each group's subgroups are ordered independently.

SUBSUMMARY REPORTS WITH NO BODY PART

In a typical subsummary report, a subsummary part serves to organize and/or present summary data about a subgroup of data that is detailed on the report. All the subsummary reports presented so far in this chapter, in fact, fit this structure.

Figure 10.16
Reordering the set by a summary field produces a group-level ranking report.

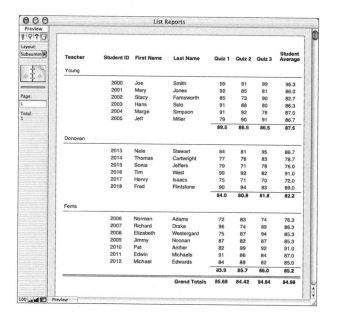

But there's no reason why you can't remove the body part from your report, thereby just presenting some sort of listing of the groups themselves. Especially if your groups consist of large record sets, simply presenting the aggregated groups may result in a report that's much more meaningful. If a more detailed view of things is required, you can either provide it in a different report or simply allow users to perform ad hoc searches.

TIP

> You can also allow users to toggle the body part "on and off" by redefining it as a subsummary by the primary key. That way, when the found set is sorted by the primary key, the faux body part is visible. When sorted by just the break field, it disappears.

Figure 10.17 shows a quiz scores report in which the body part has been removed. The absence of a body part means that it's not necessary to have both a leading and trailing subsummary part; there's nothing that would appear in between them, so it's not necessary. Similarly, the only columns of the report are the break field (Teacher) and four summary fields. It doesn't make any sense to have fields like FirstName or StudentID because those aren't representative of an entire group of records.

The subsummary techniques presented in this chapter represent just about everything you can do with a subsummary report. After you fully learn these techniques, you can pick and choose which ones you need to use to produce a given report. You'll also find that simply knowing the tools at your disposal will influence the way you design reports. The more you can design reports that work within the constraints of the tools, the easier it will be to generate those reports.

Figure 10.17
Without a body part, a subsummary report becomes a group-level list report.

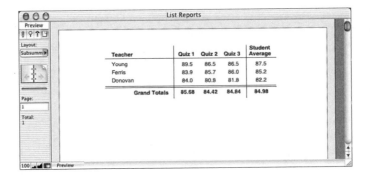

TROUBLESHOOTING

PRINTED REPORTS SHOW ONLY A SINGLE RECORD

Sometimes, my printed reports contain only the first record of data. Why is that?

Chances are that your print settings are configured to print the current record rather than the current found count. When printing from a list view, be sure to select the option to print Records Being Browsed. This configuration can be specified within a script, so be sure to set your print scripts to use this configuration as well.

SLOW GENERATION OF SUBSUMMARY REPORTS

I have built several subsummary reports, but many of them take quite a while to generate. Is there anything I can do to speed them up?

A number of factors can influence the time it takes to generate a subsummary report. The most important of these is the size of the found set. A subsummary report over a found set of 50,000 records takes considerably longer to generate than one with 100 records. Another factor is the amount of summarization the report performs. Having a half-dozen summary fields in a subsummary part requires more time than a report with a single summary field.

Another potential bottleneck is the complexity of the summarization. Summary fields that operate on plain number fields generally perform better than summary fields that operate on calculations that return number results. This is especially true if the calculations contain complex logic or aggregate functions that operate on large record sets.

There are a few things you might try to help ease the pain of slow subsummary reports. The first is to automate the reports to run during the middle of the night; you can view the results as a PDF in the morning. Another option is to pre-summarize some of the data. This might involve running a script to set plain number fields to the result of complex calculations. Or you might create utility tables where you can store summarized data. For instance, every month you might run a month-end closing routine that posts monthly totals for each product or salesperson to a utility table. Then, rather than summary reports based on granular data, you can run reports against the pre-summarized data.

FILEMAKER EXTRA: INCORPORATING REPORTS INTO THE WORKFLOW

The focus of this chapter has been on the creation of list and subsummary report layouts. There's a bit more to creating useful reports, however, than merely setting up nice looking layouts: You have to incorporate reports into the user workflow, controlling how a user both accesses and exits a report. The methods you choose may vary from solution to solution, and your choice is a function of both what the system does and the particular audience. If the users are proficient with FileMaker, they may be comfortable manually finding and sorting a set of records and navigating to the appropriate layout. More often, however, users benefit from your taking some time to set up some infrastructure to help them access the reports properly.

There are many ways you can go about building reports into the workflow of a solution. Following are some of the most common that we've seen over the years.

- **Place buttons to run reports on relevant data entry layouts.** For instance, on an Invoice Entry screen, you might have buttons for creating an Invoice Aging report, and on a Contact entry layout, there might be a Callback Report and a Contact Activity Report. Users typically are expected to find whatever data they want included in the report; the script simply goes to the correct layout, sorts, and previews.

- **In your report scripts, use Custom Dialogs to give users certain choices about how the report will be generated.** For instance, a dialog may prompt them whether they want to produce a report for the current month's data or the previous month's.

- **You can create a centralized "Report Menu" layout that can be accessed from any place in your solution.** By centralizing your reports, you can avoid having to clutter data entry layouts with report buttons. Also, you give your users one place to go any time they want a report, rather than require that they memorize which reports can be generated from where. A centralized report menu works well when the report scripts run predetermined finds.

- **As a variation on the "Report Menu" concept, you can give users control over finding and sorting the data.** You can, for example, place global fields on a layout so the user can enter a date range on which to search. The find criteria is usually specific to a certain report or group of reports, so you need to branch to the appropriate "finder" layout when a user makes a selection from the report menu.

- **You can enable users to modify the title of a report or to add a secondary header of their own choice.** This typically is done with custom dialogs, but you can also incorporate this element into a report menu or finder layout.

After the report has been generated, you'll probably want to return users to wherever they were before running the report. Try to avoid a situation where a user gets stranded on a report layout without any tools to get back to familiar territory.

10

You should also strive to have some consistency in how reports look and function in your system; this will make using them easier and more intuitive for your users. For instance, you might set up as a convention that reports are always (or never) previewed on screen, and then users are prompted whether they want to print a report or not. Similarly, place layout elements such as the title, page number, and report date and time in consistent locations on your reports so users don't have to hunt for them.

10

DEVELOPER TECHNIQUES

CHAPTER 11

DEVELOPING FOR MULTI-USER DEPLOYMENT

In this chapter

DEVELOPING FOR MULTIPLE USERS

Some of the best, most lovingly-developed FileMaker Pro systems are only ever used by a single person. A certain author's mother is a prime example: Her entire insurance sales practice is driven by a FileMaker Pro database. It is a mature system, built so "someone's mom" can use it, and lives without any expectation of being extended to include other users.

Then there are the rest of the databases out there. FileMaker Pro enjoys a graceful growth curve from single-user applications to systems that support enterprise-level workgroups and operations of hundreds of users.

This graceful transition from single-user to multi-user thankfully means that issues to take into consideration when building multi-user systems are reasonably modest. Much of what you already know about building FileMaker Pro systems—regardless of your planned deployment—also applies directly to building a multi-user application.

We'll cover two primary topics: how the FileMaker engine handles multiple users, and development techniques you need to consider when building multi-user applications. Although not technically a multi-user–only topic, we go into some depth about audit trails.

We recommend that anyone intending to deploy a system to multiple users read this chapter. Some of the issues we discuss become necessary considerations only in systems that are getting heavy use from multiple users, but they're good to have in mind nonetheless.

11

→ This chapter is a good companion to Chapter 24, "FileMaker Deployment Options," **p. 729**.

"SESSIONS" IN FILEMAKER PRO

FileMaker Pro is a client-server application (at least when being used in multi-user states). Each time someone using FileMaker Pro (a client) connects to FileMaker Server and opens an instance of the files hosted there, he creates a *session*.

In practical terms, this means that one of your users can be on layout #10 while you yourself are working with layout #2. You can run a script and nothing will happen on another user's computer; likewise, someone else can export data on her machine, while you're performing a find request in the very same database table on yours. You each have a separate connection to the database, with its own unique environment. While working with the same data, all your users can be performing separate, distinct tasks in your system. Each user can have a separate view of the database, with different active windows, active tables, or active found sets, among other things.

Generally these individual user sessions don't interfere with each other at all; however, there are cases where they can conflict—for example, when two users try to edit the same record at once. We will cover throughout this chapter various techniques for identifying and coping with such issues.

NOTE
> Keep in mind that sessions pertain only to global fields, window states, and layouts. Actual data is stored and displayed consistently for everyone.

Before approaching how to manage sessions and potential conflicts, it is important to understand what a session is and how FileMaker Pro manages multiple users. In FileMaker Pro, sessions are implicit and enjoy a state-full, persistent, always-on connection to the server. The system preserves and isolates your user experience in the FileMaker Pro client. Keep in mind that after the session is over (the user closes the database), all information about that session—what layout was in use, where windows were positioned, what the found set was—is discarded. The next time that user opens the database in question, it opens in its default state, with no preservation of how it was last left the system.

You might have heard the term *session* as applied to the Web. FileMaker Pro is quite different. On the Web, sessions are stateless. The Web server does not maintain a connection to a user; the behavior of a session is approximated by the explicit creation of an identifier for a given user when she logs in to a system. That identifier is then passed (and often stored/retrieved via a cookie) through all the page requests a person may make in a given time period. Web developers need to overtly create the mechanics of a session to preserve one's experience from page to page. Whenever you buy a book from Amazon, the developers there have no doubt labored to make sure each page you visit tracks sensibly your use of the site—especially when it comes to the multi-page shopping cart experience.

11

SESSION-SPECIFIC ELEMENTS

FileMaker Pro's sessions maintain a consistent user experience until the application itself is closed. This experience includes your log-in account (unless you specifically log out and log back in), the position and number of windows you have open, which layouts you're on, your current found set, your current sort order, and portal scroll positions. On the development side of things, custom colors you've stored in the layout tools are, unfortunately, lost at the end of a session.

GLOBAL BEHAVIOR

Globals (fields specified as having global storage) are session-specific and they deserve some additional discussion. In a multi-user client session, they utilize and store values unique to one specific user's session. This enables you as a developer to depend on globals storing different information for each user. A simple example is a displayed account name at the top of each layout set at the time of login.

→ For more details on global field storage, **see** "Storage and Indexing," **p. 82**.

At the start of a session, each global is initialized to the last value it had in single-user mode. If you run in single-user mode only, this makes the global appear to persist across sessions, but it's misleading to infer that there are multi-user and single-user types of sessions. Using global behaviors as stored across sessions for single users is a handy way to "leave things the way they were," but it also allows developers to create a "default" state for globals.

Globals are used for a range of functions in multi-user databases: They often hold images for navigation and user interface purposes, they hold temporary variables used by scripts, and they sometimes hold session information such as the current date or the active, logged-in user. It makes sense, then, that they'd be specific to a given user's experience.

 If your global fields suddenly seem to be holding wrong data, refer to "Unpredictable Global Default Values" in the Troubleshooting section at the end of this chapter.

USER ACCOUNTS AND SESSION DATA

One excellent use of global behavior in a multi-user environment is to set a global field with your currently logged-in account. This enables you to always have a central field that's easy to use in calculation formulas and scripts. One could argue that simply using the Get (AccountName) function wherever necessary would accomplish the same end, but there's a further use for storing the current account name in a global: You can drive a relationship with it into a User table.

This enables you to tie account information to data. You might want to do so if, for example, you need to store someone's real name, his preference to always start on a specific layout when the system opens, or (in a particularly abstract example) in what language he wants to use your database.

All these examples depend on your having done something with the information you store in a user table. It's useful to store someone's preference for starting layout only if you then write the requisite script that uses this as a reference.

Another possibility lies with tracking database use. Although you might debate whether or not a database (or database administrator) should be looking over someone's shoulder, you could write routines that post records to a user log table whenever users log in, log out, or even when they perform certain scripted actions (delete records, create records, run an invoice report, and so on).

One more user-friendly option is to accommodate users simply by enabling them to specify where they prefer a window to be positioned and sized.

CONCURRENCY

You might have heard of the term *concurrency* as it relates to databases. It refers to the logic and behavior of database systems when two (or more) users attempt to interact with the same information. A simple metaphor might be two people trying to use a phone book or dictionary at once. Every multi-user database platform has to address this issue.

Certainly it'd be easiest to simply restrict using the database to one user or function at a time, but clearly that's an unrealistic solution.

THE ACID TEST

To address issues of concurrency and transaction integrity, database engineers have developed what has come to be known as "the ACID test." Database software needs to pass this test to completely manage concurrency issues. ACID stands for *atomicity, consistency, isolation,* and *durability*; these four terms describe the features and requirements for processing transactions in a database system. If a system does not meet these requirements, the integrity of the database—and its data—cannot be perfectly guaranteed.

In the context of databases, the term *transaction* relates to a single logical operation comprising one or more steps that results in data being posted to the system. Examples might include committing a new record to the database, performing a script that calculates summary information, or in real-world terms, completing the multiple steps of debiting one financial account and crediting another. The ACID test exists to ensure such transactions are reliable.

FileMaker Pro databases, unfortunately, do not fully meet ACID compliance, nor is it realistic to develop a solution in FileMaker that perfectly does. FileMaker Pro scripts can be interrupted (a machine crash or a force-quit of the application) and as such it is possible to leave a transaction half completed.

We're including this section not to point out a shortcoming of FileMaker, but rather to illustrate some important guidelines on how you should consider building solutions for critical business systems for large workgroups. It is possible to go a long way toward ACID compliance in a FileMaker Pro database—if it's properly engineered. It's also quite possible to build a FileMaker Pro database that leaves wide opportunity for data integrity problems to crop up.

As consultants, we're pragmatists. Often the craftsman in all of us yearns to build the world's most perfect system, but in reality there are trade-offs in complexity, time, and flexibility to consider. We use the guidelines that follow as just that—guidelines. By identifying the criticality of certain data and using sensible safeguards to ensure its integrity to the degree possible, we are able to cover all but the most extreme cases of database failures.

- **Atomicity**—Atomicity requires that transactions be completed either in their entirety or not at all. In other words, a logical routine (say, crediting one account and debiting another) cannot be left half done. In FileMaker Pro terms, data is either committed or not committed to your database, a script needs to reach its logical conclusion, and a calculation function stores and indexes its results properly. Although a script can be interrupted, it is important to approach atomicity by writing scripts that conclude whatever routines they're designed for.

- **Consistency**—Consistency ensures that your database is left in a "legal state" at the beginning and end of any given transaction. This means that the transaction won't break any of the rules, or integrity constraints, of the system. This often can encompass business logic: An example might be that all financial credit transactions be positive numbers.

- **Isolation**—Transactions in mid-process are never exposed to other processes or users. In the credit/debit example, a user should never see a credit appear on one account before the debit has been posted. Likewise, an account balance report should not be allowed to run when a credit or debit is in the midst of being added.

11

■ **Durability**—After a transaction has been performed and completed, the information resulting from that process needs to be persistent. It should be saved with the database, and if someone pulls that computer's plug, the information is then still present in the file.

ACID is a goal of development to ensure data integrity. We encourage you, especially when writing scripts, to focus on delivering on these guidelines, especially in a multi-user environment.

SCRIPT LOG

One technique we use for verifying processes and debugging is a *script log*. By building one, you approach better atomicity and are able to identify cases where it fails.

In large, complex solutions where transaction integrity is vital, it may be warranted to create a process that causes all scripts to write log records to a separate table (often in a separate file as well) when they start and again when they are successfully completed. It's possible to track other data as well: who initiated the script, on what layout the user was, which instance of a window was in use, timestamp data for start and end (for performance and troubleshooting purposes), and potentially any data the script manipulates. This is not to be confused with an audit trail, covered later in the chapter. Audit trails enable you to record all data transactions in a database. A script log is a means of confirming that your functional routines are completed properly.

By adding a script log to your system and periodically checking it for incomplete conclusions, you can identify cases where scripts failed and manually address such issues when necessary. By definition, if a script log "start" entry doesn't have a corresponding "close" entry, it failed ACID's atomicity test and possibly the consistency test as well.

TIP

> One final note on script logs: We encourage you to create a single flag in your database that when "turned off" disables all script logging in your system.

COMMIT VERSUS CREATE AND SERIAL IDs

In FileMaker Pro 7, data is committed (saved) after a user exits the record, either by clicking outside a field or by performing a range of other actions such as running a script, changing modes, changing layouts, or hitting a "record-entry" key (the default is the Enter key, but field behaviors can be changed to allow the Return or Tab keys as well).

→ For more details on field behaviors, **see** "Field Behavior," **p. 116**.

It is possible to use the <u>R</u>ecords, <u>R</u>evert Records option to undo the creation of a record. Until a record has been committed, it exists in a temporary state. Relying on a transaction remaining unsaved until expressly committed helps ensure better ACID compliance. This is important to remember in a multi-user environment where you may be operating on assumptions established with prior versions of FileMaker Pro. For example, if you're attempting to serialize some form of data and two users create two records at the same time, it is possible that one will commit the record in an order different from that in which the records were initially created. It is also possible that a user will undo his or her changes with a "Revert Record" command and leave you with a gap in your serialization.

In the case of auto-entry serial IDs, FileMaker enables you to specify when the serial number is incremented—on creation or on commit. This enables you to control auto-enter serialization; however, it does not protect you from other assumptions. For example, if you're relying on GetSummary() calculation fields to keep track of an incremented total, remember that the calculations that control this are evaluated and displayed only after a record is committed.

RECORD LOCKING

Just as a record is not saved to your database until it is committed—maintaining an isolated state while you create new records—so too will FileMaker not allow editing by more than one person at a time. In this way, FileMaker Pro meets the isolation test of ACID for posting data. Record locking exists to ensure that no two edits collide with each other (such as when multiple users attempt to edit the same record simultaneously).

After a user begins editing a record, FileMaker locks that record from other users and script processes, and (when not captured and suppressed by a script) presents users with an error message if they attempt to enter or change any data in that record.

It's possible to place your cursor in a field and still leave the record unlocked (safe for other users to enter data into the same record), but at the point at which you actively begin typing, that record essentially becomes "yours" until you either commit or revert it.

NOTE

> For those of you familiar with prior versions of FileMaker Pro, remember that those versions locked records as soon as a user clicked in to a field. That feature has changed in this version.

Locking applies to related records in portals as well. If you are modifying a record in a portal row, that record's "parent" is also locked. This behavior occurs only when the related child record is edited in a portal; if you are simply editing the child record on its own table-specific layout, it is just that single child record that is locked.

Also keep in mind that record locking applies only to editing. You can still find those records, view reports with them included, change sort orders with locked records in your found set, and even export data. Only editing is protected.

If a user has a record locked and you get an error message, you can ask that user to release the record to you. The error dialog appears in Figure 11.1, along with a resultant message that user might see if you send one.

Figure 11.1
You see this message
if you try to edit a
record someone else
is modifying. If need
be, use the Send
Message command to
ask for control.

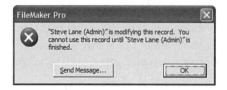

The one downside to record locking is that you cannot force a user out of a record remotely through FileMaker Pro. If someone begins editing a record and then decides to fly to Tahiti, you need to shut down the file, kick him off by using the Server Administration Tool, restart the server, or address the issue at the user's local computer.

To help with multi-user account testing, refer to "Use Re-Login for Testing Access and Sessions" in the Troubleshooting section at the end of this chapter.

TRAPPING FOR RECORD LOCKING IN SCRIPTS

A subtle way your database might prove error prone is in always making the assumption in scripts that you have access to all the records in your found set.

You can explicitly open a record for editing with the Open Record/Request script step. After you've issued that script command, the record becomes "yours," and other users who try to edit the record get a record lock error until you release the record. Because any attempt to modify a record results in the same condition, explicitly using an Open Record/Request script step may not be technically necessary, but we find it helpful to turn to nonetheless. Admittedly, the more important step is checking to see whether you are locked out.

To capture the error that results in cases where either your current privileges don't allow editing of the record in question or the record is locked by another user, we recommend testing first to see whether you can open a record. If that doesn't work, then deal with the result prior to attempting an edit. Use the Open Record/Request script step followed by a Get(LastError) check. Here's how it might look:

```
Set Error Capture [On]
Open Record/Request
Set Field [MyDataTable::gError; Get (LastError)]
If[MyDataTable::gError <> 0]
   Show Custom Dialog ["Error"; errorCodes::Message]
End If
//Execute your "real" script here... and don't forget to commit
➥your record at the end.
```

Use a Commit Record/Request script step at the end of your script to release the record back into non-edit mode and unlock it for other users.

NOTE

> Consider building error utility tables into your systems; this enables you to easily tailor error messages based on whatever value is held in gError, including those you create for yourself. The Custom Dialog step could just as easily be "Sorry, you don't currently have access to that record. It could be locked or you may not have sufficient access privileges."

Instead of checking simply for a non-zero error, you could also write a series of If -> Else If script steps checking for errors such as 301 (Record is in use by another user), 303 (Database schema is in use by another user), and so on. There are a wide range of possible errors.

→ For a reference on error codes in FileMaker Pro, refer to FileMaker Pro's online help.

MULTI-WINDOW LOCKING

Multi-window locking is closely related to multi-user record locking. It is possible to open a new window, via the Window, New Window menu command, and lock yourself out of editing a record from your original window. If you are actively editing a record that has yet to be committed and you try to edit the same record in another window, you'll see an error message that says, "This record cannot be modified in this window because it is already being modified in a different window." FileMaker tries to ensure you're not losing data or edits you're in the midst of creating.

The point here is that a user can lock himself out of a record. Someone might not realize he's left a record in an edit state before moving on to a new window. The simple answer here is simply not to try to edit a record in two places at once. A user would have to go a bit out of his way to encounter this problem. If you've scripted routines for creating new windows with a script, you may want to include a Commit Record/Request step before opening the new window.

AUDIT TRAILS IN FILEMAKER PRO

Data integrity is vital in a multi-user database. A well designed database, properly structured, will go a long way toward ensuring proper data integrity, but no database will ever be perfect. Pesky humans have a habit of introducing a certain "unpredictability" into the mix. Although $.02 may very well be a perfectly valid number as an invoice total, the truth that the invoice in question was actually $200 isn't something a database will ever be able to discern. Then there are cases where a client accidentally makes alterations across a number of records using an import or replace function.

For cases like these, you need a mechanism to first identify and then undo changes. Possible problem records might be identifiable by date, by user, or by some other criteria. In some cases, maybe only a field needs addressing. The process of undoing changes is referred to as a *rollback*, and for it to be possible, you first need an "audit trail" of logged transactions in your database to provide the breadcrumbs necessary for a series of undo steps.

Audit trails track the edits made to a database at the granular field level. Changes tracked usually include the field name, a timestamp, and user account for the person (or function) that made the change. Although FileMaker Pro doesn't have audit trail capabilities built in by default, it is entirely possible to build them. The following sections illustrate three increasingly complete techniques.

RECORD CREATE/MODIFY META DATA

The simplest way to track the evolution of one's data is to create fields for creation and modification events. This alone doesn't allow for rollbacks, but it certainly gives you visibility into the events of your database and provides a layer of accountability.

This sort of data is not related to a given business or organization, but helps describe when and by whom data is entered into a database. It is often referred to as *meta data*: data about data.

When building a system for multi-user deployment, we recommend establishing timestamps for creation and modification of records, along with account names. We don't recommend usernames. This enables you to track who's responsible and when edits have been made to your database so that you can, at a minimum, identify problems. For example, if one of your users consistently makes a data entry error, or if a bug in development led to wrong lookup values, you can isolate such records by timestamp and account name.

CAUTION

> You might have noticed that we specified *account name* rather than *username* for these meta fields. Individual users can modify their names in the preferences dialogs of FileMaker Pro clients, and there's no corresponding authentication for such. Because this data isn't reliable, we always opt to use the account name.

To explore error trapping practices, refer to "Trapping for Errors" in the Troubleshooting section at the end of this chapter.

SCRIPT-CONTROLLED EDITING

A second technique for controlling edits to your database solutions is scripting-intensive, but allows for the most control. It's conceptually straightforward: Lock down the actual fields of your database in Browse mode and have your users make edits in global fields with a Submit or Cancel button. The script attached would then move the data from temporary fields into actual fields. This allows you to control, via script, any checks you might want to make on the data, and also allows you to write records to an audit trail database to record changes.

One of the more difficult aspects of this approach is what to do with portals and related records. A technique that works well (but again will have you working in ScriptMaker quite a bit) is to use a temporary scratch table. Users place edits in its temporary child records and if they click Cancel, those records are simply discarded. Your audit trail would then need to track to which table a given row of data belonged.

This scripted approach isn't for the faint-of-heart. You'll need to be quite adept with scripting, and this sort of approach will dramatically add to the time it takes for you to deliver a solution. The upside, of course, is a solid system that does everything it can to protect against honest mistakes—both in terms of trapping data changes and providing a complete, deliberately designed user experience.

AUTO-ENTRY TECHNIQUE FOR AUDIT TRAILS

The third technique in building audit trails relies on the auto-entry options of FileMaker Pro and the capability for fields to modify themselves (see Figure 11.2). An audit trail should track when and by whom a change was made, and also the change itself.

Figure 11.2
Notice that the Audit_Log field on the bottom has a chronological (time stamped) history.

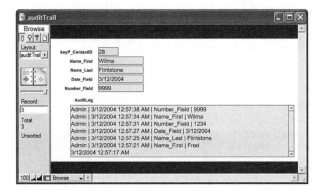

This technique might seem somewhat advanced, but it's actually quite simple. Given FileMaker's dramatically extended storage limits, you may opt to make this a standard feature in all your database solutions. You may see some performance issues arise as your database grows, so we recommend moving this data into an archive when (if) you need.

The `Audit_Trail` field displayed in Figure 11.2 is nothing more than a text field with auto-entry options enabled. Specify that you want to have a calculation result auto-populate the `Audit_Trail` field, be certain to turn off the Do Not Replace Existing Value (If Any) option, and add some "seed" data to the field as well via the another Auto Entry option (see Figure 11.3).

Define your calculation as shown in Figure 11.4.

You need to combine a few different functions and elements to assemble this auto-entry calculation:

- **Evaluate**—Evaluate returns the results from an expression passed to it. You might wonder why we're bothering with it; after all, this is a calculation entry—by definition it will be evaluated. However, any fields added to the optional properties of an evaluate function serve as triggers (much as a `Lookup` function works). When they are changed, so too will be the `Audit_trail` field. Be sure to add however many trigger fields as you'd like tracked in your audit trail.

Figure 11.3
Notice that you need two auto-entry options enabled where the timestamp seeds the field.

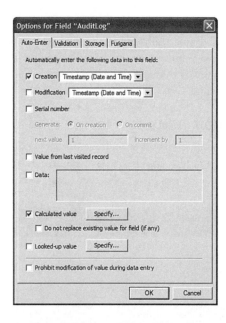

Figure 11.4
Use the Evaluate function's optional trigger field parameters to cause the Audit_Trail field to be reevaluated.

11

- **Quote**—Quote enables you to protect text from being evaluated within the Evaluate function and enables you to properly concatenate the label and text values in the function. Without the Quote used, your evaluated result would be a "?".

- **Get (CurrentAccount)**—Returns the account signed in from the database's security settings.

- **Get (CurrentTimeStamp)**—This simply returns the time and date at which the user changed one of the trigger fields. An exceedingly minor point: The timestamp occurs when the audit log field is written/committed, not when the actual edit occurred.

- **Get (ActiveFieldName)**—This Get function returns the active field name of the field being edited; because the field in question (say, for example Name_First) is also listed as a trigger in the Evaluate function, there's a brief moment as the record is being committed that FileMaker Pro resolves the Evaluate function while still recognizing the trigger field as active. It is this behavior that enables the audit trail to work.

- **Get (ActiveFieldContents)**—Just as Get (ActiveFieldName) works at the moment of a trigger to capture the edited field name, Get (ActiveFieldContents) captures the actual contents of the field in question.

- **& "¶" & AuditLog**—If you append the AuditLog field itself to the end of your calculation, you'll be able to save prior entries and simply keep adding to the top of the log. If you prefer to have your entries sorted chronologically, begin your formula with AuditLog & "¶" &.

- **[Name_First; Name_Last; Date_Field; Number_Field]**—These last elements of the formula are the optional criteria for the evaluate function. They serve as your triggers.

The seed data you added on the Auto-Entry Options dialog (creation timestamp) allows you to leave the Do Not Evaluate If All Fields Are Empty option turned on; otherwise you'd need to turn this option off to get the calculation to work the first time (when the AuditLog field was empty). Despite the triggers, it is the only actual field referenced in the calculation.

CAUTION

> If you turn off the Do Not Evaluate If All Fields Are Empty option, you'll end up with a blank row in your audit log. Somehow that didn't feel proper to us, and theoretically it's possible for someone to create a record and leave it unedited for a period of time. Adding at least the initial timestamp to "initialize" the Audit_Log then at least offers more information.

You'll want to consider some additional issues before using this technique in your database solutions. First, FileMaker Pro cannot recognize the current field name or field contents while a replace function is being performed. The audit trail will record that a change was made, but it will lack both the data itself and the field name in question. This same issue applies in the case of imports, and all script steps that don't actively mimic user actions. Set Field, for example, does not actively enter a field. In the case of using Set Field, the symptoms are identical to the case of a Replace or Import; however, presumably because Set Field exists in a script, you could opt to record whatever audit information your system required.

Second, keep in mind that your data still lives with the record in question. If you were to delete a record, you would presumably lose your audit trail. To preserve all audit trails and to ensure the capability to perform a rollback, we suggest writing a script routine that controls delete processes and properly records all data in an audit table before erasing it from your system.

Related records work in the same manner: Their audit trail routines would live in their respective records, just as in a "parent" record. If you delete a related record, you will need to store that state in an audit table of some kind.

 For help with controlling auto-entry behaviors, refer to "Making Sure Your Auto-Entry Always Edits" in the Troubleshooting section at the end of this chapter.

CREATING ROLLBACK FUNCTIONALITY

Regardless of whether or not you choose to move your audit information into its own table or leave it in each record to which it pertains, a rollback follows the same basic principles.

A rollback, true to its name, allows a database administrator, in backward fashion, to re-create the state of a database as it existed at any point in time. She can do so without having to resort to deploying a backup (which may not include the latest functionality of the system).

This involves writing a script to walk through each record's audit trail (from top to bottom as an audit trail writes its data), using Set Field script steps, and re-creating a record at a given date and time. The logic relies on a loop that tests to see whether each iterative row in your audit trail data is older than (or equal to) the point in time you've selected for rollback. If the result of the test is true, then your script would be set to parse the data at the end of the line (using the Middle function), and by referencing the stored field name in that row, it would populate your data.

CAUTION

> If your database relies on Set Field script steps (for possibly tracking various status flags or data you've scripted), don't forget that you need to re-create that information via other means. It is not just the data a user sees that needs to be rolled back.

LAUNCH FILES

One of the challenges users on a network have is actually finding the specific FileMaker files they need to use. This is a no-brainer if you have only one FileMaker Pro solution with a single file, but over time your Hosts dialog can become quite crowded in multi-user situations. This is less problematic in FileMaker 7 than in previous versions, given that FileMaker 7 allows multiple tables per file and thus requires fewer files, but in large organizations or companies with many different FileMaker Pro files, a server list can be a bit daunting.

To offer a solution to this simple problem, we often build *launch files*. These are utility files that are distributed as single-user files and sit on each individual person's computer. They have generally one layout and one script that calls an open routine in a network file.

NOTE

> We generally put a solution logo and "system loading…please wait…" message on the single layout.

Although it's tempting to put other niceties in these launch files—the capability to load clusters of files, or perhaps some sense of acknowledging the individual user logging in—we encourage you to leave things as simple as possible. You'll have dozens of these files distributed on your network with no easy means of replacing them with upgrades. The simpler you keep them, the easier they will be to maintain.

A final nice touch on launch files is that they close themselves after launching the system in question. They're no longer needed and shouldn't have to clutter the <u>W</u>indow menu.

TROUBLESHOOTING

UNPREDICTABLE GLOBAL DEFAULT VALUES

I have global fields, used for holding system settings, that have been working perfectly for weeks, but today suddenly they have different data in them. What happened?

It's likely they got reset by some script modification you've recently made, or when you had files in an offline, single-user state. In our practice, we find it difficult to remember to set globals for default states in single-user mode through the course of developing and maintaining a system. This is a common source of bugs and we've found over the years not to make any assumptions about global values; it's better to simply set them explicitly within a start-up script. It's also important to either explicitly set or test for values at the beginning of a script that depends on them.

USE RE-LOGIN FOR TESTING ACCESS AND SESSIONS

One of my users is reporting a problem that I don't see when I'm logged in. I'm getting sick of having to re-login time and again to test this. Is there an easier way to test this?

If you're having trouble testing how other users, with different access levels, might be interacting with your system, write a re-login script that enables you to hop into another account at the click of your mouse. It's even possible to store passwords when using the Re-Login step. Connect it to a convenient button or place it in the Scripts menu and you have one-click account switching.

MAKING SURE YOUR AUTO-ENTRY ALWAYS EDITS

My auto-entry function worked the first time I edited a field, but then it remains stuck and won't update again. What setting is the likely culprit?

If your auto-entry field for your audit log isn't updating—it does it once, but then never again—make sure you uncheck the Do Not Replace Existing Value For Field (If Any) option. It is always checked by default and is easy to miss.

Likewise, the Audit Log routine we described depends on there being data in the field to begin with. Either seed it with something (we use Creation TimeStamp) or turn off the Do Not Evaluate If All Referenced Fields Are Empty option. It too is enabled by default.

TRAPPING FOR ERRORS

I need to tighten my scripts, and don't want to have to code for every exception under the sun. What's the best approach for trapping for errors?

Trapping for errors is always a smart development practice. Get into the habit and you'll save yourself years of your life debugging. A simple approach is to simply use the Get(LastError) function and use a Case or If/If Else routine to display meaningful messages and logic branches to your users. You can trap for either explicit errors or just a non-zero number.

A better way to abstract your code and provide yourself with a central place to reuse error handling is to simply write an error routine once and be done with it.

There are two ways to manage error messaging. You can either set up your own errorCodes table (we strongly recommend this) or build a custom function. Setting up a table is simple and allows you to add your own custom error conditions and messages if you wish. You can do this as well with a custom function, but it's not as easy, nor can you easily set up multiple messages or attributes for an error code.

The idea is simple: Establish a global gError field in your main system and relate that to an errorID in your error table.

FILEMAKER EXTRA: DEVELOPMENT WITH A TEAM

 Sometimes systems are big enough that they warrant multiple developers in addition to multiple users. Developing as a team can be a bit complex with FileMaker Pro, but one of the best (and often unsung) features of this latest version is that database schema changes can be made while the database is live, on a server, as other users are in the system. This is an extraordinary boon for FileMaker developers and will make a real difference in all of our lives.

The idea is simple: Set up a server (far better than multi-user peer-to-peer hosting) and have as many developers as a given system needs work together.

It's important to keep a few things in mind: Only one person can adjust the schema at a time. This is true for scripts as well. If another developer is working in ScriptMaker, you can view scripts there, but you will be unable to make changes or add new scripts until your teammate is finished. This means you can have one person focused on scripting, one defining a new calculation field, and a handful of others working on different layouts all at once.

Over the years we've assembled some best practices for working on a team. Here's a list of techniques we draw on:

- **Use FileMaker Server**—Server (as opposed to simply working peer-to-peer) allows you to run frequent backups, and if any one machine crashes, the files are still protected from the crash.

- **Use FileMaker Developer**—The Script Debugger is handy to use in the multi-developer environment. When another developer is editing scripts, and you can't open a script in ScriptMaker, turn on the debugging tool and you'll at least be able to see the script in question.

- **Use Custom Functions**—Custom functions can be written while other programming activities are underway, and they provide a deep layer of possible abstraction. It's possible to have multiple developers building custom functions while others work in the core system, and it's also a great way to reuse code across a team.

- **Set up a bug tracking database**—If you're working on a multi-user system, testing, requests, random ideas, and other communication is vital. You've got some of the world's best database software at your fingertips; put it to use and build a bug tracking system for your development team and your users.

- **Build re-login scripts, toggle status area scripts, and "developer" layouts**—Giving developers access to the "back stage" area of a system is vital. Build scripts to get them there.

- **Assign a chief architect**—With creating a meal, too many cooks in the kitchen spoils the broth. Similarly, one person should ultimately be responsible for the overall technical directions the system requires.

- **Comment**—Comment. Comment. Comment. Your team will either thank or kill you, depending on how well you take this to heart.

11

CHAPTER **12**

IMPLEMENTING SECURITY

In this chapter

FILEMAKER SECURITY FEATURES OVERVIEW

Implementing sound security practices can be complicated, and the effort shouldn't be undertaken without a security plan. It's difficult to construct a good FileMaker security plan without first having an overall sense of how FileMaker's security tools work, so this chapter starts with a review of FileMaker's security features. That is followed with a methodology for using FileMaker's security tools to design and implement a database security plan.

FileMaker Pro 7's security features are radically different from the security feature set that has remained almost unchanged for the last several versions of the product. Even if you consider yourself a security expert with previous versions of FileMaker, you should read this next section and familiarize yourself with the security tools that FileMaker Pro 7 puts at your disposal. These security features are clustered into three main components:

- Accounts
- Privilege sets
- Extended privileges

Briefly, accounts control which users have access to the database; privilege sets control what logged-in users can see and do; and extended privileges control network access to the database by client copies of FileMaker Pro, and also tools such as ODBC/JDBC, the Web, and FileMaker Mobile. In addition, custom extended privileges can be created for a variety of purposes.

The following sections discuss all three components in detail. The first you should understand is the Accounts feature.

ACCOUNTS

 Accounts control user access through a login process. When a user wants to log in to the database, she must provide credentials to prove her identity. These credentials take the form of an account name and a password. After she has entered the credentials, FileMaker authenticates those credentials, which means that it checks those credentials against the file's list of authorized accounts. If (and only if) the account name matches a name in the list, and the corresponding password matches the password assigned to that account, then the user is granted access to the file. That access is further governed by a set of rules, called a *privilege set*.

When you're logged in to a database file with full access privileges, you can choose File, Define, Accounts & Privileges to bring up the Define Accounts & Privileges dialog, as shown in Figure 12.1.

The dialog contains three tabs that correspond to the three main components of FileMaker Pro's security system. The Accounts tab is highlighted. In the lower-right corner of the Define Accounts & Privileges dialog is a pop-menu that allows you to view the accounts by three different criteria: creation order, authentication order, and account name. The authentication order is the important one, because it means that if a user provides credentials that match up to more than one account (you'll see how that might happen later in the chapter), then the authentication order determines which account is logged in.

Figure 12.1
The Admin account is created automatically when you create a new file.

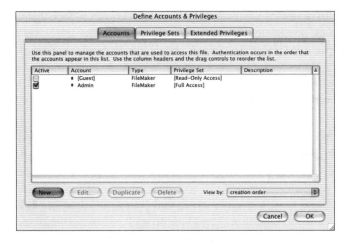

NOTE

Although accounts are usually thought of as being associated with human users, Web servers and ODBC sessions can also make use of FileMaker accounts. For the sake of this chapter, though, we'll refer to "users" as if they were always human users.

When you create a new database file in FileMaker Pro 7, the two accounts shown in Figure 12.1 are automatically created. One is an administrative account called Admin, which has full access to the database. The other is a guest account with read-only access. If you double-click on the Admin account, the Edit Account dialog opens, as shown in Figure 12.2.

Figure 12.2
Selecting the Admin account and clicking the Edit button invokes the Edit Account dialog. You can double-click the Admin account to get the same effect.

FILEMAKER ACCOUNTS

At the top of the dialog is the selection menu for the authentication method. FileMaker can either use accounts and passwords stored in the database file to self-authenticate, or use an external server for authentication. A FileMaker account is one that is stored in the file. Each FileMaker file must have at least one full-access FileMaker account.

From time to time, developers or users have been known to lock themselves out of their own databases. Sometimes the person who created the database leaves the company and the full access password is lost. Sometimes people just forget the full-access password. In previous versions of FileMaker Pro, lost passwords could be recovered by FileMaker, Inc., and by password recovery tools. That is not the case with FileMaker Pro 7. Passwords stored in the file are irreversibly encrypted and can't be recovered.

EXTERNAL ACCOUNTS

 Users need to know a lot of passwords these days. In most organizations, users need to log in to their computers before they can even launch any applications. They need to have usernames and passwords for their email accounts, and other usernames and passwords for various network resources such as file servers and even their FileMaker databases. Some organizations like to centralize their administration of user accounts and passwords so that it takes less time to maintain all these passwords. To do this, they set up an *authentication server*. It's possible to have FileMaker Pro use an authentication server to validate login credentials.

> **NOTE**
>
> External server authentication requires the use of FileMaker Server. If you're using a file in single-user mode on your local hard drive or sharing the file peer-to-peer with other copies of FileMaker Pro, you can't use an external server to authenticate accounts.

FileMaker Pro 7 is flexible in that you can mix and match account authentication methods within a single file. You can have some accounts that are authenticated by FileMaker, and other accounts that are authenticated by an external server. For deployment environments with a large number of users and a regular IT infrastructure, a good strategy would be to set up database administrator accounts that are authenticated by FileMaker, and then user accounts that are authenticated by an external server. That way, IT personnel who may not be familiar with FileMaker administration can maintain user accounts with tools that they're familiar with, and developers can still log in to the database files with full access even if they're disconnected from the network and unable to authenticate with an external server.

> **TIP**
>
> This same account configuration is also a good strategy if you need to do offline development and swap in new database files in from time to time. If user accounts are maintained outside FileMaker, you don't need to worry about any account additions or modifications that might have been made while you were making changes to a copy of the file (or files). As long as no changes have been made to groups, any user account changes are incorporated automatically as soon as you host the files with FileMaker Server.

EXTERNAL AUTHENTICATION ON MAC OS X   FileMaker Server needs to be configured to make use of an external authentication server. This process is slightly different for the Mac and Windows versions of the Server Administration Tool (SAT), so we review both methods.

→ For more on using the Server Administration Tool to configure FileMaker Server, **see** "Configuring and Administering FileMaker Server Using the SAT," **p. 746**.

On Mac OS X (version 10.2.8 or later), you need to launch the FileMaker Server Admin tool. Choose Server, Connect to FileMaker Server to bring up the Connect to FileMaker Server dialog. Depending on where you run the FileMaker Server Admin tool, you might be connecting to a copy of FileMaker Server on your local machine or somewhere out on the network. After you've connected to the server, click the Configure button. Click the right-most tab on the configuration screen, which is the Security tab. The selected Security tab is shown in Figure 12.3.

Figure 12.3
In Mac OS X, the Security tab needs to be configured if you plan to use external server authentication for clients.

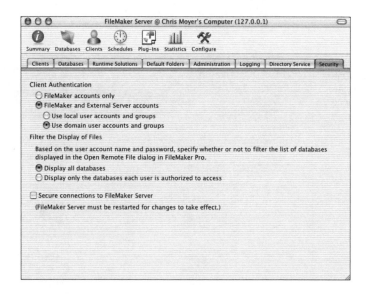

EXTERNAL AUTHENTICATION ON WINDOWS   Now let's take a look at this process for the Windows FileMaker Server Admin tool, which we're going to start abbreviating as SAT. Like the Mac OS X version of the SAT, it doesn't matter if FileMaker Server resides on the same machine as the SAT or on a machine elsewhere on the network.

Because the Windows version of the SAT runs in the Microsoft Management Console, or MMC, the standard view has no tabs as there are on the Mac. If you prefer to use a tabbed interface, you can right-click on the server name and select Properties to bring up the FileMaker Server Properties dialog shown in Figure 12.4. If instead you use the MMC, you configure the various components by using Assistants that step you through the process. Click the Security icon to run the Security Assistant, as shown in Figure 12.5.

12

Figure 12.4
The FileMaker Server Properties dialog consolidates all security options in one place.

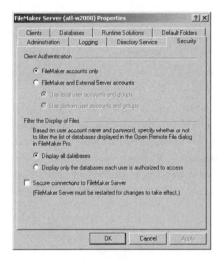

Figure 12.5
The Security Assistant steps you through the process of configuring FileMaker Server's security settings.

After a screen or two, you'll come to the screen shown in Figure 12.6. This screen shows some of the same settings you just saw on Mac OS X and on the FileMaker Server Properties dialog.

After you've decided whether to authenticate with local user accounts and groups or domain user accounts and groups, you can click through the remaining Security Assistant screen (which we'll come back to later in this chapter) and complete the Security Assistant.

FILEMAKER ACCOUNT PASSWORDS

 In earlier versions of FileMaker, it was possible to have a file that had no passwords or security restrictions at all. With FileMaker Pro 7, every file has to have an account with full access to the file. Although the default Admin account can be deleted, you still have to have at least one account with full access before you can exit the Define Accounts & Privileges dialog. The [Guest] account can't be deleted at all. In fact, throughout the Define Accounts & Privileges dialog, if you see anything wrapped in square brackets [], that means it can't be deleted.

Figure 12.6
Just as with the Mac OS X version of the SAT, the Windows version enables you to authenticate using either local or domain user accounts and groups.

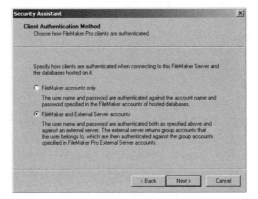

FileMaker Pro 7 makes a few things happen automatically when a new file is created. First of all, as we've seen, the Admin and [Guest] accounts are created automatically. If that was all that happened, then the file would prompt a user for a password as soon as it was re-opened after its initial creation. That doesn't happen, and if you choose File, File Options to bring up the File Options dialog shown in Figure 12.7, you can see why.

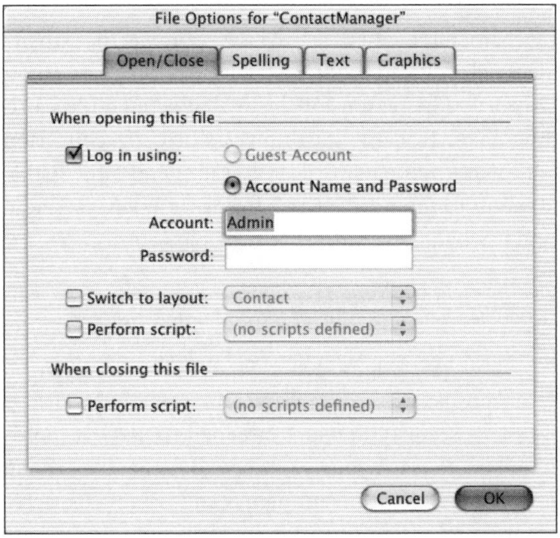

Figure 12.7
Newly created files are automatically set to open with full access.

12

The file is automatically set to open with the default Admin account. That means that as soon as you want to deploy your file with the access privileges you set up, you need to remove the automatic login behavior. The result is that the next time the file is opened, the user is presented with the login dialog shown in Figure 12.8.

Figure 12.8
When a file's default login has been disabled, users are presented with a login dialog when they attempt to open the file.

You should note that the Admin account has no password assigned to it. Actually, it's more accurate to say that it has a password, but the password is blank. Although it may be convenient in the short term to leave the password blank, it should definitely be changed before you deploy the system. The failure to change default passwords is a contributing factor in countless computer system break-ins. We'll say it once more: *Always change the default password*. Even if you want all users to have access to the file, it's rarely in your best interest to have users in there with full access. That would mean they could change the full access password, intentionally or not, and lock you out of your own file. If you want to let the world into your database, let them in with something less than full access.

Another noteworthy characteristic of FileMaker accounts is that when the account name and password are identical, you can log in to a file by leaving the account name blank and just entering the password. The reason for this is that when a file has been converted from earlier versions of FileMaker Pro, any existing passwords are converted to accounts that have the same account name and password. For example, if a file had a password called Admin, during conversion to the FileMaker 7 format, a FileMaker account called Admin would be created, and it would have Admin for the password.

To learn more about what to do if you've forgotten your password, refer to "Locked Out of Your Database" in the Troubleshooting section at the end of this chapter.

→ For more on conversion issues, **see** "Migration Choices," **p. 508**.

During a login, FileMaker displays bullet characters instead of the actual text when you type in your password. This is a security measure intended to make it more difficult for someone looking over your shoulder to learn your password. Because the account name is entered in clear text, someone who knew that account names and passwords were identical (which would be the case immediately after a file conversion) could easily learn your password by looking at your account name.

External Server Passwords

The Account Name and Password entry boxes appear only when the account is authenticated via FileMaker. If you switch the account so that it's authenticated via an external server, the Edit Account dialog changes to look like the one shown in Figure 12.9.

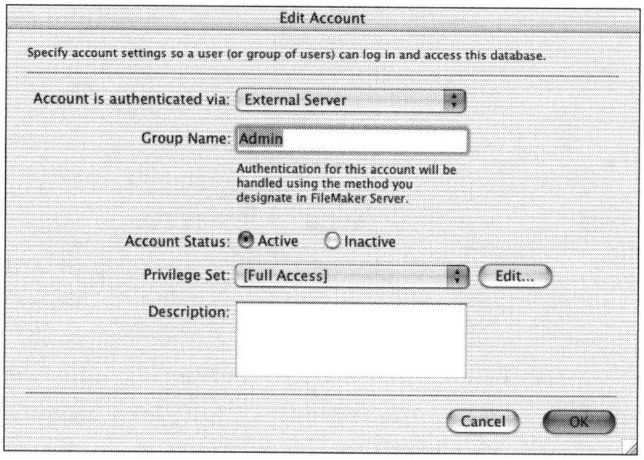

Figure 12.9
Accounts that are authenticated though an external server specify only a group name, not an account name and password.

Because the Account Name and Password information is stored in the external authentication server, you don't need to enter that information in the Edit Account dialog. When those credentials are passed to the external authentication server, what comes back is a list of groups to which the account belongs. That's why, when you switch the authentication to External Server, you get an entry box for the Group Name.

There are some implications to this, so it's a good idea to talk through a couple of examples.

Imagine that you have a user who gets authenticated by the external server. On that external server, you set up two different FileMaker groups. One is FMP Manager, and the other is FMP User. You have also set up two externally authenticated user accounts in FileMaker that specify those two groups.

The example user belongs to both groups, and thus can use either account. (This is the only way that user credentials can match up to multiple accounts, by the way. FileMaker prevents you from creating accounts that don't have unique account names or group names.) Suppose the example user logs in with her credentials and the authentication server returns FMP Manager and FMP User as the group names. What happens? To answer that question, we need to revisit the Define Accounts & Privileges dialog, which is shown in Figure 12.10.

You get to control what happens in cases where user credentials match up to more than one group account. By setting the authentication order, you can determine which account authenticates. A reasonable policy is to decide that if a user has credentials for more than one account, the account with the highest level of access should be authenticated. That's the configuration shown in Figure 12.10.

Figure 12.10
The authentication order determines which account is authenticated in cases where credentials match more than one account.

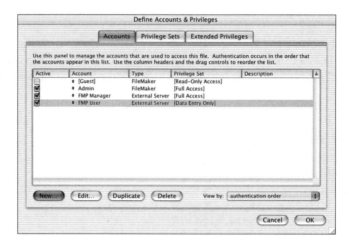

Suppose that you set your authentication order so that the accounts with the lowest level of privileges authenticate first, and that the account with the least access is authenticated by an external server. Then suppose that a well-meaning IT person accidentally assigns everyone to that group. The result would be that no one with externally authenticated accounts would be able to get in with anything other than the lowest level of access. This is also a good illustration of why your administrator-level passwords should be authenticated by FileMaker, not by an external server. If you're not careful with your group management on externally authenticated accounts and you authenticate weaker accounts first, you can, at least temporarily, lock yourself out of your database.

You could remedy this dire scenario by removing the high-level users from the low-level group on the external server (and then logging back in to the system), but we want to drive home the point that you need to put some thought into your security configurations.

If you're having problems trying to get all accounts to use an external authentication server, refer to "Can't Delete Last FileMaker Account" in the Troubleshooting section at the end of this chapter.

CONTROLLING PASSWORD CHANGES

Figure 12.2 is reproduced in Figure 12.11 so you don't have to flip pages back and forth as we discuss the rest of the Edit Account dialog. The next item to consider in the Edit Account dialog is the User Must Change Password on Next Login check box. This feature, too, has a potential pitfall. If this option is checked, but the privilege set specified by the account doesn't allow the user to change his password, the user is not allowed to log in.

That consideration aside, it's generally a good security policy to have users set their own passwords. That way, the database administrator doesn't have knowledge of any account passwords but his or her own. After they are entered, passwords can't be determined even by those with full access.

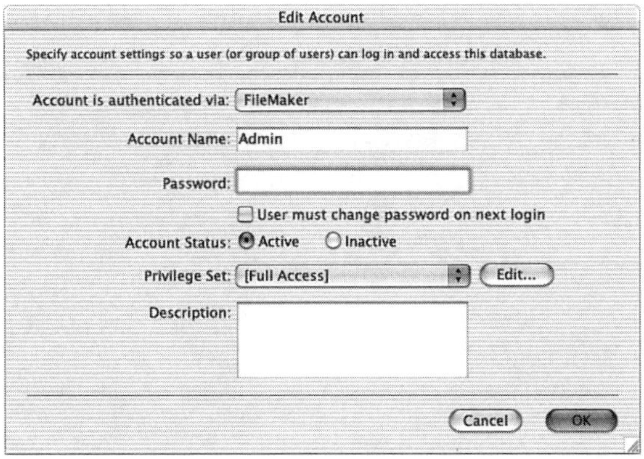

Figure 12.11
Check User Must
Change Password on
Next Login only if the
assigned privilege set
permits password
changes.

> **NOTE**
>
> For accounts that will be used by Instant Web Publishing users, you should never check the Change Password option because that feature isn't supported by Instant Web Publishing.

OTHER ACCOUNT SETTINGS

The next item is the Account Status setting. In previous versions of FileMaker, if you wanted to temporarily disable an account when someone was on leave, your only option was to completely remove the account and set it back up again later. In FileMaker Pro 7, you can set an account to be inactive and then just re-active it again at a later date.

> **TIP**
>
> If you have a large group of employees all starting on the same date, the account status feature allows the database administrator to set up all the accounts in advance without activating them. After the employees start, all that needs to be done is to set the account status to Active.

The next item is the privilege set. The privilege set controls the behavior of the account after it's been authenticated. Privilege sets are a large topic unto themselves, and are covered in detail in the next section.

The last item is the description. Especially for externally authenticated group accounts that don't necessarily match up to a person, it's often helpful to have a short description of the purpose of that account.

PRIVILEGE SETS

The second tab in the Define Accounts & Privileges dialog is the Privilege Sets tab. When you create a new database file in FileMaker Pro 7, the three privilege sets shown in Figure 12.12 are automatically created.

Figure 12.12
Three default privilege sets are automatically created whenever you create a new file.

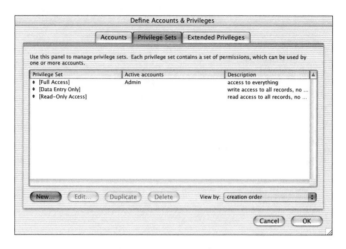

Again, anything wrapped in square brackets [] can't be deleted. In the case of these three default sets, they can't really be changed, either, although extended privileges for the three sets can be enabled.

To cope with problems using a full access account with a file hosted by FileMaker Server, refer to "Can't Access Database Hosted by FileMaker Server" in the Troubleshooting section at the end of this chapter.

CREATING A NEW PRIVILEGE SET FOR A USER

You can create a new privilege set by clicking the New button. This brings up the Edit Privilege Set dialog shown in Figure 12.13.

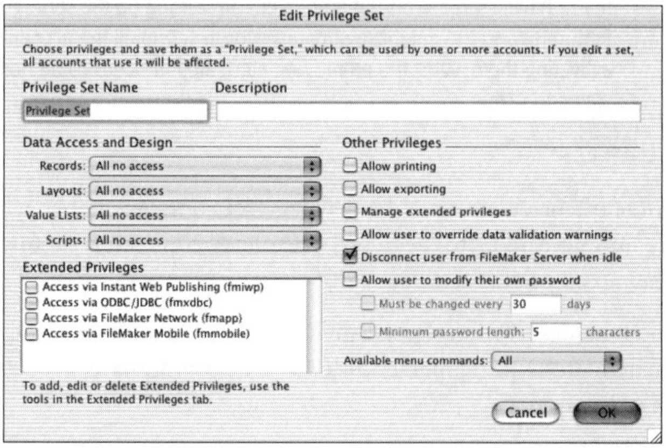

Figure 12.13
This is the default state when a new privilege set is created in FileMaker Pro 7.

Let's take a moment to contrast this with earlier versions of FileMaker Pro. Figure 12.14 shows the Define Passwords dialog from FileMaker Pro 6. If you just created a password without changing any settings, the default level of security was full access. This can be termed an optimistic level of security; all options are granted and need to be shut off if necessary. In contrast, the default state of a new privilege set in FileMaker 7 is pessimistic. All options are shut off and need to be granted if necessary.

Figure 12.14
This is the Define Passwords dialog from FileMaker Pro 6. FileMaker Pro 6 and earlier versions had security settings that defaulted to full access.

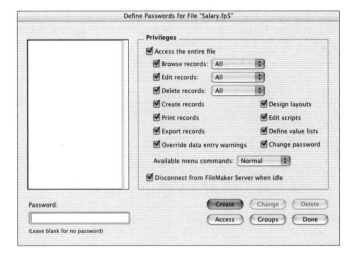

It seems like a small nuance, but the difference is an added layer of security. In earlier versions, if a database administrator forgot to uncheck an option, the result was too little security. In FileMaker 7, if a database administrator forgets to grant an option, the result is too much security, which is preferable. This is an important consideration when converting older systems into FileMaker 7. The optimistic settings of the older systems are re-created in FileMaker 7.

TIP

> When you convert systems that were created in earlier versions of FileMaker pro, be sure to review security post-conversion to make sure the settings meet your security requirements.

→ For more on addressing security issues after a conversion, **see** "Post Conversion Tasks," **p. 522**.

In the Edit Privilege Set dialog (refer to Figure 12.13), you can see that it has three distinct areas: Data Access and Design, Extended Privileges, and Other Privileges. Remember that at the beginning of the chapter we talked about developing a security plan before implementing your security settings. To do that properly, you need to be aware of the security options available to you. As we go through these settings, you should be mentally noting them as tools to help implement your security goals.

The first thing you need to do is name the privilege set. For this example, it's Salesperson, the idea being that this is the privilege set that will be assigned to any users who are salespeople.

If you click on the pop-up menu next to Records, as shown in Figure 12.15, you can see that you have a variety of options when it comes to record access. Note the list of tables at the top of the dialog. For simple systems, it's possible that some users might need to have the same type of access for all tables in the system. In systems of any complexity, though, this probably isn't going to be the case. Marketing or accounting or human resources people might have a high level of record access in marketing- or accounting or human resources–related tables, and a low level of access in other tables.

Figure 12.15
For each privilege set, you can grant full, partial, or no access to records in the database. You can also customize record access.

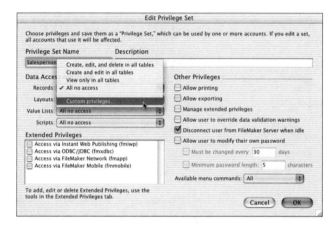

The example at hand has a very simple system with only two tables: contact and salesperson. The rules will be that each contact is "owned" by a salesperson, and salespeople can edit or delete only contact records that belong to them, although they can view contact records that belong to others.

In the Salesperson table, only a sales manager can create, edit, and delete records, although a salesperson is allowed to edit his own particular record. This sort of table-specific access requirement is very common, but it doesn't work with simple access rules that apply to all tables. To implement this scenario, you need to use Custom Privileges for record access. Selecting that option will bring up the Custom Record Privileges dialog shown in Figure 12.16.

Figure 12.16
The default state for a new privilege set is to have all access shut off.

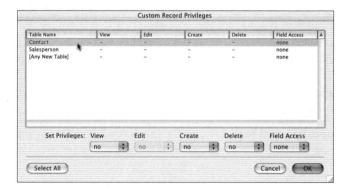

In the Custom Record Privileges dialog, you can set rules for record viewing, editing, creating, deleting, and field access on a table-by-table basis. In addition to that, you can set those rules for any future tables that haven't even been created yet. As new tables get created, they'll automatically pick up the settings specified for [Any New Table].

Notice that once again, FileMaker Pro's default security state is pessimistic. All access is shut off until you specifically grant it. If you want to apply the same setting to two or more tables, you can Shift-click tables to select a range of tables, or (⌘-click) [Ctrl+click] to select noncontiguous tables.

In the current case, you need different settings for different tables, so you need to set them up one at a time. First, select the Contact table and enable record viewing, as shown in Figure 12.17.

Figure 12.17
Record viewing can be on, off, or limited (based on calculated criteria).

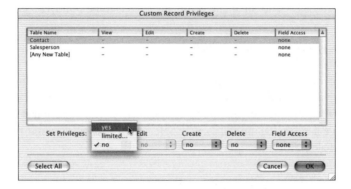

Remember that salespeople can edit and delete only Contact records that belong to them. To implement that, you need to set up limited editing. When you select the Limited option for the Editing privilege, you get the Specify Calculation dialog shown in Figure 12.18.

Figure 12.18
The criteria used for limiting privileges must be Boolean, or an expression that can be evaluated as true or false.

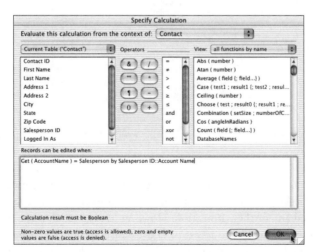

Because you want to allow editing only in cases where the contact record belongs to the current user, you need to have FileMaker check the account name of the current user to be sure it matches the account name for the salesperson that's designated as the owner of the contact. The Get (AccountName) function gives you the name of the currently logged in user, and you can see whether that equals the account name information stored in the salesperson's record in the related Salesperson database. The resulting Boolean (true or false) calculation is

```
Get ( AccountName ) = Salesperson by Salesperson ID::Account Name
```

After this is done, the privilege for creating new records needs to be set to Yes, because all salespeople are allowed to create new contact records. That process is not cut and dried, however. Because each new contact record needs to be tagged with the ID of the salesperson that created it, record creation has to be a scripted process, and the ability for salespeople to create new records using the menu commands needs to be removed. This is covered later in the chapter.

→ To learn how to script the creation of contact records, **see** "Creating a New Privilege Set for a Manager," **p. 333**, later in this chapter.

The next privilege is the Delete privilege, and that should be limited in the same way that the Edit privilege is limited. The last privilege is Field Access, and because salespeople need to be prevented from modifying the Salesperson ID to which a contact has been assigned, this privilege needs to be limited as well. Selecting that option brings up the Custom Field Privileges dialog shown in Figure 12.19.

Figure 12.19
The Custom Field Privileges dialog enables you to restrict access on a field-by-field basis.

It would be normal to assume that the Contact ID field is an auto-entered serial number with the Prohibit Modification of Value During Data Entry setting enabled, and if so, the field doesn't need any further protection. However, this is not the case for the Salesperson ID field. Because it controls the access privileges for each contact record, it needs to be locked down for salespeople. Select the field and then click the View Only radio button as shown in Figure 12.19. No other changes are necessary, so you can just click OK.

At this point, the settings for the Contact table are complete, and they should look like the settings shown in Figure 12.20.

Figure 12.20
The Custom Record Privileges are complete for the Contact table.

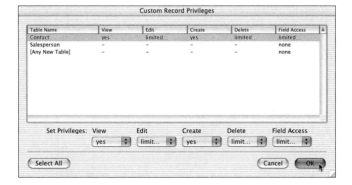

The Salesperson table has different rules. Although every salesperson can view every other salesperson's record, only a sales manager can create or delete records. A salesperson can edit his personal information on his own record, although he can't change his Salesperson ID or Account Name. To enforce these editing rules, you need to use the Limited option for the Edit privilege. The calculation will again be a Boolean calculation that makes sure the currently logged-in user has an account name that equals the value in the Account Name field, as shown in Figure 12.21.

Figure 12.21
This calculation ensures that a salesperson can edit only his own record.

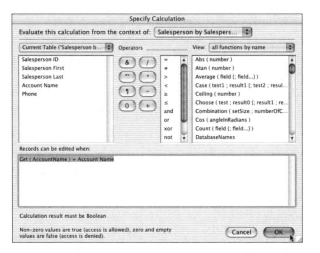

For field editing restrictions, we'll assume again that because the Salesperson ID is the primary key, it is already an auto-entered serial number with the Prohibit Modification of Value During Data Entry setting enabled. To enforce the rule that a salesperson can't edit an Account Name, you need to limit the Field Access privilege, as shown in Figure 12.22.

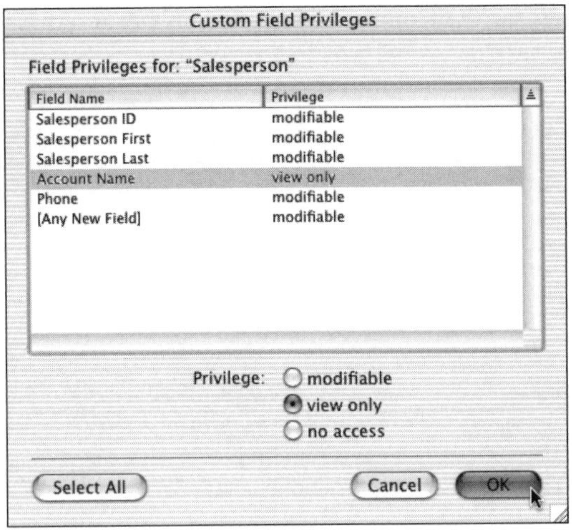

Figure 12.22
Salespeople can edit their personal contact information, but not their Account Name, which needs to match the Account Name in the security settings.

That takes care of the custom record privileges for the salesperson privilege set, but some other settings need to be adjusted. Salespeople need to have access to layouts, value lists, and scripts, although they can't edit any of these. If they can't get to a layout or make use of a value list or run the appropriate scripts, they probably won't be able to use the system properly. When a sales manager sets up a new salesperson record, the corresponding account will be established with a temporary password. That means that salespeople need to be able to change their own passwords.

They also need to be able to print, and because salespeople will be accessing the system while it's being hosted by FileMaker Server, the Access via FileMaker Network Extended privilege needs to be enabled. Later in this chapter you'll learn how to control the creation of contact and salesperson records by scripted logic. To force users to work only through the scripted process, the menu commands need to be set to Editing Only. That will prevent salespeople from using the menu commands to create new records. The result will be the settings shown in Figure 12.23.

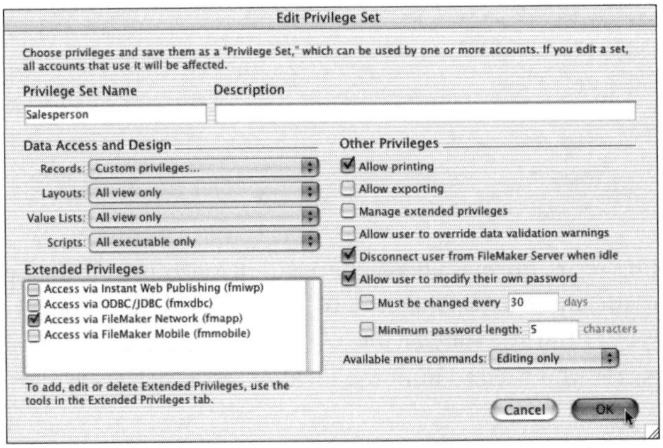

Figure 12.23
These are the final settings for the Salesperson privilege set.

Creating a New Privilege Set for a Manager

The next step is to create a privilege set for sales managers. Obviously, the sales manager privilege set enables them to do much more than a salesperson. They'll be able to create, edit, and delete records in both tables, and they'll also be allowed to export records. For the sake of this example, we'll also allow them to manage extended privileges. Sales managers can have full access to menus, but all other settings are the same as the salesperson privilege set settings. The result is shown in Figure 12.24.

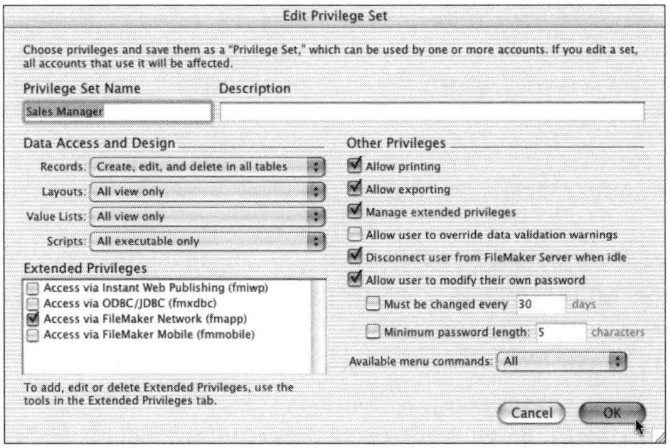

Figure 12.24
Sales managers have much more latitude in working with the system. Compare this figure to the salesperson settings in Figure 12.23.

Although that concludes the setup required for the privilege sets themselves, more work is needed to make those roles fully functional. Because salespeople are to be disallowed from using the New Record menu command to create new contacts, it's necessary to create a script that creates new contact records.

Before you get into the details of the script, you should review the logic. When a salesperson creates a new record, that record needs to have the Salesperson ID of the currently logged in salesperson automatically inserted. You need to be able to determine the appropriate Salesperson ID, and to do that, you'll create a calculation field called z_Logged In in the Contact table:

```
Get ( AccountName )
```

Get functions, when used in a regular calculation, evaluate when the record is created—or when the calculation is first created for existing records. It doesn't update when a new user logs in. The way to force the function to re-evaluate is to make it an unstored calculation by checking Do Not Store Calculation Results, as shown in Figure 12.25.

→ For more information on unstored calculations, **see** "Storage Options," **p. 221**.

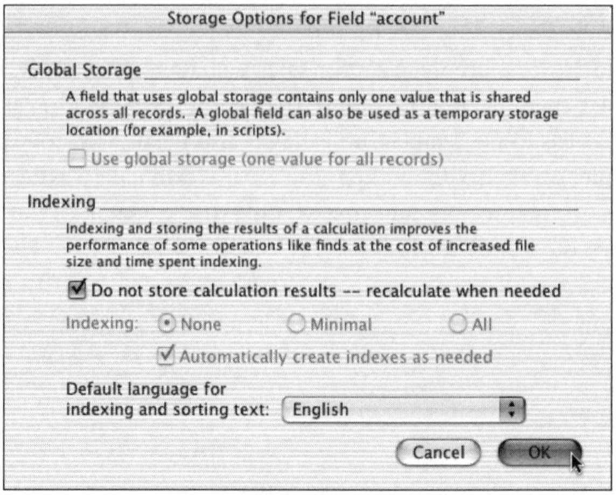

Figure 12.25
Forcing the calcula-
tion to an unstored
state ensures that it
re-evaluates each
time someone logs in.

After the calculation has been created, then you can create the script that creates new
Contact records with the salesperson's ID number. You need to test for situations where the
sales manager or database administrator is logged in, and handle those situations accordingly. The BTN: New Contact script reads as follows:

```
Go to Layout ["Contact" (Contact)]
If [IsValid (Salesperson by Account Name::Account Name)]
  #Currently logged in user has a record in the salesperson table
  New Record/request
  Set Field [Contact::Salesperson ID; Salesperson by Account
Name::Salesperson ID]
Else
  #Currently logged in user does not have a record in the salesperson table
  Show Custom Dialog ["New Contact Error"; "Because you are not
a listed salesperson,
➥ this contact record cannot be linked to you. Contact the Sales Manager
➥ to correct this situation."]
End If
```

In cases where the sales manager or the database administrator are creating new records,
they'll need to manually assign them to a specific salesperson. Another issue needs to be
considered. Remember that the salesperson privilege set was set up so that salespeople
couldn't edit the Salesperson ID field in the Contact table. For this script to set that value, it
needs to be enabled to run with full access privileges, as shown in Figure 12.26.

That takes care of creating new contacts. The next step is to take a look at the script that
will be used to create new salesperson records and add a corresponding security account.

This script needs to be much more sophisticated. It's generally a good idea to keep regular
system users—even higher-level users like a sales manager—from editing the system security
settings. To that end, this script takes the information from the Account Name field and
attempts to create a new account with it. If the account already exists, the sales manager is
notified. If the account doesn't exist, it is created with a temporary password that the salesperson is required to change on the next login. The BTN: New Salesperson script reads as
follows:

Figure 12.26
By enabling the Run Script with Full Access Privileges setting, a developer can allow scripts to perform functions that a user's privileges wouldn't allow.

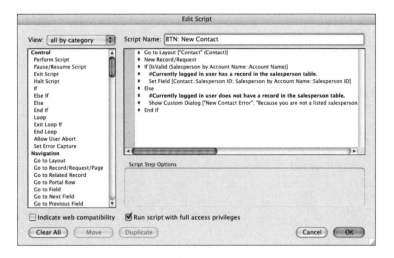

```
Set Error Capture [On]
Go to Layout ["Salesperson Detail" (Salesperson by Salesperson ID)]
If [Get ( PrivilegeSetName ) = "Sales Manager" or Get ( PrivilegeSetName ) =
"[Full Access]"
  New Record/Request
  Loop
    Pause/Resume Script [Indefinitely]
    If [IsEmpty (Salesperson by Salesperson ID::Account Name)]
      Show Custom Dialog ["Missing Account Name"; "You need to enter a unique
      ➥ account name before you can proceed."]
    Else
      Add Account [Account Name: Salesperson by Salesperson ID::Account Name;
      ➥ Password: "Temp"; Privilege Set: "Salesperson"; Expire password]
      Exit Loop If [Get ( LastError ) = 0]
      Set Field [Salesperson by Salesperson ID::Account Name; ""]
      Show Custom Dialog ["Existing Account Name"; "You need to enter a unique
      ➥ account name before you can proceed."]
    End If
  End Loop
  Commit Records/Requests[]
Else
  Show Custom Dialog ["New Salesperson Error"; "Only Sales Managers can create
  ➥ a new salesperson record."]
End If
```

Note that the script starts by setting error capture to On. This is to suppress the FileMaker error dialog that's invoked when the script attempts to create a user account that already exists. Also note the loop within the script. If the sales manager leaves the Account Name field empty or if a new account name is required, the script needs to loop back to the paused state so that the sales manager can complete the data entry.

→ For more information on looping and error trapping within scripts, **see** "Common Scripting Techniques," **p. 249**.

This should give you a good feel for the capabilities of privilege sets in FileMaker Pro, and it should also give you some ideas about how scripts can interact with privilege sets.

EXTENDED PRIVILEGES

NEW As mentioned in the previous section, extended privileges can be assigned to privilege sets to expand their functionality. There are two types of extended privileges: default and custom.

DEFAULT EXTENDED PRIVILEGES

The four default extended privileges are present automatically in any new file, and they can't be deleted. The default extended privileges, which are shown in Figure 12.27, control access to the file from other applications and technologies.

Figure 12.27
The four default extended privileges cannot be deleted.

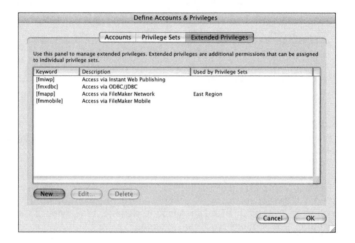

The four default extended privileges are pretty self-explanatory:

- **Access via Instant Web Publishing**—When Access via Instant Web Publishing is enabled for a privilege set, users with accounts attached to that privilege set have access to the file from a Web browser.

- **Access via ODBC/JDBC**—Access via ODBC/JDBC needs to be enabled if you want an ODBC or JDBC client to use SQL to converse with FileMaker.

- **Access via FileMaker Network**—Access via FileMaker Network needs to be enabled for privilege sets that need to access the file over the network when the file is being shared in a peer-to-peer fashion, or if it's being hosted with FileMaker Server so that FileMaker Pro clients can work with it. That isn't the only use for FileMaker Server, by the way. It's possible that you might want to host a database that will be accessed only from the Web, not from a FileMaker Pro client.

- **Access via FileMaker Mobile**—If you're using FileMaker Mobile and you want to synchronize files between FileMaker and Mobile for one or more privilege sets, you need to enable Access via FileMaker Mobile.

→ For more on using ODBC/JDBC with FileMaker, **see** "Importing From an ODBC Data Source," **p. 552** and "Accessing FileMaker Data Using ODBC/JDBC," **p. 578**.

CUSTOM EXTENDED PRIVILEGES

Although important, the default extended privileges are the least interesting aspect of extended privileges. Where things really get interesting is with custom privileges. After they are created, the Get (ExtendedPrivileges) function can be used to detect their assignment to a privilege set. After an extended privilege has been detected, scripts can branch accordingly, fields can validate based on that information, or calculated values can conditionally display values. It's important to note that custom extended privileges have no inherent functionality.

For the sake of illustration, let's suppose that you have a sales contact database with a credit rating screen that gets populated by the Credit department. In a real world example, you might compartmentalize salespeople by team or office or market, and would then grant different privilege sets to each sub-group. In the interest of keeping this scenario simple, we presume a single salesperson group with a corresponding privilege set and use an extended privilege to control access to the Credit Rating layout, even though it would be sufficient to just use the privilege set itself to control access to the layout.

To create a custom extended privilege, you need to be on the Extended Privileges tab of the Define Accounts & Privileges dialog. Click the New button to bring up the Edit Extended Privilege dialog. A custom extended privilege needs to have a name, and because this privilege is to be used to control access to a contact's credit rating, type **credit** into the Keyword box, as shown in Figure 12.28. You can add a description of what the privilege is to be used for, and also assign the privilege to any of the privilege sets. After you've finished making these settings, just click OK. The new extended privilege displays in the list of all extended privileges, as shown in Figure 12.29. Custom extended privileges can be distinguished from default extended privileges by their lack of square brackets.

Figure 12.28
The Edit Extended Privileges dialog can be used to assign the privilege to one or more privilege sets.

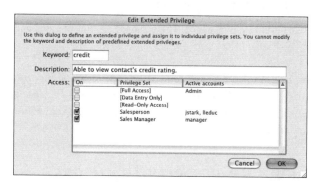

12

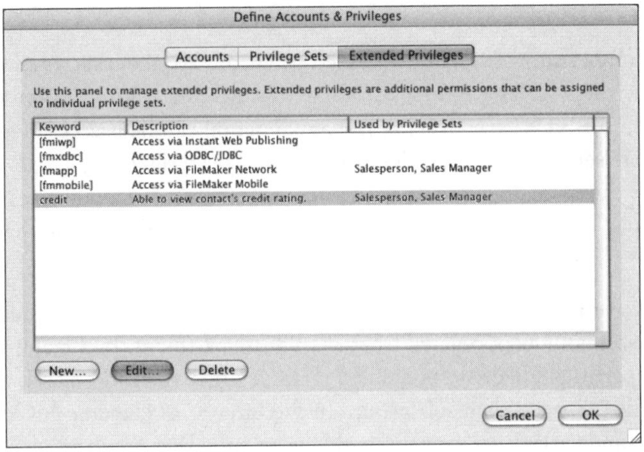

Figure 12.29
FileMaker does not allow you to wrap a custom extended privilege with square brackets.

It's important to remember that extended privileges can be assigned only to privilege sets, not to individual accounts directly. For that reason, extended privileges can be used only to modify the privileges of classes of users. If you need to do things that modify individual accounts, you need to either have different privilege sets for each account, or manage those sorts of things using scripts that test for the currently logged in account and act accordingly.

To take advantage of the newly created extended privilege, we've created a script that permits navigation to a Credit Rating layout only when the currently logged in user has been granted the credit extended privilege. Assuming the existence of the Credit Rating layout and the credit extended privilege, the Credit Rating script would look like this:

```
If [PatternCount (Get (ExtendedPrivileges); "credit")]
   Go to Layout ["Credit Rating" (Contact)]
Else
   Show Custom Dialog ["Insufficient Privileges"; "You do not have sufficient
   ➥ privileges to view the credit rating."]
End If
```

This is just a simple example of how extended privileges can be incorporated into your scripts and calculations to control navigation and field access. Because the detection of the extended privilege is calculation-based, it can also be used in field validation and even in calculated auto-entry situations.

FILEMAKER SERVER SECURITY FEATURES

We've reviewed the authentication settings for FileMaker Server, but there are additional security features built in to the Server product. Specifically, there are security settings that control who can administer a FileMaker Server. There are also security controls for the display of files in the Open Remote File dialog. As was mentioned earlier, because the Server administration tools have a different look on Windows and OS X, the following sections look at how these features are configured on both platforms.

ADMINISTRATION SECURITY

The first thing to understand is how FileMaker Server itself is administered. Using the FileMaker Server Administration tool on Windows, you can use the Administration assistant as shown in Figure 12.30.

Figure 12.30
The Administration assistant takes you through the steps required to configure FileMaker Server.

In earlier versions of FileMaker Server, if you had physical access to the server and could launch FileMaker Server Console, then you could administer the copy of FileMaker Server running on that machine. It relied on the server's security to protect administrative access. In other words, if you had enough access to use the keyboard of that server, then you had enough access to administer FileMaker Server. It was possible to password protect the administration function, but that applied only to people who were trying to administer FileMaker Server remotely.

NEW The new FileMaker Server has a more rigorous security implementation. It recognizes the fact that just because someone has access to a server—perhaps an IT worker who needs to perform backups—that doesn't mean that person should be able to administer FileMaker Server. For that reason, the administrative password can be used to authenticate local administrators who need to administer FileMaker Server while standing at the machine. The FileMaker Server administrator has the option to have this protection apply to just local administrators or both remote and local administrators simultaneously.

This security on remote administrators is important. Although the old FileMaker Server Console could be used only to administer FileMaker Server running on that machine, the new FileMaker Server Administration tool can administer installations of FileMaker Server running on that machine or anywhere on the network.

12

Another change is that FileMaker Server is more tightly integrated with network security implementations. The old FileMaker Server Console allowed you to only create a remote administration password. The new FileMaker Server Administration tool still allows you to create your own administrative password, but you can also use local server accounts or even domain user accounts as long as they have membership in a group called "fmsadmin," as shown in Figure 12.31. For organizations that have centralized control of accounts and passwords, this feature enables FileMaker to easily integrate with existing account administration functions.

Figure 12.31
A group called "fmsadmin" can be used with local or domain user accounts to allow administration of FileMaker Server.

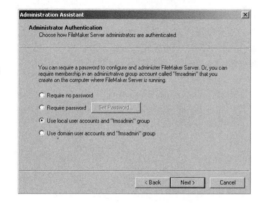

The default behavior is for this password protection to authenticate local administrative users. If you want to allow users to administer FileMaker Server over the network, you need to explicitly enable that behavior, as shown in Figure 12.32.

Figure 12.32
Administrator authentication applies only to local users unless remote administration is specifically enabled.

TIP

> A configuration option that has minor security implications is the hostname that FileMaker Server displays to remote users. It's a security issue in that the default hostname is the server's system name. If the system name is used as the hostname, that means that remote users can probably identify which physical server is acting as the database host. In cases where highly sensitive databases are being hosted, it might be preferable to obfuscate the true "home" of the data. The hostname can be changed with the same administration assistant, as shown in Figure 12.33.

Figure 12.33
Specifying an appropriate hostname can make hosted files easier to locate and can also mask the computer's physical location.

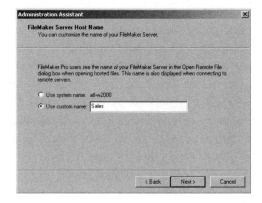

That roughly sums up the sequence of events that you'll go through when you use the Administration assistant on the Windows platform. On Mac OS X, all these steps are compressed onto the Administration tab of the Configure section of the FileMaker Server Admin tool, as shown in Figure 12.34.

Figure 12.34
This is the Mac OS X administration screen for changing the host name.

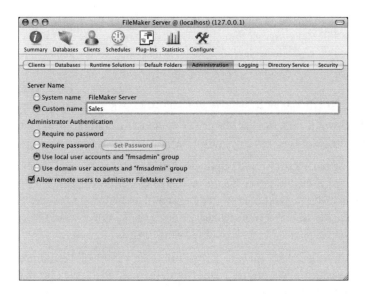

12

DIRECTORY SERVICE INTEGRATION

The next area we need to look at is FileMaker Server's integration with *Lightweight Directory Access Protocol*, or LDAP, directory servicesIntegration with an LDAP server adds a layer of security in that an LDAP server can ensure that users see hosted FileMaker databases only if they have been authorized to use them. This feature was in earlier versions of the product as well, but most FileMaker users aren't familiar with how this feature works. That being the case, this section reviews this feature in some detail. But first you need to understand exactly what LDAP is.

Those who have had to wrestle with configuring applications to work properly with LDAP services tend not to believe in its "lightweight" moniker. The term lightweight is actually in comparison to its predecessor, X.500, a richer, more complicated directory services model. A *directory server* is analogous to a search engine for your local network. It's the directory that lists where everything is. It can list contacts for your address book application, or services, such as FileMaker database services, for your FileMaker Pro application.

Although it's possible to use a directory server anonymously, the real power comes from using accounts. You can configure your Windows or Mac OS X operating system to authenticate you by using a directory server rather than the accounts built into your operating system. After you've been authenticated to the directory server, network resources, such as hosted FileMaker databases, can be made available to you depending on how your LDAP account has been configured.

In the case of FileMaker, if you're using FileMaker Pro and you need to open a database that's being hosted by FileMaker Server, an LDAP server allows you to see only the database files that have been assigned to you. If there are dozens of hosted database files, but you have access to only two, then you'll see only those two in the Hosts dialog.

Setting this up is a bit involved, but after you're finished, it's easy to use. The first step is to configure FileMaker Server. For the LDAP server to be aware of FileMaker Server (they should be two separate servers, of course), FileMaker Server needs to register with the LDAP server.

REGISTERING FILEMAKER SERVER WITH DIRECTORY SERVICES

On Windows, launch the FileMaker Server Administration tool and start the Directory Services assistant as shown in Figure 12.35.

To configure this feature, you're going to need some information from your IT department. You need to know the server's name or IP address, and you need to know a distinguished name to which FileMaker Server can register. The first thing you need to do with the assistant is give the LDAP server's name, although an IP address works just as well, as long as you can be confident that its IP address won't change.

In a Windows environment, the odds are that the server will be running Microsoft's Active Directory, which is Microsoft's LDAP product. If so, check the option that denotes that fact, as shown in Figure 12.36.

Figure 12.35
The Directory Service assistant enables you to register FileMaker Server with a directory services server such as Active Directory.

Figure 12.36
You can use either a server name or an IP address to identify a directory server.

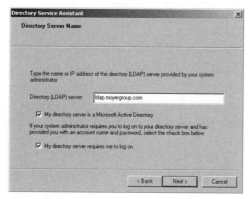

Your FileMaker server will require account credentials to register with the Active Directory server, so check the option that forces your server to require a logon. If this option is checked, the next screen asks for the logon credentials (account name and password).

The next screen asks for a distinguished name. A *distinguished name* is a kind of pointer that specifies where FileMaker Server needs to register in the directory's tree structure. This directory tree structure is an odd concept, so a different kind of example might be helpful. Think of a house. Suppose that you want FileMaker Server to sit in the first chair at your dining room table. A distinguished name would break this up into branches of a tree, starting with the end of the branch and working its way back to the trunk. In this example, a distinguished name might be ou=first, ou=chair, dc=dining room, dc=246 Sycamore Street, dc=house.

Ou stands for *organizational unit*. An organizational unit is any arbitrary unit that the directory server administrator would like to use to organize the directory. In one case, the appropriate organizational unit might be a department; in another, a sales region. It's completely up to the administrator's discretion.

Dc stands for *domain component* and is used to break down a named server's address. If you want FileMaker Server to register in the FMPServer organizational unit on a directory server named ldap.moyergroup.com, then the distinguished name would be ou=FMPServer, dc=ldap, dc=moyergroup, dc=com. It looks a little bizarre, but it makes perfect sense as soon as you understand the structure to which it's referring. This information gets entered into the Distinguished Name screen of the assistant, as shown in Figure 12.37.

Figure 12.37
You'll need to get the appropriate distinguished name information from your directory services administrator.

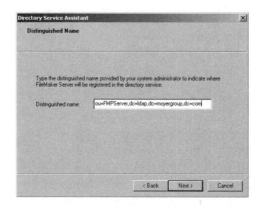

That's about it for a Windows configuration. On Mac OS X, all these screens are condensed onto a single Directory Service tab, as shown in Figure 12.38.

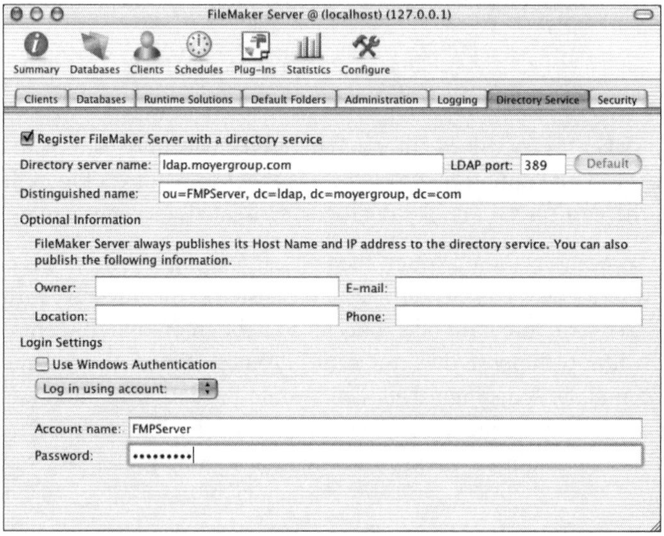

12

Figure 12.38
FileMaker Server Admin on Mac OS X has all the directory services settings listed on one screen.

CONFIGURING FILEMAKER PRO TO USE DIRECTORY SERVICES

Once FileMaker Server has been configured, the next step is to configure FileMaker Pro to make use of the directory server. In FileMaker Pro, choose File, Open Remote to bring up the Open Remote File dialog. Choose Hosts Listed by LDAP from the View pop-up, click Specify and then enter the LDAP settings as shown in Figure 12.39.

Figure 12.39
The LDAP server Search base should match the distinguished name that was used to register FileMaker Server.

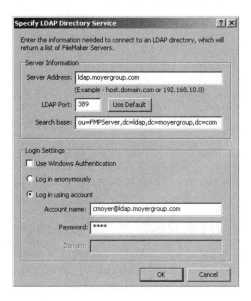

When this has been configured properly, only the database files that you're permitted to see are displayed on the right side of the Open Remote File dialog.

USING DIRECTORY SERVICES WITH THE SERVER ADMINISTRATION TOOL

If you're a database administrator, LDAP can act as your directory for all the FileMaker Server installations that you need to administer. The setup for this is similar on Windows and on Mac OS X. On Mac OS X, with the FileMaker Server Admin tool open, choose FileMaker Server Admin, Preferences. Switch from General to LDAP Directory Service, as shown in Figure 12.40.

For Windows, switch the View menu from Favorite Servers to Servers Listed by LDAP. Click the Specify button to configure directory service information.

After the LDAP preferences have been configured on Mac OS X, choose Server, Connect to FileMaker Server to bring up the Connect to FileMaker Server dialog. Switch from Favorite Servers to Servers listed by LDAP to see a list of available servers. On Windows, just click the Save button to see the list of available servers.

That wraps up the overview of FileMaker's security features. Now that you have a good handle on what security tools are available, you can use that knowledge to design an appropriate security plan for your deployment. The first step in developing that plan is to determine the security risk.

12

Figure 12.40
The LDAP directory server can list FileMaker Servers that are available for administration.

ASSESSING THE SECURITY RISK

In the same way that you need to gather specifications and plan the design of a database system, you need to assess security risks and develop a security plan before cooking up a security implementation. It's always easier to build security into a database system as it's being built than it is to add security features to a complete system, so if you're constructing a new database system, security considerations need to be factored in at the database design stage, not later on.

A security risk assessment can be performed on an existing database system right away, but if a new system is being created from scratch, you need to design the database structure before conducting the security assessment. Without the database structure, you have no way of knowing the scope of the security issues.

The first step in creating a good security implementation is to assess the security risk. The term "security risk" is a very general one. The risk can take a variety of forms:

- Your client information falls into the hands of your competitors and they begin to call on your customers.
- Your customers' credit card numbers are used by unscrupulous employees for their own purchases.
- A copy of your system is reverse-engineered by a competitor and your proprietary formulae or trade secrets are discovered, damaging or eliminating your competitive advantage.
- One or more of your employees don't know how to use the system properly, and they accidentally delete important information.
- Certain employees have the ability to edit scripts, and accidentally cause a business process to malfunction.

The concept of "data" should be thought of in broad terms. Data is certainly the data stored in the fields of a database, but it's also the organizational logic stored in the structure, scripts, and calculations of the database system itself. When you perform a security assessment, you should try to answer the following questions for each table or logical group of tables (a Purchase Order and the corresponding Purchase Order Items, for example) in the database system:

What's the worst thing that could happen if this data fell into the hands of a competitor or hostile user?

What's the worst thing that could happen if all this data were deleted?

What's the worst thing that could happen if the system were tampered with so that this process started handling data incorrectly? For example, what if the line items on an order were assigned to the wrong order?

How long would it take to detect system malfunction errors like the one just described, and how much damage would be done in the mean time?

How much data entry work could you afford to lose in the event of a system failure or malfunction?

For the system itself, you should answer:

What's the worst thing that could happen if a copy of the system fell into the hands of a competitor or hostile user?

Even if data is available from other sources such as product catalogs or the company Web site, there are still reasons to secure your database systems. Just because the data isn't sensitive doesn't mean that it wouldn't be an inconvenience or even a drag on productivity if the system stopped working properly. If a system is left completely unprotected, there's nothing to stop poorly trained users from attempting system modifications. A user who has stumbled into layout mode can easily rearrange fields on a layout, or delete them from a layout.

The point is that even if data isn't sensitive, it's a good idea to implement at least a minimal level of security just to protect the proper functioning of the database system itself. That brings us to the topic of users. While you're evaluating security risk, you also need to identify the different classes of users who work with the system. After you've gathered this information, you're ready to formulate a security plan.

DEVELOPING A SECURITY PLAN

Like the security assessment, a security plan needs to be developed after the structure of the database system is known. For existing systems, the structure is already known, but for new systems, the security plan needs to wait until the system structure plan is complete. As soon as all the tables and field structures have been determined, then you can go through that structure and determine the different levels of access that need to be used with each table and field.

System roles often match up well to job titles in an organization, but it often happens that two people with the same title need to have different roles within the system. Job titles are a good starting point for developing user categories, but don't overlook role differences just because two people have the same title.

You'll need to evaluate user categories in the context of each table. For example, members of a Sales category might need a high level of access in a Contacts table so that they can add, modify, and delete contacts, but they may have view-only access to an Accounts Receivable table. A great way to represent these table-by-table details of a security plan is to construct an access grid for each table. An example is shown in Table 12.1.

TABLE 12.1   ACCESS GRID

User Category	Administrator	Manager	Sales	Accounting
Menu Access (Full, Editing Only, None)	Full	Full	Edit Only	Edit Only
Script Access (Yes, No, Limited)				
Execute	Yes	Yes	Yes	Yes
Modify	Yes	No	No	No
Value List Access (Modifiable, View, None)	Modifiable	Modifiable	View	
Record Access				
View	Yes	Yes	Yes	Yes
Create	Yes	Yes	Yes	No
Edit	Yes	Yes	Limited	No
Delete	Yes	Yes	Limited	No
Field Access				
Contact ID	Yes	Yes	No	No
First Name	Yes	Yes	Yes	Yes
Last Name	Yes	Yes	Yes	Yes
Address 1	Yes	Yes	Yes	Yes
Address 2	Yes	Yes	Yes	Yes
City	Yes	Yes	Yes	Yes
State	Yes	Yes	Yes	Yes
ZIP Code	Yes	Yes	Yes	Yes

12

After you've developed access grids for each table in the database system, you're ready to implement the security plan.

Start by first setting up the privilege sets you're going to need, then the accounts and the extended privileges. After those pieces are in place, you can create or modify scripts and calculations that test for the various security configurations.

TROUBLESHOOTING

LOCKED OUT OF YOUR DATABASE

What can I do if I lose the master password for my database file?

If you lost the master password to your database with earlier versions of FileMaker Pro, it was possible to send your database file to FileMaker, Inc. and have them recover the password for you. That's no longer even technically possible with FileMaker Pro 7. The reason is that the new password encryption methodology renders passwords stored in FileMaker (as opposed to passwords authenticated by an external server) unrecoverable.

That means that you need to be much more careful about ensuring access to your database files than in years past. You need to make sure that a single employee isn't the only person who knows the login information required to get full access to a file. It's not unheard of for a disgruntled employee to leave a company and take the file access information with him or her. It also happens that a developer will work on a database system and then forget to pass on the full access information. She might give that information to someone who misplaces it.

Such mistakes will prevent you from ever modifying your file again with FileMaker Pro 7. You need to take precautions so that you always know who has the full access login information. It's a good idea to have at least two people who know that information so if one person leaves, the information isn't lost. That access should also be tested from time to time so that if someone changes the full access login (intentionally or unintentionally), it can be detected quickly.

CAN'T ACCESS DATABASE HOSTED BY FILEMAKER SERVER

For some reason I can't access the database hosted by FileMaker Server, even though I have a Full Access account.

Sometimes a person can create a database, set up user accounts properly, move the database to FileMaker Server, and then can't even see the database over the network. One common mistake is not enabling the file for network access. It's possible to use FileMaker Server to host files exclusively for Web or ODBC access. If you forget to enable network file sharing, you can't access the file with FileMaker Pro.

If you can see the file, but your full access account doesn't log you in, that means that you forgot to grant the fmapp extended privilege to the [Full Access] privilege set. People often get so caught up in configuring new privilege sets that they forget to grant the appropriate extended privileges to the [Full Access] privilege set.

CAN'T DELETE LAST FILEMAKER ACCOUNT

I want all accounts to use an external server, but I can't delete the last FileMaker account.

FileMaker Pro must have at least one account that's a FileMaker account, so although you can delete FileMaker accounts, even the Admin account, you need to leave one account authenticated by FileMaker. It may be your company policy to have all accounts authenticated by a authentication server, but if that server went down and all accounts were externally authenticated, the FileMaker database would be impossible to access by any means. With at least one account that's authenticated by FileMaker, you're always assured of at least one means of access should the authentication server fail.

FILEMAKER EXTRA: CONFIGURING EXTERNAL AUTHENTICATION SERVERS FOR MAC OS X

To use external server authentication, FileMaker Server must be set to use FileMaker and External Server accounts for Client Authentication. On Mac OS X, you can use either local accounts and groups that reside on the machine that FileMaker Server is running on, or domain accounts and groups. You should consult with your IT personnel in charge of security to determine which option would be preferable in your particular case. Generally, if your organization has centralized control of user accounts and passwords, that information is maintained on a domain server. If login information has not been centralized organization-wide, but you'd still like to maintain account information outside of FileMaker, you can set that up on the machine on which FileMaker is running.

If you happen to be the person responsible for setting up users and groups, you should know that you can maintain this information on either a Mac OS X Server machine or just a machine running regular Mac OS X.

FileMaker Server can run on both Mac OS X Server and the standard version of Mac OS X. Depending on which OS you're on, you need to use different tools to set up user accounts and groups. Mac OS X Server has a tool called the Workgroup Manager that enables you to maintain users, groups, and group membership. You can also use the command line, but it's much simpler to use Workgroup Manager.

The standard version of Mac OS X doesn't come with Workgroup Manager. If you don't use the command line, the usual way to maintain accounts on a non-server version of Mac OS X is to open System Preferences and use the Accounts tool to set up and maintain new accounts. The Accounts tool doesn't allow you to set up groups, however. If you launch Mac OS X's directory system utility NetInfo Manager (found in the Utilities directory), you can actually see users and groups, and group memberships, but it's not a tool for administering user and group memberships.

NOTE

> If you have Mac OS X Server, it comes with a set of Admin Tools that can be installed on a non-server version of Mac OS X, but the tools talk only to a copy of Mac OS X Server elsewhere on the network and can't be used to administer the local machine.

Because FileMaker relies on group membership for external server authentication purposes, this situation is problematic for those who aren't command-line savvy.

Fortunately, there's a donation-ware product called SharePoints (http://www.hornware.com/sharepoints/) that allows you to set up groups on the standard version of Mac OS X. Special thanks to Jonathan Reff for turning us on to this utility. It's so easy to use we won't even describe how to go about it, although you can get an idea of what it looks like in Figure 12.41. The point is that if you want to do external server authentication using local accounts and groups on a standard copy of Mac OS X, you can.

Figure 12.41
SharePoints enables you to administer group assignments on Mac OS X.

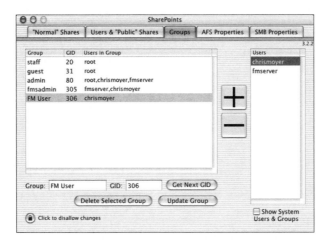

None of this is necessary on Windows servers because you can use the regular account administration tools to set up users and groups.

CHAPTER 13

ADVANCED LAYOUT TECHNIQUES

In this chapter

USER INTERFACES IN FILEMAKER PRO

Every new FileMaker Pro database essentially begins with a single, blank layout. User interface designers—and, yes, you're now one by definition—often have to approach each solution they design somewhat differently, to tailor it for the specific use in question, for the users for whom the system is ultimately intended, and in keeping with the time/budget/scope variables we all struggle with in some form or another. This chapter is not intended to present a complete user interface discourse. How to approach a user interface is a widely debated topic in both the FileMaker and computer science worlds. On the Web, as you no doubt know, what works for one site doesn't often work for another—nor should it. We won't presume to know what the world's most perfect user interface might be.

Rather than trying to present the "what" or "why" of user interface and layout design, we're going to focus on the "how." There *are* some constants in FileMaker interface design: Almost every database solution ever built has some form of navigation, meaning a button-and-script–driven means of moving from layout to layout. Data presentation—how you view and access information in your system—varies, and we explore some of the options there as well. We also examine how to approach working with multiple windows.

This chapter presents a number of different topics. Each section could comfortably stand on its own; the idea here is to present you with some ideas that you can apply to your solutions as you see fit. The chapter assumes a moderately advanced familiarity with FileMaker Pro, but beginners should be able to grasp the concepts quite easily, if they don't immediately understand the implementation.

User interfaces are central to most FileMaker databases. It is rare (though entirely possible) that a FileMaker database would serve only as a back-end data repository, with some other system providing a visual front-end. The Web is an obvious exception, but many FileMaker-based Web systems also have administrative or data-entry functions built into "native" FileMaker Pro layouts and accessed with FileMaker Pro, not to mention IWP (Instant Web Publishing) that depends on layouts being created in FileMaker. Some FileMaker systems also serve as front-end extensions of larger systems through ODBC or XML connections; one of the core reasons why organizations choose to use FileMaker in such cases is the rapidity and flexibility with which interfaces can be built. It's safe to say that not only is storing data fundamental to FileMaker Pro, so too is its presentation.

→ For more detail on Instant Web Publishing, **see** Chapter 21, "Instant Web Publishing," **p. 605**.

Figures, 13.1, 13.2, and 13.3, present some interface examples we've come across in our travels.

Figure 13.1
This is a fairly typical example of a tabbed interface in FileMaker Pro.

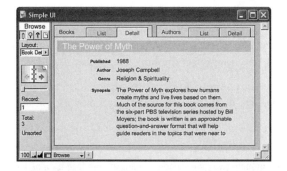

Figure 13.2
FileMaker Tasks, produced by FileMaker, Inc. itself, is a solid example of a classic design. Notice the two tiers of tabs.

Figure 13.3
Here's a different twist on user interface—lean, with lots of white space.

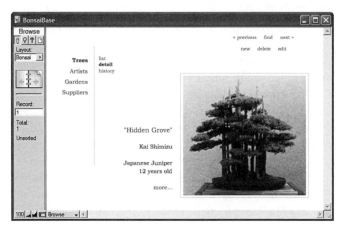

13

Primary user interface considerations include how to trigger functions specific to your database solution (for example, a series of scripts that create monthly invoices), how to manage creating and deleting records, whether or not you want to build some form of interface to help with Find requests, and how a user might run a report.

Other issues will also need to be worked out: What colors do you want the database to be? How much screen real estate do you have? What font will work for all the users in your system?

TIP

> We recommend two things when defining an interface for a new solution. First, define one. Rather than having things just evolve at random, you'll be well served by spending a few minutes up front coming up with a standard approach.
>
> Second, create a prototypical layout for your system and then test it with users before building the rest of your system. Establish a common standard for where things go, how large the screen is, how portals look, and where field labels sit, and then get buy-in from the people who will ultimately live with the database day in and day out. It's far easier to spend a little time in the beginning discovering that your boss deeply loathes the color green than having to go back and rework your database.
>
> When moving forward in your system, it will be easier to duplicate your template layout than to start from scratch each time.

FileMaker's Native User Interface

Another critical consideration for your user interface (UI) is to what degree to use FileMaker's own native elements—the Status Area, menu commands, and Scripts menu—or how to go about replacing them with your own buttons and scripts.

It is entirely possible to build a perfectly usable FileMaker database without a single button. Users rely on the layout menu in the Status Area and, for those reports and functions that require scripts, turn to the Scripts menu. This approach delivers some significant benefits in the time it takes you to build a database, and your users are likely already to understand at least some of the basics of working with a FileMaker database. This bare-bones approach can "just get it working" quite quickly. The downside, aside from simple aesthetics, is that your database may not be particularly easy for non-developers to manipulate in cases where your data structure becomes complex. Data integrity is also an issue: By leaving things "wide open," you invite trouble if you allow anyone to use Replace, Import, Export, Delete Record, and other menu commands. We strongly recommend embracing FileMaker's *raison d'etre*: flexibility. Although it's possible to pull off some quite advanced user interface systems, make sure you take on added complexity deliberately, by choice, and recognize the cost.

NOTE

> Be sure if you use a native approach in FileMaker to do so fully and make use of its security. You can still leave FileMaker's menu commands available to your users if you carefully think through your security setup.

→ For complete details on FileMaker security, **see** Chapter 12, "Implementing Security," **p. 315**.

Building Your Own Interface

The equally possible alternative to a native FileMaker approach is to completely replace the Status Area and menu functions with one's own buttons and scripts. The approach here gives you the most control, but also signs you up for the most work.

You will need to replace all the functions of the Status Area in three of the four modes (it is not possible to replicate its functions in Layout mode), and you'll likely opt to close and lock the Status Area after you've done so.

 To understand how to replicate the functionality of the Omit check box in Find mode, refer to "Omit Re-created" in the Troubleshooting element at the end of this chapter.

Interface Look and Feel

Remember that container fields and objects simply pasted onto a layout can be associated with a script or button action. This enables you to design quite complete user interface elements in the image-editing software of your choice. Buttons can be far more than simply gray rectangles, and it's quite possible to create a user experience that feels nothing like FileMaker in its native state.

We recommend that you insert all such graphical UI elements into container fields set for global storage, rather than paste them directly on layouts. If you ever need to make a change, you need only do so in one place, rather than having to paste an element back onto all the layouts on which it was used and re-apply its script or button behavior.

> **TIP**
> Remember, when you are placing a button on multiple layouts, first apply the script behavior to the element, then copy-paste on all layouts with the behavior intact.

It's even possible to create a kiosk experience in FileMaker Pro that takes complete control of the screen.

→ To learn more about creating kiosks in FileMaker Pro, **see** Chapter 26, "FileMaker Developer and Plug-ins," **p. 777**.

Single File Interface Versus Distributed Interface

We can now put to rest one of our favorite debates from prior versions of FileMaker Pro. Given FileMaker Pro 7's capability to combine tables into one file—that includes external table references to other files—it's the rare case in which you'd ever choose to distribute your user interface across multiple files. We recommend building your user interface layouts in a single file of your solution.

The only exception to this is if you undertake building a modular application—where parts of it are compartmentalized so that they can either be upgraded separately or, for a particularly challenging architecture, optionally used. You may also opt to develop two systems in parallel with an eye toward integration at a later date.

Obviously, there might be times where you have no choice: Your database might have been converted from a distributed interface system from prior versions of FileMaker, in which case you'd need to do substantial rewriting to bring the interface elements into one file.

→ To explore table architecture options, **see** Chapter 6, "Working with Multiple Tables," **p. 153**.

→ For more information on converted files, **see** Chapter 18, "Converting Systems from Previous Versions of FileMaker Pro," **p. 507**.

Navigation

Navigation implementations can come in many forms, and depending on how one defines it, can include a variety of functional elements as well. Your system might perform validation checks, run security routines, manage audit trails, and more. In FileMaker Pro 7, scripts depend on layout context to establish table context. This then means that your users won't be the only ones needing to navigate the system: Scripts will need to switch to different layouts to establish context, and return to the original to maintain the user experience. Likewise, users won't want to *only* navigate. For example, at times they'll be interested in also manipulating found sets or perhaps seeing record selections made, automatically changing modes, or having navigation include a sort command.

In addition to the wide variety of functions navigation performs, its presentation can vary as well. Tabbed interfaces are common, which boil down to simply a series of buttons on a layout that have `Go To Layout` scripts attached.

Again, we don't go into all of these options, but explore the behind-the-scenes techniques you'll find useful and can apply in a variety of ways as you see fit.

Tabbed Navigation

This is one of the classic ways to get around a FileMaker database. Regardless of whether or not you make your buttons actually look like tabs, the basic idea is that you have a series of buttons on each layout, one of which is in a "current" state, and that users can see this omnipresent navigation element as they use the system (see Figure 13.4).

Figure 13.4
The "tab" look was created by simply laying a 2-pixel line along the bottom of the button that needed to appear as a "front" or current tab.

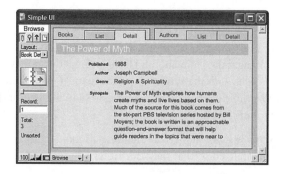

Implementation methods vary widely. At the simplest level, you need only create a button for each layout in your system and attach a Go To Layout button behavior to it. This basic approach isn't the best way to manage buttons in a database solution, but it's a perfectly serviceable method.

You should try to abstract things a bit more. First off, never attach anything other than scripts to buttons to avoid painting yourself into a corner. Second, because navigation routines are going to duplicate a good deal of functionality (ultimately it's only the destination layout that changes) and will very likely evolve over time with a given solution, try to limit the number of scripts that you have to edit when modifying the navigation routines. If you can rely on one central place for all such logic, it is relatively easy to add functionality to your database or to, say, change one layout from an old version to a new updated version.

→ For discussion on scripting best practices, **see** Chapter 9, "Getting Started with Scripting," **p. 241**.

NAVIGATION MEDIATOR AND THE GLOBAL Nav SCRIPT

By using script parameters you can drive most, if not all, of your navigation through one script. The layers of abstraction here could potentially become fairly complex, so we recommend keeping an eye on your goal: creating a simple, single routine for handling navigation. This routine might be called from a button on a layout or from another script. In either case, it needs to work. It would be a waste of effort to have to re-create navigation processes for scripts.

The basic technique is this: Attach a single Nav script to your navigation buttons and set a parameter that the button in question should pass to the script.

→ For more information on script parameters, **see** Chapter 15, "Advanced Scripting," **p. 421**.

You could certainly pass a layout name as a parameter and, within the Nav script called, use the Go To Layout script step combined with a Get(ScriptParameter) calculation. But that still means you have hard-coded layouts attached to buttons. Here's the basic script step:

```
Go to Layout [Get(ScriptParameter)]
```

Now consider where your script parameters live: attached to the however-many buttons you have in your database. If you use this approach, you will essentially hard-code all your layout names to your button assignments.

If you need to change the layout to which a particular set of buttons points, you'll be stuck editing all the parameters of those buttons. This will also be true for a simple renaming of a layout. This dependency nearly obviates the advantages of a single navigation script by giving up flexibility.

To truly abstract your process, you need to set up a *mediator table*. The goal here is to address the inflexibility of attaching layout names to buttons and provide a layer of abstraction that allows again for flexibility. If you store layout names in a data table (the mediator table), and point to specific rows in that table via script parameters, it'll be a snap to modify which layouts the buttons refer to in the future. You could accomplish the same from a large switch process of If Else script steps in a large script, but things are far simpler and more

13

flexible when you simply place your logic in a data table. We'll walk you through the process.

1. First, create a few layouts in any database. For this example, we refer to four: Book List, Book Detail, Author List, and Author Detail. It doesn't matter how many tables or layouts your system has.

2. Now create a new table, Nav, with the following fields:
   - NavCode (text, validated to be unique and required)
   - NavLayout (text)
   - NavScript (text)
   - NavReturn (text)
   - gNavCodeSelected (text, global storage)
   - gNavOriginal (text, global storage)
   - gNavTargetLayout (calculation, global storage, lookup [SelectedNav::NavLayout])
   - gNavTargetScript (calculation, global storage, lookup [SelectedNav::NavScript])
   - gNavTargetReturn (calculation, global storage, lookup [SelectedNav::NavReturn])

   The lookup fields here are global calculations—which means you can reference them without establishing table context, and therefore don't need a Go To Layout (Nav) in your script. You could accomplish the same result by taking the user to the Nav layout, but the screen flashing involved does not make it seem as elegant. To make the lookup calculations work, you need to establish a relationship from one instance of the Nav table to another: a self-join from gNavCodeSelected to NavCode. This enables you to take the script parameter code in gNavCodeSelected and match it to the appropriate row in the Nav table. The resultant lookup fields then push through the correct data.

   Keep in mind that you could just as easily use numbers or full text strings of some sort for the data in your NavCode fields. We recommend using something that can jog your memory and differentiate from other field names or script names.

3. Create a new script, called Navigate, and leave it blank for now. We'll get back to it.

4. Now add a four-button navigation group to all layouts. Assign your Navigate script to each button.

→ To explore layout tools and how they're used, **see** Chapter 4, "FileMaker Fundamentals: Working with Layouts," **p. 89**.

5. Now it's time to populate the Nav table with some data, keeping in mind that some of the system logic is now held in data (see Figure 13.5).

6. Now it's time to write the Navigate script, as shown in Listing 13.1.

Figure 13.5
The codes used both for *NavCode* and *NavScript* are completely arbitrary and internal to your routine. A user will never see them.

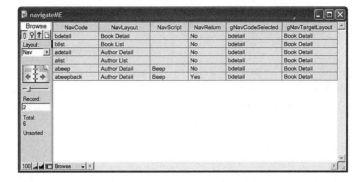

LISTING 13.1   THE Navigate SCRIPT

```
#
#    get Selected script parameter
Set Field [ Nav::gNavCodeSelected; Get (ScriptParameter) ]
#
#    trap the layout from which the script originated
Set Field [ Nav::gNavOriginal; Get ( LayoutName ) ]
#
#    go to the target layout as specified by the SelectedNav relationship
Go to Layout [ Nav::gNavTargetLayout ]
#
#    if the SelectedNav requires a sub-script, run "switch_SubScripts"
If [ not IsEmpty (Nav::gNavTargetScript) ]
Perform Script [ "_switch_SubScripts" ]
End If
#
#    test whether the SelectedNav is intended to return users
➥to the original layout
#    and do so when warranted
If [ Nav::gNavTargetReturn = "yes" ]
Go to Layout [ Nav::gNavOriginal ]
End If
#
```

After you complete this main script, you need to create a _switch_SubScripts script that calls whatever additional script you might want after the navigation routine has taken place. This script holds however many optional sub-scripts you might want, and pulls its target script from the value placed in NavScript. You can write routines that are as elaborate or as simple as you wish. The _switch_SubScripts script might look something like this:

```
If [ IsEmpty (Nav::gNavTargetScript) ]
    Exit Script
Else If [ Nav::gNavTargetScript = "beep" ]
    Perform Script [ "Beep" ]
Else If [ Nav::gNavTargetScript = "findAll" ]
    Perform Script [ "Find_All_Records" ]
Else If [ Nav::gNavTargetScript = "sortAuthorLast" ]
    Perform Script [ "Sort_by_AuthorNameLast" ]
```

13

```
Else If [ Nav::gNavTargetScript = "sortAuthorfindAll" ]
    Perform Script [ "Find_All_Records" ]
    Perform Script [ "Sort_by_AuthorNameLast" ]
End If
```

Keep in mind that we've not taken this methodology all that far at this point. You could very easily add script steps (or sub-scripts for clarity) to handle closing and locking the Status Area, maintaining window positions, or processing data integrity checks, or to include security privilege checks before taking a user to a specific layout.

This overall approach is clearly more work than simply using the Status Area Layout menu or dropping a few buttons on your layouts with Go To Layout button behaviors attached, but we think it's an approach that can grow with almost any system. If you're honestly planning only a handful of layouts in a solution, the overhead here might not be worth the result, but we suspect that if you're reading this chapter you're already working on systems that would benefit from this approach.

Branched Layout Navigation

One interesting possibility this approach also offers is the potential to branch your navigation routines based on data. Imagine building two layouts and driving users to them by either preference or privilege: You could offer two different list views, for example, and your navigation system could direct users as appropriate. The architecture fleshed out in the current example doesn't support this, but it wouldn't be difficult to extend for that purpose.

This drives home the point of this exercise as well. Imagine building this navigation scheme and having your users request exactly that which we've described: Some users want to see "version one" of a list layout, and other users need access to a "version two." If you'd built your navigation with separate, multiple scripts or attached Go to Layout script steps to buttons without the benefit of scripts, the alterations your database would require might be fairly numerous. In this abstracted navigation approach, you need only modify and test the one Navigate script, and need not modify your layouts or buttons at all.

One approach in dealing with branching layouts would be to modify the way in which the NavLayout is determined. As it stands today, that value is simply entered by an administrator or developer in data. It would be almost trivial to insert some logic here in the process whereby a second table is consulted with a concatenation of NavCode and Get(PrivilegeSetName).

Back Buttons

One of the most dreaded questions we used to hear while working with previous versions of FileMaker Pro was, "Where's the Back button?"

It's not that Back buttons were technologically that big a deal…it's just that they used to be a lot of work, and added unwelcome overhead to database solutions. In FileMaker Pro 7, they're a snap, and the new ceiling on storage limits makes overhead a complete non-issue. This is a great example of how FileMaker Pro 7 dramatically extended the horizon forward for all of us.

FileMaker Pro has two layers of navigation (a subtlety many novice users don't immediately grasp): navigation from record to record and navigation from one layout to another. Web browsers aren't troubled by such things, nor in their stateless world is there a distinction between "data" and "page." The metaphor of a Back button isn't a perfect fit in FileMaker Pro, but users will immediately understand what they do. They'll help users distinguish more easily between the book icon (or your replacement for it) and navigating from layout to layout.

The approach shown here leverages the abstracted navigation routine described in the preceding section. We hope you've been following along.

Our goal here is to track each instance of navigation that a user makes—by writing to a navigation history table—and then be able to trace backward along those historical records.

The first task you'll have is to trap the instances of navigation commands that you want to store in history. Create a NavHistory table, as shown in Figure 13.6.

Notice in the figure that you're storing AccountName with NavHistory records. If you didn't do so, you'd have no means of differentiating your back history from someone else's (assuming you've assigned one account per person).

Figure 13.6
AccountName and NavCode are the two points of data you need to track navigation history.

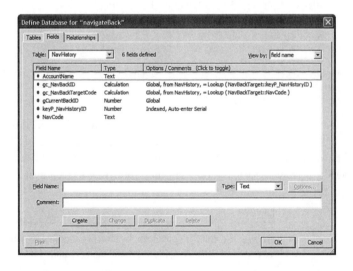

You also need to create a self-join relationship to a second table occurrence, relating gCurrentBackID to keyP_NavHistoryID (see Figure 13.7). This relationship enables you to track the current row in the history by controlling the values in gCurrentBackID. It provides the target NavCode you need if someone clicks the Back button. Keep in mind: It's the second most-recent record you need, not the first. If someone clicks the Back button, you don't want to perform the last navigation command executed. That simply takes him to the layout on which he already sits. You need to step back one record in the history. To accomplish this, simply change your relationship from an equijoin (=) to a greater than (>) relationship.

→ To learn more about the different join and relationship types, **see** Chapter 6, "Working with Multiple Tables," **p. 153**.

Figure 13.7
This relationship actually relates to all the prior records (you'd see them if you set up a portal) but FileMaker, when asked, takes values from only the first valid match it finds.

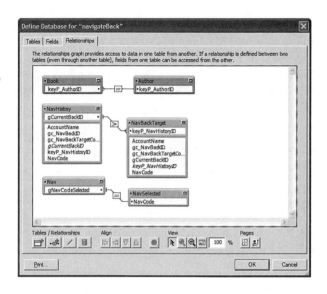

Now create a script for creating new records in the NavHistory table. You should call this script each time the user clicks on a navigation button.

```
Go to Layout [ "NavHistory" (NavHistory) ]
New Record/Request
Set Field [ NavHistory::AccountName; Get (AccountName) ]
Set Field [ NavHistory::NavCode; Get (ScriptParameter) ]
Set Field [ NavHistory::gCurrentBackID; NavHistory::keyP_NavHistoryID ]
Commit Records/Requests [ No dialog ]
Go to Layout [ original layout ]
```

Notice that this script depends on a script parameter as well. You need to set this from within your Navigate script, and it is the same parameter that was passed from the original button that was clicked for navigation. Also notice that you're establishing context with the Go to Layout ("NavHistory") step, and then returning to whatever context in which the system was at the beginning of the script.

NOTE

> The NavCode field could be populated by lookup or some other approach, but a script parameter seemed fairly straightforward and didn't require a relationship or globals.

Now you need to create the conditions by which this Create NavHistory script will be performed.

Here's your modified Navigate script:

```
#
# get Selected script parameter
Set Field [ Nav::gNavCodeSelected; Get (ScriptParameter) ]
#
# trap the layout from which the script originated
```

```
Set Field [ Nav::gNavOriginal; Get ( LayoutName ) ]
#
# go to the target layout as specified by the SelectedNav relationship
Go to Layout [ Nav::gc_NavTargetLayout ]
#
# record the navigation in the NavHistory table
If [ ( Nav::gc_NavTargetInternal ≠ "yes" ) and ( Nav::gNavBackFlag ≠ "yes" ) ]
    Perform Script [ "_record_NavHistory"; Parameter: Nav::gNavCodeSelected ]
End If
#
# if the SelectedNav requires a subscript, run it from
⮕the "switch_SubScripts" script
If [ not IsEmpty (Nav::gc_NavTargetScript) ]
    Perform Script [ "_switch_SubScripts" ]
End If
#
# test if the SelectedNav is intended to return users to the
⮕original layout, and do so when warranted
If [ Nav::gc_NavTargetReturn = "yes" ]
    Go to Layout [ Nav::gNavOriginal ]
End If
#
```

The interesting thing about this script is that it required you to add only a few steps, and the system doesn't need to know anything at all about the back function you've built. It simply needs to record navigation history.

You won't want to record some navigation: internal scripts that establish context and then return to an original layout, and the navigation that the Back button itself performs. If you add both a NavInternal attribute and a flag, gNavBackFlag, to your Nav table you can check against both when performing navigation routines. More specifically, you need to check these only when writing new NavHistory records.

NOTE

> The If condition has been included in this script for clarity, but you could just as easily have included it in the _record_NavHistory sub-script.

Now look at Figure 13.8 and note what happens now when you navigate the system.

There's one last step in creating your Back button functionality. You need a Back button and script. Fortunately, you can use the same navigation script you've already written. Here's the script you'll need:

```
Set Field [ Nav::gNavBackFlag; "yes" ]
Perform Script [ "Navigate"; Parameter: NavHistory::gc_NavBackTargetCode ]
Set Field [ NavHistory::gCurrentBackID; NavHistory::gc_NavBackID ]
Set Field [ Nav::gNavBackFlag; "" ]
```

Attach this script to a Back button. You don't need a script parameter. Notice that this script uses the Navigate script to control where it goes, and instead of passing a fixed, button-specific parameter, it simply passes the value from NavHistory.

Figure 13.8
You'll add records to this NavHistory table at a prodigious rate. We recommend writing a clean-up script that deletes all the records for a specific Account when closing the database, unless you'd like to be able to "go back" across sessions.

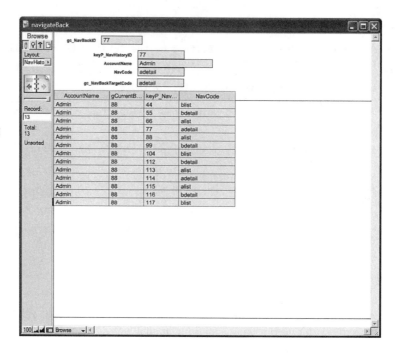

One big caveat with the work you've just read: It's incomplete. This script will not function correctly in multi-user situations, nor is there any error trapping going on whatsoever. We leave both in your hands.

 For a discussion of how to approach multi-user back button functionality, refer to "Multi-user Back Button Functionality," in the Troubleshooting section at the end of this chapter.

OTHER NAVIGATION TECHNIQUES

There are many other approaches you could use for navigation, but in general they are variations on the themes we've mapped out so far in this chapter. Scripts—however they're displayed—call Go to Layout script steps and send the user to a new layout. In an extreme case, we once ran into a database that used the four corners and edges of the screen for navigation. A degree of luck was involved because the system lacked any labels or indication that there were actually buttons there at all. Some navigation schemes are better than others, no doubt. The following are a few other approaches than the one described here.

Rather than lay buttons directly on a layout—buttons that are always present on that layout—some developers choose to create *navigation portals*. Each portal row contains a button and some attribute (the equivalent of the nav codes from the previous example) that then determines what script or layout should be the result of a button click. This could work with script parameters passing a layout name, or it would fold nicely in with the nav code approach as well.

In other cases, perhaps a simple pop-up menu and Go button can be used. In this instance, a user would make a navigation choice from a menu, then click a Go button, initiating a script that would use the menu choice to determine what navigation to perform. It could make this determination using a series of If/Else statements, or the system could be set up for some kind of data-driven navigation, as in the nav example earlier in the chapter. In this case the user's choice would be a key that would point to a data record fully describing the chosen navigation option and its logic.

A third idea is to establish buttons on their own layout and script the opening and maintaining of that window as a "navigation palette." The downside of this approach is that your users need to click twice to use it: once for the window to come forward, and once again to activate a navigation button/script; however, this is a great approach for people with different monitor resolutions (allowing those users with large monitors to place their navigation window wherever they choose), and makes navigations a distinct process, separate from other functions.

Regardless of which visual and presentation approach you prefer, we encourage you to think ahead and try to bake in some flexibility and room to grow when dealing with navigation scripts. They are more often than not some of the most interwoven and omnipresent script routines in your solutions.

MULTI-WINDOW INTERFACES

Opening a new window for your navigation elements is only the tip of the iceberg when it comes to working with multiple windows. It is now possible in FileMaker Pro 7 to strictly control multiple windows—their position, size, and title—and to present entirely new experiences for your users than in past versions of FileMaker Pro.

The simple nuts and bolts of these features can be found in the Window script step options. With them you can create new windows, close windows, select (bring to front) a specific window by name, adjust and resize windows, tile and cascade multiple windows at once, and control the availability of the Status Area as well.

Figure 13.9 shows a simple example of the script options for the New Window script step.

The possible uses for multiple windows are quite varied.

- View as many layouts at once as your screen real estate allows.
- Create multiple list view windows of the same table, with different found sets, at once.
- Use a form for editing a single record while still viewing multiple records via either list or table view.

TOOL AND FUNCTION PALETTES

As discussed previously, it's possible to build a palette for navigation, functions, or any number of options for buttons in your solution. For example, you might want to present your users with a new window containing a portal of all the possible reports in their database solutions—that also open in their own individual windows. Another idea might be to have a central "control panel" that allows you as a developer to unlock certain layouts, run test scripts, re-log in, view internal field data, and so on.

Figure 13.9
This square 500px by 500px window opens with a title of MyWindow and is positioned in the upper left of the screen.

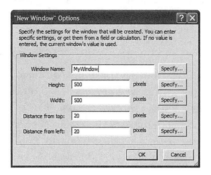

The only drawback to this approach is that users need to click twice to perform button actions: once to bring the window forward, into an active state, and a second time on the button of their choosing.

RICH DIALOG WINDOWS

Modal dialogs—windows that stay open in the foreground while waiting for some action to be performed by the user—are a common user interface standard that users will find familiar. Certainly the Show Custom Dialog script step will take care of some of your basic needs, but in cases where you'd like to control the look and feel of a dialog or need more than three simple text entry fields, you will need to turn to crafting your window dialogs.

This technique is entirely driven by scripts. You are free to build whatever type of layout and window you wish. The only stipulation here is that you give users a means of "continuing" with the process after you've brought them to a modal dialog. Your database will be in a paused state, waiting for user input. More often than not, resuming from this state is accomplished with a Continue button, or, with a bit more scripting, Submit and Cancel buttons.

Cancel buttons imply that whatever action the user has taken in the modal dialog window can be undone. One technique for managing the undo process is to use global fields for data entry and to populate "true" fields only when the user clicks Submit. Other techniques involve record-level rollbacks. (A *rollback* essentially undoes a transaction in a database, returning it to a prior state.)

→ To learn more about rollbacks and undo operations, **see** Chapter 11, "Developing for Multi-User Deployment," **p. 297**.

To build a modal dialog, follow these steps:

1. Build a layout intended to act as your pop-up dialog, called Pop Up. Size it in such a way that it is smaller than a "main" layout that is to remain behind it. You can add whatever functions and layout objects onto it that you wish. The layout can be as

simple as a single field, or it can be as complex as on that displays a subsummary report in preview mode.

2. Add a Done button to your Pop Up layout. For now, attach it to its own placeholder script with just a comment. You will return to it later.

3. Now place a button on your "main" layout. For now, create a label for it: **Open**. Attach it to the following script:

```
Allow User Abort [ Off ]
New Window [ Name: "Pop Up"; Height: 300; Width: 500; Top: 100; Left: 100 ]
Go to Layout [ "Pop Up" (MyTable) ]
Show/Hide Status Area [ Hide, Lock ]
Pause/Resume Script [ Indefinitely ]
```

It's important to disallow user abort; otherwise users can close your window without performing the action you're attempting to require. It's also a good idea to lock the Status Area. Finally, you need to hold FileMaker in a paused state so that users can't perform any other action while attending to the dialog. Generally it's a bad idea to leave a script paused—users can get stuck in limbo—but in this case it is exactly the behavior you want. The script ends, leaving the user in a paused state. You need to remember this when performing any additional scripts or when providing other functions in your Pop Up window.

 For details on the caveats and pitfalls of using this technique, refer to "Modal Dialog Dangers," in the Troubleshooting section at the end of this chapter.

Keep in mind that your users will still be able to run scripts that are visible in the Scripts menu. In solutions that use this technique, developers often opt to *not* set scripts to display in the Scripts menu, or write their scripts such that all that are visible take into account this paused state (by either refusing to run or ending gracefully so that the user's state in the modal dialog window is not disrupted).

Now return to ScriptMaker and create the Done script. You need to write whatever application logic your solution requires (for example, committing data to fields from globals, performing an evaluate function, running a report, and so on) and end your script with

```
Close Window [ Name: "Pop Up" ]
```

One final element is critical. You'll notice we haven't yet dealt with the pause state. If you add a Pause/Resume script step to the Done script, FileMaker won't know that you want it to resume a currently paused script. The behavior it respects is to overlay a new pause state on top of the earlier pause state. This is entirely as it should be: This allows you to build routines with multi-tiered pause states.

13

Multi-Tiered Pause State

A *multi-tiered pause state* can occur when you have one routine running, paused, while another runs and then hits a pause state of its own. For example, you might be running a report that pauses for a user to enter some find criteria. In performing the find sub-script, your process might turn up zero records and pause again to have the user respond to some options on what do to about the situation. These multi-layered pause routines fold into each other like Russian dolls: Each pause needs its respective resume script step performed before the outer pause state can be itself resumed.

The solution to dealing with your pause state lies with the button options attached to each button object. Select your Done button object and either right-click or navigate to the Format menu (in Layout mode) and choose the Button option. Another technique is to simply double-click on the button object in Layout mode. Refer to the Current Script options shown in Figure 13.10.

Figure 13.10
Notice the rarely used Current Script option.

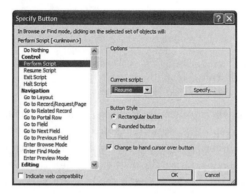

The Current Script option for the Perform Script button behavior is almost never changed. Most often its default state of pausing a currently running script while performing whatever new script is necessary will meet your needs. In this case, however, you need it to resume the current script (which will simply continue from the pause state, effectively ending it) before proceeding through the Done script and closing the pop-up window.

This then closes the pause state without creating a nested second one and allows the user back into the state of using the database solution normally. Combined with the `Close Window` script step, the user's experience will be that of clicking Done and seeing the window close. Clicking your Open button sends users back to the layout from which they began.

SPECIAL EFFECTS

Other window techniques don't seem to add much more functionality to your solution, but can certainly be fun to include for more polish (or to just show off). Calling these techniques "special effects" is probably a stretch—we hope those of you who are Flash developers will just let this section roll by for what it's worth—but we've had some fun coming up with a few tricks that you can pull off with window script steps.

MARQUEE TITLES

Using a simple loop, you can rename the title of a window with progressively scrolling text. Use a `Set Window Title` script step inside a loop. Use a number increment (stored in a global field) and apply it to a `Right` or `Left` function with the text you want to display. The script looks like this:

```
New Window [ Height: 500; Width: 500; Top: 20; Left: 20 ]
Set Field [ myTable::loopIncrement; 1 ]
Loop
```

```
        Exit Loop If [ myTable::loopIncrement = Length (myTable::windowTitleText) ]
        Set Window Title [ Of Window: Current Window; New Title: Middle
        ➥( myTable::windowTitleText; myTable::loopIncrement; myTable::
        loopIncrement) ]
        Set Field [ myTable::loopIncrement; myTable::loopIncrement + 1 ]
        Commit Records/Requests [ No dialog ]
        Pause/Resume Script [ Duration (seconds): .1 ]
End Loop
```

Not the greatest use of computer technology ever made, but you can certainly draw attention to a warning message or alert of some kind.

EXPANDING WINDOWS

By using a similar looping technique you can alter the horizontal and vertical dimensions of a window so that it appears to "grow" or expand onto the screen:

```
New Window [ Height: 500; Width: 500; Top: 20; Left: 20 ]
Set Field [ myTable::loopIncrement; 1 ]
Loop
    Exit Loop If [ myTable::loopIncrement = 500 ]
    Move/Resize Window [ Current Window; Height: myTable::loopIncrement;
    ➥Width: 500; Top: 40; Left: 40 ]
    Set Field [ myTable::loopIncrement; myTable::loopIncrement + 1 ]
    Commit Records/Requests [ No dialog ]
End Loop
```

This particular example is somewhat slow because it needs to loop 500 times to draw the window in question. Play with the increments in your Set Field [myTable:: loopIncrement] script step to make your window draw more quickly. You could just as easily set the width in a similar manner.

HIDING WINDOWS

You can use starting coordinates for a window of 9000, 9000, or negative numbers to "hide" windows off screen. On the Mac this works beautifully—users will have no idea they're there—but on Windows no matter what you do you are presented with scroll bars in the FileMaker application window.

SHOWING/HIDING CONTEXTUAL LAYOUT ELEMENTS

13

In addition to presenting various windows for your users, there are times as a developer that you'll want to control whether or not users have access to specific functions on a current layout. A simple example might be a Delete button: Not everyone who uses your database should be given delete privileges. If you have placed a button on your layouts for deleting records, you'll need to either trap for an un-authorized attempt to use it (and likely present a graceful, "you're not permitted to do that" message with FileMaker's security settings), or craft separate layouts that offer both the "full" and "limited" functionalities you need.

Creating a new layout for each case in which you want to hide or display specific layout objects is obviously a technique you'll want to use sparingly. Any change made on one of these duplicated layouts requires that you change all versions. This quickly can become a maintenance nightmare. Conversely, there are many useful applications of being able to conditionally display information and functions. Imagine a social security field that appears only for members of your HR department. Another scenario might be a tab in your user interface that only administrators can see or click. A third possibility could include Submit and Cancel buttons appearing on screen only after someone has modified available fields. You certainly won't want to have to create separate layouts for each of these cases. Pragmatism will be at odds with UI design.

To get layout objects to appear and disappear based on some programmatic condition, use portals. In addition to displaying data fields, portals can contain layout objects in FileMaker Pro. When one or more records are related to the table occurrence associated with your current layout, their rows appear in a portal, along with any buttons or other layout objects you've placed there. When there is no valid related data, neither the data itself nor layout objects appear. If a user were to click in that area of the screen, nothing would happen.

A simple example is shown in Figure 13.11.

NOTE

Although the portal displayed here has a border for clarity, in your finished solution you'd likely want to make it invisible by applying no border.

Figure 13.11
Your button simply "appears" onscreen when appropriate.

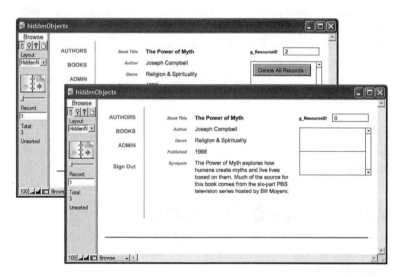

You can implement this sort of functionality in your database solutions in a variety of ways. The simplest approach is to create an "on/off" resource table (simply a table you'll use as a developer to store internal logic) with one record. When necessary, simply relate to it by populating a global in your main user interface table with perhaps a constant that matches the same in the resource table. Place whatever layout objects you need in its single portal row. Because you won't be drawing from any data in the resource table, you need only as many records as you expect to display in your "contextual" portal rows.

Another approach gives you more flexibility: Add button labels and script parameters to your resource table. To control which button appears in your portal, change the resource match key. If you use script parameters pulled from the related row, you need not bother changing the script attached to your button. Simply use an If/Else switch script to point your buttons to the appropriate scripts. If you need to add more contextual functions to your database, simply create a new resource record.

These techniques are driven by a resource key in your current table (and table occurrence as dictated by your current layout). By using a multi-key, you can offer multiple, contextual buttons when appropriate (see Figure 13.12).

→ To explore managing multi-key match fields, **see** "Multi-keys and Multi-row Selections," **p. 460**.

Figure 13.12
This portal dynamically presents functions based on security and navigation area variables.

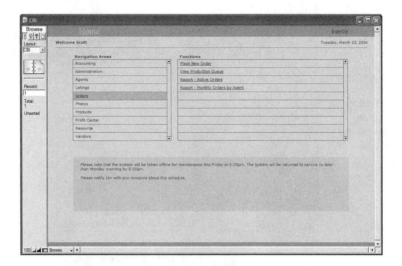

Another dimension for these techniques is working horizontally. By specifying the starting row for a portal, you can have multiple buttons appear side by side. This would work well for the resource file example (see Figure 13.13).

Another application of this technique can be even more specific to your database. Consider cases where often you don't have the screen real estate to display multiple portal rows, and would like users to have a stronger visual cue than just a darkened scroll bar for additional associated child records.

Instead of pointing to a resource database, these techniques can also be applied to actual data tables. Imagine a series of tabs appearing in cases where you, say, have more than one mailing address for a contact (see Figure 13.14). Another example might be where you want to have available multiple pieces of account information for a customer.

13

Figure 13.13
To make buttons appear horizontally, place duplicates of the same portal side by side and change its starting row.

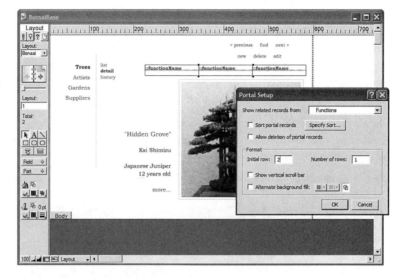

Figure 13.14
Notice that a tab appears only in cases where related data is present.

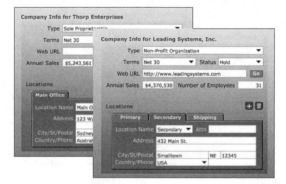

The various applications for this technique are wide ranging. We encourage you to use it once or twice so you're familiar with its implementation. After you've got it comfortably added to your toolbox, your creativity will kick in and you'll spot cases where you can use it to great effect.

DEDICATED FIND LAYOUTS

Entering Find mode and performing Find requests is a crucial part of FileMaker Pro, but it's also one of the more difficult things to manage at the user interface level. As your solutions become more complex, Find mode will not be as intuitive for users: They might not have all the fields by which they want to search on one layout, or they may want to perform find requests on related data. Although FileMaker Pro can manage this quite easily, users may be disoriented or confused by the results.

For example, say you've created a "utility" relationship that displays related data based on selected criteria or some temporary condition in the database. The fields sitting on your layout are not a "structural" one-to-many representation of your primary data architecture. Nonetheless, human users will intuitively want to hop into Find mode and have the process act on the "primary" relationship rather than your utility relationship.

Here's an example: Imagine looking at an author table with a related book title field of the most current book written by that author. By definition, only one book can be the most current. Now imagine that someone is searching for an author who wrote a given book a long time ago. She is likely to click into that field in Find mode and be baffled why it returned zero results—or worse yet, not realize her mistake. Given that the fields on the right relate only to the most current book for an author, the search would be accurate but yield undesirable results.

Furthermore, there may be dozens of fields in your database, related and otherwise, but users will want to search on only a small handful of these 90% of the time.

To make the Find process as intuitive as possible, you can create a separate find layout. An additional nicety is setting it up to open in a pop-up window. Your users will remain in context—in other words, they'll see where they were in the window behind the current one—and will intuitively understand the process going on.

You can build Find processes generally in two ways, each of which is covered in the following sections.

DEDICATED FIND MODE LAYOUTS

The first process is perhaps the most simple. Create a separate layout and populate it with all the appropriate fields specific to the table in which a Find is to be performed. Take care to place "primary" related fields on these layouts: Using the book example again, you'd place a book title from an authorID-to-authorID relationship between the Book and Author tables. The find result would then properly return authors who wrote books—any books, not just the most current—that matched the find criteria.

You can rely on users navigating to these find layouts themselves, along with entering Find mode and performing finds, or you can script the process. The scripted process would involve a button on your standard layouts to take the user to the special Find layout and enter Find mode. A second button on the Find layout itself would perform the request and return the user to the original layout and Browse mode.

This is a great way to give your users an intuitive process and shield them from unpredictable results. It's also a nice way to reduce the sheer volume of fields from which they have to choose in Find mode.

SCRIPT-DRIVEN FINDS

A more complex Find routine replaces the fields in the preceding example with globals. Instead of having users work with the related fields themselves (which in Browse mode would display actual data and pose, potentially, a problem if users didn't realize they had access to actual data), you can control access and the entire process using a script, and offer users empty global fields for entering find criteria.

13

This is a complex approach, and relies on heavy scripting. As in the example in the previous section, you need to bring users to the Find layout. This time, leave them in Browse mode. After their find criteria is entered, they need to click a Find button that then takes the system into Find mode, populates and performs the find request (by using Set Field script steps), and then returns the user to some proper results layout.

The difficulty here lies in replicating all the Find functionalities: inserting omit requests, extending found sets, constraining found sets, and working with multiple requests. We'd recommend using this technique only in rare cases when you want to fully control the user experience.

DATA PRESENTATION

Just as the functional side of your solutions has to be intuitive—navigating from layout to layout or window to window, gaining access to various functional buttons, and interacting with FileMaker's Find processes—viewing data needs to be so as well.

We don't need to cover some of the basics, such as differentiating between fields and field labels, or logically grouping information together (as in a company's street address, city, state, and zip fields) but you should take note of FileMaker's capabilities to auto-format data and manipulate text style formatting.

TEXT FORMATTING

By using the Text Formatting functions—RGB, TextColor, TextFont, TextSize, TextStyleAdd, and TextStyleRemove—you can precisely control how information is displayed in your database solutions. Consider that a status field could convey additional information through different color and text style applications. You could use FileMaker's native formatting options to cause numbers to change color when negative; and with some more work, they could also take on shades based on how close to, say, a quota they are. You might color code regions in a geographical area or want to highlight certain keywords within a body of text.

→ To get started with calculation functions, **see** Chapter 8, "Getting Started with Calculations," **p. 213**.

→ For a complete reference of all calculation functions, **see** Appendix B, "Calculation Function Reference," **p. 807**.

→ For detailed examples of Text formatting functions, **see** Chapter 14, "Specialized Calculation Functions," **p. 381**, and Chapter 17, "Troubleshooting," **p. 445**.

AUTO-FORMATTING DATA

Both Chapter 3, "Defining and Working with Fields," and Chapter 8, "Getting Started with Calculations," have covered this functionality. This auto-entry capability to reformat data on entry enables you to capture certain information and impart meaning through making it bold, red, and so on.

Just as you can apply text formatting functions by using a script or through calculation fields, your database can automatically change text formatting on entry. Figure 13.15 shows a case where an invoice amount might be wrong (it is a negative number) and changes its text to italics. In a live environment, the amounts might also be changed to red.

Figure 13.15
Note that this layout is a table view and that it preserves text formatting applied.

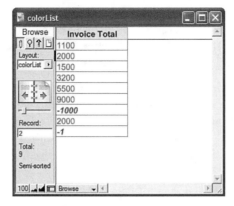

→ To understand how the auto-entry options can be applied to fields, **see** Chapter 3, "Defining and Working with Fields," **p. 63**.

WORKING WITH TABLE VIEW

There's a lot to be said for something that's free and "just works." If you're in an environment where a simple user interface is an option for your users, consider turning to Table views. They deliver a fair amount of functionality with zero development effort. Regardless of your end-users, as a developer you'll find them invaluable.

→ To learn more about Table view, **see** Chapter 2, "Using FileMaker Pro," **p. 27**.

One technique we use to make Table views even more useful can be found in the Table View Properties dialog under the Layout Setup dialog: You can opt to include header and footer parts on your layout, as well as control other aspects of your layout (see Figure 13.16).

Figure 13.16
Applying a header and footer part to your database allows you to fold in navigation and function buttons, along with a logo and other user interface elements as you prefer.

Header and footer parts can hold any FileMaker layout object you need. This includes your navigation or function buttons and whatever header might be common to the rest of your system, but most importantly it can hold fields. Your users can see a combined list-and-detail view that displays the currently selected row's data in either the header or footer.

There are a few drawbacks to using this technique. For one, you cannot overlay buttons on top of the rows—which is a handy way to allow users to navigate to detail layouts or perform other functions directly from list view. You also cannot turn off or alter the column headers. Your column headers are based directly on your field names, which, depending on your naming conventions, may be aesthetically imperfect or downright abstruse.

TROUBLESHOOTING

OMIT RE-CREATED

I am trying to create a scripted find process, so that I can keep the Status Area hidden, but the omit checkbox is tricky. What's a technique for offering the same functionality?

Most of the Status Area functions are fairly straightforward to reproduce: next record, previous record, switch mode, displays for record X of Y, sorting state, and so on. There's one that's not so obvious, though: the Omit check box in Find mode.

A scripted Find mode often takes users into Find mode and pauses the script in question (disallowing abort). The system then waits in a paused state for the user to click a button (often labeled something like Find, Continue, or Search). After the button is clicked, the script continues by utilizing the Perform Find script step. (An alternative to this is to have users enter find criteria into global fields and to manage populating find requests programmatically.)

It'd be a no-brainer to add a check box to a layout, call it "omit_flag," and test for a value in it when you've scripted a find routine. But here's the rub: If you're actually in Find mode, in a paused state as just described, what happens to that flag if you perform a find?

That's right—it'll be included in the find request itself.

The easiest way to deal with this is to simply make the checkbox a Boolean calculation with an auto-entry of "yes" or "1" (whatever the value list controlling your check box is set to.) In data terms, it serves as a constant, but in Find mode it does not affect the outcome of a Find request; it is always valid for all records. As such, you can use it as a variable against which to check in your Perform Find steps without having to worry about clearing it from your Find requests. You still need to manage the process of what to do with the flag if your users enable it, but at least the user-interface works as they (and you) would expect.

MULTI-USER BACK BUTTON FUNCTIONALITY

How do I manage a back button in a multi-user environment where I want to trace backward through the layouts only I have visited?

When designing a system for use by multiple users, to get a Back button to honor only the history one user creates, rather than all the history from all navigation in the system, simply use the `AccountName` information already stored in the NavHistory table you created. You need to modify the `NavBackTarget` relationship to include a second match condition between a global field holding the current user's account name and the `AccountName` stored in NavHistory. Your target rows will then point only to those that apply to your current user. This assumes that one person has access to one account.

MODAL DIALOG DANGERS

What are the downfalls to using the Modal Dialog technique to control what data gets posted to my solution?

Using the modal dialog technique described in this chapter isn't a foolproof way to address atomicity in FileMaker Pro.

→ Atomicity specifies that a transaction needs to either be completed in its entirety or not at all. For more information on atomicity and multi-user development, **see** Chapter 11, "Developing for Multi-User Deployment," **p. 297**.

Users can close FileMaker Pro anytime they wish. Depending on what assumptions you've made in your development and the scripts leading to opening such a dialog, your system might be left in a less-than-optimal state. We encourage you to create flags for when pop-up windows are opened and then confirm that they're then closed. In cases when such doesn't occur, you might create an error message or some other graceful form of alerting you to the fact.

FILEMAKER EXTRA: USER INTERFACE HEURISTICS

We opened this chapter by saying we'd not preach to you about what makes a good interface and what doesn't. Well, we're breaking our word here. Although we won't argue about pop-up windows versus single-pane applications, whether or not buttons should be 3D beveled or just text on the screen, here are a few guidelines we recommend to all of our clients, students, and developers alike.

- **Use real world terminology**—You should strive to speak your customer's language. Use terms they'll find familiar. In some cases you may need to retrain them, but whenever possible, leverage the body of knowledge already in place in an organization to make your system more intuitive.

- **Impart meaning with more than just labels**—Text is only one of many things your users will see on a layout. They'll also see colors, shapes, headlines, subheads, footers, and so on. Use all the objects in your toolbox to impart meaning: consider, for example, coloring find layouts differently or perhaps making navigation buttons look different from functional buttons.

- **Give users the freedom to "click around" without fear**—Users should be able to cancel out of any destructive function (delete, for example) so that they can explore your application and learn by doing.

- **Be consistent**—We can't stress this enough. Whatever colors, shapes, sizes, styles, and so on that you prefer, make sure your layouts follow whatever set of rules you establish. Name fields and buttons consistently, place them in the same positions, and give your users a visual grammar for your system they can learn.

- **Manage errors**—Errors happen. Handle them behind the scenes whenever possible, but when they're unavoidable make sure you present the user with a graceful error routine that informs them, proffers a course of action, and then returns them to what they were doing.

- **Focus your screens**—Less is more. White space is your friend. Leave the important bits on your layouts and dialogs and remove the objects that can be pushed elsewhere. If you offer focus to users, you will help them understand what to do on a given layout.

- **Remember your power users**—Contrary to all the prior advice, don't forget your power users. Offer keyboard shortcuts through "Are you sure?" dialogs, give them simple Table view access to your data, and don't bother them with wizards.

CHAPTER 14

SPECIALIZED CALCULATION FUNCTIONS

WHAT'S A SPECIALIZED FUNCTION?

Chapter 8, "Getting Started with Calculations," presented an introduction to FileMaker Pro 7 calculation formulas. Our goals there were to give you a grounding in how and where calculation functions are used, and to present what we feel are the "core" functions and formulas FileMaker Pro developers need to know and use on a daily basis.

This chapter covers functions and usages that are more specialized in nature. Think of the core functions covered in Chapter 7 as the hammers, screwdrivers, and wrenches of a developer's toolkit. They're the tools you use every day. The specialized functions covered here are the metric socket sets, the low-angled block planes, and the self-leveling laser levels of your toolkit. These might not be things that you use on every project, but they sure come in handy at times. The nice thing, of course, is that after you've made the "investment" in the specialized "tool," you'll have it handy for all future projects.

Certainly, our characterization of some functions or usages being part of a "core" and others as being "specialized" is subjective and open to debate. We do want to stress that specialized doesn't necessarily mean difficult or advanced. Nor does it mean arcane or esoteric. We think all the specialized functions presented here have very practical uses. In some cases, what's specialized isn't the function itself, but perhaps some usage of a core function that's not something you're likely to encounter on a routine basis.

We don't intend to present here a comprehensive list of functions. That can be found in Appendix B, "Calculation Function Reference." Rather, similar to our approach in Chapter 8, we take a thematic approach and focus on demonstrating practical uses of a handful of functions.

LOGICAL FUNCTIONS

The category of functions known as the *logical functions* contains a strange hodgepodge of things. Chapter 8 discussed two of them: the If and Case conditional functions. The logical functions covered here include several that are new to FileMaker Pro 7.

THE Let FUNCTION

The Let function enables you to simplify complex calculations by declaring variables to represent sub-expressions. These variables exist only within the scope of the formula and can't be referenced in other places. As an example, this is a formula that was presented in Chapter 8 for extracting the last line of a text field:

```
Right(myText; Length(myText) - Position(myText; "¶"; 1;
➥PatternCount(myText; "¶")))
```

With the Let function, this formula could be re-written as

```
Let ([fieldLength = Length(myText) ;
     returnCount = PatternCount(myText; "¶") ;
     positionOfLastReturn = Position (myText; "¶"; 1; returnCount) ;
     charactersToGrab = fieldLength - positionOfLastReturn];

Right (myText, charactersToGrab)
)
```

The Let function takes two parameters. The first is a list of variable declarations. If you want to declare multiple variables, then you need to enclose the list with square brackets and separate the individual declarations within the list with semicolons. The second parameter is some formula that you want evaluated. That formula can reference any of the variables declared in the first parameter just as it would reference any field value.

 If you experience unexpected behavior of a Let *function, the trouble might be your variable names. For more information, see "Naming Variables in* Let *Functions" in the Troubleshooting section at the end of this chapter.*

Notice in this example that the third variable declared, positionOfLastReturn, references the returnCount variable, which was the second variable declared. This capability to have subsequent variables reference previously defined ones is one of the powerful aspects of the Let function because it enables you to build up a complex formula via a series of simple ones.

It is fair to observe that the Let function is never necessary; you could write every formula that uses the Let function either as a complex nested formula or by explicitly defining or setting fields to contain sub-expressions. The main benefits of using the Let function are simplicity, clarity, and ease of maintenance. For instance, one formula that returns a person's age expressed as a number of years, months, and days is the following:

```
Year (Get (CurrentDate)) - Year(birthDate) - (DayOfYear(Get(CurrentDate))
➥ < DayOfYear(birthDate)) & " years, " & Mod ( Month(Get(CurrentDate))
➥- Month (birthDate) - (Day (Get(CurrentDate)) < Day(birthDate)); 12) &
➥" months, and " & (Get(CurrentDate) - Date (Month(Get(CurrentDate))
➥- (Day (Get(CurrentDate)) < Day(birthDate)); Day (birthDate);
➥Year (Get(CurrentDate)))) & " days"
```

This is a fairly complex nested formula, and many sub-expressions appear multiple times. Writing and debugging this formula is difficult, even when you understand the logic on which it's based. With the Let function, the formula could be rewritten as

```
Let ( [   C = Get(CurrentDate);
          yC = Year (C) ;
          mC = Month (C) ;
          dC = Day (C) ;
          doyC = DayOfYear (C) ;

          B = birthDate;
          yB = Year (B) ;
          mB = Month (B) ;
          dB= Day (B) ;
          doyB = DayOfYear (b) ;

          num_years = ( yC - yB - (doyC < doyB)) ;
          num_months = Mod (mC - mB - (dC <dB) ; 12) ;
          num_days = C - Date (mC - (dC < dB) ; dB ; yC) ] ;

          num_years & " years, " & num_months & " months, and " & num_days
          ➥& " days" )
```

14

Because of the extra space we've put in the formula, it's a bit longer than the original, but it's vastly easier to comprehend. If you were a developer needing to review and understand a formula written by someone else, we're sure you'd agree that you'd prefer seeing the Let version of this rather than the first version.

Besides simplicity and clarity, there are also performance benefits to using the Let function. If you have a complex sub-expression that you refer to multiple times during the course of a calculation, FileMaker Pro evaluates it anew each time it's referenced. Alternatively, a sub-expression in a variable is evaluated only once. In the example just shown, for instance, FileMaker would evaluate Get(CurrentDate) eight times in the first version. In the version that uses Let, it's evaluated only once. In many cases, the performance difference may be trivial or imperceptible. But other times, optimizing the evaluation of calculation formulas may be just the answer for increasing your solution's performance.

The more you use the Let function, the more likely it is that it will become one of the "core" functions that you use. To help you become more familiar with it, we use it frequently throughout the examples in the rest of this chapter.

TIP

> The Let function makes it really easy to debug calculation formulas. It used to be that if you wanted to make sure that a sub-expression was evaluating correctly, you'd need to create a separate field to investigate it. Using Let, you can just comment out the second parameter of the Let function and have the function return one or more of the sub-expressions directly. When you've got them working correctly, just comment out the test code and comment in the original code.

THE Choose FUNCTION

The If and Case functions are sufficiently robust and elegant for most conditional tests that you'll write. For several types of conditional tests, however, the Choose function is a more appropriate option. As with If and Case, the value returned by the Choose function is dependent on the result of some test. What makes the Choose function unique is that the test should return an integer rather than a true/false result. The syntax for Choose is as follows:

```
Choose (test ; result if test=0 ; result if test=1 ; result if test =2 ....)
```

A classic example of where a Choose function comes in handy is when you have categorical data stored as a number and you need to represent it as text. For instance, you might import demographic data where the ethnicity of an individual is represented by an integer from 1 to 5. The following formula might be used to represent it to users:

```
Choose (EthnicityCode; ""; "African American"; "Asian"; "Caucasian"; "Hispanic";
➥ "American Indian")
```

Of course, the same result could be achieved with the following formula:

```
Case (EthnicityCode = 1; "African American"; EthnicityCode = 2; "Asian",
➥EthnicityCode = 3; "Caucasian"; EthnicityCode = 4; "Hispanic";
➥EthnicityCode= 5; "American Indian")
```

You should consider the Choose function in several other situations. The first is for generating random categorical data. Say your third-grade class is doing research on famous Presidents, and you want to randomly assign each student one of the six presidents you have chosen. By first generating a random number from 0 to 5, you can then use the Choose function to select a president. The formula would be

```
Let ( r = Random * 6;       // Generates a random number from 0 to 5
    Choose (r, "Washington", "Jefferson", "Lincoln", "Roosevelt", "Truman",
    ➥ "Kennedy"))
```

Don't worry that r isn't an integer; the Choose function ignores anything but the integer portion of a number.

Several FileMaker Pro functions return integer numbers from 1 to n, so these naturally work well as the test for a Choose function. Most notable are the DayofWeek function, which returns an integer from 1 to 7, and the Month function, which returns an integer from 1 to 12. As an example, you could use the Month function within a Choose to figure out within which quarter of the year a given date fell:

```
Choose (Month(myDate)-1; "Q1"; "Q1"; "Q1"; "Q2"; "Q2"; "Q2"; "Q3"; "Q3"; "Q3";
➥ "Q4"; "Q4"; "Q4")
```

The –1 shifts the range of the output from 1–12 to 0–11, which is more desirable because the Choose function is zero based. There are more compact ways of determining the calendar quarter of a date, but this version is very easy to understand and offers much flexibility.

Another example of where Choose works well is when you need to combine the results of some number of Boolean tests and produce a distinct result. As an example, imagine that you have a table that contains results on Myers-Briggs personality tests. For each test given, you have scores for four pairs of personality traits (E/I, S/N, T/F, J/P). Based on which score in each pair is higher, you want to classify each participant as one of 16 personality types. Using If or Case statements, you would need a very long, complex formula to do this. With Choose, you can treat the four tests as a binary number, and then simply do a "conversion" back to base-10 to decode the results. The formula might look something like this:

```
Choose ( (8 * (E>I)) + (4 * (S>N)) + (2 * (T>F)) + (J>P);
    "Type 1 - INFP" ; "Type 2 - INFJ" ; "Type 3 - INTP" ; "Type 4 - INTJ" ;
    "Type 5 - ISFP" ; "Type 6 - ISFJ" ; "Type 7 - ISTP" ; "Type 8 - ISTJ" ;
    "Type 9 - ENFP" ; "Type 10 - ENFJ" ; "Type 11 - ENTP" ; "Type 12 - ENTJ" ;
    "Type 13 - ESFP" ; "Type 14 - ESFJ" ; "Type 15 - ESTP" ; "Type 16 - ESTJ")
```

Each less-than comparison is evaluated as a 1 or 0 depending on whether it represents a true or false statement for the given record. By multiplying each result by successive powers of 2, you end up with an integer from 0 to 15 that represents each of the possible outcomes. (This is similar to how flipping a coin 4 times generates 16 possible outcomes.)

As a final example, the Choose function can also be used anytime you need to "decode" a set of abbreviations into their expanded versions. Take, for example, a situation where survey respondents have entered SA, A, N, D, or SD as a response to indicate Strongly Agree, Agree, Neutral, Disagree, or Strongly Disagree. You could map from the abbreviation to the expanded text by using a Case function as follows:

14

```
Case (ResponseAbbreviation = "SA"; "Strongly Agree";
      ResponseAbbreviation = "A"; "Agree" ;
      ResponseAbbreviation = "N"; "Neutral" ;
      ResponseAbbreviation = "D"; "Disagree" ;
      ResponseAbbreviation = "SD"; "Strongly Disagree" )
```

You can accomplish the same mapping by using a Choose function if you treat the two sets of choices as ordered lists. You simply find the position of an item in the abbreviation list, and then find the corresponding item from the expanded text list. The resulting formula would look like this:

```
Let ( [a = "¦SA¦¦A¦¦N¦¦D¦¦SD¦" ;
       r = "¦" & ResponseAbbreviation & "¦" ;
       pos = Position (a; r ; 1 ; 1) ;
       itemNumber = PatternCount (Left (a; pos-1); "¦") / 2];

       Choose (itemNumber, "Strongly Agree"; "Agree"; "Neutral"; "Disagree";
       ➥ "Strongly Disagree")
)
```

In most cases, you'll probably opt for using the Case function for simple decoding of abbreviations. Sometimes, however, the list of choices isn't something you can explicitly test against (such as with the contents of a value list) and finding one's position within the list may suffice to identify a parallel position in some other list. Having the Choose function in your toolbox may offer an elegant solution to such challenges.

THE GetField FUNCTION

When writing calculation formulas, you use field names to refer abstractly to the contents of particular fields in the current record. That is, the formula for a FullName calculation might be FirstName & " " & LastName. FirstName and LastName are abstractions; they represent data contained in particular fields.

Imagine, however, that instead of knowing in advance what fields to refer to in the FullName calculation, you wanted to let users pick any fields they wanted to. So you set up two fields, which we'll call UserChoice1 and UserChoice2. How can you rewrite the FullName calculation so that it's not hard-coded to use FirstName and LastName, but rather uses the fields that users type in the two UserChoice fields?

The answer, of course, is the GetField function. GetField enables you to add another layer of abstraction to your calculation formulas. Instead of hard-coding field names in a formula, GetField allows you to place into a field the name of the field you're interested in accessing. That sounds much more complicated than it actually is. Using GetField, we might rewrite our FullName formula as follows:

```
GetField (UserChoice1) & " " & GetField (UserChoice2)
```

The GetField function takes just one parameter. That parameter can either be a literal text string or it can be a field name. Having it be a literal text string, though possible, is not particularly useful. The function GetField("FirstName") would certainly return the contents of the FirstName field, but you can achieve the same thing simply by using FirstName by itself.

14

It's only when the parameter of the GetField function is a field or formula that it becomes interesting. In that case, the function returns the contents of the field referred to by the parameter.

There are many potential uses of GetField in a solution. Imagine, for instance, that you have a Contact table with fields called First Name, Nickname, and Last Name (among others). Sometimes contacts prefer to have their nickname appear on badges and in correspondence, and sometimes the first name is desired. To deal with this, you could create a new text field called Preferred Name and format that field as a radio button containing First Name and Nickname as the choices. When doing data entry, a user could simply check off which name should be used for correspondence. When it comes time to make a Full Name calculation field, one of your options would be the following:

```
Case ( Preferred Name = "First Name"; First Name;
       Preferred Name = "Nickname"; Nickname) &
       " " & Last Name
```

Another option, far more elegant and extensible, would be the following:

```
GetField (PreferredName) & " " & Last Name
```

When there are only two choices, the Case function certainly isn't cumbersome. But if there were dozens or hundreds of fields to choose from, then GetField clearly has an advantage.

Building a Customizable List Report

One of the common uses of GetField is for building user-customizable list reports. It's really nothing more than an extension of the technique shown in the previous example, but it's still worth looking at it in depth. The idea is to have several global text fields where a user can select from a pop-up list of field names. The global text fields can be defined in any table that you want. Remember, in calculation formulas, you can refer to a globally-stored field from any table, even without creating a relationship to that table. The following example uses two tables: SalesPeople and Globals. The SalesPeople table has the following data fields:

> SalesPersonID
>
> FirstName
>
> LastName
>
> Territory
>
> CommissionRate
>
> Phone
>
> Email
>
> Sales_2002
>
> Sales_2003

The Globals table has six global text fields named gCol1 through gCol6.

With these in place, you can now create six display fields in the SalesPeople table (named ColDisplay1 through ColDisplay6) that will contain the contents of the field referred to in one of the global fields. For instance, ColDisplay1 has the following formula:

```
GetField (Globals::gCol1)
```

ColDisplay2 through 6 will have similar definitions. The next step is to create a value list that contains all the fields that you want the user to be able to select. The list used in this example is shown in Figure 14.1. Keep in mind that because the selection is used as part of a GetField function, the field names must appear exactly as they have been defined.

Figure 14.1
Define a value list containing a list of the fields from which you want to allow a user to select for the custom report.

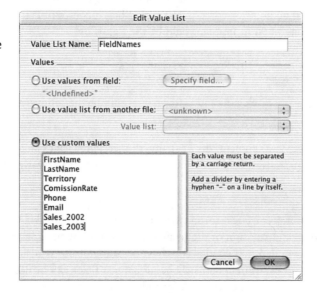

The final task is to create a layout where users can select and see the columns for their custom list report. You might want to set up one layout where the user selects the fields and another for displaying the results, but we think it's better to take advantage of the fact that in FileMaker Pro 7, fields in header parts of list layouts can be edited. The column headers of your report can simply be pop-up lists. Figure 14.2 shows how you would set up your layout this way.

Figure 14.2
The layout for your customizable list report can be quite simple. Here, the selection fields act also as field headers.

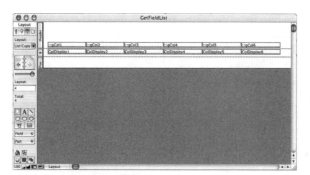

Back in Browse mode, users can now click into a column heading and select what data they want to appear there. This one layout can thus serve a wide variety of needs. Figures 14.3 and 14.4 show two examples of the types of reports that can be made.

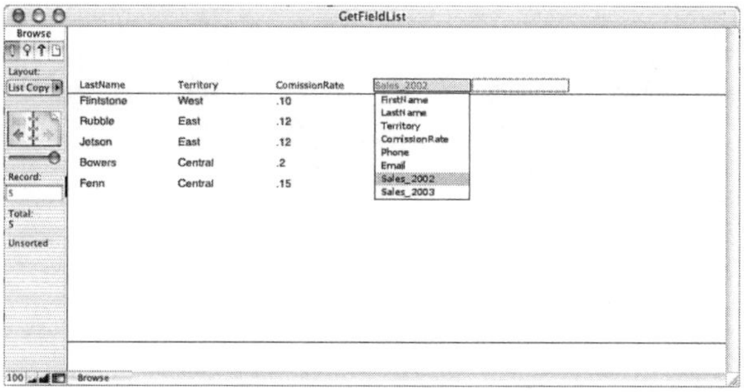

Figure 14.3
A user can customize the contents of a report simply by selecting fields from pop-up lists in the header.

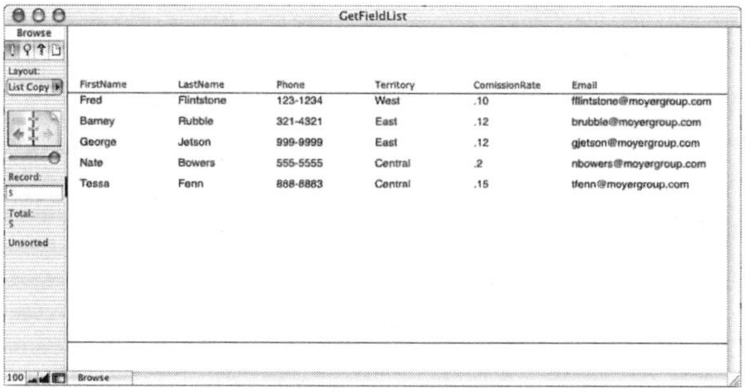

Figure 14.4
Here's another example of a how a user might configure the customizable list report.

EXTENDING THE CUSTOMIZABLE LIST REPORT

After you have the simple custom report working, there are many ways you can extend it to add even more value and flexibility for your users. For instance, you might add a subsummary part that's also based on a user-specified field. A single layout can thus be a subsummary based on any field the user wants. One way to implement this is to add another pop-up list in the header of your report and a button to sort and preview the subsummary report. Figure 14.5 shows what your layout would look like after adding the subsummary part and pop-up list. BreakField is a calculation in the SalesPeople table that's defined as follows:

```
GetField (Globals::gSummarizeBy)
```

The Preview button performs a script that sorts by the BreakField and goes to Preview mode. Figure 14.6 shows the result of running the script when Territory has been selected as the break field.

THE Evaluate FUNCTION

NEW The Evaluate function is one of the most intriguing new features of FileMaker Pro 7. In a nutshell, it enables you to evaluate a dynamically generated or user-generated calculation formula. With a few examples, you'll easily understand what this function does. It may, however, take a bit more time and thought to understand why you'd want to use it in a solution. We start with explaining the what, and then suggest a few potential whys.

Figure 14.5
A subsummary part based on a user-defined break field gives your custom report added power and flexibility.

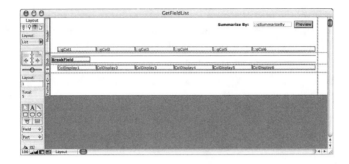

Figure 14.6
Sorting by the break field and previewing shows the results of the dynamic subsummary.

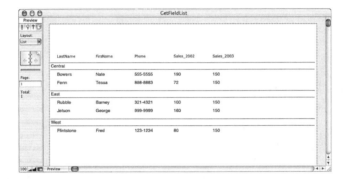

The syntax for the Evaluate function is as follows:

```
Evaluate ( expression {; [field1 ; field2 ;...]} )
```

The expression parameter is any calculation formula that you want evaluated. The optional parameter is a list of fields whose modification triggers the reevaluation of the expression.

For example, imagine that you have a text field named myFormula and another named myTrigger. You then define a new calculation field called Result, using the following formula:

```
Evaluate (myFormula; myTrigger)
```

Figure 14.7 shows some examples of what Result will contain for various entries in myFormula.

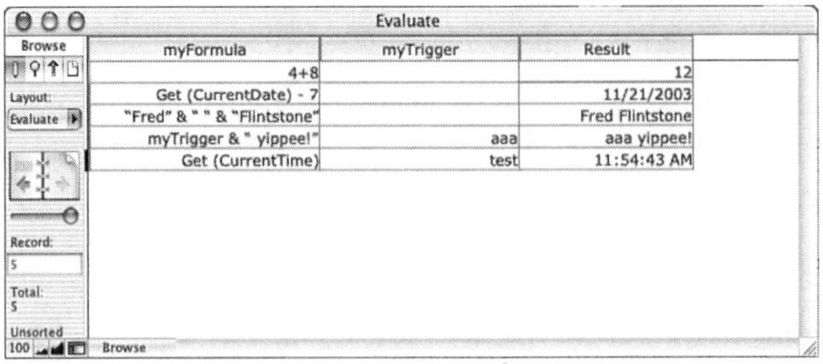

Figure 14.7
Using the Evaluate function, you can have a calculation field evaluate a formula contained in a field.

There's something quite profound going on here. Instead of having to "hard-code" calculation formulas, you can evaluate a formula that's been entered as field data. In this way, Evaluate provides an additional level of logic abstraction similar to the GetField function. In fact, if myFormula contained the name of a field, then Evaluate(myFormula) and GetField(myFormula) would return the exact same result. It might help to think of Evaluate as the big brother of GetField. Where GetField can return the value of a dynamically specified *field*, Evaluate can return the value of a dynamically specified *formula*.

USES FOR THE Evaluate FUNCTION

A typical use for the Evaluate function is to track modification information about a particular field or fields. A timestamp field defined to auto-enter the modification time is triggered any time any field in the record is modified. There may be times, however, when you want to know the last time that the Comments field was modified, without respect to other changes to the record. To do this, you would define a new calculation field called CommentsModTime with the following formula:

```
Evaluate ("Get(CurrentTimestamp)" ; Comments)
```

The quotes around the Get(CurrentTimestamp) are important, and are apt be a source of confusion. The Evaluate function expects to be fed either a quote-enclosed text string (as shown here) or a formula that yields an expression (as in the Result field earlier). For instance, if you want to modify the CommentsModTime field so that rather than just return a timestamp, it returns something like "Record last modified at: 11/28/2003 12:23:58 PM by Fred Flintstone," you would need to modify the formula to the following:

```
Evaluate ("\"Record modified at: \" & Get (CurrentTimeStamp) & \" by \" &
➡Get (AccountName)" ; Comments)
```

Here, because the formula you want to evaluate contains quotation marks, you must escape them by preceding them with a slash. For a formula of any complexity, this becomes difficult both to write and read. There is, fortunately, a function called Quote that eliminates all this complexity. The Quote function returns the parameter it is passed as a quote-wrapped text string, with all internal quotes properly escaped. Therefore, you could rewrite the above function more simply as:

```
Evaluate (Quote ("Record modified at: " & Get (CurrentTimeStamp) & " by " &
➡Get (AccountName)) ; Comments)
```

In this particular case, using the Let function further clarifies the syntax:

```
Let ( [
    t = Get ( CurrentTimeStamp ) ;
    a = Get ( AccountName );
    myExpression = Quote ( "Record modified at: " & t & " by " & a ) ] ;

  Evaluate ( myExpression ; Comments )
)
```

14

EVALUATION ERRORS

You typically find two other functions used in the vicinity of the Evaluate function: IsValidExpression and EvaluationError.

IsValidExpression takes as its parameter an expression, and it returns a 1 if the expression is valid, a 0 if it isn't. An invalid expression is any expression that can't be evaluated by FileMaker Pro, whether due to syntax errors or other runtime errors. If you plan to allow users to type calculation expressions into fields, then by all means be sure to use IsValidExpression to test their input to be sure it's well formed. In fact, you probably want to include something right within your Evaluate formula:

```
Let ( valid = IsValidExpression (myFormula) ;
    If (not valid; "Your expression was invalid" ; Evaluate (myFormula) )
```

The EvaluationError function is likewise used to determine whether there's some problem with evaluating an expression. However, it returns the actual error code of the problem. One thing to keep in mind, however, is that rather than testing the expression, you want to test the evaluation of the expression. So, as an error trap used in conjunction with an Evaluate function, you might have the following:

```
Let ( [result = Evaluate (myFormula) ;
      error = EvaluationError (result) ] ;
    If (error ; "Error: " & error ; result)
)
```

CUSTOMIZABLE LIST REPORTS REDUX

We mentioned previously that Evaluate could be thought of as an extension of GetField. In an example presented in the GetField section, we showed how you could use the GetField function to create user-customizable report layouts. One of the drawbacks of that method that we didn't discuss at the time is that your field names need to be user- and display-friendly. However, there is an interesting way to get around this limitation that also happens to showcase the Evaluate function. We discuss that solution here as a final example of Evaluate.

→ Another use of Evaluate is presented in "Passing Multi-valued Parameters," **p. 424**.

To recap the earlier example, imagine that you have six global text fields (gCol1 through gCol6) in a table called Globals. Another table, called SalesPeople has demographic and sales-related data for your salespeople. Six calculation fields in SalesPeople, called ColDisplay1 through ColDisplay6, display the contents of the demographic or sales data fields, based on a user's selection from a pop-up list containing field names. ColDisplay1, for instance, has the formula:

```
GetField (Globals::gCol1)
```

We now extend this solution in several ways. First, create a new table in the solution called FieldNames with the following text fields: FieldName and DisplayName. Figure 14.8 shows the data that might be entered in this table.

Figure 14.8
The data in `FieldName` represents fields in the SalesPerson table; the `DisplayName` field shows more "user-friendly" labels that will stand in for the actual field labels.

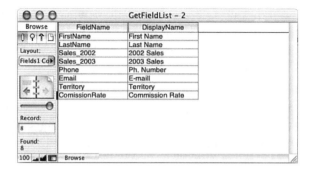

Before, we suggested using a hard-coded value list for the pop-up lists attached to the column selection fields. Now you'll want to change that value list so that it contains all the items in the `DisplayName` column of the FieldNames table. Doing this, of course, causes all the `ColDisplay` fields to malfunction. There is, for instance, no field called "Ph. Number," so `GetField ("Ph. Number")` will not function properly. What we want now is the `GetField` function not to operate on the user's entry, but rather on the `FieldName` that corresponds to the user's `DisplayName` selection. That is, when the user selects "Ph. number" in `gCol1`, `ColDisplay1` should display the contents of the `Phone` field.

You can accomplish this by creating a relationship from the user's selection over to the `DisplayName` field. Because there are six user selection fields, there need to be six relationships. This requires that you create six occurrences of the FieldNames table. Figure 14.9 shows the Relationships Graph after you have set up the six relationships. Notice that there's also a cross-join relationship between SalesPeople and Globals. This relationship allows you to look from SalesPeople all the way over to the FieldNames table.

Figure 14.9
To create six relationships from the Globals table to the FieldNames table, you need to create six occurrences of FieldNames.

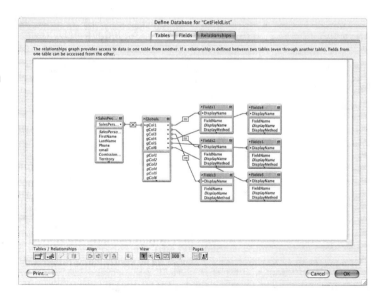

The final step is to alter the calculation formulas in the ColDisplay fields. Remember, instead of "getting" the field specified by the user, we now want to get the field related to the field specified by the user. At first thought, you might be tempted to redefine ColDisplay1 as:

```
GetField (Fields1::FieldName)
```

The problem with this is that the only way that ColDisplay1 updates is if the FieldName field changes. Changing gCol1 doesn't have any effect on it. This, finally, is where Evaluate comes in. To force ColDisplay1 to update, you can use the Evaluate function instead of GetField. The second parameter of the formula can reference gCol1, thus triggering the re-evaluation of the expression every time gCol1 changes. The new formula for ColDisplay1 is therefore

```
Evaluate (Fields1::FieldName ; Globals::gCol1)
```

There is, in fact, still a slight problem with this formula. Even though the calculation is unstored, the field values don't refresh onscreen. The solution is to refer not merely to the related FieldName, but rather to use a Lookup function (which is covered in depth in the next section) to explicitly grab the contents of FieldName. The final formula, therefore, is

```
Evaluate (Lookup (Fields1::FieldName) ; Globals::gCol1)
```

There's one final interesting extension we will make to this technique. At this point, the Evaluate function is used simply to grab the contents of a field. It's quite possible, however, to add another field to the FieldNames table called Formula, and have the Evaluate function return the results of some formula that you define there. The formula in ColDisplay1 would simply be changed to

```
Evaluate (Lookup (Fields1::Formula) ; Globals::gCol1)
```

One reason you might want to do this is to be able to add some text formatting to particular fields. For instance, you might want the Sales_2002 field displayed with a leading dollar sign. Because all the ColDisplay fields yield text results, you can't do this with ordinary field formatting. Instead, in the Formula field on the Sales_2002 record, you could type the following formula:

```
"$ " & Sales_2002
```

There's no reason, of course, why a formula you write can't reference multiple fields. This means that you can invent new fields for users to reference simply by adding a new record to the FieldNames table. For example, you could invent a new column called "Initials," defined as

```
Left (FirstName; 1) & Left (LastName; 1)
```

You could even invent a column called "Percent Increase" that calculates the percent sales increase from 2002 to 2003. The formula for that would be

```
Round((Sales_2003 - Sales_2002) / Sales_2002 *100, 2) & " %"
```

Figure 14.10 shows the contents of the FieldNames table. Note that for columns where you just want to retrieve the value of a field (for example, FirstName), the field name itself is the entire formula.

Figure 14.10
The expression in the Formula field is dynamically evaluated when a user selects a column in the customizable report.

This technique is quite powerful. You can "cook up" new columns for the customizable report just by adding records to the FieldNames table. Figure 14.11 shows an example of a report that a user could create based on the formulas defined in FieldNames. Keep in mind, Initials, $ Increase, and Percent Increase have not been defined as fields anywhere.

Figure 14.11
In the finished report, users can select from any of the "columns" defined in the FieldNames table, even those that don't explicitly exist as defined fields.

THE LOOKUP FUNCTIONS

 In previous versions of FileMaker Pro, lookups were exclusively an auto-entry option. In addition to that, in the new version, there are two lookup functions as well. They are Lookup and LookupNext, and both will become welcome additions to any developer's toolkit.

The two lookup functions operate quite similarly to their cousin, the auto-entry lookup option. In essence, a lookup is used to copy a related value into the current table. Lookups (all kinds) have three necessary components: a relationship, a trigger field, and a target field. When the trigger field is modified, then the target field is set to some related field value.

It's important to understand the functional differences between the lookup functions and the auto-entry option. Although they behave similarly, they're not quite equivalent. Some of the key differences include the following:

- Auto-entry of a looked-up value is an option for regular text, number, date, time, or timestamp fields, which are subsequently modifiable by the user. A calculation field that includes a lookup function is not user-modifiable.

- The lookup functions can be used anywhere—not just in field definitions. For instance, they can be used in formulas in scripts, record-level security settings, and calculated field validation. Auto-entering a looked-up value is limited to field definition.

- The lookup functions can be used in conjunction with other functions to create more complex logic rules. The auto-entry options are comparatively limited.

Lookup

The syntax of the `Lookup` function is as follows:

```
Lookup ( sourceField {; failExpression} )
```

The `sourceField` is the related field whose value you want to retrieve. The optional `failExpression` parameter is returned if there is no related record or if the `sourceField` is blank for the related record. If the relationship specified matches multiple related records, the value from the first related record is returned.

There are two main differences between using the `Lookup` function and simply referencing a related field in a formula. The first is that calculations that simply reference related fields must be unstored, but calculations that use the `Lookup` function to access related fields can be stored and indexed. The other difference is that changing the `sourceField` in the related table does not cause the `Lookup` to retrigger. Just as with auto-entry of a looked up value, the `Lookup` function captures the `sourceField` as it existed at a "moment in time." The alternative of simply referencing the related field results in what's known as a cascading update: When the related value is updated, any calculations that reference it are updated as well.

LookupNext

The `LookupNext` function is designed to allow you to map continuous data elements to categorical results. It has the same effect as checking the "copy next lower value" or "copy next higher value" options when specifying an auto-entry lookup. Its syntax is

```
LookupNext ( sourceField ; lower/higherFlag )
```

The acceptable values for the second parameter are `Lower` and `Higher`. These are keywords and shouldn't be placed in quotes.

An example should help clarify what we mean about mapping continuous data to categorical results. Imagine that you have a table that contains information about people, and that one of the fields is the person's birth date. You want to have some calculation fields that display the person's astrological information, such as a zodiac sign and ruling planet. Birthdates mapping to zodiac signs is a good example of continuous data mapping to categorical results: Ranges of birthdates correspond to each zodiac sign.

In practice, two small but instructive complications arise when you try to look up zodiac signs. The first is that the zodiac date ranges are expressed not as full dates, but merely as months and days (for example, Cancer starts on June 22 regardless of what year it is). This means that when you set up your zodiac table, you'll use text fields rather than date fields for the start and end dates. The second is that Capricorn wraps around the end of the year. The easiest way to deal with this is to have two records in the Zodiac table for Capricorn, one that spans Dec. 22–Dec. 31, and the other that spans Jan 1–Jan 20.

Figure 14.12 shows the full data of the Zodiac table. The StartDate and EndDate fields, remember, are actually text fields. The leading zeros are important for proper sorting.

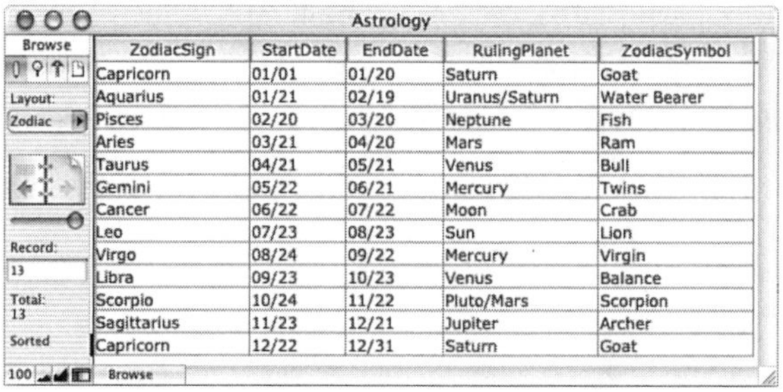

Figure 14.12
The data from the Zodiac table is looked up and is transferred to a person record based on the person's birth date.

ZodiacSign	StartDate	EndDate	RulingPlanet	ZodiacSymbol
Capricorn	01/01	01/20	Saturn	Goat
Aquarius	01/21	02/19	Uranus/Saturn	Water Bearer
Pisces	02/20	03/20	Neptune	Fish
Aries	03/21	04/20	Mars	Ram
Taurus	04/21	05/21	Venus	Bull
Gemini	05/22	06/21	Mercury	Twins
Cancer	06/22	07/22	Moon	Crab
Leo	07/23	08/23	Sun	Lion
Virgo	08/24	09/22	Mercury	Virgin
Libra	09/23	10/23	Venus	Balance
Scorpio	10/24	11/22	Pluto/Mars	Scorpion
Sagittarius	11/23	12/21	Jupiter	Archer
Capricorn	12/22	12/31	Saturn	Goat

In the Person table, you need to create a calculation formula that generates a text string containing the month and date of the person's birth date, complete with leading zeros so it's consistent with the Zodiac table. The DateMatch field is defined as follows:

```
Right ("00" & Month (Birthdate); 2) & "/" & Right ("00"& Day (Birthdate); 2)
```

Next, create a relationship between the Person and Zodiac tables, matching the DateMatch field in Person to the StartDate field in Zodiac. This relationship is shown in Figure 14.13.

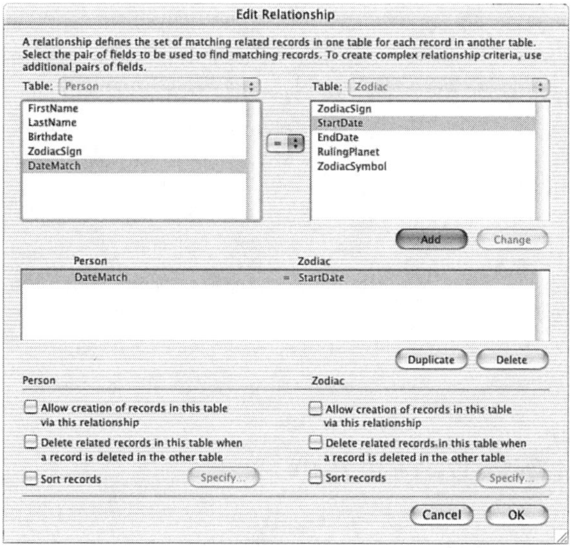

Figure 14.13
By relating the Person table to Zodiac, you can look up any information you want based on the person's birth date.

Obviously, many birthdates aren't start dates for one of the zodiac signs. To match to the correct zodiac record, you want to find the next lower match when no exact match is found. For instance, with a birth date of February 13th (02/13), there is no matching record where the StartDate is 02/13, so the next lowest StartDate, which is 01/21 (Aquarius), should be used.

In the Person table, therefore, you can grab any desired zodiac information by using the LookupNext function. Figure 14.14 shows an example of how this date might be displayed on a person record. The formula for ZodiacInfo is as follows:

```
"Sign: " & LookupNext (Zodiac::ZodiacSign; Lower) & "¶" &
"Symbol: " & LookupNext (Zodiac::ZodiacSymbol; Lower) & "¶" &
"Ruling Planet: " & LookupNext (Zodiac::RulingPlanet; Lower)
```

Figure 14.14
Using the LookupNext func-tion, you can create a calculation field in the Person table that con-tains information from the "next low-est" matching record.

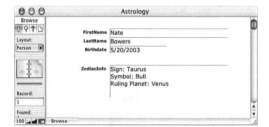

It would have been possible in the previous examples to match to the EndDate instead of the StartDate. In that case, you would simply need to match to the next higher instead of the next lower matching record.

An entirely different but perfectly valid way of approaching the problem would have been to define a more complex relationship between Person and Zodiac, where the DateMatch was greater than or equal to the StartDate and less than or equal to the EndDate. Doing this would allow you to use the fields from the Zodiac table as plain related fields; no lookup would have been required. There are no clear advantages or disadvantages of this method over the one discussed previously.

NOTE

> Other typical scenarios for using LookupNext are for things such as shipping rates based on weight ranges, price discounts based on quantity ranges, and for defining cut scores based on continuous test score ranges.

TEXT FORMATTING FUNCTIONS

In previous versions of FileMaker Pro, there was no way to affect the display of a field (that is, color, size, font, style) via calculation formulas. Developers had to come up with workarounds for seemingly simple tasks, such as having the contents of a field change color based on some conditional test. For example, a typical workaround was stacking two calcu-lation fields on top of one another, each formatted with a different text color on the layout, and then having a conditional test in each turn it "on" or "off" to simulate the effect of the text changing color.

In FileMaker Pro 7, six new text formatting functions obviate the need for many of these old workaround options. They are each discussed in detail in Appendix B, but here we demonstrate some examples of how and why you might use these functions.

TEXT COLOR, FONT, AND SIZE

The TextColor, TextFont, and TextSize functions are quite similar. The first parameter of each is the text string that you want to act upon; the second parameter contains the formatting instructions you want to apply.

For example, perhaps you have a Tasks table, and you want to have any tasks due within the next week be displayed in red. To accomplish this, you would define a calculation field called TaskDisplay with the following formula:

```
Case (DueDate <= Get (CurrentDate) + 7;
    TextColor (TaskName; RGB (255; 0; 0));    // Red
    TextColor (TaskName; 0))                  // Black
```

The TaskDisplay field displays the task name in either red or black, depending on the due date.

The second parameter of the TextColor function needs to be an integer from 0 to 16777215 (which is 256^3-1), which represents a unique RGB color. If you know the integer value of the color you want (for example, black is 0), then you can simply use that integer. More typically, you'll use the RGB function, which returns the integer representation of the color specified. Each of the three parameters in the RGB function must be an integer between 0 and 255. The first parameter represents the red component of the color, the second the green component, and the third, the blue. The RGB function determines the integer representation by the following formula:

```
((255^2) * Red) + (255 * Green) + Blue
```

TEXT STYLE

The two other text formatting functions are TextStyleAdd and TextStyleRemove. Each of these takes two parameters. The first is a text string to act upon; the second is a style or styles to apply to the text string. If listing multiple styles, you need to separate them with a plus sign (+). The style names are keywords, and should not appear in quotes. They also must be hard coded in the formula; you can't substitute a field that contains style instructions. The valid styles for both TextStyleAdd and TextStyleRemove are as follows:

Plain

Bold

Italic

Underline

Condense

14

Extend

Strikethrough

SmallCaps

Superscript

Subscript

Uppercase

Lowercase

Titlecase

WordUnderline

DoubleUnderline

AllStyles

To remove all styles from a chunk of text, you can either *add* Plain as a style, or you can *remove* AllStyles. Additionally, there are numeric equivalents for each of the text style keywords. Unlike the keywords themselves, the numeric equivalents can be abstracted as field values. Refer to Appendix B for a listing of the numeric equivalents and some sample usage.

EXAMPLES INVOLVING TEXT FORMATTING FUNCTIONS

There are many practical, everyday uses for the text formatting functions. For instance, you might have a database where you've tracked books and articles pertaining to a research project. You could define a field called `BibliographyDisplay` that performs the appropriate bibliographic formatting of the data elements.

Another use is to create tools so users can highlight and format field data without using the built-in menu commands. For this example, imagine that you have a simple layout with three text fields on it called Text1, Text2, and Text3. The end goal is to add buttons to the layout that perform some formatting action on a text snippet selected by the user, no matter in which field the user has highlighted a selection. For the example, the formatting options are limited to Bold, Underline, and Red, but you'll easily be able to extend it to perform any formatting you require. Believe it or not, you can do this with a single, one-line script!

Figure 14.15 depicts the layout, buttons, and some sample text. For now, the buttons don't do anything.

The script that does the formatting is called `Apply Format`. Its single step will be a `Set Field`. Normally with `Set Field`, you'll specify the field that you want to alter. However, with the field unspecified, the currently selected field, where the user has highlighted some text, is affected. The formula needed to actually do the formatting is as follows:

```
Let ( [
    param = Get (ScriptParameter);  // will be Bold, Underline, or Red ...
    oldText = Get ( ActiveFieldContents );
    highlightedText = Middle (oldText; Get ( ActiveSelectionStart );
    ➥Get ( ActiveSelectionSize ));
    newText = Case (param = "Red" ;
```

14

```
        TextColor (highlightedText ; RGB (255 ; 0 ; 0));
        TextStyleAdd (highlightedText; param)
) ];

    Replace (oldText; Get ( ActiveSelectionStart );
    ➥Get ( ActiveSelectionSize ); newText)
)
```

Figure 14.15
Users can highlight a section of text in any field on the layout and use the buttons at the top of the screen to format their selections.

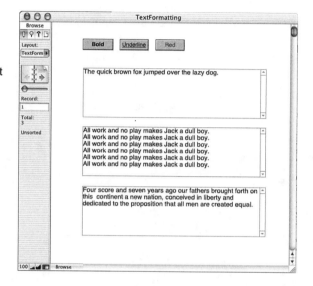

The three buttons each use a script parameter to pass in a formatting request, enabling you to use this single script to do any and all formatting. Notice also that Get(ActiveFieldContents), Get(ActiveSelectionStart), and Get(ActiveSelectionSize) are used to identify and isolate the snippet highlighted by the user. Then the appropriate formatting is applied to that snippet, and the Replace function is used to swap it into the old text.

With the script written, all that's left is to go back to the three buttons and define them to call the Apply Format script. Each button needs to pass formatting instructions (Bold, Underline, "Red") to the script through the script parameter. Creating buttons to perform additional formatting would simply be a matter of duplicating an existing button and changing its script parameter.

Figure 14.16 shows the results after some formatting has been performed on the three text fields.

Even though the example is complete as it stands, you might want to add a nice additional bit of functionality to the Apply Format script. Currently, after the formatting is applied, the user's selection is no longer highlighted. If she wants to perform multiple format operations, such as bold *and* red, then she needs to manually re-highlight the desired text. Alternatively, you can use the Set Selection script step to leave the user's selection highlighted. The Set Selection script step needs to know three things: in what field to operate, what character

14

number should start the selection, and what character number should end the selection. Just as with the Set Field, if you don't explicitly specify a field on which to act, the currently selected field is used, which is exactly what's desired in this case. For the start and end positions, you can use the Get(ActiveSelectionStart) and Get(ActiveSelectionSize) functions. The problem is that in re-formatting the field, those values are lost. Therefore, you need to capture those two values at the very beginning of the script in some way that you can refer to later. One way to do this would be simply to create two global number fields (one for each value), but because we're discussing interesting applications of functions, let's look at a method for storing and passing both values as part of a single global text field. As the first step of the Apply Format script, add a Set Field that sets some global text field (gTemp) to the following:

```
"start = " & Get ( ActiveSelectionStart ) & " ; stop= " &
➡Get ( ActiveSelectionSize ) + Get ( ActiveSelectionStart ) - 1
```

Figure 14.16
A single, one-line script is used to format the user's selection appropriately.

After this step has executed, gTemp might contain something like the following:

```
"start = 16 ; stop = 23"
```

What we've done here is captured the two values in which we're interested, in a format that can be dropped into the middle of a Let function and evaluated with the Evaluate function.

As the final step of the script, the Set Selection script step needs to be told the starting and ending positions of the selection. The starting position would be "unpacked" from gTemp by the following formula:

```
Evaluate ( "Let ([ " & TextFormatting::gTemp & " ]; start)")
```

The wonderful thing about this method is that you can pass any number of "variables" quite easily. When unpacking it for later use, you simply swap in the appropriate variable at the end of the Evaluate function.

ARRAY FUNCTIONS

Arrays are a powerful and extremely useful programming concept. If you've done any programming in languages such as C++, Perl, PHP, or Visual Basic, you're probably very familiar with both the concept of arrays and some uses for them. We think it likely, however, that most FileMaker Pro developers out there haven't had much experience with arrays and will benefit from both a formal and practical discussion of them.

Abstractly, an *array* is essentially a structure that can hold multiple values. The values are ordered within the structure and can be referenced by their position or index number. Figure 14.17 shows a representation of a simple array. The array has been defined to hold up to seven values, but only four values are present. The first element in the array is the value "red."

Figure 14.17
An array is a structure that can hold multiple values. Each value can be identified and referenced by an index number.

1	2	3	4	5	6	7
red	green	blue	white			

Arrays are useful for a wide variety of things, including storing lists of data, efficiently moving multiple values through a system, and for dealing with variable-length data structures where it's impossible to define separate fields for each data element.

FileMaker Pro doesn't have an explicit "array" data type, but fields defined to hold multiple repetitions can be regarded as arrays. More commonly, if you want to use arrays in FileMaker, you can create your own by placing into a text field multiple values separated by some delimiter.

NOTE

In FileMaker Pro 7, a new "array notation" can be used to refer to data in a repeating field. myField[3], for instance, refers to the data in the third repetition of myField. It's really just a shorthand notation for GetRepetition(myField, 3), but it makes formulas much easier to read.

Return-delimited lists pop up all over the place in FileMaker Pro. Many functions and operations in FileMaker generate return-delimited lists, including most of the Design functions and the Get (ExtendedPrivileges) function. When a user selects multiple values in a check box–formatted field, FileMaker stores that data as a return-delimited list of the selections. Additionally, the Copy All Records script step generates a return-delimited list of the data elements on the current layout for the current found set (tabs separate the elements within a record).

14

WORKING WITH RETURN-DELIMITED DATA ARRAYS

FileMaker Pro 7 has four new functions that greatly facilitate working with return-delimited data arrays such as the ones just described. These are ValueCount, LeftValues, MiddleValues, and RightValues. Syntactically, they are very similar to the four "word" functions (WordCount, LeftWords, MiddleWords, and RightWords) as well as to the four "character" functions (Length, Left, Middle, Right).

Briefly, the syntax of these functions is as follows:

- **ValueCount (text)**—Returns the number of items in a return-delimited list. Unlike its cousin the WordCount function, which interprets sequential word delimiters as a single delimiter, if you have multiple carriage returns in a row, even at the beginning or ending of a list, ValueCount treats each one as a delimiter. For example, ValueCount ("¶¶Red¶Blue¶Green¶¶White¶") returns 7. It's immaterial whether the list contains a single trailing return or not; the ValueCount is not affected by this. Multiple trailing returns affect the ValueCount.

- **LeftValues (text; numberOfValues)**—Returns a list of the first *n* elements of a return-delimited text string. The list always has a trailing return, even if you are requesting just the first item of the array.

- **MiddleValues (text; startIndex; numberOfValues)**—Returns a list of *n* elements from the middle of a return-delimited array, starting from the position specified in the second parameter. As with LeftValues, the output of this function always contains a trailing return.

- **RightValues (text; numberOfValues)**—Returns a list of the last *n* elements from a return-delimited array. This function, too, always generates a trailing return at the end of its output.

If you ever use arrays that use delimiters other than return characters, see "Working with Arrays" in the Troubleshooting section at the end of this chapter.

To demonstrate how you might use these functions in a solution, we present an example of iterating through a user's selections in a check box–formatted field and creating records for each selection in another table.

Imagine that you have a table containing information about kids coming to your summer camp, and that one of the pieces of information that you are capturing is a list of sports in which the child wants to participate. When you originally set up the table, you simply created a check box–formatted field in the CamperInfo table for this information. You now realize that it's impossible to run certain reports (for example, a subsummary by sport) with the data structured this way, and that you should have created a separate table for CamperSport data. You'd like not to have to re-enter all the data, so you want to create a script that loops through all the CamperInfo records and creates a record in the CamperSport table for each sport that's been checked for that camper.

There are many ways you can approach a challenge such as this. You might, for instance, temporarily set data from CamperInfo into global fields, navigate to a layout based on the CamperSport table, create records, and populate data from the global fields. You've chosen instead to use a portal from the CamperInfo table to the CamperSport table that allows creation of related records. This way, you avoid having to navigate between layouts for each camper, and the CamperID field is automatically set correctly in the CamperSport table.

Stepping Through an Array

A user's selections in a check box field are stored as a return-delimited array, in the order that the user checked them. There are two ways you can step from element to element in such an array. First, you can iteratively "lop off" the first element of the array until there's nothing left to process. This requires first moving the data to be processed into a scratch field where it can be cut apart without harming the original data. The other method is to use a counter to keep track of what element is being processed. You continue processing, incrementing the counter as you go, until the counter has exceeded the number of elements in the array. To some extent, it's personal preference which method you use. I had a preference for the first method in earlier versions of FileMaker Pro because it was simpler syntactically, but the new "value" functions make the second method very appealing now. Both versions of the script are presented here in Listings 14.1 and 14.2 so that you can decide for yourself which is preferable.

LISTING 14.1   METHOD 1: "LOP OFF" THE TOP ELEMENT OF THE ARRAY

```
Go to Layout ["CamperInfo" (CamperInfo)]
Go to Record/Request/Page [First]
Loop
    Set Field [Globals::gSports; CamperInfo::SportArray]
    Loop
        Exit Loop If [ValueCount (Globals::gSports) = 0]
        Go to Portal Row [Select; Last]
        Set Field [CamperSports::Sport; Let ( sport =
        ➥LeftValues (Globals::gSports; 1) ; Substitute(sport; "¶"; ""))
        Set Field [Globals::gSports; Let (count =
        ➥ValueCount(Globals::gSports); RightValues
        ➥(Globals::gSports; count-1))
    End Loop
    Go to Record/Request/Page [Next; Exit after last]
End Loop
```

Notice here that in line 8, the first element of the SportArray is pushed through the portal, where it becomes a record in the CamperSports table. In the very next line, the gSports field is then reset to be everything *after* the first line. It gets shorter and shorter with each pass through the loop, until finally there aren't any more items to process, concluding the inner loop.

14

LISTING 14.2   METHOD 2: WALK THROUGH THE ELEMENTS ONE BY ONE

```
Go to Layout ["CamperInfo" (CamperInfo)]
Go to Record/Request/Page [First]
Loop
Set Field [Globals::gCounter; 1]
    Loop
        Exit Loop If [Globals::gCounter > ValueCount (CamperInfo::SportArray)]
        Go to Portal Row [Select; Last]
        Set Field [CamperSports::Sport; Let ( sport =
        ➥MiddleValues (CamperInfo::SportArray; Globals::gCounter; 1)) ;
        ➥Substitute(sport; "¶"; ""))
        Set Field [Globals::gCounter; Globals::gCounter  + 1]
    End Loop
    Go to Record/Request/Page [Next; Exit after last]
End Loop
```

Again, the main difference with this method is that the inner loop steps through the elements of the SportArray field based on a global counter field.

NOTE

> In both cases, notice that the Substitute function has been used to remove the trailing return character generated by the LeftValues and MiddleValues functions.

THE "FILTER"-ING FUNCTIONS

 The Filter and FilterValues functions, both new additions to FileMaker Pro 7, are nifty tools for complex text comparison and manipulation. The following sections provide an example of each of them.

THE Filter FUNCTION

The syntax for the Filter function is as follows:

```
Filter (textToFilter; filterText)
```

The filterText parameter is essentially a set of characters that you want to "protect" in textToFilter. The output of the Filter function is the textToFilter string, minus any characters that don't appear in filterText. For example:

```
Filter ("This is a test" ; "aeiou") = "iiae"
```

Here, the "filter" is the set of five vowels. Therefore, the output from the function contains all the vowels from the string "This is a test". The filter is case sensitive, so if you wanted to include both upper and lowercase vowels in your output, you'd need to make the filterText parameter aeiouAEIOU. The output is ordered according to the order that characters in the filter are found in the first parameter. The order of the characters in the filter itself is irrelevant.

The Filter function is useful anytime you want to constrain the domain of possible characters that a user can enter into a field. The most common use of Filter, therefore, is as part of an auto-entry calculation for text fields. Figure 14.18 shows the auto-entry options dialog for a field called Phone. Note that the option Do Not Replace Existing Value of Field (If Any) has been unchecked. What this means is that the auto-entry calculation isn't triggered only when the record is created, but it also is triggered any time the Phone field is modified. Essentially, this means that whenever a user modifies the Phone field, his entry is replaced immediately by the result of the calculation formula specified.

Figure 14.18
The Filter function is often used as part of the auto-entry of a calculated value.

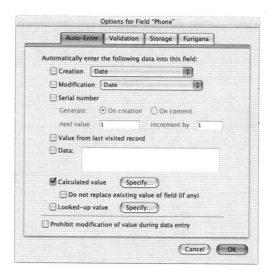

You can use the Filter function as part of the auto-entry calculation for the Phone field to remove any non-numeric characters that might have been entered by the user. The nice thing about the Filter function here is that you don't need to anticipate all the incorrect things that a user can enter (text, punctuation, spaces), but rather, you can specify what the acceptable characters are. The actual function you use to re-format the user's entry in the Phone field depends on your needs and preferences, but one option would be the following:

```
Let ( [
    ph = Filter (Phone; "0123456789");
    len = Length (ph) ;
    areaCode = Case ( len = 10; Left (ph; 3); "");
    exchange = Case ( len = 10; Middle (ph; 4; 3); Left (ph; 3)) ;
    end = Right (ph; 4) ];

    Case (
        len =10 ;   "(" & areaCode & ") " & exchange & "-" & end ;
        len =7 ;    exchange & "-" & end ;

        "Error: " & TextStyleAdd ( Phone ; Bold)
    )
)
```

The formula starts by stripping out any non-numeric characters from the user's entry. Then, if the length of the remaining string is either 7 or 10, the number is formatted with

14

punctuation and returned to the user. If it's not, then the function shows the user an "Error" message, complete with the original entry presented in bold text.

THE FilterValues FUNCTION

The FilterValues function is similar to the Filter function, except that it filters the elements in one return-delimited set by the elements in a second return-delimited set. When each of the sets consists of unique elements, then the FilterValues function essentially returns the intersection of the two sets. In Figure 14.19, you can see that FilterValues returns the items that are common to the two sets. Had the two parameters been reversed and the formula written as FilterValues (Set B; Set A), then the only difference would have been the order of the elements in the resulting list.

NOTE

> The result list always is ordered based on the first set. If an element appears multiple times in the first set (and it's included in the filter set), then it appears multiple times in the result set.

Figure 14.19
The FilterValues function returns a list of all the items of Set A that are also in Set B.

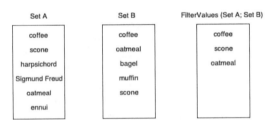

Practically speaking, FilterValues comes in handy anytime you want to see whether two lists contain any of the same elements. For instance, if you've defined any extended privileges as part of your security settings, you can see a list of all the privileges that have been granted to the current user with the Get (ExtendedPrivileges) function. If you have some routine that only users with PrivSetA or PrivSetC should have access to, you can use the formula FilterValues("PrivSetA¶PrivSetC"; Get (ExtendedPrivileges)). If the result is not empty, then the user has at least one of those two privilege sets.

As another example, imagine that you are a third grade teacher and that you have just given your students a 10-question True/False test. Rather than set up a related table for their answers, you've just entered all their responses into a return-delimited text field. By also putting the "answer key" into a global text field, you can use the FilterValues function to determine the number of correct answers each student had. Figure 14.20 shows how this might look when you're finished. The formula for the NumberCorrect field is

```
ValueCount (FilterValues (TestResults; AnswerKey) )
```

Figure 14.20
By using the `FilterValues` and `ValueCount` functions, you can count how many items in one array are contained within some other array.

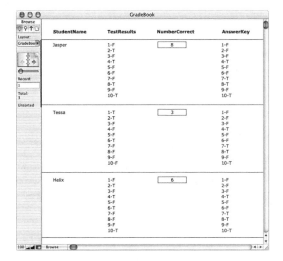

CUSTOM FUNCTIONS

In addition to all the wonderful and powerful calculation functions built into FileMaker Pro 7, you also can create your own custom functions. To create custom functions, you need to have a copy of FileMaker Developer 7. Any custom functions that you create using FileMaker Developer remain in the file and are fully usable when it's subsequently used by the regular FileMaker Pro 7 client application. You just can't edit the formula of the custom function unless you have FileMaker Developer.

As with other "objects," such as scripts, tables, and user account information, custom functions live "in" a particular file. There is—unfortunately—no way to move or import custom functions defined in one file into another one. The implications of this are obvious: If you have a solution that consists of multiple files, you need to define custom functions redundantly in all the files that need to access them, thus complicating maintenance and troubleshooting. This fact shouldn't scare you off from using custom functions—they're really quite wonderful—but it's certainly a constraint you need to be aware of.

Custom functions that have been created for a particular file show up with all the built-in functions in the list of functions within the calculation dialog. To see just the custom functions, you can choose Custom Functions from the filter above the function list. Custom functions are used in a formula just as any other function. The function name and the names of its parameters are defined by the person who writes the custom function.

USES OF CUSTOM FUNCTIONS

There are a number of reasons for using custom functions in a solution. Primarily, custom functions enable you to abstract snippets of calculation logic so that they become re-useable. Abstracting out bits of logic also makes your code easier to read and eliminates redundancy.

SIMPLIFYING COMPLEX FORMULAS

The best place to begin understanding the potential uses of custom functions is with a simple example. Imagine, for instance, that for some reason you need to generate a random integer from 10 to 50. Knowing, as you do from reading Chapter 8, "Getting Started with Calculations," that the Random function returns a random number between 0 and 1, you eventually conclude that a formula that solves this particular problem is

```
Int(Random * 41) + 10
```

With the problem solved, you write your formula and go on your merry way. Now, imagine that the next day you come back and discover you need to write another function that requires a random integer from 1 to 6. After a bit more thinking, you come up with the following:

```
Int(Random * 6) + 1
```

About this time, you'd be wishing that the engineers at FileMaker, Inc. had thought to create a function that would return a random integer from x to y. Using FileMaker Developer 7, you can in fact write your own custom functions for situations such as this. Rather than continue to solve particular problems, you can solve the general case and never again need to divert your attention to the particular.

So, what would a generalized solution to the random number problem look like? First, you'd need to have some way of abstractly representing the "from" and "to" numbers. Let's call these two numbers lowNumber and highNumber. Then the function that satisfies the general condition would be

```
Int (Random * (highNumber - lowNumber + 1)) + lowNumber.
```

For any lowNumber and highNumber you feed this function, you get back an integer between the two. We'll look in a moment at how you would physically go about setting this up as a custom function, but for now, the important thing is the concept that custom functions, just like the built-in functions you use all the time, have inputs (which are called parameters) and an output. Let's say that you decide to call this function RandomInRange. Now, to solve the first problem we looked at, finding a random integer from 10 to 50, you could just use the following function:

```
RandomInRange (10; 50)
```

And to find a number from 1 to 6, you could use this one:

```
RandomInRange (1; 6)
```

You've simplified your code by replacing a complex expression with a single function, thereby making it easier to read and maintain. You've abstracted that bit of logic out of whatever larger formula you were working on, leaving you one less thing to think about.

CUSTOM FUNCTIONS AS SYSTEM CONSTANTS

There are a few different schools of thought about when you should write a custom function to abstract your programming logic, and when you should use existing tools to solve the problem. Some hold that you should always write custom functions. Even if you use a given custom function only a single time, you've made your code more modular, thus making it easier to track down and troubleshoot problems. Plus, if you do ever need that function again, it's there, ready and waiting.

Other developers find that they use custom functions more sparingly. Their attitude is this: If you find yourself solving a particular problem more than once, then go ahead and write a custom function for it, and go back to change the original occurrence to reference the custom function instead. This process, often called *refactoring* as a general programming concept, has a certain pragmatism to it: Write a custom function as soon as it's more efficient to do so, but not sooner.

Whatever camp you find yourself falling into, you should be aware of two other common uses for custom functions. The first is for defining system constants. As an example, imagine that in your sales organization, the commission rate is 15%. In calculations where you determine commission amounts, you might find yourself writing numerous formulas where sales figures are multiplied by .15. If, heaven forbid, you ever need to change that figure to, say, .18, you'd need to sift through all your code to find all the instances where you had hard-coded the commission figure.

As an alternative, you might consider defining custom functions to represent system-wide constants such as these. In this example, you would simply have a custom function called CommissionRate that had no parameters and returned a value of .15. By abstracting out the hard-coded value, you're able to quickly and easily make global changes just by editing a single function. You should never refer directly to the "magic number" in a formula; use the custom function instead. Other examples of numbers and strings that should be abstracted out of your formulas include IP addresses, URLs, and colors.

CREATING RECURSIVE FUNCTIONS

The final common situation where custom functions are used is for making recursive functions. One of the limitations often lamented by developers over the years has been the fact that you can't create looping constructs within calculation formulas. That is, you can't instruct a regular calculation formula to keep doing something until some condition holds. Custom functions, on the other hand, can contain recursive logic. This means that a class of problems can be solved only by the creation of custom functions. This stands in stark contrast to the custom-functions-as-vehicles-for-abstraction idea discussed previously. As an abstraction tool, custom functions can always be replaced in a formula by the logic they've abstracted. No such substitution can be made when dealing with recursive functions. In those cases, using custom functions is not a convenience; it's a necessity. In the section that follows, we develop and discuss several recursive functions.

CREATING CUSTOM FUNCTIONS

Now that you understand what custom functions are and why you might want to use them, it's time to turn to the mundane subject of how to actually create them. First, recall that custom functions can be created and edited only with FileMaker Developer 7, and that

14

custom functions "live" in a file. To see a list of custom functions that have been defined in a particular file, and to define new ones, choose File, Define, Custom Functions. The resulting Define Custom Functions dialog is shown in Figure 14.21.

Figure 14.21
With FileMaker Developer 7, you have access to a Define Custom Functions dialog.

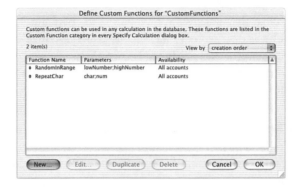

Buttons from this dialog enable you to create, edit, or delete a custom function. You also see the names of the parameters that have been defined for each function, as well as whether a function is available to all accounts or just those with the Full Access privilege set. When you go to create or edit a custom function, you're taken to the Edit Custom Function dialog, which is shown in Figure 14.22.

Figure 14.22
The parameters and formula for a custom function are defined in the Edit Custom Function dialog.

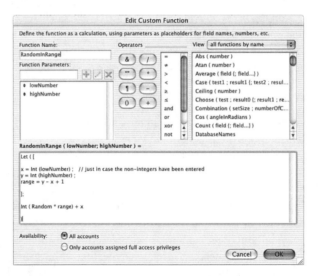

This dialog is similar in many ways to the standard calculation formula dialogs, so it shouldn't seem terribly unfamiliar. The main difference is the upper-left portion of the dialog, where instead of seeing a list of fields, you can name your function and its parameters. The restrictions for function and parameter names are the same as the those for field names: They can't contain any mathematic symbols (such as + - * / ^ =), they can't contain the words AND, OR, XOR, or NOT, they can't begin with a digit or period, and they can't have the same name as an already existing function or keyword.

> **TIP**
>
> When naming your custom functions and parameters, we think it's best to follow the same naming conventions used in the built-in functions. The initial letter of each word in a function name should be capitalized, and the name should contain no spaces or other punctuation. Parameters should be in "camel case," with the first letter in lowercase and the first letter of subsequent words capitalized (for example, numberOfCharacters, textString1).

There is no practical limit to the number of parameters you can define for a function, but most functions require anywhere from 0 to a handful. The order of the parameters is important: When you use a function and specify the input parameters, they are interpreted as being in the order in which they are listed in the Edit Custom Function dialog.

> **NOTE**
>
> If you find yourself writing a function that requires more than about four or five parameters, that's a pretty good signal that you should be break the function down into two or more smaller functions.

The other significantly new and different portion of this dialog is the Availability section at the bottom. By default, a function is available to all user accounts. Any time a user or developer has access to a calculation dialog, he or she will see and be able to use all the unrestricted custom functions. The other option available to you is to restrict the use of the function to only those users who have been assigned the "Full Access" privilege set. The latter are referred to as *private* functions, and the former can be thought of as *public* functions. We find it helpful to place an underscore at the beginning of the name of private functions so that they can be quickly and obviously identified. If access to a function has been restricted, then users who don't have full access will not ever see or have access to use that function. If these users ever view a calculation dialog that references a private function (say, in a script), the name of the function is replaced with <Private function> in the calculation dialog. Declaring a function as private has no impact on what data is displayed or accessible to a user. The functions still do their jobs and work properly. It's just the functions themselves that can't be viewed or used.

You might want to restrict access to a function for several reasons. As you will see in some of the examples in the section that follows, often when you define recursive functions, you need to define two functions to accomplish one goal. In these cases, the first function is often a public function, whereas the other is restricted, thereby keeping users from accidentally calling it directly. Another reason to define a function as private is simply to keep from confusing novice developers. Your function may not be documented anywhere, and it might not contain adequate error trapping to handle improper parameter values. By making it private, you reduce the risk that the function will be used improperly.

14

EXAMPLES OF CUSTOM FUNCTIONS

We think the best way to learn how to write your own custom functions is to study examples so you can get ideas about uses in your own solutions. Some of the example functions that follow might have intrinsic value to you, but more important than the specific formulas are the ideas and techniques. To that end, following each of the examples presented in this section, we provide commentary about the syntax and/or use of the function.

```
Hypotenuse (leg1Length ; leg2Length) =
Let ( [
    a2 = leg1Length * leg1Length;
    b2 = leg2Length * leg2Length;

    c2 = a2 + b2] ;
    Sqrt (c2)
)
```

Although FileMaker Pro provides built-in functions for many common mathematical formulas and operations, there are a number of common equations missing. The preceding Hypotenuse function uses the Pythagorean Theorem ($a^2 + b^2 = c^2$) to find the length of the hypotenuse of a right triangle given the lengths of the two legs.

Examples:

Hypotenuse (3 ; 4) = 5

Hypotenuse (5 ; 12) = 13

```
NthRoot (number ; root) =
Exp (Ln (number) / root )
```

This is another example of creating a custom function to provide an abstraction for a mathematical formula: There is a built-in function that returns the square root of a number, but no function that returns the nth root of a number. The NthRoot function uses logarithms to find this number.

Examples:

NthRoot (8 ; 3) = 2

NthRoot (256; 4) = 4

```
Quarter (myDate) =
"Q" & Ceiling ( Month (myDate) / 3)
```

This function returns the calendar quarter (Q1–Q4) of myDate. This function exemplifies the idea of custom functions being used to substitute for code chunks, making your code easier to read and maintain. The Month() function returns a number from 1 to 12, so taking the ceiling of that number divided by 3 yields an integer from 1 to 4.

Examples:

```
Quarter ("12/11/03") = Q4
Quarter ("4/1/04") = Q2
```

```
WeekEndingFriday (myDate) =
myDate + Mod (6 - DayOfWeek(mydate); 7)
```

Given a date, this function returns the date of the following Friday. This sort of functionality is often necessary in time tracking systems so that you can summarize records by week. It would be easy to alter or extend this function to be referenced to some day other than Friday. To extend it, you would just specify a second parameter in the function and replace the hard coded "6" (which is the DayOfWeek of any Friday) with a value derived from the parameter.

Examples:

```
WeekEndingFriday ("12/11/2003") = "12/12/2003"  // the 11th was a Thursday
WeekEndingFriday ("1/9/2004") = "1/9/2004" // the 9th was a Friday
```

```
RepeatText (text ; numberOfRepetitions) =
text & Case (numberOfRepetitions>1; RepeatText (text; numberOfRepetitions - 1))
```

This is the first example of a recursive function. The RepeatText function returns n repetitions of the text string passed in the first parameter. For instance, RepeatText ("t"; 3) returns the string ttt. If the concept of recursive functions isn't clear to you, then this is a good place to begin experimenting. Figure 14.23 traces through exactly what the function is asked to do when it evaluates this simple example. RepeatText ("t"; 3) is first evaluated as t and the result of RepeatText ("t"; 2). Of course, the latter is then evaluated as t and the result of RepeatText ("t" ; 1), which is simply t. The iteration stops at this point because numberOfRepetitions is not greater than 1. This is known as the function's *exit condition*; without one, you have endless recursion (picture a dog chasing its tail endlessly), which fortunately FileMaker Pro is smart enough to recover from after some large number of iterations.

CAUTION

> Be sure that any recursive function you write has some exit condition that is guaranteed to be reached.

Possible uses of the RepeatText function include creating progress bars or bar graphs. If you ever tried to do this sort of thing in previous versions of FileMaker, you know what a kludgy workaround was required to get a repeating string of characters. Another use is for padding out spaces when generating fixed-length data formats. Say you need to pad out a FirstName field to 15 characters by adding spaces at the end. In previous versions of FileMaker you would have used the formula Left (FirstName & "   " ;

14

15). Using `RepeatText`, you could simply use `FirstName & RepeatText (" " ; 15 - Length(FirstName))`. Of course, if you have a lot of padding to do, you might decide to abstract this one more layer and build the `PadCharacters` function shown next.

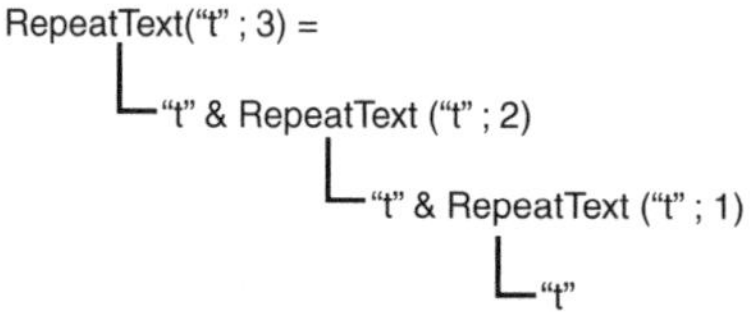

Figure 14.23
This diagram shows how the recursive custom function `RepeatText ("t" ; 3)` is evaluated.

```
RepeatText("t" ; 3) =
    └─"t" & RepeatText ("t" ; 2)
          └─"t" & RepeatText ("t" ; 1)
                └─"t"
```

Examples:

```
RepeatText ("¦" ; 10) = "¦¦¦¦¦¦¦¦¦¦"
RepeatText ("hello"; 3) = "hellohellohello"


PadCharacters (text ; padLenth; characterToPad; side) =
Let ( [
    padString = RepeatText (characterToPad; padLength - Length(text));
] ;
Case (
  Length (text) > padLength ; Left (text; padLength);
  side = "start"; padString & text;
  side = "end"; text & padString
)
)
```

Building on the preceding example, the `PadCharacters` function pads either leading or trailing characters onto a string. We've used four parameters here to gain flexibility. The third and fourth parameters specify the pad character and whether the padding should be at the "start" or "end" of the string. If you knew you always wanted to pad leading zeros, you could define this function with just two parameters and then hard-code the location and character within the formula.

Notice that this function makes a call to the `RepeatText` function to generate the `padString`. We could have included the formula for `RepeatText`, but by abstracting it out, we centralize the code for `RepeatText` (making it easier to troubleshoot) while also making the formula easier to read.

Examples:

```
PadCharacters ("foo"; 8 ; "x"; "end") = "fooxxxxx"
PadCharacters ("123"; 10; "0"; "start") = "0000000123"


TrimChar (text; removeCharacter; location) =
  // valid locations are "start", "end", "all"
Let ( [
  leftChar = Left (text; 1);
  rightChar = Right (text; 1);
  remainderLength = Length(text) -1
```

```
] ;
Case (
  (location = "start" or location = "all") and leftChar = removeCharacter;
    TrimChar (Right(text; remainderLength) ; removeCharacter; location) ;
  (location = "end" or location = "all") and rightChar = removeCharacter;
    TrimChar (Left(text; remainderLength) ; removeCharacter; location) ;
  text
)
)
```

FileMaker Pro's built-in `Trim` function removes any leading and trailing spaces from a text string. There are times, however, when you need a more generalized way of removing a specific leading or trailing character from a string. The `TrimChar` function does just this. The first parameter is the string you want to trim; the second is the character you want removed. The third parameter, `location`, is used to specify whether you want the character removed from the start or end of the string, or from both. Valid inputs are `start`, `end`, and `all`.

This function works by checking whether the first or last character in the string needs to be lopped off. If so, the remainder of the string is fed back recursively to itself. Each iteration removes at most a single character; the "loop" continues until no more characters need to be removed, at which point the shortened text string is simply returned.

Examples:

```
TrimChar ("xxThis is a testxxx", "x", "all") = "This is a test"

TrimChar ("Another test¶¶¶", "¶", "end") = "Another test"


CrossProduct (array1; array2) =
_CrossProductGenerator (array1; array2; 1)
```

This, the final custom function example, looks at a more complex recursive function. In the recursive examples shown previously, the exit condition for the recursion was based either on an explicitly passed parameter reaching a certain value (`RepeatChar`), or when some condition was no longer true (`TrimChar`). There are other situations where you want to be able to increment a counter with every iteration, and have the exit condition for the loop based on that counter reaching some threshold. The interesting part is that because the counter needs to be passed along from iteration to iteration, it must be defined as a parameter. This means, however, that anyone using the function must "initialize" the counter for you, most likely setting it simply to 1.

The other solution is that you have a private function with a counter parameter that's called by a public function without one. In this case, the public function `CrossProduct` takes only two parameters, which are both expected to be return-delimited arrays. The function is defined merely to call another function `_CrossProductGenerator`, which has three parameters. The first two inputs to `_CrossProductGenerator` are simply passed along based on the user's input. The third, however, is hard coded to 1, hence initializing a counter used there.

The syntax for the private function is `_CrossProductGenerator (array1; array2; counter)`, and it has the following formula:

14

```
Let ( [
  array1count = ValueCount (array1);
  array2count = ValueCount (array2);
  limit = array1count * array2count;

  pos1 = Ceiling (counter / array2count) ;
  pos2 = Mod (counter - 1; array2count ) + 1;

  item1 = TrimChar (MiddleValues (array1; pos1; 1); "¶" ; "end");
  item2 = TrimChar (MiddleValues (array2; pos2; 1); "¶" ; "end")
] ;

Case ( counter <= limit ;
    item1 & item2 & "¶" & _CrossProductGenerator (array1; array2; counter + 1))

)
```

The cross product of two sets is a set containing all the two-element sets that can be created by taking one element of each set. For example, if Set1 contained {A, B} and Set2 contained {P, Q, R, S}, then their cross product would consist of {AP, AQ, AR, AS, BP, BQ, BR, BS}. The number of elements in the cross product is the product of the number of elements in each of the two sets.

The _CrossProductGenerator function "loops," incrementing a counter as it goes, until the counter is no longer less than the number of elements expected in the result set. Each time it iterates, it figures out what element number to grab from each list. With Set1 and Set2 of the example, the function would iterate 8 times. If you were on iteration 5, the function would realize it needed to grab the second item from the first list (because Ceiling (5 / 4) = 2), which is "B," and the first item from the second list (because Mod (4; 4) + 1 = 1), which is "P." That's how "BP" becomes the fifth element of the result set.

Notice also that this function, besides recursively calling itself, also calls the TrimChar function created earlier in this section. From the section on working with arrays, you'll remember that the LeftValues, MiddleValues, and RightValues functions all return a trailing return after the item list; that trailing return needs to be removed before the item is processed.

Examples:

CrossProduct ("A¶B¶C" ; "1¶2¶3¶4") = "A1¶A2¶A3¶A4¶B1¶B2¶B3¶B4¶C1¶C2¶C3¶C4¶"

CrossProduct ("Red¶Yellow¶Blue" ; "-fish") = "Red-fish¶Yellow-fish¶Blue-fish¶"

TROUBLESHOOTING

NAMING VARIABLES IN Let FUNCTIONS

Can I use spaces in the names of variables used in Let functions? Are the variable names case sensitive? What happens if I name a variable the same thing as an existing field name or a function name?

First off, yes, you can use spaces in the names of variables used in Let functions. Variable names can't begin with numbers, nor can they contain certain reserved characters (such as ; ,

\ / + - * = ( ) [ ] < > & and "). You can, however, use characters such as $ and % in variable names. If you're accustomed from other programming languages to use $ to denote a text string, you may want to continue to use that as part of your naming convention.

Variable names are not case sensitive. You can use a particular name only once within a function, but names can certainly be reused in separate functions.

There are no restrictions against naming variables with the same names used for fields and functions. Be aware that any subsequent use of the name within the function refers to the local variable, not the field or function. With most functions, you don't need to worry about this, but names of functions that don't take parameters, such as Random, WindowNames, and Pi, should not be used for variables within a Let function. For instance, the formula Let (Pi = "Hello"; Pi) would return the string Hello, not the trigonometric constant Pi that you might expect.

Working with Arrays

I use arrays that have pipe characters as delimiters. Can I use the "values" functions to extract elements from these arrays?

The four "values" functions (ValueCount, LeftValues, MiddleValues, RightValues) operate only on return-delimited lists of data. If you have lists that are delimited by other characters, such as pipes or tabs, you'd first need to do a substitution to change your delimiter into a return. For example, if myArray is a pipe-delimited array, you could count the number of values in it with the following formula:

```
Let (tempArray = Substitute (myArray; "¦"; "¶"); ValueCount (tempArray))
```

Of course, one of the reasons you might not have used returns as your delimiter in the first place is that your data elements may possibly contain return characters. If that's the case, then you can't swap in returns as your delimiters and expect the structure of the array to remain unchanged. Before turning pipe characters into carriage returns, you'd want to turn any existing carriage returns into something else—something that's guaranteed not to be found in an element and that's easy to turn back into a return character if necessary. You might, for instance, use the Substitute function to turn returns into the string ***RETURN***.

FileMaker Extra: Creating a Custom Function Library

If you or your organization uses custom functions across several solutions, you'll likely want to develop some sort of centralized library of the functions you've developed. That way, when you find yourself in need of a particular function, you won't have to rack your brain remembering where it was used before. Also, centralizing the function library is a way of creating a knowledge base that can help your organization leverage its past work and can aid in the training of new developers.

Your library can take many forms. One option, of course, is to create a FileMaker Pro file for your function library. Minimally, you'll want to include fields for the function name, its parameters, its formula, and a brief description. You might also use a container field to store an example file for a particular function. Another "nice to have" would be a related table for storing information about where you've used the function.

As of the time of this writing, there's no way to move custom functions from one file to another. Cutting and pasting formulas to and from the library isn't terribly time consuming, though. Custom functions are, however, part of the Database Design Report (DDR) that can be produced by the FileMaker Developer 7. If you're handy with XML, or are looking for a fun first XML project, you might want to use the XML output of the DDR to create your function library.

Finally, if you always want to have a particular set of custom functions in your files, create a sparse template file that has them in it. Then, rather than create new files from scratch, you can just duplicate and develop on top of your template.

CHAPTER 15

ADVANCED SCRIPTING

WHAT IS ADVANCED SCRIPTING?

15

Chapter 9, "Getting Started with Scripting," presented an introduction to FileMaker Pro scripting techniques. It covered such topics as error trapping, linking scripts together via subscripts, conditional branching, looping scripts, and using custom dialogs. These are all essential scripting techniques that you should become familiar with.

This chapter explores several additional scripting techniques, including working with script parameters and managing windows. Although we think that everyone can potentially benefit from learning these techniques, they do require a good familiarity with general scripting techniques, calculation formulas, and the Relationships Graph. For this reason, we have opted to present these as "advanced" scripting techniques.

This chapter does not present a comprehensive overview of scripting techniques. Indeed, such an overview could require an entire book of its own. Rather, we have chosen techniques that highlight new features of FileMaker Pro 7 and that we think will have the broadest appeal. Appendix C, "Scripting Reference," contains a complete script reference; refer to that source for additional information about script steps used throughout this chapter.

SCRIPT PARAMETERS

Script parameters, new to FileMaker Pro 7, are a mechanism for passing inputs into scripts. This is desirable because it means that scripts can be written more abstractly and thus can be reused. By "abstractly," we mean that scripts are written to solve general problems rather than specific ones. Using script parameters saves you time, reduces the number of scripts that are necessary in your files, and makes your scripts easier to maintain.

That being said, the use of script parameters is completely optional. FileMaker developers did quite well for years without them, and there's no scenario we can think of where you couldn't still muddle through without them. Script parameters represent a considerable advance for FileMaker Pro scripting; the extent to which you want to take advantage of that depends on the needs of your users and the scope of your files.

Before getting into the details of how and why to use script parameters, a short example will give you a concrete sense of what script parameters are all about and why you want to learn this. Imagine that you want to create several navigation buttons that take users to a specified layout. One way to do this is to create a separate script that's hard-coded to go to a particular destination. You'd need as many scripts as you have destination layouts, and every time you wanted to add a new destination, you'd create a new script.

Another way to accomplish this task is to create a generic "Go to" script that navigates to a layout specified by the script parameter that was passed to it. Then, when setting up the buttons themselves, you would simply call the "Go to" script, specifying the destination as the parameter. This approach has the advantage of requiring but a single script. To add another destination in the future, you simply specify the new destination as the parameter. There is no need to add a new script or to edit the original "Go to" script.

15

It's clear from this example that extracting hard-coded values from a script and placing them instead into script parameters has a tangible benefit. Keep this example in mind as you read further about script parameters.

SPECIFYING SCRIPT PARAMETERS

Script parameters can be defined in two places: either as part of a button definition or as an option for invoking a subscript within the Perform Script script step. Figure 15.1 shows the first of these: the dialog for specifying what script should run when a button is clicked. The dialog for specifying a subscript is exactly the same.

Figure 15.1
When attaching a script to a button, you can also specify an optional script parameter, which is passed into the script.

At the bottom of this dialog, you have the option of specifying a script parameter. The parameter can be some text string you type into the space provided, or you can enter a calculation formula as the parameter. Clicking the Edit button brings up a standard calculation formula dialog box. If you use a calculation formula as your script parameter, then when the button (or subscript) is triggered, the formula is evaluated, and the results are used as the parameter.

The actual string or formula you use as your parameter depends completely on what you're trying to accomplish. Later in this section, you'll see some example applications of script parameters.

NOTE

> Only scripts that are triggered by buttons or that are called as subscripts of other scripts can have script parameters passed to them. Scripts that are triggered through the Script menu, by an external source (such as via Custom Web Publishing), or as startup/shutdown scripts (under File, File Options) cannot have script parameters passed to them.

RETRIEVING A SCRIPT PARAMETER

The Get(ScriptParameter) function can be used to retrieve the value of the script parameter passed to a script. If no parameter was specified, then this function simply returns an empty string. The value of the script parameter can be accessed anywhere from within the script in this way. It can't be changed or altered in any way, and it "expires" as soon as the script is complete.

Any subscripts called by a script can have their own independent script parameters—they do not "inherit" the parameter of the script that calls them. As an example, say that the string abc was designated as the parameter to be passed to a script called Main Script. Assume further that Main Script called a subscript called Child Script as its second step, and that the parameter xyz was specified as part of the Perform Script step. Within Main Script, Get(ScriptParameter) will always return abc. Within Child Script, Get(ScriptParameter) will always return xyz.

The parameter passed to a script can be the result of a calculation, so by using Get(ScriptParameter) as the parameter, you can pass a script's parameter down to the subscripts it calls, as shown in Figure 15.2.

Figure 15.2
If you want a subscript to "inherit" a parameter, set the parameter to Get(Script Parameter).

PASSING MULTI-VALUED PARAMETERS

The interface for specifying script parameters allows for only a single value to be passed to a script. For many situations, this is sufficient to achieve the desired outcome. Other times, however, you will find that you want to be able to pass multiple parameters to a script. Although this isn't directly possible, there are several methods to achieve such a result.

PARSING A TEXT ARRAY

The simplest way to pass multiple values in a script parameter is to specify a delimited array as the script parameter. For instance, if you wanted to send a parameter that contained the values Fred, 123, and Monkey, you could send the string Fred¦123¦Monkey, or even Fred¶123¶Monkey.

NOTE

The delimiter you use (here we've used pipe characters and carriage returns) is up to you; just choose something that you know won't be found in the data you're passing.

To retrieve a portion of the passed parameter, use the built-in text parsing functions of FileMaker Pro. If you've used carriage returns as your array delimiter, the MiddleValues function is the easiest way to extract a particular value. Say that you want to grab the third value (Monkey). From within your script, anytime you wanted access to this value, you would use the following formula:

```
Substitute (MiddleValues (Get (ScriptParameter) ; 3 ; 1), "¶", "")
```

→ For more on text parsing functions, **see** Chapter 8, "Getting Started with Calculations," **p. 213**, Chapter 14, "Specialized Calculation Functions," **p. 381**, and Appendix B, "Calculation Function Reference," **p. 807**.

NOTE

> The Substitute function is necessary because the output of the MiddleValues function always contains a carriage return at the end of it.

→ For more on the MiddleValues function, **see** "Array Functions," **p. 403**.

The nice thing about using delimited lists to pass multiple values is that you can set them up very easily. Even if some of the values are derived as calculated results, it's still quite easy to set up a formula that concatenates all the appropriate pieces together. For instance, if you wanted to pass the current layout name and the current time as the two values of your script parameter, you would use the following formula:

```
Get (LayoutName) & "¶" & Get (CurrentTime)
```

The main drawback of this method is that the burden is on you, the developer, to know what the values in the array represent. Is "Monkey" a favorite animal, a password, or a Halloween costume? There's nothing in the parameter itself that offers any assistance. This can (and should!) be clarified with script and/or calculation comments.

USING THE Let FUNCTION

Another method for passing multiple values in a script parameter involves the Let and Evaluate functions. If you have a good understanding of those functions, you'll likely appreciate the elegance of this technique.

→ For more on the Let and Evaluate functions, see "Logical Functions," **p. 382**.

Imagine that you pass as your script parameter the following string:

```
"First Name = \"Fred\"; Favorite Number = \23 ; Favorite Animal = \"Monkey\""
```

What you have here is a set of name/value pairs, separated by semicolons. Immediately you can see one of the benefits of this method over the previous one: When you pass both names and values, the parameter becomes more meaningful. In six months when you need to troubleshoot or enhance your script, you won't have to rack your brain to remember what the elements in your parameter represent. Another benefit of this method is that the order of the values doesn't matter. They'll be retrieved by name rather than by their position within the parameter.

You'll notice that within the parameter, there are back slashes before all the internal quotation marks. This process, known as *escaping* your quotes, is necessary any time you want to pass a string that contains internal quotes. For this technique, you need to escape any text values in your parameter; numeric values (such as the 123) do not need to be escaped.

You might recognize that the parameter specified previously is structured similarly to the first parameter of a Let function. This isn't a coincidence. Recall that the Let function allows you to set variables within a calculation formula. Imagine you had the following formula:

```
Let ([First Name = "Fred"; Favorite Number = 123 ; Favorite Animal =
"Monkey"] ; Favorite Animal)
```

This formula sets three local variables (First Name, Favorite Number, and Favorite Animal) and then returns the value of the Favorite Animal variable. It would, in fact, return Monkey.

By combining the Let and Evaluate functions, you can build a formula that pulls out a named value from within a script parameter. The Evaluate function executes a dynamically constructed calculation formula. Therefore, within your script, anytime you want to retrieve the value of the Favorite Animal, you would use the following formula:

```
Evaluate ( "Let ([" & Get(ScriptParameter)  & "]; Favorite Animal)")
```

As you can see, a string containing a Let function is dynamically assembled from the value of the script parameter. The Evaluate function is then used to execute it. To return one of the other variables within the script parameter, you would simply need to change the end of the formula to reference the proper variable name.

If you foresee a need to do much parsing of multi-value script parameters, you should consider creating a custom function to simplify the process even more. That way, you won't have to remember the syntax for the Let and Evaluate functions every time you need to retrieve a parameter value. Figure 15.3 shows the definition for a custom function called GetParam.

 For more on creating custom functions, **see** "Custom Functions," **p. 409**.

Figure 15.3
The custom function *GetParam* abstracts the script parameter parsing routine even more.

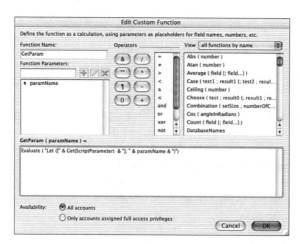

The `GetParam` function takes a single argument, `paramName`. The formula for the function is the same as the `Evaluate` formula shown previously, but with the `paramName` inserted in the place of the hard-coded parameter name:

```
Evaluate ( "Let ([" & Get(ScriptParameter)  & "]; " & paramName & ")")
```

Now, within your script, to retrieve the value of the `Favorite Animal`, you just need the following formula:

```
GetParam ("Favorite Animal")
```

This final abstraction provided by the `GetParam` custom function certainly makes the parameter parsing more convenient. After it's in place, you can pass and retrieve multi-valued script parameters with ease.

PASSING STRUCTURED DATA ELEMENTS

The final method in this discussion for passing multi-valued script parameters involves creating your own structured data elements. It's really a hybrid of the other two methods, in that it requires standard text parsing to retrieve an element (like the first method), but the elements are meaningfully named (as in the second method).

The syntax you create for naming elements is up to you. We generally prefer an XML-like structure because it's easy to use and organize. For instance, to pass the same three values discussed in the previous section, you might specify the following as your script parameter:

```
"<First Name>Fred</First Name><Favorite Number>123</Favorite Number><Favorite
Animal>Monkey</Favorite Animal>"
```

This is, of course, simply another way of specifying element names and values. But you don't need to worry about escaping any quotes, as you do with a string that will be used in a Evaluate statement. To retrieve the value of a particular element of the script parameter, you would need to use standard text parsing functions. This is best accomplished with the creation of a custom function; you then need to write the parsing logic just once. The following formula could be used as the definition for such a custom function; the function's only parameter is `paramName`:

```
Let ( [
    openElement = "<" & paramName & ">";
    closeElement = "</" & paramName & ">" ;

    startPos = Position (Get(ScriptParameter) ; openElement ; 1; 1) +
    ➥Length (openElement);
    endPos = Position (Get (ScriptParameter) ; closeElement ; 1; 1)] ;

Middle (Get(ScriptParameter) ; startPos ; endPos - startPos)
)
```

If this function were called `GetParamXML`, the value of one of the script parameter elements could then be retrieved with the function `GetParamXML("First Name")`. The custom function is hard-coded to parse out a value from a script parameter.

15

TIP

> You could easily turn this into a more generic XML parsing tool by passing a text string in which to search as another parameter.

STRATEGIES FOR USING SCRIPT PARAMETERS

Using script parameters can greatly reduce the number of scripts in a file and can make your database much easier to maintain. You should consider using script parameters in several common programming scenarios.

MODULARIZING SCRIPTS

The first—and most important—reason for using script parameters is to add a layer of abstraction to your scripts, thereby making them more modular and reusable. Rather than write scads of single-purpose scripts, if you can generalize your scripts by using script parameters, you will need fewer scripts and your solution will be easier to maintain.

Practical Script Parameter Examples

Elsewhere in this book are several examples of script parameters being used to modularize scripts. For instance, in Chapter 10, "Reporting with Grouped Data," one of the reporting techniques involved turning the column headings on a list view into buttons that would sort by the values in that column. All the buttons called a single script, passing in a different script parameter. Without script parameters, that routine would have required separate scripts for each column, each with a single hard-coded sort specification. Not only would that take longer to set up, but if the behavior ever needed to be modified, changes would need to be made to multiple scripts rather than a single, abstract script.

Script parameters were also central to the navigation routine described in Chapter 13, "Advanced Layout Techniques." There, a generalized navigation script was passed a destination layout as a script parameter.

You will know if you have encountered a situation that can potentially be simplified and strengthened by using script parameters if you find yourself writing several scripts that do basically the same thing, differing only in some specific value. In place of that specific value, use Get (ScriptParameter), then have the buttons or other scripts that trigger the script specify the particular value.

For instance, say you've developed a system that contains a calendar, and that one of your layouts shows all the scheduled appointments for a given week. You'd like to be able to place a button above each of the seven days of the week (Sunday through Saturday) that users can click when they want to create a new appointment on that particular day. Assume you have a field that contains the date of the Sunday of the week. Therefore, a script that would create a new appointment on Wednesday would do something like the following:

```
New Record/Request
Set Field [Appointments::AppointmentDate ; SundayDate + 3]
```

The scripts for creating appointments on the other days of the week would differ from what's shown in the preceding formula only by the constant that's added to the SundayDate.

You could therefore write seven scripts, link them to your buttons, and move on to your next task.

We hope you can already see how and why script parameters can be used here. In the example script, if you change the + 3 to + Get (ScriptParameter), then you need only a single script to do the work of the seven that would be required without script parameters. Each of the seven buttons calls the generic version of this Add Appointment script, passing as a parameter an integer from 0 to 6 to differentiate them from each other. By using this method, you've replaced seven hard-coded scripts with a single generalized one.

PASSING DATA BETWEEN FILES

Another situation in which script parameters can be beneficial is for passing data between files. Using script parameters for this purpose saves you from needing to create extra fields and relationships in your files.

As an example, imagine that you have a file called Transactions and another called TransactionArchive (each with a single table with the same name as the file). You periodically archive old transactions into the archive file, but occasionally you have a need to pull a record back from the archive into the main production file. Further, you'd like to avoid placing a table occurrence from the archive file in the main file because the two need to be able to function independently.

Because you can call scripts in another file without having a relationship to that file, script parameters make an ideal transfer mechanism for moving data between unrelated files. In the example scenario, you might set up a script in the TransactionArchive file that calls a subscript in the Transaction file, passing a multi-valued parameter (using one of the methods described in the previous section) that contains the pertinent data elements from the transaction. In the Transaction file, then, your subscript would create a new record and populate it, using the parsed-out parameter data.

In this example, importing the record from one file to the other would have been another solution within the defined constraints. Nonetheless, it still clearly demonstrates the role that script parameters can play in moving data around. It's certainly preferable to copying and pasting data, or even parking data in global fields for later retrieval (both of which were common techniques with previous versions of FileMaker).

PROTECTING SUBSCRIPTS

A final strategy for using script parameters is as a means of protecting subscripts from inadvertently being called improperly. Imagine that you have a pair of scripts, Script A and Script B, and that Script B is called as a subscript from Script A. As it stands, nothing would prevent another script from calling Script B, or even from Script B being called directly. In some cases, there may be undesirable consequences that can occur if subscripts are called directly.

To "protect" Script B, and ensure that it's called only as a subscript of Script A, you can pass a script parameter that "authorizes" Script B to run. It really doesn't matter what value you

15

pass. You can check at the beginning of Script B to see whether the script parameter is set correctly. If it isn't, exit the script or show a warning dialog to the user.

CAUTION

> Of course, any user who has access to the scripts in question can discover what parameter Script B expects, so this method isn't intended to be used as a security measure. It merely protects against accidental execution of subscripts (and also direct invocation from the Web).

WINDOW MANAGEMENT TECHNIQUES

NEW Among the many features introduced in FileMaker Pro 7, the capability to have multiple windows showing data from the same table stands out as one of the most important. To aid developers with managing this new feature, several new window management script steps were added to ScriptMaker. These include the following:

- New Window
- Select Window
- Close Window
- Move/Resize Window
- Set Window Title

There are also 11 `Get` functions that return data about the active window, ranging from its size and location to its name and the mode it's in. Another function that plays a role in window management is `WindowNames`, which returns a list containing the names of all the open windows, ordered according to the stacking order of the windows.

These script steps and calculation functions provide you with tremendous ability to control the user experience. The amount of window management you do may differ widely from solution to solution, but having a good grounding in the options available to you is certainly desirable.

THE ANATOMY OF A WINDOW

When you create, move, and resize windows, you have the opportunity to specify both a location for the window and its size. The unit of measure for all window manipulation is the pixel. Figure 15.4 shows the options for the `Move/Resize Window` script step.

For each parameter of the `Move/Resize Window` script step, you can either specify a literal number or supply a calculation formula whose result determines the parameter's value. If you leave any of the parameters empty, their values are inherited from the current active window. For instance, if you merely want to move the current window (without changing its size), you don't need to specify anything for the Height and Width parameters.

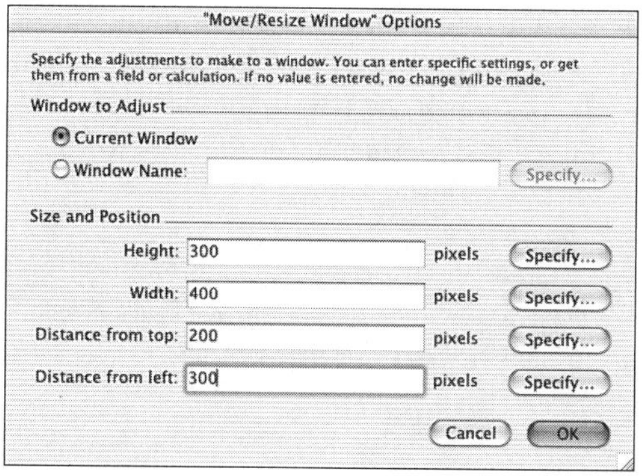

Figure 15.4
The `Move/Resize Window` script step enables you to specify the exact coordinates (in pixels) and size for any given window.

"Move/Resize Window" Options

Specify the adjustments to make to a window. You can enter specific settings, or get them from a field or calculation. If no value is entered, no change will be made.

Window to Adjust
- Current Window
- Window Name: [   ] (Specify...)

Size and Position

Height:	300	pixels	(Specify...)
Width:	400	pixels	(Specify...)
Distance from top:	200	pixels	(Specify...)
Distance from left:	300	pixels	(Specify...)

(Cancel) (OK)

Before you start creating and moving windows around the screen, however, it's important that you have a good understanding of the anatomy of a window. When you specify the Distance from Top for a new window, for instance, is that the distance from the top of the screen, or the top of the application window? Is it the distance to the window's title bar or to the layout itself? These are the types of questions that this anatomy lesson answers.

Working from the outside inward, there are four important objects for managing windows. These are the screen, the desktop, the window, and the content area.

SCREEN

The screen is the backdrop against which all window actions take place. Screen resolution can, of course, differ from user to user. You can use the `Get (ScreenHeight)` and `Get (ScreenWidth)` functions to return the absolute height and width (in pixels) of the user's screen.

If multiple monitors are hooked up to a machine, then these functions return the dimensions of whichever monitor contains the active window. If the active window straddles monitors, the active screen is considered to be the one that contains the majority of the window. You cannot programmatically alter the dimensions of the screen from within FileMaker Pro.

DESKTOP

FileMaker also has a pair of functions that return the dimensions of something called the *window desktop*: `Get (WindowDesktopHeight)` and `Get (WindowDesktopWidth)`. In a nutshell, these represent the dimensions of the FileMaker application window.

On a Macintosh, the top menu bar, which is 22 pixels high, is not considered part of the application window. The desktop height, therefore, is 22 pixels smaller than the screen height. The desktop and screen widths should be identical.

The desktop size is slightly more complicated on Windows because an application can be maximized to fill the screen, or it can float free in its own window space. The two desktop functions return the *inside* dimensions of the application window. The application title bar and the FileMaker menu bar are not considered to be part of the "window desktop" on

Windows. Scrollbars on the right and bottom of the application, however, are considered to be part of the window desktop. If you fully maximize FileMaker on Windows XP, and if the Taskbar has its default size and location at the bottom of the screen, then the desktop height is 80 pixels less than the screen height. That includes 46 pixels for the application title bar and menu bar and 34 pixels for the Taskbar.

CAUTION

> Be aware that the dimensions are slightly different in Windows 2000, and that many system settings can affect the exact pixel sizes for various screen elements. It's best to test on your own system.

You cannot programmatically set the dimensions of the desktop area, nor can you determine the placement of the desktop relative to the screen (which is interesting only on Windows when the application is not maximized).

WINDOW

The next type of object to discuss is the *window*. This is finally where you, as the developer, get to have some control over things. You can set the size, placement, and name of windows on the screen through a variety of script steps. The size of the active window—its outside dimensions—can be obtained with the Get (Height) and Get (Width) functions. These dimensions include both the window's *frame* and its *content*. These concepts are discussed in depth later in this section.

When you position a window on the screen, you specify, in effect, the coordinates for the top-left corner of the window. These coordinates are *not* relative to the overall screen dimensions. They are *mostly* relative to the window desktop. We say "mostly" here because a window positioned 0 pixels from the top and 0 pixels from the left is placed at the top-left corner within the application window. If there are no active, docked toolbars, then this window's position would, in fact, be relative to the window desktop. It's the potential presence of docked toolbars (either the Standard toolbar or the Text Formatting toolbar) that muddies the waters. Each of those can move the absolute position of (0,0), either downward or to the right, depending on where the toolbar is docked. Docked in the standard position at the top of the screen, each toolbar takes up 26 pixels on Mac and 27 pixels on Windows XP. The toolbars do not affect the size of the desktop area.

Further, the presence of the status bar (not to be confused with the status area) on Windows decreases the usable application window space by an additional 18 pixels. There's no way to test for the presence or location of the toolbars or the status bar, so it's impossible to know without experimentation the maximum size a window can be without exceeding the dimensions of the application window.

CAUTION

On Windows, a user may choose to use Normal, Large, or even Extra Large Fonts under the display properties. The status bar does not change size, but the window and application title bars both increase in height dramatically. You should be aware that the pixel sizes for various objects provided here are not true constants.

15

CONTENT

While the outside dimensions of a window are described by the Get (Height) and Get (Width) functions, the inside dimensions are described by the Get (ContentHeight) and Get (ContentWidth) functions. The content area is the most important to you, the developer, because it's the space that your layouts inhabit.

It might be helpful to think of a window like a framed picture: Much as a picture frame surrounds a picture, a window's frame surrounds the content of the window. The content dimensions refer to the dimensions of the picture, not including the frame.

The size of the window's frame differs slightly on Mac and Windows. And because you specify window size, not content size, when creating or resizing windows, this means that to display a fixed content size, you need to use a variable window size.

On Macintosh, a window's title bar takes up 22 pixels, and its left and bottom scroll bars are each 15 pixels thick. If the status area is visible, this adds 69 pixels to the window's frame.

On Windows, if the current window is maximized, then the window has no top title bar. If it's not maximized, the title bar requires 38 pixels on Windows XP, and 31 pixels on Windows 2000. The left and bottom scroll bars are each 16 pixels thick. If the window is not maximized, then there's a further border on the left and right hand sides of the window that adds 12 more pixels to the width of the frame. Finally, the status area on Windows is the same as on a Mac—69 pixels.

The content dimensions tell you only the visible content area of the active window. That is, they don't take into account "content" that you need to scroll to see.

POSITIONING A WINDOW RELATIVE TO ANOTHER WINDOW

One common window manipulation routine involves having a new window pop up at a position on the screen relative to another window. This technique can make for very effective user interface management. Even if users move a window to another part of their screen, your pop-up window appears in the same position relative to the window that called it.

 You might have difficulty when creating pop-up windows for use on Windows PCs. See "Pop-up Window Issues on a PC" in the Troubleshooting section at the end of this chapter.

The example discussed in this section is an expansion on the window pop-up technique discussed in the "Rich Dialog Windows" section of Chapter 13, "Advanced Layout Techniques." Please refer to that for more information on how to make the pop-up window behave like a modal dialog.

Figure 15.5 shows a layout from a basic contact management system; the portal at the bottom is used to collect notes associated with a particular contact.

Figure 15.5
A contact info layout with a portal into a Notes table becomes the "anchor" for a pop-up window.

Imagine that you want to create a workflow where users are not allowed to add new notes directly from the portal. Instead, you would like a pop-up window to appear in front of the portal when users click the Add Note button, regardless of where a user has positioned the contact info window. The end result of this is shown in Figure 15.6.

Figure 15.6
The "Add Note" window is positioned in front of the portal on the Contact Info layout, regardless of where that window has been positioned on the screen.

The trick to having the pop-up window follow the anchor window around the screen is referencing the position of the anchor window in the coordinates for the pop-up window. You still have to know the relative placement of the two windows. However, there's a systematic approach to this that can make the whole process quite simple.

Begin by creating a layout that contains the desired interface for the pop-up window. Use a rectangle (of any color) as the background for this layout. It's important that you use an actual rectangle rather than just change the color of the layout part, because the size of this rectangle determines the size of the pop-up window. Position the rectangle so that it's snug against the top and left borders of your layout. In the example shown in Figure 15.6, the background rectangle on the Add Note layout measures 457 pixels wide by 139 pixels high.

Your layout should contain only a body part, and you should slide the body up right to your background rectangle.

After the pop-up layout has been created, copy the background rectangle to your clipboard, switch over to the anchor layout (here, the Contact Info layout), and paste the rectangle onto this layout. Position it exactly where you want the pop-up window to be placed. Turn on the Object Size dialog (View, Object Size), and make a note of the top and left coordinates of the rectangle. In the example seen previously in Figure 15.6, these positions were 305 and 46, respectively. You can then delete the rectangle from your layout.

→ For more on using the Object Size palette, **see** "Positioning Objects on a Layout," **p. 106**.

CAUTION

> The values for the top and left pixel of an object returned by the Object Size are relative to the page margins that have been defined for your layout. The margin settings can be set explicitly on the Printing tab of the Layout Setup dialog. If you want to know the absolute position of an object, set the top and left margins to both be 0. Or subtract the top and left margin settings from the values you noted in the Object Size dialog. Your goal is to know the position of the rectangle relative to the current window, so the margins, which aren't even visible in Browse mode, must be factored out.

In the script that generates the new window, you need to use the positions you've noted for the rectangle and the position of the current window to determine the location of the new window. Remember that you need to consider the size of the new window's frame as well, and that the frame size differs on Mac and Windows. The rectangle you placed on the anchor layout determines the size of the window's content area. The size of the window itself must be derived from this.

Taking all these factors together, the parameters that you need for your new window are as follows:

Height: `139 + Case ( Get (SystemPlatform)) = -1 ; 37; 54)`

Width: `457 + Case ( Get (SystemPlatform)) = -1 ; 15; 27)`

Top: `305 + Get (WindowTop)`

Left: `46 + Get (WindowLeft)`

You'll notice that the constants at the beginning of each of these formulas come from the size and position of the pop-up window that were noted earlier. The other constants in these formulas (the ones that were determined by checking whether the user is on a Mac or a Windows PC) are needed to translate from content size to window size. Recall from the previous section that the size of the window's frame is different on each platform. The preceding calculations also make an assumption that the status area will be hidden in both the anchor window and the pop-up window. If that's not the case, you can easily adjust by adding and/or subtracting 69 (the width of the status area) to the width and distance from left values as necessary.

15

The remainder of the scripts used for the Add Note routine closely resemble those discussed in the "Rich Dialog Windows" section of Chapter 13.

The Add Note script itself is as follows:

```
Allow User Abort [Off]
If [PatternCount (WindowNames ; "Add Note")]
    Close Window [Name: "Add Note"]
End If
Set Field [Contact::gNote; ""]
New Window [Name: "Add Note"; <other paramaters as given above>]
Go to Layout ["Add Note" (Contact)]
Show/Hide Status Area [Lock; Hide]
Adjust Window [Resize to Fit]
Pause/Resume Script [Indefinitely]
```

On the Add Note layout itself, both the Cancel and Submit buttons are specified to Resume the current script. The Cancel script simply closes the current window. The Submit button, which is defined to pass the current record's ContactID as a script parameter, runs the following script:

```
If [not IsEmpty (Get (ScriptParameter))]
    If [not IsEmpty (Contact::gNote)]
        Go to Layout ["ContactNotes" (ContactNotes)]
        New Record/Request
        Set Field [ContactNotes::ContactID; Get (ScriptParameter)]
        Set Field [ContactNotes::Note; Contact::gNote]
    End If
    Close Window [Current Window]
Else
    Show Custom Dialog ["Warning"; "Invalid script parameter."]
End If
```

There are many ways you could script the actual addition of the note record. This example navigates to a layout based on the ContactNote table. Because the user entered the new note into a global field, after the new record is created, the ContactNotes::Note field can be directly set to the value of the gNote field. However, the ContactNotes::ContactID field, which is a foreign key relating back to the Contact table, needs to be set to the ContactID of whatever the active record was at the beginning of the routine. It could simply be placed in a field with global storage, but instead, we've elected to have the Submit button pass the ContactID as a script parameter to the Submit Note script.

 If you have issues with found sets not being retained when you create new windows, see "Creating New Windows Loses My Found Sets" in the Troubleshooting section at the end of this chapter.

Go to Related Record

`Go to Related Record` is one of the most useful and important script steps. In this discussion of scripting, we've focused for the most part on categories of tasks that you can perform with scripts rather than on specific steps, but `Go to Related Record`, which we'll refer to as GTRR, merits a discussion entirely its own.

The Go to Related Record Options dialog is shown in Figure 15.7. Essentially, GTRR lets you navigate to one or more records that are related to whatever record you're currently viewing. As we discuss in this section, there are several options for how and where that related set will be displayed. It may take a while for all the nuances of GTRR to sink in, but mastery of this script step is crucial for becoming an experienced script writer.

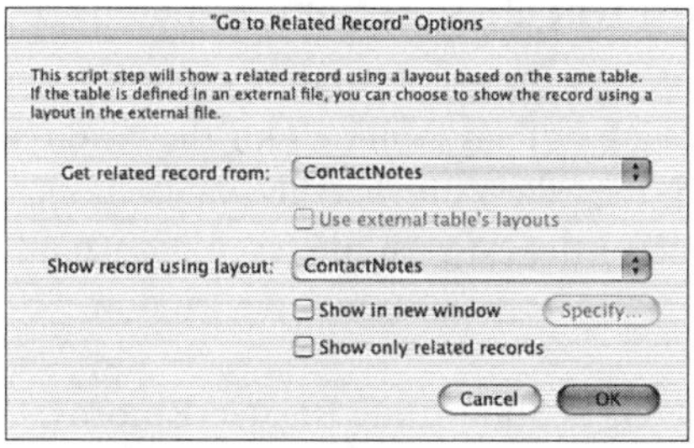

Figure 15.7
Go to Related Record is one of the most useful script steps. It's also one of the most complex.

GTRR Basics

It might be helpful to think of GTRR as a way to move or jump from one point on the Relationships Graph to another point. But *from* where, and *to* where? In the GTRR options dialog (shown previously in Figure 15.7), the first thing you specify is the destination table occurrence for this move. The starting point for the move is determined by the script's *context*. We'll use the terms *origin* and *destination* to refer to these table occurrences.

Whenever a script executes, it does so in a context determined by the active window, the active layout, the active found set, and the active record. These things can, of course, all be changed during the course of a script through the use of a wide variety of script steps. The origin for a GTRR script step is determined by whatever layout is active at the point in the script that the GTRR occurs. The active layout situates you at a particular point on the Relationships Graph. So, managing the origin of the jump is done not in the GTRR step itself, but rather through navigation (if necessary) to the appropriate layout beforehand.

As the destination for the GTRR, you can select any table occurrence on the graph, including table occurrences tied to external tables, table occurrences that aren't related to origin, and even the origin itself. This last option produces a special result that's discussed in the "Jumping to Disconnected Table Occurrences" section a little further on in this chapter.

The other pop-up list within the GTRR dialog is for specifying a layout to use for displaying whatever set of records is returned by the GTRR. Unlike the choice of a destination table occurrence, you are restricted in your choice to selecting among layouts that are tied

15

to the same table (*not* table occurrence) as the destination table occurrence. That's a convoluted way of saying that you're expected to specify an appropriate layout to display the related set of records. We'll therefore refer to this layout as the *display layout*. If (and only if) the destination table occurrence is from an external file, you'll have the option to select the Use External Table's Layouts check box. The choices for the display layout consist of those layouts in the external file that are tied to the same table as the destination table occurrence.

Another option in the GTRR dialog enables you to specify that the related set of records appear in a new window. If you select this option, you have access to the same setup parameters that you do when using the New Window script step (window name, location, size). If you don't check the Show in New Window option, one of two things happens when the GTRR is executed:

- If the display layout is in the current file, then that becomes the active layout.
- If the display layout is in a different file, then another window must be activated (windows are file specific). If there are not any windows for the required file currently open, then a new window is created (regardless of whether you've checked this option or not). If there are windows belonging to the external file (even hidden ones), then the frontmost of those in the stacking order becomes the active window.

The final option on the GTRR dialog is Show Only Related Records. You choice here partially determines what found set the display layout contains. It's easier to discuss the possible implications of selecting this option in the course of a specific example, which we do in the example that follows. For now, know that in the majority of cases, you'll want to enable this option.

GTRR—A SIMPLE EXAMPLE

As an example of GTRR in action, consider the scenario of a database that contains information about teachers and classes. Figure 15.8 shows the Relationships Graph from such a file; there is a one-to-many relationship from the Teacher table occurrence to the Class table occurrence. The relationship is defined to sort by ClassName. There are two layouts in the file—Teacher Detail and Class Detail—each tied to the obvious table occurrence.

Figure 15.8
The two table occurrences in this Relationships Graph are connected on the TeacherID field.

Say that you want to use a `Go to Related Record` script step to "find" all the classes taught by a particular teacher. To do this, begin by navigating to the record of the teacher you're interested in. Place a button on the layout that performs a `Go to Related Record` step. Because the button is on the Teacher Detail layout, the Teacher table occurrence is the context in which the GTRR will be performed; it acts as the origin for the coming jump. In the GTRR dialog, specify the Class table occurrence as the destination for the jump. Finally, specify Class Detail as the display layout.

The found set and the sort order that will actually be displayed on the Class Detail layout depend on three things: what other options have been specified for the GTRR, the existing found set on the Class Detail, and the relationship settings that link the origin and destination table occurrences. The possible outcomes are as follows:

- If you check the option to Show Only Related Records, then the found set consists of just those classes that are related to the current teacher record. Those records are sorted according the to the sort setting in the relationship, and the first record in the set is the active record.

- If the option to Show Only Related Records and Show in New Window are both unchecked, the found set on the Class Detail layout depends on whether the first related record was already part of the found set there. If it was, then that record becomes the active record and the found set remains unchanged. If not, then all records in the table are displayed, with the first related record as the active record. The sort order of the display layout (here, Class Detail) is not altered in either case. Be aware that it's only the presence of the first related record that matters. In fact, it's possible that other related records may not even be part of the found set following the GTRR step.

- If the Show Only Related Records option is not checked, but Show in New Window is checked, then all the records in the Class table will be in the found set, regardless of what found set existed there previously. The first related record is the active record.

- If there are in fact no related class records for the given teacher, then the found set and sort order on the Class Detail remain unchanged. Further, the display layout does not even become the active layout. Be on guard for this, because if your scripts assume either that you have a particular found set or that you're on a particular layout following a GTRR, you might have problems. To trap for this situation, you can test for the existence of related records prior to the GTRR by using the `Count` function to determine the number of related records. Alternatively, you can check to see whether the GTRR step generates an error. Error 101, "Record is missing," is returned if there are no related records. Finally, if you had checked the option to "Show in New Window" and there are no related records, be aware that a new window is not created.

PREDICTING THE FOUND SET

The preceding section contained an example of using GTRR to navigate to a set of classes that are related to a particular teacher. Because only one "hop" was involved in this GTRR,

15

it was very easy to conceptualize what found set would be generated by the GTRR step. A GTRR, however, is not limited to short jumps such as this. In fact, the origin and destination table occurrences can be distantly connected on the Relationships Graph. When this is the case, it can sometimes be difficult to predict exactly what set of records will be returned. A few simple rules and examples should clarify this for you.

First of all, the origin and destination table occurrences must be connected on the Graph for the GTRR to function. If they aren't, the user sees an error stating that "This operation could not be completed because the target is not part of a related table." The actual error generated is error 103, "Relationship is missing."

Assuming that there is some unique path from the origin to the destination, you really need to know just three rules to determine what found set will appear if you do a Go to Related Record script step.

- Every relationship along the path is evaluated.
- The found sets are cumulative.
- The sort setting of the final hop determines the sort order.

To discuss more concretely how these rules can be applied, it is helpful to consider some examples. Figure 15.9 contains a Relationships Graph with five table occurrences. The Teacher and Advisor occurrences are both linked to the Teacher base table. The other table occurrences—Student, Enrollment, and Class—are linked to base tables of the same names. In all the examples that follow, assume that the Show Only Related Records option is checked for all the GTRR steps. Starting from any of the table occurrences on the Relationship Graph shown in Figure 15.9, can you predict with what found set you would end up if you performed a Go to Related Record, targeting each of the other table occurrences?

Figure 15.9
From any table occurrence on this graph, you can jump to any other location on the graph using a Go to Related Records script step.

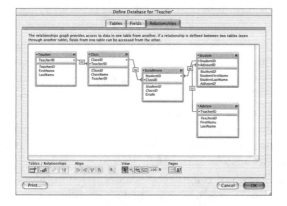

Imagine that you were on the Teacher Detail layout. In the previous section, you saw how a GTRR directed at the Class table occurrence would find all of that teacher's classes. How about if you did a GTRR directed at the Enrollment table occurrence from the Teacher Detail layout? There's a one-to-many relationship from Teacher to Class, and another one-to-many relationship from Class to Enrollment. The GTRR would need to traverse two "hops," first to the set of classes taught by the teacher, and then to the enrollment records for those classes. The first hop might result in a set of, say, three classes. The second hop is the cumulative result of going to the related enrollments for each of the three classes. The end result would be a set of all the enrollment records for all the classes taught by that teacher.

What if you went one hop further, over to the Student table occurrence? The first two hops (Teacher to Class, Class to Enrollment) would again yield all the enrollment records for that teacher. The third hop, from Enrollment to Student, would yield the set of students that those Enrollment records represent. It's as if a GTRR were performed on each record of the found set of enrollments. The set of student records would represent all students enrolled in any of that teacher's classes.

Finally, what about a GTRR from the Teacher Detail layout all the way over to the Advisor table occurrence? Following the reasoning from the other examples, that would result in the set of teachers who are advisors for the students enrolled in any of that teacher's classes.

If any of the individual hops in a multi-hop GTRR yield a null set, then the entire GTRR behaves the same as a single-hop GTRR that yields a null set. See the preceding section for a discussion of this possibility.

As stated in the third "rule" earlier, the sort order of the found set in a multi-hop GTRR is determined by the last hop. In this example, say that there was a sort defined for the relationship from Class to Enrollment. Even though a GTRR from Teacher to Enrollment would yield a sorted result, a GTRR from Teacher to Student would not, unless the relationship from Enrollment to Student was also sorted.

There's one final point to make about predicting the found set of a multi-hop GTRR. If you're ever in doubt about what records would appear or in what order, simply create a portal that displays records from the destination table occurrence. The same set of records that shows up in the portal would end up as the found set after a GTRR. Assuming that the portal itself wasn't sorted, the order of the records would even be the same.

JUMPING TO DISCONNECTED TABLE OCCURRENCES

There's one final behavior of the `Go to Related Record` step that's worth noting: It can be used to move a found set from one table occurrence of a base table to another. This even works for disconnected table occurrences. In a given window, all the layouts associated with a given table occurrence share the same found set and sort order. This is a good thing because it means that moving back and forth between, say, a list view and a form view based on the same table occurrence doesn't require any found set manipulation.

However, if two layouts are attached to different table occurrences, their found sets and sort orders are independent of each other, even if they're both occurrences of the same base table. Say you have two occurrences of a Teacher base table called Teacher 1 and Teacher 2 on your Relationships Graph (either related or unrelated to each other). Imagine that you're on a layout associated with Teacher 1 and that you've done a find for some subset of Teacher records.

Now what do you suppose would happen if from that layout you were to do a GTRR that specified Teacher 1 as the destination and a layout linked to Teacher 2 as the display layout? The origin and destination are the same table occurrence here, so the answer might not be completely intuitive. The effect of such a GTRR, assuming you had checked the Show Only Related Records option, would be that the current found set and sort order would be *transferred* to the Teacher 2 layout.

So, by using the same table occurrence for both the origin and destination of a GTRR, you can move the current found set to another layout and/or window. There's something about this behavior that defies intuition, but it's very handy nonetheless.

Troubleshooting

Pop-up Window Issues on a Windows PC

Pop-up windows don't appear in front of the current window when the current window is maximized.

On the Windows platform, when a window is maximized to fill the application window, no other windows can also be visible on the screen. That is, only a single window can be maximized, and it must be the foreground window. This means that if you try to pop up a window in front of a maximized window, the "background" window cannot remain maximized. It instead reverts to its reduced state.

If you plan on building a user interface that makes use of multiple windows, be aware of this potential pitfall. It would be better in such cases to never have any windows maximized, even though this means you have to work within a reduced space. Users may still manually maximize a window, so test your routines thoroughly to see what effect this would have. You'll likely need to add some control routines to your navigation scripts like `Adjust Window [Resize to Fit]` to get the windows back to the size you intend them to be viewed.

Creating New Windows Loses My Found Sets

Whenever I create a new window, all the found sets of the non-visible layouts are reset to show all records. What causes this behavior?

When a new window is created, either manually via the Window, New Window menu command or via script, it inherits many characteristics of the currently active window. Specifically, it keeps the same size (except when opened via script and specified otherwise), the same active layout, found set, sort order, and active record. To all appearances, it's as if it's an exact duplicate of the currently active window.

In fact, only the settings of the active layout are retained when a new window is created. All layouts that are not visible (except those tied to the same table occurrence as the active layout) lose any sense of the found set, active record, and sort order. All records are displayed, unsorted, and the first record in the table is the active record.

FILEMAKER EXTRA: RECURSIVE SCRIPTS

Chapter 14, "Specialized Calculation Functions," discusses how you could make custom functions recursive by including calls to themselves within their formulas. In a similar manner, you can use script parameters to create recursive scripts. Although this isn't something you need to do on a daily basis, there are some interesting applications for recursive scripts.

A recursive script is one that calls itself repeatedly until some exit condition is satisfied. Each time the script calls itself as a subscript, it passes a script parameter that can be used as part of an exit condition test. In many ways, recursive scripts are quite similar to looping scripts, and many of the tasks you can accomplish with one can be done as easily by the other.

As an example of a recursive script, consider the Recursive Add script below:

```
If [Get (ScriptParameter) >= 100]
    Exit Script
End If
New Record/Request
Perform Script ["Recursive Add"; Parameter: Get (ScriptParameter) + 1 ]
```

This script adds 100 new records to the current table. It's first called without a script parameter, so the first time through, the script calls itself as a subscript, passing a parameter of 1. The parameter increments each subsequent time through, until eventually the exit criteria (Get (ScriptParameter) >= 100) is met.

If there are any steps in the script after the recursive subscript call, then these are all executed, from the inside, out, after the exit criteria has been met. Try to predict what would happen if you added the following two steps to the end of the preceding script:

```
Beep
Show Custom Dialog ["The parameter is:" ; Get (ScriptParameter)]
```

The 100 records would be created exactly as they were originally. But after they were all created, you'd hear a beep and see a message telling you that the script parameter value is 99. After clicking OK, you'd then hear another beep and a message telling you that the parameter is 98. This would continue for some time, and eventually the last message you'd see is that the parameter is empty, which, of course, was the condition on the very first trip through the script.

Although it's certainly possible to create 100 new records with a looping script, that would typically require the use of a global number field to act as a counter. The recursive script requires no such additional field, and indeed this is the main advantage that recursive scripts have over looping scripts.

As a final example of recursive scripting, consider the following script, which flags duplicates among a set of records. Assume that the set contains a list of names, which has been sorted by name before this script is called:

```
If [IsEmpty (Get (ScriptParameter))]
    Go to Record/Request/Page [First]
Else
    Go to Record/Request/Page [Next; Exit after last]
```

```
        If [Get (ScriptParameter) = Contacts::Name]
            Set Field [Contacts::DuplicateFlag; "Duplicate"]
        End If
    End If
Perform Script ["Mark duplicates"; Parameter: Contacts::Name]
```

During each iteration through the script, the current record's name is compared against the value of the script parameter, which was set to the value of the previous record's name. The exit condition here is the Exit after last option on the fourth line; the script continues through the set of records, stopping only when there's no "next" record to go to.

## CHAPTER 16

WORKING WITH PORTALS

PORTALS IN FILEMAKER PRO

Portals are important tools in the FileMaker Pro toolbox. In their most basic form they display data that pertains to the essential relationships in a given system. For example, a record for a neighborhood might show all the related house records in a portal, or a record for a class might show a portal of all the students enrolled in that class. Portals in cases like this reflect the primary relationships in a database. This is especially true if you make use of portal functionality allowing for the creation of related records; they serve as the mechanism by which related records are created.

In other cases, portals serve a wide variety of user interface needs. They can be used to present a "pick list" for selecting records for various functions. They can be used to display ad hoc reports. They can even be used to present navigation or function options to users, display images, or offer alternate list views combined with form views of data.

This chapter begins by covering some basic portal details, but after we've moved through that, we get to some more meaty advanced techniques. We recommend this chapter for everyone, including beginners and advanced developers: Working with portals is a fundamental part of becoming adept with FileMaker, for whatever purpose.

PORTAL BASICS

As previously mentioned, a portal is essentially a view into a related table. In each row of your portal, you will see fields from records as they relate to the current record to which the portal is tied.

Another way to think of portals is that they offer a view into another table from a specific perspective. The match criteria you've established determine the perspective and, depending on how you've set things up, it is possible to change that perspective to useful ends.

FileMaker Pro 7 introduced new relationship operators, beyond the single equijoin ("="), and portals have become even more flexible than in the past. However, a portal's basic function of displaying one record per row from a related table remains essentially the same. A Cartesian cross-product operator (x), for instance, relates all the records in one table to all the records in another table, regardless of key values. A portal based on such a relationship would therefore display all the records of the related table. Similarly, a < operator compares the match fields on either side of your relationship and the rows in your portal will be displayed accordingly. As a final example, a ≠ operator enables you to exclude certain records from your portal.

→ To learn more about relationships and working with portals, **see** "Using a Portal to Add Related Records," **p. 164**.

One of the most important details to keep in mind is that the match field in the table from which you want to view records must be indexed (with a value index) for the relationship to properly resolve and display records in a portal. It is not the fields themselves that are matched to form a relationship; it is the comparison of the field's indexed values on one side of the relationship to those of the other.

→ To understand indexing, **see** "Storage and Indexing," **p. 82**.

Keep in mind that you can index calculations, as long as they do not reference related or un-indexed fields themselves. It is entirely possible to relate to a calculation field in another table, rather than always relying on data input by users. You cannot create records through that relationship, however. Just as users cannot modify a calculation field, neither can FileMaker Pro itself. As you may recall, portals can be set to allow for the creation of related records. A user can click on the first empty row in a portal and enter data directly. FileMaker Pro then does the equivalent of a Set Field step and rightly places the match field value—key—in the analogous field on the other side of the relationship.

Indexing is not required for the match field in your current table. You can use global fields or un-stored calculation values to create the bridge between two tables. We get into those techniques later in the chapter.

16

PORTALS VERSUS LIST VIEW/TABLE VIEW

Knowing when to use portals is often a matter of personal preference, user interface requirements, and data architecture. Quite often developers go through phases of infatuation with using various ways to display multiple records in a single view. The three tools for doing this are List views, Table views, and portals. Each has its own pros and cons, and we'd argue that all three are used for very different purposes.

We encourage laziness (it breeds a need for efficiency), so we tend to favor Table view a lot. You get a good bit of functionality for free, such as column sorting, column headers, the ability to resize and reorder columns. The main downside to Table view is that you cannot add buttons or other visual objects to your rows. You also cannot rename or modify the appearance of column headers. Table view therefore is generally used for layouts that are accessible only to developers. They're usually not suitable for end users.

For cases where control over user interface is of paramount importance, List view and portals come into play. The key difference between the two, from a user's perspective, is that a List view can dynamically represent whatever found set your table currently has and portals always display a set of related records.

List view displays records in their creation order unless a user or script explicitly sorts the records. Unless you've controlled and turned off menu access, users can omit records, show all records, and otherwise manipulate the found set in an ad hoc manner to suit their needs. List views display the number of rows that will fit on a screen, expanding as much as a user has monitor space. When printing a List view of records, all the records can be printed; page breaks are placed between records as necessary.

Portals are differently focused: They are always driven by a specific relationship and always display a fixed number of rows—only the content changes. They are always sorted (at a minimum in the order in which their related records were created, unless otherwise specified), so if you have a particularly large set of related data, your screen redraw speed may become an issue with hundreds of thousands of records. The obvious advantage of portals is that you can combine them on the same layout with data from other tables—both with fields from a related record and with other portals.

NEW PORTAL SETUP

To add a portal to a layout, use the Portal tool from the Status Area in Layout mode, and draw a rectangle that approximates how large you want your portal to be. You are then presented with the Portal Setup dialog, from which, at least, you need to choose a table occurrence on which to base the portal (see Figure 16.1).

Figure 16.1
These options enable you to govern how a specific portal behaves.

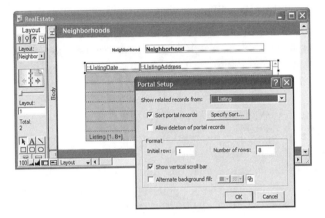

NOTE

Setting new portal options in the Portal Setup dialog does not affect other portals in your solution, regardless of whether or not others are tied to the same table occurrence.

TIP

When choosing from the list of table occurrences, note that it is not possible to create a portal showing records from an unrelated table. By definition portals show related records. If you need to display records in an unrelated manner, create a Cartesian cross-product relationship to the table occurrence in question, but this is still a relationship. It will display all the records from that table.

As a helpful reminder, in Layout mode, the name of the table occurrence to which the portal is tied is displayed in the lower left, along with its row format options. We cover those options shortly.

SPECIFYING PORTAL SORTING

You can specify the order in which the related records are displayed by specifying sort criteria in the Portal Setup dialog (see Figure 16.2). It's thus possible to create two portals side by side, based on the same table occurrence, that offer two different sort views from the same related tables.

Figure 16.2
It is possible to establish different sort options for each portal in your database.

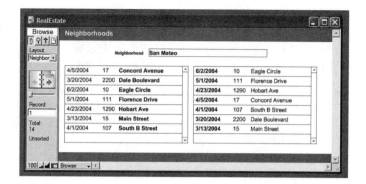

Note that the sort order is hard-coded to the portal. For users to change the sort order, they'd have to enter Layout mode and modify the Portal Setup dialog options. A technique for dynamic, user-based portal sorting is covered later in the chapter.

Note that the relationship from the current table occurrence to the destination table occurrence may have a sort defined, but a portal sort overrides the relationship sort. If the table occurrence is multiple hops away on the Relationships Graph, the last relationship is the one that determines the sort order.

ALLOWING PORTAL ROW DELETION

By enabling the Allow Deletion of Portal Records option, you enable users to select a portal row and delete a record by pressing the Delete or Backspace key. They are then prompted by FileMaker as to whether or not they want to delete the one related record in question.

Generally you will opt to overlay buttons attached to scripts in portal rows to delete related records so you can more fully control the behavior of portals. This enables you to perform your own functions prior to deleting a record, or at a minimum control the color of a selected portal row; it's not possible to alter FileMaker's default selection mask color. (It varies depending on background color and OS.)

The disadvantage of placing buttons that completely fill a portal row is that users may no longer get the visual feedback they need to see that a portal row has been selected. Using the Delete or Backspace key can still work, but the user experience isn't as clear. In the same vein as never attaching anything but scripts to buttons for the purposes of control and maintainability, we almost never use the ability to delete records in portals with FileMaker's default behavior. We opt instead to explicitly place buttons, attached to scripts, to do so.

Nonetheless, it's a handy feature to enable if you're working with a database that uses FileMaker's native user interface behaviors.

SETUP OPTIONS

FileMaker's Portal Setup options enable you to specify a starting row, how many rows (tall) a portal should be, whether to offer a vertical scroll bar, and whether to alternate row colors between that which you set for the portal itself and an alternate color.

The row choices are noteworthy. If you turn off your scroll bar, you can opt to display rows 1–8 in one portal instance and rows 9–16 in another. Keep in mind that the end point is artificial; a child table can hold potentially millions of child records. With scroll bars turned on, a portal simply allows you to scroll from the initial row downward.

> To know what pitfalls to look for in using initial rows beyond the first with portals, refer to "Portal Rows Not Displaying" in the Troubleshooting section at the end of this chapter.

RELATIONSHIP PROPERTIES

Relationship properties have a direct bearing on a portal's behavior. They were covered in some detail in Chapter 6, "Working with Multiple Tables"; however, we'd like to draw your attention to some particular aspects of the Edit Relationships dialog, shown in Figure 16.3 and in the sections that follow.

Figure 16.3
Portal behavior is affected by the options you choose in the lower portion of the dialog.

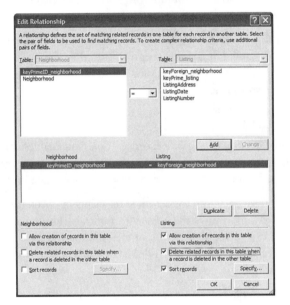

CREATING RELATED RECORDS

Notice in Figure 16.3 that one of the options you can specify for a relationship is Allow Creation of Records in This Table via This Relationship. When you check this option, a portal that's based on the relationship will contain a blank row beneath the related records, which is readily available for data entry. When a user commits data in that blank related record, FileMaker pushes the value from the current record's match key into the related match field automatically.

This behavior is possible only with equijoin (=) relationships in which FileMaker can determine exactly the foreign value to populate in the newly created record. You also need to be able to modify the field in question. If the relationship is tied to a calculation field, FileMaker Pro cannot automatically populate it with a value from a related record (see Figure 16.4).

Figure 16.4
Note that the match field, shown here in the first column, is populated automatically.

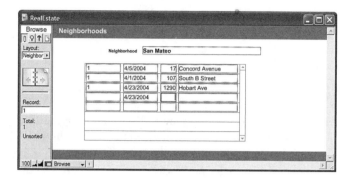

→ For more depth on relationships and relationship properties, **see** Chapter 6, "Working with Multiple Tables," **p. 153**.

CASCADING DELETION OF RELATED RECORDS

The next option is "Delete Related Records in This Table when a Record Is Deleted in the Other Table." Choosing this option ensures that when a user deletes a record in one related table, all its related records are deleted as well. This cascading effect ensures that your database doesn't orphan records by allowing a user to delete records without their respective related records. A good example might be a contact person's record and related phone number records. It is unlikely that you'd want to retain just the phone number records after deleting the contact record to which related phone records belong.

The downside, of course, is that users may not realize that along with deleting the current record they are also going to delete all the records they see displayed in a portal, or, worse yet, that they will be deleting records they may not see on screen currently.

RELATIONSHIP-BASED SORTING

The Sort Records option at the bottom of the Edit Relationship dialog enables you to define a sort order for that relationship. If set, it drives the order in which rows are displayed in portals based on this relationship. Portals themselves have their own sorting options and their options override whatever sort properties you set here; however, it's useful enough to consider this a default sort, if you wish.

STICKY PORTALS

FileMaker Pro 7 introduced a feature whereby portals can maintain their scroll position even after a record has been committed or exited. In the past, FileMaker would "pop" back to the top of a portal, regardless of how far down in a given record set a user might have scrolled. If you'd like to make use of the feature, turn off the Show Field Frames when Record Is Active option in the Layout Setup dialog (found under the Layouts menu.)

The state of your portal is honored until you refresh the screen by changing modes, close the window in question, quit FileMaker Pro, perform a sort or script, or change records. All these actions result in a screen refresh. If you change from one record to another and return

16

to the original, its portal position reverts to the top as well. Portals maintain their position when users actively edit fields in portal rows.

SCRIPTED NEW PORTAL RECORDS

It's quite common for developers to choose to disallow the creation of related records in portals. You might want to circumvent the need for users to scroll to the bottom of a portal to create new related records. You may want to have your portal serve as display only, or you may simply have too many rows and don't want to force users through a bunch of unnecessary scrolling. Doing so means having to modify the relationship itself. You cannot simply turn on and off this behavior on a case-by-case basis at the portal level.

After the option to Allow the Creation of Related Records is turned off, you've then got the task of figuring out how—other than driving users to the related table in question—to create new related records.

One approach to manage the creation of new records is to use a Set Field script step in combination with passing the necessary key match value via script parameter:

```
Go to Layout [ "Contact" (Contact) ]
New Record/Request
Set Field [ Contact::keyForeignID_company; Get (ScriptParameter)
    // keyPrimeID_company ]
Commit Records/Requests [ No dialog ]
Go to Layout [ original layout ]
```

"NEW RECORD ONLY" RELATIONSHIPS

You might not want to have to write scripts to create new related records for display in your portals. Scrolling to find them can still be an issue in some cases, and a script still requires a user action to be executed or performed.

An alternative is what we're calling "new record only" relationships. To establish them, you need to rely on the auto-entry options in FileMaker Pro, the triggering behavior of the Evaluate() function, and the order in which FileMaker Pro performs certain tasks.

The technique described here enables you to use related fields through a relationship that allows creation of new records, just as if you were planning to allow users to scroll to the end of a portal, but that don't require you to scroll to the bottom of a portal to do so. The related fields you'll use provide a data entry area outside the portal that is always available to create new related records. When users type data into the fields, a new record is instantly created, but then on committing those new edits, the relationship is immediately invalidated so that these new record fields remain blank and ready for more data input.

This then obviates the need for scripting, and opens up some possibilities for user interface and working with portals.

Consider the Relationships Graph shown in Figure 16.5, where a neighborhood is related to many houses. The second of the two relationships is set to allow for the creation of related records. Note that we have created two foreign IDs in the related table occurrences and that the two relationships are different.

Figure 16.5
This Relationships Graph represents two equijoin relationships. The temp relationship is set to allow creation of related records.

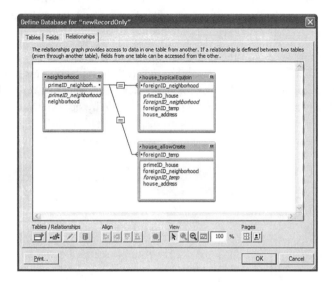

The rest of this technique relies on field definitions. The basic approach is that you allow the foreignID_temp to be populated via the Allow Creation of Related Records function, but then immediately set the field to zero when the record is committed.

This requires that two tasks happen: that the foreignID_neighborhood gets set, and that, only after this field is set, foreignID_temp is cleared.

To accomplish the first task, set foreignID_neighborhood to foreignID_temp, using an auto-entry calculation. At an instant before the temp field is cleared it will contain a proper value for this house record's neighborhood ID.

The second task, clearing the temp field, is accomplished if you set the auto-entry options for foreignID_temp, turning off the Do Not Replace Existing Value for Field (If Any), with a formula of:

```
Evaluate (
    If ( IsEmpty (foreignID_neighborhood); foreignID_temp; 0);
    foreignID_neighborhood
)
```

Notice that the foreignID_neighborhood is defined as a trigger for the Evaluate function. When foreignID_neighborhood is populated, by its own auto-entry pointing to foreignID_temp, that event then triggers foreignID_temp's auto entry—which then sets itself to zero. The technique assumes you have no records in your neighborhood table with a primeID_neighborhood of zero. Because the second relationship based on the foreignID_temp is invalidated after this process is complete, you can place data entry fields on a layout, tied to your second temp relationship, that are then cleared after a new record is committed.

"HORIZONTAL" PORTALS

Working with user interfaces and creating new records together form a large part of working with portals. Another issue developers often face is the desire to have a portal scroll from left to right rather than vertically.

Horizontal portals are one of the grails for which FileMaker developers seek. Although FileMaker Pro 7 doesn't offer the capability to scroll through columns, rather than rows, of related records (or simply scroll horizontally to view more data in a related record row), you can easily display a fixed number of related records side by side without any fuss. Use the format options in the Portal Setup dialog to display related records to control different starting rows for multiple, side-by-side portals. An example is shown in Figure 16.6.

Figure 16.6
Notice that the right-most portal has a scroll bar. That ensures that however many related records this record has, they will all be accessible to your users.

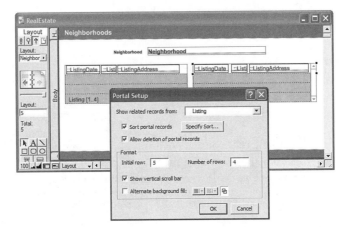

SELECTION PORTALS

We've covered the basics of portals thus far, and discussed the idea that portals are used to display records from a related table and that the records themselves, well, "relate" in a meaningful way. In other words, the related records shown in a portal correspond to the active record—Parents to their own children, Class to its attending students, Company to its own employees, Neighborhoods to houses and so on.

These relationships are often thought of as "primary." They're the relationships that you depend on to define and determine a database's core architecture. Your users, likewise, will intuitively understand the process of entering data for, say, a class and then fleshing out its roster of students. There's a direct correlation between a primary data structure and the information that users expect to view, enter, and report on.

→ For more in-depth discussion of data modeling, **see** Chapter 5, "Relational Database Design," **p. 123**.

We will now venture beyond that one function and explore other uses of portals. The other, advanced uses of portals mainly revolve around user interface choices where you might opt for a more sophisticated approach in making selections.

BASIC SELECTION PORTALS

The first advanced portal use that we discuss is what we refer to as a "selection portal." Selection portals are used to present choices to the user in lieu of a value list or menu of some kind (see Figure 16.7).

Figure 16.7
Notice that when using a value list you have to expose your internal IDs to users, and that the mechanism here can display information from only one other field.

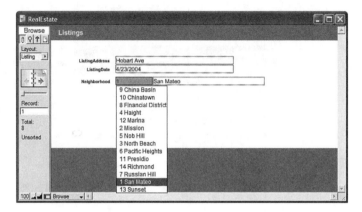

Selection portals offer an alternative to the standard approach of using value lists to choose foreign key values.

The only way two records in an equijoin become related is if they share a like value in match key fields. If you want, for example, to relate a real estate agent to a listing record, you can either manually enter the key for an agent into an AgentID field for the listing record, or you can assist data entry by providing a pop-up list or menu of options.

→ For a refresher in related value lists, **see** Chapter 3, "Defining and Working with Fields," **p. 63**.

Value lists, although a quick and easy means of giving users access to choose related records, can be limited: If you have hundreds of possible values, they can become cumbersome to scroll through. You're also able to display the contents of only two fields, the first of which needs to be the values for your match field. Some developers and designers sensitive to user interface issues feel that these key values expose too much of a database's inner workings to users who may be turned off by having to see and choose from what often are alphanumeric codes meaningful only to the database itself. Figure 16.8 offers an alternative where users never see the primary keys of a database.

Selection portals address these issues, although admittedly requiring more work to build. When a user wants to associate a record, as shown in Figure 16.8, he need only click the "Rowena Lane" row in the selection portal. Notice that the example shows the selection portal in a different pop-up window. This is a common way to display a selection portal for only as long as it is necessary. Clicking on a row above can also close the window in question.

Figure 16.8
This portal of options allows users to pick which related record they wish to associate with their current record.

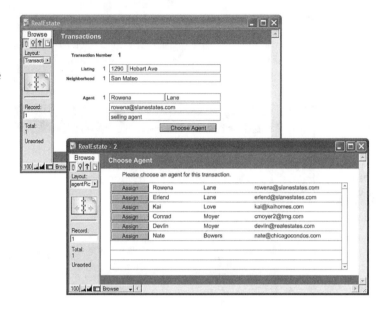

The basic concept for selection portals is fairly straightforward. The goal here is to display all the possible relatable matches for a given record, and then through scripting capture and populate its match key into the appropriate foreign match key on the other side of the relationship. The work involves two elements: creating a portal that displays all the records from the other table, and, second, writing a script that captures and populates the ID after a user has clicked on one of the portal rows available.

First define your data structure. In the example shown in Figure 16.8, agents can work with multiple listings, but a listing might have multiple agents as well: one representing the buyers and another representing the sellers. Notice that this now becomes a many-to-many relationship. At times there might be multiple agents on the buying or selling side as well. For the purposes of this example, use the Relationship Graph shown in Figure 16.9.

> **TIP**
>
> To see this process work, first create an Agent layout and add a portal for all the listings associated with that agent. We recommend displaying your match key fields until you get comfortable with this technique.

Now you need a portal that shows all the listings in the table from which users can choose. For any portal, you always first need a relationship, so create a second table occurrence and second relationship. The example in Figure 16.9 related the primeID_agent to the primeID_listing via a Cartesian cross-product operator (x).

> **NOTE**
>
> Note that it doesn't matter what fields you choose as match fields for a cross-product join. The operator doesn't make any comparison and simply relates all records to all records.

Figure 16.9
We've simplified the fields and relationships in this example to show just the primary data structure and a handful of fields necessary for the example.

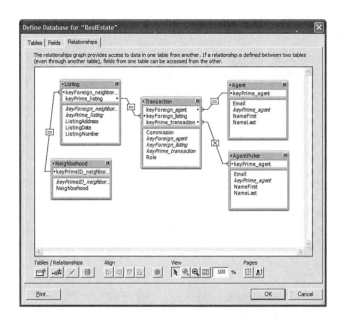

A second portal can now be placed on your existing layout or, in all likelihood, you would have these two portals displayed on a different layout expressly established for this picking process. You can even combine it with a pop-up window, as explained in Chapter 13, "Advanced Layout Techniques."

→ To review how to create a pop-up window, **see** "Rich Dialog Windows," **p. 368**.

After your cross-product selection portal is in place, you need to write a script to associate the related record. The script, which will be tied to a button that's placed in the selection portal, needs to navigate to another layout to create the association. So that information about the current record and the selected portal row can be accessible on that other layout, you need to define the button to pass the agent and listing IDs as a script parameter. Use the following:

```
Select_Listing
    #
    # establish context
    Go to Layout [ "Transaction" (Transaction) ]
    #
    # create the new record
    New Record/Request
    #
    # set the two foreign IDs required.
    # This script assumes that the button that launches the script passes the
    ➥script parameter:
    # Agent::primeID_agent & " " & select_Listing::primeID_listing
    Set Field [ Transaction::foreignID_agent; LeftWords ( Get (ScriptParameter);
    ➥ 1 ) ]
    Set Field [ Transaction::foreignID_listing; RightWords ( Get
    ➥(ScriptParameter); 1 ) ]
    #
    # commit and return to the original layout
    Commit Records/Requests [ No dialog ]
    Go to Layout [ original layout ]
```

→ To review script parameters and how to pass multiple parameters, **see** Chapter 15, "Advanced Scripting," **p. 421**.

This basic technique allows you to create a more complete user experience for your users and to expressly control the creation of related records. The advantages of this over a value list are that you can offer more than two fields of information to users, you can leave obscured the key values in your database, and generally the user interface can come across as more polished (depending, of course, on your artistic abilities).

PORTAL ROW HIGHLIGHTS

You are now exploring ways of working with portals that go beyond simply using them to display data that is related in a real-world sense. You're now establishing relationships that allow for other things. In the example in the preceding section, you related your current record to all records in another table. In this example, we establish a condition by which a single portal row can be highlighted (see Figure 16.10). This is another technique to enhance usability and extend user interface.

Figure 16.10
The highlighting gives solid feedback to users that they are acting on the row in question.

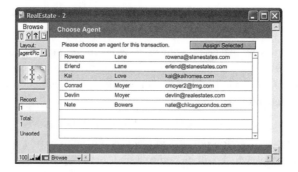

NOTE

> Notice that the Assign Selected button has been moved to the top of the portal, rather than placed on every row of the portal.

This technique involves setting a global field to the value of the primary key of whichever row the user clicks. You need three fields in all for this technique. We generally add them to the related table or a separate utility table, but keep in mind that you can use globals from any context. The following is a list of the fields you'll need for this technique.

- gHighlightColor—A global container field that holds a rectangle of the color you want to use as a highlight. You need only one such field in your database, regardless of how many portals you want to have use this technique.

- gSelectedRowID—A global number field that holds the primary key value of whichever row the user last clicked.

- HightlightRow—A calculation field that returns a container as its result:
  ```
  If ( gSelectedRowID = primeID_relatedTable;
  ➥gHighlightColor; "")
  ```

To set the global field, you need only create a script like so:

```
SelectRow_SetHighlight
    Set Field [ Listing::gSelectedRowID;
    ➥relatedTable::primeID_relatedTable ]
    Commit Records/Requests [ No dialog ]
```

This script presumes that the user has clicked on a portal row: the primeID_relatedTable is passed from that mouse click.

Notice that in cases when gSelectedRowID = the primary key of the related table, the calculation returns the value (in this case a colored rectangle) from gHighlightColor. Because you're using global fields, this solution works perfectly well in a multi-user environment. Whatever a given user has selected as her highlight row remains specific to her session.

The final element of implementing highlighted portal rows is to place the HighlightRow calculation field in the portal itself. Make the field exactly the size of the top row of the portal, and set its graphic format to Crop. (Make sure your colored rectangle is larger than the portal rows you plan on having the highlight.) Attach the field to the SelectRow_SetHighlight script. In Browse mode a button does not need to be the top-most object on the screen to work. Move fields above it and your highlight color fills in nicely in the background. You would generally turn off access to the fields in your portal in Browse mode—so that clicking on the portal row anywhere results in a highlight appearing, rather than a field being entered for data entry.

 If you're having difficulty getting the colored rectangle to display properly, refer to "Incomplete Highlight Rectangle" in the Troubleshooting section at the end of this chapter.

One additional option when storing a selected row ID and creating a highlighted portal row is that it is possible to then also create a relationship specifically for that selected record. By relating gSelectedRowID to primeID_listing, you now have a relationship that will change as a user clicks portal rows.

Consider the implications: You can display related record fields directly on your current layout, based on the selected row (see Figure 16.11).

Figure 16.11
Notice that the information on the right corresponds to the related record selected by the portal on the left.

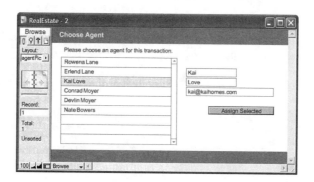

This is a great way to address a portal that is getting too crowded with fields. Instead of making each column smaller, or perhaps stacking fields in rows that might then get difficult to read, simply allow users to select a row in a portal and then display additional information about the selected, related record off to the side.

Avoid Navigation Problems

There's one flaw in the technique we've now described. When users move from record to record, what happens to the row highlight? The gSelectedRowID would still remain associated to a record in the related table, even though a subsequent record may not include it in the selection portal. This could lead to confusion at best or, at worst, data integrity problems.

You need to store the SelectedRowID in a field specific to the record you're viewing to prevent problems when navigating to different records.

This is actually a better user interface implementation, even if you're not displaying related fields based on the user's selected portal row. Maintaining a portal selection on a record-by-record basis may be something you want to apply in some cases.

If you change from a globally stored field to a record-specific field for tracking the currently selected related record, you can run into problems in a multi-user environment. Remember that global fields are session specific, whereas a standard field is not. If two users click different portal rows at the same time, one person's screen is likely to be out of sync with the actual record.

To manage displaying related data in a safe, multi-user conscious way, refer to "Multi-user Selected Data" in the Troubleshooting section at the end of this chapter.

MULTI-KEYS AND MULTI-ROW SELECTIONS

In addition to wanting to highlight a single row, as in the previous example, you may encounter the need to have multiple rows selected at once. In the Agent Listings example, for instance, you may want to allow users to click multiple rows in the listing portal and assign them all at once to the agent in question.

This is a particularly handy way of allowing users to do multiple things at once: add a batch of listings to an agent, select multiple people for form letters, apply new dates to a series of records, and so on. There are dozens of possibilities.

The technique for this is nearly identical to that already presented. However, we rely on FileMaker Pro's capability to resolve multiple match values in a single field. These multiple match value keys are often called *multi-keys*.

Consider a company table related to an agent table, as shown in Table 16.1.

TABLE 16.1 PEOPLE	
ID	**Name**
1	Rowena
2	Erlend
3	Kai

ID	Name
4	Conrad
5	Devlin
6	Nate

If you establish a relationship to this table by using a field—global or otherwise—FileMaker Pro will recognize all return-delimited match key values as though they were individual values.

For example, if your company match field holds the following:

1

3

then your valid, related records will be Rowena and Kai's.

Likewise:

5

2

6

relates to Devlin, Erlend, and Nate. It doesn't matter to FileMaker in which order the values fall, simply that they are valid.

With a multi-key match, it is possible to show multiple rows as highlighted or selected in a given portal. You can use again the same three fields you'd use to set up a single row highlight:

- gHighlightColor—A global container field that holds a rectangle of the color you want to use as a highlight.

- gSelectedRowID—A global text field that holds multiple primary key values, return delimited, of whichever rows the user last clicked. Note that a number field no longer works. You cannot insert line breaks in a number field. Happily, in this case, FileMaker Pro can relate a text field to a number field. Be wary of problems with field types, but in this case there will be no problem.

- HighlightRow—A calculation field that returns a container as its result:

```
If ( FilterValues ( gSelectedMultiRows; primeID_listing );
➥gHighlightColor; "" )
```

If you are modifying the fields from the example given earlier in the chapter, notice that the test in the calculation is now using a FilterValues function that recognizes whether or not an ID is included in your global (as opposed to simply checking whether the two fields are equal).

When setting values in gSelectedRowID, a simple Set Field script step won't do the trick any longer. Doing so would replace the contents of the field and you'd be left with just one row selected. Your script needs to look like this:

```
SelectRow_SetHighlight
#
# if the ID already exists, remove it
If [ FilterValues ( Listing::gSelectedMultiRows; select_Listing::primeID_
    ➥listing ) ]
    Set Field [ Listing::gSelectedMultiRows;
        Let ( [
        selectedRowKey = select_Listing::primeID_listing & "¶"
        ] ;
        Substitute ( Listing::gSelectedMultiRows; selectedRowKey ; "")
    ) ]
#
# if the ID doesn't exist, append it to the end
Else
    Set Field [ Listing::gSelectedMultiRows;
        Let ( [
        selectedRowID = select_Listing::primeID_listing & "¶"
        ] ;
        Listing::gSelectedMultiRows & selectedRowID
    ) ]
End If
#
Commit Records/Requests [ No dialog ]
#
```

FILTERED PORTALS

Allowing users to select rows within portals allows portals to serve multiple functions: They can both display information to the user and also, through selections, act on that data somehow. However, in this chapter thus far we have dealt only with portals that are driven by fixed relationships. The data displayed remains constant and changes only when the data itself changes (when records are added to or deleted from a database.)

A portal filter extends your capabilities to allow you to dynamically alter or constrain the rows of data displayed in a portal.

For example, imagine a case where you have hundreds of customers in a database and a portal displaying all customers. Your portal actively shows only a modest fraction of all customers in your system and forces users to scroll quite a bit. (Most users don't have monitors that can support a portal hundreds of rows tall.) To solve this usability problem, you can turn to either a List view, supported by Find mode to reduce the found set, or to a filtered portal.

Generally, filters enable users to dynamically specify a match criteria—often a status or type field of some kind—and then view only portal rows that match that criteria. In the real estate example you've been following in this chapter, listings are "active," "sale pending," or "sold." Using a portal filter, you could allow users viewing a set of listings in a portal to specify a particular status and have the contents of the portal change to reflect their choice (see Figure 16.12).

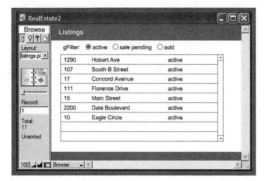

Figure 16.12
In this example, choosing from the available value list alters the rows displayed in the portal.

To create a simple filtered portal, first create a globally stored text field for holding the value a user chooses. In the example shown in Figure 16.12, a gFilter_ListingStatus will work well. When placing it on a layout, we'd recommend attaching a value list with "active," "sale pending," and "sold" for ease of use.

The second element to this technique is modifying the relationship between agents and listings to take the filter into account. The relationship was originally set up with a cross-product operator so that all listings could be displayed. If you replace that with a match of gFilter_ListingStatus to ListingStatus, only listings that match the currently specified status are considered related records (see Figure 16.13).

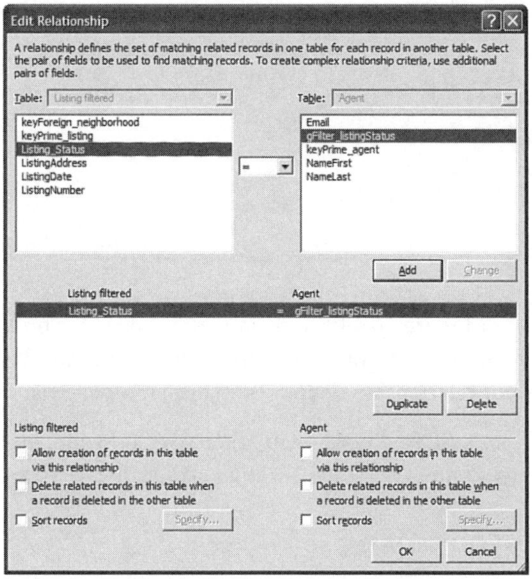

Figure 16.13
The assumption this relationship makes is that gFilter_Listing Status will change based on user preference.

NOTE

> *gFilter_ListingStatus* is a global and is therefore unindexable; however, from the perspective of its table, it is possible to use this field to relate to another table. Only the "far" table being viewed in a relationship requires an indexed match field (in this case, *ListingFiltered*).

By comparing the status field from the listing table with the *gFilter_ListingStatus*, you have created a relationship that changes based on the value a user selects in *gFilter_ListingStatus*. Keep in mind, if *gFilter_ListingStatus* is empty, so too will the portal be empty.

MULTI-VALUE "AND" FILTERED PORTALS

Consider a second scenario where you might want to filter on two criteria. To accomplish such, add a second criterion to your match relationship, as shown in Figure 16.14.

Figure 16.14
This example makes use of two match criteria.

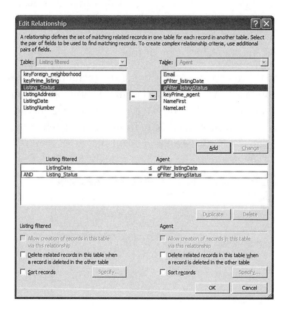

The relationship shown in Figure 16.14 filters on match values for both status and date fields. A filter acts on both fields. Notice the ≤ operator on the date. You can use a combination of match fields and relationship operators to display a wide range of related records.

This enables you to create a filtered portal with a range of possible, mutually inclusive filters. You can allow someone to select, say, all active listings for dates greater than 4/1/2004.

MULTI-VALUE "OR" FILTERED PORTALS

A natural extension to the example you've been exploring is a case wherein you want the portal to match one or another criterion but not necessarily both. For example, what if you alter the value list attached to `gFilter_ListingStatus` to include "all" as an option? Here you will want listings for an agent displayed based on his status, unless the user selects All, in which case all listings for a given agent should be displayed.

You need to apply the technique for a multi-key as discussed previously. In the previous example, the multi-key was applied to the front end of the relationship. This time we apply it to the back end.

Create a calculation field in the listings table like so:

```
listingStatus & "¶" & "all"
```

Now change the listing side of the relationship from `listingStatus` to the new calculation field. This is the only change (beyond adding the `"all"` option to your filter value list) that you need to make to turn this into an or filter. This relationship resolves where values in the status list include one of the three statuses or `"all"`.

RANGED, MULTI-VALUE "OR" FILTERED PORTALS

Multi-value or filters can become quite powerful. Consider a new example: Imagine wanting to provide users with a filtered list of contact names from a pool of hundreds or even thousands of records in a contact table. Instead of creating a value list by which to filter, allow your users to type a few characters of text into a filter field. If a user enters **co**, your (presumed) contacts returned in the portal might be a list like this:

> Coleen Neff
>
> Conrad Moyer
>
> Cordelia Henrich

If someone enters **col**, the list might return only Coleen Neff.

The way to approach this is to use the relationship operators for comparing ranges of text. Consider an example where you have the following fields in a contact table:

- `gMatchField`—A text field stored globally where users type whatever portion of text by which they'd like to match.
- `NameFirst`—The first name of your contact person.

You now need to compare the text co against some set of values to get the record for Coleen Neff to appear from the list.

Consider that a < c is a valid expression in FileMaker Pro. By relying on text string comparisons, you can create a relationship comparing your `gMatchField` to `NameField`. If you create a calculation like so:

```
NameFieldzzz, calculation = [NameField & "zzz"]
```

And then create a calculation where `gMatchField` <= `NameFieldzzz`, a portal using this example comparison will display all names that are comparatively less than "Coleenzzz."

This gets you only half of the way there. "Anthony" and "Beth" are, for example, comparatively less than "Coleenzzz." You need to create a second calculation:

NameFieldaaa, calculation = [If (IsEmpty (gMatchField); "0"; gMatchField)]

In cases where gMatchField has a value, say "co", the comparisons now would be:

- "Coleen" >= "co" and "Coleen" <= "cozzz"
- "Conrad" >= "co" and "Conrad" <= "cozzz"
- "Cordelia" >= "co" and "Cordelia" <= "cozzz"

In this example, "Anthony" and "Beth" would both not be valid match conditions. Both are comparatively less than "co."

The relationship driving a portal of this nature is shown in Figure 16.15.

Figure 16.15
Notice that relationships can accept multiple "and" criteria.

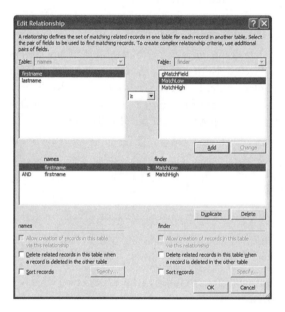

Consider the NameFieldaaa field. When empty, it returns a value that no text string will be less than 0. This then means that when gMatchField is empty, all the records in your contact table will be valid matches and all records will show in the portal.

You can opt to add further fields to drive the relationship in the portal by adding additional pairs of gMatchField and its two comparison fields. The relationship shown in Figure 16.16 demonstrates the case where both LastName and FirstName fields can be used.

EXPLODED KEY FILTERED PORTALS

The last technique is one often used with prior versions of FileMaker Pro and enables you to assemble a true "or" condition for a relationship by making use of multi-key matching. The technique still applies, and using a custom function to explode match values is even easier to utilize.

Figure 16.16
This relationship references two match fields. If a user types fractions of text in `gMatch_firstname` and `gMatch_lastname`, the portal filters on both values.

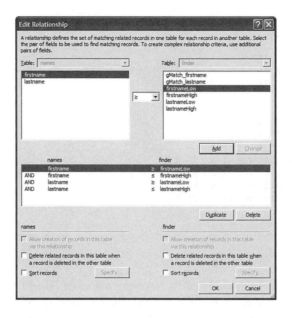

There's a large caveat to using this technique: It dramatically increases the size of your database indices. However, if you want a single `gMatchField` to operate on multiple related fields, this is a solid approach.

Consider the same example from the preceding section, where you expect a user to type some fraction of text in a `gMatchField` text field and you want your filtered portal to display matches from either a contact record's `NameFirst` field, `NameLast` field, or the domain from a `ContactEmail` field. In Figure 16.17, notice that matches are valid for all three data columns.

Figure 16.17
Notice that the filter is being applied to three fields: first name, last name, and email address. The records returned match the filter in at least one case.

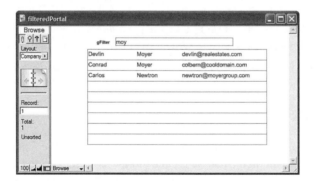

To accomplish this, use exactly the same multi-key technique. Rather than concatenate the values from one field, the match field concatenates the values from multiple fields. The calculation looks like this:

```
Let ( [
     atPosition = Position ( Email; "@"; 1; 1 ) + 1 ] ;
Left (FirstName; 4) & "¶" &
```

16

```
Left (FirstName; 3) & "¶" &
Left (FirstName; 2) & "¶" &
Left (FirstName; 1) & "¶" &
Left (LastName; 4) & "¶" &
Left (LastName; 3) & "¶" &
Left (LastName; 2) & "¶" &
Left (LastName; 1) & "¶" &
Left (Email; 4) & "¶" &
Left (Email; 3) & "¶" &
Left (Email; 2) & "¶" &
Left (Email; 1) & "¶" &
Middle (Email; atPosition; 4) & "¶" &
Middle (Email; atPosition; 3) & "¶" &
Middle (Email; atPosition; 2) & "¶" &
Middle (Email; atPosition; 1) & "¶" &
FirstName & "¶" &
LastName & "¶" &
Email & "¶" &
"all"
)
```

This calculation, if you can't already guess, resolves a match based on the first four characters of a contact's first name, last name, email address start, or email address domain (the characters following the "@" symbol). Notice the end of the calculation includes the full text of all three fields, along with an `"all"` to support users wanting to see all contacts in their databases.

Remember that the far side of a relationship requires an indexed field. This means you cannot include related data in your multi-key.

This calculation shows explicitly the values you need to assemble for a multi-key match field, and it's valuable to know how to do it as a straight calculation field, but we'd suggest building a custom function for assembling match fields. Using the recursive capabilities of custom functions and the fact that they are reusable throughout a solution, you can write one custom "explode text" function to take the parameters of however many fields you want to feed them, and never again have to write a calculation like the one we've shown here.

→ To learn more about how to build custom functions, **see** Chapter 14, "Specialized Calculation Functions," **p. 381**.

DYNAMIC PORTAL SORTING

Developers often place column labels above portals, and one of the first things we've seen users do with a newly minted database is click those ever-so-tempting column headers expecting them to sort. As discussed previously in this chapter, you can sort portals either at the portal level or at the relationship level. One of the more common requests we get as developers is to allow users to sort by whatever column they wish. Unfortunately, there's no way to programmatically define by which field a portal sorts. There is, however, a method for dynamically sorting a portal.

Using a calculation field, you provide FileMaker with the data by which you want a portal sorted. You need to create two new fields for your database: a control field, gSortPref, to hold the name of the field by which you want to sort, and a field for the actual sorting, sortCalc. We suggest you place sortCalc in the same table in which the rest of your portal fields sit. Your control field serves as a mechanism for choosing sort order. There are multiple ways to allow the user to change the values in it: You can use a value list, set by script when a user clicks on a column header, or perhaps a script available in the Scripts menu. However this field is managed, it's the end result that is important. Your sortCalc field depends on it. Here's an example of how sortCalc might be defined:

```
Case (
    gSortPref = "First Name" ; Name_first;
    gSortPref = "Last Name"; Name_last;
    gSortPref = "Email"; Email;
    "error"
)
```

If you set a portal to sort by sortCalc, notice that depending on what choice someone makes of gSortPref, the calculation returns the data by which the user expects to sort. If gSortPref = "First Name", the related portal data from sortCalc might look like

- Alex
- Beth
- Coleen

If gSortPref = "Email", sortCalc's data would change to be

- beth@email.com
- gibson_alex@email.com
- neffy@email.com

There are a few more steps to completely flesh out this technique, but these are the basics.

One remaining task to be done is managing screen refresh. Your user may change gSortPref, and sortCalc updates accordingly, but your portal doesn't actually resort until the user changes layouts or modes, or performs one of a range of other possible actions. You could write a script to take the user into Preview mode and back into Browse mode, but to force the screen to refresh with a minimum of screen flashing, reset the key that controls the front of the portal relationship. Use a Set Field () script step, and set the key field to itself. This forces the portal to refresh—because you've just altered one of the sides of its relationship—without requiring the user to navigate or change modes.

To establish sort buttons at the top of column headers, simply create as many buttons as there are fields in your portal, then attach a script that, using Set Field, controls what parameter is passed to gSortPref.

An alternative technique would be to have gSortPref hold the actual name of the field by which you want to sort, and then instead of a case statement, use a GetField function to populate sortCalc. This works well for cases where all your fields are of the same type; however, both techniques fail when you are dealing with multiple field types—for example,

NameFirst, NameLast, BirthDate, and Age. You still need a case statement, as explained in a later section.

MULTIPLE FIELD TYPE PORTAL SORTING

If you are using the technique just described, sortCalc needs to be a calculation that returns text, and so numbers and dates sort by the rules that govern text. Unfortunately, it's not possible to dynamically control what data type a calculation returns, so the following data—1, 8, 9, 12, 82—sorts like so

1

12

8

82

9

To get numbers to sort properly as text, you need to ensure that all of your numbers contain an equal number of digits. 01, 03, and 10 sort properly where 1, 3, and 10 would not.

Dates in your text calculation, likewise, sort like so:

1/12/2004

10/1/2004

10/10/2004

10/2/2004

3/1/2004

Remember that FileMaker stores dates internally as integers. This is the key to solving the puzzle. The idea here is that if the integer representations of dates are compared, then the sort works properly. sortCalc needs to be set as the following, assuming you have three fields that you want to display in your portal (myNumber, myText, and myDate):

```
Case (
    gSortPref = "Number" ; Right ( "000000000000000" & myNumber; 15 );
    gSortPref = "Text"; myText;
    gSortPref = "Date"; GetAsNumber( myDate );
    "error"
)
```

This calculation converts all your numbers into 15-digit numbers. It concatenates 15 zeros with whatever number has been entered into myNumber, then truncates the result to 15 characters. This ensures that 1, 3, 10, and 999 respectively return 000000000000001, 000000000000003, 000000000000010, 000000000000999.

Quite likely, the integer representation of your date field already uses the same number of digits. Remember that dates are stored in FileMaker as integers. 4/1/2004 is 731672. To drop below or above six digits, you'll need to be working with dates approximately prior to 274 A.D. or after 2738 A.D. Most databases are a safe bet at six digits, but if you're calculating dates for a sci-fi novel or are dealing with ancient times, feel free to use an identical approach to add digits.

DESCENDING DYNAMIC PORTAL SORTING

It's possible to extend the technique discussed in the previous section so that the portal can be sorted in either ascending or descending order. To accomplish this function, you need to sort by two fields—one ascending and one descending—instead of just one.

Recall how sorting by multiple fields works: FileMaker Pro sorts all like values from the first field in a sort request together, and then orders records with identical values in that first field by a second field. Table 16.2 shows an example where a user sorted by last name, then first name.

TABLE 16.2   CONTACTS ASCENDING

Last Name	First Name
Abrams	Alex
Abrams	Beth
Adams	Steve
Adid	Fereena
Adid	Samir

Recall also that sort fields can be set for ascending or descending behaviors. If you change the first name in Table 16.2 to sort descending, the list would look like Table 16.3.

TABLE 16.3   CONTACTS FIRST NAME DESCENDING

Last Name	First Name
Abrams	Beth
Abrams	Alex
Adams	Steve
Adid	Samir
Adid	Fereena

You can use FileMaker Pro's capability to properly sort in descending order for your sortCalc field. To toggle between the two behaviors, ensure that the first field always contains identical values when a user wants to have a portal sort by the second field—in this case set to descending order.

Here are the two fields you need:

```
sortAscend =

Case (
    gSortPref = "number-ascending" ;
        Right ( "000000000000000" & myNumber; 15 );
    gSortPref = "text-ascending"; myText;
    gSortPref = "date-ascending"; GetAsNumber( myDate );
    1
)
```

```
sortDescend =

Case (
    gSortPref = "number-descending" ;
        Right ( "000000000000000" & myNumber; 15 );
    gSortPref = "text-descending"; myText;
    gSortPref = "date-descending"; GetAsNumber( myDate );
    1
)
```

Notice that in the case that someone chooses one of the descending options, all the values in sortAscend equal 1. If you set up your sort dialog to first sort by sortAscend (ascending) and second by sortDescent (descending), your first field overrides the second when a user chooses one of the ascending options from gSortPref; otherwise that field is set to all the same values, and by definition the values in sortDescent will apply, happily making use of the descending sort behavior built into FileMaker.

To put the finishing touches on your user interface, you might consider making icons that indicate when a portal column is sorted ascending or descending. The script that sets your gSortPref can also control which images appear in container fields to provide visual feedback to the user.

TROUBLESHOOTING

PORTAL ROWS NOT DISPLAYING

I know I have a valid relationship established, but some (or all) of my portal rows aren't showing. What could be some of the issues?

You can opt to display only a specific set of rows via Portal Setup format options, but it is possible that you'd have a case of related records in your data that would never show up for a user. If you turn off vertical scroll bars and set a portal to show rows 4–8, rows 1–3 and 9+ won't display.

This applies to creating rows as well. If you've allowed the creation of related records and a portal's bottom-most row is intended to allow such, your users cannot access that feature if the row falls outside your range of visibly formatted rows. As in the example of only showing rows 4–8, there would have to be already at least three related records in the database before the "editable row" would appear for users.

CREATING RELATED ROWS FOR NON–EQUIJOIN RELATIONSHIPS

How do I create records via relationships that aren't equijoins? The option is grayed out.

When you allow creation of related records in a relationship, you may have noticed this works only for the equijoin ("=") operator. In cases where your primary relationship is driven by a different operator, we recommend still establishing an equijoin relationship with different table occurrences to create new records. If you're still not happy doing so (perhaps over concerns of cluttering your relationships graph), the only other alternative is to create a script that takes a parameter—the primary key of your parent table's current record—navigate to a layout attached to your child table occurrence, and use the create new record/request script step in combination with a manual Set Field [childTable::keyF_ParentID; Get (ScriptParameter)] for the match key.

INCOMPLETE HIGHLIGHTING RECTANGLE

My row highlight is showing in its container field, but it doesn't fill the entire portal row well. Where should I first look to address this?

If you place an image in a container field, and then have a calculation display the contents of that container field in a portal row, even when Maintain Original Proportions is enabled, your rectangle may show whitespace on either side. This is further complicated if you are trying to put something more complex than just a colored rectangle in the highlight field. FileMaker's resizing of images can be unpredictable at times.

The best way around this in many cases is to simply make the image larger than you need it to be and set the graphic format to Crop.

MULTI-USER SELECTED DATA

I have used a straight field—not a global—for storing which related record I want selected in a selection portal and related fields. In multi-user environments, this will break if two users are working with the same record at once. How do I work around that problem, while still not using globals that might display the wrong related data for a given record?

In cases where the field tracking a portal row selection is a standard field, as opposed to a global field, you will run into problems in multi-user environments. Two users might be viewing the same record at the same time and make two different row selections on a portal. Only one state would be valid (the latter of the two), but no event or screen refresh would occur for the first user.

There are two ways to deal with this. To employ the first, make certain users never end up working with the same record by either scripting a check-in/check-out approach or possibly building a one-record-only user interface for each user. This first approach is quite scripting and development intensive.

The second approach makes use again of multi-keys. To track what portal row is selected, keep track of your account name in a global field and populate a multi-key that concatenates accountName and rowID into the selectionID field. You need to use the substitute function to parse in-and-out as multiple users work with the portal, but this is multi-user–safe so long as they don't run into actual record locking problems.

FILEMAKER EXTRA: PORTALS AND RECORD LOCKING

NEW Record locking behaviors have changed with FileMaker Pro 7 from prior versions. Record and portal rows do not lock until a user begins actively editing a field or when a script performs an `Open Record/Request` script step.

At the point at which a user begins actively entering data (or modifying existing data), a record lock is established until such time as the user exits the record and commits or reverts the record.

It is important to keep this behavior in mind and to understand how it applies to portals. When a record is being modified and is related to other records viewed in a portal, it and the portal itself are locked; however, other users (or the same user in a different window) can navigate to one of the related records and edit it directly.

Portal rows and related records are created when the record is committed. FileMaker treats the entire set as a single transaction. It is possible to create a new parent record, tab from field to field entering data, tab into a portal and create a few rows (including potentially entering data into fields from a grandchild record), and either commit the entire batch at once or roll back and revert the entire batch. To support such functionality, FileMaker Pro locks the entire portal for a given record.

Record locking used to be more of an issue for both users and scripts in prior versions of FileMaker Pro. Although this new version doesn't do away with record locking—nor would we want it to for maintaining data integrity—the behavior you need to anticipate is far more localized.

TROUBLESHOOTING

WHAT IS TROUBLESHOOTING?

We hear about troubleshooting all the time. It conjures the image of a brainy technician, her utility belt bristling with tools, head stuck inside a rocket engine, muttering about how the condensers on the Apollo-96 tend to get "a little sticky" in the asteroid belt. One answer to the question "What is troubleshooting?" is simply "the art of detecting, diagnosing, and repairing problems." In our case, of course, we're concerned with problems that might appear during the operation of a piece of software.

This diagnostic flavor of troubleshooting is extremely important. This chapter introduces you to some of the broader systematic problems that can occur in a FileMaker system. We explain how to spot these and fix them, and we discuss some useful debugging tools that the FileMaker product offers you.

We're also going to try to sell you on a broader interpretation of the idea of troubleshooting. The problem that's easiest to fix, of course, is the problem that never happens. So in addition to *reactive* troubleshooting—the art of finding and fixing problems *after* they happen—we're also going to spend some time talking about *proactive* troubleshooting. To us, this means designing systems that are simply less error-prone, and designing them in such a way that any errors that do appear are caught and handled in a systematic way. The better you become at this kind of proactive troubleshooting, the less often and less severely your reactive skills are likely to be tested.

STAYING OUT OF TROUBLE

Whether you're writing applications that only you will use, that your coworkers will use, or that a client has hired you to build, the best thing to do with trouble is to avoid it. When we think of software bugs, we think of users or developers cursing the foibles of machines and wishing that "the software (or the tools) just worked better." The truth is, the overwhelming majority of problems in software are caused by human mistakes, and often those humans are programmers. So, clearly, as programmers, we should avoid making mistakes! Let's look at some typical sources of programmer mistakes.

UNDERSTAND SOFTWARE REQUIREMENTS

On the one hand, the need to understand requirements might seem obvious, and on another it might seem a bit far afield from this chapter's topic, but as far as preventing software error, understanding requirements is at the top of the food chain. If you don't know what the software you're writing is supposed to do, it's very unlikely that it will work correctly. Oh, it may work correctly from a technical perspective; it won't necessarily crash, or scramble data. But from a user's perspective it'll be just as bad. If you misunderstood how your client calculates mortgage futures, then from her perspective, the software is broken.

So *know what the program is supposed to do.* "Sort of" knowing isn't good enough, and guessing is even worse. There's often pressure—sometimes severe—to "just get started," even if all the requirements haven't been fully explored. Do not give in! FileMaker is a wonderful rapid application development (RAD) tool. It's terrifically easy in FileMaker to sit down and just start banging out screens and scripts, and it gives a wonderful feeling and appearance of productivity. But if you haven't fully understood what you're doing, this feeling is an illusion.

Sometimes it's not possible or advisable to try to scope out *all* the requirements of a project before getting started. If you determine that your project is of this type, you need a different approach. In this case we recommend you explore and familiarize yourself with some of the latest thinking on what software engineers call *agile development*, which is the art of developing a complex piece of software in small, incremental stages, or *iterations*. One popular school of agile development is called "Extreme Programming." We give some references to works on this topic in Appendix A, "Additional Resources."

The basic theory of Extreme Programming (or XP) is to break the work up into small pieces that meet two criteria. In the first place, each piece needs to be complete; that is, it needs to be large enough and inclusive enough that it constitutes a working piece of software in its own right. Think of a big program for a real estate management firm. Perhaps a portion of their requirements is a module that calculates different types of mortgages. Can this module be separated from the rest of the system and made independent? If so, you can build that module as a unit and then worry about what to build next.

The second requirement for such a unit is, of course, that it be small enough that it *is* possible to nail down all the requirements! If you can break a project up into pieces that are each complete, comprehensible, and as mutually independent as possible, you'll greatly increase your chances of success.

This book isn't intended to be a primer on software development methodologies, so for further information, refer to the readings in Appendix A. But remember this essential point: If you feel you don't quite understand what your program is supposed to do, please stop working and find out! Otherwise you're priming the pump for a later flood of software defects.

Avoid Unclear Code

As a programmer or software developer, relatively little of your time will be spent in writing new programs. Most of your time will be spent maintaining and extending old ones. This being the case, it's imperative that the programs you write be easy to extend and maintain. As much as possible, your programs should be both *readable* and *modular*.

Have you ever returned to a script you wrote six months ago, and find you have no idea what it does or how it does it? Of course you have; so have we all. And when we do this, we're in immediate violation of the "know what you're doing" rule. You *don't* know what you're doing, and you have to relearn it. You'd better have a good memory!

Much better is to write your program in a way that makes its functioning clear to whomever reads it, be that you or someone else. Two things in particular are important: giving descriptive names to the different components of your program (databases, tables, fields, layouts, and scripts, to name a few), and using comments liberally throughout your program.

CHOOSING GOOD NAMES

As much as possible, the names you choose should be descriptive and follow clear conventions where possible. We'll offer some suggestions, but they should be taken as just that: suggestions. Think of them more as examples on which you could base your own naming conventions. The most important thing here is consistency: Try to adopt clear rules for naming things, and do your best to stick to them.

DATABASES AND TABLES   Each database file (a collection of tables) should be named for its overall function. If one file contains all the tables for an invoicing module, call the database Invoicing, not Module A.

For tables, we recommend that you name the table according to the type of thing that it stores. For intermediate "join" tables, you should give thought to the function of the table and then decide what "thing" it represents. So a join table between Student and Class could be called StudentClass, but is better called Registration. A join table between Magazine and Customer is called Subscription, a join table between Book and Library is Holding, and so forth.

> **TIP**
>
> Additionally, we like our table names to be in the singular. So a table of customers is called Customer, a table of pets is called Pet, and so forth.

Some join tables don't really evoke a natural function, in which case you may need to fall back on the less descriptive name that just incorporates the names of each file: ProjectEmployee, for example, or OrderPayment.

Some tables are naturally "line item" files. The children of other files, which are generally accessed through portals, are characteristic of certain kinds of business documents. Order line items and invoice line items are common examples. Calling these OrderLine or InvoiceLine seems to make sense.

NEW FileMaker 7 presents a new naming challenge as well, with the existence of the table occurrences that populate the Relationships Graph. A number of developers feel that it's helpful to name these tables in some way that indicates their base table, so that if the same base table has multiple occurrences in the Graph, it's possible to discern this fact easily.

When it comes to field naming conventions, the debates among FileMaker developers often assume the character of holy wars (much like the arguments about bracing style among C programmers). We're not going to inject ourselves here and make any strong pronouncements—we'll just offer a few thinking points.

→ For additional discussion of field naming conventions, **see** "Field Naming Conventions," **p. 66**.

FIELDS   One of the main issues with "fields" in FileMaker is that they're a superset of what we normally think of as database fields. FileMaker fields include, of course, the classic "fields," which are those that store static data, generally entered by users. But they also include fields with global storage, which are not data fields at all, but programming variables. They include calculation fields, which are in fact small functions, units of programming logic. And they include summary fields, which are actually aggregating instructions intended for display in reports.

You, as a developer, need to decide what things you need to be able to distinguish quickly in this thicket of "fields," and devise a suitable naming scheme. Generally, we like to be able to pick out the following database elements quickly:

> User data
>
> Globally stored fields
>
> Structural database keys

Distinguishing globals and keys is easy. One common practice is to prefix global field names with a *g*, and keys with a *k*, plus another letter to describe the type of key: *kp* for primary keys, *kf* for foreign keys. When you sort your field list alphabetically, all the key names clump together and you have easy access to your fundamental structural elements.

Making a broad distinction between user fields and developer fields is harder. Those that try to do this generally adopt some kind of overall field name prefix. It's not uncommon to see a scheme where all developer fields are prefixed with an additional *z*. This puts them all together at the end of the field list, and uses an uncommon letter that's unlikely to overlap with the first letter of a user field (well, except ZIP code, which is common, but you can fudge this by calling the ZIP a "postal code" instead). In a z-based scheme, globals might be prefixed with *zg* and keys with *zkp* or *zkf*.

There are those that swear by such naming schemes, and an equal number that swear *at* them. Even the authors of this book are somewhat divided! I personally recommend that you think very carefully before deciding you don't need *some* kind of field naming scheme. Admittedly, such a scheme takes discipline to keep up. You should choose a scheme that at least makes certain things such as keys and globals clear; then you can decide whether you need more. Again, no matter which convention you choose, consistency is the important thing.

LAYOUTS   With naming layouts, again, we'd advocate that you have some clear naming scheme to distinguish between layouts your users interact with directly and those that you build for behind-the-scenes use. One general rule is to prefix the names of all "developer" layouts with `Dev_` or a similar tag.

As with table names, FileMaker 7 gives a new twist to layout naming because layouts are associated with an underlying table occurrence and base table. Some developers have argued that it's a good idea to include the base table name in all layout names, as an easy way to indicate what kind of records will display on the layout.

SCRIPTS   With scripts, it's hard to provide any clear guidelines, especially because—unlike the Create Database field listing—script names can't be sorted, and so you can't take great advantage of any clever naming scheme. You should try to keep your scripts grouped, using dummy "divider" scripts to create the groups. Other organizational tricks include adding prefixes to scripts, such as Btn: for scripts intended to be called by pressing a button, Nav: for scripts whose function is navigational, and so on. In some ways the script organization problem is more daunting in FileMaker 7 because scripts that used to live in multiple files might all now live in one single file.

OTHER ELEMENTS   There are, of course, still other areas where improper names can sow confusion, such as the naming of value lists, extended privileges, and custom functions. Function and parameter naming are especially important, so we'll touch on that area as well.

It pays to take care when naming custom functions, custom function parameters, and also the temporary "local" variables you create in a Let statement. A few simple choices here can greatly add to the clarity of your code or greatly detract from it.

Suppose you have a custom function intended to compute a sales commission, with a single parameter, intended to represent a salesperson's gross sales for the month. To be fully descriptive, you should call this parameter something like grossMonthlySales. That might seem like a lot to type, but if you call it something short and efficient like "gms" you'll be scratching your head over it in a few months' time. The longer name will stay descriptive.

NOTE

> Notice the capitalization. For custom function parameters and Let variables, we like to use a style called "camel case," popular among Java programmers, in which the first letter of the first word is lowercase and all other words in the name begin with uppercase. We don't use this convention for field names by the way—there we prefer title case.

→   For additional discussion of custom functions, **see** "Custom Functions," **p. 409**.

USING COMMENTS WISELY

A *comment* is a note that you, the programmer, insert into the logic of your program to clarify the intent or meaning of some piece of it. You can use comments many different ways, but we strongly suggest you find ways that work for you, and use them.

 FileMaker 7 offers significantly expanded commenting facilities compared to previous versions. Whereas in previous versions of the product you could add comments only to scripts, you can now add them onto field definitions, and inside the body of calculations as well.

To add a comment to a field, just type your note into the Comment box in the field definition dialog. To view comments, you need to toggle the Comments/Options column of the field list—the list can display comments or options, but not both at once.

Comments can be useful for almost any field. They can be used to clarify the business significance of user data fields, or to add clarity to the use of global and summary fields. Figure 17.1 shows a field list with comments liberally applied.

 Also new in FileMaker 7 is the capability to insert comments into the text of calculations and custom functions. We recommend you make use of this new feature to clarify complex calculations.

Figure 17.1
Adding comments to your field definitions can provide useful clarification.

→ For more information on how to insert comments into the text of calculations and custom functions, **see** "Using Comments Effectively," **p 1025**.

Finally, FileMaker enables you to add comments to your scripts. Some developers have elaborate script commenting disciplines. They may create an entire "header" of comments with space for the names of everyone who's worked on it, the creation date, and even a full modification history. Figure 17.2 shows an example of such a commenting style.

Figure 17.2
Using script comments to keep a copious revision history for a script.

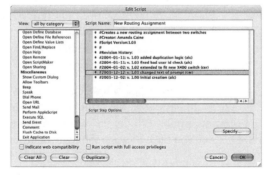

Other developers use script comments more sparingly, reserving them for places where the flow of the script is less than self-explanatory, or for guiding the reader through the different cases of a complex logic flow. Short, pointed comments throughout a lengthy script can add a great deal to its clarity.

Some developers scorn comments altogether, swearing that they can instantly understand their own programs even if they come back to them cold six months or a year later. Well, even if that were true (it surely is for some people), it ignores the fact that you need to write programs to be read not only by you, but by anyone who comes after you. Someday, someone else will probably have to maintain and extend what you wrote. Of course, if they can't make heads or tails of it, they're much more likely just to conclude that it's simpler to scrap it and rewrite it.

TIP

> Commenting increases the longevity of your code, and we recommend you learn about the different commenting options that FileMaker allows.

→ For more information on how to use comments, **see** "Using Comments Effectively," **p. 1025**.

WRITING MODULAR CODE

"Modularity" is one of those popular buzzwords for which it seems every programmer has a different interpretation. To us, a modular program is one that avoids unnecessary duplication of effort. Much as the concept of database normalization encourages that each piece of information be stored once and only once in a database, you should try to program in such a way that you avoid (as much as possible) writing multiple routines that do the same or similar things. Try instead to write that routine or piece of logic once and then draw on it in many places.

MODULARITY IN SCRIPTS   As a simple example, let's say you're working with a system that prints a lot of reports. Many of the reports need to be printed to a special printer, on legal-size paper, with certain paper-handling options specific to the printer. Well, naturally, you'll have scripts to print each of the reports, and you could simply have a Print Setup step in each script that sets up the printer and page handling correctly. But there are two problems with this. In the first place, you'll have to set up those print options for each and every script in which you want to use them. The more times you do this, the greater the odds that you'll make a mistake. Further, if you ever need to change those options, you need to track down every place you've set them up and change them there.

A better practice would be to write a single script called "Print Setup Report Legal" or something to that effect. All the script does is set the print options—nothing more. When you need to call up that set of print options, call the script. When you need to change the options, change the script. This way you have to write the logic once, and you only ever need to change it in one place.

FileMaker 7 offers several powerful new features that can greatly increase the modularity of your code if used with discipline. Two of the most important are custom functions and script parameters. These topics have been covered thoroughly in their respective chapters, but it's worthwhile to bring them up here again. You should thoroughly understand the mechanics and uses of custom functions and script parameters, and use them aggressively to make your code more general and extendable. (Bear in mind that custom functions can be created only with FileMaker Developer 7, not with the regular FileMaker Pro 7 product.)

→ For more on custom functions, **see** "Creating Custom Functions," **p. 411**.

→ For more on script parameters, **see** "Script Parameters," **p. 422**.

Like other areas in FileMaker, even seasoned developers can disagree on the best way thing to do things. Some developers use custom functions more aggressively, some less so. To finish off this section let's look at an example of the aggressive use of custom functions to make code more abstract.

MODULARITY USING CUSTOM FUNCTIONS   Let's say we're dealing with a simple problem: We have a system that deals with billing of some kind, and our client has asked that bills that are more than 30 days old appear with their date written in a red color in the billing list.

FileMaker's new text formatting calculations make that a snap. Let's say the table has a field called DueDate and another called DueDateDisplay. If the DueDate is less than 30 days ago, the DueDateDisplay field contains the date in a black color; otherwise it contains the date in a red color. It's easy enough to write a calculation for DueDateDisplay that does all these things:

```
Case( Get(CurrentDate) - DueDate <= 30; GetAsText(DueDate); TextColor
➡(GetAsText(DueDate); RGB ( 255 ; 0 ; 0 ) ))
```

Well, that works, but there are things that could be better about it. For one thing, it hard-codes quite a number of different elements: What if the rules change so that "Past Due" happens at 45 days? What if they want the color to be a different shade of red? If those things are being used in multiple places, you'll have to hunt them all down and change them. The second problem with this setup is that it works only for the specific field called DueDate. If you wanted to perform similar logic elsewhere, you'd have some duplication to do.

Let's tackle these issues one at a time, using custom functions. Chapter 14, "Specialized Calculation Functions," discusses the possibility of using custom functions for "system constants" to abstract out hard-coded values. That's a good place to start. Define one custom function, called getOverDueLimit. That function takes no parameters, and always returns 30. The next thing is to define another custom calc called getOverdueHighlight, and define it to always return RGB(255;0;0).

So far, so good. This abstracts out some of the hard-coded values. Next, you need a generic way to determine whether a record is overdue. You could write a custom function called isOverdue(dateValue), defined as follows:

```
Case( dateValue + getOverdueLimit < Get(CurrentDate); 0; 1)
```

This function takes a dateValue, compares it to the current date and the value from getOverdueLimit, and returns a 0 or 1 depending on whether or not the date is overdue.

The next function is called colorIfOverdue(dateValue, textValue, rgbColor). This function's job is to take a date, a piece of text, and a color, and apply the color to the text if the date is overdue. The definition looks like this:

```
Case( not IsOverdue ( dateValue ); textValue;
➡TextColor ( textValue ; rgbColor) )
// last parameter needs to be an RGB color value, i.e. the result of RGB(x,y,z)
```

(Notice, by the way, that this function uses a comment to clarify the data type of the third parameter.) This function draws on the previously created isOverdue function to do its work. Notice also that this function doesn't assume anything about the color to apply to the text, or even what the text is—it just applies *a* color to *a* text string based on a date.

With these custom functions created, it's finally time to do some work based on actual fields. So the DueDateDisplay field can now be redefined very simply as

```
colorIfOverdue ( GetAsText(DueDate); DueDate, getOverdueHighlight() )
```

It might seem like that was a lot of work, but look at the advantages. If you decide you want a different color for all your overdue highlights, you need to change only the definition of getOverdueHighlight. If you decide to let bills go 45 days instead of 30, you need to change only the definition of isOverdue(). And if you need additional fields to highlight according to whether a record is overdue, you don't need to replicate any of the core logic; just create another display field like DueDateDisplay that references a different base field, and you're in business.

That's an example of what we'd call fairly aggressive use of custom functions to achieve a high degree of modularity and flexibility. As with any technique, it's possible to overdo it. As a general rule of thumb, try to abstract out those elements of the logic that seem to have the most potential to change or be duplicated. As another general rule of thumb, additional layers of abstraction can make a program harder to understand at first glance. Make sure you provide sufficient comments for later readers to understand your elegant abstraction.

PLANNING FOR TROUBLE

The previous sections suggested a few approaches you can follow to make your programming easier to troubleshoot. But errors *will* happen. As you build systems, you need to expect errors, and plan for how to handle them. Many programmers (too many) make the mistake of assuming that things will always work correctly. Their programs behave perfectly well, as long as nothing unexpected happens. But when a user enters data they didn't expect, or a network connection drops, suddenly the program ceases to behave gracefully, and its behavior becomes what we call (charitably) "undefined."

Let's take a simple example. You have a FileMaker system that periodically needs to import data from some other source. Imagine that the FileMaker system contains a table of manufacturers, and the manufacturer data is actually being fetched from an Oracle system via an XML Import. The update is intended to be a "destructive" update, meaning that the new data completely replaces the old. You want to perform all this work via a script, so you write the following (naïve) script:

```
Go to Layout ["Manufacturers"]
Show All Records
Delete All Records [No dialog]
Import Records [No dialog: http://my.mfg.com/mfg_update?code=3]
```

That *seems* right. Find all the current manufacturers, delete them, and import the new ones. But it's not right; it's dead wrong. What if the import step fails (for example, because the

Web server at `http://my.mfg.com` is down for maintenance)? Well, you've already deleted all your manufacturers, and now you have no way to fetch new ones, for who knows how long. Much better to go on with a slightly outdated manufacturer list than none at all.

The deletion step could fail as well—for example, if users had one or more records locked. If this happens and you don't catch it, you end up with duplicate manufacturers, which could be a serious problem.

The right way to do this, of course, is to perform the import *first*. If and only if it succeeds, you can then find the old records and delete them. The script should look like Listing 17.1

LISTING 17.1   CORRECT IMPORT SCRIPT

```
Import Records [No dialog: http://my.mfg.com/mfg_update?code=3]
If[ Get( LastError ) <> 0 ]
    Exit Script
Else
    Show Omitted Only
    Delete All Records [No dialog]
End If
```

17

This still isn't perfect, but it's much better. To make it better still, you'd need to examine what the exact error was during the import, to decide whether some records had been imported and needed to be deleted. But it prevents the worst case, which is an empty manufacturer table.

→ For more on FileMaker's XML Import feature, which we posited as a possible source for the data in this example, **see** "XML Import: Understanding Web Services," **p. 653**.

It's easy to produce other examples of this kind. They all boil down to the same logical error: the unwarranted assumption that a specific step is going to work. The only time that it's okay to make this assumption is if there's no significant penalty for being wrong. For example, imagine you have a script that finds all invoices over 30 days old and changes their status from "Current" to "Past Due." It's possible that the search will fail and find no records. But in that case it's innocuous to go on and perform the Replace step—it will operate on a found set of zero records and will have no effect.

So, one of the most important ways to avoid software defects (the graceful term for bugs) is to be aware of all the possible failure points in your system, and, most importantly, *calculate the consequences of failure*. Good programmers do this instinctively. They always have a clear sense of what will happen if some element of their program fails. The question is never a surprise to them, and they always know the answer.

TROUBLESHOOTING SCRIPTS AND CALCULATIONS

There are many specific areas of potential trouble in FileMaker, and we'll get to those in the next section. Here, though, we want to discuss some general principles for dealing with errors in scripts and calculations.

HANDLING ERRORS IN SCRIPTS

Many FileMaker actions can result in an error. "Error" in this context can mean any exceptional condition that needs to be reported to the user. This can be something as simple as a search that returns no records or a field that fails to pass validation, or it can be a more esoteric error involving something like a missing key field. In general, in the normal operation of FileMaker, these errors get reported to the user via a dialog box of some kind, often with some sort of choice as to how to proceed.

For example, as shown in Figure 17.3, if a user performs a search that finds no records, she gets a dialog alerting her to the error and she has the option to go back and redefine her search.

Figure 17.3
FileMaker generally provides a lot of feedback on error conditions, such as this "no records found" message.

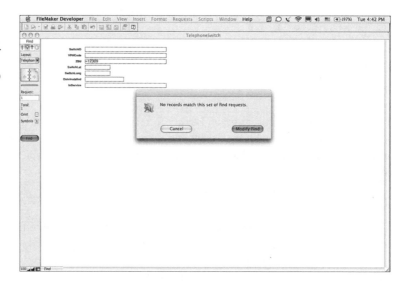

This is fine, up to a point. But you, the developer, may not want the user to see this default FileMaker dialog. You may want to present a different message, or none at all. Well, if your user performs her searches by dropping into Find mode, filling in some search criteria, and clicking the Find button, there's not much you can do. But if your user is performing a find via a script that you've written, you can intervene in such situations.

There's a very important script step called Set Error Capture. It's worth your while to become very familiar with it. This step allows you to tell FileMaker whether or not to suppress error messages while your script is running. The use of the step is shown in Figure 17.4.

If this step is not present in a script, or if it's present and set to "off," then FileMaker reports errors to the user directly. If your script performs a search, and no records are found, your users see the usual FileMaker dialog box for that situation (shown in figure 17.3). However, if you have error capture set to "on," the user sees no visible response of any kind. After you've set the error capture state (on or off), this setting is carried down through all subscripts as well, unless you explicitly disable it by using Set Error Capture [Off] somewhere down in a subscript.

Figure 17.4
The Set Error Capture script step is useful for controlling how FileMaker errors are displayed to the user.

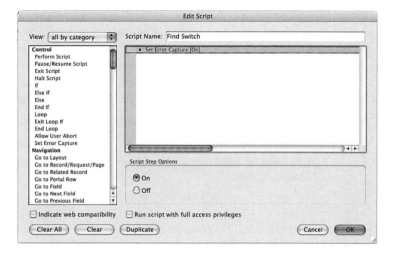

In general, you don't just turn error capture on and walk away. In fact, error capture obliges you to do a lot more work than you normally might. With error capture on, FileMaker error dialogs are suppressed, so it's up to you to check for errors and either handle them or inform the user of those that are important.

As an example of custom error handling, suppose you've built a system that primarily stores text content in a variety of forms: press releases, biographies, articles, and so on. If a user does a search in one area and finds no results, you'd like to offer the option to search in other areas as well. Rather than let FileMaker intervene and show the standard No Records Found dialog, you want to pop up a custom dialog that allows the user to run a different scripted search on a different table or just give up. The script might look like the one in Figure 17.5.

Figure 17.5
Within a script, you can use Set Error Capture to hide the usual error messages and display custom feedback to the user.

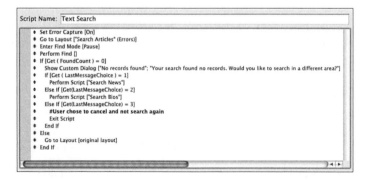

Here, Set Error Capture is turned on and the script is configured to check whether the user's search found any records. If so, he's sent to the article list. If not, the custom dialog with other search choices is offered. If he picks a different type of search, the appropriate script runs; otherwise the script is exited and he is left where he was.

In addition to checking for specific conditions (such as a found count of zero), it's also possible to check more generically to determine whether the previous script step produced an error. This technique was shown in Listing 17.1, which used the Get(LastError) function. This function returns whatever error code was produced by the most recent operation. An error code of 0 means "no error." Otherwise, an error of some kind has occurred. In Listing 17.1, as written, it didn't matter too much exactly which error had occurred—it was enough to know that *some* error had happened.

NOTE

The FileMaker online help provides a complete listing of error codes and their more verbose descriptions.

Get(LastError) can be tricky. It reports on the most recent action taken no matter whether the action was triggered directly by a user or by a script. Let's say you have the following script fragment:

```
Set Error Capture [On]
Perform Find[]
Go To Layout ["Search Results"]
If[ Get(LastError)<>0 ]
    Show Message ["An error has occurred"]
End If
```

This is not going to do quite what you would hope. If the Perform Find script step found no records, then at that point the "last error" would be 401 (the code for "no records found"). But after the Go To Layout step runs, that error code no longer applies. If that step runs successfully (which it might not if, for example, the particular user didn't have privileges to view that layout), then the last error code would now be 0. So, if you want to check for errors, check for them at the exact point of possible failure, not a couple of steps down the road.

Note also that the concept of "last error" is relative to each client session. This means that if another user, in his session, generates an error, this has no effect on the "last error" status in other sessions.

TRACKING DOWN ERRORS

Suppose, despite your best efforts at defensive programming, some aspect of your system just doesn't work right. (Actually, you don't need to suppose. This *will* happen, and what's more, it'll happen after the software is delivered. That's not cynicism; it's reality.)

When this happens, of course, you'll want to track the problem down and fix it. There are a couple of verbs you'll want to keep in mind: *reproduce* and *isolate*.

REPRODUCING ERRORS

The first thing to do with any problem is to render it reproducible. Bugs that occur only occasionally are a programmer's worst nightmare. Often the circumstances are clear and entirely reproducible: "If I hit Cancel in the search script, I end up on some goofy-looking utility layout, instead of back at the main search screen." At other times, the problem is more slippery: "Sometimes, when I mark an invoice as closed, the system creates a duplicate of that invoice!"

If the bug is not transparently reproducible, you need to gather as much data on the bug as you can. Who experienced it? What type of computer and what operating system? Has it been experienced by one user, or several? Does it appear consistently? Look for hidden patterns. Does it occur more at certain times of day? Only from specific computers? Only for a particular account or privilege set? Only during the last week of the fiscal quarter? And so on.

Reproducing the bug should be your first priority, because you can't isolate it until it's reproducible, and isolating it is your best means of fixing it.

You might find that you, yourself, are unable to make the bug happen. This may be a sign that you are using the software differently from your users. Your usage pattern might never cause the bug to happen. One way to leap this hurdle is just to sit down with a user and watch him work. You might find that he's using a feature of the software differently than you had intended or expected, or that he performs functions in a different order. This may give you the clue you need.

What if, despite all these efforts, the bug remains elusive? You can see its tracks but can't catch it. Well, you have a few choices. One is to program around it. If users report that, very occasionally, they get duplicate invoices when they close an invoice, you can rewrite the invoice-closing script to check for duplicates and eliminate an extra one when it appears. This doesn't eliminate the bug, but it does repair the effects. This is a distinctly less-than-perfect solution, but if it solves the problem and makes the system work again, that's what counts. But the bug is still in there, possibly causing other mischief.

Another possibility is to try to do some kind of logging. For example, in the duplicate invoice case, you could add some logic to the Close Invoice script. In addition to all the work it normally does, it would also create an entry in a new Log table. It would write out the time the script was run, the username, the system IP address, and the platform. Then, at the end of the script, it would check for duplication and log the findings. Even if you were programming around the bug at this point, to buy time, you could still use this log information to try to pin down the bug. Let the system run for a month, then look at the log and try to pick out any patterns in when the bug happens.

DEBUGGING CALCULATIONS

After you've reproduced the bug (you hope), it's time to *isolate* it. Let's think about calculations for a moment. Suppose you have a complex calculation like the one in Listing 17.2. This calculation expresses a person's age (the DOB field) as something like "38 years, 5 months, 9 days."

LISTING 17.2   COMPLEX CALCULATION EXAMPLE

```
Let (  [ Today = Get(CurrentDate); DOBDay=Day(DOB); TodayDay = Day(Today) ] ;

GetAsText(Year(Today) - Year(DOB) - Case(Today< Date(Month(DOB);
➥DOBDay; Year(Today)); 1; 0)) & " Years, " &

GetAsText(Mod(Month(Today) - Month(DOB) + 12 -
➥Case(TodayDay <> DOBDay; 1; 0); 12)) & " Months, " &

GetAsText(TodayDay - DOBDay + Case(TodayDay >= DOBDay; 0; Day(Today- TodayDay)
< DOBDay; DOBDay; Day(Today - TodayDay))) & " Days")
```

Actually, as written, the calculation does have a bug, and will generally give the wrong value for the "days" element. How do you debug this lengthy calculation?

NOTE

Lengthy though this calculation is, FileMaker 7's Let statement makes the formula much more elegant than it would be in previous versions of the product.

One nice thing about this calculation is that it's actually three smaller calculations merged into one. To isolate the problem in this calculation, you need to pull out each individual piece and see whether it gives the expected result. Here you could pull out just the piece that computes the "days" value, like so:

```
Let (  [ Today = Get(CurrentDate); DOBDay=Day(DOB); TodayDay = Day(Today) ] ;

GetAsText(Mod(Month(Today) - Month(DOB) + 12 - Case(TodayDay <> DOBDay; 1;
➥ 0); 12)))
```

Turn this snippet into its own calculation and see how it behaves. You'll find it behaves the same way when isolated from the rest of the calculation, and now your problem has shrunk in size. It shouldn't take you long to find that the <> (not equals) in the second line is a slip of the hand, and should just be < (less than).

As a general rule, we recommend that you debug complex calculations by breaking them down into smaller pieces and pulling those pieces into their own calculations if possible, for testing purposes. This suggestion contains a strong implication for how you should build complex calculations in the first place: Define and test the smaller pieces of functionality in their own calculations first, then merge them into the larger one. Or, if there's anything at all reusable in the smaller pieces, don't just fold them into a larger calc, but define them as custom functions instead.

TIP

> For easy debugging of "calculation fragments" like the one shown previously, define two new fields in the problem table: a `CalcSource` field (which holds a calculation fragment), and a `CalcEval` field (well, the names can be whatever you like) that's a calculation defined as `Evaluate(CalcSource)`. Anything you cut and paste from the problem calc into the `CalcSource` field will be evaluated by the `CalcEval` field. This beats defining entirely new fields to hold your calculation fragments.

The key to the idea of "isolation" is specifically to isolate the broken part. Pull out the pieces that are known to work. As you test each piece, remove it if it tests out correctly. As you do this, the area that contains the problem grows smaller and smaller.

DEBUGGING SCRIPTS

The principle of isolation applies to scripts as well as to calculations. Your problem may lie inside of one script, or you may have a complex chain of scripts and subscripts that's exhibiting failure. By far the best tool available for this now is the Script Debugger, which is part of FileMaker Developer 7.

→ For a full treatment of FileMaker Developer 7 and the Script Debugger, **see** "Script Debugger," **p. 778**.

The Script Debugger vastly simplifies the process of script debugging, which used to rely chiefly on the insertion of numerous Pause Script and Show Message script steps! But debugging scripts is still not an automatic process. A few points are worth noting.

PLACING BREAKPOINTS   The Script Debugger enables you to place a breakpoint in a script so that execution stops there and you can see what's happening. In theory, if you have a troublesome script or script chain, you could place a breakpoint at the very start and step through the script. But if this is a lengthy script chain, much less one than contains a loop that might run many times, this may not be very time effective.

Consider a case where you have a complex set of scripts that call each other—let's say that there are three scripts total. Somewhere in the middle of that script, a date field on the current record is getting wiped out, but you don't know where.

In a case like this, you can use a classic isolation technique called "binary search." If you have no idea where the problem is happening, place a breakpoint more or less in the middle of everything, say halfway through script #2. Turn on the Script Debugger, let the script run, and see whether the field has been wiped out by the time you stop at the breakpoint. If the problem has already occurred, move the breakpoint to around the midpoint of the first half of the script chain (that is, 25%) and try again. If it hasn't happened by the 50% mark, move the breakpoint to 75%. Repeat until you narrow the possible range to one or two lines. This may sound like it's not much of a time-saver, but using this technique can find the error in a script of over 1000 lines using at most ten of these check-and-move operations.

TIP

> If you have to a debug a looping script, it's worthwhile to try to reduce the number of records on which the script runs. In general, if you need to debug the loop itself, one internal breakpoint should suffice at first, either at the beginning or end of the loop.

INSPECTING VALUES   One of the most important uses of a debugger is to watch certain values and see how they change. These could be database fields, global variables, or aspects of FileMaker state such as the current layout.

Checking which layout is current while you're debugging is easy, but it may be harder to inspect certain values in which you're interested. If they're present on layouts, and the script executes on those layouts, you're fine. Otherwise you might need to create special "debug layouts" that show the fields in which you're interested. You can then alter the script to show that layout, where possible.

CAUTION

> Be aware of the potential for error here—make sure these layouts keep the appropriate table context, or they could greatly alter the script's behavior.

TROUBLESHOOTING IN SPECIFIC AREAS: PERFORMANCE, CONTEXT, CONNECTIVITY, AND GLOBALS

The individual troubleshooting sections in each chapter of this book cover particular isolated "gotchas" that we've wanted to highlight. In this section, we want to do two things: We want to talk generally about broad areas of potential FileMaker trouble and how to diagnose them, and we want to talk about a number of specific areas that don't pop up in the other chapters, or at least don't get a comprehensive treatment.

PERFORMANCE

"The system is slow!" Performance is a critical part of the user experience. What can you do if things seem slow? Well, first of course, it's important to *isolate* the problem. Is just one area of the system slow, or one particular function? Or does the system generally seem sluggish? In general here, we're assuming that your solution is a multi-user solution hosted under FileMaker Server, but most remarks (except those entirely specific to Server) apply equally to Server and non-Server configurations.

GENERAL SLOWNESS

If a FileMaker application seems generally sluggish and slow to respond, the leading candidates are insufficient hardware (client, server, or both), improper server configuration, or insufficient network resources. The last two apply only when the files are being hosted on FileMaker Server.

Hardware is a straightforward issue. Read and understand the hardware requirements for the client and server computers. If you plan on having many users on the server, please don't skimp on the server hardware! Get the very best machine you can afford. Likewise, on the desktop, try to meet or exceed the stated standards.

If you're not hosting the files on FileMaker Server, but rather have a peer-to-peer configuration, and things seem slow, you should seriously consider moving to Server.

If you're working with FileMaker Server, you also need to make sure your server settings are configured correctly for your situation. In particular, you'll want to look at things such as the percentage of cache hits, the frequency with which the cache is flushed, and the amount of RAM dedicated to the file cache size. (FileMaker Server's default is 8MB for the cache size but you may well need to raise that number.)

→ For a full treatment of FileMaker Server 7 settings, **see** "Configuring and Administering FileMaker Server Using the SAT," **p. 746**.

If you're using Server and all the hardware seems reasonable, it's time to look at your network. You should know your network's exact topology. What connections are there, at what speeds? Where are the routers, switches, and hubs? What other traffic besides FileMaker traffic flows over the network? FileMaker is fastest over a LAN at speeds of 10 megabits and higher. In general it's better not to try to run FileMaker over a network link that's slower than T1 speed (1.544 megabits). All other things being equal, a fully switched network is better than not, and of course a 100-megabit LAN is better than a 10-megabit LAN, if they're both built correctly. FileMaker, like any networked service, also suffers from competition with other services running over the same wire.

You should also be familiar with your firewall situation. Does FileMaker traffic need to pass through any firewalls or packet filters? This can slow things down as well.

A last point is that FileMaker Server can be set to encrypt traffic between the client and the server. This encryption is somewhat processor-intensive and may impose a performance penalty. If you're experiencing slowness in a client-server environment, and you're using client-server encryption, you may want to disable the encryption and see whether that makes a difference. If so, you may need to consider investing in faster hardware.

SLOWNESS IN SEARCHING AND SORTING

Searching and sorting are among the operations that, in a Server configuration, are handled chiefly by the server. So it's possible the slowness in searching or sorting is symptomatic of some general networking issue of the type discussed in the previous section.

It's also possible that there's a problem with the search or sort itself. In terms of performance, the cardinal sin is to execute a search or a sort based on one or more *unindexed* fields. This, of course, means that there's no index for the field, which in turn condemns FileMaker to examining each and every record in the database—somewhat akin to trying to find a word in a dictionary where the order of the words is random.

As you might recall, some fields in FileMaker can be unindexed merely because the designer chose to leave them that way, perhaps to save space. For certain fields, this setting can be changed, and FileMaker can be permitted to index the field. Other fields, though, such as globals, or any calculation that references a global or a field in another table, *cannot* be indexed under any circumstances. If your search or sort includes such a field, the operation will never go quickly, and in fact its performance degrades linearly as the database grows in size.

NOTE

> You should allow an unindexed search only if you're sure the set of searchable records is always going to remain fairly small, and there's no other way to achieve the result you need. In general, programming a search or sort on unindexed fields should be considered a design error and should be avoided.

Note too that "unindexable-ness" has a certain viral character to it, where calculations are concerned. Suppose you have a calculation A, which references calculation B, which references fields 1, 2, and 3. For reasons of saving space, you decide at some point to eliminate the index on field 3. Immediately, calculations A, B, and C all become unindexed as well, for the simple reason that they now all depend on an unindexed field. Any searches or sorts that use these will now potentially run quite slowly. Be aware of this issue of cascading dependencies when working with indexes.

→ For additional discussion of indexes, **see** "Storage and Indexing," **p. 82.**

SLOWNESS IN EXECUTING CALCULATIONS

If you have a calculation that seems to execute very slowly, there are a few avenues you can explore. In general, the greater the number of fields and other calculations that your calculation references, the slower it'll be. It's possible to build up quite lengthy chains of dependencies, or to have dependencies with a non-obvious performance impact. Consider the previous example, with a calculation C that references a calculation B that references a calculation A. Every time A or B changes, C gets re-evaluated as well. So the calculation contains more work than you might expect. It's very easy to create elaborate chains of such dependencies, so watch out for them. If you find such chains, see whether there are ways to restructure the chain, perhaps in a way that allows some of the intermediate data to be stored, or set by a script.

Likewise beware if your calculations reference any custom functions with recursive behavior. A recursive function is like a little looping script. How long it loops for any case all depends on the inputs. If you're referencing these in your calculations, be aware of this fact.

→ For more information on recursion, **see** "Creating Custom Functions, **p. 411.**

Finally, if your calculation references related fields, it may be a bit slower than a calculation that looks only at fields in the same table.

SLOWNESS IN SCRIPTS

You can do almost anything in a script, so in some sense a slow script could be caused by anything that could cause slowness elsewhere in FileMaker. But there's one additional point we want to make here: You can often speed things up by using some of FileMaker's complex built-in functionality from a script, rather than building things up from simpler script steps.

USE REPLACE RATHER THAN LOOP   Assume you have a batch of records representing library books. Once a day you want to scan the book list, find all those that were due yesterday and are still checked out, and mark them overdue. Well, you could solve this with a loop: Find the right records, go to the first one, loop through the whole set, and perform a Set Field on each record. But there's a quicker and easier way: Use the Replace Field Contents script step. This step lets you specify a field and a value to put into the field. The value can be a hard-coded value, or the result of a calculation, possibly quite a complex one. (The latter technique is called a *calculated replace*—an essential tool in a FileMaker developer's toolkit.)

In any case, a Replace Field Contents, calculated or otherwise, has almost exactly the same effect as a Loop/Set Field combination, and is often much faster. In simple tests that we've performed, Replace seems to run about twice as fast as Loop.

GO TO RELATED RECORDS VERSUS SEARCHING   The Go To Related Records script step is one of FileMaker's most powerful tools. Using this step, you can navigate from a starting point in one table to a related set of records in some other table, via the relationships defined in the Relationships Graph. (Technically, you are navigating from one table occurrence to another via the graph.)

CREATING RECORDS   Under certain circumstances, creating records can be a slow process. Specifically, record creation will be slower the more indexes you have on a FileMaker table. Indexes on a table are updated every time a table record changes, and each index on that table may potentially need to be updated. As a general rule, indexes cause searches to run faster, but may cause record creation to be slower.

CONNECTIVITY AND RELATED ISSUES

There are many scenarios in which FileMaker's behavior may be affected by network and connectivity considerations. Unless you are working alone with a FileMaker database that lives on one single computer, and is used on only that computer, you're likely going to find yourself in a situation where FileMaker data is being distributed over a network. This situation offers a number of potential problems.

INABILITY TO CONTACT THE SERVER

What happens if you're running FileMaker Server and your users can't see your files? There could be any number of reasons for this turn of events, but this list contains a few of the most common reasons.

- **Server is down**—Verify that the server is running via inspection or a network utility such as "ping."
- **Server is up, but FileMaker service is not responding**—Verify that *both* the FileMaker Server and FileMaker Server Helper processes are running. (Without the Helper process, clients cannot connect to the server.)

17

- **The server machine is working and the processes are running correctly, but the files have not been correctly set for network hosting**—Make sure that you have granted network access to the files for at least some users.

- **The files have been placed on the server but are not opened for sharing on the server**—Even if the files are on the server, with appropriate network hosting, it's still necessary to instruct FileMaker Server to open the files for sharing. If the files don't appear in the Files area in the Server Administration Tool, they are not open for hosted sharing.

- **Users may not have appropriate permissions to see the hosted files**—In the FileMaker Network Settings dialog, it's possible to specify that the file will be visible for network sharing only to users with certain privilege sets. Users with insufficient privileges could thus in theory have no privileges that would allow them to see any of the hosted files.

→ Making files available via network access is covered fully; **see** Chapter 25, "FileMaker Server," **p. 737**.

- **Firewall problems**—If there's a firewall between your server and any of your users, the firewall needs to pass traffic on port 5003. If this port is blocked, users will probably not even be able to see the server, much less access any files on it.

CROSSTALK

If a user comes to you and says that all of last week's sales data has disappeared, there are a number of possible causes for this effect. It's possible, of course, that last week's sales data really *is* gone (in which case you'll want to price tickets to Nome). But it's also possible you've been bitten by a case of *crosstalk*.

Crosstalk had the potential to be a serious problem in previous versions of FileMaker. FileMaker 7's new File Reference feature has taken a lot of the sting out of the problem, but the potential for trouble remains.

→ For a full discussion of file references, **see** "Working with Multiple Files," **p.197**.

 The trouble stems from the way FileMaker Pro resolves external file references. To access any content from another file, you must first create a file reference to it. You need to do this to add tables from an external file to the relationships graph, or to call a script from that file, or to use a value list from that file. In FileMaker 7, you create and manage file references explicitly. In previous versions of the product, FileMaker managed them for you, behind the scenes, making it easy to lose track of what you were doing. FileMaker also had an "automatic" search routine, so that if it couldn't find a file in the first place it looked, it might look elsewhere, and come up with the wrong copy of the file.

FileMaker 7 does not perform this sort of automated search for your files. Instead, it looks to the file references you've set up. If it exhausts the search path for a file, it stops looking. However, if you specify a multi-element search path for a file, you could still get into trouble.

Suppose you're developing a system that has one file for Customers and another for Orders, each containing a cluster of tables to support its function. You're developing the files locally, on your own computer, so to bring the Order file into the Relationship Graph in the Customers file, you'd create a local reference in the Customers file, as shown in Figure 17.6.

Figure 17.6
A file reference with one local entry.

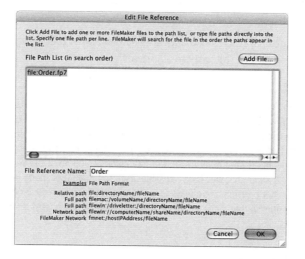

Now suppose you deploy the files to FileMaker Server. Now you'd like to add an element to the Order reference's search path that points to the copy of the file on the Server. You place it before the local reference, so that FileMaker looks to the server first, as shown in Figure 17.7. This has become a bit dangerous! If FileMaker can't find that file on the server, it looks for it on a user's local hard drive, and if it finds it, it opens it up and uses it. At the very least, you the developer need to be quite careful in this scenario about which version of the file you're working with.

Figure 17.7
A file reference with multiple search locations defined.

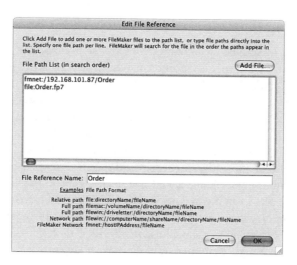

Other users aren't likely to have a copy of the file locally. But suppose you had made a reference instead to a shared network drive? That could cause a real headache—the server goes down, the network drive is still in the search path, and clients begin to access and enter data into the non-served copy.

Again, the elegance of file references makes this danger much less severe than in the past, but it still pays to be aware of the issue to avoid any pitfalls.

NOTE

If you've got a system that's being hosted on a network, and you are still doing development work on another copy of the system, there are several anti-crosstalk precautions you can take. In the first place, make sure to work in single-user mode. One useful practice is to add scripts to every file you create, to toggle between single-user and multi-user mode. In the case of multi-file (not multi-table) solutions, it's possible to create a single master script that flips between single-user and multi-user mode for a whole file set. And the other precaution is always to archive your old working copies by some form of compression, so that they can't be accidentally opened and hosted on the network.

CONTEXT DEPENDENCIES

The idea of *context* covers a lot of ground. Speaking generally, it refers to the fact that many actions that occur in FileMaker don't happen in a vacuum. The effect of certain script steps, calculations, or references can vary depending on "where you are" in the system. "Where you are" means specifically what layout you're on, what window you're in, what mode you're in (Browse, Find, Layout, or Preview), and what record you're on in the current table. Each of these dependencies has its own pitfalls, and each one is discussed in the sections that follow.

LAYOUT DEPENDENCIES

Be aware, when writing scripts, that a number of script steps might not function as you intend, depending on what layout is currently active. Most of these steps require certain fields to be present on the current layout. These include the Go To Field, virtually all the editing functions (Undo, Cut, Copy, Paste, Clear, Set Selection, Select All, Perform Find/Replace), all the Insert steps, Replace Field Contents, Relookup Field Contents, and Check Selection. These are all script steps that act on a field on the current layout. You can run each of them without specifying a field, in which case they run on whatever field is current. They can also be run with a particular field specified. If you specify a field, and for some reason the script is invoked on a layout that doesn't contain the field, the desired action doesn't take place. Even if you don't specify a field, the odds are very strong that you have a specific layout on which you intend that script to be run. In general, these script steps are somewhat fragile and you should use them with care. If you do use them, you should be sure that your logic guarantees that the correct layout will be current when the script step runs.

Table Context

You're certainly familiar with table context if you've read much of the rest of this book. The topic was introduced in Chapter 6, "Working with Multiple Tables," and it plays an important role in most other chapters as well.

→ For a full discussion of table context, **see** "Understanding Table Context," **p. 161.**

NEW FileMaker 7 databases, unlike those in previous versions of the product, can contain multiple tables. For many actions in FileMaker, then, it's necessary to specify which table is the "current" one. For new records, to what table does the new record get added? When I check the current found count, for which table am I checking it? And so forth.

Table context introduces a new kind of layout dependency, and one which, in our opinion, dwarfs the old layout dependencies of earlier versions of FileMaker. If you're not aware of table context and don't handle it correctly, your FileMaker solutions may appear to be possessed. They will almost certainly not behave as you expect, unless your system is extremely simple.

There are quite a number of areas in FileMaker 7 where table context comes into play. A brief recap of each of these is provided here.

CAUTION

As with other kinds of dependencies, it's important to make sure that the context is correct for an operation before trying to perform that operation. This is a special pitfall for scripts, which can easily change context during script operation via a Go To Layout step. If your script steps are context sensitive, make very sure to establish the proper context first!

Table context is probably one of the trickiest areas of the new FileMaker: powerful, but full of pitfalls for the unwary.

LAYOUTS   A layout's table context is determined by the table occurrence to which it's tied. Table context governs which records the layout displays. Note that the link is to a table occurrence, not to a base table—this is significant if you'll be working with related fields, or navigating to related record sets (via the Go to Related Record step). In that case, the choice of table occurrence can make a difference in the contents of related fields.

→ For a discussion of table occurrences and their implications for related fields, **see** Chapter 6, "Working with Multiple Tables," **p. 153** and Chapter 8, "Getting Started with Calculations," **p. 213**.

IMPORTING RECORDS   When you import records into FileMaker, the target table is determined by the current table context, which is of course determined by the current active layout. Before importing records, manually or via a script, be sure to go to the appropriate layout to set the context correctly.

EXPORTING RECORDS   Exporting records is also context dependent. Furthermore, if you're exporting related fields and you're exporting from a base table with multiple table occurrences, the choice of table occurrence from which to export might also make a difference. As in the case of importing, make sure you establish context before an export.

CALCULATIONS   Calculations can also be context dependent, in very specific circumstances. If a calculation lives in a base table that appears multiple times in the Relationships Graph (that is, there are multiple occurrences of that table in the Graph), *and* the calculation references related fields, then the table context matters. The Calculation dialog in FileMaker 7 has a new menu choice at the very top, where you can choose the context from which to evaluate the calculation. If the calculation matches the criteria just mentioned, you should make sure you get the context right. In other cases, you can ignore it.

VALUE LISTS   Like calculations, value lists can also access and work with related data, via the options to Also Display Values From Second Field and/or Include Only Related Values. Here again, if the value list lives in a base table that appears with multiple occurrences, *and* it works with related data, the table context will be an issue and you should make sure it's set correctly.

SCRIPTS   Every script executes in a particular table context, which is determined by the table context of the current layout in the active window. (FileMaker 7 can have several windows open within the same file, and they might even display the same layout.) A large number of script steps in FileMaker 7 are context-dependent. If you fail to set the context correctly, or change it inadvertently during a script (by switching layouts or windows), you could end up deleting records in the wrong table, to take an extreme case. Interestingly, FileMaker 7 currently doesn't offer a Set Context script step. You need to establish your context explicitly by using a Go To Layout step to reach a layout with the appropriate context.

MODE DEPENDENCIES

A variety of actions in FileMaker depend on the current mode. In other words, things taking place in scripts (which is where these dependencies occur) don't happen in a vacuum; they depend on the current state of the application and the user interface. To take an easy example, some script steps don't work if the application is in Preview mode, including especially the editing steps such as Cut, Copy, and Paste, and others such as Find/Replace and Relookup. If you have a script that's trying to execute a Relookup step, and some other script has left the application in Preview mode, your Relookup won't happen.

NOTE

> The Copy command does actually have one meaningful and useful behavior in Preview mode. If no target field is selected, a Copy command executed in Preview mode copies the graphic image of the current "page" to the Clipboard.

Most of these mode dependencies are really "Browse mode dependencies," because in general it's Browse mode that's required. But a few other mode-based quirks are also important to remember. A few script steps have different meanings in Find mode than in Browse mode. In Find mode, the Omit script step causes the current Find request to become an Omit request, whereas New Record and Delete Record create and delete Find requests respectively. These three steps work differently in Browse mode, where they respectively omit a record from the current found set, or create or delete a record.

If you're using such script steps, the answer's the same here as elsewhere: Explicitly set the context if you're using script steps that depend on it. In this case, you should use an explicit Enter Browse Mode script step when using steps that depend on this mode.

> **NOTE**
>
> Some FileMaker dogmatists go so far as to suggest that *every* script you write should begin with an Enter Browse Mode, unless otherwise required. We think this policy may be a bit much in practice, but the spirit of it is dead-on: Be aware of these dependencies, like others, and handle them explicitly.

Finally, there are also mode dependencies that occur outside the context of scripting. A number of FileMaker's presentation features are dependent on Layout mode. These include the capability to display data in multiple columns, the capability to show the effects of any "sliding" options you may have set, and the capability to show summary parts and summary fields.

→ To find full detail on these Preview-dependent layout features, **see** "Working with Objects on a Layout," **p. 103**, Chapter 4, "FileMaker Fundamentals: Working with Layouts," **p. 89** and "Summarized Reports," **p. 281**.

THE RECORD POINTER

In addition to all the other elements of context, there's one other important one. Quite a number of scriptable actions depend on what record you're currently "on." You might remember that this is a function of two things: what layout you're on (which in turn translates to a table occurrence, which in turn translates to a base table), and which *window* you're in. FileMaker 7, you may remember, supports multiple windows open onto the same layout, each with its own found set.

Within each found set, FileMaker keeps track of something called the "record pointer"—in other words, on which record of the set you actually are. This is indicated both by the record number in the status area, and possibly by the small black bar that appears to the left of each record in list views. Figure 17.8 shows both of these indicators.

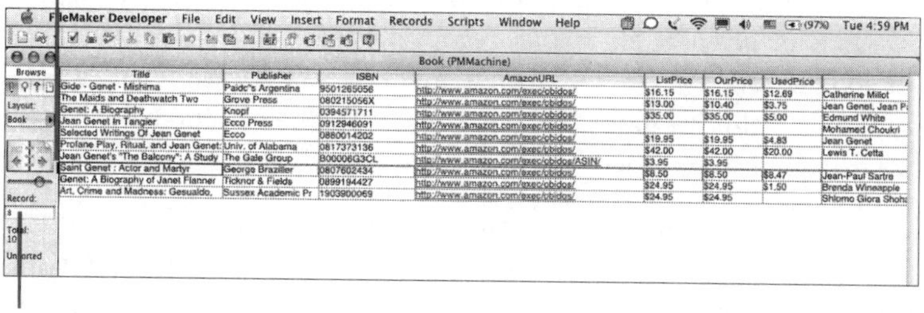

Indicates the position of the record pointer

Figure 17.8
The small black bar in a list view indicates the record pointer's position. The status area also shows the current record number.

The current record number

Some script steps *are affected* by the record pointer, while others *affect* it. Obvious cases of the former are Delete Record and Set Field. The record that gets deleted, and the field that gets set, depend on which record you were on to start with. These kinds of cases are clear and trivial.

Less clear are the steps that affect the record pointer—in other words, that move it. Say you have a found set of 7 found records and you navigate to number 5 and delete it. Which record do you end up on? Old number 6, or old number 4? Old number 6 is the answer: Deletion *advances* the record pointer (except, of course when you delete the last record of a set). The omission of one or more records from the found set is treated like deletion as far as the record pointer is concerned.

What about adding or duplicating a record? Is the additional record created immediately after the current record? Just before it? At the end or beginning of all records? Well, it turns out to depend on whether the current record set is sorted. If the record set is unsorted, new or duplicate records are added at the very end of the found set. (More exactly, the set is then sorted by creation order, so of course the newest records fall at the end.) But if the record set is sorted, things are different. New records are created right after the current record. A duplicate is created at its correct point in the sort order, which could be immediately after the current record, or possibly several records farther along.

The bottom line is that you need to be aware of which script steps move the record pointer. This is a particular pitfall inside looping scripts that perform these kinds of actions, such as a looping script that deletes some records as it goes. If, on a given pass through the loop, you don't delete a record, you need a Go to Record/Request/Page [Next] to advance the record pointer; but if you delete a record on one pass, the pointer advances automatically, and unless you skip the "go to next record" step this time around, you'll end up one record ahead of where you want to be.

GLOBALS

 Global fields (which in FileMaker 7 are more exactly called "fields with global storage" because "Global" is no longer really a field type) have long been a powerful feature of FileMaker Pro. But there are a few non-obvious facts about globals that can cause problems and confusion.

Unlike data values that are placed in record fields, the values of global fields are specific to each database user (if the databases are being run in a multi-user configuration). That is, if you have an invoicing system with an Invoice Date field, every logged-in user sees exactly the same invoice date for invoice record number 1300. By contrast, if you have a globally stored field called gFlag, it's possible that every single user could see a different value for that global field. If a global field gets set to a value of 1300 by one user, that value isn't seen by other users. They each have their own "copy" of the field, unlike a non-global data field.

It's helpful to remember that when a file containing globally-stored fields is first opened, all global fields are set to the last values they had when the files were last open in single-user mode. This means that users in a multi-user environment can't "save" the values of global fields. When a user closes a file, all global fields associated with that file's tables are wiped clean. (In effect, they disappear.) If the same user reopens the file, all the globals will have reverted to the server defaults. This is an important troubleshooting point. If you are relying on global fields to store important session information such as user preferences, be aware that if the user closes the file containing those globals, all those session settings disappear, and reopening the file does not, by itself, bring those stored global values back.

From a troubleshooting perspective, it's important to remember that globals are volatile and session-specific.

FILE MAINTENANCE AND RECOVERY

A corrupted database system is every developer's nightmare, as well as every user's. Database systems are complex, and very sensitive to the integrity of their data structures. Errors in the way data is written to a database can damage a system, or in the worst case render it unusable. Periodic maintenance can help you avoid file structure problems. In the worst case, if one of your files does become corrupted, FileMaker has tools to help you recover from this situation as well.

FILE MAINTENANCE

As you work with a database file, the file can become slowly more fragmented and less efficient over time. Large deletions can leave "holes" in the file's data space. Heavy transaction loads can cause indexes to become fragmented. If your databases are large or heavily used, it's a good idea to perform periodic file maintenance.

The File Maintenance feature is available only in FileMaker Developer 7. File maintenance can be performed only on files that are open locally. It can't be performed on files that are hosted. To invoke it, choose File, File Maintenance. You'll see a dialog like the one in Figure 17.9, which allows you to choose to compact the file, optimize the file, or both. We recommend you execute both of these steps when performing file maintenance.

Figure 17.9
Periodic file maintenance (a feature of FileMaker Developer) is a good idea if your files are large or heavily used.

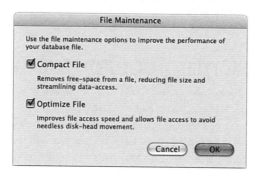

There isn't a firm rule of thumb for when and how often to perform file maintenance. A general rule might be that if you have a database file over 20–30 megabytes in size, or that is changed hundreds of times daily, it might be wise to perform a file maintenance every few months. If your file sizes rise into the hundreds of megabytes, or your activity rises into the thousands of records changed daily, you may want to perform maintenance monthly, or even more frequently.

FILE RECOVERY

It might occasionally happen that a FileMaker file becomes so badly damaged it cannot be opened. When this happens it's usually because the file's host (either the FileMaker client or the FileMaker Server) suffered a crash. If a file is damaged in this way, it's necessary to use the File, Recover command available in any copy of FileMaker Pro. This command tries to rebuild the file and repair the damage in such a way that the file can again be opened and its data accessed. The recovery process can take from a few seconds to many minutes or occasionally hours, depending on the size of the file and how many indexes it contains.

The recovery process is not intended to repair a damaged file fully. *Files that have been damaged badly enough to require recovery should not be put back into service.* The recovery process is intended to bring the file back to a state in which the data can be moved into a "clean" copy of the file. You need to create that clean copy by taking a recent backup (you do have a backup, don't you?) of the file, opening it, and choosing File, Save A Copy As, then choosing to save it as Clone (No Records). This creates an empty copy of the file, containing all the structural elements such as table definitions, scripts, layouts, and the like. From here, you should run an import to fetch in the data from the recovered file.

CAUTION

> This is so important we're going to repeat it here. Do *not* use a file that has been recovered! Even assuming the recovery proceeded without errors, this does not constitute a guarantee that all damage to the file has been repaired. If you go on using it, eventually the recovered copy will propagate throughout your backups and you'll no longer have access to a truly clean copy. If there later turns out to be hidden damage remaining, you'll be out of luck.

FILEMAKER EXTRA: OTHER TOOLS OF THE TRADE

A number of the important tools you can use to avoid or diagnose trouble in your FileMaker systems were touched on in this chapter. Many of these are development practices, and a few, such as the Script Debugger, are available within the FileMaker product line. But there are also a number of third-party tools that can provide valuable diagnostics. As a rule, these tools analyze the structure and logic of a FileMaker system and produce output that warns you about potential difficulties with the files. Not all these tools were known to be available for FileMaker 7 at the time of this writing, but we fully expect them all to make to leap to 7 soon after the product is released. In general, these tools analyze an existing FileMaker file set and produce an interactive report (either in HTML or as a set of FileMaker databases).

- **Analyzer**—Analyzer, from Waves in Motion (http://www.wavesinmotion.com) is a tool that, well, analyzes your FileMaker solutions and produces a FileMaker-based report. Analyzer documents the entire internal structure of your system. Among the output it produces are notes about errors encountered within the system structure. The most common type of errors involves missing elements, such as missing fields, layouts, or related table occurrences, as well as relationships that are invalid or suspect.

- **Metadata Magic**—Metadata Magic, from New Millennium Communications (http://www.nmci.com), is a FileMaker plugin that performs solution analysis and returns the results as a set of FileMaker databases, as does Analyzer. MdM is able to document a variety of problem areas in a FileMaker database. Of particular interest is its capability to note whether a file has been recovered, and if so, how many times.

- **Brushfire**—From Chaparral Software (http://www.chapsoft.com) produces an HTML-based report that, like the other two products mentioned here, shows complete details about the structure of a FileMaker solution, as well as highlighting possible trouble spots. Among its noteworthy features are the capability to find "obsolete" items that are no longer used or referenced, and the capability to find objects with improper names.

These tools are all worth serious consideration. Each has strengths and weaknesses. As a FileMaker developer it's worth your while to invest in at least one of this type of tool, or possibly several, depending on your needs.

## CHAPTER 18

CONVERTING SYSTEMS FROM PREVIOUS VERSIONS OF FILEMAKER PRO

In this chapter

MIGRATION CHOICES

If you've never touched FileMaker Pro prior to version 7, the material in this chapter may not be of much use to you. On the other hand, anyone who has ever built or currently maintains systems in previous versions of FileMaker Pro faces a significant set of decisions regarding whether and how to migrate those systems to FileMaker Pro 7.

You've likely heard, read, or discovered on your own that FileMaker Pro 7 is tremendously different from previous versions of the product. The last time the product experienced such a fundamental change was in moving from version 2.1 to 3.0. If you were working with FileMaker back then (way back in 1995), you probably remember that there was a lot of unlearning, relearning, converting, and rebuilding that had to take place. For the first time, in FileMaker Pro 3.0, the product contained such important tools as relationships and portals. It took quite a while for developers proficient with FileMaker 2.1 to fully understand relational database concepts and the benefits that portals and related fields offered over repeating fields and lookups. It was possible to convert solutions from 2.1 to 3.0 without loss of functionality, but to take advantage of the powerful new features required either extensive redevelopment or, in some cases, rebuilding the files from scratch. The same holds true of the migration from 6.0 to 7.0.

The features introduced in versions 4.x, 5.x, and 6 can perhaps be described as more evolutionary than revolutionary. Web publishing, plug-ins, and data exchange via ODBC all were important extensions to FileMaker, but none of them required fundamental mind-shifts, nor was there any concern that a converted solution might not function exactly as it had previously.

FileMaker Pro 7, on the other hand, represents a revolutionary shift from its predecessors. The ability to place multiple tables in a single file, the addition of an entirely new security model, the ability to create relationships based on multiple match fields, the ability to have multiple windows open in a file, server-based Web publishing tools, and custom functions are some of the biggest changes, but there are myriad subtle changes as well, ranging from being able to add comments to fields and calculation formulas to changes in how alphabetic characters placed in number fields are interpreted.

Because of the sweeping changes, conversion of existing solutions into FileMaker Pro 7 becomes a complex issue. There are circumstances where it will be a better idea to rewrite a solution completely rather than convert it; even if you do convert, you may need to do considerable development work and testing before the converted solution can be deployed. In the end, the effort to do either is well worthwhile. This chapter helps you identify the migration strategy that makes the best sense for your solution and how to go about it.

FACTORS INFLUENCING YOUR MIGRATION STRATEGY

By the term *migration*, we mean simply the concept of moving a solution from a previous version of FileMaker to version 7. You can employ two primary strategies to effect a migration. The first is to *convert* your solution using the built-in routines in FileMaker Pro 7. The other is to *rewrite* your solution as a fresh set of FileMaker Pro 7 files.

The decision about how (and indeed whether) to migrate your solution will be informed by a number of factors, including your future needs, the benefits you hope to reap through migration, the complexity of your solution, and your timeline and available resources. You may decide that some of your solutions can simply be converted; other solutions may be better off being rewritten from scratch.

MIGRATION BENEFITS

Of all the new features and benefits of FileMaker Pro 7, there will undoubtedly be some features that matter more to you than others. For some people, support for Unicode may be a compelling reason to upgrade, whereas others may not find this feature relevant. Some people will choose to migrate to use the new security features; others for the new Instant Web Publishing. For existing solutions, determine what specific benefits you hope to achieve by migrating to FileMaker Pro 7; if you decide to migrate, you'll then need to determine whether those benefits can best be attained by conversion or rewriting. Sometimes the desired benefits will completely drive the migration strategy; other times they will play less of a role in the decision.

Centralized security is a good example of a reason to rewrite rather than convert. Anyone who's maintained complex security settings in a 50-file solution will welcome the ability to assign accounts and privileges for all the tables in a file. When you convert a relational solution, however, each file in the existing systems turns into a one-table file in the new system, and there's no easy way to consolidate tables into the same file. So, after converting a 50-file solution, even if everything works flawlessly, you'll still need to manage accounts and privileges in 50 different places. If centralized security is a crucial feature for you, you may prefer to rewrite your solution as a single-file application.

 If you do attempt to consolidate tables, there are some potential issues you should be aware of. See "Repointing Table Occurrence References" in the Troubleshooting section at the end of this chapter.

Many other benefits will be just as achievable through straight conversion as through a rewrite. Examples of these include the new larger field and file size limits, the ability to put binary data into container fields, support for Unicode, and encrypted data transfer between FileMaker Server and client applications.

Another class of benefits can be achieved by a rewrite or through a hybrid of conversion and subsequent development. For instance, your solution may have work-arounds to get around limitations of previous versions of FileMaker. After conversion, those work-arounds will still be in place, but they may no longer be necessary; your converted solution may be FileMaker Pro 7 *compatible* but it may not be FileMaker Pro 7 *optimized*. Examples of features that you won't use unless you rewrite or do post-conversion development include custom functions, script parameters, text formatting functions, and relationships based on complex match criteria.

COMPLEXITY

Complexity is such a subjective and nebulous concept that it's hard to pin down the effect of solution complexity on the decision to convert or rewrite. All other things being equal—which of course they never are—the more complex a solution is, the more likely it is that you'll prefer to rewrite from scratch rather than convert.

To some extent, complexity can be measured by sheer numbers: number of scripts, number of files, number of relationships, and number of layouts. But there are qualitative measurements of complexity that may override the quantitative: Having a hundred simple navigation scripts is less complex than having a hundred scripts that do, well...complex things. Complexity also may involve interactions with external systems, or simply very complicated business logic.

So why is it better to rewrite than to convert a complex solution? If some features don't work properly in a complex system after conversion, it can be very time consuming to find and fix the problems. Further, it can be almost impossible in complex systems to systematically test every button and script to ensure that it functions as it's supposed to. It's possible that some conversion issues won't be easy to discover, resulting in problems well down the road.

When you create a system from scratch, you test components as you go, so it's less likely that there will be lingering issues after the system is deployed. Also, in a rewritten FileMaker Pro 7 system, it's almost always possible to achieve your previous functionality with significantly fewer objects: fewer fields because you won't need as many unstored calculations; fewer scripts because of script parameters and being able to define multiple different finds and sorts within a single script; fewer relationships because they're all inherently bi-directional.

It will also be easier and more efficient to maintain a complex solution in FileMaker Pro 7 if it's been rewritten than if it's been converted. Figure 18.1 shows the Relationships Graph of a very large, complex file after conversion. Keep in mind, of course, that you'll have similarly impenetrable graphs in many—if not all—of the files in your solution. It's going to be very difficult to groom all those graphs into something that can be efficiently maintained. A rewrite, on the other hand, gives you the opportunity to systematically plan how to arrange tables in your graphs; you can also choose the file architecture that's best for your solution rather than passively accepting the one-table-per-file architecture obtained through conversion.

NOTE

Each relationship in the previous file is converted into a table occurrence in the new file, named by the relationship name from the old system.

Figure 18.1
After conversion, each file in your solution will have a hub-and-spoke design graph with the current file at the top center of the graph.

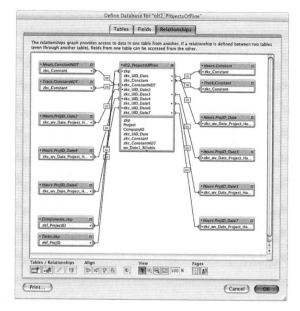

CONDITION OF THE EXISTING SYSTEM

The condition of your existing system can have an impact on your migration decision. Plenty of systems out there have grown more like weeds than well-tended gardens. Such systems exhibit inconsistent naming conventions, have fields, scripts, and layouts that are no longer needed, use inefficient and/or idiosyncratic processes, and usually have data integrity problems to boot.

Converting these systems often accomplishes little more than paving the cow path: It's using a new technology to do things the same, inefficient way they've always been done. Chances are that you'll end up disappointed in the new product because it doesn't solve any of your inveterate problems. It will also be very difficult to do proper post-conversion testing and development on such systems, as you'll always be plagued by the detritus from the old system.

On the other hand, if your solution has been well tended over the years, or has recently been overhauled, there's a good chance it will convert well and be easy to maintain going forward. A well-tended solution will have consistent, intuitive naming conventions, will have a minimum of unnecessary objects, and will have ample data protection in place. If that's not a description of your system, you may want to use the upgrade to FileMaker Pro 7 as your excuse to do the rewrite that your system needs. Rather than blindly replicating the existing system, take the time to design and build it correctly from the start.

FUTURE NEEDS

Your future needs for a particular solution may influence your decision whether to convert or rebuild. If you have a solution that does x, y, and z, and all you need to have it do going forward is x, y, and z, conversion might be the best path for you. In such cases, your primary motivation for conversion is likely something like the larger file size limit, or the ability to make schema and privilege changes without kicking users out of the system. Even if it takes kludgy work-arounds to do x, y, and z, if you don't foresee a likely need to do much future development or maintenance work on the system, it's probably just fine to leave those kludgy work-arounds in place.

At the other end of the continuum is a solution (and likely an organization) that's in constant flux. You need a system that's easy to maintain and is nimble enough to adapt to changing needs and conditions. Or maybe your current solution is phase one of a larger, grander application. If for these or any other reasons you foresee a need to do considerable post-conversion development for a solution, it's likely that you'll be better off rewriting your solution. If you don't, you'll probably end up with a stratified solution, where old features and objects are noticeably "B.C." (before conversion) and new work is noticeably "A.C." (after conversion). Such a system will invariably be more difficult to build upon and maintain than one developed entirely in FileMaker Pro 7.

TIME AND COST

There's little question that rewriting a solution from scratch requires more time and/or cost than simply converting a solution. Be aware that conversion itself isn't without time and cost requirements: You always need to do significant testing before deploying a converted solution and often need to do some post-conversion maintenance as well.

Estimating the time and cost requirements for either migration strategy is difficult because you won't know what issues you'll face until after you're underway. Conversion is like a home remodeling job in many ways. After you tear down a few walls you may be faced with a bigger problem than you anticipated. Similarly troublesome, rewriting is prone to the "while-we're-at-it" factor (that is, "as long as we're rewriting the solution, let's hire a designer to create a new interface while we're at it", or "while we're at it, let's build those hooks into the accounting and shipping solutions we've always talked about adding").

Rewriting a solution from scratch certainly sounds like it will involve more significant time and cost than conversion. Keep in mind, though, that you have your original solution as a blueprint, and that you'll be able to copy significant portions of the system, including layouts, scripts, and calculation functions. It certainly won't require the same resources as it did to build the system originally.

It's important also when you think about the time and cost of migration that you take a long view. What might be more time- and cost-efficient in the short term might have significantly higher costs in the long run because of inefficiency and lost productivity. For example, it may take longer to add new features in the future to a converted solution. Or, if your present system has inefficient processes, an initial time and cost outlay to rewrite your systems may result in a steady stream of cost savings in the future.

There's another way that time plays into your migration plan, and that's the timeliness of your need. If you have a solution that's on the verge of the old file size limit, or if you have been teetering along with an unstable, crash-prone solution, you probably want to migrate as quickly as possible. It's calendar time, not programming time that matters the most to you, and conversion is your best course of action. Even if you decide that your solution needs to be rewritten in the future, you may opt to deploy a converted solution as a stopgap until a more permanent solution can be achieved.

THE BOTTOM LINE

You might have noticed that nowhere in the preceding discussion did we ever recommend conversion or rewriting absolutely. We instead pointed out factors that might cause you to prefer one method to another. In the real world, of course, you must figure out how to weigh all these factors against each other. You might have a very clean, very complex system that won't need much future development. Or you might have a simple solution that's used by a hundred users, each with a separate password. There are no simple rules you can follow to determine which path is best, but to make an informed decision, it certainly helps to have all the issues on the table.

CONVERTING FILES

The actual conversion of files from previous versions of FileMaker is a very simple task. Even if you have decided to do a total rewrite of a solution, you will still end up performing a conversion so that you can salvage scripts and layouts. You'll probably also do another conversion to move the data to the new version. From here on out, though, we're going to assume that you've decided to migrate your solution via conversion, and will focus on the process and methods to accomplish this.

18

NOTE
> FileMaker Pro 7 can directly convert files from versions 3, 4.x, 5.x, and 6. If you have files created in FileMaker Pro 1 or 2.x, you need to convert them first to version 3 or higher before converting to 7.

It's quite likely—and even expected—that you will need to perform multiple conversions on a solution during the course of migration. Typically, the first conversion is a throwaway that you'll use for research and experimentation. We usually refer to this as the "alpha" conversion. We've found that each solution behaves a bit differently after conversion, and rather than theorizing and guessing what features will or won't convert well, just convert them and do some poking around. You may quickly discover you need to disable startup scripts that check for the presence of plug-ins, or that you can't open the solution because you don't remember the case of your passwords. (They're case sensitive in FileMaker Pro 7, but not in previous versions.) If necessary, make minor adjustments to the source files and make a new alpha conversion set. The goal at this stage is simply to have a set of FileMaker Pro 7 files that you can open and dissect. These files will never see the light of day, so experiment freely.

Later in this chapter, we'll discuss some pre-conversion tasks that can make the migration process go more smoothly. When you've completed these tasks and are ready to proceed, you'll convert your files once again, this time creating what we call the "beta" conversion set. These are the files that will eventually be deployed as your new solution. Some solutions require significant post-conversion testing and tweaking. It's important that you make frequent backups of your beta files during this process so that if you make mistakes, you can roll back to a stable version without having to re-convert the files.

NOTE

> The types of mistakes that can necessitate a rollback include things like deleting file references before you've re-specified any objects that use them, and removing tables or table occurrences from your files without accounting for the impact on scripts or layouts.

In cases where the testing and other post-conversion work takes days or weeks to perform, you are likely to need to do another conversion of your original system so that you can import fresh data before deploying the converted solution.

CAUTION

> Be sure to take the old files offline during this conversion and data migration to prevent users from making additional modifications.

For this final conversion, the only thing you care about is the raw data; the solution doesn't need to function beyond letting you open the files and show all records. You can skip converting the indexes for this conversion; they won't be necessary for the final transfer.

It's also possible merely to export data from your old system and import into your new one. There's no way to import directly from the old files into FileMaker Pro 7, though. The main drawback with exporting and importing is that you'll not be able to transfer any data in container fields. You will also lose text styling information that might have been applied to bits of text within individual fields. For these reasons, we prefer to do the final import from a freshly converted set of files.

CONVERTING SINGLE-FILE SOLUTIONS

There are a few ways to actually go about converting files. If you have a multi-file system, it's important that you convert all the files at the same time so that links between the files are properly preserved. The method for converting multi-file solutions is covered in the next section.

A single-file solution is one that has no links to other FileMaker databases, whether those links are relationships, external scripts, imports, or value lists. You can convert such files simply by launching FileMaker Pro 7, choosing File, Open, and selecting your old file. When you do so, you see a dialog similar to the one in Figure 18.2, asking whether you'd like to rename the old file.

Figure 18.2
When converting a single file, you'll have the option to rename the existing file. There's no need to do so.

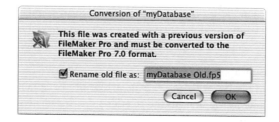

There's no particular need to rename the old file. During conversion, the old file is left unaltered and is still fully functional; a brand new, FileMaker Pro 7 file is created for you. You have the opportunity to name the converted file and specify a location for it as well.

TIP

> If your file contains a large amount of data, it may take considerable time to convert your file. For the alpha conversion, it's helpful to have all the data, but for the beta conversion, consider creating a clone of your file. This speeds up both your conversion and your post-conversion development work.

CONVERTING RELATIONAL SOLUTIONS

When you convert a multi-file relational solution, it's important that you convert all the files at once. If you don't, and instead use the method outlined in the previous section to convert each file individually, you are forced to wade through potentially numerous "File Not Found" messages as each file converts and opens. Also, if you don't specify the correct file name for the converted files (by removing the `Converted` suffix appended by default), you may have a hard time fixing your file references later on.

To convert a set of files all at once, simply select them all and drag them on top of the FileMaker Pro 7 application icon. You can achieve the same thing by choosing multiple files from the File, Open dialog. Hold down the (⌘) [Ctrl] key to do this.

You aren't prompted to rename your old files, nor to name your new ones. Instead, you are presented with the dialog shown in Figure 18.3, in which you're asked to select a directory in which to place the converted files. We recommend setting up a new directory for each set of converted files; if you simply place them in the same folder where your old files live, it gets a bit confusing, particularly if you're performing multiple conversions.

Figure 18.3
When converting multiple files, your new files are given the same names as the old ones. You aren't prompted for filenames the same way you are when converting single files.

As with single-file conversion, your old files are unaltered during conversion and can still be used. Nonetheless, it's certainly good practice to make sure you have backups of your old system in case of accidents such as deleting or renaming the wrong files.

For each file in your old solution, the conversion routine creates a new FileMaker Pro 7 file, named the same as the old file but with an .fp7 file extension. Each converted file contains a single table, named the same as the file. All the relationships are turned into external table occurrences on your Relationships Graph (with the exception of self-relationships, which are local table occurrences).

 If your databases don't open correctly immediately after conversion, see "Disabling Startup Scripts" in the Troubleshooting section at the end of this chapter.

Pre-Conversion Tasks

You can and should do a number of things before converting existing solutions to FileMaker Pro 7. Your pre-conversion tasks vary somewhat from solution to solution, but some categories of tasks are still common to most solutions.

Our comments here are aimed at people who are converting relational systems of some complexity. The purpose of doing any pre-conversion work at all is to make the post-conversion work go more smoothly; for single-file and simple relational solutions, you might not need to have rigorous conversion plans like this in place.

Also, by "conversion" here, we mean beta conversion rather than alpha conversion. In fact, many of the pre-conversion tasks that we discuss will cause you to want to make new alpha sets of the files. The simple difference between alpha and beta conversion files (as you'll recall from earlier in the chapter) is that alpha files are meant to be experimented with and thrown away, whereas beta files are turned into your new solution.

Prepare for Conversion

Converting a solution entails much more than the physical creation of new, upgraded files; you need to prepare both yourself and your environment for the conversion. The process goes faster and smoother if you spend a bit of time up front planning out the details. The specific preparation tasks you should do include the following:

- **Set up a test environment**—Install FileMaker Pro 7 on the machine that you plan to use to actually perform the conversion and do testing. If you are networking your solution, having FileMaker Server 7 installed on a non-production server is important during testing.

- **Acquire any necessary hardware and software**—You may need to upgrade machines and/or operating systems before you can deploy a FileMaker Pro 7 solution. Be sure that you get the ball rolling on this task early on in your conversion process because it can cause deployment delays. If you use plug-ins in your solution, check with their vendors to learn about any compatibility issues.

- **Learn FileMaker Pro 7**—We strongly recommend that you spend a fair amount of time learning FileMaker Pro 7 and perhaps even develop a few new solutions entirely with it prior to converting your old systems. The learning curve is considerable; if a conversion project is your first exposure to FileMaker Pro 7, it is certain to take you longer and be more difficult than if you had previous experience.

- **Read the conversion documentation**—In the Electronic Documentation folder within your FileMaker Pro 7 folder, you'll find a PDF called "FM 7 Converting Databases." It discusses many of the same issues raised in this chapter and also details all the exact behavior changes that can be expected in FileMaker Pro 7. It's a great resource during conversion, and certainly should be read before you get too far into the process. Look for migration whitepapers on FileMaker's Web site (`www.filemaker.com`) as well.

DOCUMENT YOUR SOLUTION

The more familiar you are with a solution, the better your conversion will go. Even if you're the sole creator of a system, having up-to-date documentation comes in handy during the conversion process. We recommend having at least the following items:

- **An ER diagram**—If you've never taken the time to formally create an ER diagram of your system, now's the time. For a refresher on creating ER diagrams, please see Chapter 5, "Relational Database Design."

- **Printouts of field definitions, scripts, and layouts**—You may balk at the thought of actually printing out and organizing all these documents, and some people may indeed find that creating PDFs rather than printing works well for them. Many subtle changes take place during conversion, and it's very helpful when looking at a script or calculation formula to be able to compare it with the original. One nice thing about hard copies, of course, is that you can annotate them as you go. You may, for instance, check off buttons on screen shots of layouts as you test them, noting whether everything worked as planned or needs post-conversion attention. The printouts become both your testing plan and your post-conversion audit trail.

- **An access privilege matrix**—This is simply an overview of the privilege settings in your current files. Create it in a database, spreadsheet, or text document—it really doesn't matter.

If you have FileMaker Developer, you may want to create a Database Design Report of your old solution as part of your documentation process. Third-party tools such as Brushfire (from Chaparral Software) and Analyzer (from Waves in Motion) also are excellent documentation tools and are both highly recommended.

→ For more information on third-party documentation tools, **see** Appendix D, "Documenting FileMaker Pro Systems," **p. 1023**.

18

FIX FILE REFERENCES

Whenever you link one FileMaker Pro file with another, FileMaker uses a *file reference* stored in File A to locate File B. The operations that may require file references include defining relationships, performing external scripts, creating value lists based on the contents of fields in another file, performing an Open script step, and scripting an import from another file.

 File references are visible and editable in FileMaker Pro 7 for the first time. In previous versions, they existed, but were hidden "under the hood." When you convert files created in earlier versions, all the old file references are suddenly visible. You may be in for a bit of shock, in fact, when you examine file references in a converted solution and discover a hornet's nest you never knew existed.

ABSOLUTE PATHS

To understand how that hornet's nest was created and why it can be difficult to untangle, you must understand how FileMaker managed file references in previous versions of the product. Prior to FileMaker Pro 5.5, all file references were stored as *absolute* paths: When you define a link from File A to File B, FileMaker remembers the full path to File B. On Mac OS X, that might look like /Macintosh HD/Documents/myDatabases/File B. On Windows, the full path could be something like C:/myDatabases/File B. If the link were to a hosted file, the link might include the IP address of the hosted file, as in 192.168.100.87/File B. If the hosted file were on the same subnet as the person defining the link, then the IP address wouldn't be stored; an asterisk would appear in the file reference instead.

The main problem with absolute references is that they tend to cause problems when you move files from one machine to another or rename files or folders. In those cases, FileMaker would pop up a message to the user saying, in effect, "I can't find File B...where is it?" You would re-establish the reference by pointing to the moved or renamed file. But rather than replace the previous reference, FileMaker would store the new path as an additional search path for the given link. If you had a file that had been developed over the course of many years and/or on many different machines, you may have had dozens of absolute paths stored in your files. If you ever had problems in previous versions where FileMaker would seemingly irrationally open the wrong copy of a given file, it was likely because there was an obsolete file reference higher up in the search order.

Another problem with file references in previous versions of FileMaker is that different linking operations might produce entirely new references. For instance, say you had created a relationship from File A to File B while the files were both open on your local computer. A file reference containing the path to File B would be stored. Then you moved the files to a server where they were hosted with FileMaker Server, and from your desktop you created a script in File A that called a subscript in File B. An entirely new file reference was created for the external script call.

RELATIVE PATHS

FileMaker Pro 5.5 introduced the option to store only a *relative* path when creating links between files. This went a long way to solve the problems caused by renaming or moving files. Rather than locate File B with a full path reference, a relative reference simply indicates the path to get to File B *from* File A. For example, the relative path may be `../File B`, which would indicate that FileMaker should look for File B in File A's parent directory.

CONVERSION OF FILE REFERENCES

So what happens to all of these obsolete and redundant file references during conversion? The conversion routine does try to do some consolidating and eliminating of file references that are no longer needed, but in most cases, you'll still end up with a bit of a mess. As an example, Figure 18.4 shows the file references from a converted solution. The names of converted file references are simply set to the filename plus a counter if there are multiple references to a given file. Notice that there are no less than five separate references to the Mainmenu file. The fact that there isn't a "Mainmenu 3" or "Mainmenu 4" makes it clear that in fact the conversion routine did identify those as unneeded. The conversion log also explicitly identifies any file references that are removed during conversion.

Figure 18.4
In a solution that's been around for a few years, it's likely that you have a lot of redundant and obsolete file references.

There are several potential problems that you may experience using a converted solution with file reference problems. The first is speed: FileMaker looks for files in the locations specified by the file references, in the order in which they appear. A complex solution with obsolete file references may take many times longer to open than one with "clean" file references.

After conversion, you can, of course, manually change all the obsolete paths to updated, relative paths. In a complex solution, this may require manually editing hundreds of references. After you're finished, you'll have solved the problem of obsolete references, but not that of redundant references.

The problem with redundant references is maintenance. If you have five file references that all point to the same file, every time you set up a link to a file, you have to choose which of those five references to use. If you ever need to update the reference, you need to update it in five places. That may be an acceptable short-term solution, but eventually, you'll want to eliminate the redundant file references.

Simply deleting redundant file references can have potentially disastrous consequences. Every link that uses that reference, be it an external table occurrence, a value list, or an external script call, will be broken and will need to be repaired manually. The proper way to remove redundant file references is as follows:

1. Pick one of the set that is to survive the consolidation.

2. Rename all the other file references in the set so that they include an easily identifiable text phrase. "DELETE ME" works well.

3. Run a DDR report using FileMaker Developer 7.

4. Open the DDR report in a text editor or word processor and search for your text phrase to find all the objects that use a redundant file reference.

5. In your converted files, manually change the file reference used by these objects to the canonical reference for that set.

6. Run a new DDR report to make sure you haven't missed any references.

7. Delete the file references that are no longer needed.

Be sure to make a backup of your system before you start playing with file references; a small mistake such as deleting the wrong one can have far-reaching consequences.

METADATAMAGIC TO THE RESCUE

Cleaning up file references in a converted solution can be a very time-consuming and frustrating process. Thankfully, there's a tool called MetadataMagic, distributed by New Millennium Communications (www.nmci.com), which enables you to clean up file references in your system prior to conversion. The File Reference Fixer, one of the tools of MetadataMagic, provides several options for modifying file references. If you use the Auto-Fix function, only the most recently created relative path to a file is retained, and all internal links are updated to use that reference. Obsolete file references are then removed from the files.

In a complex solution, you may be better off using the Consolidate and/or Set Relative-Only functions. For instance, if you have files that span multiple FileMaker Servers or are located in multiple folders, the Consolidate function simply changes multiple and/or redundant references to a single file references.

If you clean up file references in your old solution, the conversion process takes less time and you're left without a severe post-conversion headache. Figure 18.5 shows the post-conversion file references of the same file depicted in Figure 18.4, but this time the file references were cleaned up before conversion with MetadataMagic.

Figure 18.5
If you run File Reference Fixer before conversion, the file references in your new files are much easier to troubleshoot and maintain.

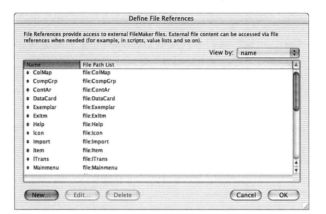

It's easy to see the improvement here. All the file references are now simple relative paths, equally well suited for deployment as a single-user solution or by FileMaker Server. Before using File Reference Fixer, be sure to read the documentation and practice on a set of test files.

Do Some Housekeeping

In addition to file references, other potential post-conversion problems can be avoided if you do a bit of pre-conversion work. You can actually identify much pre-conversion work by examining the alpha conversion files. You may, for instance, discover you have objects with illegal names, which are placed in between curly brackets during conversion. These can be changed in the original system so that by the time you're ready to do your beta conversion, they're no longer an issue. By doing as much work as possible in the pre-beta conversion stage, you'll reduce the amount of time and work required to get your converted files ready for production.

If there are scripts, layouts, relationships, passwords, value lists, or fields that you know are no longer used or needed, try to eliminate these before conversion. If there has been case inconsistency in the entry of passwords in your current system, take the time to standardize them. These efforts will be rewarded by shorter conversion time and less to test after conversion. Any other housekeeping can only be beneficial, including organizing scripts, editing object names, and archiving old data.

18

POST-CONVERSION TASKS

As discussed in the previous sections, you can avoid many potential post-conversion problems by doing some pre-conversion work on your old system. However, a number of tasks can only be done post-conversion.

> **NOTE**
>
> The actual tasks vary from system to system; many of the tasks listed here may not be applicable to your particular solution.

You should begin a list of post-conversion tasks during your exploration of the alpha files. You'll spot problems and potential areas of improvement. Anything that can't easily be fixed through pre-conversion work should go on your post-conversion task list. Keep in mind that you'll end up destroying the alpha files, so don't spend too much time or effort fixing problems. Some fixes are necessary just so you can continue your exploration; you may opt to do other fixes just so you can test out the results.

To know what tasks you'll need to do after conversion, you need to understand what actually happens to your files during conversion. The following sections look at five different aspects of your files: security, relationships, scripts, fields, and data. For each, we discuss what happens during conversion and what potential post-conversion tasks you need to perform.

> **TIP**
>
> One vital post-conversion task that goes almost without saying is testing. Before deploying a converted solution, it's vital that you do sufficient testing to identify any problems.

 If your databases don't open correctly immediately after conversion, see "Disabling Startup Scripts" in the Troubleshooting section at the end of this chapter.

SECURITY

Depending on whether and how passwords and groups were set up in your solution, you may have some post-conversion work to do involving security. During conversion, passwords in your previous system are turned into accounts, and groups are turned into privilege sets. Accounts in FileMaker Pro 7, of course, have both an account name and a password. For each account in a converted system, the account name and password will both be the same as the old password. So, a password of "test123" in your old system turns into an account named "test123" with a password of "test123."

Post-conversion, you should change all the account names to something other than their default conversion value. Account names are visible on screen during login, so if you don't do this it will be very easy for people to discover their co-workers' passwords. Be sure you distribute the new account information prior to deployment.

The conversion of groups into privilege sets is more complex than the conversion of passwords into accounts. The number of privilege sets may be more or less than the number of groups in the old system. The following list explains the rules for determining how groups relate to privilege sets:

- If there are multiple groups with identical settings, only the first group is converted and the others are discarded.

- If there are passwords not assigned to any groups, new privilege sets are created based on the properties of the passwords. The first one is named "Privilege Set," the second "Privilege Set 2," and so on. Any passwords with the same properties are assigned to the same privilege set.

- Any groups not assigned to any passwords (other than master passwords) are not converted into privilege sets.

- If a password is assigned to multiple groups that have different access privileges, a new privilege set is created that has the privileges of both groups. The name of the privilege set is a combination of the names of the groups used for its formation. For instance, if a password "foo" was associated with groups "bar" and "baz," each of which had different access rights, the new account named "foo" would be associated with a privilege set named "bar/baz."

- Master passwords are associated with the "[Full Access]" privilege set.

TIP

> The `Status(CurrentGroups)` function is turned into `Get (PrivilegeSetName)` during conversion. However, if the function tests for the presence of literal text strings, you may need to change the strings to the new privilege set names; these aren't modified at all during conversion. For instance, if you used `PatternCount (Status (CurrentGroups), ("masterGroup"))` in a script or calculation formula, after conversion you need to manually edit this to be `Get (PrivilegeSetName) = "[Full Access]"`. Because accounts can be associated with only one privilege set (whereas passwords can be associated with multiple groups), the `PatternCount` function is no longer needed.

DEFAULT PASSWORDS

If you specified a default password in the document preferences in your old file, the converted solution has a default account specified in the File Options. As in previous versions of FileMaker Pro, you can force the account/password dialog to be shown by holding down the (Option) [Shift] key as the file opens.

(no password)

Previous versions of FileMaker allowed you to specify a blank password as a valid way of gaining access to a file. As shown in Figure 18.6, this is represented in the password list as (no password). During conversion, a file with a blank password has the Guest account activated. It is associated with whatever privilege set is appropriate. When the Guest account is active, in the login dialog, users have the option of selecting the Guest Account radio button. It is grayed out if that account isn't active.

Figure 18.6
In previous versions of FileMaker Pro, you could specify no password as a valid password.

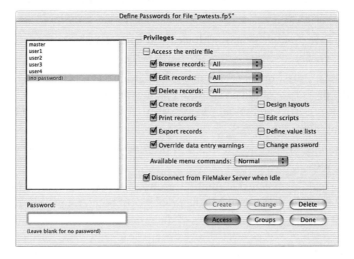

FILES WITH NO PASSWORD

If you convert a file that has absolutely no passwords in it, the converted file has an account named Admin with a blank password. It is assigned the [Full Access] privilege set, and is set as the default login under File, File Options. This is shown in Figure 18.7. A guest account is created as well, but it is inactive.

Figure 18.7
In the File Options dialog, you can specify an account to use as a default login.

EXTENDED PRIVILEGES

If a file is set to be Multi-User or Multi-User (Hidden), all the privilege sets will have the fmapp extended privilege enabled when it is converted to FileMaker Pro 7. This is required for accounts to be able to open files hosted by FileMaker Server or shared peer-to-peer. You can certainly enable or disable this extended privilege after conversion as fits your deployment needs.

RELATIONSHIPS

During conversion, relationships are turned into table occurrences. For instance, if you have a relationship from File A to File B called "File B by someKey," when you convert these files, the Relationships Graph for File A will have an external table occurrence called "File B by someKey." The number of table occurrences in the converted file will be equal to the number of relationships in the old file. Settings from the relationship, such as cascading delete and the ability to add records through the relationship, will be retained in the converted solution.

As illustrated previously in Figure 18.1, the Relationships Graph in a converted solution is always in a hub-and-spoke configuration. The hub is a table occurrence associated with the file's base table; it is named the same as the table (and the file itself). All the other table occurrences are connected to the hub as spokes are connected to a wheel. All the layouts in the file are associated with the hub table occurrence, which means that it is always the context for all scripts, calculations, imports, and exports.

NOTE

> Remember that each file in a relational solution is turned into a file in FileMaker Pro 7 during conversion. Each has its own hub-and-spoke Relationships Graph.

If you plan on doing any future development in your converted system, you'll likely want to spend some time organizing the Relationships Graphs. This may simply mean repositioning and resizing table occurrences to make particular relationships easier to locate. You might also consider using color as a means of organizing the graphs. Finally, depending on what sort of conventions you used to name your relationships, you may want to change the names of the table occurrences to better reflect their purposes.

Down the road, consider making some more significant changes to the converted Relationships Graph. Many of the relationships from previous versions of FileMaker either could be implemented differently or are not required at all in FileMaker Pro 7. For instance, many developers used relationships based on constants as a means for setting and retrieving global field values from other files. In FileMaker Pro 7, fields with global storage can be accessed from any table occurrence, even ones disconnected from the current context. Likewise, relationships built with multi-line and/or concatenated keys could be built in FileMaker Pro 7 with join types other than equi-joins and/or multiple match criteria. These aren't changes you need to make prior to deployment, but they do make the converted solution easier to maintain and extend in the long run.

SCRIPTS

Many script steps in FileMaker Pro 7 have slightly different parameters or behavior than in previous versions, and as such, you need to be vigilant in regard to a few potential post-conversion issues. The conversion routine actually adds steps to your scripts in some cases as a way to compensate for functional changes.

Some of the changes, and the issues that arise from them, include the following:

- The Go To Layout script step no longer has an option to Refresh Window. If you had checked this option, a Refresh Window script step is inserted during a conversion, directly after the Go To Layout step.

- The Refresh Window script step no longer has an option to Bring to Front. A Select Window [Current Window] step is added to scripts that had this option specified. This can cause some extra "screen flashing" in some instances, so you may need to remove Select Window steps to achieve the behavior you want.

- The Perform Script step no longer has the option not to perform sub-scripts. This was a feature that was infrequently used, so chances are that you won't miss it. In FileMaker Pro 7, sub-scripts are always run. The conversion routine does nothing to account for this, nor does anything in the conversion log alert you of any Perform Script steps where the sub-scripts button was unchecked. If this was a feature you relied on in your solution, you may need to rework some of your scripts during post-conversion testing.

- In previous versions of FileMaker, when an external script was called as the last step of a script, the external file's window would become active, having the effect of "leaving" the user in the other file. The same holds true of Go to Related Record steps. That's no longer the case in FileMaker Pro 7. To accommodate this change, the conversion routine inserts a Select Window step following certain Perform Script and Go to Related Records steps. If a script ends with a call to an external subscript or with a Go to Related Records step, the conversion routine adds a Select Window [Name: "NameOfOtherFile"]. When these steps are not found at the end of a script, a Select Window [CurrentWindow] is added. The selection of another file's window, however, can be a bit fragile because the name of the window is hard-coded as the filename itself. If no window by that name exists, control isn't passed properly to the external file. You may need to edit the Select Window steps—or perhaps even delete some of them—for your script to function as it did previously.

- There is no longer a Show Message script step in FileMaker Pro 7. During conversion, it is changed into a Show Custom Dialog step. The default title of the dialog is simply "Message," and the message itself is the text of your old script. You need to make no post-conversion changes to these; simply be aware of the change that occurs.

- The settings stored on the Windows operating system for Print and Print Setup script steps may not convert properly. Be sure to test, and if necessary re-specify, the print settings after conversion. It may help to go back to your previous solution and take screen shots of the settings stored for particular scripts so that you can easily restore them post-conversion.

- The `Open File` script step in FileMaker Pro 7 always activates the file being opened. In previous versions, the `Open` script step would do this only if it were the last step in the script. Any additional steps would cause the calling file to remain active. For example, say you have a script in File A that has two steps: `Open ["File B"]` and `Exit Record/Requests`. When performed in a previous version of FileMaker Pro, File A would remain the active file throughout the script. To retain this behavior in FileMaker Pro 7, you need to add a `Select Window [Current Window]` after the `Open File` script step.

- FileMaker Pro 7 requires much greater attention to the opening and committing (saving) of records than previous versions did. Consequently, some of your scripts may require some post-conversion tweaking so they behave as desired. For instance, if a script ends with a step that modifies a record, such as a `Set Field`, the record isn't committed when the script ends. This may cause users not to see "refreshed" data until they manually commit the record. If the script in question was called as a subscript, there may be other unintended behaviors because the edited record would still be locked. The fix for this is to add a `Commit Record/Request` step at the end of any script that modifies data.

NOTE

> Because `Exit Record/Request` converts into `Commit Record/Request`, you can also fix many of these problems as pre-conversion tasks.

18

- In previous versions of FileMaker Pro, the `Go to Field` step would generate an error if the record was locked, so it was common to use this step as a test in scripts that needed to be able to modify records. In FileMaker Pro 7, simply entering a field no longer attempts to place a lock on a record, so it doesn't generate errors that you can rely on. You should therefore find and change any `Go to Field` step that serves this need into an `Open Record/Request` step (which does explicitly try to lock the record).

- FileMaker Pro 7 handles summary field sorting differently than previous versions of FileMaker Pro did. Instead of being able to specify only a single summary field as one of your sort criteria, in FileMaker Pro 7 you can re-sort any number of sort criteria based on summary fields. During conversion, scripts that store sorts that include summary fields are altered so that the summary field is attached to the last non-summary field in the sort criteria. For instance, say you have a summary report of customers and invoices where you sort by `CustomerName`, then by `InvoiceDate`, and finally by `TotalInvoiced` (a summary field). Your report would not list customers alphabetically, but rather from lowest to highest, based on the total you had invoiced. After conversion, your script's sort would have two criteria: `CustomerName` and `InvoiceDate`. The latter would be reordered by `TotalInvoiced`. You would need to manually adjust the sort criteria so that the `TotalInvoiced` summary was applied to the `CustomerName` field rather than `InvoiceDate` for your report to display the way it did previously.

- In previous versions of FileMaker Pro, after sorting a set of records, the active record was always the first one in the sorted set. In FileMaker Pro 7, the active record is whatever it was prior to sorting. Because this could have adverse impact on scripts that expect to be on the first record after a sort, a `Go To Record/Request/Page[First]` step is automatically added after every `Sort` script step during conversion.

- If you've specified scripts to execute when a file opens or closes, these preferences are retained in the converted file. Be aware, however, that they may be triggered at slightly different times in FileMaker Pro 7. Startup scripts execute the first time that a window for a particular file becomes visible. For instance, if File A has relationships to File B, when File A is opened, File B appears in the list of hidden files in parentheses, meaning that there are no windows for that file, hidden or active. If you were to select that file from the list, the startup script for that file would run. Shutdown scripts run when the last window for a given file is closed. The `Close File` script step closes any windows for that particular file, thereby triggering the shutdown script. In both of these cases, however, if files that have relationships to the file you just closed are still open, the file name still appears in the list of hidden windows in parentheses. Thus, a file is not truly closed until all files that reference it are closed as well.

FIELDS AND FORMULAS

There are some subtle (and some not so subtle) differences in FileMaker Pro 7 regarding fields and formulas. As with scripts, you'll find that the conversion routine does a good job at heading off many problems by modifying your code a bit. Still, a few things can go awry in a converted solution that you'll need to deal with during post-conversion testing.

- FileMaker Pro 7 has new reserved words that didn't have the same significance in previous versions. For instance, "Bold" and "Italic" are potential parameters in the new `TextStyleAdd` and `TextStyleRemove` functions; you would be warned in FileMaker Pro 7 that these are illegal file names. If you used any reserved words or illegal names in your old system, anytime they were used in calculation formulas they are enclosed, upon conversion, with the symbols `${ }` to avoid confusion with the reserved words. A field named "Bold" in your previous solution would appear as `${Bold}` in formulas in FileMaker Pro 7. The conversion log also lists this as a "Poor field name."

- FileMaker Pro 7 uses a new shortcut evaluation method to speed up the processing of calculation formulas. This can cause problems in a converted system if you were relying on every portion of a formula being evaluated. As an example, say you have the formula `If (Length(myField) > 10 and Left (myField, 1) = "X", 1, 2)`. When FileMaker evaluates the first part of the test, `Length(myField) > 10`, if that does not return True, then it doesn't bother evaluating the other half of the test. It immediately knows that the False result must be returned. In previous versions of FileMaker, external function calls to plug-ins were often placed in innocuous places in functions; it's possible they may not be invoked after conversion to FileMaker Pro 7. For instance, in the formula `If ( 1 or External ("myPlugin", "someParameter"), 1, 2)`, the plug-in would never be invoked because the first part of the test is sufficient to establish which value should be returned.

- The Today function is no longer supported in FileMaker Pro 7. During conversion, references to Today in scripts and validation checks are converted into Get (CurrentDate). If it's used in stored calculation fields, a new date field called Today is added to your database; it is set to auto-enter the creation date. Additionally, a new script called Update Today Field is added to the file; it's shown in Figure 18.8. This script is set as the file's startup script, or, if it already has a startup script, that script is modified so that it calls the Update Today Field script as its first step.

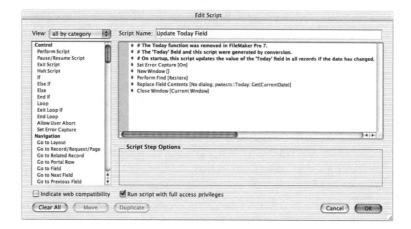

Figure 18.8
The conversion routine automatically adds this script to your file if you have fields that use the Today function.

- The results returned by DatabaseNames and Status(CurrentFileName) included file extensions in previous versions of FileMaker Pro. In FileMaker Pro 7, DatabaseNames and Get (FileName) do not return file extensions. You may need to edit scripts and fields that presume the presence of a file extension. For instance, you might check to see whether a file "foo.fp5" is open by using the formula PatternCount (DatabaseNames, "foo.fp5"). This formula always returns 0 in FileMaker Pro 7. Be aware also that no existing data is affected during conversion. If you have a field that auto-enters the results of Status (CurrentFileName) into the field (or even a stored calculation with the same formula), then after conversion all your data will still contain a file extension, but any new data you create won't. This sort of inconsistency should be avoided; it may have adverse consequences down the road.

- The indexing rules have changed slightly in FileMaker Pro 7. For instance, non-alphanumeric characters weren't indexed in previous versions but are in FileMaker Pro 7. One of the consequences of the new indexing rules is that hyphens are considered word breaks for the first time. For instance, WordCount ("testA-testB") returns "2" in FileMaker Pro 7 but only "1" in previous versions. Some text parsing routines may need to be changed to account for this.

- Alphabetic characters, spaces, colons, and plus signs are not acceptable separators in date fields in FileMaker Pro 7. If your previous files use any of these as separators, your converted dates will be invalid. You can test for invalid dates after conversion by doing a find for ? in date fields. You can clean up invalid dates using a calculated Replace that uses the Substitute function.

- Previous versions of FileMaker interpret text strings placed in a number field one of three ways. If the text string begins with the letters "Y" or "T" (representing "Yes" and "True"), it is considered to have a value of 1. Text strings beginning with an "N" or "F" (representing "No" and "False") are considered to have a value of 0. With any other starting character, the value is considered blank. In FileMaker Pro 7, all text strings are regarded as having no numeric value. Frequently, developers captured Yes/No radio button responses in number fields, knowing they could perform math as if these were 1 and 0. In a converted solution, any formula that relies on this behavior returns incorrect values. You can either edit these formulas so they explicitly regard "Y" and "T" as 1 and "N" and "F" as 0, or you can perform a Find/Replace action to modify your legacy data.

- With the exception noted in the previous bullet, text placed in number fields was ignored by previous versions of FileMaker Pro. If, for instance, a number field called myNum contained a value of "23 skidoo", then Length (myNum) would return 2. In FileMaker Pro 7, text functions recognize text characters found in number fields, so this function would return 9. To correct for this, all number fields used as parameters in text functions are wrapped with a GetAsNumber function, which strips out any non-numeric characters. Don't be surprised if you see GetAsNumber sprinkled throughout your field definitions after conversion. It may not be needed, but it's a case of better safe than sorry.

- The contents of container fields are preserved during conversion, but depending on what platform you do the conversion, you may have some post-conversion work before they can be displayed properly cross-platform. In previous versions of FileMaker Pro, when the Store Compatible Graphics option was selected in a file's document preferences, both Windows Metafile and PICT images were stored in a single container field. The Windows Metafile data is not immediately accessible if you use a Mac for the conversion. You can restore it by opening the files on a PC and viewing each record with a container field. If, on the other hand, you use a PC for the conversion, be sure that QuickTime is installed or else the PICT data is not preserved.

TIP

> If you think you may have issues with container fields, be sure that you test your alpha conversion files on both platforms. If it's convenient, perform the final conversion on a PC with QuickTime to avoid this issue altogether.

- The Mod function in FileMaker Pro 7 handles negative numbers differently than previous versions did. For example, in previous versions, Mod (-10, 3) would return -1, but it returns 2 in FileMaker Pro 7.

TROUBLESHOOTING

DISABLING STARTUP SCRIPTS

I've converted a solution, but it won't open properly.

Because of the changes that take place during conversion, there are many reasons your files may not open properly after conversion. The typical cause for this is a startup script that attempts to validate for conditions that no longer are true. For instance, a startup script may check that a certain plug-in is available. If you haven't installed the plug-in in FileMaker Pro 7, or if the interface to it has changed, your script might not be able to get by the validation check.

Another typical problem in startup scripts is checking to see that some set of related files is open. The DatabaseNames function used to return file extensions of open files, but doesn't do this in FileMaker Pro 7. Validating that "foo.fp5" is open, for instance, may cause a startup script to deny entry into the system.

If you experience problems opening a converted solution, try disabling the startup scripts in the pre-converted files and try again.

REPOINTING TABLE OCCURRENCE REFERENCES

After conversion, I've attempted to consolidate tables from multiple files into a single file, but the relationships, scripts, and portals all get pointed to the wrong fields when I repoint the table occurrence references.

One of the most difficult post-conversion tasks you can attempt is to consolidate tables from multiple files into a single file. Typically, you would begin by creating a second table in one of your files, with fields named the same as those in one of your other files. On the Relationships Graph, when you repoint table occurrences from the external table to the new internal table, the match fields involved in the relationship may change, even if you've taken great care to keep all the field names exactly the same.

This happens because the match fields don't resolve by name, but rather by field ID. Therefore, if you create the fields in a different order, or have ever deleted fields, thereby leaving "holes" in your field IDs, the relationships won't match up right. This also affects portals and scripts that reference fields through the changed table occurrences.

If you ever need to repoint a table occurrence from one base table to another, be aware that you may have these problems. In some solutions, it may be simple to respecify all the affected objects manually. In more complex solutions, you need to make sure that the field IDs in the two tables match correctly. The best way to do this is to use a tool called FMrobot, from New Millennium Communications (www.nmci.com). FMrobot automates the process of creating tables and fields. Other third-party tools may also become available to help with the issue of consolidation.

After consolidating tables into a single file, be aware that you still need to move all your layouts, scripts, value lists, privilege settings, and data into the new file. None of these is a trivial activity. If consolidation of tables into a single file is one of the goals you hope to achieve from migrating to FileMaker Pro 7, you may be better off rewriting your system.

FILEMAKER EXTRA: CONVERTING WEB-ENABLED DATABASES

If your existing solutions are Web-enabled, then you have a few additional concerns when migrating to FileMaker Pro 7. The Web capabilities of FileMaker Pro 7 are considerably different from previous versions; your migration plan depends mainly on the technology you used to Web-enable your solution.

INSTANT WEB PUBLISHING

No Instant Web Publishing (IWP) configuration options are retained during conversion of a solution to FileMaker Pro 7. IWP is so greatly improved in FileMaker Pro 7 that the previous configuration options are irrelevant and unnecessary. Where you were limited to a handful of layouts and themes before, IWP now has a status area that is very similar to that in FileMaker Pro itself, and it allows a user to potentially access any layout in a file. More than 70 script steps are IWP compatible (compared to about a dozen before), making IWP a very powerful and flexible Web technology. Even though no IWP settings are preserved during conversion, if you used IWP in your previous solution, you'll be up and running again within a matter of minutes.

Security is handled just as it is for FileMaker users—via accounts and privilege sets—so you can easily create special accounts for Web users and restrict them to Web-friendly layouts.

→ **See** Chapter 21, "Instant Web Publishing," **p. 605**, for more information on how to use IWP to Web-enable a database.

CUSTOM WEB PUBLISHING

The other methods for Web-enabling FileMaker solutions are often grouped under the banner of "Custom Web Publishing" (CWP). However, your migration path depends on what flavor of CWP you use.

CDML

CDML (Claris Dynamic Markup Language) is no longer supported in FileMaker Pro 7. FileMaker has instead focused its CWP efforts on XML/XSLT. You can, thankfully, convert your CDML format files to XSLT stylesheets by using the CDML to XSLT Conversion Tool, which comes with FileMaker Server 7 Advanced.

We strongly suggest that you use the conversion tool only after you have gained some proficiency working with XML and XSLT stylesheets. Even if the converted pages work flawlessly, without some knowledge of how they work, you'll be hard pressed to fix problems or extend the solution.

XML/XSLT

If you previously used the XML output from FileMaker as part of a custom Web publishing solution, your previous code should require only minor programming changes to work with

FileMaker Pro 7. The biggest change you'll face will likely be understanding and setting up the new Web publishing components. There is, of course, no longer a FileMaker Unlimited or a Web Companion. All custom Web publishing ties directly into FileMaker Server 7 Advanced via the Web Publishing Engine.

There are also some changes to the query syntax and to the XML grammars that FileMaker can return; you can read about these in detail in Chapter 23, "Custom Web Publishing." You need to learn about the changes and make modifications to your code as necessary.

PHP

PHP has become a popular tool for Web-enabling FileMaker Pro databases. Most people using PHP as part of their FileMaker Web publishing strategy make use of the FX.php class, developed and distributed for free by Chris Hansen (www.iviking.org). When PHP exchanges data with FileMaker, it does so via XML, but the FX class makes all of this transparent to the developer.

Because of the changes to the query syntax and XML grammars, you need to swap in an updated copy of FX.php for use with your converted files. If you rename files, layouts, or fields, you may have a bit of programming to do, but the changes should be minimal.

18

DATA INTEGRATION AND PUBLISHING

## CHAPTER 19

IMPORTING DATA INTO FILEMAKER PRO

In this chapter

WORKING WITH EXTERNAL DATA

FileMaker Pro can work with data from a variety of other sources. It's possible to bring data directly into FileMaker from a number of different flat-file formats, as well as from remote databases and XML-based data sources. In many cases, you can open data files from other applications simply by dropping them onto the FileMaker Pro application as though they were native FileMaker files. FileMaker can also import data that resides on other computers (such as data from a remote database or a Web-based XML data source), or even from devices such as a digital camera.

→ Additional information bearing on the topic of FileMaker data exchange can be found in Chapter 20, "Getting Data Out of FileMaker," **p. 563**, and Chapter 22, "FileMaker and Web Services," **p. 639**.

FLAT-FILE DATA SOURCES

Flat file is a generic term that refers to a file containing data in row-and-column format. If you think of a spreadsheet that holds data about personal contacts, the spreadsheet will have some number of columns, for attributes such as first name, last name, address, and so forth, and some number of rows, each one representing a single contact.

The formats of flat files can vary. Some might separate one column from the next by tabs, and one row from the next by carriage returns (a tab-delimited file). Another might use commas to separate column values. Some might include a first row that gives a name to each column, whereas others might not. Some might be in a plain text format that you could read with any text editor, whereas others might be in specialized file formats (such as FileMaker Pro or Microsoft Excel). In general, though, all flat-file data sources represent some variation on the idea of row-and-column data.

CHOOSING THE TARGET TABLE

As you can tell from the previous description, a flat data file maps well onto the concept of a database table. And indeed, in FileMaker Pro, we do import data into only one table at a time. FileMaker chooses this target table for you automatically, based on the prevailing table context.

Current Table Context
The current table context is determined by the active layout. You can examine the table context for a given layout by choosing View, Layout Mode, then choosing Layouts, Layout Setup and inspecting the Show Records From menu. Be sure to switch back to Browse mode before trying to import records, though.

→ For a full discussion of table context, **see** "Understanding Table Context," **p. 161**.

INITIATING THE IMPORT

We give the example of importing tab-separated data because it's a good example of a typical text-based flat-file format. Many of the other text-based formats vary from tab-separated text only in small details. We'll note those differences further on.

Like other types of data, a tab-separated data file can be imported in one of three ways:

- Choose File, Import Records, then navigate to the file and select it.
- Choose File, Open, then navigate to the file and select it.
- Drag and drop the file directly onto the FileMaker Pro application.

Importing and opening non-FileMaker files are very similar actions in FileMaker Pro. The main difference is that the "open" action creates a new FileMaker file, whereas the "import" action is used to bring more data into an existing file. Importing can also be used to bring in images from a digital camera, or data from multiple files in a folder—neither of these is possible if you use either variation of the Open command.

THE IMPORT FIELD MAPPING DIALOG

When you're importing data, after you've chosen your source file you'll be presented with the Import Field Mapping dialog box, shown in Figure 19.1. This dialog lets you choose how the records in your source file will be imported, and in what order.

Figure 19.1
FileMaker's Import Field Mapping dialog. All importing processes pass through this dialog at some point.

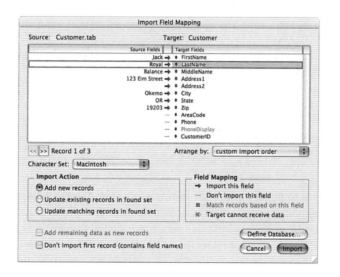

The Field Mapping dialog lists two file names at the top, called Source and Target. Source is the file from which you're importing, and Target refers to the current table in the current file—in other words, the one that's receiving the imported data.

CHOOSING AN IMPORT ACTION

One of the things you need to choose in the Import Field Mapping dialog is called the Import Action. It's visible in the lower left of the dialog box. This choice tells FileMaker whether to try to *add* new records in the target table (one record per row of source data), or whether to try to *update* the existing FileMaker records with the source data. Updating on import is a topic in its own right, which we deal with later in this chapter. For now, we'll cover what happens when we want to create new FileMaker records based on the source data.

ALIGNING SOURCE AND TARGET FIELDS

You also need to decide which fields in the target are to receive data, and from which source columns they'll receive data. Figure 19.2 shows the field structure for a FileMaker table designed to hold customer information. It consists mostly of text fields, with the exception of the PhoneDisplay field, which is meant to create a formatted display from the AreaCode and Phone fields.

Figure 19.2
The field structure for a basic table of customer information.

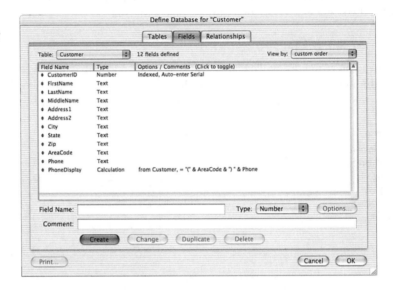

Assume you want to import some data into this customer table. The source file is a tab-separated file containing first name, middle name, last name, address1, address2, city, state, and zip. (Notice the order is a little different from the field order on the FileMaker side). To do this, you'd choose File, Import Records, File. From the Show menu choose Tab-Separated Text, then navigate to your file and select it. The result is shown in Figure 19.3.

If we look at the way the source fields line up with the target fields, something isn't right. We have a record for someone named Jack Royal Balance. But this record will be imported into the system as Jack Balance Royal if nothing is changed in the import order. In the FileMaker creation order, middle name comes after last name, but in the source file, it comes before. It's not possible to manipulate the ordering of the fields on the left (the source fields), but you can use the black "up-down" arrows next to each target field to change the target ordering manually. In this case you'd just drag the MiddleName field up one line to make it change places with LastName.

Figure 19.3
Another look at the Import Field Mapping dialog. Note that the source and target fields don't quite line up correctly. Jack R. Balance is about to enter the system as Jack B. Royal.

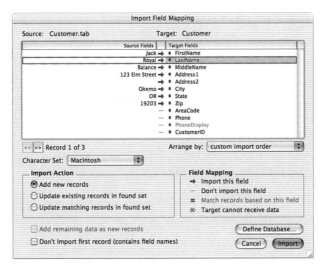

CAUTION

When you change the target field ordering by dragging a field manually, the field you drag *changes places* with the field you drop it on. Often you might want to drop the field you're moving "between" two others in the import ordering, so that it pushes all the fields underneath it down a step, but this is *not* how the manual ordering works.

DECIDING WHERE THE DATA GOES

After all the target fields are correctly aligned with the source fields, you need to make sure they're all set to receive data. Between the columns of source and target fields is a column of field mapping indicators. The possible indicators are shown in the Import Field Mapping dialog, in the section at the lower right called Field Mapping, which is shown in Figure 19.4.

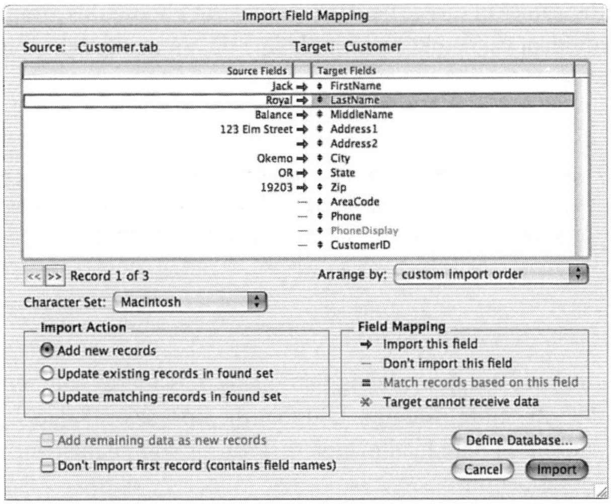

19

Figure 19.4
FileMaker's Import Field Mapping indicators.

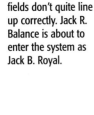

The meaning of the different indicators is as follows:

- **Arrow**—Data from the source field will be imported into the target field.
- **Straight line**—Data from the source field will not be imported into the target field.
- **Equals sign**—The source and target fields are being used as part of a match criterion. This choice is available only if you've chosen one of the "update" import actions. We discuss the update options fully in the following section (see "Updating Records with Imported Data").
- **Red x**—This indicates that the target field *cannot* receive data. Typical causes are that the target field is a calculation or summary field.

To sum up, you'll want to make sure that all your target fields are aligned with the correct source fields, and that the mapping indicators are set so as to allow data to flow into the fields you intend to receive it.

WAYS OF AUTO-ALIGNING SOURCE AND TARGET FIELDS

In the Import Field Mapping dialog, you might have noticed a menu at the middle right called Arrange By. This menu simply governs the ordering of the target fields in the column on the right. It may be that you can line the target fields up with the source fields by putting the target fields in creation order, for example, or in alphabetical order by name. If you choose one of these options, FileMaker rearranges the target fields in the order you've chosen, then does its best to set the mapping indicators accordingly. Most likely you'll need to do some manual adjustment of the result, but these choices can often eliminate a lot of tedious hand labor.

One very useful choice in this menu is the first one, called Matching Field Names. This choice is available only when the source file has some kind of data in it that attaches names to each of the source fields. Examples of such files are actual FileMaker files (of course), or flat data files with field names in the first row. If your source file contains field names that correspond to the names of target fields, then you can choose this arrangement option and all the fields with identical names will simply line up, no matter what position they have in their respective files.

NOTE

> This doesn't guarantee that the target fields will be able to accept data. If a source field has the same name as a calculation field in the target table, the two will line up, but it will still be impossible to import any data into the target field.

SCANNING THE DATA BEFORE IMPORTING

When the Import Field Mapping dialog first opens, the Source column shows data from the first record in the source file. You may find that the first record's data is not enough to remind you of the appropriate field mapping. That, or you might want to scan through the source data for other reasons.

Directly under the source column, you'll notice forward-arrow and back-arrow buttons, and a display that shows the total number of inbound records, as well as the record you're currently viewing. You can use the forward and back arrow buttons to scan through the inbound data, either to verify that you have the correct mapping of source to target, or to examine it for other reasons.

PERFORMING THE IMPORT

After you've verified all your field mappings and made your choice of import action (so far we've looked only at adding records), pressing the Import button starts the import proper. When the import completes, FileMaker displays a dialog box telling you how many records were imported, and whether there were any errors in the import process.

Depending on how you have your field validation set up, the inbound data may or not be acceptable. Under certain circumstances, FileMaker may reject imported records for this reason. See "Imports and Validation" in the Troubleshooting section at the end of this chapter for more information.

Assuming there were no serious errors and at least some records were imported, the newly-imported records are isolated in their own found set after the import is complete. This is an important point, because if there's something seriously amiss with the imported data you have an opportunity to delete the whole set and start over. Or, more optimistically, the records are all there in one set if you need to perform any other operations on them as a group.

UPDATING RECORDS WITH IMPORTED DATA

When you import data into a FileMaker Pro table, you have a choice as to whether the source data should be used to create new records, or whether it should be added into records that already exist.

As an example, suppose you have a FileMaker file with a table of records about people. This table contains a name, address, Social Security number, and other information about each person. Let's say that you periodically want to import the most current address for each person, from some other source outside of FileMaker, and apply the most current address to each of your FileMaker records, without changing anything else about the record.

Assume your table of personal data looks something like the data shown in Figure 19.5.

Then assume that you can get a data file from some other source, possibly governmental, that contains (among other things) a field for Social Security number and a few fields of address information. You'd like to match up the records in the source file with the records in your FileMaker table. Two records will be considered to match if they have the same Social Security number. If there's a record on the FileMaker side that doesn't have a match in the source file, you'd expect it to be left alone. If there's a record in the source file that doesn't have a matching FileMaker record, you'd want to ignore the source record altogether.

All these goals are easily accomplished with FileMaker's import options. Figure 19.6 shows the necessary settings in the Import Field Mapping dialog.

19

Figure 19.5
Data structure for a table containing personal information.

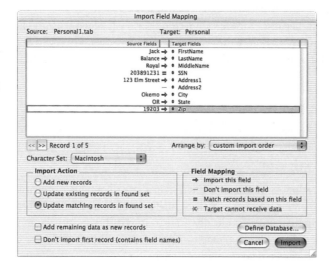

Figure 19.6
The Import Field Mapping dialog, preparing to import address data for records with matching Social Security numbers in the source.

Here the action Update Matching Records In Found Set has been selected. This tells FileMaker that you're going to specify at least one pair of fields as matching fields. This pair of fields acts a lot like a match field in a FileMaker relationship: Each row (or record) in the source is matched with any corresponding records in the target.

FileMaker's Update Matching Records feature can be tricky. For an overview of some of the potential pitfalls, see "Matching Imports" in the Troubleshooting section at the end of the chapter.

In addition to choosing the Update Matching Records setting, it's also been chosen to bring in just the address fields. So these particular settings update just the address information, leaving all the other fields untouched.

As a final note on update importing, you should be aware that the update affects only records in the current found set on the target side. If a record on the target matches a record in the source, but the target record is outside the current found set, it is *not* affected by the import.

UPDATING RECORDS WITHOUT USING MATCH FIELDS

You've probably noticed that another "update" option is available in the Import Action section. It's called Update Existing Records In Found Set, and it's simpler than the Update Matching Records choice. When this action is selected, rather than matching records based on a match field or fields, FileMaker matches records based purely on their position: The first record in the source updates the first record in the current found set on the target side, the second source record updates the second found target record, and so on.

If the number of records in the source doesn't exactly equal the number of records in the target found set, FileMaker takes account of this. If there are more source records than target records, the "extra" source records are skipped. If there are more target records than source records, the "extra" target records are left untouched. In either case, FileMaker provides an extra message to tell you what happened.

The only exception occurs if you check the box labeled Add Remaining Data As New Records. In that case, if there are "extra" records on the source side, they are imported into the target as brand new records.

SPECIAL FLAT FILE FORMATS

All the flat file formats that are available for import into FileMaker have many similarities. They are generally text-based, row-and-column data files, suitable for import into a single target FileMaker table. Two of the possible formats are worth special mention.

IMPORTING FROM ANOTHER FILEMAKER PRO FILE

As you might expect, it's possible to import from other FileMaker Pro files. If you choose FileMaker Pro as your source format, you also need to specify a table in the source file from which you want to draw data. This choice is available in the Import Field Mapping dialog, as shown in Figure 19.7.

Importing from a FileMaker file can be particularly convenient in that it allows you to use the Matching Field Names option for lining up the source and target fields.

→ For some other uses of the FileMaker-to-FileMaker import feature, **see** "FileMaker Extra: Exploiting the FileMaker-to-FileMaker Import," at the end of this chapter (**p. 561**).

IMPORTING FROM A MICROSOFT EXCEL FILE

FileMaker Pro has some special capabilities for importing data from Microsoft Excel documents. FileMaker is aware of multiple worksheets within an Excel document, and is also aware of any *named ranges* (a group of cells that's been given a specific name). When you select an Excel file for import, if it contains multiple worksheets or named ranges,

19

FileMaker prompts you to select either a worksheet or a named range as the source for the data, as shown in Figure 19.8.

Figure 19.7
When importing from a FileMaker database with multiple tables, it's necessary to pick the source table from which you want to draw data.

Figure 19.8
When you import data into FileMaker from an Excel document, you can import from a specific tab or a named Excel range.

After you've chosen the specific part of the Excel document you want to import, the rest of the import proceeds.

If you're bringing Excel data into FileMaker by choosing File, Open, and selecting an Excel file to open, FileMaker creates a new FileMaker file, as it does when opening other "importable" file types. In this situation, FileMaker can apply a little extra intelligence to creating the new FileMaker file. If a column in the Excel file contains only one type of data (numbers, text, dates), FileMaker assigns a suitable field type to the resulting FileMaker field. If the data in the column are somehow "mixed"—that is, the column contains some data that look like numbers, and other data that look like dates, for example—then the resulting FileMaker field will be a Text field.

NOTE

> When importing from an Excel file, FileMaker brings in only the raw data it finds in the file. FileMaker does not import Excel formulas, only their results. FileMaker also does not import any graphics or charts, nor does it import notes. Programming logic, such as Visual Basic macros, is also not imported into FileMaker.

IMPORTING MULTIPLE FILES FROM A FOLDER

FileMaker can import data from several files at once. In this "batch" mode, FileMaker takes the data from a file and imports it into one or more fields in a FileMaker table. FileMaker can also bring in information about each file's name and directory path.

FileMaker can work with two types of data when performing a folder import: image files and text files. In the case of image files, FileMaker can bring the image data from each file into a container field so that each image can be viewed inside FileMaker. In the case of text files, FileMaker brings the entire contents of the file into a specified text field.

CAUTION

> FileMaker can store a maximum of 2 gigabytes of data in a single field. This may seem like a lot, and it *is* a lot compared to the limit of 64K that was in force in previous versions of FileMaker! But it follows from this that you shouldn't import text or image files into FileMaker if any single imported file will be larger than two gigabytes.

IMPORTING TEXT FILES

Assume you have a folder with a number of plain text files in it. Assume also that you have a FileMaker database that has a table in it with fields called `TextContent`, `FileName`, and `FilePath`. If you select File, Import Records, Folder, you'll see FileMaker's Folder of Files Import Options dialog box, shown in Figure 19.9.

Figure 19.9
FileMaker kicks off the Import From Folder process with a special initial dialog box.

In the upper area you can choose the folder from which to import data. You can also choose whether to confine the import to files at the first level inside the folder, or whether to drill into all the subfolders that might be below the top level.

After you've chosen a folder from which to import, choose the file type. To import from text files, choose the Text Files option and click Continue. You'll then see a folder import dialog box, similar but not identical to the regular Import Field Mapping dialog box, shown in Figure 19.10.

Figure 19.10
When importing from a folder of files, the source fields have a special name and meaning.

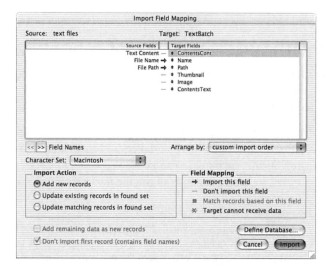

When you're doing a folder import, the names and contents of the source fields on the left are fixed: They depend on the type of file from which you're importing. When you're importing from text files, the source fields are called Text Content, File Name, and File Path. These fields contain, respectively, the actual text content of the field, the name of the individual file from which the data is coming, and the full name of the path to the file. As with any other data source, you can choose to import some or all of these fields, and you can choose how to map them to fields in the FileMaker table that's the target of the import.

Unlike imports from other kinds of flat-file data sources, FileMaker's batch text import brings the *entire* contents of each text file into a single FileMaker field.

After importing, you might have a data set that looks like the data seen in Figure 19.11.

Determining File Type

When you choose to import files from a folder, FileMaker scans the files in the directory to determine which ones are of the right type to import. So for each file in the folder, FileMaker decides whether it's an image file (if you're importing images) or a text file (if you're importing text). But how does it make this determination?

If you're familiar with the way file types are handled in Mac OS X and Windows, you know that the file's suffix (.html, .jpeg, and so on) often has a lot to do with it. Often, applications use the file suffix to determine whether an application "owns" that file type and can try to open it.

FileMaker's batch import determines file type differently, depending on platform. On Mac OS X, FileMaker looks first at the file's *type* and *creator*–special information (also called *metadata*) that Mac OS X stores with each file. If a file has no type or creator (for example, if it was created on a non-Macintosh platform), then FileMaker falls back on the file suffix.

Windows, by contrast, has no file type metadata, so FileMaker simply relies on the file suffix to determine whether a file is "eligible" for a batch import.

What this means is that FileMaker has no other innate "intelligence" about file types. If you take an image or PDF file in Windows and give it a .txt file suffix, FileMaker considers it eligible for a text import and tries to bring its content into a text field. Likewise, if you strip out file type and creator on the Mac and manipulate the suffix, it's possible to confuse FileMaker about the file type.

To see a file's type and creator in Mac OS X, if you have the Apple Developer Tools installed, you can use the command line tool /Developer/Tools/GetFileInfo to see file metadata, and /Developer/Tools/SetFile to change the metadata. Or you can use a shareware tool such as Xray (http://www.brockerhoff.net/xray/).

Figure 19.11
This is a sample data set resulting from a batch import of three text files from a folder.

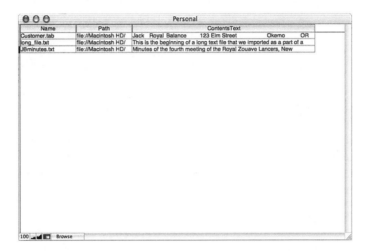

IMPORTING IMAGE FILES

Importing image files from a folder is quite similar to importing text files. See Figure 19.12 for a look at the folder-import options that apply to images. As with text files, you need to choose a source folder, and decide whether to drill down into any subfolders as well.

IMAGES OR REFERENCES?

In the past, FileMaker's usefulness as a tool for storing entire files (sometimes referred to as *asset management*) was somewhat limited by the 2GB maximum size of an individual FileMaker file. With FileMaker 7, the file size limit is reckoned in terabytes, so it's tempting to try to use FileMaker as a tool for managing large amounts of non-FileMaker data such as image files.

Still, image data can take up a great deal of storage space, and it may not make sense to try to store thousands of high-resolution images inside a FileMaker file. Accordingly, FileMaker offers you the option (when importing images from a folder), to import only a *reference* to each file, rather than the entire contents of the image. If you choose to import a reference, FileMaker "remembers" where the image is stored on disk, and refers to it when necessary.

19

Figure 19.12
These are the special Import Field Mapping options for importing from a folder of images.

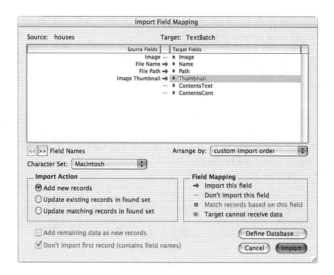

→ There are some additional considerations when using container fields in conjunction with FileMaker's Instant Web Publishing: **see** "Container Fields," **p. 626**.

The benefit of storing references is, of course, that they take up much less space in the database. The disadvantage is that if the original files are moved or renamed in any way, FileMaker will no longer be able to find them, and the images will not display in FileMaker nor be otherwise usable.

This is especially problematic if the file containing the images is hosted for multi-user access. Each user of the system needs to "see" the image directory via the same network path. Because Windows and Macintosh handle server paths differently, creating a unified server structure to work in both environments could be challenging.

In the end, the decision as to whether to import whole image files or just references is up to you, keeping in mind the tradeoff between the flexibility of having all images stored directly in the database, versus the increased capacity that comes from working with the file references alone.

IMAGES VERSUS THUMBNAILS

When you import data from text files, you can bring in up to three pieces of data: the filename, the full path to the file, and the text contents of the file. With image files, it is possible to bring in four pieces of data. As with text files, you can bring in the filename and file path. You can bring in the full contents of the image file (into a container field, presumably), and you can also bring in a smaller version of the image if you choose, called a *thumbnail*. See Figure 19.12, shown previously, for a possible import configuration for a batch import of images.

Naturally, a full-sized image can take a lot of space, so FileMaker gives you the option of bringing in only a smaller thumbnail instead. You can bring in the thumbnail in addition to the larger image, or instead of it. (Of course, you could choose to import just the filename and path if that suited your purpose.)

TIP

> FileMaker doesn't give you any control over how it creates thumbnails during the image import process. You may find that although you do want to store only a smaller copy of the image in the database, FileMaker's thumbnail process doesn't give you what you want. You might want the thumbnails a little smaller or larger, or with some kind of color adjustment. If so, you will want to experiment with creating your own thumbnails first, and import those instead.

Manipulating Images

With a tool such as Adobe Photoshop, it's possible to create batch-processing scripts (called *actions* in Photoshop) that can apply a series of transformations to every image in a folder. You might want to create an action to shrink every image to 120 pixels wide, 72 dots per inch, and save it as a high-quality JPEG with a two-pixel black border. You could then batch-import the resulting "custom thumbnails." In doing so, you'd want to make sure to import the image data rather than the thumbnail data: If you asked FileMaker for the thumbnail data, your classy custom thumbnails would be further scrunched down into thumbnails of thumbnails—not the desired effect.

IMPORTING PHOTOS FROM A DIGITAL CAMERA

In Mac OS X, FileMaker is able to import photos from a digital camera, or a similar device such as a memory card reader. This procedure is fairly thoroughly covered in the manual, so we'll be content with a brief overview.

If you choose File, Import Records, Digital Camera on Mac OS X, with a compatible digital device connected to the computer and powered on, you'll see the dialog box shown in Figure 19.13. Here you'll have the opportunity to specify which photos you want to import from the camera or device, as well as the choice whether to import entire images or just image references. (See the earlier section titled "Images or References?" for details.)

TIP

> If you choose the option to Specify Images in this dialog box, not only will you be able to select individual images for import, but you'll also be able to specify whether imported thumbnails should be small, medium, or large—an option that's not available when importing many images from a folder.

After you've decided on which photos to import, and whether to import them as images or full references, you'll proceed to the standard Import Field Mappings dialog. Just about everything here is as you expect it, but there's one possible difference, as you can see in Figure 19.14.

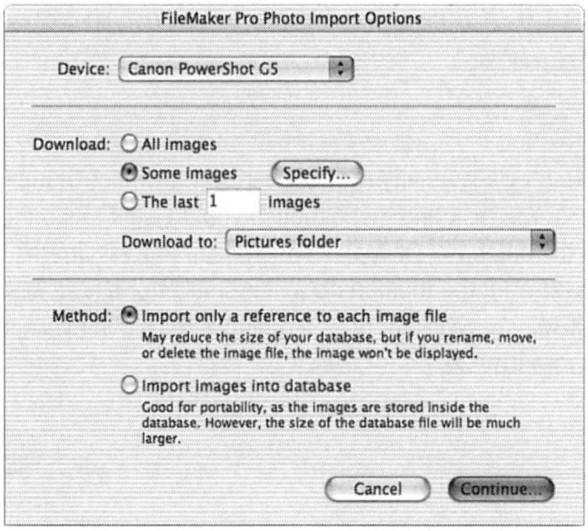

Figure 19.13
FileMaker has a variety of options for importing from a digital camera.

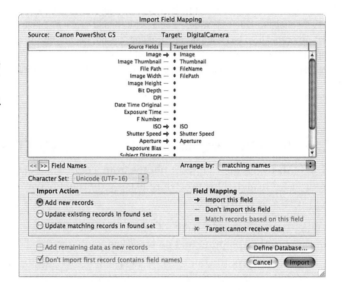

Figure 19.14
FileMaker can read and import EXIF data from a digital camera, in addition to the regular filename and path and image fields.

If the images you're importing contain EXIF (Exchangeable Image File) data, FileMaker can read and import that data as well. This data can include information such as the time of day, shutter speed, aperture, and film speed for the images, as well as many other pieces of data. The photos being imported in Figure 19.14 do contain EXIF data, as the long list of source fields shows; any or all of these fields are available for import. Many digital cameras capture EXIF data with each image.

IMPORTING FROM AN ODBC DATA SOURCE

In addition to importing data from resources on a local disk drive, such as individual flat files or folders of text or image files, FileMaker Pro can also access data sources that may be visible only over a network of some kind. One such type of remote data source is represented by remote databases, which FileMaker can access using a widespread technology known as *Open DataBase Connectivity (ODBC)*.

HOW ODBC WORKS

A full discussion of ODBC technologies is beyond the scope of this book. We'll have to be content with a fairly thorough overview.

Many database configurations are referred to as *client-server* configurations. Numerous *clients* (usually individual workstations) somehow connect to a database housed on a single master *server* (usually a powerful, centrally-located computer). Each client interacts directly with the server to request data, or to submit changes to the database. Because there are ostensibly only two layers in this architecture (the client and the server), this kind of setup is also called a *two-tier architecture*.

FileMaker Pro, you may be aware, when coupled with FileMaker Server, represents a classic two-tier, client-server architecture. FileMaker Pro is the client, of course, and FileMaker Server is, well, the server. FileMaker Pro and FileMaker Server communicate via a special FileMaker network protocol that isn't shared or understood by other applications. Figure 19.15 illustrates the FileMaker client-server architecture.

Figure 19.15
A sketch of FileMaker's two-tier client-server architecture.

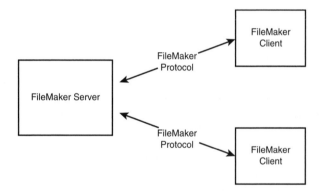

19

There are, of course, many other kinds of relational database servers in existence. Like FileMaker Server, each other product communicates using its own specialized protocol. But to overcome all this rampant disparity, a number of database and software vendors worked together to develop some more standard protocols for accessing database servers, so that rather than access databases a dozen different ways, clients can rely on a more consistent access method.

The result has been the ODBC standard. With ODBC, rather than having a client and a server communicate via a specific vendor protocol, the two sides can agree to communicate via ODBC instead. In this way, a client application that can use ODBC (such as FileMaker), can potentially communicate with any of the dozens of database products that use ODBC as well. Figure 19.16 illustrates the notion that a single client can communicate with many servers.

Figure 19.16
Using ODBC drivers and protocols, a single client application can communicate with many different types of ODBC-enabled servers.

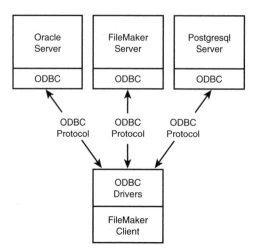

The ODBC standard is generally used with database servers that speak the SQL (Structured Query Language) database language, but some non-SQL database servers (such as FileMaker Server, for instance!) can also be accessed via ODBC.

→ This chapter covers techniques for bringing data *into* FileMaker via ODBC. Chapter 20, "Getting Data Out of FileMaker," **p. 563**, covers how it's possible to extract data *from* FileMaker via ODBC.

INSTALLING ODBC

For a client and server to be able to communicate via ODBC, both sides need some special preparation. Many database servers can communicate via ODBC with no additional configuration. Some may require that special modules be added or certain settings be configured. For the purposes of this chapter we're going to assume that you need access to a server that has already been correctly configured for ODBC.

Second, to participate in an ODBC communication, the client side must also be configured correctly. Generally, an individual client machine needs to have a special *driver* installed to allow it to communicate with a particular kind of database server. The driver is a piece of software, installed via the client's operating system, that knows how to talk to a particular kind of data source.

For example, if you want ODBC access to an Informix database from a client machine running Windows 2000, two things need to happen. First, of course, the Informix server needs to be configured for ODBC access. Second, though, you need an Informix ODBC driver that works under Windows 2000. If you want to perform similar access from a Mac OS X client, you need a separate Informix ODBC driver for Mac OS X. ODBC drivers are not generally transferable, either across database servers or across operating systems: You need a driver that's specific both to the database you want to access and to the operating system you're working from.

CAUTION

One of FileMaker's most powerful appeals is that it's fully cross-platform (well, as long as the platforms under consideration are Mac or Windows). ODBC connectivity, by contrast, does not have as gleaming a record in the cross-platform arena. The Mac has historically lagged behind Windows in terms of ODBC support; it often used to take a long time, if ever, for the Mac to be able to use the latest ODBC drivers for a given database. The drivers for a version 8 of a certain database might appear on Windows, and not be followed by version 8 Mac drivers for months, or longer.

With the advent of Mac OS X, especially version 10.2 ("Jaguar"), the ODBC connectivity picture for the Mac is much improved. OS X is of course a flavor of Unix under the hood, opening the path for the porting and adoption of a wide range of Unix-based ODBC tools.

The bottom line, though, is still "buyer beware." If you want or need to delve into ODBC, be aware that there remain differences in the nature and extent of ODBC support on the different FileMaker target platforms.

CREATING A DSN

After your ODBC drivers are installed, the next step is to create one or more DSNs (Data Source Names). This is also somewhat beyond the scope of a book on FileMaker, but we'll touch on some of the major points.

NOTE

The exact mechanics of installing ODBC drivers vary depending on the particular drivers being installed and on the target operating system. Going into great detail on driver installation is outside the scope of this book. We're going to assume that your FileMaker client machine or machines have ODBC drivers installed on them for the databases or data sources you want to access via ODBC.

19

Both the Mac OS X (version 10.2 and greater) and Windows operating systems have built-in tools for working with ODBC drivers and DSNs. On the Mac, Apple ships a tool called ODBC Administrator, which can be found in the Application, Utilities folder. On Windows, there's a shortcut to the ODBC Data Administrator located in Start, Settings, Control Panel, Administrative Tools, Data Sources (ODBC).

To create a DSN to access a particular ODBC-based data source, you need to have a driver for that particular data source installed on the computer you're working from. Figure 19.17 shows the Mac and Figure 19.18 shows the Windows ODBC tools with a list of available drivers. Windows systems tend to have a great many ODBC drivers installed by default. Mac OS X, by contrast, doesn't install any ODBC drivers by default.

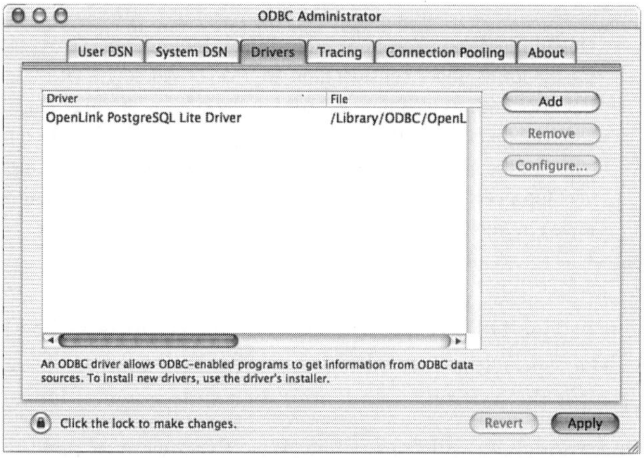

Figure 19.17
The Mac OS X ODBC Administrator.

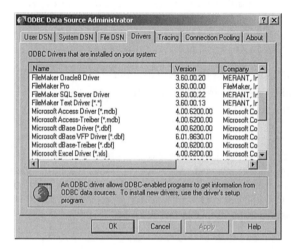

Figure 19.18
The Windows 2000 ODBC Data Source Administrator.

You need to create a DSN that uses the appropriate driver for the data source you're trying to work with. You probably also need to do some configuration of the DSN. Depending on the type of data source you're using, the DSN configuration can vary widely. To access a SQL database, for example, you'd generally need to configure the DSN with the hostname or IP address of the database server, a username, a password, and possibly the name of a specific SQL database. We show a sample DSN configuration screen in Figure 19.19, but in general, each DSN needs to be configured differently, and we can't give any general guidelines in a book of this nature. You'll need to consult the documentation for the particular ODBC driver you're using, and you may need to enlist the aid of someone, such as a database administrator, who's aware of the configuration settings for the data source you're trying to access.

NOTE

You have a choice between creating a User DSN and creating a System DSN. These two kinds of DSNs differ only in who can access them: System DSNs are meant to be accessible to all users on a system, whereas a user DSN is meant to be accessible only to the user that created it. FileMaker can work with either type, though it respects the access restrictions: You'll be able to access a user DSN from FileMaker only if the DSN is accessible to you.

Figure 19.19
Defining a DSN for the Postgresql open source database in Mac OS X.

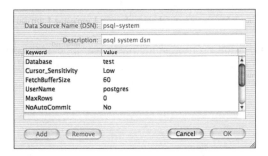

PERFORMING THE ODBC IMPORT

After you have a working DSN for the ODBC data source you want to access, importing from the data source is simply a matter of selecting File, Import Records, ODBC Data Source. You'll see a list of available DSNs, as shown in Figure 19.20.

Figure 19.20
When you begin an import from an ODBC data source, FileMaker prompts you to choose an ODBC DSN.

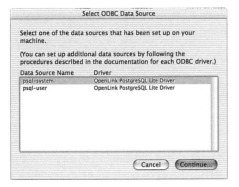

Here, two DSNs are available: a user DSN and a system DSN, both of which make connections to a Postgresql database. (Postgresql is an extremely powerful open source SQL database).

If the data source to which you're connecting requires authentication, you might see a password prompt like the one shown in Figure 19.21.

19

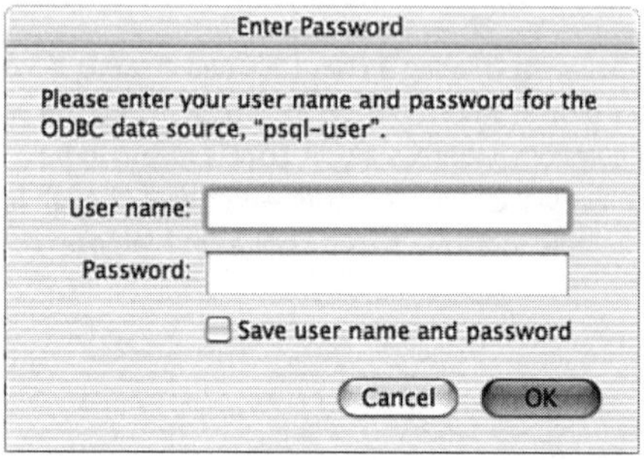

Figure 19.21
Some ODBC data sources may prompt you for authentication.

After you pass the authentication prompt, you'll likely see some additional dialog boxes, depending on the type of ODBC data source you're accessing. For SQL-based data sources, for example, you'll likely see a dialog that helps you formulate a SQL query, such as the one shown in Figure 19.22.

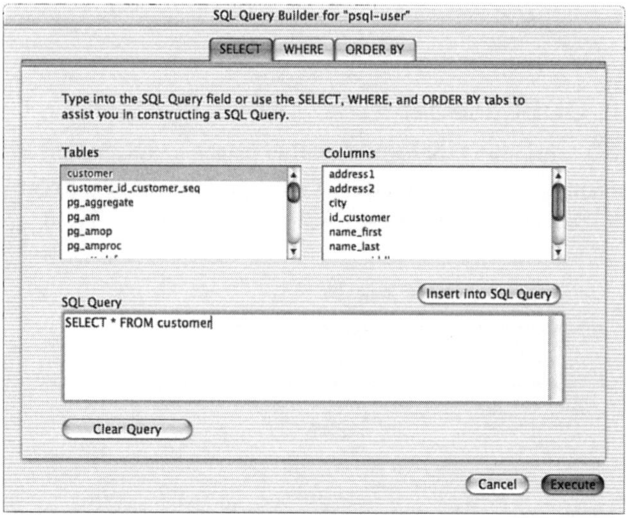

Figure 19.22
When importing from a SQL-based ODBC data source, you'll probably need to formulate a SQL query via a wizard like this one.

Here we're fetching data from a table called "customer" in a remote Postgresql database. The SQL query instructs the ODBC driver to fetch all fields from the customer table.

After this query is run, you'll be confronted with FileMaker's Import Field Mappings dialog, with which we've dealt extensively in this chapter. The dialog lets you map the fields from the SQL data source onto the fields in the FileMaker table.

Again, the options for ODBC import can vary widely depending on the particular driver and data source you're using. It's a bit beyond the scope of this book to provide a full overview of ODBC, SQL, or particular drivers. You may need to experiment a bit, or consult with the oft-mentioned "local systems expert" (in case it isn't you!) to arrive at the correct configuration for importing ODBC data.

IMPORTING FROM AN XML DATA SOURCE

Importing data from an XML data source is a large topic—so large, in fact, that we devote an entire chapter to it, in the more general context of discussing how FileMaker can interact with Web services.

→ For a full explanation of FileMaker's XML Import capabilities, **see** Chapter 22, "FileMaker and Web Services," **p. 639**.

USING A SCRIPT TO IMPORT DATA

Like most other actions in FileMaker Pro, importing data can be triggered from a script. It's possible to save your import settings in a script for later reuse as well.

A scripted import has a few steps and options that are slightly different from the regular File, Import Records method. To import records from within a script, choose the Import Records script step and add it to your script. ScriptMaker gives you several choices, as shown in Figure 19.23.

Figure 19.23
FileMaker enables you to save a number of options when you import records from within a script.

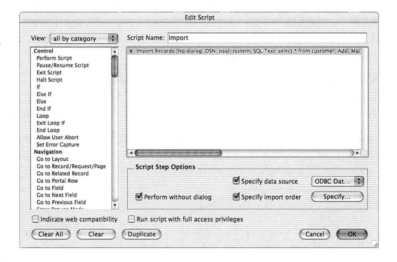

The Specify Data Source menu at the lower right gives you access to a set of options identical to those you see when you choose File, Import Records. Using this selection, you can save all the important information about your data source. For files, this means mainly the file name. For folders, it includes the file type, and the choice of whether to save references or not. For ODBC data sources, it includes the DSN information, password, and other data such as a SQL query.

The Specify Import Order button at the lower right gives you access to the Import Field Mapping dialog, where you can set any or all of the relevant import mapping features.

Finally, as with other script steps in FileMaker, you have the choice of performing the import with or without dialogs. If you choose to run the import with dialogs, the user can re-specify any aspect of the data source or import order on the fly. If you choose to run it without dialogs, the import is a "canned" process that uses all the saved options you've specified.

TIP

> When performing a complex import, you may want to save "drafts" of the import into a script as you go. That way if you make a mistake or need to change things, you don't run the risk of FileMaker "forgetting" the import specification you worked so hard on.

TROUBLESHOOTING

MATCHING IMPORTS

I can't get an import to work using the "update matching records" option. The outcome is never what I expect.

When you choose to "update matching records" when importing data into a FileMaker table, FileMaker tries to match records in the source to records in the target, based on the specified match field or match fields. We've been assuming that there will be at most one source record and one target record that share the same match criteria. But what happens if there are multiple matches on either or both sides?

Assume you're doing a matching import based on a Social Security number. If there are several records in the source data with the same Social Security number, the data from the *last* of these records is used to update matching records in the target (assuming there are any).

On the other hand, if there are multiple records with the same Social Security number on the target side, they are *all* updated with whatever turns out to be the matching data from the source side. So all target records with the same value in their match field(s) are updated with the same data from the source, whether that means updating two target records or two thousand.

If you put both scenarios together, and multiple records in both the source and target share the same Social Security number, the outcome is as follows: Data from the *last* such record in the source will be used to update *all* the matching records in the target. If four matching records were in the source, and nineteen in the target, data from the fourth matching source record would be used to update all nineteen matching target records.

IMPORTS AND VALIDATION

I imported data, but some of it turns out to be invalid. I have field validation rules set up, but it seems as though FileMaker is ignoring them.

In previous versions of FileMaker, field validation and data imports didn't mix well. FileMaker simply didn't perform any field validation at all on data that was imported. Even if you marked a field as having to be not empty, for example, it was perfectly possible to import records that had no value in that field. This could be an annoying back door around your carefully-constructed validation rules.

The situation is better in FileMaker 7, but there are still pitfalls. Everything depends on your field validation settings. When you apply validation to a field in FileMaker 7, you can choose to validate the data Only During Data Entry, or Always. If you select the first option, the behavior is similar to previous versions of FileMaker: Imported data is *not* checked for validity, and it's up to you to handle the consequences. On the other hand, if you choose Always for the data validation on a field, imported records *are* checked. If this is the case, any record that does not pass a validation check is rejected, and the dialog box that appears at the end of the import tells you how many records were rejected (thought not *which* ones, unfortunately).

FILEMAKER EXTRA: EXPLOITING THE FILEMAKER-TO-FILEMAKER IMPORT

You saw earlier that it's possible to import data into one FileMaker table from another. Those tables can be in the same FileMaker file or different ones. This capability has a number of useful and interesting applications.

DUPLICATING A FOUND SET

Occasionally, you'll encounter situations where you want to duplicate a found set of records. Of course, as with most things in FileMaker, there are several approaches. You could write a script that would start at the beginning of the found set and loop through it, duplicating as it went. But you'd quickly find you had some tricky record-position issues to deal with. (Duplicating records can change which record is the "current" one, so it can be hard to keep your place when looping through a found set.)

One general rule for speeding up FileMaker operations goes something like this: *Where possible, replace scripts, especially looping scripts, with built-in FileMaker operations.* FileMaker's Replace command is much quicker than a script that loops over a group of records and performs a Set Field step on each record. FileMaker's Delete Found Records command is quicker than a script that loops over a set of records and deletes each one. And so on.

Another choice is to export these records to a separate table, then import them right back into the original table again. A single script can control both the export and the import, and the logic is much easier to read and understand.

DUPLICATING BETWEEN TABLES

Suppose you have a simple order tracking database. The database has tables for customers, orders, order lines, and products. Each order, of course, has one order line per product on the order.

Suppose also that users have said that they want to create new orders by checking off a number of products from a list and then having a new order be created with one line for each selected product. So a user would check off Screwdrivers, Milk, and Roofing Tar in a product list, click a button that says Make Order, and see a new order with lines for the three selected products.

Again, you can do a number of things with scripts, but one elegant solution is to gather up the selected products into a found set and then simply import that found set (well, the relevant fields from it, anyway) into the Order Lines table, thus creating one new order line per selected product.

19

CHAPTER 20

GETTING DATA OUT OF FILEMAKER

In this chapter

REASONS FOR EXPORTING DATA

Users need to get data out of FileMaker Pro for a lot of reasons. They range from using data in slide presentations to charting numbers in a spreadsheet to sending data to another database system. This chapter covers the various techniques that can be employed to move data out of FileMaker Pro. Exporting data is the most commonly used technique, but there are others. Instant Web publishing and custom Web publishing using XML are two other popular methods. Those two topics are so broad that they each warranted their own chapters and aren't covered in this chapter.

→ For more on instant Web publishing, **see** Chapter 21, "Instant Web Publishing," **p. 605**.

→ For more information on custom Web publishing using XML, **see** Chapter 23, "Custom Web Publishing," **p. 671**.

This chapter also covers the use of ODBC for moving data out of FileMaker systems. First, though, we cover all the different ways that data can be exported from FileMaker Pro.

CAUTION

A quick word about security: When data is moved out of FileMaker Pro by means of an export or some other method, it is not secure. Many people go to a lot of trouble securing their database systems, but then they leave data that is exported from the system unprotected. If you need to export sensitive data from a secure system, at least take the trouble to compress and password protect the exported data with a ZIP or SIT utility.

FUNDAMENTALS OF EXPORTING DATA

Some general rules apply when exporting data out of FileMaker Pro and FileMaker Developer.

The active window controls the export process because the active window displays a specific layout, and that layout is based on a specific table occurrence, and that table occurrence is based on a specific table. In the simplest type of export where no related fields are included in the export, the data comes from that specific table. It's a key concept in FileMaker Pro 7: The active window determines the table for export. The active window controls other aspects of exporting as well, but those will be considered in the next section. For now, we consider the simplest type of export.

The number of records that you can export is controlled by the found set in the window that's active at the time of the export. If you have 500 records in your Customer table, but the currently active Customer layout is showing only a found set of 33, then you'll be able to export data from only those 33 records. If you want to export all your Customer records, you need to select Records, Show All Records first. If the found set of records has a sort order, that order is preserved in the export process.

The simplest type of export is one in which you export the contents of a single FileMaker table. After you have a found set containing the records you want to export, the export process itself is very simple to perform as long as your access privileges permit exporting.

→ For more on how privilege sets are used to control a user's ability to export, **see** Chapter 12, "Implementing Security," **p. 315**.

Choose File, Export Records to bring up the Export Records to File dialog. Enter a file name, then click on the Save as Type pop-up list on the bottom of the dialog box and note the various formats that are available, as shown in Figure 20.1.

Figure 20.1
FileMaker Pro can export data to a variety of formats.

Typically, the format that you use is determined by the application into which you need to import the data. When in doubt, it's hard to go wrong with tab- or comma-separated text files.

After you enter a file name, select a format, and click Save, the Specify Field Order for Export dialog comes up, as shown in Figure 20.2.

The list on the left side of the dialog contains fields that are available for export. Although it's possible to export related fields, just consider the fields in the current table (determined by the active window) for now. Double-clicking a field or selecting a field and then clicking Move causes that field to move into the Field Export Order. Fields in the Field Export Order will be included in the export. This mechanism enables you to include or exclude certain pieces of data if you so desire.

NOTE

> It's important to realize that only the FileMaker export format supports the exporting of data that's contained in container fields. An export using any other export file format does not allow you to move container fields into the Field Export Order.

Figure 20.2
Most export formats don't allow the inclusion of a container field in the export order.

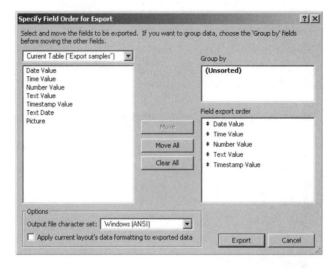

Container fields can't be included in most export file formats. If you're not exporting to the FileMaker format, you need to use a script containing the Export Field Contents script step, or the Export Field Contents menu command to export the contents of a container field.

Note that the fields listed in the Field Export Order have double-headed arrows in front of each line. Clicking and dragging those arrows enables you to re-order the Field Export Order. If the field order is at all critical in your exported file, this mechanism enables you to set the order according to your requirements.

The Group By option is available only if you sort the database prior to exporting your data. This option is investigated in more detail later in the chapter. The Options box at the bottom of the dialog enables you to set the character set of the exported file. The option to Apply Current Layout's Data Formatting to Exported Data is covered in the next section.

After you have the Field Export Order set the way you want, click Export to create the export file.

EXPORTING WITH LAYOUT FORMATTING

Many of FileMaker's export formats can be set to use the format settings of the layout from which you're exporting. That means, for example, that if you have a date field that contains the value 11/17/2004, and it's set to display as Wednesday, November 17, 2004, you can enable the Apply Current Layout's Data Formatting to Exported Data option in the Specify Field Order for Export dialog, and then the date value is exported in that format. Special formatting options applied to date, time, or number fields are carried through in the export if this option has been enabled. The formatting options also apply to calculated fields with date, time, or number results.

NOTE

In Layout mode you can apply date and time formatting to a time stamp field, but those settings are carried through in an export only if you use the XML format.

The formats that support the application of layout settings are Tab, Comma-separated (CSV), BASIC, Merge, HTML, FileMaker, and XML.

WKS/WK1 partially applies the current layout style. Number formats come through with formatting, but time and date values are converted to time and date functions, the result being that they appear as unformatted times and dates when opened in a spreadsheet application.

SYLK, DBF, and DIF do not support the application of layout styles at all.

A quick example demonstrates the kinds of data formatting that can be achieved through using the Apply Current Layout's Data Formatting to Exported Data option. Suppose a FileMaker Pro 7 file has the following fields defined:

> Date Value [Date]
>
> Time Value [Time]
>
> Number Value [Number]
>
> Text Value [Text]
>
> Picture [Container]

And suppose that the file contains the values formatted as shown in Figure 20.3.

Figure 20.3
The date, time, number, and text values have all had custom formats applied. The container field is not shown.

This data with the layout formatting settings shown in Figure 20.3 can yield a variety of different exported results, depending on the export file format chosen. Samples of several of the formats are shown in Table 20.1, along with some notes about each format.

20

TABLE 20.1   EXPORT FILE FORMATS

Text

Tab	Tab-separated text. Container fields cannot be exported. Layout formatting can be applied. A great all-purpose format that works with almost any application that can import text files. Container fields cannot be exported. Layout formatting can be applied.

Sample exported Tab data:

Saturday, April 17, 2004   9:32 $34.21   The Big Dog jumped high.   4/17/2004 9:32:53 AM

Comma-Separated (CSV)	Works with almost any application that can import text files. Extension can be .txt or .csv. Carriage returns within field values are converted to vertical tab values. Group separator character between repeating field values. Any non-number characters in number fields (such as letters or currency symbols) are stripped out during the export process, although if number formatting options have been applied, those are preserved if current layout settings are applied during the export. Regular quotation marks (not smart quotes) convert to single quotes.

Sample exported CSV data:

"Saturday, April 17, 2004","9:32","$34.21","The Big Dog jumped high.","4/17/2004 9:32:53 AM"

BASIC	This format works with Microsoft BASIC programs. Carriage returns within text fields are converted to spaces. Group separator character between repeating field values. Exports only the first 255 characters of text fields. Regular quotation marks (not smart quotes) convert to single quotes.

Sample exported BASIC data:

"Saturday, April 17, 2004","9:32",34.21,"The Big Dog jumped high.","4/17/2004 9:32:53 AM"

Merge	Used for mail merge applications with word processors. This format retains field names.

Sample exported Merge data:

Date Value,Time Value,Number Value,Text Value,Timestamp Value

"Saturday, April 17, 2004","9:32","$34.21","The Big Dog jumped high.","4/17/2004 9:32:53 AM"

HTML Table	Exports data as an HTML table that can be viewed by a Web browser and copied into the HTML for another Web page. Fields become table columns; records become table rows; repeating values become nested tables.

Sample exported HTML Table data:

```
<HTML>
<HEAD><META HTTP-EQUIV="Content-Type" CONTENT=
"text/html;CHARSET=ISO-8859-1"></HEAD>
<BODY><TABLE BORDER=1>
<TR>
<TH>Date Value</TH>
<TH>Time Value</TH>
<TH>Number Value</TH>
```

```
<TH>Text Value</TH>
<TH>Timestamp Value</TH>
</TR>
<TR>
<TD>Saturday, April 17, 2004</TD>
<TD>9:32</TD>
<TD>$34.21</TD>
<TD>The Big Dog jumped high.</TD>
<TD>4/17/2004 9:32:53 AM</TD>
</TR>
</TABLE></BODY></HTML>
```

XML   FileMaker can export XML in two different grammars: FMPXMLRESULT and FMPDSORESULT. This is the only format (and only when the FMPXMLRESULT grammar is in use) that can apply date and time layout styles to timestamp fields.

Sample exported XML data:

```
<?xml version="1.0" encoding="UTF-8" ?><FMPXMLRESULT xmlns=
"http://www.filemaker.com/fmpxmlresult">

<ERRORCODE>0</ERRORCODE><PRODUCT BUILD="02-10-2004"

NAME="FileMaker Pro" VERSION="7.0v1"/>

<DATABASE DATEFORMAT="M/d/yyyy" LAYOUT="Export samples" NAME="Export
samples.fp7" RECORDS="1" TIMEFORMAT="h:mm:ss a"/>

<METADATA>

<FIELD EMPTYOK="YES" MAXREPEAT="1" NAME="Date Value" TYPE="DATE"/><FIELD
EMPTYOK="YES" MAXREPEAT="1" NAME="Time Value" TYPE="TIME"/>

<FIELD EMPTYOK="YES" MAXREPEAT="1" NAME="Number Value" TYPE="NUMBER"/>

<FIELD EMPTYOK="YES" MAXREPEAT="1" NAME="Text Value" TYPE="TEXT"/>

<FIELD EMPTYOK="YES" MAXREPEAT="1" NAME="Timestamp Value" TYPE="TIMESTAMP"/>

</METADATA>

<RESULTSET FOUND="1">

<ROW MODID="5" RECORDID="1">

<COL><DATA>Wednesday, November 17, 2004</DATA></COL>

<COL><DATA>9:32</DATA></COL>

<COL><DATA>$34.21</DATA></COL>

<COL><DATA>The Big Dog jumped high.</DATA></COL>

<COL><DATA>April 17, 2004 9:32:53</DATA></COL>

</ROW></RESULTSET></FMPXMLRESULT>
```

20

continues

TABLE 20.1   CONTINUED

Text

| DIF | Field names are retained in the export. Format has a column (vector)/row (tuple) structure. FileMaker Pro conforms to DIF restrictions during export. Group separator character is inserted between repeating field values during export. Cannot apply layout format settings to data during export. |

Sample exported DIF data:

TABLE

0,1

"Export samples.fp7"

VECTORS

0,5

""

TUPLES

0,00000001

""

LABEL

1,0

"Date Value"

LABEL

2,0

"Time Value"

LABEL

3,0

"Number Value"

LABEL

4,0

"Text Value"

LABEL

5,0

"Timestamp Value"

DATA

0,0

""

-1,0

BOT

1,0

"11/17/2004"

1,0

"9:32:21 AM"

0,34.21

V

1,0

"The Big Dog jumped high."

1,0

"4/17/2004 9:32:53 AM"

-1,0

EOD

Binary Formats (no examples because these aren't text formats)

DBF	dBase format. This format is compatible with dBase III and IV, but not dBase II. The nice thing about this format is that field names are preserved in the process, but with some caveats. There's a limit of 10 characters per field name, and any spaces are converted to the underscore character. The field name is uppercase. This truncation can lead to inadvertent duplicate field names, which are illegal and which FileMaker resolves by prepending under score characters to the names. For example, First Name of the Dog, First Name of the Cat, and First Name of the Lizard fields export as FIRST_NAME, _FIRST_NAME, and __FIRST_NAME. This format can have a maximum of 128 fields, a maximum of 254 characters per field, a maximum of 400 bytes per record, and exports only the first value in a repeating field. Layout format settings cannot be applied to the export. This format does not support the Macintosh character set.
SYLK	Only the first value in repeating fields can be exported, and the layout format settings cannot be applied to the export.
WKS/WK1	A spreadsheet format, this format can be imported by Lotus 1-2-3 and most other spreadsheet applications. Only 240 characters per field. Date and time fields are exported as functions, not fields. Lotus supports dates from only 1900 through 2099, so dates outside this range are exported as text. Only the first value in a repeating field is exported. Layout formatting applies to number and time fields, but not date fields. The export format is WK1 on Win, and WKS on the Mac, although the file extension is WK1.

20

Generally, FileMaker can export two broad types of files: text files and binary files. Different types of text files are internally organized in different ways, but they are all text-based documents. Binary files are not stored in a text format. As a result, it's possible to show sample data for only the text file formats in Table 20.1, but not for the binary formats.

 If you have fields that you use to store lengthy notes or comments, you may find that those notes get truncated when they are exported to certain file formats. To learn how to deal with these situations, see "Data Gets Truncated with Certain Export Formats" in the Troubleshooting section at the end of this chapter.

N O T E

If you export data to the XML format, the Specify Field Order for Export dialog is preceded by the Specify XML and XSL Options dialog shown in Figure 20.4.
The FMPXMLRESULT grammar is the only export format that can incorporate date formatting options applied to a timestamp field. After you've selected a grammar and clicked Continue, the usual Specify Field Order for Export dialog comes up.

Figure 20.4
FileMaker can export two different XML grammars: FMPXMLRESULT and FMPDSORESULT.

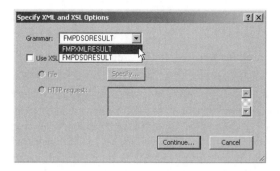

→ For information on importing XML data, **see** "Importing from an XML Data Source," **p. 559**.

FIXED-LENGTH FIELD EXPORTING

FileMaker users often have to exchange data with other database systems. Some older systems, especially governmental systems, still use fixed-length records. A fixed length record is one in which each field has been allotted a certain number of characters, and the combination of all fields in a record always results in a record that is a fixed number of characters long.

For example, suppose that a payment database has a First Name field that requires 10 characters, a Last Name field that requires 15 characters, and a Payment Amount field that requires 8 characters. Typically, number fields that hold currency values do not permit decimal characters. In this case, if a payment amount is $123.43, the properly formatted number value is 00012343. Notice that any blank spaces need to be padded with zeros, and notice also that currency symbols, commas, or decimal characters are not included. The system that receives this record will know that it needs to divide the number value by 100. Just as number values are typically padded with zeros, so text values are typically padded with spaces. The first name of "Gilbert" would use the characters of the name "Gilbert" and then follow that with three space characters. Text values are usually followed by the padding character, whereas number values are usually preceded by the padding character.

As you saw in the last section, FileMaker doesn't have an export file format specifically for fixed-length exporting. That's not a problem, though, because you can use a calculation field to construct a fixed-length record export like this. Given the fields previously mentioned, the calculation to create a fixed length export would be

```
Left (First Name & "          "; 10) & Left (Last Name & "               "; 15)
➥ & Right ( "00000000" & Filter (Payment Amount; "0123456789"); 8)
```

The basic concept is simple. For a text field of a given length, say 10 characters, you take the field value and append 10 spaces to the end of it. You then take the left 10 characters of that to get a string that contains the field value and the correct number of spaces. The process is reversed for numbers. Zeros are added to the left of the number, and then the rightmost characters are used. These field strings are used as building blocks to construct a full record. You can create a single calculation field (let's call it Fixed Length Export) that uses this calculation and returns a text result, as shown in Figure 20.5.

Figure 20.5
You can construct a fixed-length export record by concatenating and trimming various fields together to form one long field.

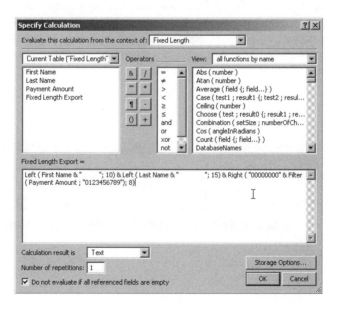

To create a fixed-length export file, you need to find the records you want to export, and then export just this one field in a tab-delimited format. Because you're exporting only one field, no tabs are inserted into the file; the carriage return delimiter that's used in the tab export format (and others) is the same delimiter typically used to set fixed length records apart from each other.

FileMaker also ships with an XSLT stylesheet that can produce fixed-length output with all columns the same length. This stylesheet is easy to modify and use for columns of differing (fixed) lengths as well. The stylesheet is part of the XML Examples.

EXPORTING FIELD CONTENTS

Selecting File, Export Records isn't the only way to export data out of FileMaker. It's possible to export the contents of a single field on a specific record. All you need to do is put the cursor into any field—even a container field—and select Edit, Export Field Contents. For container fields, the Export Field Contents menu item is grayed out unless the container field contains either a file or a reference to a file. FileMaker objects, such as rectangles, that have been copied and pasted into a container field cannot be exported. After you've selected the Export Field Contents menu item, the Export Field to File dialog comes up. All you need to do is specify a name and location for the resulting file and click Save.

EXPORTING GROUPED DATA

Sometimes you don't need to export all the raw data that resides in your database. You might need to export only grouped or summarized information, the kind that you might display in a summary report. For example, you might want to list a count of the number of customers in each state, rather than listing all customers. A summarized export is also a great way to "de-duplicate" data. Suppose you want to create a master vendor list from a database that contains every vendor transaction that has ever been. Any one vendor might have several transactions. You want to get a list that shows each vendor only once. For the sake of this example, let's also suppose that you'd like to get a count of the number of transactions for each vendor.

The first step is to create a new summary field called Transaction Count, as shown in Figure 20.6.

Figure 20.6
A summary field can be used to count the number of members in a group of data.

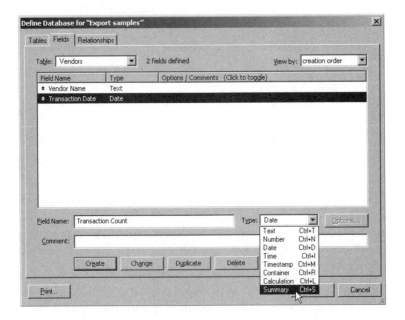

Click Create to open the Options for Summary Field dialog shown in Figure 20.7.

Figure 20.7
Summary fields can
be used to compute
values across a found
set of records.

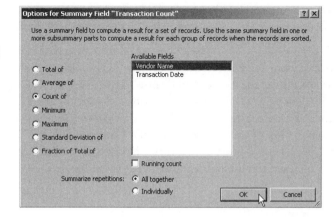

Many of the summary options, such as Total of or Average of, can work only with number
fields. The Count of option can work with any type of field, as long as there is a value in
that field. Empty fields are not counted. Click the Count of option, select Vendor Name,
and click OK to exit the Options for Summary Field dialog. Click OK again to exit the
Define Database dialog.

→ For more information on field types, **see** "Working with Field Types," **p. 69**.

The next step is to get the appropriate found set of Transaction records (in this case, all
records) and then sort them by Vendor Name. Next, select File, Export Records to bring up
the Export Records to File dialog. For this particular example, it would be logical to export
the data in the FileMaker format because the FileMaker format preserves the names of
fields during export and because the exported data will ultimately be used in a FileMaker
format. Select FileMaker Pro as the Type, name the file, and click Save to bring up the
Specify Field Order for Export dialog shown in Figure 20.8.

Figure 20.8
When the database
has been sorted, the
Group By box lists the
fields used in the cur-
rent sort order.

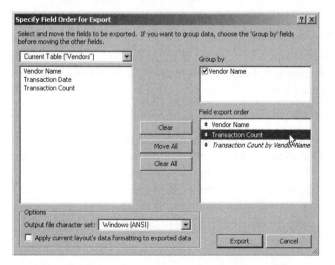

The Group By box has Vendor Name in it because the database was sorted by Vendor Name prior to starting the export. Check Vendor Name. Move Vendor Name and Transaction Count into the Field Export Order by double-clicking them. Notice that as soon as Transaction Count moves into the export order, it spawns another field called Transaction Count by Vendor Name.

If we were to leave both Transaction Count fields in the export order, the Transaction Count field would display the count of all records in the found set on each exported record. The Transaction Count by Vendor Name field would display the number of records for that particular Vendor Name, which is the result you want. Select the Transaction Count field and clear it from the export order, leaving only the Vendor Name and Transaction Count by Vendor Name fields. Click Export to export the database. Open the exported file and view it in table view. The result should look like the file shown in Figure 20.9.

Figure 20.9
The summarized data displays each distinct value only once, along with a count of the number of records associated with that value.

Vendor Name	Transaction Count by Vendor Name
Vendor A	8
Vendor B	14
Vendor C	22

SCRIPTED EXPORTS

That covers just about all the possibilities for manually exporting data from FileMaker. It often happens that the same kind of export needs to be done repeatedly. Examples might be the sending of sales reports to a home office, or perhaps generating a telephone contact list. In cases where an export operation needs to be done on a regular basis, it makes sense to use a script to automate the process. There are additional issues to consider when setting up a scripted export. Take another look at the database shown in Figure 20.1. The same export can be automated so that users can run it by just clicking a button. That makes it possible for people who have no expertise with FileMaker or even your data requirements to successfully export a properly formatted file.

To create such a script, select Scripts, ScriptMaker to bring up the Define Scripts dialog. Create a new script called **Export Tab File** and add an Export Records script step to it, as shown in Figure 20.10.

Check Specify Output File to bring up the Specify Output File dialog shown in Figure 20.11.

The Specify Output File dialog controls the file format that gets exported, and it controls the potential locations to which it can be exported by means of the Output File Path List. The Output File Path List is a powerful tool (available only for scripted exports, not manual exports) that allows a single script to work properly in a variety of user environments. A user might log on to a database from a home computer, or at the office, or from a Terminal Server session, and in each case might have different drive configurations, even while using the same database.

Figure 20.10
The Export Records script step can be set to run with more or less user interaction.

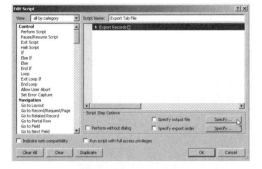

Figure 20.11
The Output File Path List can be used to allow a single script to adapt to multiple user export environments.

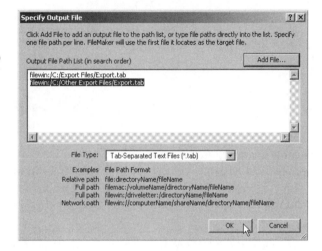

As a developer, you can set up an output file path for every possibility by clicking the Add File button. When the script is run, FileMaker works through the list to see whether any of the file paths are valid. The first valid path that it finds is the one it will use to export the file. You can rearrange the order of the file paths to force FileMaker to check one location before it checks another. If none of the paths are valid, you get the error dialog shown in Figure 20.12.

Figure 20.12
If none of the scripted Output File Paths are valid, FileMaker displays this error message.

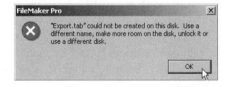

You cannot suppress this dialog by using the Set Error Capture script step. It always displays if none of the file paths are valid. After the Output File Paths and the File Type have been specified, click OK to exit the Specify Output File dialog and return to the Edit Script dialog.

Check Specify Export Order to bring up the Specify Field Order for Export dialog, as shown in Figure 20.13.

Figure 20.13
When you script an export, you use the same Specify Field Order for Export dialog that you use when you perform the export manually.

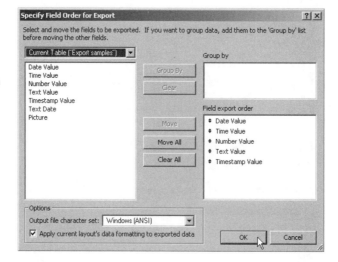

After you've set the Field Export Order, Group By, and Layout Formatting options, click OK to exit the Specify Field Order for Export dialog. Click OK again to exit the Edit Script dialog, and your script is ready for use. Be sure to test it from the various user environments so you can be sure it will function properly when different directories are available.

The Export Field Contents script step works in an identical fashion. It has the same option to set multiple output file paths. The only difference is that the Export Field Contents script step applies to only a single field on a single record. It doesn't export field contents for every record in a found set. If you need that functionality, you can put the Export Field Contents script step inside a looping script that moves from record to record.

→ For more information on constructing looping scripts, **see** "Common Scripting Techniques," **p. 249**.

ACCESSING FILEMAKER DATA USING ODBC/JDBC

In the preceding chapter, you learned the basics of how to use ODBC to import data into FileMaker Pro. In this chapter, you're going to learn how to use Open Database Connectivity (ODBC) and a similar technology, Java Database Connectivity (JDBC), to move data out of FileMaker. Both technologies use SQL as their query language. JDBC is designed for use with Java, whereas a variety of programming languages and tools can be used to access the ODBC interface.

CAUTION

NEW

> We need to start off with an important piece of information: As of this writing, only the Windows versions of FileMaker Pro, FileMaker Developer, and FileMaker Server 7 Advanced can act as ODBC/JDBC hosts. The Mac OS X versions of the products do not have this functionality, although that is expected to change in the future. All the instructions that follow refer to only the Windows versions of these products.

This section covers two main methods for moving data out of FileMaker. The first is ODBC/JDBC publishing, where FileMaker Pro, FileMaker Developer, or FileMaker Server 7 Advanced act as a host for ODBC clients. You might think of this as a "pull" method, where another application is pulling data from FileMaker. In this scenario, FileMaker Pro and FileMaker Developer have identical ODBC/JDBC functionality, so for this rest of this section, references to FileMaker Pro should also be considered valid for FileMaker Developer as well.

The second method is a "push" method, with FileMaker Pro/FileMaker Developer use ODBC—but not JDBC—to send data to another application. We begin with the first method, and then combine it with the second in a single example.

SETTING UP FILEMAKER PRO TO HOST AN ODBC/JDBC SESSION

It's possible for you to host a database file that has no content. For example, if you launch FileMaker Pro and create a new file called Contact_Management.FP7, you don't really need to create any fields or new tables for it to be useful for ODBC purposes. A more typical case would be a fully fleshed out database system that would then be queried with ODBC, but that scenario is considered later in this chapter. For now, it's worth creating a FileMaker file that is only a shell so that ODBC can be used to create tables within the shell. An important aspect of FileMaker Pro ODBC/JDBC hosting is that FileMaker Pro accepts only local ODBC/JDBC connections from an ODBC/JDBC client application such as Crystal Reports or the Microsoft Query Tool. The client application needs to be on the same computer as FileMaker Pro. If you need to have remote ODBC/JDBC applications get access to FileMaker files, then you have to use FileMaker Server 7 Advanced.

NOTE

> As of this writing, FileMaker's ODBC functionality does not handle spaces in file names properly. For any files that you might use for ODBC purposes, be sure to use an underscore rather than a space in the file name.

20

To enable the file for ODBC/JDBC sharing, all you need to do is select Edit, Sharing, ODBC/JDBC, as shown in Figure 20.14.

Figure 20.14
ODBC/JDBC sharing is currently available only in the Windows versions of FileMaker Pro and FileMaker Developer.

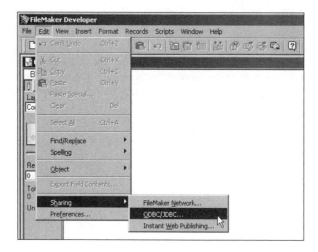

The ODBC/JDBC Sharing Settings dialog opens (see Figure 20.15). This dialog has two parts. The upper section, labeled ODBC/JDBC Settings, controls ODBC/JDBC access to this copy of FileMaker Pro. When ODBC/JDBC Sharing is set to On, FileMaker Pro responds to ODBC/JDBC queries.

Figure 20.15
ODBC/JDBC access to a file can be set for any file that FileMaker Pro is hosting, but not for files that are being hosted by FileMaker Server and that FileMaker Pro has open as a guest.

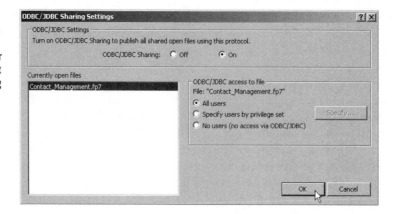

The lower part of this dialog controls ODBC/JDBC access on a file-by-file basis, but only for files that are hosted by FileMaker Pro. FileMaker Pro can't act as an ODBC/JDBC host for files that are being hosted by FileMaker Server.

If you have multiple files open, you can Control+click to select multiple files so that settings changes can apply to several files at once. The settings on the right apply to the currently selected file or files. If you don't want a file to be available for ODBC/JDBC access, you can set the file access to No Users. If the file is set to All Users, the ODBC/JDBC extended privilege gets granted to all privilege sets.

Select File, Define, Accounts & Privileges, as shown in Figure 20.16.

Figure 20.16
Accounts, privileges, and extended privileges are accessed via the Accounts & Privileges menu.

The Define Accounts & Privileges dialog appears. If you click on the Extended Privileges tab, you'll notice that the [fmxdbc] privilege, which controls ODBC/JDBC access to the file, is now in use by all privilege sets. Double-clicking the [fmxdbc] privilege brings up the Edit Extended Privilege dialog, as shown in Figure 20.17.

Figure 20.17
The Edit Extended Privilege dialog shows that every existing privilege has been enabled for ODBC/JDBC access.

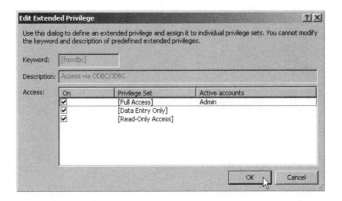

By setting the file to All Users in the ODBC/JDBC Sharing Settings dialog, you turn access on for every privilege set in the file. Any new privilege sets automatically pick up the [fmxdbc] extended privilege as well. Click OK to exit the Edit Extended Privilege dialog, then click the Privilege Sets tab. Double-click the [Full Access] privilege set to bring up the Edit Privilege Set dialog shown in Figure 20.18.

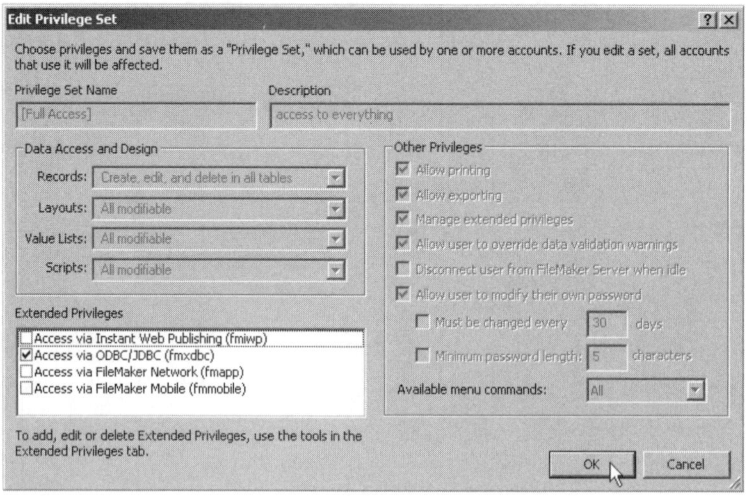

Figure 20.18
The Access via
ODBC/JDBC extended
privilege is automati-
cally enabled when
the All Users option is
selected in the
ODBC/JDBC Sharing
Settings dialog.

The Access via ODBC/JDBC extended privilege is selected in this dialog as well. It's worth noting that extended privileges can be selected and de-selected in two different places—three if you count the sharing dialogs that are accessible from the Edit menu.

Ordinarily, if you're just going to enable an ODBC client application to add, delete, and update records, you should create a privilege set for that purpose. It should have the same settings as the privilege set shown in Figure 20.19.

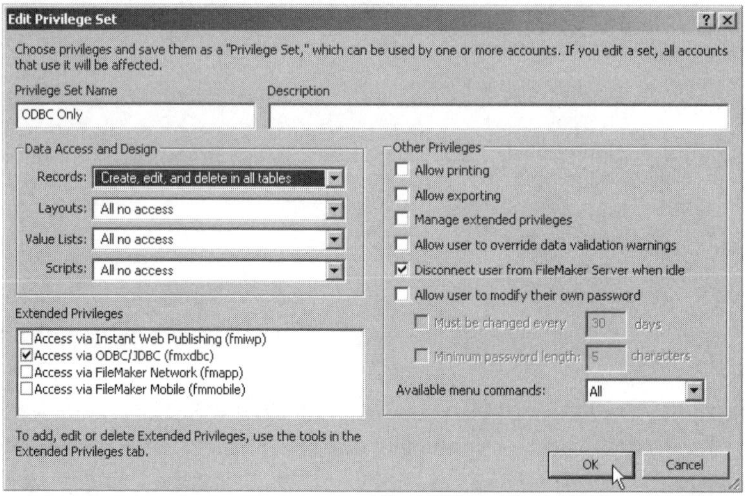

Figure 20.19
For an ODBC/JDBC
client to insert,
update, and delete
records, the privilege
set needs to have only
full record access. No
layout access is
required.

The access to records needs to be Create, Edit, and Delete in All Tables, but no Layout, Value List, or Script access is required. Scripts cannot be called via ODBC/JDBC, so there's no point in enabling access to them.

If you want to allow an ODBC client to use CREATE TABLE, DROP TABLE, or ALTER TABLE to make schema changes, then the account that the ODBC/JDBC client uses needs to be tied to the [Full Access] privilege set. That's the only privilege set that allows schema changes. From a security standpoint, you should assign an ODBC/JDBC account to the [Full Access] privilege set only if that account needs to make schema changes. Otherwise, the best policy is to restrict the level of access to just the minimum privileges required.

To that same point, you shouldn't leave ODBC access open to all users unless literally everyone on the network needs ODBC access to the FileMaker file. A more secure configuration would be to restrict ODBC/JDBC sharing to specific privilege sets, as shown in Figure 20.20. When that option is chosen in the ODBC/JDBC Sharing Settings dialog, the Specify Users by Privilege Set dialog comes up. This dialog enables you to assign or un-assign ODBC/JDBC access to specific privilege sets.

Figure 20.20
ODBC/JDBC access can be granted to specific privilege sets— a more secure configuration than allowing access to All Users.

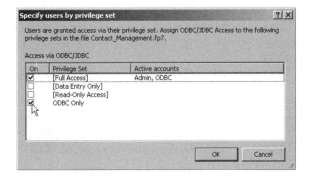

At this point, the file is ready for access. ODBC or JDBC client applications on that same computer can access the file. If you need to have remote ODBC/JDBC applications access the file via the network, then you need to host the file with FileMaker Server 7 Advanced.

Setting up FileMaker Server 7 Advanced to Host Multiple ODBC/JDBC Sessions

Because the Contact_Management.FP7 file has already been enabled for ODBC/JDBC access with FileMaker Pro, it can just be moved to FileMaker Server 7 Advanced. (The regular version of FileMaker Server is not able to host files for ODBC/JDBC access.) The file needs to be moved into the Databases directory in the Data directory in the root level of FileMaker Server 7 Advanced. When it is there, the file can be opened with the FileMaker Server Administration tool, or SAT.

Use the SAT to connect to FileMaker Server 7 Advanced and click the Files item in the Databases item in the left pane of the console. The file should be listed. If the SAT was already open at the time you moved your file in, you probably need to refresh the window. With Files still selected, select Action, Refresh. You can also right-click the right pane and choose Refresh from the pop-up menu. After you locate your file, right-click it and choose Open, as shown in Figure 20.21.

20

Figure 20.21
In the Server Administration tool, you can right-click on a file to open, close, or pause it.

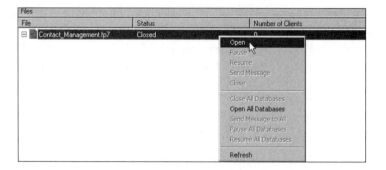

After the file is up and running, you need to enable FileMaker Server 7 Advanced to allow ODBC/JDBC client connections. To do so, select the server itself, as shown in Figure 20.22.

NOTE

You don't need to have any files hosted to allow FileMaker Server 7 Advanced to accept ODBC/JDBC client connections. You could enable the client connections first, and then host databases.

Figure 20.22
You need to select the server before you can change server properties.

With the server chosen, select <u>A</u>ction, <u>P</u>roperties to bring up the Properties dialog shown in Figure 20.23. If not already selected, click on the Clients tab.

FileMaker Server 7 Advanced can have a maximum of 50 ODBC/JDBC connections, and those connections can coexist with regular FileMaker Pro connections. The total number of FileMaker Pro/ODBC/JDBC connections is 250. FileMaker Server has dynamic memory management, so you can max out the connection limits and FileMaker will use memory only as it needs it. To enable ODBC/JDBC access, click Enable Client Services to bring up the Enable Client Services dialog, shown in Figure 20.24.

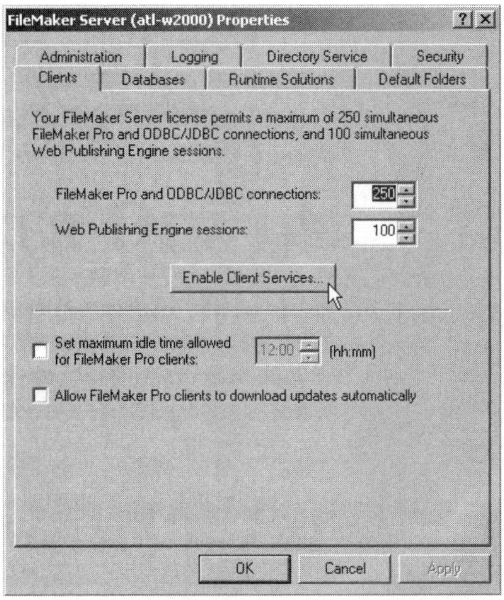

Figure 20.23
FileMaker Server 7 Advanced can host a maximum of 50 ODBC/JDBC connections.

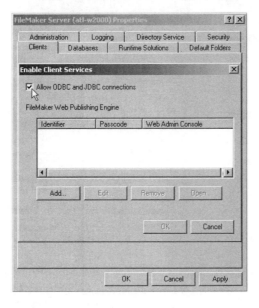

Figure 20.24
The Allow ODBC and JDBC Connections option enables the xDBC plug-in.

Check Allow ODBC and JDBC Connections and click OK to exit the Enable Client Services dialog. FileMaker Server 7 Advanced is now ready to accept ODBC/JDBC connections.

NOTE

> ODBC/JDBC connectivity on FileMaker Server 7 Advanced is actually implemented by a plug-in called xDBC, but it doesn't behave like a regular plug-in and can't be enabled with the plug-in section of the SAT. Using the Enable Client Services dialog is the only way to enable and disable the xDBC plug-in.

20

CONFIGURING A DATA SOURCE NAME FOR ODBC

To connect to either FileMaker Pro or FileMaker Server 7 Advanced, a client ODBC application needs to use a Data Source Name, or DSN. A DSN is a configuration file. ODBC has four components: a host, a client, a driver, and a driver manager. The driver is used to connect to a specific type of host, such as a FileMaker host or a PostgreSQL host. The driver manager is used to create specific configurations for the drivers. These configurations, or data source names, contain information such as the address of the server, the name of the specific database to which you want to connect, port information, and sometimes login information. You need a separate DSN for each database file to which you want to connect.

On Windows, the driver manager is a control panel called Data Sources (ODBC). You can locate it by selecting Start, Settings, Control Panel, Administrative Tools, Data Sources (ODBC), as shown in Figure 20.25.

Figure 20.25
The Data Sources (ODBC) control panel is used to manage ODBC driver configurations.

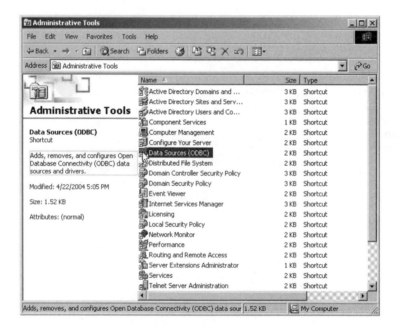

The ODBC driver for FileMaker requires a separate installation. When that is done, double-click the Data Sources (ODBC) control panel to bring up the ODBC Data Source Administrator dialog. Click on the Drivers tab. If your FileMaker ODBC driver installed correctly, you should see a driver called DataDirect 32-BIT SequeLink 5.4, as shown in Figure 20.26. If the driver isn't in the list of drivers, see the "FileMaker Extra: Installing and Troubleshooting the ODBC Client Driver" section at the end of this chapter.

After you're sure that the driver is there, you can use that driver to create a DSN. Click on the User DSN tab and click Add, as shown in Figure 20.27.

Figure 20.26
The DataDirect 32-BIT SequeLink 5.4 driver comes with the Windows versions of FileMaker Pro, FileMaker Developer, and FileMaker Server 7 Advanced. It has a separate installer application.

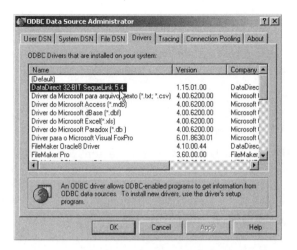

Figure 20.27
Click Add to create a new User DSN.

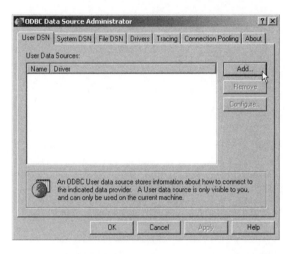

This brings up the Create New Data Source dialog. Select the DataDirect 32-BIT SequeLink 5.4 driver and click Finish, as shown in Figure 20.28.

Figure 20.28
Although it doesn't say anything about FileMaker, the DataDirect 32-BIT SequeLink 5.4 driver is included with various FileMaker products for use in connecting with FileMaker databases.

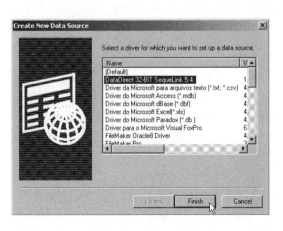

20

Ironically, after you click Finish, you get to start configuring the ODBC driver. The Finish button brings up the DataDirect SequeLink for ODBC Setup dialog. You need to enter a name for the Data Source Name, but the description is optional. The description is useful if you have multiple Data Source Names that connect to the same server, but to different files on that server.

Because there are no translator .DLLs included with the driver, clicking Translate to bring up the Select Translator dialog won't get you very far.

Leave the Use LDAP option unchecked. For the SequeLink Server Host, you need to enter the address of the server on which FileMaker Server 7 Advanced is running. If it's the same machine as the DSN, just use localhost. The SequeLink Server Port is 2399. That port number is the same whether you're using ODBC or JDBC to connect to a FileMaker file, so commit that to memory. After you have the name, host address, and port number entered, you can click the button to browse files available for ODBC access, as shown in Figure 20.29.

Figure 20.29
You can enter the Server Data Source manually, but you can also browse to find out which files are available.

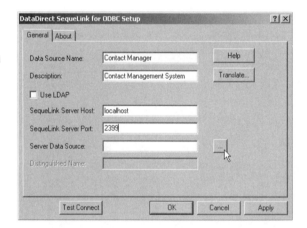

Clicking the Browse button brings up the Server Data Sources dialog shown in Figure 20.30. This is where spaces in the filename cause a problem. If you have a filename with a space in it, you can select it in the Server Data Sources dialog. The problem comes immediately after that point, because the result substitutes the string %20 for any spaces in the filename, and the connection does not test correctly. In Figure 20.30, the filename uses an underscore instead of a space, so it does work properly. After you've selected the file, click OK to exit the Server Data Sources dialog.

Back in the DataDirect SequeLink for ODBC Setup dialog, click Test Connect to bring up the Logon to the SequeLink Service dialog. Remember that to perform schema changes via ODBC, the account needs to have the [Full Access] privilege set specified. Enter the FileMaker username and password credentials for the ODBC access account and click OK, as shown in Figure 20.31.

Figure 20.30
The Server Data Sources dialog lists hosted FileMaker files that have been enabled for ODBC access.

Figure 20.31
You need to enter FileMaker account credentials when testing the ODBC connection.

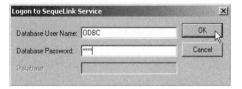

As long as the account credentials are correct, you get a message from the SequeLink ODBC Driver stating that the test was successful, as shown in Figure 20.32. If something is wrong with credentials, or the file isn't being hosted properly, you get an error message. This is where the error message occurs for files that use spaces in the filename.

Figure 20.32
The SequeLink ODBC Driver returns the results of the connection test.

Click OK to exit the SequeLink ODBC Driver dialog, then click OK to exit the DataDirect SequeLink for ODBC Setup dialog. You should now see your new DSN in the list, as shown in Figure 20.33. You can now use it to make ODBC connections to the designated FileMaker file.

Figure 20.33
The new DSN is now available for use by client ODBC applications.

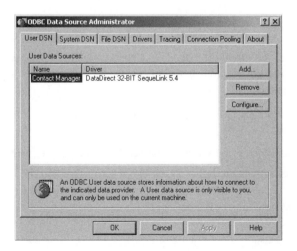

In this case, you created a DSN to connect to a file hosted by FileMaker Server 7 Advanced, but the process would have been virtually identical to create a DSN to connect to a file hosted by FileMaker Pro. The only difference is that a DSN for FileMaker Server 7 Advanced can be created anywhere on the network, whereas a DSN for FileMaker Pro needs to be created on the same computer as the one on which FileMaker Pro is running.

USING FILEMAKER PRO AS AN ODBC CLIENT

FileMaker Pro has the capability of acting as a client to an ODBC host. That ODBC host might be Microsoft SQLServer, Oracle, mySQL, or even FileMaker Server 7 Advanced. It could also be a FileMaker 6 database, which could be useful in some conversion scenarios.

→ For more information about using ODBC to import data into FileMaker Pro, **see** "Importing From an ODBC Data Source," **p. 552**.

For the purposes of this example, FileMaker Pro acts as an ODBC client to FileMaker Server 7 Advanced. This is only to demonstrate FileMaker as an ODBC host and client at the same time. In practice, you wouldn't need to do this because FileMaker Pro is a much more fully functioning client when you use a regular client connection to connect to FileMaker Server 7 Advanced. You would be much more likely to have FileMaker Pro acting as the client to some other ODBC host.

For the record, FileMaker, Inc., doesn't support this configuration, meaning that you won't be able to get assistance from technical support if you have trouble getting this configuration to work, but it works fine for our purposes. That doesn't mean that if you try this, you'll never be able to get technical support again. It just means that they won't help you set this up.

At this point, you know how to set up a file for ODBC access on both FileMaker Pro and FileMaker Server 7 Advanced. If you have a FileMaker file that's available for ODBC access, you can use SQL to create and modify tables within that file. To try this out, launch FileMaker Pro and create a new file called ODBC Example. It doesn't need to have any fields in it—yet.

CREATE TABLE

CREATE TABLE is a SQL command that is used to specify the name and fields for a new database table. It can be used by FileMaker Pro's Execute SQL script step to set up tables in other database systems.

To try this out, select Scripts, ScriptMaker to bring up the Define Scripts dialog. Click New to bring up the Edit Script dialog.

→ For more detailed information about creating scripts, **see** "Common Scripting Techniques," **p. 249**.

Name the script Create Contact Table. In the list of script steps on the left, scroll all the way to the bottom and select Execute SQL. Click Move, as shown in Figure 20.34, to move the script step to the right side of the dialog.

Figure 20.34
The Execute SQL script step can be used to run SQL statements against any host specified by a DSN on that same computer.

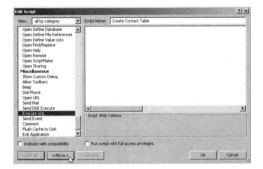

After the Execute SQL step is on the right side (and selected), click Specify to bring up the Specify SQL dialog shown in Figure 20.35.

Figure 20.35
Use the Specify button to link the SQL step to a specific DSN.

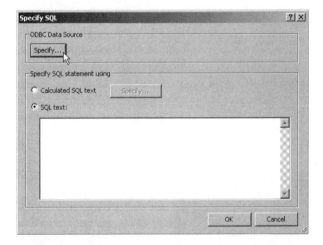

Click Specify in the ODBC Data Source section to bring up the Select ODBC Data Source dialog shown in Figure 20.36.

Figure 20.36
The Select ODBC Data Source dialog lists any User or System DSNs that have been created.

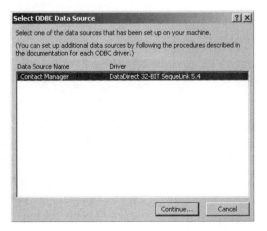

20

Select the DSN you want to use and click Continue to exit the Select ODBC Data Source dialog and bring up the Enter Password dialog shown in Figure 20.37.

Figure 20.37
By checking the Save User Name and Password option, you enable the script to authenticate itself every time it executes.

Enter the credentials for the ODBC-enabled FileMaker account that you want to use. In this case, you're about to create a SQL statement that creates a table, which is a schema change. For that statement to execute correctly, the account needs to have the [Full Access] privilege set specified. Unless you check the Save User Name and Password option as shown, you are prompted for login credentials every time this script executes. Click OK to exit the Enter Password dialog and return to the Specify SQL dialog.

Enter the following text into the SQL text box:

```
CREATE TABLE "Contact" ("Contact ID" Decimal primary key,
"First Name" VarChar(20), "Last Name" VarChar,
"Organization" VarChar, "Address" VarChar, "City" VarChar,
"State" VarChar(2), "Zip" VarChar)
```

Figure 20.38
SQL statements can be entered into an Execute SQL script step by hand, as in this case, or they can be drawn from a field.

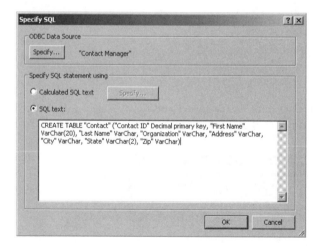

You might have noticed some inconsistencies in this SQL statement. Several of the fields were specified as VarChar, or variable-length character fields. Only two, though—the First Name field and the State field—had a field length specified. This is intentional. With FileMaker (Pro or Server 7 Advanced), field lengths can be explicit or undefined. You'll see the effect of this in a moment. It's also worth pointing out that the Contact ID field has been defined as the primary key. You'll see the effect of this as well. One last point: When using SQL with FileMaker, table and field names must be enclosed in double quotes. Note that these are straight quotes, not curly quotes.

Click OK to exit the Specify SQL dialog, then click OK to exit the Edit Script dialog and return to the Define Scripts dialog. With the Create Contact Table script still selected, click Perform. In this case, no news is good news. If no error dialog comes up, you can assume that the script executed properly. To see the result of the script's execution, open Contact_Management as a guest of FileMaker Server 7 Advanced. Select File, Define, Database to bring up the Define Database dialog. Select the Fields tab and select Contact from the table list. You should see the list of fields shown in Figure 20.39.

Figure 20.39
The Contact table and the fields within it were created via ODBC.

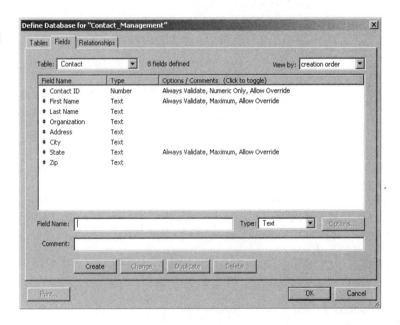

Notice that the Contact ID, First Name, and State fields all have validation applied to them. Select the Contact ID field and click Options to bring up the Options for Field dialog. Click the Validation tab and take a look at the validation settings. They should look like Figure 20.40.

20

TIP

> Remember that the Contact ID field had two specifications. One was decimal, and the other was primary key. The decimal type is enforced with FileMaker's Numeric Only validation. The primary key designation had no effect, and was ignored by FileMaker. Although functional primary keys can be created in FileMaker Pro, there is no explicit setting to designate a field as a primary key in any formal sense. The primary key designation causes no harm when present, but because it has no effect, there's no point in using it in a CREATE TABLE statement.

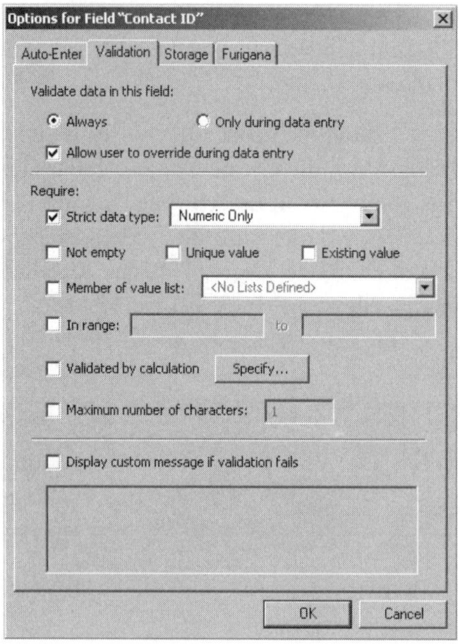

Figure 20.40
Fields specified as decimal in a CREATE TABLE statement end up with Numeric Only validation in FileMaker.

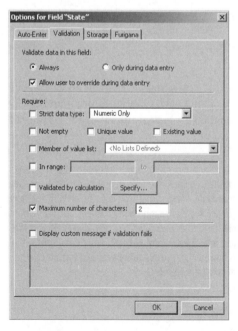

→ For more information about creating primary keys in FileMaker Pro, **see** "Working with Keys and Match Fields," **p. 158**.

The First Name and State fields were both VarChar fields with specified length. Take a look at the validation setting for the State field, shown in Figure 20.41. You can see that the maximum number of characters has been set at 2.

Figure 20.41
Fields specified as VarChar with a fixed number of characters in a CREATE TABLE statement end up with Maximum Number of Characters validation in FileMaker.

If you exit the Options for Field dialog and click on the Relationships tab, you can see that a table occurrence for the Contact table was created. However, if you click OK to exit the Define Database dialog and switch into Layout mode, you'll find that a layout was not automatically created. When you use ODBC to create tables, you need to create layouts to display data from those tables by hand.

Switch back to your ODBC Example file and try running the Create Contact Table script again. You should get a duplicate name error message like the one shown in Figure 20.42.

Figure 20.42
If you try to create a table with the name of a table that already exists, you get a Duplicate Name ODBC error.

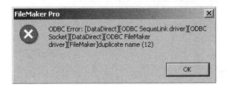

It's good to get feedback when things go wrong, but it's also good to get feedback when things go right. The Create Contact Table script can and should be modified so that the user is clear on the result of the script action. As it stands right now, when the script works properly, no message is given to the user.

To change this, select Scripts, ScriptMaker to bring up the Define Scripts dialog. Select the Create Contact Table script and click Edit to bring up the Edit Script dialog. Change the script so that after the Execute SQL step, it reads:

```
If[Get ( LastError ) = 0]
  Show Custom Dialog ["SQL Action Status"; "Create table
executed successfully. "]
End If
```

Click OK to exit the Edit Script dialog. The script now gives the user notification when it runs properly and when it encounters an error. To test it, you need to get rid of the Contact table so you can try to re-create it. To use SQL to delete a table, you use the DROP TABLE command. Like the CREATE TABLE command, this needs to be executed from an Execute SQL script step.

DROP TABLE

DROP TABLE is a SQL command used to delete a table. When you drop a table, you delete all the data that resides in that table, as well as the table itself. The DROP TABLE command can be used by FileMaker Pro's Execute SQL script step.

To try using it, select the Create Contact Table script and click Duplicate to create a copy of the script. The Create Contact Table Copy script should be selected, so click Edit to bring up the Edit Script dialog. Rename the script to Drop Contact Table. Double-click the Execute SQL script step to bring up the Specify SQL dialog. Change the SQL text to

```
DROP TABLE "Contact"
```

Because this script is a copy of the Create Contact Table script, the ODBC Data Source has already been specified and doesn't need to be changed. Click OK to exit the Specify SQL dialog. Next, double-click the Show Custom Dialog step and change the message so that it says, Drop table executed successfully. Click OK to exit the Show Custom Dialog Options dialog. The result should look like Figure 20.43

Figure 20.43
The DROP TABLE statement is used to delete a table.

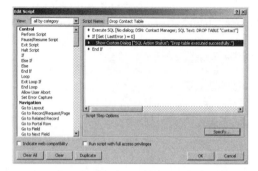

Click OK again to exit the Edit Script dialog. Run the script to drop the Contact table. You should get your message saying that DROP TABLE executed successfully. Now you can run your Create Contact Table script again to make sure that you get the Create table executed successfully message.

INSERT INTO

INSERT INTO is a SQL command that inserts data into a database table. The command can be used by FileMaker Pro's Execute SQL script step.

Now that you have a table, you can load it with data. Usually when you use FileMaker as an ODBC client, most of the activities involve querying records that already exist on the ODBC host. Sometimes, though, you need to create a new record in FileMaker and add it to the set of records on the host. Consider a scenario where FileMaker Pro is running a database that mirrors the structure of an ODBC host. To replicate that structure with your ODBC Example file, add a Contact table with the following fields:

> Contact ID (number, auto-entered serial)
>
> First Name (text)
>
> Last Name (text)
>
> Address1 (text)
>
> City (text)
>
> State (text)
>
> Zip (text)

An INSERT INTO SQL command needs to incorporate the field values from the current record. You can do that in one of two ways. One way is to create a calculation field in the

Contact table that assembles the SQL statement, but that clutters up the table. A better way is to put the calculation inside the Execute SQL script step.

Once again, select Scripts, ScriptMaker to bring up the Define Scripts dialog. Select the Create Contact Table script and click Duplicate to create a copy of the script. Click Edit to edit the copy. Rename the script to Insert Contact. Double-click the Execute SQL script step to bring up the Specify SQL dialog. Click the radio button in front of Calculated SQL text to bring up the Specify Calculation dialog. Given the fields specified above, this calculation creates the appropriate INSERT statement:

```
"INSERT INTO " & Quote ("Contact") & "(" & Quote ("Contact ID") & ", " &
Quote ("First Name") & ", " & Quote ("Last Name") & ", " & Quote ("Address") &
", " & Quote ("City") & ", " & Quote ("State") & ", " & Quote ("Zip") & ")
VALUES ('" & Contact::Contact ID & "', '" & Contact::First Name & "', '" &
Contact::Last Name & "', '" & Contact::Address1 & "', '" & Contact::City & "',
'" & Contact::State & "', '" & Contact::Zip & "')"
```

This calculation is also shown in Figure 20.44.

Figure 20.44
The Quote function is very useful for putting quotation marks in the appropriate places.

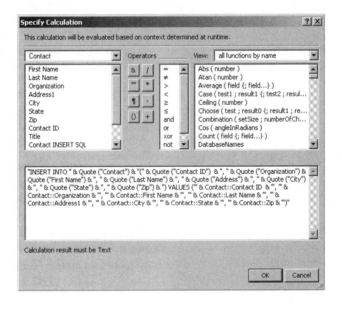

The calculated result of this formula would look something like this:

```
INSERT INTO "Contact"("Contact ID", "Organization", "First Name", "Last Name",
"Address", "City", "State", "Zip") VALUES ('1', 'Vegan Steakhouse', 'Scott',
'Stevenson', '1326 Old County Rd.', 'Mentor', 'OH', '44060')
```

Again, a word about quotation marks. When you use SQL in an ODBC client application to connect to FileMaker files, the names of tables and fields need to be in double quotes, whereas values—even number values—need to be enclosed in single quotes.

After the calculation has been entered, click OK to exit the Specify Calculation dialog and return to the Specify SQL dialog. It should now look like Figure 20.45, with the ODBC Data Source already specified.

20

Figure 20.45
The Specify SQL dialog gives you the option to manually enter a SQL statement or to calculate one.

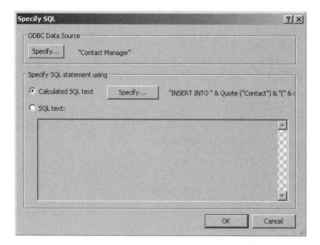

Click OK to exit the Specify SQL dialog and return to the Edit Script dialog. Double-click the Show Custom Dialog step and change the message so that it says, Record Insert executed successfully. Click OK to exit the Show Custom Dialog Options dialog. Click OK to exit the Edit Script dialog, and your script is complete. This script can be called in a looping script to load all the records in a found set into an ODBC host table.

UPDATE

The UPDATE SQL command is used to change data in an existing table record. This command can be used by FileMaker Pro's Execute SQL script step.

After records have been loaded into a table, it may be necessary to edit them. Changes made in FileMaker need to get pushed up to the ODBC host. To do that, duplicate the Insert Contact script and modify the Execute SQL script step so that the Calculated SQL text reads as follows:

```
"UPDATE " & Quote ("Contact") & " SET " & Quote ("Organization") & " = '" &
Contact::Organization & "', " & Quote ("First Name") & " = '" &
Contact::First Name & "', "
& Quote ("Last Name") & " = '" & Contact::Last Name & "', "
& Quote ("Address") & " = '" & Contact::Address1 & "', "
& Quote ("City") & " = '" & Contact::City & "', "
& Quote ("State") & " = '" & Contact::State & "', "
& Quote ("Zip") & " = '" & Contact::Zip & "' WHERE " & Quote ("Contact ID") &
    " = '" & Contact::Contact ID & "'"
```

The calculated result of this formula will look like this:

```
UPDATE "Contact" SET "Organization" = 'Vegan Steakhouse', "First Name" =
'Scott', "Last Name" = 'Stevenson', "Address" = '1326 Old County Rd.',
"City" = 'Mentor', "State" = 'OH', "Zip" = '44060' WHERE "Contact ID" = '1'
```

This SQL statement has an important element: the WHERE clause. The WHERE clause functions like a find in FileMaker Pro. WHERE introduces a set of search criteria. The WHERE clause can have multiple criteria, such as WHERE "State" = 'Washington' AND "County" = 'Lake'.

If the WHERE clause is left off, then the UPDATE acts like a Replace function in FileMaker, and it updates every record in the table with the specified information. Similarly, if the WHERE criteria matches multiple records, all those records are all updated in the same fashion.

 FileMaker does not support the SELECT FOR UPDATE syntax, so it's not possible to lock a record with a SQL query. To avoid running into another user's record update while you're updating a record, see "An Alternative to Updating with a Record Lock" in the Troubleshooting section at the end of this chapter.

DELETE

DELETE is a SQL command that can be used to delete one or more records from a table. The command can be used by FileMaker Pro's Execute SQL script step.

The DELETE command is quite simple. You just need to specify the table and which rows to delete. If the rows aren't specified, the contents of the entire table are deleted. Like the other examples, it can be embedded in an Execute SQL script step. An example of a DELETE statement might look like this:

```
DELETE FROM "Contact" WHERE "Contact ID" = '53'
```

Again, if there is no WHERE clause, the DELETE applies to every record in the table. This is another statement that you would best assemble by calculating a value from the current record. This means that if you want to delete a record in FileMaker and in the ODBC host, you need to execute the SQL statement first, and only then delete the local FileMaker record.

TROUBLESHOOTING

DATA GETS TRUNCATED WITH CERTAIN EXPORT FORMATS

After I export data from my database, I noticed that some fields exported only part of the information that they contain. How can I export all the data?

If you have fields that you use to store lengthy notes or comments, you may find that those notes get truncated when being exported to certain file formats.

Several of FileMaker's export formats have limitations on the amount of data that can be exported. The BASIC export file format truncates data from any single text field beyond 255 characters. The DBF supports only 254 characters, and only 4000 bytes per record. The WK1 format exports only 240 characters per field. If you need to export extensive notes data on a regular basis, these limitations can be problematic. One possible solution is to move your notes into a separate table. You can enter notes into separate rows of a portal, and any especially long notes can be broken up among multiple notes records. They'll all still relate to the same parent record, and it actually gives you some additional flexibility in managing those notes. You can attach separate dates and times to each note, for example, and sort or search on that criteria.

An Alternative to Updating with a Record Lock

How can I make sure that other users can't change information that I'm editing when I'm using an ODBC client application?

FileMaker does not support the SELECT FOR UPDATE syntax, so it's not possible to lock a record with a SQL query.

Because you can't lock a record prior to updating it with ODBC, it's necessary to come up with an alternate plan to avoid overwriting another user's changes. One option is to query the record contents into a set of temporary fields before editing the record. With some effort, you can construct a calculation that constructs the UPDATE statement so that it updates only the fields that you changed. The result is that you and another user can have your record changes merge together.

FileMaker Extra: Installing and Troubleshooting the ODBC Client Driver

The DataDirect ODBC driver that's used to connect to FileMaker Pro, FileMaker Developer, or FileMaker Server 7 Advanced is not installed during the regular FileMaker installation process. It requires a separate installation.

Remember that FileMaker Pro and FileMaker Developer can act as xDBC hosts only for client applications running on the same computer. If you want to use Microsoft Excel, for example, to connect to a database hosted by FileMaker Pro, then the ODBC client driver needs to be installed on the same computer as that on which FileMaker Pro is installed.

If the database is being hosted by FileMaker Server 7 Advanced, and a client application elsewhere on the network needs to use ODBC to access that database, then the ODBC client driver needs to be installed on the same computer as that on which the client application is installed.

You need to use a FileMaker Pro, FileMaker Developer, or FileMaker Server 7 Advanced installation CD to perform the installation of the ODBC driver on the client computer.

On the FileMaker Pro install CD, for example, you need to click the eyeglasses button, as shown in Figure 20.46.

Clicking the eyeglasses button enables you to explore the CD content. The xDBC directory, which is shown in Figure 20.47, contains the installation programs for the ODBC and JDBC drivers. It also contains extensive documentation on how to install and use both the ODBC and JDBC drivers.

Figure 20.46
Click the eyeglasses button to access the installation CD content.

Figure 20.47
Double-click the xDBC directory to get to the ODBC and JDBC client driver installers.

After you've found the ODBC client driver installer, run it as you would any other software installer. At the end of the process, you should have three new ODBC drivers installed. To verify this, select Start, Settings, Control Panel to bring up the Control Panel window. Double-click Administrative Tools to bring up the Administrative Tools window. Double-click Data Sources (ODBC) to bring up the ODBC Data Source Administrator dialog. Click on the Drivers tab to see the list of installed ODBC drivers. The DataDirect 32-BIT SequeLink 5.4 driver should be among them, as shown in Figure 20.48.

20

Figure 20.48
After you've run the DataDirect ODBC client installer, the DataDirect 32-BIT SequeLink 5.4 driver should be visible in your list of ODBC drivers.

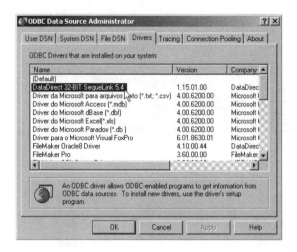

Two other drivers get installed at the same time. One is the FileMaker Oracle8 Driver, and the other is the FileMaker Text Driver. If you ran the installer properly and these drivers are not visible in your ODBC Data Source Administrator dialog, then you probably have a problem with some of your registry values. This problem is more likely to happen on Windows XP.

To fix this problem, launch the Command prompt and type **regedit** and then Return to bring up the Registry Editor. Find the Registry entry called

HKEY_LOCAL_MACHINE\SOFTWARE\ODBC\ODBCINST.INI

as shown in Figure 20.49.

Click each entry by clicking on it once. The first item for each entry should be Default, and it should have some value displayed, even if that value is value not set. If your DataDirect driver isn't showing up in the driver list, though, odds are it has a null or blank value, as shown in Figure 20.49, instead of (value not set).

If the Default has a null value, press the Delete key to clear it. You get a Confirm Value Delete dialog asking you to confirm the deletion, as shown in Figure 20.50.

Click Yes, and the null value changes to (value not set), as shown in Figure 20.51.

Go through all the entries in the HKEY_LOCAL_MACHINE\SOFTWARE\ODBC\ODBCINST.INI key to make sure that none of the Default entries has a null value. When you've finished, close RegEdit and restart the machine. The DataDirect 32-BIT SequeLink 5.4 driver, Oracle8 driver, and FileMaker Text driver will now appear in the Drivers tab of the ODBC control panel.

Registry Edit View Favorites Help
My Computer
HKEY_CLASSES_ROOT
HKEY_CURRENT_USER
HKEY_LOCAL_MACHINE
HARDWARE
SAM
SECURITY
SOFTWARE
SYSTEM
HKEY_USERS
HKEY_CURRENT_CONFIG
My Computer\HKEY_LOCAL_MACHINE\SOFTWARE

Figure 20.49 ODBC registry entries are in the `SOFTWARE` section of `HKEY_LOCAL_MACHINE`.

Confirm Value Delete
Are you sure you want to delete this value?
Yes
No

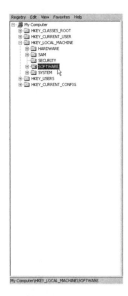

Figure 20.50 You need to confirm deletion of a null value.

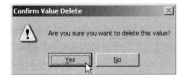

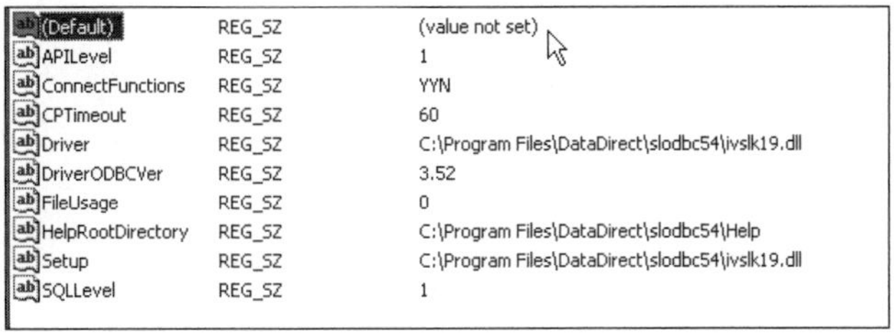
(Default) REG_SZ (value not set)
APILevel REG_SZ 1
ConnectFunctions REG_SZ YYN
CPTimeout REG_SZ 60
Driver REG_SZ C:\Program Files\DataDirect\slodbc54\ivslk19.dll
DriverODBCVer REG_SZ 3.52
FileUsage REG_SZ 0
HelpRootDirectory REG_SZ C:\Program Files\DataDirect\slodbc54\Help
Setup REG_SZ C:\Program Files\DataDirect\slodbc54\ivslk19.dll
SQLLevel REG_SZ 1

Figure 20.51 After the null value has been cleared, the Default entry should say `(value not set)`.

CHAPTER 21

INSTANT WEB PUBLISHING

INSTANT WEB PUBLISHING—AN OVERVIEW

Instant Web Publishing (IWP) has been a feature of FileMaker Pro since its introduction years ago in version 4.0. In its earlier incarnations, IWP was never quite the robust tool that one hoped it would be. Its main benefits were that it was utterly simple to enable and configure, and that it turned FileMaker layouts into Web pages without any CGI programming or HTML coding whatsoever. There were, however, many limitations, particularly with the number of layouts you could use and with script behavior, making IWP unsuitable for all but the most basic of Web applications.

In FileMaker Pro 7, IWP retains its amazing ease of setup and use, but for the first time, it has enough features and flexibility that it can be used as part of a serious business application. We think that the new IWP will revolutionize the way that FileMaker Pro systems are developed and deployed. Whether you're new to FileMaker Pro development or just haven't looked at IWP in a while, it's well worth your time to investigate and learn about this tool.

WHAT IS IWP?

Broadly speaking, Instant Web Publishing is one of several options for sharing data from a FileMaker database to the Web. The other options include exporting static HTML, exporting XML and transforming it into HTML with a style sheet, and Custom Web Publishing (CWP), which involves doing HTTP queries of the Web Publishing Engine and transforming the resulting XML into HTML.

→ For more on XML export, **see** "FileMaker and XML," **p. 641**.

→ For more on custom Web publishing, see Chapter 23, "Custom Web Publishing," **p. 671**.

The goal of IWP is to translate to a Web browser as much of the appearance and functionality of a FileMaker Pro database as possible, without requiring that a developer do any additional programming. FileMaker layouts are rendered in the user's browser almost exactly as they appear to users of the FileMaker Pro desktop application. To give you an idea of what this looks like from the user perspective, Figures 21.1 and 21.2 show an example of a layout rendered both in FileMaker Pro and through IWP in a Web browser.

Figure 21.1
Using Instant Web Publishing, the layouts that you create in FileMaker are dynamically turned into Web pages for you.

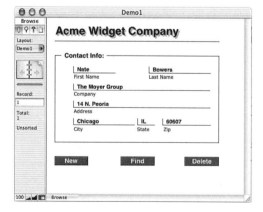

Figure 21.2
Instant Web Publishing renders FileMaker layouts almost flawlessly as Web pages.

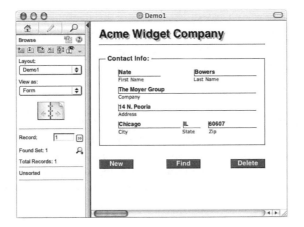

IWP is more, though, than simply rendering your layouts as Web pages. IWP users have much, if not all, of the same application functionality through their browsers as do FileMaker Pro users. They can run scripts and view, create, edit, and delete data just like traditional FileMaker Pro users.

IWP IMPROVEMENTS IN FILEMAKER PRO 7

There are numerous improvements to IWP in FileMaker Pro 7. For those readers who have used IWP in previous versions, we'll run through some of the most significant changes.

First, there is no longer a configuration wizard where you pick themes and views that determine the look and functionality of a status area. Instead, IWP now has a status area that looks and functions similar to its FileMaker counterpart. And there are no restrictions on the number of layouts that can be accessed. The only layout restrictions are those that you, the developer, choose to put in place. We'll discuss this concept more in the "Designing for IWP Deployment" section later in this chapter.

Another major difference in the new IWP is script support. Previous versions of IWP had severe restrictions on the type and length of scripts that could be run from a browser. Now, over 70 script steps are supported, and there are no length constraints. We discuss script support in detail later in this chapter as well.

Perhaps the biggest change to IWP in FileMaker 7 is how it's deployed. In earlier incarnations, IWP was part of the Web Companion, which meant that a client copy of FileMaker Pro or FileMaker Pro Unlimited acted as the Web host. That client was able to share files that it had opened as a guest of FileMaker Server. Frequently, this architecture proved to be unstable and required a fairly high degree of maintenance.

FileMaker Pro can still act as the host for IWP sharing (for up to five concurrent users), but now, FileMaker Server 7 Advanced can also be a Web host. Not only does the latter allow greater stability and a greater number of connections, but you can also use FileMaker Server's SSL encryption capabilities to better secure your data.

21

Finally, the new IWP is session-based. We'll explore this concept more closely later in the chapter; the session capability is one of the ways that IWP is able to function very similarly to the FileMaker desktop application. It allows IWP to have a semblance of persistence in an otherwise "stateless" environment.

SCENARIOS FOR IWP

There are two primary scenarios in which IWP is a deployment option you may wish to consider: first, for providing remote users access to your files, and second, for creating or integrating with a database-driven Web site. In each case, IWP is a less costly and an easier-to-implement choice than alternative options. We think it's helpful before diving into the implementation details to have a good understanding of how IWP stacks up against these alternatives.

REMOTE USERS

First, let's consider the idea of providing remote users access to a FileMaker database. By "remote," we mean any users who are not physically connected to the same local area network as the FileMaker Pro (or FileMaker Server) application that is hosting a given file. It is certainly possible for remote users to use FileMaker's built-in networking to connect to a hosted database, which is of course what users on the local area network would do. The benefits of this are that there are no functionality differences experienced between remote and local users and that you don't have any additional costs or development work. The remote users need to have a copy of the FileMaker Pro desktop application, and that's it. The drawback of this as an option for remote users is performance. A networked FileMaker solution is highly network intensive and needs lots of bandwidth to operate well. Remote users may find client-server performance to be unacceptable, especially when using large files and for reporting functions.

One alternative you might consider is setting up Citrix with Terminal Services, or even just Terminal Services by itself, for your remote users. Essentially, when remote users start a Citrix session, their FileMaker Pro application are running locally on the same network as FileMaker Server, and are hence very fast. All that's shipped across the network are keystrokes, mouse clicks, and screen images. Citrix/Terminal Services is an appropriate solution when you have multiple offices or lots of remote users who need to access a centralized FileMaker database, but it comes with a fairly steep price tag and requires not insignificant amounts of configuration and maintenance.

NOTE

Check out www.citrix.com for more information on using Citrix for deploying FileMaker to remote users.

Other remote access emulation technologies are worth considering, such as Timbuktu and gotomypc.com. These can be excellent low-cost solutions for organizations with just a few remote users, but do not allow multiple simultaneous client connections.

Instant Web Publishing offers a reasonable alternative to both FileMaker's built-in networking and to remote access emulation products as a means for providing database access for remote users. It might provide faster access to data than using FileMaker's networking, and it comes with much lower cost and maintenance requirements than a Citrix deployment. There are limitations of IWP that need to be weighed against these benefits, but for its functionality, speed, cost, and ease of use, it's certainly worth trying.

CREATING A DATABASE-DRIVEN WEB SITE

There are two general techniques for incorporating data from a FileMaker database into a Web site. On the one hand, you can create "static" views of data by exporting HTML or XML from your database. This works especially well for "read-only" sites where the content doesn't change often. For instance, you might want to publish data from an event database on your Web site. It might be suitable simply to find and export some portion of the data on a periodic basis, and then to move the resulting HTML document to your Web site.

→ Exporting XML and transforming it into other formats via XSLT is covered in Chapter 22, "FileMaker and Web Services"; **see** "Transforming XML," **p. 646**.

The alternative to publishing "static" data is to publish data "dynamically," which means that the Web user is somehow interacting with the database in real time. This allows up-to-the-second data accuracy and also enables users to easily add, edit, and delete data directly from their browsers.

Creating dynamic connections from Web pages to a FileMaker database can be a complex and time consuming task. This process is often referred to as *Custom Web Publishing (CWP)*. For now, it's enough that you know a few of the pros and cons of CWP. On the plus side, using CWP, you can create robust, complex, and professional Web applications. The drawback of CWP is the same as with most Web application development: It's a fairly complex skill to learn and is therefore costly in terms of time and/or money.

→ Please **see** Chapter 23, "Custom Web Publishing," **p. 671**, to learn more about Custom Web Publishing and how it compares to IWP.

Instant Web Publishing offers a reasonable alternative to CWP as a means for building a dynamic Web application. You can design layouts in your FileMaker solution that fit nicely with the rest of a site, or you can even create a whole Web site out of FileMaker layouts if you're so inclined. With IWP, you don't need to learn HTML or any middleware languages, and maintaining your site is as simple as editing some scripts and layouts. However, these "strengths" of IWP also become its weaknesses when attempting to develop especially complex Web applications. You have no ability to modify how IWP behaves at a low level: It does what it does, and that's it. You can't look "under the hood" at the code and manipulate it.

GETTING STARTED WITH IWP

21

After you've decided that IWP is something you want to try, there isn't too much that you'll need to do to get started. There are two ways to deploy IWP. You can use the regular FileMaker Pro 7 desktop application, in which case you're limited to publishing a maximum of 10 database files to, at most, 5 concurrent users. Alternatively, you can use FileMaker

Server 7 Advanced, which allows for significantly more files and users. The configuration for each of these options is covered in detail in the next section.

The host machine—whether running FileMaker Pro 7 or FileMaker Server 7 Advanced—of course needs to have an Internet (or intranet) connection. Ideally, it will be a persistent connection (for example, T1, DSL), and the host machine needs to have a static IP address. If you don't have a static IP address on the host machine, remote users can have a difficult time accessing your solution. Finally, any databases you want users to access via IWP need to be open on the host machine.

TIP

Consider setting up a domain name for the IWP host machine. This enables your users to go to something like databases.mycompany.com instead of a difficult-to-remember IP address. Your ISP or a networking specialist can help you with that task. If you ever need to change machines or IP addresses, you can repoint the domain name to the new address without your users being affected by the change.

To access your IWP-enabled files, remote users need to have an Internet connection and a compatible browser. Because IWP makes heavy use of Cascading Style Sheets, the browser restrictions are important, and are something you need to consider carefully if you intend to use IWP as part of a publicly accessible Web site.

On Windows, users must have Internet Explorer version 6.0 (or higher). On Mac OS X 10.2.8, they'll need Internet Explorer 5.1 or 5.2. On Mac OS X 10.3, Safari 1.1 will work as well. Obviously, these options may change with new releases of browsers and new versions of operating systems, so consult the www.filemaker.com Web site for the latest configuration guidelines. Whichever approved browser is used, JavaScript needs to be enabled, and the cache settings should be set to always update pages.

CAUTION

Some organizations forcibly disable JavaScript in all browsers. If you, or any of your remote users, work for such an organization, be aware of this and its ramifications for your Web publishing strategy.

ENABLING AND CONFIGURING IWP

To publish databases to the Web via IWP, you need to enable and configure IWP on the host machine, and you need to set up one or more database files to allow IWP access. Each of these topics is covered in detail in the sections that follow.

CONFIGURING FILEMAKER PRO FOR IWP

Using FileMaker Pro 7, you can share up to 10 databases with up to 5 users. To share more files or share with more users, you need to use FileMaker Server 7 Advanced as your IWP host. FileMaker Pro 7 can serve only files that it opens as a host. That is, it's not possible for FileMaker Pro to open a file as a guest of FileMaker Server 7 Advanced and to further share it to IWP users.

Figure 21.3 shows the Instant Web Publishing setup screen in FileMaker Pro. In Windows, you get to this screen by choosing Edit, Sharing, Instant Web Publishing. On Mac, choose FileMaker Pro, Sharing, Instant Web Publishing. The top half of the Instant Web Publishing dialog box relates to the status of IWP at the application level; the bottom half details the sharing status of any currently open database files. The two halves function independently of one another and are discussed separately here. For now, we're just concerned with getting IWP working at the application level and therefore limit our discussion to the options on the top half of the Instant Web Publishing dialog box.

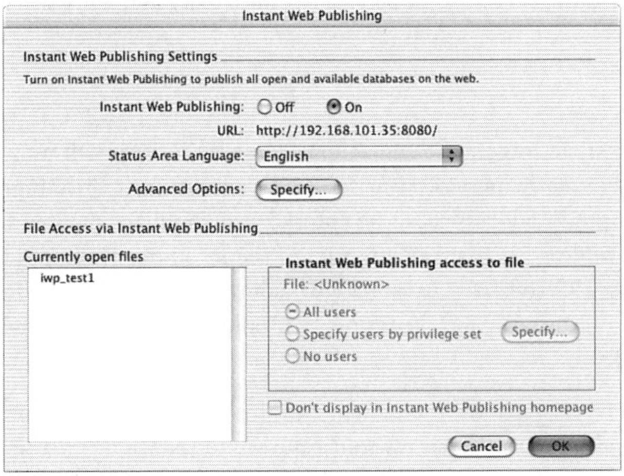

Figure 21.3
To enable Instant Web Publishing, simply select On on the IWP configuration screen.

Turning Instant Web Publishing on and off is as simple as toggling the Off/On selection. Selecting On enables this particular copy of FileMaker Pro to act as an IWP host. You can choose the language that will be used on the IWP Database Homepage and in the status area. You can also configure a handful of advanced options, as shown in Figure 21.4.

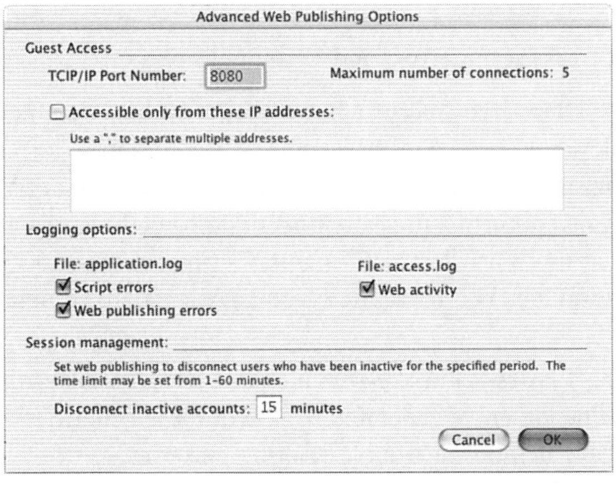

Figure 21.4
On the Advanced Web Publishing Options dialog box, you can configure the port number, logging options, IP restrictions, and the session disconnect time.

21

PORT NUMBER

By default, IWP is configured to use port 80 on the host machine. If another application, such as a Web server, is already using that port, you see an error message and are asked to specify a different port to use. FileMaker, Inc. has registered port 591 with the Internet Assigned Numbers Authority (IANA), so that's the recommended alternate port number. The only downside of using a port other than 80 is that users need to explicitly specify the port as part of the URL to access IWP. For instance, instead of typing "127.0.0.1," your users would need to type "127.0.0.1:591" (or whatever port number you specified).

NOTE

> If you are using Mac OS X, you may be asked to type your computer's pass phrase if you attempt to change the port number when configuring IWP within the FileMaker client.

SECURITY

If you know the IP addresses of the machines your IWP users will use when accessing your solution, you can greatly increase your solution's security by restricting access to only those addresses. Multiple IP addresses can be entered as a comma-separated list. You can use an asterisk (*) as a wildcard in place of any part of the IP address (except for the first part). That is, entering 192.168.101.* causes any IP address from 192.168.101.0 to 192.168.101.255 to be accepted. Entering 192.* allows access to any user whose IP address begins with 192.

If you don't set IP restrictions, then anyone in the world who knows the IP address of your host machine and has network access to it can see at least the IWP Database Homepage (which lists IWP enabled files), and if you've enabled the Instant Web Publishing extended privilege on the Guest privilege set, the files could be used as well. This is, of course, exactly the behavior you'd want when IWP is used as part of a publicly accessible Web site.

LOGGING

You can enable two activity logs for tracking and monitoring your IWP solution: the application log and the access log.

The application log tracks script errors and Web publishing errors.

- **Script Errors**—These errors occur when a Web user runs a script that contains non-Web-compatible script steps. See the section titled "Scripting for IWP," later in this chapter, for more information about what particular steps are not Web compatible. A script error can also occur if a user attempts to do something (via a script) that's not permitted by that user's privilege set. Logging script errors—especially as you're testing an existing solution for IWP friendliness—is a great way to troubleshoot potential problems.

- **Web Publishing Errors**—These errors include more generic errors, such as "page not found" errors. The log entry generated by one of these generic errors is very sparse and may not be terribly helpful for troubleshooting purposes.

The access log records all IWP activity at a granular level: Every "hit" is recorded, just as you'd find with any Web server. As a result, the access log can grow quite large very quickly, and there are no mechanisms that allow for automatic purging of the logs. Be sure to check the size of the logs periodically and to prune them as necessary to keep them from eating up disk space. (A knowledgeable system administrator can configure both Windows and Mac OS X to periodically trim or rotate logs to prevent uncontrolled log growth.)

NOTE

Each of the two logs can be read with any text editor, but you may find it helpful to build a FileMaker database into which you can import log data. It will be much easier to read and search that way.

ENDING A SESSION

The final option on the Advanced Web Publishing Options dialog box is the setting for the session disconnect time. As mentioned previously, one of the new features in FileMaker Pro 7 is that IWP establishes a unique session for each Web user. This means that as a user interacts with the system, things such as global values, the current layout, and the active found set are "remembered." Rather than just treat requests from the Web as discrete and unrelated events, as was the case in previous incarnations of IWP, the host maintains session data on each IWP user.

Because only five sessions can be active at any given time when using FileMaker Pro as an IWP host, it's important that sessions be ended at some point. A session can be ended several ways:

- A user can click the Log Out button in the status area.
- The Exit Application script step ends an IWP session and returns the user to the Database Homepage.
- You can terminate a session after a certain amount of inactivity. The default is 15 minutes, but you can set it to anything from 1 to 60 minutes.

 Are your IWP sessions not ending when you think they should? See "Problems Ending IWP Sessions" in the Troubleshooting section at the end of this chapter.

Clicking on the "house" icon in the status area to return to the database home page does not end a session. If a user re-enters the file from the database home page without ending his session, he returns to exactly the same place he left, even if a startup script or default layout is specified for the file.

CONFIGURING FILEMAKER SERVER 7 ADVANCED FOR IWP

One of the best new features of the FileMaker 7 product line is the capability to do Web publishing directly from files hosted by FileMaker Server 7 Advanced. Using FileMaker Pro 7 as an IWP host works well for development, testing, and some limited deployment situa-

21

tions, but for many business applications, you'll find that you want the added power and stability that come from using FileMaker Server 7 Advanced for this purpose.

Using FileMaker Server Advanced as your IWP host provides several significant benefits. The first is simply that it scales better. With FileMaker Pro 7, you are limited to five concurrent IWP sessions; with FileMaker Server 7 Advanced, you can have up to 100 IWP sessions. FileMaker Server 7 Advanced can also host up to 125 files, compared to FileMaker Pro's 10. Even more important, you have the option to use SSL for data encryption when using FileMaker Server Advanced as the Web host. FileMaker Server 7 Advanced is a more reliable Web host as well. It is more likely that the shared files will always be available for Web users, that they'll be backed up on a regular basis, and that the site's IP address won't change when you use FileMaker Server. (Even in organizations that use dynamic addressing for desktop machines, servers are typically assigned static IP addresses.)

Chapter 25, "FileMaker Server," covers in detail the various components and installation options of FileMaker Server and the Web Publishing Engine. Chapter 23, "Custom Web Publishing," also contains a good deal of installation and configuration information. Here, we'll assume that you have all the required components in place and will merely touch on the relevant configuration screens in the FileMaker Server *Web Publishing Administration Console (WPAC)*. WPAC is a Web-based configuration tool that allows you to attach a Web Publishing Engine to a FileMaker Server and configure it. As shown in Figure 21.5, you turn on Instant Web Publishing for FileMaker Server simply by toggling the On/Off buttons on the Publishing Engine Configuration page. This page is—by design, of course— quite similar to the IWP configuration dialog in the FileMaker Pro 7 desktop application.

Figure 21.5
Use the Web Publishing Administration Console to allow FileMaker Server Advanced to host IWP-enabled databases.

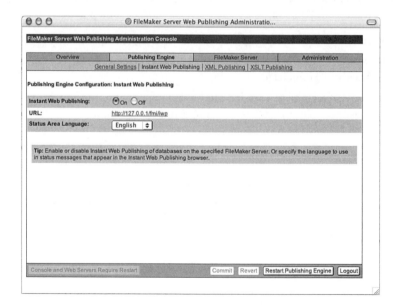

On the General Settings page, as shown in Figure 21.6, you can specify logging and session disconnection settings. These are analogous to their FileMaker Pro counterparts, which were discussed in depth in the previous section. Refer back to that section if you need additional information about what is contained in the logs or the significance of the session disconnection setting. The logs are written as text files in the following directory on the Web server:

Mac OS X: `/Library/FileMaker 7/Web Publishing/logs`

Windows: `\Program Files\FileMaker\FileMaker Server 7\Web Publishing\logs`

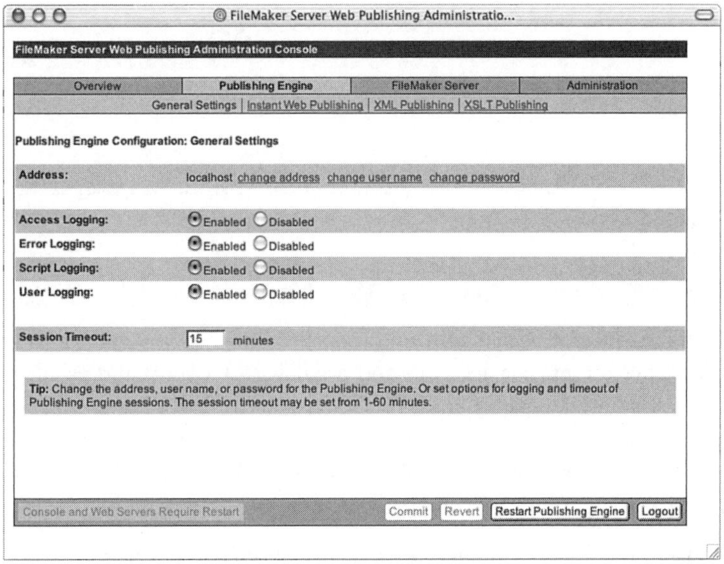

Figure 21.6
Logging and session disconnection options are specified on the General Settings page.

You can see a list of the databases that are accessible via IWP on the server by going to the FileMaker Server Published Databases page, shown in Figure 21.7. For a database to be IWP-accessible, one or more privilege sets needs to have the fmiwp extended privilege enabled. There's no configuration or setup that you need to do in WPAC nor to the files themselves before hosting them with FileMaker Server. In fact, even while a file is being hosted by FileMaker Server, a user with the privilege to manage extended privileges can use FileMaker Pro to open the file remotely and edit the privilege sets so that the file is or isn't IWP accessible.

NOTE

If you want a file to be accessible via IWP, but not to show up on the Database Homepage, you need to open the file with FileMaker Pro (open it directly, that is, not simply as a guest of FileMaker Server) and go into the Instant Web Publishing configuration screen. After you are there, select the file and then check the Don't display in Instant Web Publishing homepage check box. You do not need to actually enable IWP or add any extended privileges to privilege sets to have access to this setting.

21

Figure 21.7
WPAC lists all of Web-accessible databases on the server, but you don't need to do any configuration here at the file level to allow something to be shared to IWP.

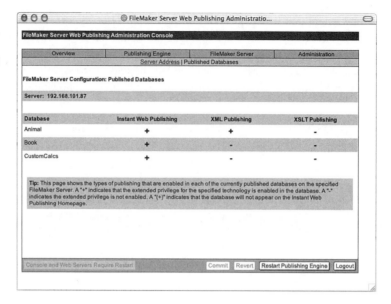

SHARING AND SECURING FILES VIA IWP

Security for Instant Web Publishing users is managed the same way it's managed for FileMaker Pro users: via accounts and privileges. Accounts and privileges also dictate which database files are accessible via IWP. To be shared via IWP, a particular file needs to be open, and one or more privilege sets in that file needs to have the fmiwp extended privilege enabled. This is true regardless of whether you plan to use FileMaker Pro 7 or FileMaker Server 7 Advanced as the Web host.

You assign the fmiwp extended privilege to a privilege set in any of three ways:

■ Go to File, Define, Accounts & Privileges. On the Extended Privileges tab, you'll see a list of the various extended privileges (EPs) and be able to assign fmiwp to any privilege sets you want.

→ For more information on what extended privileges are and how to assign them to a privilege set, **see** "Extended Privileges," **p. 336**.

■ Also in File, Define, Accounts & Privileges, on the Privilege Set detail screen, you can select fmiwp as an extended privilege for the currently active privilege set.

■ On the Instant Web Publishing setup screen (refer to Figure 21.3), the bottom half of the screen shows a list of open database files. When you select a particular database, you can manage the fmiwp extended privilege right from this screen. If you select All Users or No Users, the fmiwp extended privilege is granted or removed from all privilege sets in the file. You can also select Specify Users By Privilege Set to select those privilege sets that should have access to IWP. Though the words "extended privilege" and "fmiwp" never appear on this screen, it functions exactly the same as the Extended Privilege detail screen. This screen is intended to be more user friendly and convenient, especially when working with multiple files.

NOTE

To assign extended privileges in any of these ways, a user must be logged in with a password that grants rights to Manage Extended Privileges.

→ For information on setting up privilege sets and restricting access to manage extended privileges, **see** "FileMaker Security Features Overview," **p. 316**.

The other sharing option you can configure on the Instant Web Publishing setup screen is whether or not the database name appears on the Database Homepage. In a multi-file solution, you may wish to have only a single file appear there so that users are forced to enter the system through a single, controlled point of entry.

NOTE

Any changes that are made in the sharing settings and privileges for a file take effect immediately; you do not need to restart FileMaker or close the file.

When users type the IP address (or domain name) of the IWP host in their browsers, the first thing they'll see is the IWP Database Homepage, an example of which is shown in Figure 21.8). The Database Homepage lists, in alphabetical order, all files on the host machine that have at least some privilege sets with the fmiwp extended privilege enabled. The Database Homepage cannot be altered in any way or suppressed.

Figure 21.8
The Database Homepage provides users with a list of accessible files.

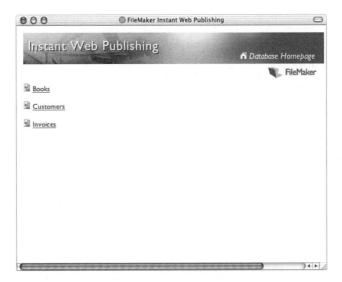

Users aren't prompted for a password on their way to the Database Homepage. The password prompt occurs (with an exception noted below) when they first try to interact with a database. IWP uses a standard HTTP authentication dialog for entering a username and password. To be authenticated, users must enter an active, valid username and password, and their accounts must be associated with a privilege set that has the fmiwp extended privilege enabled.

You should know a number of things about how accounts and privileges are authenticated under IWP:

- The username and password are case sensitive.

- IWP ignores any default login account information that's been set up under File Options.

- IWP does not support the Account option to require users to change their passwords after the next successful login. Changing passwords is not a feature supported by IWP. If this option has been set, the Web user who tries to log in with that username and password receives an Error 211, Password Has Expired, and cannot enter the system.

- IWP-enabled accounts must use FileMaker Pro as their authentication method. IWP cannot authenticate a password against an external server as FileMaker Pro can.

- If the Guest account has been activated and given the fmiwp extended privilege, then users are not prompted for a username/password to access the database. They automatically have the privileges of the Guest account. This setting would typically be used only for Web sites that need to be accessed by the general public.

 If you're having difficulty getting past the password prompt from the IWP homepage, see "Logging into an IWP-Enabled Database" in the Troubleshooting section at the end of this chapter.

TIP

> You can create a script that uses the new account management script steps to create your own customized login routine. Users would use Guest privileges to get to your login screen, and then your script would use the Re-login step to re-authenticate them as different users.

After a user is authenticated as a valid user of the file, that user's privilege set then controls which actions can be performed, just as it does for users of the FileMaker Pro desktop application. Field and layout restrictions, record level access, creation and deletion of records...all of these are managed exactly the same for IWP users as for FileMaker Pro users. This "unified" security model is truly one of the best innovations of FileMaker Pro 7 and makes it much simpler to deploy robust and secure IWP solutions.

→ For more information about setting up user accounts and privileges, **see** "FileMaker Security Features Overview," **p. 316**.

You will likely want to restrict your IWP users to some set of IWP-friendly layouts. If you have users who sometimes access your file via FileMaker (when they're in the office) and sometimes via IWP (from home), consider setting up two separate accounts for those people: one that has the fmiwp extended privilege and one that doesn't.

DESIGNING FOR IWP DEPLOYMENT

The previous section discussed how to enable IWP at the application level and how to set a file so that users can access it via IWP. Although this is enough for IWP to function, there are usability issues to consider as well. Not all layouts and scripts translate well to the Web, and some FileMaker features simply don't work via IWP. This section discusses the constraints that you, as a developer, must be aware of when deploying an IWP solution. We also discuss a number of development techniques that can make an IWP solution feel more like a typical Web application.

CONSTRAINTS OF IWP

Most of the core functionality of FileMaker Pro is available to IWP users. This includes being able to view layouts, find and edit data, and perform scripts attached to buttons. There are, however, a number of FileMaker features that are not available to IWP users. It's important to keep these in mind, especially when trying to port an already existing solution to the Web.

- IWP users have no database development tools. This means IWP users can't create new files, define tables, fields, and relationships, alter layouts, manage user privileges, or edit scripts.

- IWP users can't use any of FileMaker Pro keyboard shortcuts. Be sure that you leave the status area visible or provide your users with ample scripted routines for tasks such as executing finds and committing records.

- There is no capability to import or export data from an IWP session. In general, any action that interacts with another application or the operating system is not possible via IWP.

- IWP has no Preview mode. This means that sliding, sub-summary reports, and multi-column layouts, all of which require being in Preview mode to view, are not available to IWP users. Similarly, printing is not supported. IWP users can choose to print the contents of the browser window as they would any other Web page, but the results will not be the same as printing from FileMaker Pro. (That is, headers and footers won't appear on each page, page setups will not be honored, and so on.)

- There are a few data entry differences for IWP users. For instance, Web users can't edit rich text formatting in fields. That is, they can't change the style, font, or size of text in a field. They can generally, however, see rich text formatting that has already been applied to a field.

- Most window manipulation tools and techniques do not translate well to IWP. The user's browser can show only the contents of the currently active window in the virtual FileMaker environment. That environment can maintain multiple virtual windows and switch between them, but a user can't have multiple visible windows in the browser, and cannot resize or move windows.

- None of the FileMaker Pro toolbars are available via IWP. IWP does offer its own "toolbars" in the status area, however, and these contain some of the same functionality found in the FileMaker Pro toolbars.

21

- Spell Checking is not available via IWP.

- Many graphical layout elements are rendered differently, or not at all, on the Web. This includes diagonal lines, rounded rectangles, rotated objects, ovals, and fill patterns. The sections that follow discuss this topic in greater detail.

- IWP users can't edit value lists through a Web browser.

- There is no built-in way for users to change their passwords via IWP, even if they have the privilege to do so. If you need this sort of functionality, you need to use the Account management script steps and come up with your own scripted routine.

SCRIPTING FOR IWP

One of the greatest advances in the current version of Instant Web Publishing is script support. In previous versions, only a handful of script steps could be executed from the Web, and scripts could be no more than three steps long. Under those severe restrictions, it was quite difficult to build anything but the most basic Web applications.

Now, IWP supports more than 70 script steps, and scripts can be of any length and complexity. Also, because the new IWP is session based, scripts that are executed from the Web operate within what might be thought of as a virtual FileMaker environment. This means that changes to the environment (active layout, found set, and so on) are persistent and affect the browser experience, which is a good thing.

Even though IWP script support has come a long way, there are still some behaviors, constraints, and techniques that you should be aware of.

UNSUPPORTED SCRIPT STEPS

Given the great number of supported script steps, it's easier to talk about what's not supported under IWP. In general, anything that requires that the user interact with a dialog box is unsupported, as are any steps that interact with the operating system or other applications. The list of unsupported steps is shown in Table 21.1.

TABLE 21.1   UNSUPPORTED SCRIPT STEPS

Script Category	Script Step
Navigation	Enter Preview Mode
Editing	Perform Find/Replace
Fields	Insert from Index
	Insert Picture
	Insert QuickTime
	Insert File
	Export Field Contents
Records	Import Records
	Export Records

Script Category	Script Step
Windows	Adjust Window
	Move/Resize Windows
	Arrange All Windows
	Freeze Window
	Refresh Window
	Scroll Window
	Show/Hide Text Ruler
	Set Zoom Level
Files	All steps are unsupported
Spelling	All steps are unsupported
Open Menu Item	All steps are unsupported
Miscellaneous	Show Custom Dialog
	Allow Toolbars
	Beep
	Speak
	Dial Phone
	Send Mail
	Perform AppleScript
	Send Message
	Execute SQL
	Send Event
	Flush Cache to Disk

Additionally, the option to perform with dialog is not supported in a number of supported script steps. These include Delete Record/Request, Replace Field Contents, Omit Multiple Records, and Sort Records. These steps are always performed without dialog via IWP, regardless of which option has been selected.

The ScriptMaker itself has a new option that makes identifying unsupported script steps quite easy. When you check the Indicate Web Compatibility check box, all the unsupported script steps are dimmed. This affects both the list of script steps and the steps in whatever script you're viewing. Figure 21.9 shows an example of what script step dimming looks like. The Web compatibility check box has no effect other than showing you which steps are not supported; how you choose to use that information is up to you (although unsupported script steps are dimmed out, you can still add them to a script). Additionally, its status is not tied to any particular script. That is, it is either turned on or off for the entire file, and it remains that way until a developer changes it. We point this out explicitly because the check box right next to it, Run Script With Full Access Privileges, is a script-specific setting.

21

Figure 21.9
When writing scripts that will be used via IWP, turn on the Indicate Web Compatibility check box to be sure your scripts will execute as intended.

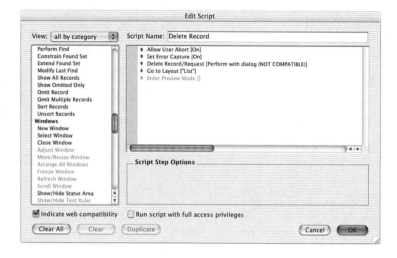

ERROR CAPTURE

The outcome of running a script (from the Web) that contains unsupported script steps depends on the whether Allow User Abort has been turned on or turned off. If it's not explicitly specified, a script executes on the Web as if Allow User Abort had been turned on. So, not specifying any setting is the same as explicitly turning it on.

If user abort is on (or not set at all), then script execution halts when an unsupported step is encountered. Steps prior to the offending script step are performed as normal. If you've chosen to log script errors, then the offending step is logged as an error in the application log. The user does not see any error message or have any knowledge that anything is amiss.

If user abort has been turned off, then a script will simply bypass any unsupported scripts and attempt to perform subsequent steps. It's performed as if the offending step is simply not there. No error is logged to the application log when this occurs.

Scripts steps with the unsupported perform with dialog options discussed earlier are not affected at all by the error capture setting. These script steps will always be performed as if Perform Without Dialog had been checked, regardless of error capture.

COMMITTING RECORDS

If a script run via IWP causes a record to be altered in any way (such as using a Set Field script step), then be sure that you explicitly save the change by using the Commit Record/Request step sometime before the end of the script. If you don't, your Web user will be left in Edit mode and, provided the status area is visible, will have the option to Submit or Cancel the changes, which is likely not an option you want to offer at that point. Canceling would undo any changes made by the script.

STARTUP AND SHUTDOWN SCRIPTS

If you have specified a startup script for a file, it is performed for IWP users when the session is initiated. Similarly, IWP also switches to a particular layout on startup if you've selected that option.

The shutdown script is performed when the user logs out, even if the logout is the result of timing out.

CAUTION

> The startup script executes only once per session, when the user navigates there from the Database Homepage (or follows an equivalent link from another Web page). The startup script is not run if a file is activated through the performance of an external script.

PERFORMING SUBSCRIPTS IN OTHER FILES

A script can call a subscript in another file, but that file needs to be open and enabled for IWP for the subscript to execute. Calling a subscript does not force open an external file, as happens in the FileMaker Pro desktop application.

If your subscript activates a window in the external file, the IWP user sees that window in the browser. Unless you provide navigation back to the first file, a user has no way of returning, except by logging out and logging back in. You should be sure to make sure that any record changes are fully committed before navigating to a window in another file. It's possible that the record will remain in an uncommitted, locked state, even though the IWP user has no idea this has occurred.

TESTING FOR IWP EXECUTION WITHIN A SCRIPT

If you have a solution that will be accessed both by FileMaker Pro desktop users and IWP users, chances are that they'll use some of the same scripts. If those scripts contain unsupported script steps, you might want to add conditional logic to them so that they behave differently for IWP users than they do for FileMaker users. You can do this by using the Get (ApplicationVersion) function. If the words "Web Publishing" are found within the string returned by this function, that means the person executing the script is a Web user. It's not possible to discriminate between an IWP user and a CWP user with this function; you simply know you have a Web user. The actual syntax for performing the test is as follows:

```
PatternCount (Get (ApplicationVersion); "Web Publishing")
```

LAYOUT DESIGN

Most layouts that you design in FileMaker Pro will be rendered almost perfectly in a Web browser via Instant Web Publishing. IWP does this by using the absolute positioning capability of Cascading Style Sheets, Level 2. The CSS requirements of IWP are the reason there are browser restrictions for its use. We've already mentioned a few layout elements

21

that don't translate well to IWP—we'll recap them here as well—but there are several additional things to keep in mind when creating or modifying layouts for IWP use.

GRAPHIC ELEMENTS

Rounded rectangles, ovals, diagonal lines, rotated objects, and fill patterns are not rendered properly in the Web browser and should be avoided. In some cases, IWP displays altered versions of the objects; in other cases the objects simply do not show up.

Figure 21.10 shows a test layout in FileMaker that we filled with various shapes and objects; Figure 21.11 shows how it renders in a Web browser. As you can see, IWP does a great job with vertical and horizontal lines of varied widths, with rendering non-standard fonts, with overlapping text, and with stylized boxes. However, it completely ignored the circle and diagonal line, and altered the rotated text, rounded rectangle, and fill pattern. As well, multi-column check box and radio button fields don't maintain their columnar alignment.

Figure 21.10
It's important to be aware of which layout elements don't render properly via IWP.

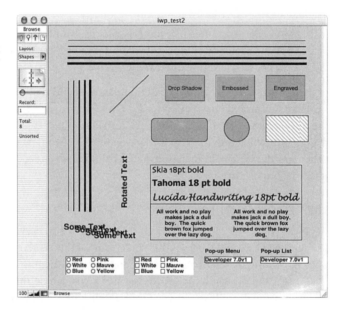

TAB ORDER

The tab order that you set for a layout within FileMaker does not carry over to the Web browser. Instead, tab order in the browser is determined by the stacking order of the fields on the layout, with the back-most field being first in the tab order. Be sure that you test tab order and alter your layouts accordingly before deploying an IWP solution. There's no quick and easy way to see or edit the stacking order; mostly you need to use the Arrange, Send Backward and Arrange, Bring Forward commands to rearrange things manually.

Figure 21.11
Most elements of the test layout render properly in a browser, but a few are either displayed differently or not at all.

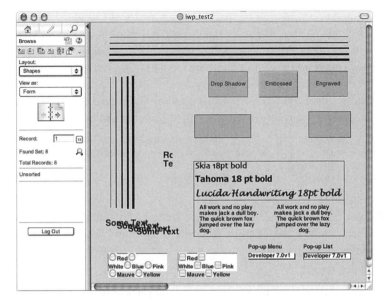

CAUTION

IWP does not support the new field behavior options to go to the next field by using the Return or Enter key rather than the Tab key. Navigation from field to field occurs via the Tab key, just as it would for any browser-based form.

"VIEW AS" OPTIONS

Web users have the same ability that FileMaker desktop users have to switch between View As Form, View As List, and View As Table on a given layout, unless you restrict that ability at the layout level. To do so, go into the Layout Setup options, shown in Figure 21.12 and simply uncheck any inappropriate views. The additional Table view options that can be specified all translate well to IWP, except for resizable and reorderable columns.

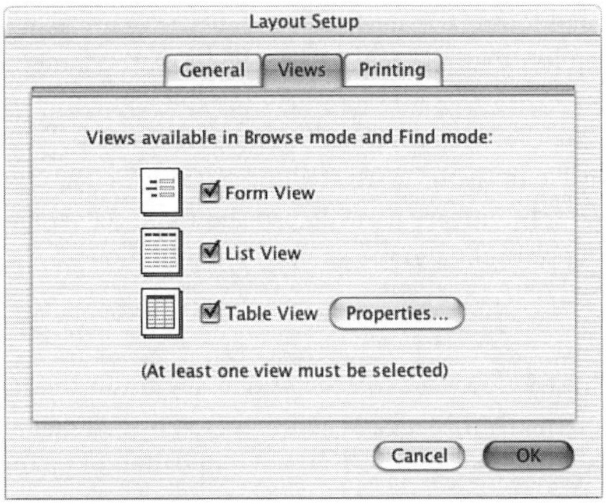

Figure 21.12
In Layout Setup, you can specify to which views a user should be able to switch for a given layout.

You should be aware of a few special characteristics of List and Table view in IWP. By default, View As List maximally shows a set of 5 records, and View As Table maximally shows a set of 20 records. You cannot change these settings. Also, while in List or Table view, whenever a user clicks on a record to edit it, the active record jumps to the top of the set. This can be slightly disconcerting for users who are habituated to working with lists of records in FileMaker. For instance, if a user is viewing records 6–10 of a set as a list, and clicks on record 8, record 8 jumps to the top, and the screen then displays records 8–12.

→ **See** the "FileMaker Extra: Building Your Own Next and Previous Page Buttons" section of this chapter, **p. 636**, to learn how to build your own Next and Previous navigation routine for use with List and Table views when the status area is hidden.

LAYOUT PARTS

IWP can render any and all parts that comprise a layout. There are a few differences, however, between how and when parts display in IWP and how and when they display in the FileMaker desktop application.

First of all, in form view, the vertical size of a part displayed via IWP is the size that the part was defined to be. It doesn't stretch to fill the vertical space. This is different from how FileMaker Pro behaves. In FileMaker Pro, the last visible part "expands" to fill any remaining vertical space. Say, for instance, that you have a layout that consists of only a single, colored body part. Via IWP, if a user resizes a browser window so that it's larger (vertically) than the body part, the space between the bottom of the part and the bottom of the browser is a white void. This also means that if your layout has a footer part, it won't necessarily (indeed, won't likely) be displayed at the bottom of the browser.

View As List in a browser also has some differences from its FileMaker counterpart. In FileMaker, a header or footer part is "locked" on the screen at the top or bottom. The area in between displays as many body records as space permits. In FileMaker, leading and trailing grand summary parts display in list view, but title header, title footer, and subsummary parts do not (in Browse mode).

As we've mentioned, in a browser, List view always contains five records (except, of course, when the found set is smaller than five or if the active record is one of the last four of the found set). The header and footer are not fixed elements as they are in FileMaker. If the five records of the list take up less than the full browser window, the footer simply shows up in the middle of the screen; if they take up more than the full window, a user would need to scroll to see the footer. Another major difference is that title header, title footer, and subsummary parts are all visible in the browser at all times (in list view). Even if the database is sorted properly, however, subsummary parts do not show correct values—they show the same values that a leading or trailing grand summary would show.

CONTAINER FIELDS

There are a few special restrictions and considerations when using container fields in an IWP solution. Most importantly, there is no ability to add or edit data in a container field via IWP; these fields are strictly view-only. Entry and updating of pictures, sounds,

QuickTime movies, files, and objects is available only to users of a FileMaker Pro desktop interface.

The visibility and/or accessibility of a container field's contents are dependent on the types of objects they are and how they were entered into the container field in the first place.

- Graphic images that have explicitly been stored in a container field (that is, not stored as a reference) are visible through a browser. Images should be stored as pictures, not as files.

- Graphic images that have been stored as a reference are visible to IWP users only if the image is stored in the Web folder of the FileMaker Pro application (if FileMaker Pro is the IWP host) or if they are stored in the root folder of the Web server (if FileMaker Server is the IWP host).

- QuickTime movies can't be accessed directly from the Web browser. If you insert them as files rather than as QuickTime, however, a user can play or download them.

- Files explicitly stored in a container field are rendered to an IWP user as a hyperlink. Clicking on the link begins a download of the file. No icon or other graphic representation of the file is visible to Web users.

- Sounds that have been recorded in container fields cannot be played via IWP.

APPLICATION FLOW

We've discussed many of the technical limitations and details of how various FileMaker features translate to the Web. We turn now to more practical development matters. There are certain routines and development habits that work well in the FileMaker desktop application that don't work as well from a Web browser. The following sections discuss how the constraints of IWP will influence how you develop solutions.

Web-based applications generally have a different application flow than FileMaker applications, and you may consequently find that you need to rethink some things when you share a solution to IWP. By application flow, we mean broadly how a user actually interacts with the application. For instance, one of the typical flows for Web applications is search->hitlist->detail. Think about google.com or amazon.com and how those sites essentially boil down to this pattern. A user enters search criteria, sees a list of matching records, usually in chunks of 10 or 20 at a time, and then drills down to a detail record by clicking on a link from the hitlist.

Such an application flow is rare in FileMaker solutions. More often, users spend most of their time on a detail record. They drop into Find mode when they need to locate records. They then flip through the records one by one, or perhaps they switch to a list view where they can scroll through to locate a particular record. An application flow like this can indeed work via IWP; our point is merely that it's not a traditional Web application flow. Depending on your solution and your users' experiences, they may expect a more Web-like flow.

21

When it comes down to it, we've discovered that it's actually easier to make FileMaker mimic the Web flow than the other way around.

TIP

> If you're designing a new solution and you know that you'll have IWP users, you might consider thinking about how you would develop the solution if it were a Web application. Because there are more constraints placed on designing for the browser, anything you build for the browser should work well for FileMaker users as well.

EXPLICIT RECORD COMMITS

Many of the application flow differences described in the previous section stem from the fact that HTTP—the underlying protocol of the Web—is a "stateless" protocol. This means that every request that a browser makes to a Web server is separate and independent from every other request. Put differently, the Web server doesn't maintain a persistent connection to the Web client. After it has processed a request from someone's browser, it simply stands by waiting for the next request to come in. To make HTTP connections appear to be persistent, Web programmers need to add information to each request from a single client, and then let some piece of Web server middleware keep track of which client is which, based on this extra request data. This technique is referred to as *session management*.

The client/server connection between FileMaker Pro and FileMaker Server is persistent. The two are constantly talking back and forth, exchanging information and making sure that the other is still there. FileMaker Server is actively aware of all the client sessions. When FileMaker Server receives new record data from any client on the network, it immediately broadcasts that information to all the other clients. And when a user clicks into a field and starts editing data, FileMaker Server immediately knows to consider that record as "locked," and to prevent other users from modifying the record.

The fact that IWP is now capable of performing session management means that FileMaker maintains information about what's happening on the Web in a virtual FileMaker environment. Even though this doesn't change the fact that HTTP is stateless, using sessions gives IWP a semblance of persistence. Essentially, the server stores a bunch of information about each IWP user; each request from a user includes certain session identifiers that enable the server to recognize the IWP guest and to know the context by which to evaluate the request. One of the benefits of this session model is that IWP users can lock records, and they are notified if they try to edit a record that a regular FileMaker Pro user has locked.

Still, the statelessness of the Web makes the application flow for something even as basic as editing a record much different in IWP than it is in FileMaker. In FileMaker, of course, a user just clicks into a field, starts typing away, then clicks out of the field to commit the change. On the Web, editing a record involves two distinct transactions. First, by clicking on an editable field or using the Edit Record button in the status area, the user generates a request to the server to return an "edit form" for that record and to mark the record as locked. As we discussed earlier in this chapter, Edit mode in the browser is distinctly different than Browse mode.

21

The second transaction occurs when the user clicks the Commit button in the status area (or clicks a similar button you've provided for this purpose). No actual data is modified back in FileMaker until and unless the record is submitted explicitly.

This transaction model for data entry may feel very alien to users who are accustomed to working with a FileMaker interface. As you evaluate the Web-friendliness of existing layouts or build new layouts for IWP users, try to make the application flow work well as a series of discrete and independent transactions. One common way to do this is by having tightly controlled routines that users follow to accomplish certain tasks. For instance, rather than let users just create new records anywhere they want, create a "new record" routine that walks users through a series of screens where they enter data and are required to click a Next Screen or Submit button to move forward through the routine.

Lookups and Portal Filters

Because of the transactional nature of the Web, two common FileMaker development tools—lookups and portal filters—don't work well in IWP.

Consider first how a lookup works in FileMaker. When a value in a trigger field is edited (usually by a user), the values of one or more target fields change. For instance, when creating an invoice, it's typical to enter a Product ID for a line item and have a description and price for that item appear as soon as the user Tabs out of the field. It's not important here whether the description and price are actually looked up or are simply related fields. The point is that from a user perspective, Tabbing out of the field caused something to happen.

→ For more on lookups, **see** "Auto-Entry Field Options," **p. 75**.

Using IWP, to trigger an action such as a lookup or the display of related data, a user must actually submit the change as an edit to the trigger field and then wait for a reply. It works, but it's a far cry from being able to just Tab out of a field and have data appear.

Portal filters suffer from the same problem. The typical portal filter works by having a user choose some value in a field that anchors one end of a relationship. After the selection is made, the portal data updates to reflect the matches to the filter. Via IWP, the user would again need to explicitly submit the filter value as a record edit for the portal to refresh.

→ For more information about creating portal filters, **see** "Filtered Portals," **p. 462**.

As a more Web-like alternative to triggered events like these, you might consider calling great attention to the fact that something needs to be submitted before the user can continue with entry. For instance, Figure 21.13 is an example of a layout for creating a new invoice. Notice that as step 1, users are asked to enter a Customer ID and to click Find Customer. After this is done, the related customer data is displayed, and they move on to step 2, where they're asked to enter the product code of an item to add to the invoice. Behind the scenes they're actually entering a value into a global field at that point; the Submit button creates a related line item record, filling in the description and quantity, and then returns users to Edit mode so they can enter another product. By leaving users almost perpetually in Edit mode, you'll cut in half the number of transactions they have to explicitly trigger during repetitive data entry like this.

21

Figure 21.13
If you have a routine that requires triggered events, make the submission of the triggers a very explicit part of the process. That is, draw more attention to them rather than less.

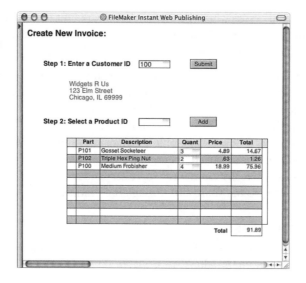

HIDING THE STATUS AREA

As when designing a solution for FileMaker users, you have the option to leave the status area visible for your IWP users or to hide it from them. And unless you lock it open or closed, users can toggle it themselves.

By default, the status area is visible for your IWP users. The script step Show/Hide Status Area enables you to programmatically control the visibility of the status area. Typically, if you want to hide the status area, you do so as part of a start-up script.

There are certainly benefits to having the status area visible. Most importantly, the status area provides a wealth of functionality for the IWP user. Navigation, complex searching, and a host of record manipulation tools are all features that "come for free" in the status area. Also, the status area heightens the "FileMaker-ness" of the user experience. If one of your goals is to make your IWP deployment feel like FileMaker to your users, then the status area can certainly help accomplish this.

There are also reasons that developers want to hide the status area from users. The first is simply to constrain users' activities by forcing them to use just the tools you give them. This is generally the reason why developers hide the status area for FileMaker desktop deployments as well. Hiding the status area also makes your application more "Web-like." If you are integrating IWP into an existing Web site or plan to have the general public access your site, then you'll probably want to hide the status area.

If you do decide to hide the status area, you must provide buttons in your interface for every user action, including committing records, submitting find requests, and logging out of the application. Because users have no keyboard shortcuts—including using the Enter key to do things like submit Find requests and continue paused scripts—and no pull-down menus, you'll probably need even more buttons than you would when designing without the status area for FileMaker users.

CREATING LINKS TO IWP FROM OTHER WEB PAGES

The IWP Database Homepage provides a convenient access point for entering Web-enabled databases. It's possible also to create your own links into a file from a separate HTML page, which is perhaps more desirable for publicly accessible sites. To do this, you simply create a URL link with the following syntax:

```
http://<ip address>:<port number>/fmi/iwp/cgi?-db=<database name>&-loadframes
```

CAUTION

> This syntax is different than it was in previous versions of FileMaker, so be sure to update external links if you're upgrading an IWP solution to FileMaker Pro 7.

If you are using FileMaker Pro as your IWP host, you can place static HTML files and any images that need to be accessible to IWP users in the Web folder inside the FileMaker Pro folder. The Web folder is considered the root level when FileMaker Pro acts as a Web server. If you had, for example, an HTML page called foo.html in the Web folder, the URL to access that page would be the following:

```
http://<ip address>:<port number>/foo.html
```

If you develop a solution that uses FileMaker Pro as the host and later decide to migrate to FileMaker Server Advanced, you should move the entire contents of the Web folder (if you've put any documents or images there) to the root folder of your Web server.

PORTALS

Instant Web Publishing does an astonishingly good job of displaying portals in a browser, complete with scroll bars, alternating row colors, and the capability to add data through the last line of a portal (providing, of course, that the relationship allows it). Another nice thing about portals in IWP is that you can edit multiple portal rows at once and submit them together as a batch.

When designing an IWP application that requires displaying search results as a list, consider whether you can use a portal instead of a list view. A portal gives you flexibility as far as the number of records that are displayed, and you can use the space to the left or right of it for other purposes. Figure 21.14 shows an example of what a search results screen might look like if you used a portal instead of List view.

21

Figure 21.14
For many search results screens, a portal makes a good alternative to using List view to display the found records.

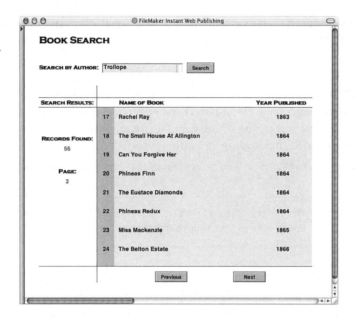

The best way we've found for having a portal display an ad hoc set of records (such as those returned by a user search) is to place all the record keys of the found set into a return-delimited global text field (using the Copy All Records script step), and then to establish a relationship between that field and the file's primary key. Because you can let the portal scroll, you don't strictly need to create Next and Previous links, but it would make your application more Web-like if you did. One option to do this is to take the return-delimited list of record IDs and extract the subset that corresponds to a given "page" worth of IDs. The MiddleValues function comes in handy for this. You'd simply need to have a global field that kept track the current page number. Then this function:

```
MiddleValues (gRecordKeys; (gPageNumber-1) * 8 + 1; 8)
```

would return the 8 record IDs on that page. Substitute a different number of records per page in place of 8, of course, if you want to have a hitlist with some other number of records on it. The scripts to navigate to the next and previous pages then simply need to set the page number appropriately and refresh the screen.

NOTE

To see the example from this section in action, locate `PortalExample.fp7` on the CD-ROM accompanying this book.

USING AN IWP SOLUTION

The focus of this chapter is on what a developer needs to know to create and share databases to the Web using Instant Web Publishing. One crucial piece is an understanding of what IWP looks like and how it functions from the user's perspective.

BROWSE MODE

If you've hidden the status area from your users, you have complete control over what a user can do and how it's done. With the status area active, however, a user has access to a great many "built-in" features, including the ability to conduct complex finds, sort records, navigate to other layouts, and manipulate data. Even so, you can still constrain a user's options by placing restrictions on the privilege sets assigned to IWP users.

TIP

> To avoid a user navigating to a non IWP-friendly layout, edit the layout options of the IWP-enabled privilege sets. Mark any layouts you want them to avoid as No Access.

Figure 21.15 shows the status area a user sees while in Browse mode. Unless you explicitly lock the status area either open or closed, a user can toggle it open and closed while in any mode.

Figure 21.15
The IWP status area in Browse mode contains a number of record manipulation and navigation tools.

While in Browse mode, providing that they have the proper privileges, users can create, edit, duplicate, and delete the current record. They can also sort, find all, omit one record, omit multiple records, and show only the omitted records. Any buttons whose functionality is not permitted by the users' privilege sets are dimmed and inactive.

21

Edit Mode

As we've discussed, one of the biggest differences between the user experience in IWP versus the FileMaker Pro desktop application is the formal distinction between being in Browse mode and Edit mode. A user can enter Edit mode in several ways:

- By clicking on any field (except container and calculation fields) where the Field Behavior is set to allow entry while in Browse mode.
- By running a script that opens a record and doesn't commit it.
- By clicking the Edit Record button in the status area.

Buttons on a layout are active regardless of whether a user is in Browse, Edit, or Find mode. Executing a script via a button does not change the mode unless a mode changing step is in the script.

CAUTION

> The Enter Browse Mode script step does not return an IWP user from Edit mode to Browse mode. Use the Commit Record/Request script step for this purpose.

Find Mode

Users can enter Find mode in IWP either by clicking on the magnifying glass icon in the status area or by clicking on a button of your creation that leaves them in Find mode. The status area as it appears in Find Mode is shown in Figure 21.16. Users can enter their search criteria and execute the find by clicking on the appropriate buttons in the status area. Just as in the FileMaker Pro desktop application, users can create multiple find requests, pick from a set of find operators, choose to omit found records, and extend or constrain the current found set.

Figure 21.16
In Find mode, the IWP status area contains all the tools necessary for users to create complex ad hoc searches.

CAUTION

> If you are using the Perform Find, Constrain Found Set, or Extend Found Set script steps to execute a find, be aware that if no records are found, IWP does not display an error message to users. You need to trap for that error yourself and take appropriate action, such as navigating to a layout that has a "No records found" message.

SORTING RECORDS

The Sort button in the status area takes users to a pop-up sort dialog that looks and functions much like its FileMaker Pro counterpart. It's shown in Figure 21.17. The only way to get to this dialog is through the status area; there's unfortunately no way you can write a script to get here.

Figure 21.17
The Sort dialog in IWP appears as a pop-up window.

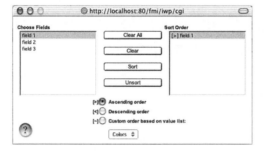

Unlike the sort dialog in the FileMaker Pro desktop application, which lets users choose any field from the current layout's table, the IWP sort dialog allows them to choose only from fields that are physically present on the current layout.

TROUBLESHOOTING

PROBLEMS ENDING IWP SESSIONS

FileMaker Pro thinks that there are active IWP sessions, but you know that all the users have closed their browsers.

Closing the browser window and/or quitting the browser application do not end a session, so be sure to train your users to click the Log Out button (or an equivalent button that you provide). One of the problems you could run into is that an IWP user might quit his browser but still have a record lock. Until the session times out, no other user can modify that record.

If you experience this problem, try reducing the session timeout setting to something like five minutes.

LOGGING INTO AN IWP-ENABLED DATABASE

You keep trying to log in to a file from the IWP homepage, but can't get past the prompt for a user-name and password.

IWP doesn't provide any sort of error message to users when an invalid username and password are entered. They are simply taken back to the IWP home page. This can be a bit frustrating when you think you're entering the proper credentials but keep getting thrown back to where you started. Keep in mind that passwords are case sensitive and that IWP users must belong to a privilege set that has the fmiwp extended privilege enabled.

A related problem is the unfriendly error message that users see if their accounts have been set to require a password change on the next login. If a user ever mentions seeing an Error 211 when trying to log in to an IWP database, this is almost invariably the problem.

FILEMAKER EXTRA: BUILDING YOUR OWN NEXT AND PREVIOUS PAGE BUTTONS

When a user views records via a browser as a list or table, the flipbook navigation tool in the status area changes its behavior slightly. Rather than move from record to record, as it does for Form views, it performs Next Page/Previous Page navigation, jumping by either 5 records (for list view) or 20 records (for table view). If you have hidden the status area from your users, you need to create your own Next Page/Previous Page buttons and place them in the header or footer part.

The concept is fairly simple: You need a script that jumps ahead or backward by some number of records. One thing you need to consider, however, is what should happen when the user is already on the first or last page. That is, if you are on record 1 and try to go backward, what happens? And, if you're viewing records 20–24 of a set of 24 records and you and click Next, what happens?

It turns out that you don't need to worry too much about the first case. If you feed the Go To Record/Request/Page script step a negative number or 0, you simply end up on record 1, which is perfectly acceptable behavior. However, in the latter case, if you're viewing records 20–24 of 24 found, and you try to jump to record 25, you end up on a page consisting only of record 24. It's not the end of the world, but it's also not what users expect. It would be better if the Next Page script were smart enough to know when it would exceed the record count, in which case it shouldn't do anything at all.

You can create different scripts for the Next and Previous buttons, and you can hardcode the jump size to either 5 or 20 depending on whether it's a list or table view, but you can also use script parameters and conditional logic to do everything, including the check for exceeding the found count, in a single, one-line script. That step would be Go To Record/Request/Page [By Calculation], and would use the following formula:

```
Let ( [
  curRec = Get ( RecordNumber );
  jumpSize =
```

```
  Case (
   Get ( LayoutViewState ) = 1; 5;  // it's in List view
   Get ( LayoutViewState ) = 2; 20; // it's in Table view
   1) ;     // it's in Form View
  direction =
   Case (
    Get (ScriptParameter) = "Next"; 1;  // jump forwards
    Get (ScriptParameter) = "Prev"; -1 );  // jump backwards
  newRec = curRec + (jumpSize * direction) ] ;

  Case ( newRec > Get ( FoundCount ) ; curRec ; newRec)
)
```

You might want to add one other finishing touch to your Next and Previous buttons. It's common that the Previous link appears dimmed out when you're on the first page, and that the Next link behaves similarly when you're on the last page. One way to accomplish this is to use the TextColor function to conditionally gray out the link text in those situations. The logic needed is virtually the same as in the navigation script above. For the Next link, for instance, you could define an unstored calculation field with the following formula:

```
Let ( [
  curRec = Get ( RecordNumber );
  jumpSize =
   Case (
    Get ( LayoutViewState ) = 1; 5;  // it's in List view
    Get ( LayoutViewState ) = 2; 20; // it's in Table view
    1) ;      // it's in Form view
  newRec = curRec + (jumpSize ) ] ;

  Case ( newRec > Get ( FoundCount ); TextColor ("Next"; RGB (120;120;120));
  ➥TextColor ("Next"; 0))
)
```

You can simply place this field in the header and define it to be a button, or you can place it on top of a graphic element to make it look like a button. If you do the latter, you need to be sure to group the two elements as a single button to avoid having them function independently. Do not use Merge fields for the text because calculated text colors in Merge fields do not show up properly via IWP.

The logic for the Previous link is similar. Rather than test whether the new record number would exceed the found count, test instead whether it would be less than one.

FILEMAKER AND WEB SERVICES

22

ABOUT WEB SERVICES

So what is a Web service? It's certainly a popular buzzword, but what does it mean? Well, loosely speaking, the term refers to the ability of computers that are remote from each other to exchange information and messages over the World Wide Web (which we'll generally refer to simply as "the Web").

As an example, let's say there's a computer out there somewhere on the Internet that knows the current temperature at various points all over the world. If you send that computer a latitude and longitude, in the correct format, the remote computer sends back the nearest current temperature it can find. Such a transaction is shown in Figure 22.1.

Figure 22.1
A desktop PC queries a remote server for temperature data over the Web, and receives an answer in XML format.

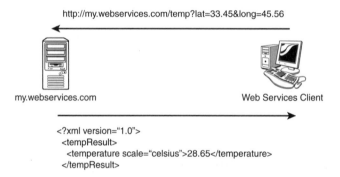

http://my.webservices.com/temp?lat=33.45&long=45.56

my.webservices.com

Web Services Client

```
<?xml version="1.0">
  <tempResult>
    <temperature scale="celsius">28.65</temperature>
  </tempResult>
```

You'll notice a couple of things about this picture. The machine making the request, which we've called the Web Services Client, has sent its request in the form of a URL (a *Uniform Resource Locator*, the standard way of making a request for content over the Web). And the responding computer has sent the requested information back in a tagged message format that you may recognize as XML.

The important thing about this transaction is that it doesn't require any specialized communication protocols to exist between the two machines. The request and response both use standard HTTP, the well-established protocol that powers the entire Web. And the data returned by the server is presented as XML—a standardized and widely-accepted way to present data.

So that's our definition: a *Web service* is a means of exchanging information and messages between two computers, which uses XML data sent over the Web via HTTP. Not all Web services involve sending XML over HTTP. But many do, and it's a suitable way to think about Web services for the purpose of working with FileMaker Pro.

Before you can delve very far into how FileMaker works with Web services, though, you need to learn some of the basics of how FileMaker can work with XML data. For the first half of this chapter we discuss how FileMaker interacts with XML, and in the second half, we apply that knowledge to working with actual Web services.

FileMaker and XML

Before you can appreciate FileMaker's Web service capabilities, you need to learn more about the things FileMaker can do with XML data. To put it briefly, FileMaker can both *import* and *export* data as XML. This capability has several interesting uses: For one thing, it means FileMaker can participate in Web services transactions, as you'll see in this chapter. For another, it means FileMaker can exchange data with other applications via XML. Before we delve deeper, though, a brief overview of XML may be useful.

The Basics of XML

XML is a large topic, on which many books have been written. We'll have to content ourselves with a quick overview; you can find further reading suggestions in Appendix A.

XML is a text-based means of representing data, which is at the same time *rich* and *portable*. By "rich," we mean that the data is more than mere text: An XML document is capable of describing its own structure, so that in looking at an XML document you can tell a chapter heading from a bullet point, or a personnel ID from a health-insurance deductible. By *portable*, we mean that XML documents are stored as plain text and can be read by a wide variety of programs on a wide variety of computers and operating systems.

As an example, consider the XML document that appears in Listing 22.1. This is a short document containing information about motors. You'll notice the document is full of tags (called *markup*) that might look superficially familiar to you if you've seen some HTML before. You'll notice that the tags always occur in pairs, with some content between them, and you'll notice that the tags seem to describe the data they contain. These tag pairs are known in XML jargon as *elements*.

Listing 22.1   A Small XML File Containing Motor Data

```
<?xml version="1.0" encoding="UTF-8" ?>
<motors>
    <motor>
        <model>Rotary 17</model>
        <weight>1200</weight>
        <part_number>M3110A-3</part_number>
        <volume>312</volume>
    </motor>
</motors>
```

This XML document is rich, in the sense that it contains two kinds of information: It contains raw data, but it also contains tags telling a reader what the data *means*. In this document, M3110A-3 is not just a string of numbers and letters; it's specifically a part number.

The document is also portable in the sense that it's stored as plain text, meaning you don't need a special "motor processing" application to read it. Any tool or program that can read plain text can work with this data.

XML documents have to follow some simple rules. Each must begin with an XML declaration, like the first line of Listing 22.1. Each must have a single outermost, or "document," element—in Listing 22.1, the document element is called `motors`. Each tag must be properly closed—if you have a `<model>` tag, you'd better have its closing counterpart, called `</model>`. And, although tags may be nested (for example, in Listing 22.1, the `weight` element is completely enclosed within the `motor` element), it is not permissible for tags to overlap. Therefore, something like

```
<model>Rotary<weight>500</model></weight>
```

would not be allowed, because the `weight` tag, rather than being completely enclosed in the `model` tag, instead overlaps it.

XML documents that follow these few simple rules, as well as some rules about allowable characters, are said to be *well-formed*.

NOTE

> XML is a rigorous standard, with plenty of technical documents that describe it in exact detail. In this book we opt for clarity over rigor, so we encourage you to get hold of additional resources to explore the full details of XML concepts such as well-formedness. The description we've given is fairly complete, but the last word can be found at
> `http://www.w3.org/TR/2004/REC-xml-20040204/#sec-well-formed`.

FILEMAKER'S XML GRAMMARS

XML syntax rules, as you may have noticed, don't say anything about *how* to mark up your data. XML doesn't force you to use a `motor` element when talking about motors, nor would it specify what other elements a motor element should contain. If you're designing an XML document, the exact structure of the document, as far as what data it contains and how that data is marked up, remains up to you, the designer.

FileMaker is capable of presenting its data as XML, and when it does so, it uses its own, FileMaker-specific set of elements to describe its data. FileMaker can actually present its data in either of two XML structures, called *grammars*; you, as the user or developer, get to choose which one suits your current situation best.

EXPORTING FILEMAKER DATA AS XML: THE FMPDSORESULT GRAMMAR

Suppose you have some product data in a FileMaker table, which looks like Figure 22.2.

To export these records as XML, choose File, Export Records, then choose a file type of XML in the following dialog. When you do this, before seeing the familiar Export dialog, you see an XML options dialog, as shown in Figure 22.3.

Figure 22.2
Some sample "widget" data in a FileMaker table.

Figure 22.3
FileMaker's XML/XSL export options dialog.

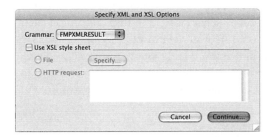

Here you can choose which of FileMaker's XML "grammars" to apply. (You can also apply an XSL stylesheet to the output, which is an important topic we'll deal with in its own section later in this chapter.) If you're trying this for the first time, you might want to choose FMPDSORESULT. From there, you'll see the familiar Export dialog, where you can choose which fields to export, and in what order.

If you open the resulting exported file, you'll see something like the document in Listing 22.2.

LISTING 22.2   RECORDS EXPORTED USING FILEMAKER'S FMPDSORESULT GRAMMAR

```xml
<?xml version="1.0" encoding="UTF-8" ?>
<!-- This grammar has been deprecated - use FMPXMLRESULT instead -->
<FMPDSORESULT xmlns="http://www.filemaker.com/fmpdsoresult">
  <ERRORCODE>0</ERRORCODE>
  <DATABASE>Widget.fp7</DATABASE>
  <LAYOUT/>
  <ROW MODID="1" RECORDID="1">
    <WidgetID>W1</WidgetID>
    <Description>Medium Frobisher</Description>
    <Color>Mauve</Color>
    <Weight>12.2</Weight>
  </ROW>
  <ROW MODID="1" RECORDID="2">
    <WidgetID>W2</WidgetID>
    <Description>Gosset Socketeer</Description>
    <Color>Red</Color>
    <Weight>4</Weight>
```

continues

LISTING 22.2   CONTINUED

```
    </ROW>
    <ROW MODID="0" RECORDID="3">
      <WidgetID>W3</WidgetID>
      <Description>Triple Hex Ping Nut</Description>
      <Color>Steel</Color>
      <Weight>2.3</Weight>
    </ROW>
</FMPDSORESULT>
```

FileMaker has applied its own XML structure to the exported data—in this case the FMPDSORESULT structure. An FMPDSORESULT document has a document element (the top-level element) called <FMPDSORESULT>. That element in turn contains elements for ERRORCODE (generally 0 unless there was some error in the export process), for DATABASE (to tell us which database file the data was drawn from) and LAYOUT, as well as one <ROW> element for each record in the table from which we're exporting. The <ROW> elements in turn contain additional elements, named for the fields that were selected for export.

About the FMPDSORESULT Grammar

You might have noticed, in Listing 22.2, that the second line of the generated XML contains a warning: "This grammar has been deprecated—use FMPXMLRESULT instead." *Deprecation* is a term used in computer languages to indicate that a language's designers are actively discouraging you from using an element or feature. This is generally because the language designers believe that newer features represent an improvement on the deprecated feature. The old feature continues to work (as does FMPDSORESULT in FileMaker 7), but you are discouraged from using it and encouraged to use a different or newer feature instead.

Although FMPDSORESULT is now formally deprecated, we chose to use it here anyway, because of its value in teaching XML. It's a verbose grammar that creates XML element names based on FileMaker field names. This makes it very easy for an XML novice to see how the FileMaker data maps onto the XML output, and this makes FMPDSORESULT a very useful teaching tool.

So what's wrong with FMPDSORESULT? Three things, all of them tied to the fact that FileMaker generates the element names for this grammar directly from FileMaker field names. In the first place, if your FileMaker field names are of any length, the XML element names are similarly long, and the generated files can become massive. Second, the element structure of an FMPDSORESULT document obviously varies depending on the FileMaker field names that lie behind it. All such documents will have an FMPDSORESULT element, containing one or more ROW elements, but within each ROW element there's no way to predict what the sub-elements will be. This makes it impossible to validate these documents via a single Document Type Definition document, or DTD. (We don't deal with DTDs much in this book, but many XML environments and workflows make significant use of them, and the ability to conform to a single DTD is useful.)

The third and most serious problem with FMPDSORESULT, though, is that it can generate XML that is literally invalid. To take a simple example, XML element names may not begin with a number. There's no such restriction on FileMaker field names. A FileMaker file with a field named 2004Results will generate an FMPDSORESULT XML document with elements called <2004Results>. That's not a valid XML element name, and any XML parser that tries to process a document containing such a name will generate an error.

So, pay careful attention to the fact that this grammar is deprecated. Although we used it in this section for teaching purposes, we recommend that you begin using the FMPXMLRESULT grammar as soon as you feel comfortable with this more complex grammar.

Exporting FileMaker Data as XML: The FMPXMLRESULT Grammar

The FMPDSORESULT grammar is considered to be FileMaker's more "readable" export grammar. It's a bit more legible to humans, but it's not the one FileMaker uses most heavily. That honor is reserved for the other grammar, called FMPXMLRESULT. If you were to export the widget data as XML with this grammar, you'd see something like the document in Listing 22.3.

Listing 22.3 Data Exported Using FMPXMLRESULT Grammar

```
<?xml version="1.0" encoding="UTF-8" ?>
<FMPXMLRESULT xmlns="http://www.filemaker.com/fmpxmlresult">
  <ERRORCODE>0</ERRORCODE>
  <PRODUCT BUILD="01-07-2004" NAME="FileMaker Pro" VERSION="7.0v1"/>
  <DATABASE DATEFORMAT="M/d/yyyy" LAYOUT="" NAME="Widget.fp7"
➥RECORDS="3" TIMEFORMAT="h:mm:ss a"/>
  <METADATA>
    <FIELD EMPTYOK="YES" MAXREPEAT="1" NAME="WidgetID" TYPE="NUMBER"/>
    <FIELD EMPTYOK="YES" MAXREPEAT="1" NAME="Description" TYPE="TEXT"/>
    <FIELD EMPTYOK="YES" MAXREPEAT="1" NAME="Color" TYPE="TEXT"/>
    <FIELD EMPTYOK="YES" MAXREPEAT="1" NAME="Weight" TYPE="NUMBER"/>
  </METADATA>
  <RESULTSET FOUND="3">
    <ROW MODID="1" RECORDID="1">
      <COL>
        <DATA>W1</DATA>
      </COL>
      <COL>
        <DATA>Medium Frobisher</DATA>
      </COL>
      <COL>
        <DATA>Mauve</DATA>
      </COL>
      <COL>
        <DATA>12.2</DATA>
      </COL>
    </ROW>
    <ROW MODID="1" RECORDID="2">
      <COL>
        <DATA>W2</DATA>
      </COL>
      <COL>
        <DATA>Gosset Socketeer</DATA>
      </COL>
      <COL>
        <DATA>Red</DATA>
      </COL>
      <COL>
        <DATA>4</DATA>
      </COL>
    </ROW>
    <ROW MODID="0" RECORDID="3">
      <COL>
        <DATA>W3</DATA>
```

continues

LISTING 22.3 CONTINUED

```
      </COL>
      <COL>
        <DATA>Triple Hex Ping Nut</DATA>
      </COL>
      <COL>
        <DATA>Steel</DATA>
      </COL>
      <COL>
        <DATA>2.3</DATA>
      </COL>
    </ROW>
  </RESULTSET>
</FMPXMLRESULT>
```

The most obvious difference from the FMPDSORESULT grammar is that whereas FMPDSORESULT provides element names within each row that correspond to field names, FMPXMLRESULT wraps all the database data in generic-looking <COL> and <DATA> elements. There's also a <METADATA> element, which you can see contains sub-elements for each field that give a lot of information about the field, such as its data type, whether it's a repeating field, and whether it's allowed to be empty. The data within the <ROW> elements then matches up to the field descriptions in the <METADATA> section based on position: The value Mauve in the first row is the third data element, and when you consult the <METADATA> section you can see that this means it corresponds to the Color field.

TRANSFORMING XML

By itself, the capability to turn FileMaker data into XML is not terribly useful. The reason is that FileMaker emits the XML in one of its specialized grammars. Even though other applications can *read* the file containing the exported data, they may not be able to make much sense of the FMPDSORESULT or FMPXMLRESULT grammars. In fact, this is a general issue with XML-aware applications: They all work with different formats and structures of XML.

Let's say there exists a tool (call it WidgetPro) that can read information about widgets from an XML file, so long as the XML file looks like what's shown in Listing 22.4.

LISTING 22.4 THE "WIDGETPRO XML" FORMAT

```
<?xml version="1.0" encoding="UTF-8" ?>
<widgetset>
    <widgetrecord index="1">
        <id>789</id>
        <widget_description>Large Flanger</widget_description>
        <widget_color>blue</widget_color>
        <widget_weight>45</widget_weight>
    </widgetrecord>
    <widgetrecord index="2">
        <id>790</id>
```

```
        <widget_description>Granite Auger</widget_description>
        <widget_color>Slate</widget_color>
        <widget_weight>715</widget_weight>
    </widgetrecord>
</widgetset>
```

We can get widget data from FileMaker, and we can get it as XML, but the two XML documents have different structures—the same data, but expressed with different tag names and tag structures.

This is an important point to understand about XML: XML is not in itself a language or a file format. Using XML, the same data can be described ("marked up," as it's often said) in many different ways. For applications to share data via XML, it's not enough for each application to support reading and writing data in its own, specific XML format. There has to be some means to translate between different forms of XML as well. In the widgets example, this means that we need to take the "FileMaker widget XML" and make it look like "WidgetPro widget XML." This leads to the concept of *XML transformations*.

Figure 22.4 illustrates the idea of an XML transformation. From the FileMaker Pro database of widget information, we first need to export the widget data in an FMPXML structure. Next, we need to *transform* that XML so that it looks like WidgetPro's XML structure instead. Finally, we bring the transformed XML into WidgetPro. Figure 22.4 sketches what this process would look like.

Figure 22.4
An XML transformation pipeline. FMPXMLRESULT (emitted by FileMaker) is transformed into WidgetPro XML (accepted by WidgetPro).

FileMaker   FMPXML   Transformation   WidgetPro XML   WidgetPro

INTRODUCING XSL STYLESHEETS

It turns out that XML already has a transformation technology available for us. That technology is called XSL, which stands for eXtensible Stylesheet Language. The *stylesheet* turns out to be the transformer. In much the same way that a word processing or page layout stylesheet can take ordinary text and transform it into formatted text, an XSL stylesheet can take one form of XML and transform it into another (or into any other text-based format, actually), as shown in Figure 22.5.

Figure 22.5
An XML transformation pipeline that uses an XSL stylesheet to accomplish the transformation.

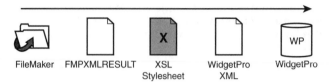

FileMaker   FMPXMLRESULT   XSL Stylesheet   WidgetPro XML   WidgetPro

> **NOTE**
>
> You might often see the terms XSL and XSLT (which stands for XSL Transformations) used interchangeably. Technically they're distinct; XSLT is in fact a subset of XSL. But when people speak of XSL they're generally referring to XSL transformations, so we won't make a major point of distinguishing between the two terms.

So what is an XSL stylesheet? It's a series of commands that describe how to transform XML input into some new form. The new form can also be XML (and often is), but it's possible to use a stylesheet to transform your XML into other text-based formats as well: tab-separated text, HTML, or more complex formats such as PDF and RTF. Interestingly, the XSL transformation language is itself a variety of XML, so XSL stylesheets are also valid XML documents in their own right.

Here's an example of an XSL stylesheet that would transform the "FileMaker widget XML" into "WidgetPro XML" (see Listing 22.5).

LISTING 22.5   AN XSL STYLESHEET

```xml
<?xml version="1.0" encoding="UTF-8" ?>
<xsl:stylesheet version="1.0"
➥xmlns:fmp="http://www.filemaker.com/fmpxmlresult"
➥xmlns:xsl="http://www.w3.org/1999/XSL/Transform"
➥exclude-result-prefixes="fmp">
  <xsl:output indent="yes" method="xml"/>
  <xsl:template match="fmp:FMPXMLRESULT">
    <widgetset >
      <xsl:for-each select="fmp:RESULTSET/fmp:ROW">
        <widgetrecord index="{position()}">
          <xsl:for-each select="fmp:COL">
            <xsl:choose>
              <xsl:when test="position()='1'">
                <id>
                  <xsl:value-of select="fmp:DATA"/>
                </id>
              </xsl:when>
              <xsl:when test="position()='2'">
                <widget_description>
                  <xsl:value-of select="fmp:DATA"/>
                </widget_description>
              </xsl:when>
              <xsl:when test="position()='3'">
                <widget_color>
                  <xsl:value-of select="fmp:DATA"/>
                </widget_color>
```

```
            </xsl:when>
            <xsl:when test="position()='4'">
              <widget_weight>
                <xsl:value-of select="fmp:DATA"/>
              </widget_weight>
            </xsl:when>
          </xsl:choose>
        </xsl:for-each>
      </widgetrecord>
    </xsl:for-each>
  </widgetset>
  </xsl:template>
</xsl:stylesheet>
```

Our goal, remember, is to take the original XML output from FileMaker (Listing 22.3), and translate that output into a new form of XML that contains much the same information, but in a different structure (Listing 22.4).

The stylesheet in Listing 22.5 contains two kinds of statements: On the one hand there are XSL commands (which you can tell by their xsl: prefix), and on the other hand are the actual XML tags that the stylesheet will output. The stylesheet's job is to pick through the original XML document and decide which pieces of it to output, and in what order.

ANALYZING A STYLESHEET

If you've never read through an XSL stylesheet before, this section may be useful. We'll go through the stylesheet in Listing 22.5 line by line to illustrate its inner workings.

THE XML DECLARATION

```
<?xml version="1.0" encoding="UTF-8" ?>
```

Every XML document begins with an XML declaration—and XSL stylesheets are XML documents. Simple enough.

THE STYLESHEET STATEMENT

```
<xsl:stylesheet version="1.0"
➥xmlns:fmp="http://www.filemaker.com/fmpxmlresult"
➥xmlns:xsl="http://www.w3.org/1999/XSL/Transform">
```

The xsl:stylesheet statement announces the document as an XSL stylesheet. The stylesheet statement also declares two XML *namespaces* (that's what the xmlns stands for). Namespaces are an important XML concept, but like most of the finer points of XML, namespaces are a bit too complex a topic for us to spend much time on in this book. Suffice it to say that both the namespaces declared here are necessary. The second namespace, which is abbreviated xsl, is common to all XSL stylesheets, and is used to distinguish all the XSL stylesheet commands from other forms of XML. (These commands, again, begin with the same xsl: prefix that's specified by the namespace.) And the fmp namespace declaration is crucial as well because it matches the namespace declaration that appears at the start of any XML document output by FileMaker. We'll have a bit more to say about the FileMaker namespace farther on.

NOTE

> Notice also that the stylesheet declaration includes a statement called `exclude-result-namespaces`. This rather important command prevents namespaces declared in the source document from being carried through to the output document. In general, we recommend you use this command in the `<xsl:stylesheet>` element of your stylesheets to strip all FileMaker-specific namespaces from your output. The `exclude-result-namespaces` attribute uses a space-delimited list of namespace prefixes to decide what to strip out. In Listing 22.5 just one namespace is being stripped, so it says `exclude-result-prefixes="fmp"`. If there were multiple namespaces to strip (as there often are in FileMaker's Custom Web Publishing), you would say something like `exclude-result-prefixes="fmp fml fmr fmrs"`. This would exclude all four namespaces from the stylesheet's output.

→ FileMaker's Custom Web Publishing is covered in depth in Chapter 23, "Custom Web Publishing," **p. 671**.

SPECIFYING THE OUTPUT TYPE

```
<xsl:output indent="yes" method="xml"/>
```

The `xsl:output` statement tells the XSL processor what type of document is being output. If you're trying to produce XML output, you need to include a statement like this one so that the XSL processor adds the appropriate XML declaration to the final document. The output statement also includes an attribute called `indent`—when this is set to `yes`, the XSL processor tries to format the XML output in a pleasing and readable way.

USING A TEMPLATE TO FIND THE RESULT SET

```
<xsl:template match="fmp:FMPXMLRESULT">
        <widgetset>
        [... code omitted ...]
        </widgetset>
```

The concept of a *template* is crucial to XSL. Templates are a way for the stylesheet writer to specify which parts of the source document she's interested in. In this case, we're telling the processor we want to find the element called `<FMPXMLRESULT>` in the source document and do something with it. You'll notice that this template takes up all the rest of the stylesheet—so the rest of the stylesheet tells what to do with the `<FMPXMLRESULT>` after we've found it.

Just inside the `xsl:template` statement is some actual XML, in the form of a `<widgetset>` tag. This tag is matched by the `</widgetset>` tag at the very end of the template instruction (almost at the end of the document). These two tags, unlike the `xsl:` commands, aren't instructions at all—they represent XML that will be output. So the `xsl:template` here is saying "When you find a `<RESULTSET>` tag, output a `<widgetset>` ... `</widgetset>` tag pair, and then go on to do some other things inside it."

Of course, inside the `<widgetset>` tag we want the stylesheet to emit XML that describes the individual widget records, which is what the next part of the stylesheet does.

USING `xsl:for-each` TO LOOP OVER A RESULT SET

```
<xsl:for-each select="fmp:RESULTSET/fmp:ROW">
        <widgetrecord index="{position()}">
```

The `<xsl:for-each>` tag is a *looping construct*. Right now, we're inside the XSL template that matches an `<FMPXMLRESULT>` tag, so the command tells the XSL processor to find all `<ROW>` elements that are children of `<RESULTSET>` elements inside the `<FMPXMLRESULT>`. The additional commands inside the `<xsl:for-each>...</xsl:for-each>` tag pair furnish instructions on what to do with each `<row>` element that we find.

For each `<ROW>` in the original FileMaker XML, we want to output a `<widgetrecord>` element, and that's what the next line does. Additionally, the `<widgetrecord>` element needs to have an attribute called `index`, which shows the numerical position of the widget, in sequence. The `position()` function that's used in that line gives the position of the current element. (We wrap the function call in curly braces so that the XSL process knows it's a command, and not literal text to be output with the XML.)

USING `xsl:choose` TO DETERMINE OUTPUT

```
<xsl:for-each select="fmp:COL">
                  <xsl:choose>
                      <xsl:when test="position()='1'">
                          <id>
                              <xsl:value-of select="fmp:DATA"/>
                          </id>
                      </xsl:when>
                      [other columns omitted for brevity]
```

At this point, we're inside the `<ROW>` element in the original FileMaker XML, and from an output standpoint, we're inside the `<widgetrecord>` element in the output XML. (Read that sentence a few times if it doesn't sink in right away!) Given what we know the output is supposed to look like, all that's left is to find the four data elements from this `<ROW>` in the FileMaker XML, and output each one wrapped in a tag that correctly names its data field.

This is a little trickier, because in the FileMaker XML, a `<ROW>` contains only `<COL>` elements, with no mention of the actual field name in question. (You might recall that field names, in the `FMPXMLRESULT` output grammar, appear near the top of the document in the `<METADATA>` section.) We have to loop through all the `<COL>` elements inside the row, and for each one, we decide how to output it based on its position in the group.

Once again we use `<xsl:for-each>` to loop over a set of elements, in this case all the `<COL>` elements inside the current `<ROW>`. For each `<COL>` element we process, we need to make a choice as to how to output it. If it's in the first position, we output it as an `<id>` element, if it's in the second position, we output it as a `<widget_description>` element and so forth.

22

If we were trying to program this type of multiple choice in a FileMaker calculation, we'd use a Case() statement, or perhaps a Choose(). Here we use the XSL equivalent, which is called <xsl:choose>. Like FileMaker's Case statement, xsl:choose lets you choose among several options, each one corresponding to a logical test of some kind. The <xsl:choose> element contains one or more <xsl:when> statements. Each one corresponds to a particular choice, and each choice is associated with a logical test. In the code we showed in the preceding section, the first test inside the <xsl:choose> element is the test for columns whose position equals 1. In this case, we go on to output the <id>...</id> tag pair, with the data value inside it. To do this, we use the <xsl:value-of> element, which can pull out a piece of the source XML document to output. In this case, each <COL> element in the FileMaker source XML has a <DATA> element inside it, and it's that element we want to grab and add to the output.

The rest of the <xsl:when> statement contains the remaining tests, for the columns in positions 2, 3, and 4 of the output. At this point, we're done! The rest of the code consists of emitting closing XML tags that match the opening tags we've already sent, and of closing up our XSL constructs, like <xsl:for-each>.

APPLYING AN EXPORT TRANSFORMATION TO FILEMAKER XML

FileMaker lets you use XSL stylesheets to transform your data when moving data into or out of FileMaker with XML. Let's consider the export example first. If you have a table of FileMaker data (such as the widget data we've been using, for example), and you choose to export the data as XML, you'll see the dialog box shown in Figure 22.6.

Figure 22.6
When exporting XML from FileMaker, you may also choose to apply a stylesheet to transform the outbound XML.

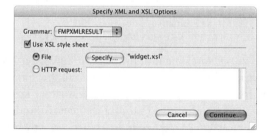

Here you can choose your XML export grammar, as we've already seen, but you can also choose whether to apply an XSL stylesheet to transform the XML as it's being output. If you want to apply a stylesheet, you can pick a local file (in other words, a file resident on your local hard drive or on a mounted server volume). You can also pick a stylesheet file that's available over HTTP (namely, on a Web server somewhere).

Working with Remote Stylesheets

The HTTP feature was a very smart choice on the part of FileMaker's development team. It's very important in a multi-user FileMaker deployment, where many users use the same solution files hosted by a single server. If the only option for stylesheet use was to use a file from the user's locally accessible hard drive or drives, you'd either have to distribute the stylesheet to all system users and make sure they put it in the right location on their hard drives, or else you'd have to have a common server volume that all users would have to mount. With the capability to pull a stylesheet from a Web server, you can create one single stylesheet and place it on a central Web server, and accessed by all users.

One important qualification to this capability is that FileMaker currently supports remote access to stylesheets via only the HTTP protocol. HTTPS (secure HTTP) is not currently supported.

Using XSL stylesheets in the export process in this way, you can transform FileMaker data into a wide variety of output formats: other variants of XML, or HTML, or XML suitable for import into applications such as Excel or Quark Xpress, or even a complex text format such as PDF.

XML IMPORT: UNDERSTANDING WEB SERVICES

In addition to FileMaker's capability of exporting data via XML, either with or without an XSL stylesheet, FileMaker also has the capability of working with remote XML data sources, often referred to under the umbrella term "Web services." This is a capability that was added in FileMaker version 6 and is a significant addition to FileMaker's XML strengths. Using this capability, you can bring data from a variety of remote data sources directly into FileMaker, as we'll discuss in the sections that follow.

FILEMAKER'S XML IMPORT CAPABILITY

The concept of XML exporting ought to seem fairly straightforward: Take some FileMaker data, pick an XML "grammar" for the export, and optionally apply an XSL stylesheet to transform the XML data as it heads out. But what about the concept of *importing* XML? What does this mean, and what is it good for?

Stated simply, FileMaker can import any XML data that conforms to the FMPXML grammar. FileMaker reads the <METADATA> section of the document to determine the field structure, and reads the individual row and column data to figure out the actual data values that should be imported.

To demonstrate this for yourself, find some suitable FileMaker data and export it as XML, using the FMPXMLRESULT grammar, without applying any XSL stylesheet to it. Starting from the same file and table, go back and re-import the file you just exported, treating it as an XML data source—you'll see that FileMaker correctly reads the field structure and data from the XML document. Or, to test it in a different way, drag the new XML file onto the FileMaker application icon to "open" it. FileMaker should, without intervention from you (except for choosing a file name for the new file), open the XML file, read its structure, and create a new FileMaker file with a new table containing the correct fields, field types, and data values.

NOTE

> One of the things developers have often wanted from FileMaker is a way to save a file's field structure as a text document, then use that text document to move the field structure somewhere else and re-create it. The capability to open an XML document and have it create a new FileMaker file might seem to make that possible, but there are caveats. The XML export doesn't preserve important information about your field structure, such as the definitions of calculation fields and summary fields. In the XML output, these fields are treated simply as their underlying data types, so a calculation that produces a number is treated in the XML metadata as a simple number field, without preserving the calculation's definition.

So, FileMaker can import any XML data file that conforms to the FMPXMLRESULT grammar. Additionally, as you might have seen, this XML data stream can come from a local file, or it can come from a file available over HTTP—in other words, a file from somewhere on the Web. This is where things get interesting, so let's delve further into the concept of a Web service.

 If you try to import data that doesn't conform to the FMPXMLRESULT *grammar, FileMaker gives you an error. For more information, see "Wrong XML Format" in the Troubleshooting section at the end of this chapter.*

NOTE

> As was the case with using remote stylesheets for XML export, FileMaker is also unable to work with data from an HTTPS data source when importing XML. If the data source from which you want to import is available only over secure HTTP, FileMaker isn't able to import it.

WEB SERVICES REVIEWED

We started this chapter by saying that "Web services" was a term referring to the sharing of data between computers via the Web's HTTP protocol, and that the data was often exchanged in XML format. Imagine you have two computer systems that need to exchange data. One is a large student information system that resides on a mainframe computer. The other is a system that generates complex forms for each student, to conform to governmental guidelines. Periodically, the forms application needs to consult the mainframe application to see whether any new students have been added, so that those students are accounted for in the forms system.

There are many ways to make this kind of sharing happen. The mainframe programmer could export a file of new students every night, in some plain text format, and the forms programmers could write routines to grab the file and process it in some way. Or the mainframe could be made accessible via a technology such as ODBC, and the forms application could be configured to make ODBC requests to the mainframe.

→ For more information on ODBC, **see** Chapter 19, "Importing Data into FileMaker Pro," **p. 537**, and Chapter 20, "Getting Data Out of FileMaker," **p. 563**.

Another option, though, is to make it possible to send queries to the mainframe via HTTP, and get XML back in response. This is simpler than either of the previous scenarios: It doesn't require any complicated processes like writing and then fetching an actual file, nor does it involve the client-side complexities of ODBC transactions. It uses the widely (almost universally) available HTTP protocol, and requires only that one side be able to generate a form of XML, and the other side be able to read it. Don't get us wrong—Web services transactions can still be plenty complicated, but standards such as XML and HTTP make them less complex than they might be otherwise. Refer back to Figure 22.1 for a sketch of a possible Web services transaction.

Let's say that, in our example, the forms application was written in FileMaker. And let's assume the mainframe student information system was accessible as a Web service, meaning that you could send a request via HTTP and get back a listing of new students in some XML format (that would likely *not* conform to the FMPXMLRESULT grammar). To import that data into FileMaker, you could perform an XML import, use the URL of the student information system as the data source, and apply an XSL stylesheet that would transform the "new student XML" into FMPXMLRESULT. The concept is sketched out in Figure 22.7. To retrieve student data from this mainframe, make a request to a URL that's able to produce an XML representation of the student, and then bring that XML back through a stylesheet into FileMaker.

Figure 22.7
This is a graphical representation of the process of retrieving data via XML.

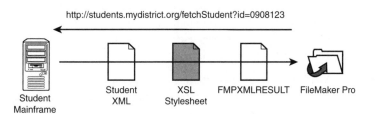

A Stylesheet for XML Import

For the sake of argument, assume that we have an XML *data stream* representing new students. (We use the term "data stream" rather than "file" as a reminder that the data need not come from a file, but can also come from a networked data source over HTTP). Listing 22.6 shows what that data might look like.

LISTING 22.6   SAMPLE XML FILE CONTAINING DATA

```
<?xml version="1.0" encoding="UTF-8"?>
<newStudentSet count="4" date="11/1/2003">
    <student id="414">
        <nameFirst>Jonathan</nameFirst>
```

continues

LISTING 22.6 CONTINUED

```
                <nameLast>Middlesex</nameLast>
                <nameMiddle>A</nameMiddle>
                <address>123 Oak Way</address>
                <city>Bensenville</city>
                <state>AK</state>
                <zip>09080-1001</zip>
                <county>Hightower</county>
                <district>Sparta</district>
                <school>Bensenville Junior High</school>
                <grade>4</grade>
                <parents>
                    <parent>
                        <nameFirst>Sharon</nameFirst>
                        <nameLast>Middlesex</nameLast>
                        <relationship>Parent</relationship>
                    </parent>
                    <parent>
                        <nameFirst>Martin</nameFirst>
                        <nameLast>Middlesex</nameLast>
                        <relationship>Parent</relationship>
                    </parent>
                </parents>
        </student>
</newStudentSet>
```

It's a simple enough structure, consisting of a `<newStudentSet>` filled with one or more `<student>` elements, where each `<student>` has a number of fields associated with it. The only wrinkle has to do with parent information: Clearly a student can have more than one parent, so each student contains a `<parents>` element with one or more `<parent>` elements inside it. We'll have to think about what to do with that.

That's the XML file that the hypothetical data source can put out. But remember, for FileMaker to import this XML data, it has to be structured in the FMPXMLRESULT format. Such a structure would look like Listing 22.7.

LISTING 22.7 DATA IN THE IMPORTABLE FMPXMLRESULT FORMAT

```
<?xml version="1.0" encoding="UTF-8" ?>
<FMPXMLRESULT xmlns="http://www.filemaker.com/fmpxmlresult">
    <ERRORCODE>0</ERRORCODE>
    <PRODUCT BUILD="11-05-2003" NAME="FileMaker Pro" VERSION="7.0v1"/>
    <DATABASE DATEFORMAT="M/d/yyyy" LAYOUT="" NAME="Student.fp7" RECORDS="1"
            TIMEFORMAT="h:mm:ss a"/>
    <METADATA>
        <FIELD EMPTYOK="YES" MAXREPEAT="1" NAME="NameFirst" TYPE="TEXT"/>
        <FIELD EMPTYOK="YES" MAXREPEAT="1" NAME="NameLast" TYPE="TEXT"/>
        <FIELD EMPTYOK="YES" MAXREPEAT="1" NAME="NameMiddle" TYPE="TEXT"/>
        <FIELD EMPTYOK="YES" MAXREPEAT="1" NAME="Address" TYPE="TEXT"/>
        <FIELD EMPTYOK="YES" MAXREPEAT="1" NAME="City" TYPE="TEXT"/>
        <FIELD EMPTYOK="YES" MAXREPEAT="1" NAME="State" TYPE="TEXT"/>
        <FIELD EMPTYOK="YES" MAXREPEAT="1" NAME="Zip" TYPE="TEXT"/>
        <FIELD EMPTYOK="YES" MAXREPEAT="1" NAME="County" TYPE="TEXT"/>
```

```
                <FIELD EMPTYOK="YES" MAXREPEAT="1" NAME="District" TYPE="TEXT"/>
                <FIELD EMPTYOK="YES" MAXREPEAT="1" NAME="School" TYPE="TEXT"/>
                <FIELD EMPTYOK="YES" MAXREPEAT="1" NAME="Parents" TYPE="TEXT"/>
        </METADATA>
        <RESULTSET FOUND="1">
            <ROW MODID="0" RECORDID="1">
                <COL><DATA>Jonathan</DATA></COL>
                <COL><DATA>Middlesex</DATA></COL>
                <COL><DATA>A</DATA></COL>
                <COL><DATA>123 Oak Way</DATA></COL>
                <COL><DATA>Bensenville</DATA></COL>
                <COL><DATA>AK</DATA></COL>
                <COL><DATA>09080-1001</DATA></COL>
                <COL><DATA>Hightower</DATA></COL>
                <COL><DATA>Sparta</DATA></COL>
                <COL><DATA>Bensenville Junior High</DATA></COL>
                <COL><DATA>Sharon Middlesex(Parent),
                ➥Martin Middlesex (Parent)</DATA></COL>
            </ROW>
        </RESULTSET>
</FMPXMLRESULT>
```

Web services scattered through the ether are unlikely to emit XML that conforms to the FMPXMLRESULT grammar. So before bringing that data into FileMaker, we need to *transform* it into FMPXMLRESULT. And the tool for doing that is, of course, an XSL stylesheet. This is exactly the reason FileMaker lets you apply a stylesheet to *inbound* XML (in other words, on import). Odds are that the XML data source does not produce the FMPXMLRESULT grammar directly, so it's our job to translate the source XML into the form that FileMaker can read.

We need an XSL stylesheet to make that transformation. The stylesheet needs to make sure to output all the initial information found in an FMPXMLRESULT file, such as database name, and all the metadata describing the field structure. Then, in the context of a <RESULTSET>, we need to output the actual student data.

Listing 22.8 shows what the stylesheet for transforming student data prior to importing it into FileMaker should look like.

LISTING 22.8   AN XSL STYLESHEET

```
<?xml version="1.0" encoding="UTF-8" ?>
<xsl:stylesheet version="1.0" xmlns:xsl="http://www.w3.org/1999/XSL/Transform">
 <xsl:output indent="yes" method="xml"/>
 <xsl:template match="newStudentSet">
   <FMPXMLRESULT xmlns="http://www.filemaker.com/fmpxmlresult">
     <ERRORCODE>0</ERRORCODE>
     <PRODUCT BUILD="11-05-2003" NAME="FileMaker Pro" VERSION="7.0v1"/>
     <DATABASE DATEFORMAT="M/d/yyyy" LAYOUT="" NAME="Student.fp7"
     ➥RECORDS="{@count}" TIMEFORMAT="h:mm:ss a"/>
     <METADATA>
       <FIELD EMPTYOK="YES" MAXREPEAT="1" NAME="NameFirst" TYPE="TEXT"/>
       <FIELD EMPTYOK="YES" MAXREPEAT="1" NAME="NameLast" TYPE="TEXT"/>
```

continues

22

LISTING 22.8   CONTINUED

```
        <FIELD EMPTYOK="YES" MAXREPEAT="1" NAME="NameMiddle" TYPE="TEXT"/>
        <FIELD EMPTYOK="YES" MAXREPEAT="1" NAME="Address" TYPE="TEXT"/>
        <FIELD EMPTYOK="YES" MAXREPEAT="1" NAME="City" TYPE="TEXT"/>
        <FIELD EMPTYOK="YES" MAXREPEAT="1" NAME="State" TYPE="TEXT"/>
        <FIELD EMPTYOK="YES" MAXREPEAT="1" NAME="Zip" TYPE="TEXT"/>
        <FIELD EMPTYOK="YES" MAXREPEAT="1" NAME="County" TYPE="TEXT"/>
        <FIELD EMPTYOK="YES" MAXREPEAT="1" NAME="District" TYPE="TEXT"/>
        <FIELD EMPTYOK="YES" MAXREPEAT="1" NAME="School" TYPE="TEXT"/>
        <FIELD EMPTYOK="YES" MAXREPEAT="1" NAME="Grade" TYPE="TEXT"/>
        <FIELD EMPTYOK="YES" MAXREPEAT="1" NAME="Parents" TYPE="TEXT"/>
      </METADATA>
      <RESULTSET FOUND="{@count}">
        <xsl:for-each select="student">
          <ROW MODID="0" RECORDID="{position()}">
            <COL><DATA><xsl:value-of select="nameFirst"/></DATA></COL>
            <COL><DATA><xsl:value-of select="nameLast"/></DATA></COL>
            <COL><DATA><xsl:value-of select="nameMiddle"/></DATA></COL>
            <COL><DATA><xsl:value-of select="address"/></DATA></COL>
            <COL><DATA><xsl:value-of select="city"/></DATA></COL>
            <COL><DATA><xsl:value-of select="state"/></DATA></COL>
            <COL><DATA><xsl:value-of select="zip"/></DATA></COL>
            <COL><DATA><xsl:value-of select="county"/></DATA></COL>
            <COL><DATA><xsl:value-of select="district"/></DATA></COL>
            <COL><DATA><xsl:value-of select="school"/></DATA></COL>
            <COL><DATA><xsl:value-of select="grade"/></DATA></COL>
            <COL><DATA><xsl:for-each select="parents/parent">
                <xsl:value-of select="nameFirst"/>
                <xsl:text> </xsl:text>
                <xsl:value-of select="nameLast"/>
                <xsl:text> (</xsl:text>
                <xsl:value-of select="relationship"/>
                <xsl:text>)</xsl:text>
                <xsl:if test="position() != last()">
                  <xsl:text>, </xsl:text>
                </xsl:if>
              </xsl:for-each></DATA></COL>
          </ROW>
        </xsl:for-each>
      </RESULTSET>
    </FMPXMLRESULT>
  </xsl:template>
</xsl:stylesheet>
```

We won't spend as much time dissecting this stylesheet as we did with the last one. The mechanics should be pretty easy to discern. After the usual declarations, we declare a template that matches to the source document's <newStudentSet> element. (It's the root element, so there will only be one.) That's the occasion to output all the header-type information particular to the FMPXMLRESULT grammar, including the field structure metadata. We then go on to output a <RESULTSET>...</RESULTSET> tag pair, and do some more work inside of that.

Within the resultset tags, we use an <xsl:for-each> to loop over all the <student> elements inside the <newStudentSet>. For each one, we output the corresponding <ROW> element.

Each <ROW>, in turn, is a collection of <COL><DATA>...</DATA></COL> tag pairs. We output one of these for each inbound field, and insert the correct data into it, using <xsl:value-of>.

The only thing at all noteworthy is the treatment of the parent information. The inbound student information is not completely "flat." The nested <parents> element almost implies a new table, in relational database terms. We could choose to handle it that way, and bring the parent information into a separate table, but we chose instead to "flatten" the parent data into a single field. This was more to illustrate a particular technique than because it's actually a good idea to do that. Whether it really is a good idea depends on the application.

In any case, the technique here is to loop over the individual <parent> elements, using <xsl:for-each>. For each parent, we output the first name, last name, and the family relationship in parentheses. You might notice that we use the <xsl:text> command liberally, to output the spaces between words and the parentheses around the relationship. The reason for this is that XML treats certain characters, such as white space, specially. White space, in particular, XML ignores. Wrapping it in an <xsl:text> tag ensures that the processor treats it as real white space and outputs it as such.

The last wrinkle here is that we want the parent list to be comma separated. So we write a little piece of logic that requests that a comma and its following white space be output, but only if the current <parent> element is not the last one in the group. The check is performed with <xsl:if>.

As you can see, the stylesheet isn't too complicated. The hardest part is getting all the FMPXMLRESULT-specific elements and attributes correctly included.

TIP

> It's irritating, if not impossible, to remember all the specifications for the FMPXMLRESULT grammar every time you need to write a new import stylesheet. To save yourself the trouble, first make sure the FileMaker table you're using to receive the data is correctly built and has the right structure. Then add a sample record or two to the table, and export the table as FMPXMLRESULT. The result is exactly what any inbound XML needs to look like (well, the data itself is likely to be different!). You should be able to copy large chunks of this XML output and paste them into your stylesheet to get yourself started.

After you've written the stylesheet, you would apply it in the course of the import. If everything goes smoothly, the stylesheet is successfully applied, it emits pure FMPXML, and this is cleanly imported into FileMaker.

 If your stylesheet contains a programming error, FileMaker presents an error dialog and tries to alert you as to where in the stylesheet the problem occurred. For more information, see "Errors in Stylesheets" in the Troubleshooting section at the end of this chapter.

You might need to do a bit of work to make sure the fields get lined up correctly on import. The easiest way to assure this is to write your XSL stylesheet in such a way that the field names in the resulting <METADATA> section of the XML are exact matches for your FileMaker field names. If that's the case, you need to specify only that fields should import based on "matching names." If for any reason there's a discrepancy between the field names that are used in the resultant FMPXMLRESULT, and the field names in the target table, you have to specify the import matching by hand.

→ For more details about specifying import field mappings, **see** "The Import Field Mapping dialog," **p. 539**.

 Of course, the import may not go smoothly. See "Correct Stylesheet, Failed Import" in the Troubleshooting section at the end of this chapter for some tips on how to handle stylesheets that don't perform as expected.

WORKING WITH WEB SERVICES

The previous section, on importing XML via a stylesheet, tells you more or less all you need to know to work effectively with Web services in FileMaker. The only other thing you need is a real Web service to work with.

It can actually be a bit difficult to find interesting Web services to play with. Many of the really meaty Web services, because they're providing useful information, charge an access or subscription fee of some kind. (These might include Web services that provide current weather information from satellites, or financial information, for example.) Many of the free Web services, by contrast, are either of limited scope, or else represent hobby work, student programming projects, and the like.

Happily, there are a few exceptions. We're going to take a look at Amazon.com's Web service offerings. Amazon, of course, has a user interface, presented via HTML, that you can use to conduct Amazon searches by pointing and clicking with your mouse in a Web browser. But Amazon has also been a pioneer in offering XML-based Web services that let you do the same thing, allowing you to integrate Amazon data into other applications.

Suppose you have a FileMaker database containing information about books. For each book you'd like to be able to check whether it's available from Amazon, and if so, at what price. With FileMaker's XML Import capability, you can do this fairly easily.

ACCESSING THE AMAZON WEB SERVICES

Working with Amazon's Web services is straightforward, but you need to do a couple of things first. You should visit http://www.amazon.com/webservices; there, you'll be able to download the Web services developer's kit, which provides useful documentation, and you'll also be able to apply for a "developer's token," which is a special personal key you'll need to send along with your Web service requests for validation. (There's no charge for either the developer's kit or the token.)

NOTE

> If you don't want to take the trouble to apply for your own developer's token, you can use one that we requested for use in this book. That token is D1AT17BPIA1PX7.

Types of Web Services

As you browse the Internet looking for Web services, and as you look at the Amazon material, you may see a lot of references to different types of Web services, using terms such as SOAP or XML-RPC. Here's what you need to know about this: Though all the Web services we're interested in work by sending and receiving XML over an HTTP protocol, there are several different ways to do this. HTTP requests are divided into broad categories, called GET and POST. A GET request passes information in the URL: If you've ever seen a long, ugly-looking URL in your browser, like

`http://my.ecommerce-site.com/cartApp.astj?userID=ED45jUiJJ&sessKey=6a45Rtfe4`, you're looking at information being sent via a GET request. On the other hand, if you've ever filled out an HTML form and pressed the Submit button, odds are the data were being sent behind the scenes, in what's called a POST request.

Web services may work with either GET or POST requests. FileMaker's XML Import feature, however, can make only a GET request. But a number of the most common Web services techniques work exclusively via POST.

SOAP is an example of such a Web services protocol. SOAP transactions send a complex XML request to the server via a POST operation. Many Web services are available only via SOAP. A good example is the Google Web service, which lets you interface directly to the Google search engine. Because Google is SOAP-based, there is no direct way for FileMaker to interact with the Google Web service at the moment.

In looking for FileMaker-ready Web services, then you're looking for Web services that support simple XML over HTTP via GET requests.

The developer's kit comes with documentation that shows how to formulate various types of HTTP requests for data. Here's an example URL:

```
http://xml.amazon.com/onca/xml3?t=xxx&dev-t= D1AT17BPIA1PX7
&PowerSearch=title:Genet&mode=books&type=lite&page=1&f=xml
```

This searches Amazon for books with the word "Genet" in the title. Try entering the above URL in Internet Explorer 5 or greater (which renders the resulting XML nicely), and you'll see what the returned results look like. This returns data in Amazon's "lite" format, which has less information than the corresponding "heavy" format.

Amazon's XML formats, whether "lite" or heavy, are clearly not FileMaker's FMPXMLRESULT. So if you want to bring this book data back into FileMaker via an XML import, you need a stylesheet to transform it appropriately on the way in.

WRITING A STYLESHEET TO IMPORT AMAZON DATA

Let's say we have a book database with the field structure shown in Figure 22.8.

Figure 22.8
Field structure for a
database of book
information.

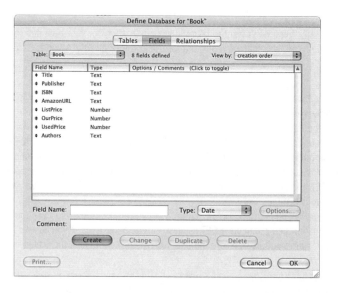

We can bring Amazon data into this FileMaker structure by performing an import from an
XML data source, and applying a stylesheet to the inbound data. The stylesheet looks and
works a lot like the one in Listing 22.8. We show it here, for completeness, as Listing 22.9.

LISTING 22.9 STYLESHEET FOR TRANSFORMING AMAZON XML INTO FMPXMLRESULT XML

```xml
<?xml version="1.0" encoding="UTF-8" ?>
<xsl:stylesheet version="1.0" xmlns:xsl="http://www.w3.org/1999/XSL/Transform">
  <xsl:output indent="yes" method="xml"/>
  <xsl:template match="ProductInfo">
    <FMPXMLRESULT xmlns="http://www.filemaker.com/fmpxmlresult">
      <ERRORCODE>0</ERRORCODE>
      <PRODUCT BUILD="11-05-2003" NAME="FileMaker Pro" VERSION="7.0v1"/>
      <DATABASE DATEFORMAT="M/d/yyyy" LAYOUT="" NAME="Student.fp7" RECORDS="10"
➥ TIMEFORMAT="h:mm:ss a"/>
      <METADATA>
        <FIELD EMPTYOK="YES" MAXREPEAT="1" NAME="Title" TYPE="TEXT"/>
        <FIELD EMPTYOK="YES" MAXREPEAT="1" NAME="Publisher" TYPE="TEXT"/>
        <FIELD EMPTYOK="YES" MAXREPEAT="1" NAME="ISBN" TYPE="TEXT"/>
        <FIELD EMPTYOK="YES" MAXREPEAT="1" NAME="AmazonURL" TYPE="TEXT"/>
        <FIELD EMPTYOK="YES" MAXREPEAT="1" NAME="ListPrice" TYPE="NUMBER"/>
        <FIELD EMPTYOK="YES" MAXREPEAT="1" NAME="OurPrice" TYPE="NUMBER"/>
        <FIELD EMPTYOK="YES" MAXREPEAT="1" NAME="UsedPrice" TYPE="NUMBER"/>
        <FIELD EMPTYOK="YES" MAXREPEAT="1" NAME="Authors" TYPE="TEXT"/>
      </METADATA>
      <RESULTSET FOUND="10">
        <xsl:for-each select="Details">
          <ROW MODID="0" RECORDID="{position()}">
            <COL>
              <DATA>
                <xsl:value-of select="ProductName"/>
```

```
            </DATA>
          </COL>
          <COL>
            <DATA>
              <xsl:value-of select="Manufacturer"/>
            </DATA>
          </COL>
          <COL>
            <DATA>
              <xsl:value-of select="Asin"/>
            </DATA>
          </COL>
          <COL>
            <DATA>
              <xsl:value-of select="url"/>
            </DATA>
          </COL>
          <COL>
            <DATA>
              <xsl:value-of select="ListPrice"/>
            </DATA>
          </COL>
          <COL>
            <DATA>
              <xsl:value-of select="OurPrice"/>
            </DATA>
          </COL>
          <COL>
            <DATA>
              <xsl:value-of select="UsedPrice"/>
            </DATA>
          </COL>
          <COL>
            <DATA>
              <xsl:for-each select="Authors/Author">
                <xsl:value-of select="."/>
                <xsl:if test="position() != last()">
                  <xsl:text>, </xsl:text>
                </xsl:if>
              </xsl:for-each>
            </DATA>
          </COL>
        </ROW>
      </xsl:for-each>
    </RESULTSET>
  </FMPXMLRESULT>
  </xsl:template>
</xsl:stylesheet>
```

This is extremely similar to the earlier stylesheet, even down to the treatment of book authors, which occur in nested groups: Here, we loop over authors in the same way we looped over parent records, flattening them into a single text field.

22

BUILDING A MORE FLEXIBLE INTERFACE TO A WEB SERVICE

The previous section concentrated on the stylesheet that you would use to import data from Amazon. But so far, we've just assumed FileMaker is issuing some hard-coded URL to perform an Amazon search. In fact, we probably want our users to be able to compose their own queries and submit them to Amazon.

There's no great mystery to this. The Amazon developer's kit documents the different types of search strings that the Amazon Web service can accept. (If we're just searching for books, a lot of the more interesting options can be found as part of the overall "power search" option.)

So far, we've imported XML only from data sources we specified via a hard-coded URL. It's also possible, though, when importing XML into FileMaker via a script, to draw the XML from a data source specified by a calculation. Figure 22.9 shows the relevant dialog choice.

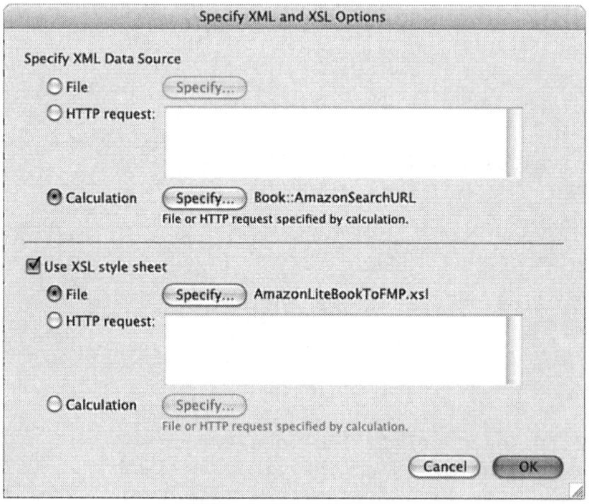

Figure 22.9
When importing XML into FileMaker via a script, you can use a calculation to create the source URL on the fly.

This makes it possible to compose the Amazon URL on the fly based on user input. For example, if we wanted to search for books by Naguib Mafouz, published by (say) Farrar Straus & Giroux, the Amazon URL would look like this:

```
http://xml.amazon.com/onca/xml3?t=xxx&dev-t=D1AT17BPIA1PX7&PowerSearch=
➥author:Mafouz and publisher:giroux&mode=books
➥&type=lite&page=1&f=xml
```

(In the real URL, you would use your Seller ID, if you had one instead of the nonsense string xxx.) To compose this URL dynamically, you'd need to offer the user a couple of global fields to type into. Assume the user called gAuthorSearch and gPublisherSearch. You could then define a calculation field that would look something like this:

```
http://xml.amazon.com/onca/xml3?t=xxx&dev-t=D1AT17BPIA1PX7
➥&PowerSearch=author:" & gAuthorSearch & " and publisher:"
➥& gPublisherSearch & "&mode=books&type=lite&page=1&f=xml"
```

And, as shown in Figure 22.9, you can instruct FileMaker to derive the URL from a calculation, which could point directly to this dynamic field. This snippet is really useful only as an example of how you might go about this conceptually. In reality, you'd need to do some work to build a really nice interface to Amazon. You'd want to add fields for all the types of Amazon searches (there are about seven). You'd also want to provide for the fact that the user might choose to search on some but not all criteria, making it a good idea to omit the unused search types from the URL. You'd have to account for the fact that it's possible for searches to have multiple words, in which case they need to be enclosed in quotes. And you'd want to account for the different search types Amazon allows, such as searching by exact match or initial match.

USING FILEMAKER AS A WEB SERVICES SOURCE

So far in this chapter, we've mainly discussed how to get data *from* Web services, *into* FileMaker. But it's possible to do this the other way around as well. Let's say that you have some order data in FileMaker Pro. Let's also suppose that there's a central mainframe computer that needs to have access to the FileMaker orders, as they're completed.

There are a number of ways to skin this particular cat, but let's suppose for the sake of example that the mainframe system is capable of requesting data from a Web service. In other words, the mainframe can make a request for data over HTTP, and expects to get some form of XML back in return.

The strategy for handling this with FileMaker is straightforward. First, you need to make the relevant FileMaker database available over the Web. This means you need to have a copy of FileMaker Server with the appropriate Web publishing technologies enabled, and you need to have the particular database in question available for Web access.

→ For more information on configuring Web publishing on your FileMaker Server, **see** "Configuring FileMaker Server 7 Advanced for IWP," **p. 613**, as well as "Setting up the Server-side Components for CWP," **p. 676**.

Assuming your FileMaker databases are correctly configured for Web access, the procedure for allowing FileMaker to act as a Web services server is relatively straightforward. All that's necessary is to make potential Web services clients aware of the correct URLs to use. You'll provide one or more URLs that will publish FileMaker data to an XML format. You could provide a URL that would provide "raw" XML in one of FileMaker's built-in XML grammars. For example:

```
http://192.168.123.101/fmi/xml/fmresultset.xml?-db=products-lay=sales&-findall
```

Or you could provide a URL that would first format the outbound XML with a stylesheet, like this:

```
http://192.168.123.101/fmi/xsl/my_template/my_stylesheet.xsl?-grammar=
➥fmresultset&-db=mydatabase &-lay=mylayout&-findall
```

As you'll learn in Chapter 23, "Custom Web Publishing," it's possible to include access validation logic in your stylesheets that could (for example) check to make sure that

Web services requests came from only a select set of IP addresses, or perform some other kind of validation.

In general, though, using FileMaker as a Web services provider falls under the heading of Custom Web Publishing, which we cover thoroughly in Chapter 23.

TROUBLESHOOTING

WRONG XML FORMAT

I'm trying to import an XML file someone gave me, but I can't even get to the Import Field Mappings dialog. FileMaker says there's an "unknown element" in the document.

FileMaker can import only XML that's in the FMPXMLRESULT grammar. If you got the XML document from some source other than FileMaker, it's very unlikely to conform to FMPXML-RESULT. You'll need to apply a stylesheet to the XML as you import it to transform it into valid FMPXMLRESULT XML.

ERRORS IN STYLESHEETS

FileMaker says there's a "parse error" in my XSL stylesheet.

There's a lot of programming in an XSL stylesheet—and XSL and XML are fairly unforgiving languages. A single bracket out of place in your stylesheet, and the XML parser rejects it as being ill-formed. You need to be able to track down the syntax error and fix it. A good XML development environment, such as Oxygen for the Macintosh or XMLSpy for the PC, can be a big help in tracking down such problems.

CORRECT STYLESHEET, FAILED IMPORT

My XML development tool tells me my stylesheet is valid and correct, but when I use it in the process of importing XML into FileMaker I still get strange errors from FileMaker.

It's perfectly possible to write a stylesheet that's correct in itself, but does not produce correct output. When you're importing into FileMaker, the inbound data has to be in correct FMPXMLRESULT format. Any deviation from that format, and FileMaker rejects the data. You might have written a stylesheet that is correct and runs perfectly without an error, but that nonetheless doesn't produce correct FMPXMLRESULT output as you intended. Here again, you need to figure out what went wrong and how to fix it.

There are other possible errors as well. For example, if you are fetching either your XML data or an XSL stylesheet from an HTTP server, you get an error if that server isn't available to you when you try to perform the import.

Unfortunately, FileMaker isn't much of an XML debugger. If you run into either of the errors we just discussed, FileMaker gives you a fairly terse error message, which may possibly lead you to the line of the file that produced the problem. If the problem is that you produced bad XML from your stylesheet, you may not even get that much information.

This is no fault of FileMaker's. XML development is a big area and it's not in the scope of FileMaker's capabilities to be a full-fledged development environment for generating and debugging XML files. But if you're at all serious about using FileMaker and XML together, you'll want to invest in such a tool.

An XML development tool generally consists of an XML editor that provides a lot of assistance in writing XML and XSL files. It may include features such as tag balancing (automatically closing tags when it seems right to do so), command completion (for example, being able to finish your XSL commands for you after you type a few letters), automatic indentation, and, of course, document validation and debugging.

To use such a tool to develop an export stylesheet for FileMaker, for example, you could first do a sample XML export from your FileMaker database, into a test file. You could bring this FileMaker XML file into your XML development tool. Then you could write up your XSL stylesheet, have the tool check its syntax to make sure it's technically correct, and then have the tool apply the stylesheet to the FileMaker XML. You could then inspect the result for correctness.

We strongly recommend you look into such a tool if you plan on doing much XML work with FileMaker. On the Mac, the Oxygen XML editor is fairly full-featured (http://www.oxygenxml.com). On the PC, Altova's XMLSpy is highly regarded (http://www.altova.com).

FILEMAKER EXTRA: WRITE YOUR OWN WEB SERVICES

We generally think of Web services as being something that someone else has, and that we want access to. But Web services have many other uses as well. They can provide a powerful way to extend the capabilities of your FileMaker application.

For example, suppose you needed to compute a Fourier transform, based on some measured signal data. FileMaker has no built-in facility for such analysis—computing the transform requires complex mathematics. (Well, with enough diligence, you might be able to write a FileMaker script to perform a Discrete Fourier Transform, but its cousin the Fast Fourier Transform requires mathematical operations FileMaker can't perform.)

NOTE Don't worry if Fourier transforms don't ring a bell; its just a data example. A Fourier transform is an advanced mathematical technique for taking a complex signal, such as a sound or radio wave, and decomposing it into a series of simpler signals.

FileMaker already provides a number of extension mechanisms to developers. Many problems can be solved with a custom function. Those that can't may be addressed by a plug-in already in existence.

→ For more details about installing and using FileMaker plug-ins, **see** "Plug-ins," **p. 789**.

Web services provide another way to extend FileMaker's capabilities. They are, in our view, easier to write than plugins, which require knowledge of a low-level programming language such as C++, and knowledge of how to program in each specific client environment supported by FileMaker 7, namely Windows and the Mac OS. Web services, by contrast, can be written in the "lighter-weight" scripting languages, which we feel are easier to learn, and because they execute in a server environment, they don't require that you have any knowledge of how to program specifically for the Mac or Windows.

Of course, this points up one of the hurdles involved in writing your own Web service: You still have to know how. Web services can be written in a wide variety of programming languages, such as PHP, Perl, JSP, ASP, Visual Basic, Tango, Lasso, or any of many other "Web scripting languages," not to mention hard-core languages such as Java, C, or C++. There's literally no limit to the kinds of work you can perform with Web services written in these languages. The only catch is, again, you have to know how.

Of the languages discussed, we feel the "Web scripting" languages are probably the most approachable. PHP is a superb general-purpose Web scripting language. JSP has a Java base, whereas ASP and Visual Basic are particular to a Windows server environment. Tango and Lasso were once exclusively FileMaker-aware Web tools, but have since grown into more general-purpose languages. All these languages presume some familiarity with the fundamentals of computer programming, and familiarity with the specific language in question.

Let's return again to the hypothetical example. Let's say you're importing signal data from an electronic instrument of some kind. You have the raw data, and you want to compute a Discrete Fourier Transform of the samples. Our strategy for doing this is twofold: First we write a Web service capable of doing the math, then we call that Web service from FileMaker, hand it our data, and get our results back in return.

In a book of this kind, we can't explain in detail how to write the kind of Web service that would do this. Conceptually, if you know a language like PHP, you can write a PHP program, designed to be accessed over the Web, which expects to receive a vector of numbers in the request. You would call the Web service via a URL, which might look something like this:

```
http://webservices.my-company.net/DFT.php?samples=
➥"1.0, .45, 3.2, -.23, 1.76, 1.55, 2.01, 1.23, .34, -.78, -.64, -.09"
```

The "samples" represent the actual data you are sending to the Web service for processing. You would compose the URL dynamically in FileMaker, much as we demonstrated for the Amazon example earlier in this chapter. The URL accesses the Web server at webservices.my-company.com, requests access to the Discrete Fourier Transform program, and passes the DFT program a series of sample values. The DFT program processes the information, and returns some information. For the purposes of getting the resulting data back into FileMaker, we want to work through the FileMaker XML Import feature, so the DFT program should output XML of some sort—either straight FMPXML that we can import back into FileMaker, or some other XML flavor that we can transform with a stylesheet.

22

So what's DFT.php? Well, it would be a program, written in the PHP language, that knows how to compute a Discrete Fourier Transform from a vector of numbers, and output the results in XML. You might choose to write the program in straight PHP. For more advanced math, though, such as the more complex Fast Fourier Transform, you might choose to use PHP to call a code library on the Web server computer, which would perform the complex math in a very fast language such as C.

The one downside to using Web services in this way (besides the need to learn one or more additional languages) is that the Web service functionality doesn't really live "in FileMaker"; it lives on a server someplace, so if you are creating standalone FileMaker applications that are meant to work in a single-user, non-hosted environment, or possibly an environment with no network or Internet connection, then home-brew Web services are probably not the way to go.

There are relatively few limits to the kinds of programming tasks you can accomplish "in FileMaker," just by hooking FileMaker up to the appropriately-written Web service. Of course, those services are not trivial to produce in practice. But if you have the knowledge to do so (or access to someone with such knowledge), the potential uses are almost limitless.

To recap, Web services can provide a way to extend the capabilities of FileMaker. The range of possible functionality is much wider than that afforded by custom functions, and programming Web services is, in general, easier than programming FileMaker plug-ins (which requires writing platform-specific compiled code).

CHAPTER 23

CUSTOM WEB PUBLISHING

In this chapter

ABOUT CUSTOM WEB PUBLISHING

 Custom Web Publishing is one of two technologies you can use to dynamically publish your FileMaker data on the World Wide Web. (The other is Instant Web Publishing, which you can read about in Chapter 21). Custom Web Publishing in FileMaker 7 replaces the technology that was known as CDML (Claris Dynamic Markup Language) in previous versions of FileMaker Pro.

One of the most significant advances in FileMaker Web publishing technologies is that, in FileMaker 7, it's possible to publish FileMaker data to the Web without using a copy of the FileMaker Pro client. In previous versions of the product, it was necessary to use FileMaker Unlimited, which was a specially enabled version of the client software. In the FileMaker 7 product line, the Web publishing technologies are built directly into the Server products and run as true standalone server-side processes.

NOTE

> In FileMaker 7, it's still possible to use Instant Web Publishing to publish data from a client copy of FileMaker Pro. IWP can also be used in the server-only mode as well, though, and can support many more users in a server configuration.

NOTE

> As you can read in more detail in Chapter 25, "FileMaker Server," the FileMaker Server product line has two different flavors, FileMaker Server and FileMaker Server Advanced. It's necessary to purchase FileMaker Server Advanced to gain the capability to do server-side Web publishing.

Server-side Web publishing works through an intermediate server called the Web Publishing Engine (which we'll call the WPE for short). The WPE is installed in a way that binds it to a Web server (Apache and Internet Information Server are the supported Web servers), and is able to make calls directly against a copy of FileMaker Server. Figure 23.1 shows the flow of a server-side CWP request (this flow actually applies to both Instant and Custom Web Publishing).

Figure 23.1
The Web Publishing Engine mediates between a Web server and a copy of FileMaker Server.

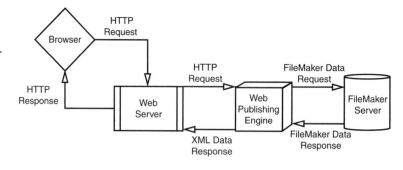

The WPE is responsible for accepting a request for FileMaker data that comes in over the Web and for relaying that request to a copy of FileMaker Server. The WPE then receives the server's response and (this is important!) converts the data into an XML format before sending it back.

The last part bears repeating, and is a significant break with the CDML technology that characterized previous versions of FileMaker: Custom Web Publishing in the FileMaker 7 product line is completely XML-based. Requests to the CWP engine can return either "raw" XML—meaning that it's presented in one of FileMaker's built in XML grammars—or they can return the results of an XSLT transformation applied to the XML. This leads to the possibility of transforming the XML into HTML, PDF, or any other text-based format before the data is returned to the client.

→ You can read about FileMaker's XML grammars in "FileMaker's XML Grammars," **p. 642**, and you'll learn more about them in the course of this chapter as well.

CUSTOM WEB PUBLISHING VERSUS INSTANT WEB PUBLISHING

If you've read about Instant Web Publishing already (in Chapter 21), you'll be aware that the IWP capabilities of FileMaker 7 represent a big advance over those in previous versions. The advance is so significant, in fact, that you might wonder whether IWP would suffice for all your Web publishing needs. It certainly seems simpler than working with a lot of XML and XSL data files.

But CWP has a number of important advantages over IWP. Here are some of the most significant ones:

- IWP works very hard to replicate the look and feel of your FileMaker layouts, so it is guaranteed to work with only a few browsers (Internet Explorer, as well as Safari 1.1 or better on Mac OS 10.3). By contrast, if you are publishing XML data as HTML, you can create HTML that is compatible with as wide (or narrow) a range of browsers as you choose.

- If you are converting previous solutions that were written in CDML, FileMaker offers a conversion path from CDML to FileMaker 7's CWP, via the CDML Conversion Tool that is discussed later in this chapter.

→ For more on converting from CDML to CWP, **see** "The CDML Converter," **p. 722**, later in this chapter.

- With CWP, it's straightforward to integrate FileMaker data with other Web sites, or provide FileMaker data to others in the form of a Web service. CWP makes a strong distinction between the raw data (which is returned as XML) and the final presentational form (which can result from applying an optional XSLT stylesheet). By contrast, in IWP, data and presentation are combined in a way that makes it all but impossible to use the data itself in other contexts.

- CWP is best for sites that need to conform to the conventions of the World Wide Web. IWP presents data in a FileMaker-driven way: It's fairly easy, using IWP, to reproduce a

23

fairly complex FileMaker layout on the Web, but it would be quite difficult to, for example, display a set of search results in a two-column list, or break a large set of search results up into multiple results "pages"—both of which are common presentation styles on the Web.

- IWP has a number of built-in limitations. For instance, it cannot reproduce FileMaker's Preview mode, so it can't be used to display subsummary reports on the Web. Also, the IWP list and table views are limited to displaying 5 and 20 records at a time, respectively. These are limits that CWP can overcome.

In general, IWP is best for making some portion of the functionality of an existing FileMaker database accessible to remote users. IWP's chief strength is in bringing the FileMaker experience into a Web browser. The most likely targets for this technology are remote users of a FileMaker system who may not be able to be in the same building or same site as the server, but require ready access. This is likely to cater to a relatively small group of users (hundreds, say, rather than the thousands and tens of thousands that a public Web site can reach).

CWP, on the other hand, is best when FileMaker data needs to be presented in a "non-FileMaker" style, either as familiar-looking Web pages or in some other text-based form. It enables you to make FileMaker data available over the Web as raw XML, to integrate FileMaker data into an existing Web site, or to build a new Web site around FileMaker data while preserving all the conventions of Web presentation.

Custom Web Publishing Versus XML Export

At first view, Custom Web Publishing might sound a lot like the XML Export capability we discussed in Chapter 20, "Getting Data Out of FileMaker." There are some similarities, but there are also many significant differences. The main ones are these:

- XML export is a "push" technology rather than a "pull" technology. New data becomes available to potential clients only when you decide to "publish" the data by performing a new export, possibly manually, possibly via an automated script. CWP is a server-side technology that can be made available on demand, enabling clients to "pull" new data at any time by accessing a specific URL that you provide.

- Using CWP, you can publish your FileMaker data in a new XML grammar, called fmresultset. This new grammar has the richness of the FMPXMLRESULT grammar, while being easier to work with for stylesheet writers. The grammar is available only through CWP.

- CWP is a server-side technology, which means you don't need a copy of the FileMaker client to take advantage of CWP. All necessary programming occurs on the server side. On the other hand, exporting XML can take place only from a client application.

To sum up: Use XML export for occasional exports of FileMaker data as raw or transformed XML that you trigger through a client copy of FileMaker Pro. Use CWP when you want to provide live, on-demand access to FileMaker data via a Web interface.

GETTING YOUR DATABASES READY FOR CUSTOM WEB PUBLISHING

To get your FileMaker databases ready for Custom Web Publishing, you need to do a few specific things with access privileges in each file you want to share via Custom Web Publishing.

If you're familiar with previous versions of FileMaker Pro, you'll recall that the various "publishing" options for a database (Web sharing, local ODBC, remote ODBC) were all accessed via a file's "sharing" options. Enabling or disabling a sharing method was simply a matter of checking or unchecking a sharing option.

 In FileMaker 7, access to a database via either XML or XSLT is handled via the security and privilege system. This is much more flexible than in previous versions because you can allow or deny XML or XSLT access to a file based on whether a user has the appropriate privilege.

Unfortunately, with this flexibility comes some additional work. To enable Custom Web Publishing in a file, you must create, by hand, a new Extended Privilege for each type of CWP access you want to allow. To allow access to data from the file as raw XML, create an extended privilege with the keyword `fmxml`. To allow access via XSLT, create an extended privilege with the keyword `fmxslt`. Figure 23.2 illustrates the creation of these extended privileges.

Figure 23.2
You'll need to add Extended Privileges by hand to enable Custom Web Publishing with XML and XSLT.

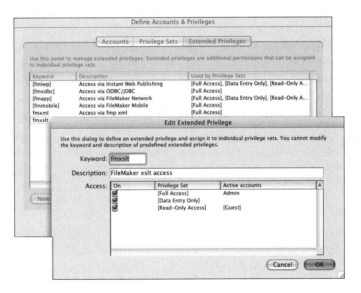

NOTE

In earlier versions of FileMaker Pro, Web sharing in any of its forms could not be enabled or disabled while a database was being served by FileMaker Server. In FileMaker 7, the extended privileges for CWP can be added while the databases are being hosted, and these privileges can be added to or removed from privilege sets on the fly as well.

To recap, each database that you want to share via CWP needs to have the appropriate extended privileges created and added to one or more privilege sets.

If you expect to see a database served via Custom Web Publishing and it doesn't appear, check to make sure the appropriate extended privileges are enabled. See the section on "Getting the Right Privileges" in the Troubleshooting section at the end of this chapter.

Setting Up the Server-Side Components for CWP

Three distinct server-side components make up the CWP "publishing chain." Requests for FileMaker data via CWP come first to a Web server—either Apache (on Mac OS X) or Internet Information Server (on Windows). The Web server then routes that request to a Web Publishing Engine, a standalone server process that sits in between the Web server and FileMaker Server. The Web Publishing Engine processes the Web request, makes the appropriate call to a copy of FileMaker Server Advanced, and formats the returned data into XML, which it then sends back to the client via the Web server.

In theory, all three server-side components (Web server, Web Publishing Engine, and FileMaker Server), can be run on the same machine. In practice, this is not a good idea. We recommend that you use at least two machines for your CWP setup: one for the Web server and another for FileMaker Server. The Web Publishing Engine can be installed on either of those two machines. If you want, you can spread the deployment across three machines, and have the Web Publishing Engine sit on its own machine in the middle. We see the biggest gain in moving from a one-machine setup to either of the two-machine configurations.

If you have any firewalls anywhere in your network architecture, be aware of this: If any of the machines in your Custom Web Publishing setup are separated from the others by a firewall, certain ports in that firewall may need to be open. See "Dealing with Firewalls" in the Troubleshooting section at the end of this chapter.

Installing the Web Publishing Engine

We're going to assume that you already have a Web server running (Apache and IIS, again, are the only choices here), and a working installation of FileMaker Server. You'll also need to have access to the FileMaker Server Web publishing components, either by having purchased a full version of FileMaker Server Advanced, or by having purchased the FileMaker Server Advanced Option Pack to add Web publishing capabilities to an existing installation of FileMaker Server.

NOTE

If you're adding Web publishing capabilities to an existing FileMaker Server, you need to update the license key for that server installation. You do this via the Server Administration Tool.

→ For more information on the Server Administration tool, **see** "Configuring and Administering FileMaker Server Using the SAT," **p. 746**.

There are actually two separate items to install: The Web server plugin and WPE administrative console constitute one piece and the WPE itself the other. Unless you're installing the WPE on a machine different from the Web server, you can install all these components at once, on the same machine. If the Web server and WPE are on different machines, you need to install the Web server module and the admin console on the Web server machine, and then install the WPE on whichever other machine you've designated for that purpose. Figure 23.3 shows how these components work together.

Figure 23.3
FileMaker's Custom Web Publishing consists of a number of server-side components. The Web Publishing Engine may or may not be installed on the same machine as your Web server.

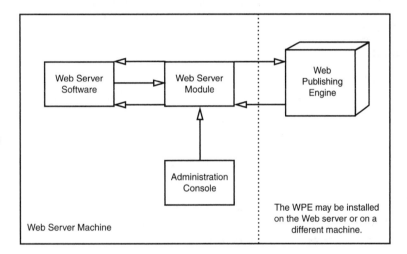

The Web server module is an add-on to your Web server (Apache or IIS) that allows the Web server to communicate with the Web Publishing Engine. The Administration Console is a Web-based application, installed on the same machine as the Web server, that allows you to configure and control a WPE via a Web browser.

NOTE

For best results, shut down your Web server processes (not the server machine itself, but the Web server processes) before installing the Web server module and admin console.

NOTE

The WPE, if you're curious, is based on Tomcat, a popular open-source Web application platform based on Java servlets, and the Web server module (different for each server) enables the Web server to communicate directly with a Tomcat installation.

CONFIGURING THE WEB PUBLISHING ENGINE

The Web Publishing Engine is configured via the Administration Console, which is a Web-based application that gets installed when you install the Web server module on the Web server of your choice. After you've completed that install, and you've also installed a Web Publishing Engine (either on the same machine as the Web server or elsewhere), you can configure the Web Publishing Engine by opening a browser and pointing it to
`http://<server-ip>/fmi/config/`.

SETTING UP AUTHENTICATION

When doing this for the first time, you'll be prompted to configure administrative access to the Console, via a screen like the one shown in Figure 23.4.

Figure 23.4
You'll need to configure the Administration Console with a username and password when you access it for the first time.

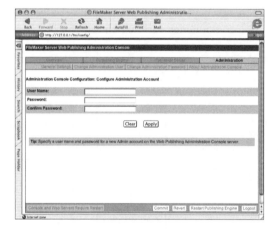

When this is done, you'll be prompted for the IP address of the Web Publishing Engine, as shown in Figure 23.5. (If the Web Publishing Engine is on the same machine as the Web server, just enter the word **localhost**.)

Figure 23.5
You need to specify the address of the machine on which your Web Publishing Engine is located.

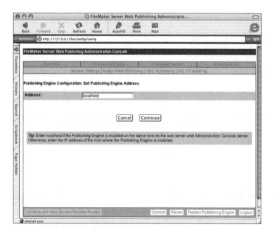

The third step is to configure authentication for the Publishing Engine. This authentication is separate from the administrative access you configured in step one. The screen is shown in Figure 23.6.

Figure 23.6
You need to set a username and password that are specific to one Publishing Engine.

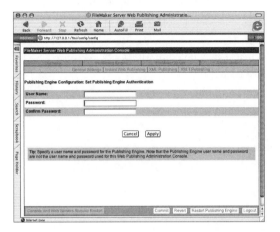

At this point, you should see an Overview screen like the one in Figure 23.7. In this shot we see a setup with the Web server and the Web Publishing Engine on a single machine. The WPE has been fully configured here for all three kinds of access: Instant Web Publishing, XML, and XSLT. (You'll see shortly how to do this.) In this image, the connection to FileMaker Server hasn't yet been configured.

Figure 23.7
The overview screen provides a look at all installed components of the Custom Web Publishing chain.

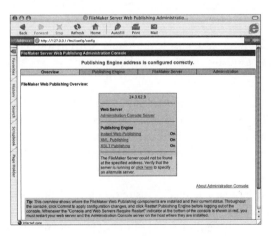

CONFIGURING DIFFERENT TYPES OF ACCESS TO THE WEB PUBLISHING ENGINE

You need to configure the Web Publishing Engine for each different type of Web access you want to support. The Publishing Engine tab of the Administration Console has four sub-tabs, one for General Settings and three more for the three flavors of Web access. Chapter 21 discusses how to configure the Web Publishing Engine for Instant Web Publishing.

→ For more information on configuring the WPE for Instant Web Publishing, **see** "Configuring FileMaker Server 7 Advanced for IWP," **p. 613**.

The configuration screen for XML access is so simple we won't show it here. It consists of a single radio button that turns XML access on or off. If XML access is off it isn't possible to serve XML data from the Web Publishing Engine, regardless of any privileges the attempting user may have.

The same is true for XSLT access. The configuration screen for XSLT-CWP is more complex and is shown in Figure 23.8

Figure 23.8
You might need to consider many options when configuring the Web Publishing Engine for XSLT access.

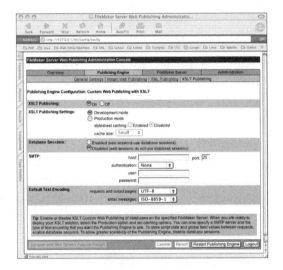

This screen, of course, allows you to enable or disable XSLT publishing. As with XML and IWP publishing, you can globally disable the publication of data via XSLT from the Web Publishing Engine.

Next, you can choose between "development" and "production" modes. In development mode, the Web Publishing Engine returns HTML screens with detailed error messages, including a specific error number and the exact position in the XSL stylesheet that generated the error (if known). In production mode, your users don't see these formidable messages, but instead see a friendlier, more generic message.

Next, you can enable "stylesheet caching." This option is available only in Production mode. It causes the Web Publishing Engine to store stylesheets in memory after they're initially accessed, which speeds up repeated uses of the stylesheet. You can also set the cache's maximum size. We recommend enabling this option whenever you go to Production mode (unless you feel strapped for RAM, in which case you probably need a beefier server for the Web Publishing Engine anyway). We recommend setting the cache to the maximum size necessary for the solutions you'll serve, but no larger. The Small option covers up to 25 stylesheets, Medium covers 25–100 stylesheets, and Large is for more than 100.

TIP

> During development and debugging, you should turn stylesheet caching off. With caching turned on, any changes you make to your stylesheets won't be reflected until the cached copy expires.

Your next choice is whether or not to use database sessions. This is a complex concept that is covered more fully later in this chapter, in the section titled "About Sessions."

Next, you can specify a mail server that will be used for any emails you send from your stylesheets. FileMaker's Custom Web Publishing offers you the capability to have your Web application send emails. If you create such a Web application, this area is where you'd specify the parameters of the SMTP server you're using for outbound mail.

Last, you have the opportunity to set the default text encoding for stylesheets and emails. Text encoding is a large topic that we don't cover fully in this book. The FileMaker defaults are generally adequate for an American or Western European environment. If you're working in an Asian environment you may need to change these settings.

CONFIGURING THE CONNECTION WITH FILEMAKER SERVER

The Web Publishing Engine and FileMaker Server now need to be made aware of each other. There's work to be done on both sides. In the Administration Console, you need to specify the IP address of the FileMaker server. You also need to give your Web Publishing Engine an *identifier* and an optional *passcode*. The Web Publishing Engine uses these two keys to identify itself when it makes requests to FileMaker Server.

FileMaker Server, in turn, needs to be configured to accept requests from a specific Publishing Engine. To do this, you need to open the Server Administration Tool and connect to the relevant FileMaker Server.

→ For more information on the Server Administration tool, **see** "Configuring and Administering FileMaker Server Using the SAT," **p. 746**.

Of course, you need to have FileMaker Server set up to allow some number of Web Publishing Engine sessions. The relevant dialog from the Server Admin Tool is shown in Figure 23.9.

Additionally, after you click the Enable Client Services button, you have two more options. The first allows you to enable ODBC/JDBC connections to the Server, but the second is what we're interested in here. You can configure FileMaker Server to be aware of more than one Publishing Engine. Figure 23.10 shows a copy of Server that's been configured to know about two different Publishing Engines.

→ For more information on ODBC/JDBC connectivity, **see** "Accessing FileMaker Data Using ODBC/JDBC," **p. 578**.

Notice that we don't say "work with" two different Engines. Only one of the Engines can be checked at a time, and this is the only Engine from which that copy of Server will accept connections (based on the identifier and optional passcode).

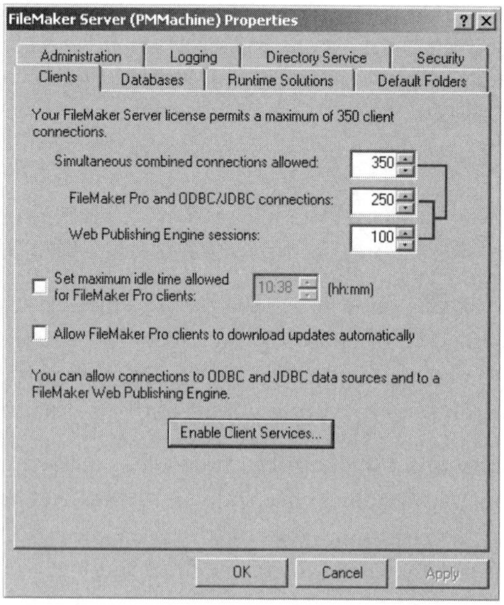

Figure 23.9
FileMaker Server also needs to be configured to accept connections from a specific Web Publishing Engine.

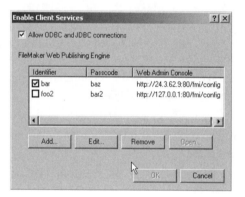

Figure 23.10
FileMaker Server can be aware of several Publishing Engines at once, though it can accept connections from only one at a time.

After you enable the connection to the Server from both sides, you should be able to access the FileMaker Server tab in the Administration Console. Then go to the Published Databases subtab and see a list of all databases on the chosen Server that are enabled for some form of Web publishing, as shown in Figure 23.11.

SAVING YOUR CHANGES

As you move through the Administration Console, remember to press the Commit button where necessary to save your changes. (Somewhat confusingly, not all screens have a Commit button. In some cases your entries are saved when you press Continue.)

Certain changes require you to restart the Publishing Engine. If a screen requires this, you have a Restart Publishing Engine button available at the lower right. Additionally, some changes require that you restart the entire Web server. If this is the case, a red message to this effect appears at the lower left of the window.

Figure 23.11
The Administration Console lets you see at a glance which databases are enabled for Custom Web Publishing.

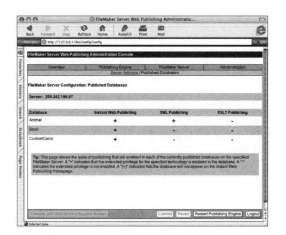

PUBLISHING FILEMAKER DATA AS XML

Custom Web Publishing falls into two broad categories: CWP with XML and CWP with XSLT. The former technique allows you to publish FileMaker data as raw XML over the Web. The latter technique is XML-based as well, but involves applying additional *transformations* to the XML to turn it into other data formats such as HTML. Because XML publishing is the basis for both of these "flavors" of CWP, we begin with a thorough discussion of FileMaker data publishing with XML.

INTRODUCTION TO XML PUBLISHING

To publish FileMaker data as XML via the Web Publishing Engine, you need several things:

- A Web server with the appropriate Web server module and the Administration Console installed.

- A running copy of the Web Publishing Engine, with XML publishing enabled. (See the previous section, "Configuring the Web Publishing Engine.")

- A copy of FileMaker Server Advanced that's configured to work with the Web Publishing Engine.

- One or more FileMaker databases that are enabled for XML access via the appropriate extended privilege, and are being served by the server mentioned in the preceding bullet.

If—and only if—all these pieces are in place, you can draw XML data from a served database by opening a Web browser and entering a URL like the following:

`http://192.168.100.101/fmi/xml/fmresultset.xml?-db=Animal&-lay=web&-findall`

This URL, 192.168.100.101, is the address of the Web server that we've configured to work with the Web Publishing Engine. The path to `fmresultset.xml` indicates that we want the results returned in the `fmresultset` grammar. URL also instructs the WPE to access a database called Animal, via a layout called Web, and then find all records and return them in the selected `fmresultset` grammar.

NOTE

> Note that it's not necessary to include the filename suffix (.fp7) when referencing the database name in the URL.

If you indeed had a database called Animal open under FileMaker Server, and if it had privilege sets with the extended privilege for XML enabled, and it had a layout called Web, then the Web Publishing Engine would return an XML document to your browser. If you're using a browser capable of displaying XML (the major ones at the time of writing were later versions of Mozilla/Netscape and Internet Explorer 5 or later), you'd see something like the code in Listing 23.1.

LISTING 23.1   XML FORMATTED WITH THE fmresultset GRAMMAR

```
<?xml version="1.0" standalone="no"?>
<!DOCTYPE fmresultset PUBLIC "-//FMI//DTD fmresultset//EN"
➥ "/fmi/xml/fmresultset.dtd">
<fmresultset xmlns="http://www.filemaker.com/xml/fmresultset" version="1.0">
    <error code="0">
    </error>
    <product build="12/10/2003" name="FileMaker Web Publishing Engine"
    ➥ version="7.0v1" />
    <datasource database="animal" date-format="M/d/yy" layout="web"
    ➥ table="Animal" time-format="h:mm:ss a" total-count="17" />
    <metadata>
        <field-definition auto-enter="no" global="no" max-repeat="1"
        ➥ name="date_birth" not-empty="no" result="date" type="normal" />
        <field-definition auto-enter="yes" global="no" max-repeat="1"
        ➥name="id_animal" not-empty="yes" result="text" type="normal" />
        <field-definition auto-enter="no" global="no" max-repeat="1"
        ➥ name="id_father" not-empty="no" result="text" type="normal" />
        <field-definition auto-enter="no" global="no" max-repeat="1"
        ➥ name="id_mother" not-empty="no" result="text" type="normal" />
        <field-definition auto-enter="no" global="no" max-repeat="1"
        ➥ name="name" not-empty="no" result="text" type="normal" />
        <field-definition auto-enter="no" global="no" max-repeat="1"
    ➥ name="weight_birth" not-empty="no" result="number" type="normal" />
        <field-definition auto-enter="no" global="no" max-repeat="1"
    ➥ name="weight_current" not-empty="no" result="number" type="normal" />
        <field-definition auto-enter="no" global="no" max-repeat="1"
        ➥ name="HerdID" not-empty="no" result="text" type="normal" />
        <field-definition auto-enter="no" global="no" max-repeat="1"
        ➥name="gender" not-empty="no" result="text" type="normal" />
    </metadata>
    <resultset count="17" fetch-size="17">
        <record mod-id="6" record-id="1">
            <field name="date_birth">
                <data>4/23/1994</data>
            </field>
            <field name="id_animal">
                <data>A1</data>
            </field>
            <field name="id_father">
                <data></data>
```

```
            </field>
            <field name="id_mother">
                <data></data>
            </field>
            <field name="name">
                <data>Great Geronimo</data>
            </field>
            <field name="weight_birth">
                <data>107</data>
            </field>
            <field name="weight_current">
                <data>812</data>
            </field>
            <field name="HerdID">
                <data>H1</data>
            </field>
            <field name="gender">
                <data>Male</data>
            </field>
        </record>
        [ ... multiple additional records ...]
    </resultset>
</fmresultset>
```

In general, when you want to access XML data from an appropriately-configured FileMaker file, you do so by entering a URL in the following format:

<protocol>//*<server-ip>*[:*<port>*]/fmi/xml/*<grammar>*.xml?[*<query-string>*]

Protocol indicates a Web protocol, either HTTP or HTTPS.

Server-IP is the IP address of the Web server that serves as the point of entry to the Web Publishing Engine. Note that if by chance the Web Publishing Engine is installed on a different machine from the Web server, you must specify the IP address of the Web server machine here—providing the address of the Web Publishing Engine does not work.

Port is an optional part of the URL. In general, your Web server will be running on the default HTTP port of 80 or the default HTTPS port of 443. If for any reason you've configured your Web server to run on a different port than the protocol default, you need to specify that port number here. This port has nothing to do with any of the WPE-specific ports (in the 16000 range) or the FileMaker Server port (5003) that you may have encountered in the Web Publishing Engine documentation; it refers strictly to the port on which your Web server accepts incoming requests.

Grammar refers to one of three FileMaker xml grammars: FMPXMLRESULT, FMPXMLLAYOUT, or fmresultset.

NOTE

Note that only the first one of these is available via XML Export: the second two are available only via Custom Web Publishing. The FMPDSORESULT grammar that's available with XML Export is not available with Custom Web Publishing.

Query-string refers to a series of one or more specific pieces of information you pass to the Web Publishing Engine to form the substance of your request. Among the pieces of information you would pass in the query string are the name of the database to access, the name of the layout you want to work with, and the name of a database *action* (such as "find all records", expressed in the example URL by the -findall command).

In general, then, you'll use specially-formatted URLs to access FileMaker data as XML via Custom Web Publishing. These URLs can be manually entered in a Web browser, or they can be linked from a Web page, or they can be used by other processes or applications that want to consume FileMaker data as XML.

UNDERSTANDING QUERY STRINGS

A lot of the action in a Custom Web Publishing URL occurs inside the *query string*—that odd-looking set of commands at the end of the URL. Here again is the example URL from the previous section:

```
http://192.168.100.101/fmi/xml/fmresultset.xml?-db=Animal&-lay=web&-findall
```

The query string is the portion of the URL that comes after the question mark. A query string consists of multiple *name-value pairs*, with each name-value pair taking the form *name=value*. If there are multiple name-value pairs in a URL, additional pairs are separated from the first one by an ampersand character (&).

NOTE

> Query strings are not peculiar to FileMaker or to Custom Web Publishing—they're an HTTP standard for passing information to a server-side program via a URL.

In the example URL, we've passed three name-value pairs. Table 23.1 shows the names and their corresponding values.

TABLE 23.1 NAME-VALUE PAIRS IN A SAMPLE CWP URL

Name	Value	Meaning
-db	Animal	Which FileMaker database to access
-lay	Web	Which layout in the specified database to use
-findall	(no associated value)	What action to perform

In general, any Custom Web Publishing URL needs to specify at least a database name, a layout name, and a database action to perform. (In fact, the database name and layout name can also be omitted in the case of a few specialized database actions). So at a minimum, you will usually provide a -db value, a -lay value, and the name of some database action.

A few more notes on query string syntax: The *order* of the name-value pairs within the query string doesn't matter, as long as all the required pairs are present. The initial dash (-)

in the various names *is* significant, however, and can't be omitted. You'll notice that the database action consists of a name without a value (which is perfectly legitimate in an HTTP URL query string); database actions always consist of a name with no value attached.

 If you have spaces in your field, layout, or database names, this will cause trouble. See "Dealing with Spaces" in the Troubleshooting section at the end of this chapter.

PERFORMING SPECIFIC SEARCHES WITH CWP URLS

The CWP URLs we've looked at so far are simply querying a FileMaker database table, finding all records, and returning the results as raw XML according to the selected XML grammar. But what if you want to query different tables within the chosen database, or select only certain records rather than all records, or apply a sort order to the results? All these things are possible with CWP.

SPECIFYING THE TABLE

One of the reasons it's so important to supply a layout name with your CWP URLs (via the -lay parameter) is that, in FileMaker 7, the active table is determined by the active layout, via that layout's *table context*. You may recall that, in the Layout Setup dialog for each layout, there's a choice labeled Show Records From. This enables you to select a table occurrence that will provide the layout's table context. When you specify a layout in a CWP URL, you are implicitly setting the active table as well. All commands in the query string are considered to be applied to whatever table underlies the chosen layout.

→ For a refresher on the idea of table context, **see** "Understanding Table Context," **p. 161**.

FINDING SPECIFIC RECORDS

The Custom Web Publishing URL can also be used to search for specific records. To do this, use -find as the database action, instead of -findall. You also need to specify one or more search criteria, which are also supplied as name-value pairs.

For example, if you're working with a database of animals, and there's a field called *name* for the animal's name, you can use the following URL to search for any animals named Hector:

```
http://192.168.100.101/fmi/xml/fmresultset.xml?-db=animal&-lay=web
➥&name=Hector&-find
```

> **NOTE**
>
> The database in question has only a single table, also called Animal, and that table is the table context for the Web layout.

This code snippet specifies a database action of -find, and adds one more parameter to the query string. We say name=Hector to cause the Web Publishing Engine to search for only records where the name is Hector. If there are any such records, they'll be returned in the chosen XML grammar. If there are no matching records, we get back a response that looks a bit like Listing 23.2.

LISTING 23.2   SAMPLE ERROR RESPONSE

```
<?xml version="1.0" encoding="UTF-8" standalone="no" ?>
<!DOCTYPE fmresultset (View Source for full doctype...)>
<fmresultset xmlns="http://www.filemaker.com/xml/fmresultset" version="1.0">
    <error code="401" />
    <product build="12/10/2003" name="FileMaker Web Publishing Engine"
    ➥ version="7.0v1" />
    <datasource database="" date-format="" layout="" table="" time-format=""
    ➥ total-count="0" />
    <metadata />
    <resultset count="0" fetch-size="0" />
</fmresultset>
```

You can see that in the case where no records are found, the XML returned by the Web Publishing Engine contains an error code appropriate to the situation. In this case, the code is a standard "no records found" error. (Note that the exact format of the error response varies depending on which XML grammar you specified in the URL.)

SPECIFYING AN EXACT MATCH WHEN SEARCHING

In the previous example, the search appeared to be for all animals named Hector. This is not exactly true. The previous URL will have exactly the same effect as entering Find mode in the regular FileMaker client, typing **Hector** into the name field, and performing the search. FileMaker, when searching text fields, searches on a "starts with" basis, so this search actually finds animals named Hector, Hector II, Hectorax, and so on. To specify that you want an exact match, rather than a "starts with" match, you need a bit more precision. In FileMaker's regular Find Mode, you'd type **=Hector** in the search field, with the equals sign indicating an exact match. In a CWP URL, you'd write:

```
http://192.168.100.101/fmi/xml/fmresultset.xml?-db=animal&-lay=web&name=Hector
➥&name.op=eq&-find
```

Another parameter has been added to the query string here. The new parameter specifies what kind of *operator* we want to apply to one of the search fields. The syntax for this new parameter is

```
<field-name>.op=<operator>
```

Here, *field-name* is the field to which you want to apply the operator, and *operator* is a short character string indicating one of nine different possible operators. Here, the operator we've chosen is eq for an exact match. Other possible operators are cn for "contains", bw for "begins with" (the default), and ew for "ends with." So, if you wanted to find all animals with a name ending in "tor", you could use this URL:

```
http://192.168.100.101/fmi/xml/fmresultset.xml?-db=animal&-lay=web&name=tor
➥&name.op=ew&-find
```

This query string instructs the Web Publishing Engine to treat the search on the name field as an "ends with" search.

NOTE

The operators available to you in Custom Web Publishing are similar to, but not identical to, the list you would find in the FileMaker client if you entered Find Mode and clicked on the symbol list in the status area. FileMaker Find Mode and the Custom Web Publishing find syntax each contain operators that are not available in the other. Table 23.2 lists all the operators available in Custom Web Publishing .

TABLE 23.2   COMPARISON OPERATORS FOR THE -find COMMAND

Operator	Significance	FileMaker Find equivalent
eq	Equals	=value
cn	Contains	*value*
bw	begins with	value*
ew	ends with	*value
gt	greater than	>value
gte	greater than or equal	>=value
lt	less than	<value
lte	less than or equal	<=value
neq	not equal	(omit checkbox)

PERFORMING A NUMERICAL COMPARISON SEARCH

Consider a database that contains some numerical fields. The Animal database used as an example so far contains a field called weight_birth for an animal's birth weight. Suppose you want to find all animals with a birth weight less than 100 pounds. The following URL would do it:

```
http://127.0.0.1/fmi/xml/fmresultset.xml?-db=animal&-lay=web&weight_birth=100
➥&weight_birth.op=lt&-find
```

Here, 100 is specified for the weight_birth search field, but we go on to say that the *operator* for that search field is the "less than" operator, symbolized by the code lt.

SEARCHING ON MULTIPLE CRITERIA

Suppose we want to construct a more narrowly tailored search. You want to find all *male* animals with a birth weight less than 100. (This is the equivalent of filling in two fields in FileMaker's Find Mode, instead of just one.) You'd use a URL like the following:

```
http://127.0.0.1/fmi/xml/fmresultset.xml?-db=animal&-lay=
➥web&weight_birth=100&gender=Male&weight_birth.op=lt&-find
```

Here we've simply added one more search field: gender=Male. This constitutes a further limit on the search you saw in the previous example. This search finds only records for male animals with birth weight less than 100.

CREATING MULTIPLE FIND REQUESTS

The preceding example showed how to use multiple criteria to narrow a search. But what if you want to use multiple criteria to *broaden* a search? We've searched for animals with birth weight less than 100. What if you also want to find, in the same search, any animals who have a current weight less than 500? (You might recognize this as the equivalent of creating additional Find requests in the regular FileMaker Pro software.)

To explain this kind of search, you need to introduce the concept of a *logical operator*. In the search demonstrated previously, for a record to be included in the search, *all* the search criteria in the query string had to be true. That is, an animal would not be included in the search results unless it was both male *and* had a birth weight less than 100. This kind of search is thus often referred to as an "and" search or an "all-true" search.

On the other hand, when you think about also finding animals with current weight less than 500, you have a situation where an animal will be included in the search results if *any* of the search criteria are true. In other words, a record will be found if the animal had a birth weight of less than 100, *or* it has a current weight of less than 500. This type of search is thus often called an "or" or an "any-true" search.

By default, the Web Publishing Engine treats all searches as "and" searches. To perform an "or" search, you'd use a URL like this one:

```
http://127.0.0.1/fmi/xml/fmresultset.xml?-db=animal&-lay=web&weight_birth=100
➥&weight_current=500e&weight_birth.op=lt&weight_current.op=lt
➥&-lop=or&-find
```

Here you supply two search criteria. You also need to supply the field-level operator for each search field. In both cases, you're performing a "less-than" search, so you need to specify an operator of lt for each field. The new element in the query string is the -lop parameter, which stands for "logical operator". -lop can have a value of "and" (the default) or "or" (the one we're using here). The -lop parameter here instructs the Web Publishing Engine to treat the search as an "or" search.

NOTE

> In FileMaker proper, you can construct a search that's a complex mixture of "and" and "or" searches by entering multiple Find requests, each with more than one field filled in. Such searches can't readily be reproduced with Custom Web Publishing: the -lop command can be applied only to all the search fields taken together. There is also no way to invoke the additional FileMaker search options of Constrain or Extend Found Set.

SPECIFYING A SORT ORDER FOR SEARCH RESULTS

When you make a request to the Web Publishing Engine, you can specify how the results should be sorted. You can specify one or more fields to sort on, as you can in the regular FileMaker application, and you can specify whether each sort field should be sorted in ascending or descending order. Consider a URL that will find all records in the Animal table, and ask that the records be sorted by name:

```
http://192.168.101.100/fmi/xml/fmresultset.xml?-db=Animal&-lay=web
➥&-sortfield.1=name&-findall
```

The new query string command here is called `-sortfield`. You'll notice we also added the suffix `.1` to this parameter. This indicates the sort field's *precedence*. The concept of precedence is meaningful only if you have more than one sort field, as you'll see in a moment. Despite this fact, you can't omit the sort precedence, even for a one-item sort, or the records won't be sorted at all.

Suppose you wanted the records to be sorted by gender, and within each gender to be sorted by current weight from highest to lowest. You'd do that like this:

```
http://127.0.0.1/fmi/xml/fmresultset.xml?-db=Animal&-lay=web
➥&-sortfield.1=gender&-sortfield.2=weight_current&-sortorder.2=
➥descend&-findall
```

Here two sort fields are specified. The first sort is by `gender`, the second by `weight_current`. There's also a new parameter, called `-sortorder`. Like `-sortfield`, `-sortorder` also takes a numeric suffix. Here, it's used to indicate which sort field is being referred to. By default, each field will be sorted in ascending order. If you supply a value of `descend` for the second sort field, you ensure that the animals will be sorted, within each gender group, from heaviest to lightest.

APPLICATIONS OF CUSTOM WEB PUBLISHING WITH XML

The current section shows how to use the Web Publishing Engine to query a database and "publish" the results as raw XML in one of several XML grammars. But what use is the capability, exactly?

Well, the most obvious significant use is to allow FileMaker to act as a Web service provider. In Chapter 22, "FileMaker and Web Services," we cover how to use FileMaker to pull data from other Web services on the Internet. But FileMaker can also act as a Web service. If you provide a Web service client with an appropriate URL, remote services and programs can query your FileMaker database via the Web Publishing Engine and extract whatever information you choose to let them see.

Additionally, the URL query syntax discussed in this section is also at the heart of the more sophisticated form of Custom Web Publishing that's made possible by the application of XSLT style sheets, which is the topic of the next section.

23

Using XSLT with Custom Web Publishing

The previous section discusses how to use FileMaker to produce plain XML, distributed over HTTP. This section builds on the previous one and demonstrates how to use XSL transformations (XSLT) to manipulate that raw XML further.

About Server-Side XSLT

The previous section demonstrates how to query a FileMaker database via the Web Publishing Engine, and return the results as some form of raw XML. But, as you'll know if you've worked with XSLT before, or if you've already read Chapter 22 of this book, XML becomes even more interesting when you begin to transform it with XSLT stylesheets.

→ For an overview of XML and XSLT basics, **see** "FileMaker and XML," **p. 641** and "Transforming XML," **p. 646**. (Chapter 22)

If you've already read Chapter 22, you'll have become familiar with the distinction between *client-side* and *server-side* XSL transformations. When using FileMaker's XML Export capability, it's the client copy of FileMaker that performs any XSL transformations you specify, hence the term *client-side transformation*. On the other hand, with Custom Web Publishing, the transformation is performed by the Web Publishing Engine (server-side), and only the transformation result is sent back to the client (in this case a Web browser).

In the world of Custom Web Publishing, all XSLT transformations are server-side transformations. Stylesheets are placed in one or more predetermined locations within the Web Publishing Engine install hierarchy and accessed by the Web Publishing Engine as necessary.

Where to Put Your Stylesheets

When using Custom Web Publishing with XSLT, your stylesheets live on the same machine as the Web Publishing Engine. All the stylesheets you write need to be located at or beneath a certain point in the Web Publishing Engine directory hierarchy. On Mac OS X, the root directory is /Library/FileMaker Server 7/Web Publishing/xslt-template-files. On Windows, the root directory is located by default at c:\Program Files\FileMaker\ FileMaker Server 7\Web Publishing\xslt-template-files, but you have the option to change the install directory on Windows, so be aware of where you installed your Web Publishing Engine and plan accordingly.

Getting Started with XSLT in CWP

To use XSLT style sheets in your Custom Web Publishing project, you need several things. A number of them are also prerequisites for using Custom Web Publishing with plain XML. The only significant additional points are that the Web Publishing Engine must be configured with XSLT publishing enabled (see the section titled "Configuring the Web Publishing Engine" earlier in this chapter), and all FileMaker databases that you want to make accessible must have the fmxslt extended privilege created, and assigned via a privilege set to one or more activated user accounts (see the section titled "Getting Your Databases Ready for Custom Web Publishing" earlier in this chapter).

A SIMPLE STYLESHEET TO DISPLAY SEARCH RESULTS

Suppose that, rather than have data come out of FileMaker Server as raw XML, you'd like to return it in nicely formatted HTML. For convenience, let's continue working with the example of a simple listing of herd animals. A simple database lists the animals, and you'd like them to appear in a browser formatted as shown in Figure 23.12.

Figure 23.12
We'd like to produce a simple HTML listing from a database.

So you need an XSLT stylesheet that will transform FileMaker's XML into formatted HTML.

You'll probably remember that, before you can write a stylesheet to transform FileMaker XML, you need to know in what grammar that XML will be presented. When you're using Custom Web Publishing, you can request the XML from the Web Publishing Engine in whichever one of the available FileMaker grammars you prefer. Here you're going to request the data in the `fmresultset` grammar and write the stylesheet accordingly. (For an example of this CWP-only grammar, see Listing 23.1.) A stylesheet that will do this is shown in Listing 23.3.

LISTING 23.3   CSS-FORMATTED HTML STYLESHEET

```
<?xml version="1.0" encoding="UTF-8"?>
<xsl:stylesheet version="1.0"
➥ xmlns:fmrs="http://www.filemaker.com/xml/fmresultset"
xmlns:xsl="http://www.w3.org/1999/XSL/Transform">
 <xsl:output doctype-public="-//W3C//DTD HTML 3.2 Final//EN"
➥ indent="yes" method="html"/>
 <xsl:template match="/fmrs:fmresultset">
  <html>
   <head>
    <title>Animal Listing</title>
    <STYLE MEDIA="screen" TYPE="text/css">
```

continues

23

LISTING 23.3 CONTINUED

```
      H3 { font-weight:800; font-size:12.5pt;
      ➥ font-family:verdana,helvetica,arial; color:#333333;}
      .name { font-weight:800; font-size:10pt;
      ➥ font-family:verdana,helvetica,arial; color:#333333;
      ➥background-color:silver }
      .label {font-weight:800; font-size:9pt;
      ➥font-family:verdana,helvetica,arial; color:#000099;}
      .data {font-weight:300; font-size:9pt;
      ➥ font-family:verdana,helvetica,arial; color:#000000;}
    </STYLE>
  </head>
  <body>
   <H3>Bison Herd Listing</H3>
   <table border="0">
    <xsl:for-each select="/fmrs:fmresultset/fmrs:resultset/fmrs:record">
     <tr>
      <td class="name" colspan="3">
       <b>
        <xsl:value-of select="fmrs:field[@name='name']/fmrs:data"/>
       </b>
      </td>
     </tr>
     <td>
      <span class="label">Born:</span>
      <span class="data">
       <xsl:value-of select="fmrs:field[@name='date_birth']/fmrs:data"/>
      </span>
     </td>
     <td>
      <span class="label">Birth Weight:</span>
      <span class="data">
       <xsl:value-of select="fmrs:field[@name='weight_birth']/fmrs:data"/>
      </span>
     </td>
     <td>
      <span class="label">Current Weight:</span>
      <span class="data">
       <xsl:value-of select="fmrs:field[@name='weight_current']/fmrs:data"/>
      </span>
     </td>
    </xsl:for-each>
   </table>
  </body>
 </html>
 </xsl:template>
</xsl:stylesheet>
```

The mechanics of the stylesheet are straightforward enough. It declares a namespace called fmrs, to match up with the fmresultset namespace. It does an initial template match on the fmresultset element, where it outputs all the initial HTML elements, including a small CSS stylesheet. After this is done, it uses <xsl:for-each> to loop over all the <fmrs:record> elements, and outputs two formatted HTML table rows for each record: one containing the name, the other containing the other three fields of interest. You'll notice that the fmresultset grammar is easier to work with than the FMPXMLRESULT grammar because you can reference field names directly, instead of having to refer to them by their position within the <METADATA> element.

FORMAT OF THE XSLT URL

The previous section demonstrated a simple server-side stylesheet, but it didn't explain exactly how the stylesheet would be applied to XML coming out of FileMaker Server. Just as with XML Custom Web Publishing, you invoke the stylesheet from a Web browser, via a specially formatted URL. For the previous section's stylesheet, an example URL might be

```
http://192.168.101.100/fmi/xsl/animal/animal-fmresult.xsl?-lay=web
➡&-db=Animal&-grammar=fmresultset&-findall
```

The general format of an XSLT URL is somewhat similar to that for XML. It looks like this:

```
<protocol>//<server-ip>[:<port>]/fmi/xsl/[<path>/]<stylesheet.xsl>
➡[?<query string>]
```

Many of these elements have the same significance as in the plain XML URL. Rather than reference the /fmi/xml path on the server, though, we reference /fmi/xsl. We follow this immediately with the name of the stylesheet, but note that this assumes the stylesheet is immediately inside the root XSL directory in your Web Publishing Engine installation directory. You have the option, though, of creating additional subdirectories inside that root directory, and if you do this, you need to reference those intermediate folders in the path as well. In the URL shown previously, we've created a subdirectory inside the XSLT root directory, called "animal", and inside that directory is the stylesheet, called animal-fmresult.xsl. So you need to include the intermediate /animal folder in the path in the URL.

NOTE

> If you're used to working with the Web Companion in FileMaker 6 or earlier, you're probably used to seeing the names of your program files passed as a -format parameter inside the query string. The -format parameter is now obsolete. Whereas before you would access the CGI program called FMPRo in the URL, and add the file name in the query string, you now access the stylesheet itself directly.

After the name of the stylesheet, a query string is supplied that's very similar to the XML query string (because you can request the identical actions and search options). One difference, though, is that you need to pass a parameter called -grammar, and set it to be equal to the name of the grammar you intend to use. The earlier stylesheet was written with the fmresultset grammar in mind, so this needs to be specified in the URL. It's an error to omit the -grammar parameter. And of course, if you specify a grammar different from the one the stylesheet expects, you'll get unexpected results.

NOTE

It's actually possible to omit the entire query string when using XSLT with Custom Web Publishing! The reason is that XSLT-CWPT has a special command for embedding the query parameters inside the stylesheet itself. You'll see more on this in the following section.

EMBEDDING QUERY PARAMETERS IN A STYLESHEET

One of the difficulties with allowing your FileMaker data to be accessed via a URL is that a canny user can easily experiment with the URL elements to try to create effects other than those you intended—for example, by displaying forbidden records, or even sending a command to delete a record.

Custom Web Publishing has a method for embedding query parameters in the body of a stylesheet. To do this, you use a special XML construct called a *processing instruction*. A processing instruction is a command to a specific XML processor. If you pass a processing instruction that your processor doesn't understand, it is ignored.

To embed query parameters in a stylesheet, you could add a line like the following to a stylesheet:

```
<?xslt-cwp-query params="-grammar=fmresultset&-db=Animal&-lay=web&-findall"?>
```

What this processing instruction means is that any values for `-grammar`, `-db`, `-lay`, or the database action that are passed via the URL will be overridden by the values supplied in this processing instruction. So no one can ever point the page to a different database, or demand a different database action (such as record deletion!).

CAUTION

You should be aware that this query string in the processing instruction does not simply *replace* the query string that might be present in a URL. It *overrides* it, one parameter at a time. What this means is that if the URL contains a parameter (such as a search field or sort order) that isn't mentioned in the processing instruction, that parameter will still be in force. If you want to block any possibility that a user can supply a "rogue query parameter," you need to specify that parameter explicitly in your static processing instruction.

It's a good idea to use this technique wherever you can to increase the security of your databases and your Web application. Also, embedding at least the expected grammar in the stylesheet prevents you from ever having a mismatch between the grammar you choose in a URL and the one for which the stylesheet is written.

BUILDING WEB APPLICATIONS WITH XSLT-CWP

All of the examples shown so far consist of one query at a time. And so far the examples have all been oriented toward displaying search results. In this section, we'll demonstrate some techniques for building multi-screen sites that allow you to navigate smoothly between different views of your data, and allow you to create, edit, and delete records as well.

BUILDING A "VIEW DETAIL" LINK

Suppose you envision something more interesting—for example, the capability to click a View link in the list view and come to a new screen with more detailed information on the record.

To do this, the View link needs to consist of another Custom Web Publishing URL, one that links to a stylesheet that searches for one specific record, and displays information about it. That URL will look like this:

```
<a href="animal-detail.xsl?-recid=2&-find">View</a>
```

(This assumes, by the way, that the animal_detail.xsl file is in the same directory as the list view file, so as to be accessible via a relative URL.) What's new in this URL is the -recid parameter. FileMaker stores a unique identifier of its own for each database record. This identifier is internal to FileMaker and is in addition to any primary key fields you may define. In Custom Web Publishing, the fmresultset grammar (among others), contains the record ID for each returned record (it's in the record-id attribute of the <record> element)—so you have access to the record ID in your stylesheets. Additionally, if your XSL URL contains the -recid parameter, and a database action of -find, the Web Publishing Engine attempts to find that specific record, which is exactly the behavior you want.

Figure 23.13 shows how you might like the new Web page to look.

Figure 23.13
You might like to add a simple View link to the HTML list.

The strategy, then, is to retool the earlier record list stylesheet so that it contains links to the detail stylesheet. Each link needs to reference a specific record ID. Second, a stylesheet needs to be written for the detail view.

The first thing to consider is the modified stylesheet that includes a View link. It's presented as Listing 23.4.

LISTING 23.4 STYLESHEET FOR A LIST WITH A VIEW LINK

```
<?xml version="1.0" encoding="UTF-8"?>
<xsl:stylesheet version="1.0"
    xmlns:fmrs="http://www.filemaker.com/xml/fmresultset"
    xmlns:xsl="http://www.w3.org/1999/XSL/Transform">
    <?xslt-cwp-query params="-grammar=fmresultset&-db=Animal&-lay=web
➡&-findall"?>
    <xsl:output doctype-public="-//W3C//DTD HTML 3.2 Final//EN"
➡ indent="yes" method="html"/>
    <xsl:template match="/fmrs:fmresultset">
        <html>
            <head>
                <title>Animal Listing</title>
                <STYLE MEDIA="screen" TYPE="text/css">
    H3 { font-weight:800; font-size:12.5pt;
            ➡font-family:verdana,helvetica,arial; color:#333333;}
    .name { font-weight:800; font-size:10pt;
            ➡font-family:verdana,helvetica,arial; color:#333333;
            ➡background-color:silver }
    .label {font-weight:800; font-size:9pt;
            ➡font-family:verdana,helvetica,arial; color:#000099;}
    .data {font-weight:300; font-size:9pt;
            ➡font-family:verdana,helvetica,arial; color:#000000;}
    .edit-cell { border-color:silver; background-color:silver;
            ➡text-align:right; font-weight:300; font-size:8pt;
            ➡font-family:verdana,helvetica,arial; color:#000099;}
    </STYLE>
</head>
<body>
 <H3>Bison Herd Listing</H3>
 <table border="0">
  <xsl:for-each select="/fmrs:fmresultset/fmrs:resultset/fmrs:record">
   <tr>
    <td class="name" colspan="2">
     <b>
      <xsl:value-of select="fmrs:field[@name='name']/fmrs:data"/>
     </b>
    </td>
    <td class="edit-cell">
     <a>
      <xsl:attribute name="href">animal-detail.xsl?-recid=
          ➡<xsl:value-of select="@record-id"/>
      </xsl:attribute>View</a>
    </td>
   </tr>
   <td>
    <span class="label">Born:</span>
    <span class="data">
```

```
        <xsl:value-of select="fmrs:field[@name='date_birth']/fmrs:data"/>
       </span>
      </td>
      <td>
       <span class="label">Birth Weight:</span>
       <span class="data">
        <xsl:value-of select="fmrs:field[@name='weight_birth']/fmrs:data"/>
       </span>
      </td>
      <td>
       <span class="label">Current Weight:</span>
       <span class="data">
        <xsl:value-of select="fmrs:field[@name='weight_current']/fmrs:data"/>
       </span>
      </td>
     </xsl:for-each>
    </table>
   </body>
  </html>
 </xsl:template>
</xsl:stylesheet>
```

The code is similar to Listing 23.3. The main difference is in the added link, which is placed in its own table cell (we added some additional CSS styling for this cell as well). The text View is wrapped in an <a>...</a> tag pair. To output the href attribute, we use the <xsl:attribute> tag. For the href, we provide the name of the stylesheet we'll be using to view the record detail, which we've named animal-detail.xsl. We've also added a query string that picks the record-id attribute out of the current <record> element and adds a database action of -find.

Now consider what animal_detail.xsl might look like. It's a straightforward stylesheet, and appears as Listing 23.5.

LISTING 23.5   STYLESHEET TO PRODUCE A DETAIL VIEW

```
<?xml version="1.0" encoding="UTF-8"?>
<xsl:stylesheet version="1.0"
    ➥ xmlns:fmrs="http://www.filemaker.com/xml/fmresultset"
    ➥ xmlns:xsl="http://www.w3.org/1999/XSL/Transform">
 <?xslt-cwp-query params="-grammar=fmresultset&-db=Animal&-lay=web&-find"?>
 <xsl:output doctype-public="-//W3C//DTD HTML 3.2 Final//EN"
    ➥ indent="yes" method="html"/>
 <xsl:template match="/fmrs:fmresultset">
  <html>
   <head>
    <title>Animal Detail</title>
    <STYLE MEDIA="screen" TYPE="text/css">
    H3 { font-weight:800; font-size:12.5pt;
        ➥font-family:verdana,helvetica,arial; color:#333333;}
    TH { text-align:left;}
    .name { font-weight:800;  font-size:10pt;
        ➥font-family:verdana,helvetica,arial; color:#333333;
        ➥background-color:silver }
```

continues

23

LISTING 23.5 CONTINUED

```
    .label {font-weight:800; font-size:9pt;
        ➥font-family:verdana,helvetica,arial; color:#000099;}
    .data {font-weight:300; font-size:9pt;
        ➥font-family:verdana,helvetica,arial; color:#000000;}
  </STYLE>
</head>
<body>
 <H3>Bison Record Detail</H3>
 <table border="0">
  <xsl:for-each select="/fmrs:fmresultset/fmrs:resultset/fmrs:record">
   <tr>
    <td class="name" colspan="2">
     <b>
      <xsl:value-of select="fmrs:field[@name='name']/fmrs:data"/>
     </b>
    </td>
   </tr>
   <tr>
   <th>
    <span class="label">Born:</span></th>
    <td> <span class="data">
     <xsl:value-of select="fmrs:field[@name='date_birth']/fmrs:data"/>
    </span>
   </td></tr>
   <tr>
   <th>
    <span class="label">Gender:</span></th>
    <td> <span class="data">
     <xsl:value-of select="fmrs:field[@name='gender']/fmrs:data"/>
    </span>
   </td></tr>
   <tr>
   <th>
    <span class="label">Birth Weight:</span></th>
      <td> <span class="data">
     <xsl:value-of select="fmrs:field[@name='weight_birth']/fmrs:data"/>
    </span>
   </td></tr>
   <tr><th>
    <span class="label">Current Weight:</span></th>
      <td> <span class="data">
     <xsl:value-of select="fmrs:field[@name='weight_current']/fmrs:data"/>
    </span>
   </td></tr>
  </xsl:for-each>
 </table>
 </body>
 </html>
 </xsl:template>
</xsl:stylesheet>
```

It was relatively easy to take the list view stylesheet and move a few things around to get the stylesheet shown in Listing 23.5. In addition to changing the styling and formatting of the data somewhat, and adding the Gender field, the only other significant change is in the setup of the static query parameters, where we've changed the database action from `-findall` to `-find`. Remember that the stylesheet still uses any additional parameters coming in unless the static parameters override them. Because we don't override the inbound `-recid`, the stylesheet accepts it and uses it as the basis for the database search.

USING TOKENS TO SHARE DATA BETWEEN STYLESHEETS

Suppose you wanted to build a list-and-detail page arrangement like the one in the previous section, but you wanted to add the capability to page through records in "detail" mode. You'd like to have a Next and a Previous link on the detail screen, so that you can flip between records without having to go back through the list view. The Web page might appear as in Figure 23.14.

Figure 23.14
A detail view of an animal record with links added to allow paging between records.

Well, the links to do this will presumably look just like the links used to get from the list view to an individual detail view. Those links, again, look like this:

```
<a href="animal-detail.xsl?-recid=2&-find">View</a>
```

The Next and Previous links will look just like this, but will reference the record IDs of the next and previous records. You might think at first glance that you need to pass these record IDs from the list stylesheet over to the detail stylesheet, but this doesn't quite work. After you begin paging through the records in detail view, you'll quickly "use up" the record IDs that were passed in, and you won't know where to go next.

To do this correctly (well, *more* correctly), you need to change the way the detail page works. Previously we accessed the detail page with a `-recid` parameter and a `-find` action, instructing the Web Publishing Engine to search for one specific record ID, and display just that record. What you want to do now is ask instead for a `-findall` action, but only *display* the one chosen record. Because you'll have access to all the records in the set, you'll still be able to pull out the next and previous record IDs to use in the Next Record and Previous Record links.

To do things this way, you don't want to pass in the record ID as a `-recid` parameter anymore. The action specified for the detail page is going to be a `-findall`, so passing an explicit `-recid` could be confusing (to a programmer if not to the software!). You need another means to pass along the record ID.

To do this, you can use a CWP tool called a *token*. A token is a named piece of information (much like a variable) that you can pass in a CWP URL and that the target stylesheet can then extract. A URL that included a token for the specific record ID to show might look like this:

```
<a>href="animal-detail-links.xsl?-token.rec-to-show=3
```

Tokens in the URL are denoted by the `-token` parameter, with a suffix that gives the token its own unique name. You need to provide a `-token` parameter and a unique name for each token you want to pass.

NOTE

> There's no limit to the number of tokens you can pass, or to the size of the data you can pass with them, except for that imposed by the HTTP standard. If you're passing tokens via the URL itself (an HTTP GET request), you're probably limited to at most a few hundred characters in the URL. If you're passing the tokens via a form, there should be no limit to the number of tokens nor the amount of data passed.

To do this in the list/detail arrangement, you need to modify the View links in the list page to include a token for the current record ID. Then you need to modify the detail page to cause it to find all records, limit the display to the record ID corresponding to the passed token, and generate Next and Previous links based on the record IDs of the records before and after the record displayed.

Listing 23.6 contains a code fragment showing how you can rewrite the View link from Listing 23.5 to pass the current record ID as tokens.

LISTING 23.6   A RECORD DETAIL LINK CONTAINING A RECORD ID TOKEN

```
<a>
  <xsl:attribute name="href">animal-detail-links.xsl?-token.rec-to-show=
  ➥<xsl:value-of select="@record-id"/>
  </xsl:attribute>View
</a>
```

Now that you have a link that passes along the current record ID as a token, you need to add some code to the detail view that will extract these tokens, as well as some code to generate Next and Previous links based on the current record ID. This is actually a bit tricky. It turns out that the Web Publishing Engine provides a way for you to access *any* request parameter from within a stylesheet. You could use this technique to access a token value, or the specific values of search criteria, or the name of the requested database—anything that was sent in the query string that was part of the calling URL.

The Web Publishing Engine passes all this information to every stylesheet via an *XSL parameter*. XSL parameters look a lot like function parameters: They're values that are passed in to your stylesheet "from the outside" and are available to you under specific names.

→ For details on functions and function parameters, **see** "Exploring the Calculation Dialog Box," **p. 216**.

Suppose you access the detail stylesheet with this URL:

```
http://192.168.101.100/fmi/xsl/animal/animal-detail.xsl?-token.rec-to-show=3
```

If you then issue the following command within the stylesheet:

```
<xsl:param name="request-query" />
```

this creates an XSL variable, called $request-query, which contains the following XML document fragment:

```
<query action="animal-detail.xsl" xmlns="http://www.filemaker.com/xml/query">
   <parameter name="-token.rec-to-show">3</parameter>
</query>
```

Note that the <query> element defines a new namespace! To access this document fragment, you need to add a matching namespace declaration at the top of your stylesheet. Assume you add the following namespace declaration:

```
xmlns:fmq="http://www.filemaker.com/xml/query"
```

You can then access your token via an expression of the following type:

```
$request-query/fmq:query/fmq:parameter[@name = '-token.rec-to-show']
```

NOTE

As we get into more advanced Custom Web Publishing, we'll be getting into more advanced XSLT as well. We'll touch on a number of the major significant XSLT topics as we go, but this book is no substitute for a solid grounding in XSLT, and you'll need that grounding to get the most out of Custom Web Publishing. XSL variables and XSL parameters are somewhat more advanced XSL concepts. We recommend you study them thoroughly in the XML reference guide of your choice. See Appendix A, "Additional Resources," for a list of recommended readings.

To see how to use these tokens in the detail page, it's best just to see the whole page and then look at it piece by piece. It's shown as Listing 23.7.

LISTING 23.7   STYLESHEET SHOWING A SINGLE RECORD WITH "NEXT" AND "PREVIOUS" LINKS

```
<?xml version="1.0" encoding="UTF-8"?>
<xsl:stylesheet version="1.0" xmlns:fmq="http://www.filemaker.com/xml/query"
 xmlns:fmrs="http://www.filemaker.com/xml/fmresultset"
 xmlns:xsl="http://www.w3.org/1999/XSL/Transform">
 <?xslt-cwp-query
 params="-grammar=fmresultset&-db=Animal&-lay=web&-findall"?>
 <xsl:output doctype-public="-//W3C//DTD HTML 3.2 Final//EN" indent="yes"
   method="html"/>
```

continues

Listing 23.7   Continued

```
<xsl:param name="request-query"/>
<xsl:variable name="rec-to-show">
 <xsl:value-of select="$request-query/fmq:query/fmq:parameter
 [@name = '-token.rec-to-show']"/>
</xsl:variable>
<xsl:variable name="document-path">
➥http://127.0.0.1/fmi/xsl/animal/animal-detail-links.xsl</xsl:variable>
<xsl:template match="/fmrs:fmresultset">
 <html>
  <head>
   <title>Animal Detail</title>
   <STYLE MEDIA="screen" TYPE="text/css">
   H3 { font-weight:800; font-size:12.5pt;
    font-family:verdana,helvetica,arial; color:#333333;}
    TH { text-align:left;}
    .name { font-weight:800; font-size:10pt;
    font-family:verdana,helvetica,arial;
    color:#333333; background-color:silver }
    .label {font-weight:800; font-size:9pt;
    font-family:verdana,helvetica,arial; color:#000099;}
    .data {font-weight:300;
    font-size:9pt; font-family:verdana,helvetica,arial;
    color:#000000;}
    record-link { text-align:center; font-weight:300;
    font-size:8pt; font-family:verdana,helvetica,arial;
    color:#000099;}
   </STYLE>
  </head>
  <body>
   <H3>Bison Record Detail</H3>
   <table border="0">
    <xsl:for-each select="/fmrs:fmresultset/fmrs:resultset/fmrs:record
    ➥[@record-id=$rec-to-show]">
     <xsl:variable name="rec-previous">
      <xsl:value-of select="preceding-sibling::fmrs:record/@record-id"/>
     </xsl:variable>
     <xsl:variable name="rec-next">
     <xsl:value-of select="following-sibling::fmrs:record/@record-id"/>
     </xsl:variable>
     <tr>
      <td class="name" colspan="2">
       <b>
        <xsl:value-of select="fmrs:field[@name='name']/fmrs:data"/>
       </b>
      </td>
     </tr>
     <tr>
      <th>
       <span class="label">Born:</span>
      </th>
      <td>
       <span class="data">
        <xsl:value-of select="fmrs:field[@name='date_birth']/fmrs:data"/>
       </span>
      </td>
```

```
       </tr>
       <tr>
        <th>
         <span class="label">Gender:</span>
        </th>
        <td>
         <span class="data">
          <xsl:value-of select="fmrs:field[@name='gender']/fmrs:data"/>
         </span>
        </td>
       </tr>
       <tr>
        <th>
         <span class="label">Birth Weight:</span>
        </th>
        <td>
         <span class="data">
          <xsl:value-of select="fmrs:field[@name='weight_birth']/fmrs:data"/>
         </span>
        </td>
       </tr>
       <tr>
        <th>
         <span class="label">Current Weight:</span>
        </th>
        <td>
         <span class="data">
          <xsl:value-of select="fmrs:field[@name='weight_current']/fmrs:data"/>
         </span>
        </td>
       </tr>
       <tr>
        <td class="record-link">
         <xsl:if test="$rec-previous !=''">
          <a>
           <xsl:attribute name="href"><xsl:value-of select="$document-path"/>
           ➥?-token.rec-to-show=<xsl:value-of select="$rec-previous"/>
           ➥</xsl:attribute>Previous Record </a>
         </xsl:if>
        </td>
        <td class="record-link">
         <xsl:if test="$rec-next !=''">
          <a>
           <xsl:attribute name="href">
           <xsl:value-of select="$document-path"/>
           ➥?-token.rec-to-show=<xsl:value-of select="$rec-next"/>
           ➥</xsl:attribute>Next Record </a>
         </xsl:if>
        </td>
       </tr>
      </xsl:for-each>
     </table>
    </body>
   </html>
  </xsl:template>
 </xsl:stylesheet>
```

This stylesheet shows off quite a number of new XSLT-CWP techniques. We go through them one by one.

In the first place, we've added a new namespace declaration:

```
xmlns:fmq="http://www.filemaker.com/xml/query"
```

As we said before, this is mandatory if you're going to be able to access individual request parameters, as you'll see shortly.

Next, we've changed the statically-encoded database action from -find to -findall. This is in keeping with our new strategy, which is to fetch all the records and then sift through them to find a particular one.

CAUTION

In general, fetching all records here would not be a good idea. You'd want to use some combination of the -max and -skip parameters to fetch the records in groups. See Table 23.3 for some notes on -max and -skip.

Next, we declare one stylesheet *parameter* and two XSL *variables*, as shown in Listing 23.8.

LISTING 23.8   EXTRACTING A TOKEN FROM A REQUEST

```
<xsl:param name="request-query"/>
 <xsl:variable name="rec-to-show">
  <xsl:value-of select="$request-query/fmq:query/fmq:parameter
➥[@name = '-token.rec-to-show']"/>
 </xsl:variable>
 <xsl:variable name="document-path">
➥http://127.0.0.1/fmi/xsl/animal/animal-detail-links.xsl</xsl:variable>
```

The <xsl:param> statement provides access to the data passed to the stylesheet under the name request-query. The following <xsl:variable> statement reaches into the XML that's contained in the request-query variable, and digs out the parameter called -token.rec-to-show, which is the token passed from the list view. This value is now available under the name rec-to-show. Finally, we set up another variable, called document-path, which contains the path to the detail stylesheet. We need to use it in several places later, and it's always a better idea to pull out such "magic values" and keep them in one place, instead of having to update them in several places if something changes.

The next change is in the <xsl:for-each> selector used to pick out the record of interest. In the previous version, we simply looped over all instances of the <record> element, knowing there would only be one. Here, because the action is -findall, all the records are available, and we need to make sure to select only the one we're interested in. We do it like this:

```
<xsl:for-each select="/fmrs:fmresultset/fmrs:resultset/fmrs:record
➥[@record-id=$rec-to-show]">
```

The expression in square brackets is known in XSL as a *predicate*. It's a logical test that has the effect of limiting the previous expression to just those elements that match the predicate expression. So, rather than selecting all <record> elements, it selects only those whose `record-id` attribute is equal to the `rec-to-show` variable (which we already set equal to the token passed from the list view).

At the same spot, we take the opportunity to look at the records before and after the one we're displaying, and store their respective record IDs in different XSL variables, as shown in Listing 23.9.

LISTING 23.9   USING THE "SIBLING" AXES

```
<xsl:variable name="rec-previous">
     <xsl:value-of select="preceding-sibling::fmrs:record/@record-id"/>
     </xsl:variable>
     <xsl:variable name="rec-next">
     <xsl:value-of select="following-sibling::fmrs:record/@record-id"/>
     </xsl:variable>
```

To make this technique work, we use some special XSL *axes* called preceding-sibling and following-sibling. These expressions enable us to step back or forward one record within the `<resultset>` element, and then reach in and grab the `record-id` attribute. If we're on the first or last `<record>` element, these expressions won't find anything, and we'll end up with a blank value, which is fine.

All that's left is to write some code that creates the Next and Previous links, based on whether the next and previous record IDs are empty or not (see Listing 23.10). If not (meaning we're on the first or last record), no link is generated.

LISTING 23.10   XSL CODE FOR NEXT AND PREVIOUS LINKS

```
<tr>
     <td class="record-link">
      <xsl:if test="$rec-previous !=''">
       <a>
        <xsl:attribute name="href"><xsl:value-of select="$document-path"/>
        ➥?-token.rec-to-show=<xsl:value-of select="$rec-previous"/>
        ➥</xsl:attribute>Previous Record </a>
      </xsl:if>
     </td>
     <td class="record-link">
      <xsl:if test="$rec-next !=''">
       <a>
        <xsl:attribute name="href">
        <xsl:value-of select="$document-path"/>
        ➥?-token.rec-to-show=<xsl:value-of select="$rec-next"/>
        ➥</xsl:attribute>Next Record </a>
      </xsl:if>
     </td>
    </tr>
```

To generate each link, we use `<xsl:if>` to test whether the relevant record ID is empty or not. If it's empty, we output nothing. Otherwise we output an HTML link with a URL based on our `document-path` variable, which also passes the correct record ID in the `-token.rec-to-show` parameter.

This example introduced a fair number of additional XSL constructs, such as stylesheet parameters, XSL variables, and some of the more advanced expression axes. It also introduced a number of concepts peculiar to XSLT-CWP, such as token passing and the capability to extract request parameters within a stylesheet. We recognize that these are advanced concepts, so we suggest you start by understanding the supplied demo files and begin modifying them to experiment with these techniques.

USING A STYLESHEET TO DELETE A RECORD

So far, all our actions have involved searching for records. But it's also possible to send the Web Publishing Engine a URL with a query string that contains a command to create, edit, or delete a record as well.

Suppose you have a list view in HTML, like those you've already looked at, and you want to add a link to each row that enables to delete the record. Let's also say you want to see some kind of confirmation screen before you actually perform the delete, and you further want some way to know the deletion has been performed. This can be done with three separate Web pages: the list view, a page that shows a yes/no confirmation message, and a page that confirms that the deletion has actually occurred. The flow of the pages might look like Figures 23.15, 23.16, and 23.17.

Figure 23.15
A new list view of animals with a Delete link.

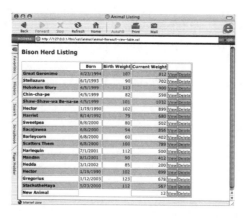

Figure 23.16
A small screen to prompt the user to confirm the deletion.

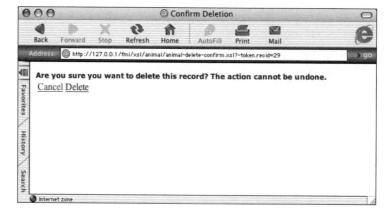

Figure 23.17
A final screen to confirm the deletion and enable the user to return to the list.

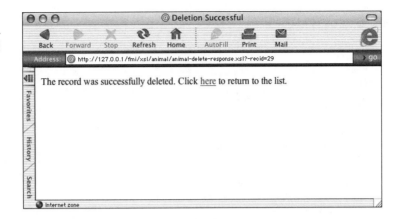

To accomplish this, you need a link in the list view that passes the user over to `delete-confirm.xsl`, and passes the record ID as a token. The `delete-confirm.xsl` page does very little: It just interrogates the user as to whether to proceed with the deletion. If the user decides not to delete, she's returned to the main list view. If she decides to go ahead with it, she's brought to `delete-response.xsl`, which is the page that actually performs the deletion and informs the user of the results.

Take a look at the code for the three pages. First is the code for the list view. We've modified the page so that it presents the records in an ordinary table grid, with View and Delete links at the end of each line. We've also added a little code to color alternate rows. The code is shown in Listing 23.11.

LISTING 23.11   STYLESHEET FOR A TABLE WITH VIEW AND DELETE LINKS

```
<?xml version="1.0" encoding="UTF-8"?>
<xsl:stylesheet version="1.0"
xmlns:fmrs="http://www.filemaker.com/xml/fmresultset"
xmlns:xsl="http://www.w3.org/1999/XSL/Transform">
<?xslt-cwp-query params="-grammar=fmresultset&-db=Animal&-lay=web&-findall"?>
 <xsl:output doctype-public="-//W3C//DTD HTML 3.2 Final//EN"
   indent="yes" method="html"/>
 <xsl:template match="/fmrs:fmresultset">
  <html>
   <head>
    <title>Animal Listing</title>
    <STYLE MEDIA="screen" TYPE="text/css">
     H3 { font-weight:800; font-size:12.5pt;
     font-family:verdana,helvetica,arial; color:#333333;}
     .label {font-weight:800;  font-size:9pt;
     font-family:verdana,helvetica,arial; color:#000099;}
     .data {font-weight:300; font-size:9pt;
        font-family:verdana,helvetica,arial;
     color:#000000;}
     .number-data {font-weight:300; font-size:9pt;
       font-family:verdana,helvetica,arial;
     color:#000000; text-align:right;}
      .view-cell { text-align:right; font-weight:300; font-size:8pt;
```

continues

23

LISTING 23.11 CONTINUED

```
     font-family:verdana,helvetica,arial; color:#000099;}
  </STYLE>
 </head>
 <body>
  <H3>Bison Herd Listing</H3>
  <table border="1">
   <tr>
    <th>
     <xsl:text> </xsl:text>
    </th>
    <th class="label">Born</th>
    <th class="label">Birth Weight</th>
    <th class="label">Current Weight</th>
    <th colspan="2">
     <xsl:text> </xsl:text>
    </th>
   </tr>
   <xsl:for-each select="/fmrs:fmresultset/fmrs:resultset/fmrs:record">
    <tr>
    <xsl:if test="position() mod 2 = 1">
     <xsl:attribute name="bgcolor">#cccccc</xsl:attribute></xsl:if>
     <td class="data">
     <b>
      <xsl:value-of select="fmrs:field[@name='name']/fmrs:data"/>
     </b>
     <td class="data">
      <xsl:value-of select="fmrs:field[@name='date_birth']/fmrs:data"/>
     </td>
     <td class="number-data">
      <xsl:value-of select="fmrs:field[@name='weight_birth']/fmrs:data"/>
     </td>
     <td class="number-data">
      <xsl:value-of select="fmrs:field[@name='weight_current']/fmrs:data"/>
     </td>
     </td>
     <td class="view-cell">
     <a>
      <xsl:attribute
        name="href">animal-detail.xsl?-recid=<xsl:value-of select=
        ➥"@record-id"/>
      </xsl:attribute>View</a>
    </td>
     <td class="view-cell">
     <a>
      <xsl:attribute
        name="href">animal-delete-confirm.xsl?-token.recid=<xsl:value-of
        ➥ select="@record-id"/>
      </xsl:attribute>Delete</a>
    </td>
    </tr>
   </xsl:for-each>
  </table>
 </body>
</html>
</xsl:template>
</xsl:stylesheet>
```

There's not a great deal that's new in this stylesheet, other than the reformatting into a table layout, and the addition of the Delete link. You'll notice that this link points to a page called `animal-delete-confirm.xsl`, and passes the record ID of the current record across to that page in a token called `-token.recid`.

With that in mind, now look at the code for the deletion confirmation page, which is presented in Listing 23.12. This page performs no database actions; it merely confirms that the user wishes to perform the specified deletion.

LISTING 23.12   A STYLESHEET FOR A DELETION CONFIRMATION PAGE

```
<?xml version="1.0" encoding="UTF-8"?>
<xsl:stylesheet version="1.0"
 xmlns:fmq="http://www.filemaker.com/xml/query"
  xmlns:fmrs="http://www.filemaker.com/xml/fmresultset"
   xmlns:xsl="http://www.w3.org/1999/XSL/Transform">
   <?xslt-cwp-query params="-grammar=fmresultset&-process"?>
   <xsl:output doctype-public="-//W3C//DTD HTML 3.2 Final//EN
   indent="yes" method="html"/>
   <xsl:param name="request-query"/>
   <xsl:variable name="rec-to-delete">
 <xsl:value-of select="$request-query/fmq:query/fmq:parameter
➥[@name = '-token.recid']"/>
   </xsl:variable>
   <xsl:template match="/fmrs:fmresultset">
 <html>
   <head>
   <title>Confirm Deletion</title>
   <STYLE MEDIA="screen" TYPE="text/css">
     .label {font-weight:800; font-size:9pt;
     font-family:verdana,helvetica,arial; color:#000099;}
   </STYLE>
   </head>
   <body>
   <span class="label">Are you sure you want to delete this record?
       The action cannot be undone.</span>
   <table>
     <tr>
     <td>
       <a href="http://127.0.0.1/fmi/xsl/animal/
       ➥animal-fmresult-view-table.xsl">Cancel</a>
     </td>
     <td>
       <a>
       <xsl:attribute
       name="href">http://127.0.0.1/fmi/xsl/animal/animal-delete-response.xsl?
         ➥-recid=<xsl:value-of select="$rec-to-delete"/>
       </xsl:attribute>Delete</a>
     </td>
     </tr>
   </table>
   </body>
 </html>
   </xsl:template>
</xsl:stylesheet>
```

23

This stylesheet is a little different from those you've worked with thus far, in that it doesn't perform any database action. This is signified by the statically-encoded -process action in the `<?xslt-cwp-query?>` processing instruction. The -process command tells the XSL processor to process the stylesheet without interacting with FileMaker Server at all. This is useful in stylesheets that don't need to touch a database: It keeps the load on the server from being heavier than it needs to be.

This stylesheet contains code to extract the -token.recid from the query parameters. The code is identical to that in Listing 23.8.

The stylesheet presents an HTML page that asks the user whether he wants to perform the deletion, and gives two choices, each one formatted as an HTML hyperlink. The first link, Cancel, takes the user back to the list view and performs no action. The second, Delete, passes the selected record ID along to a page called animal-delete-response.xsl.

Let's now look at the code for the third page, presented as Listing 23.13.

LISTING 23.13 A STYLESHEET FOR A "DELETION RESPONSE" PAGE

```
<?xml version="1.0" encoding="UTF-8"?>
<xsl:stylesheet version="1.0"
xmlns:fmrs="http://www.filemaker.com/xml/fmresultset"
xmlns:xsl="http://www.w3.org/1999/XSL/Transform">
  <?xslt-cwp-query params="-grammar=fmresultset&-db=Animal&-lay=web&-delete"?>
  <xsl:output doctype-public="-//W3C//DTD HTML 3.2 Final//EN"
      indent="yes" method="html"/>
  <xsl:template match="/fmrs:fmresultset">
<xsl:variable name="error-code">
  <xsl:value-of select="fmrs:error/@code"/>
</xsl:variable>
<xsl:variable name="doc-title">
  <xsl:choose>
  <xsl:when test="$error-code !=0">Deletion Error</xsl:when>
  <xsl:otherwise>Deletion Successful</xsl:otherwise>
  </xsl:choose>
</xsl:variable>
<html>
  <head>
  <title>
    <xsl:value-of select="$doc-title"/>
  </title>
  <STYLE MEDIA="screen" TYPE="text/css">
    .label {font-weight:800; font-size:9pt;
    font-family:verdana,helvetica,arial; color:#000099;}
  </STYLE>
  </head>
  <body>
<xsl:choose>
  <xsl:when test="$error-code !=0">
  <span class="label">Sorry, there was an error deleting the records.
      (Error code =
  <xsl:value-of select="$error-code"/>)</span>
  </xsl:when>
  <xsl:otherwise>The record was successfully deleted.</xsl:otherwise>
```

```
    </xsl:choose> Click <a
    href="http://127.0.0.1/fmi/xsl/animal/animal-fmresult-view-table.xsl">here
    </a> to return to the list. </body>
  </html>
    </xsl:template>
</xsl:stylesheet>
```

There are a few new twists in this stylesheet. By the time this page is reached, the user has confirmed that she does indeed want to perform a deletion. The ID of the record to delete has been passed to the page, this time in the standard -recid query parameter. We've statically coded the rest of the query parameters, including the database name, layout, and the database action, which now is called -delete. The -delete action looks for an inbound -recid, and if it finds it, it tries to delete that record.

There's something new in this stylesheet that really should be present in every stylesheet you write, namely error handling. In general, it's a bad idea to assume that a database operation will succeed. Even for a simple search, the search might contain no valid criteria, or you might misspell a database name, or the connection between the Web Publishing Engine and FileMaker Server could be down. Any of these circumstances would cause your stylesheet to generate an error.

CAUTION

> For stylesheets (or indeed any kind of program!) that are going to be deployed in production, careful error checking is mandatory. You should develop some standard techniques for checking errors in your XSLT-CWP stylesheets.

The error test here is pretty simple. We create an XSL variable called error-code and populate it with whatever error code the underlying XML contains. (In the fmresulset grammar, this can be found at /fmrs:fmresultset/fmrs:error/@code, assuming the namespace has been abbreviated as fmrs.) This code will be either 0 (no error) or some non-zero numeric value, indicating an error of some kind.

Based on the error code, we create another variable, called doc-title, because we want to cause the page to appear with different titles, depending on whether the deletion worked or not.

Finally, in the body of the stylesheet, we use an <xsl:choose> construct that checks the error code variable and decides which confirmation message to display. In all cases we present the user with a link back to the list view.

USING STYLESHEETS TO CREATE AND EDIT RECORDS

It's also possible, using techniques similar to those we demonstrated for record deletion, to make stylesheets that can create records (with the -new action) or edit them (with the -edit action). Space prevents us from giving detailed examples (a full treatment of Custom Web Publishing could fill a book of its own!) but we can discuss them generally.

Both record creation and record editing can be thought of as requiring two different pages. The first page consists of a data entry form where the user either enters or updates some data. As in the deletion example in Listing 23.13, the other page is responsible for actually performing the database action and reporting on the result. (The deletion example contained a third intermediate page where the user was prompted for confirmation of this more dangerous database action.)

To form a better idea of how record creation and editing work, we recommend that you use the Site Assistant to generate a full suite of XSLT stylesheets for a simple database, and then inspect those of the generated stylesheets that handle adding and updating records. The Site Assistant generates three stylesheets that handle these actions: `addrecord.xsl`, `editrecord.xsl`, and `browserecord.xsl`. Here's an overview of what these generated pages do:

- `addrecord.xsl`—Displays an HTML form enabling the user to add values for all fields of an animal record. The form's action targets the `browserecord.xsl` page, and sends along the `-db`, `-lay`, and `-grammar` parameters, as well as the `-new` command. Sending the `-new` command ensures that the `browserecord.xsl` stylesheet will take care of creating the new record before trying to display it.

> **TIP**
>
> We recognize that it's odd to think of the "browse" page as being the place the *creation* of the record happens, but this is a common occurrence in Web programming. Often a destination page needs to do *two* things: take an action, and then report on the result. The `addrecord.xsl` page can't actually create the record, because the user's data entries aren't known at the time the page is loaded.

- `editrecord.xsl`—This page displays an HTML form populated with the current values of an animal record. This page is accessible only from the `browserecord.xsl` page, and is accessed with a `-find` command and a specific `-recid`. This page actually performs no editing (just as `addrecord.xsl` didn't actually add the record). All this page does is find the record and display the field contents in an HTML form. When the user presses the Save Record button, this sends all the edited information over (once again) to the `browserecord.xsl` page, along with the `-edit` command and the specific `-recid`.

- `browserecord.xsl`—This is something of a hybrid page. It can be targeted in two different ways. When the page is targeted from the `addrecord.xsl` page, the URL contains a `-new` command, causing `browserecord.xsl` to create a new record based on the field values that also got sent over from `addrecord.xsl`. When the page is targeted from `editrecord.xsl`, the URL contains an `-edit` command, the specific `-recid` of the record to edit, and the field values for the updated record. Regardless of whether it's performing a `-new` or an `-edit` action, `browserecord.xsl` then displays the new or updated record.

What Happens Where in Web Programming

If you're new to Web programming, you may find it confusing that none of these pages seems to do what its name suggests. Again, this is because of the one-step-at-a-time nature of Web interactions. When adding a record, you want to perform three steps: specify the data, add the record, view the result. Of those three, only the first can be performed on the Add page. The record can't be created until the user presses Save Record on the Add page. By that time, the user is headed off to the destination page (`browserecord.xsl`), so in addition to displaying the record, `browserecord.xsl` also needs to be responsible for creating it. If you wanted your stylesheet names to follow a "truth in advertising" concept, you could perhaps name them thusly: `addform.xsl`, `editform.xsl`, and `add-or-edit-and-then-browse.xsl`!

23

We've depicted the relationships among these three pages in Figure 23.18, which should help to clarify how commands and data flow among the three pages.

Figure 23.18
The flow of data and commands among the three Site Assistant pages.

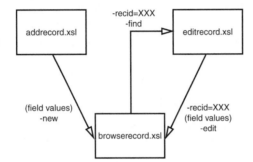

OTHER CUSTOM WEB PUBLISHING COMMANDS AND PARAMETERS

In addition to the commands covered so far, XSLT-CWP has a lengthy list of other commands and parameters that you can pass as part of the query string. This section lists and explains them briefly.

OTHER QUERY COMMANDS

As you know, each Custom Web Publishing URL contains a query string, and that query string can supply at most one database command. Commands covered so far include `-find`, `-findall`, `-delete`, `-new`, and `-edit`. Commands are supplied as a single name with no associated value. Table 23.3 contains the full list.

TABLE 23.3   CUSTOM WEB PUBLISHING DATABASE ACTION COMMANDS

Command Name	Command Effect
-dbnames	Returns an XML document containing the names of all databases available on the given FileMaker Server that are enabled for Custom Web Publishing.
-delete	Deletes a specific record. Requires that a -recid parameter be sent to identify the record to delete.
-dup	Duplicates a specific record. Requires that a -recid parameter be sent to identify the record to duplicate.
-edit	Updates a record, according to whatever name-value pairs are passed with the request (generally taken from an HTML form). Requires a -recid parameter indicating which record to edit.
-find	Performs a search, either based on field values sent as name-value pairs, and/or on a specified -recid. Can be modified by optional parameters for sort order, field operators, and logical operators.
-findall	Finds all records in the database.
-findany	Finds a random record.
-layoutnames	Requires a -db parameter to specify a database to query. Returns an XML document with a list of names of all the layouts in the specified database.
-new	Creates a new record based on whatever name-value pairs accompany the request.
-process	Can be used only with XSLT stylesheets, and causes the stylesheet to be processed without any interaction with FileMaker Server.
-scriptnames	Like -layoutnames, but provides a list of all script names in a database.
-view	Requires that -db and -lay be specified. If the requested grammar is FMPXMLLAYOUT, this command retrieves detailed layout information for the specified layout (this includes things such as the contents of value lists). If the FMPXMLRESULT or fmresultset grammar are specified, this retrieves just the metadata section of the XML document.

OTHER QUERY PARAMETERS

In addition to a single database command, Custom Web Publishing URLs can contain other parameters. Some are mandatory, such as -db, and (generally) -lay and -grammar. Others, such as -lop and -sortfield, are particular to specific commands. Table 23.4 shows a full list.

TABLE 23.4 OTHER CUSTOM WEB PUBLISHING URL PARAMETERS

Parameter Name	Parameter Effect
-db	Name of the database on which to act. Mandatory for all commands except for -dbnames and -process. Do *not* include a filename extension (such as .fp7) when using this parameter.
-encoding	Use this to specify the encoding for an XSLT stylesheet.
-field	Use the -field parameter with the name of a *container* field to request the contents of the container field.
fieldname	Use plain unadorned field names as query parameters when sending data for use with the -new, -find, and -edit commands. See "Performing Specific Searches with CWP URLs," earlier in this chapter.
Fieldname.*op*	Sets the comparison operator for *fieldname* when performing a search. (See the table of operators earlier in this chapter.)
-grammar	For XSLT stylesheets, specifies the grammar of the underlying XML.
-lay	Specifies which layout (and hence which table context) to use for the request. Mandatory with all commands except –process, –dbnames, –layoutnames, and –scriptnames.
-lay.response	Enables you to use one layout for processing the command contained in a URL, and a different layout for generating the XML that comprises the response. For example, you might want to process your request (an Add, say) via a layout with certain hidden fields on it, but process the response via a layout that omitted those fields. Data could thus be added to the hidden fields, but that hidden data would then be omitted from the response.
-lop	Used with the -find command, specifies whether to treat the search as an "and" search or an "or" search.
-max	Used with the -find command, specifies the maximum number of records to return. Sending a parameter of -max=all permits all records to be returned. (This is the default.)
-modid	FileMaker's modification ID is an internal number that increments every time a record is changed. Use the -modid parameter to ensure that the record you're editing has not been edited since the time you last checked the modification ID. This is useful for prohibiting different users' changes from overwriting each other.
-recid	Specifies which record should be affected by a given action. This parameter is mandatory with -edit, -delete, and -dup, and can also be used with -find.

continues

23

23

TABLE 23.4   CONTINUED

Parameter Name	Parameter Effect
`-script`	Use this parameter to run a FileMaker script during the processing of the request. By default the script runs after the query command and any sorting have occurred. For example, to run a script in your FileMaker solution after each new record is created, you can create a URL with the `-new` command that also includes the `-script` parameter for that "post-creation" script.
`-script.prefind`	If your command URL involves any kind of find request, use this parameter to request a script to be run before the specified search takes place.
`-script-presort`	If your command URL involves any kind of find request and a sort, use this parameter to request that a script be run after the specified search takes place, but before sorting.
`-skip`	Used with the various search commands, specifies that records should be returned starting elsewhere than at the first record. If you specify `-skip=10`, the records are returned starting with the eleventh record.
`-sortfield.[1-9]`	Specify any of up to nine different fields to sort by.
`-sortorder.[1-9]`	For a given sort field, specify whether it should sort ascending or descending.
`-styletype`	Used in conjunction with `-stylehref`. Use these two parameters to specify a client-side stylesheet for additional processing. The most common choices would likely be CSS and XSLT. For these choices, you would specify `-styletype=text/css` or `-styletype=text/xsl`.
`-stylehref`	Use this in conjunction with `-styletype` to specify the location of a stylesheet for client-side processing. Note that this option and the previous one are effective only when the user's client (generally a browser) supports some form of client-side stylesheet processing.
`-token.[string]`	Use to pass additional data from one stylesheet to another. See "Using Tokens to Share Data Between Stylesheets," earlier in this chapter, for more detailed information.

ABOUT THE FILEMAKER XSLT EXTENSIONS

All XSL transformations need to be performed by an XSL *processor* of some kind. An XSL processor should conform to some standard flavor of XSL (currently 1.0). But XSL processors are also free to add their own extensions; like proprietary extensions to Web browsers, this practice stands to increase the range of actions you can perform with a given XSL stylesheet, but risks the creation of stylesheets that work well with only one XSL processor. Stylesheets for CWP work well in only a FileMaker environment anyway, so this is not a serious concern.

The Web Publishing Engine's XSLT processor obviously adds some extensions because it's capable of triggering FileMaker database actions. But it also has a host of other extended capabilities. Some of these you've seen already, such as the capability to access all the parameters of the HTTP request that invoked the stylesheet. With similar syntax, you can get access to the user's IP address, username, and password, as well as the address of the server from which the stylesheet is being served.

FileMaker also provides XSL extensions to handle a host of other common Web programming tasks. There's a rich library of string-manipulation functions, as well as a set of functions to send email, a set of functions to create and maintain user sessions, and functions to deal with HTTP headers and cookies. Unfortunately, a full treatment of all these areas is beyond the scope of this book, but the documentation that accompanies FileMaker Server Advanced describes these functions fairly thoroughly.

23

The point to be aware of here is that FileMaker's XSL implementation is actually a full-featured Web programming language as well, and has many of the features of powerful modern Web programming languages such as Perl, PHP, or JSP. After you're familiar with the basics of combining XSL stylesheets with FileMaker database actions, you can delve further into the other rich features of the CWP XSL implementation.

ABOUT SESSIONS

If you've read Chapter 21, "Instant Web Publishing," you've already read some discussion of the concept of *sessions*. To recap briefly: The connection between a Web browser and the Web Publishing Engine is very much *unlike* the connection between a client copy of FileMaker and the FileMaker Server. FileMaker Server can at any time reach out and "push" data to any connected client. It knows at all times what its connected clients are, where they are in the system, and at what network address they can be found. A Web server, by contrast, retains no memory of a client from one connection to the next.

This is not a good thing for database work! I need my Web site to remember the contents of my shopping cart as I shop around the site. This is possible only with *session management*. Session management is generally a middleware feature. Web programming languages such as PHP and JSP offer the programmer different means of managing sessions. In general, under session management, each incoming Web request is associated with a key of some kind. The key may be passed in the URL (if you've ever seen a long ugly string like ?jsession=A9238Ajasdj9mAEd in a Web URL, odds are you're looking at a session key), or it may be passed behind the scenes in an HTTP cookie. (FileMaker's Custom Web Publishing session implementation lets you choose between these two methods.)

Whatever the means, the middleware on the Web server has a way of associating that key to other information about the client. In the shopping cart example, the key might hook up to a database record that stores the actual contents of your cart as you navigate around the site.

FileMaker's Custom Web Publishing, like other middleware solutions, enables you to manage sessions for your users behind the scenes. You would use this capability any time you wanted to store important information about the user that would be carried from screen to screen. An experienced HTML programmer could get away with passing a lot of data from page to page via the URL, or via an HTML form. But there are limits to the amount of data than can be passed by URL, and there are limits to the *type* of data that can be passed by either method—generally just plain text strings.

FileMaker's session implementation is quite elegant because it allows you to pass around XML fragments behind the scenes. This allows for much richer data structures than you could pass with regular HTML.

In addition to passing around XML information by means of sessions, FileMaker's session implementation allows you to keep track of the state of the FileMaker client session as well. This is the distinction described previously in the "Setting Up the Server-side Components for CWP" section: The XSLT configuration screen allows you to enable or disable database sessions. Database sessions are an additional capability on top of regular session management. In addition to "sessionizing" user information of your choice, they enable you to also keep track of FileMaker-specific information such as global fields or the current "script state."

So, for example, if your stylesheets modify a global field, and you have database sessions enabled, the global field retains its new value, for the specific current user, as that user navigates from page to page. Or, if you used a script to change some aspect of the user's state (for example, by using the Relogin script step to change the user's privileges), this state is maintained across sequential requests.

Session management is a large topic and we don't have space to do it justice. The FileMaker documentation helps you get a better grip on the specific functions and commands that Custom Web Publishing uses for session management. As for the issue of whether to configure the Custom Web Publishing to use database sessions, your decision will depend on how you construct your XSLT-CWP solution. If you intend to make heavy use of global variables, or call scripts from your stylesheets that would change the state of a user's privileges, you should configure the Web Publishing Engine to enable database sessions.

TROUBLESHOOTING

GETTING THE RIGHT PRIVILEGES

I can connect to my Web Publishing Engine and FileMaker Server via the Administration Console, but I don't see the databases I expect to see.

Make sure that for every database you want to make available via XML-CWP or XSLT-CWP, you have created an appropriate Extended Privilege (fmxml or fmxslt) and attached it to at least one privilege set.

DEALING WITH FIREWALLS

My Web requests mysteriously time out, as though something were blocking them.

If you can get to the Administration Console, but your Custom Web Publishing URL requests appear to get no response, you may have a firewall in your way. If you suspect a firewall may be involved, consult your network administrator to explore this question. If it turns out that your machines are set up such that your Web server is on one side of a firewall, and your Web Publishing Engine machine or FileMaker Server machine is on the other, you need to open certain ports in the firewall. The rules are these:

- When the Web server and Administration Console are on one machine, and the Web Publishing Engine on another, traffic must be able to flow between the two machines on ports 16016 and 16018.

- When the Web Publishing Engine is on a different machine from FileMaker Server, traffic must be able to flow between the two machines on port 5003.

DEALING WITH SPACES

The Web Publishing Engine doesn't seem to see my entire URL. I enter a long URL and the Web server appears to truncate it and reports that the shorter URL can't be found.

If (despite the cautionary notes in this chapter) you have left any of your databases, fields, or layouts with spaces (or indeed any other non-alphanumeric characters) in their names, your Custom Web Publishing URLs may very well break. If a Web server or browser encounters a space in a URL, it assumes the URL ends there. Other non-alphanumerics have different but equally irritating effects.

If you must work with URLs with spaces in them, you can get by with replacing all spaces with the string %20 whenever you need to write out a URL. Your stylesheet then might generate an HTML page with the following link:

```
<a href="http://192.168.101.100/fmi/xsl/process-this.xsl?
➥-db=Too%20Many%20Spaces&-lay=Spaces%20Here%too&-findall
```

If at all possible, we strongly encourage you to use only alphanumeric characters for database, layout, and field names and to avoid the use of whitespace. Extend this caution to script names if you are planning to call scripts from the Web.

FILEMAKER EXTRA: ABOUT THE CUSTOM WEB PUBLISHING TOOLS

FileMaker Server Advanced comes with a couple of extremely useful tools for kick-starting your work with FileMaker XSL. These are the CDML Converter and the Site Assistant. They're not installed automatically—you need to install them separately if you want to use them.

THE CDML CONVERTER

 The CDML Converter is designed to do what its name implies. It does its best to take a set of FileMaker-based Web pages written in CDML (which was the custom Web publishing option in previous versions of FileMaker Pro) and convert these files to a set of XSLT-CWP stylesheets. As of FileMaker Pro 7, CDML is no longer an available Web publishing option for FileMaker, so if you want to use an existing CDML solution with FileMaker 7, you need to convert it somehow, and the CDML Converter is probably the best place to start.

The CDML Converter converts all your CDML files into XSLT-CWP stylesheets. A reasonable conversion path exists for most CDML constructs, but not all CDML is converted correctly. There are, for example, a few CDML commands that the Web Publishing Engine no longer supports, such as -dbopen and -dbclose. CDML also, like XSLT-CWP, supported custom functions for sending email, but these tags won't be converted correctly and you'll probably need to rewrite your email functionality with the new XSLT-CWP tools.

As the CDML Converter converts your CDML files, it writes out a conversion log describing the conversion process. If there were any errors during conversion, the Converter writes an entry into the log describing the error. It also adds a comment to the affected XSLT file, if possible, pointing you to the exact location and description of the error.

The documentation that accompanies FileMaker Server Advanced has a thorough description of the CDML conversion process, and a detailed list of all potential trouble areas. To ensure the smoothest conversion of your CDML files, we recommend you read the conversion specification carefully before beginning. Take note of any potential trouble areas. The documents offer specific guidance in rewriting any CDML "trouble spots."

Whether or not you do any rewriting, it's a good idea to verify that your CDML files actually work (under FileMaker 6 or whichever version they're built for). After you have a working CDML system that you've vetted for possible conversion problems, make a copy of the system and try out the CDML Converter. From there, you'll want to refer to the conversion log, inline comments, and the detailed conversion documentation to iron out any remaining difficulties.

THE SITE ASSISTANT

The Site Assistant is likely to have much wider application for you than the CDML Converter. Think of the Site Assistant as an XSLT "wizard" of sorts. You point the Site Assistant to a hosted database, tell it what kinds of stylesheets you want to generate (search, edit, summary report, and so on), and where to put the files. It then generates the files, and you're free to use them as is, or modify them further. If so instructed, the Site Assistant generates a "home page" with links to the different stylesheets, and can add navigational elements to each page as well. If you have the Site Assistant generate a full suite of pages for a database, you'll end up with a fairly full-featured little Web site that allows you do almost anything you need to via XSLT-CWP.

Using the Site Assistant is simple. When run, the Site Assistant asks to be pointed to a running Web Publishing Engine. After you give it the Web Publishing Engine's address, it queries the Web Publishing Engine for a list of hosted databases that have XSL publishing enabled. You then choose one, and continue to the next screen. This first step is shown in Figure 23.19.

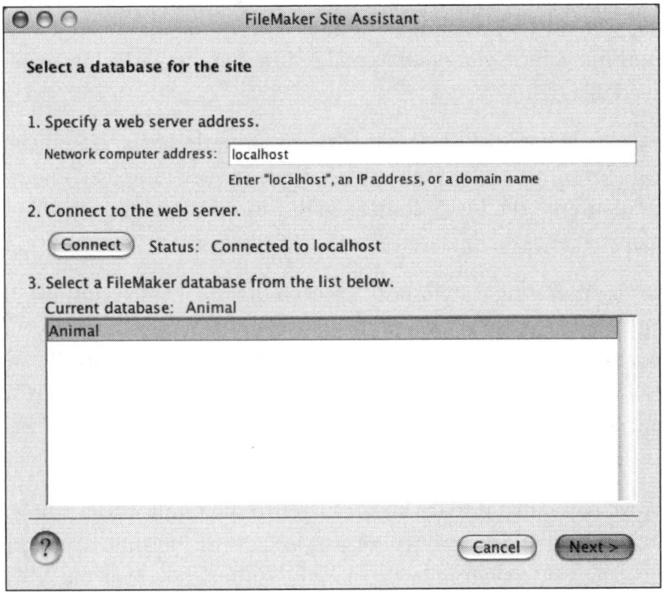

Figure 23.19
Choosing a database for use with the Site Assistant.

After you've picked your file, you're presented with a screen that allows you to choose up to seven different kinds of stylesheets. The screen is shown in Figure 23.20.

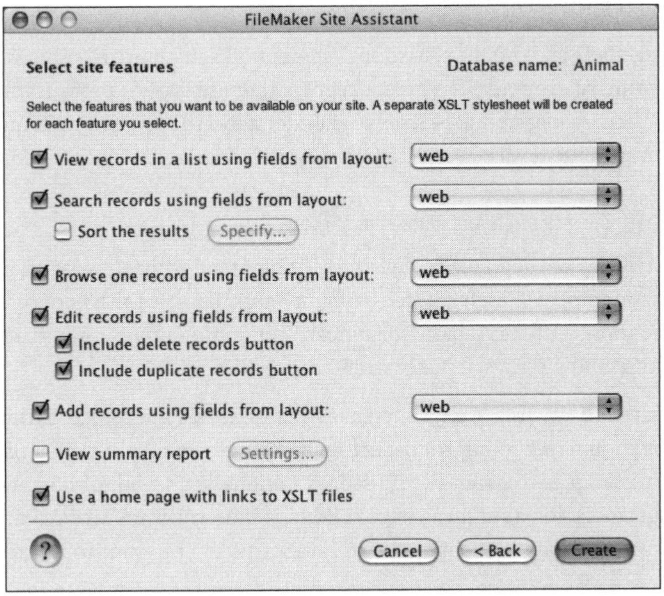

Figure 23.20
Choosing which stylesheets you'd like the Site Assistant to generate.

Most of these choices involve specifying a layout against which the stylesheet should run. Remember that this also amounts to choosing the affected *table*, because each layout's table context determines the target table.

There are a few pitfalls to be aware of when using the Site Assistant. The generation process really works well only when all your actions involve the same base table. If your database contains multiple tables, you need to make sure that all the layouts you reference are based on the same table.

There are also a few mutual dependencies among stylesheets. If you choose Search Records Using Fields From, you should also select View Records In List. The generated search stylesheet tries to use the list stylesheet to display its search results, but unless you ask the Site Assistant to generate that stylesheet, it won't exist.

In addition to generating a stylesheet for each of your chosen options, the Site Assistant generates a "utilities" file called, appropriately enough, `utilities.xsl`. Even if you never use the Site Assistant again, it's worth your while to generate this file and inspect it carefully. It includes a number of powerful techniques for working with XSLT-CWP. If you can thoroughly understand the XSLT techniques contained in this file, you'll have some very useful additions to your XSLT-CWP toolkit.

In general, we recommend that you try to get to the point where you write your own files from scratch. The one place we feel otherwise is with subsummary reports. Subsummary reporting is famously irritating to do in XSL—so much so that the XSL 2.0 proposal contains specific features for making it easier. For subsummary reporting, we recommend you rely heavily on the files generated by the Site Assistant. Learn how the selected options translate into the final HTML page, and learn which pieces of the page are specific to the Site Assistant's "mini-site" functionality (which you can replace) and which ones are at the core of the report.

One caveat, though: The Site Assistant's generated subsummary reports support only one level of summary grouping. To create reports that are two or more levels deep, you need to read the wizard-generated files carefully, understand the applied techniques, and extend them to your multi-level report.

LEARNING HOW TO PROGRAM WITH CWP

In general, we're not big fans of "wizards." They tend to both obscure the way things actually work and impose a limit on the flexibility and power of the underlying tools. We find them to be most useful as a basis for quickly generating an example that you can then dissect by hand to see how things actually work.

One danger with wizards, though, is that because they're automated, they often tend to assume that you're *not* going to inspect or modify the results. So they often use quite advanced techniques to generate pleasing functionality. Think of how most typical graphical Web design tools generate JavaScript rollovers: The rollovers work beautifully, but the tool usually generates some extremely dense JavaScript. If you want to use the tool's output without modifications, you're in great shape. If you want to use the output as a basis for learning, you need to deal with some advanced code.

This is more or less the case with the XSL stylesheets generated by the Site Assistant. The generated stylesheets are quite powerful, and are packed with complex functionality—especially the record list view and the subsummary reports. But they do *not* generate simple XSL! You need to have a good grasp of intermediate-to-advanced XSL to be able to read the output.

But of course, you need to be a strong XSL programmer in any case to get the best use out of Custom Web Publishing. If you're an XML/XSL novice, here's the learning path we'd recommend:

1. Write some simple queries that use plain old XML-CWP. In other words, get accustomed to writing the query strings that the Web Publishing Engine uses to bring back FileMaker data. Experiment with various search criteria and sort fields.

2. Write some simple stylesheets to process search results. We recommend beginning with stylesheets that display search output in a variety of list formats.

3. Generate a set of stylesheets with the Site Assistant. Pay special attention to the files that perform database actions other than searches. Read and understand the utilities.xsl file.

4. Experiment with adding capabilities to the Site Assistant files.

5. Read up on the advanced features of XSLT-Custom Web Publishing in the supplied documentation and expand your knowledge. Practice with features such as email, cookies, and sessions.

Custom Web Publishing is a rich programming environment, and this chapter only scratches the surface. As you progress with CWP, you'll want to deepen your mastery of XSL and XML by reading, experimenting, and participating in online forums. The recommended readings listed in Appendix A are a good place to start.

23

PART V

DEPLOYING A FILEMAKER SOLUTION

CHAPTER **24**

FILEMAKER DEPLOYMENT OPTIONS

In this chapter

FILEMAKER DEPLOYMENT OPTIONS

One of the strengths of FileMaker is that a solution can be deployed in a variety of ways. With this flexibility, FileMaker can fit many different needs, and it can change and adapt as your organization evolves. This chapter offers a brief overview of eight ways a FileMaker database can be deployed. Several of these are discussed in depth in their own chapters elsewhere in the book, but we bring them all together here to give you a broad view of the deployment landscape.

Your deployment decisions depend on a number of factors. How many users will need access to the database? Where are they located? Are they all on the same local area network? Do other systems or applications need access to the data? Some of the deployment decisions may involve additional investment in hardware, or learning new skills. Some deployment options depend on others. There's no way to do Custom Web Publishing, for example, without using FileMaker Server. Finally, most of the deployment options are not mutually exclusive. You might have both FileMaker Pro clients and Web clients accessing the same files hosted by FileMaker Server.

24

SINGLE USER

The most basic way of deploying a solution is as a single-user application. In any organization that uses a lot of FileMaker, there are likely dozens or hundreds of single-user databases scattered on computers throughout the organization. The typical single-user solution is something that a knowledge worker cooked up to meet an ad hoc need. Perhaps it's a database for the office football pool or to keep track of gifts from a baby shower. Maybe someone needed a tool to clean up the ugly data sent by one of your customers. In many cases, the creator of such a database could have met the need with another tool, such as Microsoft Excel, but chose FileMaker Pro instead because of its simplicity and attractive user interface.

Single-user solutions like these are typically not well planned out, nor constructed according to rigorous development standards. These databases usually grow organically, have little or no security, and sparse or idiosyncratic user interfaces. Single-user databases are typically a developer's first foray into the world of FileMaker; these solutions frequently exhibit the evolving skills of the creator.

There are a few risks to be aware of with single-user solutions. First, it's unlikely that such solutions have been integrated into a rigorous backup strategy. If you, or users in your organization, store important data in or fulfill important business needs through single-user solutions, be sure to periodically burn a backup on CD or copy it to an external device, or to some networked volume that you're sure is being backed up on a periodic schedule.

Another common risk of single-user deployments is that they may not be suitable for evolution into workgroup or organization-wide solutions. It's trivial to share the files peer-to-peer, or to move them to a FileMaker Server for hosting, but if a solution was originally designed with a single-user mentality, you may end up with a difficult-to-maintain and/or fragile solution.

→ For more information on good multi-user design, **see** Chapter 11, "Developing for Multi-User Deployment," **p. 297**.

Peer-to-Peer Hosting

Peer-to-peer deployment enables a small number of workers to share a solution, without the cost of setting up and maintaining a dedicated server. You can turn any single-user solution into a peer-to-peer solution simply by turning on FileMaker Networking and adding the fmapp Extended Privilege to one or more privilege sets.

→ To learn more about Extended Privileges, **see** Chapter 12, "Implementing Security," **p. 315**.

Peer-to-peer deployment is often found in small organizations or departments where only a handful of users need access to shared data. The database usually physically lives on one person's machine or on a file server. The first person to open the file is known as the *host*; other users who access it are *clients*. Provided they have proper privileges for the file, both the host and clients can modify field definitions, access privileges, scripts, and layouts. Development teams therefore often use peer-to peer sharing during construction of large systems.

Several of the risks of single-user deployments also pertain to peer-to-peer deployments. Files are likely to be backed up sporadically rather than systematically; development standards are frequently non-existent or not enforced. Solutions that are shared peer-to-peer often fly beneath the radar of IT departments as well, which might be a good or bad thing depending on your perspective. As the creator or user of a system, it's nice to be in control of your own project, but our experience is that IT departments generally prefer that shared systems are centrally controlled and managed.

Using peer-to-peer sharing, you are restricted to sharing up to 10 databases with up to 5 concurrent users. If you need to expand beyond these constraints, you need to use FileMaker Server to deploy your solution.

CAUTION

> Because the host of a peer-to-peer shared solution is a user's workstation, you may face stability and performance concerns. For instance, the user's machine may crash, she might need to disconnect clients to reboot her machine, or she may perform actions in other applications that cause slow client performance. FileMaker Server is the remedy to all these problems.

FileMaker Server

FileMaker Server 7 is the correct deployment option for most business-critical solutions. Databases hosted by FileMaker Server are always "open," and can therefore be accessed by guests without concern that the host is unavailable (which is a concern with peer-to-peer sharing). FileMaker Server allows access for up to 250 concurrent FileMaker Pro clients.

FileMaker Server also has a number of built-in tools to aid with database administration. For instance, you can (and should!) schedule regular backups. You can also do things such as disconnect idle guests to free up resources and enable clients to automatically download updates of plug-ins. Data exchanged between FileMaker Server and clients can be encrypted with SSL, making FileMaker Server a secure deployment option as well.

→ For more information on these and other features of FileMaker Server, **see** Chapter 25, "FileMaker Server," **p. 737**.

The connection between FileMaker Server and FileMaker Pro clients is network intensive, so this deployment option is most appropriate when all the clients are connected to the server via a fast network. Remote client connections are possible, but performance may not be sufficient to meet users' needs and expectations. In cases where remote users need access to your FileMaker data, you need to consider Web publishing, or using a remote access tool such as Citrix/Terminal Services (discussed later in this chapter) as part of your deployment strategy.

WEB PUBLISHING

A FileMaker database can be deployed to Web users in several ways. One is to simply export data as either HTML or XML so that it can be statically accessed through a Web server. For dynamic interaction with your database, the deployment options are Instant Web Publishing (IWP) and Custom Web Publishing (CWP).

Both FileMaker Pro client and FileMaker Server 7 Advanced can provide access to databases via IWP. FileMaker Pro supports up to 5 concurrent IWP connections; FileMaker Server 7 Advanced supports up to 100. In both cases, setup is trivial. With IWP, your existing FileMaker layouts are dynamically rendered as Web pages. Most scripts will function correctly as well, meaning that designing a solution for IWP deployment requires no Web programming skills. Because of the browser restrictions for using IWP, we don't recommend using IWP for public Web sites. It's a more proper deployment option for remote users who would otherwise be connecting to your databases via a slow FileMaker Pro client connection.

→ For more information on Instant Web Publishing, **see** Chapter 21, "Instant Web Publishing," **p. 605**.

Custom Web Publishing is an appropriate deployment option when you need to integrate FileMaker data into an existing Web site, to provide FileMaker data to other applications in the manner of a Web service, or when you simply require more flexibility than IWP affords. CWP requires that a database be hosted by FileMaker Server 7 Advanced. You must also set up a Web Publishing Engine and have a suitable Web server available (Apache or Internet Information Server). Using CWP, appropriately formatted HTTP requests can be interpreted by the Web Publishing Engine and passed on to FileMaker Server. The server responds to these requests via XML, which can be transformed into HTML with an XSL style sheet or simply parsed by some other middleware application. Unlike IWP, CWP requires some knowledge and experience with Web application development.

→ For more information on Custom Web Publishing, **see** Chapter 23, "Custom Web Publishing," **p. 671**. For more information on Web Services, **see** Chapter 22, "FileMaker and Web Services," **p. 639**.

ODBC/JDBC

ODBC (which stands for Open Database Connectivity) and JDBC are standards that were developed to facilitate data exchange between disparate data sources. FileMaker can access remote data via ODBC/JDBC (sometimes referred to jointly as "xDBC"), and it can act also as an ODBC/JDBC data source for other applications. The latter is a deployment option you should consider if you need your FileMaker data to feed other applications in your organization.

TIP

> ODBC and JDBC are standards, not languages or applications. Different applications are compliant with these standards to varying degrees. SQL (Structured Query Language) is the language used to exchange data via ODBC/JDBC.

24

To make FileMaker data available via xDBC, you must be using the Windows version of FileMaker Pro 7 or FileMaker Server 7 Advanced. Configuring a database to be accessible via xDBC is similar to configuring it to be accessible via the Web: You need to add the fmxdbc Extended Privilege to one or more privilege sets, and you need to turn ODBC/JDBC Sharing on. After doing this, you need to set up data sources (DSNs) for other applications to use when accessing your FileMaker databases. After everything has been configured properly, other applications can send SQL queries to FileMaker.

You might want to consider xDBC as part of your deployment strategy for many reasons. For instance, you might set up report templates and charts in Microsoft Excel that pull data from FileMaker via ODBC. Similarly, you can design Java applets that interact with FileMaker databases via JDBC. Other potential uses include integration with JSP pages, ASP or ASP.NET pages, and query tools.

→ For more information on using ODBC/JDBC with FileMaker, **see** Chapter 20, "Getting Data Out of FileMaker," **p. 563**, and Chapter 19, "Importing Data into FileMaker Pro," **p. 537**.

CITRIX/TERMINAL SERVICES

As discussed previously, the connection between FileMaker Server and FileMaker Pro clients is network intensive. Users outside your local area network may not find client/server performance to be satisfactory for their needs.

One solution to the remote user deployment dilemma is to use remote access software, such as Citrix MetaFrame and Terminal Services. The hardware and software licensing costs for such a solution are not inconsequential, but neither are the performance benefits it provides. Remote users establish a network connection to the Citrix/Terminal Services server, which in turn opens a FileMaker Pro client connection to FileMaker Server. The only data flowing between the remote user and the Citrix server are screen refresh information, keystrokes, and mouse clicks. Because the Citrix server and the FileMaker Server are located on the same local area network, the client performance is outstanding.

TIP

> There are several less expensive remote access options you may want to consider. These include Timbuktu, PCAnywhere, and gotomypc.com. None of these offer all the features of Citrix/Terminal Services, such as local printer mapping, nor do they allow for multiple concurrent remote connections. On a budget, though, or for the occasional remote access need, these are fantastic tools.

RUNTIME SOLUTIONS

For some solutions, the best deployment option is as a bound, runtime solution. A *runtime solution* can be distributed to users who can run it without having a copy of FileMaker Pro on their machine. Runtime solutions are created with the Developer Utilities, which are available only in FileMaker Developer 7.

A typical example of a solution that might be deployed as a runtime solution is a product catalog. Perhaps you've developed a gorgeous FileMaker database of all your products, and you want to send it to all your customers on a CD. You could create a runtime version of the files and do just this. Your customers would be able to browse and search for items, maybe even print or email orders to you, all without having a copy of FileMaker on their machines.

The downside to runtime deployment is often version control. After you distribute stand-alone copies to myriad users, if you need to make a change to the solution, you might need to distribute new copies to those users. Moving data from the old solution to the new solution can be a bit troublesome, both for you and your users. If version control of distributed solutions is likely to be a problem for you, consider Web enabling your database or providing remote access via Citrix/Terminal Services as alternate deployment methods.

TIP

> If you need to distribute a runtime solution to both Mac and PC users, you must bind a separate version for each platform, and you therefore need access to both a Mac and a PC during development.

Runtime solutions are primarily designed to be run as single-user applications. A runtime solution can't be shared peer-to-peer. You can, however, host a runtime solution with FileMaker Server; users would need FileMaker Pro to access it, just as they would for any other hosted file.

Another deployment option that's available via the Developer Utilities is to create a *kiosk* from your FileMaker solution. When run as a kiosk, a solution takes up the entire screen. Users don't have access to any menu commands, which means you must provide buttons for every conceivable action they might perform.

→ For more information on the Developer Utilities, creating runtime solutions, and creating kiosks, **see** Chapter 26, "FileMaker Developer and Plug-ins," **p. 777**.

DEPLOYING TO HANDHELD DEVICES

If you have users who are on the road a lot, or who are just hooked on handheld devices, a deployment option you may want to consider is FileMaker Mobile. FileMaker Mobile enables you to easily synchronize data between a FileMaker database and a handheld device.

NOTE

In previous versions of the product, both Palm OS and Pocket PC devices were supported. As of the time of this writing, a new version of FileMaker Mobile was not available.

When a database is deployed to FileMaker Mobile, you can specify which fields should be available and how they should appear to users (for example, text field, check box field, popup list). None of your FileMaker layouts or scripts is actually available on the handheld device.

FileMaker Mobile is not the only option for using handheld devices with FileMaker. Citrix makes an ICA client for Pocket PC, which means that if you have a wireless network available to you, you can use a FileMaker solution directly from a handheld device. The display on a handheld device has a different form factor than regular monitors, so you'd likely need to design handheld-friendly layouts.

A final option for handheld deployment is via the Web. Using Custom Web Publishing and wireless Web protocols such as WML and WAP, you can design handheld solutions that interact with FileMaker databases.

24

CHAPTER **25**

FileMaker Server

In this chapter

ABOUT FILEMAKER SERVER

You'll use FileMaker Server to make your FileMaker Pro databases available to many users at once across a network. On its own, the FileMaker Pro software can host files for networked access from up to five users at a time, in what's called a *peer-to-peer* configuration. In practice, except for developmental configurations, or production deployments to very small groups, peer-to-peer sharing is unlikely to be a suitable choice for making files available to multiple networked users. Unless you're in that rather small minority of situations, you'll want to look at FileMaker Server instead.

THE FILEMAKER SERVER PRODUCT LINE

Three separate products are available under the name FileMaker Server:

- **FileMaker Server**—FileMaker Server is used to provide concurrent access to as many as 250 networked users running FileMaker Pro client software.

- **FileMaker Server Advanced**—You'll need FileMaker Server Advanced if you wish to make FileMaker data available via ODBC, JDBC, Instant Web Publishing, or Custom Web Publishing. FileMaker Server Advanced supports networked access from up to 250 FileMaker Pro or ODBC/JDBC clients, as well as an additional 100 Web clients. (Under certain circumstances, there may be no limit on the number of Custom Web Publishing clients. The number of Instant Web Publishing clients will always be limited to 100.)

→ For a discussion on ODBC and JDBC, **see** Chapter 20, "Getting Data Out of FileMaker," **p. 563.**

→ To find out about Instant Web Publishing, **see** Chapter 21, "Instant Web Publishing," **p. 605**.

→ Custom Web Publishing is discussed in Chapter 23, "Custom Web Publishing," **p. 671**.

- **FileMaker Server Advanced Option Pack**—This upgrade adds FileMaker Server Advanced capabilities (ODBC/JDBC and Web connectivity) to an existing installation of FileMaker Server.

The essential distinction here is between Server and Server Advanced. Server allows connections from only FileMaker Pro clients. To allow access from ODBC, JDBC, or Web clients, you need to purchase Server Advanced, or use the Option Pack to upgrade an existing copy of Server.

Installing and working with the components of FileMaker Server Advanced is covered extensively in other chapters. This chapter focuses on the administration and configuration tools and techniques that pertain to the core Server product.

FILEMAKER SERVER VERSUS PEER-TO-PEER DATABASE HOSTING

There are some major differences between FileMaker Server and peer-to-peer database hosting. We've alluded to the differences between these methods in the preceding chapter. The limitations of the peer-to-peer sharing method are fairly severe: With peer-to-peer sharing, no more than ten database files may be served, to no more than five clients at a time. The peer-to-peer method uses a regular copy of FileMaker Pro as the database host, so a deployment of this type also forgoes important features of FileMaker Server, especially the ability to make regular, scheduled backups of the databases. Though such schedules could be created with operating-system-level scripting technologies, it's much simpler to use FileMaker Server's built-in tools.

Additionally, peer-to-peer configurations tend to be run on less capable hardware than Server-based configurations. In some cases, we've even seen peer-to-peer configurations hosted on an individual's personal workstation, in constant daily use for many tasks. Neither lower-end hardware nor constant competition for machine resources is a good foundation for a stable multi-user deployment.

If you do choose to begin with a peer-to-peer configuration for multi-user database sharing, we recommend that you still treat this situation as a "server-type" deployment as far as possible. Give the database host its own dedicated machine on which to run—one that people won't casually use for other daily tasks; make sure you have a reliable solution for regular backups; make sure the machine at least meets the minimum specifications for the FileMaker Pro client software, and add a bit more RAM if you possibly can.

Backing Up Open Files

If you're backing up hosted FileMaker files by hand, please be aware that you should never make a copy of a FileMaker file while it is open—even if it's not hosted, and is in use by only a single user. FileMaker can guarantee that a database file is in a fully consistent state on disk only if the file has been closed. Otherwise, there might be database transactions that exist only in RAM, that have not yet been committed to disk.

In previous versions of FileMaker, a database that had been copied from an open file would display a warning the next time it was opened, stating that the file had been closed improperly and was being checked for consistency. This warning no longer necessarily appears in FileMaker 7 when you open a file that has been copied from an open file. Don't let this fact lure you into thinking that it's now okay to copy an open file. It's not.

As you'll read in a later section, FileMaker Server's built-in backup capability handles the details of closing the files before backing them up. If you're working in a peer-to-peer setting, you don't have that luxury. You'll need to make sure that any automated solution you put into place takes into account the need to close each database file before backing it up.

25

The extremely limited scalability and lack of backup automation capabilities ought to discourage you from using FileMaker's peer-to-peer sharing for production use. For the cost of a handful of copies of the FileMaker Pro client, you can host your databases on a solid server platform (FileMaker Server) that can handle 125 database files (potentially comprising thousands of tables) and up to 250 users.

FileMaker Server Capabilities

We've talked about some of the features that set the FileMaker Server product line apart as a hosting solution: much greater scalability than the plain FileMaker Pro software, and the capability to perform automated tasks such as backups. There are quite a number of other distinguishing features as well. Here are some of the most important:

■ **Centralized Remote Administration**—FileMaker Server comes with the Server Administration Tool (SAT), which is an application that can be used to administer one or several instances of FileMaker Server, potentially all running on different machines from the machine where the SAT is installed.

■ **Plug-in Management**—FileMaker Server can be configured to download plug-ins to FileMaker Pro clients in response to programmed requests from the clients, assuring that clients will always have the latest versions of plug-ins installed on their own machines.

■ **External Authentication**—FileMaker Server can be configured to check user credentials against a networked authentication source, such as a Windows Active Directory server or a Mac OS X Open Directory server.

■ **Secure Transfer of Data**—When FileMaker Pro clients are used in conjunction with FileMaker Server, the transfer of data can be encrypted with SSL (Secure Socket Layer).

In addition to these features, FileMaker Server offers a large number of other important functions as well, such as the capability to send messages to guests, to disconnect idle guests, to limit the visibility of database files based on user privileges, to be run in a scripted fashion from the command line, and to capture a variety of usage statistics and server event information for logging and analysis. All of these features are discussed in the sections to come.

FILEMAKER SERVER REQUIREMENTS

Like any piece of server software, FileMaker Server has certain minimum hardware and software requirements. You'll achieve the best results with a dedicated server; as with any piece of server software, it's best if FileMaker Server is the only significant server process running on a given machine. Forcing FileMaker Server to compete with other significant processes, such as mail services or domain controller services, is likely to hurt Server's performance.

File Sharing and FileMaker Server

A special word is in order about file sharing and file servers. FileMaker, Inc., recommends that all file sharing should be disabled on a machine running FileMaker Server. This has long been the official position, and in the past, a number of different reasons have been advanced for this. For instance, FileMaker Server uses its own techniques for managing concurrent access to files, and it's been said that contention between FileMaker Server's file access and the operating system's file sharing could lead to file corruption.

Another troublesome fact about file sharing is that it opens the possibility that users could mount the volume containing the hosted database files on their own computers, and open the files directly with FileMaker Pro, at the same time that other users were accessing the files via Server. This is a clear recipe for disaster and is almost certain to lead to file corruption.

In practice, it's often been difficult to disable file sharing completely on the server machine. It's often desirable to have at least part of the server machine published as a share point to move new FileMaker databases up to the server or to copy local backups to remote storage.

At the very least, if you feel you *must* have an operating system–level share point somewhere on the server, make very sure that the OS-level file sharing does not directly cover the directories where the "live" FileMaker files are kept. (Later sections in this chapter discuss the location of those files.)

And as a best practice, try to disable OS-level file sharing altogether on the server machine, and use one of the many good remote administration tools available instead—tools such as Terminal Services (Windows), Apple Remote Desktop (Mac OS), or Timbuktu (cross-platform commercial).

The server machine, in addition to being dedicated as far as possible to FileMaker Server, and having the minimum amount of file sharing enabled (preferably none), also needs the things discussed in the following sections.

STATIC IP ADDRESS(ES)

The server machine needs to be enabled for TCP/IP networking with one or more static IP addresses. (Earlier versions of FileMaker Server supported the IPX/SPX protocol in addition to TCP/IP, but this has not been the case for several versions of Server.) Note, by the way, that in contrast with earlier versions of FileMaker Server, FileMaker Server 7 is capable of *multi-homing*, meaning that it can take full advantage of multiple physical network interfaces, each with its own IP address. FileMaker Server listens on all available network interfaces. As far as we know, it's not possible to configure FileMaker Server to ignore one or more of the available interfaces; if the interface is available, FileMaker Server tries to bind to port 5003 on that interface and begins listening for FileMaker traffic. (The FileMaker client-server port number, 5003, is also not configurable.)

FAST HARD DRIVE

 Like any database, FileMaker Server is capable of being extremely disk-intensive. For some database operations, particularly those involving access to many records—such as a large update or a report—the speed of the server's hard disk may be the limiting factor. RAID (Redundant Array of Inexpensive Disks) technologies (whereby multiple physical disks are combined into a single *disk array*, for greater speed, greater recoverability, or both) are becoming ever cheaper, and some sort of RAID array may well be the right answer for you. (It probably goes without saying, but we're talking about a hardware-based RAID, not a software-based RAID.) Otherwise, consider a high-RPM SCSI disk, or one of the relatively new Serial ATA disks. Serial ATA boasts impressive speeds, and it's a bit cheaper than SCSI, but it's a newer technology, so the full picture of its reliability may not have emerged yet.

FAST PROCESSOR(S)

 This is a fairly obvious requirement for a server machine. But it's worth noting that FileMaker Server 7, unlike previous versions, now can take full advantage of multiple processors.

LOTS OF RAM

 Again an obvious requirement, and again an area in which FileMaker Server 7 represents a big advance over previous versions. Earlier versions of Server would use a maximum of

40MB of RAM, no matter how much RAM was installed. Server 7 uses as much RAM as you choose to throw at it, up to the limits of what the operating system itself can manage. Large amounts of RAM become even more desirable if you're running components of FileMaker Server Advanced on the same machine as Server itself. (Those components can be installed on the same machine as Server, or a different machine, as discussed in Chapter 23.)

FAST NETWORK CONNECTION

 FileMaker is a client-server application, which means that FileMaker Pro clients remain in constant contact with a database host such as FileMaker Server. FileMaker Server constantly *polls* (attempts to contact) any connected clients to determine what they're doing and whether they're still connected. In addition, although Server 7 is capable of handling a great many more tasks than its predecessors, it still needs to send quite a lot of data to the client for processing in certain kinds of operations. All this means that FileMaker is an extremely network-intensive platform that benefits greatly from increased network speed. Best results will be achieved on fast network connections of T1 speed or greater. A 10Mbps LAN is an improvement, and 100Mbps is even better. Of course, there's no point in spending money on machines with Gigabit Ethernet interfaces if the intervening network and the individual client machines don't support such a high speed.

SUPPORTED OPERATING SYSTEM

FileMaker Server 7 supports the following operating systems: Mac OS X Server, Mac OS X client, Windows 2000 Server, and Windows 2003 Server. On the Mac OS X side, Mac OS X Server is listed as the "recommended" choice. FileMaker, Inc., has indicated that this means they have not tried to verify the acceptability of the regular Mac OS X operating system for loads greater than 50 connected FileMaker users.

DATA CENTER ENVIRONMENT

Though not strictly a "requirement" for running FileMaker Server, proper care and housing of server equipment is a necessity, one that's often overlooked, especially in the small- and medium-sized business sectors, some areas of education, and among non-profit groups. These are all key groups of FileMaker users, ones that do not always have sufficient resources to build and maintain anything like a data center. Ideally, a server of any kind should be housed in a physically secure and isolated area, with appropriate cooling and ventilation, with technical staff on hand 24 hours a day to troubleshoot any issues that arise, and with automated monitoring software that periodically checks key functions on the server and notifies technical personnel by email or pager if any services are interrupted. Some organizations are fortunate enough to be able to house their FileMaker Servers in such an environment. But even if you can't provide all those amenities, you can see to the key areas. The server should minimally be up off the floor, well ventilated, and under lock and key if possible. And some sort of monitoring software is nice, and need not break the bank: the open source package Nagios (http://www.nagios.org) is a popular and powerful open-source monitoring package.

NOTE

> Nagios runs on Unix, but can monitor servers running on almost any platform. Many server monitoring packages exist for Windows deployment as well.

NOTE

> It's sometimes a point of confusion, but it's important to know that FileMaker Server 7 will not run on a machine running an earlier version of FileMaker Server at the same time. If you want to run Server 7 and Server 6 at the same time, you need two machines to do so.

INSTALLING FILEMAKER SERVER

FileMaker Server consists of several components. When you install the product, you may choose to install the FileMaker Server software, the Server Administration Tool (SAT), or both. You may install either component without the other: FileMaker Server can run on a machine that does not have the SAT installed, and the SAT can be used to administer multiple instances of FileMaker Server, none of which needs to be installed on the same machine as the SAT.

The installation process is straightforward and is well covered by the supplied documentation and by the installer screens. On Windows, all installed files, both FileMaker Server itself and the SAT, are installed in a directory called `Program Files\FileMaker\FileMaker Server 7`. On the Mac OS, the FileMaker Server components are installed in `/Library/FileMaker Server 7`, and the SAT and documentation are installed in `/Applications/FileMaker Server 7`. The default install location can be changed on Windows, but not on the Mac OS.

RUNNING FILEMAKER SERVER

Installing FileMaker Server installs two separate components, both of which run as services: FileMaker Server and the FileMaker Server Helper. These appear as two separate services (Windows) or processes (Mac OS). FileMaker Server does not function correctly without the FileMaker Server Helper service also running.

STARTING AND STOPPING FILEMAKER SERVER

When you install FileMaker Server, you can choose whether to have these services start automatically (in which case they are started every time the server itself starts up) or manually (in which case you need to start the services by hand). On Windows you can start and stop the services with the tools available in the Services console. On the Mac OS, it's a bit trickier.

On Mac OS X, there is no tool that corresponds to the Windows Services console. If you chose to have the services start automatically, a directory called `/Library/StartupItems/FileMakerServerHelper` was created on the server machine. This directory contains a simple

25

shell script that controls automatic starting of the service on Mac OS X. To see the specific command line syntax for starting and stopping the server, read the startup script, which is contained in `/Library/StartupItems/FileMakerServerHelper/FileMakerServerHelper`. Currently the command to start the FileMaker Server services looks like this:

```
/Library/FileMaker\ Server\ 7/Tools/fmserver_helperd
```

And the command to stop the services looks like this:

```
/Library/FileMaker\ Server\ 7/Tools/fmserver_helperd stop
```

HOSTING DATABASES

FileMaker Server can host up to 125 FileMaker databases. When the server starts, it looks for files in the default database file directory, and in the alternate database directory if one has been specified. (We discuss how to specify the alternate directory later.) It also tries to open any databases found in the first directory level within either of those two top-level directories. Databases in more deeply nested directories are not opened. The main database directory can be found at `Program Files\FileMaker\FileMaker Server 7\Data\Databases` (Windows) and `/Library/FileMaker Server 7/Data/Databases` (Mac OS X).

Care should be taken to place these directories on hard drives that are local to the server machine. It's not at all a good idea to host files from a mapped or networked drive. In such a configuration, every database access needs to be translated into a network call and passed across the network. At the very least this approach is likely to cause significant loss of performance.

USING THE SERVER ADMINISTRATION TOOL

In previous versions of FileMaker Server, a given instance of FileMaker Server could be administered only from the console of the machine on which the server software was installed. FileMaker Server 7 introduces the Server Administration Tool, a separate piece of software that can administer multiple remote instances of FileMaker Server. You can't configure FileMaker Server without using the SAT, though you can perform many routine administrative tasks from the command line.

When you open the SAT, you are prompted to connect to a server. You can choose a server that's available on your local network, a server you've stored in a list of "Favorite Servers," or a server that's registered with an LDAP server. (We cover the LDAP registration process later in the chapter.) The connection screen is shown in Figure 25.1.

Assuming the server you specify exists and is available, after you've connected, you'll see the main SAT interface. When working with the SAT, on Windows you have a choice between using a wizard-like interface (reached by clicking the server name in the left SAT pane) and using the more specialized tool available in the left SAT pane. The wizard-like interface is useful for simple configuration, but a number of features can be accessed only by using the tools in the left pane. For quick access to all configuration options, right-clicking the server name opens the Server Properties dialog, giving quick access to all configuration options. Figure 25.2 shows the Server Properties dialog in the Windows version of the SAT.

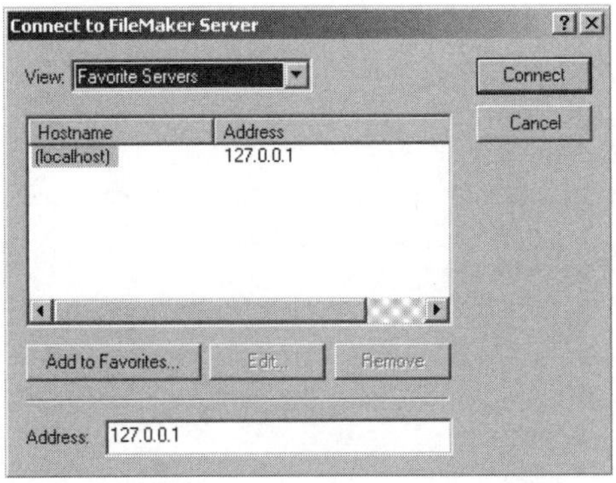

Figure 25.1
When you open the SAT, you must first connect to a specific FileMaker server.

Figure 25.2
Right-click the server name and select Properties to have quick access to all of FileMaker Server's configurable properties (Windows SAT only).

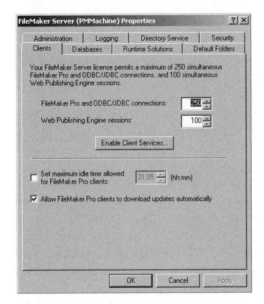

When using the SAT on Mac OS X, there is no equivalent to the various wizards available on Windows. All configuration options can be reached by clicking the Configure tool at the top of the SAT window, which gives access to a set of configuration tabs that mirror those in the Properties box in Windows. Figure 25.3 shows the Configuration window on Mac OS.

Figure 25.3
Select the Configure icon to have quick access to all FileMaker Server's configurable properties when using the Mac OS version of the SAT.

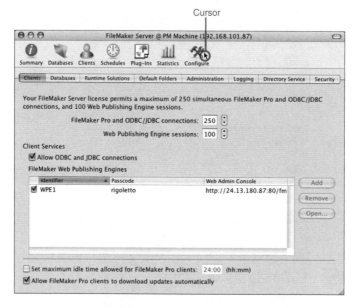

Cursor

CONFIGURING AND ADMINISTERING FILEMAKER SERVER USING THE SAT

You use the SAT tool to set up and maintain a number of important properties of a FileMaker Server installation. We cover here what we consider to be the most critical areas. The supplied documentation provides comprehensive coverage of the remaining features.

SERVER ADMINISTRATION SETTINGS

On the Administration tab of the SAT you can set some options that control administrative access to the server. In particular, you can choose the method by which administrators must authenticate, as well as specify whether remote administration of FileMaker Server is possible, as shown in Figure 25.4.

You should always require a password for server administration (and this should go without saying). You have the option, though, of using a non-FileMaker authentication source. You can instruct FileMaker Server to authenticate administrators against a user group called fmsadmin. You can choose to look for such a group among the accounts that are local to the specific machine, or to look among the accounts for whatever domain in which the server machine participates, if any.

Also on this tab you can control whether to allow remote administration of this instance of FileMaker Server. If this box is unchecked, FileMaker Server can be administered only by a copy of SAT running on the same machine. You need to enable this option if you want to administer FileMaker Server from a copy of the SAT running on a remote machine.

Figure 25.4
Use the Administration area of the SAT to control administrative access to the server.

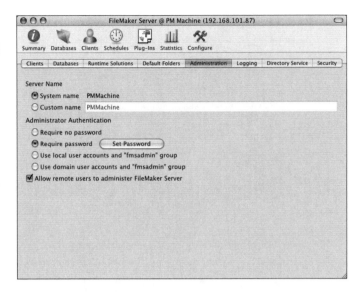

RESOURCE USAGE SETTINGS

The SAT has a number of settings that control the resources that FileMaker Server sets aside for certain tasks. On the Clients tab of the SAT, you can specify the maximum number of FileMaker Pro and Web clients that can be connected at one time, and on the Databases tab you can control the maximum number of files that FileMaker Server will try to open. (The Clients tab was shown previously in Figure 25.2. The Databases tab is shown in Figure 25.5.) All these numbers have a hard upper limit: 250 for simultaneous FileMaker Pro or ODBC/JDBC users, 100 for simultaneous Web clients, and 125 for the maximum number of open files. If you know that your loads will be lower than those figures, though, you can lower the numbers. If you'll never need to have more than 50 files open, or more than 25 users, you can set these thresholds lower. Doing so frees up resources, such as RAM, that FileMaker Server would otherwise need to keep in reserve for the possible higher loads. As a general rule, you should set these three numbers as low as you can.

You can also specify the amount of RAM to set aside for a database cache. This value is configured on the Databases tab. The SAT lets you know what it thinks the maximum allowable cache size is, based on total available RAM.

It's tempting to think you should just set the database cache to the largest possible size, but this isn't always the best option. Setting aside too large a cache can take RAM from other areas, such as the operating system, without necessarily being beneficial to FileMaker Server. It's probably safe to say that your cache should never need to be much bigger than the total size of all your served databases. So if you're serving files that total 100 megabytes in size, there's probably not much point to a 300-megabyte cache, even if you have enough RAM to support a cache of that size.

25

Figure 25.5
Use the Databases
area to control file
hosting and cache
size limits.

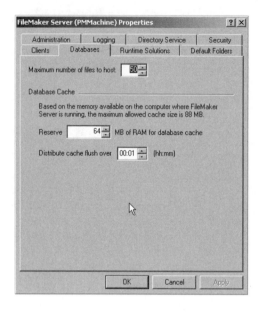

CLIENT CONNECTIVITY SETTINGS

The Clients tab of the SAT also lets you specify additional connectivity options for an
installation of FileMaker Server Advanced. Here you can allow or disallow ODBC and
JDBC connections, and configure connections to a Web Publishing Engine. These options
are fully explored in other chapters.

→ For a discussion on ODBC and JDBC, **see** Chapter 20, "Getting Data Out of FileMaker," **p. 563**.

→ To find out about Instant Web Publishing, **see** Chapter 21, "Instant Web Publishing," **p. 605**.

→ Custom Web Publishing is discussed in Chapter 23, "Custom Web Publishing," **p. 671**.

MANAGING CLIENTS

Using the SAT, you can see a list of all currently connected FileMaker Pro clients. You can
also see which databases they currently have open. Any Administrative sessions (that is, connections from the SAT) are shown. ODBC, JDBC, and Web connections are not shown.
The display of connected clients is shown in Figure 25.6.

From this display, by (Control-clicking) [right-clicking] on an individual user, or by selecting the user and going to the _A_ction menu, you can choose to send that individual user a
message (asking him to log out, for example, or to call you to discuss the large number of
files he has open). You can also choose to disconnect the user from the server. You also have
the option to send a message to all users, or to disconnect all users, if you choose. (On the
Mac OS version of the SAT, these options appear only if no specific clients are selected. On
Windows, they are always available.)

Figure 25.6
Use the SAT to monitor connected clients.

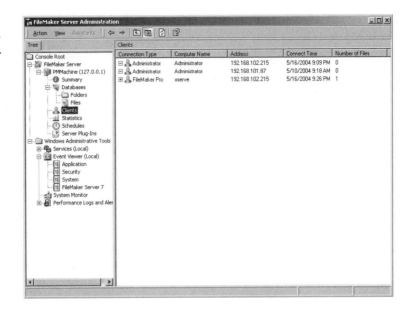

MANAGING DATABASES

The Databases area of the SAT is somewhat similar to the Clients area. Here, you can see a list of all open databases, grouped by directory if you so choose. (On Windows, choose the Files node within the Databases area to see files without directory groupings; on the Mac OS, choose Action, Database, Hide Folders.) See Figure 25.7 for a look at the database monitoring area on Windows. By (Control-clicking) [right-clicking] a database in the list, or selecting a database in the list and then choosing an option from the Action menu, you can open a closed database (making it available to clients). You may also close or pause an open database. The Pause option does not fully close the database (which would forcibly disconnect any users who might be connected to the database), but it does prevent the database from being read or written to until the Resume command is given for that database. The Pause command also synchronizes the database cache, rendering the database file consistent on disk so that it can be backed up.

When working with databases in the SAT, you also have the option to close, open, pause, or resume all databases at once.

25

Figure 25.7
Use the database monitoring area to inspect hosted databases.

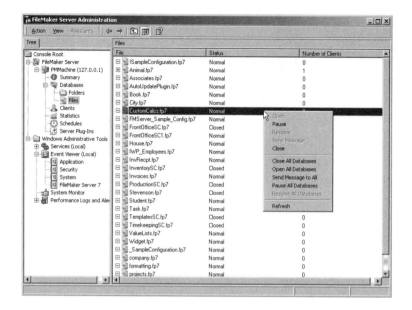

ADMINISTRATION FROM THE COMMAND LINE

So far we've looked at how to configure and administer FileMaker Server with the Server Administration Tool. But many of these tasks can be accomplished at the command line as well, with a command-line utility called fmsadmin that's installed alongside FileMaker Server. If you're comfortable at the command line, you can administer FileMaker Server without ever installing the SAT. Like the SAT, the fmsadmin tool can administer instances of FileMaker Server that are running remotely, as well as those running on the same machine.

> **CAUTION**
>
> This section assumes you're fairly familiar with working at the command line on your chosen platform. It assumes you have some familiarity with setting system paths, writing batch scripts, and executing scheduled tasks.

Command-line administration is accomplished by passing arguments to the fmsadmin command. Consider the following code:

```
fmsadmin send -m "You have work to do!"
```

This command sends the message "You have work to do!" to all clients connected to the database on the local machine.

ABOUT SYSTEM PATHS

If you've worked much at the command line, you know that tools such as fmsadmin are easier to use if they're somewhere in the system path. If the command is not somewhere in the system path, it can be invoked only if the full path to the command is specified, as in this example:

```
/Library/FileMaker\ Server\ 7/Tools/fmsadmin send -m "You have work to do!"
```

(This is a Mac OS-style path, and the backslashes in the path are necessary to "escape" the spaces in the FileMaker Server install directory path on the Mac OS.) Alternatively, you can call the command from its installed location by saying

```
./fmsadmin send -m "You have work to do!"
```

where the dot (.) indicates the current working directory. Neither of these is very desirable, so it's best for the fmsadmin command to be available via the system path.

On Mac OS X Server, this happens automatically. On Mac OS X Server, fmsadmin is installed in /usr/bin, which is generally part of the system path. On regular Mac OS X, as well as Windows, fmsadmin is installed outside the default system paths. In this case, there are two choices: either copy it to a location within the default system path, such as /usr/bin on Mac OS, or C:\WINNT on Windows, or edit the system path to include the fmsadmin install directory. The latter choice is probably the better option because it keeps the system path directories unencumbered.

The correct way to edit the system paths varies depending on operating system, and each operating system generally provides several ways to accomplish this goal. On Windows, you can choose Start Menu, Settings, Control Panel, then open the System icon, select the Advanced tab, click the Environment Variables button, then select and edit the Path variable in the System Variables window. On Mac OS, you can edit a file such as /etc/profile to add your custom path commands. (Which file you edit depends on which command shell you and your users are using. If you're not very sure which file to edit, it's best to consult with a system administrator.)

A third option, on the Mac OS, is to create a *symbolic link* to the fmsadmin command from someplace on the system path. This installs a file in the system path that points to the true install location of fmsadmin. Such a command would look like this:

```
ln -s /Library/FileMaker\ Server\ 7/Tools/fmsadmin /usr/bin/fmsadmin
```

COMMAND LINE REFERENCE

The FileMaker Server documentation doesn't document the command line syntax very well (an odd lapse in what's otherwise a very good document). Instead, it refers you to the online help. Table 25.1 contains a list of all the commands and options you can use with fmsadmin.

TABLE 25.1 fmsadmin COMMANDS AND OPTIONS

Name	Meaning	Usage
backup	Back up databases	fmsadmin BACKUP [FILE...] [PATH...] [-diopuwy]
close	Close databases	fmsadmin CLOSE [FILE...] [PATH...] [-imptuwy]

continues

TABLE 25.1   CONTINUED

Name	Meaning	Usage
delete	Delete a schedule	fmsadmin delete schedule [SCHEDULE #] [-ipuwy]
disable	Disable plug-ins or schedules	fmsadmin DISABLE TYPE [PLUG-IN #] [SCHEDULE #] [-ipuwy]
disconnect	Disconnect a client	fmsadmin disconnect client [CLIENT #]
enable	Enable plug-ins or schedules	fmsadmin ENABLE TYPE [PLUG-IN #] [SCHEDULE #] [-ipuwy]
files	List open databases (deprecated)	fmsadmin FILES
list	List clients, files, plug-ins, or schedules	fmsadmin LIST TYPE [-ipsuwy]
open	Open databases	fmsadmin OPEN [FILE...] [PATH...] [-ipuwy]
pause	Pause databases	fmsadmin PAUSE [FILE...] [PATH...] [-ipuwy]
reload	Re-load preferences	fmsadmin RELOAD [-ipuvy]
resume	Resume paused databases	fmsadmin RESUME [FILE...] [PATH...] [-ipuvy]
run	Run a schedule	fmsadmin RUN SCHEDULE [SCHEDULE #] [-ipuwy]
send	Send a message	fmsadmin SEND [-cimpuwy] [CLIENT #] [FILE...] [PATH...]
status	Show status of guests and files	fmsadmin STATUS TYPE [-ipuvy] [ID #] [FILE]
stop	Shut down the server	fmsadmin STOP [-fimptuwy]

COMMAND OPTIONS

Command options are additional parameters you can add to a command invocation to alter its behavior. The fmsadmin tool supports a number of standard options, and also several options that apply only to certain specific commands. The "usage" column in each of the previous descriptions lists possible command options in square brackets. Many options have a long form that appears preceded by a double hyphen. The long form can be used to increase readability, for example in scripts. See Table 25.2 for the available options.

TABLE 25.2   COMMAND OPTIONS

General Options

Option	Description
-h, --help	Print the usage page.
-i address, --ip address	Specify the IP address of a remote server.
-p pass, --password pass	Password to use to authenticate with the server.
-u user, --user user	Username to use to authenticate with the server.
-w seconds, --wait seconds	Specify time in seconds for command to time out.
-v, --version	Print the version information.
-y, --yes	Automatically answer "yes" to all prompts.

Command-Specific Options

Option	Description
-d PATH, --dest PATH	Specify a destination path for a backup.
-f, --force	Close databases or shut down the server forcefully, without waiting for clients to disconnect gracefully.
-m message, --message message	Specify a text message to send to clients.
-o, --offline	Perform an offline backup.
-s, --stats	Return additional detail about clients or files.
-t, --grace-time	Specify time in seconds before clients will be forcibly disconnected.

25

SCRIPTING FILEMAKER SERVER ADMINISTRATIVE TASKS

Using the capabilities of the fmsadmin tool, an experienced system administrator can use command-line scripts to control many aspects of FileMaker Server functioning. These scripts may be executed manually, or run at scheduled times via a system utility such as cron (Mac OS) or the Task Scheduler (Windows). As you'll see further on, in the section on "Scheduled Tasks," FileMaker Server can also be configured to run system scripts on a schedule.

Using scripted administration, you can even perform a few tasks that cannot directly be performed via the SAT. Suppose you have a database system with several distinct files. The database is partitioned into different files because different tables in the database have widely differing usage patterns. One very large table is read-only, and consists of data that's imported nightly from another system. Other tables are smaller, but are updated constantly and contain critical data. You'd like to back the smaller tables up once an hour, but the larger table can be backed up as infrequently as once a day. If you establish a FileMaker Server backup schedule via the SAT, each schedule must back up an entire directory at a time—you can't pick and choose among files within a directory. It would be easy enough to put the large file in one directory, the smaller files in another, and establish FileMaker Server-based backup schedules. If this organization is not desirable, though, you need to write two backup scripts—one for the large file, another for the smaller files—and use the operating system's task scheduling facilities to run them at different times. Each script would be fairly simple. They might look like this:

```
#hourly backup script for the transaction files
fmsadmin backup transaction.fp7 customer.fp7 orders.fp7

#daily backup script for the products file
fmsadmin backup product.fp7
```

You could also extend the scripts to use other operating system facilities. For example, you could compress the files after they had been backed up, or notify an administrator via email if the backup failed—neither of which is possible with FileMaker Server backups established via the SAT.

WORKING WITH EXTERNAL SERVICES

FileMaker Server can take advantage of certain external services to help centralize the management of information such as server location and user authentication credentials. If you or your organization maintain such services, you can configure FileMaker Server to use them. You can use external services to centralize two types of information:

- Information about the location of machines running FileMaker Server. You can use one or more directory servers to maintain information about the names and locations of FileMaker Servers throughout your organization, rather than having your users keep track of server names or addresses.

- Information about user credentials. You can use the authentication services built into Windows and the Mac OS to map users' network credentials directly onto FileMaker accounts and privileges.

REGISTERING WITH AN LDAP SERVER

Suppose you work with a large organization, where the network is divided into several subnets, and there are a number of instances of FileMaker server running on different machines throughout the network. For a user on one subnet to access a FileMaker Server on another, the user must know the machine name or IP address of the server, and must add that information to her list of favorite servers.

Rather than ask users and administrators to keep track of multiple machines and machine names, it's possible to use a *directory server* to maintain this information in a central location. The FileMaker Pro or FileMaker Developer client and the SAT can both be configured to look for available servers via a directory server. As soon as the client or the SAT is configured to work through a directory server, any new FileMaker Servers registered with the directory server automatically become visible to those clients.

FileMaker Server is capable of registering itself with directory servers that implement LDAP (Lightweight Directory Access Protocol). Such servers include Active Directory (Windows), Open Directory (Mac OS), and OpenLDAP (Unix/Linux).

Configuring the interaction with a directory server has three steps:

1. Configure the directory server.
2. Configure an instance of FileMaker Server to register itself with the directory server.
3. Configure one or more copies of FileMaker Pro, FileMaker Developer, or the SAT to search the directory server for available instances of FileMaker Server.

The registration process is relatively complex, and is best attempted by administrators with experience in managing the type of directory server in question. We'll walk through the critical steps in this section, without pretending to give a full introduction to the complex world of LDAP.

LDAP is a very flexible and very complex protocol. There are probably a great many ways to configure an LDAP server in such a way as to enable registration of FileMaker Server instances. We'll show you just one way, which involves creating a new *organizational unit* on the LDAP server and registering servers beneath it. We use Windows Active Directory to illustrate the process.

CONFIGURING AN ACTIVE DIRECTORY SERVER

To register a FileMaker Server with an Active Directory server, begin by adding a new Organizational Unit (OU) to the server. Choose Start, Programs, Administrative Tools, Active Directory Users and Computers. In the new window, right-click on the name of the LDAP server machine and choose New, Organization Unit. This operation is shown in Figure 25.8. Give the new OU a name; we call ours fmp-ldap.

Figure 25.8
To set up a FileMaker registry under Active Directory, begin by creating a new Organizational Unit.

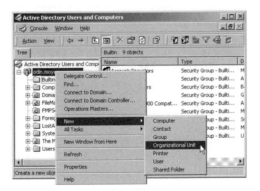

You need to associate a user with the new OU. You may want to create a new user just for this purpose. In that case, right-click the Users directory and choose New, User. This operation is shown in Figure 25.9. Take note of the username and password; they'll be necessary later when accessing the directory server remotely.

Figure 25.9
You'll probably want to create a new user to whom you want to delegate rights over the new OU.

You next need to delegate certain privileges over the new OU to the user you just created. Right-click on the OU name and choose Delegate Control. You then see the Delegation of Control Wizard. On the second screen, choose the new user you just created. On the following screen, labeled Tasks to Delegate, choose the Create a Custom Task to Delegate radio button. On the following screen, choose to delegate control of This Folder, Existing Objects in This Folder, and Creation of New Objects in This Folder. On the next screen titled Permissions, choose Full Control in the Permissions area. On the screen that follows, click Finish to complete the act of delegation. That completes the configuration of the Active Directory Server.

> **NOTE**
>
> It is probably possible to create a workable configuration by delegating less than Full Control to the user in question. If you create a user specifically for this purpose, though, and grant him minimal or no rights elsewhere on the server, there is probably little risk in giving that user full rights to the OU.

REGISTERING WITH AN ACTIVE DIRECTORY SERVER

With the Active Directory configuration complete, you next need to register one or more servers with the directory server. You use the SAT to do this. In the SAT, connect to the server you want to register and go to the Directory Service tab. Figure 25.10 shows the necessary configuration. Here are the important settings:

- **Directory server name**—The host name or IP address of the Active Directory server you just configured.

- **LDAP port**—Use the default port of 389 unless your server has been configured differently.

- **Distinguished name**—It's important to get this exactly right. In Figure 25.10 Active Directory is configured with an OU, so the distinguished name looks like ou=<your OU name> and then a series of dc= directives, which refer to the individual components of the machine name. If your machine name is adserver.mycompany.com and your OU is named fmp-ou, the distinguished name would be ou=fmp-ou,dc=adserver,dc=mycompany,dc=com.

- **Login settings**—Choose to use Windows authentication. For the account name, it's important to use the form <account-name>@<server-name>.

Figure 25.10
You need to do a bit of work to fill in all the items necessary to register FileMaker Server with an LDAP server.

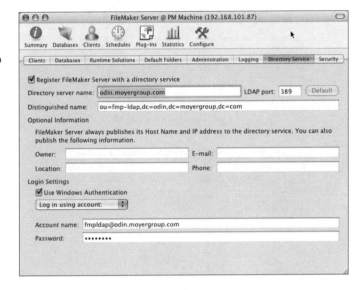

After you've filled these settings in, the SAT automatically tries to register the FileMaker Server with the Active Directory Server. This is the moment of truth!

One good way to check on the success of this operation is to look at the event log for the server you're trying to register. A registration failure generates only one or two events—one of them an error. A common error is one of insufficient privileges. This error may mean that you didn't supply the right logon credentials (bad username or password). It may also mean that you didn't delegate sufficient privileges over the OU to the chosen user. Such an error is shown in Figure 25.11.

If registration did succeed, you should see quite a long list of events as each piece of information about the directory service is communicated to the server, culminating in an event with EventID 206, "Registration with directory service succeeded."

Successful registration also is visible on the Active Directory server, though it can take a while for the change to be visible there. Each registered server appears below the OU in which you registered it. The result is shown in Figure 25.12.

Figure 25.11
Configuring your delegated user with insufficient privileges over the Organization Unit is a common source of problems.

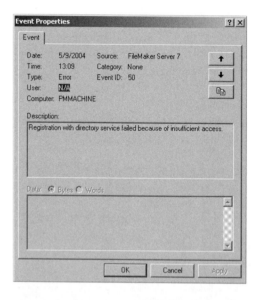

Figure 25.12
After FileMaker Server is successfully registered with the Active Directory server, the FileMaker server appears under the OU in Active Directory.

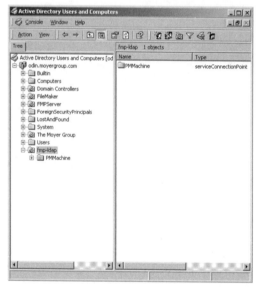

TIP

In the Mac OS version of the SAT, you can set up a preferred LDAP configuration. Choose FileMaker Server Admin, Preferences, then choose LDAP Directory Service from the popup menu in the resulting dialog. You are given a screen where you can enter a default server address, port, search base, and login credentials.

LOOKING FOR SERVERS VIA LDAP

After you've successfully registered your FileMaker Server with the Active Directory server, you can then use the Active Directory server when looking for hosts from FileMaker Pro, FileMaker Developer, or the SAT.

In FileMaker Pro, for example, if you choose File, Open Remote, you can then choose Hosts Listed by LDAP from the View menu. You can then click the Specify button to specify a directory service to connect to. Fill in the service information in the Specify LDAP Directory Service dialog. Possible settings are shown in Figure 25.13.

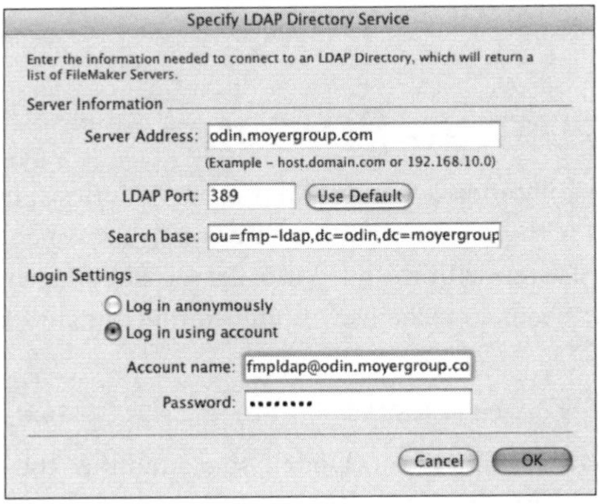

Figure 25.13
Use settings similar to those already used to register the server to look for registered FileMaker Servers.

The settings are very similar to those you used when registering a FileMaker Server. For Search Base, fill in the same string you supplied in the Distinguished Name field in the SAT when registering the FileMaker Server earlier.

If all has gone well, the Open Remote File dialog should now show a list of all FileMaker Servers registered with the chosen directory server. From here, you may work directly with those servers, or click Add to Favorites to add them to your list of preferred servers. These choices are shown in Figure 25.14.

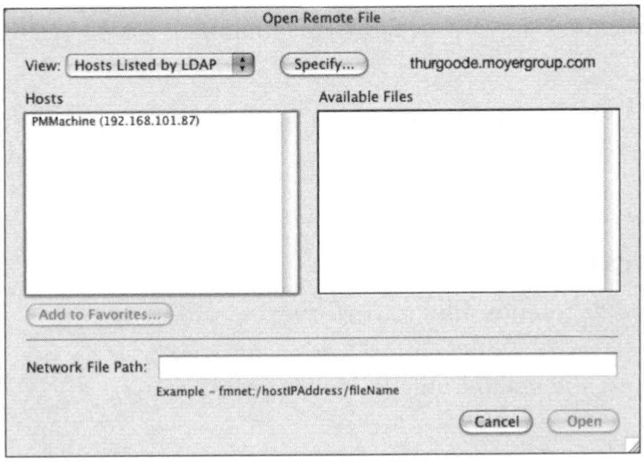

Figure 25.14
After you've successfully connected to an LDAP server, you should see a list of all FileMaker Servers registered with that directory service.

There are quite a few things that can go wrong in the complex process of configuring and con-necting to an LDAP server. To learn about some of them, see "Trouble with LDAP" in the Troubleshooting section at the end of this chapter.

USING EXTERNAL AUTHENTICATION SERVICES

You can configure FileMaker Server to work with external authentication services. If your organization maintains a directory of usernames and passwords, and you'd like to be able to reuse these credentials, it's possible to configure FileMaker Server to do so. The mechanics of configuring both FileMaker Pro and FileMaker Server to do this are covered in Chapter 12, "Implementing Security."

→ For a discussion of how to configure external authentication, **see** "External Accounts," **p. 318**.

AUTOMATICALLY UPDATING PLUG-INS

Using plug-ins has become commonplace in FileMaker Pro solutions, both big and small. One of the perceived issues with plug-in use has traditionally been the difficulty of distribut-ing them to client machines. Even with the advent of server-side plug-ins in FileMaker Pro 7, every client machine that needs to make use of plug-in functionality must have the plug-in installed and enabled.

→ For a full discussion of using plug-ins with FileMaker Pro, **see** "Plug-ins," **p. 789**.

FileMaker Server 7 has a feature called Auto Update that simplifies the distribution of plug-ins to client machines. The concept is very simple. Place your plug-ins in a designated folder on the server. When a user makes a client connection to a file hosted by FileMaker Server, you can have a script execute that checks the user's machine to see whether she has version such-and-such of such-and-such plug-in. If she doesn't, the script can automatically download the plug-in from the server. The plug-in is placed in the appropriate directory (the Extensions folder within the FileMaker Pro folder) and enabled. The server thus pro-vides "automatic updates" to client machines that request them, obviating the need to manu-ally distribute plug-ins.

There's a bit of setup and scripting you have to do to make use of this feature, but it's cer-tainly not more than an hour's work per solution. The time you'll save not having to run around to all the machines on your network updating plug-ins is certainly worth the invest-ment of an hour.

There are essentially three tasks that you need to perform to use the auto update feature. These are

- Prepare FileMaker Server
- Prepare FileMaker Pro
- Add scripts to your solution files to perform the auto update

These tasks are covered in detail in the following sections.

PREPARING FILEMAKER SERVER

To prepare FileMaker Server to provide automatic downloads of plug-ins, you must enable the option and put the plug-ins in the appropriate folder on the server.

You can turn on Auto Update within the Client Connections Assistant of the Server Administration Tool. It's simply a matter of checking a check box. There's only one check box on the screen, so you shouldn't have any trouble locating it. That same check box can be accessed on the Clients tab of the FileMaker Server Properties window, shown previously in Figure 25.2. You do not need to restart FileMaker Server after enabling the Auto Update feature.

The other task you need to do on the server is placing the plug-ins in an appropriate directory. Inside the Database directory, you should have a folder called AutoUpdate. That's where your plug-ins go. You create a folder within the AutoUpdate directory for each plug-in that you want to be downloaded to client machines. Name the folder the same as the plug-in itself, sans extension.

Within that folder, create a folder for each version of the plug-in that you want to make available. You can name the folders anything you like, but it's recommended that you simply use the version number of the plug-in. For example, within the MyPlugin folder, you might have a folder called 1.0 and another named 1.1.

Finally, place the actual plug-ins within the appropriate version folder. If you have both Mac and Windows users, you need to place both the Mac OS X and Windows versions of the plug-in in this same version-specific directory. If you are using a Windows version of FileMaker Server and need to allow Mac OS X clients to download plug-ins, be aware that you must compress the Mac version of the plug-in as a `.tar` archive. (See the "Mac Plug-ins on a Windows Server" Sidebar that follows to learn how to do this.)

25

Mac Plug-ins on a Windows Server

If you need to make Macintosh versions of your plug-ins available from a Windows version of FileMaker Server, you need to compress the Mac plug-in as a `.tar` archive and place the archive on the server. This ensures that Macintosh-specific file information is not lost during the transition of the file from one platform to another.

Tar, which stands for tape archiver, was originally developed to create tape backups on Unix systems. It's now commonly used for compressing files for all sorts of purposes. You can use the Terminal application on OS X to create a `.tar` archive that contains your plug-in.

From the command-line prompt in the Terminal application, navigate to the directory where the plug-in is located on your machine by using the `cd` command. (You can learn more about changing directories by typing in **man cd** at the command prompt.)

Say that the plug-in you are working with is called `foo.fmplugin`. You want to turn this into an archive called `foo.fmplugin.tar`. To do this, you would type the following at the command line:

```
tar -cf foo.fmplugin.tar foo.fmplugin
```

Take the `.tar` file and place that in the appropriate directory on your Windows server. The archive is automatically expanded when Mac clients download the archive.

CAUTION

> If you are using a Mac OS X version of FileMaker Server, then you need to make sure that any plug-ins you place on the server are owned by the "fmsadmin" group and have group read permissions.

A sample plug-in is installed with FileMaker Server so you can see the directory and naming structures that you need to follow. There's also a sample FileMaker Pro database that contains scripts to download the sample plug-in. These are both valuable resources the first time you go about setting up an auto upload routine.

To give you an additional, more "real-world" example, we walk through the steps you'd take to build an auto update routine for a different plug-in. The plug-in that we've chosen as our guinea pig is UPLOADit, from Comm-Unity Networking Systems (www.cnsplug-ins.com). There's nothing special about this choice; we merely wanted to use something other than the sample plug-ins that ship with FileMaker. You follow the same steps for any plug-in that you use.

When you download UPLOADit, you'll get a folder full of demo files, instructions, and of course, the plug-ins themselves. The Mac version is called UPLOADit_OSX.fmplugin, and the Windows version is called UPLOADit_Win.FMX. The tasks you would need to undertake to prepare FileMaker Server to download these to client machines are as follows:

1. Create directories in the AutoUpdate folder on the server (\FileMaker Server 7\Data\Databases\AutoUpdate\) called UPLOADit_OSX and UPLOADit_Win. You need to have both because the plug-ins have different names on the two platforms.

2. Create a directory within each of these folders called simply 1.0.

3. Compress the Mac version of the plug-in into a .tar archive called UPLOADit_OSX.fmplugin.tar (see previous Sidebar titled "Mac Plug-ins on a Windows Server").

4. Copy the .tar archive and the Windows version of the plug-in to the appropriate 1.0 folder.

After those steps have been taken, and assuming the auto update feature of FileMaker Server has been enabled, client connections to the server can now begin requesting the UPLOADit plug-in. The actual download process is covered in the following sections.

PREPARING FILEMAKER PRO

For a FileMaker Pro client to download plug-ins from FileMaker Server, the client needs to have the AutoUpdate plug-in installed and enabled. This plug-in is part of the typical installation of FileMaker Pro, so unless you've disabled the plug-in for some reason, chances are that the client application will be all prepared to download plug-ins.

As with all plug-ins, the AutoUpdate plug-in should be placed in the Extensions folder within the FileMaker Pro application directory. To confirm that the plug-in is enabled, go to the Plug-ins tab of the Preferences dialog, which is shown in Figure 25.15.

Figure 25.15
The AutoUpdate plug-in must be enabled on a workstation for it to be able to retrieve downloads of other plug-ins from FileMaker Server.

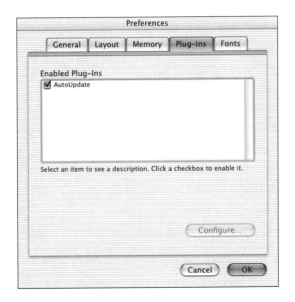

As part of the routine for performing the actual download—which is described in detail in the next section—you'll write a script that checks that the AutoUpdate plug-in is installed and active. If it's not, you can show users a dialog telling them to call the database administrator or giving them instructions on how to obtain and enable the AutoUpdate plug-in.

PERFORMING THE AUTO UPDATE

The actual downloading of a plug-in from the server to the client machine is triggered by a script executed on the client machine. The AutoUpdate plug-in, which was discussed in the preceding section, has three functions, which all play a role in an auto update routine. These three functions are

- `FMSAUC_Version (0)`—Returns a string containing the name and version number of the AutoUpdate plug-in itself. Currently, this value is `"FileMaker Auto Update Plugin Version 7.0"`.

- `FMSAUC_FindPlugin ( plug-in_name )`—Returns a space-delimited list of the folder names on the server within the directory specified by the *plug-in name* parameter. The list, however, returns only folders that contain the specified plug-in. If there's no folder in the AutoUpdate directory on the server that's named the same as the specified parameter, then this function returns a -1.

- `FMSAUC_UpdatePlugin ( plug-in_name_and_version)`—This is the function that actually obtains the plug-in from the server. A string containing both the plug-in name and version should be used as the parameter. If the plug-in downloads with no error, the function returns a 0. Table 25.3 shows the other values that may be returned.

TABLE 25.3   ERROR CODES RETURNED BY FMSAUC UpdatePlugin

Error Code	Description
-1	The file to be downloaded is missing from the temporary folder.
-2	The Extensions\Saved folder to contain the backup of the outdated plug-in or support file couldn't be created.
-3	The file to be replaced on the client computer couldn't be deleted from the Extensions folder.
-4	The file to be replaced couldn't be moved to the Extensions\Saved folder.
-5	The downloaded file can't be copied to the Extensions folder.
-6	The download file must be a plug-in file.
3	The Auto Update plug-in is disabled in the FileMaker Server Administration Client Connections Assistant, FileMaker Server Properties (Windows), or Configure, Clients (Mac OS).
5	The download file can't be found in the AutoUpdate folder on the FileMaker Server computer.
6	An error occurred on the computer running FileMaker Server as the file was being downloaded.
100	The external function definition for FMSAUC_UpdatePlugIn contains an invalid or empty parameter.
101	The function call from the client computer to the computer running FileMaker Server failed. The server computer might be running a previous version of FileMaker Server.

To download a plug-in from the server, a user must first open a client session of a file that resides on the server. It will not work from a locally hosted file.

A typical auto update routine consists of three tasks:

- Checking to see what version of the plug-in, if any, already resides on the client's workstation.
- Checking whether the server has a more recent version.
- If necessary, downloading the plug-in to the client workstation.

If a certain plug-in is required for a file to operate as designed, then you will want to have the auto update routine be part of the file's startup script. That way, if for some reason the user isn't able to retrieve the plug-in, you can prevent her from entering the system. Whether you write the routine using just a single script or split it into three (or more) subscripts that are called from a master script is a matter of personal preference. In the example that follows, we use a single script: it's a bit easier to follow the logic. First, however, we briefly discuss each of the parts of the routine independently.

CHECK WHAT'S ALREADY ON THE WORKSTATION

Every plug-in should contain a function that returns the name and version number of the plug-in itself. By calling that "identity" function, you'll know not only whether the user's workstation already has the plug-in, but also what version of the plug-in they have (thereby possibly obviating the need to download the plug-in again). You need to manually install and enable the plug-in on a workstation so that you can find out what this function is supposed to return when everything is up to date.

In the case of the UPLOADit plug-in that is serving as our example, this function is called `Upld_Version`, and the version we're working with returns the string `UPLOADit v.1.0.0`. A quick call to this function at the beginning of your auto update routine informs you whether the workstation already has everything it needs. If it returns nothing, or if it returns a different version number, then the script needs to proceed with the update routine.

Of course, if the user's workstation doesn't have the AutoUpdate plug-in installed and enabled, there's no chance that a download can occur. You therefore need to check the version number of that plug-in as well; you do this with the function `FMSAUC_Version (0)`. As long as this function returns something—indeed, anything—then the plug-in is active and you can proceed. If not, then you'll want to provide users with some feedback on what they need to do (such as calling the database administrator).

CHECK WHAT'S ON THE SERVER

You can check what version(s) of a plug-in are available for download from the server by using the function `FMSAUC_FindPlugin`. The parameter you pass should be the name of a folder you've set up on the server to contain plug-ins. If a folder with the specified name can't be found, the function returns a -1. If it is found, then the function returns a string containing a space-delimited list of the version numbers of the plug-ins of that name that are available.

The version number string returned by this function contains the names of the folders you've created within the plug-in's directory; these may or may not correspond to the actual version numbers of the plug-in. That is, you can name the folder anything you want. As long as it's in the plug-in's directory and contains the specified plug-in, the folder name is included in the response generated by the `FMSAUC_FindPlugin` function. For the example plug-in, the functions `FMSAUC_FindPlugin ("UPLOADit_OSX")` and `FMSAUC_FindPlugin ("UPLOADit_Win")` would both be expected to return `1.0`.

There's one other thing to know about the list of version numbers returned by the `FMSAUC_FindPlugin` function. It returns only the names of folders that actually contain a version of the plug-in that's appropriate for the client's operating system. That is, if you have a Mac version of the plug-in in a folder called 1.0.1, and a Windows version in a folder called 1.0.2, Mac clients "see" only the 1.0.1 directory and Windows clients the 1.0.2 directory. If both directories contain versions for both platforms, then the function returns the string `1.0.1 1.0.2`.

25

CAUTION

> Because the FMSAUC_FindPlugin function returns a space-delimited string, you should avoid using spaces in the names of the folders you create on the server. It is impossible to parse one folder name from another if they contain spaces.

After you've determined the version numbers that are available on the server, you need to compare that to what the client already has to determine whether a new version should be downloaded. There are many ways you can go about comparing the local and remote version numbers, and there's no single "right" way that will work in all cases. You'll probably need to extract the numeric portion of the local version, using the GetAsNumber function or one of the text parsing functions. Set up the name of the version folders on the server to facilitate easy comparison with what's actually returned.

TIP

> It's rare that you'll ever need or want to have multiple versions of a plug-in available on the server. If you have only one version, then you can simply check whether the local version equals the server version.

25

Download the Plug-in

If the workstation either doesn't have the plug-in, or if your comparison of the local and server versions reveals that the local version needs to be updated, then you'll use the FMSAUC_UpdatePlugin function to download the plug-in to the workstation. The parameter you pass to this function should contain both the plug-in name and the version number, separated by a space. For instance, to download the Mac version of the UPLOADit plug-in, you would use the following function:

```
FMSAUC_UpdatePlugin ("UPLOADit_OSX 1.0")
```

If desired, you can use FileMaker's string manipulation functions to dynamically build a string to pass as this parameter, using the results from the FMSAUC_FindPlugin function. If you know the name and version number you want, though, you can also hard-code it as has been done here.

If the user's machine already has a version of the plug-in, it is automatically moved to a directory named Saved (within the Extensions folder). The new plug-in is placed in the Extensions folder and is enabled for immediate use. There should be no user intervention necessary before, during, or after the download.

It's good practice to include a final check at the end of your update routine to ensure that the plug-in is indeed active. This would consist of another call to the version function of the particular plug-in. Assuming all's well, your startup script can proceed with any other desired tasks.

PUTTING IT ALL TOGETHER

The preceding sections have discussed the tasks and principles involved in a typical auto update routine. It should nonetheless be helpful to see a complete example script from start to finish. The example again uses the UPLOADit plug-in and assumes a directory structure on the server as described in the "Preparing the Server" section. Because the names of the Mac and Windows versions of the plug-ins are different, it's necessary to have some conditional logic that takes the client platform into consideration. Assume in the following script that gLocalVersion, gRemoteVersion, and gError are all globally stored text fields. Finally, in this script we're simply interested in getting the version 1.0.0 plug-in on the user's machine. You could add more complex logic to automatically test for updates; this script would need to be edited slightly if an updated plug-in became available.

```
Set Field [ AutoUpdatePlugin::gLocalVersion; Upld_Version ]
If [ RightWords (AutoUpdatePlugin::gLocalVersion; 1) ≠ "1.0.0" ]
    If [IsEmpty (FMSAUC_Version (0))]
        Show Custom Dialog [ Title: "Warning"; Message: "You do not have the
        ➥ Auto Update plug-in installed on your workstation.  Please
        ➥ call Jasper, the database administrator, immediately";
        ➥ Buttons: "OK" ]
        Halt Script
    End If
Set Field [ AutoUpdatePlugin::gRemoteVersion;
    Let ([paramName = Case ( Get (SystemPlatform) = -2;
            "UPLOADit_Win" ; "UPLOADit_OSX");
        versionString = FMSAUC_FindPlugin (paramName) ];
        RightWords (versionString; 1)) ]
    If [ IsEmpty (AutoUpdatePlugin::gRemoteVersion) ]
        Show Custom Dialog [ Title: "Warning"; Message: "The UPLOADit plug-in
        ➥ could not be found on the server.  Please call Jasper, the
        ➥ database administrator, immediately"; Buttons: "OK" ]
        Halt Script
    End If
Set Field [ AutoUpdatePlugin::gError;
    Let ( [pluginName = Case (Get (SystemPlatform) = -2;
            "UPLOADit_Win"; "UPLOADit_OSX");
        version = AutoUpdatePlugin::gRemoteVersion;
        paramName = pluginName & " " & version] ;
        FMSAUC_UpdatePlugin (paramName)) ]
    If [AutoUpdatePlugin::gError ≠ 0 ]
        Show Custom Dialog [ Title: "Error Downloading Required Plug-in";
        ➥ Message: "There was an error encountered during an attempt
        ➥ to download a plug-in required by this database.  ERR = " &
        ➥ AutoUpdatePlugin::gError; Buttons: "OK" ]
        Halt Script
    End If
End If
```

As you can see, this script has three error traps in it. You'd want to change the error handling to be appropriate for your solution. We've just put Halt Script steps in here, but you may want to exit the application or take the user back to a main menu layout.

 If you're having problems getting the auto update feature to work, check the troubleshooting section at the end of this chapter, titled "Problems with Auto Update."

SCHEDULED TASKS

FileMaker Server 7 has a built-in capability for executing scheduled tasks. The three types of tasks that can be scheduled are database backups, execution of batch scripts, and sending messages to connected users.

The Server Administration Tool (SAT) is used to create scheduled tasks. On Windows, you use the Task Scheduling Assistant, which walks you through a series of seven screens, prompting you for a few bits of information about the schedule on each screen. On Mac OSX, you can click the New button while viewing the schedule list, or you can select Action, Schedules, New Schedule. The new task dialog on Mac OSX is shown in Figure 25.16.

Figure 25.16
When creating a new task, you specify information such as the type of task and the frequency with which it should be executed.

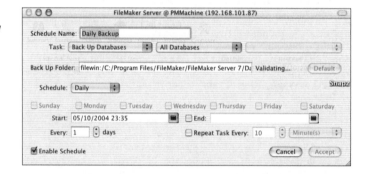

The information you are asked to provide when setting up a schedule is quite obvious and intuitive; we don't need to go over every option here. There are, however, a few important facts and tips that are worth knowing. First, you can create no more than 50 scheduled tasks. We've never seen anyone get anywhere near this limit, so it shouldn't be an area of concern for you. Second, new tasks are set to be "enabled" by default. Finally, if you need to create many similar scheduled tasks, it's best to create one and then duplicate it, changing each copy as appropriate to get the desired variation (backup schedules that vary only by the day of the week, for example).

You can see a list of all the tasks that are scheduled by navigating within the SAT to the Schedules screen, which is shown in Figure 25.17.

From the schedule list you can see a lot of useful information about the status of your scheduled tasks. For instance, you can see the date and time the task was last executed, as well as the date and time of the next scheduled execution. A check mark at the beginning of the line indicates that a task is enabled.

TIP

> If you ever need to suspend task execution because of system maintenance or other troubleshooting activities, it's better to simply disable any tasks that are waiting to be run rather than to delete them.

Figure 25.17
The Schedules screen contains a list of all the schedules and shows information such as the task's name, status, and next and last execution times.

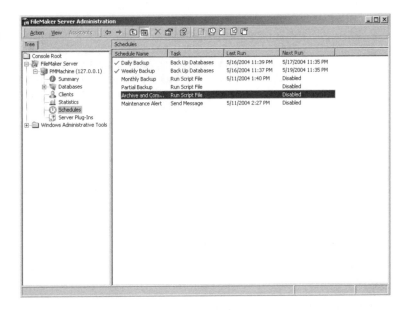

You can edit any task's options by double-clicking on it from the task list. If you right-click (Windows) or Control-click (Mac), you will see a list of other actions you can perform. These include running the task immediately, enabling or disabling the task, and duplicating the task. You can also delete a task this way.

If you schedule tasks in such a way that one task isn't finished by the time the next one is ready to begin, the second task is delayed until the first one has finished executing.

SCHEDULING BACKUPS

The most commonly scheduled tasks are database backups. The frequency of backups is dependent on your business needs. Some organizations back up their data once a day; others back up every hour during the day. The general rule of thumb is that your backup frequency should be based on how much data you're willing to lose. If you always base your assumptions on worst-case scenarios, you'll probably be well covered in the event such a scenario comes about.

When you set up a backup schedule, you can specify whether all databases should be backed up or just those in a particular folder. Typically, you'll choose to backup all of the databases. The main reason to back up just those in a particular directory is if you have some number of very large files that don't change often, such as a data archive or large lookup table. You can place those databases in their own directory and back them up on a less frequent basis than your main production files. This results in less time required to perform the backup, but more importantly, the backups take up less hard drive space.

You also must specify a directory in which the backup files are placed. When you install FileMaker Server, a folder called Backups is automatically set up for you within the Data directory. You can use that directory for your backups, or specify another valid directory path if that's preferable.

TIP

> If space permits on your hard drive, it's a good idea to have multiple destination folders set up for your backups so that they don't overwrite one another. For instance, if you back up daily, then have a Monday folder, a Tuesday folder, and so on, and set up separate schedules for each day's back up. This ensures that you always have several backups of varying ages if there's ever a problem. Sometimes you'll discover a data problem days after it occurs, so being able to go back to older backups comes in handy.

If the drive to which you are backing up runs out of space during the backup, the backup is aborted, any partial files that have been created are deleted, and an error is written to the server logs. Be sure to periodically check (once a month, at least) that your backups are being created as expected and that you have adequate drive space.

FileMaker Server 7 performs backups slightly differently than previous versions of FileMaker Server did. It used to be the case that databases were put into a paused state during a backup. Users would commonly experience a coffee-cup icon if they attempted to access a paused database.

 FileMaker Server 7 performs a "live" backup that requires significantly less time when the databases are unavailable. At the beginning of the backup process, FileMaker Server flushes the cache so that any data saved in memory is written to disk. Then it creates a "dirty" copy of the file. Users can still access and modify the original file while this copy is being made. After that's finished, the live database is paused and compared to the dirty copy; incremental changes are made to the copy so that it reflects the current state of the live file. The pause required for the incremental update is usually quite short and may not even be perceptible to users.

Running Scripts

In addition to database backups, you can also use FileMaker Server to schedule the execution of script files. On Windows, script files might be batch files or something like a WinBatch executable file. On Mac OS X, script files might be AppleScript applets or Unix batch files. Scripts must be placed within the Scripts directory, which is located in the Data folder.

Script files are typically used to perform activities such as copying backup files to remote drives and compressing copies of backup files. Pretty much anything that you can do from the command line on either platform can be done through a batch file. You can even use FileMaker Server's command line interface commands to have your batch scripts act upon FileMaker Server itself. See the section called "Administration from the Command Line" in this chapter to learn more about the types of activities this enables.

Sending Messages to Users

The final type of task that can be scheduled directly from FileMaker Server are messages to users. Messages can be sent either to all users connected to the server or just those using databases in a certain folder.

Sending messages via the server is useful for notifying users of scheduled downtime for the server or to remind them of periodic events.

MONITORING FILEMAKER SERVER

If you administer one or more machines running FileMaker Server, you'll want to take advantage of some of the tools that are available for monitoring resource usage and application events. We look at each of these areas in turn.

WORKING WITH USAGE STATISTICS

If you click the Statistics icon in the SAT, you'll see a table of information concerning six key usage parameters on the server. For each parameter, you can see the current, average, low, and peak values. Here's a list of what's monitored.

- **Network KB/sec**—Average data transfer per second. This number tells you the extent to which the raw network bandwidth of the machine is being used up.

- **FileMaker Pro Clients**—This tells you the number of connected FileMaker Pro clients. It's useful to see it here in the summary view, but clicking the Clients icon in the SAT gives you more detailed information on connected clients.

- **Files**—This tells you the number of open files. Again, clicking the Database icon gives more detailed information.

- **Disk KB/sec**—This gives you some idea of how much data is actually being written to disk over a given period. This is to some extent a measure of the extent to which the database files are being changed. If the files are being predominantly read from, the disk write activity should be low. If the files are constantly being written to, disk activity will be high. Keep an eye on this number if you expect that hard disk performance may be a bottleneck.

- **Cache Unsaved %**—Like many database servers, FileMaker Server sets aside an area of RAM (of a size configured by the administrator) to use as a cache. When a user makes a request for data, FileMaker Server checks first to see whether the data is in the cache, and if so, it fetches it from the cache, more quickly than it could fetch it from disk. Over time, the contents of the cache are written out to disk. The period over which this occurs is governed by a setting on the Databases tab of the server properties (Windows) or Configure icon (Mac OS). The setting is called Distribute Cache Flush Over. For example, if that value were set to one minute, FileMaker would attempt to write the whole cache out to disk over the course of a minute. The Cache Unsaved % should ideally be around 25% or lower. If it's much above that, you may want to shorten the length of the cache flush period. Having too much data unsaved in the cache increases the odds of data corruption in the event of a crash.

- **Cache Hit %**—This number indicates how often FileMaker Server is finding the data it's looking for in the cache. Here you want to see a number over 90%. Much less than that, and FileMaker is looking to the disk too often. In that case, it's a good idea to increase the size of the RAM cache (also on the Database tab under Properties (Windows) or Configure (Mac OS)). If the RAM cache is already as high as it can reasonably go, you may want to consider adding more RAM to the machine.

25

WORKING WITH APPLICATION EVENTS

FileMaker Server uses the event-logging facilities of the operating system on which it's installed. On the Windows platform, FileMaker Server events can be viewed with the Windows Event Viewer, whereas on the Mac the events are written to a file called Event.log.

WORKING WITH APPLICATION EVENTS ON WINDOWS

On Windows, you can access the Event Viewer from the left pane of the SAT by choosing Windows Administrative Tools, Event Viewer, FileMaker Server 7. The Event Viewer is shown in Figure 25.18.

Figure 25.18
It's a good idea to become familiar with the server event log.

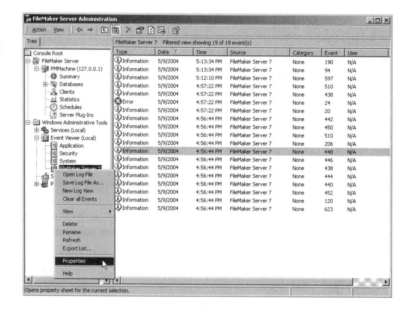

In this view you'll see a list of application events, sortable by any column. Double-clicking an event brings up additional detail about the event. Icons in the left margin indicate events that constitute errors.

Right-clicking on the log name enables you to manipulate the log in a variety of ways, such as clearing it or exporting it. Choosing Properties enables you to set some important logging parameters, such as the maximum size of the log and the filtering conditions that govern how the log is displayed. These choices are shown in Figure 25.19.

WORKING WITH APPLICATION EVENTS ON MAC OS X

On the Mac, events are written to the file /Library/FileMaker Server 7/Data/Logs /Event.log. This is a plain text file that you can view with any text editor. You can also view it in the Console application to get a "live" view of the log while the server is running. The Mac OS X event log is shown in Figure 25.20.

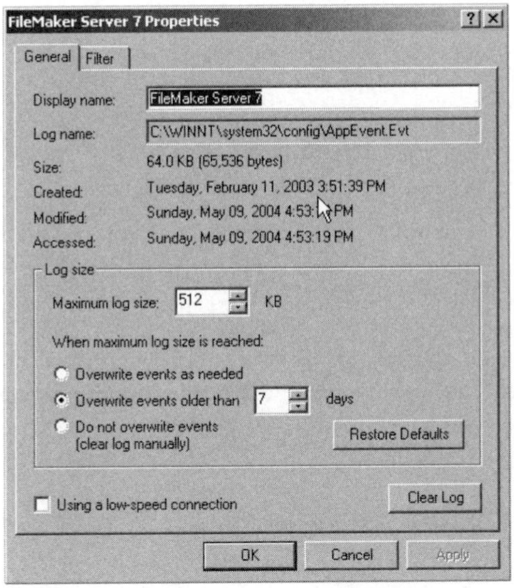

Figure 25.19
On Windows, you can configure a number of useful parameters pertaining to event logging.

Figure 25.20
On Mac OS X, the event log is a plain text file.

The FileMaker Server event login model is fairly verbose. It logs all current configuration options when it starts up. It logs each database as it opens, and each client connection on a per-client per-file basis. The Event log should always be one of the first sources of information that you draw on when troubleshooting a problem with FileMaker Server.

TROUBLESHOOTING

TROUBLE WITH LDAP

I think I configured my Active Directory server correctly, but when I try to use the SAT to register a server there, I get an error message reading "insufficient access privileges" in the Server event log.

There are several possible reasons for this. It's possible that you've specified an incorrect username or password in the Directory Services tab of the SAT. When connecting to Active Directory, make sure the username is in the form <username>@server, and make sure to verify the password as well.

It's also possible that you've delegated insufficient privileges over the organization unit you created. You shouldn't run into this problem if you grant your chosen user full access over the OU.

I tried to register with an Active Directory server but I got a "Server Down" message in my FileMaker Server event log.

This indicates that connection to the server has failed for some reason. First verify that you have the correct server name. Next, verify that you know on what port the directory service is running—389 is the default port for LDAP, but a server administrator can change the port. If the server name and port are configured correctly in the Directory Service tab of the SAT, make sure that any and all intervening firewalls are configured to pass traffic on the correct directory service port.

PROBLEMS WITH AUTO UPDATE

On some of our workstations, the auto update process seems to take a really long time, and in the end it doesn't work. The FMSAUC_FindPlugin *function when called from these workstations returns a question mark.*

Check to see what version of FileMaker Pro 7 is installed on those machines. There was a bug with auto update in the v1 release of FileMaker Pro 7.0. You can see the version number on the splash screen when the application launches, or you can just go to the About screen. The v2 update cleared up the auto update problem.

FILEMAKER EXTRA: BEST PRACTICES CHECKLIST

Much of the work of server maintenance and administration consists of diligently following a routine. For each server or service you maintain, there should be a checklist of necessary tasks. Some of these you need to do only once, when you set things up. Others are recurring tasks that should be attended to carefully. In this section, we present a series of considerations for setting up and maintaining a FileMaker Server installation.

If you're working with network staff or administrators who don't have previous experience with FileMaker, offer them this list as a handy overview of the essentials of maintaining a FileMaker Server.

Determine Network Infrastructure

You'll want to run FileMaker traffic over the fastest network possible. Before doing anything about a server machine proper, make sure you have a handle on prevailing networking conditions. What's the topology of the network over which FileMaker will run? Is it fully switched, or are hubs involved? What's the minimum speed of links within the network? With what other services will FileMaker traffic be competing? Knowing the answers to all these questions can help you make the right hardware choices, and will give you a leg up on diagnosing any later problems that appear to be network-related.

Purchase Hardware

We discussed ideal hardware characteristics earlier in the chapter. Simply put, buy the best machine you can afford. Get a machine with one or more fast processors (ideally, 2GHz and up), a healthy dose of RAM (1GB and up), fast disk storage (SCSI or Serial ATA, and consider a hardware RAID configuration), and a networking capability that matches the prevailing speed of your network. Expandability is also a good idea: Additional drive bays, external hard drive connectivity, and multiple slots (for additional or upgraded networking capability, for example) are all desirable.

All this might sound expensive, but hardware power these days is reasonably priced. For example, at the present time (mid-2004), $2750 will get you a PowerMac G5 with dual 1.8GHz processors, 1GB of RAM, and a 160GB Serial ATA drive. And $2600 will get you a Dell PowerEdge 1600SC with dual 2.4GHz Xeon processors, 1GB RAM, and a 73GB SCSI hard drive. If you want to spend less, you could reduce the amount of available hard drive space, use a bit less RAM (but not much less!) or drop back to a single processor.

Install Software

Use the latest version of an approved operating system, with all relevant patches and updates. Avoid enabling any other services on the machine except for those strictly necessary for system administration. In particular, avoid file sharing as much as possible. If it can't be avoided, make *sure* you do not enable file sharing for those areas that contain the hosted database files—otherwise you run the risk of file corruption.

Install FileMaker Server and make sure all appropriate updates are applied. Make sure your version of FileMaker Server is compatible with both the operating system and, if applicable, the service pack level of the operating system.

Configure FileMaker Server

Configure FileMaker Server to a level appropriate for your expected usage (see the detailed notes earlier in the chapter). Bear in mind that it's worthwhile to try to use only those resource levels (for example, maximum numbers of connected clients and hosted files) that you think you'll need.

DEPLOY DATABASES AND SCHEDULE BACKUPS

Decide on your database directory structure—that is, how you'll group databases into directories on the server. Decide whether to use an alternate database directory. Regardless of your choice, establish backup schedules that provide you and your organization with an appropriate level of security. How much data can you afford to lose? Decide on the answer and back up accordingly. Remember that local backups by themselves are not sufficient security: You should make provisions to transfer this data to offline storage such as a tape backup.

MONITOR USAGE STATISTICS

Keep a careful eye on usage statistics, especially early on when usage patterns are being established. Be alert for signs of inappropriate configuration, such as a low cache hit percentage or a high amount of unsaved data in the cache. Make sure that your network bandwidth continues to be adequate.

MONITOR EVENT LOGS

Check the application event logs periodically to make sure things are operating smoothly. If you want to be especially proactive, and have some facility with operating system scripting, write a batch script that scans the event log for errors and emails you if errors appear in the log.

PERFORM REGULAR FILE MAINTENANCE

It's probably a wise idea to run the File Maintenance tool, available in FileMaker Developer, periodically. How often to run it depends on how heavily used your files are. A good rule of thumb is probably to perform file maintenance once per month. If your databases experience thousands or tens of thousands of transactions a month, you may wish to optimize your files as often as every couple of weeks.

KEEP CURRENT WITH SOFTWARE UPDATES

It should go without saying, but you'll want to keep current with all updates and patches to your operating system, and to all software packages installed on the server, including, of course, FileMaker Server itself.

CHAPTER 26

FILEMAKER DEVELOPER AND PLUG-INS

FileMaker Developer

As you evolve as a FileMaker developer, your need to extend FileMaker into different arenas will grow; your work may evolve to supporting mission-critical data applications, or you may run into a circumstance that FileMaker Pro alone cannot solve but might be extended to address. You might find yourself, for example, needing to build an asset management system with file plug-ins, exploring ways to manage drawing charts in FileMaker, wanting to deploy a specialized kiosk, or developing a library of functions that you can reuse and refine across a large solution.

This chapter explores FileMaker Developer and covers the variety of functions it offers. We recommend whenever possible using it as your authoring tool: The debugging tool is quite handy, and custom functions are an invaluable tool for nearly any solution. Although your end users will be fine working with FileMaker Pro, for any job that requires significant development, you will find having a copy of Developer on hand invaluable.

Although we cover using and deploying plug-ins, we do not go into the details of actually writing FileMaker plug-ins. Developer includes FileMaker's plug-in API and documentation.

NOTE

> If you are interested in authoring a plug-in, be sure to confirm that you're versed in how plug-ins work within FileMaker Pro and are familiar with writing software in C++.

Script Debugger

Software development is a challenge, and the mark of good developers is not how few bugs they let by, but rather how quickly they can isolate and deal with them. This isn't exaggeration; we'll take a good critical thinker and debugger any day. It's rare that something works on the first try—it's crossing the line to the second try that takes experience, skill, and a little help from FileMaker Developer.

The Script Debugger provides two valuable functions. First, after turning it on, you can launch a script (via the Scripts menu or a button) and then click the ScriptMaker icon at the upper right of the debugger dialog to be taken directly into ScriptMaker with the script in question selected. There's no need to go into Layout mode or scroll through all the scripts you've written.

Second, the Script Debugger enables you to step through a script and see it unfold just as if you were driving it manually. By "manually" we're referring to the idea that scripts in FileMaker essentially mimic and automate actions that you as a user could be taking. If you use the Script Debugger, you can control a script step by step just as though you were executing the script's actions yourself by hand. This is an effective way to spot problems. Notice in Figure 26.1 that two break points have been set. Breakpoints persist with scripts until they are cleared by the user.

Step (this script only)

Step into (includes subscripts)

Step out (back to calling script)

Figure 26.1
The Script Debugger
enables you to watch
and control the flow
of a script and by
demonstration
enables you to spot
problems.

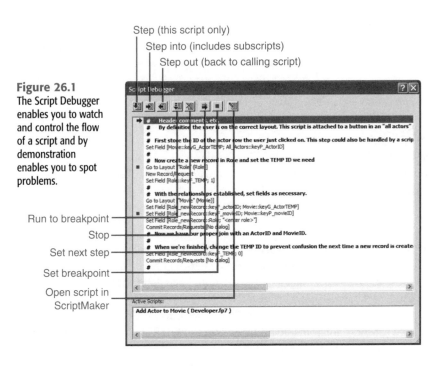

Run to breakpoint

Stop

Set next step

Set breakpoint

Open script in
ScriptMaker

Using the Script Debugger should be fairly straight-forward. Setting breakpoints (by clicking to the left of a given script step) enables you to skip ahead to trouble areas. Notice that the bottom pane of the dialog shows active scripts.

> **TIP**
>
> It's useful to begin and end every script with a comment. This then allows you to explicitly review a script when it is entered and exited (as a sub-script) before FileMaker performs an action.

→ To learn more about scripting, **see** Chapter 9, "Getting Started with Scripting," **p. 241**, and Chapter 15, "Advanced Scripting," **p. 421**.

→ To explore further the intricacies of script debugging, **see** "Troubleshooting Scripts and Calculations," **p. 485**.

Using the debugger, you'll step through each discrete step in a script. Behind the Script Debugger dialog you'll be able to see what happens as the script runs. Some of your scripts may be quite complex and include loops, If[] branches, and sub-scripts. The debugger's Step Into and Step Out controls enable you to follow the script routine into sub-scripts as you wish, and you can use breakpoints to skip through a loop that you know already works. (To do so, you set a breakpoint on the step following the conclusion of a loop and then click the Run to Breakpoint function.)

Set Next Step is quite helpful: It enables you to skip down to a particular point in your script, ignoring however many steps precede it. Simply select a script step and click the Set

Next Step button. The blue indicator moves from the top of the script (if you've just initiated the script) to whatever step you have selected. (All the intervening parts of the script are executed, of course.)

 For more help with diagnosing script problems with the Script Debugger, refer to "Script Debugger Control" in the Troubleshooting section at the end of this chapter.

DATABASE DESIGN REPORT

Documentation is always critically helpful in debugging as well, and additionally helps you simply come to understand a database with which you may not be familiar. The *Database Design Report*, or DDR, is a feature of FileMaker Developer that identifies every file reference, relationship, layout, script, value list, custom function, and security setting in a given set of files.

You can choose to export the report into XML or HTML, and we fully expect that by the time this book is in your hands, some third-party developers will have built tools to provide a DDR import into FileMaker Pro. Such a database would likely help with finding particular elements of a database (such as errors) by using FileMaker's find capabilities, and we'd expect more facile navigation than the DDR's HTML pages offer. We'd encourage you to hop online and see what tools are available for extending the DDR. It's a great resource and we fully expect tools surrounding it to evolve.

TIP

> You can also import the report into a FileMaker database yourself, after you get adept at writing style sheets for XML Import, as we describe in Chapter 22, "FileMaker and Web Services."

The DDR generates at least two output files: a summary file and a document for each of your database files. When running it you'll have the option of including and excluding files and functions as you need.

The DDR can be quite lengthy. The best way to make use of it is by performing searches for various specific elements. You can look for scripts that include a dependency on a given field, or look for relationships that use a given key field.

→ For a reference on some of the third party tools available, **see** Appendix A, "Additional Resources," **p. 799**.

The DDR is most frequently used in three main ways:

- To help familiarize yourself with a database that you didn't design or build.
- To help identify detritus that is no longer used in a given system (unused fields, old scripts).
- As a means of searching for all instances where a given element (script, field, relationship, table occurrence) is used.

The HTML-based version of the DDR is excellent for simply creating documentation for a solution. (We find that clients are favorably impressed if at the end of a project we hand them a DDR.)

Using either the XML or HTML version, it often also helps to search for explicit errors. Search for the strings <missing>, <unknown>, and so on.

If you're preparing to convert an old solution into FileMaker 7, the DDR is an invaluable way to troubleshoot and gain insight into both the old version and new version of your files. Searching for specific strings allows you to spot uses of bad characters, problematic uses of the Today function, and other trouble spots for conversion.

→ To learn more about migration issues and strategies, **see** Chapter 18, "Converting Systems from Previous Versions of FileMaker Pro," **p. 507**.

DEVELOPER UTILITIES

FileMaker Developer allows you to perform a range of functions on a grouped set of files; check Developer Utilities under the File menu. This third primary function of FileMaker Developer focuses largely on modifying your files in preparation for deployment. These options vary from renaming files to building a runtime kiosk. Review Figure 26.2 for an overview of the options available.

Figure 26.2
In the Developer Utilities dialog you're able to work with a group of files and apply various options or rename them.

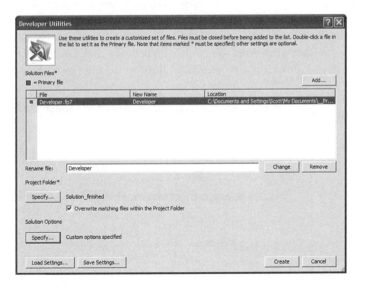

The mechanics of the dialog are fairly simple: Add all the files in a given solution to the dialog (they need to be closed for you to do so) and then specify a destination project folder. FileMaker Pro creates new files any time you use these utilities, so it needs to know where to put them.

You can opt to save your Solution Utility settings. Often solutions require multiple developer utility settings. By using the Load Settings and Save Settings buttons, you'll be able to save yourself the trouble of having to reenter all the various settings. This is quite helpful: This dialog includes a number of different options, and development and testing often requires running through the process multiple times.

RENAMING FILES

This might sound trivial, but don't let the apparent simplicity here deceive you. Multi-file solutions in FileMaker depend on filenames to maintain internal references. If you arbitrarily rename one of the files in a given solution via your operating system, FileMaker prompts you with a `File could not be found` error when it next tries to resolve a reference to that file. You can risk breaking table occurrence references, script references, value list references, and more. We very strongly recommend against manually renaming files.

> **TIP**
>
> If you run across a file that shows signs of having been incorrectly renamed or lost altogether, the DDR is a great place to turn in order to root out "file missing" problems.

→ To explore issues of file references in converting files from prior versions of FileMaker Pro, **see** "Fix File References," **p. 518**.

Rename your files by using the Developer Utilities dialog. Notice, as in Figure 26.3, you will need to add all the files for a given solution to the dialog. This is important: You need to add both the file you want to rename and all those files that reference it. Then set new names for however many files you require. When you click Create, FileMaker generates new files in your destination project folder, leaving the old files unchanged.

Figure 26.3
The files in this example have been prepared for renaming.

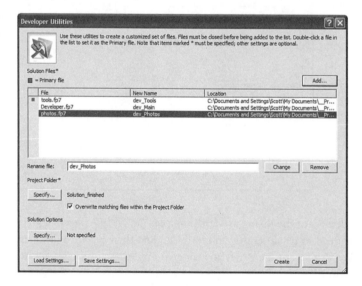

To learn how to manually address file name and reference problems, refer to "File Reference Errors" in the Troubleshooting section at the end of this chapter.

SOLUTION OPTIONS

Under the Solution Options button you'll find a range of actions that FileMaker Developer can perform as it creates a new solution (and a new set of files). All these options generally pertain to readying your files for deployment; they are not necessarily something you'd use during development, but rather at the end when you're preparing files to hand off to users (see Figure 26.4).

Figure 26.4
Solution options enable you to prepare a set of files for deployment with options beyond simply posting to a server.

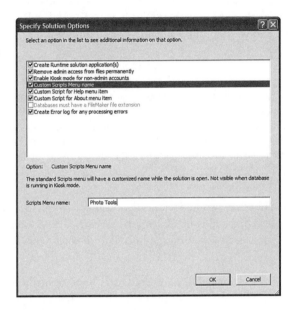

CREATE RUNTIME APPLICATION

FileMaker Developer enables you to bind a set of files into a *runtime application*—one that includes the FileMaker "engine" and does not require that the user buy a copy of FileMaker Pro to make use of the solution you've built. This is a great way to create distributable software with FileMaker Pro, and FileMaker, Inc.'s licensing terms allow you to do so without further obligation.

> **NOTE**
>
> FileMaker Developer's licensing details for runtime solutions can be found in the Licensing PDF you'll find in the root folder of your FileMaker Developer installation.

You'll need to keep some conditions in mind. A bound runtime version does not support development, works only with the files bound with it, and is single-user only. If end users want to share the files, they need to turn to FileMaker Server and standard copies of FileMaker Pro. To be specific, the resultant runtime application you create does not include Layout mode, ScriptMaker, and the Define Database functions, thus disallowing further editing of the files.

26

The changes illustrated thus far do not, however, significantly alter your FileMaker files from the originals. The database files within the application remain FileMaker Pro files, accessible from FileMaker Pro proper (assuming you've not disabled such access via the Remove Admin Access solution option that is covered later in this section). You can continue to work with your files, add features, and simply deploy the files themselves without having to recreate a runtime solution each and every time a change is called for. Likewise, you can have some users make use of the runtime applications and still others access separate copies of the files (or share files) with full versions of FileMaker Pro. It's rare that you'd build a database that could be used in both single-user and multi-user modes, but the point here is that it's possible.

> **NOTE**
>
> Some bound runtime solutions require a good bit of data entry prior to their being ready to distribute to a wide audience. It can be convenient to host the files—just as they are— on a FileMaker Server to allow multiple people to enter data. The fact that the FileMaker files themselves are unaltered by the binding process means you can swap them between a bound runtime application and FileMaker Pro or Server as needed.

Binding into a runtime imposes two important modifications to the files: Your files will be renamed with a new file suffix, and your files will be associated with a bind key. There are other options as well, but these two settings are mandatory when you've opted to create a runtime solution.

BIND KEYS   To have the runtime application recognize its associated files, the *bind key* in a given file needs to match the bind key of the application. This simple pairing ensures that a given application will "authorize" use of specific FileMaker Pro files. Notice in Figure 26.5 that FileMaker Developer inserts a timestamp by default as a bind key.

Figure 26.5
Runtime solutions depend on you to specify a "bind key" and allow you to add a customized closing image as well.

To replace or add a file to a solution that has already been bound, use the same bind key when preparing that new file, and users will be able to drop the file in question directly into their solution folders. You need not replace their entire solutions.

Consider cases where you'd want to be able to add files to a solution to upgrade functionality or address bugs. This introduces the complex issue of upgrade paths in a FileMaker Pro solution. You need to remember that after someone begins using your solution, he will be adding and storing data in your files. If you were to simply replace those files with no concern for exporting or managing that data, users would open their applications and discover an empty shell waiting again for the first records to be created.

In addition to managing bind keys, runtime solutions also enable you to define a custom closing image users will see for some matter of seconds before the application closes. If you choose to include a custom closing image, size it for 382×175 pixels at 72 dpi. JPEG and GIF both work best in cross-platform environments; others we don't recommend.

One last note: The process of creating a runtime solution is platform specific. The Windows version of FileMaker Developer creates a Windows runtime application, and likewise the Mac OS X version creates a runtime that works only on Mac OS X. These platform dependencies apply to only the runtime application itself: FileMaker files themselves remain completely cross-platform.

DATABASE EXTENSION   The extension for FileMaker-bound runtime solutions determines, in both Mac OS X and Windows, what application becomes associated with your individual solution files—which by definition is the runtime application you're in the process of creating. Think of the extension as quite similar to your bind key, but rather than work internally with the FileMaker runtime, they apply at the operating system level. These file extensions simply help identify the application that should open your files and differentiate them from other FileMaker Pro documents.

Mac OS X uses four-character extensions (creator codes) and FileMaker simply inserts an uppercase *F* after the first character. (usr becomes uFsr.) On Mac OS X, we recommend registering your creator code with Apple: http://developer.apple.com/dev/cftype/find.html.

On Windows a somewhat incomplete check can be found directly via http://shell.windows.com/fileassoc/0409/xml/redir.asp?Ext=fp7 (where the last three letters are the extension you want to investigate.) Another source of information can be found at http://filext.com/.

REMOVING ADMIN ACCESS

This function often goes hand-in-hand with creating a runtime solution, but doesn't necessarily have to. To prevent anyone—including yourself—from changing the files in a given solution (regardless of whether or not you intend to bind them into a runtime), it is possible to remove all admin (or better, perhaps, "developer") access to a set of files.

26

CAUTION

There's no going back after you've removed the access, so be certain you have all the kinks worked out of your solution, and keep your original files backed up!

You'll remove access to the dialogs for Define Database, Value Lists, File References, Accounts & Privileges, and Custom Functions. Access to Layout mode and ScriptMaker are also removed.

In addition, removing admin access removes any accounts set up explicitly with the [Full Access] privilege set. This is quite important because it actually modifies the account and privilege settings of your files. Your "developer" account will be removed. If you have written scripts that depend on a certain account being there, you need to be careful in how you accomplish such functions. You also need to ensure you *yourself* have a password that will allow you into the solution after you've run this process.

It's possible to define an account and assign a custom privilege set that has the equivalent of all access without assigning it to the built-in [Full Access] set, but keep in mind that, again, the ability to use all editing functions will be removed from the files. Those menu options, regardless of the account you used to sign in, will be grayed out.

→ For a complete understanding of security in FileMaker 7, **see** Chapter 12, "Implementing Security," **p. 315**.

TIP

We recommend, at a minimum, making certain there's a good way to export all data from a solution before removing admin access. Just write a scripted routine that saves all records to XML files. This at least ensures that you can extract data from a "locked down" version of your system.

ENABLING KIOSK MODE

Kiosks are good ways to present users with completely encapsulated user experiences. One of our favorite projects was building a wine recommendation service for grocery stores using touch-screen input.

Kiosk mode allows FileMaker Pro to open full-screen, with no toolbars or menus. On Windows and Mac OS X, the Taskbar and Dock, respectively, become unavailable as well. This has the effect of taking over the entire computer environment and allowing you to build complete appliances that serve a specific purpose. If you combine kiosk mode with an alternate means of data input—touch screen input, bar code readers, or other devices—the result can be something that very much departs from what you might think of as a "database."

Securing Kiosk Mode

Kiosk mode does not completely lock down a computer. On Windows, users can still Alt-Tab to different running processes. The way to avoid this is to simply establish FileMaker Pro as the only running application. Also, on Windows a Ctrl+Alt+Delete calls forward Windows' task manager, and the Windows key on current keyboards brings forward the Start menu. You need to take additional steps to lock down Windows.

If you plan on deploying many kiosks, this would be tedious, but you can use a system utility such as `gpedit` on Windows XP to lock access to various elements such as the Alt key, Start menu, and so on.

Another approach is to use a third-party utility such as WinControl:
`http://www.salfeld.com/body_details_win_control.htm`.

On Mac OS X, this is not as much an issue. Kiosk mode properly takes control of the computer environment, but there are still back-doors, not the least of which is simply pulling the power cable of the computer in question.

In general, though, keep in mind that kiosk mode is meant to facilitate a storefront experience especially geared toward touch-screen input, and is not focused on delivering perfect security.

When preparing a solution for kiosk mode, you need to consider a number of unique issues, not the least of which are important user interface elements. Because FileMaker's menus are inaccessible in kiosk mode, a vital requirement is to offer users a means for at least exiting the application. Without a scripted quit routine, users have to force-quit the application and may lose data as a result.

Being able to exit the application, though, is just the first requirement. Any function you'd like users to be able to perform needs to have been scripted and attached to a layout object (such as a button). You can opt to leave the FileMaker Status Area open if you wish, but none of FileMaker's native keyboard shortcuts will work (for, say, creating or deleting records).

Most kiosks offer a complete set of scripted functions attached to a custom-crafted user interface, and very rarely do developers opt to leave the Status Area open. Therefore, you need to create scripts and buttons for navigating from layout to layout, for creating records, for managing any importing or exporting of data, and for dealing with upgrading the files themselves, if necessary.

Here again we've introduced layers of complexity: After a kiosk is deployed to end users (it need not be a kiosk—it could just be a copy of a FileMaker database you're distributing widely), you leave the world of modifying and managing workgroup solutions and enter the world of commercial development where your ability to "tweak things" becomes exponentially more difficult. This then means that a solution either needs to be completely tested and perfect before it goes out the door or that you craft and implement an upgrade strategy that allows you to pass new functionality to your users without leaving them lost, with no means of preserving whatever data they may have input. This strategy could be as simple as exporting all data from the old version and importing into the new, or you could build a distributed file system where it's possible to replace certain files without altering the data itself.

→ For ideas on user interface approaches, **see** Chapter 13, "Advanced Layout Techniques," **p. 353**.

26

SOLUTION CUSTOMIZATION

When distributing a custom solution, you can better tailor its look-and-feel by creating a custom Script menu name, and assigning specific scripts to both the Help and About menu options.

These custom scripts allow you a fair degree of control over your solution: You could write a complete help system that might include opening a FileMaker Pro file or interface in itself. Users might then be able to perform find requests and employ other familiar approaches to using your system. The About menu could be as simple as a window with an image or logo that is brought forward, or you could get as fancy as a QuickTime movie that is played from within a container field.

The opportunity FileMaker Developer gives you is to truly customize a solution so that it takes on an identity of its own.

TIP

> This might seem a minor point, but we've found that if you take pains to give your solutions a name and add even simple levels of customization, end users more easily accept the system that they will then presumably spend a good percentage of their work lives using.
>
> It's also somewhat helpful in getting users and IT folk to differentiate FileMaker Pro—the technology—from your specific solution. If you name and modestly customize it, you foster a better sense of differentiation by creating an identity other than "the FileMaker database."

ERROR LOG

A good habit to run in all cases, the error log lists problems that arose while FileMaker Developer performed its functions in the creation of new files. To generate a log, simply turn on this option while utilizing developer utilities. A text file named `LogFile.txt` is created in your solution folder. Some of the developer utility processes run into errors that don't prompt dialogs, and thus it's a good idea to check the log before wrapping up a solution for end users.

The errors you'll find in the log are

- `Updating File Specs for this destination file skipped due to a previous fatal error.`

- `Destination file could not be created, and all further processing on it was skipped. File:`

- `Skipped runtime generation, due to missing or damaged resources.`

- `Destination folder could not be created, and all further processing was skipped. Folder name:`

As you can see, these aren't particularly illuminating and generally indicate you have a significant problem with the interaction between your OS and FileMaker's processes. In testing for these conditions, a full hard drive was the cause for some of these issues.

CUSTOM FUNCTIONS

FileMaker Developer enables you to create custom functions that then work just as other calculation functions do: You can pass parameters to them and get an evaluated result in return. Although they are authored in FileMaker Developer, conceptually they belong with calculation functions.

→ To learn about authoring custom functions and how to put them to use, **see** "Custom Functions," **p. 409**.

To create a custom function, simply go to the File menu, choose Define and then Custom Functions. You first see a dialog that lists all the custom functions you've defined thus far, and that allows you to add a new function to your list or edit an existing one.

Custom functions can be defined only with FileMaker Developer, but they can be used by any FileMaker Pro application or runtime.

Keep in mind that they're file specific. If you have a multi-file solution, you need to re-create the functions you plan on using in each file where they'll be needed.

FILE MAINTENANCE

File Maintenance, under the File menu, offers two additional functions in FileMaker Developer: Compact File and Optimize File. Their explanations are fairly clear: Compact File removes any unused space and Optimize File performs essentially a defragmentation of a file's internal structure and also re-indexes the indices in a file. The two can be performed together and lead to improved performance for disk-related access to a given file. We recommend doing this periodically.

For more details on when to use File Maintenance, refer to "File Maintenance and Performance Slow-Downs" in the Troubleshooting section at the end of this chapter.

→ To explore indices and understand how they relate to data architecture, **see** "Storage and Indexing," **p. 82**.

PLUG-INS

Plug-ins extend FileMaker Pro's capabilities and are quite varied. Their offerings range from charting functionality, OS-level file manipulation, bar code readers, scientific math functions, credit card authentication, help systems, telephony, and more.

NOTE

We encourage you to visit `http://www.filemaker.com/plugins/index.html` to explore the full breadth of plug-ins.

We won't describe specific plug-ins here; a wide range of professionally supported plug-ins are available, many of which we use frequently in our consulting practice, but one could write an entire book on that topic alone. For the purposes here, we cover briefly the concepts you need to keep in mind for all plug-ins.

Plug-ins are written and compiled in accordance with FileMaker Pro's plug-in API. They're not something many FileMaker developers will ever need to create, and you generally do not have access to the code from which they're built.

If you want to delve into writing your own plug-ins, you need to be an expert in either the C or C++ languages. (We don't recommend a FileMaker plug-in as your first C++ project!) You also need a development environment, such as CodeWarrior for the Mac or Visual Studio for Windows, and the plug-in API documentation and example files that ship with FileMaker Developer. Plug-ins are platform specific, so if you want your plug-in to work on both Mac and Windows, you need to do at least some re-engineering to get your code to compile and run correctly on both Mac and Windows.

As in all third-party software products, we recommend you get to know a given plug-in well and test it along with the rest of your solution before deploying. Another obvious consideration is cost: Some of your clients might benefit from utilizing a plug-in, but remember that this is third-party software and many require purchasing licenses.

UNDERSTANDING PLUG-INS

Plug-ins work by adding external functions to your calculation functions list. Generally, but not always, they take a single text parameter. The result of the plug-in is then delivered in the form of a calculation result.

Here's the general approach:

```
Set Field [table::fieldname; External ("Plug-in_Function"; "Text_Parameter")]
```

In the case of FileMaker's example plug-in, an actual external call looks like this:

```
XMpl_Add( numberInput1; numberInput2 )
```

If you use this plug-in function, it returns two numbers added together.

The plug-in function is a string specific to the plug-in with which you're working. Its syntax is governed by the plug-in, and (if it followed proper FileMaker, Inc., conventions) includes the name of the plug-in as well. In this case, XMpl_ is the prefix FileMaker chose for its example plug-in. Likewise the expected parameters passed as text vary widely from none to complex data arrays. FileMaker Pro 7's new data storage limit of 2GB per field means that we could be facing some quite complex programming within the realm of a single text field. One of our favorite charting plug-ins requires that a complex array of information be passed to both format and then populate the charts it returns.

When called, the results of a plug-in are returned as a calculation result, but often some other action may be performed as well. For example, a dialog may appear. Often the calculation field simply serves as a means for passing error conditions.

For example, a plug-in might copy an image file from one directory to another. Or it might display a dialog of some kind. Or it might create a chart image and place it on your clipboard. The possibilities are nearly endless and we recommend, again, exploring available plug-ins to understand specific cases.

USING FILEMAKER'S SAMPLE PLUG-IN

FileMaker Developer includes a sample plug-in, including the C++ library and code necessary for building it. It offers some basic functions that should get you thinking about what plug-ins are capable of.

- XMpl_Add—Adds two numbers together. Totally superfluous when you'd always use a calculation to do so, but serves as the most basic example of a plug-in function.

- XMpl_Append—Appends the contents of one text field to another. You can continue to add parameters to the function. It simply appends all those that you pass it. Again, redundant with the "&" operator.

- XMpl_NumToWords—Converts a number (1111) to words (One Thousand, One Hundred and Eleven).

- XMpl_StartScript—Initiates a script as specified by filename and script name.

- XMpl_UserFormatNumber—Reformats a number based on user preference. The plug-in's default is a standard (111) 222-3333 North American phone number.

The sections that follow discuss the process of installing and configuring plug-ins in FileMaker.

INSTALLING PLUG-INS

There are two distinct types of plug-ins: server based and client based. Deployment is consistent between the two: To enable a plug-in, it needs to be placed in the Extensions folder with the FileMaker application folder for each client, regardless of whether or not it is a server- or client-based plug-in. In addition to each client, server-based plug-ins need to be deployed to the Extensions folder on the server as well. (This is true for both Windows and Mac OS X platforms.)

 If your plug-in is not responding, refer to "Plug-in Not Responding or Not Installing" in the Troubleshooting section at the end of this chapter.

DEPLOYING PLUG-INS VIA FILEMAKER SERVER

FileMaker Server offers auto-update functionality that copies a plug-in from the server machine onto a client computer when a requisite plug-in is either out of date or missing altogether on the client. This saves a great number of headaches and makes it possible to seamlessly fold a plug-in into a workgroup solution.

The functions that manage auto-update are called by scripts and require, ironically, that the Auto-Update plug-in be installed and enabled on all client computers. (Fortunately it is installed and enabled by default with FileMaker Pro and FileMaker Developer.)

26

→ For a full discussion of using plug-ins with FileMaker Server, **see** "Automatically Updating Plug-ins,"
p. 760.

CONFIGURING AND ENABLING PLUG-INS

To enable a particular plug-in, visit the Preferences dialog within your FileMaker Pro (or Developer) application. Notice that to use a given plug-in you need to explicitly enable it (by marking its respective check box), as shown in Figure 26.6.

Figure 26.6
Plug-ins are enabled and configured via the Preferences dialog.

Notice also that your Auto Update plug-in is enabled in this list as well. It is here that you can find all the plug-ins available for a given client.

Some plug-ins offer configuration choices (see Figure 26.7). Every plug-in is different; here we're using the example plug-in that ships with FileMaker Developer, FM.

Figure 26.7
FileMaker's Example plug-in gives users the option to specify a number format for one of its functions in its configuration attributes.

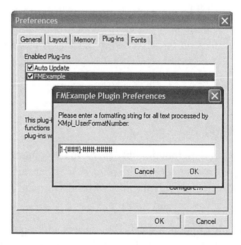

If you've just enabled or installed a plug-in, you'll need to close and restart your FileMaker Pro client to gain access to its external functions.

TROUBLESHOOTING

SCRIPT DEBUGGER CONTROL

Even with the Script Debugger turned on, it's difficult to see what my script is doing until it's too late and the action is already finished. How can I make it more clear?

By definition, the Script Debugger helps iron out problems with scripts, but if you're having difficulty seeing how scripts and sub-scripts flow, insert some benign comments into your scripts, so that it is possible to see your script advancing and stepping into and out of sub-scripts without having to actually perform actions until you're ready to see them.

It's helpful to place the fields your scripts are interacting with on layouts so that you can visually confirm that the scripts are working as you'd predict.

FILE REFERENCE ERRORS

I renamed my files, but still seem to have problems with missing files. How can I manipulate my file references by hand?

If you encounter problems with file references, where you get "file missing" error messages when FileMaker Pro opens your database solution or you notice such in your DDR, we recommend first working with the Define File References dialog, (Define, File References, under the File menu). You may be able to simply re-point a file reference to repair some issues. In other cases you may need to manually reestablish connections; to identify all such places where that will be necessary, refer to the DDR.

Again this is a symptom of a file having been manually renamed at the OS level. The Rename Files function in FileMaker Developer is a great way to rename files all you like; we encourage you to use it whenever this is necessary.

FILE MAINTENANCE AND PERFORMANCE SLOW-DOWNS

When should I use the File Maintenance functions?

If you find that disk access is slowing down your database, we recommend using the File Maintenance functions. It's useful to do so periodically, but you should certainly use the function after deleting a large batch of records, prior to archiving a given file, after deleting a number of fields, or perhaps after moving around large chunks of data by whatever means (import, export, a long loop, for example).

PLUG-IN NOT RESPONDING OR NOT INSTALLING

My plug-in isn't working. Where do I start to diagnose and fix the problem?

Issues with plug-ins can be difficult to troubleshoot. If a plug-in isn't responding, check first to see that you have the latest version, and make sure that it is enabled on your client computer. Restarting FileMaker Pro (or Developer) after adding a plug-in to the extensions folder is also a necessary first step.

Beyond that, your testing has to encompass the functionality of the plug-in itself. You may, for example, be struggling with a plug-in written for a prior version of FileMaker Pro. FileMaker Pro 7's plug-in API is largely compatible with FileMaker 6 and earlier, but not perfectly.

When using the Auto Update feature, one of the most common mistakes to make is forgetting to turn on the Auto Update option at the server itself.

FILEMAKER EXTRA: THE LIMITS OF CUSTOMIZATION

Using the tools in FileMaker Developer, you can customize your solutions to a considerable degree. However, there are still some limitations on what you can accomplish in using FileMaker Developer to create something like a "shrink-wrap" software experience. This section explores some of those limitations and what you can do to overcome them.

LACK OF MULTI-USER CAPABILITY

As we mentioned earlier, FileMaker solutions that are bound into runtime applications cannot be shared among multiple users. Each copy of a bound runtime application can be installed and used on only one computer, and multiple copies of the same runtime application can't share data.

There is an exception to this rule. If you have a copy of FileMaker Server and you configure it to allow the hosting of runtime solutions, you can then share a bound solution such that users with the FileMaker Pro software can open and work with the files. This technique, of course, removes much of the reason for creating a bound runtime in the first place, because one goal is to allow the distribution of FileMaker-based software to users who don't have a copy of FileMaker Pro.

Ironically, bound FileMaker runtime applications once had multiuser capabilities (back in the days of FileMaker 3!), but those capabilties were removed from bound solutions starting around FileMaker 4. If you feel (as many do) that this is an important and useful feature, by all means start lobbying FileMaker, Inc., to add the feature back in. You also might want to decide what you think the feature is worth to you or should cost. In all likelihood, there was an element of revenue protection in FileMaker, Inc.'s decision to remove the feature, so give some thought to what you think a fair pricing structure might look like, because they're sure to ask!

LACK OF MENU CUSTOMIZATION

Developers often bemoan the lack of much menu customization in FileMaker. Using FileMaker's Accounts and Privileges, you can perform some limited customization of menus: You can limit users to "editing" menu commands only (Cut, Copy, Paste, Clear, and so on), or you can inhibit access to all menu items. Of course, what many developers would like is the ability to enable or disable individual menu items selectively based on user privileges.

FileMaker Developer doesn't really improve on that situation. Kiosk mode will completely remove the menu bar, of course, and you can also rename the Scripts menu and attach specific scripts to the Help and About menu items. However, that's the extent of the extra menu capabilities afforded by Developer.

Further customization of menus *is* possible, though, using third-party plug-ins. SecureFM and MenuMagic, both from New Millennium Communications (www.nmci.com), address these issues, as does MenuControl from Dacons (www.dacons.net).

NOTE

> As with all plug-ins, you'll want to look at these carefully and weigh whether they have the right features you need. Plug-ins aren't guaranteed in any way by FileMaker, Inc., so do your homework! Also, be sure to check out www.filemaker.com/plugins/ for a large database of currently available plug-ins.

LACK OF EVENT TRIGGERS

The term *event triggers* refers to the ability to associate program logic (such as running a script) with specific kinds of user interaction events (such as tabbing out of a field while doing data entry). In a system that supports event triggers, it would be possible to specify that a particular script be run every time a user exited a field, or every time a user submitted or deleted a record.

FileMaker doesn't yet support event triggers (though we hope they're toiling away on them behind the scenes!), but this doesn't mean that such functionality can't be achieved. Again, you'll want to look into a plug-in that can accomplish some or all of this task. Several useful candidates are listed in the Scripting section of the FileMaker, Inc., plug-ins list (www.filemaker.com/plugins/Scripting.html). Each of these plug-ins will have its strengths and limitations, so here again, due diligence is called for.

26

PART **VI**

APPENDIXES

ADDITIONAL RESOURCES

In this appendix

GENERAL INFORMATION ON RELATIONAL DATABASES

"A Relational Model of Data for Large Shared Data Banks," by E. F. Codd. The relational model was first conceived by E. F. Codd and presented in this paper. This is the paper that started the entire relational database industry. Originally published in 1970 in CACM 13, No. 6, this paper is now available online ($10 at the time of this writing) as a PDF file through the ACM Digital Library:

http://portal.acm.org/citation.cfm?id=362685&coll=portal&dl=ACM&CFID=16185674

We didn't delve too deeply into relational database theory in this book. If you'd like to read up on the roots of the relational model (set theory and predicate logic), a pretty readable math book is *Discrete Mathematics* by Richard Johnsonbaugh (ISBN: 0-13-089008-1). We have found it to be very succinct on the topics of set theory and predicate logic.

An Introduction to Database Systems by C.J. Date (ISBN: 0-32-119784-4) is a classic overview of database systems with an emphasis on relational database systems. You should consider it essential reading if you want to know your craft well.

DATA MODELING AND DATABASE DESIGN

Data Modeling for Information Professionals by Bob Schmidt (ISBN: 0-13-080450-9). This gets into much more than just data modeling, but the content is great.

The Data Modeling Handbook by Michael Reingruber and William Gregory (ISBN: 0-471-05290-6). This book gets a lot more into the data modeling design process.

Handbook of Relational Database Design by Candace Fleming and Barbara von Halle (ISBN: 0-201-11434-8). This book has full coverage of design methodologies.

The Rational Unified Process, An Introduction, by Philippe Kruchten (ISBN: 0-201-70710-1) or *The Unified Modeling Language User Guide* by Grady Booch, James Rumbaugh, and Ivar Jacobson (ISBN: 0-201-57168-4). The Rational Unified Process, or RUP, is an end-to-end methodology for software design. It's overkill for most FileMaker projects, but it can be mined for many useful insights that apply to smaller projects.

Extreme Programming Explained, by Kent Beck (ISBN: 0-201-61641-6) and *Extreme Programming in Practice*, by James Newkirk and Robert C. Martin (ISBN: 0-201-70937-6). Although FileMaker Pro database development isn't completely compatible with Extreme Programming, there are many useful ideas to be had here, especially in the area of estimating time required to complete tasks.

Code Complete, by Steve McConnell (ISBN: 1-5561-5484-4). It's ten years old, but still an extremely solid, fundamental book on good programming practices. It's oriented toward languages like C, but includes plenty of useful information for developers in any language. Anything by McConnell is likely to be very good. You might also try his more recent *Rapid Development* (ISBN: 1-5561-5900-5) or *Professional Software Development* (ISBN: 0321193679).

Practical Software Requirements, by Benjamin L. Kovitz (ISBN: 1-884777-59-7). An extremely useful and readable book about developing requirements for software, including plenty of information useful to database developers. Nice discussions of data modeling, among many other topics.

RUNNING A FILEMAKER CONSULTING PRACTICE

Managing the Professional Service Firm by David H. Maister (ISBN: 0-684-83431-6). Maister is The Man. If you run or work in a consulting company, this is an essential book that will open your eyes. It explores every aspect of the running of a service firm.

The Trusted Advisor by David H. Maister, Charles H. Green, and Robert M. Galford (ISBN: 0-743-21234-7). More conceptual than the other book, it still offers plenty of food for thought for database consultants.

GENERAL RESOURCES FOR TIPS AND TRICKS

The Moyer Group: `http://www.moyergroup.com/`

Pridian Consulting: `http://www.pridianconsulting.com/`

The home sites of the authors of this book, these sites contain white papers and how-to files.

FileMaker Pro Advisor: `http://filemakeradvisor.com/`

For years, FileMaker Advisor has been the place to look for product announcements, news about upcoming FileMaker conferences, product reviews, and tips and tricks.

ISO FileMaker Magazine: `http://www.filemakermagazine.com/`

ISO Productions has been publishing tips and tricks longer than just about anyone. This site has two levels of content: one for the general public and one for subscribers only.

A FileMaker Affliction: `http://www.afilemakeraffliction.com/`

LeSaux Media Services has a great site full of useful free articles and examples, along with sneak peeks at guides and training videos they have available for purchase.

Database Pros: `http://www.databasepros.com/index.html`

Database Pros has the largest collection of FileMaker templates and technique examples on the Internet. Especially if you're still learning FileMaker Pro, you should bookmark this site.

FileMaker TechInfo database: `http://www.filemaker.com/support/techinfo.html`

FileMaker, Inc., publishes its own technical support database online. It contains thousands of articles to help you troubleshoot problems and to help you learn the important details about seldom-visited corners of FileMaker Pro's feature set.

Data Concepts Tips: `http://www.dwdataconcepts.com/dwdctips.htm`

Don Wieland has created dozens of tips in the form of free downloadable example files. He has separate versions for Windows and Mac.

A

FileMaker World Web Ring: http://1.webring.com/hub?ring=fmpring

This Web Ring links together more than 150 Web sites with FileMaker-themed content.

FileMaker Developers: http://www.filemaker.com/developers/fsa_members.html

Trying to find a FileMaker developer or trainer in your part of the world? This site has a list of consultants and trainers in more than 20 different countries.

HOSTING FILEMAKER DATABASES ON THE WEB

FileMaker ISPs: http://www.filemaker.com/support/isp.html

After you've created a FileMaker-based Web solution, you need to host it on a server that's connected to the Internet. If you or your client doesn't have such a server, you can find a FileMaker Pro Web Hosting provider at this link.

FILEMAKER NEWS SOURCES

FileMaker Now: http://www.filemaker.com/news/newsletter.html

FileMaker Now is a Web-based newsletter published by FileMaker, Inc. It contains news about product announcements and upcoming events, as well as a tech support Q&A.

FM NewsWire: http://www.fmnewswire.com/

Another service provided by ISO Productions, the FM Newswire is exactly what it sounds like. It lists training announcements, product update announcements, and other FileMaker-related news stories.

FMPro.org: http://www.fmpro.org/

The Hot FileMaker Pro News section lists FileMaker-related product announcements and user group meetings.

PLUG-INS

FileMaker Plug-in Directory: http://www.filemaker.com/plugins/

FileMaker's own site has the most complete listing of available plug-ins. If you need to find out whether a specialized plug-in even exists, this is the place to start. Although there are many plug-in developers, the following publishers have some of the largest selections.

New Millenium Communications: http://www.nmci.com/Products.htm

New Millennium has revised versions of all of their plug-ins to make them compatible with FileMaker Pro 7. They will also be maintaining a Web page that lists all plug-ins that are on the market (not just theirs), with a field for their FileMaker Pro 7 status (FileMaker Pro 7-compatible version available, FileMaker Pro 7 version announced, FileMaker Pro 7 version not announced) along with URLs for the sites of the developers. The URL is `http://www.filemakerplugins.com`.

As of this writing, New Millenium anticipated the following plug-ins would be available at the same time as the release of FileMaker Pro 7, or within a month of the release:

SecureFM: Allows developers to disable menus and keyboard shortcuts in FileMaker Pro.

SecureFM with MenuMagic: Has the same functionality as SecureFM, but with the additional capability to customize FileMaker Pro menus.

DialogMagic: Allows for enhanced control of standard FileMaker Pro dialogs.

ExportFM: Enables developers to export images, sound, and movie files in their native formats.

Troi Automatisering: `http://www.troi.com/`

Troi Activator Plug-in: Controls scripts on different computers, includes scheduling capabilities.

Troi Coding Plug-in: Adds capability to use DES encryption to encrypt and decrypt fields.

Troi Dialog Plug-in: Allows use of dynamic dialogs, including calculation-based progress bars and up to nine input fields.

Troi File Plug-in: Works with files from within a database. Enables saving and reading of files and the capability to use file and folder information.

Troi Serial Plug-in: Adds the capability to read and write to serial ports.

Troi Text Plug-in: Includes XML parsing and a variety of powerful text manipulation tools.

Troi URL Plug-in: Fills in Web forms and retrieves raw data from any HTTP URL.

Troi ClipSave Plug-in: Saves and restores the clipboard.

Troi Grabber Plug-in: Records images and video from a video camera and puts them in container fields.

Troi Graphic Plug-in: Adds color container creation, screen shot capture, and thumbnail creation.

Troi Number Plug-in: Adds Dynamic Balance Functions.

Troi Ranges Plug-in: Generates date and number ranges between endpoints.

Waves in Motion: `http://www.wmotion.com`

Most of the not-revised plug-ins will continue to work in FileMaker 7. The following plug-ins will be enhanced or re-engineered for compatibility with FileMaker 7:

Charts: Current version will continue to work. Users should specify the table name, not the filename.

A

eAuthorize: Allows users to authorize credit cards securely from within FileMaker. The current version supports U.S. protocols; the FMNext version will support credit card processing in England and Australia as well.

Events: Triggers scripts based on specified scheduling. Re-engineering for FileMaker 7 will ensure additional reliability.

Date & Time: Allows for extended indexing of data and time data, includes a reservation system.

String Functions: Allows for complex string manipulation and management.

Portal Filter: Allows developers to use specific criteria to filter portals.

Smartcard: Integrates Smart Card media with FileMaker Pro for additional security or data portability.

FileTools: Provides complete file management for file-related tasks.

Variables: Creates dynamic memory variables that can be used to store temporary data.

DEVELOPER TOOLS

Chaparral Software: http://www.chapsoft.com/

Chaparral Software publishes two tools that assist developers with the analysis of existing database solutions as well as the migration of data:

Brushfire: Creates an easy-to-read HTML document illustrating script relationships, designed to aid in refactoring. Aids in migration from FileMaker 6 to FileMaker 7.

EZxslt: Produces perfectly formatted Microsoft Word documents by generating XSLT stylesheets based on templates. Allows for a better way to do mail merges, contracts, and more.

ERwin: http://www3.ca.com/Solutions/Product.asp?ID=260

ERwin is a Windows-only data modeling tool published by Computer Associates.

Visio: http://www.microsoft.com/office/visio/prodinfo/default.mspx

Visio, published by Microsoft, is a Windows-only technical diagramming tool that does a great job on entity-relationship (ER) diagrams.

OmniGraffle: http://www.omnigroup.com/applications/omnigraffle/

OmniGraffle, published by The Omni Group, is a Mac OS X–based diagramming and charting tool that also does a great job on ER diagrams.

WinA&D & MacA&D: http://www.excelsoftware.com

WinA&D and MacA&D, published by Excel Software, are CASE tools, useful for generating ER diagrams.

A

MetadataMagic: http://www.nmci.com/Products.htm

MetadataMagic, published by New Millenium, is an outstanding database analysis tool. The File Reference Fixer feature is an essential tool for assisting with migration of pre-FileMaker 7 databases to the FileMaker 7 format.

Password Administrator: http://www.nmci.com/Products.htm

Password Administrator (possibly to be renamed as Account Administrator), also published by New Millenium, provides the capability to manage accounts and privilege sets across a multi-file solution, and it enables developers to ensure that all passwords in a multi-file solution are identical by case (all lower case, or a consistent mix of upper and lower case, and so on).

Conversion Problem Report Tool: http://www.nmci.com/Products.htm

Conversion Problem Report Tool, published by New Millenium, imports the conversion log that is generated when files are converted. It presents the important issues to the user, with appropriate ranking of significance, and provides an interface so that they can be grouped by category of problem, rather than only by file, as is the default.

WEB PROGRAMMING

If you're going to venture into Web deployments of FileMaker, you'll find it beneficial to be well read on Web programming technologies. Even if you're using only Instant Web Publishing, it helps to be very familiar with how the Web works. A good—though very exact and technical—discussion is *HTTP: The Definitive Guide*, (O'Reilly) by David Gourley, Brian Totty, et al. (ISBN: 1-56592-509-2). You can also consult the *HTTP Developer's Handbook* (SAMS) by Chris Shiflett (ISBN: 0-67232-454-7).

If you're getting into Custom Web Publishing, you'll likely be well served by a solid reference library on the fundamental Web technologies: HTML, JavaScript, and CSS. In general, we've found the books from O'Reilly Press (http://www.oreilly.com) to be impeccable. SAMS also has a strong lineup in this area. You can also sign up for a nifty e-book subscription service, Safari (http://safari.informit.com) to take these and other hefty volumes for a test drive.

XML/XSL

FileMaker XML Central: http://www.filemaker.com/xml. Here you'll find access to discussion groups and other resources for using XML with FileMaker, as well as a range of sample files.

XML.com: http://www.xml.com/. This site gives access to a wide range of XML resources.

Jeni Tennison's site: http://www.jenitennison.com/xslt/. Jeni Tennison is a very sharp XML author and consultant, and her personal pages contain many useful links, documents, and references.

A

We find a lot of the books from (the now defunct) Wrox Press to be quite good. You might want to look into *Beginning XML*, by David Hunter, et al. (ISBN: 0764543946) as well as *Professional XML*, by Mark Birbeck, et al. (ISBN: 1861003110), and *Beginning XSLT*, by Jeni Tennison (ISBN: 1861005946).

After you get further into XSLT you might also look at *Professional XSL*, by Kurt Cagle, et al. (ISBN: 1861003579) or *XSLT:Programmer's Reference*, by Michael Kay (ISBN: 0764543814). These books, even the beginning ones, are meaty and do presume some hands-on experience with some form of Web programming such as HTML, or similar experience and familiarity with Web technology. Out of all of these, Jeni Tennison's XSLT book may be the best starting point. She's extremely knowledgeable about the subject and a very effective writer. Her book is most likely out of print, but is probably available used. The other Wrox books, especially the multi-author ones, tend to mingle generally useful chapters with more specialized ones. As a reference work, though not a tutorial, you might consult *The XML Companion* (Addison-Wesley) by Neil Bradley (ISBN: 0-20177-059-8). The same goes for *Definitive XSLT and Xpath* (Prentice Hall PTR), by G. Ken Holman (ISBN: 0-13065-196-6). For a tour of the esoteric power of XSLT, check out *XSLT and XPath On The Edge* (Wiley) by Jeni Tennison (ISBN: 0-76454-776-3).

ODBC/JDBC

OpenLink: http://demo.openlinksw.com/

If you don't already have the appropriate drivers, OpenLink Software is the place to go for ODBC drivers for both Windows and Mac platforms. They have 30-day trial downloads so you can try before you buy.

JDBC: http://java.sun.com/products/jdbc/index.jsp

JDBC is Sun's Java-based cross-platform database access technology. Sun's main JDBC page gives a nice overview of the technology. You'll also find a link to Sun's driver database. It lists available drivers for dozens of different databases.

A

CALCULATION FUNCTION REFERENCE

Abs()

Category: Number

Syntax: Abs (number)

Parameters: number—any expression that resolves to a numeric value.

Description: Returns the absolute value of number; absolute value is always a positive number.

Examples:

Abs (Get (CurrentPlatform))

Returns 1 for MacOS and 2 for Windows.

Abs (RetailPrice - WholeSalePrice)

Returns the difference between the two prices, regardless of which is larger.

Atan()

Category: Trigonometric

Syntax: Atan (number)

Parameters: number—any expression that resolves to a numeric value.

Description: The arc tangent of a number is the angle (measured in radians) whose tangent is the specified number. The range of values returned by the Atan function is -(pi/2) to pi/2.

Examples:

Atan (0) = 0

Atan (1) = .785398163

which is pi/4 radians, or 45 degrees.

Comments:

If `Atan (x) = y`, then `Tan (y) = x`.

`Atan (x) = Atan (-x)`.

`Average()`

Category: Aggregate

Syntax: `Average ( field { ; field...} )`

Parameters: `field`—any related field, repeating field, or set of non-repeating fields that represent a collection of numbers. Parameters in curly braces { } are optional.

Description: Returns a numeric value that is the arithmetic mean of all non-blank values in the set designated by the parameter list. The arithmetic mean of a set of numbers is the sum of the numbers divided by the size of the set. Blank values are not considered as part of the set.

Examples:

`Average (field1 ; field2 ; field3 )`

Returns 2, when `field1` = 1, `field2` = 2, and `field3` = 3.

`Average (repeatingField)`

Returns 2, when `repetition1` = 1, `repetition2` = 2, and `repetition3` = 3.

`Average (Customer::InvoiceTotal)`

Returns $450, when a customer has three related invoice records with invoice totals of $300, $500, and $550.

Comments:

When the parameter list consists of 2 or more repeating fields, `Average()` generates a repeating field in which the corresponding repetitions from the specified fields are averaged separately. So, if a field `Repeater1` has two values, 16 and 20, and another field, `Repeater2`, has two values, 14 and 25, `Average (Repeater1; Repeater2)` would return a repeating field with values 15 and 22.5.

`Case()`

Category: Logical

Syntax: `Case ( test1 ; result1 { ; test2 ; result2 ; defaultResult ...} )`

Parameters: `test(n)`—an expression that yields a Boolean result; `result(n)`—the value to return if corresponding test is true; `defaultResult`—the value to return if all tests are false. Parameters in curly braces { } are optional.

Description: The `Case` function returns one of several possible results based on a series of tests.

Each test expression is evaluated in order, and when a True expression is found, the value specified in the result for that expression is returned. The function stops evaluating as soon as it finds a True test.

The default result at the end of the parameter list is optional. If none of the tests evaluate to True, the function returns the value specified for defaultResult. If no default result is specified, the Case function returns an "empty" result.

Examples:

```
Case ( IsEmpty ( Contact_Name ) ; 1)
```

Returns 1 if the Contact_Name field is empty. Note that a default value is not required, making the usage of Case() shorter than If().

```
Case(
  Get(SystemLanguage) = "French" ; "Bienvenue";
  Get(SystemLanguage) = "Italian" ; "Benvenuto" ;
  Get(SystemLanguage) = "German" ; "Willkommen" ;
  Get(SystemLanguage) = "Swedish" ; "Välkommen" ;
  Get(SystemLanguage) = "Spanish " ; "Bienvenido", ;
  Get(SystemLanguage) = "Dutch" ; "Welkom" ;
  Get(SystemLanguage) = "Japanese" ; "Irashaimasu" ;
  "Welcome" // default value
)
```

Returns a welcoming message in the language determined by the Get (SystemLanguage) function.

Comments:

Consider using hard returns in long Case() statements to make them more readable. Note that this example makes repeated calls to Get(SystemLanguage); in practice it might be better to use Let() to make a single call to Get(SystemLanguage) so that it needs to be evaluated only once.

Ceiling()

Category: Number

Syntax: Ceiling (number)

Parameters: number—any expression that resolves to a numeric value.

Description: Returns number rounded up to the next integer.

Examples:

```
Ceiling ( 1.05 ) = 2
Ceiling ( -4.6 ) = -4
Ceiling ( 3 ) = 3
```

Comments:

One common use for the Ceiling function is finding out how many pages will be required to print x items if y items fit on a page. The formula for this is Ceiling (x / y). For instance, if you have 16 items, and 5 can print per page, you would need Ceiling (16/5) = Ceiling (3.2) = 4 pages.

Choose()

Category: Logical

Syntax: Choose (test ; result0 { ; result1 ; result2...})

Parameters: test—an expression that returns a number greater than or equal to zero; result(n)—the expression that is evaluated based on the result of test. Parameters in curly braces {} are optional.

Description: Returns one of the result values, according to the integer value of test. FileMaker Pro evaluates test to obtain an index number, which is used to choose the corresponding ordinal result.

Because the Choose function is a 0-based list, the first item on the list is indexed 0 and the second item on the list is indexed 1. For example, if test evaluates to 2, then result2 is chosen. Any fractional value of test is ignored when obtaining the index number.

Examples:

```
Choose( DayOfWeek( Get (CurrentDate)) ; ""; "Sun"; "Mon"; "Tue"; "Wed"; "Thu";
➥"Fri"; "Sat")
```

Returns a three-letter day name abbreviation for today's date.

The following formula converts decimal values to fractional notation, rounded to the nearest eighth.

```
Let ([
    n = myNumber; int = int(n); decimal = mod(n ; 1);
    numberOfEighths = Round(decimal / .125 ; 0);
    intDisplay = If (int; int & If(decimal ; " - "; ""); "")] ;
    Choose(numberOfEighths;
        Floor (n);
        intDisplay & "1/8";
        intDisplay & "1/4";
        intDisplay & "3/8";
        intDisplay & "1/2";
        intDisplay & "5/8";
        intDisplay & "3/4";
        intDisplay & "7/8" ;
        Ceiling(n))
)
```

If myNumber contained 3.45, this function would return 3 - 1/2.

Comments:

If the index value returned by test exceeds the number of results available, the Choose function will not return a result. There is no way to define a default value to use when the index value exceeds the number of results available.

Combination()

Category: Number

Syntax: Combination (setSize ; numberOfChoices)

Parameters: setSize—any expression that returns a non-negative numeric value; numberOfChoices—any expression that returns a non-negative numeric value.

Description: Returns the number of ways to uniquely choose numberOfChoices items from a set of size setSize.

The values returned by this function are referred to as *combination coefficients*. They form Pascal's triangle. This function is useful in statistics, combinatorics, and polynomial expansions.

The formula used to determine the Combination value is n! / (n-x)! * x!, where n = set size, x = number of choices.

Examples:

Combination (4 ; 2)

Returns 6, because there are 6 ways of selecting 2 items from a set of 4 items. Given set {A, B, C, D}, these subsets would be {AB, AC, AD, BC, BD, CD}.

Combination (x ; 0)

Returns 1 for any x, representing the empty set.

Combination (x ; x)

Returns 1 for any x.

(13 * 12 * Combination(4;2) * Combination(4;3)) / Combination(52;5)

Returns 0.00144057..., which is the probability of being dealt a full house in 5-card poker (less than a 1% chance).

Comments:

The numbers returned by the Combination function are the coefficients of the binomial expansion series. For instance,

$(x + y)^4 = 1x^4 + 4x^3y + 6x^2y^2 + 4xy^3 + 1y^4$

Combination (4 ; 0) = 1

Combination (4 ; 1) = 4

Combination (4 ; 2) = 6

Combination (4 ; 3) = 4

Combination (4 ; 4) = 1

B

`Cos()`

Category: Trigonometric

Syntax: `Cos ( number )`

Parameters: `number`—any expression that resolves to a numeric value that represents an angle measured in radians.

Description: Returns the cosine of the angle represented by the value of the parameter, measured in radians. `Cos` is a periodic function with a range from -1 to 1.

Examples:

```
Cos (0) = 0
Cos (Pi / 4) = .707106781 (which is 1 / Sqrt (2))
Cos (Radians (60)) = .5
```

Comments:

In any right triangle, the cosine of the two non-right angles can be obtained by dividing the length of the side adjacent to the angle by the length of the hypotenuse.

You can convert an angle measured in degrees into radians by using the `Radians()` function, or by multiplying the value by Pi / 180. 1 radian is slightly more than 57 degrees.

`Count()`

Category: Aggregate

Syntax: `Count ( field { ; field...} )`

Parameters: `field`—any related field, repeating field, or set of non-repeating fields; or an expression that returns a field, repeating field, or set of non-repeating fields. Parameters in curly braces {} are optional.

Description: Returns the number of fields (or repetitions, in the case of repeating fields) in the parameter list that have valid non-blank values.

Examples:

```
Count ( field1 ; field2 ; field3 )
```

Returns 2 when `field1` and `field2` contain valid values, and `field3` is empty.

```
Count ( repeatingField )
```

Returns 2 when repetitions 1 and 2 contain valid values, and repetition 3 is empty.

```
Count ( InvoiceItem::InvoiceID )
```

Returns 2 when the current record is related to two `InvoiceItem` records. When using the `Count()` function to count the number of related records, be sure to count a field that is guaranteed not to be blank, such as the table's primary key.

Comments:

When the parameter list consists of 2 or more repeating fields, Count() returns a repeating field in which the corresponding repetitions from the specified fields are counted separately. So if a field Repeater1 has three values, 16, 20, and 24, and another field, Repeater2, has two values, 14 and 25, Count (Repeater1; Repeater2) would return a repeating field with values 2, 2, and 1.

DatabaseNames()

Category: Design

Syntax: DatabaseNames

Parameters: None.

Description: Returns a carriage return–delimited list of currently open databases, whether open as a client of another machine or open locally. File extensions are not included in the result.

Examples:

DatabaseNames might return

Customers¶Invoices¶Invoice_Line_Items

PatternCount (DatabaseNames ; "Customers")

Returns 1 if the Customers database is open.

Comments:

Use caution when checking for open databases with hard-coded strings. In the second example, the check fails if someone changes the name of the Customers database. Get (FileName) can be used in conjunction with a startup script to see whether a filename has been changed.

Date()

Category: Date

Syntax: Date (month ; day ; year)

Parameters: month—the month of the year (a number from 1 to 12); day—the day of the month (a number from 1 to 31); year—the year (four digits between 0001 and 4000).

Description: Returns a valid date of data type date represented by the three parameters. The Year parameter should be passed as a four-digit number.

Values for month and day outside of normal ranges will be interpreted correctly. For instance, a month value of 13 returns a date in January of the following year. A day value of 0 returns the last day of the preceding month.

B

Examples:

Date (1 ; 1 ; 2000)

Returns January 1, 2000 (formatting is determined on the layout).

Math can be performed on dates:

```
Date( 1 ; 1 ; 2000 ) - 1
```

Returns December 31, 1999.

The parameters in a Date function can be calculated:

```
Date ( Month ( Get ( CurrentDate )) ; 1 ; Year ( Get ( CurrentDate )))
```

Returns the date of the first of the current month; if today is August 12, 1965, then August 1, 1965 is returned.

The parameters in a Date function can be fields:

```
Date ( pickMonth ; 1 ; Get ( CurrentDate ))
```

Returns the date of the first of a month specified by the value in the field pickMonth.

Comments:

Parameters to date functions can be calculation expressions or fields; as long as the final result is valid, the date function will work correctly. Dates are stored internally as numbers (a unit of "1" represents one day); whole number math can be done on dates.

Be sure when returning dates as the result of calculation fields that you specify a calculation result of Date. If you were to define a field as Date (1 ; 1 ; 2000) and were to set the calculation result as Number, then you would see 730120 as the calculation value. Internally, FileMaker stores dates as the number of days since January 1, 0001, and that internal representation is returned if you incorrectly specify the return data type.

Day ( )

Category: Date

Syntax: Day (Date)

Parameters: Date—Any valid date (1/1/0001–12/31/4000), expression that returns a date, or field that contains a date.

Description: Returns the day of month (1–31) for any valid date.

Examples:

```
Day ( "1/15/2000" ) = 15
```

Other functions can be referenced in Day():

```
Day ( Get ( CurrentDate ))
```

returns the day of month for today.

Parameters in Day() can be calculated:

```
Day ( Get ( CurrentDate ) - 90 )
```

returns the day number for the date 90 days before today, which may not be the same as today's day number.

DayName()

Category: Date

Syntax: DayName (Date)

Parameters: Date—Any valid date (1/1/0001–12/31/4000), expression that returns a date, or field that contains a date. The parameter can also be the numeric representation of a date (1–1460970).

Description: Returns a text string containing the name of a weekday for any valid date (1/1/0001–12/31/4000).

Examples:

DayName ("11/24/2003")

Returns Monday.

DayName (dateField)

Returns the day of week for the date stored in the field dateField.

DayName (Get (CurrentDate) - 30)

Returns the day name for the date 30 days prior to today.

DayOfWeek()

Category: Date

Syntax: DayOfWeek (Date)

Parameters: Date—Any valid date (1/1/0001–12/31/4000), expression that returns a date, or field that contains a date. The parameter can also be the numeric representation of a date (1–1460970).

Description: Returns a number from 1 to 7, representing the day of week (Sunday = 1, Saturday = 7) for any valid date (1/1/0001–12/31/4000).

Examples:

DayOfWeek ("11/24/2003")

Returns 2 (Monday)

DayOfWeek (dateField)

Returns the day of week for the date stored in the field dateField.

DayOfWeek (Date (12 ; 25 ; Year (Get (CurrentDate))))

Returns the day of week on which Christmas falls this year.

B

Comments:

DayOfWeek() can be used to perform conditional tests on days of week without concern for localization issues. The number returned is always the same regardless of what language version of FileMaker Pro the user is using. The number value returned by DayOfWeek() can also be used in mathematical calculations.

DayOfYear()

Category: Date

Syntax: DayOfYear (Date)

Parameters: Date—Any valid date (1/1/0001–12/31/4000), expression that returns a date, or field that contains a date. The parameter can also be the numeric representation of a date (1–1460970).

Description: Returns a number representing the day of year (1–366) for any valid date (1/1/0001–12/31/4000).

Examples:

DayOfYear ("12/31/2000")

Returns 366 (leap year).

DayOfYear ("12/31/2001")

Returns 365 (non–leap year).

DayOfYear ("1/24/2004")

Returns 24.

DayOfYear (dateField)

Returns the day number for the date stored in dateField.

DayOfYear (Get (CurrentDate) + 30)

Returns the day of year for a date 30 days from now.

Comments:

You can use the DayOfYear function to check whether a particular year is a leap year. Given a field Year, the formula DayOfYear (Date (12 ; 31 ; Year)) would return 366 if Year was a leap year, and 365 if it wasn't.

Degrees()

Category: Trigonometric

Syntax: Degrees (number)

Parameters: number—a number representing an angle measured in radians.

Description: Converts an angle measured in radians to its equivalent in degrees. There are 2×Pi radians in 360°, so 1 radian is just over 57°.

Examples:

`Degrees ( 0 )`

Returns 0

`Degrees ( Pi / 4 )`

Returns 45

`Degrees ( 2 * Pi )`

Returns 360

`Degrees ( 4 * Pi )`

Returns 720

`Degrees ( -Pi / 2 )`

Returns -90

Comments:

Another way to convert radians to degrees is to multiply by 180/Pi.

`Div()`

Category: Number

Syntax: `Div ( numer ; denom )`

Parameters: numer—any expression that resolves to a numeric value; denom—any expression that resolves to a numeric value.

Description: Returns the quotient resulting from the division of the numerator numer by the denominator denom.

Examples:

`Div ( 30 ; 4 )`

Returns 7 because 30/4 is 7, remainder 2.

`Div ( 51 ; 8 )`

Returns 6 because 50/8 is 6, remainder 3.

Comments:

The `Div` function is equivalent to `Floor ( numer / denom )`.

To obtain the remainder when a numer is divided by denom, use the `Mod` function.

`Evaluate()`

Category: Logical

Syntax: `Evaluate ( expression { ; [ field1 ; field2 ; ...] } )`

Parameters: `expression`—any valid calculation formula, field containing a valid formula, or expression returning a valid formula; `field(n)`—a list of fields upon which the expression is dependent; the expression re-evaluates when any of the fields are updated.

Parameters in curly braces { } are optional. The optional field list must be enclosed by square brackets when there are multiple parameters.

Description: The `Evaluate()` function returns the results obtained by evaluating `expression`.

The optional second parameter is a list of fields on which the calculation is dependent. When any of those fields are modified, the `Evaluate()` function re-evaluates the expression specified by the first parameter.

Examples:

`Evaluate(MyFormula)`

Returns 8, if `MyFormula` contains the string 5+3.

`Evaluate(MyFormula)`

Returns 4, if `MyFormula` contains the string `Length (FirstName)` and `FirstName` contains Fred.

`Evaluate("MyFormula")`

Returns 5+3, if `MyFormula` contains the string 5+3.

```
Evaluate(Quote ("The comment field was last updated on " &
➡Get (CurrentDate) & " by " & Get (AccountName)) ; CommentField)
```

Returns a string containing information about the date and user who last modified the `CommentField`.

Comments:

Uses of the `Evaluate()` function are covered in depth in Chapter 14, "Specialized Calculation Functions."

The `Evaluate()` function expects that the first parameter passed to it is a string that contains a formula of some sort. If you are passing a literal string, as in the fourth of the preceding examples, using the `Quote()` function ensures that any quotation marks in the formula itself are properly encoded. If the first parameter is a field name or an expression, that field or expression is expected to return a formula, which the `Evaluate()` function then evaluates. In a nutshell, if the first parameter is *not* surrounded by quotation marks, the *result* of whatever field or expression is provided is evaluated.

B

EvaluationError()

Category: Logical

Syntax: EvaluationError (expression)

Parameters: `expression`—any FileMaker calculation formula.

Description: Returns an error code, if any, from `expression`. There are two types of errors: syntax errors and runtime errors. A syntax error indicates an invalid calculation. A runtime error, such as `Field missing` or `Record missing`, occurs when the calculation currently being run is valid but cannot properly execute.

The `EvaluationError()` function must enclose the `Evaluate()` function to return any syntax errors.

Examples:

`EvaluationError ( myFunction )`

Returns any runtime error codes that would arise from evaluating the expression in `myFunction`.

`EvaluationError(Evaluate(myFunction))`

Returns any error codes that would arise from evaluating the expression in `myFunction`.

Exact()

Category: Text

Syntax: `Exact ( originalText ; comparisonText )`

Parameters: `originalText`—any text expression, text field, or container field; `comparisonText`—any text expression, text field, or container field.

Description: Compares the contents of any two text or container expressions. This function is case sensitive. If the expressions match, the result is 1 (True); otherwise the result is 0 (False). For container fields, not only must the data be the same, but it must also be stored in the same manner (either embedded or stored by file reference).

Examples:

`Exact ( "Smith" ; "smith" )`

Returns 0 (False).

`Exact ( Proper ( Salutation ) ; Salutation)`

Returns 1 if the contents of the `Salutation` field begin with initial caps.

`Exact ( Zip_Lookup::City_Name ; City_Name )`

Returns 1 if the value of `City_Name` is exactly the same as the one stored in a related ZIP code table.

Comments:

Remember that `Exact()` considers the case of the two strings, whereas the = operator does not. If you need to compare two values in a conditional test, consider using `If ( Exact ( A ; B ); ...` instead of `If ( A = B ; ...`.

Exp()

Category: Number

Syntax: Exp (number)

Parameters: number—any expression that resolves to a numeric value.

Description: Returns the value of the constant *e* raised to the power of *number*. The Exp() function is the inverse of the Ln() function.

Examples:

Round (Exp (5) ; 3)

Returns 148.413.

Exp (Ln (5))

Returns 5.

Comments:

To return the value of the constant *e* itself, use Exp (1), which returns 2.7182818284590452. You can use the SetPrecision() function to return *e* with up to 400 digits of precision.

Extend()

Category: Repeating

Syntax: Extend (non-repeatingField)

Parameters: non-repeatingField—any non-repeating field (a field defined to contain only one value).

Description: Allows a value in non-repeatingField to be used in every repetition in a calculation defined as repeating. Without Extend(), only the first repetition of a repeating calculation field can use the value of a non-repeating field.

Examples:

Given a number field RepCommission, defined to hold 3 repetitions, a non-repeating number field (SalePrice), and repeating calculation field (SalesCommission), defined as follows:

Round (RepCommision * Extend (SalePrice) ; 2)

RepCommission	SalePrice	SalesCommission
.10	18.00	1.80
.12		2.16
.15		2.40

Without the Extend() function, only the first repetition of SalesCommission would have returned the correct value.

External()

Category: External

Syntax: External (nameOfFunction ; parameter)

Parameters: nameOfFunction—the name of the external function being called; parameter—the parameter that is being passed to the external function.

Description: The External() function is used to call functions defined within a plug-in. A plug-in must be installed (located in the Extensions folder) and enabled (under the Plug-Ins tab of Preferences) for you to have access to its functions.

Examples:

External ("myPlugin" ; "param1¦param2¦param3")

External ("myPlugin" ; myParmField)

Comments:

The function name and parameter syntax for an external function is defined by the plug-in developer. When calling external plug-ins, be sure to use the exact syntax specified in the documentation for the plug-in. The external function parameter can generally be passed as a field, as long as the contents of the field conform to the requirements set forth by the plug-in developer.

Factorial()

Category: Number

Syntax: Factorial (number { ; numberOfFactors })

Parameters: number—any expression that resolves to a positive integer; numberOfFactors—any expression that resolves to a positive integer that represents how many factors to include in the multiplication.

Parameters in curly braces { } are optional.

Description: Returns the factorial of number, stopping either at 1 or stopping at the optional numberOfFactors. The factorial of a number n is defined as $n \times (n-1) \times (n-2) \times (n-3) \ldots \times 1$. Factorials are useful in statistics and combinatorics. In mathematics, factorials are usually represented by an exclamation mark. 4! = Factorial (4) = 4×3×2×1 = 24.

Examples:

Factorial (3)

Returns 6, which = 3×2×1.

Factorial (10 ; 3)

Returns 720, which = 10×9×8.

B

Comments:

One application of factorials is to determine how many unique ways a set of objects can be ordered. For instance, a set of three objects {A, B, C} can be ordered 3! = 6 ways: {ABC, ACB, BAC, BCA, CAB, CBA}.

FieldBounds()

Category: Design

Syntax: FieldBounds (fileName ; layoutName ; fieldName)

Parameters: fileName—name of the file where the field resides; layoutName—name of the layout where the field resides; fieldName—name of the field open.

Description: Returns the physical position and rotation of a field that is described by the parameters. Note that the parameters are text and must either be references to fields or enclosed in quotation marks. Results are returned as a space-delimited text string in the form of "Left Top Right Bottom Rotation." The first four of these values represent the distance in pixels from either the left margin of the layout (in the case of Left and Right) or the top margin (in the case of Top and Right). The Rotation value will be 0, 90, 180, or 270, depending on the field's orientation on the layout.

Examples:

FieldBounds (myFile ; myLayout ; myField)

might return 444 84 697 98 0.

Comments:

The values returned are delimited by spaces; the MiddleWords() function can easily be used to parse them.

Be aware that changing the name of a file, layout, or field may cause literal references to them to be broken in functions that use FieldBounds.

The field name that is passed to FieldBounds() must be the name from Define Database (not the field label); if a field appears on layout more than once, the one that is lowest in the layering order will be used.

Related fields must be referenced by RelationshipName::FieldName or FileName::FieldName.

FieldComment()

Category: Design

Syntax: FieldComment (fileName ; fieldName)

Parameters: fileName—the name of the open file where the field is located; fieldName—the name of the field for which to return comments.

Description: Returns the contents of any comment that has been entered in Define Database for the specified field. The syntax Table::fieldName is required to reference fields outside of the current table context. (The safest approach is to use this method in all cases.)

Examples:

```
FieldComment ( "myDatabase" ; "Contacts::FirstName")
```

Returns the comment, if any, for the FirstName field as it appears in the table definition.

Comments:

FieldComment() is useful for documenting a database. Care must be taken, however, because literal references to fields can be broken when file, table, or field names are changed. FieldNames() and TableNames() can be used to dynamically investigate all field names and load the results from FieldComment() into tables for browsing.

FieldIDs()

Category: Design

Syntax: FieldIDs (fileName ; layoutName)

Parameters: fileName—the name of the open FileMaker database from which to return IDs; layoutName—the name of the layout from which to return field IDs.

Description: Returns a list of all field IDs in fileName and layoutName, separated by carriage returns. Fields outside the current table context are returned as TableID::RelatedFieldID. If layoutName is empty, then the field IDs of the first table created (the "default" table) are returned.

Examples:

```
FieldIDs ( "Invoices" ; "List View" )
```

returns IDs of all unique fields, including related fields, on the List View layout in Invoices.

Comments:

Calls to FieldIDs() can be broken when file and layout names are changed. Field IDs are assigned by FileMaker and cannot be changed.

FieldNames()

Category: Design

Syntax: FieldNames (fileName ; layout/tableName)

Parameters: fileName—the name of an open FileMaker database from which to return field names; layout/tableName—the name of the layout or table to reference.

Description: Returns a carriage return–delimited list of field names. Note that if you want to generate a list of field names for a table, you must not have a layout with the same name as the table. FileMaker checks for layouts of that name first.

Examples:

```
FieldNames ( Get ( FileName ) ; "Customers" )
```

Returns a list of fields found in the table named Customers in the current database.

B

Comments:

FieldNames() can be used to dynamically generate database structure information about any open FileMaker database.

When information about fields in a table is returned, the results are ordered according to the creation order of the fields. When the names of the fields on a particular layout are returned, the results are ordered according to the stacking order of the fields, from back to front. If an object appears on a layout more than once, it appears multiple times in the result list. Related fields appear as RelationshipName::FieldName.

FieldRepetitions()

Category: Design

Syntax: FieldRepetitions (fileName ; layoutName ; fieldName)

Parameters: fileName—the name of the open file where the field to be referenced is located; layoutName—the name of the layout where the field to be referenced is located; fieldName—the name of the field for which to return repetition information.

Description: Returns a space-delimited string that indicates the number of repetitions and orientation of the field in question. Note that you must pass a layout name. (A table name does not work.) The data is returned in the format of "NumRepetitions Orienation."

Examples:

FieldRepetitions (Get (FileName) ; "Invoice_Detail" ; "Payment_History")

might return a string like 3 vertical.

Comments:

The MiddleWords() function can be used to extract either component of the result.

If literal names of objects are used, calls to the function may be broken when file or object names are changed. Functions such as Get(FileName), LayoutNames(), and FieldNames() can be used to dynamically return information about a database. Also remember that only the number of repetitions that appear on the layout are returned, not the number of repetitions defined in Define Database. Use FieldType() to return the number of repetitions specified in Define Database.

FieldStyle()

Category: Design

Syntax: FieldStyle (fileName ; layoutName ; fieldName)

Parameters: fileName—the name of the open file where the field is located; layoutName—the name of the layout where the field is used; fieldName—the name of the field for which to return results.

Description: Returns a space-delimited string indicating the field style and any associated value list. The field styles are

Standard

Scrolling

Popuplist

Popupmenu

Checkbox

RadioButton

Examples:

`FieldStyle ( Get ( FileName ) ; "Invoice_Detail" ; "Notes" )`

might return `Scrolling` for a notes field that has scrollbars turned on.

`FieldStyle ( Get ( FileName ) ; "Invoice_Detail" ; "Paid" )`

might return `RadioButton Yes_No` for a field formatted as a radio button that uses a value list called Yes_No.

Comments:

Calls to `FieldStyle()` that rely on literal object names may be broken if file, layout, or field names are changed.

FieldType()

Category: Design

Syntax: `FieldType ( fileName ; fieldName )`

Parameters: `fileName`—the name of the open file where the field is located; `fieldName`—the name of the field for which to return results.

Description: Returns a space-delimited string indicating the field type of the field specified by `fieldName`. There are four components to the string, each of which can contain several possible values. The possible values for each item are

Item 1: `standard`, `storedcalc`, `summary`, `unstoredcalc`, or `global`

Item 2: `text`, `number`, `date`, `time`, `timestamp`, or `container`

Item 3: `indexed` or `unindexed`

Item 4: Number of repetitions (1 for a non repeating field)

`fieldName` must be specified as `Table::Field` when referencing fields in tables outside of the current table context.

Examples:

`FieldType ( Get (FileName) ; "Contacts::ContactID" )`

might return values that look like this: `standard number indexed 1`.

`FieldType ( Get (FileName) ; "Contacts::gTempName" )`

might return values that look like this: `global text unindexed 1`.

B

Comments:

Using the `Table::Field` method for referencing fields as a matter of course avoids broken references when the current table context changes.

Filter()

Category: Text

Syntax: `Filter ( textToFilter ; filterText )`

Parameters: `textToFilter`—any expression that resolves to a text string; `filterText`—the characters to preserve in the specified text.

Description: Returns from `textToFilter` only those characters specified in `filterText`, in the order that they were originally entered in `textToFilter`. If `filterText` doesn't have any characters, an empty string is returned. The `Filter()` function is case sensitive.

Examples:

```
Filter ( "ab123"; "abc")
```

Returns ab.

```
Filter ( PhoneNum ; "0123456789" )
```

Would strip any non-numeric characters from the `PhoneNum` field.

Comments: The `Filter()` function is frequently used to ensure that users have entered valid data into a field. The `textToFilter` parameter should contain any valid characters; the order of the characters within `textToFilter` isn't important.

FilterValues()

Category: Text

Syntax: `FilterValues ( textToFilter ; filterValues )`

Parameters: `textToFilter`—a return-delimited text string or expression that generates a return-delimited text string; `filterValues`—a return-delimited text string or expression that generates a return-delimited text string representing values that you want to preserve in the specified text.

Description:

`FilterValues()` produces a return-delimited list of items in `textToFilter` that are included among the specified `filterValues`. The items must match exactly to be returned, with the exception of case; `FilterValues()` is not case sensitive.

Values are returned in the order they appear in `textToFilter`. If `filterValues` is an empty string, or if no items in `textToFilter` are contained in the `filterValues` list, then an empty string is returned.

Examples:

```
FilterValues(Offices ; "Atlanta¶Chicago¶Detroit")
```

Returns `Chicago¶Atlanta` when Offices contains: `Chicago¶Atlanta¶San Mateo`.

Comments:

`FilterValues()` can be used to determine whether a particular item is part of a return-delimited array. For instance, the `WindowNames()` function produces a return-delimited list of windows. If you wanted to know whether a window named Contact Detail existed, you could use the following formula:

```
ValueCount (FilterValues( WindowNames ; "Contact Detail"))
```

If the value count is anything other than zero, that means the window name was found. The benefit of using `FilterValues` for this rather than `PatternCount()` is that `Contact Detail - 2` would not be returned if `Contact Detail` were the filter.

Floor()

Category: Number

Syntax: `Floor ( number )`

Parameters: `number`—any expression that resolves to a numeric value.

Description: Returns `number` rounded down to the next lower integer.

Examples:

```
Floor (1.0005 )
```

Returns 1.

```
Floor ( -1.0005 )
```

Returns -2.

Comments:

For positive numbers, `Floor()` and `Int()` return the same results; however, for negative numbers, `Int()` returns the next larger integer, whereas `Floor()` returns the next smaller integer.

FV()

Category: Financial

Syntax: `FV ( payment ; interestRate ; periods )`

Parameters: `payment`—the nominal amount of the payment; `interestRate`—the per-period interest rate; `periods`—the number of periods in the duration of the investment.

Description: Returns the future value of a periodic investment based on the payments and interest rate for the number of periods specified.

B

Examples:

```
FV ( 50 ; .10 ; 2 )
```

Returns 105, indicating the amount of money you would have after making 2 periodic deposits of $50 into an investment that paid 10% per period.

If the investment compounds monthly, divide the annual interestRate by 12 to express the periods as a number of months.

To figure out the future value of monthly investments of $250, earning 8% interest, for 10 years, you would use the formula:

```
FV ( 250 ; .08/12 ; 10 * 12)
```

which returns 45736.51

Comments:

The FV() function doesn't account for the present value of your investment, and it assumes that payments are made at the end of each period.

Get(AccountName)

Category: Get

Syntax: Get (AccountName)

Parameters: none

Description: Returns the name of the authenticated account being used by the current user of the database file. If a user is logged in under the default Admin account, Admin is returned. If a user is using the FileMaker Pro guest account, then [Guest] is returned.

For external server authentication, Get(AccountName) returns the name of the authenticated account being used by the current user of the database file, not the group to which the user belongs. (The group name appears in the Account list when you define accounts and privileges in FileMaker Pro.) If an individual belongs to more than one group (account), the first group name listed when you View By Authentication Order while defining accounts and privileges determines access for the user.

Examples:

```
Get ( AccountName )
```

Returns sales when the current user is logged in with the sales account.

Comments:

Get (AccountName) can be used to retrieve the account name of the current user for purposes of logging or auditing database access.

B

Get(ActiveFieldContents)

Category: Get

Syntax: Get (ActiveFieldContents)

Parameters: none

Description: Returns the contents of the field in which the cursor is currently inserted. The contents of the field need not be highlighted.

Examples:

Get (ActiveFieldContents)

Returns Fred when the current field contains the name Fred.

Comments:

Get (ActiveFieldContents) can return the contents of fields of any data type, but the field in which you place those contents may need to be of the same data type for it to display properly.

When using Get() functions within field definitions, in most cases you should set the storage option to be "unstored" so that the field always displays current data.

Get(ActiveFieldName)

Category: Get

Syntax: Get (ActiveFieldName)

Parameters: none

Description: Returns the name of the field that currently contains the cursor.

Examples:

Get (ActiveFieldName)

Returns Name_First when the cursor is in the Name_First field.

Comments:

Even when the active field is a related or unrelated field from another table, Get (ActiveFieldName) simply returns the field's name. It does *not* use the double-colon syntax "relationshipName::FieldName."

When using Get() functions within field definitions, in most cases you should set the storage option to be "unstored" so that the field always displays current data.

B

Get(ActiveFieldTableName)

Category: Get

Syntax: Get (ActiveFieldTableName)

Parameters: none

Description: Returns the name of the table occurrence of the field that currently contains the cursor.

Examples:

```
Get ( ActiveFieldTableName )
```

Might return Contacts2.

Comments:

Note that the table occurrence name (from the Relationships Graph) is returned, rather than the base table name.

When using Get() functions within field definitions, in most cases you should set the storage option to be "unstored" so that the field always displays current data.

Get(ActiveModifierKeys)

Category: Get

Syntax: Get (ActiveModifierKeys)

Parameters: none

Description: Returns the sum of the constants that represent the modifier keys that the user is pressing on the keyboard. The constants for modifier keys are as follows:

1—Shift

2—Caps lock

4—Control

8—Alt (Windows) or Option (Mac OS)

16—Command key (Mac OS only)

Examples:

```
Get ( ActiveModifierKeys )
```

Returns 4 if the Control key is being held down, and returns 7 if the Shift, Caps Lock, and Control keys are being held down.

The following formula can be used to show text values for keys being held down; it can be used in a calculated field or a custom function:

```
Let (keys = Get (ActiveModifierKeys);
Case (Mod (keys;2); "Shift ") &
Case (Int (Mod (keys;4)/2); "Caps Lock ") &
Case (Int (Mod (keys;8)/4); "Control ") &
Choose ( 2 * (Int (Mod (keys;16)/8)) + (Abs (Get(SystemPlatform)) - 1) ;
    "";""; "Option "; "Alt ")&
Case (keys>=16; "Command")
)
```

If the user is holding down the Shift, Caps, and Control keys when this function runs, the text values for those keys are returned in the form of Shift, Caps Lock, and Control.

Comments:

When using Get() functions within field definitions, in most cases you should set the storage option to be "unstored" so that the field always displays current data.

Get(ActiveRepetitionNumber)

Category: Get

Syntax: Get (ActiveRepetitionNumber)

Parameters: none

Description: Returns the number of the active repetition (the repetition in which the cursor is) for a repeating field. Repetition numbers start with 1. If the cursor is not in a field, 0 is returned.

Examples:

Get (ActiveRepetitionNumber)

Would return 2 when a user was clicked into the second repetition of a field.

Comments:

When using Get() functions within field definitions, in most cases you should set the storage option to be "unstored" so that the field always displays current data.

Get(ActiveSelectionSize)

Category: Get

Syntax: Get (ActiveSelectionSize)

Parameters: none

Description: Returns the number of characters that are highlighted in the current field. The function returns 0 if no characters are highlighted, and returns null if no field is active. When multiple windows are open (which leads to the possibility of multiple highlighted selections), only the active window is considered.

Examples:

Get (ActiveSelectionSize)

Would return 10 if a user had highlighted 10 characters in any field in the active window.

Comments:

Carriage returns, tabs, spaces, and other invisible characters are counted by
Get (ActiveSelectionSize).

When using Get() functions within field definitions, in most cases you should set the storage option to be "unstored" so that the field always displays current data.

B

Get(ActiveSelectionStart)

Category: Get

Syntax: Get (ActiveSelectionStart)

Parameters: none

Description: Returns the position of the first character in the highlighted text of the current field. If no text is highlighted (that is, the user has simply clicked into a block of text), then the current position of the cursor is returned. It returns null if no field is active. When multiple windows are open, only the active window is considered.

Examples:

Get (ActiveSelectionStart)

Returns 1 if the user has selected an entire field, or if the insertion point is at the beginning of a field.

Comments:

Remember that carriage returns, tabs, spaces, and other invisible characters are taken into account when evaluating Get (ActiveSelectionStart).

Used in conjunction with Get (ActiveSelectionSize), you can determined the string that a user has highlighted in any field, using the formula:

```
Middle ( Get (ActiveFieldContents) ; Get (ActiveSelectionStart) ;
➥    Get ( ActiveSelectionSize ))
```

Get(AllowAbortState)

Category: Get

Syntax: Get (AllowAbortState)

Parameters: none

Description: Returns 1 if Allow User Abort is On; returns 0 if Allow User Abort is Off.

Examples:

In the following script:

```
Allow User Abort [Off]
Show Custom Dialog [Get ( AllowAbortState ) ]
```

the custom dialog would display 0.

In the following script:

```
Allow User Abort [On]
Show Custom Dialog [Get ( AllowAbortState ) ]
```

the custom dialog would display 1.

B

Comments:

If the setting for User Abort hasn't been explicitly set, a script runs as if Allow User Abort is On. `Get (AllowAbortState)` returns 1 in such cases.

Get(ApplicationLanguage)

Category: Get

Syntax: `Get ( ApplicationLanguage )`

Parameters: none

Description: Returns a text string representing the current application language. The possible results are as follows:

English
French
Italian
German
Swedish
Spanish
Dutch
Japanese

Examples:

`Get ( ApplicationLanguage )`

Would return `English` for users using an English language version of FileMaker Pro.

Comments:

The string returned will always be in English, even in versions of the product based on other languages. That is, it returns `German`, not `Deutsch`, in a German language version of FileMaker.

Get(ApplicationVersion)

Category: Get

Syntax: `Get ( ApplicationVersion )`

Parameters: none

Description: Returns a text string representing the application and version:

`Pro` for FileMaker Pro.

`Developer` for FileMaker Developer.

`Runtime` for FileMaker Runtime.

`Web Publishing Core` for FileMaker Web Client.

`Web Publishing Engine` for FileMaker Web Server.

B

Examples:

```
Get ( ApplicationVersion )
```

Returns Developer 7.0v1 for FileMaker Developer 7.0v1

Comments:

If you have allowed Web access to a database, you may want to add conditional tests within some of your scripts so that they will behave differently for Web and FileMaker Pro clients. To identify Web users, use either of the following formulas:

```
PatternCount ( Get ( ApplicationVersion ) ; "Web")

Position ( Get ( ApplicationVersion); "Web" ; 1 ; 1)
```

If either of these return anything other than 0, the user is a Web client.

Get(CalculationRepetitionNumber)

Category: Get

Syntax: Get (CalculationRepetitionNumber)

Parameters: none

Description: Returns the current repetition number of a calculation field. If the calculation is not set to allow more than one value, Get (CalculationRepetitionNumber) returns 1.

Examples:

```
Get ( CalculationRepetitionNumber )
```

Returns 1 in the first repetition of a repeating field, 2 in the second repetition, and so on, up to the maximum number of repetitions the field has been defined to hold.

A calculation field defined to hold 5 repetitions and that has the following formula:

```
Get (CalculationRepetitionNumber) ^ 2
```

returns the repetition values 1, 4, 9, 16, 25.

Comments:

Get (CalculationRepetitionNumber) is really nothing more than the repetition number. It's the repeating field analog of the Get (PortalRowNumber) and Get (RecordNumber) functions.

You can use the repetition number in conditional tests involving repeating fields. For instance, the following formula:

```
If (Get (CalculationRepetitionNumber) < 4; "foo"; "bar")
```

returns a repeating calculation field with values foo, foo, foo, bar, bar, etc.

B

Get(CurrentDate)

Category: Get

Syntax: Get (CurrentDate)

Parameters: none

Description: Returns the current date according to the system calendar.

The format of the result varies based on the date format that was in use when the database file was created. In the United States, dates are generally in the format MM/DD/YYYY. You can change a computer's date format in the Regional Settings Control Panel (Windows 2000), the Date and Time Control Panel (Windows XP), or the Date & Time System Preference (Mac OS X).

If the result is displayed in a field, it is formatted according to the date format of the field in the current layout.

Examples:

DayName (Get (CurrentDate) - 30)

Returns the day name for the date 30 days prior to today.

Get (CurrentDate) - InvoiceDate

Returns the number of days outstanding for a given invoice.

Get(CurrentHostTimestamp)

Category: Get

Syntax: Get (CurrentHostTimestamp)

Parameters: none

Description: Returns the current date and time according to the host's system clock, to the nearest second.

Examples:

Returns 1/1/2004 11:30:01 AM when the system clock on the host machine shows January 1, 2004, 11:30:01 AM.

Comments:

Get (CurrentHostTimeStamp) returns the date and time from the host machine, regardless of the date and time settings on the client machine. Get (CurrentHostTimestamp) is therefore useful for storing information about when records are created or edited because it disregards differences in time zones or improper settings of the client machines.

Function calls that run on the server may impact a network user's performance, especially when they are used in unstored calculations.

Get(CurrentTime)

Category: Get

Syntax: Get (CurrentTime)

Parameters: none

Description: Returns the current time from the local system clock (on the client machine.)

Examples:

Get (CurrentTime) + 3600

Returns the time one hour from now.

Get (CurrentTime)

returns the current time from the local system clock.

Comments:

Note that the Time data type is stored internally as the number of seconds since midnight. Math can be performed on all Time() functions using multiples of seconds (60 = 1 minute, 3600 = 1 hour).

Remember that the time returned by Get (CurrentTime) is the local time on the system clock of the client machine. In cases where clients are accessing a database from different time zones, this data may be less useful than time extracted from the host machine's system clock with the Get (CurrentHostTimeStamp) function.

Get(CurrentTimestamp)

Category: Get

Syntax: Get (CurrentTimestamp)

Parameters: none

Description: Returns the current date and time according to the local system clock, to the nearest second.

Examples:

Get (CurrentTimeStamp)

Might return 1/25/2004 8:28:05 PM.

Truncate (Get (CurrentTimeStamp)/ 86400 ; 0) + 1

Extracts the date from a timestamp.

Mod (Get (CurrentTimeStam); 86400)

Extracts the time from a timestamp.

B

Comments:

Note that a timestamp is stored internally as an integer that represents the number of seconds since 1/1/0001. Therefore, calculations that use seconds as the base unit can be performed on timestamp data types.

Get (CurrentTimeStamp) uses the date and time settings of the local machine (client) and may be less useful than Get (CurrentHostTimeStamp) in a database that is accessed by clients from different time zones.

Get(ErrorCaptureState)

Category: Get

Syntax: Get (ErrorCaptureState)

Parameters: none

Description: Returns 1 if Set Error Capture has been set to On, and 0 if Set Error Capture was either not set or set to Off.

Examples:

In the following script:

```
Set Error Capture [Off]
Show Custom Dialog [ Get (ErrorCaptureState) ]
```

the custom dialog displays 0.

In the following script:

```
Set Error Capture [On]
Show Custom Dialog [ Get (ErrorCaptureState) ]
```

the custom dialog displays 1.

Comments:

It is not possible to tell with the Get (ErrorCaptureState) function whether Error Capture was explicitly turned off or simply not set.

Get(ExtendedPrivileges)

Category: Get

Syntax: Get (ExtendedPrivileges)

Parameters: none

Description: Returns a list of keywords, separated by carriage returns, identifying the extended privileges available to the account being used by the current user of the database file. Extended privileges are additional access rights assigned to a privilege set; they control such things as access via the Web, via ODBC/JDBC, and via FileMaker Networking.

B

If the user's privilege set doesn't have any extended privileges enabled, `Get( ExtendedPrivileges )` returns an empty list.

Examples:

If the currently logged in account uses a privilege set that includes the extended privileges of Access via Instant Web Publishing (keyword fmiwp) and Access via FileMaker Network (keyword fmapp).

```
Get (ExtendedPrivileges)
```

Returns `fmiwp¶fmapp`.

Comments:

To test whether a user has a certain extended privilege, use one of the following formulas:

```
PatternCount (Get (ExtendedPrivileges) ; "fmiwp")
```

If this function returns anything other than 0, then the user has the `fmiwp` extended privilege

The `Position()` function can also be used:

```
Position (Get (ExtendedPrivileges) ; "fmiwp"; 1; 1)
```

In this case, any value greater than 0 indicates the presence of the specified privilege.

`Get(FileName)`

Category: Get

Syntax: `Get ( FileName )`

Parameters: none

Description: Returns the filename of the current database file, without the file extension.

Examples:

```
Get (FileName)
```

Returns the value `HR` when the current database file is named HR.fp7.

```
GetNextSerialValue (Get (FileName); "Contacts::PrimaryContactID")
```

Returns the next `PrimaryContactID` from the Contacts table in the current file.

Comments:

`Get(FileName)` is useful in function calls that require a filename, even if the current file is being referenced. This way, if the filename changes, you don't need to change any of your calculation formulas.

If a field in file `A.fp7` contains the formula `Get (FileName)`, and that field is displayed on a layout in another file, `B.fp7`, via an external table occurrence, the field value will still return `A`.

B

Get(FilePath)

Category: Get

Syntax: Get (FilePath)

Parameters: none

Description: Returns the full path to the currently active database file, including the file extension.

Returns file:/driveletter:/databaseName for local files in Windows.

Returns file://volumename/myfoldername/databaseName for remote files in Windows.

Returns file:/path/databaseName for local and remote files in the Mac OS.

Returns fmnet:/networkaddress/databaseName for FileMaker Pro networked files.

Examples:

Get (FilePath)

Returns the current file path.

Left (Get (FilePath) ; Position (Get (FilePath) ; Get (FileName) ; 1 ; 1) -1)

Returns just the path to the current file directory. The Position() function truncates the path before the filename.

Comments:

Remember that Get (FilePath) includes the filename and extension. Text parsing functions can be used to extract just the file path from the results returned by Get (FilePath). This can be useful for building dynamic paths to objects that are in the same directory as the current file.

If a field in file A.fp7 contains the formula Get (FilePath), and that field is displayed on a layout in another file, B.fp7, via an external table occurrence, the field value will still return the file path for file A.

Get(FileSize)

Category: Get

Syntax: Get (FileSize)

Parameters: none

Description: Returns the size of the current file in bytes.

Examples:

If the current file size is 1,404,928 bytes Get (FileSize) returns 1404928.

Round (Get (FileSize) / 1024 ; 0)

Returns 1372, the file size in KB.

B

```
Round (Get (FileSize) / 1048576 ; 2)
```

Returns 1.34, the file size in MB.

Get(FoundCount)

Category: Get

Syntax: Get (FoundCount)

Parameters: none

Description: Returns a number that represents the number of records in the current found set.

Examples:

If 240 records are in the found set, Get (FoundCount) returns 240.

Comments:

If multiple windows are open in the current database file, each window can have its own found set. If the Get (FoundCount) function is used in a script, it returns the found count of the active layout in the active window.

Get (FoundCount) is often used in scripts, following finds, to determine navigation paths. In the following script, if one record is found, the Detail layout is shown. If multiple records are found, the List layout is shown. Finally, if no records are found, the script notifies the user with a dialog box.

```
If[Get(FoundCount)=1]
  Go To Layout[Detail]
Else If[Get(FoundCount)>1]
  Go To Layout[List]
Else
  Show Custom Dialog ["Empty Set"; "No Records Found"]
End If
```

Get(HighContrastColor)

Category: Get

Syntax: Get (HighContrastColor)

Parameters: none

Description: Windows only: returns the name of the current high-contrast default color scheme. Returns an empty value (null) if Use High Contrast is unavailable, inactive, or if the function is used on the Mac OS.

Examples:

```
Get (HighContrastColor)
```

Returns High Contrast White (large) when the Use High Contrast option in Windows 2000 is active and Black on White is selected.

Returns `High Contrast Black (large)` when the Use High Contrast option in Windows 2000 is active and White on Black is selected.

Returns the name of the custom color scheme when the Use High Contrast option in Windows 2000 is active and a custom color scheme is selected.

Returns null if the Use High Contrast option is not selected or if the computer is a Macintosh.

Comments:

Use High Contrast is an option under Control Panel, Accessibility Options, Display tab. The standard options increase default font sizes and heighten screen contrast to assist users with impaired vision.

Get(HighContrastState)

Category: Get

Syntax: Get (HighContrastState)

Parameters: none

Description: Windows only: Returns a number representing the state of the Use High Contrast option in the Accessibility Options control panel.

Returns:

0 if Use High Contrast is unavailable, inactive, or if the function is used on the Mac OS.

1 if Use High Contrast is available and active.

Examples:

If you have users with impaired vision, you might create alternate versions of your layouts that are easier for them to use. If so, you can test in your navigation scripts whether Use High Contrast is active and go to an appropriate layout or zoom the window.

```
If [ Get (HighContrastState) = 1 ]
    Go to Layout ["ContactDetail (HC)"]
Else
    Go to Layout ["ContactDetail"]
End If
```

Get(HostName)

Category: Get

Syntax: Get (HostName)

Parameters: none

Description: Returns the registered name on the computer that is hosting the database file.

To change the registered name on a computer:

B

On Windows, the computer name is found on the Network Identification tab of the System Properties control panel. The Full computer name option displays the current registered name.

On Mac OS, the computer name is found within System Preferences, under the Sharing settings.

Examples:

If the computer is named "Gandalf"

```
Get(HostName)
```

results in Gandalf.

Comments:

If a client connects to a file hosted by FileMaker Server, Get (HostName) returns the name of the server. The host name can be configured with the Server Administration Tool. By default, FileMaker Server uses the system's name, but a custom name can be supplied instead.

Get(LastError)

Category: Get

Syntax: Get (LastError)

Parameters: none

Description: Returns the number of the error generated by the most recent script step. If there was no error, then Get (LastError) returns 0. Use this function in combination with Set Error Capture [On] to trap and handle errors raised in scripts.

Examples:

Consider the following script:

```
Set Error Capture [On]
Print Setup[Restore]
Get (LastError)
```

If the user cancels out of the Print Setup dialog, Get (LastError) returns 1 (user canceled action). If the Print Setup step executes successfully, Get (LastError) returns 0.

Comments:

The Get (LastError) function returns the error code from only the most recently executed script step. For example, in this script:

```
Perform Find
If (Get(ErrorCaptureState) = 1)
    Show Custom Dialog (Get (LastError))
End If
```

B

The Get (LastError) step returns the result of the execution of the If statement, not the error code generated by the Find step.

A full list of error codes is available in the FileMaker Help system under Get(LastError).

Get(LastMessageChoice)

Category: Get

Syntax: Get (LastMessageChoice)

Parameters: none

Description: Returns a number corresponding to the button clicked in the Show Custom Dialog.

Returns:

1 for the default button.

2 for the second button.

3 for the third button.

Examples:

For the following script step, where the default button is labeled OK, the second button is labeled Maybe, and the third button is labeled Cancel:

```
Show Custom Dialog ["test";"Proceed?"]
```

If the user chooses OK, Get (LastMessageChoice) returns 1.

If the user chooses Maybe, Get (LastMessageChoice) returns 2.

If the user chooses Cancel, Get (LastMessageChoice) returns 3.

You can then use an If() statement to handle each possibility appropriately.

Comments:

Though it has a value of 1, the default button on a dialog is always on the far right side. For example, if there are three buttons, they will appear in 3-2-1 (Cancel, Maybe, OK) order.

Get(LastODBCError)

Category: Get

Syntax: Get (LastODBCError)

Parameters: none

Description: Returns a string that shows the ODBC error state (SQLSTATE), as published by ODBC standards, based on ISO/IEF standards.

The ODBC error state is cleared before the next ODBC-related script step is performed. Anytime before that happens, you can check to see whether an ODBC error was generated.

Examples:

When attempting to execute a SQL statement with an invalid field name, Get (LastODBCError) returns S0022.

If no error is encountered, Get (LastODBCError) returns 00000.

Comments:

By setting Error Capture to On, you can suppress the error messages that a user sees during execution of a script that uses ODBC functions.

Get(LayoutAccess)

Category: Get

Syntax: Get (LayoutAccess)

Parameters: none

Description: Returns a number that represents the current user's record access privileges level for the current layout. Privileges are assigned in the Custom Layout Privileges dialog box (File, Define, Accounts & Privileges).

Examples:

Get(LayoutAccess)

Returns 0, if the custom layout privileges of an account's privilege set allow "no access" to records via this layout.

Returns 1, if the custom layout privileges of an account's privilege set allow "view only" access to records via this layout.

Returns 2, if the custom layout privileges of an account's privilege set allow "modifiable" access to records via this layout.

Comments:

The Get (LayoutAccess) function can be used to alert users of restricted privileges at the layout level. Note that Get (LayoutAccess) returns information about only the current layout. Record access privileges for any other layout are not represented.

Note also that Get (LayoutAccess) does not return information about whether or not the layout itself is accessible, but rather what access the user has to edit record data via the current layout.

The Get (RecordAccess) function evaluates record access privileges independent of the Get (LayoutAccess) function. To fully evaluate record access, evaluate the return values of both the Get (LayoutAccess) and Get (RecordAccess) functions.

B

`Get(LayoutCount)`

Category: Get

Syntax: `Get ( LayoutCount )`

Parameters: none

Description: Returns the total number of layouts in the current file.

Examples:

`Get(LayoutCount)`

Returns 3 when there are three layouts in a database file.

Comments:

`Get(LayoutCount)` returns the total number of layouts within a file, including hidden layouts and layouts the user doesn't have privileges to see.

`Get(LayoutName)`

Category: Get

Syntax: `Get ( LayoutName )`

Parameters: none

Description: Returns the name of the layout currently displayed in the active window.

Examples:

`Get(LayoutName)`

Returns `Data Entry` when the Data Entry layout is displayed.

Returns `Invoice List` when the Invoice List layout is displayed.

Comments:

To change the name a layout, in Layout mode, go to Layouts, Layout Setup, General. Layouts do not need to be uniquely named.

`Get(LayoutNumber)`

Category: Get

Syntax: `Get ( LayoutNumber )`

Parameters: none

Description: Returns the number of the layout currently displayed in the active window. The order of layouts can be set in the Layouts, Set Layout Order menu.

Examples:

`Get (LayoutNumber)`

Returns 6 when the sixth layout on the Set Layout Order list is active.

Comments:

Get (LayoutNumber) can be used to keep track of the last layout a user visited. The following script takes a user from one layout to another, allows the user to complete other tasks, and then returns the user to the original layout:

```
Set Field [temp; Get(LayoutNumber)]
Go to Layout ["Other Layout"]
[perform script, process, etc]
Go to Layout [temp]
```

Because the layout you navigate to might be associated with a different table than the calling layout, the temp field used to store the layout number should be set to have global storage.

Get(LayoutTableName)

Category: Get

Syntax: Get (LayoutTableName)

Parameters: none

Description: Returns the name of the table occurrence (not the base table) from which the current layout shows records.

Examples:

Get(LayoutTableName)

Returns Invoices when the current layout is attached to the table occurrence named Invoices.

Returns Employees when the current layout is attached to the table occurrence named Employees.

Comments:

Because there is no way of retrieving the name of the base table with which a layout is associated, consider prefixing the names of table occurrences with an abbreviation that represents the base table. For instance, you might name a table occurrence INV|CustomerInvoices. You can then use text parsing functions to retrieve the base table name from the results returned by the Get (LayoutTableName) function.

Get(LayoutViewState)

Category: Get

Syntax: Get (LayoutViewState)

Parameters: none

Description: Returns a number that represent the view mode for the current layout in the active window:

Examples: Get (LayoutViewState) returns 0, 1, or 2, depending on the current layout's view state:

0 = View as Form

1 = View as List

2 = View as Table

Comments:

Get (LayoutViewState) is useful in scripts to test the state of the current layout. Unless a layout has been restricted not to be viewable in another state, users can manually change the state of the current layout, provided they have access to menu commands. You can detect whether the layout is in the proper state, and if necessary, change it with the View As script step.

Get(MultiUserState)

Category: Get

Syntax: Get (MultiUserState)

Parameters: none

Description: Returns a number that represents the FileMaker networking status for the current file.

Examples:

Get (MultiUserState)

Returns 0 when network sharing is off, or when network sharing is on but no privilege sets have the [fmapp] keyword enabled.

Returns 1 when network sharing is on, the database file is accessed from the host computer, and some or all users have the [fmapp] keyword enabled.

Returns 2 when network sharing is on, the database file is accessed from a client computer, and some or all users have the [fmapp] keyword enabled.

Get(NetworkProtocol)

Category: Get

Syntax: Get (NetworkProtocol)

Parameters: none

Description: Returns the name of the network protocol that FileMaker Pro is using on the current machine.

Examples:

Get (NetworkProtocol)

Returns TCP/IP.

B

Comments:

Unlike in previous versions of FileMaker, the only network protocol supported by FileMaker Pro 7 is TCP/IP. Get (NetworkProtocol) always returns TCP/IP, even if FileMaker Network sharing is off.

Get(PageNumber)

Category: Get

Syntax: Get (PageNumber)

Parameters: none

Description: When printing or previewing a document, this function returns the current page number. If nothing is being printed or previewed, Get (PageNumber) returns 0.

Examples:

Imagine you have an unstored calculation with the formula:

`"Page " & Get (PageNumber)`

When printing a multi-page report, this field could be placed in the footer of the layout and it would return the proper page number when the report was previewed or printed.

Comments:

If you are printing a report of unknown length and you want to determine the number of pages, you can have a script go to the last page and capture the value returned by Get (PageNumber) in a global field. This would then allow you to have something like "Page 2 of 5" appear in the footer of your report.

Get(PortalRowNumber)

Category: Get

Syntax: Get (PortalRowNumber)

Parameters: none

Description: Returns the number of the currently selected portal row. When no portal row is selected, Get (PortalRowNumber) returns 0.

Examples:

When the user clicks on the third row of a portal,

`Get (PortalRowNumber)`

returns 3.

When the user clicks out of the portal onto the layout itself,

`Get (PortalRowNumber)`

returns 0.

Comments:

Get (PortalRowNumber) is frequently used in scripts that need to loop through a set of records displayed in a portal. You can set the current portal row number into a global field, perform some set of operations outside the portal, then return to the proper row of the portal by using the Go to Portal Row [by Calculation] step.

Get(PrinterName)

Category: Get

Syntax: Get (PrinterName)

Parameters: none

Description: Returns information about the currently selected printer.

In Windows, Get (PrinterName) returns a text string containing the printer name, driver name, and printer port, separated by commas.

In Mac OS, Get (PrinterName) returns a text string with the name or IP address of the printer, as it appears in the Print Center.

Examples:

In Windows,

Get (PrinterName)

might return \\server1\Lexmark Optra M412 PS3, winspool,Ne02:.

In Mac OSX,

Get (PrinterName)

may return the IP address 255.5.5.255.

Or it may return the name of the current printer (if the printer is not networked). For example, hp LaserJet 4200.

Comments:

If there are certain print jobs that require that a specific printer be selected, you can test for Get (PrinterName) within a script and ask the user to select a different printer if necessary.

Get(PrivilegeSetName)

Category: Get

Syntax: Get (PrivilegeSetName)

Parameters: none

Description: Returns the name of the privilege set assigned to the current user.

B

Examples:

`Get (PrivilegeSetName)`

returns [`Full Access`] if you haven't modified the security settings of a new database.

`Get (PrivilegeSetName)`

returns `Sales` if the current user is logged in with an account assigned the Sales privilege set.

Comments:

Every account must be assigned one, and only one, privilege set.

`Get(RecordAccess)`

Category: Get

Syntax: `Get ( RecordAccess )`

Parameters: none

Description: Returns a number that represents the current user's access privileges for the current record. Record privileges are assigned via privilege set.

Examples:

`Get ( RecordAccess )`

returns `0` if the user does not have View or Edit privileges for the current record.

Returns `1` if the user has view-only access to the current record. This could mean the View is set to Yes for the current table, or that View is set to Limited and that the calculation defined for Limited access returns a value of True.

Returns `2` if the user has edit access for the current record. This could mean that Edit is set to Yes for the current table, or that Edit is set to Limited and that the calculation defined for Limited access returns a value of True.

Comments:

The `Get (RecordAccess)` function can be used to alert users of restricted privileges at the record level. Note that `Get (RecordAccess)` returns information only about global record privileges. Record access may be restricted through the layout access as well. However, in scripts, record access privileges overrule layout access restrictions.

To fully evaluate current record access, evaluate both the return values of `Get (LayoutAccess)` and the `Get (RecordAccess)` function.

`Get(RecordID)`

Category: Get

Syntax: `Get ( RecordID )`

Parameters: none

Description: Returns the unique ID number of the current record. This number is generated automatically by FileMaker Pro and does not change.

Examples:

Get (RecordID)

returns 275 when the FileMaker record ID is 275.

Comments:

The record ID is assigned sequentially within each table, beginning at 1. Record IDs are not re-used; if a record is deleted, its ID is not reassigned.

When files are converted from previous versions, record IDs from the original file are preserved.

The record ID is required for editing and deleting records via Custom Web Publishing, as this is how the record to be changed or deleted must be identified.

Get(RecordModificationCount)

Category: Get

Syntax: Get (RecordModificationCount)

Parameters: none

Description: Returns the total number of times the current record has been modified. A record change must be committed before the modification count updates.

Committing multiple field changes at once is considered a single record modification. Each time a change is committed, the modification count increases.

Examples:

Get (RecordModificationCount)

returns 0 if a record has never been modified.

Returns 17 if a record has been modified 17 times since it was originally created.

Comments:

Get (RecordModificationCount) can be used by custom Web applications to ensure that one user's changes do not overwrite another's. At the time the record is loaded into the Web browser, the record modification count can be stored. When the record is saved, the current record modification count can be checked against the stored one to see whether another user has updated the record in the meantime.

Duplicated records retain the same record modification count as the record from which they were created; the count is not reset to zero. There's no way to alter or reset the modification count.

B

Get(RecordNumber)

Category: Get

Syntax: Get (RecordNumber)

Parameters: none

Description: Returns a number that represents the position of a record in the current found set. This value changes depending on the found set and the sort order.

Examples:

Get (RecordNumber)

returns 1 for the first record in the found set.

Returns 83 for the 83rd record in a found set of 83 records.

Comments:

Get (RecordNumber) tells you a record's position within the found set. This is useful in situations where you want to hide the status area but still want to allow users to see where they are within a set.

To determine a unique and permanent record ID, use Get (RecordID).

Get(RequestCount)

Category: Get

Syntax: Get (RequestCount)

Parameters: none

Description: Returns the total number of find requests defined in the current window.

Examples:

If the current find request asks for invoices with values greater than $200.00,

Get (RequestCount)

returns 1.

If the current find request asks for invoices with values greater than $200 or invoices with dates after 1/1/2004,

Get (RequestCount)

returns 2.

Comments:

Get (RequestCount) can be used in scripted find routines to see whether the user has added any find requests to the default request. It is also useful as a boundary condition if you ever need to loop through all the find requests and either capture or set search parameters.

Get(ScreenDepth)

Category: Get

Syntax: Get (ScreenDepth)

Parameters: None

Description: Returns the number of bits needed to represent the color or shade of gray of a pixel on the user's monitor. A value of 8 represents 256 (equal to 2^8) colors or shades of gray.

Examples:

Get (ScreenDepth)

returns 32 on a display showing millions (2^32) of colors.

Returns 16 on a display showing thousands (2^16) of colors.

Returns 4 on a VGA display.

Returns 1 on a black-and-white display.

Comments:

Use Get (ScreenDepth) to alert users if their monitor color settings are set too low to view images correctly. For example:

```
If[Get(ScreenDepth)<32]
  Show Custom Dialog ["Color";"Your monitor should be set to "Millions
  of colors" to display images correctly"]
End If
```

Get(ScreenHeight)

Category: Get

Syntax: Get (ScreenHeight)

Parameters: none

Description: Returns the number of pixels that are displayed vertically on the current screen. When the active window spans more than one screen, this function calculates the value for the screen that contains the largest percentage of the window.

Examples:

Get (ScreenHeight)

returns 854 on a monitor set to display at 1280×854.

Comments:

Use Get (ScreenHeight) and Get (ScreenWidth) to check minimum resolution settings on a user's computer.

B

```
If [Get (ScreenHeight)<600 OR Get (ScreenWidth)<800]
  Show Custom Dialog ["Resolution";"This application requires a minimum
  of 800 x 600 screen resolution."]
  Perform Script ["Close All Files"]
End If
```

Get(ScreenWidth)

Category: Get

Syntax: Get (ScreenWidth)

Parameters: none

Description: Returns the number of pixels that are displayed horizontally on the active screen. When the active window spans more than one screen, this function calculates the value for the screen that contains the largest percentage of the window.

Examples:

Get (ScreenWidth)

returns 1280 when the user's monitor is set to display at 1280×854 resolution.

Comments:

See Get (ScreenHeight).

Get(ScriptName)

Category: Get

Syntax: Get (ScriptName)

Parameters: none

Description: Returns the name of the current script. When no script is running, Get (ScriptName) returns an empty string.

Examples:

Get(ScriptName)

returns Calculate Invoice if the current script is Calculate Invoice.

Comments:

One use of Get (ScriptName) is to capture errors. In this example, the Log Error script takes the script name as a parameter.

```
If [Get(LastError) <> 0]
  Perform Script ["Log Error"; Parameter: Get (ScriptName)]
End If
```

Passing the current script's name as a script parameter can be useful anytime a subscript can be called by multiple scripts.

B

Get(ScriptParameter)

Category: Get

Syntax: Get (ScriptParameter)

Parameters: none

Description: Retrieves the parameter that was passed to the current script.

Examples:

In this example, the Navigate script is called, with the parameter "West":

Perform Script ["Navigate"; "West"]

Within the Navigate script, the script parameter value ("West") is assigned to a field ("Direction") through the use of the following script step:

Set Field ["Location::Direction"; Get (ScriptParameter)]

Direction now equals West.

Comments:

The value of a script parameter can be retrieved anywhere within the script, regardless of subscript calls. Script parameters cannot be altered during execution of a script.

Subscripts do not inherit the script parameter of the calling script. Rather, they can be passed parameters of their own that exist only for the duration of the subscript. If you want a subscript to inherit a script parameter, pass Get (ScriptParameter) as the subscript's parameter.

Only one value can be passed as a script parameter, but that value can contain a delimited list, thus allowing multiple values to be passed.

→ For more information on how to pass and parse multi-valued script parameters, **see** Chapter 15, "Advanced Scripting," **p. 421**.

Script parameters can be specified when scripts are performed via buttons and via subscripts, but not when scripts are called manually from the Scripts menu or via a startup or shutdown script.

Get(SortState)

Category: Get

Syntax: Get (SortState)

Parameters: none

Description: Returns a number that represents the sort state of the active window.

Examples:

Get (SortState)

returns 0 if the found set in the active window is not sorted.

B

Returns 1 if the found set in the active window is sorted.

Returns 2 if the found set in the active window is partially sorted (semi-sorted).

Comments:

Get (SortState) can be used in a customized interface where the status area is normally hidden from the user. Also, Get (SortState) can be used to correctly display sort icons in a customized interface.

A sorted found set becomes semi-sorted if new records are created. Omitting or deleting records does not cause the sort status to change, however. Subsummary reports may not show expected results when the found set is semi-sorted.

Get(StatusAreaState)

Category: Get

Syntax: Get (StatusAreaState)

Parameters: none

Description: Returns a number that represents the state of the status area of the active window.

Examples:

Get(StatusAreaState)

returns 0 if the status area is hidden.

Returns 1 if the status area is visible.

Returns 2 if the status area is visible and locked.

Returns 3 if the status area is hidden and locked.

Comments:

If you want a single test that will tell you whether the status area is hidden (regardless of whether it's locked or not), use Mod (Get (StatusAreaState) ; 3). When this returns 0, the status area is hidden; when it's anything else, the status area is visible.

Get(SystemIPAddress)

Category: Get

Syntax: Get (SystemIPAddress)

Parameters: none

Description: Produces a return-delimited list of the IP addresses of all the machines connected to a NIC (Network Interface Controller) card.

Examples:

Returns 202.27.78.34, for example, when only one machine is connected.

Get(SystemLanguage)

Category: Get

Syntax: Get (SystemLanguage)

Parameters: none

Description: Returns the language setting of the user's machine.

Examples:

Get (SystemLanguage)

returns English on a system set to use English.

Get(SystemNICAddress)

Category: Get

Syntax: Get (SystemNICAddress)

Parameters: none

Description: Produces a return-delimited list containing the hardware addresses of all the NIC (Network Interface Controller) cards connected to the machine.

In Windows, you can find this address by typing **ipconfig /All** from a command prompt. On Mac OS X, you can find the NIC address by using the Apple System Profiler utility.

Examples:

Get (SystemNICAddress)

returns 00:30:65:cf:df:98.

Comments:

If the user's machine has multiple NIC cards, Get (SystemNICAddress) generates a return-delimited list of all their addresses. You might, for instance, have both a built-in Ethernet card and a wireless networking card installed in a laptop. Or, a server might have multiple built-in Ethernet ports. In both of these cases, Get (SystemNICAddress) returns the addresses of both devices.

Get(SystemPlatform)

Category: Get

Syntax: Get (SystemPlatform)

Parameters: none

Description: Returns a number that represents the current platform.

B

Examples:

`Get (SystemPlatform)`

returns `-1` if the current platform is Mac OS X.

Returns `-2` if the platform is Windows 2000 or Windows XP.

Comments:

Because FileMaker tends to change or add to the values in the platform-checking function (as new versions of operating systems become supported), checks against this function should be performed in a single, central location for ease of future updates. The results of the function may be stored in a global field during startup, and then referred to for subsequent platform checks throughout the rest of the database.

The reason that this function returns negative numbers is for backward compatibility. Positive 1 and 2 were used for operating systems that are no longer supported by FileMaker Pro.

`Get(SystemVersion)`

Category: Get

Syntax: `Get ( SystemVersion )`

Parameters: none

Description: Returns the current operating system version level.

Examples:

`Get (SystemVersion)`

returns `10.3.3` for Mac OS X version 10.3.3.

Returns `5.0` for Windows 2000.

Returns `5.1` for Windows XP.

Comments:

The values returned by `Get (SystemVersion)` will change as new versions of operating systems become available. As with checks against `Get (SystemPlatform)`, you should try to perform tests of the system version in a single, central location within your files so that it will be easy to update in the future.

`Get(TotalRecordCount)`

Category: Get

Syntax: `Get ( TotalRecordCount )`

Parameters: none

Description: Returns the total number of records in the current table, regardless of the state of the found set.

Examples:

`Get (TotalRecordCount)`

returns 283 when there are 283 records in the current table, regardless of the size of the current found set.

Comments:

The `Get (TotalRecordCount)` function is most often used in unstored calculations and scripts. Be sure to navigate to a layout that establishes the correct table context before referencing the function.

The total record count includes records that have been created but not yet committed. If such records are reverted, the total record count is decreased.

`Get(UserCount)`

Category: Get

Syntax: `Get ( UserCount )`

Parameters: none

Description: Returns the number of clients currently accessing the file, including the current user.

Examples:

`Get (UserCount)`

returns 1 if FileMaker Network sharing is turned off.

If a file is hosted by FileMaker Server 7, `Get (UserCount)` returns the number of client connections to the current file.

Comments:

Only FileMaker Pro client connections are counted by the `Get (UserCount)` function. Web, ODBC, and JDBC connections are not counted.

`Get(UserName)`

Category: Get

Syntax: `Get ( UserName )`

Parameters: none

Description: Returns the username that has been established for the current user's copy of FileMaker Pro. This is specified on the General tab of the Preferences dialog, and can be set to return either the system name or a custom name.

Examples:

`Get (UserName)`

returns `Delilah Bean` when the user-specified name is "Delilah Bean."

Comments:

The returned name is the same for anyone opening any database on the machine, regardless of what account name and password they've used. It's an application-level setting, not a document-level setting. The username can always be manually changed, regardless of whatever security you've set up.

For greater security, use `Get (AccountName)` to track and manage user access; a user cannot change the account name used to log in to a database file.

`Get(WindowContentHeight)`

Category: Get

Syntax: `Get ( WindowContentHeight )`

Parameters: none

Description: Returns the height, in pixels, of the content area of the current window. The content area is the area inside a window's frame, and doesn't include the title bar, scroll bars, or the status area.

Examples:

`Get (WindowContentHeight)`

on the Mac OS, returns 563 when the current window height is 600. The title bar and bottom scroll bar make up the other 37 pixels.

Comments:

The relationship of the content area dimensions to the overall window dimensions are different on each platform.

→ For a thorough discussion on the differences, **see** the discussion of window management techniques in Chapter 15, "Advanced Scripting," **p. 421**.

`Get(WindowContentWidth)`

Category: Get

Syntax: `Get ( WindowContentWidth )`

Parameters: none

Description: Returns the width, in pixels, of the content area of the current window. The content area is the area inside a window's frame, and doesn't include the title bar, scroll bars, or the status area.

Examples:

`Get(WindowContentWidth)`

on the Mac OS, returns 782 when the current window width is 800 and the status area is not showing.

B

Comments:

The relationship of the content area dimensions to the overall window dimensions are different on each platform.

→ For a thorough discussion on the differences, **see** the discussion of window management techniques in Chapter 15, "Advanced Scripting," **p. 421**.

`Get(WindowDesktopHeight)`

Category: Get

Syntax: `Get ( WindowDesktopHeight )`

Parameters: none

Description: Returns the height, in pixels, of the desktop space.

In Windows, the desktop space is the FileMaker Pro application window. `Get (WindowDesktopHeight)` measures the total vertical space used by the application window. If the application is maximized, the application window height is the screen height, minus the height of the Start menu (if it's placed on the bottom of the screen).

On Mac OS X, the desktop space includes everything on the screen except the top menu bar.

Examples:

`Get (WindowDesktopHeight)`

returns 746 in the Mac OS when the current monitor's resolution is set to 1152×768. The menu bar accounts for the other 22 pixels of height.

Comments:

You cannot programmatically set the window desktop height or width, nor on Windows can you tell where the application window has been positioned on the user's monitor.

`Get(WindowDesktopWidth)`

Category: Get

Syntax: `Get ( WindowDesktopWidth )`

Parameters: none

Description: Returns the width, in pixels, of the desktop space.

In Windows, the desktop space is the FileMaker Pro application window. `Get (WindowDesktopWindow)` measures the total horizontal space used by the application window. If the application is maximized, the application window width is the screen width, minus the width of the Start menu (if it's placed on the side of the screen).

On Mac OS X, the desktop space includes everything on the screen except the top menu bar.

B

Examples:

Get (WindowDesktopWidth)

returns 1152 in the Mac OS when the current monitor's resolution is set to 1152×768.

Comments:

You can not programmatically set the window desktop height or width, nor on Windows can you tell where the application window has been positioned on the user's monitor.

Get(WindowHeight)

Category: Get

Syntax: Get (WindowHeight)

Parameters: None

Description: Returns the total height, in pixels, of the current window. The current window is usually the active window, but it's also possible for a script to run in a window that isn't the active foreground window.

Examples:

Get (WindowHeight)

returns 541 when the window that is being acted upon is 541 pixels tall.

Comments:

The window height and width return the outside dimensions of a window. So, if you make a new window and specify a height and width of 300, then the Get (WindowHeight) and Get (WindowWidth) would both return 300.

Be aware that the window height and width is different from the window content height and width, which return the inside dimensions of a window.

Get(WindowLeft)

Category: Get

Syntax: Get (WindowLeft)

Parameters: None

Description: Returns the horizontal distance, in pixels, from the outer left edge of a window to the left edge of the application window.

Examples:

Get (WindowLeft)

returns 0 when the left edge of the window being acted upon is flush with the left edge of the application window.

B

Comments:

See Get (WindowDesktopHeight) for a discussion of how the application window is defined for each platform.

If any docked toolbars are placed along the left edge of the application window, the position of the origin shifts inward. The Get (WindowLeft) function is relative to the inside edge of the application window, inclusive of docked toolbars.

Get (WindowLeft) can return negative numbers. This may indicate the window is located on a second monitor positioned to the left of the first, or it may mean that a portion of the left-hand side of the window is hidden.

Get(WindowMode)

Category: Get

Syntax: Get (WindowMode)

Parameters: None

Description: Returns a number that indicates in what mode the active window is.

Examples:

Get (WindowMode)

returns 0 for Browse mode.

Returns 1 for Find mode.

Returns 2 for Preview mode.

Returns 3 if printing is in progress.

Comments:

Notice that this function can never return a value indicating that a window is in Layout mode. If a script ever attempts to operate within the context of a window that is in Layout mode, the window is automatically switched to Browse mode and the script continues as expected.

Get(WindowName)

Category: Get

Syntax: Get (WindowName)

Parameters: None

Description: Returns the name of the active window.

Examples:

Get (WindowName)

returns Contacts if the window being acted upon is named Contacts.

Comments:

The name of a window is the text string that appears in the window's title bar. A window's name can be specified when it is created with the New Window script step. It can also be altered with the Set Window Title script step.

Window names do not need to be unique. If a user manually creates a new window, the name of the new window will be the same as the active window at the time the user selected New Window, but will have a - 2 (or higher number if necessary) appended to it.

Get(WindowTop)

Category: Get

Syntax: Get (WindowTop)

Parameters: None

Description: Returns the vertical distance, in pixels, from the top edge of a window to the inside of the top of the application window.

Examples:

Get (WindowTop)

returns 0 when the top edge of a window is positioned flush to the top of the application window.

Comments:

See Get (WindowDesktopHeight) for a discussion of how the application window is defined for each platform.

If any docked toolbars are placed along the top of the application window, this shifts the location of the inside edge of the application window.

Get (WindowTop) can return negative numbers. This may indicate the window is located on a second monitor positioned above the first, or it may mean that a portion of the top of the window is hidden.

Get(WindowVisible)

Category: Get

Syntax: Get (WindowVisible)

Parameters: None

Description: Returns a number indicating whether the current window is visible or hidden.

Examples:

Get (WindowVisible)

Returns 1 if the window is visible.

Returns 0 if the window is hidden.

Comments:

When you call a subscript in another file, it operates from the context of the front-most window in that file, but that window does not need to become the active window. The current window can therefore be different from the active, foreground window, and it can either be hidden or visible.

Get(WindowWidth)

Category: Get

Syntax: Get (WindowWidth)

Parameters: None

Description: Returns the total width, in pixels, of the current window. A window retains all its properties, such as height and width, even if it is hidden.

Examples:

Get (WindowWidth)

Returns 650 when the window that is being acted upon is 650 pixels wide.

Comments:

The window height and width measures the outside dimensions of a window, whereas the window content height and window content width measure the inside dimensions of a window.

Window height and width can be assigned when creating and resizing windows.

GetAsCSS()

Category: Text

Syntax: GetAsCSS (text)

Parameters: text—any expression that resolves to a text string

Description: GetAsCSS()returns a representation of the specified text string, marked up with CSS (Cascading Style Sheet) tags. CSS can capture rich text formatting that has been applied to a text string.

Examples:

The field myField contains Go Team and has manually been formatted as follows:

Font = Helvetica, Font Size = 36 points, Font Color = red, Font Style = bold.

GetAsCSS (myField) returns

```
<SPAN STYLE= "font-size: 36px;color: #AA0000;font-weight: bold;
➥> text-align: left;"Go Team</SPAN>
```

Comments:

Representing formatted text as CSS means that you can export stylized text and have it rendered properly by CSS-aware applications, such as Web browsers.

GetAsCSS() is also useful within FileMaker itself, because you can determine what special formatting, if any, has been applied to a field.

GetAsDate()

Category: Text

Syntax: GetAsDate (text)

Parameters: text—any text expression or text field that returns a date, formatted the same as the date format on the system where the file was created.

Description:

GetAsDate() interprets a text string that contains a date as an actual date. Anytime you use a date constant within a calculation formula, you should use the GetAsDate() or Date() functions to ensure that the date is interpreted correctly.

Examples:

GetAsDate ("1/1/2004")

Returns 1/1/2004 stored internally as a date.

GetAsDate ("1/1/2004") + 8

Returns 1/9/2004. In this case, had the GetAsDate() function not been used, "1/1/2004" + 8 would have returned 112012.

GetAsNumber()

Category: Text

Syntax: GetAsNumber (text)

Parameters: text—any valid text expression that contains numbers.

Description: GetAsNumber() returns only the numbers from a text string, as a data type number. All non-numeric characters are dropped from the string.

Examples:

GetAsNumber ("abc123")

Returns 123.

GetAsNumber ("$100.10")

Returns 100.1.

B

Comments:

Use GetAsNumber() to strip all non-numeric characters out of a text string. For instance, you might have a phone number field to which you want to apply some formatting. GetAsNumber (PhoneNumber) returns just the numeric characters from the field, stripping all punctuation and spaces, so that you can then apply whatever new formatting you wish.

GetAsNumber() can also be applied to date and time fields to coerce the data into its integer representation. For instance,

GetAsNumber (Get (CurrentDate))

would return 731689 when the date was 4/18/2004.

GetAsSVG()

Category: Text

Syntax: GetAsSVG (text)

Parameters: text—any expression that resolves to a text string.

Description: GetAsSVG() returns a representation of the text string, marked up in SVG (Scalable Vector Graphics) format. SVG can capture rich text formatting that has been applied to a text string.

Examples:

The field myField contains two phrases, Go Team and Hello World!, each with some text formatting applied to it.

GetAsSVG (myField)

might return:

```
<StyleList>
<Style#0>"font-size: 36px;color: #AA0000;font-weight: bold;text-align: left;",
➡ Begin: 1, End: 8</Style>
<Style#1>"color: #000000;font-weight: normal;font-style:normal;text-align:
➡ left;", Begin: 9, End: 20</Style>
</StyleList>
<Data>
<Span style="0">Go Team </Span>
<Span style="1">Hello World!</Span>
</Data>
```

Comments:

SVG format can be used to transfer formatted text from FileMaker to other applications. You can also test a SVG-formatted version of a text string to determine what, if any, formatting has been applied to the string.

B

GetAsText()

Category: Text

Syntax: GetAsText (data)

Parameters: data—any field or expression that returns a number, date, time, timestamp, or container.

Description: GetAsText() returns the text equivalent of data in any other data type. You can then manipulate the data as you would any other text string.

When applied to a container field that stores a reference to an object, GetAsText() returns the path to the container data. If the container data is embedded in the database, GetAsText() returns a question mark.

Examples:

GetAsText (Get (CurrentDate))

Might return 3/8/2004.

Comments:

One frequent use of GetAsText() is to get the path and filename information for container data stored as a reference. You can then parse the path information and build links to other objects in the same location.

In most cases, you do not need to explicitly coerce number, date, and time data into text before performing text operations on the data. Text functions operate on numbers, dates, and times as if they were text strings, even if you don't wrap the data with GetAsText().

GetAsTime()

Category: Text

Syntax: GetAsTime (text)

Parameters: text—any text expression or text field containing a time.

Description: GetAsTime() returns the data specified in the text string as data-type time. The value can then be manipulated like any other time data.

Examples:

GetAsTime ("01:30:30")

Returns 1:30:30 AM when you specify Time as the calculation result.

GetAsTime ("01:30:30")

Returns 1/1/0001 1:30:30 AM when you specify Timestamp as the calculation result.

GetAsTime (48000)

Returns 8:53:20.

B

Use GetAsTime() when working with literal time strings in calculation formulas:

GetAsTime ("15:30:00") - FinishTime

would yield the elapsed time between 3:30pm and the FinishTime.

Comments:

GetAsTime() can be used to convert an integer representing a number of seconds into an elapsed time, as demonstrated in the third of the preceding examples.

GetAsTimestamp ( )

Category: Text

Syntax: GetAsTimestamp (text)

Parameters: text—any text string or expression that returns a text string that contains a timestamp.

Description: GetAsTimestamp() converts a timestamp contained in a text string into a data-type timestamp. It can then be used in formulas as any other timestamp would be.

Examples:

GetAsTimestamp ("1/1/2004 1:10:10")

Returns 1/1/2004 1:10:10.

GetAsTimeStamp (61997169000)

Returns 8/12/1965 7:50:00 p.m..

Comments:

GetAsTimestamp() also converts numbers into timestamps. See the Timestamp() function for more information on how timestamps can be represented as numbers.

Use GetAsTimestamp() anytime you include a literal string containing a timestamp. For instance, to find out the amount of time that has elapsed between a fixed time in the past and now, you would use the following formula:

Timestamp (Get(CurrentDate); Get (CurrentTime) - GetAsTimestamp
➡("6/29/1969 4:23:56 PM"))

GetField ( )

Category: Logical

Syntax: GetField (fieldName)

Parameters: fieldName—a text string, or field or expression that returns a text string, which contains the name of a field.

Description: Returns the contents of the fieldName field.

B

Examples:

```
GetField ("myField")
```

Returns the contents of myField.

```
GetField (myField)
```

Returns the contents of FirstName, when myField contains the string "FirstName".

```
GetField (MiddleValues (fieldList; counter ;1))
```

Returns the contents of the LastName field, when fieldList is a return-delimited list of field names containing "FirstName¶LastName¶City¶State¶Zip" and counter is 2.

Comments:

Essentially, GetField() provides a level of abstraction when retrieving the contents of a field. Instead of saying "Give me the value of the FirstName field," for instance, it's like saying "Give me the value of the field whose name is in the gWhatField field." By putting a different field name in the gWhatField field, you can retrieve the contents of a different field.

The Evaluate() function can always be used in place of the GetField(). In this example, for instance, Evaluate (gSelectColumn) and GetField (gSelectColumn) both return the same result. The opposite is not true, however. Evaluate() can perform complex evaluations and can have trigger conditions defined, whereas GetField() can retrieve only the contents of a field.

```
GetNextSerialValue()
```

Category: Design

Syntax: GetNextSerialValue (fileName ; fieldName)

Parameters: fileName—a string or text expression that represents the name of an open file; fieldName—a string or text expression that represents the name of the field for which to return results.

Description: Returns the next value for a field defined to auto-enter a serialized value.

Examples:

```
GetNextSerialValue ("Invoices" ; "InvoiceID")
```

might return 5435.

```
GetNextSerialValue ( Get (FileName) ; "Contacts::ContactID")
```

might return 84.

Comments:

It's good practice to use TableOccurrence::FieldName syntax to reference the field in this formula so that it can be evaluated in any context. Without explicitly naming a table occurrence, this function assumes the field can be found in the current context, which may not be the case. Because the auto-entered serial number is defined at the table level, it doesn't matter which of a table's occurrences you reference; they will all return the same result.

GetRepetition()

Category: Repeating

Syntax: GetRepetition (repeatingField ; repetitionNumber)

Parameters: repeatingField—any repeating field, or an expression that returns a reference to a repeating field; repetitionNumber—a positive integer representing the repetition number to retrieve.

Description: Returns the contents of the specified repetition of a repeating field.

Examples:

GetRepetition (RepPercentage ; 2)

Returns the contents of the second repetition of the RepPercentage field.

If you had a repeating text field called QuoteOfTheDay that contained 20 repetitions, you could extract a random quote using the following formula:

```
Let (repNumber = Ceiling (Random * 20) ;
   GetRepetition (QuoteOfTheDay ; repNumber)
)
```

Comments:

A new shorthand notation can be used in place of the GetRepetition() function. The repetition number can be placed in square brackets after the name of the repeating field. For instance, GetRepetition (myField ; 6) is the same as myField[6].

GetSummary()

Category: Summary

Syntax: GetSummary (summaryField ; breakField)

Parameters: summaryField—a field of type summary, or an expression that returns a reference to one; breakField—a field, or an expression that returns a reference to one.

Description: The GetSummary() function returns the value of summaryField when summarized by breakField. The found set must be sorted by breakField for GetSummary() to return the proper value.

When the summaryField and the breakField are the same field, GetSummary() returns a grand summary representing the entire found set of records.

Examples:

Given the following record set, sorted by Country, and a summary field called Sum_Sales defined as the Total of Sales:

B

Country	Region	Sales
U.S.	North	55,000
U.S.	South	45,000
China	North	35,000
China	South	40,000

A field `SalesByCountry` defined as

`GetSummary (Sum_Sales ; Country)`

returns `100,000` for the two U.S. records and returns `75,000` for the two China records.

Comments:

`GetSummary()` returns the same values that you would see if you were to place the specified summary field in a subsummary report. `GetSummary()` is necessary when you need to use summarized values in calculation formulas or for display purposes while in Browse mode.

To calculate a grand summary value, use the same summary field for both the summary field and the break field parameters.

→ **See** Chapter 10, "Reporting with Grouped Data," **p. 269** for more practical examples and commentary on the `GetSummary()` function.

`Hour()`

Category: Time

Syntax: `Hour ( time )`

Parameters: `time`—any valid time value or expression that returns a valid time value.

Description: The `Hour()` function returns an integer representing the number of hours specified by the time parameter.

Examples:

`Hour ("10:45:20") = 10`

`Hour ("12:15 am") = 0`

`Hour ("11:15 pm") = 23`

`Hour ( Get ( CurrentTime ))`

will return a value from 0 to 23.

Comments:

When its parameter represents a specific time of day, the `Hour()` function returns a value from 0 to 23. To map this into the more familiar 1 to 12 range, you can use the following formula:

`Mod ( Hour (time) -1 ; 12 ) + 1`

The `Hour()` function can return an integer value outside of the 0 to 23 range when its parameter represents a duration rather than a specific time of day. For instance, `Hour ("65:12:53")` returns 65.

If()

Category: Logical

Syntax: `If ( test ; result1 ; result2 )`

Parameters: `test`—a logical expression that returns True (1) or False (0); `result1`—the expression to evaluate if test is true; `result2`—the expression to evaluate if test is false.

Description:

The `If()` function returns one of two possible results depending on whether the test supplied as the first parameter is true or false. `Result1` is returned if the test is true; `Result2` is returned if the test is false.

The test parameter should be an expression that returns a numeric or Boolean result. For numeric results, zero and null are both considered false; all other values are considered true.

Examples:

```
If( DayOfWeek (Get (CurrentDate))) = 1 ;
    "It's Sunday, no work!" ; // true result
    "Get back to work!" // false result
)
If ( myFlagField ; graphicTrue ; graphicFalse)
```

Looks for a true value (non zero, non blank) in `myFlagField`, and displays the correct graphic container.

```
If (not IsEmpty (Taxable) and TaxRate > 0;
    Price + (Price * TaxRate);
    Price
)
```

Comments:

If the test contains multiple conditions separated by "and" or "or," FileMaker stops evaluating the conditions as soon as it can determine the overall truthfulness of the test. For instance, if the test parameter is `IsEmpty(FieldA) and IsEmpty(FieldB)`, if Field A is not empty, then there's no way that the entire expression could be true. FileMaker will not evaluate the other condition involving FieldB, and will return the false result.

You can nest `If()` statements within one another, but it is usually more efficient to use a `Case()` statement rather than an `If()` in such cases.

Int()

Category: Number

Syntax: `Int ( number )`

Parameters: `number`—any expression that resolves to a numeric value.

Description: Returns the whole number (integer) part of number without rounding. Digits to the right of the decimal point are dropped.

Examples:

`Int (1.0005)`

Returns 1.

`Int (-1.0005)`

Returns -1.

Comments:

Note that for positive numbers, `Floor()` and `Int()` return the same results, however, for negative numbers, `Int()` returns the next larger integer, whereas `Floor()` returns the next smaller integer.

There are many practical uses for the `Int()` function. For instance, given any date, to find the date of the Sunday preceding it, use the formula `GetAsDate (Int (myDate/7) * 7)`. Similarly, to test whether an integer is odd or even, you can test whether `Int (num/2) = num/2`.

`IsEmpty()`

Category: Logical

Syntax: `IsEmpty ( expression )`

Parameters: `expression`—typically a field name, but can be any valid FileMaker Pro calculation formula

Description: Returns 1 (True) if the referenced field is empty or if the expression returns an empty string. Returns 0 (False) if the field or expression is not empty.

Examples:

`IsEmpty (myField)`

Returns 1 if `myField` is empty.

`IsEmpty (Name_First & Name_Last)`

Returns 1 if the result of concatenating the two fields together is an empty string.

Comments:

Remember that zero is a valid entry for a number field. If a number field contains a 0, it is not considered to be empty.

B

`IsValid()`

Category: Logical

Syntax: `IsValid ( expression )`

Parameters: expression—typically a field name, but can be any valid FileMaker Pro calculation formula.

Description: Returns either a 1 (True) or a 0 (False), depending on whether the field or expression returns valid data.

IsValid returns a 0 if there is a data type mismatch (that is, text in a date field) or if FileMaker cannot locate the table or field that is referenced.

Otherwise it returns 1, indicating that the data is valid.

Examples:

IsValid (myField)

Returns 1 (True) when myField is present and contains data appropriate to its defined data type.

IsValid (Contacts::Name)

Returns 0 (False) if the current record has no related records in the Contacts table.

IsValidExpression()

Category: Logical

Syntax: IsValidExpression (expression)

Parameters: expression—a text string containing a calculation expression, or a field or expression that returns a text string that contains a calculation expression.

Description: Returns 1 (True) if the expression syntax is correct. Returns 0 (False) if the expression has a syntax error.

Examples:

IsValidExpression ("Length (SideA)")

Returns 1 (True) as long as there is, in fact, a field named SideA.

IsValidExpression ("Middle (myField ; 1)")

Returns 0 (False) because the Middle function requires three parameters to be considered valid syntax.

IsValidExpression (myFormula)

Returns 1 (True) if the contents of myFormula would be considered a valid calculation expression.

Comments:

B

The IsValidExpression() function is often used in conjunction with the Evaluate() function to ensure that Evaluate() is passed a valid expression. For instance, if users are allowed to enter a formula into a field called myFormula, and you want to have another field express the results of that formula, you could use the following:

```
If (IsValidExpression (myFormula) ; Evaluate (myFormula) ; "Invalid formula: "
➥& TextColor (myFormula ; RBG (255 ; 0 ; 0)))
```

An expression is considered invalid if it contains syntax errors or if any of the referenced fields cannot be found. Errors that might occur only during execution of the expression, such as record access restrictions, are not detected by the IsValidExpression() formula.

Last()

Category: Repeating

Syntax: Last (field)

Parameters: field—any repeating field or related field.

Description: If the specified field is a repeating field, Last() returns the last valid, non-blank value in the field. If the specified field is a related field, it returns the last non-blank value from the set of related records. The order of the set of related records is determined by the sort order of the relationship. If no sort order has been specified, then the creation order is used.

Examples:

When RepPercentage is a repeating field with the values .04, .05, and .06, Last (RepPercentage) returns .06.

```
Last (PhoneNumber::Number)
```

Returns the most recent phone number entry, assuming no sort is specified for the relationship.

LayoutIDs()

Category: Design

Syntax: LayoutIDs (fileName)

Parameters: fileName—a string or text expression that represents the name of an open file. It can include a file extension, but doesn't need one.

Description: Returns a carriage return–delimited list of layout IDs for the specified file. The list is ordered according to the current layout order, not the creation order.

Examples:

```
LayoutIDs (Get(FileName))
```

Might return a list of values that looks like this:

```
3
9
10
24
13
28
```

Comments:

LayoutIDs are assigned in sequential order beginning at 1. The original file's LayoutIDs are retained when older databases are converted to FileMaker Pro 7.

LayoutNames()

Category: Design

Syntax: LayoutNames (fileName)

Parameters: fileName—a string or text expression that represents the name of an open file. It can include a file extension, but doesn't need one.

Description: Returns a carriage return–delimited list of layout names for the specified file.

Examples:

LayoutNames (Get (FileName))

Might return a list of values that looks like this:

Contact_List
Contact_Detail
Invoice_List
Invoice_Detail

Comments:

As with the LayoutIDs() function, the order of the layout names is determined by the current order of the layouts, not their creation order.

If you wanted to find out a particular layout's ID (say, the Contact_Detail layout), you can use the LayoutNames() and LayoutIDs() functions together, as follows:

```
Let ( [
  LNs = LayoutNames (Get(FileName));
  LIs = LayoutIDs (Get(FileName));
  pos = Position (LNs; "Contact_Detail" ; 1 ; 1);
  num = PatternCount (Left(LNs, pos) ; "¶") + 1 ] ;
  GetAsNumber (MiddleValues (LIs; num ; 1))
)
```

Left()

Category: Text

Syntax: Left (text ; numberOfCharacters)

Parameters: text—any expression that resolves to a text string; numberOfCharacters—any expression that resolves to a positive integer.

Description: Returns a string containing the first *n* characters from the specified text string. If the string is shorter than numberOfCharacters, the entire string is returned. If numberOfCharacters is less than 1, an empty string is returned.

B

Examples:

```
Left ("Hello" ; 2)
```

Returns He.

```
Left (FirstName ; 1)
```

Returns the first character of the FirstName field.

Comments:

The Left() function is commonly used in text parsing routines to extract portions of a text string. It is often used in conjunction with other text functions. For example, to extract the City portion of a field (called "CSZ") containing "City, State Zip" data, you could use the following formula:

```
Let (commaPosition = Position (CSZ; "," ; 1 ; 1) ; Left (CSZ ;
➥commaPosition - 1))
```

LeftValues()

Category: Text

Syntax: LeftValues (textToFilter ; numberOfValues)

Parameters: textToFilter—a return-delimited text string or expression that returns a return-delimited text string; numberOfValues—any positive number or expression that returns a positive number.

Description: Returns the specified number of items from the beginning of the textToFilter parameter.

Examples:

```
LeftValues("A¶B¶C¶D¶E";3)
```

Returns the following list:

A
B
C

```
LeftValues (WindowNames;1)
```

Returns the name of the active window.

Comments:

The LeftValues() function returns the first *n* items from a return-delimited array. The items will themselves be a return-delimited array, and there will always be a trailing return at the end of the last item.

You can remove the trailing return in a number of ways. If you are extracting a single item from the beginning of a list, you can use the Substitute() function to remove any return characters—for instance, Substitute (LeftValues (text ; 1) ; "¶" ; ""). You would not use this method when returning multiple items because the internal delimiters would be lost as well. Instead, the following function returns everything except the last character of the extracted list:

```
Let (x = LeftValues (text; n) ; Left (x ; Length (x) - 1 ))
```

Another option is the following:

```
LeftWords (LeftValues (text ; n) ; 999999)
```

This function takes advantage of the fact that the `LeftWords()` function ignores any leading or trailing delimiters. Be aware that this function also ignores leading or trailing delimiters (including punctuation symbols) from the actual items in the array, so in some cases this function does not return the desired result. The safest function to use in all cases is the `Let()` function (described ahead).

LeftWords()

Category: Text

Syntax: `LeftWords ( text ; numberOfWords )`

Parameters: `text`—any expression that resolves to a text field; `numberOfWords`—any positive number or expression that returns a positive number.

Description: Returns the first *n* number of words in a text expression, where *n* is the number specified in the `numberOfWords` parameter.

Examples:

```
LeftWords("the quick brown fox jumps" ; 3)
```

Returns `the quick brown`.

```
LeftWords(FullName ; 1)
```

Returns `Joe` when `FullName` contains `"Joe Smith"`.

Comments:

Be aware of what symbols are considered to be word breaks by FileMaker Pro. Spaces, return characters, and most punctuation symbols are considered to be word breaks. Multiple word breaks next to each other (for example, two spaces, a comma and a space) are considered as a single word break.

Certain punctuation symbols are word breaks when separating alpha characters, but not when separating numeric characters. These include the colon (:), slash (/), period (.), comma (,), and dash (-). For instance, `LeftWords ("54.6" ; 1)` returns `54.6`, but `LeftWords ("x.y" ; 1)` returns `x`. The reason for this behavior is that those symbols are valid date, time, and number separators.

Leading and trailing punctuation around a word may be ignored by the `LeftWords()` function. For example, `LeftWords ("John Q. Public, Jr."; 2)` returns `John Q`, but `LeftWords ("John Q. Public, Jr."; 3)` returns `John Q. Public`.

B

Length()

Category: Text

Syntax: Length (text)

Parameters: text—any expression that resolves to a text string.

Description: Returns the number of characters in the specified text string. Numbers, letters, punctuation, spaces, and carriage returns are all considered as characters.

Examples:

Length ("Hello there!")

Returns 12.

Length (LastName)

Returns 8 when LastName contains "Humphrey".

Length (Get (CurrentDate))

Returns 9 when the date is 3/27/2004.

Note that in previous versions of FileMaker, this last example would have returned 6, because the serialized numeric value for the current date would have been used (as opposed to the "3/27/2004)" formula). To achieve that same result, use the following formula:

Length (GetAsNumber (Get (CurrentDate)))

Comments:

The Length() function is often used as part of data validation rules. For instance, if you want to make sure that users enter phone numbers with either 7 or 10 digits, you could set up a validation by calculation rule as follows:

Length (Phone) = 7 or Length (Phone) = 10

Let()

Category: Logical

Syntax: Let ({[}var1=expression1 {; var2=expression2...]} ; calculation)

Parameters: var(n)—any valid variable name. The rules for naming variables are the same as for defining fields. expression(n)—any calculation formula, the results of which are assigned to the var(n) variable. calculation—any calculation formula.

Parameters in curly braces { } are optional.

Description: The Let() function enables you to declare local variables within a calculation formula. The variables exist only within the boundaries of the Let() function itself.

The first parameter of the Let() function is a list of variable names and expressions. If multiple variables are declared, the list needs to be enclosed in square brackets. The items in the list are separated by semicolons. The variables are set in the order in which they appear.

B

This means that you can use previously defined variables as part of the expression to define another variable.

The final parameter, `calculation`, is some calculation formula that you want to evaluate. That formula can reference any of the variables declared in the first half of the function.

Duplicate variable names are not allowed, but variables can be named the same as existing fields. If this happens, the value assigned to the variable, not the field, will be used in future references to the variable within the `Let()` function.

Examples:

The following formula extracts the domain name from an email address:

```
Let( [
   start = Position (eMail ;"@" ;1 ;1);
   numberOfCharacters = Length (eMail) - start];
   Right ( eMail ; numberOfCharacters)
)
```

The following example produces a summary of a student's grades:

```
Let ([
   TotalGradePoints = Sum (Grades::GradePoints);
   CreditPoints = Sum (Classes::CreditPoints);
   GPA = Round (TotalGradePoints/CreditPoints ; 2)] ;
   "Total Grade Points: "& TotalGradePoints & "¶" &
   "Available Credit Points: " & CreditPoints & "¶" &
   "Your GPA is: " & GPA
)
```

The final example formula returns the volume of a pyramid:

```
Let(
   SideOfBase = 2 * Sqrt(2 * SlantHeight^2 - Height^2;
   SideOfBase^2 * Height/3
)
```

Comments:

`Let()` can be used to simplify complex, nested calculation formulas. In the case where a subexpression is used many times within a formula, the `Let()` function may also provide a performance benefit because the subexpression is evaluated only once, when it is assigned to the variable.

Lg()

Category: Number

Syntax: `Lg ( number )`

Parameters: `number`—any expression that resolves to a positive numeric value.

Description: Returns the base-2 logarithm of `number`. Negative values for `number` return an error.

Examples:

```
Lg (1) = 0
Lg (2) = 1
Lg (32) = 5
```

Comments:

The base-2 logarithm (often called the *binary logarithm*) of a number is the power of 2 that you would need to generate the number. Thus, if 2^x = y, then Lg(y) = x. The value returned by the Lg() function is increased by 1 every time that *x* is doubled.

Ln()

Category: Number

Syntax: Ln (number)

Parameters: number—any positive number or expression that returns a positive number.

Description: Returns the natural logarithm of the specified number. The natural logarithm uses the transcendental number *e* as its base. The value of *e* is approximately 2.71828.

Examples:

```
Ln (2.7182818)
```

Returns .9999999895305023.

```
Ln (Exp(1))
```

Returns 1.

```
Ln (100)
```

Returns 4.6051701859880914.

```
Ln (Exp(5))
```

Returns 5.

Comments:

Exp() and Ln() are inverse functions of one another.

The Log() and Lg() functions produce base-10 and base-2 logarithms, respectively. The Ln() function produces base-*e* logarithms, but it can also be used to solve a logarithm of any base. The log, base-*x*, of *y*, is equivalent to the Ln (y) / Ln (x).

Log()

Category: Number

Syntax: Log (number)

Parameters: number—any positive number or expression that returns a positive number.

Description: Returns the base-10 logarithm of number.

Examples:

`Log (1)`

Returns 0, because $10^0 = 1$.

`Log (100)`

Returns 2, because $10^2 = 100$.

`Log (1000)`

Returns 3, because $10^3 = 1000$.

Comments:

Logarithms are used to determined the power to which a number must be raised to equal some other number. If $x^n = y$, then $n = Log_x(y)$. The Log() function assumes a base (the variable x in the preceding formula) of 10. The Lg() function uses a base of 2, whereas the Ln() function uses a base of e.

Lookup()

Category: Logical

Syntax: `Lookup ( sourceField { ; failExpression } )`

Parameters: sourceField—any related field; failExpression—an expression to evaluate and return if the lookup fails. This is an optional parameter.

Description: Returns the contents of sourceField, or if no related record is found, the result of the failExpression. The table containing the sourceField must be related to the table where the Lookup() is defined.

A calculation field that contains a Lookup() function can be stored or unstored. If it is unstored, then anytime the sourceField changes, the calculation field updates. If the calculation is stored, which is typically why you want to use a Lookup in the first place, then changes to the sourceField do not cascade automatically through to the calculation field. Lookup() is retriggered when any of the relationship's match fields (in the current table, not the source table) are modified, or when a relookup is triggered on any of those fields.

Examples:

Imagine you have a stored calculation field in an Invoice table called CustomerNameLookup, defined as follows:

`Lookup (Customer::CustomerName;"<Missing Customer>")`

Assume that the Invoice and Customer tables are related on the CustomerID. Whenever the CustomerID field is modified in the Invoice table, this triggers the lookup, and the name of the customer is copied into CustomerNameLookup. If an invalid CustomerID is entered, <Missing Customer> is returned. Because CustomerNameLookup is stored, indexed searches can be performed on it.

B

Be aware, however, that if the `CustomerName` field is updated in the Customer table, the change does not cascade automatically through to the Invoice table.

Comments:

`Lookup()` is invaluable for addressing performance issue caused by interacting with related (and hence unindexed) values.

`LookupNext()`

Category: Logical

Syntax: `LookupNext ( sourceField ; lower/higher Flag )`

Parameters: `sourceField`—any related field; `lower/higher Flag`—keyword that indicates whether to take the next lower or higher value if no direct match is found.

Description: Returns the contents of `sourceField`, or if no related record is found, the next lower or higher match value. The table containing the `sourceField` must be related to the table where the `LookupNext()` is defined.

The `LookupNext()` function is very similar to the `Lookup()` function; they differ only in how they handle the case of no matching record. The `Lookup()` function returns a fail expression in such cases, whereas the `LookupNext()` returns the value associated with the next lower or higher match.

The `Lower` and `Higher` flags are keywords and should not be placed in quotation marks.

Examples:

`Lookup (ShipRates::ShippingCost ; Higher)`

Returns the contents of the `ShippingCost` field from the ShipRates table. If no exact match is found, the next highest match is returned.

Comments:

See the `Lookup()` function to learn about how a lookup is triggered and how the storage options determine how often the `LookupNext()` function is to be refreshed.

Looking up a value from the next higher or lower matching record is desirable when mapping a continuous variable onto a categorical variable. Think, for instance, of how student grades typically map to letter grades. A grade of 90 to 100 is considered an A, 80 to 89 is a B, 70 to 79 is a C, and so on. The percentage value is a continuous variable, whereas the letter grades are categorical.

Using the `Lookup()` function, if you wanted to use the student's percentage score to retrieve the letter grade, you would need to have records for every possible combination of percentage and letter grade.

The `LookupNext()` function makes it possible to have records representing only the border conditions. For student grades, you would need to have 5 records in your lookup table: 90 is

B

an A, 80 is a B, 70 is a C, 60 is a D, and 0 is an F. You could then relate a student's percentage score to this table, and define the following formula as the StudentLetterGrade:

LookupNext (GradeLookup::LetterGrade; Lower)

Given a percentage score of 88, which has no exact match, the next lower match would return a letter grade of B.

Lower()

Category: Text

Syntax: Lower (text)

Parameters: text—any expression that resolves to a text string.

Description: Returns an all-lowercase version of the specified text string.

Examples:

Lower ("This is a test")

Returns this is a test.

Lower (Name)

Returns mary smith when the Name field contains "MARY Smith".

Comments:

The Lower() function is one of three functions FileMaker has for changing the case of a text string. The other two are Upper() and Proper().

The following formula can be used to test whether a given text string is already written with all lowercase characters:

Exact (text ; Lower(text))

Max()

Category: Aggregate

Syntax: Max (field { ; field...})

Parameters: field—any related field, repeating field, or set of non-repeating fields that represent a set of numbers. Parameters in curly braces {} are optional.

Description: Returns the largest valid, non-blank value from the set of values specified by the field parameter.

Examples:

Max (44; 129; 25)

Returns 129.

Max (repeatingField)

Returns 54 (when repetition 1 = 18, repetition 2 = 10, and repetition 3 = 54).

B

```
Max (Invoice:InvoiceAmount)
```

Returns the largest invoice amount found in the set of related Invoice records.

Comments:

When the parameter list consists of 2 or more repeating fields, `Max()` returns a repeating field in which the corresponding repetitions from the specified fields are evaluated separately. So, if a field `Repeater1` has three values, 16, 20, and 24, and another field, `Repeater2`, has two values, 14 and 25, `Max (Repeater1; Repeater2)` would return a repeating field with values 16, 25, and 24.

Because dates, times, and timestamps are represented internally as numbers, the `Max()` function can be used to compare data of these data types. For instance, to return the later of two dates, you could use the following type of formula:

```
GetAsDate (Max (Date (4; 1; 2005); Get (CurrentDate)))
```

This would return either 4/1/2005 or the current date, whichever is greater.

Middle()

Category: Text

Syntax: `Middle ( text ; startCharacter ; numberOfCharacters )`

Parameters: text—any expression that resolves to a text string; startCharacter—any expression that resolves to a numeric value; numberOfCharacters—any expression that resolves to a numeric value.

Description: Returns a substring from the middle of the specified text field. The substring begins at startCharacter and extracts the numberOfCharacters characters following it. If the end of the string is encountered before the specified number of characters has been extracted, the function returns everything from the start position though the end of the string.

Examples:

```
Middle ("hello world"; 3 ; 5)
```

Returns llo w.

```
Middle (FirstName ; 2 ; 99999)
```

Returns everything except the first character of the first name.

Comments:

The `Middle()` function is often used in conjunction with other text functions as part of text parsing routines. For instance, if you had a field containing city, state, and ZIP data where the entries were consistently entered as "city, state zip", you could extract the state portion of the string with the following formula:

```
Let ([commaPosition = Position(CSZ; "," ; 1 ; 1); Middle
➡(CSZ ; commaPosition + 2 ; 2))
```

MiddleValues()

Category: Text

Syntax: MiddleValues(textToFilter ; startingValue ; numberOfValues)

Parameters: textToFilter—any return-delimited string or expression that generates a return-delimited string; startingValue—any positive integer or expression that returns a positive integer; numberOfValues—any positive number or expression that returns a positive integer.

Description: Returns the specified number of items from the middle of the textToFilter parameter, starting at the value specified in the startingValue parameter.

Examples:

MiddleValues ("A¶B¶C¶D¶E"; 2; 3)

Returns the following:

B

C

D

MiddleValues (test; 3; 1)

Returns the following:

C

when test contains

A

B

C

D

Comments:

The MiddleValues() function returns a slice from the middle of a return delimited array. The output itself will be a return delimited array, and there will always be a trailing return at the end of the last item.

See the LeftValues() function for a discussion of methods to remove the trailing return from the output of the MiddleValues() function.

The MiddleValues() function is used frequently in scripts to loop over the items in an array. Each time through the loop, you can extract the next value from the array by incrementing a counter. For instance:

```
Set Field [myTable::gCounter ; 1]
Loop
   Set Field [myTable:gItem ; MiddleValues (myTable::myArray ; myTable::
   ➥gCounter ; 1)
```

B

```
[ ... some set of operations involving the extracted item]
    Exit Loop If [myTable::gCounter = ValueCount (myTable::myArray)]
End Loop
```

MiddleWords()

Category: Text

Syntax: MiddleWords (text ; startingWord ; numberOfWords)

Parameters: text—any expression that resolves to a text string; startingWord—any positive number or expression that returns a positive number; numberOfWords—any positive number or expression that returns a positive number.

Description: The MiddleWords() function extracts a substring from the middle of a text string. The substring begins with the *n*th word of the text string (where *n* represents the startingWord parameter) and extends for the number of words specified by the third parameter.

Examples:

MiddleWords ("the quick brown fox jumps" ; 3 ; 2)

Returns brown fox.

MiddleWords (FullName" ; 2 ; 1)

Returns Allan when FullName contains "Edgar Allan Poe."

Comments:

MiddleWords(text; 1 ; 1) and LeftWords (text; 1) are equivalent functions.

Be aware of what symbols are considered to be word breaks by FileMaker Pro. Spaces, return characters, and most punctuation symbols are considered to be word breaks. Multiple word breaks next to each other (for example, two spaces, a comma and a space) are considered as a single word break.

Certain punctuation symbols are word breaks when separating alpha characters, but not when separating numeric characters. These include the colon (:), slash (/), period (.), comma (,), and dash (-). The reason for this behavior is that those symbols are valid date, time, and number separators.

Leading and trailing punctuation around a word may be ignored by the MiddleWords() function. For example, MiddleWords ("John Q. Public, Jr."; 2 ; 1) returns Q, but MiddleWords ("John Q. Public, Jr."; 2; 1) returns Q. Public.

Min()

Category: Aggregate

Syntax: Min (field { ; field...})

Parameters: field—any related field, repeating field, or set of non-repeating fields that represent a set of numbers. Parameters in curly braces { } are optional.

Description: Returns the lowest valid, non-blank value from the set of values specified by the field parameter.

Examples:

```
Min (44; 25; 129)
```

Returns 25.

```
Min (repeatingField)
```

Returns 10 (when repetition 1 = 18, repetition 2 = 10, and repetition 3 = 54).

```
Min(Invoice:InvoiceAmount)
```

Returns the lowest invoice amount found in the set of related Invoice records.

Comments:

When the parameter list consists of two or more repeating fields, Min() returns a repeating field in which the corresponding repetitions from the specified fields are evaluated separately. So, if a field Repeater1 has three values, 16, 20, and 24, and another field, Repeater2, has two values, 14 and 25, Min (Repeater1; Repeater2) would return a repeating field with values 14, 20, and 24.

Because dates, times, and timestamps are represented internally as numbers, the Min() function can be used to compare data of these data types. For instance, to return the earlier of two dates, you could use the following type of formula:

```
GetAsDate (Min (Date (4; 1; 2005); Get (CurrentDate)))
```

This would return either 4/1/2005 or the current date, whichever is less.

Minute()

Category: Time

Syntax: Minute (time)

Parameters: time—any valid time value or expression that returns a valid time value.

Description: The Minute() function returns an integer representing the number of minutes from the given time value.

Examples:

```
Minute ("10:45:20")
```

Returns 45.

```
Minute ("12:07 am")
```

Returns 7.

```
Minute (Get (CurrentTime))
```

Returns a value from 0 to 59.

B

Comments:

The `Minute()` function always returns an integer in the range from 0 to 59. If you want the output of this function to always be expressed as a two-character string (for example, `07` instead of 7 when the time is 4:07 p.m.), use the following formula:

```
Right ("00" & Minute (time) ; 2)
```

`Mod()`

Category: Number

Syntax: `Mod ( number ; divisor )`

Parameters: `number`—any expression that resolves to a numeric value; `divisor`—any expression that resolves to a numeric value.

Description: Returns the remainder after `number` is divided by `divisor`.

Examples:

```
Mod (7 ; 5)
```

Returns 2.

```
Mod (-7 ; 5)
```

Returns 3.

```
Mod (13 ; 3)
```

Returns 1.

```
Mod (1.43 ; 1)
```

Returns .43.

Comments:

`Mod()` is related to the `Div()` function; `Div()` returns the whole number portion of x divided by y, whereas `Mod()` returns the remainder.

There are many practical uses for the `Mod()` function. For instance, when x is an integer, `Mod (x ; 2)` returns 0 if x is even, and 1 if x is odd. `Mod (x ; 1)` returns just the decimal portion of a number.

`Month()`

Category: Date

Syntax: `Month ( Date )`

Parameters: `Date`—Any valid date (1/1/0001–12/31/4000). The parameter should be a string containing a date (for example, `"3/17/2004"`), an expression with a date result (for example, `Date (6, 29, 1969)`), or an integer that represents a serialized date value (for example, `718977`).

Description: Returns the month number (1–12) for any valid date (1/1/0001–12/31/4000).

Examples:

```
Month ("5/1/2000")
```

Returns 5.

```
Month (718977)
```

Returns 6.

```
Month (Get (CurrentDate))
```

Returns 3 (if the current date is in March).

Comments:

The numeric value returned by Month() can be used in mathematical calculations as well as within the Date() function to construct a new date.

One common use of the Month() function is to build a formula that returns the quarter of a given date:

```
Case(
   Month(myDate)<4, "First Quarter",
   Month(myDate)<7, "Second Quarter",
   Month(myDate)<9, "Third Quarter",
   "Fourth Quarter"
)
```

MonthName()

Category: Date

Syntax: MonthName (Date)

Parameters: Date—Any valid date (1/1/0001–12/31/4000). The parameter should be a string containing a date (for example, "3/17/2004"), an expression with a date result (for example, Date (6, 29, 1969)), or an integer that represents a serialized date value (for example, 718977).

Description: Returns the month name of the specified date.

Examples:

```
MonthName ("1/1/2000")
```

Returns January.

```
MonthName ("5/20/2003")
```

Returns May.

```
MonthName (Get (CurrentDate) )
```

Might return March.

B

Comments:

The MonthName() is frequently used for display purposes in subsummary reports. Although you display the name of the month, be sure that you summarize based on the month number (obtained with the Month() function). If you don't, your report will be summarized alphabetically by month rather than chronologically by month.

NPV()

Category: Financial

Syntax: NPV (payment ; interestRate)

Parameters: payment—a repeating field that contains one or more values representing loan and payment amounts; interestRate—an interest rate, expressed as a decimal number.

Description: Returns the Net Present Value of a series of unequal payments made at regular intervals, assuming a fixed interestRate per interval. The repeating field specified in the first parameter should contain all loan and payment amounts.

Examples:

Imagine someone borrows $300.00 dollars from you and repays you $100, $50, $100, and $125 at regular intervals.

Assuming an interest rate of 5%, the NPV() function can tell you the actual profit, in today's dollars, that will be realized from this transaction. To calculate this, you would place the following values in a repeating number field: -300, 100, 50, 100, and 125. Then, use the formula:

```
Round (NPV (Payments; .05)),
```

which returns $28.39. Your actual profit on the transaction would be $75 (simply the sum of the payments minus the original loan). That $75, however, is collected over time, so the present value is discounted by the assumed interest rate. The higher the interest rate, the less the NPV of the $75.

PatternCount()

Category: Text

Syntax: PatternCount (text ; searchString)

Parameters: text—any expression that resolves to a text string; searchString—any expression that resolves to a text string, representing the substring for which you want to search within the text string.

Description: Returns the number of times that searchString appears in the text string. PatternCount() returns 0 if the searchString is not found.

Examples:

```
PatternCount ("This is a test"; "is")
```

Returns 2.

```
PatternCount (WindowNames; "¶") + 1
```

Returns the number of carriage returns in the list returned by the `WindowNames()` function. This could be used to determine the number of windows that are available. The `ValueCount()` function could also be used for this purpose.

```
PatternCount ("abababa" ; "Aba")
```

Returns 2.

Comments:

Only non-overlapping occurrences of `searchString` are counted by `PatternCount()`. `PatternCount()` is not case sensitive.

Even though `PatternCount()` is designed to answer the question "how many?", it is often used simply to determine whether one string is contained within another. If it returns any value other than zero, the search string is found.

Pi

Category: Trigonometric

Syntax: Pi

Parameters: None

Description: Returns the value of the trigonometric constant Pi, which is approximately 3.1415926535897932. Pi is defined as the ratio of the circumference to the diameter of any circle.

Examples:

```
Pi / 2
```

Returns 1.5707963267948966.

```
SetPrecision (Pi; 25)
```

Returns 3.141592653589793238462634.

Comments:

`Pi` is most often used in conjunction with other trigonometric functions, such as `Sin()`, `Cos()`, and `Tan()`, which each require an angle measured in radians as a parameter. There are 2×Pi radians in 360 degrees.

PMT()

Category: Financial

Syntax: PMT (principal ; interestRate ; term)

Parameters: principal—a number (or numeric expression) representing the initial amount borrowed. interestRate—a decimal number (or numeric expression), representing the monthly interest rate used to amortize the principal amount. Given an annual interest rate, you can divide by 12 to get the monthly interest rate. `term`—a number (or numeric expression) representing the period of loan, expressed in months.

Description: Returns the monthly payment that would be required to pay off the principal based on the `interestRate` and term specified.

Examples:

Someone borrows $1,000 from you, and you want to set up a payment schedule whereby the loan is paid off in 2 years at an interest rate of 6%. To determine the monthly payment:

```
PMT (1000 ; .06/12 ; 24)
```

Returns $44.32.

Comments:

The PMT calculation makes it easy to see the effect of interest rates on the monthly payment of an installment loan. For instance, buying a $20,000 car at 6.9% for 48 months would require a $478.00 monthly payment, but at 3.9%, the payment would be $450.68.

```
Position()
```

Category: Text

Syntax: `Position ( text ; searchFor ; startingAt ; occurrence )`

Parameters: `text`—any expression that resolves to a text string in which you want to search; `searchFor`—any expression that resolves to a text string for which to search; `startingAt`—an integer representing the character number at which to begin searching; `occurrence`—an integer representing which occurrence of `searchFor` to locate. A negative number causes the search to proceed backward from the `startingAt` character.

Description: Returns the character number where the `searchFor` string is found within the specified text string. If the `searchFor` string is not found, the `Position()` function returns a 0.

Examples:

```
Position ("This is a test"; "is";  1 ; 1)
```

Returns 3.

```
Position ("This is a test"; "is";  1 ; 2)
```

Returns 6.

```
Position ("
  Let (myString = "This is a test"; Position (myString; " " ; Length (myString);
  ➥ -1))
```

Returns 10, which is the position of the last space in `myString`.

B

Comments:

In most cases, the Position() function is used to find the first occurrence of some substring within a string. Both the startingAt and occurrence parameters will simply be 1 in such instances.

To find the *last* occurrence of a substring within a string, set the startingAt parameter to be the length of the string and the occurrence parameter to be -1, indicating that the function should search backward from the end of the string for the first occurrence of the substring.

The Position() function is not case sensitive.

Proper()

Category: Text

Syntax: Proper (text)

Parameters: text—any expression that resolves to a text string.

Description: Returns the specified text string with the initial letter of each word capitalized and all other letters as lower case.

Examples:

Proper ("this is a TEST")

Returns This Is A Test.

Proper (Address)

Returns 123 Main Street when Address contains "123 main street".

Comments:

The Proper() function is one of three case-changing functions in FileMaker Pro 7. The other two are Lower() and Upper().

The Proper() function is often used as part of an auto-entered calculation formula to reformat a user's entry with the desired case. For instance, in a City field, where you would expect the first letter of each word to be capitalized, you could set up an auto-entry option to enter Proper(City) and uncheck the option to not replace existing value. Then, if a user were to type SAN FRANCISCO, upon exiting the field the entry would be reset to San Francisco.

PV()

Category: Financial

Syntax: PV (payment; interestRate; periods)

Parameters: payment—a number (or numeric expression) representing a payment amount made per period. interestRate—a decimal number (or numeric expression) representing the interest rate per period. periods—the number of periods of the loan.

B

Description: The Present Value formula tells you what money expected in the future is worth today. The `PV()` function returns the present value of a series of equal payments made at regular intervals, and assumes a fixed `interestRate` per interval.

Examples:

Imagine you have won $1,000,000 in a lottery. You have been offered either $50,000 per year for the next 20 years, or a one-time lump sum payment now of $700,000. Which option should you choose?

Assuming an inflation rate of 3% per year, the present value of the future payments is determined by

`PV (50000 ; .03 ; 20)`

which returns `743873.74`.

If you assume a 4% inflation rate, the present value of the future payments decreases to `679516.31`. So, depending on your assumptions about inflation rates, you may or not be better off taking the lump sum payment.

As another example, consider the question of whether it would be better for someone to give you $10 today, or $1 per year for the next 10 years. You can use the `PV()` function to tell you the present value of receiving $1 for 10 years. Assuming an inflation rate of 3%, the formula `PV (1, .03, 10)` shows that the present value of the future income is only $8.53.

Quote()

Category: Logical

Syntax: `Quote ( text )`

Parameters: `text`—any expression that resolves to a text string.

Description: The `Quote()` function returns the specified text string enclosed in quotation marks. To escape any special characters within the text string, such as quotation marks and double backslashes, place a backslash before them in the text string.

Examples:

If the `FullName` field contains the name Billy "Joe" Smith, then `Quote (FullName)` would return `"Billy \"Joe\" Smith"`. The absence and presence of quotation marks here is deliberate; the quotation marks are part of the returned string.

Comments:

The `Quote()` function is used primarily in conjunction with the `Evaluate()` function, which can evaluate a dynamically generated formula. If the formula you are assembling contains a literal text string enclosed by quotation marks, or if it includes field contents that may potentially have quotation marks in it, then use the `Quote()` function to ensure that all internal quotation marks are escaped properly.

B

`Radians()`

Category: Trigonometric

Syntax: `Radians ( number )`

Parameters: `number`—A number representing an angle measured in degrees.

Description: The `Radians()` function converts an angle measured in degrees into an angle measured in radians.

Examples:

`Radians (60)`

Returns `1.0471975511965977` (= Pi / 3).

`Radians (180)`

Returns `3.1415926535897932` (= Pi).

Comments:

The trigonometric functions `Sin()`, `Cos()`, and `Tan()` all take an angle measured in radians as their parameter. To find, say, the cosine of a 180° angle, you could use the formula `Cos ( Radians (180))`. There are 2×Pi radians in 360°.

Random

Category: Number

Syntax: `Random`

Parameters: None

Description: Returns a random number between zero and one. When used in a field definition, a new value is generated when the formula is updated. It is also updated anytime the formula re-evaluates, such as when other field values referenced in the formula change. In an unstored calculation, the `Random()` function re-evaluates each time the field is displayed.

Examples:

`Round (Random ; 5)`

Might return `.07156`.

Comments:

If you want to generate a random integer in a certain range, multiply the result returned by the random function by the range you want to produce, then use the `Int()`, `Floor()`, `Ceiling()`, `Round()`, or `Truncate()` functions to remove the decimals.

For instance, to return a random number from 1 to 6 (as in the roll of a die), use the formula:

`Ceiling (Random * 6)`

B

If you need to specify a lower bound for the random number, just add the bound to the results of the random number. For instance, to return a random number between 10 and 100, inclusive, use the following formula:

```
Int (Random * 91) + 10
```

RelationInfo()

Category: Design

Syntax: `RelationInfo ( fileName ; tableOccurance )`

Parameters: `fileName`—a string or text expression representing the name of an open file; `tableOccurence`—a string or text expression representing the name of a particular table occurrence in `fileName`.

Description: Returns a list of information about all the table occurrences that are related to the specified `tableOccurrence`.

The results are formatted as

```
FileName
Related Table Reference::Related Field
Local Related Field
Options for "right" side of relationship ( "Delete", "Create" and/or "Sorted")
```

Repeat above four lines for each relationship.

Examples:

```
RelationInfo (Get(FileName);"Contacts 2")
```

might return values that look like this:

```
MyDatabase

Invoice_Line::ContactID_fk

ContactID_pk

Delete Sorted

MyDatabase

Phone_Nums::ContactID_fk

ContactID_pk

Delete
```

Comments:

The `RelationInfo()` function returns four lines for each table occurrence that's related to the one you specify. If there are no options selected on the "right" side of the relationship, the fourth line is blank.

Note that the first line tells you the name of the file where the base table resides, but does not tell you the name of the table occurrence itself. If multiple match criteria are defined for the relationship, only the first one is listed by the `RelationInfo()` function. Similarly, there is no indication about the join operator used.

Replace()

Category: Text

Syntax: `Replace ( text ; startingAt ; numberOfCharacters ; replacementText )`

Parameters: `text`—any expression that resolves to a text string; `startingAt`—any positive number or expression that returns a positive number; `numberOfCharacters`—any positive number or expression that returns a positive number; `replacementText`—any expression that resolves to a text string.

Description: The `Replace()` function extracts a segment of a text string and replaces it with some other string. The segment to extract begins with the `startingAt` character number and extends for `numberOfCharacters`. The replacement string is specified by the `replacementText` parameter.

The extracted segment and the replacement text do not need to be the same length.

Examples:

`Replace ("abcdef"; 4; 2; "TEST")`

Returns abcTESTf.

`Replace ("Fred Smith" ; 1 ; 4 ; "Joe")`

Returns Joe Smith.

Comments:

The `Replace()` and `Substitute()` functions are often confused with one another. `Substitute()` replaces all occurrences of a particular substring with another string, whereas `Replace()` replaces a specified range of characters with another string.

`Replace()` is often used for manipulation of delimited text arrays. There is no function that will directly replace the contents of a particular item in an array with another. The `Replace()` function can do this by finding the appropriate delimiters and inserting the replacement item. For instance, if you have the a pipe-delimited list of numbers (for example, 34¦888¦150¦43) and you wish to increase the third item in the list by 18, you could use the following formula:

```
Let ([
    item = 3;
    increase = 18;
    start = Position (myArray ; "¦" ; 1 ; (item-1)) + 1;
```

B

```
      end = Position (myArray; "¦" ; 1 ; item);
      itemValue = Middle (myArray ; start ; end-start);
      newValue = itemValue + increase ];
      Replace (myArray ; start ; end-start ; newValue)
)
```

Given the example string as myArray, this would produce the string 34¦888¦168¦43. Typically, the item and increase values would be supplied by other fields and not hard-coded into the formula.

RGB ( )

Category: Text Formatting

Syntax: RGB (red ; green ; blue)

Parameters: red—any number or numeric expression containing a value ranging from 0 to 255; green—any number or numeric expression containing a value ranging from 0 to 255; blue—any number or numeric expression containing a value ranging from 0 to 255.

Description: Returns a number that represents a color.

To calculate this integer, the red, green, and blue values are combined using the following formula:

```
(red * 256²) + (green * 256) + blue
```

Examples:

Table B.1 lists the RGB values of some common colors.

TABLE B.1   RGB VALUES

Function	Integer Result	Color
RGB (255 ; 0 ; 0)	16711680	Red
RGB (0 ; 255 ; 0)	65280	Green
RGB (0 ; 0 ; 255)	255	Blue
RGB (255 ; 255 ; 255)	16777215	White
RGB (0 ; 0 ; 0)	0	Black
RGB (24 ; 162 ; 75)	1614411	Dark Green
RGB (7 ; 13 ; 78)	462158	Dark Purple
RGB (23 ; 100 ; 148)	1533076	Bright Blue

Comments:

Use the RGB() function in conjunction with the TextColor() function to format text.

If a number above 255 is supplied as the parameter, the formula in the example still computes a result. If the result of the formula returns a value above the expected 0 to 16777215 range, the Mod (result; 16777216) is used to map the result into the expected range. So RGB (255; 255 ; 256), which returns a value one higher than white, returns the color black, just as 0 does.

Right()

Category: Text

Syntax: Right (text ; numberOfCharacters)

Parameters: text—any expression that resolves to a text string; numberOfCharacters—any expression that resolves to a numeric value.

Description: Returns a string containing the last *n* characters from the specified text string. If the string is shorter than numberOfCharacters, the entire string is returned. If numberOfCharacters is less than 1, an empty string is returned.

Examples:

```
Right ("Hello" ; 2)
```

Returns lo.

```
Right (FirstName ; 1)
```

Returns the last character of the FirstName field.

Comments:

The Right() function is commonly used in text parsing routines to extract portions of a text string.

RightValues()

Category: Text

Syntax: RightValues (textToFilter ; numberOfValues)

Parameters: textToFilter—any return-delimited text string or expression that generates a return-delimited string; numberOfValues—any positive number or expression that returns a positive number.

Description: Returns the specified number of items from the end of the textToFilter parameter.

Examples:

```
RightValues("A¶B¶C¶D¶E";3)
```

Returns the following:

```
C
D
E
```

```
RightValues(test;1)
```

Returns C when test contains

A

B

C

Comments:

The RightValues() function returns the last *n* items from a return-delimited array. The items themselves will be a return-delimited array, and there will always be a trailing return at the end of the last item.

See the LeftValues() function for a discussion of methods to remove the trailing return from the output of the RightValues() function.

RightWords()

Category: Text

Syntax: RightWords (text ; numberOfWords)

Parameters: text—any expression that resolves to a text string; numberOfWords—any positive number or expression that returns a positive number.

Description: Returns the last *n* number of words in a text expression, where *n* is the number specified in the numberOfWords parameter.

Examples:

RightWords ("the quick brown fox jumps" ; 3)

Returns brown fox jumps.

RightWords (FullName ; 1)

Returns Smith when the FullName field contains Joe Smith.

Comments:

Be aware of what symbols are considered to be word breaks by FileMaker Pro. Spaces, return characters, and most punctuation symbols are considered to be word breaks. Multiple word breaks next to each other (for example, two spaces, a comma and a space) are considered as a single word break.

Certain punctuation symbols are word breaks when separating alpha characters, but not when separating numeric characters. These include the colon (:), slash (/), period (.), comma (,), and dash (-). For instance, RightWords ("54.6" ; 1) returns 54.6, but RightWords ("x.y" ; 1) returns y. The reason for this behavior is that those symbols are valid date, time, and number separators.

Leading and trailing punctuation around a word will be ignored by the RightWords() function. For example, RightWords ("John Q. Public, Jr."; 2) returns Public, Jr, and RightWords ("John Q. Public, Jr."; 3) returns Q. Public, Jr.

`Round()`

Category: Number

Syntax: `Round ( number ; precision )`

Parameters: `number`—any expression that resolves to a numeric value; `precision`—any number or numeric expression, representing the number of decimal points to which to round the number.

Description: Returns the specified `number` rounded off to the number of decimal points specified by the `precision` parameter. The `Round()` function rounds numbers from 5 to 9 upward, and from 0 to 4 downward.

Examples:

`Round (62.566 ; 2)`

Returns `62.57`.

`Round (62.563 ; 2)`

Returns `62.56`.

`Round (92.4 ; 0)`

Returns `92`.

`Round (32343.98 ; -3)`

Returns `32000`.

`Round (505.999 ; -1)`

Returns `510`.

Comments:

A precision of 0 rounds to the nearest integer. A negative number for the precision causes the number to be rounded to the nearest ten, hundred, thousand, and so on.

`ScriptIDs()`

Category: Design

Syntax: `ScriptIDs ( fileName )`

Parameters: `fileName`—a string or text expression that represents the name of an open file.

Description: Returns a carriage return–delimited list of script IDs from the specified file.

Examples:

`ScriptIDs ("myFile")`

Returns a list of script IDs for the current file that might look like this:

`21`

`22`

B

24

25

Comments:

ScriptIDs are assigned sequentially by FileMaker, starting at 1 for each new file. The results returned by the ScriptIDs function are ordered according to the current order within ScriptMaker, not the creation order of the scripts.

When you convert a solution developed in an earlier version of FileMaker, the ScriptIDs of the original file are retained after conversion.

Any scripts that are set to "no access" for the current user's privilege set are not included in the list.

ScriptNames()

Category: Design

Syntax: ScriptNames (fileName)

Parameters: fileName—a string or text expression that represents the name of an open file.

Description: Returns a carriage return–delimited list of script names from the specified file.

Examples:

ScriptNames (Get (FileName))

Returns a list of script names for the current file that might look like this:

Contact_Nav

Invoice_Nav

-

Contact_New

Invoice_New

-

Contact_Delete

Invoice_Delete

Comments:

As with the ScriptIDs() function, the order of the list returned by ScriptNames() is the current order of the scripts within ScriptMaker.

Any scripts that are set to "no access" for the current user's privilege set are not included in the list.

B

`Seconds()`

Category: Time

Syntax: `Seconds ( time )`

Parameters: `time`—any valid time value or expression that returns a valid time value.

Description: The `Seconds()` function returns an integer representing the number of seconds specified by the `time` parameter.

Examples:

`Seconds ("10:45:20")`

Returns `20`.

`Seconds ("12:15 am")`

Returns `0`.

Comments:

This function always returns a value from 0 to 59.

If you want to express the output of this function as a two-character string rather than as an integer (for example, `03` rather than 3), use the following formula:

`Right ("00" & Seconds (Time) ; 2)`

If the `time` parameter has a seconds value greater than 59, the `Seconds()` function returns the Mod-60 result of that value. For instance, `Seconds ("12:42:87")` returns `27`. Note that the "overflow" of the seconds value is applied to the minutes value: `Minute ("12:42:87")` returns `43`.

`SerialIncrement()`

Category: Text

Syntax: `SerialIncrement ( text ; incrementBy )`

Parameters: `text`—any text or text expression that contains an alpha-numeric string; `incrementBy`—a number or numeric expression with which to increment the text value.

Description: Returns the combined text and number from the text value, where the numeric portion of the text has been incremented by the value specified in the `incrementBy` parameter.

The `incrementBy` value is truncated to an integer when incrementing. Positive and negative numbers are accepted.

Examples:

`SerialIncrement ("test1" ; 2)`

Returns `test3`.

B

SerialIncrement ("moyergroupv12.3" ; -1)

Returns moyergroupv12.2.

SerialIncrement ("2hithere3" ; 3)

Returns 2hithere6.

SetPrecision()

Category: Number

Syntax: SetPrecision (expression ; precision)

Parameters: expression—any number or expression that returns a number; precision—an integer from 1 to 400.

Description: FileMaker normally computes decimals with 16 digits of precision. The SetPrecision() function allows you to specify with up to 400 digits of precision.

The expression specified in the first parameter is rounded at the digit specified by the second parameter.

Examples:

SetPrecision(Pi;28)

Returns 3.1415926535897932384626433833.

SetPrecision(Pi;29)

Returns 3.14159265358979323846264338328.

Comments:

The trigonometric functions do not support extended precision.

You can specify a number below 17 as the precision, but FileMaker still returns 16 digits of precision regardless. Use the Round() function instead to specify a precision up to 16.

Sign()

Category: Number

Syntax: Sign (number)

Parameters: number—any expression that resolves to a numeric value.

Description: Returns a value that represents the sign of number:

-1 when number is negative
0 when number is zero
1 when number is positive

Examples:

Sign (0)

Returns 0.

```
Sign (100)
```

Returns 1.

```
Sign( -100)
```

Returns -1 for the formula `If (Sign (BalanceDue) = -1 ; "Please pay now!" ; "Thanks for your payment!").`

Comments:

For any x other than 0, multiplying x by `Sign(x)` yields the `Abs(x)` .

Sin()

Category: Trigonometric

Syntax: `Sin ( number )`

Parameters: number—any number or numeric expression representing the size of an angle measured in radians.

Description: Returns the sine of the specified angle. Sine is a periodic function that has a range from -1 to 1.

Examples:

```
Sin ( 0 )
```

Returns 0.

```
Sin ( Pi / 2)
```

Returns 1.

```
Sin ( Radians (-30))
```

Returns -.5.

Comments: In any right triangle, the sine of the two non-right angles can be obtained by dividing the length of the side opposite the angle by the length of the hypotenuse.

Sqrt()

Category: Number

Syntax: `Sqrt ( number )`

Parameters: number—any expression that resolves to a positive number.

Description: Returns the square root of number.

Examples:

```
Sqrt (64)
```

Returns 8.

```
Sqrt (2)
```

Returns 1.414213562373095.

B

StDev()

Category: Aggregate

Syntax: StDev (field { ; field...})

Parameters: field—any related field, repeating field, or set of non-repeating fields that represent a collection of numbers. Parameters in curly braces { } are optional.

Description: Returns the standard deviation of the non-blank values represented in the parameter list. Standard deviation is a statistical measurement of how spread out a collection of values is. In a normal distribution, about 68% of the values are within one standard deviation of the mean, and about 95% are within two standard deviations of the mean.

Examples:

There are several ways you can manually calculate the standard deviation of a set of numbers. One is to take the square root of the sum of the squares of each value's distance from the mean, divided by n-1, where n is the number of values in the set.

For instance, given the set of numbers 8, 10, and 12, the mean of this set is 10. The distances of each value from the mean are therefore -2, 0, and 2. The squares of these are 4, 0, and 4. The sum of the squares is 8. The standard deviation of the population is Sqrt (8/(3-1)), which is 2.

StDev (8; 10; 12)

Returns 2.

Given a portal that contains a field called Scores with the following values (64, 72, 75, 59, 67),

StDev (People::Scores)

returns 6.35.

Comments:

The difference between the StDevP() and StDev() functions is that StDev divides the sum of the squares by n-1 instead of by n.

StDev() can also be calculated as the square root of the Variance() of a set of numbers.

StDevP()

Category: Aggregate

Syntax: StDevP (field { ; field...})

Parameters: field—any related field, repeating field, or set of non-repeating fields that represent a collection of numbers. Parameters in curly braces { } are optional.

Description: Returns the standard deviation of a population represented by the non-blank values represented in the parameter list. Standard deviation is a statistical measurement of how spread out a collection of values is. In a normal distribution, about 68% of the values are within one standard deviation of the mean, and about 95% are within two standard deviations of the mean.

Examples:

There are several ways you can manually calculate the standard deviation of a population. One is to take the square root of the sum of the squares of each value's distance from the mean, divided by the number of values.

For instance, given the set of numbers 8, 10, and 12, the mean of this set is 10. The distances of each value from the mean are therefore -2, 0, and 2. The squares of these are 4, 0, and 4. The sum of the squares is 8. The standard deviation of the population is Sqrt (8/3), which is 1.633.

StDevP (8; 10; 12)

Returns 1.633.

Given a portal that displays the heights of a set of people (64, 72, 75, 59, 67),

StDevP (People::Heights)

Returns 5.68.

Comments:

The difference between the StDevP() and StDev() functions is that StDev() divides the sum of the squares by *n*-1 instead of by *n*.

StDevP() can also be calculated as the square root of the VarianceP() of a set of numbers.

Substitute()

Category: Text

Syntax: Substitute (text ; searchString ; replaceString)

Parameters: text—any text string or expression that returns a text string; searchString—any text string or expression that returns a text string; replaceString—any text string or expression that returns a text string.

Description: Returns a text string in which all instances of searchString in the text parameter are replaced with the replaceString.

Examples:

Substitute ("Happy Anniversary!" ; "Anniversary" ; "Birthday")

Returns Happy Birthday!.

Substitute ("This is a test"; "i" ; "q")

Returns Thqs qs a test.

B

Comments:

Multiple substitutions may occur in the same Substitute() function:

Substitute ("This is a test"; ["i"; "q"]; ["s"; "$"])

Returns Thq$ q$ a te$t.

The Substitute() function is case sensitive.

Sum()

Category: Aggregate

Syntax: Sum (field { ; field...})

Parameters: field—any related field, repeating field, or set of non-repeating fields that represent a collection of numbers. Parameters in curly braces { } are optional.

Description: Returns the sum of all valid values represented by the fields in the parameter list.

Examples:

Sum (field1 ; field2 ; field3)

Returns 6 (when field1 = 1, field2 = 2, and field3 = 3).

Sum (repeatingField)

Returns 6 (when repetition 1 = 1, repetition 2 = 2, and repetition 3 = 3)

Sum (repeatingField1 ; repeatingField2)

Returns a repeating calculation field that contains 6;12;24, when the referenced repeating fields each contain three values.

Sum (Customer::InvoiceTotal)

Returns 420 (when the sum of InvoiceTotal in the related set of data is 420).

Comments:

The Sum() function is most often used to add up a column of numbers in a related table.

TableIDs()

Category: Design

Syntax: TableIDs (fileName)

Parameters: fileName—a string or text expression that represents the name of an open file.

Description: Returns a carriage return–delimited list of table occurrence IDs from the specified file.

B

Examples:

`TableIDs (Get (FileName))`

Returns a list of table occurrence IDs for the current file that might look like this:

```
100021
100049
100002
```

Comments:

Note that `TableIDs()` returns the IDs of table occurrences from the Relationships Graph, not the actual data tables. A database table may appear in the Relationships Graph more than once.

A unique `TableID` is assigned by FileMaker whenever a table occurrence is added to the Relationships Graph. The order of the IDs in the list is based on the alphabetic ordering of the table occurrence names themselves.

TableNames()

Category: Design

Syntax: `TableNames ( fileName )`

Parameters: `fileName`—a string or text expression that represents the name of an open file.

Description: Returns a carriage return–delimited list of table occurrence names from the specified file.

Examples:

`TableNames (Get (FileName))`

Would return a list of table occurrence names for the current file that might look like this:

```
Contacts
Contact2
Invoices
Invoice_Lines
```

Comments:

Note that `TableNames()` returns the names of table occurrences from the Relationships Graph, not the actual data tables. A database table may appear in the Relationships Graph more than once.

The list returned by the `TableNames()` function is ordered alphabetically.

B

`Tan()`

Category: Trigonometric

Syntax: `Tan ( number )`

Parameters: `number`—any number representing the size of an angle measured in radians.

Description: Returns the tangent of the specified angle.

Examples:

`Tan (0)`

Returns 0.

`Tan (Pi / 6)`

Returns .5773502691896257.

`Tan (Radians (45))`

Returns 1.

Comments: The tangent of an angle can also be obtained by dividing the sine of the angle by its cosine. In any right triangle, the tangent of the two non-right angles can be obtained by dividing the length of the side opposite the angle by the length of the adjacent side.

`TextColor()`

Category: Text Formatting

Syntax: `TextColor ( text; RGB ( red; green; blue ) )`

Parameters: `text`—any text string or expression that returns a text string; `RGB (red;green;blue)`—a function that accepts three parameters from 0 to 255 and returns a number representing a color. See the `RGB()` definition.

Description:

Returns the text string in the color specified by the RGB parameter.

Examples:

`TextColor ("this text will be blue"; RGB (0;0;255))`

Returns this text will be blue, formatted in blue.

`TextColor ("this text will be red"; 16711680)`

Returns this text will be red, formatted in red.

Comments:

Use the `TextColor()` function within text expressions to emphasize words:

`"We will have " & TextColor (NumberItems;RGB (255;0;0)) & " errors per cycle.
➥Unacceptable!"`

B

TextColor() can also be used for conditional text formatting. The following calculation highlights losses in red:

```
Let (Profit = GetAsText (Earnings - Expenditures);
   Case (
      Profit > 0; TextColor (Profit; RGB(0;0;0));
      Profit < 0; TextColor (Profit; RGB(255;0;0));
      "")
)
```

If a field is formatted in the Number Format dialog, some options override the TextColor() function. For example, conditional color for negative numbers overrides TextColor, unless the user has clicked into the field being formatted.

TextFont()

Category: Text Formatting

Syntax: TextFont (text; fontName {; fontScript})

Parameters: text—any text string or expression that returns a text string; fontName—any font name available on the system. Must be enclosed in quotation marks. fontScript—the name of a character set (for example, Cyrillic, Greek, Roman). This is an optional parameter; quotation marks should not be used around the script name. Parameters in curly braces { } are optional.

Description: Changes the text font to the specified fontName and optional fontScript. Font names are case sensitive.

If no matches for the specified font and script exist, FileMaker first looks for the font script and associated font in the Fonts tab of the Preferences dialog box. If the script is not specified in the Fonts tab, the TextFont() function uses the default font for the system. This font script might not be the same as the specified script.

A list of font scripts is available in the online help system.

Examples:

```
TextFont ("testing 123" ; "Courier")
```

Results in the string testing 123 in Courier font.

Comments:

When TextFont() is used as part of the definition of a calculation field, the calculation should be set to return a text result. Text formatting options are lost if the data type returned is anything other than text.

TextSize()

Category: Text Formatting

Syntax: TextSize (text ; fontSize)

B

Parameters: text—any text string or expression that returns a text string; fontSize—any font size expressed in pixels as an integer.

Description: Returns the text string at the specified font size.

Examples:

TextSize ("Hello, world!" ; 8)

Results in Hello, world!

TextSize ("Large print book" ; 18)

Results in Large print book.

Comments:

When TextSize() is used as part of the definition of a calculation field, the calculation should be set to return a text result. Text formatting options are lost if the data type returned is anything other than text.

TextStyleAdd()

Category: Text Formatting

Syntax: TextStyleAdd (text; style(s))

Parameters: text—any text string or expression that returns a text string; style—any named style or list of styles separated by a plus (+) sign, or an integer that represents a combination of styles. Named styles should not be placed in quotation marks and cannot be passed as field contents.

Description: Returns a text string that has the specified style(s) applied to it.

Examples:

TextStyleAdd ("word underline."; WordUnderline)

Results in word underline.

TextStyleAdd ("bold italic!"; bold+italic)

Results in *bold italic!*

TextStyleAdd ("Plain text"; Plain)

Removes all styles from the text. If the "Plain" style is combined with any other styles, it is ignored.

Comments:

The style names are reserved keywords in FileMaker Pro and should not be placed within quotes. You cannot, however, place a keyword in a field and use the field as the style parameter within TextStyleAdd(). Styles can be specified as local variables within Let functions.

All the style names have numeric equivalents that you can use instead of the names. To combine multiple styles, simply add the numeric equivalents together. The numeric equivalent can be specified by a field, so use this method if you need to dynamically specify a text style.

The list of styles and their numeric equivalents is shown in Table B.2:

TABLE B.2   STYLE NAMES AND NUMERIC EQUIVALENT

Style Name	Numeric Equivalent
Plain	0
Strikethrough	1
Smallcaps	2
Superscript	4
Subscript	8
Uppercase	16
Lowercase	32
Titlecase	48
Wordunderline	64
Doubleunderline	128
Bold	256
Italic	512
Underline	1024
Condense	8192
Extend	16384
Allstyles	32767

TextStyleRemove()

Category: Text Formatting

Syntax: `TextStyleRemove ( text ; style(s) )`

Parameters: `text`—any text string or expression that returns a text string; `style`—any named style or list of styles separated by a plus (+) sign, or an integer that represents a combination of styles. Named styles should not be placed in quotation marks and cannot be passed as field contents.

Description: Removes the specified styles from formatted text.

Examples:

`TextStyleRemove ("word underline"; WordUnderline)`

Removes the word underline formatting from the phrase `"word underline"`.

B

```
TextStyleRemove ("bold italic!" ; bold+italic)
```

Removes the bold and italic formatting from the phrase "bold italic!"

```
TextStyleRemove (sampleText ; AllStyles)
```

Removes all formatting styles from the contents of the variable sampleText.

Comments:

Removing AllStyles with TextStyleRemove() accomplished the same thing as adding Plain with TextStyleAdd().

See TextStyleAdd() for a complete list of styles and a discussion of their numeric equivalents.

Time()

Category: Time

Syntax: Time (hours ; minutes ; seconds)

Parameters: hours—a number representing the hours portion of the desired time value; minutes—a number representing the minutes portion of the desired time value; seconds—a number representing the seconds portion of the desired time value.

Description: Returns a time value built from the specified hours, minutes, and seconds parameters. The resulting value accurately calculates the effect of fractional parameters. Similarly, although the typical range for the minutes and seconds parameters is from 0 to 59, any values above or below are compensated for in the resulting time value.

Examples:

```
Time (8 ; 34; 15)
```

Returns 8:34:15.

```
Time (15.25 ; 0 ; 0 )
```

Returns 15:15:00.

```
Time (22 ; 70 ; 70 )
```

Returns 23:11:10.

```
Time (12 ; -30 ; 0)
```

Returns 11:30:00.

Comments:

The Time() function is often used in conjunction with the Hour(), Minute(), and Seconds() functions. For instance, the following formula takes the current time and returns the time of the next lowest hour:

```
Time (Hour (Get (CurrentTime));0;0)
```

B

Timestamp()

Category: Timestamp

Syntax: Timestamp (date ; time)

Parameters: date—any calendar date or expression that returns a date. The date parameter can also be an integer from 1 to 1460970, representing the number of days since January 1, 0001. time—any time value or expression that returns a time value. The time parameter can also be an integer representing the number of seconds since midnight.

Description: Returns a timestamp from the two parameters, in the format "12/12/2005 10:45:00 AM".

Examples:

Timestamp ("10/11/2005"; "10:20 AM")

Returns 10/11/2005 10:20 AM.

Timestamp ("10/11/2005"; "20:20:20")

Returns 10/11/2005 8:20:20 PM.

Timestamp (Date (10;11;2005); Time (10;20;00))

Returns 10/11/2005 10:20 AM.

Timestamp (laborDay; 0)

Returns 9/5/2005 12:00:00 AM when laborDay is equal to 9/5/2005.

Timestamp (1; 0)

Returns 1/1/0001 12:00 AM.

Comments:

You can use text parsing functions or mathematical operations to extract the pieces of a timestamp. You can also use the GetAsDate() and GetAsTime() functions to retrieve just the date or time.

Internally, FileMaker Pro stores timestamp data as the number of seconds since 1/1/0001 12:00 a.m. You can use the GetAsNumber() function to see the numeric representation. For instance, GetAsNumber (Timestamp ("4/18/2004"; 12:00pm)) returns 63217886400.

You can manually calculate the integer value of a timestamp by using the following formula:

(GetAsNumber (myDate)-1) * 86400 + GetAsNumber (myTime)

Trim()

Category: Text

Syntax: Trim (text)

Parameters: text—any expression that resolves to a text string.

B

Description: Returns the specified text string with any leading or trailing spaces removed.

Examples:

```
Trim ("  This is a test  ")
```

Returns This is a test.

Comments:

The Trim() function removes only leading and trailing spaces and not any other characters (such as carriage returns).

Trim() can be used to reformat data where users have inadvertently typed spaces at the end of an entry. This happens frequently with fields containing first names. To automatically have the entry reformatted when the user exits the field, have the field auto-enter Trim (FirstName) and uncheck the option not to replace any existing value in the field. Thus, if a user enters "Fred " into the FirstName field, it is replaced with "Fred" when the user exits the field.

Trim() is also used frequently to clean up fixed-width data that has been imported from some other data source. In such cases, fields have been padded with leading or trailing spaces to be a certain length. Remove them after importing by doing calculated replaces in the appropriate fields.

```
Truncate()
```

Category: Number

Syntax: Truncate (number ; precision)

Parameters: number—any expression that resolves to a numeric value; precision—any expression that resolves to a numeric value.

Description: Returns the specified number truncated to the specified number of decimal places (precision). Unlike the Round() function, the Truncate() function simply discards further digits without performing any sort of rounding.

Examples:

```
Truncate (Pi ; 6)
```

Returns 3.141592.

```
Truncate (Amount ; 2)
```

Returns 54.65 when Amount contains 54.651259.

```
Truncate (1234.1234 ; 0)
```

Returns 1234.

```
Truncate (-1234.1234 ; 0)
```

Returns -1234.

B

Comments:

Truncating a number by using a precision parameter of 0 has the same effect as taking the Int() of that number. Truncate (x ; 0) = Int (x).

Negative values can be used for the precision parameter in the Truncate() function. For instance, Truncate (1234.1234 ; -1) returns 1230. Truncate (1234.1234 ; -2) returns 1200.

Upper()

Category: Text

Syntax: Upper (text)

Parameters: text—a string or text expression.

Description: Returns a completely uppercase version of the specified text string.

Examples:

Upper ("This is a test")

Returns THIS IS A TEST.

Upper (AccessCode)

Returns 1ABC-2XYZ when AccessCode contains "1abc-2XYz".

Comments:

The Upper() function is one of three functions FileMaker Pro has for changing the case of a text string. The other two are Lower() and Proper().

The Upper() function is often used to reformat user-entered data to ensure consistent data entry. Sometimes when exporting data that is to be used by external applications, you need to format the data entirely as uppercase characters to be consistent with data in the other system.

The following formula checks whether a given text string is already written in all uppercase characters:

Exact (text ; Upper(text))

ValueCount()

Category: Text

Syntax: ValueCount (text)

Parameters: text—any return-delimited string or expression that generates a return-delimited list.

Description: Returns a count of the number of values in the text provided.

B

Examples:

ValueCount ("A¶B¶C¶D¶E")

Returns 5.

ValueCount (officeList)

Returns 3 when officeList is equal to

Atlanta
Chicago
San Francisco

Comments:

The presence or absence of a trailing return after the last item in the return-delimited list does not affect the result returned by ValueCount. For instance, ValueCount ("Blue¶Green") and ValueCount ("Blue¶Green¶") both return 2.

If there are multiple returns at any point in the list, the ValueCount() function recognizes the empty items as valid items. For instance, ValueCount ("¶¶Blue¶¶Green¶¶") returns 6. Note that this behavior is different from how the WordCount() function treats multiple delimiters. There, multiple delimiters in a row are considered to be a single delimiter.

ValueListIDs()

Category: Design

Syntax: ValueListIDs (fileName)

Parameters: fileName—a string or text expression that represents the name of an open file.

Description: Returns a carriage return–delimited list of value list IDs from the specified file.

Examples:

ValueListIDs (Get (FileName))

Returns a list of value list IDs for the current file that might look like this:

21
92
90
108
15

Comments:

FileMaker assigns a serial number to each value list created in a file. The order of the list returned by the ValueListIDs() function is the same as that in which the value lists are ordered in the Define Value Lists dialog when the order is set to Custom Order. Changing the Custom Order changes the way the results are ordered, but selecting one of the other choices (Creation Order, Source, Value List Name) does not affect the order.

ValueListItems()

Category: Design

Syntax: ValueListItems (fileName ; valueListName)

Parameters: fileName—a string or text expression that represents the name of an open file; valueList—the name of a value list in fileName.

Description: Returns a carriage return–delimited list of the items in the specified value list.

Examples:

ValueListItems (Get (FileName);"Phone_Label")

Returns a list of values from the value list Phone_Label in the current file that might look like this:

Home

Work

Cell

Fax

Comments:

The ValueListItems() function is often used to consolidate information about a set of related records. For instance, in an invoice file, you might have a value list called Products_Ordered that's defined to return the ProductName field from a related set of records in the InvoiceItem table. ValueListItems (Get (FileName); "Products_Ordered") would return a list of all the products ordered on the current invoice.

ValueListNames()

Category: Design

Syntax: ValueListNames (fileName)

Parameters: fileName—a string or text expression that represents the name of an open file.

Description: Returns a carriage return–delimited list of value list names from the specified file.

Examples:

ValueListNames (Get (FileName))

Returns a list of value list names from the current file that might look like this:

Phone_Label

Location

Type

Category

B

Comments:

The order of the list returned by the `ValueListNames()` function is the same as that in which the value lists are ordered in the Define Value Lists dialog when the order is set to Custom Order. Changing the Custom Order changes the way the results are ordered, but selecting one of the other choices (Creation Order, Source, Value List Name) does not.

`Variance()`

Category: Aggregate

Syntax: `Variance ( field { ; field...} )`

Parameters: `field`—any related field, repeating field, or set of non-repeating fields that represent a collection of numbers.

Description: Returns the variance of the non-blank values represented in the parameter list. Variance is a statistical measure of how spread out a set of values is.

Examples:

The `Variance` of a set of numbers can be calculated by summing the squares of the distance of each value from the mean, then dividing by n-1, where n is the number of values.

For instance, given the set of number 8, 10, and 12, the mean of the set is 10. The distance of each value from the mean is -2, 0, and 2. The squares of these distances are 4, 0, and 4, and the sum of the squares is 8. The `Variance` is 8 divided by (3–1), which is 4.

`Variance (8; 10; 12)`

Returns 4.

`Variance (7; 11; 15)`

Returns 16.

Comments:

The `StDev()` of a set of numbers is the square root of the `Variance()` of the set.

The difference between the `Variance()` and `VarianceP()` functions is that the `Variance` divides the sum of the squares by n-1 instead of by n.

`VarianceP()`

Category: Aggregate

Syntax: `VarianceP ( field { ; field...} )`

Parameters: `field`—any related field, repeating field, or set of non-repeating fields that represent a collection of numbers.

Description: Returns the variance of a population represented by the non-blank values in the parameter list. Variance of population is a statistical measure of how spread out a set of values is.

Examples:

The variance of a population represented by a set of numbers can be calculated by summing the squares of the distance of each value from the mean, then dividing by *n*, where *n* is the number of values.

For instance, given the set of number 8, 10, and 12, the mean of the set is 10. The distance of each value from the mean is -2, 0, and 2. The squares of these distances are 4, 0, and 4, and the sum of the squares is 8. The VarianceP is 8 divided by (3), which is 2.67.

VarianceP (8; 10; 12)

Returns 2.67.

VarianceP (7; 11; 15)

Returns 10.66.

Comments:

The StDevP() of a set of numbers is the square root of the VarianceP() of the set.

WeekOfYear()

Category: Date

Syntax: WeekOfYear (Date)

Parameters: Date—any valid date (1/1/0001–12/31/4000). The parameter should be a string containing a date (for example, "3/17/2004"), an expression with a date result (for example, Date (6, 29, 1969)), or an integer that represents a serialized date value (for example, 718977).

Description: Returns the week number of the specified date. Weeks are defined as starting on Sunday and ending on Saturday. A partial week at the beginning of the year is considered as week 1, so the WeekOfYear() function can return values from 1 to 54.

Examples:

WeekOfYear ("3/12/2004")

Returns 11.

WeekOfYear ("12/31/2001")

Returns 53.

Comments:

WeekOfYear() can be used to return the approximate number of weeks between two dates in the same year. For instance, WeekOfYear("6/1/2001") - WeekOfYear("5/1/2001") returns 4.

January 1st of any given year is always part of week 1, no matter on what day of the week it falls.

B

WeekOfYearFiscal()

Category: Date

Syntax: WeekOfYearFiscal (Date ; StartingDay)

Parameters: Date—any valid date (1/1/0001–12/31/4000). The parameter should be a string containing a date (for example, "3/17/2004"), an expression with a date result (for example, Date (6, 29, 1969)), or an integer that represents a serialized date value (for example, 718977). StartingDay—a numeric value between 1 (Sunday) and 7 (Saturday).

Description: The WeekOfYearFiscal() function returns an integer from 1 to 53 that represents the week number of the year of the specified date. Weeks are defined as starting on the day of week specified by the StartingDay parameter.

The first week of a year is defined as the first week that contains four or more days of that year. For instance, January 1, 2004 was a Thursday. Using a StartingDay of 5, the first fiscal week of the year would be considered as 1/1/2004 through 1/7/2004. The second fiscal week would begin on Thursday, 1/8/2004. However, if you used a StartingDay of 1 (Sunday), then the first day of the fiscal year would be 1/4/2004. In the previous week (12/28/03–1/3/2004), only three days are in 2004, so that would be considered as the 53rd fiscal week of 2003.

Examples:

WeekOfYearFiscal ("3/21/2004", 4)

Returns 12.

WeekOfYearFiscal ("1/1/2004", 1)

Returns 53.

WeekOfYearFiscal ("1/1/2004", 2)

Returns 1.

Comments:

WeekOfYearFiscal() and WeekOfYear() often yields different results. WeekOfYear() is always based on a week defined as Sunday through Saturday, whereas WeekOfYearFiscal() can begin on whatever day you specify. Even when it begins on Sunday, however, you might have discrepancies because of the rule that the first week must have four or more days in the current year. Whereas WeekOfYearFiscal("1/1/2004") returns 53, WeekOfYear("1/1/2004") returns 1.

WindowNames

Category: Design

Syntax: WindowNames

Parameters: None

Description: Returns a carriage return–delimited list of open window names.

Examples:

WindowNames might return a list of values that looks like this:

```
Customers
Invoices
myDatabase
Invoices - 2
```

Comments:

Note that WindowNames returns window names from all open FileMaker files. Window names do not need to be unique. The order of the list is determined by the stacking order of the windows, with the topmost window (the active window) listed first. Hidden windows are listed, but not any window that appears in the window list surrounded by parentheses. This indicates a file that is open but that doesn't have any windows, hidden or visible. Visible windows are listed first, then minimized windows, then hidden windows.

WordCount()

Category: Text

Syntax: WordCount (text)

Parameters: text—any expression that resolves to a text string.

Description: Returns a count of the number of words in text.

Examples:

WordCount ("The quick brown fox jumps over the lazy dog.")

Returns 9.

WordCount (FullName)

Returns 4 when FullName contains "John Q. Public, Jr."

Comments:

Spaces, return characters, and most punctuation symbols are considered to be word breaks by FileMaker Pro. Multiple word breaks next to each other (for example, two spaces, a comma, and a space) are considered as a single word break.

Certain punctuation symbols are word breaks when separating alpha characters, but not when separating numeric characters. These include the colon (:), slash (/), period (.), comma (,), and dash (-). For instance, WordCount ("54.6") returns 1, but WordCount ("x.y") returns 2. The reason for this behavior is that those symbols are valid date, time, and number separators.

B

`Year()`

Category: Date

Syntax: `Year ( Date )`

Parameters: `Date`—any valid date (1/1/0001–12/31/4000). The parameter should be a string containing a date (for example, "3/17/2004"), an expression with a date result (for example, `Date (6, 29, 1969)`), or an integer that represents a serialized date value (for example, `718977`).

Description: Returns the year portion of the `Date` parameter.

Examples:

`Year ("1/1/2004")`

Returns `2004`.

`Year (Get(CurrentDate))`

Returns the current year.

`Year (myBirthdate)`

Returns the year portion of the field `myBirthdate`.

Comments:

The `Year ()` function is often used in conjunction with the `Date ()` function to assemble new date values. For instance, if you have a field called `DateOfBirth` that contains someone's birthdate, you can calculate the date of that person's birthday in the current year as follows:

`Date (Month (DateOfBirth), Day (DateOfBirth), Year (Get (CurrentDate)))`

B

C

SCRIPT STEP REFERENCE

ABOUT THE SCRIPT STEP REFERENCE

The script step reference is a detailed guide to all the FileMaker Pro script steps. It is similar in layout to FileMaker's online help system, but adds more detailed examples and commentary where possible. The listing for each script step also indicates its platform compatibility, any menu equivalent, and whether the script step is Web compatible. A number of Web-compatible steps are marked with an asterisk. This indicates that though the step as a whole is Web compatible, one or more specific options of the step are not. So far, the only non-Web-compatible options we've seen are those that display a dialog box to the user when the step executes.

ADD ACCOUNT

Compatibility: Mac: yes   Windows: yes   Web: yes

Menu Equivalent: None

Syntax:

```
Add Account [Account Name: <account name>; Password: <password>; Privilege Set:
➥"<privilege set>"; Expire password]
```

Options:

Account Name is the account name. Literal text can be entered or Specify can be clicked to create a new account name from a calculation.

Password is the new password. Literal text can be entered or Specify can be clicked to create a new password from a calculation.

Privilege Set allows you to assign a preexisting privilege set for the user or to create a new one. (Full Access cannot be assigned via this script step. Accounts with Full Access must be created manually.)

User Must Change Password on Next Login: When selected, this option forces users to change their password the next time they log in to the database.

Examples:

```
Add Account [Account Name: "User_Account"; Password: "User_Password"; Privilege
➥Set: "[Data Entry Only]"; Expire password]
```

Description: This script step adds an account name, password, and privilege set to a database's security configuration. Account and password text may be defined in a calculation or typed into the script step itself. The account name must be unique, and full access to the file is required to execute this step.

Comments: It might be desirable to allow access to this functionality via a script, if certain users or user groups have limited access to the FileMaker menus because of security configurations. See the `Change Password` script step for a fuller discussion.

ADJUST WINDOW

Compatibility: Mac: yes   Windows: yes   Web: no

Menu Equivalent: None

Syntax:

```
Adjust Window [Resize to fit/Maximize/Minimize/Restore/Hide]
```

Options:

Resize to Fit shrinks a window to the minimum possible size while including all layout elements.

Maximize expands the current window to the size of the user's screen.

Minimize minimizes the current window to an icon.

Restore returns the current window to the size it was before the last resize.

Hide hides the current database window.

Examples:

```
Go to Layout ["Detail"]
Adjust Window [Maximize]
```

Description:

This script step hides or otherwise controls the size of the current database window. It is important to note that in a single-user environment, the size and position of a window cannot be relied upon unless one has explicitly set it or users are explicitly prohibited from modifying it.

ALLOW TOOLBARS

Compatibility: Mac: yes   Windows: yes   Web: no

Menu Equivalent: None

C

Syntax:

```
Allow Toolbars [<On/Off>]
```

Options:

On allows FileMaker's native toolbars to be utilized.

Off hides and makes inaccessible FileMaker's toolbars as well as the toolbar submenu options in the view menu.

Examples:

```
Allow Toolbars [Off]
```

Description: This script step hides and shows the FileMaker Pro toolbars and menu options. This is often used to control the amount of screen space available in a given database screen. This script step takes effect only while the file that calls this script is active. This option has no effect in Kiosk mode because toolbars are always hidden in Kiosk mode.

ALLOW USER ABORT

Compatibility: Mac: yes   Windows: yes   Web: yes

Menu Equivalent: None

Syntax:

```
Allow User Abort [<on or off>]
```

Options:

On allows users to halt the execution of a script by pressing the Esc key (or ⌘-period on Mac OS machines).

Off disables the halting of scripts by users.

Examples:

```
Allow User Abort[Off]
```

Description: Allow User Abort is used to control the user's ability to cancel scripts by using the Esc key (or the ⌘-period key combination on Mac OS systems). This script step is usually used in scripts whose operation should not be arbitrarily canceled by the user, such as login logic or data import/export. Most of FileMaker's menu options are also unavailable while a script is in the Allow User Abort [Off] state.

Comments: If a script involves any processes that could work with large record sets, such as sorting, looping, or running a Replace script step, the user sees a progress dialog for the duration of that operation. If Allow User Abort is on, as it is by default, users can cancel the script and disrupt those operations, leaving them partially complete. If a script contains any process that must not be interrupted before completion, it should use Allow User Abort[Off] to ensure that these processes are able to finish without user interruption.

ARRANGE ALL WINDOWS

Compatibility: Mac: yes   Windows: yes*   Web: no

Menu Equivalent: Window, (various choices)

Syntax:

```
Arrange All Windows [Tile Horizontally/Tile Vertically/Cascade Window/Bring All
➥to Front]
```

Options:

Tile Horizontally positions open windows from left to right across the screen. They are resized to avoid any overlaps.

Tile Vertically positions open windows from top to bottom down the screen. They are resized to avoid any overlaps.

Cascade Window positions windows overlapping diagonally from upper left to lower right. The idea of this arrangement is, presumably, to allow the reading of the title bar of each window. The windows are resized to fit the available screen space.

Bring All to Front (Mac OS only) brings all open windows to the front without resizing or otherwise moving or rearranging them. In the event that any open FileMaker windows have been hidden by (that is, are behind) any other application's windows, this step ensures that all FileMaker windows are above other application windows.

Examples:

```
New Window [Name: "Trees"; Height: 200; Width: 600; Top: 16; Left: 16]
Arrange All Windows [Tile Vertically]
```

Description: This script step resizes and/or repositions open windows, but does not affect which window has focus. The active record also remains the same.

BEEP

Compatibility: Mac: yes   Windows: yes   Web: no

Menu Equivalent: None

Syntax:

```
Beep
```

Options:

None

Examples:

```
Set Error Capture [On]
Perform Find [Restore]
If [Get (FoundCount) = 0]
   Beep
   Show Custom Dialog ["No records were found that match your find criteria."]
End
```

Description: This script step plays a beep noise. The beep is played at the default volume of the machine on which it is played.

Comments: You may want to use the beep as an extra alert noise. (We've even heard of an intrepid FileMaker developer, on the road without an alarm clock, who programmed himself an alarm clock in FileMaker with the Beep step.)

CHANGE PASSWORD

Compatibility: Mac: yes   Windows: yes   Web: yes*

Menu Equivalent: File, Change Password

Syntax:

```
Change Password [Old Password: <old password>; New Password: <new password>;
➥No dialog]
```

Options:

Old Password is the current account's current password. It can be the result of a specified calculation or typed in.

New Password is the desired new password for the current account. It can be the result of a specified calculation or typed in.

Perform Without Dialog suppresses the FileMaker Pro confirmation dialog for this action.

Examples:

```
Change Password [Old Password: '0ldpassw0rd'; New Password: New_Password;
➥No Dialog]
// Change Password can be used in conjunction with "Show Custom Dialog" to
➥cascade password changes throughout several files:
Allow User Abort [ Off ]
Set Error Capture [ On ]
#
Show Custom Dialog [ Title: "Password Change"; Buttons: "OK", "Cancel";
➥Input #1: zgPassword_Old. t, "Old Password:";
➥Input #2: zgPassword_New. t, "New Password:" ]
#
If [ Get(LastMessageChoice)=1 ]
  Change Password [ Old Password: zgPassword_Old. t;
➥New Password: zgPassword_New. t ]
  # send password change to other files
  Perform Script [ "Change Password"; from file "Contacts" Parameter:
➥zgPassword_Old. t&"¶"&zgPassword_New. t ]
  Perform Script [ "Change Password"; from file "Invoices" Parameter:
➥zgPassword_Old. t&"¶"&zgPassword_New. t ]
End If
# be sure to clear the globals for security reasons
Set Field [zgPassword_Old. t; ""]
Set Field [zgPassword_New. t; ""]
```

Description: This script step changes the password for the current account. By default, a Change Password dialog is displayed unless the Perform Without Dialog option is selected. If error capture has been enabled (in the Set Error Capture script step) and Perform

Without Dialog is not selected, then the user is given five attempts at changing his or her password. If error capture has not been enabled and Perform Without Dialog is not selected, then the user is given only one attempt at changing the password. Run Script With Full Access Privileges enables a user to change the password for the current account even if he or she lacks the explicit permission to do so.

Comments: A number of FileMaker script steps perform functions similar or identical to choices that are available in the FileMaker menus. For reasons of security or solution design, a developer might choose to limit user access to the FileMaker menus. (Menu access can be configured differently for each privilege set in a file. See Chapter 12, "Implementing Security," for more information on creating and editing privilege sets.) If access to menus is limited, it may be necessary or desirable to reproduce some functionality available through menus by creating a scripted interface instead. A user without access to menus might instead then see a Change Password button or clickable link, which invokes the Change Password script step.

When programming for the Web, be sure to select Perform Without Dialog. Leaving the box unchecked is not Web compatible and does not work on the Web.

CHECK FOUND SET

Compatibility: Mac: yes   Windows: yes   Web: no

Menu Equivalent: Edit, Spelling, Check All

Syntax:

```
Check Found Set
```

Options:

None

Examples:

```
Perform Find [Restore]
Check Found Set
```

Description: This script step uses FileMaker Pro's spelling checker to check the spelling of the contents of text fields in all the records currently being browsed. The step checks spelling in all fields of type Text, and all calculation fields with a calculation result type of Text. It is an interactive script step that displays the familiar spelling dialog for every questionable spelling that the system finds.

Comments: This option is normally available via the FileMaker menus. If one or more users have limited access to menu items, it may be necessary to write scripts that give them access to functionality normally available through menus, such as spell check functions. See the Change Password script step for further discussion of this point.

CHECK RECORD

Compatibility: Mac: yes   Windows: yes   Web: no

Menu Equivalent: Edit, Spelling, Check Record

Syntax:

```
Check Record
```

Options:

None

Examples:

```
Go to Record/Request/Page [First]
Loop
    Check Record
    Go to Record/Request/Page [Next; Exit after last]
End Loop
```

Description: This script step uses FileMaker Pro's spelling checker to check the spelling of the contents of text fields in every record in the current record. The step checks spelling in all fields of type Text, and all calculation fields with a calculation result type of Text. It is an interactive script step that displays the familiar spelling dialog for every questionable spelling that the system finds. See also the Check Found Set script step for further discussion.

Comments: This option is normally available via the FileMaker menus. If one or more users have limited access to menu items, it may be necessary to write scripts that give them access to functionality normally available through menus, such as spell check functions. See the Change Password script step for further discussion of this point.

CHECK SELECTION

Compatibility: Mac: yes   Windows: yes   Web: no

Menu Equivalent: Edit, Spelling, Check Selection

Syntax:

```
Check Selection [Select; table::field]
```

Options:

Select Entire Contents checks the spelling of the entire contents of the designated field. If this option is not chosen, then only the text that has been selected (highlighted) is checked.

Go to Target Field allows for the selection of the field to spell check.

Examples:

```
Check Selection [Select; Product::Description]
```

Description:

This script step uses FileMaker Pro's spelling checker to check the spelling of the contents of a single field. The step can check spelling in all fields of type Text, and all calculation fields with a calculation result type of Text. It is an interactive script step that displays the familiar spelling dialog for every questionable spelling that the system finds.

Comments:

This option is normally available via the FileMaker menus. If one or more users have limited access to menu items, it may be necessary to write scripts that give them access to functionality normally available through menus, such as spell check functions. See the `Change Password` script step for further discussion of this point.

CLEAR

Compatibility: Mac: yes   Windows: yes   Web: yes

Menu Equivalent: Edit, Clear

Syntax:

```
Clear [Select; <table::field>]
```

Options:

Select Entire Contents allows for the deletion of the entire contents of a field, regardless of what portion of its contents have been selected (highlighted).

Go to Target Field specifies which field is to have its contents or selected contents deleted.

Examples:

```
#The following example clears the values in a repeating field with
➥three repetitions.
Clear [Select, table::field[3]]
Clear [Select, table::field[2]]
Clear [Select, table::field]
```

Description:

This script step removes either the entire contents of a field (if the `Select Entire Contents` option has been designated) or the selected portion of a field (if the `Select Entire Contents` option has not been designated). It is important to note that `Clear` is distinct from the `Cut` operation in that it does not place the deleted content on the clipboard. In a Web-published database, it is necessary to use a `Commit Record/Request` script step to update the record that had one (or more) of its fields cleared.

Comments:

`Clear` is one of a number of script steps that depend on the presence of specific fields on the current layout. For these steps to take effect, the targeted field must be present on the current layout and the current mode must be Browse mode. Note, however, that these script steps take effect even if the field has been marked as not enterable in Browse mode. Other script steps with the same limitations include `Cut`, `Copy`, `Paste`, and `Set Selection`.

CLOSE FILE

Compatibility: Mac: yes   Windows: yes   Web: no

Menu Equivalent: File, Close

Syntax:

```
Close File [Current File/"<filename>"]
```

Options:

Specify allows you to select a FileMaker Pro file to close from among the list of existing predefined file references.

Add File Reference allows the selection of a file to close while at the same time adding it to the list of pre-defined file references.

Define File References allows for existing file references to be modified or deleted.

Examples:

```
Close ["Line_Items.fp7"]
```

Description:

This script step closes the specified file. The target file may be specified via a file reference. If no file reference is designated, then the file in which the script is running is closed. (This also has the effect of halting the execution of the script that contains the Close File step.)

Comments:

If you used File, File Options to specify a script that should run when a file is closed, that script is triggered when the Close File script step is run.

CLOSE WINDOW

Compatibility: Mac: yes   Windows: yes   Web: yes

Menu Equivalent: None

Syntax:

```
Close Window [Current Window or Name: <name of window>]
```

Options:

Specify allows you to choose a window to close, either by typing its name explicitly, or by drawing the name from a calculation.

Examples:

```
Close Window [Name: "Sales records"]
```

Description:

This script step closes either the currently active window or a window designated by name. The name may be a string literal typed into the script itself or generated as the result of a calculation.

Comments:

Closing the last open window in a database closes the database and halts execution of the currently running script. This also triggers any script that has been set to run when the file closes.

COMMENT

Compatibility: Mac: yes   Windows: yes   Web: yes

Menu Equivalent: None

Syntax:

```
#<comment text>
```

Options:

Specify allows for the entry of comment text in a dialog box.

Examples:

```
# Clear Globals for Login
#
# Script authored by : Tom
# Last modified on 1/12/2004
#
Clear [Select, table::gCurrentUserID]
Clear [Select, table::gCurrentUserName]
Clear [Select, table::gCurrentUserEmail]
```

Description:

This script step allows for the addition of comments to scripts. You can see these comments only when a script is viewed in ScriptMaker, or when a script is printed and the comments are bold text preceded by a #. Comments print as italics.

Comments:

Properly commented code helps greatly in legibility and debugging. For more discussion of this point see Chapter 9, "Getting Started with Scripting" and Chapter 17, "Troubleshooting." Script comments are somewhat different from calculation comments, in that calculation comments are inserted in the body of a calculation's text, and can be preceded with // or wrapped in /* . . . */ comment delimiters.

COMMIT RECORDS/REQUESTS

Compatibility: Mac: yes   Windows: yes   Web: yes*

Menu Equivalent: None

Syntax:

```
Commit Records/Requests [No dialog]
```

C

Options:

Skip Data Entry Validation overrides any data entry validation options set for fields and commits the record anyway. This option skips validation only for fields set with the Only During Data Entry validation option in the Options for Field dialog box; fields set to Always Validate still validate, even if the Skip Data Entry Validation option is selected.

Examples:

```
Show Custom Dialog ["Commit record?";
"Click 'Commit' to save your changes."]
If [Get(LastMessageChoice) = 1]
   Commit Records/Requests
Else
   Revert Record/Request [No dialog]
End
```

Description:

This script step *commits* a record. In other words, it exits the current record or find request and updates the field data for the record. It has the effect of causing the user to exit the record, in the sense that no field will be active on the current layout once the record is committed. Note: exiting a record will also have the effect of committing any changes made to it. Exiting a record can be accomplished in many non-scripted ways, including changing to another record or merely clicking on a layout outside of any field so that no field is selected. See the Revert Record/Request script step for more discussion.

Comments:

While a user is editing a record, any changes she makes to the record can't be seen. Only when she commits the record are her changes saved to the database and broadcast to other users. This script step has wide applicability. Any time you change data in a record via a script, it's a good idea to commit the record explicitly. This is especially true if the changes will result in significant screen updates. For example, if data changes in a record would lead to different data being displayed in a portal on the current layout, it's very important to make sure the data changes are explicitly committed. As a best practice we recommend using this step in any script where record data is altered. It's also necessary to add this script step to scripts that are called from the Web, if those scripts change record data.

When programming for the Web, be sure to select Perform Without Dialog. Leaving the box unchecked is not Web compatible and does not work on the Web.

CONSTRAIN FOUND SET

Compatibility: Mac: yes   Windows: yes   Web: yes

Menu Equivalent: Requests, Constrain Found Set

Syntax:

```
Constrain Found Set [Restore]
```

Options:

Specify Find Requests creates and stores a find request with the script step. See the Perform Find script step for more information.

Examples:

```
# Find all employees older than 60 years of age.
Enter Find Mode [ ]
Set Field [Age; ">60" ]
Perform Find []
# Find which of these want early retirement
Enter Find Mode [ ]
Set Field [Early_Retire; "Yes" ]
Constrain Found Set[]
```

Description:

This script step specifies a find request that will be used to narrow the current found set. This is equivalent to applying the last find request with the new find request appended via a logical AND operator.

Comments:

Constrain[] is useful when searching unindexed fields as part of a complex find. If a search includes criteria for both stored and unstored fields, a performance gain may be achieved by first performing a find on the indexed fields, and then using Constrain[] to limit the search for the unindexed criteria to the smaller found set.

CONVERT FILE

Compatibility: Mac: yes   Windows: yes   Web: no

Menu Equivalent: None

Syntax:

```
Convert File ["<filename>"]
```

Options:

Specify Data Source allows for the designation of a data source to be converted into a FileMaker Pro 7 file.

The possible data sources are

File

XML

ODBC

Examples:

```
Convert File ["datafile.fp5"]
```

Description:

This script step converts a file from a variety of supported formats into a FileMaker 7 file. This command works on only one file at a time. Supported data formats are BASIC format, Comma-Separated Text format, dBase III and IV DBF format, DIF format, FileMaker Pro format, HTML Table format, Lotus 1-2-3 WK1/WKS formats, Merge format, Microsoft Excel format, SYLK format, Tab-Separated Text format, and XML format. Designation of various data sources follows the same procedures as an import. See the `Import Records` script step for further discussion.

Comments:

This step is analogous to the effects of using File, Open to open a non-FileMaker 7 file. A variety of formats can be opened/converted, each with its own set of options. See Chapter 18, "Converting Systems from Previous Versions of FileMaker Pro" and Chapter 19, "Importing Data into FileMaker Pro."

Copy

Compatibility: Mac: yes   Windows: yes   Web: yes

Menu Equivalent: Edit, Copy

Syntax:

```
Copy [Select; <table::field>]
```

Options:

Select Entire Contents copies the entire contents of a field to the Clipboard rather than just the selected portion of the designated field's contents.

Go to Target Field or **Specify** allow you to select the field from which you wish to copy the contents to the clipboard. If no field is specified and nothing is selected, FileMaker Pro copies the values from all fields of the current record.

Examples:

```
Go To Layout[ "Customer Entry" (Customer)]
Copy [Select; CustomerTable::Shipping_Address]
Paste [Select; CustomerTable::Billing_Address]
```

Description:

This script step places the contents of the specified field on to the clipboard. If no field is specified, all fields from the current record are copied, causing the step to function identically to the Copy Record step.

Comments:

`Copy` is generally a poor way to move data within scripts. It requires that the current layout contain the field to be copied. (This is fragile because the script malfunctions if the field is removed.) Additionally, the contents of the clipboard are overwritten, without the consent of the user. `Copy` does have some interesting uses, however. When in Preview Mode, `Copy` takes an image of the screen, and this image can then be pasted into a container field. Copy is one of a number of script steps that depend on the presence of specific fields on the current layout. Other script steps with the same limitations include Cut, Copy, Paste, and Set Selection.

COPY ALL RECORDS/REQUESTS

Compatibility: Mac: yes   Windows: yes   Web: yes

Menu Equivalent: None

Syntax:

Copy All Records/Requests

Options:

None

Examples:

```
# Copy Current Record
Go To Layout ["Detail"]
Copy All Records/Requests
# Place all records in log field
Go To Layout ["Log"]
New Record/Request
Paste [Select; Log Table::Log]
```

Description:

This script step copies the values of all fields in all the records in the current found set to the clipboard in a tab-delimited export format. Styles and formatting are not copied. The field values are exported in the order in which they appear on the current layout. Only those fields that appear in the current layout are included. With a record, individual fields are separated by tabs, and records are delimited by carriage returns. Repeating field values are separated by a group separator character between each repetition. Carriage returns within a field are copied to the clipboard as the "vertical tab" character (ASCII value 11), just as they are when being exported.

Comments:

Copy All Records/Requests is one of a number of script steps that depend on the presence of specific fields on the current layout. Other script steps with the same limitations include Cut, Copy, Paste, and Set Selection.

In previous versions of FileMaker it was often necessary to use this script step to copy a set of record keys and paste them into a field that would act as a "multikey," capable of relating to many records in another file at once. This technique was often used to navigate multi-step relationship chains. The new relational capabilities of FileMaker 7 make it unlikely that this step will need to be used in this way.

COPY RECORD/REQUEST

Compatibility: Mac: yes   Windows: yes   Web: yes

Menu Equivalent: None

Syntax:

```
Copy Record/Request
```

Options:

None

Examples:

```
# Copy Current Record
Go To Layout ["Detail"]
Copy Record/Request
# Place record in log field
Go To Layout ["Log"]
New Record/Request
Paste [Select; Log Table::Log]
```

Description:

This script step copies the values of all fields in the current record to the clipboard in a tab-delimited export format. Styles and formatting are not copied. The field values are exported in the order in which they appear on the current layout. Only those fields that appear in the current layout are included. With a record, individual fields are separated by tabs, and records are delimited by carriage returns. Repeating field values are separated by a group separator character between each repetition. Carriage returns within a field are copied to the clipboard as the "vertical tab" character (ASCII value 11), just as they are when being exported.

Comments:

`Copy Record/Request` is one of a number of script steps that depend on the presence of specific fields on the current layout. Other script steps with the same limitations include `Cut`, `Copy`, `Paste`, and `Set Selection`.

CORRECT WORD

Compatibility: Mac: yes   Windows: yes   Web: no

Menu Equivalent: Edit, Spelling, Correct Word

Syntax:

```
Correct Word
```

Options:

None

Examples:

```
Check Selection [Select; Product::Description]
Correct Word
```

Description:

This script step opens the spelling dialog box to allow for the correction of the spelling of a word that has been identified as having been misspelled by the FileMaker Pro spell check operation. The option to Check Spelling as You Type must be selected. A word can be corrected only if FileMaker has identified it as being misspelled.

Comments:

This option is normally available via the FileMaker menus. If one or more users have limited access to menu items, it may be necessary to write scripts that give them access to functionality normally available through menus, such as spell check functions. See the Change Password script step for further discussion of this point.

Cut

Compatibility: Mac: yes   Windows: yes   Web: yes

Menu Equivalent: Edit, Cut

Syntax:

```
Cut [Select; <table::field>]
```

Options:

Select Entire Contents copies the entire contents of a field to the Clipboard, rather than just the selected portion of the designated field's contents. The field is cleared of its contents.

Go to Target Field or **Specify** allow you to select the field from which you wish to cut the contents to the clipboard. If no field is specified and nothing is selected, FileMaker Pro cuts the values from all fields of the current record.

Examples:

```
Enter Browse Mode [ ]
Cut [Select, Table1::Recent Notes]
Paste [Table1::Previous Notes]
```

Description:

This script step places the contents of the selected field (or of all fields on the current layout if no field is selected or designated within the script itself) onto the clipboard and then clears the contents of that field.

Comments:

Cut is generally a script step that bears avoiding. It requires that the current layout contain the field to be cut. (This is fragile because the script malfunctions if the field is removed.)

Additionally, the contents of the clipboard are overwritten, without the consent of the user. Think carefully about whether the intended effect could be accomplished in a layout-independent, less intrusive fashion. Other script steps with the same limitations include Copy, Paste, and Set Selection.

DELETE ACCOUNT

Compatibility: Mac: yes   Windows: yes   Web: yes

Menu Equivalent: None

Syntax:

Delete Account [Account Name: <account name>]

Options:

Specify allows for the selection or input of the account to be deleted.

Examples:

Delete Account [Account Name: "Guest Access account"]

Description:

This script step deletes the specified account in the current database. Full access is required to complete this operation and an account with full access may not be deleted with this script step. It is possible to specify Run Script with Full Access Privileges to ensure that any user can execute this script. However, care must be taken to ensure that such usage does not create a security hole. After Run Script with Full Access Privileges has been checked, any user who can see the script can run it, including those who have external access from other FileMaker files and Web access.

Comments:

It might be desirable to allow access to this functionality via a script, if certain users or user groups have limited access to the FileMaker menus because of security configurations. See the Change Password script step for a fuller discussion.

DELETE ALL RECORDS

Compatibility: Mac: yes   Windows: yes   Web: yes*

Menu Equivalent: Records, Delete All Records

Syntax:

Delete All Records [No dialog]

Options:

Perform Without Dialog allows for the deletion of all records in the current found set without user intervention.

Examples:

```
Perform Find [Restore]
// use a custom dialog to warn user before deleting all records
Allow User Abort [ Off ]
Set Error Capture [ On ]
Show Custom Dialog [ Title: "Delete All Records";
➥Message: "Are you really sure you want to delete all records?"; Buttons:
➥ "Cancel", "Delete" ]
If [Get(LastMessageChoice)=2 ]
# the user still wants to delete
  Show Custom Dialog [ Title: "Delete All Records";
  ➥Message: "Do you have a current backup?"; Buttons: "No", "Yes" ]
If [ Get(LastMessageChoice)=2 ]
 # after they confirmed twice, go ahead with delete
 Show All Records
 Delete All Records[ No dialog ]
 End If
End If
```

Description:

This script step deletes all records in the current found set. It can be set to operate without user approval if you select the Perform Without Dialog option. Special care should be exercised in the use of this script step because it is not possible to undo the operation after it has been completed.

Comments:

Note that any records that are "in use" by other users are not deleted by this step. Records are considered to be in use if other users are actively editing them and have not committed/saved their changes. You may want to check explicitly whether this has occurred, either by examining the found set, or by using Get(LastError) to check for a script error. You should also decide how you want to handle cases where the step doesn't execute completely for reasons such as these. Note that this script step is context-dependent. The current layout determines which table is active, which determines from which table the records are deleted.

When programming for the Web, be sure to select Perform Without Dialog. Leaving the box unchecked is not Web compatible and does not work on the Web.

DELETE PORTAL ROW

Compatibility: Mac: yes   Windows: yes   Web: yes

Menu Equivalent: None

Syntax:

```
Delete Portal Row [No dialog]
```

Options:

Perform Without Dialog allows for the deletion of the current related record without user approval.

Examples:

```
Go to Portal Row [Last]
Delete Portal Row [No dialog]
```

Description:

This script step deletes the current portal row. In other words, it deletes a record that's related to the current record. It can be set to operate without user approval if you select the Perform Without Dialog option. Special care should be exercised in the use of this script step because it is not possible to undo the operation after it has been completed.

Comments:

Performance of this step can be inhibited if the record represented by the specified portal row is in use by another user. See the Delete All Records script step for further discussion. Note that this script step deletes a portal row even if the Allow Deletion of Portal Records check box in the Portal Setup dialog box is unchecked.

When programming for the Web, be sure to select Perform Without Dialog. Leaving the box unchecked is not Web compatible and does not work on the Web.

DELETE RECORD/REQUEST

Compatibility: Mac: yes   Windows: yes   Web: yes

Menu Equivalent: Records, Delete Record/Request

Syntax:

```
Delete Record/Request [No dialog]
```

Options:

Perform Without Dialog allows for the deletion of the current record or find request without user approval.

Examples:

```
Go to Record/Request [Last]
Delete Record/Request [No dialog]
```

Description:

This script step deletes the current record or find request record. It can be set to operate without user approval if you select the Perform Without Dialog option. Special care should be exercised in the use of this script step because it is not possible to undo the operation after it has been completed.

Comments:

If the current layout has a portal and a portal row is selected, the user is prompted to specify whether the master record or the related record should be deleted. If the step is performed without a dialog, the action automatically applies to the master record. If a portal row is selected and the portal is not set to Allow Deletion of Portal Records, the option to delete a related record never appears. Note that this is in contrast to the `Delete Portal Row` step, which deletes an active portal row regardless of whether `Allow Deletion of Portal Records` is enabled or not. Performance of this step can be inhibited if the record is in use by another user. See the `Delete All Records` script step for further discussion. Note that this script step is context-dependent. The current layout determines which table is active, which determines from which table the record is deleted.

When programming for the Web, be sure to select `Perform Without Dialog`. Leaving the box unchecked is not Web compatible and does not work on the Web.

DIAL PHONE

Compatibility: Mac: no   Windows: yes   Web: no

Menu Equivalent: None

Syntax:

`Dial Phone [No dialog; <phone number>]`

Options:

Perform Without Dialog prevents the Dial Phone dialog from displaying when this script step executes.

Specify displays the Dial Phone options.

- **Phone Number** allows the entry of a telephone number.
- **Specify** allows the creation of a calculation to generate the telephone number to be dialed.
- **Use Dialing Preferences** applies the pre-established telephone dialing preferences to the number to be dialed, based on the designated location information.

Examples:

`Dial Phone [No Dialog, Contacts::Phone_Home]`

Description:

This script step allows FileMaker Pro to dial a telephone number from within a script. The number to be dialed may be entered within the script itself, contained within a field, or generated by a specified calculation. Current telephone dialing preferences can be applied optionally based on location information. Letters within telephone numbers are translated into the appropriate numbers (q and z being, of course, omitted). Note: This script step does not work on Mac OS.

Comments:

You might use this script step if you want to be able to dial the phone numbers of people or organizations whose contact information is stored in FileMaker. You might also use it to perform more low-level serial-line tasks, in conjunction with a plug-in that can communicate directly with a computer's serial port.

DUPLICATE RECORD/REQUEST

Compatibility: Mac: yes   Windows: yes   Web: yes

Menu Equivalent: Records, Duplicate Record/Request

Syntax:

```
Duplicate Record/Request
```

Options:

None

Examples:

```
Go to Portal Row [Last]
Duplicate Record/Request
```

Description:

This script step duplicates the current record while in Browse mode and the current find request in Find mode. Fields with auto-entry options are not duplicated; new values are generated for these fields, according to the details of the specific auto-entry options. If this script step is used after the Go to Portal Row script step has been executed and the portal relationship allows for the creation of related records, then the related record is duplicated, rather than the master record.

Comments:

If there are certain fields you want to make certain are never duplicated, you can set them to auto-enter an empty string (""). On duplication, the auto-entry option will take effect and clear the field in the new record.

EDIT USER DICTIONARY

Compatibility: Mac: yes   Windows: yes   Web: no

Menu Equivalent: Edit, Spelling, Edit User Dictionary

Syntax:

```
Edit User Dictionary
```

Options:

None

Examples:

```
Show Custom Dialog ["Edit the user dictionary?"]
If [Get (LastMessageChoice) = 1]
   Edit User Dictionary
End If
```

C

Description:

This script step opens the User Dictionary dialog box. This is often used to display the User Dictionary dialog box when user privileges do not allow for the dialog to be chosen directly from the FileMaker menus.

ELSE

Compatibility: Mac: yes   Windows: yes   Web: yes

Menu Equivalent: None

Syntax:

```
Else
```

Options:

None

Examples:

```
If [gUsername = "Tom"]
   Show Custom Dialog ["Hello Tom"]
Else If [gUsername =  "Raul"]
   Show Custom Dialog ["Hola Raul"]
Else If [gUsername = "Guido"]
   Show Custom Dialog ["Ciao Guido"]
Else
   Show Custom Dialog ["I don't know who you are!"]
End If
```

Description:

This script step can be placed after an If or Else If statement and immediately before an End If statement. The designated code block for the Else statement is executed only if all the previous If and Else If statements have evaluated as false. It is thus often used as a way to deal with values that do not fit within expected parameters or as a default action.

ELSE IF

Compatibility: Mac: yes   Windows: yes   Web: yes

Menu Equivalent: None

Syntax:

```
Else If [<Boolean calculation>]
```

Options:

Specify allows for any available fields, functions, and operators to be used to enter the Boolean calculation into the Specify Calculation dialog box. Only a zero (0), false, or null (empty) result is construed as a Boolean false.

Examples:

```
If [gUsername = "Tom"]
   Show Custom Dialog ["Hello Tom"]
Else if [gUsername =  "Raul"]
   Show Custom Dialog ["Hola Raul"]
Else If [gUsername = "Guido"]
   Show Custom Dialog ["Ciao Guido"]
Else
   Show Custom Dialog ["I don't know who you are!"]
End If
```

Description:

This script step must follow the If script step or the Else If script step. It performs an action or actions based on the value of the Boolean calculation. The statements in the Else If block are executed only if none of the previous If or Else If statements are true.

Comments:

There can be an arbitrary number of Else If statements between an If statement and an End If statement. Their Boolean calculations are evaluated in the sequence in which they appear. If one should happen to evaluate to True, then its code block is executed and all subsequent Else If and Else clauses that appear before the End If are ignored.

ENABLE ACCOUNT

Compatibility: Mac: yes   Windows: yes   Web: yes

Menu Equivalent: None

Syntax:

Enable Account [Account Name: <account name>; Activate/Deactivate]

Options:

Specify displays the Enable Account Options dialog box.

- **Account Name** allows either the manual entry of or designation of a calculation to generate an account name.
- **Activate Account** enables the specified account.
- **Deactivate Account** disables the specified account.

Examples:

Enable Account [Account Name:"UserAccount"; Activate]

Description:

This script step enables or disables a specific pre-existing account. For this script step to be performed, the user must be assigned the Full Access privilege set or the Run Script with Full Access Privileges option must be selected. Accounts with Full Access may not be deactivated with this script step.

Comments:

It might be desirable to allow access to this functionality via a script if certain users or user groups have limited access to the FileMaker menus because security configurations. See the Change Password script step for a fuller discussion.

END IF

Compatibility: Mac: yes   Windows: yes   Web: yes

Menu Equivalent: None

Syntax:

End If

Options:

None

Examples:

```
If [gUsername = "Tom"]
   Show Custom Dialog ["Hello Tom"]
Else If [gUsername =  "Raul"]
   Show Custom Dialog ["Hola Raul"]
Else If [gUsername = "Guido"]
   Show Custom Dialog ["Ciao Guido"]
Else
   Show Custom Dialog ["I don't know who you are!"]
End If
```

Description:

This script step designates the end of an [If][Else If][Else] structure. See Else and Else If for more information.

END LOOP

Compatibility: Mac: yes   Windows: yes   Web: yes

Menu Equivalent: None

Syntax:

End Loop

Options:

None

Examples:

```
Set Field [Table1::gCounter; "0"]
Loop
   New Record/Request
   Set Field [Table1::gCounter; Table1::gCounter + 1]
   Exit Loop If [gCounter > 10]
End Loop
```

Description:

This script step marks the end of a Loop structure. The steps between Loop and End Loop are executed until the loop is explicitly exited. This step passes control to the step immediately following the Loop command preceding it.

Comments:

Note that this step doesn't cause a loop to stop executing. Without termination logic, a loop will run forever. Use the Exit Loop If script step to establish the conditions under which the loop will stop running and control will pass to the script step immediately following.

ENTER BROWSE MODE

Compatibility: Mac: yes   Windows: yes   Web: yes

Menu Equivalent: View, Browse Mode

Syntax:

```
Enter Browse Mode [Pause]
```

Options:

Pause stops the script step's execution to allow for user data entry and record navigation. The user may resume the script by clicking the Continue button in the Status Area, or by executing a Resume Script script step through a button or directly through the FileMaker Scripts menu.

Examples:

```
Allow User Abort [Off]
Set Error Capture [On]
Go To Layout ["Monthly Report"]
Enter Preview Mode [Pause]
Go to Layout [Original Layout]
Enter Browse Mode []
```

Description:

This script step places the current file into Browse mode.

ENTER FIND MODE

Compatibility: Mac: yes   Windows: yes   Web: yes

Menu Equivalent: View, Find Mode

Syntax:

```
Enter Find Mode [Restore; Pause]
```

Options:

Pause stops the script step's execution to allow for user data entry and record navigation. The user may resume the script by clicking the Continue button in the Status Area, or executing a Resume Script script step through a button or directly through the FileMaker Scripts menu.

Specify Find Requests enables you to create and edit find requests for use with the script step.

Examples:

```
#an example of a find that is executed from requests stored with the script
Go to Layout ["Detail View"]
Enter Find Mode [Restore]
Perform Find []
#this example waits for the user to enter find criteria and execute the find
Go to Layout ["Detail View"]
Enter Find Mode [Pause]
Perform Find[]
```

Description:

This script step places the current layout into Find mode. In Find mode, find requests may be created, edited, deleted, and duplicated. In addition, find requests can be stored with the script step if you check the Restore check box and using the Specify dialog. String multiple find requests together to create complex find requests. A single find request may either omit records from or add them to the existing found set.

Comments:

Enter Find Mode is one of several script steps that are capable of saving complex options along with the script step. Other such script steps are Perform Find, Sort Records, Import Records, Export Records, and Print Setup. See Chapter 9, "Getting Started with Scripting", for more discussion of saved script step options. Use the Pause option if you want the user to be able to enter his own search criteria, or modify a search that's saved with the script. If the status area is visible, the user sees a Continue button, as well as a Cancel button if Allow User Abort is set to "on" in the script. Be sure to set Allow User Abort to "off" if you don't want to offer an option to cancel the script at that point. If the status area is hidden, these buttons won't be accessible, and the user needs to either show the status area or use keyboard equivalents for Continue (Enter or Return) or Cancel (Escape or ⌘-period).

ENTER PREVIEW MODE

Compatibility: Mac: yes   Windows: yes   Web: no

Menu Equivalent: View, Preview Mode

Syntax:

```
Enter Preview Mode [Pause]
```

Options:

Pause stops the script step's execution to allow for user inspection of the preview for the designated layout. The user may resume the script by clicking the Continue button.

Examples:

```
Enter Preview Mode [Pause]
```

Description:

This script step places the current layout into Preview mode, where an approximation of what a layout will look like when it is printed out is displayed. Preview mode is helpful for viewing layouts that use special layout parts for reporting, title headers, leading grand summaries, subsummaries, trailing grand summaries, and title footers. Preview is the only FileMaker mode that displays all layout parts correctly. (Subsummary parts do not display correctly in Browse mode.)

Comments:

Use the `Pause` option if you want the user to be able to spend time in Preview mode working with the displayed data. If the status area is visible, the user sees a Continue button, as well as a Cancel button, if `Allow User Abort` is set to "on" in the script. Be sure to set Allow User Abort to "off" if you don't want to offer an option to cancel the script at that point. If the status area is hidden, these buttons aren't accessible, and the user needs to either show the status area or use keyboard equivalents for Continue (Enter or Return) or Cancel (Escape or ⌘-period). For more information on Preview mode, see Chapter 4, "FileMaker Fundamentals: Working with Layouts," and Chapter 10, "Reporting with Grouped Data."

Execute SQL

Compatibility: Mac: yes   Windows: yes   Web: no

Menu Equivalent: None

Syntax:

```
Execute SQL [No Dialog; ODBC: <datasource name>; <native SQL or calculated SQL>]
```

Options:

Perform Without Dialog prevents the Specify SQL dialog box, the Select ODBC Data Source dialog box, and the Password dialog box from displaying when the script step executes.

Specify displays the Specify SQL dialog box, where you can set the following options:

- **Specify** displays the `Select ODBC Data Source` dialog box. This allows for the selection of an ODBC connection and allows for the entry of the appropriate username and password.
- **Calculated SQL Text** allows for the creation of a calculation to generate the desired SQL query.
- **SQL Text** allows for the direct entry of a text SQL query.

Examples:

```
Execute SQL [No Dialog; ODBC: SQL_Server; "UPDATE Customers SET Status = '" &
➡Customer::Status & "' where CustID = '" & Customer::CustomerID & "' ;"]
```

Description:

This script step executes a designated SQL query over a selected ODBC connection. This allows for manipulation of SQL data sources through standard queries. A script can contain multiple Execute SQL steps that act on different SQL data sources.

Comments:

The Execute SQL step opens a great many avenues in FileMaker development. For a thorough discussion, see Chapter 20, "Getting Data Out of FileMaker."

EXIT APPLICATION

Compatibility: Mac: yes   Windows: yes   Web: yes

Menu Equivalent: FileMaker Pro, Quit FileMaker Pro (Mac OS); File, Exit (Windows)

Syntax:

```
Exit Application
```

Options:

None

Examples:

```
Exit Application
```

Description:

This script step closes all open files and exits the FileMaker Pro Application.

Comments:

The Exit application triggers the closing scripts of any files that have a closing script attached.

EXIT LOOP IF

Compatibility: Mac: yes   Windows: yes   Web: yes

Menu Equivalent: None

Syntax:

```
Exit Loop If [<Boolean calculation>]
```

Options:

Specify allows for the definition of the Boolean calculation that decides whether the loop is exited or not.

Examples:

```
Set Field [Table1::gCounter; "0"]
Loop
   New Record/Request
```

```
    Set Field [Table1::gCounter; Table1::gCounter + 1]
    Exit Loop If [gCounter > 10]
End
```

Description:

This script step terminates a loop if the Boolean calculation evaluates to True (non-zero and non-null). Upon termination, control is passed to the next script step after the End Loop script step that applies to the current script step. If the Boolean calculation evaluates to False (zero or null), then control is passed to the next script step, or to the step at the beginning of the loop if no further steps are specified within the loop.

Comments:

You'll probably want to have at least one Exit Loop If script step inside any loop you write. Without at least one such statement, it's difficult to exit the loop, except by performing a subscript that performs a Halt Script.

EXIT SCRIPT

Compatibility: Mac: yes   Windows: yes   Web: yes

Menu Equivalent: None

Syntax:

Exit Script

Options:

None

Examples:

```
Perform Find [Restore]
If [Get (CurrentFoundCount)=0]
    Show All Records
    Go to Layout ["Detail View"]
    Exit Script
Else
    Print []
End
```

Description:

Exit Script forces the current script to stop executing. No further script steps in the current script will execute. If the current script was called by another script, the remaining script steps in the calling script will continue to execute.

Comments:

It's important to distinguish this script step from the related script step Halt Script. Halt Script forces the termination of *all* currently running scripts, whereas Exit Script simply exits the current script.

C

EXPORT FIELD CONTENTS

Compatibility: Mac: yes   Windows: yes   Web: no

Menu Equivalent: Edit, Export Field Contents

Syntax:

```
Export Field Contents [<table::field>; "<filename>"]
```

Options:

Specify Target Field allows for the specification of the field whose contents are to be exported.

Specify Output File allows the desired filename and file path for the exported data to be specified.

Examples:

```
Go to Layout [Pictures::Agent_Picture]
Export Field Contents [Pictures::Picture_Full; Pictures::filename]
```

Description:

Export Field Contents creates a named file on disk with the contents of the specified field.

Comments:

Export Field Contents is a very powerful and flexible command when used in conjunction with container fields. FileMaker Pro allows the user to store a file of any type in a container field (including FileMaker Pro files). Export Field Contents writes the file out to disk in its native format, where the file can then be opened with the appropriate application. Any type of file, including images, of course, can be saved in a FileMaker database and written out to disk. For more information on exporting, see Chapter 20, "Getting Data Out of FileMaker."

EXPORT RECORDS

Compatibility: Mac: yes   Windows: yes   Web: no

Menu Equivalent: File, Export Records

Syntax:

```
Export records [No dialog; "<output filename>"]
```

Options:

Perform Without Dialog prevents dialog boxes from displaying when the script step executes that lets the user set new export criteria.

Specify Output File allows the desired filename and file path for the exported data to be specified as well as its file type. If XML Export is selected, then the XML Export Options dialog is displayed and allows the selection of an appropriate XML grammar and stylesheet for the export.

Specify Export Order displays the export order that was in effect when you added the script step. The last export order used in the file appears as the default and can be edited or deleted.

Examples:

```
Export Records [No dialog, "Contracts"]
```

Description:

This script step exports records from the current found set to a specified file in a specified format. The current sort order of the found set is used for the export order of the records. Note that Group By works only for fields that are included in the current sort order. (Sorted fields appear in the Group By box; check off any fields by which you want to group by.)

Comments:

Because it's possible to create FileMaker field names that are not valid names for XML elements, use extreme caution when exporting in the FMPDSORESULT grammar; the resulting XML may be invalid. FMPDSORESULT is deprecated in this version of FileMaker Pro and should probably be avoided. For more information, see "About the FMPDSORESULT Grammar" in Chapter 22, "FileMaker and Web Services."

Exporting data from FileMaker is a large and complex topic. For more information on exporting, see Chapter 20, "Getting Data Out of FileMaker."

EXTEND FOUND SET

Compatibility: Mac: yes   Windows: yes   Web: yes

Menu Equivalent: Requests, Extend Found Set

Syntax:

```
Extend Found Set [Restore]
```

Options:

Specify Find Requests allows for the creation and storage of find requests with the script step.

Examples:

```
#This script finds employees that are local or have a specific zip code
Set Error Capture [On]
Allow User Abort [Off]
Enter Find Mode [ ]
Set Field [Local; "Yes"]
Perform Find [ ]
Enter Find Mode [ ]
Set Field [Zip; "94965"]
Extend Found Set[]
```

Description:

This script step allows the current found set to be extended if you append additional search criteria to the previous search, or, put differently, if you apply designated search criteria only to records *not* included in the current found set. (This is equivalent to a logical OR search combined with the results of the previously executed search.)

Comments:

Similar to the Constrain Found Set script step, this step enables you to combine the results of more than one search. Whereas Constrain Found Set enables you to limit the results of one found set by the results of a second search (an operation known as an *intersection*), the Extend Found Set command enables you add the results of one search to the results of another search (an operation known as a *union*).

FLUSH CACHE TO DISK

Compatibility: Mac: yes   Windows: yes   Web: no

Menu Equivalent: None

Syntax:

Flush Cache to Disk

Options:

None

Examples:

```
Replace Field Contents [Line_Items::ProductID; Line_Items::NewProductID]
Flush Cache to Disk
```

Description:

This script step causes FileMaker Pro's internal disk cache to be written to disk. This operation is normally performed periodically or after structural changes such as defining fields or modifying calculation definitions. Flush Cache to Disk enables the developer to explicitly write out the contents of memory.

Comments:

Note that this script step flushes the contents of the cache for a local client copy of FileMaker Pro. It has no effect on the cache of any instance of FileMaker Server. See Chapter 25, "FileMaker Server," for more information on configuring and flushing the FileMaker Server cache.

FREEZE WINDOW

Compatibility: Mac: yes   Windows: yes   Web: no

Menu Equivalent: None

Syntax:

```
Freeze Window
```

Options:

None

Examples:

```
Freeze Window
Replace Field Contents [Line_Items::ProductID; Line_Items::NewProductID]
Sort [Restore; No Dialog]
Refresh Window
```

Description:

This script step halts the updating of the active window as script steps are performed. The window resumes refreshing either at the end of the script where it was frozen or after a `Refresh Window` script step is executed within a script.

Comments:

`Freeze Window` is useful in creating more professional-looking applications because it prevents the screen from flashing or redrawing while other script steps execute (for example, those that navigate to "utility" layouts, perform some work there, and then return to a main interface layout). It's also possible to realize some performance gains from freezing a window; scripts that would otherwise cause changes to the contents or appearance of the active window run more quickly if the active window doesn't need to be refreshed.

GO TO FIELD

Compatibility: Mac: yes   Windows: yes   Web: yes

Menu Equivalent: None

Syntax:

```
Go to Field [Select/perform; <table::field>]
```

Options:

Select/Perform directs FileMaker to select all contents of the designated field. If an action is associated with that field (such as playing a movie or sound file) then that action is performed.

Go To Target Field allows for the specification of the field to go to, using the standard FileMaker Pro field selection dialog box.

Examples:

```
Enter Browse Mode []
Go to Layout ["Contracts"]
New Record/Request
Go to Field [Contracts::Signatory]
```

Description:

This script step selects a specified field in the current layout. If the `Select/Perform` option is selected, then if an action is associated with a field, that action is performed. (Actions would be associated with container field types, such as sound files or movies—in these cases the associated action would be to play the sound or movie file.) In cases where there is no implied action, the entire contents of the field are selected.

Comments:

`Go to Field` allows the developer to insert the cursor into a specific field after a record has been created from a script.

Like other script steps such as `Cut`, `Copy`, and `Paste`, this step depends on the specified field being present on the current layout.

GO TO LAYOUT

Compatibility: Mac: yes   Windows: yes   Web: yes

Menu Equivalent: None

Syntax:

```
Go to Layout ["<layout name or layout number>"]
```

Options:

Specify allows the target layout to be selected. The following choices are available.

- **Original Layout** refers to the layout that was active when the script step was executed.
- **Layout Name by Calculation** enables you to enter a calculation that generates the name of the desired layout.
- **Layout Number by Calculation** enables you to enter a calculation that will generate the number of the desired layout. Layout numbers correspond to the order in which layouts are listed.

An existing layout may also be specified by name.

Examples:

```
Go to Layout ["Contracts"]
Copy [Select; DataTable1::ID_Number]
Go To Layout [Original Layout]
```

Description:

This script step makes the specified layout active in the current file. This step can navigate only to layouts in the currently active file. In the case where multiple layouts have the same name, the first match is selected for a calculated layout name.

Comments:

It's also possible to draw either the name or the number of a layout from a calculation. For an extended example of the use of this script step in a custom navigation mechanism, see Chapter 13, "Advanced Layout Techniques."

GO TO NEXT FIELD

Compatibility: Mac: yes   Windows: yes   Web: yes

Menu Equivalent: None

Syntax:

```
Go to Next Field
```

Options:

None

Examples:

```
Go to Field [Table1::First Name]
Set Field [Table1::gCounter; "0"]
Loop
    Set Field [Table1::gCounter; Table1::gCounter + 1]
    Exit Loop If [gCounter > Table1::ActiveField]
    Go To Next Field
End Loop
```

Description:

This script step moves to the next field in the established tab order for the current layout. If no field is selected, the first field in the established tab order for the current layout is selected. If the user regains control, either by pausing in Browse mode or by exiting the script, the cursor remains in the selected field. If there is no tab order on the layout, the fields are traversed in the order in which they were added to the layout.

Comments:

Note that this script can override the effect of field behaviors that prevent entry into a field.

GO TO PORTAL ROW

Compatibility: Mac: yes   Windows: yes   Web: yes

Menu Equivalent: None

Syntax:

```
Go to Portal Row [<first/last/previous/next/by calculation>]
```

Options:

First selects the first row of the designated portal.

Last selects the last row of the designated portal.

Previous selects the previous row of the designated portal. If the `Exit After Last` option is selected, then an exit loop action is performed when the first row in the designated portal is reached.

Next selects the next row of the designated portal. If the `Exit After Last` option is selected, then an exit loop action is performed when the last row in the designated portal is reached.

By Calculation selects the row number determined by the designated calculation.

Examples:

```
Go to Portal Row [Select, First]
```

Description:

This script step allows navigation among related records in the active portal on the current layout. If no portal is active, then the first portal in the layout stacking order is assumed. This step attempts to maintain the selected portal field when it changes rows. If no field is selected, the first modifiable field is selected in the new row.

Go to Previous Field

Compatibility: Mac: yes   Windows: yes   Web: yes

Menu Equivalent: None

Syntax:

```
Go to Previous Field
```

Options:

None

Examples:

```
Go to Previous Field
```

Description:

This script step moves focus to the previous field in the current layout's tab order. If no field is selected, then the last field in the current layout's tab order is selected. If the user regains control, either by pausing in Browse Mode or by exiting the script, the cursor will remain in the selected field. If there is no tab order on the layout, the fields are traversed in the order in which they were added to the layout.

Comments:

Note that this script can override the effect of field behaviors that prevent entry into a field.

Go to Record/Request/Page

Compatibility: Mac: yes   Windows: yes   Web: yes*

Menu Equivalent: None

Syntax:

```
Go to Record/Request/Page [<first/last/previous/next/by
calculation>]
```

Options:

First moves to the first record in the current found set, displays the first find request, or moves to the first page of the currently displayed report if in Preview mode.

Last moves to the last record in the current found set, displays the last find request, or moves to the last page of the currently displayed report.

Previous moves to the previous record in the current found set, displays the previous find request, or moves to the previous page of the currently displayed report. If the Exit After Last option is selected and the script is currently performing a loop, then an exit loop action is performed when the first record is reached; otherwise no action is taken. If the record pointer is already on the first page, FileMaker generates an error code of 101, which is not reported to the user.

Next moves to the next record in the current found set, displays the next find request, or moves to the next page of the currently displayed report. If the Exit After Last option is selected and the script is currently performing a loop, then an exit loop action is performed when the last record is reached; otherwise no action is taken. If the record pointer is already on the last page, FileMaker generates an error code of 101, which is not reported to the user.

By Calculation selects the record, find request, or report page determined by the designated calculation.

Examples:

```
# A very inefficient way of counting records
Go To Record/Request/Page [First]
Set Field [Contacts::gCount; "0"]
Loop
    Set Field [Contacts::gCount; Contacts::gCount + 1]
    Go To Record/Request/Page [Next; Exit After Last]
End Loop
# Contacts::gCount now contains the number of records in the found set.
# This could have been more easily accomplished by:
# Set Field [Contacts::gCount; Get(FoundCount)]
```

Description:

This script step moves to a record in the found set if the file running the script is in Browse mode, to a find request if it is in Find mode, and to a report page if it is in Preview mode. This step can also be configured to exit a loop when either the first or last record has been reached.

Comments:

When programming for the Web, be sure to select Perform Without Dialog. Leaving the box unchecked is not Web compatible and does not work on the Web.

GO TO RELATED RECORD

Compatibility: Mac: yes   Windows: yes   Web: yes

Menu Equivalent: None

Syntax:

```
Go to Related Record [From table: "<table name>";Using layout "<layout name>"]
```

Options:

Get Related Record From allows the selection of a table that's related to the current table. If an appropriate table is not in the list or if you need to add or change a relationship, Define Database displays the Define Database dialog box, where you can create or edit relationships.

Use External Table's Layouts opens the file containing the external table you specify and displays any related record(s), using the specified layout in that file.

Show Record Using Layout displays related record(s), using the specified layout in the current file.

Show Related Records Only creates a found set in the related table containing only related records. For example, if you use this script step on a relationship that has four matching records in Table B for the current record in Table A, this option replaces any current found set in Table B with a new found set of just these four records. If the relationship has a sort order applied in the table occurrence to which you're navigating, this option causes the found set to be sorted by the relationship's sort criteria. If the Show Related Records Only option is not selected, the resulting found set is not sorted.

Examples:

```
#The following example goes to a related record in the table "LineItems" and
➥shows a found set of related records only.
Go to Related Record [Show only related records;
From table: "LineItems"; Using layout: "List View"]
```

Description:

This script step goes to the table designated by the relationship selected in the script step, bringing its window to the foreground and selecting the first related record in the process. This step also works with portals. If a portal row is selected and the Go to Related Record step—specifying the portal's relationship—is executed, then the related table is brought to the forefront and the row that was selected in the portal corresponds to the record that is selected in the related table. This step may also use relationships to external files so that when the step is executed, the selected external file is opened and brought to the forefront, with its found set consisting of related records only. Further, if a layout was selected, then the records are displayed in that layout.

C

Comments:

This script step goes to a record in a related table (that is, a table that is related to the currently active table by one or more relationships in the Relationships Graph). There are a number of options to this script step, and they relate in somewhat complex ways. If more than one record in the target table is related to the current record in the table where the script is being called, FileMaker selects the first related record in the target table. If the relationship has a sort order on the target table, that sort order is used to determine which is the first of several related records. For example, if you have a table of Customers and a table of Orders, and a relationship between the two that is sorted on the Order side by OrderDate ascending, then the "first" related record when navigating from a specific customer to related orders is a given customer's earliest order. If the relationship has no sort order specified on the target table, then the first record is determined based on the creation order of the related records.

As part of this script step, you need to determine the layout that should be used to display the related records. Most likely, you'll want it to be a layout tied to a table occurrence that's based on the target table. If the target table is part of an externally referenced file, you may choose to display the records on a layout in the external file. If you choose to do so, that file comes to the forefront. You may also choose to display the related record set in a new window. If you choose to do so, you can specify a set of new window options, such as the window name, height, width, and screen position. One unfortunate limitation is that you can't direct the related records to appear in an existing window other than the currently active one. If you had to have that effect, you could select the desired target window, capture its name, dimensions, and positions into global fields, then close that window and create a new window with exactly the same dimensions and use that as the target of this script step.

If the option to Show Related Records Only is checked, FileMaker creates a found set in the target table that contains only those records that are related to the current record in the table in which the script is executing. For example, given a table of Salespeople and a table of Orders related to Salespeople by a SalespersonID field, if you issue a Go to Related Record[Show only related records; From table:"Orders"] while on a record in Salespeople, you end up with a found set of only those Orders related to the current Salesperson by the SalespersonID. If the option to Show Only Related Records is unchecked, the behavior is more complex: If there's a found set on the target layout and the first related record is within that found set, the found set is unchanged. If there's a found set on the target layout and the first related record is outside that found set, all records in the target table are found (though only the first related record is selected). If there is no found set on the target layout (that is, all records are currently found), that remains the case. No matter whether Show Related Records Only is checked or not, and no matter what the state of any found set on the target layout is, the first related record is always selected. If there are no related records, no navigation takes place, and a FileMaker Error of 101 is generated.

→ For further discussion of the Go To Related Records script step, **see** "Go To Related Record," **p. 437**.

HALT SCRIPT

Compatibility: Mac: yes   Windows: yes   Web: yes

Menu Equivalent: None

Syntax:

```
Halt Script
```

Options:

None

Examples:

```
# Example of using 'Halt Script' to return control immediately back to the user.
Show Custom Dialog ["Print Report?"]
If [Get (LastMessageChoice) = 2]
   Halt Script
End If
Print[]
```

Description:

This script step causes all script activity to stop immediately. All scripts, subscripts and external scripts are cancelled and the system is left in whatever state it was in when the Halt step was executed. Halt Script is different from Exit Script in that the latter merely aborts the current subscript and allows the script that called the subscript to continue running, whereas the former stops all script activity, whether it is run from a subscript, a sub-sub-script, and so on.

IF

Compatibility: Mac: yes   Windows: yes   Web: yes

Menu Equivalent: None

Syntax:

```
If [<Boolean calculation>]
```

Options:

Specify allows the definition of the Boolean calculation by which the If step determines its branching.

Examples:

```
If [gUsername = "Tom"]
   Show Custom Dialog ["Hello Tom"]
Else if [gUsername =  "Raul"]
   Show Custom Dialog ["Hola Raul"]
Else If [gUsername = "Guido"]
   Show Custom Dialog ["Ciao Guido"]
Else
   Show Custom Dialog ["I don't know who you are!"]
End If
```

Description:

The If step introduces a block of conditional logic. It needs to be used with an End If statement, and, optionally, one or more Else and Else If statements. This script step contains a calculation, which should perform a logical true/false test. If the specified Boolean calculation results in a 1 (or any number greater than 1), the specified action(s) will be performed. If the specified Boolean calculation results in a 0 (or nothing or any non-number), then the specified action(s) will be skipped and control passed to the next Else If or Else clause. If there are no more such clauses, then control passes to the End If step and proceeds to any subsequent steps. Else If and Else clauses are optional. End If is required when If is used.

Comments:

If you don't provide a Boolean test in the If step, it defaults to a result of False.

IMPORT RECORDS

Compatibility: Mac: yes   Windows: yes   Web: no

Menu Equivalent: File, Import Records

Syntax:

```
Import Records [No dialog; "<source or filename>"; Add/Update existing/Update
➝matching; <platform and character set>]
```

Options:

Perform Without Dialog prevents the display of FileMaker Pro's Import Records dialog box, which enables the user to select a file from which to import, to set new import criteria, to map fields from import to target fields, and to see a summary of facts about the import after it has been successfully completed.

Specify Data Source allows for the selection of the source for the data to be imported. Data can be imported into FileMaker Pro from a file, a folder of files, a digital camera (Mac OS), an XML data source, or an ODBC data source.

Specify Import Order allows the order in which FileMaker imports records to be set. The last import order used is used as the default for the subsequent import. This option allows control of how FileMaker is to handle repeating field data, either by splitting it among new records or keeping it together as a repeating field in the destination table. Also, the import can be made to add new records with the imported data, to replace the records in the found set with the imported data, or to attempt to reconcile data by matching keys (ID fields).

Examples:

```
Import Records [Restore; No dialog; "Contacts"; Mac Helvetica]
```

Description:

This script step imports records from another file or data source specified either dynamically through the Import Records dialog or within the script step configuration itself. Import order can be specified as either manually defined or based on matching fields names.

(It is important to note that when import source fields and target fields are mapped with matching names, field name matching is performed dynamically each time the script step is performed.)

→ For a full description of FileMaker's importing options, **see** Chapter 19, "Importing Data into FileMaker Pro," **p. 537**.

Insert Calculated Result

Compatibility: Mac: yes   Windows: yes   Web: yes

Menu Equivalent: None

Syntax:

```
Insert Calculated Result [Select; <table::field>; <formula>]
```

Options:

Select Entire Contents replaces the contents of a field. If this option is not selected, Insert Calculated Result replaces only the selected portion of the current field, or inserts the result at the insertion point. The default insertion point is at the end of the field's data.

Go To Target Field allows the selection of the field into which the contents of the clipboard are to be inserted. The specified field must be available for modification on the current layout for this script step to operate properly.

Calculated Result allows the definition of a calculation whose result is inserted into the specified target field by this script step.

Examples:

```
Insert Calculated Result [Books::Author; Get(AccountName)]
```

Description:

This script step pastes the result of a calculation into the current (or specified) field on the current layout.

Comments:

In a Web-published database, use a Commit Record/Request script step after an Insert Calculated Result script step to update the record in the browser window. All of the Insert... functions depend on the presence of fields on the current layout. If the correct field is not present, FileMaker will generate an internal error of 102.

Insert Current Date

Compatibility: Mac: yes   Windows: yes   Web: yes

Menu Equivalent: Insert, Current Date

Syntax:

```
Insert Current Date [Select; <table::field>]
```

Options:

Select Entire Contents replaces the contents of the selected field with the current date. If this option is not selected, then the current date is appended to the end of the current contents of the field.

Go To Target Field allows for the selection of the field into which the current date will be inserted.

Examples:

```
New Record/Request
Go To Layout ["Invoice"]
Insert Current Date [Select; Invoices::Invoice Date]
```

Description:

This script step pastes the current system date into the specified field on the current layout.

Comments:

In a Web-published database, use a `Commit Record/Request` script step after an `Insert Current Date` script step to update the record in the browser window. All the `Insert...` functions depend on the presence of fields on the current layout. If the correct field is not present, FileMaker generates an internal error of 102.

INSERT CURRENT TIME

Compatibility: Mac: yes   Windows: yes   Web: yes

Menu Equivalent: Insert, Current Time

Syntax:

```
Insert Current Time [Select; <table::field>]
```

Options:

Select Entire Contents replaces the contents of the selected field with the current time. If this option is not selected, then the current time is appended to the end of the current contents of the field.

Go To Target Field allows for the selection of the field into which the current time is to be inserted.

Examples:

```
New Record/Request
Go To Layout ["Invoice"]
Insert Current Date [Select; Invoices::Invoice Date]
Insert Current Time [Select; Invoices::Invoice Time]
```

Description:

This script step pastes the current system time into the specified field on the current layout.

Comments:

In a Web-published database, use a Commit Record/Request script step after an Insert Current Time script step to update the record in the browser window. All the Insert... functions depend on the presence of fields on the current layout. If the correct field is not present, FileMaker generates an internal error of 102.

INSERT CURRENT USER NAME

Compatibility: Mac: yes   Windows: yes   Web: yes

Menu Equivalent: Insert, Current User Name

Syntax:

```
Insert Current User Name [Select; <table::field>]
```

Options:

Select Entire Contents replaces the contents of the selected field with the current username. If this option is not selected, then the current username is appended to the end of the current contents of the field.

Go To Target Field allows for the selection of the field into which the current user name is to be inserted.

Examples:

```
New Record/Request
Go To Layout ["Invoice"]
Insert Current Date [Select; Invoices::Invoice Date]
Insert Current Time [Select; Invoices::Invoice Time]
Insert Current User Name [Select; Invoices::Entered_By]
```

Description:

This script step pastes the current username into the specified field on the current layout.

Comments:

In a Web-published database, use a Commit Record/Request script step after an Insert Current User Name script step to update the record in the browser window. All the Insert... functions depend on the presence of fields on the current layout. If the correct field is not present, FileMaker generates an internal error of 102.

INSERT FILE

Compatibility: Mac: yes   Windows: yes   Web: no

Menu Equivalent: Insert, File

Syntax:

```
Insert File [Reference; <table::field>; "<filename>"]
```

Options:

Store Only a Reference instructs FileMaker Pro to store only a link to a file in the container field, rather than the entire file. This option may reduce the size of your FileMaker Pro file, but if you move or delete the file being referenced, FileMaker Pro can't display it.

Select Go To Target Field or click Specify to specify the container field into which to insert the selected file.

Select Specify Source File or click Specify to designate the file to be inserted.

Examples:

```
Go To Field [Photos::Thumbnail]
Insert File ["house_thumb.jpg"]
```

Description:

This script step inserts a file into a selected container field on the current layout. Files may be stored in their entirety within FileMaker Pro, or you may choose to store only a file reference. File references certainly take up much less space within the database but they remove an element of control over a database's behavior. Files stored by reference can be moved or deleted while this is much more difficult to achieve within FileMaker itself.

Comments:

All the Insert... functions depend on the presence of fields on the current layout. If the correct field is not present, FileMaker generates an internal error of 102.

INSERT FROM INDEX

Compatibility: Mac: yes   Windows: yes   Web: no

Menu Equivalent: Insert, From Index

Syntax:

```
Insert From Index [Select; <table::field>]
```

Options:

Select Entire Contents replaces the contents of the selected field. If this option is not selected, then the selected index value is appended to the end of the current contents of the field if the field does not contain the cursor, or at the current cursor position if it does.

Go To Target Field allows for the selection of the field into which the selected index value is to be inserted.

Examples:

```
Enter Find Mode [ ]
Insert From Index [Users::User_Name]
Perform Find [ ]
```

C

Description:

This script step displays the index (if one exists) of the designated field and allows one of its values to be inserted into the field. If the `Select Entire Contents` option is selected, the contents of the field will be replaced with the selected value. If this option is not selected, then the value is inserted either at the position of the cursor in the field or appended to the end of the field's contents, depending on whether or not the field has the cursor in it. Note: If the specified field does not exist on the layout where the script is being performed or indexing has been disabled for the selected field, `Insert From Index` returns an error code which can be captured with the `Get(LastError)` function.

Comments:

All the `Insert...` functions depend on the presence of fields on the current layout. If the correct field is not present, FileMaker generates an internal error of 102.

INSERT FROM LAST VISITED

Compatibility: Mac: yes   Windows: yes   Web: yes

Menu Equivalent: Insert, From Last Visited Record

Syntax:

```
Insert From Last Visited [Select; <table::field>]
```

Options:

Select Entire Contents replaces the contents of the selected field. If this option is not selected, then the value from the last visited field is appended to the end of the current contents of the field if the field does not contain the cursor or at the current cursor position if it does.

Go To Target Field allows for the selection of the field into which the last visited field value is to be inserted.

Examples:

```
Go to Record/Request/Page [Next]
Go to Field [Vendor Name]
Insert From Last Visited []
#Will use vendor from previous record
```

Description:

This script step pastes the value of the specified field from the same field in the last active record. This step is compatible with both Find and Browse mode. A record is considered as having been active if it has been operated upon by FileMaker Pro in some way.

Comments:

In a Web-published database, use a `Commit Record/Request` script step after an `Insert From Last Visited` script step to update the record in the browser window. All the `Insert...` functions depend on the presence of fields on the current layout. If the correct field is not present, FileMaker generates an internal error of 102.

INSERT OBJECT

Compatibility: Mac: no   Windows: yes   Web: no

Menu Equivalent: Insert, Object

Syntax:

```
Insert Object ["<object type>"]
```

Options:

Specify displays the Insert Object dialog box.

Object Type allows the selection of the type of object to embed or link from the list of available file and application types.

Create New embeds a blank object of the specified object type.

Create from File allows the specification of the name of an existing file as the object to be embedded or linked.

When Create from File has been selected, Link can be selected to indicate that the object should be a linked object. When Link is not selected, the object is embedded instead.

Display As Icon tells FileMaker Pro not to display the embedded or linked object completely, but to display an icon that represents the object. The Change Icon button can be used to select a different icon for display. When Display As Icon is not selected, the complete object is displayed in the container field.

Examples:

```
Go to Field [Profile::Greeting]
Insert Object ["Video Clip"]
```

Description:

This script step allows the user, through the Insert Object dialog box, to select an OLE Object and insert it into the current container field. If the specified object/file does not exist on the computer on which the script is being run, Insert Object returns an error code that can be captured with the Get(LastError) function.

Comments:

All of the Insert... functions depend on the presence of fields on the current layout. If the correct field is not present, FileMaker generates an internal error of 102. Insert Object works only on the Windows platform. Insert Object returns an error code if run on the Mac OS.

INSERT PICTURE

Compatibility: Mac: yes   Windows: yes   Web: no

Menu Equivalent: Insert, Picture

Syntax:

```
Insert Picture [Select; <table::field>]
```

C

Options:

Store Only A Reference To The File allows graphics to be stored by file system reference, thereby alleviating the need to store the actual image in the database. However, if the file is moved from the designated file path, FileMaker Pro can no longer display it.

Specify Source File or **Specify** allow the designation of the file path to the desired image file.

Examples:

```
Go to Field [Profile::Greeting]
Insert Picture ["headshot.jpg"]
```

Description:

This script step imports an image file into the current container field. The desired field must be selected before this script is run. If the desired image file has not been specified, the user is given the Insert Picture dialog box.

Comments:

All the `Insert...` functions depend on the presence of fields on the current layout. If the correct field is not present, FileMaker generates an internal error of 102.

INSERT QUICKTIME

Compatibility: Mac: yes   Windows: yes   Web: no

Menu Equivalent: Insert, QuickTime

Syntax:

```
Insert QuickTime ["<filename>"]
```

Options:

Specify Source File or **Specify** allow the designation of the file path to the desired QuickTime file.

Examples:

```
Go to Field [Profile::Interview]
Insert Picture ["Interview_Video"]
```

Description:

This step imports a QuickTime movie or sound file into the current container field. A container field must be selected before this step can function. If an appropriate QuickTime file has not been designated, a dialog box is presented to the user, through which he or she may select and preview the file to be imported. This step requires that QuickTime be installed on the system being used to import the desired file.

Comments:

All the `Insert...` functions depend on the presence of fields on the current layout. If the correct field is not present, FileMaker generates an internal error of 102.

INSERT TEXT

Compatibility: Mac: yes   Windows: yes   Web: yes

Menu Equivalent: None

Syntax:

```
Insert Text [Select; <table::field>; "<text>"]
```

Options:

Select Entire Contents replaces the contents of a field. If this option is not selected, Insert Text inserts the specified value at the end of the field's data.

Use **Go To Target Field** or click **Specify** to specify the field to receive the pasted information. If no field is selected, the Insert Text command places the specified text after the insertion point. If no field is active at the time the command executes, it has no effect. If the selected field is not present on the current layout, the Insert Text command has no effect.

Specify displays the Specify dialog box where you can enter the text to be pasted.

Examples:

```
Insert Text [Select; Profile::Favorite_Color; "Red"]
```

Description:

This script step inserts text into the selected text field in the current record. If the Select Entire Contents option has not been selected, then the designated text is inserted at the cursor position or at the end of the field's contents, depending on whether or not there is a cursor in the field. The text to be inserted needs to be specified explicitly. If you want to insert variable text data, use the Insert Calculated Result script step or the Set Field script step.

Comments:

In a Web-published database, use a Commit Record/Request script step after an Insert Text script step to update the record in the browser window. All the Insert... functions depend on the presence of fields on the current layout. If the correct field is not present, FileMaker generates an internal error of 102.

LOOP

Compatibility: Mac: yes   Windows: yes   Web: yes

Menu Equivalent: None

Syntax:

```
Loop
```

Options:

None

C

Examples:

```
# Create 10 new blank records
Set Field [Table1::gCounter; "0"]
Loop
   New Record/Request
   Set Field [Table1::gCounter; Table1::gCounter + 1]
   Exit Loop If [gCounter > 10]
End
```

Description:

This script step marks the beginning of a Loop structure. The end of the Loop structure is defined by a corresponding End Loop step. Script control passes from the Loop step through all intervening steps to the End Loop step and back again until an Exit Loop directive is encountered or until a Halt Script or Exit Script step is encountered. The Exit Loop directive is available as an option with the Exit Loop If step, the Go To Record/Request/Page step, and the Go To Portal Row step. Loops are often used to perform an action over a group of records or portal rows.

MODIFY LAST FIND

Compatibility: Mac: yes   Windows: yes   Web: yes

Menu Equivalent: Records, Modify Last Find

Syntax:

```
Modify Last Find
```

Options:

None

Examples:

```
Modify Last Find
Set Field [Contacts::Birthdate; "1/1/1974...1/1/1985"]
Perform Find[]
```

Description:

This script step activates Find mode and then recalls the last find requests used. The find requests may then be modified and executed with the Perform Find script step.

MOVE/RESIZE WINDOW

Compatibility: Mac: yes   Windows: yes   Web: no

Menu Equivalent: None

Syntax:

```
Move/Resize Window [Current Window or Name: <name of window>; Height: <n>; Width
➥: <n>; Top: <n>; Left: <n>]
```

Options:

Specify allows the setting of the move/resize options.

Current Window causes the changes to be performed on the current window.

Window Name causes the changes to be performed on an open window, specified by name. Literal text may be entered or Specify clicked to create a window name from a calculation.

Height is the height of the adjusted window in pixels. A number may be entered or Specify clicked to generate a number from a calculation.

Width is the width of the adjusted window in pixels. A number may be entered or Specify clicked to generate a number from a calculation.

Distance From Top is the adjusted window's distance in pixels from the top of the screen (Mac OS) or top of the FileMaker Pro window (Windows). A number may be entered or Specify clicked to generate a number from a calculation.

Distance From Left is the adjusted window's distance in pixels from the left of the screen (Mac OS) or left of the FileMaker Pro window (Windows). A number may be entered or Specify clicked to generate a number from a calculation.

Examples:

```
Move/Resize Window [Name:Invoices ; Height: 400; Width: 600; Top: 16; Left: 16]
```

Description:

This script step adjusts the size and location of the selected window. Every other aspect of the window, including found set, current table, and current record remain unchanged. Where an option is left without a value, the current value of that option is used. If position or size options exceed or fall below allowable minimums or maximums for a machine's particular operating system and configuration, the allowed minimums or maximums are used instead of the chosen values. In multiple monitor environments, the use of negative position values makes it possible to position a window on alternate monitors. Note for Windows: FileMaker Pro orients the moved window to the top left corner of the visible part of the application window. Note that this may not be the (0, 0) point of the window, depending on how the current file window is positioned (for example, if half of the file window extends past the left border of the application window, you would need to scroll to the left to see the [0, 0] point of the application window).

NEW FILE

Compatibility: Mac: yes   Windows: yes   Web: no

Menu Equivalent: File, New Database

Syntax:

```
New File
```

Options:

None

C

Examples:

```
New File
```

Description:

This script step enables the user to create a new database file in FileMaker Pro's usual Create New File Named dialog box. If the `Show Templates in New Database Dialog Box` preference is selected, then the script step shows the New Database dialog box.

Comments:

The user is taken to the Define Database dialog. When he's finished defining the new database, and has closed the Define Database dialog, the script that invoked the `New File` command continues. The new database stays open, but it is not activated.

New Record/Request

Compatibility: Mac: yes   Windows: yes   Web: yes

Menu Equivalent: Records, New Record

Syntax:

```
New Record/Request
```

Options:

None

Examples:

```
# Create 10 new blank records
Set Field [Table1::gCounter; "0"]
Loop
   New Record/Request
   Set Field [Table1::gCounter; Table1::gCounter + 1]
   Exit Loop If [gCounter > 10]
End
```

Description:

This script step creates a new, blank record if the system is in Browse mode, and a new find request if the system is in Find mode.

Comments:

Note that this script step is context-dependent. The current layout determines which table is active, which determines in which table the record is created.

New Window

Compatibility: Mac: yes   Windows: yes   Web: yes

Menu Equivalent: Window, New Window

C

Syntax:

```
New Window [Name: <name of window>; Height: n; Width: n; Top: n; Left: n]
```

Options:

Specify allows the setting of options for the new window.

Window Name is the name specified for the new window. Literal text may be entered or Specify clicked to create a window name from a calculation.

Height is the height of the new window in pixels. A number may be entered or Specify clicked to generate a number from a calculation.

Width is the width of the new window in pixels. A number may be entered or Specify clicked to generate a number from a calculation.

Distance From Top is the new window's distance in pixels from the top of the screen (Mac OS) or top of the FileMaker Pro window (Windows). A number may be entered or Specify clicked to generate a number from a calculation.

Distance From Left is the new window's distance in pixels from the left of the screen (Mac OS) or left of the FileMaker Pro window (Windows). A number may be entered or Specify clicked to generate a number from a calculation.

Examples:

```
New Window [Name: "Profile"; Height: 500; Width: 700; Top: 25; Left: 25]
```

Description:

This script step creates a new window based on the current window. The new window is the same as the current window except in the specified options. In the case where an option is left without a value, the default value (as specified in the Window menu, New Window command) for that option is used. If position or size options exceed or fall below allowable minimums or maximums for a machine's particular operating system and configuration, the allowed minimums or maximums are used instead of the chosen values. In multiple monitor environments, the use of negative position values makes it possible to position a window on alternate monitors. Note for Windows: FileMaker Pro orients the moved window to the top-left corner of the visible part of the application window. Note that this may not be the (0, 0) point of the window, depending on how the current file window is positioned. (For example, if half of the file window extends past the left border of the application window, you would need to scroll to the left to see the [0, 0] point of the application window.)

OMIT MULTIPLE RECORDS

Compatibility: Mac: yes   Windows: yes   Web: yes

Menu Equivalent: Records, Omit Multiple

Syntax:

```
Omit Multiple Records [No dialog; <number of records>]
```

Options:

Perform Without Dialog prevents a dialog box from displaying when the script step executes. Without this option selected, the user sees a dialog that allows the user to enter the number of records to be omitted.

When `Perform Without Dialog` is selected, if a number of records to omit is not specified, only the current record is omitted.

Selecting **Specify Records** or clicking **Specify** allows the entry of the exact number of records to omit. The `Specify` button may also be clicked in the Options dialog box to allow for the entry of a calculation. The calculation result must be a number.

Examples:

```
Perform Find [Restore]
# Omit only the current record
Omit Multiple Records [No Dialog]
```

Description:

This script step omits the specified number of records from the found set, leaving the next available record as the current record. Omitted records are not deleted; they are just excluded from the found set. They remain in the database, as can be easily verified if you re-execute the Find Request that generated the found set in the first place.

Comments:

When programming for the Web, be sure to select `Perform Without Dialog`. Leaving the box unchecked is not Web compatible and does not work on the Web.

OMIT RECORD

Compatibility: Mac: yes   Windows: yes   Web: yes

Menu Equivalent: Records, Omit Record

Syntax:

```
Omit Record
```

Options:

None

Examples:

```
# Omit records marked for omission
Go To Record/Request/Page [First]
Loop
 If [Contacts::Omit]
   Omit Record
 End If
 Go To Record/Request/Page [Next; Exit After  Last]
End Loop
```

Description:

This script step omits the current record from the current found set when executed in Browse mode. The next available record becomes the new current record. Omitted records are not deleted. They are merely removed from the current found set. If this script step is executed while in Find mode, the current find request's Omit check box is toggled. (If it was checked, it will be unchecked and if it is unchecked it will be checked.) A find request that has the omit checkbox checked becomes an omit request that subtracts rather than adds to the found set.

OPEN DEFINE DATABASE

Compatibility: Mac: yes   Windows: yes   Web: no

Menu Equivalent: File, Define, Database

Syntax:

```
Open Define Database
```

Options:

None

Examples:

```
If [Get (LastMessageChoice) = 1]
   #1=Yes, 2=No
   Open Define Database
End If
```

Description:

This script step opens the Define Database dialog box, where the user can create or edit tables, fields, and relationships. This script step is not performed if the user's account does not have the Full Access privilege set. (The script may be set to Run Script With Full Access Privileges in the ScriptMaker menu.) When the user closes the dialog box, the remaining steps in the script, if any, are executed.

OPEN DEFINE FILE REFERENCES

Compatibility: Mac: yes   Windows: yes   Web: no

Menu Equivalent: File, Define, File References

Syntax:

```
Open Define File References
```

Options:

None

Examples:

```
Show Custom Dialog ["Do you want to create or edit a file
reference?"]
```

```
If [Get (LastMessageChoice) = 1]
   #1=Yes, 2=No
   Open Define File References
End If
```

Description:

This script step opens the Define File References dialog box, where the user can create or edit references to files used throughout the database. This script step is not performed if the user's account does not have the Full Access privilege set. (The script may be set to Run Script With Full Access Privileges in the ScriptMaker menu.) When the user closes the dialog box, the remaining steps in the script, if any, are executed.

OPEN DEFINE VALUE LISTS

Compatibility: Mac: yes   Windows: yes   Web: no

Menu Equivalent: File, Define, Value Lists

Syntax:

```
Open Define Value Lists
```

Options:

None

Examples:

```
Show Custom Dialog ["Do you want to create or edit a value list?"]
If [Get (LastMessageChoice) = 1]
   #1=Yes, 2=No
   Open Define Value Lists
End If
```

Description:

This script step opens the Define Value Lists dialog box, where the user can define new or edit existing value lists. This script step is not performed if the user's account does not have the Full Access privilege set. (The script may be set to Run Script With Full Access Privileges in the ScriptMaker menu.) When the user closes the dialog box, the remaining steps in the script, if any, are executed.

OPEN FILE

Compatibility: Mac: yes   Windows: yes   Web: no

Menu Equivalent: File, Open

Syntax:

```
Open File [Open hidden; "<filename>"]
```

Options:

Open Hidden causes FileMaker Pro to open the specified database hidden (with its window minimized.)

Specify allows the selection of a FileMaker Pro database to be opened. Within the Specify menu, Add File Reference provides a dialog box to assist in the location and selection of a filename. After a file is selected, it is added to the Specify list. In the same menu, Define File References allows one to modify or delete a file reference already added to the list.

Examples:

```
Open File [Open Hidden; "Tempfile.fp7"]
```

Description:

This script step opens the specified file or allows the user to select a file to open in the Open File dialog box. The Open File Dialog box is invoked when no file is specified in the script step or if the specified file cannot be found. The active file before the Open File step is executed remains active after it has completed.

OPEN FILE OPTIONS

Compatibility: Mac: yes   Windows: yes   Web: no

Menu Equivalent: Open, File Options

Syntax:

```
Open File Options
```

Options:

None

Examples:

```
Show Custom Dialog ["Open File Options dialog box?"]
If [Get (LastMessageChoice) = 1]
   #1=Yes, 2=No
   Open File Options
End If
```

Description:

This script step opens the File Options dialog box to the General preferences area. This script step is not performed if the user's account does not have the Full Access privilege set. (The script may be set to Run Script With Full Access Privileges in the ScriptMaker menu.)

OPEN FIND/REPLACE

Compatibility: Mac: yes   Windows: yes   Web: no

Menu Equivalent: Edit, Find/Replace, Find/Replace

Syntax:

```
Open Find/Replace
```

Options:

None

Examples:

```
Show Custom Dialog ["Open the Find/Replace dialog box?"]
If [Get (LastMessageChoice) = 1]
   #1=Yes, 2=No
   Open Find/Replace
End If
```

Description:

This script step opens the Find/Replace dialog box. The remaining steps in the script, if any, are executed after the user closes the dialog box or completes a search.

OPEN HELP

Compatibility: Mac: yes   Windows: yes   Web: no

Menu Equivalent: Help, FileMaker Pro Help

Syntax:

```
Open Help
```

Options:

None

Examples:

```
Show Custom Dialog ["Do you want to open onscreen Help?"]
If [Get (LastMessageChoice) = 1]
   #1=Yes, 2=No
   Open Help
End If
```

Description:

This script step opens the FileMaker Pro Help system. By default, the user is placed in the Help System Contents screen.

Comments:

The Help dialog is non-modal, so any additional script steps after the Open Help step execute right away, possibly pushing the help window into the background.

OPEN PREFERENCES

Compatibility: Mac: yes   Windows: yes   Web: no

Menu Equivalent: Edit, Preferences (Windows) or FileMaker Pro, Preferences (Mac OS)

Syntax:

```
Open Preferences
```

Options:

None

Examples:

```
Show Custom Dialog ["Open Preferences dialog box?"]
If [Get (LastMessageChoice) = 1]
    #1=Yes, 2=No
    Open Preferences
End If
```

Description:

This script step opens the Preferences dialog box. The General Preferences area is selected by default.

Comments:

When the user closes the dialog box, the remaining steps in the script, if any, are executed.

OPEN RECORD/REQUEST

Compatibility: Mac: yes   Windows: yes   Web: yes

Menu Equivalent: None

Syntax:

```
Open Record/Request
```

Options:

None

Examples:

```
Perform Find [Restore]
Go to Record/Request/Page [First]
Open Record/Request
If [ Get(LastError) = 200 or Get(LastError) = 300]
    Show Custom Dialog ["An error has ocurred. This record is locked or you do
    ➥not have sufficient permission to access it."]
End If
```

Description:

This script step attempts to acquire exclusive access to the current record. Exclusive access prevents other users from editing the record. It has the same effect as a user selecting a data field on a layout (by clicking or tabbing) and then beginning to enter or edit field data. These actions either give exclusive access to that user, or, if another user has already acquired exclusive access (otherwise known as a "lock"), the user attempting to gain control of the record sees an error message with a warning that another user has control of the record. It can be useful to try to gain exclusive access to a record in the course of a script. If you are looping over records and need to change each one, if a user is editing one of the records, your script may be prevented from changing it. Open Record/Request cannot override another user's access, but if the script step fails it generates an error that your script can inspect with the Get(LastError) statement.

OPEN REMOTE

Compatibility: Mac: yes   Windows: yes   Web: no

Menu Equivalent: File, Open Remote

Syntax:

```
Open Remote
```

Options:

None

Examples:

```
Show Custom Dialog ["Do you want to look for a networked database?"]
If [Get (LastMessageChoice) = 1]
   #1=Yes, 2=No
   Open Remote
End If
```

Description:

This script step opens the Open Remote dialog box to allow the opening of a shared FileMaker Pro database over a network connection.

Comments:

When the user closes the dialog box, the remaining steps in the script, if any, are executed.

OPEN SCRIPTMAKER

Compatibility: Mac: yes   Windows: yes   Web: no

Menu Equivalent: Scripts, ScriptMaker

Syntax:

```
Open ScriptMaker
```

Options:

None

Examples:

```
Show Custom Dialog ["Open ScriptMaker?"]
If [Get (LastMessageChoice) = 1]
   #1=Yes, 2=No
   Open ScriptMaker
End If
```

Description:

This script step opens the ScriptMaker dialog box, which enables a user to create, edit, rename, and duplicate scripts. When this script step is performed, FileMaker halts the current script because if any currently-executing scripts were to be edited, the resulting behavior could be unpredictable.

OPEN SHARING

Compatibility: Mac: yes   Windows: yes   Web: no

Menu Equivalent: Edit, Sharing, FileMaker Network (Windows) or FileMaker Pro, Sharing, FileMaker Network (Mac OS)

Syntax:

```
Open Sharing
```

Options:

None

Examples:

```
Show Custom Dialog ["Do you want to open the sharing dialog?"]
If [Get (LastMessageChoice) = 1]
   #1=Yes, 2=No
   Open Sharing
End If
```

Description:

This script step opens the FileMaker Network Settings dialog box where users can configure network database sharing.

OPEN URL

Compatibility: Mac: yes   Windows: yes   Web: yes

Menu Equivalent: None

Syntax:

```
Open URL [No dialog; <URL>]
```

Options:

Perform Without Dialog prevents the Open URL Options dialog box from displaying when the script step executes.

Specify may be selected to display the Open URL Options dialog box, where the URL can be typed directly into the text entry area or created by a calculation.

Examples:

```
Open URL [No dialog; "http://www. apple. com/"]
Open URL [No dialog; "file://c:/addresses. txt"]
Open URL [No dialog; "mailto:no-one@name. net"]
Open URL [No dialog; "fmp7://system:password@192. 168. 10. 46:591/WebDB"]
 #Note about the last example: "system" is the FileMaker Pro account name,
 ➥ "password" is that account's password, and "WebDB" is
 ➥ the FileMaker Pro filename.
```

Description:

This script step allows a URL to be opened in the appropriate application. Supported schemes include HTTP, FTP, file, mailto, and HTTPS. FileMaker consults the operating system preferences to help decide which application to use to service a particular URL scheme.

Comments:

This could be one effective means to an asset management solution. If the solution stores only references to the files, and the files are stored in a Web server directory, FileMaker can construct a full URL to the file based on the reference in the database, and bring the file up in the user's browser with an Open URL command.

When programming for the Web, be sure to select Perform Without Dialog. Leaving the box unchecked is not Web compatible and does not work on the Web.

PASTE

Compatibility: Mac: yes*   Windows: yes   Web: yes

Menu Equivalent: <u>E</u>dit, <u>P</u>aste

Syntax:

```
Paste [Select; No style; <table::field>]
```

Options:

Select Entire Contents replaces the contents of a field with the contents of the Clipboard. If Select Entire Contents is not used, Paste copies the contents of the Clipboard to the currently selected portion of the field.

Paste Without Style tells FileMaker Pro to ignore all text style and formatting associated with the Clipboard contents.

Select **Go To Target Field** or click **Specify** to specify the field into which to paste.

Link If Available (Windows only) tells FileMaker Pro to choose a link over other formats on the clipboard. If both a link and an embedded object are present on the clipboard, the link is selected. If a link is available, it is selected over other formats.

Examples:

```
Go to Record/Request/Page [First]
Copy [Select; Customer::ZipCode]
Loop
  Go to Record/Request/Page [Next; Exit after last]
  Paste [Select; No style; Customer::ZipCode]
End Loop
```

Description:

This script step pastes the contents of the clipboard into the specified field in the current record. If the data type of the data being pasted does not match the type of the field being pasted into, FileMaker Pro displays the customary validation alert when the record is committed. (It's also possible that the script that calls the Paste step may leave the record in an uncommitted state, in which case the error dialog appears later, when the record is committed.) If the field is not on the current layout, FileMaker Pro returns an error code, which can be captured with the Get(LastError) function. In a Web-published database, use a Commit Record/Request script step after a Paste script step to update the record in the browser window.

Comments:

Paste is one of a number of script steps that depend on the presence of specific fields on the current layout. Other script steps with the same limitations include Cut, Copy, Paste, and Set Selection.

PAUSE/RESUME SCRIPT

Compatibility: Mac: yes   Windows: yes   Web: yes

Menu Equivalent: None

Syntax:

```
Pause/Resume Script [Duration (seconds) <n>]
```

Options:

Specify displays the Pause/Resume Options dialog box, where the following options can be set.

Select **Indefinitely** to pause the script until the user clicks the Continue button in the Status Area.

Select **For Duration** to enter the number of seconds to pause the script.

Select **For Duration** and click **Specify** to create a calculation that determines the number of seconds to pause.

Examples:

```
Perform Find [Restore]
Pause/Resume Script [Indefinitely]
Set Field [Contacts::Status; "Ready for Review"]
```

Description:

This script step pauses a script for a specified period of time or indefinitely. This enables the user to perform data entry or other tasks before continuing the script. This step brings the active window of the file in which the script step is running to the foreground if it is not already there. The duration of a pause must be a number and represents the number of seconds that the pause will last before resuming execution for the script. Most FileMaker Pro menu options are not available to users while in a paused script. While paused, a script displays a Continue button in the status bar. The pause is terminated when a user clicks this button. There is also a Cancel button, which appears only if the Allow User Abort option is set to On. This button exits the currently running script. In the case where the status bar is hidden, the Enter key performs the same function as the Continue button. Buttons that run other scripts function while the current script is paused. Thus a button may be linked to a script that executes the Resume Script step. A script run in this way is run as a subscript of the paused script.

Perform AppleScript

Compatibility: Mac: yes   Windows: no   Web: no

Menu Equivalent: None

Syntax:

```
Perform AppleScript ["<applescript text>"]
```

Options:

Specify to display the Perform AppleScript Options dialog box, where the following options can be set:

Calculated AppleScript lets you draw the AppleScript code from the result of a calculation.

Native AppleScript allows you to enter an AppleScript by hand (up to 30,000 characters long).

Examples:

```
#This example sets the primary monitor to its minimum bit depth.
Perform AppleScript ["tell application "Finder" to set bounds of window
➥"My Files" to {100, 100, 100, 100}"]
```

Description:

This script step sends AppleScript commands to an AppleScript-aware application. The AppleScript may be typed in manually or generated as the result of a specified calculation. Calculated scripts are compiled every time the script is run, whereas typed-in scripts are compiled only when the script is edited. Obviously, the latter is a faster process, but creating AppleScript code via a calculation provides much greater flexibility.

Comments:

Perform AppleScript is supported only on the Mac OS. The script step generates an error on Windows. For more information on AppleScript and AppleEvents, see the "Apple Events Reference" included with FileMaker Pro.

Perform Find

Compatibility: Mac: yes   Windows: yes   Web: yes

Menu Equivalent: None

Syntax:

```
Perform Find [Restore]
```

Options:

Select **Specify Find Requests** or click **Specify** to create or edit one or more find requests that will be stored with the script steps.

New opens a dialog box that enables you to create and specify a new find request to be stored with the script step.

Edit opens a selected find request from the existing list for editing.

Duplicate duplicates one or more selected find requests from the list and adds them to the stored set.

Delete deletes one or more selected find requests from the list.

Use the **Edit Find Request** dialog box to work with find request criteria.

Use **Find Records** or **Omit Records** to specify the behavior of the request. Selecting Omit Records is equivalent to checking the Omit check box in a find request in Find mode. Finding records adds them to the current found set. Omitting records excludes them. As in Find mode, use multiple requests if it's necessary to both find and omit records in the course of a single stored search.

Find Records When (or **Omit Records When**) shows a list of the fields in your current table. To construct a find request, begin by selecting a field from this list.

To select a field from a related table, click the name of the current table at the top of the list and select the related table you want. Select a related field from this new list.

Change the value in Repetition to specify a particular cell of a repeating field.

Type the search criteria for the selected field in the Criteria area.

Click Add to add criteria to the find request.

To change existing criteria, select the line containing the field and criteria from the top of the dialog box, and make the changes to the field and/or criteria. Click Change to store changes.

To delete existing criteria, select the line containing the field and criteria from the top of the dialog box and click Remove.

Examples:

```
Set Error Capture [On]
Perform Find [Restore]
#check for a "no records" error
If [Get (LastError) = 401]
   Show Custom Dialog ["Sorry, no records were found. "]
End If
```

Description:

This script step places the system in Find mode and performs the search request(s) that have been designated for this step. If no find requests have been designated, then the last find request(s) that the system performed is performed. If the system is in Find Mode when Perform Find is executed, then the currently entered find request is performed. This behavior is often used in conjunction with the Enter Find Mode step with the Pause option selected to allow a user to define a search request or group of search requests and then perform them. If FileMaker Pro doesn't find any records that match the find criteria when a script is performed, the script can be stopped, execution of the script can be resumed with

C

zero records in the current found set, and the find criteria can be changed. With the Set Error Capture script step and the Get(LastError) function, a script to handle such situations can be written.

PERFORM FIND/REPLACE

Compatibility: Mac: yes   Windows: yes   Web: no

Menu Equivalent: None

Syntax:

```
Perform Find/Replace [No dialog; "<text to be found>"; "<replacement text>";
➥Find Next/Replace & Find/Replace/Replace All]
```

Options:

Perform Without Dialog inhibits the display of the Find/Replace Summary dialog box at the end of the Find/Replace operation. This option also prevents display of the confirmation dialog box when a Replace All operation is executed.

If it is desired that the user be able to enter find or replace criteria, use the Open Find/Replace script step.

Specify displays the Specify Find/Replace dialog box, where search options, as well as the type of find/replace operation to be performed, can be set.

Examples:

```
Perform Find/Replace ["hte"; "the"; Replace All]
```

Description:

This script step finds the specified text, and, if directed, replaces it with either literal text or the result of a calculation. The scope of the operation can be defined to be the current record or the entire found set. The Find/Replace can span all fields in a layout or just the current field. The operation can be defined to proceed forward or backward in the current found set (as sorted). Finally, options are available for the matching of whole words only instead of parts of words, and for the matching of case.

PERFORM SCRIPT

Compatibility: Mac: yes   Windows: yes   Web: yes

Menu Equivalent: None

Syntax:

```
Perform Script ["<script name>"; Parameter: <parameter>]
```

Options:

To select a script, click Specify and choose the script from the list.

Specify a script parameter using the optional script parameter choice. You can specify the parameter as text, or click Edit and specify the parameter by means of a calculation formula.

Examples:

```
Go to Layout ["Detail"]
Perform Script ["Find Contact"; Parameter:
Contact::ContactID]
```

Description:

This script step performs a script either in the current file or in another FileMaker Pro file. Scripts can be as simple or as complex as is required, but it is often more efficient to break larger scripts into smaller subscripts for ease of re-use and debugging. Script parameters allow scripts to communicate with one another without having to use database fields or globals. The script parameter may be accessed with the Get(ScriptParameter) function. It is important to note that script parameters exist only within a script into which they have been explicitly passed. For a subscript to have access to the parameter of the script that called it, it must, in turn, be passed into the subscript. Script parameters exist for only as long as the script to which they are passed exists. Parameter strings can contain many pieces of information as long as they are properly separated. Carriage returns and separator characters are common ways to pass many pieces of information in a parameter string.

→ For more information using script parameters and subscripts in programming, **see** Chapter 15, "Advanced Scripting," **p. 421**.

PRINT

Compatibility: Mac: yes   Windows: yes   Web: no

Menu Equivalent: File, Print

Syntax:

```
Print [Restore; No dialog]
```

Options:

Perform Without Dialog prevents a dialog box from displaying when the script step executes. Ordinarily, users would see a dialog box permitting them to use their own settings. When this option is selected, FileMaker Pro uses the print settings that are stored with the script step.

Select **Specify Print Options** or click **Specify** to open the Print dialog box and set generic printing options, including the printer, number of copies, and the pages to print. FileMaker Pro can also set printing options such as printing the current record, printing records being browsed, or printing a blank record.

Examples:

```
Go To Layout ["Detail View"]
Show All Records
Sort Records [Restore; No dialog]
Print Setup [Restore; No dialog]
Print []
```

Description:

This script step prints selected information from a FileMaker Pro file. This information can include field contents, reports, and field or script definitions. Print setup is stored with the script step, but may be changed with the `Print Setup` script step. Multiple `Print` steps may be used in a single script.

Comments:

Printer settings generally do not transfer well between platforms. Unless your settings are very generic, you may need separate `Print` or `Print Setup` steps for each platform you intend to support. You may need to check the current user's platform with `Get(SystemPlatform)` and use separate print setups for each different platform.

Print Setup

Compatibility: Mac: yes   Windows: yes   Web: no

Menu Equivalent: File, Print Setup

Syntax:

```
Print Setup [Restore; No dialog]
```

Options:

Perform Without Dialog prevents a dialog box from displaying when the script step that lets the user enter new printing options executes. When this option is selected, FileMaker Pro uses the print settings that are stored with the script step.

Select **Specify Print Options** or click **Specify** to open the Print dialog box and set generic printing options, including the printer, number of copies, and the pages to print. FileMaker Pro can also set printing options such as printing the current record, printing records being browsed, or printing a blank record.

Examples:

```
Go To Layout ["Detail View"]
Show All Records
Sort Records [Restore; No DIalog]
Print Setup [Restore; No dialog]
Print []
```

Description:

This script step sets printing options such as printer, print layout, number of copies, and so on, which can all be stored within the script step. There is the option to allow the user to modify the print setup by presenting him or her with the Print Setup dialog box. Multiple `Print Setup` steps may be used in a single script.

Comments:

Printer settings generally do not transfer well between platforms. Unless your settings are very generic, you may need separate `Print` or `Print Setup` steps for each platform you intend to support. You may need to use Get(SystemPlatform) to check the current user's platform and use separate print setups for each different platform.

RE-LOGIN

Compatibility: Mac: yes   Windows: yes   Web: yes

Menu Equivalent: None

Syntax:

```
Re-Login [Account Name: <account name>; Password: <password>; No dialog]
```

Options:

Perform Without Dialog prevents the Open File dialog box from displaying when the script step executes. When this option is unchecked, users see a normal FileMaker authentication dialog. When this option is checked, FileMaker Pro uses the account and password information that is stored with the script step, or derives the information from calculations.

Click **Specify** to display the Re-Login Options dialog box, where you can set the following options:

Account Name is the name of the account to be authenticated. This may be entered as literal text, or Specify can be clicked to create a new account name from a calculation.

Password is the password for this account. Literal text may be entered or Specify clicked to create a new password from a calculation.

Examples:

```
Re-Login [Account Name:"User"; Password:"Password"; No
dialog]
```

Description:

This script step allows a user to log in to the current database with a different account name and password. This does not require the database file to be closed or re-opened. Privileges assigned to the new account take effect immediately, including access to tables, records, layouts, scripts, and value lists. Users get five attempts to enter an account and password, unless the Set Error Capture script step is enabled. If the Set Error Capture script step is enabled, users get a single attempt to enter an account and password. If a user fails the allotted number of times, she must close and re-open the database file before she can try to access the database again.

Comments:

When programming for the Web, be sure to select Perform Without Dialog. Leaving the box unchecked is not Web compatible and does not work on the Web.

C

RECOVER FILE

Compatibility: Mac: yes   Windows: yes   Web: no

Menu Equivalent: File, Recover

Syntax:

```
Recover File [No dialog; "<filename>"]
```

Options:

Perform Without Dialog prevents a dialog box from displaying after the script step completes. Ordinarily, users would see a dialog box that shows how many bytes of data were recovered, the number of records and field values skipped, and the number of field definitions recovered.

Select **Specify Source File** or click **Specify** to display a dialog box where you can select the file to be recovered. If you don't select a source file, the Open Damaged File dialog box displays when the script is run.

Examples:

```
Recover File [No Dialog; "DataFile.fp7"]
```

Description:

This script step recovers damaged FileMaker Pro files. In the recovery process, FileMaker Pro attempts to repair and recover as much of the information in a damaged file as is possible. It then creates a new file and saves it to the selected directory. The original file is not deleted or replaced. The new recovered file is named exactly as the damaged file except "Recovered" is appended to its filename, before any extenders. For example, the recovery of DataFile.fp7 would produce the file DataFile Recovered.fp7.

Comments:

Recover File is intended only to recover data from a corrupted file. It does not remove any corruption that may be present in the file, nor does it render the file fit for production use again. You should *never* re-use a file that has been recovered! Import the extracted data into the most recent clean backup of the file and discard the recovered version.

REFRESH WINDOW

Compatibility: Mac: yes   Windows: yes   Web: no

Menu Equivalent: None

Syntax:

```
Refresh Window
```

Options:

None

Examples:

```
Freeze Window
Go to Record/Request/Page [First]
# Give everyone a 10% raise.
Loop
   Set Field [Employee::Salary; Employee::Salary * 1. 1]
   Go to Record/Request/Page [Next; Exit after last]
End Loop
Refresh Window
```

Description:

This script step updates the active FileMaker Pro document window. Use Refresh Window after Freeze Window to update a window.

Comments:

This step may also be used to force a portal to refresh after match fields (such as keys or other IDs) have been modified. It may also happen that complex related data is slow to refresh in a window, or user interaction—such as a mouse click—may be required to show the changed data. If you find such behavior, you may be able to cure it with an explicit Refresh Window step.

RELOOKUP FIELD CONTENTS

Compatibility: Mac: yes   Windows: yes   Web: yes*

Menu Equivalent: Records, Relookup Field Contents

Syntax:

```
Relookup Field Contents [No dialog; <table::field>]
```

Options:

Perform Without Dialog prevents a dialog box from displaying when the script step that lets the user confirm field information executes.

Select **Go To Target Field** or click **Specify** to specify the field that is the match field of the relookup operation. FileMaker Pro moves the cursor to the field you specify. This must be the match field for the relationship upon which the lookup is based, not the lookup source or target field. If no field is selected, Relookup Field Contents returns an error code.

Examples:

```
Relookup Field Contents [No dialog, Invoice::Customer ID]
```

Description:

Use Relookup to "refresh" values that are copied from one place to another via the Lookup field option. It's important to realize that you must specify the field that's the *match field* for the lookup operation, rather than any of the fields that will receive the newly copied data. As an example, imagine you have a system with a Customer table and an Invoice table. The two tables are related by a shared CustomerID. The Invoice table also has fields for Customer

Name and Customer Address, which are defined to look up the corresponding fields from the related Customer record. To "refresh" the customer name and address information on one or more invoices, it would be necessary to specify the Customer ID field in Invoices, which is the match field that links the two tables, rather than specify either of the two fields intended to receive the refreshed. Note that the relookup operates only on records in the current found set.

Comments:

When programming for the Web, be sure to select `Perform Without Dialog`. Leaving the box unchecked is not Web compatible and does not work on the Web.

REPLACE FIELD CONTENTS

Compatibility: Mac: yes   Windows: yes   Web: yes*

Menu Equivalent: Records, Replace Field Contents

Syntax:

```
Replace Field Contents [No Dialog; <table::field>; Current contents/Serial
➥ numbers/Calculation results]
```

Options:

Perform Without Dialog prevents display of the Replace Field Contents dialog box when the script step executes.

Select **Go To Target Field** or click **Specify** to specify the target field for the replace operation.

Click **Specify** to display the Replace Contents dialog box, where you can determine the settings required for the Replace Field Contents command so that they'll be stored in the script.

Replace With Current Contents uses the current value in the specified field as the replacement value to place in that field in every other record in the current found set.

Replace With Serial Numbers updates the field with new serial numbers in every record in the current found set.

Entry Options consults the underlying database structure to determine how to serialize records. In particular, it causes the Replace step to use the database field settings for Next Value and Increment by, as stored in the field options for that field.

Custom Values lets you enter a value to be used as a starting point for the serialization, as well as a value by which to increment each serialized field in the current found set.

Update Serial Number In Entry Options resets the serial number value in the entry options for the field, so that the next serial number that is automatically entered follows the records you have reserialized with this script step. If this option is not used, the serial value in Entry Options is not changed, and may not be in sequence with the newly reserialized records. This may lead to duplicated serial numbers or data validation errors.

C

If the field to be replaced was set up for auto-entry of a serial number and Prohibit Modification of Value is not selected, FileMaker Pro still puts sequential numbers in the selected field, but does so starting with the next number to be automatically entered.

Replace With Calculated Result displays the Specify Calculation dialog box, where you can enter a calculation to be used as the replacement value.

Examples:

```
# Fill in full names
Replace Field Contents [No Dialog; Contacts::FullName; FirstName & " " &
➥LastName]
```

Description:

This script step replaces the contents of a selected field in the current record or every record in the found set with either a designated field's value or a calculated result. This step can also be used to reserialize a field in every record in the found set. Note that if the specified field does not exist on the layout where the script is being performed, `Replace Field Contents` returns an error code which can be captured with the `Get(LastError)` function.

Comments:

It may be helpful to think of this step as being akin to filling in multiple cells in a spreadsheet column. Replace is particularly powerful when used in conjunction with a calculation (a technique often known as a *calculated replace*). The calculation can reference fields, which refer to the field values in whichever is the current record. So in a database with fields for FirstName and LastName, you could create an additional text field called FullName, and use a calculated replace to insert the results of a formula concatenating first and last names together with a space in between.

RESET ACCOUNT PASSWORD

Compatibility: Mac: yes   Windows: yes   Web: yes

Menu Equivalent: None

Syntax:

```
Reset Account Password [Account Name: <account name>; New Password: <password>;
➥Expire password]
```

Options:

Click **Specify** to display the Reset Account Password Options dialog box.

Account Name is the name of the account with the password to be reset. You can enter literal text or click Specify to create a new account name from a calculation.

New Password is the new password for this account. Literal text may be entered or Specify clicked to create a new password from a calculation.

When **User Must Change Password On Next Login** is selected, this option forces users to change their password the next time they log in to the database.

Examples:

```
Reset Account Password [Account Name:"Guest User"; New Password:"guestpassword";
➥ Expire password]
```

Description:

This script step resets the account password for the selected account. The selected account must be existing. The Full Access privilege set is needed to perform this script step. The Run with Full Access Privileges option may be selected in the ScriptMaker dialog box to circumvent this restriction for all users.

Comments:

Be aware that using **User Must Change Password On Next Login** does not work correctly when users log in to a solution via the Web. It's also important to make sure that any user with that restriction can modify his password.

REVERT RECORD/REQUEST

Compatibility: Mac: yes   Windows: yes   Web: yes*

Menu Equivalent: Records, Revert Record

Syntax:

```
Revert Record/Request [No dialog]
```

Options:

Perform Without Dialog inhibits the display of a confirmation dialog when the script step executes.

Examples:

```
Show Custom Dialog ["Do you want to save your changes?";
"Click 'Save' to save your changes, or 'Revert' to
return the record to its original state."]
#1 = Save, 2 = Revert
If [Get(LastMessageChoice) = 1]
Commit Records/Requests
Else
    Revert Record/Request [No dialog]
End If
```

Description:

This script step discards changes made to a record and its fields, assuming the record has not been saved. After changes have been committed, such as through use of the Commit Records/Requests script step, they can no longer be reverted. This is also true if a user has clicked outside of any field.

Comments:

Note that record reversion applies not only to the current record on whatever layout is being viewed, but also to any records in related tables that are displayed in a portal on the current layout. If a user has edited one or more records in a portal, the `Revert Record/Request` script step, if carried out, undoes all uncommitted changes to portal records, as well as any uncommitted changes to the current record.

When programming for the Web, be sure to select `Perform Without Dialog`. Leaving the box unchecked is not Web compatible and does not work on the Web.

SAVE A COPY AS

Compatibility: Mac: yes   Windows: yes   Web: no

Menu Equivalent: File, Save a Copy As

Syntax:

```
Save a Copy as ["<filename>"; copy/compacted/clone]
```

Options:

Specify Output File displays the Specify Output File dialog box, which allows specification of the name and location of the resulting copy. If a save location is not specified in the script, FileMaker Pro displays a regular Save As dialog box so the user can specify copying options.

Use **Specify** to choose a save format: copy of current file, compacted copy (smaller), or clone (no records).

Examples:

```
Save a Copy as ["Customers.bak"]
```

Description:

This script step saves a copy of the current file to the designated location. If no location is designated, a dialog box is presented to the user. Three types of copies are available. **Copy** creates an exact replica of the current file. **Compressed** also creates a copy of the current file, but the copy will be compressed to utilize space more efficiently. This sort of copy takes longer to create but is generally smaller than the original. **Clone** creates a file that's structurally identical to the current database but contains no data. This is useful for backup purposes because clones are very compact.

SCROLL WINDOW

Compatibility: Mac: yes   Windows: yes   Web: no

Menu Equivalent: None

Syntax:

```
Scroll Window [Home/End/Page Up/Page Down/To Selection]
```

Options:

Use **Specify** to choose a scrolling option.

Home, **End**, **Page Up**, or **Page Down** scrolls the window to the beginning, to the end, up a page, or down a page.

To Selection brings the current field into view (similar to tabbing into a field).

Examples:

```
Go to Field[ "Scroll Right"]
Scroll Window [To Selection]
#The next step just makes sure we leave the "scroll to" field
Commit Records/Requests
```

Description:

This script step scrolls a window to its top or bottom, up or down, or to a specified field.

Comments:

You may want to use this script step for rapid, easy scrolling within a window. For example, if you've had to design a layout that's wider than some users screens, you can put dummy "scroll left/scroll right" fields at the far left and right sides of the layout. If you make the field small and forbid entry, the user will not notice them. Then a script like the example above scrolls quickly to the right side of the window (assuming the field is placed somewhere to the right).

SELECT ALL

Compatibility: Mac: yes   Windows: yes   Web: yes

Menu Equivalent: Edit, Select All

Syntax:

```
Select All
```

Options:

None

Examples:

```
Go To Field [Contacts::Statement]
Select All
Copy []
Go To Field [Contacts::PreviousStatement]
Paste[]
```

Description:

This script step selects the entire contents of the current field.

SELECT DICTIONARIES

Compatibility: Mac: yes   Windows: yes   Web: no

Menu Equivalent: Edit, Spelling, Select Dictionaries

Syntax:

```
Select Dictionaries
```

Options:

None

Examples:

```
Select Dictionaries
Check Record
```

Description:

This script step opens the Select Dictionaries dialog box. This is often used to give users access to the Select Dictionaries dialog box when access to the FileMaker Pro menus has been restricted.

SELECT WINDOW

Compatibility: Mac: yes Windows: yes Web: yes

Menu Equivalent: None

Syntax:

```
Select Window [<name of window>]
```

Options:

Current Window brings the active window of the file that contains the script to the foreground.

Otherwise, click **Specify** to select the window FileMaker Pro should bring to the foreground. The name may be typed as literal text, or derived from a calculation.

Examples:

```
Select Window [Name: "Contract Players"]
```

Description:

This script step specifies a window by name and makes it the current window. FileMaker Pro script steps are always performed in the foreground table. It is, therefore, sometimes necessary to bring a specific window to the front. Use this script step when working with scripts in multi-table files to make certain that a script step is performed in the intended table. (You may also need to use a Go to Layout step to establish context correctly.) The Select Window script step does not open a window of a related file when the related file is open in a hidden state, such as when a file is opened, because it is the source file of a related field. The related file must be explicitly opened with the Open File script step before its windows are allowable targets for the Select Window step.

C

SEND DDE EXECUTE

Compatibility: Mac: no   Windows: yes   Web: no

Menu Equivalent: None

Syntax:

```
Send DDE Execute [<topic text or filename>; <service name>]
```

Options:

Click **Specify** to display the Send DDE Execute Options dialog box.

Service Name is the name of the application that executes the commands. Refer to the documentation of the application being specified for the valid service name. The service name may be entered directly as text or Specify clicked to create the service name from a calculation.

Topic is a filename or text string that describes the topic on which the application executes the commands. Refer to the documentation of the application specified in the Service Name for valid topics. Enter the topic name directly as text, or click Specify to create the topic name from a calculation.

Commands are calculated values or text strings that specify what the application does. Refer to the documentation of the application specified in the Service Name for valid commands and formats. Enter the commands directly as text or click Specify to create the commands from a calculation.

Examples:

```
Send DDE Execute [Service Name: "iexplore"; Topic: "WWW_OpenURL"; Commands:
➥"www.moyergroup.com"]
```

Description:

This script step sends a DDE (Dynamic Data Exchange) command to another DDE-aware application. FileMaker sends DDE commands but does not receive them. When a FileMaker Pro script first establishes a DDE connection, the connection stays open to execute subsequent script steps for the same service name and topic. If the script includes another DDE Execute script step that specifies a different service name or topic, FileMaker Pro closes the current connection and opens another with the new service name and topic. All open connections close when the script is completed.

SEND EVENT (WINDOWS)

Compatibility: Mac: no   Windows: yes   Web: no

Menu Equivalent: None

Syntax:

```
Send Event ["<aevt>"; "<event name>"; "<filename>"]
```

Options:

Click **Specify** to display the Send Event Options dialog box.

For **Send The *<Event Name>* Message**, select

- **Open Document/Application** to tell FileMaker Pro to open a document file or application. The application that Windows has associated with the document's file type is used to open it.

- **Print Document** to tell FileMaker Pro to print a document in another application.

Select **File** or click **Specify** to specify a document/application to open or a document to print.

Select **Calculation** or click **Specify** to create a message from a calculation.

Select **Text** to manually enter text for the message to be sent.

Select **Bring Target Application To Foreground** to activate the target application and display it on the screen. Displaying the target application can slow down the performance of a script. If Bring Target Application To Foreground is not selected, the event is performed in the background.

Examples:

```
#To launch the Notepad application, select the open document/application
➥message, click File, and specify notepad.exe. The following script step
➥appears in the Script Definition dialog box:
Send Message ["NOTEPAD.EXE", "aevt", "odoc"]
```

Description:

This script step communicates with other Windows applications. It can instruct them to either open or print a document in its associated application. Custom code written in a language such as C or BASIC can be executed this way.

Send Event (Mac OS)

Compatibility: Mac: yes   Windows: no   Web: no

Menu Equivalent: None

Syntax:

```
Send Event ["<Target Application>"; "<Event Class>"; "<Event ID>", "<Document or
➥ Calculation or Script Text>"]
```

Options:

Click **Specify** to display the Send Event Options dialog box.

Send The *<Value>* Event With offers a choice between the following:

- **Open Application** tells FileMaker Pro to open an application. Click Specify Application to select the application.

- **Open Document** tells FileMaker Pro to open a document in the target application. You can also specify a calculated value or script.

- **Do Script** tells FileMaker Pro to perform a script in the language of the target application. Click Specify Application to select an application, and use Document to select the document to use with the target application. Or select Script Text and enter script text or type in the name of the script. (Make sure it is one that will be recognized by the target program.)

- **Other** displays the Specify Event dialog box, where you can manually enter the Apple Event class and Event ID.

Select **Document** or click **Specify** to select the document you want used with the target application.

Select **Calculation** or click **Specify** to create a calculation that generates a value you want to send with the event.

Bring Target Application to Foreground activates the target application and displays it on the screen. Displaying the target application can slow down the performance of a script. If Bring Target Application to Foreground is not selected, the event is performed in the background.

Wait for Event Completion Before Continuing tells FileMaker Pro to wait until the event is finished before continuing. If you don't want to wait until the event is completed, deselect this option.

Copy Event Result to the Clipboard copies the resulting events data to the Clipboard, from which it can later be retrieved. This option is disabled if Bring Target Application to Foreground is selected.

Click **Specify Application** to display a dialog box where you can select the target application.

Examples:

```
Send Event ["TextEdit", "aevt", "oapp"]
```

Description:

This script step sends an Apple Event to another Apple Event–aware application. The desired event is selected in the Send Event Options dialog box. When FileMaker Pro sends an Apple event, it sends text (not compiled) data. You must know what information the target application expects to receive with an event. Each Send Event script step sends one event. You can include more than one Send Event in a script.

SEND MAIL

Compatibility: Mac: yes   Windows: yes   Web: no

Menu Equivalent: None

Syntax:

```
Send Mail [No dialog; To: <to>; CC: <CC>; BCC: <BCC>; Subject: <subject>;
➥Message: <message>; "<attachment>"]
```

Options:

Perform without dialog instructs FileMaker Pro to put the composed email message in the email application's Out box, ready to be sent. If this option is not selected, the composed message is left open in the email application so that it can be reviewed. In Microsoft Outlook Express or Microsoft Entourage on the Macintosh operating system, the new message is left in the Drafts folder.

Click **Specify** to display the Specify Mail dialog box, where options for mail can be set. For each of the following options, one can enter text directly, or click > to enter values from an address book, field, or calculation.

- Select **Specify Email Addresses** to select an email address from the email application's address book.
- Select **Specify calculation** to create an address (or subject or message text) from a calculation.
- Select **Specify Field Name** to choose a single field that contains the desired value.
- If the **Specify Field Name** option is used to specify a value for the To:, CC:, or BCC: entries, one can also select Get Values from Every Record in Found Set to specify that all the values from this field in the current found set be used (to address a message to multiple recipients).

To stores the address(es) of the recipient(s).

CC stores the address(es) of the carbon copy recipient(s).

BCC stores the address(es) of the blind carbon copy recipient(s).

Subject indicates the title for the email message.

Message indicates the text of the email message. The message may be typed as text, designated as a field value, or created by a calculation.

Select **Attach File** to select a file to send as an attachment to the mail message.

Examples:

```
Perform Find [Restore]
# Send the same email to everyone in the found set.
Send Mail [To: sContacts::email; Subject: "This is a test email"; Message:
➥"Testing..."]
```

Description:

The Send Mail script steps allow you to send email to one or more recipients via a client-side email application. The following things are necessary to send mail from FileMaker:

- Windows: A [Mail] section in the Win.ini file, and Microsoft Exchange or another email application that is MAPI-compliant, installed and configured to work with an existing email account.
- Mac OS: Mac OS X Mail or Microsoft Entourage installed and configured as the default email application.

Comments:

To send mail, you must have an Internet connection and a correctly-configured email client (see the previous Description section for configurations). It's not possible to use the Send Mail step to send email via an SMTP server.

SET ERROR CAPTURE

Compatibility: Mac: yes   Windows: yes   Web: yes

Menu Equivalent: None

Syntax:

```
Set Error Capture [<on or off>]
```

Options:

Setting Error Capture to **On** suppresses most FileMaker Pro alert messages and some dialog boxes. If the error result is 100 or 803, then certain standard file dialog boxes are suppressed, such as the Open dialog box.

Setting Error Capture to **Off** re-enables the alert messages.

Examples:

```
Perform Find [Restore]
Go to Record/Request/Page [First]
Open Record/Request
if [ Get(LastError) = 200 or Get(LastError) = 300]
   Show Custom Dialog ["An error has ocurred. This record is locked or you do
➥not have sufficient permission to access it."]
End If
```

Description:

This script step suppresses or enables the FileMaker Pro error dialogs and messages. This provides the developer with the opportunity to write scripts to handle errors in a manner that is customizable and appropriate to the functions being performed. The Get(LastError) function, when used immediately after a script step is executed, gives the code of the error that was encountered, if an error was encountered.

SET FIELD

Compatibility: Mac: yes   Windows: yes   Web: yes

Menu Equivalent: None

Syntax:

```
Set Field [<table::field>; <value or formula>]
```

Options:

Select **Specify Target Field** or click **Specify** to specify the field whose contents you want to replace. If no field is specified and a field is already selected in Browse mode or Find mode, that field is used.

Click **Specify** to define a calculation, the results of which will replace the current contents of the target field.

Examples:

```
Freeze Window
Go to Record/Request/Page [First]
# Give everyone a 10% raise.
Loop
   Set Field [Employee::Salary; Employee::Salary * 1.1]
   Go to Record/Request/Page [Next; Exit after last]
End Loop
Refresh Window
```

Description:

This script step replaces the contents of the designated field on the current record with the result of the specified calculation. The result of the calculation must match the field type of the target field, or the results may be unexpected. Unlike many other script steps that deal with field contents, Set Field does not require that the field being targeted be on the active layout. If the result of the calculation doesn't match the target field type, and the Validate option for the field is set to Always, the field is not set and an error code is returned (which can be captured with the Get(LastError) function).

Comments:

When possible, the Set Field script step makes the record active and leaves it active until the record is exited or committed. Scripts that use a series of Set Field script steps should thus group these steps together if possible, so that subsequent Set Field script steps can act on the record without having to lock the record, synchronize data with the server, index the field, and so on, after each individual Set Field script step. Synchronization, indexing, and record-level validation are performed after the record has been exited or committed.

SET MULTI-USER

Compatibility: Mac: yes   Windows: yes   Web: no

Menu Equivalent: None

Syntax:

```
Set Multi-User [On/On (Hidden)/Off]
```

Options:

Select **On** to allow network access via FileMaker Network Sharing. This is the same as enabling Network Sharing and selecting All Users in the FileMaker Network Settings dialog box.

Select **On (Hidden)** to allow network access but prevent the name of the shared database from appearing in the Open Remote File dialog box. This is the same as enabling Network Sharing and selecting the All Users and Don't Display in Open Remote File dialog options in the FileMaker Network Settings dialog box.

Select **Off** to disallow network access. This is the same as selecting No Users in the FileMaker Network Settings dialog box.

Examples:

```
If [Get (MultiUserState) = 0]
  Show Custom Dialog ["Would you like to enable network sharing?"]
  If [Get (LastMessageChoice) = 1]
    Set Multi-User [On]
  End If
End
```

Description:

This script step allows or disallows network access to the current database. The Hidden option allows a file to be accessed by other files and in dialogs but not through the Open Remote dialog.

Comments:

If FileMaker's Network Sharing is currently set to Off, both of this script step's On options will also enable network sharing. This could possibly enable sharing access to other files than just the one in which this script step is run. The converse is not true: The Off option to this script step does not also turn off FileMaker Network Sharing. It's sometimes helpful to have `Set Multi-User On/Off` script steps in all the files of a multi-file solution. By means of a single master script in one of the files, all these individual files can execute their Set Multi-User On/Off scripts. This makes it possible to fully enable or fully disable multi-user access to a set of files with just a single script.

SET NEXT SERIAL VALUE

Compatibility: Mac: yes   Windows: yes   Web: yes

Menu Equivalent: None

Syntax:

```
Set Next Serial Value [<table::field>; <value or formula>]
```

Options:

Select **Specify Target Field** or click **Specify** to specify the serial number field on which the script step is to operate. The field specified must be defined as an auto-entry serial number field.

C

Calculated Result: Click **Specify** to enter the next serial value or create a calculation to determine the next serial value.

Examples:

```
Find All
Set Next Serial Value [Contacts::ContactID;Contacts::MaxContactID + 1]
# Note: MaxContactID would be a summary field defined as the max of the serial
➥field ContactID
```

Description:

This script step resets the Next Serial Value for an auto-enter serial number field. This is especially useful to ensure that there are no duplicate serial numbers when a large number of records have been imported into a backup clone of a system. It is also useful for importing records when it is not desirable to allow auto-enter calculations. The calculated result always evaluates to a text result. Note this script step can operate on multiple files. If a field in another file is specified, then FileMaker Pro attempts to update the serial number for the specified field in the other file. To specify a field in another file, define a relationship to that file and use **Specify Target Field** to select a field from that file. Also, if a serial number is not strictly a number, special care must be taken to ensure that the newly set serial number matches the format of the existing serial numbers.

Comments:

This script step does not change any field data. Instead, it changes the definition of the target field. Specifically, it changes the Next Serial Number you see in the Field Options dialog for that field.

SET SELECTION

Compatibility: Mac: yes   Windows: yes   Web: yes

Menu Equivalent: None

Syntax:

```
Set Selection [Start Position: <n>; End Position: <n>]
```

Options:

Select **Go To Target Field** or click the **Specify** button by the check box to specify the field whose contents you want to select.

The second **Specify** option lets you set the starting and ending positions of a selection, either by entering the start and end numbers directly or by using a calculation to determine them.

Examples:

Description:

This script step makes it possible to "select" some or all of a field's contents without direct user intervention. It's possible to specify the start and end positions (in terms of numbers of characters) for the new selection. You might do this to "set up" additional operations that act on the current selection, such as cut or copy. You might also choose to transform the selection, for example by removing it and substituting a styled version of the same text. This script step allows the setting of the starting and ending position of a selection within a field. These values may be entered literally or generated as the result of a specified calculation. This step does not operate on container fields. Data that is out of the visible portion of a layout or field is scrolled into view to show the newly selected contents. The start and end values must be integers between 1 and the number of characters in the target field. If the start position number is valid and the end position number is invalid, then the selection goes from the start position number to the end of the field contents. If the start position number is invalid and the end position is valid, the cursor (or insertion point) is placed at the specified end position with no characters selected. If neither the start nor the end numbers are valid, then the cursor is placed at the end of the fields' contents.

Comments:

Set Selection is one of a number of script steps that depend on the presence of specific fields on the current layout. Other script steps with the same limitations include Cut, Copy, and Paste.

Set Use System Formats

Compatibility: Mac: yes   Windows: yes   Web: no

Menu Equivalent: None

Syntax:

Set Use System Formats [On]

Options:

Use System Formats may be set to **On** or **Off**.

Examples:

```
If [Get (SystemLanguage) <> "English"]
   Set Use System Formats [On]
End If
```

Description:

FileMaker Pro databases store date, time, and number format preferences. These are taken from the computer on which the database was created. These creation settings may differ from those in use on other machines on which the database may be open. This script step can be used to determine whether a file draws its time display settings from those stored in the file, or those in effect on the local machine.

SET WINDOW TITLE

Compatibility: Mac: yes   Windows: yes   Web: yes

Menu Equivalent: None

Syntax:

```
Set Window Title [Current Window or Name: <name of window>; New Title:
➥<new window name>]
```

Options:

Click **Specify** to set all the options for this script.

Window to Rename tells FileMaker Pro which window to rename. Current Window renames the current window. You may also specify a different window, either by typing the window name in plain text or deriving the window name from a calculation.

New Name is the new title for the window. Here again, you can enter literal text or click **Specify** to derive a name from the result of a calculation.

Examples:

```
Set Error Capture [On]
Allow User Abort [Off]
Perform Find [Restore]
Set Window Title [Get(FoundCount) &" Contacts Found"]
```

Description:

Set Window Title sets the name of the current window or the window specified by name.

Comments:

Window names aren't case sensitive when you select them in this way, so be sure not to rely on case sensitivity in window names.

SET ZOOM LEVEL

Compatibility: Mac: yes   Windows: yes   Web: no

Menu Equivalent: None

Syntax:

```
Set Zoom Level [Lock; 25%...400%/Zoom In/Zoom Out]
```

Options:

Lock prohibits users from making changes to the zoom level.

Specify lets you select a zoom level:

- Specific reduction values: 100%, 75%, 50%, or 25%.
- Specific enlargement values: 150%, 200%, 300%, or 400%.
- Zoom In: reduces the screen image by one zoom level.
- Zoom Out: enlarges the screen image by one zoom level.

Examples:

```
Allow User Abort [Off]
Set Error Capture [On]
If[ // the screen resolution to too low// Get (ScreenHeight) < 600]
  Set Zoom Level [Lock; 100%]
Else
  Set Zoom Level [100%]
End
```

Description:

Set Zoom Level enlarges or reduces the image on the screen and optionally locks screen scaling. It is equivalent to using the magnification icons beneath the status area.

SHOW ALL RECORDS

Compatibility: Mac: yes   Windows: yes   Web: yes

Menu Equivalent: Records, Show All Records

Syntax:

```
Show All Records
```

Options:

None

Examples:

```
Allow User Abort [Off]
Set Error Capture [On]
Enter Find Mode [Pause]
Perform Find []
If[// no records were found// Get(CurrentFoundCount) = 0]
  Show Message ["No Records Found"; "Sorry, no records that match your find
  ➥criteria were found."]
  Show All Records [ ] // don't leave the user on an empty found set
```

Description:

Displays all the records in the current table and leaves the user on the current record. Show All Records is used in Browse mode or Preview mode. If you perform this step in Find mode or Layout mode, FileMaker Pro switches to Browse mode after the records have been found.

SHOW CUSTOM DIALOG

Compatibility: Mac: yes   Windows: yes   Web: no

Menu Equivalent: None

Syntax:

```
Show Custom Dialog [<title>; <message text>; Table1::input field 1;. . . ]
```

Options:

Click **Specify** to display a dialog box, where you can set the dialog box title, message text, and buttons, and specify up to three fields to use for input or display.

General options:

Title lets you specify the title of the custom dialog box. You can enter literal text or click Specify to create the dialog box title from a calculation.

Message lets you specify the message of the dialog box. You can enter literal text or click Specify to create the message text from a calculation.

Button Labels let you specify how many buttons (up to three) to display in the custom dialog box and labels for these buttons. If you leave a button label blank, the button does not appear in the custom dialog box. If you leave all button titles blank, an OK button displays in the lower-right corner of the custom dialog box.

Input Field options:

Select **Show input field <n>** to activate an input field.

Select **Specify** to choose the field for input. Each input area maps to one field.

Select **Use Password Character** (*) to mask text as it is entered, or as it is displayed from the database. This option obscures data being input into the custom dialog box or being displayed, but does not alter the actual data as it is stored in the database.

Use **Label** to specify a field label (the text that will identify this input to the user). You can enter literal text or create the label from a calculation.

Examples:

```
Allow User Abort [ Off ]
Set Error Capture [ On ]
#
Show Custom Dialog [ Title: "Password Change"; Buttons: "OK", "Cancel";
Input #1: zgPassword_Old. t, "Old Password:";
Input #2: zgPassword_New. t, "New Password:" ]
#
If [ /* user did not cancel the dialog */ Get(LastMessageChoice)=1 ]
  Change Password [ Old Password: zgPassword_Old. t;
  ➥New Password: zgPassword_New. t ]
  # send password change onto other files
  Perform Script [ "Change Password"; from file "Contacts" Parameter:
  ➥zgPassword_Old. t&"¶"&zgPassword_New. t ]
  Perform Script [ "Change Password"; from file "Invoices" Parameter:
  ➥zgPassword_Old. t&"¶"&zgPassword_New. t ]
End If
# be sure to clear the globals for security reasons
Set Field [zgPassword_Old.t; ""]
Set Field [zgPassword_New.t; ""]
```

Description:

Show Custom Dialog enables you to display a custom message dialog box. The dialog box is modal, with from one to three buttons, each with a custom title. The custom message

C

window can also display up to three input fields, each with a custom label. Each of these input fields corresponds to a FileMaker data field. When the window is opened, each input area displays the most recent contents of the corresponding field. When the user closes the window, the button clicked can be determined by the Get(LastMessageChoice) function. A result of 1 represents the first button on the right, whereas 2 and 3 would represent the middle and leftmost buttons if they were used. Button 1, the rightmost, is the default. It's also the only button that, when clicked, causes the data from any input fields to be written back to the corresponding FileMaker fields.

Comments:

If values entered into any input fields don't match the field type of the underlying FileMaker field, a validation error message displays. The user must resolve validation errors before the dialog box can be closed. The fields you specify don't need to appear on the current layout. Show Custom Dialog input fields are independent of layouts, similar to the Set Field script step. And as with the Set Field script step, Show Custom Dialog bypasses the Allow Entry Into Field field formatting option. Data entry via the Show Custom Dialog script step is limited by any access privilege rules that may be in place. In other words, users can't use a custom dialog to edit data in fields that they can't normally change because of access restriction. If you select Run Script With Full Access Privileges, this restriction is lifted. On Windows, you can create a keyboard shortcut for a custom dialog box button by placing an ampersand before the shortcut key letter in the button label. For example, to create a keyboard shortcut D (Alt+D) for a button labeled Done, type the label **&Done**.

Show Omitted Only

Compatibility: Mac: yes   Windows: yes   Web: yes

Menu Equivalent: Records, Show Omitted Only

Syntax:

Show Omitted Only

Options:

None

Examples:

```
// reduce found set to zero
Show All Records
Show Omitted Only
```

Description:

Show Omitted Only "inverts" the found set to show records that are currently not displayed, and omits records that are currently displayed.

SHOW/HIDE STATUS AREA

Compatibility: Mac: yes   Windows: yes   Web: yes

Menu Equivalent: None

Syntax:

```
Show/Hide Status Area [Lock; Show/Hide/Toggle]
```

Options:

Lock prohibits the user from using the status area control button to manually show or hide the status area.

Show tells FileMaker Pro to show the status area.

Hide tells FileMaker Pro to hide the status area.

Toggle switches between showing and hiding the status area (equivalent to clicking the status area control button).

Examples:

```
Allow User Abort [Off]
Set Error Capture [On]
Go to Layout ["Invoice"]
Show/Hide Status Area [Lock; Show] // show status area so the user can click
➥'Continue'
Enter Preview Mode [Pause]
Show/Hide Status Area [Lock; Hide] // shut the status area back down
Enter Browse Mode [ ]
Go To Layout [Original Layout]
```

Description:

`Show/Hide Status Area` allows for control of the status area from scripts.

Comments:

In databases where it's important to tightly control the user's navigation, it may be desirable to prevent users from using the status area either to page through records or to change layouts. Hiding and locking the status area may well be the right thing to do in such a case.

SHOW/HIDE TEXT RULER

Compatibility: Mac: yes   Windows: yes   Web: no

Menu Equivalent: View, Text Ruler

Syntax:

```
Show/Hide Text Ruler [Show/Hide/Toggle]
```

Options:

Show tells FileMaker Pro to show the text ruler.

Hide tells FileMaker Pro to hide the text ruler.

Toggle switches between showing and hiding the text ruler.

Examples:

```
Allow User Abort [Off]
Set Error Capture [On]
If[ // the screen resolution to too low// Get (ScreenHeight) < 600]
  Show/Hide Text Ruler [Hide]
End
```

Description:

Hides or shows the text ruler. Choosing the Toggle option switches the current state of the ruler. The Text Ruler is used with text fields, and also to aid in design in Layout mode. It can be used to set tabs and indents for a text area. Hiding the text ruler is sometimes required to save screen space. Unless you have disabled access to menus, users are generally able to enable the text rulers by choosing View, Text Ruler, and it may later be desirable to disable the rulers again to save room.

SORT RECORDS

Compatibility: Mac: yes   Windows: yes   Web: yes*

Menu Equivalent: Records, Sort Records

Syntax:

```
Sort Records [Restore; No dialog]
```

Options:

Perform Without Dialog prevents display of a dialog box that lets the user enter a different set of sort instructions.

Select **Specify Sort Order** or click **Specify** to create a sort order and store it with the script step. When Specify Sort Order is not selected, FileMaker Pro uses the most recently executed sort instructions.

Examples:

```
Allow User Abort [Off]
Set Error Capture [On]
# find overdue invoices
Perform Find [Restore]
# sort by due date and customer
Sort [Restore]
Go to Layout ["Invoice"]
Enter Preview Mode [Pause]
Enter Browse Mode [ ]
Go To Layout [Original Layout]
Unsort
```

C

Description:

Sort Records sorts the records in the current found set according to specified criteria. Be sure to perform any operations that might change the found set before calling Sort Records. If you sort a repeating field, FileMaker Pro sorts on only the first entry in that field. Note that in previous versions of FileMaker Pro, only one sort order could be saved with a script. However, in the current version, sort criteria are saved with individual Sort Record script steps, so any number of sorts can be saved with a single script.

Comments:

Note that saved sort criteria are relative to the current table context. If the table Contact was the active table when the sort criteria were entered, and fields from Contacts are used in the sort order, then that table must be active when the sort is executed. If your sort step makes field references that are not valid at the time the step is executed, the invalid field references are ignored. Table context is controlled by the current layout; to change table context, navigate to a layout that is used by the table in question.

When programming for the Web, be sure to select Perform Without Dialog. Leaving the box unchecked is not Web compatible and does not work on the Web.

SPEAK

Compatibility: Mac: yes   Windows: no   Web: no

Menu Equivalent: None

Syntax:

Speak [<text to be spoken>]

Options:

Click **Specify** to display the Speak Options dialog box, where you can set the following options.

You can enter the text to be spoken directly by hand, or draw the text from a calculation.

Use Voice lets you select from the various voices available on your computer.

Wait for Speech Completion Before Continuing tells FileMaker Pro to wait until the speech is completed before continuing with the next script step. If you leave this option unchecked, the script continues while the text is being spoken.

Examples:

```
Speak ["Hello"]
Speak[Get(CurrentDate)]
```

Description:

Speaks the specified text. You can specify which voice synthesizer to use and whether or not FileMaker Pro is to wait for the speech to be completed before continuing with the next script step. On a computer without speech capabilities, the script can still be edited, but only the default voice synthesizer is available. Speak script steps are not executed when the script is run on a computer without speech capability.

Spelling Options

Compatibility: Mac: yes   Windows: yes   Web: no

Menu Equivalent: File, File Options, Spelling

Syntax:

```
Spelling Options
```

Options:

None

Examples:

```
# a button on a layout calls this script step directly:
Spelling Options
```

Description:

Opens the Spelling tab of the File Options dialog box. Use this script step to open the File Options dialog box for users if you have restricted their access to FileMaker Pro menus.

Undo

Compatibility: Mac: yes   Windows: yes   Web: yes

Menu Equivalent: Edit, Undo

Syntax:

```
Undo
```

Options:

None

Examples:

```
Undo
```

Description:

Undo acts the same as choosing Undo from the edit menu: The most recent edits to the record are reversed.

Unsort Records

Compatibility: Mac: yes   Windows: yes   Web: yes

Menu Equivalent: None

Syntax:

```
Unsort Records
```

Options:

None

Examples:

```
Allow User Abort [Off]
Set Error Capture [On]
Enter Browse Mode []
Unsort Records
Go to Record/Request/Page [First]
```

Description:

Unsort Records restores the found set to its natural order (order in which records were created).

UPDATE LINK

Compatibility: Mac: no   Windows: yes   Web: no

Menu Equivalent: None

Syntax:

```
Update Link [<table::field>]
```

Options:

Select **Go to Target Field** or click **Specify** to specify the field to be updated.

Examples:

```
Set Error Capture [On]
Allow User Abort [Off]
Update Link [Contact::Resume]
If [//an error occured// Get(LastError)]
  Show Message ["An error occurred updating the resume link"]
End If
```

Description:

Update Link updates the OLE link in the specified container field. If the field does not contain an OLE link, then Update Link returns an error. Both manual and automatic links are updated.

VIEW AS

Compatibility: Mac: yes   Windows: yes   Web: yes

Menu Equivalent: View, View As Form/List/Table

Syntax:

```
View As [Form/List/Table/Cycle]
```

Options:

View as Form tells FileMaker Pro to display records page by page on the current layout, so that only one record at a time is shown.

View as List tells FileMaker Pro to display records as records in a list, so that the user can see multiple records at once in a list.

View as Table tells FileMaker Pro to display the records on screen in a spreadsheet-like grid.

Cycle switches from the current view type to the next type.

Examples:

```
Set Error Capture [On]
Allow User Abort [Off]
Go to Layout ["Contact List"]
View As [View As List]
```

Description:

View As sets the view mode for the current layout. Note that Layout Setup can be used to limit which views are accessible via the View menu, but the View As script step can override those settings and enable you to view a layout in any of the three styles.

DOCUMENTING FILEMAKER PRO SYSTEMS

In this appendix

WHY IS DOCUMENTATION IMPORTANT?

There are two general types of software documentation: *user documentation* and *system documentation*. User documentation is a resource to assist people who need to use or administer a system. System documentation is a resource for developers who need to make functional changes to a system. This appendix focuses on techniques for creating system documentation for FileMaker-based projects.

Creating high-quality documentation is an important yet often neglected activity in the software development process. Because FileMaker is such an intuitive tool, it is easy for developers to put off the documentation process. But sometimes a system that began as a simple contact management tool grows into a monster system with hundreds of layouts and thousands of fields and scripts. When the time comes to modify a feature that you haven't looked at in months or even years, documentation will be your best friend.

It can be tempting to delay documentation preparation until a system is complete. But in many projects there simply isn't time (or money, if the project has a specific budget) left when the project is finished to create documentation, and your memory of the system details at that point can also become fuzzy. So because it's often too late to initiate documentation at the end of the project, it is important that you adapt your workflow to include practices that contribute to creating good documentation as you work. The most important of these are developing consistent naming conventions and making liberal use of comments. We'll discuss both of these practices further in the course of this appendix, but one constant consideration is to make sure to budget a little extra time to create and maintain your documentation as you go.

One of the points we'll make here more than once is that good documentation begins at the beginning of a project. Some of these techniques become more difficult to put into place in a system that's already built.

DEVELOPING NAMING CONVENTIONS

To have a well-documented system, it is extremely important to create meaningful names for elements such as fields, table occurrences, layouts, and scripts. Each developer has personal ideas about what constitutes a meaningful name. Some developers like to embed metadata into names such as `zr_Created_Date.d` (where the `.d` suffix indicates that the field is a date field). Others prefer a simpler approach, with names like `CreationDate`.

Each project may have unique requirements for naming conventions because of factors such as the complexity of the project, number of developers, developer turnover rate, or perhaps the need to interface with external systems. In general, the more complex your project, or the greater the number of developers involved (either at one time, or across time because of a higher turnover rate), the more essential a consistent naming convention is. A good naming scheme can significantly lessen the amount of time it takes to bring a new developer "up to speed" on the system. The particular style used is less important than consistency throughout each project. Define your standards at the beginning of a project and stick with them.

USING COMMENTS EFFECTIVELY

Most programming and development environments give you some way to add comments to a system. *Comments* are descriptive information that you, the developer, supply throughout the system to clarify the meaning and usage of programming constructs. Previous versions of FileMaker allowed you to add comments to scripts. FileMaker 7 includes several additional features to enable developers to include comments throughout a system. The following sections look at these in detail.

ADDING COMMENTS FOR FIELDS

In FileMaker 7, you can now add a comment for each field in the Fields tab of the Define Database dialog box. The comments can each be up to 30,000 characters in length. The selected field's comment is displayed beneath the field name. View all comments by clicking the Options/Comments column header at the top of the field list. Field comments are included in the Database Design Report (covered later in this chapter) and are also accessible via the Get(FieldComment) function. Figure D.1 shows an example of field comments.

Figure D.1
Field comments can be displayed in the Fields tab of the Define Database dialog.

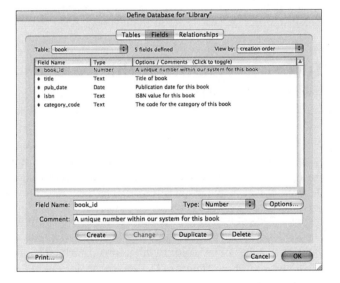

COMMENTING WITHIN FORMULAS

Formulas are defined in various places, including calculation fields, field validation, and some script steps such as If, Set Field, and Replace Field Contents. FileMaker 7 now allows comments within formulas. C-style and C++-style comments are both supported. C-style comments begin with the characters /* and end with the */ characters. C-style comments can span multiple lines and can be nested within other comments. C++-style comments begin with // and continue through the end of the line, as in the following example:

```
/* concatenate author's name in the form last, first
    example:  Smith, John     */

name_last &

Case(WordCount(name_first) and WordCount(name_last);
", ")  //don't include comma if either field is empty

& name_first
```

SCRIPTS

The Comment script step can be added anywhere within a script. Up to 30,000 characters may be included in the dialog box. Within ScriptMaker, the Comment script step appears in bold text, preceded by a # character. When a script is printed, the Comment script step is in italic.

ADDING DESCRIPTIONS IN THE ACCOUNTS & PRIVILEGES DIALOG

NEW Accounts, privilege sets, and extended privileges can each have associated descriptions. Enter a description when defining these items in the Accounts & Privileges dialog box. Up to 30,000 characters may be included for each. The descriptions appear in their respective lists and are also included in the Database Design Report.

DOCUMENTING THE RELATIONSHIPS GRAPH

The Relationships Graph does not have a built-in feature for adding comments or descriptions. However, there are a few things you can do to document the Relationships Graph. Always make table occurrence names descriptive and follow a consistent naming scheme. Some developers like to begin the name of a table occurrence with the name of the source table. This practice can be quite helpful when selecting a table occurrence from a list. Table occurrences are alphabetized when displayed in a list, and therefore all occurrences for a particular table that use that naming convention are grouped together in the list.

You also might want to use color to develop a scheme that adds meaning to table occurrences. Table occurrences for data tables, utility tables, and system tables can have different colors. You might also choose to use color to differentiate each table occurrence group. The HTML and XML versions of the Database Design Report include the color of the table occurrences, and display that color in the report output. You can add more table occurrences as group headers or comments. See the example in Figure D.2. A table occurrence name can contain up to 100 characters. The Relationships Graph can be spread across many pages if this is helpful for readability. Use plenty of whitespace and place logical groups of table occurrences on separate pages to make large Relationships Graphs easier to understand and maintain.

Figure D.2
Use "dummy" table occurrences as a means of documenting the Relationships Graph.

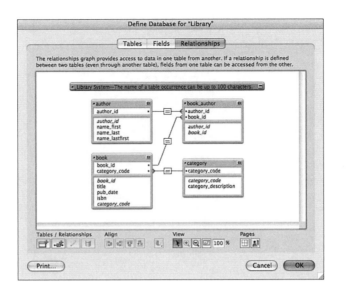

CAUTION

Be aware that these "dummy" table occurrences will still appear in any list of table occurrences anywhere in your system, so you need to name them in a way that indicates their special purposes (possibly with a leading asterisk or other special character). It's very possible that upcoming versions of FileMaker will provide some improvements in Relationships Graph management, and this practice could easily become a thing of the past.

USING THE DATABASE DESIGN REPORT

→ For additional discussion of the Database Design Report, **see** "Database Design Report," **p. 780**.

As soon as your solution has been filled with comments, descriptions, and meaningful element names, it is time to begin pulling the documentation together. FileMaker Developer 7 includes a Database Design Report (DDR) feature that is quite useful and may very well stand as the centerpiece for your system documentation. The report includes an overview of the system, along with detailed information about your database schema, including tables, fields, relationships, layouts, value lists, scripts, accounts, privilege sets, extended privileges, and custom functions. The report can be created as an integrated set of linked HTML documents or as a set of XML files. (The option to export the DDR as a FileMaker file, which was available in the previous version of FileMaker Developer, is no longer available in FileMaker Developer 7.)

CREATING A DDR

Creating a Database Design Report is a simple task. First, you must have FileMaker Developer and you must open all the files that you want to include in the report. The files must be opened with an account that has full access privileges. After the files have been opened, choose File, Database Design Report from the File menu to display the dialog box that you see in Figure D.3.

Figure D.3
FileMaker Developer's Database Design Report can document many aspects of your FileMaker databases.

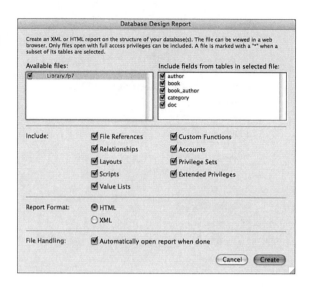

By default, all tables in all available files are included in the report. You can uncheck files or tables that you do not want to include. You can also specify the types of information to include for each file. Choose either HTML or XML for the report format. Finally, click the Create button and specify the location to save the report files.

If you're not sure whether the HTML or XML version of the DDR is more useful to you, think of it this way: The HTML version produces a set of linked Web pages that you can open and navigate immediately in a browser. The XML output is more appropriate if you need the data in a raw form and plan to manipulate it in some way before viewing or presenting it. One type of manipulation might consist of writing one or more XSLT stylesheets to transform the DDR XML data into a form suitable for importing into a FileMaker database.

WORKING WITH THE DDR IN HTML

The HTML version of the DDR includes a `Summary.html` document along with three additional HTML documents (`<filename>_ReportFrame.html`, `<filename>_TOCFrame.html`, and `<filename>.html`) for each of the FileMaker files in your solution. These three files all work together to create a frame-based view of database information for each database file. A `Styles.css` file is also created. This file includes formatting information used by all the HTML documents. To view the report, open the `Summary.html` file in any frames-capable Web browser. See Figure D.4 for an example of the Report Overview. Each of the solution's files is listed, along with counts of elements within those files. Click on a filename or any of the element counts to view details. All the details for a particular file are included on one (possibly lengthy) page. Use the navigation frame at the left side of the window to quickly move to the section you are interested in. You might also use your browser's Find feature to locate a particular element within the report.

D

TIP

> If you want to distribute the HTML-based DDR, one way is, of course, to host the files on a Web server and distribute the URL (making sure you give it only to people who should be allowed to see the internals of your database!) If you feel that hosting the files on the Web is insecure, or Web hosting is impractical for other reasons, you can distribute the HTML files as a group. If you do this, make sure to keep all the files together, in the same relative positions and with the same filenames as they had when they were first generated.

Figure D.4
FileMaker Developer can produce a Database Design Report in an HTML format.

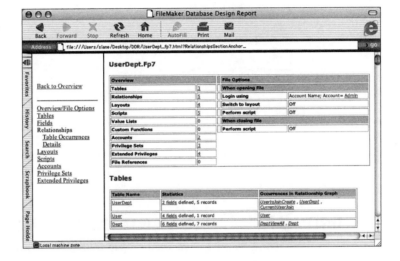

The DDR includes many hyperlinks that make it easy to navigate the report. For instance, the Fields section lists every layout, relationship, script, and value list that uses each field. Each of the listed items is a link that displays the element.

USING THE XML VERSION

When you choose to generate the DDR as XML, you'll get a file called Summary.xml, and an additional file called <filename>.xml for each database file that you choose to analyze. The XML version of the DDR includes all the information in the HTML version, as well as many more details. (In particular, you get a great deal more information about the position and styling of layout objects.) Although the XML DDR can be viewed in any text editor, you will likely prefer to use a program that understands XML (for example, an XML-aware Web browser such as Internet Explorer or Mozilla, or an XML editor such as Oxygen or XMLSpy.) You may also want to use an XSL style sheet to format or transform the raw XML. Figure D.5 shows an overview of an XML DDR viewed with most of the entities collapsed. The XML DDR contains an extensive amount of data broken down into ten sections: BaseTableCatalog, RelationshipGraph, LayoutCatalog, ValueListCatalog, ScriptCatalog, AccountCatalog, PrivilegesCatalog, ExtendedPrivilegeCatalog, CustomFunctionCatalog, and Options. Each of these sections contains information about one area of the database. The XML element names in each section are relatively self-explanatory.

Figure D.5
FileMaker Developer
can produce a
Database Design
Report in an XML
format.

Figure D.5
FileMaker Developer can produce a Database Design Report in an XML format.

USING THIRD-PARTY DOCUMENTATION TOOLS

In recent years, several programs have emerged to help fill the need for documenting FileMaker systems. These tools offer features for quickly identify missing or unknown elements, tracking dependencies, reporting differences between two solutions, script tracing, and more. Various tools extract information from FileMaker systems in different ways. They may use the Database Design Report, Apple Events, or even read data directly from the FileMaker files.

Each of the tools has strengths and weaknesses. For example, there can be substantial differences in the time required to extract data from solutions. The amount of information detail and the features included for using that information vary considerably from tool to tool as well. Having one or more of these types of tools can be very helpful for debugging and documenting systems. Check these publishers' Web pages for the latest details on their tools for FileMaker 7.

Analyzer by Waves in Motion—http://www.wmotion.com

Brushfire by Chaparral Software—http://www.chapsoft.com

MetaDataMagic by New Millenium—http://www.nmci.com

You'll be well repaid by looking at each of these tools and becoming familiar with their capabilities. Each has useful features. Analyzer, for example, has a nice set of "canned" reports you can run after your solution has been processed. Brushfire is quite fast, and offers a nice script cross-referencing feature. MetaData Magic has some very useful extras, such as the File Reference Fixer, which can repair and consolidate file references in databases designed in previous versions of FileMaker to better prepare the files for conversion to FileMaker 7.

PUTTING THE FINISHING TOUCHES ON YOUR DOCUMENTATION

In addition to the items described previously in this appendix, several other kinds of documentation may be useful to include in your system documentation package. Many of these items can be derived from the work that was done in the project's initial analysis and design phase. These documents can be printed or kept as electronic documents, such as PDF files.

- **Data Model**—A complete data model is essential for understanding how the database structure has been designed. An entity-relationship diagram (ERD) is one of the most popular data models.

→ For additional discussion of creating and using an ERD, **see** Chapter 5, "Relational Database Design," **p. 123**.

- **Documenting the Relationships Graph**—All the facts found on the Relationships Graph can be derived from the DDR report. However, the visual representation of the Relationships Graph provides an additional means for developers to gain insight into the system. The Relationships Graph can be printed or saved as a PDF file.

- **User Interface Diagrams**—For a complex system or a system with many subsystems, the overall navigation and use of the system should be documented. Depending on the scope and complexity of the system, it may be appropriate to include flow charts, storyboards, or other diagrams to indicate how users interact with the system and access its features.

- **System Flowchart**—The system flowchart should document the overall structure of the entire system. It should show how the various parts of the system interconnect and relate to each other. The system flowchart should also show manual processes and external systems or agents that the FileMaker system depends upon.

- **Process Descriptions**—Complex processes should be decomposed and documented thoroughly with written descriptions. Decision trees, charts, and tables can provide additional details.

- **Screens and Reports**—A complete set of documentation should include copies of all screens and reports used in the system. In some cases it may be helpful to produce two sets: one created with sample data in Browse mode and another that is created in Layout mode with field names.

- **Test Data**—Representative test data that shows both typical and extreme values can be a great asset in your documentation. Test data is especially helpful to those who are not familiar with the system. The test data can help to eliminate assumptions about expected data and prevent misunderstandings between clients and developers.

Final Thoughts on Documentation

This appendix has covered a variety of methods for documenting FileMaker systems. The specifics of the documentation standards that you adopt may vary with every project. Ideally, system documentation should contain enough information for another developer to completely re-create the system, using the documentation that you've created as his or her only information source. Clearly, maintaining complete and up-to-date documentation is a time-consuming task. However, many systems that you create will exist longer than expected. Systems are likely to outlive your association with the project. As a developer, you need to thoroughly understand the importance of system documentation and convey its necessity to your client or employer. Developing a workflow with a goal of producing quality documentation can produce substantial benefits in the life of each project.

INDEX

G

L

M

S

X